Chronology of American Popular Music, 1900–2000

Chronology
of American
Popular Music,
1900–2000

FRANK HOFFMANN

Routledge
Taylor & Francis Group
New York   London

Routledge
Taylor & Francis Group
270 Madison Avenue
New York, NY 10016

Routledge
Taylor & Francis Group
2 Park Square
Milton Park, Abingdon
Oxon OX14 4RN

© 2008 by Taylor & Francis Group, LLC
Routledge is an imprint of Taylor & Francis Group, an Informa business

Printed in the United States of America on acid-free paper
10 9 8 7 6 5 4 3 2 1

International Standard Book Number-13: 978-0-415-97715-9 (Hardcover)

Library of Congress Cataloging-in-Publication Data

Hoffmann, Frank W., 1949-
  Chronology of American popular music, 1900-2000 / by Frank Hoffmann.
     p. cm.
     Includes bibliographical references (p.) and index.
     ISBN 978-0-415-97715-9 (hardcover) -- ISBN 978-0-203-94176-8 (ebook) 1. Popular music--United States--Chronology. 2. Popular music--United States--20th century--History and criticism.. I. Title.

ML3477.H64 2007
781.640973--dc22
                                                                    2007032231

Visit the Taylor & Francis Web site at
http://www.taylorandfrancis.com

and the Routledge Web site at
http://www.routledge.com

Contents

❄

Preface

❄

Chronological outlines have proven to be successful when applied to rock music (e.g., *Rock Movers and Shakers*) and classical music. In an era fascinated by popular culture, particularly of a concise factual nature (witness the appeal of the Trivial Pursuit genre of games, television quiz shows, radio audience participation programming, and newspaper and magazine factoid sections), such works have been widely purchased by libraries and lay enthusiasts alike. However, such works have generally not succeeded as serious reference sources and curriculum-related guides in a formal academic setting. The intent of the proposed work is to cross-over into these fields by providing

- A wide-ranging, in-depth survey of popular music history which encompasses all notable genres, artists, and related socio-cultural trends;
- Well-organized access to this chronologically arranged information by means of a comprehensive index.

This work is—in essence—a chronology of the key dates in American popular music history between 1900 and 2000. Popular music is defined here as including all genres that place a greater emphasis on mass acceptance and commercial success as opposed to overriding aesthetic considerations or single-minded self expression. More specifically, the book embraces Tin Pan Alley pop (and related styles such as musical theater, the minstrel tradition, and vaudeville selections); jazz phases beginning with ragtime (which many consider to be a precursor of the jazz idiom), followed by Dixieland (or the traditional New Orleans Sound), small combo "hot" jazz, big band, bebop, cool jazz (including the West Coast and Third Stream spin-offs), free jazz, fusion, and smooth jazz; commercial folk music; the blues, rhythm and blues, soul, funk, and black contemporary; country and western; and rock 'n' roll with its myriad by-products, including progressive rock, punk and new wave, disco, postpunk, alternative rock, and rap/hip hop, just a name a few.

Perhaps the most challenging aspect of compiling a volume of this type relates to establishing the criteria for inclusion. Countless titles are presently available from retailers and libraries that emphasize the trivial aspects of pop music, particularly since the rise of rock 'n' roll. These books devote considerable space to the birthdates of musicians and other music industry figures (despite the fact that later biographical events are what would make them important), marriages to people of no significance to the pop music scene, and drug busts and other extra-curricular activities having little impact on music history (and often receiving scant media attention). This work has attempted to focus on events that have made an impact on the evolution of popular music, most notably,

- Milestone accomplishments, whether pertaining to an individual career or the music industry as a whole;
- Death dates, which serve as a the summation of a career;
- Events or creations that prove influential or widely imitated;
- Significant chart or sales activity, especially achieving the number one ranking on a particular chart;
- Awards or special recognition for achievements; and
- Oddities that serve to illustrate or symbolize a prevailing attitude or movement.

A few points are worth noting in order to better understand the logic behind the inclusion of certain entries. Sound recordings, live performances, and the broadcast media were the primary channels for disseminating pop music to the public at large. Charts—which typically measure record sales, radio airplay, and jukebox popularity—were not produced in trade publications, most notably *Billboard* (the leading entertainment weekly), until the mid-1930s. While charts exist for virtually every software format and music genre, *Billboard*'s singles (known as the Hot 100 since August 1958) and album charts—which focus on mainstream, mass market hits, including crossover recordings from the country and rhythm and blues fields—have received the bulk of attention. However, British hits from 1964 onwards are frequently noted as well due to that nation's importance in shaping music trends stateside. Since redundancy is avoided in the interests of both aesthetics and saving space, it is advised that users of this volume consult the index to ascertain additional information about a given artist, work, and ongoing event.

ACKNOWLEDGMENTS

I greatly appreciate the Newton Gresham Library and Computer Services staff, Sam Houston State University, for providing the resources needed to compile my entries for the book. The Music Librarian, Bruce Hall, was particularly helpful in this regard. Bruce's energy and insght in chasing down hard-to-find data knows no boundaries! Without him, this project would have been greatly dimished in scope and quality. Lynn Goeller and her associates at EvS Communication Networx, who were contracted by Routledge to edit the book, proved endlessly resourceful and patient in assiting me through the projects many stages. I can't thank them enough—they were a delight to work with!

1900

❆

January 31. Sousa's Band kicks off their first tour for the year at the Kreuger Auditorium, Newark, New Jersey. The itinerary will range as far west as Lincoln, Nebraska, while taking in the northern tier states of Michigan, Wisconsin, and Minnesota along with and Montreal, Canada, as well as the southern states West Virginia and Maryland.

March 19. The highly successful musical production, *The Casino Girl*, debuts at the Casino Theatre, New York City.

March 28. The Haydn Quartet records several songs for Berliner as the Gramophone Minstrels. The group, which first recorded for Berliner on June 27, 1898 ("Little Alabama Coon"), and would ultimately make approximately seventy discs for the label, appears to have been motivated by the wish to conform to minstrel show conventions, both in name and in mode of presentation.

April 7. Sousa's Band ends its first 1900 tour with a performance at the Newburgh, New York Academy of Music.

April 25. Sousa's Band sets sail for Europe. Their first tour of that continent will entail 175 concerts in thirty-four cities.

May. Emile Berliner sees Francis Barraud's painting of Nipper in the London office of his Gramophone Company. Berraud had delivered the painting to Barry Owen, an executive with The Gramophone Company on October 17, 1899. Nipper, a bull-terrier cross, appears to have been born in Bristol in 1884. When his original owner, scenery painter Mark Henry Barraud, died in 1887, his brother Francis, took in the dog. Barraud would occasionally record his voice via a cylinder-playing phonograph; Nipper's reaction to hearing his master's voice coming out of the black horn spurred the Liverpool-based artist to capture the image in a now-famous watercolor painting. When Owen agreed to purchase the work on September 21, 1899, he made it conditional on two modifications: the black enamel horn be replaced by a more striking brass version, and the cylinder machine by a disc-player. Berliner contacted Barraud, asking him to make a copy of the painting. Berliner brought the work back to the United States, and within a couple of years, the painting was being used to adorn record supplement publications, ads, and record labels.

May 5. Sousa's Band perform in Europe for the first time, a Matinee show at the Palais des Beaux Arts, Paris.

July 3. Sousa's Band perform at the unveiling of the Washington Monument in Paris.

July 4. Sousa's Band perform at the unveiling of the Lafayette Monument, premiering the Sousa march, "Hail to the Spirit of Liberty." After performing at the dedication of the American Pavilion, the band parades through Paris accompanied by the mounted unit of the Garde Republicaine and the American Guard—one of only eight times they marched during forty years of existence.

July 10. The U.S. patent office grants The Gramophone Company rights to the painted image of Nipper. With the formation of the Victor Talking Machine Company, Berliner passes the trademark on to his former partner Eldridge R. Johnson, who goes on to extend his rights to the image to Central and South America as well as the Far East and Japan.

July 20. Arthur Collins records seven tracks—accompanied by a pianist—for Victor. It was his first session for the label.

July 21. Arthur Collins records eight tracks for Victor, accompanied by the Metropolitan Orchestra. He appears to have been the first vocalist at one of the label's sessions to be accompanied by more than a piano.

September 6. One of the year's most popular musicals, *Fiddle-dee-dee*, opens at the Weber and Fields Music Hall in New York City.

September 24. Sousa's Band begin their first six-day segment performing four times daily at the Pittsburgh Exposition. The second segment takes place October 15–20.

October 1. *San Toy*, one of the top-grossing musical productions for the year, is first performed at the Daly's in New York City.

October 8. Sousa's Band begin their first six-day segment performing two times daily at the Merchants and Manufacturers Exposition, Boston. The second segment takes place October 22–27.

October 26. The Haydn Quartet records for Victor for the first time; the resulting track, "Negro Wedding in Southern Georgia," is issued as A-42 in the seven-inch disc configuration.

November 10. The Broadway season's biggest hit, *Floradora*, opens at the Casino Theatre. Owen Hall and Leslie Stuart's musical comedy—best known for its sextette of "typewriter girls"—would go on to run for 505 performances.

December 18. A U.S. patent is granted for the moulded cylinder to the Lambert Company of Chicago. Made of pink celluloid, they had first been produced earlier in the year, allowing the mass production of cylinders from a master. With the major problems of production solved, Edison followed in 1901 with the "gold-moulded" cylinder. As noted by the *Guinness Book of Recorded Sound* (1984), while the cylinder peaked in popularity in 1901, the rise of the disc pointed to the inevitable eclipse of the format:

> Edison correctly felt that cylinder reproduction was superior to that of the disc: the former's hill-and-date drove was not distorted by being bent sideways round the central blank area, as an disc, and playing time was less limited. The ease with which flat discs could be mass-produced by the stamper method had meant that production costs were lower than with the pantographic and other cumbersome methods of making cylinder copies.

1901

❄

January 3. Sousa's Band kick off their first tour of the year with a Brooklyn, New York Academy of Music performance. Covering the continental United States, it ends March 31 at New York City's Metropolitan Opera House.

April 7. Sousa's Band begin a second tour at the Metropolitan Opera House, New York City. It covers New England, the Midwest, and Ontario, ending with a June 10–July 6 residency at the Pan-American Exposition, Buffalo, New York.

August 29. Irish-born tenor Roger Harding dies of a viral infection in his early forties. He performed in minstrel shows, musical comedies, and opera prior to recording for many of the phonograph companies beginning in the 1890s. His repertoire included sentimental songs, lullabies, comic selections, and musical comedy hits.

September 11. Will F. Denny records twenty-four takes (covering ten songs) for Victor—his only session for that label.

September 30. Metropolitan Opera baritone Giuseppe Campanari listens to Harry McClaskey (aka Henry Burr) sing, and recommends that he go to New York for musical training.

October 3. The Victor Talking Machine Company is created—under the leadership of Eldridge R. Johnson—out of the merger and reorganization of two companies: the U.S. division of Emile Berliner's Berliner Gramophone Company, which was producing discs, and Johnson's Consolidated Talking Machine Company, then producing the machines for playing these discs. Victor would become the major commercial force within the fledgling record industry in short order, in the process assuring the ascendancy of the flat disc format over the cylinder. The label maintained its dominance throughout much of the twentieth century on the strength of best-selling artists like Billy Murray, Paul Whiteman, Perry Como, and Elvis Presley, despite being purchased by the Radio Corporation of America in 1927 and the German media firm, Bertelsmann, in 1985.

October 4. Sousa's Band perform at London's Albert Hall. Following an October 7–November 2 residency at the Glasgow (Scotland) Exposition, they tour England, ending with a December 13 concert at Southampton's Philharmonic Hall.

1902

❄

January 11. Sousa's Band begin their first tour of the year with a performance at the 22nd Regiment Armory, New York City. It covers New England, the South, and the Midwest before ending with an April 2 concert at the Krueger Auditorium, Newark, New Jersey.

May 11. Sousa's Band inaugurate a second 1902 tour with the performance at the Metropolis Theater, New York City. It proceeds to Detroit before cutting back through Canada and New England, and ends with a May 30–June 15 residency at the Willow Grove (Pennsylvania) Park.

June 28. Sousa's Band start a final 1902 tour with a residency at the Atlantic City, New Jersey, Steel Pier through August 31. It takes in much of the continental United States before ending with a December 14 concert at New York City's Casino Theater.

October 29. The Dinwiddie Colored Quartet records three songs—"Down on the Old Camp Ground" (Victor 1714/Monarch 1714), "Poor Mourner" (Victor 1715), and "Steal Away" (Victor 1716)—without instrumental accompaniment for Victor in New York City. They are believed to be the first group to record black gospel material in an authentic manner. They would return to the studio on October 31 to cut three more songs: "My Way Is Cloudy" (Victor 1724), "Gabriel's Trumpet" (Victor 1725), and "We'll Anchor Bye-and-Bye" (Victor 1726). The single-sided Victor discs may all have been issued on Monarch; however, none but #1714 have ever been proven to exist. Race recordings—that is, records performed in African American secular and religious song styles for a black audience—would not reappear until the early 1920s, when established labels began to branch out (albeit, tentatively at first) into this field in search of further profits.

October 31. Arthur Collins is paired with Byron G. Harlan for the first time in a Victor recording session—Harlan's first session with the label. They would become the most successful recording duo of the acoustic era.

December. The National Phonograph Company discontinues publication of the *Phonogram*. The monthly trade bulletin had a circulation of sixty thousand, and featured listings of the new Edison cylinder releases.

1903

❄

1903. The American Telegraphone Co. is founded by Danish engineer Valdemar Poulsen and P. O. Pedersen. The firm was committed to the commercial exploitation of the telegraphone—the first wire recorder, invented by Poulsen in 1898—which consisted of a brass cylinder, with a helical groove cut into its surface into which the wire would fit. Originally promoted as a dictation and telephone message machine, poor audio reproduction compared with cylinders—and later, magnetic tape—necessitated the use of earphones.

January. Minstrel singer Billy Golden returns to the National Phonograph Company roster with three releases: "Turkey in the Straw" (#8293), "Roll on the Ground" (#8298), and "Mixed Ale Party" (#8311).

January 2. Sousa's Band kicks off a European tour with an eight-day residency at London's Queen's Hall. Other nations on the itinerary include France, Belgium, Germany, Poland, Bohemia, Denmark, Holland, and Ireland. It ends July 30 with a concert at the Hippodrome, Blackpool, England.

January 20. *The Wizard of Oz* premieres at New York's Majestic Theatre. Featuring music by Paul Tietjens and A. Baldwin Stone and lyrics and book by L. Frank Baum, the musical would run for 293 performances. It was adapted to film in 1939 with a new score by Harold Arlen and E. Y. Harburg. A black spinoff, *The Wiz*, would open on Broadway in 1975, and itself be made into a movie in 1978 (starring Diana Ross and Michael Jackson).

January 30. The U.S. Circuit Court, Western District of Pennsylvania, restrains the Kaufmann Bros. of Pittsburgh from violating Edison patents by cutting prices on the company's phonographs, records, and blanks.

March. *The Edison Phonograph Monthly*, begins publication with the professed aim of keeping the National Phonograph Co. "in closer touch with the Jobbers and Dealers."

March. An Edison Phonograph ad featuring the heading, "Use Edison Moulded Records Make Records of your own," runs in the following mass circulation publications: *Leslie's Popular Monthly*, *McClure's Magazine*, *Munsey's Magazine*, *Scribner's Magazine*, *Argosy*, *Harper's Magazine*, *Everybody's Pearson's*, *Ainslie's*, *Smart Set*, *Good Housekeeping*, *Success*, *Lippincott's*, *National Magazine*, *Overland*, *Metropolitan*, *Booklovers' Magazine*, *Saturday Evening Post*, *Collier's Weekly*, *Life*, *Town Topics*, *Outlook*, and the *New Era Magazine Supplement* (reproduced in the largest daily papers in fifty major U.S. cities).

March 1. To commemorate the opening of the Industrial Exposition at Osaka, Japan, Thomas Edison presents the Emperor of Japan with a specially finished phonograph.

March 3. Arthur Collins records duets with Joe Natus—the last Victor session for the duo—before cutting selections with Byron G. Harlan.

April 1. Releases by Edison Moulded Records include W.H. Thompson's "The Song Bird of Melody Lane" (#8378), Byron G. Harlan's "Somebody's Waiting For Me" (#8380), Edward Favor's "The Beer That Made Milwaukee Famous" (#8381), Julian Rose's "Hebrew Vaudeville Specialty" (#8383), W. H. Thompson and Albert Campbell's "It's the Man in the Soldier Suit" (#8384), Harry MacDonough's "Heidelberg (Stein Song)" (#8385), Collins & Harlan's "When the Winter Time Comes 'Round" (#8386), Arthur Collins' coon song, "I Wonder Why Bill Bailey Don't Come Home" (#8389), and "When Our Lips in Kisses Met" (#8390), by Miss Morgan and Mr. Stanley.

May. *National Magazine* includes an interview (reprinted in the *Edison Phonograph Monthly*) of Thomas Edison by Joe Mitchell Chapple. When asked about his favorite invention, Edison replies:

> The phonograph—the phonograph, by all means! It has been a long time since the first phonograph, as we count time nowadays, and improvements come every day; but I think I have accomplished more the past year on it than in any of the years before. My ambition is to have it so perfect that it will reproduce your Boston symphonies to perfection, giving the distinct intonation of every instrument.

May 1. Releases by Edison Moulded Records include Arthur Collins' "My Little Pansy" (#8393), a Frank P. Banta piano solo, "Violets" (#8394), Byron G. Harlan's "The Banquet in Misery Hall" (#8397), Edward

Favor's "Hamlet Was a Melancholy Dane" (#8400), and Collins & Harlan's "Waltz Me Down the Alley Sallie" (8402).

June 1. Releases by Edison Moulded Records included the Arthur Collins coon song, "Won't You Roll Dem Eyes" (#8405), a Vess Ossman banjo solo, "The Mississippi" (#8408), Edward M. Favor's "Julie" (#8411), J. F. Hopkins' "Down Where the Wurzburger Flows Medley" (#8412), and Harry MacDonough's "Down at Lover's Roost" (#84150).

July. In an article entitled "Odd Uses for the Phonograph," the *Edison Phonograph Monthly* documents that sound recordings can lessen pain while having teeth extracted, elicit "pleasant" expressions from patrons in photography studios, and turn pet stop parrots into mimics.

July 1. Releases by Edison Moulded Records included Harry MacDonough's "Hiawatha" (#8425), Miss Morgan and Mr. Stanley's "'Deed I Do" (#8435), the Edison Male Quartette's "Massa's in the Cole, Cold Ground" (#8436), Len Spencer's "Reuben Haskins of Showhegan, Maine" (#8441), and Collins & Harlan's "Hurrah for Baffin's Bay" (#8447).

August. The National Phonograph Co. announces the establishment of a record-making plant in London. Plans exist for locating more plants in the chief cities of six other European countries.

August 1. The *Edison Phonograph Monthly* advertised the release of the first national releases by a twenty-six-year-old tenor, Billy Murray: "I'm Thinking of You All the While" (Edison two-minute cylinder #8452) and "Alex Busby, Don't Go Away" (Edison two-minute cylinder #8453). Both records—which fell within the then-popular genre category of "coon songs"—were immediate hits. Although it appears that he had been making cylinders as early as 1897 for the San Francisco-based Edison distributor, Bacigalupi Brothers (which, allegedly, were in great demand on the West Coast and Pacific region), Murray become an overnight success, making records for all the major (Edison, Columbia, and Victor) and independent labels within the next year or so. In addition to possessing a powerful voice and lucid diction ideally suited to the limitations of acoustic era recording, he exhibited an extraordinary comic touch. In short order, his repertoire had expanded to include Broadway musicals, love songs and sentimental ballads, comic songs, vaudeville sketches, ethnic material, topical songs, and more faddish fare such as the jungle and cowboy songs in vogue in the first decade of the twentieth century. The finest songwriters of the day—George M. Cohan, Irving Berlin, and the Von Tilzer brothers, among others—were delighted to have their material interpreted by Murray for the record-buying public. Classic songs that received a definitive interpretation from Murray included "Alexander's Ragtime Band," "By the Light of the Silvery Moon," "Casey Jones," "Give My Regards to Broadway," "The Grand Old Flag," "In My Merry Oldsmobile," "Meet Me in St. Louis, Louis," "Moonlight Bay," "Over There," and "Yankee Doodle Boy." His popularity was such that one biographer estimated that the singer's solo and collaborative efforts outsold the releases of all other popular artists combined between 1910 and 1920. While this may represent something of an exaggeration, it is clear that Murray—in an era when recording artists were accorded minimal publicity and critical respect—played a key role, like Caruso in the classical music sector, in legitimizing the recording medium. He continued to make records through 1943; his forty-six-year recording career has rarely been equaled over the years.

August 30. Sousa's Band begins a second 1903 tour with an eight-day residency at the Willow Grove (Pennsylvania) Park. It proceeds to Chicago and back, ending October 4 at New York City's Carnegie Hall.

September 1. Releases by Edison Moulded Records included Collins & Harlan's "Parody on Hiawatha" (#8475), Billy Murray's coon song, "I Could Never Love Like That" (#8477), Billy Golden's "Medley of Coon Songs" (#8491), and "Mountain Echoes" (#8495), a violin and flute duet by Jaudas & Atz.

September 2. Already a best-selling Edison artist, Billy Murray participates in his first Victor recording session. The following matrixes were produced:

> B-386 I'm Thinking of You All of the While (released as #2467)
> B-387 Alec Busby, Don't Go Away (unissued)
> B-388 Won't You Kindly Hum Old "Home, Sweet Home" to Me (unissued)
> B-389 Up in a Cocoanut Tree (#2453)
> B-390 My Little 'Rang Outang (#2454)

September 11. Collins & Harlan record "It Was the Dutch" (Victor 2451); it is believed to be the last Victor Monarch record to have a spoken announcement (done by Collins).

September 27. In a letter sent to the *Edison Phonograph Monthly*, F. K. Wilson writes that an Edison cylinder entitled "Hiawatha" was played 1,525 times, mostly at the "slot machine gallery at a Coatsville, Pennsylvania park before wearing out. The editor notes that most moulded records should be just as durable.

October. The *Edison Phonograph Monthly* announces that recording artist Cal Stewart just had a book published, *Uncle Josh Weathersby's "Punkin Centre" Stories*. It contains all his humorous sketches, augmented by illustrations.

October 1. Releases by Edison Moulded Records included Miss Corrinne Morgan's "Happy Days" (#8499), the Edison Military Band's "American Standard March" (#8500), Collins & Harlan's "It Was the Dutch" (#8509), Harlan & Stanley's "Waiting for the Dinner Horn to Blow" (#8511), Billy Murray's "Won't You Kindly Hum Old Home Sweet Home to Me" (#8521), and Harry MacDonough's "My Cosy Corner Girl" (#8522).

October 13. *Babes In Toyland* premieres at New York's Majestic Theatre. Featuring music by Victor Herbert and lyrics and book by Glen MacDonough, the musical had a run of 192 performances. The work was adapted to screen twice: the 1934 version featured Laurel and Hardy, and the 1961 edition included Ray Bolger and Ed Wynn.

November 1. Releases by Edison Moulded Records included Arthur Collins' coon song, "Any Rag" (#8525), Harry MacDonough's "By the Sycamore Tree" (#8526), Dan W. Quinn's "I Like You, Lil, for Fair" (#8534), the Invincible Quartette's "Nigger Stew" (#8537), Fred Van Epps' banjo solo, "The Lobster's Promenade" (#8540), and Billy Murray's coon song, "Under a Panama" (#8541).

November 11. Dr. A. L. Kroeber, affiliated with the University of California Department of Anthropology, finishes a month-long project documenting Mojave customs, language, ceremonies, etc., on more than one hundred phonographic cylinders through the assistance of two Mohave Indians, Captain Joe Nelson and Captain Jack Jones.

November 24. Arthur Pryor's Band enters the studio for the first time, recording two takes of "Mr. Black Man" (one of which is issued as Victor 2557). According to Rudi Blesh (*They All Played Ragtime*. Alfred Knopf, 1950), Pryor's ensemble "played with far more syncopation than any other brass band."

November 28. Jules Levy dies at age forty-five. Widely considered "the world's greatest cornet player" during the latter decades of the nineteenth century, Levy was also the first prominent musician to be recorded on a regular basis. His biggest hit was "My Country 'Tis of Thee" (North American 470; 1893).

November 30. Frank P. Banta, age thirty-three, dies at his home in New York City. He had supplied to piano accompaniment (both arrangements and playing) to more than half the recordings then listed in the Edison catalog.

December 1. Releases by Edison Moulded Records included Billy Murray's "Bedelia, an Irish Coon Serenade" (#8550) and "Up in the Cocoanut Tree" (#8564), Will F. Denny's "Trixie" (#8552), Byron G. Harlan's "Down Where the Swanee River Flows" (#8561), the Edison Quartette's "Keep on A-Shining Silv'ry Moon" (#8571), and Harry MacDonough's "The Maid of Timbuctoo" (#8572).

1904

❄

January 1. Releases by Edison Moulded Records included Billy Murray's "Under the Anheuser Bush" (#8575) and "Mary Ellen (#8597), Harry MacDonough's "Peggy Brady" (#8579), Collins & Harlan's "What Would the Neighbors Say" (#8588), S. H. Dudley's "The Whistling Bowery Boy" (#8593), and Albert Benzler's "Pretty as a Butterfly" (#8595).

January 5. John E. Finney writes that a Savannah, Georgia theater, lacking the services of a live orchestra, utilizes an Edison Triumph Phonograph both before and during the intermission of the play, *Isis*. The venue's management was sufficiently impressed with the experiment to continue it the following week.

February. The *Edison Phonograph Monthly* states that Edison today—and in recent months—makes 50 percent more cylinders than any other company.

February 1. Releases by Edison Moulded Records included Bob Roberts' "Wouldn't It Make You Hungry" (#8602) and "The Woodchuck Song" (#8617), Len Spencer's "Clancy's Prize Waltz Contest" (#8604) and "Reuben Haskins' Ride on a Cyclone Auto" (#8619), and Collins & Harlan's "Barney" (#8608) and ""I Ain't Got No Time" (#8621).

The Collins & Harlan discs were the first ever made at the Edison laboratory with orchestral accompaniment.

February 4. Various newspapers report that a phonographic record of German Emperor William's voice will be the first European deposit made in the phonetic archives to be maintained as Harvard University and in the Congressional Library and National Museum in Washington, D.C.

March 1. Releases by Edison Moulded Records included Arthur Collins' "Maydee (Pretty South Sea Island Lady)" (#8625) and "Hannah Won't You Open That Door" (#8637), Harry Anthony's "I'm Longing for My Old Kentucky Home" (#8633), the U.S. Marine Fife & Drum Corps' "Medley of National Airs" (#8638), and Harlan and Belmont's "Beautiful Birds Sing On" (#8639).

March 7. Mendlow Brothers ran an ad in the Lynn, Massachusetts, *Daily Evening Item* comparing prices for Edison Phonographs and Records between 1900 and 1904. There had been no discernable price change over that period; the players continued to retail at $10, $20, $30, $50, and $75, while the cylinder still cost 50 cents apiece ($5.00 per dozen).

April 1. Releases by Edison Moulded Records included Harry MacDonough's "In Zanzibar (My Little Chimpanzee)" (#8651), Len Spencer's "Uncle Tom's Cabin (Flogging Scene)" (#8656), Billy Murray's "Dear Sing Sing" (#8668), and the Edison Military Band's "Mr. Black Man (Cakewalk)" (#8669) and "Navajo Medley" (#8673).

May 1. Releases by Edison Moulded Records included Edward M. Favor's "Cordalia Malone" (#8675) and "The Irish, The Irish" (#8686), violinist Charles D'Alaine's "Pop Goes the Weasel Medley" (#8678), Collins & Harlan's "Good-bye, Fedora" (#8679) and "'Possum Pie (or the Stuttering Con)" (#8697), Billy Murray's "That Is a Habit I Never Had" (#8689), and William M. Redmond's "On a Good Old Trolley Ride (Out With My Pearlie, My Steady Young Girlie)" (#8696).

April 2. Sousa's Band begin their first tour of the year with a performance at the Asbury Park, New Jersey Pavilion. It ends with an April 30–June 4 residency at the St. Louis World's Fair (Louisiana Purchase Exposition).

May 16. Edison announces that the price of Gold Moulded Records would be reduced to 35 cents (from 50 cents) effective July 18. The company's rationale was the recent increases in production capacity that made the strategy of seeking a larger market share feasible.

June 1. Releases by Edison Moulded Records included Byron G. Harlan's "All Aboard for Dreamland" (#8700) and "It's the Band" (#8718), the Mendelssohn Mixed Quartette's "Evening Chimes" (#8701), James F. Harrison's "Then and Now" (#8714), and Billy Murray's "Meet Me in St. Louis, Louis (Meet Me at the Fair)" (#8722).

July.   Edison revives *Phonogram* as a monthly publication. By including a list of the imminent record releases, it functions as a promotional vehicle for phonograph jobbers and dealers. The first issue had a circulation of 100,000, which was increased to 110,000 and 135,000 for the August and September installments, respectively. By March 1906, circulation had reached 360,000 copies.

July 1.   Releases by Edison Moulded Records included Vess L. Ossman's "The St. Louis Rag" (#8726), Campbell and Roberts' "An Interrupted Courtship on the Elevated Railway" (#8731), Campbell and Harrison's "My Old New Hampshire Home" (#8734), Billy Murray's "Hannah" (#8737), the Edison Concert Band's "A Bit o' Blarney" (#8742), the Edison Male Quintette's "The Old Cabin Home" (#8744), and cornetist Bohumir Kryl's "Kryl's Favorite" (#8745).

August 1. Releases by Edison Moulded Records included Campbell and Roberts' "Michael Clancy as a Policeman" (#8754), Harry Anthony's "Little Rustic Cottage by the Stream" (#8758), Harry MacDonough's "Mississippi Mamie" (#8762), Billy Murray's "Alexander" (#8765), clarinetist William Tuson's "Minstrel Boy" (#8769), James F. Harrison's "Two Eyes of Brown" (#8770), and Bob Roberts' "When the Coons Have a Dreamland of Their Own" (#8771).

August 28. Sousa's Band kick off a second 1904 tour with a nine-day residency at the Willow Grove (Pennsylvania) Park. Covering the continental United States, it ends December 5 at the Krueger Auditorium, Newark, New Jersey.

September 1. Releases by Edison Moulded Records included Bob Roberts' "Tippecanoe" (#8775), W. H. Thompson's "Old Folks at Home" (#8781) and "The Maple Leaf Forever" (#8799), Harlan and Stanley's "Dixie" (#8784), Billy Murray's "Old Mother Goose" (#8785), and George Seymour Lenox's "The Bloom is on the Rye" (#8793).

October 1. Releases by Edison Moulded Records included two coon songs by Bob Roberts ("Teasing," #8804; "Here's My Friend," #8824), Harry Tally's "Seminole" (#8808), Collins and Harlan's "Down Where the Sweet Potatoes Grow" (#8810), Miss Nelson and Mr. Stanley's "What Colored Eyes Do You Love" (#8814), and MacDonough and Biehling's "Bye and Bye You Will Forget Me" (#8817).

October 11. The National Phonograph Co. declines acceptance of a Gold Medal for its Phonograph exhibition at the St. Louis World's Fair. President William E. Gilmore stated that it ran counter to company policy to pursue "awards of any character."

November. The *Edison Phonograph Monthly* looks at the phonograph clubs phenomena. As offered by various retailers, the concept enables financially strapped indiiduals to obtain a phonograph and recordings through an installment plan format.

November 7. *Little Johnny Jones*, George M. Cohan's third musical (and first hit), premieres at the Liberty Theatre in New York City. Cohan not only wrote the music, lyrics, and book, but directed and starred in the work. Featuring the songs "The Yankee Doodle Boy" and "Give My Regards to Broadway"—both of which were hit records at the time as recorded for a variety of labels by Billy Murray—the musical had an initial run of 52 performances; following a road tour, the show returned to Broadway twice for a total run of twenty weeks.

November 20. Releases by Edison Moulded Records included two songs by Irving Gillette (aka Henry Burr)— "Shine On, Oh Stars" (#8827) and "Star of Bethlehem" (#8853), Billy Murray's "Save It for Me" (#8830), Campbell and Harrison's "Rock of Ages" (#8839), the Ossman Banjo Trio's "I've Got a Feelin' for You" (#8841), the Edison Symphony Orchestra's "Edison Tennessee Barn Dance" (#8844) and "My Little Canoe" (#8851), and Frank C. Stanley's "Birthday of a King" (#8852).

December 20. Releases by Edison Moulded Records included the Edison Concert Band's "The Auto Race" (#8856), Miss Grace Nelson's "My Little Canoe" (#8858), Billy Murray's "Mr. Wilson, That's All" (#8863) and "Come Take a Trip in My Airship" (#8874), the Criterion Quartette's "Little Tommy Went a Fishing" (#8866), the Edison Instrumental Quintette's "Loving Hearts" (#8871), and Arthur Collins' "Abraham" (#8873).

1905

❄

January. The first issue of *Talking Machine World* is published. Due to its intelligent and unbiased coverage, it is immediately recognized as the preeminent recording industry journal.

January 4. Henry Burr makes his first recordings for Victor. Two cuts from the session—"Daddy" (4239) and "Loch Lomond" (#4240)—are issued in March.

January 6. Sousa's Band begin a British tour with a performance at Liverpool's Philharmonic Hall. It ends May 9 at the same venue.

January 23. Releases by Edison Moulded Records included Irving Gillette's "My Dreams" (#8904), Billy Murray's "Yankee Doodle Boy" (#8910), Fred G. Rover's "Those Songs My Mother Used to Sing" (#8911), Murray & Roberts' "Dan, Dan, Dan-u-el" (#8913), and Arthur Collins' "Gimme de Leavins'" (#8917).

February 25. Releases by Edison Moulded Records included Irving Gillette's "Oh Promise Me" (#8929), Collins & Harlan's "Oh, Oh, Sallie" (#8935), the Edison Military Band's "Darkie Tickle" (#8937), Murray & Roberts' "Can't You See My Heart Beats All for You" (#8942), and Miss Ada Jones' "My Carolina Lady" (#8948).

March. The *Edison Phonograph Monthly* includes the warning, "Jobbers are cautioned against allowing their sample Records each month to permanently leave their possession, or to be sold either to Dealers or to the public ahead of the receipt of their stock orders." In the May issue of *EPM*, it was noted that the National Phonograph Co. decided to stop furnishing one jobber with promotional cylinders in the future.

March 25. Releases by Edison Moulded Records included Billy Murray's "If Mister Boston Lawson Has His Way" (#8954), Miss Ada Jones' "He's Me Pal" (#8957), Irving Gillete's "In the Shade of the Old Apple Tree" (#8958), Harry MacDonough's "Billy" (#8964), and the Edison Concert Band's "Yankee Patrol" (#8971).

April 23. The Schenectady (NY) *Sunday Press* reports that Rev. Henry C. Slade delivered his own funeral sermon via phonograph on March 9, at Rideout, Kentucky.

April 25. Releases by Edison Moulded Records included Collins and Harlan's "Tammany" (#8979), Miss Ada Jones' "You Ain't the Man I Thought You was" (#8989), Murray and Roberts' "I've Got a Little Money and I've Saved It All for You" (#8991), Irving Gillette's "Good Night, Little Girl, Good Night" (#8995), Billy Murray's "When Father Laid the Carpet on the Stairs" (#8998), and Arthur Collins' "Preacher and the Bear" (#9900).

May 4. Victor begins featuring Billy Murray as lead vocalist for the Haydn Quartet in dance and novelty number. Harry Macdonough continues as frontman on sentimental ballads, old standards, and gospel hymns.

May 10. Bass vocalist George H. Broderick dies of pneumonia, at age fifty, at his home in Chicago. He recorded for all of the major record labels at the turn of the century, including Berliner and Edison. The first numbered record of the Consolidated Taking Machine Company (later renamed Victor) featured him reciting the Eugene Field poem, "Departure"; recorded on June 28, 1900, it was assigned the catalog number "A-1."

June 1. Releases by Edison Moulded Records included Billy Murray's "Paddy's Day" (#9009), Anthony & Harrison's "O Morning Land" (#9010), Ada Jones & Len Spencer's "Ev'ry Little Bit Helps" (#9016), and "South Carolina Minstrels" (#9024), by the Edison Minstrels (featuring Len Spencer, Billy Murray and a chorus by the Edison Quartette with orchestra accompaniment).

July 1. The National Phonograph Co. announces the establishment of the Edison Commercial System for installing the Edison Business Phonograph. The advantages cited include centralization of the office typewriting force and the ability to render department heads free of clerical routine.

July 1. Releases by Edison Moulded Records included Cyrus Pippins' "Courting Matilda" (#9030), "Shame on You!" (#9033), by Tascott, the white coon, Rubel and Tuson's "Two Little Bullfinches Polka" (#9035), Ada Jones and Len Spencer's "Antomy and Cleopatra" (#9036), Billy Murray's "Me an' de Minstrel Ban'" (#9037), and Miss Nelson and Mr. Stanley's "Sambo and Dinah" (#9043).

August 1. Releases by Edison Moulded Records included Miss Clarice Vance's "Mariar" (#9051), the Knickerbocker Quintette's "The Rosary" (#9052), Edgar L. Davenport's "Jim Bludsoe" (#9053), Billy Murray's "My Irish Molly O" (#9063), and Ada Jones and Len Spencer's "Louis and Lena at Luna Park" (#9064).

September 1. Releases by Edison Moulded Records included Hebert L. Clarke and John Hazel's "Swiss Boy" (#9077), Ada Jones and Len Spencer's "Chimmie and Maggie at the Hippodrome" (#9079), Miss Marie Narelle's "Killarney" (#9081), Irving Gillette's "Little Girl You'll Do" (#9094), and Billy Murray's "Give My Regards to Broadway" (#9095).

October. The *Edison Phonograph Monthly* reports on the popularity of slot phonographs in penny arcades across the nation.

October 1. Releases by Edison Moulded Records included Bob Roberts' "Everybody Works But Father" (#9100), Theo. Van Yorx's "I Wait For Thee" (#9102), Miss Elene Forster's "The Village Seamstress" (#9103), Samuel Siegel's "Evening on the Plaza" (#9113), and Billy Murray's "Hiram Green, Good-Bye" (#9118).

November 1. Releases by Edison Moulded Records included Billy Murray's "In Timbuctoo" (#9127), Byron G. Harlan's "Wait 'Till the Sun Shines, Nellie" (#9130), Ada Jones' "I'm the Only Star That Twinkles on Broadway" (#9135), Edward Barrow's "The Irish Girl I Love" (#9140), Edward M. Favor's "Fol-the-rol-lol" (#9142).

December. *Variety* begins publication. The trade weekly focuses on the entertainment business, including vaudeville, theater, the cinema, and other mass media.

December 1. Releases by Edison Moulded Records included Hans Kronold's "Traumerei" (#9149), Andrew Keefe's "I'm Old but I'm Awfully Tough" (#9152), Collins and Harlan's "Nigger Loves His Possum" (#9160), Frank Bush's "Short Stories by Frank Bush" (#9163), Billy Murray's "Sympathy" (#9164), and the Edison Male Quartette's "Silent Night" (#9168).

1906

❄

January. The *Edison Phonograph Monthly* includes a response by the National Phonograph Co. to occasional inquiries that their recordings include print-outs of the lyrics to the songs. The company deems it to be cost prohibitive due to reproduction costs and the likelihood that song publishers would demand financial reimbursement.

January 1. Releases by Edison Moulded Records included the Edison Concert Band's "The Choristers" (#9170) and "It Blew! Blew! Blew! Schottische" (#9185), MacDonough and Biehling's "Good-Bye 'Dixie' Dear" (#9187), Billy Murray's "Yankee Boodle" (#9188), and Spencer and Holt's "Barnyard Serenade" (#9190).

January 7. Sousa's Band kick off their first tour of the year at New York City's Hippodrome. It winds through New England, the South, and the Midwest (including Toronto) before ending with another Hippodrome concert April 8.

February 1. Releases by Edison Moulded Records included Eugene Rose's "'Genevieve' Waltz Medley" (#9197), Joe Belmont's "College Life March" (#9203), Billy Murray's "Lazy Moon" (#9204), Madge Maitland's "Is Everybody Happy?" (#9210), Arthur Collins' "Robinson Crusoe's Isle" (#9211), and Ada Jones and Len Spencer's "The Original Cohens" (#9215).

March. The *Edison Phonograph Monthly* includes a National Phonograph Co. announcement that jobbers and dealers would do well to advertise the seventy-four recordings—termed "cut-outs—that were eliminated from the February 1st *Record Catalogue*. The firm states, that while these selections "are quite as attractive as anything in the catalogue," it is necessary to trim stock with approximately three hundred new titles being released annually.

March 1. Releases by Edison Moulded Records included Andrew Keefe's "Uncle Josh Weathersby in a Department Store" (#9221), Ada Jones' "Just a Little Rocking Chair and You" (#9222), Bob Roberts' "My Name is Morgan, but It Ain't J.P." (#9227), Billy Murray's "Forty-Five Minutes from Broadway" (#9231), and Edward Meeker's "What's the Use of Knocking (When a Man is Down)" (#9234).

March 26. The New York Circuit Court of Appeals issues an injunction against the National Phonograph Co. from selling phonographs and records in violation of contracts granted the New York Phonograph Company by the now defunct North American Phonograph Company in 1896. Edison continues to do business in that state, contending that the rights outlined in this prior agreement had long since expired, and promising to protect its jobbers and dealers with the best legal representation money can buy.

April 1. Releases by Edison Moulded Records included Irving Gillette's "When the Whip-poor-will Sings, Marguerite" (#9243), Spencer and Porter's "Flanagan's Night Off" (#9244), Miss Hoy and Mr. Anthony's "I Would Like To Marry You" (#9248), Albert Benzler's "Ching Chang—Chinese Galop" (#9253), Billy Murray's "You're a Grand Old Rag" (#9256).

April 15. Sousa's Band begin their second tour of the year at New York City's Hippodrome. Limited to venues in New England and Montreal, it ends May 6 at the Hippodrome.

April 18. San Francisco suffers major damage from an earthquake. Edison's West Coast jobber, Peter Bacigalupi, provides an eyewitness account of the event in the July issue of the *Edison Phonograph Monthly* (pp. 10–12).

May 1. Releases by Edison Moulded Records included Ada Jones' "My Little Dutch Colleen" (#9267) and "So Long, Mary" (#9288), Harlan G. Harlan's "Keep on the Sunny Side" (#9271), the Edison Minstrels' "At the Minstrel Show—Nos. 1-6" (#s 9275-9280), and Collins and Harlan's "Traveling" (#9287).

June 27. Releases by Edison Moulded Records included Alan Turner's "In Happy Moments" (#9291), Leopold Moeslein's "Sailor's Hornpipe Medley" (#9293), Billy Murray's "If Washington Should Come To Life" (#9300), Irving Gillete's "Lonesome Little Maid" (#9303), Will F. Denny's "Nothing Like That in Our Family" (#9306), and George P. Watson's "Chas. T. Ellis' Baby Song" (#9308).

July. Implementing a proposal by Guglielmo Marconi (inventor of the wireless spark transmitter) made during his visit to the American Graphophone Company's Bridgeport plant, Columbia introduces the Velvet-Tone thin, flexible laminated shellac record, which features a paper core. The format demonstrates a reduction in surface noise compared with standard shellac discs.

July 27. Releases by Edison Moulded Records included Ada Jones' "Waiting at the Church" (#9315), Anthony and Harrison's "Heaven Is My Home" (#9319), Spencer and Porter's "The Morning After" (#9326), Billy Murray's "I'm Up in the Air About Mary" (#9329), and Ada Jones and Len Spencer's "Bashful Henry and His Lovin' Lucy" (#9335).

August 27. Releases by Edison Moulded Records included Billy Murray's "Waltz Me Around Again, Willie" (#9340), John Kimmble's "American Calk Walk" (#9341), Harry MacDonough's "Where the River Shannon Flows" (#9344), Edward M. Favor's "The Umpire is a Most Unhappy Man" (#9352), and the Edison Mixed Quartette's "I Surrender All" (#9353).

September. John Philip Sousa contributes an article, "The Menace of Mechanical Music," to *Appleton's Magazine*. He warns that records could cause a deterioration of musical taste and put many musicians out of work. He goes on to say that the desire to study music would be diminished, with future Mozarts and Wagners losing their incentive to create new work.

September 8. The New York *Evening Post* publishes a reply to John Philip Sousa's attack on all mechanical playing devices in the September issue of *Appleton's Magazine*:

> "Canned music" is the epithet applied by Mr. Sousa to the music made by phonographs and "piano-players." He strongly objects to it on the ground that it tends to blunt our national music sense. But it is a little difficult to see what there is to blunt in the musical sense of a nation which makes a hero of a Sousa, paying him $50,000 for a mediocre march not worth $50. The phonographs help make life more worth living to farmers and villagers.

September 16. Following an August 12 to September 3 residency at the Willow Grove (Pennsylvania) Part, Sousa's Band kicks off a final 1906 tour at the Cumberland, Maryland, Academy of Music. It will cover the Midwest, Boston, and New York state before ending October 28 at New York City's Hippodrome.

September 27. Releases by Edison Moulded Records included Helen Trix's "Is Your Mother In, Molly Malone?" (#9365), Hans Kronold's "Simple Confession" (#9366), Miss Hinkle and Mr. MacDonough's "Softly and Tenderly" (#9367), Ada Jones' "If the Man in the Moon were a Coon" (#9372), and Billy Murray's "Come Take a Skate with Me" (#9380).

October. Newspaper magnate William Randolph Hearst deploys cylinder recordings of his speeches while campaigning for the governor's office in the state of New York. The wax Graphophone masters are manufactured by Columbia in New York City, electroplated and molded, and distributed for playback at public gatherings and circulation by libraries.

October. Paris-based Pathe Records begins producing shellac-based records after experimenting with single-sided discs with a recording in wax on top of a cement base. The company's output, however, remains unique in that the vertically cut grooves are wider than those employed by other labels. In addition, they rotated at 90 rpm—rather than the usual 78–80 rpm—and started on the inside near the center of the disc, spiraling out to the edge. The irregularities—which required Pathe playback equipment, limited the firm's ability to compete in the U.S. or U.K. markets.

October 15. A letter, written by "Veritas," is published by the *Talking Machine News* which questions whether Thomas Edison invented the phonograph. Another letter in the same vein, signed by Henry Seymour, is included in the journal's November 1 issue. Frank L. Dyer, General Counsel of the National Phonograph Co., composes a lengthy reply reasserting Edison's claim as the inventor of the talking machine, which is published in the London edition of the *Edison Phonograph Monthly* for January 1907. It is reprinted in the February issue of *EPM*'s American edition. The company continued to use its commercial and political muscle to press the Edison perspective until forced out of business by the Great Depression.

October 27. Releases by Edison Moulded Records included Billy Murray's "Are You Coming Out To-night, Mary Ann?" (#9395), Harry MacDonough's "Not Because Your Hair Is Curly" (#9398), Harlan and

Stanley's "The Rube and the Country Doctor" (#9399), Florence Hinkle's "Lover and the Bird" (#9400), and the Edison Male Quartette's "Since Nellie Went Away" (#9408).

November. The *Edison Phonograph Monthly* provides a tour (with photos) of Edison's start-of-the-art Recording Department, opened in mid-1905 on the seventeenth floor of the Knickerbocker building, Manhattan. Included is a description of the acoustic recording process.

November 27. Releases by Edison Moulded Records included Collins & Harlan's "Camp Meeting Time" (#9415), Ada Jones' "Hottentot Love Song" (#9418), Arthur Collins' "Abraham Jefferson Washington Lee" (#9423), Billy Murray's "My Mariuccia Take-a Steamboat" (#9430), and Ada Jones and Len Spencer's "Down on the Farm" (#9431).

December 1. The *Sioux City* (Iowa) *Tribune* reports that a Council Bluffs resident, Rudolph Walter, received a phonograph recording that day from his parents, who were then in England. In addition to talking to him, they had his sister sing one of his favorite songs. Walter indicated that he would return the favor for the Christmas holidays.

December 6. A John Philip Sousa article in New York's *Town Topics* describes a fictitious concert played by a stage full of phonographs conducted by a "Professor Punk" and tells of a performance of *Faust* by an all-star cast at the home of the "Automated Opera." He notes that the event ushered in a new era in which mechanical devices would completely replace conventional instruments.

December 25. The Christmas 1906 issue of *Musical Trades* includes an article written by John Philip Sousa entitled "My Contention." He argues that the wording of the existing copyright law is ambiguous and is being interpreted by record producers to their advantage.

December 27. Releases by Edison Moulded Records included Harlan and Stanley's "Tramp! Tramp! Tramp! (#9439), W. H. Thompson's "Why Can't a Girl Be a Soldier" (#9446), Collins and Harlan's "Arrah Wanna" (#9447), Mrs. Alice Shaw and Twin Daughters' "Spring-Tide Revels" (#9448), and Billy Murray's "When Tommy Atkins Marries Dolly Gray" (#9451).

1907

❄

January 28. Releases by Edison Moulded Records included the Vassar Girls Quartette's "Kentucky Babe" (#9460), Billy Murray's "A Lemon in the Garden of Love" (#9462) and "Alice, Where Art Thou Going?" (#9474), Collins & Harlan's "Good-a-bye John!" (#9463), Andrew Keefe's "Uncle Josh in a Chinese Laundry" (#9466), Miss Hinkle and Miss Keyes' "Looking This Way" (#9467), James F. Harrison's "Good Bye, Sweet Maryland" (#9468), J. W. Myers' "Night Time" (#9470), and "Whistle It" (#9471), a selection from *The Red Mill* interpreted by Miss Trix and Messrs. Meeker and Murray.

February. The *Edison Phonograph Monthly* publishes an article entitled "Doubtful Points Legally Interpreted." Intended to serve as an ethical and commercial for Edison jobbers and dealers, it provides lengthy responses to the following questions:

1. What constitutes a proper initial order from a new Dealer, and what is meant by a suitable store?
2. Can an authorized Dealer sell out his business to another party, provided his successor continues the sale of our goods?
3. Can a Dealer who was sold out his business open up in another town without placing the initial order required of a new Dealer?
4. Is a Dealer allowed a pay a commission, and may the commission be paid in Records?
5. Can Jobbers or Dealers enter into contracts with newspapers to handle premium machines and exchange such machines for Edison machines, and also enter into a Contract with a subscriber for the purchase of Edison Records as a part consideration for the delivery of the premium machine without violating the Conditions of Sale?

February 27. Releases by Edison Moulded Records included Ada Jones' "My Irish Rosie" (#9484), the Edison Venetian Trio's "Memories of Home" (#9485), Steve Porter's "Flanagan's Troubles in a Restaurant" (#9495), Billy Murray's "Waiting for a Certain Girl" (#9496), Collins 7 Harlan's "Bake Dat Chicken Pie" (#9499), and S. H. Dudley's "Merry Whistling Darkey" (#9502).

March 27. Releases by Edison Moulded Records included a harp solo, "Angel's Serenade" (##9509), by Charles Schuetze, Louise Le Baron's "That's What the Rose Said to Me" (#9518), Collins & Harlan's "My Kickapoo Queen" (#9519), Billy Murray's "Ida-Ho!" (#9520), and Edward Meeker's "Do, Re, Mi, Fa, Sol, La, Si, Do" (#9526).

April. The *Edison Phonograph Monthly* reports that the National Phonograph Co.'s volume of business for the 1906–1907 fiscal year increased 50 percent over the preceding year.

April 27. Releases by Edison Moulded Records included Bob Roberts' "No Wedding Bells for Me" (#9538), Edith Helena's "The Last Rose of Summer" (#9546), Billy Murray's "San Antonio" (#9547), Frederick H. Potter's "Let Me Hear the Band Play, 'The Girl I Left Behind'" (#9548), and Will F. Denny's "Ask Me Not" (#9551).

May. The *Scientific American* describes a time-controlled phonograph—consisting of a spring which trips a lever attached at one end to an ordinary alarm clock, while at the other end a cord which passes over a pulley is connected to the starting lever of a phonograph—invented by Dr. J. E. Hett of Berlin, Ontario. The mechanism appears to have been created to function primarily as a more pleasant form of alarm clock.

May 27. Releases by Edison Moulded Records included Billy Murray's "In Washington" (#9558), Collins & Harlan's "Reed Bird (The Indian's Bride)" (#9559), W. H. Thompson's "It's a Long Way Back to Dear Old Mother's Knee" (#9560), the Edison Vaudeville Co.'s "Mrs. Clancy and the Street Musicians" (#9564), and Ada Jones and Len Spencer's "Becky and Izzy" (#9572).

June 25. Victor and G&T (The Gramophone and Typewriter Co.), a London offshoot of the Washington D.C.-based Berliner Gramophone Co., sign an agreement which divides the world into two distinct trading sectors. The contract would remain in effect until 1957.

June 27. Releases by Edison Moulded Records included the Edison Military Band's "Dream of the Rarebit Fiend" (#9585) and "Shoulder Arms March" (#9601), Billy Murray's "Because I'm Married Now" (#9586), Bob

Roberts' "You' Have to Wait Till My Ship Comes In" (#9590), Frank C. Stanley's "Hymns of the Old Church Choir" (#9592), and Edward Meeker's "Save a Little Money for a Rainy Day" (#9596).

July. The *Edison Phonograph Monthly* heralds the appearance of a "new type of Edison phonograph," the Alva, designed to meet the demand for a player that can be operated by alternating current widely used in most communities. Listing for $80, it is similar to Edison's Triumph model, possessing the same cabinet and general mechanism (except the motor).

July 27. Releases by Edison Moulded Records included Reinald Werrenrath's "My Dear" (#9604), Billy Murray's "He Goes To Church On Sunday" (#9612), August Molinari's "Street Piano Medley" (#9615), Edward Meeker's "Harrigan" (#9616), and Murry K. Hill's "In the Good Old Steamboat Days" (#9619).

August 8. Sousa's Band begin their 1907 tour with a performance at the Asbury Park, New Jersey, Casino. Covering the continental United States, it ends December 14 at the Albany, New York, Armory.

August 27. Releases by Edison Moulded Records included Ada Jones' "Jack and Jill" (#9627), Manuel Romain's "When the Bluebirds Nest Again, Sweet Nellie Gray" (#9628), Billy Murray's "I'd Rather Two-Step Than Waltz, Bill" (#9634), Edward Meeker's "I Think I Oughtn't Ought to Any More" (#9638), and Harlan and Belmont's "The Blue Jay and the Thrush" (#9648).

September 27. Releases by Edison Moulded Records included Reed Miller's "The Birds in Georgia Sing of Tennessee" (#9658), Ada Jones and Billy Murray's "Will You Be My Teddy Bear?" (#9659), Lilian Doreen's "Take Me Back to New York Town" (#9666), Joe Belmont's "Snow Bird Mazurka" (#9667), Billy Murray's "In the Land of the Buffalo" (#9668), and the Edison Minstrels' "Dixie Minstrels" (#9672).

October. In an article titled, "Collections of Rare Records," the *Edison Phonograph Monthly* states "there is no doubt but that as home recording becomes more understood and carefully studied, collections of records will be made just as today collections of rare autographs arouse much interest and obtain enormous prices when put up at auction."

October 28. Releases by Edison Moulded Records included Billy Murray's "Who? Me?" (#9680), Irving Gillette's "June Moon" (#9682), Ada Jones and Billy Murray's "Kiss, Kiss, Kiss" (#9683), Arthur Collins' "If I'm Goin'to Die, I'm Goin' to Have Some Fun" (#9684), and the Edison Vaudeville Company's "At the Village Post Office" (#9687).

November 1. G&T changes its name back to The Gramophone Co. Ltd. (which had last been employed in December 1900). Firm headquarters—formerly at 31 Maiden Lane, London—are relocated to the new factory at Hayes, Middlesex.

November 27. Releases by Edison Moulded Records included Collins & Harlan's "In Monkey Land" (#9700), Irving Gillette's "Some Day When Dreams Come True" (#9702), Ada Jones' "Wouldn't You Like to Have Me for a Sweetheart?" (#9706), the Edison Vaudeville Company's "Three Rubes Seeing New York" (#9707), James Brockman's "Marianina" (#9712), and Len Spencer and Gilbert Girard's "Old Dog Sport" (#9715).

December 23. Releases by Edison Moulded Records included Frederic Rose's "Down in the Old Cherry Orchard" (#9723), Ada Jones and Billy Murray's "Smile, Smile, Smile" (#9724), James Brockman's "Mariutch" (#9730), Mr. and Mrs. Waterous' "O, Moment That I Bless" (#9731), and Billy Murray's "Dixie Dan" (#9742).

1908

❋

January 5. Sousa's Band begin their first tour of the year with a performance at the New York City Hippodrome. Covering New England, the South, and the Midwest, it ends March 3 at the Providence, Rhode Island Infantry Hall.

January 25. Releases by Edison Moulded Records included Billy Murray's "Somebody's Been Around Here Since I've Been Gone" (#9747), Stella Tobin's "Will He Answer 'Goo-Goo'?" (#9758), Steve Porter's "Imitation of Amateur Night at the Vaudeville" (#9764), and Arthur Collins' "Much Obliged to You" (#9768).

February. U.S. Circuit Court for the Eastern District of Pennsylvania determines in the case of the New Jersey Patent Company and National Phonograph Company vs. Fred G. Schaefer that Edison's selling contracts should be upheld, and enjoins the illegal sale of records at cut prices.

February 1. Seven Edison recordings by Scotch comedian Harry Lauder are released. They include some of his best-known material such as "I Love a Lassie" (#19178) and "Stop Yer Ticklin', Jock" (#19179).

February 25. Releases by Edison Moulded Records included Florence Hinkle's "Golden Sails" (#9774), the Edison Symphony Orchestra's "The Teddy Bears' Picnic" (#9777), Billy Murray's "I'm Afraid to Come Home in the Dark" (#9780), Frederic Rose's "The Heart You Lost in Maryland You'll Find in Tennessee" (#9782), and Steve Porter's "Flanagan's St. Patrick's Day" (#9790).

March. The *Edison Phonograph Monthly* denies a report circulating in the Midwest that Ada Jones recently died. It reports that she is in good health and making records for Edison each month.

March 1. Russian author Leo Tolstoy writes Thomas Edison thanking him for the gift of a phonograph for use "as a labor saving device."

March 25. Releases by Edison Moulded Records included Billy Murray's "Under Any Old Flag at All" (#9796), Charles D'Almaine's "Hornpipe Medley" (#9797), Ada Jones and Billy Murray's "When You Steal a Kiss—or Two" (#9799), Edward M. Favor's "I'm Looking for the Man That Wrote 'The Merry Widow Waltz'" (#9806), and Arthur Collins' "I Got to See de Minstrel Show" (#9812).

April 25. Releases by Edison Moulded Records included Ada Jones and Len Spencer's "Chimmie and Maggie at 'The Merry Widow'" (#9820), Edward M. Favor's "The Girl Who Threw Me Down" (#9831), Billy Murray's "One! Two! Three! All Over" (#9832), Edward Meeker's "Stuttering Dick" (#9836), and Ada Jones' "Pass It Along to Father" (#9838).

May. The *Edison Phonograph Monthly* includes the comments made by Frank L. Dyer, general counsel for the National Phonograph Co., at the congressional hearings for a proposed copyright bill:

> The National Phonograph Co. have signed no agreement providing for a two-cent royalty… Admitting that copyright protection can constitutionally extend to talking-machine records, and that public interests require new legislation on the point, my client, the National Phonograph Co., is willing to agree to any fair and reasonable arrangement. I am convinced, however, that the scheme is neither constitutional nor expedient.

May 25. Releases by Edison Records included Alan Turner's "Good-Bye, Sweetheart, Good-Bye" (#9843), Ada Jones and Billy Murray's "When the Song of Love is Heard" (#9844), the Edison Concert Band's "Humoresque on 'The Merry Widow Waltz'" (#9851), Spencer and Mozarto's "Krausmeyer's Birthday Party" (#9853), the Edison Military Band's "Nigger in the Barnyard" (#9856) and "Harry Lauder Medley" (#9865), Ada Jones; "All She Gets From the Iceman is Ice" (#9859), and Billy Murray's "Big Chief Smoke" (#9862).

June 1. Edison releases ten records by William Jennings Bryan. They include such orations as "The Labor Question" (#9915) and "Immortality" (#9923).

June 25. Releases by Edison Records included Ada Jones' "Smarty" (#9872), Ada Jones and Billy Murray's "When We Are M-A-Double-R-I-E-D" (#9875), Frederick Potter's "Topeka" (#9882), and Collins & Harlan's "Nothing Hardly Ever Bothers Me" (#9883).

July. Zon-o-phone issues Will F. Denny's "All the Girls Look Good to Me" (#1048). This appears to have been his last recording to be produced for any label.

July 25. Releases by Edison Records included Dorothy Kingsley's "It Always Comes With the Summer" (#9892), William Craig's "Lady Binnie and the Shores of Lake Erie" (#9893), Billy Murray's "Yankee Doodle Comes to Town" (#9895), Arthur Collins' "Mother Hasn't Spoke to Father Since" (#9898), Will Oakland's "When the Autumn Moon is Creeping Thro' the Woodlands" (#9902), and Ada Jones and Billy Murray's "A, B, C's of the U.S.A." (#9903).

August 3. William H. Taft records 12 speeches for Edison Records. Selections include "Irish Humor" (#9997) and "Rights and Progress of the Negro" (#10007). Along with the William Jennings Bryan recordings made earlier in the year, they are heavily promoted during the presidential campaign season.

August 16. Sousa's Band kicks off its final 1908 tour with a twenty-three-day residency at the Willow Grove (Pennsylvania) Park. Covering Ohio, West Virginia, Maryland, Virginia, and New Jersey, it ends with a concert at the New York City Hippodrome on October 18.

August 25. Releases by Edison Records included Len Spencer and Mozarto's "Sim and Sam, the Musical Coons" (#9923), Matt Keefe and George Stricklett's "Mother's Lullaby" (#9932), Ada Jones and Billy Murray's "I've Taken Quite a Fancy to You" (#9933), Billy Murray's "Starlight Maid" (#9938), and Collins & Harlan's "Down in Jungle Town" (#9941).

September 25. Releases by Edison Records included Ed Morton's "Don't Take Me Home" (#9949), Ada Jones and Billy Murray's "Cuddle Up a Little Closer, Lovey Mine" (#9950), the Edison Minstrels' "Jubilee Minstrels" (#9953), Frederic C. Freemantel's "Ah! So Pure" (#9962), Billy Murray's "Pride of the Prairie" (#9968), and the New York Military Band's "Genee Waltzes from 'The Soul Kiss'" (#9971).

October 1. Edison's wax Amberol series, with two hundred windings per inch—the first narrow-groove cylinders, double the previous standard, and capable for running for four minutes—is first issued. The extended playback capabilities led Edison to exploit the operatic repertoire and market the newly developed Amberola Phonograph with an enclosed horn. The Amberols were brittle, however, causing problems with rough handling; this led to Edison's introduction of the Blue Amberol configuration in 1912, which were constructed of durable (reputed to survive three thousand plays when used with the Edison Diamond Reproducer), relatively silent-surfaced plastic. Although the Blue Amberols never challenged the hegemony of the flat disc, they continued to be used in rural areas of North America until Edison shut down all phonograph-related operations on November 1, 1929. The first fifty issues include Steve Porter's "Flanagan and 'The Reillys' at a Baseball Game" (#4), Arthur Collins' "The Preacher and the Bear" (#18), Gu Reed's "Asleep in the Deep" (#20), Steve Porter's "A Police Court Scene" (#37), and Cal Stewart's "A Busy Week at Pumpkin Center" (#43).

October 2. Will Denny dies in Seattle at age forty-eight. He had suffered a seizure September 22 while touring the Pantages Circuit. The Boston native was a prolific artist during the first two decades of commercial recording: his biggest hits were "The Pretty Red Rose" (New England cylinder, 1892) and "Any Old Place I Hang My Hat Is 'Home Sweet Home' to Me" (Gram-o-Phone 956; 1901).

October 14. Nat M. Wills participates in his first Victor recording session. One track produced at the time, "'No News' or 'What Killed the Dog'" (#5612; reissued on 17222) becomes his biggest it, remaining in the Victor catalog until remade by Frank Crumit in 1927.

October 25. Releases by Edison Records included Amy Butler's "It's the Pretty Things You Say" (#9974), the American Symphony Orchestra's "Golden Blonde" (#9979), Thomas Chalmers' "Evening Star" (#9982), Steve Porter's "A Morning in Mrs. Reilly's Kitchen" (#9988), and the Knickerbocker Quartette's "Come Where My Love Lies Dreaming" (#9994).

November 25. Edison Standard (Two-Minute) Record releases include Cal Stewart's "Uncle Josh's Arrival in New York City" (#10016) and "Last Day of School at Pumpkin Centre" (#10021), Billy Murray's "I'm Glad I'm Married" (#10018) and "My Rosy Rambler" (#10022), and Ada Jones and Billy Murray's "Oh, You Coon! (#10025). Edison Amberol (Four-Minute) Record releases include Marshall P. Wilder's "A Few Short Stories" (#54) and "Stories About a Baby" (#57), Ada Jones' "When Grandma was a Girl" (#55), and Cal Stewart's "The County Fair at Pumpkin Center" (#59).

December 1. With the introduction of the new Amberol format, two hundred Edison Standard (Two-Minute) Records are withdrawn from the company catalogue.

December 24. Edison Standard Record releases include Cal Stewart's "Uncle Josh's New Year's Pledge" (#10034) and "Uncle Josh in a Roller Skating Rink" (#10048), Billy Murray's "Good Evening, Caroline" (#10038), Ada Jones and Billy Murray's "Rainbow" (#10049), and the Metropolitan Quartette's "Darling Nellie Gray" (#10053). Edison Amberol Record releases include the Empire Vaudeville Co.'s "Aunt Dinah's Golden Wedding" (#63) and Miss Chapman and Mr. Anthony's "Sing Me to Sleep" (#67).

1909

❄

January 25. Edison Standard Record releases include Cal Stewart's "Uncle Josh in Society" (#10058) and "Jim Lawson's Horse Trade" (#10070), Billy Murray's "Sullivan" (#10060), June Rossmore's "I Don't Like You" (#10062), and Ada Jones and Billy Murray's "A Can't Say You're the Only One" (#10069). Edison Amberol Record releases include Cal Stewart's "Uncle Josh Keeps House" (#75), Edith Chapman's "Mona" (#76), Ada Jones and Billy Murray's "Cohan's Pet Names" (#78), and Miss Stevenson and Mr. Stanley's "Battle Hymn of the Republic" (#79).

February 25. Edison Standard Record releases include Sallie Stembler's "Ev'rything's Funny to Me" (#10081), Cal Stewart's "Uncle Josh on a Fifth Avenue Bus" (#10085) and "Ground Hog Dog at Pumpkin Centre" (#10093), and Ada Jones and Billy Murray's "Oh, You Kid!" (#10090). Edison Amberol Record releases include Cal Stewart & Company's "Uncle Josh's Huskin' Bee" (#83) and the National Guard Fife and Drum Corps' "On Parade Medley" (#92).

March 25. Edison Standard Record releases include "Happy Days March" (#10097), by Maurice Levi and his Band, the American String Quartette's "Solitude of the Shepherdess" (#10100), Billy Murray's "Jennie" (#10107), and Ada Jones and Billy Murray's "I'm Looking for a Sweetheart and I Think You'll Do" (#10114). Edison Amberol Record releases include the Peerless Quartette's "Choruses of Six Popular Songs" (#110) and Golden and Hughes' "My Uncle's Farm" (#111).

April 24. Edison Standard Record releases include William Craig's "Sterling Castle and Harvest Dance" (#10120), Press Eldridge's "A Confidential Chat" (#10121), Harbert Payne's "Ayesha, My Sweet Egyptian" (#10125), Billy Murray's "I Used to Be Afraid to Go Home in the Dark" (#10127). Harry Fay's "I Don't Care if There's a Girl There" (#10133), and Ada Jones and Billy Murray's "Shine On, Harvest Moon" (#10134). Edison Amberol Record releases include Mabel McKinley's "Golden Rod" (#122), Billy Murray's "I'm Awfully Strong for You" (#130), and the Metropolitan Quartette's "Come Where the Lilies Bloom" (#131).

May 25. Edison Standard Record releases include "Brooke's Triumphal March (#101037), the label debut for the United States Marine Band, Ada Jones and Billy Murray's "Isn't Love a Grand Old Thing" (#10150), and "Denver Town" (#10155), the first offering by the Premier Quartette (aka American Quartet when recording for Victor).

Edison Amberol Record releases include Grace Cameron's "Adam and Eve" (#136) and "Gavotte – Caprice" (#152), a mandolin/guitar duet by Samuel Siegel and Roy H. Butin.

June 25. Edison Standard Record releases include Ada Jones and Billy Murray's "Blue Feather" (#10162), Billy Murray's "It Happens in Many Families" (#10167), and the Premier Quartette's "Good Night, Moonlight" (#10174). Edison Amberol Record releases include Digby Bell's "The Tough Kid on the Right Field Fence" (#156), Billy Murray's "When a Fellow's on the Level with a Girl That's on the Square" (#164), and Frederick Gunster's "Where is My Wandering Boy To-Night?" (#167).

July 24. Edison Standard Record releases include Nat M. Wills' "Parody 'Down in Jungle Town'" (#10178), Josie Sadler's "He Falls for the Ladies Every Time" (#10179), the Premier Quartette's "Little Willie" (#10186), and Ada Jones and Billy Murray's "Can't You See I Love You?" (#10190). Edison Amberol Record releases include Len Spencer's "The Arkansas Traveler" (#181), Arthur S. Witcomb's "Believe Me If All Those Endearing Young Charms" (#183), John Barnes Wells' "Good Night, Dear" (#187), and Eugene A. Jaudas' "Garry Owen Medley" (#189).

August 15. Sousa's Band begin their 1909 tour with a twenty-three-day residency at the Willow Grove (Pennsylvania) Park. It covers the continental United States as well as Quebec and Ontario before ending with a December 21 concert at Jackson's Theater, Bridgeport, Connecticut.

August 24. Edison Standard Record releases include Alexander Prince's "Scotch Reels" (#10200), Ada Jones and Billy Murray's "I'm Awful Glad I Met You" (#10202), Arthur Osmond's "I Played My Concertina" (#10209), and Billy Murray's "Take Me Up with You Dearie" (#10213). Edison Amberol Record releases include Miss Ray Cox's "The Baseball Girl" (#196), Pete Murray's "Lily of the Prairie" (#207), and Ada Jones and Billy Murray's "Googy-oo" (#211).

September 1. Edison introduces the mahogany-sided Cygnet Horn, which promotional literature claims combines attractiveness with fidelity and functionality.

September 13. *The Chocolate Soldier* premieres at New York's Lyric Theatre. Featuring music by Oscar Strauss and lyrics and book by Stanislaus Stange, it would run for 296 performances. The musical represented an English translation of *Der Tapfere Soldat* (originally presented in Vienna in 1908), which was adapted from the George Bernard Shaw play, *Arms and the Man*.

September 25. Edison Standard Record releases include the Whitney Brothers Quartette's "Santa Lucia" (#10230), Arthur C. Clough's "When the Meadow Larks Are Calling, Annie Laurie" (#10233), and Collins & Harlans "Down at the Huskin' Bee" (#10234). Edison Amberol Record releases include Billy Murray's "I've Got Rings On My Fingers" (#218), P. J. Frosini's "Seneca Waltz" (#223), Earl Cartwright's "Two Grenadiers" (#251), and Ernest Pike & Peter Dawson's "Ever of Thee" (#258).

October 25. Edison Amberol Record releases—placed ahead of the two-minute cylinders for first time in the *Edison Phonograph Monthly*—include the "Stars and Stripes Forever March" (#285), the label debut for Sousa's Band, Victor Herbert and his Orchestra's "Selections from 'Little Nemo'" (#287), and Collins & Harlan's "Run, Brudder Possum, Run!" (#301). Edison Standard Record releases include Olly Oakley's "Oakley Quickstep" (#10244) and Cal Stewart's "Uncle Josh at the Opera" (#10253).

November 24. Edison Amberol Record releases include Ada Jones and Len Spencer's "The Golden Wedding" (#312), Billy Murray's "Good Luck, Mary" (#314), and Elizabeth Wheeler and Harry Anthony's "The Garden of Dreams" (#315). Edison Standard Record releases include the Premier Quartette's "Swanee Babe" (#10263) and Billy Murray's "Foolish Questions" (#10273).

December 24. Edison Amberol Record releases include John F. Burckhardt's "Annie Laurie and Home, Sweet Home" (#327), the Jorda-Rocabruna Instrumental Quintette's "Monte Cristo Waltz" (#333), and Ada Jones and Billy Murray's "Emmaline" (#343). Edison Standard Record releases include Bessie Wynn's "It's Hard To Find a Real Nice Man" (#10278), Jack Pleasants' "I Said 'Hooray'" (#10293), and the Premier Quartette's "Wedding Bells" (#10294).

1910

❄

January 25. Edison Amberol Record releases include Harvey Hindermeyer's [sic] "Hello, Mr. Moonman, Hello!" (#348), Collins & Harlan's "Slip on Your Gingham Gown" (#358), and Ada Jones and Billy Murray's "I'm Glad I'm a Boy and I'm Glad I'm a Girl" (#362). Edison Standard Record releases include Stella Mayhew's recording debut, "I'm Looking for Something to Eat" (#10298) and the Vienna Instrumental Quartet's "The Tin Soldier" (#10303).

February 25. Edison Amberol Record releases include the Manhattan Mixed Trio's "D They Think of Me at Home?" (#367), Billy Murray's "The Hat My Father Wore Upon St. Patrick's Day" (#382), "The Bonnie Blue Flag" (#389), by Polk Miler's Old South Quartette, and Harry Lauder's "The Bounding Sea" (#12119) and "When I Get Back Again to Bonnie Scotland" (#12132). Edison Standard Record releases include Marie Dressler's "I'm a Goin' to Change My Man" (#10318), H. Benne Henton's "Laverne" (#10321) and Ada Jones and Billy Murray's "What Makes the World Go 'Round" (#10330).

March 25. Edison Amberol Record releases include Edgar L. Davenport's "Sheridan's Ride" (#297) and Golden and Hughes' "The Two Happy Darkey Boys" (#403). Edison Standard Record releases include Cal Stewart's "Uncle Josh in a Chinese Laundry" (#10343) and Ada Jones and Billy Murray's "The Belle of the Barbers' Ball" (#10344).

April 1. John Yorke Atlee dies at age sixty-eight. Known as the "artistic whistler," he was one of the earliest recording stars with such hits as "The Mocking Bird" (Columbia, 1891), "Home, Sweet Home" (Columbia, 1891), and "After the Ball" (Columbia, 1893).

April 25. Edison Amberol Record releases include Billy Murray's "Has Anybody Here Seen Kelly?" (#416), Joe Maxwell's "I'd Like to Be the Follow that Girl is Waiting For" (#427), Ada Jones and Len Spencer's "The Suffragette" (#428), and "The Cubanola Glide" (432), by Collins & Harlan with the New York Military Band. Edison Standard Record releases include Billy Murray's "He's a College Boy" (#10354), Miss Marvin and Mr. Anthony's "Some Day" (#10355), Sophie Tucker's "That Lovin' Rag" (#10360), and Ada Jones' "By the Light of the Silvery Moon" (#10362).

May 25. Edison Amberol Record releases include Marie Florence's "My Hero" (#437), Billy Murray's "Casey" (#450), and Premier Quartette's "Farmyard Medley" (#451). Edison Standard Record releases include Roxy P. LaRocca's "Annie Laurie" (#10368) and Billy Murray's "What's the Matter With Father" (#10369).

June 25. Edison Amberol Record releases include "Patriotic Songs of America" (#457), by the New York Military and Premier Quartette, and Billy Murray's "Mister Pat O'Hare" (#464). Edison Standard Record releases include Vess L. Ossman's "The Moose March" (#10383) and Steve Poster's "Flanagan in Central Park" (#10390).

July 25. Edison Amberol Record releases include Stella Mayhew's "The Grizzly Bear" (#479), Pike and Kirkby's "Just for To-Night" (#486), Billy Murray's "The Morning After the Night Before" (#488), and the Premier Quartette's "A Night Trip to Buffalo" (#492). Edison Standard Record releases include J. Scott Skinner's "The Birlin Reels" (#10402) and Billy Murray's "I'm On My Way to Reno" (#10405).

August 13. Sousa's Band begin their first tour of the year with a performance at the Great Auditorium, Ocean Grove, New Jersey. Covering Pennsylvania and New York venues, it ends with a September 19–24 residency at the Pittsburgh Exposition.

August 25. Edison Amberol Record releases include Charles Daab's "Irish and Scotch Melodies" (#498), Maude Raymond's "Phoebe Brown" (#505), Billy Williams' "My Old Armchair" (#510), and the Premier Quartette's "Carry Me Back to Old Virginny" (#512). Edison Standard Record releases include "The Lady Bugs' Review" (#10421) and the Long Acre Quartette's "That Fussy Rag" (#10423).

August 30. *Madame Sherry* premieres at the New Amsterdam Theatre, in New York City. Featuring music by Karl Hoschna and lyrics and book by Otto Haurbach (changed to Harbach during World War I), it had a run of 231 performances. Notable songs included "Every Little Movement" and "Put Your Arms Around Me Honey."

September 24. Edison Amberol Record releases include Miss Barbour and Mr. Anthony's "Where the Daisies Bloom" (#522), Jere Sanford's "Yodling and Whistling Specialty" (#523), and Billy Murray's "Come Be My Sunshone, Dearie" (#531). Edison Standard Record releases include Edward Meeker's "Play That BarberShop Chord" (#1043) and the Knickerbocker Quartet's "Oft in the Stilly Night" (#10435).

October 25. Edison Amberol Record releases include "Red Wing" (#541), by Frederic Potter, Chorus and New York Military Band and Billy Murray's "Way Down in Cotton Town" (#543). Edison Standard Record releases include Billy Murray's "Nix on the Glow-Worm, Lena" (#10437) and Stella Mayhew and Billie Taylor's "That Beautiful Rag" (#10438).

November 6. Sousa's Band kick off a second 1910 tour with a concert at New York City's Metropolitan Opera House. Covering New England, Canada, the Midwest, and the Southeast, it ends with a December 14–20 residency at the Cement Exposition, Madison Square Garden, New York City.

November 7. *Naughty Marietta* premieres at the New York Theatre, in New York City. Featuring music by Victor Herbert and lyrics and book by Rida Johnson Young, it had a run of 136 performances. The classic work owed much to producer Oscar Hammerstein—forced into musical theater due to mounting debts associated with his operatic ventures—who brought in Herbert and two of his star opera singers, Emma Trentini and Orville Harrold. A movie version, starring Jeanette MacDonald and Nelson Eddy, was made in 1935.

November 25. Edison Amberol Record releases include Helen Clark's "The Man in the Silvery Moon" (#570), the New York Military Band's "By the Light of the Silvery Moon Medley" (#574), and Ada Jones and Billy Murray's "Silver Bell" (#576). Edison Standard Record releases include Will Oakland's "There's a Clock Upon the Mantel Striking One, Two, Three" (#10447) and Sophie Tucker's "Reuben Rag" (#10449).

December 12. Frank C. Stanley (real name: William Stanley Grinsted) dies of pleuro-pneumonia—the result of a cold contracted at the Waldorf-Astoria recital in New York City—at age forty-one. Widely considered the top bass vocalist in the acoustic era, he began his career playing the banjo, accompanying Arthur Collins on others on recordings in the late 1890s. He went on to fame as leader—and manager—of the Peerless Quartet. His hits included "Blue Bell" (Edison 8655; 1904) and "Tramp! Tramp! Tramp!" (Victor 16531; 1910).

December 24. Edison Amberol Record releases include Will Oakland's "Mother Machree" (#583) and Ada Jones' "You'se Just a Little Nigger, Still You'se Mine, All Mine" (#588). Edison Standard Record releases include Ada Jones and Billy Murray's "You're Mine, All Mine" (#10458) and Collins & Harlan's "Cotton Time" (#10464).

December 31. Edison discontinues five hundred Standard Records from its catalogue.

December 31. The Edison Sales Department Bulletin No. 59 outlines a new record exchange plan to take effect January 1, 1911. Among its provisions:

1. Dealers may return to Jobbers to the extent and under the conditions hereinafter indicated, any Edison (Domestic and Foreign) Records—Standard, Amberol or Grand Opera—listed more than one year previous to such return, receiving full credit at the rate of 21 cents for each Standard record, 30 cents for each Amberol record, 47 cents for each Standard Grand Opera record, 60 cents for each Amberol Grand Opera $1.00 record, 90 cents for each Amberol Grand Opera $1.50 record and $1.20 for each Amberol Grand Opera $2.00 record.

2. Dealers may return records o their Jobbers for credit as above to the extent of 10 percent of their record purchases for every three months as advised by Jobber...

1911

❄

January 2. Sousa's Band perform at Queen's Hall, London, the first of a six-day engagement featuring two daily concerts. They kick off a 352-day world tour covering 47,346 miles—"the most extensive tour undertaken by a musical organization of that size." (Paul Edmund Bierley. *The Incredible Band of John Philip Sousa*. University of Illinois Press, 2006)

January 6. George Walker dies of syphilis in Islip, New York. Along with Bert Williams, he was part of a popular comedy team from the mid-1890s up through their last performance together in Louisville in February 1909.

January 25. Edison Amberol Record releases include Miss Spencer and Mr. Ormsby's "Alma" (#601), Reinald Werrenrath's "Asthore" (#602), and Berick von Norden's "The Lord Is My Light" (#612). Edison Standard Record releases include Ada Jones and Billy Murray's "Oh, You Dream" (#10472) and the Weber Male Quartet's "In Absence" (#10474).

February 25. Edison Amberol Record releases include the Premier Quartet's "Down on the Mississippi" (#626) and "The Jingle of Jungle Joe" (#638), Billy Murray's "Gee! But It's Great to Meet a Friend from Your Home Town" (#631), and Arthur C. Clough's "Let Me Call You Sweetheart" (#637). Edison Standard Record releases include Leon Rice's "When the Roses Bloom" (#10479) and W.H. Thompson's "Dreams, Just Dreams" (#10481).

March 18. Copyright is assigned to the Irving Berlin composition, "Alexander's Ragtime Band."

March 24. The *Louisville Times* publishes an article about the life of railroad engineer, John Luther Jones, who achieved immortality when an old round-house African American, Wallace Saunders, composed a song about Casey's fatal train accident on March 18, 1900. With some fifty to seventy-five verses added via the public domain, and a Broadway reinterpretation by T. Lawrence Seibert and Eddie Newton, Saunders continues to shovel coal and wipe engines for the Illinois Central railroad.

March 25. Edison Amberol Record releases include Billy Murray's "Stop, Stop, Stop" (#648), Ada Jones and Billy Murray's "Come Josephine in My Flying Machine" (#655), and Cal Stewart's "The Revival Meeting at Pumpkin Center" (#657). Edison Standard Record releases include Agnos Noll's "Sweet Red Roses" (#10487) and the Peerless Quartet's "Way Down East" (#10489).

April 17. Vaudeville and musical comedy star Emma Carus introduces "Alaexander's Ragtime Band" on stage.

April 25. Edison Amberol Record releases include Frank H. Doyle's "I Love the Name of Mary" (#667), Billy Murray's "Piano Man" (#673) and "Let Me Live and Stay in Dixieland" (#674), Marcus Kellerman's "Danny Deever" (#682), and the Empire Vaudeville Company's "Mother Goose Days" (#685). Edison Standard Record releases include the biggest selling Amberol recording of the past six months, "Silver Bell" (#10492), by Ada Jones and Billy Murray, and "That Girl" Quartet's "Honeymooning, Honey, in Bombay" (#10494).

May 25. Edison Amberol Record releases include Sophie Tucker's "Some of These Days" (#691), Ada Jones and Billy Murray's "There's Something About You, Dear, that Appeals to Me" (#695) and "Rainbow" (#699), the latter already one of biggest sellers in the Standard catalog, Guido Gialdini's "Birds of the Forest" (#701), and Karel Bondam's "Spinning Song" (#707). Edison Standard Record releases—all of which are make-overs previously issued in the Amberol format—include Billy Murray's "Casey Jones" (#10499) and Collins & Harlan's "The Cubanola Glide" (#10500).

June 24. Edison Amberol Record releases include Ada Jones' "All Alone" (#725), the National Promenade Band's "Huskin' Bee Medley" (#727), and the Knickerbocker Quartet's "Old Black Joe" (#738). Edison Standard Record releases—all make-overs from the Amberol catalog—include Ada Jones' big seller, "Any Little Girl, That's a Nice Little Girl, Is the Right Little Girl for Me" (#10502) and Ada Jones and Billy Murray's "Come, Josephine, in My Flying Machine" (#10505).

June 26. The Six Brown Brothers—a saxophone vaudeville act actually formed as a quintet comprised of Tom, William, Verne, Alex, and Fred Brown in 1910—make their first recordings in New York. The session results in "American Patrol"/"The Bullfrog and the Coon" (Columbia A-1041).

July. The *New Phonogram* celebrates its seventh anniversary. More than five hundred thousand copies of each issue are now being distributed to Edison owners worldwide.

July 10. Edison officially unveils the Edison Disc Phonograph at the Fifth Annual Convention of the National Association of Talking Machine Jobbers, Milwaukee, Wisconsin.

July 25. Edison Amberol Record releases include Anna Chandler's "In the Land of Harmony" (#741), the Metropolitan Quartet's "My Hula Hula Love" (#742), Guido Deiro's "My Sweetheart" (#743), "Yankee Doodle" (745), by the Premier Quartet and New York Military Band, Frederick Weld's "By the Saskatchewan" (#755), and the Garde Republicaine Band's "Hungarian Serenade (#757). Edison Standard Record releases include Billy Murray's reworking of the Ada Jones Amberol hit, "All Alone" (#10509) and the Whitney Brothers' Quartet's "Forsaken" (#10510).

August 19. A full-page ad in *Variety* taken out by the Snyder Company terms its song, "Alexander's Ragtime Band" "The Song Sensation of the Century…" Recordings would flood the marketplace, including versions by Collins & Harlan, the Victor Military Band, and Billy Murray.

August 25. Edison Amberol Record releases include Dr. Franklin Lawson's "Tell Her I Love Her So" (#769), Walter Van Brunt's "I'm Just Pinin' for You" (#771) and "Any Girl Looks Good in Summer" (#775), and Stanley Kirkby's "Your Eyes Have Told Me So" (#781). Edison Standard Record releases include Sousa's Band's "The Lion Chase" (#10511) and Marie Narelle and Mary Jordan's "Every Little Movement" (#10512).

September 25. Edison Amberol Record releases include Fred Van Epps' "Dixie Medley" (#804), Evan Baldwin's "Oh Tiny, Play That 'Traumerei'" (#805), and Bessie Volckmann's "Good-Bye, Sweet Day" (#809). Edison Standard Record releases include Manuel Romain's "Down in Sunshine Valley" (#10519) and the Vienna Instrumental Quartet's "In Vienna – Serenade" (##10520).

October 9. Harry Lauder begins his fourth American tour at the Manhattan Opera House.

October 25. Edison Amberol Record releases include Billy Murray's "Alexander's Ragtime Band" (#817), Walter Van Brunt's "The Old Town is Looking Mighty Good Tonight" (#825) and "I Want a Girl" (#832), and the Premier Quartet's "The Washington Waddle" (#827). Edison Standard Record releases include Billy Murray's "Alexander's Ragtime Band" (#10522)—the first instance of a simultaneous issue in both cylinder formats—and the Premier Quartet's "When I'm Alone I'm Lonesome" (#10523).

November 25. Edison Amberol Record releases include the third saxophone solo recording to be included in the firm's catalog, Harry S. Barbour's "Tyrolienne Serenade" (#843), Henri Scott's "O'er the Fresh Green Fields" (#844), Billy Murray's "The Oceana Roll" (#846), Roland Hogue's "You're the Queen in the Kingdom of My Heart" (#850), and R. Festyn Davies' "Open the Gates of the Temple" (#858). Edison Standard Record releases include the National Military Band's "With Sword and Song March" (#19526) and Ethel Hepburn's "Will the Roses Bloom in Heaven? (#10527).

December 10. Sousa's Band end their 1911 world tour with performances at the New York City Hippodrome.

December 23. Edison Amberol Record releases include Billy Murray's "Any Place the Old Flag Flies" (#875), Charles R. Hargreaves' "O'er the Blue Waters" (#878), Mary Hissem-de Moss's "Ecstasy" (#883), the Frank Croxton Quartet's "Flora's Holiday" (#884), Lottie Gilson's "Can't You Take It Back and Change It for a Boy?" (#890), and the Premier Quartet's "That Mysterious Rag" (#893). Edison Standard Record releases include Ada Jones'"You've Got to Take Me Home To-night" (#10533) and the Premier Quartet's "The Red Rose Rag"(#10535).

1912

❄

January 24. Edison Amberol Record releases include Nevada Van der Veer-Miller's "Trust in the Lord" (#898), Joseph A. Phillips' "The Chase" (#901), and the Premier Quartet's "Oh, That Navajo Rag" (#917) and "Oh You Beautiful Doll" (#921). Edison Standard Record releases include Walter Van Brunt's "There's a Dixie Girl Who's Longing for a Yankee Doodle Boy" (#10538) and a make-over of Amberol #693—"That Mysterious Rag" (#10539), by the Premier Quartet—one of the big novelty hits of the season.

February 24. Edison Amberol Record releases include the 5th Eve. Presbyterian Church Choir's "23rd Psalm" (#929), Maurice Burkhart's "After the Honeymoon" (#932), and Manhatten Ladies' Quartet's "Pussy's in the Well" (#941). Edison Standard Record releases include the New York Military Band's "Silver Star" (#10541) and "La Paloma" (#10544), by the Trio Instrumental "Arriga."

February 26. Edison issues nine Amberol Records (#s 978-986) featuring the Fisk University Jubilee Quartet singing Negro religious and plantation songs.

March 25. Edison Amberol Record releases include three vaudeville-style selections by Irene Franklin—"I've Got the Mumps" (#950), "The Talkative Waitress" (#951), and "I Want to be a Janitor's Child" (#952)—Billy Murray's "Rum Tum Tiddle" (#954), the Premier Quartet's "Moonlight Bay" (#962) and "Ragtime Violin" (#966), and Elsie Baker's "Your Smile" (#971). Edison Standard Record releases include companion releases of Muray's "Rum Tum Tiddle" (#10548) and the Premier Quartet's "Moonlight Bay" (#10550).

April 25. Edison Amberol Record releases include the Premier Quartet's "That Coontown Quartet" (#996) and "That Hypnotizing Man" (#1001), Fred Van Epps' "Alexander Ragtime Band Medley" (#1002), and Andre Benoist's "Old Folks at Home, with Variations" (#1006). Edison Standard Record releases include Elsie Baker's "Pickaninny's Lullaby" (#10552) and Walter Van Brunt's make-over of Amberol #910, "I Want "a Regular Pal" for a "Gal" (#10553).

May 25. Edison Amberol Record releases include Collins & Harlan's "The Darkies' Ragtime Ball" (#1020), Charles Daab and William Dorn's "'So So' Polka" (#1021), the Metropolitan Quartet's "Golden Deer" (#1027), and Julius Spindler's "Long, Long Ago – with Variations" (#1034). Edison Standard Record releases include Elizabeth Spencer's "Absent" (#10557) and Byron G. Harlan's "They Gotta Quit Kickin' My Dawg Aroun'" (#10559).

June 25. Edison Amberol Record releases include Donald Chalmers' debut selection, "Till the Sands of the Desert Grow Cold" (#1043), Bill Murray's "The Gaby Glide" (#1049) and "Mammy's Shufflin' Dance" (#1051), and Irene Armstrong's "My Laddie" (#1055). Edison Standard Record releases include "Santa Lucia March" (#10561), by the H.M. Irish Guards Band, and Billy Williams' "My Father was Born in Killarney" (#10562).

July. Columbia terminates all cylinder production, opting hereafter to focus exclusively on the disc medium.

July 25. Edison Amberol Record releases include Harriet Bawden's "Ma Curly-Heady Babby" (#1066), Charles W. Harrison's "Oriental Rose" (#1068), George P. Watson's "Sauerkraut Is Bully Medley" (#1076), and Mildred Graham Reardon's "Embarrassment" (#1084). Edison Standard Record releases include Ada Jones' "Oh, Mr. Dream Man" (#10567) and Harvey Hindermyer and Donald Chalmers' "The Roses, The Robins and You" (#10569).

August 1. Edison introduces its new Home Recording Outfit, consisting of a four-minute recorder, three blank records, and a hand shaving machine.

August 24. Edison Amberol Record releases include Hugh Allan's "I Know a Lovely Garden"/"Because" (#1105), "Opera Burlesque, on Sextette from 'Lucia'" (#1107), by Billy Murray and Mixed Chorus), and Ada Jones' "Whistle It" (#1118), from *The Wall Street Girl*. Edison Standard Record releases include Walter Van Brunt's "I'd Love to Live in Loveland With a Girl Like You" (#10572) and the Premier Quartet's Amberol make-over, "The Skeleton Rag" (#10575).

September 25. Edison Amberol Record releases include Harry E. Humphrey's "Buck Fanshaw's Funeral" (#1127), the Cathedral Choir's "By the Old Cathedral Door" (#1128), the Heidelberg Quintet's "Under the Love

Tree" (#1131), Collins & Harlan's "Waiting for the Robert E. Lee" (#1144), Archie Anderson's "Will Yo No Come Back Again" (#12471), and William Davidson's "O Sing to Me the Auld Scotch Sangs" (#12474).

October 1. Edison introduces the new Blue Amberol configuration. From this point onward, all Edison Phonographs will be of the four-minute type only.

October 25. Edison Blue Amberol Record releases include Fred Van Eps' "Darkies' Dream"/"Darkies' Awakening" (#1544), the Empire Vaudeville Co.'s "Aunt Dinah's Golden Wedding" (#1563), Billy Murray's "Everybody Two Step" (#1587), "I'm the Guy" (#1592), and "Kentucky Days" (#1597), and Mary Carson's "O Dry Those Tears" (#1593).

November 20. Edison Blue Amberol Record releases—many of which are reissues than first appeared in the Amberol format—include Grace Kerns' "Roses Bloom for Lovers" (#1504), Ada Jones and Male Quartet's "By the Light of the Silvery Moon" (#1521), Ada Jones and Billy Murray's "Silver Bell" (#1524), the Emos Quartet's "Good-Night, Good-Night, Beloved" (#1548), and Billy Murray's "Casey Jones" (#1550), "When I Get You Alone Tonight" (#1602), and "Sweetheart Let's Go A-Walking" (#1607).

December. The *Edison Phonograph Monthly* comes out solidly in favor of price cutting in articles like "New Line-Cuts and a Few Suggestions" and "The Cut Prices Will Clean Up Your Stock."

1913

❅

January 1. A pubescent Louis Armstrong is picked up by the New Orleans police for firing a pistol the previous evening. He is sent to a reform school, the Coloured Waifs' Home, where he was allowed to join the band, eventually taking up the cornet.

February 1. Edison Blue Amberol Record releases include Collins & Harlan's "Row, Row, Row (#1529), Spindler, Santangelo and Giammatteo's "Dialogue for Three" (#1616), Arthur C. Lichty's "Sleepy Rose" (#1617), Edna Brown's "I'll Sit Right on the Moon" (#1623), and Royal Fish's "You're the Flower of My Heart, Sweet Adeline" (#1625).

March 15. Edison Blue Amberol Record releases include Helen Clark and Edwin Skedden's "When I Met You Last Night in Dreamland" (#1627), the Neapolitan Instrumenta Quartet's "How Could I Forget Thee" (#1630), Charles Hackett's "Mattinata" (#1636), Ferdinand Himmelreich's "Nearer, My God, to Thee" (#1647), and Albert A. Wiederhold's "Gipsy John" (#1649).

April 15. Edison Blue Amberol Record releases include "Medley of Country Dances" (#1716), by E.A. Jaudas, Charlotte Kirwan and Harvey Hindermyer's "Sympathy" (#1717), and Joseph Parsons' "Deep Down in My Heart" (#1727).

May 15. Edison Blue Amberol Record releases include Anna Chandler's "All Night Long" (#1739), the Edison Light Opera Co.'s "Favorite Airs from the Geisha" (#1740), and Campbell and Gillette's "Always Take a Girl Named Daisy" (#1762).

May 24. President Woodrow Wilson delivers an address to North American Indians via the Edison Phonograph at the White House.

June. The *Edison Phonograph Monthly* announces the first catalog of Blue Amberols and updated phonograph model catalog.

July 15. Edison Blue Amberol Record releases include the Premier Quartet's "You're a Great Big Blue Eyed Baby" (#1792), "Ragtime Violin" (#1806), and "And the Green Grass Grew All Around" (#1808), Ada Jones and Billy Murray's "Oh, You Silv'ry Bells" (#1800), the Edison Concert Band's "Glowworm" (#1807), and "Aloha Oe" (#1812), by Toots Paka's Hawaiians.

August 1. The debut of the inaugural Edison Disc Records list. The material is culled from Blue Amberol masters; recording artists are not listed. List prices range from $1 to $3 per disc. Releases include "Moonlight in Jungleland"—Baritone and Tenor Duet/"Below the Mason-Dixon Line"—Baritone Solo (#50001), "Home, Sweet Home"—Mixed Quartet/"The Swallow"—Mixed Quartet (#82033), and "Bird on the Wing"—Mixed Quartet/"Silent Night" – Soprano, Tenor and Baritone (#82040).

August 15. Edison Blue Amberol Record releases include Mrs. Clarence Eddy's "Kathleen Mavourneen" (#1828), Vernon Archibald's "Down by the Old Mill Stream" (#1829), Elizabeth Spencer and E. Eleanor Patterson's "I Would That My Love" (#1831), and Van Avery's "Just Plain Dog" (#1840). Many of the one hundred added monthly selections are reissues of four-minute Amberol masters.

September 15. Edison Blue Amberol Record releases include "Funny Doings at Sleepy Hollow" (#1929), by Harlan E. Knight and Co., Ada Jones and Billy Murray's standard, "Come, Josephine, in My Flying Machine" (#1949), and saxophonist H. Benne Henton's "The Kiss Waltz" (#1966).

October. Edison announces its first disc line, renamed the Edison Diamond-Disc in June 1914. Although the label continued to produce Blue Amberol cylinders until ceasing the productions of phonographs and records on November 1, 1929, it was clear that the format was losing ground fast as a commercially viable product. In contrast to the laterally cut grooves employed by the other American record companies, Edison's records employed the process first utilized by cylinders. According to Roland Gelatt (*The Fabulous Phonograph*),

> The combination of vertical-cut recording, individually ground diamond styli, and Edison's usual high standards of construction acted to make these instruments superior acoustically to any competing talking machine.

October 25. Edison Blue Amberol Record releases include Marie Kaiser's "Villanelle – Oft Have I Seen the Swift Swallow" (#2015), Ada Jones and Billy Murray's "Snow Deer" (#2021), and Steve Porter's "Alderman Doolin's Campaign Speech" (#2037).

November 18. Henry Burr, Albert Campbell, and countertenor Will Oakland cut "I'm On My Way to Mandalay" (Victor 17503)—apparently the first time three tenors sing together on a recording.

November 25. Edison Blue Amberol Record releases include T. Foster Why's "Thy Sentinel Am I" (#2065), Elizabeth Spencer and Billy Murray's "The Doll Girl" (#2066), and the National Promenade Band's "The Horse Trot" (#2076).

December 24. Edison Blue Amberol Record releases include Charlotte Kirwan and Kathryn Staats' "The Lord is My Shepherd" (#2117), Ernst Albert Couturier's "A Dream" (#2119), Emory B. Randolph's "When the Song Birds Sing No More" (#2120), Eliabeth Spencer and Walter Van Brunt's "Be My Little Baby Bumble Bee" (#2140), and Owen J. McCormack's "The Lass from the County Mayo" (#2142).

1914

❄

January. The Columbia Stellar Quartet's debut disc, "Sally in Our Alley"/"The Girl I Left Behind Me" (#1440) issued. The group—which specialized in popular and Broadway songs, was founded in late 1913 with members Charles Harrison and John Barnes Wells (tenors), baritone Andrea Sarto, and bass Frank Croxton.

February. Edison Blue Amberol Record releases include Henry Heidelberg's "The Nightingale" (#2149), George Wilton Ballard's "When the Twilight Comes to Kiss the Rose Good-night" (#2150), and Edward Sterling Wright's "A Little Christmas Basket"/"Howdy! Honey! Howdy! (#2152) and "When De Co'n Pones' Hot"/"Possum" (#2153).

March 19. Fred Van Eps—a minstrel-styled banjoist who first recorded on brown wax cylinders in the 1890s, makes his first ensemble dance recordings in New York for Victor.

August 6. Patrick Conway's Band record the first Victor disc to bear include the designation "Fox Trot." Composed by black ragtime composer Joe Jordan and titled "Sweetie Dear," it would be followed in short order by literally thousands of similarly described recordings.

October. The New York-based Little Wonder Record Company, founded by Henry Waterson of the music publishing firm Waterson, Berlin and Snyder, introduces single-sided 5½-inch discs listing for 10 cents. The first release features Henry Burr's "Ben Bolt"; he would appear on more Little Wonder records than any other vocalist.

December 15. Len (Leonard Garfield) Spencer, reputed to have been America's first nationally-known recording star, dies at age forty-seven. His career embraced a dizzying array of styles—sentimental ballads, minstrel songs, dramatic recitations, and comic duets—which enabled him to assume many ethnic roles. His hits included "Ta-Ra-Ra-Boom Der E" (Columbia, 1892), "Little Alabama Coon" (Columbia 7156; 1895), and "Arkansas Traveler" (Victor 1101, 1902; remake of his 1900 Columbia hit and the biggest seller of the pre-1905 era).

1915

✳

May. Henry Burr forms his own label, the Paroquette Record Manufacturing Co.

May. Victor Emerson announces the formation of the Emerson Phonograph Company, Inc. His business strategy would consist of exploiting the low-priced market and contracting out as much work as possible.

September 15. Jelly Roll Morton's "Jelly Roll Blues" is published—along with instrumental parts—in Chicago by Will Rossiter. Arranged by pianist Mel Stitze, it appears to have been the published jazz arrangement.

November. A Sergeant Dwyer, VC, records his eyewitness account of World War I conditions in the trenches for Regal, British Columbia's budget-priced subsidiary label. It was the first recording to address the conflict beyond comments made by notable politicians and other key figures. After returning to the front, from the leave which enabled him to provide his recorded insights, the young officer would be killed in action.

1916

❉

February 4. Having made many solo recordings in the past, Vess Ossman cuts his first tracks as the leader of Vess Ossman's Banjo Orchestra in Camden, New Jersey. The session produces one release, "Kangaroo Hop"/"Merry Whirl" (Victor 35536).

March 3. The Original Dixieland Jazz Band opens at Schiller's Café in Chicago, going on to achieve considerable success.

May 5. Jaudas's Society Orchestra makes its first recordings in New York for Edison.

August. Emerson announces plans to discontinue the manufacture of vertically cut records, focusing instead on universal-cut disc.

August. The Brooklyn-based Lynn Phonograph Company advertises the new Flemish record player in *Talking Machine World*.

September 18. Jim Europe enlists in the 15th New York Infantry. He would pass an officer's exam and was about to take command of a machine gun company when a colonel induces him to organize a military band.

September 25. Joseph C. Smith's Orchestra first records for Victor. One selection would end up on the "B" side of Stewart James's twelve-inch release, "Songs of the Night" (#35593). His group would specialize in dance renditions of songs and medleys from popular Broadway shows.

October. The Harmonola Company, headquartered in Philadelphia, advertises the new Harmonola phonograph in *Talking Machine World*.

October 31. Original Dixieland Jazz Band clarinetist Alcide Nunez is replaced by Larry Shields. Combined with the ouster of drummer Johnny Stein a few months earlier, and subsequent hiring of Tony Sbarbaro, the group's classic lineup is now set; other members include cornetist Nick La Rocca, pianist Henry Ragas, and trombonist Eddie Edwards.

December 1. Collins & Harlan become the first recording act to refer to the new music style called "jas." The song, "That Funny Jas Band from Dixieland," is issued in April 1917 as Blue Amberol 3140, itself a dub of Diamond Disc 50423 (released in July 1917).

1917

❄

January. Exclusive patent rights held by Edison, Columbia, and Victor begin to expire. As a result, new record companies begin entering the American marketplace, including Okeh, Brunswick, Vocalion, Pathe (France), and Emerson. The latter's introduction of an entirely new process for encoding audio data in record grooves (known as "hill-and-dale") enabled the label to avoid legal constraints.

January. The Emerson Dance Orchestra records for the first time in New York. The lineup would also be billed on some records as either the Emerson Military Band or the Emerson Symphony Orchestra; nevertheless, the material remained in dance band genre.

January 27. The Original Dixieland Jazz Band—and the new style of music they were paying—are propelled to the forefront of the entertainment business by means of a highly successful stint at Reisenweber's Restaurant in Manhattan. The band members—leader Nick LaRocca (cornet, composer of "Tiger Rag," "Livery Stable Blues," and other hit recordings), trombonist Eddie Edwards, pianist Harry Ragas, drummer Tony Sbarbaro, and clarinetist Larry Shields—got together and began playing in New Orleans, where jazz had been incubating for decades before the Eastern media anointed it the "next big thing."

February. The Columbia Graphaphone Co. is registered in Great Britain, listing Louis Sterling as manager and Sir George Croydon Marks as chairman. The venture was organized under the financial control of the U.S.-based parent company (which bore the same name effective January 28, 1913).

February 14. Borbee's Jazz Orchestra make their recording debut with the fox trot "It's a Long, Long Time" and the one-step "Just the Kind of a Girl You'd Love to Make Your Wife" (a Harry Von Tilzer composition). Issued as Columbia A2233 in July, the third "jass" group to appear on record.

February 26. The Original Dixieland Jazz Band become the first jazz act to record studio tracks, beginning with "Livery Stable Blues"/"Dixie Jass Band One-Step." Their recordings were huge sellers for a few years they were superseded by more innovative musicians such as Joe "King" Oliver, Kid Ory, Louis Armstrong, Jellyroll Morton, Fats Waller, and Duke Ellington in the 1920s.

March 7. The first jazz record, the Original Dixieland Jazz Band's "Livery Stable Blues"/"Dixie Jass Band One-Step" (Victor 18255) is released. It sells more than one million copies over the next eight years, drastically changing the course of popular music history in the process. Ironically, the Columbia label actually had recorded the Original Dixieland Jazz Band on January 30—about a month prior to the quintet's first studio date with Victor. The circumstances surrounding these developments were succinctly outlined by *The Guinness Book of Recorded Sound* (1984):

> Columbia had no idea how to record a quintet of cornet, trombone, clarinet, piano, and drums, nor did their musical director realise they were at their best playing the numbers they had worked out between them. Columbia insisted on their recording two popular dance tunes of the time, "Darktown Strutters' Ball" and "Indiana," but on hearing the results, decided against issue. Victor stepped in with superior recording and better understanding of what exactly was setting New York nightlife on fire, and though Columbia reversed the rejection decision, it was too late. Try as they might to find a similar band to pit against the Dixieland Jazz Band, they failed. As early as 1917–18 in the history of jazz, the talent simply was not there.

April 20. Dave Montgomery dies at age forty-six. He was half of the musical comedy duo, Montgomery and Stone, popular in Broadway shows, vaudeville, and minstrel shows. Partner Fred Stone died March 6, 1959, at age eighty-five.

April 26. Joe Natus dies at age fifty-seven. A member of the Big Four Quartet, he had a top-selling cylinder as a solo artist, "The Song That Reached My Heart" (North American, 1892).

May. Pathe releases the first record by Wilbur C. Sweatman and His Jass Band. They are the second jazz act to appear on a disc.

May 10. The first jazz cylinder, the Frisco Jazz Band's "Canary Cottage," is recorded by Edison, and issued in

August on its Blue Amberol series. Another song from the session, "Johnson 'Jass' Blues" (Blue Amberol 3254), is released the following month.

May 15. *Talking Machine World* announces a "new singing act now touring the Eastern States and featuring the well-known record makers, Billy Murray, Henry Burr, the Sterling Trio, Peerless Quartet, Collins & Harlan, with Theodore Morse as pianist." First referred to as the Phonograph Singers, their name would evolve into the Eight Popular Victor Artists by the 1920s. Through varying lineups (with Murray and Burr the only mainstays), the troupe would remain active until 1928.

June 4. Earl Fuller's Famous Jazz Band cuts "Slippery Hank" and "Yah-De-Dah." They are released as Victor 18321 in September. With the Original Dixieland Jazz Band refusing to record for Victor for a year following their sensational debut, the company relied on Fuller's ensemble to met the sudden demand for "jass" material.

September 21. Harry A. Yerkes makes his first recordings as a bandleader in New York. The resulting tracks— "Happy Sammies"/"That's It" (Columbia A-2482)—are credited to the Jazarimba Orchestra.

December 9. Humorist Nat Wills dies of an apparent suicide at age forty-four. He started out in the 1890s as end man of the Ideal Minstrels in Washington; by 1900, he'd found major success as a vaudeville comedian called the "gentlemanly tramp." Considered a master of parody writing and singing, his first recording—"No News" or "What Killed the Dog" (Victor 5612; 1909)—became his biggest seller.

December 10. Joseph M. Knecht—who served as musical director to the Waldorf Astoria Hotel, and from 1925 directed the B. F. Goodrich Silvertown Cord Orchestra—make his first recording in New York for Victor.

1918

❋

January. The Chicago-based Cable-Nelson Piano Co. begins producing the Dulcitone phonograph. The trademark will be filed April 14, 1919.

January. Emerson Records adds a line of nine-inch records selling for 75 cents. The label was founded in 1916 by Victor H. Emerson, who had been employed by Columbia Records as recording manager since the 1890s. He had been the co-developer of the extremely popular 10 cent Little Wonder disc. Early releases—available on seven-inch (retailing for 25 cents) and 5½-inch (ten cents) discs—concentrated on popular songs, dance numbers, and patriotic marches performed by small groups of unnamed musicians based in the New York area. After World War I, the company entered an ambitious expansion period, hiring "big name" artists such as Eddie Cantor, the Six Brown Brothers, and the Louisiana Five. However, the company would soon find itself overextended and went into receivership in 1921.

February 1. *Oh, Lady! Lady!!* premieres at the Princess Theatre in New York City. Featuring music by Jerome Kern and lyrics by P. G. Wodehouse—who also wrote the book with Guy Bolton—the musical had a run of 219 performances.

February 5. The trademark is filed for the Kimball phonograph, manufactured by the Chicago-based W.W. Kimball Company.

February 14. *Sinbad* premieres at New York City's Winter Garden. Featuring music by Sigmund Romberg, lyrics and book by Harold Atteridge, the musical—which had a run of 388 performances—was essentially a one-show show built around Al Jolson. Utilizing his customary blackface makeup, Jolson would frequently interpolate songs between different adventures, most notably "Rock-a-Bye Your Baby With a Dixie Melody" (m. Jean Schwartz-w. Sam Lewis, Joe Young) and "Swanee" (George Gershwin's first hit composition).

March 25. The trademark (in use since November 1, 1916) is filed for the Nightingale phonograph, produced by the Chicago-based Nightingale Manufacturing Company.

May. Thornell-Manton, based in New York City, advertises its new Recruit phonograph in *Talking Machine World*.

May 22. The assets—including thirty thousand discs—of Henry Burr's Par-o-ket (Paroquette) label are unloaded at a public auction in Brooklyn. The firm was hurt by the fact that few phonographs at the time were equipped to play vertical-cut records.

June. Emerson first uses the shield label design and treble clef trademark on nine- and ten-inch discs. They are marketed as Gold Seal records, although the label color is actually blue (nine-inch) or black (ten-inch).

June 18. *Ziegfeld Follies* premieres at the New Amsterdam Theatre in Manhattan. The twelfth annual edition of this extratravaganza focused on World War I with its vaudevillian mix of sketches, production numbers, and songs. Starring such luminaries as Marilyn Miller, Eddie Cantor, W.C. Fields, and Will Rogers, it had a run of 151 performances.

July. The Bush and Lane Piano Company, based in Holland Michigan, advertises the new Cecilaphone phonograph in *Talking Machine World*. It is named after Saint Cecilia, the patron saint of music.

July. Milo Rega makes his first recordings as a bandleader—under the moniker, Rega's Novelty Dance Orchestra—in New York for Okeh. Notable sidemen over the years would include Nathan Glantz, Bennie Krueger, Joe Green, Rudy Wiedoeft, and singer Jack Kaufman.

September. The Bush and Lane Piano Company advertises the new Bush and Lane phonograph in *Talking Machine World*.

September. Emerson announces the creation of Emerson International, a division devoted to ethnic and foreign-language recordings, under the direction of Louis D. Rosenfield.

September. Okeh—founded in 1916 by German-American Otto K.E. Heinemann, then U.S. branch manager for the German-owned Odeon Records—begins marketing its own record line. Centered in New York, the company would switch from the vertical to the lateral cut method 1919. Early on, it concentrated on ethnic fare geared to U.S. immigrants as well as mainstream popular recordings. When Mamie Smith's blues records became successful in 1020, the label began exploiting the African American market. Okeh pioneered "location recording" in 1922, and began sending mobile recording trucks to record performers in cities such as New Orleans, Atlanta, San Antonio, St. Louis, Kansas City, and Detroit.

September. The Los Angeles-based Southern California Hardwood and Manufacturing Company advertises the new Hawthorn phonograph in *Talking Machine World*.

October. The Chicago-based Shell-O-Phone Talking Machine Company advertises its new Shell-O-Phone phonograph in *Talking Machine World*. The product employs a conch shell for a speaker horn.

October 1. The Chicago-based Cole and Dumas Music Co. begins producing the Olympian phonograph. The trademark will be filed August 6, 1920.

October 12. William F. Hooley dies at age fifty-seven. The bass singer anchored the sound of both the Haydn Quartet (1898–1914) and American Quartet (1909–1918). His biggest solo recording was "Gypsy Love Song" (Edison 7163; 1899).

November. Louis Armstrong starts working on Louisiana riverboats.

December. The Crippen Company, based in New York City, begins producing the Crippen phonograph. The trademark will be filed December 6, 1919.

December 27. Rudy Wiedoeft and the Master Saxophone Sextette first record in New York for Columbia. Both masters, including his signature song, "Saxophobia," are rejected.

1919

❄

January. The Green Brothers—George Hamilton Green and brother Joe, who performed on drums, vibes, xylophone, and marimba—first record in New York for Aeolian Vocalion as the Xylophone Orchestra. They remain active in the studio—together and apart—through a Decca session on March 22, 1939.

January. Joseph Samuels makes his first recordings as a bandleader in New York for Pathe.

February. Emerson signs the popular white jazz group, the Louisiana Five.

February 4. Rudy Wiedoeft and the Master Saxophone Sextette enter a recording studio for the second time, this time in Edison's New York facility. His take of "Saxophobia"—as well as "Rainy Day Blues"—will again be rejected. Later in the month, both songs will be recorded again for Paramount, and issued as #22068.

February 14. Al Bernard first records for Edison; "Hesitation Blues" is issued as Blue Amberol 3738 in June and as Diamond Disc 50524 in July.

March. Jim Europe participates in three recording sessions for Pathe after returning from World War I military duty. These studio dates—combined with a fourth in May—produce eleven vertical-cut discs notable for their syncopation and other jazz flourishes.

May. Louis Armstrong departs New Orleans to join Fate Marable's black dance orchestra sailing on the Streckfus riverboat line based in St. Louis. He remained with them for two years, learning to read music and play a varied repertoire.

May. Al Bernard's "St. Louis Blues" (Emerson 9163) is released—his debut as a solo artist. He would also record the song for Edison and Brunswick in 1920.

May 9. Jim Europe dies at age thirty-nine after being stabbed backstage during a concert in Boston's Mechanic Hall. He was the first African American to lead his own band on records issued by a major company.

Son of a former slave, Europe's family relocated from his birthplace of Mobile, Alabama, to Washington, D.C. when he was nine. Continuing music lessons on piano, violin, and mandolin, he lived for a time just houses away from John Philip Sousa, whose march compositions and U.S. Marine Corps Band dominated American musical tastes. Moving to New York City around 1903, he began directing black dance ensembles and—when opportunities presented themselves—working in musical comedy.

In 1913 Europe achieved renown in New York society when his Exclusive Society Orchestra—one of the earliest jazz bands to perform at public venues—was frequently employed by the highly popular dance team of Vernon and Irene Castle. Collaborating with the Castles in early 1914, he played a key role in creating and popularizing the fox-trot. Hoping to capitalize on the popularity of the Castles, Victor signed Europe to record four titles on December 29, 1913, and February 10, 1914, respectively. His bestselling disc appears to have been "The Castles in Europe One-Step"/"Congratulations Waltz" (Victor 35372; 1914), issued in the twelve-inch configuration and retained in the company's monthly catalog for five years.

Enlisting in the 15th New York Infantry on September 18, 1916, Europe was induced to organize and lead a military band to boost troop morale. After the Armistice, he signed a recording contract with the New York-based Pathe Freres Phonograph Company. Four sessions—three in March and one in May 1919—produced eleven discs in the military band tradition, albeit punctuated by syncopation and other jazz effects. Their popularity, however, was limited because Pathe employed the vertical-cut process (often termed "hill-and-dale"), as opposed to lateral-cut technology, which was soon to dominate the marketplace. Actively collaborating with such major talents as Noble Sissle and Eubie Blake, Europe's promising career was prematurely ended when one of his drummers stabbed him in the neck backstage during a Boston concert, just two days after recording his last six sides for Pathe.

June. Sidney Bechet joins Will Marion Cook's New York Syncopated Orchestra (he'd already played some stateside gigs with the group earlier that year) for a European tour. After hearing them perform "Characteristic

Blues," Swiss conductor Ernest Ansermet would write the following review (*Revue Romande*, October 1919):

> There is in the Southern Syncopated Orchestra an extraordinary clarinet virtuoso who is, it seems, the first of his race to have composed perfectly formed blues on the clarinet. I've heard two of them which he had elaborated at great length…They are equally admirable for their richness of invention, force of accent, and daring in novelty and the unexpected. Already, they gave the idea of a style, and their form was gripping, abrupt, harsh, with a brusque and pitiless ending like that of Back's second Brandenburg Concerto. I wish to set down the name of this artist of genius: as for myself, I shall never forget it—it is Sidney Bechet.

Ansermet would conclude that clarinetist's style "is perhaps the highway the whole world will swing along tomorrow."

June. Emerson introduces ten-inch discs retailing for 85 cents. The company also launches its own trade magazine, *The Emersonian*.

July. A *Talking Machine World* ad paid for by Emerson International exclaims, "The foreigner buys big all the Time. Get his business."

July 18. Ben Selvin—violinist, vocalist, composer, and probably the most prolific recording bandleader prior to World War II—cuts his first tracks in New York for Victor.

September. Emerson discontinues its nine-inch line of discs, opting for standard ten-inch pressing in all musical categories.

September 5. Ted Lewis makes his first recordings as a bandleader—"Wond'ring" (Columbia A-2857) and "Blues My Naughty Sweetie Gives to Me" (Columbia A-2798)—in New York, which are released under the moniker "Ted Lewis Jazz Band."

September 15. Art Hickman and his Orchestra make the first recordings in what would later be recognized as the Big Band style. As the leader of the resident dance ensemble for the St. Francis Hotel in San Francisco, Hickman created a novel, richly textured sound which featured a saxophone choir providing counterpoint to the brass and rhythm sections. While in New York to fulfill an engagement, the band enters the Columbia studios to record a number of songs that were popular at the time.

October. Emerson takes out a full-page *Talking Machine World* ad announcing that Arther Fields and Irving and Jack Kaufman, three of the leading freelance recording artists of the day, had signed exclusive contracts.

October-November. Carl Fenton and His Orchestra first records in New York. Two records result from these sessions: "Karavan"/"Romance" (Brunswick 2011) and "La La Lucille"/"My Cuban Dream" (Brunswick 2012). Fenton's dance band would continue to record regularly into the early 1930s.

October 1. Joseph C. Smith's Orchestra—featuring Harry Rederman and his Laughing Trombone—records "Yellow Dog Blues" (Victor 18618). It becomes the most popular recording of a W. C. Handy composition up to this time.

November. Clarinetist/saxophonist Paul Biese records for the first time in New York. "Dardanella" (Vocalion 14002)—credited to Paul Biese—is released from the session.

November. Emerson introduces a twelve-inch disc line, although few would actually be produced.

December. Vaughn De Leath performs for a small group of listeners before a radio microphone in Lee De Forest's laboratory. De Leath--who would henceforth be known as "The (Original) Radio Girl"—would go on to star as recording artists, and radio and television pioneer.

December 7. Humorist Cal Stewart dies at age sixty-three. He was close to forty before first recording; his early life was spent working on trains and in circuses, medicine shows, and vaudeville. His records made fictional New England farmer, "Uncle Josh Weathersby," and the town of Punkin Center (allegedly created by another vaudeville performer) leading symbols of Americana by the late 1890s. His hits included "Uncle Josh's Arrival in New York" (Columbia 14000; 1898) and "Uncle Josh on an Automobile" (Columbia 1518; 1903).

1920

❄

January. The Cincinnati-based Amerinola Company advertises the new Amerinola phonograph in *Talking Machine World.*

January. Brunswick introduces a new line employing the lateral cut system then in the process of becoming the de facto pressing format. Within a few years, the label becomes one of the Big Three record companies stateside, along with Victor and Columbia.

January 9. Vincent Lopez makes his first recordings as a bandleader in New York for Edison, with Lopez and Hamilton's Kings of Harmony Orchestra. Their first release is "Peggy" (Edison Diamond Disc 50648/ Blue Amberol 4006).

January 9. Harry Raderman's Jazz Orchestra makes its first recordings in New York for Edison. Raderman had previously directed a November 1919 session for Lyric, which would be credited to the Bal Taberin Jazz orchestra.

January 10. Vocalist Mamie Smith, providing her own piano accompaniment, cuts her first song, "That Thing Called Love"—a trial recording that will remain unissued—in New York City for Victor. However, Okeh recruits her for a February 14 session, which results in two takes—a new version of "That Thing Called Love" (Matrix 7275-E0 and "You Can't Keep a Good Man Down" (Matrix 7276-D)—coupled for release #4113 (she is allegedly accompanied by the Rega Orchestra, although there is evidence to suggest that support was really provided by the all-white Hagar's Orchestra). She is generally recognized as the first true blues singer to be featured on a phonograph record. Nevertheless, much of her material will exhibit strong pop leanings, an approach typifying many other African American blues artists (e.g., Ethel Waters) interested in reaching a wider audience. Smith would continue to record for Okeh on a regular basis through February 19, 1931; she also did sessions for Ajax c. September 1924 and Victor on August 27 and 31, 1926.

c. February. Bennie Krueger makes his first recordings as a bandleader in New York for Gennett.

February. Emerson opens new studios and offices at 206 Fifth Avenue, New York City.

March. The Newport Society Orchestra makes its first recordings in New York for Paramount. Headed by studio conductor Ben Selvin, group recorded frequently during the 1920s for many record companies. The moniker also functioned as a pseudonym for Selvin's regular band on Banner and associated labels.

April 28. Sam Lanin makes his first recordings, "Oh! By Jingo"/"Rose of Chile" (Columbia A-2943), as Lanin's Roseland Orchestra. Discography expert Brian Rust states that he probably produced more dance records than any other bandleader during the 1920s, an estimated four hundred sessions between 1920 and 1931, for almost every existing New York label.

May. The Detroit-based Adora Phonograph Company advertises the new Adora record player in *Talking Machine World.*

May 12. Emerson files a trademark application for the Melodisc imprint, claiming use of the brand since February of that year.

June. Isham Jones makes his first recordings as a bandleader in Chicago for Brunswick.

July. The Racine (Wisconsin) Phonograph Company advertises the new Blandin record player in *Talking Machine World.*

July 1. Billy Murray becomes an exclusive Victor recording artist. The contract remains in effect until July 1, 1927.

August. The American Talking Machine Co., located in Bloomsberg, Pennsylvania, advertises the new Americanola phonograph in *Talking Machine World.*

August. Emerson introduces a new line of phonographs incorporating the all-spruce Music Master internal horn, apparently influenced by the Starr Piano Company's all-spruce "singing throat."

August 9. Paul Whiteman participates in his first recording session in New York City. The date came about after key Victor personnel had seen Whiteman and His Ambassador Orchestra at Atlantic City's Ambassador Hotel while attending the National Association of Talking Machine Jobbers' convention, held June 28–30, 1920 at the nearby Hotel Traymore. Whiteman—along his supporting group, which consisted of Ferde Grofe on piano, banjo player Mike Pingitore, drummer Harold McDonald, trombonist Buster Johnson, trumpeter Henry Busse, tuba payer J. K. Wallace, and saxophonists Hale Byers, Sammy Heiss, and Gus Mueller—would have two more Victor recording dates that month; the three sessions would result in various takes of six songs, which comprised his first three discs:

> "Avalon—Just Like a Gypsy"/"Best Ever Medley" (Victor twelve-inch disc 35701)
> "Whispering"/"The Japanese Sandman" (Victor ten-inch disc 18690)
> "Anytime, Anyday, Anywhere"/"Wang-Wang Blues" (Victor ten-inch disc 18694)

The first two records were announced in Victor's November 1920 supplement, the third in the December 1920 supplement. The second record (#18690) was a huge seller, propelling Whiteman's ensemble to the forefront of the dance band craze. His popularity owed much to an emphasis on innovative arrangements. Whiteman carefully controlled the arrangements employed by his musicians, a fact that was duly noted in the program notes to his February 12, 1924 Aeolian Hall Concert:

> Paul Whiteman's orchestra was the first organization to especially score each selection and to play it according to the score. Since then practically every modern orchestra has its own arranger or staff of arrangers.

August 10. Vaudeville and blues singer Mamie Smith records "Crazy Blues," the first blues by a black singer. Released by Okeh (b/w "It's Right Here for You"), it sold seventy-five thousand copies during a one-month period in Harlem alone, encouraging record companies to search for other blues singers and jazz musicians, and to begin issuing "race" records.

September. Emerson unveils a lavishly furnished showroom and auditorium at its Fifth Avenue headquarters.

September 20. The Benson Orchestra of Chicago record for the first time at Victor's Camden, New Jersey studio. All four matrices are rejected by the label; however, four records will result from the session held over the next five days. The band will record prolifically for Victor through May 23, 1925.

October. Vaughn De Leath's debut recording, "I Love the Land of Old Black Joe" (Edison Blue Amberol 4097) is released.

November 1. Albert Campbell, Henry Burr, John Meyer, and Frank Croxton—and the groups of which they are members: the Sterling Trio and the Peerless Quartet—become exclusive Victor artists. Competing labels such as Columbia and Okeh possessed enough unissued Burr material to continue release his recordings as late as April 1922 ("Little Town in the Ould County Down"; Okeh 4537).

November 2. The Westinghouse-owned radio station, KDKA, goes on the air so as to broadcast the Harding-Cox presidential election returns.

December 10. Overexpansion, stiff competition, and an unhealthy level of debt force the Emerson organization into receivership.

December 14. Tenor George J. Gaskin dies of heart failure in New York City at age 57. Nicknamed "The Irish Thrush," the Belfast native may well have been the most popular recording artist of the 1890s. He interpreted a wide range of styles, including comedy, sentimental, patriotic, sacred, and an occasional operatic air. Among his biggest hits were "Slide, Kelly, Slide" (North American), "Sweet Marie" (New Jersey), "Down in Poverty Row" (Berliner), "Sweet Rosie O'Grady" (Edison), and "On the Banks of the Wabash" (Columbia).

1921

❄

January 10. Leo Reisman and His Orchestra first record in New York for Columbia.

January 15. *Talking Machine World* notes that saxophonist Nathan Glantz "recently went to Canada to record for Berliner…[and] is now playing for practically all the record companies."

March. Nathan Glantz records for the first time under his own name. He was an extraordinarily prolific session player who specialized in the alto and tenor saxophones.

March. Adrian Schubert records under his name—Schubert's Dance Orchestra—for the first time in New York for Paramount. He was Musical Director for the Plaza group of labels for much of the 1920s, and made countless discs. His work would appear under many pseudonyms, some of which have yet to be ascertained.

March 21. Ethel Waters records for the first time, accompanied by Albury's Blue and Jazz Seven. Her first release is "The New York Glide" (Cardinal 2036).

March 24. Coon-Sanders' Novelty Orchestra first record in Kansas City. At the following session on April 5, 1924, they will be billed as Coon-Sanders' Original Nighthawk Orchestra.

May 23. *Shuffle Along* premieres at the 63rd Street Music Hall in New York City. Featuring music by Eubie Blake, lyrics by Noble Sissle, and book by Flournoy Miller and Aubrey Lyles, it was the first successful musical written, directed, and acted by African Americans. The score is best remembered for the classic "I'm Just Wild About Harry." The cast would also include Paul Robeson and Josephine Baker for a brief time.

June. *Talking Machine World* announces that the contents of the Southern States Phonograph Company plant, a regional pressing and distribution facility for the Emerson label, is being offered for sale by the Atlanta-based Dixie Paper & Box Company.

June 6. Edison issues the first Diamond Disc with a paper label: "Sunnyside Sal" (#50818). Prior to that time—beginning in 1912, when the format was first issued—Diamond Discs had molded labels, whereby a prepared plate was pressed into the record surface, resulting in an engraved, solid black impression (the earliest issues had a gray background that contrasted with the lettering). The company wanted to switch to paper sooner, but was held back by concerns relating to "pressure-bonding" the label to the disc. The problem was not evidently completely solved as record buyers would continue to be plagued by labels falling off Edison records. In contrast, Edison's domestic competitors—Victor and Columbia—never exhibited this tendency. It appears likely that Edison opted not to use label technology implemented by another company in order to avoid paying the associated fees.

June 21. The prolific Edison recording band, the Broadway Dance Orchestra, record for the first time in New York. This session yields "My Sunny Tennessee"/"When the Honeymoon Was Over" (Diamond Disc 5082); the former was also issued on Blue Amberol 4394.

June 21. The fifteenth annual *Ziegfeld Follies* premieres at New York's Globe Theatre. The revue included such stars as Fanny Brice, W. C. Fields, Raymond Hitchcock, and Van & Schenck. Featuring the song classics "Second Hand Rose" (music by James Hanley/words by Grant Clarke) and "My Man" (music by Maurice Yvain/words by Channing Pollock), it would have a run of 119 performances.

July. *Talking Machine World* announces that singer/songwriter Vaughn De Leath had "signed a contract to make Okeh records exclusively."

August 16. A trademark is filed by Abraham Culp, representing the New York City-based Culp Phonograph Company, for the Culptone record player. The machine had been in distribution since October 1918.

August 23. The studio band, the Columbians, first record in New York. The session yields "Say It With Music" (Columbia A-3472).

September 22. *Music Box Revue* premieres at New York's Music Box. Featuring music and lyrics by Irving Berlin and sketches by miscellaneous writers, it had a run of 440 performances. Subsequent *Music Box Revues*—1922, 1923, and 1924—were almost as successful.

September 29. *Blossom Time* premieres at the Ambassador Theatre in New York City. Featuring music by Sigmund Romberg (based on compositions by Franz Schubert—the first Broadway musical to utilize classical material in this manner) and lyrics and book by Dorothy Donnelly, it had a run of 516 performances. The work was not only a huge success in its own right—with four road companies sent out soon after opening night, and five Broadway revivals through 1943—but spawned many other musicals utilizing scores derived from classical works.

October. The American Phonograph Co., located in Grand Rapids, Michigan, advertises the new American record player in *Talking Machine World*.

October. A.C. Gilbert Co., based in New Haven, Connecticut, advertises the new Bobolink phonograph in *Talking Machine World*.

October 18. James P. Johnson records the stride piano masterpiece, "Caroline Shout" (which he'd first recorded as a piano roll in 1918). The number was a definitive influence on a youthful Duke Ellington, who learned to play it by copying the fingerings on his player piano.

October 20. Arthur Collins suffers serious injuries falling through a trapdoor accidentally left open during an Edison Tone Test demonstration at the Princess Theater in Medina, Ohio. He had been exiting the stage in the dark so the audience could guess whether the singing heard came from the singer himself or a Diamond Disc machine.

November. The General Phonograph Manufacturing Company, headquartered in Elyria, Ohio, advertises the new General record player in *Talking Machine World*.

November 17. The highly successful dance orchestra, the California Ramblers (also known as the Golden Gate Orchestra), enter a recording studio for the first time. The New York session produces "The Sheik" and two takes of "Georgia Rose"; the former and matrix 8266 of the latter are coupled as Vocalion 14275, while the other version of "Georgia Rose" is issued as Vocalion M-1025.

December. The Newport News, Virginia-based Granby Phonograph Corporation advertises the new Granby record player in *Talking Machine World*.

December 7. The Garber-Davis Orchestra, featuring violinist Jan Garber and pianist Milton Davis, record for the first time in New York for Columbia.

1922

❄

January. Banner Records is launched by the Plaza Music Company of New York City. Focusing on the popular music of the day, the label's New York studio featured Adrian Schubert as recording director and conductor of the house band. In 1928, Banner would merge with Pathe and Cameo to form the American Record Corporation. ARC would continue the Banner imprint through 1938.

January-February. The Cameo Dance Orchestra begin recording in Cameo's New York studio. The prolific Bob Haring, Cameo's musical director, would head the group for much of its existence through the 1920s.

February 12. Paul Whiteman and his band are heard on WJZ (then based in Newark, New Jersey). This was his first documented appearance on the radio. From 1925 through the 1940s, he would work regularly on radio.

c. March. Bob Haring—director of the Cameo Records house ensemble from the label's beginnings in 1922 until its merger with Pathe and Plaza in 1929—makes his first recordings as a bandleader in New York.

March 2. The International Novelty Orchestra, directed by Nat Shilkret, first record in New York for Victor.

March 4. Bert Williams dies at age forty-seven. Criticized in his time for helping to perpetuate certain African American stereotypes, he was nevertheless the first of his race to become a Broadway headliner. He and partner George Walker debuted on the New York stage in 1896, remaining a popular comedy team until the latter's death in 1910. Williams continued to work in vaudeville, the Ziegfeld Follies (1910–1918), and as a recording artist. His hits included "Good Morning, Carrie" (Victor 997; 1902), his composition "Nobody" (Columbia 3423; 1906), and "O Death, Where Is Thy Sting?" (Columbia 2652; 1919).

March 21. Zez Confrey and His Orchestra first record in New York for Victor. Their take of Confrey's signature tune, "Kitten on the Keys," is rejected. Following another rejected take from an April 27 session, the May 4 rendition is released as Victor 18900.

May. Investors Benjamin Abrams and Rudolph Kararek purchase Emerson for $50,000. They go on to sell the label to the Scranton Button Company in 1924. The parent firm would halt production of records in 1928, using the Emerson name for a line of radios.

May 2. Ada Jones dies in an automobile accident. Regarded as the leading female recording artist of the acoustic era, the contralto was unsurpassed in her sense of comic timing and use of ethnic and national dialects.

May 4. Harry Reser—one of the most widely recorded banjo soloists of the 1920s—cuts his first band tracks in New York for Columbia.

June. Vaughn De Leath's first Gennett discs—"I'm Just Wild About Harry" (#4905) and "Nobody Lied" (#4907)—are released. She would continue to record for the label intermittently until 1927.

June 24. Paul Specht—the pioneer radio bandleader who also actively recorded with Specht's Jazz Outfit and a "hot" band-within-a-band, the Georgians—produces his first big band recordings in New York for Columbia.

June 30. Fiddler A. C. "Eck" Robertson cuts "Sallie Gooden" and, together with fiddler Henry C. Gilliland, "Arkansaw Traveler." Issued on Victor 18956, they are the first country recordings produced by a commercial label.

August 8. Paul Whitman records what will turn out to be his biggest hit during the acoustic era, "Three O'Clock in the Morning" (Victor 18940).

November. The Coon-Sanders Novelty Orchestra begins regular radio broadcasts on the clear channel radio station, WDAF, Kansas City. Perhaps the first band of note to become mainstays on the new medium, they first recorded for Columbia ("Some Little Bird," 1921) and went on to record sixty-five tracks for Victor from 1924–1932.

November 14. The Troubadours—featuring director/drummer Eddie King—make their first recordings in New York for Victor.

1923

❄

c. January. Bessie Smith—widely considered the greatest female blues singer ever—makes her first recording for Okeh in New York City. The only track known to come out of the session, a hot combo cover of the Tin Pan Alley chestnut "I Wish I Could Shimmy Like My Sister Kate," went unissued. She was back in the same New York City studios c. February 15–16 to cut five tracks for Columbia (limited to piano accompaniment by Clarence Williams); two of them, "Down Home Blues"/"Gulf Coast Blues" (Matrices 80863-5/80864-3; #A3844), would go on to sell more than one million copies. On April 11, Columbia would utilize Her Down Home Trio in a backup role, and would later recruit such jazz notables as Fletcher Henderson, Coleman Hawkins, Don Redman, and Louis Armstrong for support. While Smith was never able to repeat the success of her debut release, she continued recording for the label through November 24, 1933. She continued to tour right up to her death—caused when the car she occupied was hit by a commercial truck—in 1937. Her recording inactivity in the last years of her life was largely due to the Great Depression; her prime audience—rural blacks—lacked sufficient disposable income to purchase many records. (The only other company to issue a record (#J1016) by Smith in her lifetime, Circle, dubbed the title track—in four parts—from the soundtrack of the film, *St. Louis Blues*, in late June 1929.)

January 2. Paul Whiteman recorded "Mister Gallagher and Mister Shean" (Victor 19007), his first selection to include a vocal refrain, in this case Billy Murray. Murray (who was not credited on the label when the record was released in March) was featured on more Whiteman sides than any other singer during the acoustic era.

April 5–6. Louis Armstrong first records as a member of King Oliver's Creole Jazz Band. The group cuts nine tracks for Gennett in its Richmond, Indiana, studio.

April 14. The Meyer Davis Orchestra first record in New York for Columbia. The March 26, 1925, session is particularly memorable among acoustic era collectors due to the presence of vocalist Billy Murray on the record "All Aboard for Heaven"/"Let It Rain, Let It Pour" (Victor 19630/His Master's Voice B-2039).

April 24. Vocalist Lizzie Miles (real name: Elizabeth Mary Pajaud, nee Landreaux) makes a trial recording of "Tishomingo Blues" for Victor in New York City. It is the label's first attempt at recording blues material. She returned to record "You're Always Msssin' Round With My Man" (Matrix #28025-2; issued as Victor 19083/HMV B1703) on May 23 and, on July 19, "Keep Yourself Together Sweet Papa (Mama's Got Her Eyes On You)" (Matrix #28297-2; issued as Victor 19158) and "Cotton Belt Blues" (Matrix #28298-1; issued as Victor 19124). Victor also worked with two more singers—Rosa Henderson and Ethel Ridley—during this same period. Henderson waxed thirteen songs in New York City through October 18, beginning with two unissued trial recordings (believed to include piano accompaniment by Fletcher Henderson) on May 5. Ridley laid down 4 tracks; two unissued trial recordings, June 13, in Camden, New Jersey, and "Memphis, Tennessee"/"If Anybody Here Wants A Real Kind Mamma (Here's Your Opportunity)"—released as Victor 19111—June 26, in New York City. After this brief flirtation with the genre, Victor doesn't produce any more race records until returning with a renewed commitment in July 1926.

June. Ward Seeley reports in "Will the Great Artists Continue?" (*The Wireless Age*) that Victor would not allow artists exclusive to the company to perform on the radio. The firm would soon change that policy, creating a biweekly radio concert series featuring their artists first aired on New Year's Day in 1925.

c. June 14. Okeh records blues singers Lucille Bogan and Fannie Goosby as part of a field trip to Atlanta. Both will make additional recordings for the label that year in New York City.

July 17. Jelly-Roll Morton cuts his first solo piano pieces in Richmond, Indiana. Two tracks are issued by Gennett as singles: "King Porter – A Stomp" (#5289) and "New Orleans (Blues) Joys" (#5486). He also performs with the New Orleans Rhythm Kings—this is the first documented case of an integrated recording band.

Juy 26. Abe Lyman makes his first recording as a bandleader in New York: "Honey Babe" (Brunswick 2563). He continued to record into the post-World War II era, his group typically known as Abe Lyman's California Ambassador Hotel Orchestra and Abe's Lyman's California Orchestra.

July 30. Sidney Bechet makes his first surviving studio recordings (in New York); an earlier session utilizing Bessie Smith was lost. Led by pianist/songwriter/producer Clarence Williams, the session featured "Kansas City Man Blues."

August 9. Fletcher Henderson makes his earliest recordings, recording two takes of "Dicty Blues," which featured a figure played on chimes.

August 13. Paul Whiteman is crowned "King of Jazz" by the Buescher Band Instrument Co. at a reception held on the S.S. *Leviathan* dock, where he and his band had disembarked after returning from his first tour of England. The event is widely covered by the mass media.

September. Trumpeter Bubber Miley begins working with Duke Ellington's Washingtonians. He would be responsible for bringing the growling trumpet sound to the band.

October. Okeh records Bennie Moten's Kansas City Orchestra both in a featured and supporting role—for blues singers Ada Brown and Mary Bradford—as part of a St. Louis field trip.

October 15. Fred Waring's Pennsylvanians make their first recordings in Camden, New Jersey, for Victor.

October 16. Art Kahn and His Orchestra make their first recordings in Chicago for Columbia.

October 19. Victor's record supplement notes that Paul Whiteman "has been crowned 'King of the Jazz'," further assuring that the appellation will be forever associated with the bandleader.

October 26. The Vagabonds—the name used by the California Ramblers when recording for Gennett—make their first recordings in New York.

November. Columbia begins marketing its rapidly expanding blues, gospel, and jazz catalog through a specifically designated "race series." First numbered as the 13000-D series, it runs to only 13007-D. This series is immediately superceded by the 14000-D sequence in December; it will run to April 1933 (the last number being 14680-D). Previously, the label's race material—which included such luminaries as Bessie Smith, Clara Smith, and Edith Wilson—was placed in the A3365 (April 1921) to A4001 (November 1923) sequence as part of the popular series.

November 3. Jazz pianist Earl Hines makes his first recording, his own "Congaine," performed by Deppe's Serenaders.

November 28. Vaughn De Leath plays Signora Calvaro in the opening of *Laugh, Clown, Laugh* at New York's Belasco Theatre.

November 30. Ted Weems and His Orchestra first record in Camden, New Jersey, for Victor.

December 8. Vess Ossman dies at age fifty-five. The most recorded ragtime musician from the original ragtime era, he was also known as "King of the Banjo" from the 1890s to World War I.

December 12. Henry Whitter records "The Wreck on the Southern Old 97," his first Okeh disc (issued early the following year as #40015, backed by "Lonesome Road Blues") He was one of the pioneers of country music, and is considered to be the first folk-styled guitarist to make records.

December 29. Reed Miller dies at age forty-three. The concert tenor had a string of hits with Frederick Wheeler (billed as "James Reed and James F. Harrison") and as a member of the Columbia Stellar Quartet. His biggest solo hit was "It's Always June When You're in Love" (Columbia 924; 1911).

1924

❄

February 12. Paul Whiteman and his Palais Royal Orchestra headline a concert at Manhattan's Aeolian Concert Hall. Billed as "An Experiment in Modern Music," the event would introduce *Rhapsody in Blue*, with composer George Gershwin at the piano.

March 10. Guy Lombardo and His Royal Canadians first record for Gennett in Richmond, Indiana. Lombardo would become perhaps the most successful sweet bandleader of the 1930s, and remain an American institution—reappearing on television for every new year's eve countdown—through much of the twentieth century.

March 14. Lou Gold and His Orchestra first record in New York for Cameo. He continues to make recordings at a prolific rate through early 1932.

c. March 15. Okeh records two tracks with blues singer Lela Bolden, "Southern Woman Blues" and "Seawall Special Blues" (issued as #8139) in New Orleans, kicking off a southern field trip that would apparently end in early April in Atlanta. While in New Orleans, the label would also wax blues vocalist Ruth Green ("Sad and Lonely Blues" and "Mama's Got Something, I Know You Want It"; released as #8140) on March 17 and the gospel group, Original Valentin Choral Club Quintette (unaccompanied renditions of "Sing On" and "Give Me That Old Time Religion"; coupled on #8134) on c. March 18. In Atlanta, Okeh recorded more blues artists: vocalist Sara Martin (with accompaniment from Sylvester Weaver on banjo and guitar) on March 19 and 21, singer Viola Baker (backed by Fanny Goosby, piano, c. March 20, and Eddie Heywood, piano, c. March 24), and vocalist/guitarist Ed Andrews in late March or early April.

March 24. Philip Spitalny and His Orchestra first record in Cleveland for Victor.

March 27. Jean Goldkette and His Orchestra—capable of interpreting anything from hot jazz to light dance material—record for the first time in Detroit for Victor. At one time or another, his band would include such luminaries as the Dorsey brothers, Joe Venuti, Don Murray, and Bix Beiderbecke.

April. Gene Austin begins studio work with country artist George Reneau (guitar, mouth harp) on a series of recordings through February 1925 for Vocalion, most notably, "The Wreck on the Southern 97"/"Lonesome Road Blues" (#14809) and "You'll Never Miss Your Mother Until She Is Gone"/"Life's Railway to Heaven" (#14811). Edison also has the duo record many of the same songs in September.

May 16. George Olsen and His Music—featuring Red Nichols on trumpet—first record in New York.

June. At the urging of future wife, Lil Harden, Louis Armstrong leaves Joe Oliver and goes out on his own. Harden follows in September. Oliver continues with a group called the Dixie Syncopators. By 1928 his trumpet technique had greatly deteriorated due to gum troubles.

June 4. An ensemble led by Jack Shilkret records "Africa" (Victor 19394), the first performance on disc credit to "Shilkret's Orchestra." He and brother Nat remained active in the recording fields well as radio and film well into the 1940s.

June 10. Paul Whiteman records Gershwin's *Rhapsody in Blue* with the composer performing on piano. Issued on Victor 55225, it is a poor seller.

August 16. *Billboard* reports that Gene Austin is employed as a songwriter and contact man with record companies by music publisher Jack Mills, Inc.

August 27. Okeh returns to Atlanta where blues singer Wayman "Sloppy" Henry, accompanied by Eddie Heywood on piano, lays down two songs: "Tom Cat Rag" (Matrix 8715-A) and "Cannon Ball Blues" (Matrix 8716-A). The tracks—his first ever recordings—are combined for 78 rpm release (#8178). Henry will continue to record for the label through March 12, 1939.

c. September 19. Billy James' Dance Orchestra make their first recordings in New York for the Banner label group. They appear to have been an ARC-Plaza studio band for a time in the late 1920s.

October. Clarinetist Sidney Bechet, cornetist Louis Armstrong, and trombonist Charles Irvis participate in a

Clarence Williams recording date. The most notable resulting track is "Texas Moaner Blues," which features a soprano saxophone solo by Bechet.

October 7. Louis Armstrong makes his first recordings with Fletcher Henderson's band, soloing on the novelty number, "Go 'Long Mule."

October 25. Minstrel-styled performer Emmett Miller cuts his first records, "Anytime" (Okeh 40239).

October 26. Lew Dockstader dies at age sixty-eight. The vaudeville and minstrel show comedian was a major star from the 1870s to the early 1900s. He had one notable hit record, "Everybody Works but Father" (Columbia 3251; 1905).

November. Duke Ellington makes his first jazz recordings as pianist/arranger/director with The Washingtonians. The New York session nets "Choo Choo (Gotta Hurry Home)" and "Rainy Nights (Rainy Days)," initially issued as Blu-Disc T-1002.

November 8. Louis Armstrong records with the Red Onion Jazz Babies for the first time. The resulting track, "Of All the Wrongs You Done to Me" is issued as Gennett 5627.

c. November 19. Hal Kemp makes his first stateside recordings as a bandleader—with the Carolina Club Orchestra—for Pathe. He first recorded in London during August with the same ensemble.

November 25. Jack Stillman makes his first recordings as a bandleader in New York for Edison.

December 22. Vaughn De Leath cuts her first Columbia record, "Nobody Knows What a Red Head Mama Can Do"/"I Ain't Got Nobody to Love" (#271-D). She would make additional recordings for the firm through October 1928.

1925

❄

January 8. Louis Armstrong and Sidney Bechet are featured in a frenetic duel in Clarence Williams recording of "Cake Walkin' Babies From Home." It is now considered a masterpiece of the New Orleans style.

January 26. Jazz cornet virtuoso Bix Beiderbecke records with his own ensemble for the first time. The Richmond, Indiana, session produces "Toddlin' Blues," "Davenport Blues," "Magic Blues," and "Nobody Knows What It's All About"; the first two takes are issued as Gennett 5654, while the others are rejected.

January 27. Francis Craig and His Orchestra—who will release a number one hit as late as 1947—first record in Atlanta. Columbia will reject the two takes recorded during the session.

March 10. Roger Wolfe Kahn and His Orchestra first record in New York for Victor.

March 12. Gene Austin records his first hit of note, "Yearning"/"No Wonder" (Victor 19625).

March 22. The Boswell Sisters—Connie, Helvetia "Vet," and Martha—make their first recordings. The New Orleans session nets "You Can Call Me Baby All the Time," "I'm Gonna Cry (Crying Blues)," and "Pal O' Mine." "I'm Gonna Cry" is issued as Victor 19639; the other two takes are rejected.

April 4. Waring's Pennsylvanians record "Collegiate" (Victor 19648; b/w "Look at Those Eyes"), which becomes their biggest hit.

May 16. The Regent Club Orchestra make their first recordings in New York for Brunswick.

May 20. The American Quartet record their last release, "Alabamy Bound" (Victor 19680). An acoustic recording issued in August 1925, it remained in the label's catalog for only fourteen months.

June 8. *The Garrick Gaieties* premieres at New York's Garrick Theatre. Featuring music by Richard Rodgers, lyrics by Lorenz Hart, and sketches by miscellaneous writers, the musical had a run of 211 performances. The songs included Rodgers and Hart's first hit, "Manhattan."

July 27. Charlie Poole, a banjo player and vocalist specializing in old time music, accompanied by the North Carolina Ramblers (Posey Rorer, fiddle, and Norman Woodlief, guitar), are brought to New York where they would record their first four tracks for Columbia Records. The label chose to couple "Can I Sleep in Your Barn"/"Don't Let Your Deal Go Down Blues" as the first 78 rpm release. It sold 102,000 copies, an incredible total for the time; according to researcher Pat Harrison, "any record in this style selling 5,000 copies was reckoned to be a good seller and one that sold 20,000, a hit." Born March 22, 1892, in Randolph County, North Carolina, Poole—who had allegedly recorded as early as 1924 for Okeh with his group—was one of the first authentic interpreters of rural American music. More importantly, he proved that authentic recreations of this rural music heritage were a salable commodity. Up until this time, when record companies had seen fit to issue music geared to this audience, they had used mainstream popular artists such as Collins and Harlan and light opera singer Vernon Dalhart to ape old time music conventions, smoothing out its rough edges in the process. Poole and his cohorts would serve as models for the first generation of country music stars, most notably the Singing Brakeman, Jimmie Rodgers, and the Carter Family, who are credited with ushering in the modern era of the style during the 1927 Bristol, Tennessee recording sessions presided over by Victor field-recording engineer and A&R man Ralph Peer.

August 13. Johnny Hamp's Kentucky Serenaders make their first recordings in New York for Victor.

September. *Talking Machine World* includes an advertisement for a second Peerless Quartet, consisting of three former members of the original group—Albert Campbell, John H. Meyer, and Frank Croxton—along with Charles Harrison. In an attempt to compete with the Eight Popular Victor Artists, this group recruited saxophonist Rudy Wiedoeft, pianist-composer Lieutenant Gitz Rice, and Baritone Arthur Fields to perform as the Peerless Entertainers.

September 16. *No, No, Nanette* premieres at the Globe Theatre in New York City. Featuring music by Vincert Youmans, lyrics by Irving Caesar, and book by Otto Harbach and Frank Mandel, the musical had a run of 321 performances. Featuring the hit songs "Tea for Two" and "I Want To Be Happy," it would be made into a movie in 1930 (starring Bernice Claire and Alexander Grey) and 1940 (with Anna Neagle and Victor Mature).

September 18. *Dearest Enemy* premieres at the Knickerbocker Theatre in New York City. Featuring music by Richard Rodgers, lyrics by Lorenz Hart, and book by Herbert Fields, the musical had a run of 286 performances.

September 21. *The Vagabond King* premieres at the Casino Theatre in New York City. Featuring music by Rudolf Friml, lyrics by Brian Hooker, and book by Hooker, Russell Janney, and W.H. Post., the musical had a run of 511 performances. It would be made into two different films: in 1930 with Dennis King and Jeanette MacDonald, and the 1950 treatment with Oreste and Kathryn Grayson.

September 22. Fred Rich makes his first band record recordings in New York for Harmony, billed as Fred Rich and His Hotel Astor Orchestra. His name would also be used a pseudonym for other studio projects.

September 22. *Sunny* premieres at the New Amsterdam Theatre in New York City. Featuring music by Jerome Kern and lyrics and book by Otto Harbach and Oscar Hammerstein II, the musical would run for 517 performances. It would be adapted to film in 1930 (with Marilyn Miller reprising her Broadway role) and 1940 (starring Anna Neagle).

October 23. The Peerless Quartet records for the first time with three new members—first tenor Carl Mathieu, baritone James Stanley, and bass Stanley Baughman—joining lead vocalist Henry Burr.

October 30. The Ipana Troubadours, directed by Sam Lanin, make their first recordings in New York for Columbia.

November 12. Louis Armstrong and his Hot Five—including trombonist Kid Ory, clarinetist Johnny Dodds, pianist/vocalist Lil Armstrong, and Johnny St. Cyr on the banjo—make their first recordings. The Chicago session nets "My Heart" and "Yes! I'm in the Barrel" (issued as Okeh 8320 and 8261, respectively).

c. December-January. Blind Lemon Jefferson travels to Chicago to record his first tracks. The first releases from this session would be gospel songs—"I Want to be Like Jesus in My Heart" and "All I Want is That Pure Religion"—credited on the label to Deacon L. J. Bates.

December 8. *The Cocoanuts* premieres at the Lyric Theatre in New York City. Featuring music and lyrics by Irving Berlin and book by George S. Kaufman, the musical would run for 276 performances. The Marx Brothers would appear in the 1929 screen version as well, the first feature film in which they would appear.

December 28. *Tip-Toes* premieres at the Liberty Theatre in New York City. Featuring music by George Gershwin, lyric by Ira Gershwin, and book by Guy Bolton and Fred Thompson, the musical would run for 194 performances. A film adaptation would be made in England in 1928, starring Dorothy Gish and Will Rogers.

1926

❄

January 2. The first issue of *The Melody Maker* appears on the newsstands in Great Britain. The monthly bills itself for "all who are interested in the production of popular music." It will remain an important music industry publication into the twenty-first century, constantly adapting to changing fashions. It became required reading in the United States in the aftermath of the British Invasion in the 1960s.

January 20. One of the more notable dance band leaders of the early electric era, Irving Aaronson, records for the first time on January 20 in New York. The resulting release, "Don't Wake Me Up (Let Me Dream)"/ "I Dare Not Love You" (Edison 51685), is credited to "Irving Aaronson and the Crusaders." By the third studio session, his backup group is called the "Commanders."

January 30. The highly successful vaudeville comedian, Billy Golden, dies at age sixty-seven. Although he remained active in recording up to the World War I era, his biggest success—"Turkey in the Straw" (Columbia, 1891)—came during the infancy of the industry.

February 2. Carmichael's Collegians—featuring pianist/director Hoagy Carmichael, composer of such standards as "Stardust," "Georgia On My Mind," and "Lazy River"—first enter a recording studio. The Richmond, Indiana, session produces two tracks; both a rejected by Gennett.

February 10. The Broadway Bell-Hops, including such notably jazz musicians as Red Nichols and Miff Mole, record for the first time in New York. Two releases come out of this session: "But I Do – You Know I Do"/"Let's Talk About My Sweetie" (Harmony 120-H) and "Wimmin – Aaah!" (Harmony 121-H).

February 28. Louis Armstrong records the hit, "Heebie Jeebies," which features his scat singing of nonsense syllables. A myth arose that the song sheet had slipped out of Armstrong's hand, forcing him to improvise. Mezz Mezzrow would offer the following assessment in his *Really the Blues*:

> All the hi-de-ho, vo-de-o-do, and the boop-boop-a-doo howlers that later sprouted up around the country like a bunch of walking ads for Alka-Seltzer were mostly cheap commercial imitations of what Louis did spontaneously, and with perfect musical sense, on that historic record…For months after that you would hear cats greeting each other with Louis' riffs when they met around town. "I got the Heebies," one would yell out, and the other would answer "I got the Jeebies."

March. Blind Lemon Jefferson has a second recording session for Paramount. The first release under his own name, "Booster Blues"/"Dry Southern Blues," becomes a hit, leading to the release of two more songs from that date, "Got the Blues"/"Long Lonesome Blues"—a major success, with six-figure sales. He would go on to record about one hundred tracks prior to his death in 1929.

March. Joe Oliver and His Dixie Syncopators record the jazz classic, "Snag It."

April 1. George Hall's Arcadians make their first recordings in New York for Edison. All masters are rejected, but their March 11, 1927, session for Pathe Actuelle nets a couple of releases.

April 20. Vitaphone Co. signs a contract with AT&T to develop film soundtracks utilizing Western Electric's electrical recording system. The process consists of 16-inch acetate-coated shellac discs recorded at a speed 33 1/3 revolutions per minute via electric motors in synch with the film reel.

April 29. B.A. Rolfe and His Palais D'Or Orchestra make their first recording in New York. Formerly a trumpet soloist with Vincent Lopez, Rolfe worked exclusively with Edison until that label ceased operations on November 1, 1929.

May. Paramount has Blind Lemon Jefferson re-record his hit, "Got the Blues"/"Long Lonesome Blues," in superior facilities at March Laboratories; subsequent issues would feature that version. Various modern Jefferson compilations often have included both versions for comparative purposes.

May 24. After moving the Vitaphone studio to the Manhattan Opera House earlier in the month, Warner Bros. makes *Volga Boatman* and other short subject musical films.

July 16. Bandleader Nathaniel Shilkret records under his name for the first time—as Nat Shilkret and the Victor Orchestra—in New York. The resulting single, "Barcelona"/"On the Riviera" (Victor 20113), features Billy Murray as vocalist on the "A" side. Shilkret was Victor's Director of Light Music between 1915 and 1945, and recorded hundreds of dance records for the label through 1932.

August 6. Warner Bros. releases *Don Juan*, the first full-length film with recorded sound in the musical scenes.

September. Joe Oliver and His Dixie Syncopators record the jazz classic, "Someday, Sweetheart."

September 14. Ben Pollack makes his first recordings as bandleader in Chicago for Victor.

November 11. Columbia Records purchases controlling interest in the Okeh label. The imprint was continued until 1935, and revived in 1940 when Columbia lost the rights to the Vocalion name (by dropping the Brunswick label). After discontinuing Okeh pressings in 1946, Columbia would revive the name again in the 1950s, using it sporadically through the 1990s. The name remains active into the twenty-first century largely as a CD reissue label.

December. Negotiations are finalized for Victor head Eldridge Johnson to sell his 45 percent interest in the company to the two New York banking houses of Speyer and Seligman. The following month, outstanding Victor stock—including shares held by stockholders other than Johnson—are sold to Speyer and Seligman at $115 per share for a total of $30 million, giving then a majority interest in the firm. The shares were then offered on the New York Stock Exchange, making Victor a public entity for the first time.

December 22. The tenor balladeer, Manuel Romain, dies at age fifty-six. He starred in vaudeville and minstrel shows during the first two decades of the twentieth century, and recorded such hits as "When I Lost You" (Columbia 1288; 1913), "I Miss You Most of All" (Columbia 1454; 1914), and "You're More Than the World to Me" (Columbia 1577; 1914).

1927

❄

February 4. Bix Beiderbecke joins with saxophonist Frankie Trumbauer's combo to record "Singin' the Blues." Budd Johnson would state in the February 8, 1968, issue of *Down Beat*: "Everybody memorized (Trumbauer's opening) solo … At that time, Frankie Trumbauer was the baddest cat around."

March 5. Enoch Light makes his first recordings as a bandleader—heading Enoch Light's Blue Jay Orchestra—in New York. His would go on to his greatest success in the early 1960s when his Light Brigade recorded a succession of best-selling LPs that helped popularize stereo effects.

March 7. Bing Crosby cuts his first record as a solo artist, "Muddy Water," with accompaniment by the Whiteman Orchestra, for Victor.

April 1. Jazz guitar virtuoso Eddie Lang makes his first recordings in New York. The resulting songs—including piano accompaniment by Arthur Schutt—include "Eddie's Twister" and "April Kisses," issued as Okeh 40807.

April 7. Duke Ellington first records his milestone jazz composition, "Black and Tan Fantasy," in New York with The Washingtonians.

April 22. Horace Heidt and His Orchestra make their first recordings in San Francisco for Victor.

May 7. Louis Armstrong and his Hot Seven—including trombonist John Thomas, clarinetist Johnny Dodds, pianist/vocalist Lil Armstrong, drummer Baby Dodds, and Pete Briggs on bass brass—record for the first time. The Chicago session nets "Willie the Weeper" and "Wild Man Blues," issued as Okeh 8482 and 8474, respectively.

August 25. Drummer Chick Webb records for the first time as a bandleader (Chick Webb's Harlem Stompers). The resulting track, "Low Levee – High Water," is rejected by Vocalion.

September 14. Gene Austin records his composition, "My Blue Heaven" (Victor 20964). The release—which capitalized on the crooner craze of the day, which had been fueled by the rise of radio and electronic recording—sold millions of copies. The hit helped make Austin—who'd previously played piano in his own dance band, worked the vaudeville circuit, and started out recording old time music with Vocalion in 1924—the most popular singer of the late 1920s. Although he lost ground in the early 1930s to the next generation of romantic male vocalists, most notably, Rudy Vallee, Russ Columbo, and Bing Crosby, Austin would enjoy a revival in the post-World War II period when Universal Records acquired the rights to his masters in 1948 and began reissuing them on 45 and 33 1/3 rpm discs and "The Gene Austin Story" was broadcast by NBC in 1956.

September 18. Jean Goldkette's groundbreaking dance band breaks up. Many key members—including Bix Beiderbecke, Frankie Trumbauer, and arranger Bill Challis—end up in Paul Whiteman's highly successful ensemble.

October 20. Veteran recording artist Arthur Fields enters the studio for the first time as a bandleader, waxing "Is It Possible?"/"Someday You'll Say 'O.K.'" (Edison Diamond Disc 52123) with His Assassinators. The former is also released as Blue Amberol cylinder 5431.

October 31. Hoagy Carmichael and His Pals record "Stardust" in Richmond, Indiana. Issued by Gennett (#6311), it becomes arguably the most popular song of the twentieth century. Interpreters over the years have included Artie Shaw, Nat "King" Cole, Nino Tempo and April Stevens, and Willie Nelson.

December 4. Duke Ellington opens at the Cotton Club. Thanks to the radio broadcasts emanating from the venue, his band became famous nationwide. He remained there for much of the next five years.

1928

❄

January 7. Vaughn De Leath is the first female artist to record "Can't Help Lovin' Dat Man" from Jerome Kern's classic musical, *Show Boat* (Columbia 1284-D).

January 23. Benny Goodman produces his first recordings as a featured player. The ensemble—billed as Benny Goodman's Boys with Jim and Glenn (cornetist Jimmy McPartland and trombonist Glenn Miller)—cuts "A Jazz Holiday" and "Wolverine Blues," issued as Vocalion 15656.

February 14. The Dorsey Brothers' Orchestra record for the first time. The New York session produces "Mary Ann" and "Persian Rug," released as Okeh 40995.

March. Django Reinhardt records for the first time accompanying—on the banjo—an accordionist and slide whistle player in four popular tunes.

March 19. Nora Bayes (real name: Dora Goldberg) dies at age forty-seven. Following a Broadway debut in 1901, she becomes a star in shows teaming her with husband Jack Norworth. They compose many pop standards, including "Shine On, Harvest Moon." Her biggest hit recordings were "Over There" (Victor 45130; 1917) and "Make Believe" (Columbia 3392; 1921).

April 12. Bandleader Gus Arnheim makes his first recordings in Los Angeles : "I Can't Do Without You" (Okeh 41057) and "If I Can't Have You (I Want to be Lonesome – I Want to be Blue)" (Okeh 41037). Over the next few years he will utilize a number of famous vocalists, including Russ Columbo, the Bing Crosby-Al Rinker-Harry Barris trio, Eddie Cantor, and Joan Crawford.

May. Paul Whiteman's band shift to the Columbia label.

May 25. Joe Venuti makes his first recordings fronting for a big band—initially known as Joe Venuti and His New Yorkers—in New York for Okeh. He had already made a name performing in "hot" jazz combos featuring guitarist Eddie Lang as well as his own Blue Four.

June 29. Henry Busse and His Orchestra first record in New York for Victor. Prior to his foray into dance music, the trumpeter recorded hot jazz with Busse's Buzzards, a small group operating within the 1925 edition of the Paul Whiteman Orchestra.

August 29. Rudy Vallee and His Connecticut Yankees first record in New York for Harmony. Vallee—greatly assisted by radio—will soon become the most popular crooner of the day, before being eclipsed by Bing Crosby in the mid-1930s.

September 20. The Bethel Quartet—comprised of tenors Norman Chestang and W. W. Coleman, baritone B. McCants, and bass Robert Joseph—records two gospel songs in Memphis for Victor; they cut six more tracks the following day. These sessions were part of Victor field excursion from August-November 1928 that also included stops at Nashville, Tennessee, Atlanta, and Bristol, Tennessee. Three singles would be issued containing this material: "So Glad I've Got the Stone"/"Jesus, Light of the World" (#21736), "On My Knees"/"Walk Through the Valley the Peace" (#V38510), and "Brother Cain Struck Abel"/"Moses Gonna Chunk Dat Melon Down" (#V38530). While this group does not appear to have made any more recordings, Victor applied the name to a number of other acts during the early decades of the twentieth century. In 1909, the label recorded a Fisk University ensemble that employed a more mannered European approach in their treatment of gospel material. In 1923, Victor released gospel records credited to the Bethel Jubilee Quartet; however, little regarding content or style is known about them.

November 10. Tommy Dorsey records for the first time heading his own ensemble. The New York session produces "It's Right Here for You" and "Tiger Rag," issued as Okeh 41178.

November 16. Lawrence Welk makes his first recordings as a bandleader in Richmond, Indiana, for Gennett.

November 26. Kay Kyser and His Orchestra first record in Camden, New York, for Victor.

December. Pathe is sold to English Columbia, while its American assets are purchased by the American Record Corporation.

December 3. Vaughn De Leath is the featured vocalist, along with Franklyn Baur, on the inaugural broadcast of the highly popular *Voice of Firestone* radio show.

December 8. Jazz pianist Earl Hines enters a recording studio for the first time. The Long Island City session produces eight solo takes: "Blues in Thirds (Caution Blues)"/"Off Time Blues" (QRS R-7036), "Chicago High Life"/"A Monday Date" (QRS R-7037), "Stowaway"/"Chimes in Blues" (QRS R-7038), and "Panther Rag"/"Just Too Soon" (QRS R-7039). These selections reveal him introducing and breaking stride rhythms at will, introducing turbulent runs and unexpected dissonances in performances nevertheless notable for their constant swing.

1929

❄

January. The Radio Corporation of America acquires the Victor Talking Machine Company. The firm will be known as RCA Victor until the latter part of the name is no longer used as part of the label logo in the 1960s.

January 24. Art Kassel and His "Kassels-in-the-Air" first record in Chicago for Victor.

January 28. The Victor Minstrels—including Henry Burr, Billy Murray, Frank Crumit, James Stanley, and others with orchestral accompaniment—cut a twelve-inch Victor record, "Minstrel Show of 1929" (#35961). An effort to recreate the ambience of an old-time minstrel show, the disc is not a big seller.

March 1. Fats Waller makes some of his best solo piano recordings, including "Handful of Keys" and "Numb Fumblin'," a humorous reference to his heavy drinking.

March 14. Bing Crosby makes his first solo recording for Columbia, "My Kinda Love"/"Till We Meet."

April 10. Smith Ballew and His Orchestra make their first recordings in New York. The popular vocalist/bandleader continues to record at a prolific rate through mid-1935.

May 6. Sousa's Band perform on the radio for the first time; the *General Motors Family Party* (NBC) features soprano Martha Atwood and a male chorus on the "U.S. Field Artillery March." The strong public response led to fourteen more appearance on the program between May 13 and November 25, 1929.

June 13. Jimmy Dorsey produces his first recordings heading his own ensemble. The New York session produces "Beebe" and "Praying the Blues," issued as Okeh 41245.

July. The American Record Corporation (also known as ARC) is created out of the merger of Regal Records, Cameo Records, Banner Records, the U.S. branch of Pathe Records, and the Scranton Button Company, the firm in control of Emerson Records. ARC would take advantage of the depressed market in the 1930s, buying failing labels at bargain prices to exploit their catalog.

July 1. The Decca Record Company is launched with three releases: the British National Anthem, conducted by Julian Clifford; a pop selection featuring Billy Cotton, Ambrose and his Orchestra, Gwen Farrer, and Billy Mayerl; and a classical set including Delius's *Sea Drift*, Offenbach's *Orpheus in the Underworld* Overture; and Grainger's *Jutish Medley*. The firm had been founded by musical instrument manufacturers Barnett Samuel and Sons Ltd., which ran a front-page ad for its first offering—the Decca Dulcephone portable gramophone—in the July 16, 1914, issue of the London *Daily Mail*. The company had been renamed the Decca Gramophone Company by the time stockbroker Edward Lewis purchased it in early 1929. Pressing its records at the recently acquired Duophone factory located in New Malden, Surrey, U.K., Decca embarked on an ambitious program of expansion, acquiring British distribution rights to the German Polydor label (1930), purchasing the Edison Bell Company (1933), forming the U.S. Decca division (1934), and absorbing the Crystalate company in March 1937.

August 3. Inventor and record company executive Emile Berliner dies of a heart attack at age seventy-eight. He was perhaps best known for developing the disc recording format at a time when his competitors were committed exclusively to cylinders. After establishing the Berliner Gramophone Company in 1895, he would join forces with engineer Eldridge R. Johnson to found the Victor Talking Machine Company.

August 21. Will Osborne and His Orchestra first record in New York for Columbia.

August 24. Ted Fiorito and His Edgewater Beach Hotel Orchestra first recordings in New York for Columbia. Their next session takes place on November 21, in Chicago, for Victor, now billed as "Ted Fiorito and His Orchestra. They remain popular on recordings well into the 1940s.

October. Count Basie records for the first time with the Bennie Moten band.

October. Herbert Yates, head of the Consolidated Film Company, takes control of ARC from Louis G. Sylvester, the former CEO of the Scranton Button Company.

October 1. The Memphis-based Cannon's Jug Stompers record four tracks in their hometown; "Walk Right In"—coupled with "Whoa! Mule, Get Up in the Alley"—is issued as Victor V-38611. A remake of the song by the folk-pop trio, The Rooftop Singers, tops the Hot 100 in early 1963.

October 29. The Casa Loma Orchestra enter the studio for the first time. The New York session produces "Love is a Dreamer" (Okeh 41329) and "Lucky Me, Loveable You"/"Happy Days Are Here Again" (Okeh 41339).

November 19. Wayne King and His Orchestra first record in Chicago for Victor.

November 25. Henry Burr begins work as director of the Artist's Bureau of the newly established Columbia Broadcasting Company in New York.

November 29. Sousa's Band performs on the *Bond Bakers* Thanksgiving program along with ten European bands and orchestras.

December. Blind Lemon Jefferson dies penniless in Chicago. Rumors state that a jealous lover poisoned his coffee, but it appears more likely he died from a heart attack (or froze to death) after being disoriented during a snowstorm. Paramount Records would pay for the return of his body to Texas by train, accompanied by pianist Will Ezell. Jefferson would be buried at Wortham Negro Cemetery; his grave was unmarked, but a Texas Historical Marker was erected in the general area of his plot in 1967.

1930

❄

January 16. West Coast bandleader Art Hickman dies at age forty-three. His group recorded many hits in the early 1920s, most notably, "Hold Me" (Columbia 2899; 1920) and "The Love Nest" (Columbia 2955; 1920).

January 21. Baritone singer Bob Roberts dies at age fifty-one. He specialized in comic novelties, including the hit "Ragtime Cowboy Joe" (Victor 17090; 1912).

February. Philip Spitalny makes his first Hit of the Week records in New York. They would be issued under various names, including Hit of the Week Orchestra, Hotel Pennsylvania Music, Hotel Pennsylvania Orchestra, the New York Twelve, Statler Pennsylvanians, and Philip Spitalny's Music.

April. Brunswick Balke Collender sells Brunswick Records to Warner Brothers, who hope to make their own soundtrack recordings for their sound-on-disc Vitaphone system.

April 5. Gene Greene, known as "the Ragtime King" on the vaudeville circuit, dies at age fifty-two.

May 20. Russ Morgan makes his first recordings as a bandleader in New York.

June 28. Joe Schenck dies at age thirty-nine. Together with Gus Van, he formed a comic duo popular in vaudeville, radio, and Broadway shows. Their long string of hits included "For Me and My Gal" (Victor 18258; 1917), "Ain't We Got Fun?" (Columbia 3412; 1921), and "Carolina in the Morning" (Columbia 3712; 1923).

August 15. Albert L. Thuras files patent no. 1,869,178 for the bass-reflex principle. The application is granted July 26, 1932. As an employee of Bell Labs, Thuras plays a part in other audio speaker advances.

August 29. Ozzie Nelson makes his first recordings as a bandleader in New York, resulting in the release, "I Still Get a Thrill (Thinking of You)"/"I Don't Mind Walking in the Rain" (Brunswick 4897).

October 1. Jack Teagarden and His Orchestra first record in New York for the Banner label group.

October 3. Fletcher Henderson records "Somebody Loves Me," an early example of his use of arrangements by alto saxophonist/trumpeter Benny Carter.

October 25. The first ARC-Brunswick studio band recordings are produced in New York City. Two Melotone records are released from the session: "(I Am Only the Words) You Are the Melody"/"Three Little Words" (#M-12001), credited to Mark Fisher and his Orchestra, and "Ukulele Moon"/"On a Little Balcony in Spain" (#M-12006), attributed to Sleepy Hall and his Collegians. The recordings—which were made through March 7, 1936—were credited to many bandleaders who contributed little or nothing to the sessions. They included Gene Austin and his Orchestra, Smith Ballew and his Orchestra, Ralph Bennett and his Seven Aces, Bob Causer and his Cornellians, Lou Gold and his Orchestra, Vic Irwin and his Orchestra, Art Kahn's Orchestra, Ralph Kirberry and his Orchestra, Ed Kirkeby and his Orchestra, Ed Lloyd and his Orchestra, Mills' Music Makers, Les Peabody and his Memphis Ramblers, Vincent Rose and his Orchestra, Milt Shaw and his Detroiters, and Paul Small and his Orchestra. In addition, a considerable number of releases utilized pseudonyms. The collective personnel employed included trumpeters Sylvester Ahola, Bunny Berrigan, Sterling Bose, Frank Guarente, and Bob Effros; trombonists Tommy Dorsey, Charlie Butterfield, and Jack Teagarden; clarinetists/saxophonists Jimmy Dorsey, Chester Hazlett, Sid Stoneburn, Arnold Brilhart, Larry Binyon, and Mutt Hayes; violinists Joe Venuti, Harry Hoffman, Walter Edelstein, and Lou Kosloff; pianists Joe Meresco and Arthur Schutt; guitarists/banjo players Eddie Lang, Carl Kress, Dick McDonough, Perry Botkin, and Tommy Felline; bassists Joe Tarto, Hank Stern, Artie Bernstein, and Dick Cherwin; and drummers Stan King and Larry Gomar.

December 3. The Chocolate Dandies—a constantly changing group of jazz musicians active between the late 1920s and early 1940s—record five tracks, including two classics, "Bugle Call Rag" and "Dee Blues." Participants in the session included clarinetist Benny Carter, saxophonist Coleman Hawkins, trombonist Jimmy Harrison, and trumpeter Bobb Stark.

1931

❄

January 8. Dick Robertson and His Orchestra first record dance music in a New York studio for Melotone. Robertson was a leading vocalist on record and radio beginning in 1927; he was not a bandleader in the conventional sense, but rather the featured vocalist with studio groups.

January 22. Clyde McCoy and His Orchestra makes its recording debut in New York, resulting in the classic "Sugar Blues" (Columbia 2389-D), backed by "Readin', Ritin', Rhythm."

March 5. Victor Young and the Brunswick Orchestra—which includes such luminaries as Bunny Berigan, the Dorsey Brothers, Joe Venuti, and Eddie Lang—make their first recordings in New York for Brunswick.

April. The Philadelphia Orchestra, conducted by Leopold Stokowski, employs a vertical-cut recorder equipped with a moving coil pickup and sapphire stylus developed at Bell Labs by Arthur C. Keller to improve the dynamic range of cellulose acetate discs pressed from gold-sputtered wax masters. Following a playback of the Berlioz overture, *Roman Carnival*, made on the same equipment at the Bell Labs, New York City, on December 1, Stokowski calls it the finest recording he has ever heard.

April 9. Sousa's Band appear on the *Standard Oil of Indiana* CBS radio program. Featured performers include Will Rogers and Louise Homer.

September 26. Harry Macdonough (real name: John S. MacDonald) dies at age sixty. The sweet-voiced tenor was surpassed in popularity only by Henry Burr as a balladeer during the acoustic era. His solo career was complemented by widespread recording activity as a member of the Victor Light Opera Co. and the Edison, Haydn, Lyric, and Orpheus quartets. He was employed as a record company executive after World War I. Macdonough's major hits included "Absence Makes the Heart Grow Fonder" (Victor 907; 1901), "Shine On, Harvest Moon" (Victor 16259; 1909), "Down By the Old Mill Stream" (Victor 17000; 1911), and "The Girl on the Magazine" (Victor 17945; 1916).

October 31. Sousa's Band appears on NBC's *Goodyear Hour* for the first time along with the Revelers Quartet. They will be featured on twenty programs up through March 9, 1932, three days after Sousa's death.

November 12. EMI opens the largest recording studio in the world at its Abbey Road complex in London. It utilizes the binaural (stereo) recording system developed and patented by Alan Blumlein in place of the established Western Electric process.

December. Warner Brothers leases Brunswick Records, Vocalion Records, and associated companies to ARC.

1932

❄

February 8. Victor obtains masters featuring the duo Eddie and Oscar (Eddie Chafer and Oscar Woods, known as the Shreveport Home Wreckers) as part of a field trip to Dallas to record promising regional blues musicians. On the following day, the label will cut material by Pete Dickson and Ramblin' Thomas (real name: Willard Thomas). Walter Davis and James "Stump" Johnson will be recorded on February 10. The trip is continued in Atlanta, where Victor captures Ruby Glaze and Hot Shot Willie (believed to be Kate and Blind Willie McTell) on February 22. Pinetop and Lindberg (real names: Aaron and Milton Sparks) also cut tracks there on February 25.

February 22. Baritone George MacFarlane dies at age fifty-four. In addition to performing on Broadway and in operettas, his recording—"A Little Bit of Heaven (Shure, They Call It Ireland)" (Victor 60132; 1915)—was a major hit.

March 3. Eddy Duchin and His Central Park Casino Orchestra first record in New York for Columbia. The pianist/bandleader would remain very popular well into the 1940s as one of the leading exponents of the "sweet band" sound.

March 5. John Philip Sousa dies at age seventy-seven. Sousa played violin in a number of orchestras prior to assuming the post of U.S. Marine Band director (1880–1891). His reputation rested the series of marches he composed during the last quarter of the nineteenth century. Due to his lack of interest in recorded music, his band was largely conducted by trombonist Arthur Pryor, with additional support from cornetists Walter B. Rogers and Herbert L. Clarke in the studio. Sousa preferred the concert medium; his band is reputed to have given more than ten thousand concerts around the world. His top-sellers included "El Capitan March" (Columbia, 1895), "Washington Post March (Columbia, 1895), and "The Stars and Stripes Forever" (Columbia 532; 1897).

March 9. Sousa's Band is broadcast on the *Goodyear Hour*, their last radio appearance. Arthur Pryor conducts with vocal support provided by the Revelers Quartet. Had Sousa not died on March 6, it is likely that his band would have continued to appear regularly on the radio. After overcoming an initial aversion to the medium, Sousa's Band had made thirty-eight appearances over the last thirty-four months of his life.

March 18. Tenor Chauncey Olcott dies at age seventy-four. He began his career in1890s minstrel shows prior to achieving success in Broadway musicals. He also won acclaim as a composer of Irish ballads (e.g., "When Irish Eyes Are Smiling," "My Wild Irish Rose," "Mother Machree"). His biggest recording successes were "When Irish Eyes Are Smiling" (Columbia 1310; 1913) and "Too-Ra-Loo-Ra-Loo-Ra (That's an Irish Lullaby)" (Columbia 1410; 1913).

May 3. Carleton Coon dies at age thirty-eight. Along with Joe Sanders (d. May 14, 1965; 70), he led the Kansas City-based Coon-Sanders Orchestra. Although best known through their NBC radio program, they also had many hit records during the 1920s, most notably, "Some Little Bird" (Columbia 3403; 1921).

May 4. Joe Haymes and His Orchestra first record in Camden, New Jersey, for Victor.

August 24. Freddy Martin and His Orchestra first record in New York. Two singles—"Goodbye to Love"/"We Just Couldn't Say Goodbye" (Columbia 2703-D) and "Three on a Match"/"Nightfall" (Columbia 2708-D)—come out of the session.

November 28. Red Nichols and His Orchestra make the first of a series of dance records (through June 11, 1940) in Chicago. This session follows the last of the legendary jazz recordings waxed by Nichols' Five Pennies.

1933

❄

January. Brunswick releases "You're Getting To Be A Habit With Me"/"Young and Healthy" (#6472), by Bing Crosby with accompaniment by Guy Lombardo & His Royal Canadians, both of which are taken from the hit film *Forty-Second Street*. While the "A" side was probably the crooner's most popular recording for the year, he continued to dominate popular music on a variety of fronts: in films, in live venues, and on the radio. His 1933 recordings cut across a wide array of styles, including pop ballads ("You're Beautiful Tonight, My Dear"), jazz ("I've Got the World On a String," which featured backing by Bunny Berigan, Tommy Dorsey, Benny Goodman, and Eddie Lang, among others), and western music ("Home on the Range").

March 3. Radio personality Phil Harris—a longtime associate of comedian Jack Benny—makes his first recordings as a bandleader for Columbia.

March 21. Jazz pianist Art Tatum makes his first issued recordings. By then—having previously recorded as an accompanist for singer Adelaide Hall and cut a version of "Tiger Rag," unissued until after his death, that seems to turn his piano into an orchestra—he already was well known within the jazz music scene.

July. Victor releases "Love Is the Sweetest Thing" (#24333), by Ray Noble & His Orchestra. The record will become the first major American hit for Noble, who fronted the most popular British band of the 1930s. The multi-talented bandleader was also an accomplished pianist, arranger, and songwriter—his compositions included "Love Is the Sweetest Thing," "The Very Thought of You," and "The Touch of Your Lips."

c. July 16–20. Huddie Ledbetter, better known as "Leadbelly," makes his first recordings for the Library of Congress at the Louisiana State Penitentiary, Angola. The tracks—which feature his vocals and own guitar accompaniment—include "The Western Cowboy," 2 takes of "Honey Take a Whiff on Me," two takes of "Angola Blues," "Frankie and Abert," 3 takes of "Irene," "You Cain' Lose Me Cholly," and "Ella Speed." Leadbelly proved to be an intelligent and responsive interpreter of folk material as well as a gifted songwriter in his own right—his compositions included "Goodnight Irene," "Midnight Special," and "Rock Island Line." As a result, he was in great demand as a recording artist. Library of Congress archivist Alan Lomax was so taken with Leadbelly that he helped obtain a pardon from the Louisiana governor to enable the performer to reach a wider audience. Amidst a full slate of concert dates, Leadbelly recorded for the Library of Congress through May 1942 as well as many commercial labels, including the American Record Company, Banner, Musicraft, Victor, Bluebird, Biograph, Asch, Melodisc (England), and Disc from the mid-1930s through 1943. These, and later recordings up to his death in 1950, have appeared on countless album compilations worldwide up to the present day.

August. *Fortune* reports that Duke Ellington's band is earning $250,000 per year. The article also notes that Ellington is working on a five-part suite bearing the titles "Africa," "The Slave Shop," "The Plantation," and "Harlem," indicating that he was already planning on breaking new ground artistically.

August 3. Arthur Collins dies at age sixty-nine. A direct product of the minstrel tradition, Collins was considered the leading dialect comedy singer of the acoustic era. He was surpassed only by Henry Burr and Billy Murray as a hitmaker prior to World War I; his duo collaboration with Byron G. Harlan was one of the most successful in recording history. He was also a member of the Peerless Quartet (1906–1917) and the Big Four Quartet. His bestselling solo hits included "Kiss Me, Honey, Do" (Edison 5462; 1899), "Bill Bailey, Won't You Please Come Home" (Columbia 872; 1902), and "Any Rags?" (Victor 2519; 1903).

August 15. Xavier Cugat and His Waldorf-Astoria Orchestra make their first recordings in New York for Victor. Cugat would play a major role in popularizing Latin styles in the United States.

September 30. *As Thousands Cheer* premieres at the Music Box in New York City. The revue—which would have a run of four hundred performances—featured music and lyrics by Irving Berlin and sketches by Moss Hart. The show is structured in the form of a newspaper, with each story (preceded by a blowup of a headline) depicted via songs, dances, and skits.

October 9. Charlie Barnet and His Orchestra first record in New York. Tracks released from the session include "What Is Sweeter?"/"Buckin' the Wind" (Banner 32876), "I'm No Angel" (Banner 32875), and "I Want You, I Need You" (Domino 155).

November 18. *Roberta* premieres at the New Amsterdam Theatre in Manhattan. Featuring music by Jerome Kern and lyrics and book by Otto Harbach, the musical would have a run of 295 performances. Notable songs include "Smoke Gets in Your Eyes" and "Yesterdays." The 1935 film adaptation would Irene Dunne, Fred Astaire, and Ginger Rogers.

December. Prohibition is repealed; as a result, countless bars and cocktail lounges spring up nationwide. A significant percentage of these establishments introduce jukeboxes, which contribute to an upswing in record sales.

1934

❄

January. Jimmie Lunceford's band enjoy their first hit with "White Heat."

May 14. Willie "The Lion" Smith records his first tracks, "Finger Buster" and "I've Got to Have My Moments." The American Record Corporation rejects both solo piano pieces.

May 22. Jazz bandleader Teddy Wilson records for the first time; in this case, unaccompanied on the piano. All four tracks are rejected by Columbia.

June. *Billboard* begins printing a weekly survey of the most frequently played songs on network radio.

June 1. Joe Reichman and His Orchestra make their first recordings in New York for the Banner group of labels.

August 8. Bing Crosby becomes the first artist to sign with the newly founded Decca, headed by Jack Kapp.

August 31. Russ Columbo participates in a recording session for the last time, concluding with the Allie Wrubel-Mort Dixon composition, "I See Two Lovers."

September. Decca Records embarks on a large-scale promotional campaign centered on its roster of artists—most notably, Bing Crosby and Guy Lombardo—and a 35-cent record price. Aided by the upsurge in jukebox receipts, the record business slowly moves back towards the level of sales enjoyed in the 1920s.

September 2. Russ Columbo is fatally shot by an antique dueling pistol in an accident involving lifelong friend Lansing V. Brown Jr.

October 19. Archie Bleyer and His Orchestra make their first recordings in New York for Vocalion. Bleyer will go on to establish Cadence Records in the early 1950s, whose roster will include the Chordettes, the Everly Brothers, and Andy Williams.

1935

❄

February 9. Ray Noble and His Orchestra record in the United States for the first time. Two singles come out of the New York session: "Clouds"/"Sonny's Little Lullaby" (Victor 24879) and "Soon"/"Down By the River" (Victor 24879). The band was best known for English vocalist Al Bowlly—a romantic heartthrob on the order of a youthful Frank Sinatra—who was tragically killed during a German air raid in World War II.

April 2. Bandleader Bennie Moten died unexpectedly during a botched tonsillectomy. Relative Buster Moten briefly leads his group, but it would soon disband. Count Basie would step into the vacuum late that year, hiring key members of the Moten organization such as bassist Walter Page, trumpeter Hot Lips Page, and baritone saxophonist Jack Washington.

April 20. Bing Crosby's "Soon" (Decca 392) reaches number one on the pop music charts.

April 20. "Your Hit Parade" premieres on the radio. It will remain a broadcast media fixture (switching over to TV in the early 1950s) until going off the air on April 24, 1959. It also sets a precedent as the first independent (i.e., non-record label) ranking mechanism regarding the popularity of sound recordings.

April 27. "It's Easy to Remember" (Decca 391), by Bing Crosby with the Rhythmettes and Three Shades of Blue, accompanied by the George Stoll orchestra, tops the pop music charts.

May 4. The Dorsey Brothers Orchestra begin a two-week stint at number one on the pop charts with "Lullaby of Broadway" (Decca 370). The recording, which features Bob Crosby as vocalist, is culled from the film, *Gold Diggers of 1935*.

May 4. Eddy Duchin peaks at number one on the pop charts with "I Won't Dance" (Victor 24871), remaining there for three weeks. The recording appears in the film, *Roberta*.

May 18. "What's the Reason (I'm Not Pleasin' You)" (Decca 393), by Guy Lombardo & His Royal Canadians, begin a two-week stint atop the pop charts.

June 1. Bob Crosby and His Orchestra makes its first recordings in New York for Decca.

June 1. Ruth Etting's "Life is a Song" (Columbia 3031) reaches number one on the pop charts, remaining there for two weeks.

June 12. Sixteen-year-old singer Ella Fitzgerald records "Stompin' at the Savoy" and "Don't Be That Way" with Chick Webb's band, infusing the mediocre material with her trademark crystalline timbre and buoyant swing. Webb would nurture her artistry, helping her become a big star. When he died in 1939, Fitzgerald led the band until 1942.

June 15. Glen Gray & the Casa Loma Orchestra begin a four-week stay atop the pop charts with "When I Grow Too Old to Dream" (Decca 349). The recording, which features Kenny Sargent as vocalist, is culled from the film, *The Night is Young*.

June 22. Victor Young's Orchestra climbs to number one on the pop charts with "She's a Latin from Manhattan," remaining there for four weeks.

June 29. The Dorsey Brothers Orchestra, featuring Bob Eberle as vocalist, begin a three-week run atop the pop charts with "Chasing Shadows" (Decca 476).

July. Benny Goodman records for the first time with his trio, featuring drummer Gene Krupa and pianist Teddy Wilson.

July 13. Bob Crosby & His Orchestra, featuring Frank Tennille (father of Toni Tennille aka The Captain and Tennille), peak at number one on the pop charts with "In a Little Gypsy Tea Room" (Decca 478), remaining there for three weeks.

July 20. Ray Noble & His Orchestra begin a two-week stint atop the pop charts with "Let's Swing It" (Victor 25070).

August 3. Jimmie Lunceford & His Orchestra go number one with "Rhythm Is Our Business."

August 10. Fred Astaire's "Cheek to Cheek" (Brunswick 7486) begins an eleven-week run atop the pop charts.

August 10. Ray Noble & His Orchestra reach number one on the pop charts with "Paris in the Spring" (Victor 25040).

August 17. Ozzie Nelson & His Orchestra peak at number one on the pop charts with "And Then Some" (Brunswick 7464).

August 21. Benny Goodman—then in the midst of a coast-to-coast tour in which he had achieved a lukewarm response to the "safe" sweet band arrangements advocated by his handlers—lets loose with the swing charts he'd been wanting to play all along, causing the Palomar Ballroom, Los Angeles, crowd to erupt with enthusiasm. This event is widely viewed as the launching pad for his career and the swing era.

August 24. Tom Coakley & His Palace Hotel Orchestra, featuring Carl Ravassa as vocalist, begin a two-week stint atop the pop charts with "East of the Sun (And West of the Moon)" (Victor 25069).

September 7. Little Jack Little's "I'm in the Mood for Love" reaches number one, remaining there for three weeks.

September 23. DeWolf Hopper dies at age seventy-seven. Although popular in musical comedy for years, he was best known for the monologue, "Casey at the Bat" (Victor 31559; 1906), first performed onstage in 1888 and reprised by him an estimated ten thousand times.

October 16. Al Donahue and His Orchestra makes their first recordings in New York for Decca. The tenor saxophonist would remain popular through the 1940s.

October 19. Fats Waller's "Truckin'" begins a three-week stay atop the pop charts.

November. *Billboard* first publishes the major record companies' best-seller charts.

November 2. Eddy Duchin & His Orchestra peak at number one with "You Are My Lucky Star" (Victor 25125), remaining there for three weeks. The recording appears in the film, *Broadway Melody of 1936*.

November 28. Charlie Parker performs professionally for the first time, earning $1.25.

November 30. Guy Lombardo & His Royal Canadians begin a four-week run atop the pop charts with "Red Sails in the Sunset" (Decca 554). The song is included in the Broadway musical, *Provincetown Follies*.

December 13. Trumpeter Bunny Berigan heads his own group—His Blue Boys—in the recording studio for the first time in New York. Two releases come out of the session: "You Took Advantage of Me"/"Chicken and Waffles" (Decca 18117) and "I'm Coming, Virginia"/"Blues" (Decca 18116).

December 21. Bing Crosby, accompanied by Victor Young's Orchestra, reaches number one on the pop charts with his own version of "Red Sails in the Sunset" (Decca 616), remaining there for two weeks.

December 21. Tommy Dorsey & His Orchestra have their first hit, going number one with "On Treasure Island" (Victor 25144). His group, which includes the heart of the Joe Haymes ensemble, is fronted here by vocalist Edythe Wright.

December 28. Fats Waller's "A Little Bit Independent" begins a two-week stint atop the pop charts.

1936

❄

January 4. *Billboard* publishes a pop music chart that ranks records on national sales for the first time.

January 4. Tommy Dorsey & His Orchestra, featuring vocalist Edythe Wright, begin a five-week run atop the pop charts with "The Music Goes Round and Round" (Victor 25201). The novelty song is included in the film, *The Music Goes 'Round*.

January 4. The Riley-Farley Orchestra reach number one on the pop charts with their version of "The Music Goes Round and Round," remaining there for three weeks.

January 10. Edward M. Favor dies in Brooklyn at age seventy-nine. He starred in vaudeville and Broadway musical comedies before making his first recording for Columbia in 1893. He specialized in Irish and comic songs, most notably nonsense materials such as "Mr. Dooley" (Columbia 876 and Edison 8125; 1902) and "Fol-the-Rol-Lol" (Victor).

January 13. Baritone Steve Porter dies at age seventy-one. He started out as a vaudeville comedian in the 1890s, and went on to become a member of the Columbia Male (1904–1905), Peerless (1906–1909), and American Quartets (1909–1919).

February 1. Eddy Duchin & His Orchestra, featuring vocalist Lew Sherwood, begin a three-week stay atop the pop charts with "Moon Over Miami" (Victor 25212).

February 8. Tommy Dorsey & His Orchestra, featuring vocalist Cliff Weston, goes number one on the pop charts with "Alone" (Victor 25191), remaining there for six weeks. The song is included in the Marx Brothers film, *A Night at the Opera*.

February 26. Red Norvo—who'd previously made a number of small jazz combo recordings—records his first big band sides in New York.

February 29. Jan Garber's "A Beautiful Lady in Blue" begins a two-week stint atop the pop charts.

March 14. Benny Goodman & His Orchestra, featuring vocalist Helen Ward, reach number one on the pop charts with "Goody-Goody" (Victor 25245), remaining there for six weeks.

March 21. Eddy Duchin & His Orchestra, featuring vocalist Lew Sherwood, climb to the summit of the pop charts with "Lights Out" (Victor 25212), a feat accomplished the prior month by the disc's flip side.

April 4. Fred Astaire's "I'm Putting All My Eggs in One Basket" (Brunswick 7609) peaks at number one on the pop charts.

April 11. Les Brown first records as a bandleader—with His Duke (University) Blue Devils—in New York for the Thesaurus label.

April 11. "It's Been So Long" (Victor 25245), by Benny Goodman & His Orchestra, featuring vocalist Helen Ward, joins the disc's flip side at the top the pop charts, remaining there for two weeks.

April 28. Silas Leachman dies at age seventy-sex. The minstrel singer was one of the most popular artists during the first decade of commercial recording. Based in Chicago, he abruptly stopped recording activities in 1902 when faced with the imperative of moving East (where the studios of the major labels were located). His biggest hit came with "Dem Golden Slippers" (Columbia, 1894).

May 2. Guy Lombardo & His Royal Canadians begin a two-week stint atop the pop charts with "Lost" (Victor 25271).

May 9. Jan Garber's "A Melody From the Sky" reaches number one on the pop charts, remaining there for three weeks.

May 18. Shep Fields and His Rippling Rhythm make their first recordings in New York for Bluebird. Fields would remain popular well into the 1940s.

May 23. Tommy Dorsey & His Orchestra climb to the summit of the pop charts with "You" (Victor 25291), taken from the film, *The Great Ziegfeld*.

May 30. Benny Goodman & His Orchestra, featuring vocalist Helen Ward, begin a six-week run atop the pop charts with "The Glory of Love" (Victor 25316).

June 6. Jimmy Dorsey & His Orchestra, featuring vocalist Bob Eberly, head up the pop charts with "Is It True What They Say About Dixie?" (Decca 768), remaining there for four weeks.

June 6. Fat Waller's "All My Life" reaches number one on the pop charts.

June 11. Artie Shaw makes his first big band recording in New York for Brunswick.

June 30. Billie Holiday records "I Cried for You"; considered her first "hit" by record producer Michael Brooks, it reportedly goes on to sell fifteen thousand copies.

July 11. Hal Kemp's "There's a Small Hotel" begins a two-week stint atop the pop charts.

July 18. Eddy Duchin & His Orchestra, featuring vocalist Jerry Cooper, ascend to the summit of the pop charts with "Take My Heart" (Victor 25343), remaining there for two weeks.

July 25. Fats Waller's "It's a Sin to Tell a Lie" begins a four-week run atop the pop charts.

August 1. Benny Goodman & His Orchestra, featuring vocalist Helen Ward, reaches number one on the pop charts with "These Foolish Things Remind Me of You" (Victor 25351), remaining there for two weeks. The song first appeared in the London musical, *Spread It Around*.

August 15. Hal Kemp's "When I'm With You" begins a two-week stay atop the pop charts.

August 22. Andy Kirk's "Until the Real Thing Comes Along" goes number one on the pop charts, remaining there for two weeks.

August 29. Shep Fields & His Rippling Rhythm Orchestra, featuring vocalist Charles Chester, begin a four-week run atop the pop charts with "Did I Remember?" (Bluebird 6476). The song appears in the film, *Suzy*.

September 5. Fred Astaire reaches number one on the pop charts with "A Fine Romance" (Brunswick 7716), remaining there for five weeks.

September 10. Soprano Grace Kerns dies at age fifty. She had approximately a dozen hits between 1911–1917, most notably, "Love Has Wings" (Columbia 5574; 1914) with Chales Harrison, and "Chinatown, My Chinatown" (Columbia 1624; 1915), with John Barnes Wells.

September 11. Byron G. Harlan dies at age seventy-five. In addition to achieving renown with the ragtime and minstrel comedy team, Collins and Harlan, he was extremely successful as a solo recording artist, specializing in sentimental ballads. His biggest hits included "Hello Central, Give Me Heaven" (Edison 7852; 1901), "All Aboard for Dreamland" (Edison 8700; 1904), and "Wait Till the Sun Shines, Nellie" (Columbia 3321; 1906).

October 3. Fred Astaire's "The Way You Look To-night" (Brunswick 7717) begins a six-week stay atop the pop charts.

October 10. Guy Lombardo & His Royal Canadians climb to the summit of the pop charts with "When Did You Leave Heaven?" (Victor 25357), remaining there for two weeks.

November 6. Woody Herman and His Orchestra make their first recordings in New York for Decca.

November 9. John Hammond oversees the recording of four tracks by a Count Basie-led quintet for Columbia's Vocalion division. They are the first recordings to include Lester Young, and are issued under the names of drummer Jo Jones and trumpeter Carl Smith to circumvent Basie's draconian Decca contract.

November 14. Benny Goodman & His Orchestra begin a two-week stint atop the pop charts with "You Turned the Tables On Me" (Victor 25391). The instrumental appears in the film, *Sing, Baby, Sing*.

November 23. Blues great Robert Johnson makes his earliest recordings during the American Record Company's three-month field trip to San Antonio. The tracks include "Kind Hearted Woman Blues" (Matrices SA-2580-1 and SA-2580-2), "I Believe I'll Dust My Broom" (SA-2581-1), "Sweet Home Chicago" (SA-2582-1 and SA-2582-2), "Ramblin' On My Mind" (SA-2583-1, SA-2583-2 and SA-2583-3), "When You Got A Good Friend" (SA-2584-1), "Come On In My Kitchen" (SA-2585-1 and SA-2585-2),

"Terraplane Blues" (SA-2586-1), and "Phonograph Blues" (SA-2587-1 and SA-2587-2). Undoubtedly recognizing the magnitude of Johnson's talent, ARC brought him back for an additional twelve takes on November 26–27. The label captured the singer/guitarist on an additional nineteen tracks during a field trip to Dallas June 19–20, 1937. When legendary talent scout John Hammond traveled to Johnson's home base in Mississippi the following year, hoping to arrange more recording sessions, he found that the artist had died under somewhat mysterious circumstances (most music historians believe he was poisoned by the jealous lover of a woman he had shown an interest in at a roadside honky tonk). Johnson would languish in obscurity until Columbia issued an LP compilation of his tracks in 1961; it would become one of the most influential blues recordings ever, helping provide the stimulus for the 1960s blues revival. Artists like Eric Clapton and Cream, Fleetwood Mac, and the Rolling Stones, among others, owed a particular debt to Johnson, performing and recording his material early in their careers.

Thanksgiving Day. Sixteen-year-old Charlie Parker and his band associates are involved in a car accident that results in three broken ribs and the death of a friend. Many have surmised that he first used heroin as a painkiller at this time; shortly afterward, he showed his wife how he shot the drug into his veins.

November 28. Bing Crosby, accompanied by Georgie Stoll & His Orchestra, begins a ten-week run atop the pop charts with "Pennies From Heaven" (Decca 947), the theme song from the film of the same name.

December 5. Eddy Duchin & His Orchestra, featuring vocalist Jimmy Newell, reach number one on the pop charts with "I'll Sing You a Thousand Love Songs" (Victor 25393).

December 12. Shep Fields & His Rippling Rhythm Orchestra begin a two-week stint atop the pop charts with "In the Chapel in the Moonlight" (Bluebird 6640).

1937

❄

January 2. Eddy Duchin & His Orchestra begin a two-week stint atop the pop charts with "It's De-Lovely" (Victor 25432). The song is culled from the Broadway musical, *Red, Hot and Blue*.

January 17. Following a series of guess appearances beginning in the fall of 1936, Gene Austin is billed as a regular cast member on the *Joe Penner Show*. He remains a mainstay on the national program (broadcast by WABC) for two full seasons.

January 21. Count Basie records his first big band track, "Honeysuckle Rose."

February 6. Benny Goodman & His Orchestra reach number one on the pop charts with "Goodnight, My Love" (Victor 25461), remaining there for four weeks. The recording—which features vocalist Ella Fitzgerald and trumpeter Harry James—is included in the film, *Stowaway*.

February 20. Henry Busse's "With Plenty of Money and You" climbs to the summit of the pop charts.

February 20. Hal Kemp's "This Year's Kisses" begins a four-week run atop the pop charts.

February 27. Benny Goodman & His Orchestra, featuring vocalist Jimmy Rushing and trumpeter Bunny Berrigan, reaches number one on the pop charts with "This Year's Kisses" (Victor 25505), remaining there for three weeks. The song appears in the film, *On the Avenue*.

March 27. Tommy Dorsey & His Orchestra, featuring vocalist Jack Leonard, begin a two-week stint atop the pop charts with the million-selling "Marie" (Victor 25523).

April 3. Guy Lombardo & His Royal Canadians peak at number one on the pop charts with "Boo Hoo" (Victor 25522), remaining there for five weeks.

April 14. *Babes In Arms* premieres at New York's Shubert Theatre. Featuring music by Richard Rodgers and lyrics by Lorenz Hart (they also wrote the book), it would run for 289 performances. The work featured more hits than any other Rodgers and Hart musical, including "I Wish I Were in Love Again," "Johnny One Note," "The Lady Is a Tramp," "My Funny Valentine," and "Where or When." It would be made into a film in 1939, starring Judy Garland and Mickey Rooney.

April 14. Swing and Sway with Sammy Kaye make their first recordings in New York for Vocalion.

April 17. Bing Crosby, accompanied by Lani McIntyre & His Hawaiians, begins a ten-week stay atop the pop charts with "Sweet Leilani" (Decca 1175).

April 19. Edward Meeker dies at age sixty-three. Best known to pioneer recording aficionados as Edison's song announcer and sound effects specialist from the early years of the century to the 1920s, he also was a successful solo artist. His biggest hits came with "Harrigan" (Edison 9616; 1907) and "Take Me Out to the Ball Game" (Edison 9926; 1908).

April 24. Bing Crosby reaches number one on the pop charts with "Too Marvelous for Words" (Decca 1185), culled from the film, *Ready, Willing, and Able*.

May 1. Fred Astaire ascends to the summit of the pop charts with "They Can't Take That Away from Me" (Brunswick 7855).

May 6. The last California Ramblers recording date—which utilizes the entire Charlie Barnet Orchestra—takes place in New York.

May 15. Teddy Wilson & His Orchestra, featuring vocalist Billie Holiday, begin a three-week run atop the pop charts with "Carelessly" (Brunswick 7867).

May 26. Blue Barron and His Orchestra first record in New York. One release comes out of the session: "I'm Feelin' Like a Million"/"Yours and Mine" (Vocalion 3772).

June 5. Guy Lombardo & His Royal Canadians reach number one on the pop charts with "September in the Rain" (Victor 25526), remaining there for four weeks. The song appears in the films *Stars Over Broadway* and *Melody for Two*.

June 14. Claude Thornhill and His Orchestra make their first recordings in New York for Vocalion.

July 3. Guy Lombardo & His Royal Canadians begin a five-week stay atop the pop charts with "It Looks Like Rain in Cherry Blossom Lane" (Victor 25572).

July 3. Russ Morgan & His Orchestra, featuring vocalist Jimmy Lewis, go number one on the pop charts with "The Merry-Go-Round Broke Down" (Brunswick 7888), remaining there for two weeks.

July 7. Count Basie records "One O'Clock Jump" for Decca. His opening solo becomes part of the tune to musicians who admired his clever use of dissonance.

July 17. Shep Fields & His Rippling Rhythm Orchestra begin a two-week stint atop the pop charts with "The Merry-Go-Round Broke Down" (Bluebird 7015).

July 24. Hal Kemp's "Where or When" reaches number one on the pop charts.

July 31. Horace Heidt & His Orchestra, featuring vocalist Larry Cotton, peak at number one on the pop charts with "Gone with the Wind" (Brunswick 7913).

July 31. Fats Waller's "Smarty" begins a two-week stint atop the pop charts.

August 7. Guy Lombardo & Royal Canadians climb to the summit of the pop charts with "A Sailboat in the Moonlight" (Victor 25594), remaining there for three weeks.

August 9. Count Basie records Eddie Durhams's "Time Out" and "Topsy." The tracks reveal him to be progressing in the utilization of his recently expanded big band resources.

August 21. Tommy Dorsey & His Orchestra begin a three-week stay atop the pop charts with the instrumental, "Satan Takes a Holiday" (Victor 25570).

September 4. Bob Crosby & His Orchestra reach number one on the pop charts with "Whispers in the Dark" (Decca 1346), remaining there for four weeks. The song appears in the film, *Artists and Models*.

September 11. Tommy Dorsey's Clambake Seven begin a two-week stint atop the pop charts with "The Big Apple" (Victor 25652).

September 11. Guy Lombardo & His Royal Canadians peak at number one on the pop charts with "So Rare" (Victor 25626).

September 25. Bing Crosby begins a four-week run atop the pop charts with "The Moon Got in My Eyes" (Decca 1375). The single is included in the film, *Double or Nothing*.

September 26. Bessie Smith—widely considered the best blues singer ever—dies at age forty-two from loss of blood in an apparent effort to secure hospital admittance following an auto accident. She toured with Ma Rainey prior to recording her debut disc, the million-selling "Down-Hearted Blues" (Columbia 3844; 1923). Her hits, recorded between 1923 and 1929, played a key role in saving Columbia from bankruptcy. They remain vital to the present day, due not only to the unrivalled depth and power of her vocal style, but for the frequent presence of the era's leading jazz musicians (e.g., Louis Armstrong) as accompanists.

October 9. Sheps Fields & His Rippling Rhythm Orchestra go to number one on the pop charts with "That Old Feeling" (Bluebird 7066), remaining there for four weeks. The song is included in the film, *Vogues of 1938*.

October 10. Charles Adams Prince dies at age sixty-eight. Originally a pianist and celesta player, he served as musical director of Columbia Records from the turn of the century to the early 1920s. In that capacity, his band backed virtually every vocalist recording for that label. Prince's Orchestra also had their own hits, including "Ballin' the Jack" (Columbia 5595; 1914) and "Hello, Hawaii, How Are You?" (Columbia 5780; 1916).

October 16. Teddy Wilson & His Orchestra, featuring tenor saxophonist Vido Musso, begin a two-week stint atop the pop charts with the instrumental, "You Can't Stop Me from Dreaming" (Brunswick 7954).

October 17. Larry Clinton and His Orchestra records for the first time in New York for Victor.

November 2. *I'd Rather Be Right* premieres at the Alvin Theatre, in New York City. Featuring music by Richard Rodgers, lyrics by Lorenz Hart, and book by George S. Kaufman and Moss Hart, the musical would run for 290 performances. Stanley Green's *Broadway Musicals* (1994) would call it "the most anxiously awaited theatrical event of the decade" because the central character was Franklin Delano Roosevelt, and the part was played by George M. Cohan (his first musical in ten years, and the only one he appeared in where he hadn't been the composer).

November 6. Bing Crosby reaches number one on the pop charts with "Remember Me?" (Decca 1451), remaining there for three weeks. The single in included in the film, *Mr. Dodd Takes the Air*.

November 20. Rudy Vallee's "Vieni, Vieni" heads up the pop charts.

November 27. Tommy Dorsey & His Orchestra, with vocal quartet accompaniment, begin a seven-week stay atop the pop charts with "Once in a While" (Victor 25686).

November 27. Tommy Dorsey & His Orchestra, featuring vocalist Edythe Wright, settles in at number one on the pop charts with the novelty number, "The Dipsy Doodle" (Victor 25693), remaining there for six weeks.

November 27. *Pins and Needles* premieres at the Labor Stage, in New York City. Featuring music and lyrics by Harold Rome and sketches by miscellaneous writers, it would run for 1,108 performances, passing *Irene* as the long-run record holder.

December 1. *Hooray For What!* premieres at the Winter Garden, in New York City. Featuring music by Harold Arlen, lyrics by E. Y. Harburg, and book by Howard Lindsay and Russel rouse, it would run for two hundred performances.

December 1. Harry James and His Orchestra record for the first time. The New York session produces "When We're Alone"/"Life Goes to a Party" (Brunswick 8035) and "Jubilee"/"(I Can Dream) Can't I" (Brunswick 8038).

December 3. Al Bowlly and His Orchestra record in New York for Bluebird (the sides will be released by His Master's Voice in Great Britain). These are the only recordings where the popular vocalist is listed as a bandleader.

December 11. Bing Crosby and Connee Boswell, accompanied by John Scott Trotter's Orchestra top the pop charts with "Bob White (Whatcha Gonna Swing Tonight?)" (Decca 1483).

1938

❄

January 1. Fred Astaire, accompanied by Ray Noble & His Orchestra, reaches number one on the pop charts with "Nice Work If You Can Get It" (Brunswick 7983). The song appears in the film, *A Damsel in Distress*.

January 15. Sammy Kaye & His Orchestra, featuring vocalist Tommy Ryan, begin a two-week stint on the pop charts with "Rosalie" (Vocalion), adapted from the film of the same name.

January 16. Benny Goodman triumphs in a sold-out concert at New York's Carnegie Hall. Joined by stars of the Count Basie and Duke Ellington bands, it is the first full evening of jazz at the famed venue, and with an integrated cast.

January 22. The Andrews Sisters, accompanied by trumpeter Bobby Hackett, begin a five-week run atop the charts with "Bel Mir Bist Du Schoen" (Decca 1562). The novelty song is adapted from the 1933 Yiddish musical, *I Would If I Could*.

January 29. Dolly Dawn makes the summit of the pop charts with "You're a Sweetheart."

February 26. Shep Fields & His Rippling Rhythm Orchestra, featuring vocalist Bob Goday, begin a four-week stay atop the pop charts with "Thanks for the Memory" (Bluebird 7318), adapted from the film, *The Big Broadcast of 1938*.

March 19. Benny Goodman & His Orchestra peaks at number one on the pop charts with the instrumental, "Don't Be That Way" (Victor 25792), remaining there for five weeks.

March 19. Horace Heidt & His Orchestra, featuring vocalists Lysbeth Hughes and Larry Cotton, begins a six-week run atop the pop charts with the Spanish song, "Ti-Pi-Tin" (Brunswick 8078).

April 8. King Oliver, the "king" of New Orleans jazz cornet during the post-World War I period, dies in Savannah, Georgia. His was the first black jazz band to record commercially; their biggest sellers included "Dipper Mouth Blues" (Okeh 4918; 1924), which featured then sideman Louis Armstrong, and "St. James Infirmary" (Victor 22298; 1930).

April 11. Vaudeville comedian Eddie Morton dies at age sixty-seven. While his most popular recording was "You Ain't Talking To Me" (Columbia 777; 1910), his "Oceana Roll" (Victor 16908; 1911) achieves far wider distribution in that it appeared on the flip side of Collins & Harlan's mega-seller, "Alexander's Ragtime Band."

April 14. Gene Krupa and His Orchestra make their first recordings in New York for Brunswick.

April 23. Duke Ellington & His Orchestra—featuring solos by Johnny Hodges, Barney Bigard, Harry Carney and Lawrence Brown—go number one on the pop charts with the instrumental "I Let a Song Go Out of My Heart" (Brunswick 8108), remaining there for three weeks.

May 7. Red Norvo & His Orchestra begin a two-week stint atop the pop charts with "Please Be Kind" (Brunswick 8088).

May 14. Sammy Kaye & His Orchestra, featuring vocalist Tommy Ryan, reach number one on the pop charts with "Love Walked In" (Vocalion 4017), remaining there for three weeks. The song is adapted from the film, *Goldwyn Follies*.

May 21. Larry Clinton & His Orchestra, featuring vocalist Bea Wain, begin a four-week stay atop the pop charts with "Cry, Baby, Cry" (Victor 25819).

May 28. Shep Fields & His Rippling Rhythm Orchestra, featuring vocalist Jerry Stewart, peak at number one on the pop charts with "Cathedral in the Pines" (Bluebird 7553), remaining there for three weeks.

June 11. Benny Goodman, featuring vocalist Martha Tilton, ascends to the summit of the pop charts with "I Let a Song Go Out of My Heart" (Victor 25840).

June 18. Red Norvo & His Orchestra begin a four-week run atop the pop charts with "Says My Heart" (Brunswick 8135).

June 25. Ella Fitzgerald, with Chick Webb & his Orchestra, heads up the pop charts with "A-Tisket, A-Tasket" (Decca 1840), enjoying a three-week run. The song is selected for the NARAS Hall of Fame.

July 16. Tommy Dorsey & His Orchestra, featuring vocalist Edythe Wright, begin a six-week stay atop the pop charts with "Music Maestro, Please" (Victor 25866).

August 16. Blues singer/guitarist Robert Johnson is allegedly poisoned by a jealous rival for a woman's affection while performing at a small roadhouse in Mississippi. His record company, Columbia, would not hear of his death until legendary executive John Hammond attempted to locate him the following spring. While Johnson's style of rural acoustic blues was considered anachronistic when his seminal recordings were made in the mid-1930s, he exerted a profound influence on key artists of the 1960s blues revival like Eric Clapton, The Rolling Stones, and Led Zeppelin.

September 17. Fred Astaire, accompanied by Ray Noble & His Orchestra, goes number one on the pop charts with "Change Partners" (Brunswick 8189), remaining there for two weeks. The song appears in the film, *Carefree*.

September 24. Bing Crosby and Connee Boswell, with a spoken introduction by Eddie Boswell, enjoy a two-week stint atop the pop charts with "Alexander's Ragtime Band" (Decca 1887).

October 1. Larry Clinton & His Orchestra, featuring vocalist Bea Wain, peaks at number one on the pop charts with "My Reverie" (Victor 26006), remaining there for eight weeks. The recording is an adaptation of Debussy's 1895 piece.

October 1. Bing Crosby begins a four-week run top the pop charts with "I've Got a Pocketful of Dreams" (Decca 1933), from the film, *Sing You Sinners*.

October 15. Jimmy Dorsey & His Orchestra, featuring vocalist Bob Eberly, head up the pop charts with "Change Partners" (Decca 2002), remaining there for two weeks. The song appears in the film, *Carefree*.

October 29. Larry Clinton & His Orchestra, featuring vocalist Bea Wain, ascend to the summit of the pop charts with "Heart and Soul" (Victor 26046).

October 29. Russ Morgan & His Orchestra begin a two-week stint atop the pop charts with "I've Got a Pocketful of Dreams" (Decca 1936). The song appears in the film, *Sing You Sinners*.

November 5. Artie Shaw & His Orchestra reaches number one on the top charts with Cole Porter's "Begin the Beguine" (Bluebird 7746), residing there for six weeks. From the Broadway musical, *Jubilee*, a *Billboard* disc jockey poll would vote the million-selling instrumental third best all-time record and fifth all-time song. Essentially a serious musician, Shaw would be troubled by fame and by the fact that he was discouraged following his more progressive instincts.

November 7. Dan Quinn dies at age seventy-nine. Reputed to have recorded 2,500-odd songs over a twenty-year career, he—along with George J. Gaskin and Len Spencer—was one of three major vocal recording stars of the 1890s. His hits included "Daddy Wouldn't Buy Me a Bow-Wow" (New Jersey, 1892) and "The Sidewalks of New York" (Columbia, 1895).

December. ARC is purchased from Consolidated Film for $700,000 by the Columbia Broadcasting System. As a result, the rights to the Brunswick and Vocalion labels return to Warner Brothers, which then assigns them to Decca.

December 17. Fats Waller's "Two Sleepy People" begins a two-week stint atop the pop charts.

December 31. Bing Crosby, accompanied by Bob Crosby's Orchestra, heads up the pop charts with "You Must Have Been a Beautiful Baby" (Decca 2147), enjoying a two-week run.

December 31. Andy Kirk begins a two-week stint atop the pop charts with "I Won't Tell a Soul (I Love You)."

1939

❄

January 7. Artie Shaw & His Orchestra, featuring vocalist Helen Forrest, peak at number one on the pop charts with "They Say" (Bluebird 10075), remaining there for two weeks.

January 14. Al Donohue's "Jeepers Creepers" begins a five-week stay atop the pop charts.

January 14. Artie Shaw & His Orchestra, featuring vocalist Helen Forrest, reach number one on the pop charts with the movie title song, "Thanks for Ev'rything" (Bluebird 10055).

February 4. Kay Kyser & His Orchestra, featuring vocalists Ginny Simms and Harry Babbitt, ascend to the summit of the pop charts with "The Umbrella Man" (Brunswick 8225).

February 11. Larry Clinton & His Orchestra, featuring vocalist Bea Wain, begin a nine-week run atop the pop charts with "Deep Purple" (Victor 26141).

March 9. Baritone Ernest Hare dies at age fifty-five. Together with tenor Billy Jones (d. November 23, 1940; 51), he formed The Happiness Boys, extremely popular radio team in the 1920s and 1930s. Also a successful recording act prior to the Great Depression, their hits included "Barney Google" (Columbia 3876; 1923) and "I Miss My Swiss (My Swiss Miss Misses Me)" (Victor 19718; 1925).

March 18. Guy Lombardo & His Royal Canadians peak at number one on the pop charts with "Penny Serenade" (Decca 2291).

April 15. *Billboard* reports that the traveling tent show, "Star-O-Rama of 1939," featuring Gene Austin, opened in Moultrie, Georgia (dateline April 8). Austin takes over the tour on July, and becomes embroiled in legal difficulties involving back taxes and payments due.

April 22. Glen Gray & the Casa Loma Orchestra, featuring vocalist Clyde Burke, begin a two-week stint atop the pop charts with "Heaven Can Wait" (Decca 2321).

May 6. Tommy Dorsey & His Orchestra head up the pop charts with "Our Love" (Victor 28202), which is adapted from a melody in Tchaikovsky's *Romeo and Juliet*.

May 13. Benny Goodman & His Orchestra—featuring vocalist Martha Tilton and trumpeter Ziggy Elman— begin a five-week stay atop the "And the Angels Sing" (Victor 26170). The recording is an adaptation of the traditional Hebraic song.

May 20. Kay Kyser & His Orchestra—featuring vocals by Ginny Simms and Harry Babbitt—reach number one on the pop charts with "Three Little Fishes" (Brunswick 8368).

June 3. Will Glahe's "Beer Barrel Polka" begins a four-week run atop the pop charts.

June 10. Glenn Miller & His Orchestra go number one on the pop charts with "Wishing (Will Make It So)" and remain there for four weeks.

July 8. Glenn Miller & His Orchestra begin a four-week stay atop the pop charts with "Stairway to the Stars" (Bluebird 10276), based on a theme from "Park Avenue Fantasy."

August. Benny Goodman hires both trumpeter Cootie Williams and electric guitarist Charlie Christian on the recommendations of John Hammond. Williams contributed to the rich texture of the Goodman band while Christian—primarily through his participation in the New York City jam sessions at Minton's— helped consolidate the be-bop revolution.

August 12. Glen Gray & the Casa Loma Orchestra, featuring pianist/composer Frankie Carle, peak at number one on the pop charts with "Sunrise Serenade" (Decca 2321), remaining there for two weeks.

August 12. Glenn Miller & His Orchestra, featuring vocalist Ray Eberle, begin a four-week run atop the pop charts with "Moon Love" (Bluebird 10303), adapted from the second movement of Tchaikovsky's *Fifth Symphony*.

August 16. Tenor Harry Tally dies at age seventy-three. He had numerous hits during the first two decades of the twentieth century, most notably, "Wait Till the Sun Shines, Nellie" (Victor 4551; 1906). He also was a member of the Empire City Quartet, who achieved major success on the vaudeville circuit.

September 9. Glenn Miller & His Orchestra, featuring Marion Hutton, reach number one of the pop charts with "The Man with the Mandolin" (Bluebird 10358), remaining there for three weeks.

September 9. Glenn Miller & His Orchestra begin a seven-week stay atop the pop charts with an adaptation of the featured song from the film, *The Wizard of Oz*, "Over the Rainbow" (Bluebird 10366).

September 19. The Dixie Hummingbirds record sixteen songs, without instrumental accompaniment, for Decca in New York City. The tracks will be coupled and released over time as eight 78 rpm discs, beginning with "When the Gates Swing Open"/"Joshua Journeyed To Jericho" (#7645). The gospel quartet—originally comprise of lead vocalist James B. Davis, tenor Fred Baker, baritone Barney Parks, and bass Jimmy Bryant—will resume recording in the mid-1940s for independent labels such as Apollo, Gotham, and Peacock. Many rock music listeners will be introduced to the group through their support role on Paul Simon's 1973 Top Five hit, "She Loves Me Like a Rock" (Columbia).

September 30. Glenn Miller & His Orchestra, featuring Tex Beneke on tenor saxophone, ascend to the summit of the pop charts with "Blue Orchilds" (Bluebird 10372).

October 11. Coleman Hawkins, having recently returned to New York following an extended stay in Europe, records his most famous performance, a restless solo on "Body and Soul" that demonstrates his harmonic ingenuity, use of double time, and intricate development of rhythmic motifs.

October 15. *Down Beat* publishes a letter from Billie Holiday under the caption, "Les Young Wasn't Carved." She argued that Young was not bested by Coleman Hawkins in a recent jam session bout featuring both tenor saxophonists.

October 21. Bob Crosby & His Orchestra, featuring vocalist Helen Ward, goes number one on the pop charts with "Day In, Day Out" (Decca 2703).

November 4. Shep Fields & His Rippling Rhythm Orchestra, featuring vocalist Hal Derwin, begin a five-week run atop the pop charts with "South of the Border (Down Mexico Way)" (Bluebird 10376).

November 11. Ink Spots peak at number one on the pop charts with "Address Unknown" (Decca 2707).

November 25. Frankie Masters' "Scatter-Brain" begins an eight-week stay atop the pop charts.

December 22. Ma Rainey—her real name was Gertrude Malissa Pridgett—dies at age fifty-three. Although the pioneer blues singer had only one mainstream bestseller—"See See Rider Blues" (Paramount 12252; 1925), she greatly influenced Bessie Smith.

December 24. Walter B. Rogers dies at age seventy-four. He was the featured cornetist in Sousa's band, and conducted on some of the famed bandleader's recordings. He also directed the Victor Light Opera Co. and Victor Military Band as well as conducting the orchestral accompaniment for virtually all Victor artists between 1908 and 1916.

1940

❄

January 18. Tony Pastor and His Orchestra make their first recordings in New York for Bluebird.

January 27. Tommy Dorsey & His Orchestra, featuring vocalist Jack Leonard, begin a two-week stint atop the pop charts with "All the Things You Are" (Victor 26401). The song appears in the Broadway musical, *Very Warm for May*.

February. Charlie Parker returns to Kansas City following a year in New York City, joining Jay McShann's newly formed big band.

February 3. Glenn Miller & His Orchestra reach number one on the pop charts with "Careless" (Bluebird 10520), remaining there for five weeks.

February 10. Glenn Miller & His Orchestra begin a twelve-week run atop the pop charts with "In the Mood" (Bluebird 10416). Based on a riff originating in Wingy Manone's "Tar Paper Stomp," the recording includes solos by tenor saxophonists Tex Beneke and Al Klink, and trumpeter Clyde Hurley. The million seller would be selected for the NARAS Hall of Fame.

February 18. Rudy Wiedoeft dies in Flushing Hospital, Queens, New York, at age forty-seven. Perhaps the most dynamic saxophonist of his days, his recordings and concert appearances from the World War I era through the 1920s played a major role in popularizing the instrument within the pop and jazz fields.

February 24. Tommy Dorsey & His Orchestra, featuring vocalist Jack Leonard, peak at number one on the pop charts with 1919 song, "Indian Summer" (Victor 26390).

February 29. Sherman Houston Dudley, an American African performer best known as a featured member of the touring vaudeville and musical comedy company, The Smart Set, dies. Due to the use of his initials for his stage name, he was sometimes confused with Victor recording artist, S. H. Dudley.

March 6. Duke Ellington records the mid-tempo "Ko-Ko" (Victor), intended as a number for a never completed opera, *Boola*. According to Lewis Porter and Michael Ullman (*Jazz*. Prentice-Hall, 1993), the instrumental work was startling for its time: at times dissonant to an extreme, a piece without a singable melody that is powerfully, unforgettably evocative."

March 16. Benny Goodman & His Orchestra, featuring vocalist Mildred Bailey and pianist Fletcher Henderson, ascends to the summit of the pop charts with "Darn That Dream" (Columbia 35331). The song is adapted from the Broadway musical, *Swingin' the Dream*.

March 30. Glenn Miller & His Orchestra begin a five-week stay atop the pop charts with "When You Wish Upon a Star" (Bluebird 10570). The single, which features a tenor sax solo by Tex Beneke, is adapted from the Disney animated feature, *Pinocchio*.

May 1. Benny Goodman performs the Mozart *Concerto for Clarinet* with conductor Leopold Stokowski.

May 4. Glenn Miller & His Orchestra go number one on the pop charts with "Tuxedo Junction" (Bluebird 10612), remaining there for nine weeks. The million-selling instrumental features solos by Dale McMickle on muted trumpet, trumpeter Clyde Hurley, and pianist Chummy MacGregor.

May 4. Glenn Miller & His Orchestra, featuring vocalist Marion Hutton, begin a seven-week run atop the pop charts with "The Woodpecker Song" (Bluebird 10598), adapted from the song, "Reginella Campagnola."

June 17. Vaughn Monroe and His Orchestra make their recording debut in New York. The session produces two singles: "I'm Home Again"/"I'll Wait for You Forever" (Bluebird B-10767) and "The Gentleman Need a Shave"/"If You See Margie" (Bluebird B-10798).

June 22. Glenn Miller & His Orchestra reach number one on the pop charts with "Imagination" (Bluebird 10622), remaining there for three weeks.

July. *Billboard* magazine begins publishing a national popular music chart. The first number one single is Tommy Dorsey's "I'll Never Smile Again" (Victor).

July. Benny Goodman is forced to disband his group due to a back injury.

July 10. Mitchell Ayres & His Fashions in Music begin a two-week stint atop the pop charts with "Make-Believe Land" (Bluebird).

July 20. Glenn Miller & His Orchestra peak at number one on the pop charts with "Fools Rush In (Where Angels Fear to Tread)" (Bluebird 10728). The song is frequently revived, most notably by Brook Benton (1960) and Rick Nelson (1963).

July 27. Tommy Dorsey & His Orchestra, with vocals by Frank Sinatra and the Pied Pipers, begin a twelve-week stay atop the pop charts with "I'll Never Smile Again" (Victor 26628).

August 24. Charlie Barnet & His Orchestra heads up the pop charts with "Where Was I?" (Bluebird 10669), remaining there for two weeks. The song appears in the film, 'Til We Meet Again.

September 7. Jimmy Dorsey & His Orchestra, featuring vocalist Bob Eberly, reach number one on the pop charts with "The Breeze and I" (Decca 3150). The single is adapted from the Spanish song, "Andalucia."

September 14. Bing Crosby, accompanied by John Scott Trotter's Orchestra, begins a four-week run atop the pop charts with the 1916 song, "Sierra Sue" (Decca 3133).

October. Benny Goodman reassembles his band, albeit with a new agenda. He now employed new arrangements by Eddie Sauter and Mel Powell less geared to dancing than in the past.

October 19. Bing Crosby peaks at number one on the pop charts with "Only Forever" (Decca 3300), remaining there for nine weeks. The song appears in the film, *Rhythm on the River*.

November 7. Duke Ellington records "Star Dust" live at a Fargo, North Dakota, ballroom. It is distinctive for the Ben Webster saxophone solo built over three choruses.

November 23. Glenn Miller & His Orchestra ascends to the summit of the pop charts with "Blueberry Hill" (Bluebird 10768). The song is frequently revived, most notably by Louis Armstrong and Fats Domino.

November 28. The Andrews Sisters begin a three-week stint atop the pop charts with "Ferryboat Serenade" (Decca 3328).

November 30. Bing Crosby, accompanied by Dick McIntyre's Orchestra, reaches number one on the pop charts with "Trade Winds" (Decca 3299), remaining there for four weeks.

November 30. Eight of Jay McShann's musicians—including Charlie Parker—participate in some informal recordings at a Wichita radio station. Known as the Wichita transcriptions (the tracks were long thought to have been made for radio broadcasts, but Bob Davis would report in the December 1990 issue of *Down Beat* that they were made just for fun), they were among Parker's first recordings. The earliest appear to have been two tunes recorded by fans at a cub the previous August.

December 15. Creole clarinetist George Bacquet reflects on cornetist Buddy Bolden's seminal role in the evolution of jazz in *Down Beat*:

> I'd never heard anything like that before. I'd played "legitimate" stuff. But this, it was something that pulled me in. They got me on the stand and I played with them. After that I didn't play legitimate so much.

December 21. Artie Shaw & His Orchestra begin a thirteen-week stay atop the pop charts with the million-selling instrumental adaptation of the Mexican song, "Frenesi" (Victor 26542).

1941

❄

January 13. Charlie Spivak and His Orchestra make their first recordings in New York for Okeh.

January 18. The Ink Spots reach number one on the pop charts with "We Three (My Echo, My Shadow, and Me)" (Decca 3379), remaining there for three weeks.

January 23. *Lady in the Dark* premieres at New York's Alvin Theatre. Featuring music by Kurt Weill, lyrics by Ira Gershwin, and book by Moss Hart, the musical would have a run of 467 performances. The 1944 film adaptation starred Ginger Rogers and Ray Milland.

February 6. Vaughn Monroe & His Orchestra begin a three-week stay atop the pop charts with "There I Go" (Bluebird 10848).

March 1. Sammy Kaye & His Orchestra, featuring vocalist Tommy Ryan, go to the summit of the pop charts with "Dream Valley" (Victor 26795). The song is included in the London musical, *New Faces*.

March 15. Glenn Miller & His Orchestra peaks at the number one on the pop charts with "Song of the Volga Boatman" (Bluebird 11029). The instrumental—an adaptation of the universally beloved Russian folk song—features solos by trumpeter Billy Man and alto saxophonist Ernie Caceres.

March 29. "Amapola" (Decca 3629)—as recorded by Jimmy Dorsey & His Orchestra, featuring vocals by Bob Eberly and Helen O'Connell—begin a ten-week run atop the pop charts. An adaptation of a Spanish song which would be featured in the film, *First Love*, it was arguably Dorsey biggest hit ever. 1941 was the bandleader's most successful year as a recording artist, with seven chart-toppers and twelve top ten hits.

c. April. *Cash Box* magazine is founded as an entertainment trade weekly competitor to *Billboard* and *Variety*. During its existence to 1997, *Cash Box* would pass through three stages of development. During World War II, it was a mimeographed tip sheet two or three pages in length catering to distributors of coin-operated music and game machines. It provided information on issues concerning jukeboxes, pinball games, slot machines, and pool halls.

In the post-war era, *Cash Box* was a key forum for the integration of the hardware end of the music business with sound recordings. Recognizing that jukebox operators accounted for more than ninety percent of all records purchased during the 1930s and 1940s, the publication attempted to reflect this state of affairs in its record reviews and sales charts. Coverage of nonmusic vending machines, however, remained one of its primary concerns.

Beginning in the early 1950s, *Cash Box* redirected its focus to covering consumer record buying habits, most notably at private sector impact points such as retail outlets, entertainment films, and the broadcast media. Geared to record company executives, booking agents, artists and musicians, talent agents and managers, music publishers, and other music industry organizations, the magazine employed a standard trade weekly format, incorporating feature stories, news briefs divided by various genre headings and software formats, record and concert reviews, directories, specialized columns, and advertisements and classifieds. Like *Billboard*, chart listings held a prominent place in each issue. Although eschewing blatantly negative forms of criticism typifying some consumer publications, *Cash Box* didn't hesitate to take a philosophical stance on controversial issues (e.g., racism, payola, censorship).

The publication was privately owned and published by three men (in varying combinations)—Joe Orleck, William Gersh, and George Albert—throughout its existence. This circumstance left it ill-equipped to compete with corporate publications such as *Billboard* and *Variety*. The failure to adequately track—and incorporate—new technological advances (e.g., the UPC bar code data provided by the music research firm, SoundScan Inc., to document actual sales from a representative sampling of retail outlets, thereby resulting in more accurate chart listings) led to a further loss of prestige in the 1980s and 1990s. With the death of Albert, the surviving family members decided to cease publication of the magazine. However, they have continued to explore possible publishing projects utilizing the *Cash Box* name. In mid-2006, it was revived as an electronic journal.

April 5. Jimmy Dorsey & His Orchestra, featuring vocalist Bob Eberly, reach number one on the pop charts with "I Hear a Rhapsody" (Decca 3570), remaining there for two weeks.

April 6. Henry Burr (real name: Harry H. McClaskey) dies in Chicago of cancer at age fifty-nine. Considered the top balladeer of the acoustic era, he began recording for national labels in 1903. He is reputed to have appeared on approximately twelve thousand recordings, as a soloist, in duets with countless partners, and as a member of the Columbia Male Quartet, Peerless Quartet, and the Sterling Trio. When his recordings stopped selling in the late 1920s, he shifted his energies to radio; he was part of the regular cast on NBC's National Barn Dance at the time of his death. His top-selling recordings included "Love Me and the World Is Mine" (Columbia 3499; 1906), "I Wonder Who's Kissing Her now" (Columbia 707; 1909), and "Just a Baby's Prayer at Twilight" (Victor 18439; 1918).

April 19. Jimmy Dorsey & His Orchestra, featuring vocalist Bob Eberly, begin a two-week stint atop the pop charts with "High on a Windy Hill" (Decca 3585).

April 19. Benny Goodman & His Orchestra, featuring vocalist Louise Tobin, peaks at number one on the pop charts with "There'll Be Some Changes Made" (Columbia 35210), remaining there for four weeks. The 1924 composition was recorded by Goodman on August 10, 1939, and revived in the 1941 film, *Playgirl*.

April 30. Jay McShann's band record "Hootie Blues" for Decca. Charlie Parker's short solo—notable for its narrative, speech-like looseness—causes a sensation among jazz musicians across the country.

June 7. Jimmy Dorsey & His Orchestra, featuring vocalist Bob Eberly, begin a two-week stay atop the pop charts with "My Sister and I" (Decca 3710).

June 14. Jimmy Dorsey & His Orchestra, featuring vocalist Bob Eberly, go number one on the pop charts with "Maria Elena" (Decca 3698), remaining there for six weeks. The song originated in Mexico, but was adapted with English lyrics for this recording.

June 21. "Daddy" (Victor 27391), as recorded by Sammy Kaye & His Orchestra, begin an eight-week run atop the pop charts.

June 28. Tommy Dorsey & His Orchestra, featuring vocals by Frank Sinatra and the Pied Pipers, climb to the summit of the pop charts with "Dolores" (Victor 27317). The song is included in the film, *Las Vegas Nights*.

July 5. Guy Lombardo & His Royal Canadians, featuring vocals by Kenny Gardner and the Leonardo Trio, begin a two-week stint atop the pop charts with "The Band Played On" (Decca 3675). The song is featured in the film, *Strawberry Blonde*.

July 20. Moses Schanfield—aka Lew Fields—dies at age seventy-five. He was part of the vaudeville team Weber & Fields, active from the 1880s through World War I. They also starred in several Broadway productions and released several bestsellers, most notably, "The Baseball Game" (Columbia 2092; 1917).

August 2. Guy Lombardo & His Royal Canadians reach number one on the pop charts with the instrumental, "Intermezzo (Souvenir De Vienne)" (Decca 3674).

c. August 24–31. McKinley Morganfield makes his first recordings ever for the Archive of Folk Song, Library of Congress under the direction of Alan Lomax and John Work. The field recordings include Morganfield's vocals, spoken passages, and guitar, augmented by comments from Son Simms (who also contributes guitar), Lomax, and Work. Two selections, "Country Blues" (Matrix 4770-A-1a) and "I Be's Troubled" (Matrix 4770-A-2a), have been issued on numerous LP compilations, including the Archive of American Folk Song 18, the Archive of Folk Song L4, Testament T2210, Bounty BY6031, and English Polydor 236574. Morganfield would also participate in a later field session for the Library of Congress on July 24, 1942 (it is also possible, though unsubstantiated, that he recorded material as part of this trip July 20–23). Many of the tracks captured at this time would also appear on the LPs noted above. They would be reissued on compact disc in the late 1990s as the *Plantation Recordings*. Morganfield would begin making commercial recordings in the mid-1940s first as James "Sweet Lucy" Carter, and later, as Muddy Waters. Under the latter pseudonym, he'd be recognized as one of the foremost purveyors of the country blues tradition.

August 30. Jimmy Dorsey & His Orchestra, featuring vocals by Bob Eberly and Helen O'Connell, begin a four-week stay atop the pop charts with "Green Eyes" (Decca 3698). The million-selling disc, which features chart-topping "Maria Elena" on the flip side, is an adaptation of a 1931 Cuban song, "Aquellos Ojos Verdes."

September 27. Jimmy Dorsey & His Orchestra, featuring vocalist Bob Eberly, peak at number one on the pop charts with "Blue Champagne" (Decca 3775).

October 1. *Best Foot Forward* premieres at the Ethel Barrymore Theatre in New York City. Featuring music and lyrics by Hugh Martin and Ralph Blane, and book by John Cecil Holm, the musical would have a run of 326 performances. It was adapted to film in 1943, starring Lucille Ball and original cast members June Allyson and Nancy Walker.

October 4. "Piano Concerto in B Flat" (Bluebird 11211), an adaptation of the Tchaikovsky concert hall mainstay by Freddy Martin & His Orchestra, begin an eight-week stay at number one on the pop charts. The million-selling instrumental featured a longtime Martin sideman, Jack Fina, on the piano.

October 20. Countertenor Richard Jose dies in San Francisco at age seventy-nine. He was one of the best-selling artists for Victor at the outset of the twentieth century when its releases were issued under the "Monarch" and "Grand Prize" imprints. Although the label did not record any new material with him after 1906, several of his records remained in the Victor catalog until 1919, most notably his big hit, "Silver Threads Among the Gold" (#31342).

October 25. Kay Kyser & His Orchestra—with vocals by Harry Babbitt, Ginny Simms, Max Williams, and Jack Martin—go number one on the pop charts with "(Lights Out) 'Til Reveille" (Columbia 36137), remaining there for two weeks.

October 29. *Let's Face It!* premieres at New York's Imperial Theatre. Featuring music and lyrics by Cole Porter, and book by Herbert and Dorothy Fields, the musical would have a run of 547 performances. It would be Danny Kaye's first starring vehicle; he would be succeeded in the midst of the run by Jose Ferrer. The 1943 cinematic version would star Bob Hope and Betty Hutton.

November 8. Glenn Miller & His Orchestra begin a five-week run atop the pop charts with "You and I" (Bluebird 11215).

November 29. Glenn Miller & His Orchestra jump to number one on the pop charts with "Chattanooga Choo Choo" (Bluebird 11230), remaining there for nine weeks. It becomes the first record formally certified as a million seller.

December 13. Horace Heidt & His Orchestra—with vocals by Larry Cotton, Donna Wood, and Don Juans—begin a three-week stint atop the pop charts with "I Don't Want to Set the World on Fire" (Columbia 36295).

December 20. Glenn Miller & His Orchestra, featuring vocals by Ray Eberle and the Modernaires, reach number one on the pop charts with "Elmer's Tune" (Bluebird 11274).

1942

❋

January 2. Jay McShann's band opens at the Savoy Ballroom, Manhattan. Bandmember Charlie Parker becomes enamored of the after-hours music scene, and breaks his association with McShann in July rather so as not to leave New York.

February 7. Glenn Miller & His Orchestra begin a two-week stint atop the pop charts with the "A String of Pearls" (Bluebird 11382). The million-selling instrumental includes solos by cornetist Bobby Hackett, tenor saxophonist Tex Beneke, alto saxophonist Ernie Caceres, and tenor saxophonist Al Klink.

February 10. Glenn Miller is the first artist to be awarded a gold record, for his recording of "Chattanooga Choo Choo."

February 14. Woody Herman & His Orchestra reach number one on the pop charts with "Blues in the Night" (Decca 4030), remaining there for four weeks. The song appears in the film of the same name.

February 28. Glenn Miller & His Orchestra begin a ten-week run atop the pop charts with "Moonlight Cocktail" (Bluebird 11401). The million seller features solos by pianist Chummy MacGregor and tenor saxophonist Tex Beneke.

March 14. Kay Kyser & His Orchestra peak at number one on the pop charts with "(There'll Be Bluebirds Over) The White Cliffs of Dover" (Columbia 36445).

March 21. Tony Martin & His Orchestra, featuring vocalist Eddie Stone, begin a two-week stint atop the pop charts with "Rose O'Day (The Filla-Da-Gusha Song)" (Buebird 11286).

May 2. Alvino Rey's "Deep in the Heart of Texas" ascends to the summit of the pop charts.

May 9. "Tangerine" (Decca 4123), as recorded by Jimmy Dorsey and His Orchestra, begin a six-week run at the top of the pop charts. One of four Dorsey songs from the film, *The Fleet's In*, to become a best-seller, it features vocals by band mainstays Bob Eberly and Helen O'Connell.

May 9. Harry James & His Orchestra, featuring vocalist Helen Forrest, head up the pop charts with "I Don't Want to Walk Without You" (Columbia 36478), remaining there for two weeks. The song appears in the film, *Sweater Girl*.

May 29. Bing Crosby records the Irving Berlin composition, "White Christmas." It will go on to become the biggest-selling single of all time.

June 6. Benny Goodman & His Orchestra, featuring vocalist Peggy Lee and trumpeter Billy Butterfield, begin a three-week stay atop the pop charts with "Somebody Else Is Taking My Place" (Okeh 6497).

June 13. Benny Goodman & His Orchestra reach number one on the pop charts with the instrumental, "Jersey Bounce" (Okeh 6590), remaining there for four weeks.

June 18. Bandleader/composer Arthur Pryor dies at age seventy-one. He first won acclaim as principal trombonist in John Philip Sousa's band; due to the latter's dislike of the recording medium, he also served as conductor on most of the Sousa releases. In the early years of the twentieth century, he guided his own outfit to great success both on discs and as a concert attraction. His notable hits included "Meet Me in St. Louis Medley" (Victor 2960; 1904) and "Hearts and Flowers" (Victor 31371; 1905).

June 20. Harry James & His Orchestra begin a four-week run atop the pop charts with "Sleepy Lagoon" (Columbia 36549), adapted from a symphonic piece by Eric Coates.

July 18. Kay Kyser & His Orchestra, featuring vocalists Julie Conway and Harry Babbitt, go number one on the pop charts with "Jingle, Jangle, Jingle" (Columbia 36604), remaining there for eight weeks. The million seller appears in the film, *The Forest Rangers*.

July 25. Glenn Miller & His Orchestra—featuring vocals by Marion Hutton, Tex Beneke, and the Modernaires—begins a two-week stint atop the pop charts with "Don't Sit Under the Apple Tree (With Anyone Else But Me)" (Bluebird 11474). The song is included in the Broadway musical, *Yokel Boy*, and film, *Private Buckaroo*.

July 31. James Caesar Petrillo's edict, issued on behalf of the members of the American Federation of Musicians, takes effect. It calls for the termination of commercial recording until record companies pay royalties to the AFM on each record sold. Until an industry-wide agreement is reached in late 1944, record labels limited to stockpiled masters, new material produced by vocalists, and the output in marginal genres such as blues and country music.

August 29. Kay Kyser & His Orchestra, featuring vocals by "Trudy" and Harry Babbitt, peak at number one on the pop charts with the million-selling "Who Wouldn't Love You" (Columbia 36526), remaining there for two weeks.

September 26. Kay Kyser & His Orchestra, featuring vocalist Harry Babbitt, begin a four-week stay atop the pop charts with "He Wears a Pair of Silver Wings" (Columbia 36604).

October 23. Murry K. Hill (real name: Joseph T. Pop) dies. The vaudeville comedian was an Edison mainstay during the first decade of the twentieth century. His most successful recording was "In the Good Old Steamboat Days" (Edison 9619' 1907).

October 24. Glenn Miller & His Orchestra reach number one on the pop charts with "(I've Got a Gal in) Kalamazoo" (Victor 27934), remaining there for eight weeks. The million seller includes vocals by Marion Hutton and the Modernaires, and solos by trumpeter Billy May and tenor saxophonist Tex Beneke.

October 31. Bing Crosby, accompanied by the Ken Darby Singers, begins an eleven-week run atop the pop charts with "White Christmas" (Decca 18429). Culled from the hit film, *Holiday Inn*, it becomes the biggest-selling single ever—with over thirty million copies sold by the late 1980s—and is selected for the NARAS Hall of Fame.

November 5. George M. Cohan dies at age sixty-four. He rose from the Four Cohans family vaudeville act to create a brash new style of American musical comedy which placed a greater emphasis on the dramatic dimension. He wrote, managed, and starred in a series of Broadway successes from the turn of the century to 1937. He recorded a number of his compositions prior to World War I (ironically, though, none of his more famous songs); his biggest seller was "Life's a Funny Proposition, After All" (Victor 60042; 1911).

December 19. Vaughn Monroe & His Orchestra top the pop charts with "My Devotion" (Victor 27925).

December 26. "Strip Polka" (Columbia 36656)—the "A" side of a double-disc hit by Kay Kyser and His Orchestra, featuring Jack Martin as the vocalist—begins a two-week stint at number one (the flip, "Ev'ry Night About This Time," reaches number eighteen). It concluded Kyser's most successful year as a recording artist. He placed eleven singles on the pop survey, including five chart-toppers. One of his 1942 releases, "Praise the Lord and Pass the Ammunition!" (Columbia 36640), would become the first number one hit of the following year. However, he would then go more than three-and-a-half years before reaching the summit of the charts again.

1943

❄

January 9. "Praise the Lord and Pass the Ammunition!" (Columbia 36640)—as recorded by Kay Kyser & His Orchestra, with vocals by the Glee Club—begins a three-week run atop the pop charts.

January 15. The Earl Hines band—featuring saxophonist Charlie Parker and trumpeter Dizzy Gillespie—open a national tour at the Apollo Theater. Parker and Gillespie help spread bop techniques and principles through numerous after-hours jam sessions.

January 16. Tommy Dorsey & His Orchestra, featuring Frank Sinatra and the Pied Pipers, reach number one on the pop charts with the million-selling "There Are Such Things" (Victor 27974), remaining there for six weeks.

January 30. Harry James & His Orchestra begin a two-week stint atop the pop charts with "Mister Five By Five" (Columbia 36650). The song appears in the film, *Behind the Eight Ball*.

February 13. Harry James & His Orchestra peak at number one on the pop charts with "I Had the Craziest Dream" (Columbia 36659), remaining there for two weeks. The song is included in the film, *Springtime in the Rockies*.

February 13. Vaughn Monroe & His Orchestra begin a three-week stay atop the pop charts with "When the Lights Go On Again (All Over the World)" (Victor 27945).

February 20. Russell Hunting dies at age seventy-eight. He began as a dramatic actor in the Boston Theatre Co. After becoming famous for his "Casey" Irish comedy recordings (where he frequently assumed multiple parts and supplied a variety of sound effects), Hunting went on to work as an Edison Bell executive and the recording head of the Pathe company. His top-selling cylinders included "Michael Casey as a Physician" (New York, 1891), "Michael Casey at the Telephone" (Columbia, 1892), "Michael Casey Taking the Census" (Columbia, 1892), "Casey as Insurance Agent" (New Jersey, 1894), and "Casey at Denny Murphy's Wake" (Columbia, 1894).

March 6. "I've Heard That Song Before" (Columbia 36668), as recorded by Harry James and His Orchestra, begins a 13-week run atop the pop charts. Featuring vocalist Helen Forrest, the song was culled from the film, *Youth On Parade*. The "A" side of a double-disc hit (the flip, "Moonlight Becomes You," peaked at number fifteen), it continued the hottest chart run in his distinguished career—two of the previous three chart-toppers had also been James records ("Mister Five By Five" and "I Had the Craziest Dream").

March 31. *Oklahoma!* premieres at New York's St. James Theatre. Featuring the initial collaboration between composer Richard Rodgers and Oscar Hammerstein II (lyrics and book), the landmark musical would have a run of 2,212 performances, setting a long-run record until overtaken by *My Fair Lady* fifteen years later. Stanley Green, in *Broadway Musicals: Show By Show* (4th edition), would address the impact of this work:

> …the production not only fused story, songs, and dances, but introduced the dream ballet to reveal hidden fears and desires of the principal characters. In addition, the musical continued in the paths of *Show Boat* and *Porgy and Bess* by further expanding Broadway's horizons in its depiction of the pioneering men and women who had once tilled the cattle of the American Southwest.

The 1955 film version would star Gordon MacRae and Shirley Jones.

April 17. Bing Crosby goes number one on the pop charts with "Moonlight Becomes You" (Decca 18513), remaining there for two weeks. The song appears in the film, *The Road to Morocco*.

May 28. Vaughn De Leath (real name: Leonore Vonderleath) dies in Buffalo, New York at age forty-six. Considered to be the first woman to sing on radio, De Leath performed more than fifteen thousand songs on two thousand broadcasts from the early 1920s to the mid-1930s. Also thought by some to be the first "crooner," her biggest hit recordings were "Ukelele Lady" (Columbia 361; 1925) and "Are You Lonesome Tonight?" (Edison 52044; 1927).

May 29. Glenn Miller & His Orchestra, featuring Skip Nelson and the Modernaires, ascend to the summit of the pop charts with "That Old Black Magic" (Victor 1523). The song appears in the film, *Star-Spangled Rhythm*.

June 12. Benny Goodman & His Orchestra, featuring vocalist Helen Forrest and trumpeter Cootie Williams, begin a three-week stay atop the pop charts with "Taking a Chance on Love" (Columbia 35869). Recorded on November 29, 1940, the song appeared in the Broadway musical and film, *Cabin in the Sky*.

June 26. Rudy Vallee's "As Time Goes By" reaches number one on the pop charts, remaining there for four weeks.

July 3. The Song Spinners begin a three-week stint atop the pop charts with "Comin' In On a Wing and a Prayer."

July 17. The Mills Brothers' "Paper Doll" (Decca 18318) enters the pop charts, spending 12 weeks at number one beginning November 6. The "A" side of a double-disc hit (the flip, "I'll Be Around," rose to number seventeen), it remained on the survey for an extraordinary thirty-six weeks. It would sell more than six million copies, and be ranked as the top non-holiday recording of the decade.

July 24. Dick Haymes begins a seven-week run atop the pop charts with "You'll Never Know" (Decca 18556). The song appears in the film, *Hello, Frisco, Hello*.

July 24. Vaughn Monroe & His Orchestra, featuring the Four Lee Sisters, head up the pop charts with "Let's Get Lost" (Victor 1524), remaining there for three weeks.

August 4. *The Merry Widow* begins a fifth Broadway revival at New York's Majestic Theatre. It would feature the same songs (music by Franz Lehar; lyrics by Adrian Ross) with an updated book by novelist Sidney Sheldon and Ben Roberts. It would have a run of 322 performances, before returning in October 1944 for additional 32 shows.

August 21. "In the Blue of the Evening" (Victor 27947), recorded by Tommy Dorsey & His Orchestra June 17, 1942 (shortly before the American Federation of Musicians ban on band recordings), begins a three-week stay atop the pop charts. It would be Dorsey's seventeenth chart-topper, the last in his illustrious career.

September. Decca comes to terms with the demands of the American Federation of Musicians.

September 4. Dick Haymes goes number one on the pop charts with "It Can't Be Wrong" (Decca 18557).

September 7. Frank Crumit dies at age fifty-three. He had a very successful run as a recording artist in the 1920s—his hits included "Sweet Lady" (Columbia 3475; 1921) and "A Gay Caballero" (Victor 21735; 1928)—even though his "small" voice was not felt to be suited to acoustic recording. A talent composer, he was best known for his work in Broadway musicals and the radio show he co-hosted with wife Julia Sanderson from 1929 to1943.

September 11. Bing Crosby, accompanied by the Ken Darby Singers, begins a seven-week run atop the pop charts with the million-selling "Sunday, Monday, or Always" (Decca 18561).

September 11. Frank Sinatra and Harry James' Orchestra reach number one on the pop charts with the reissued "All or Nothing at All" (Columbia 35587), remaining there for two weeks. The song was originally recorded September 17, 1939.

October 7. *One Touch of Venus* premieres at New York's Imperial Theatre. Featuring music by Kurt Weill, lyrics by Ogden Nash, book by Nash and S. J. Perelman, and starring Mary Martin, it would have a run of 567 performances. It would be made into a film, released in 1948, with Ava Gardner, Robert Walker, and Dick Haymes in the leading roles.

October 30. Al Dexter's "Pistol Packin' Papa" begins an eight-week stay atop the pop charts.

November. Blue Note accedes to the royalty demands of the American Federation of Musicians.

November 27. The Mills Brothers begin a twelve-week run atop the pop charts with "Paper Doll" (Decca 18318). Initially released in the fall of 1942 (and becoming a minor hit), it goes on to achieve sales of more than six million, making it the biggest non-holiday hit of the 1940s.

December 2. *Carmen Jones* premieres at the Broadway Theatre in New York City. The musical would feature a libretto adapted by Oscar Hammerstein II from the original 1875 production (by Meilhac and Halevy) of Bizet's *Carmen*, updated to a World War II setting. A film adaptation, starring Dorothy Dandridge, Harry Belafonte, and Diahann Carroll, would be released in 1954.

1944

❄

January 11. Charles King dies at age forty-nine. A veteran of many Broadway musicals from 1911 to 1930, he also recorded a string of hits prior to the Jazz Age, including "Let Me Live and Stay in Dixieland" (Victor 5843; 1911) and "My Own Iona" (Columbia 2059; 1916).

January 15. The Andrews Sisters begin a nine-week run atop the pop charts with "Shoo-Shoo Baby" (Decca 18572). The song appears in the film, *Three Cheers for the Boys*.

January 28. *Mexican Hayride* premieres at the Winter Garden in New York City. Featuring music and lyrics by Cole Porter, and book by Herbert and Dorothy Fields, the musical would have a run of 481 performances. The highlight of the Latin-tinged score was the hit ballad, "I Love You." The 1948 film adaptation would star Abbott and Costello (sans Porter songs).

January 29. Glen Gray & the Casa Loma Orchestra reach number one on the pop charts with "My Heart Tells Me" (Decca 18567), remaining there for five weeks. The song is included in the film, *Sweet Rosie O'Grady*.

February. Dizzy Gillespie participates in a studio date led by Coleman Hawkins. Widely considered the first true bop recording session, two notable tracks are produced: Hawkins's "Disorder at the Border" and Gillespie's "Woody 'n' You," named for bandleader Woody Herman.

March 4. Jimmy Dorsey & His Orchestra, featuring vocalists Bob Eberly and Kitty Kallen, begin a seven-week stay atop the pop charts with "Besame Mucho" (Decca 18574).

March 18. The Merry Macs peak at number one on the pop charts with the nonsense-words novelty "Mairzy Doats" (Decca 18588), remaining there for five weeks.

April. Dizzy Gillespie and Charlie Parker—hired as music director and head of the reed section, respectively—make their first recordings with the Billy Eckstine band.

April 8. *Follow the Girls* premieres at the New Century Theatre in New York City. Featuring music by Phil Charig, lyrics by Dan Shapiro and Milton Pascal, and book by Guy Bolton, Eddie Davis, and Fred Thompson, the musical would have a run of 882 performances.

April 16. Woody Guthrie records a few songs for Moe Asch at his studio on West 46th Street. Three days later he would return with Cisco Houston and Sonny Terry to record 63 songs. Several more marathon sessions would follow over the next few weeks. These tracks would constitute a substantial portion of Guthrie's recorded legacy.

April 22. Bing Crosby begins a five-week run atop the pop charts with "San Fernando Valley" (Decca 18586).

April 22. Guy Lombardo & His Royal Canadians, featuring vocalist Skip Nelson, head up the pop charts with "It's Love-Love-Love" (Decca 18589), remaining there for two weeks. The song appears in the film, *Stars on Parade*.

April 23. Marion Harris dies at age forty-eight. She was a veteran of Broadway musicals in addition to being perhaps the leading female singer in the last decade of the acoustic era. Her biggest hit recordings included "After You've Gone" (Victor 18509; 1919), "Look for the Silver Lining" (Columbia 3367), and "Tea for Two" (Brunswick 2747; 1925).

May 6. Bing Crosby's "I Love You" (Decca 18587) begins a five-week stay atop the pop charts. The song was adapted from the Broadway musical, *Mexican Hayride*.

June 10. Harry James & His Orchestra, featuring vocalist Dick Haymes, reach number one on the pop charts with "I'll Get By (As Long As I Have You)" (Columbia 36698), remaining there for six weeks. The recording was made April 7, 1941, and released on Columbia 36285; it is featured in the film, *Follow the Boys*.

July 1. Bing Crosby's "I'll Be Seeing You" (Decca 18595)—adapted from the 1938 Broadway musical, *Right This Way*—begins a four-week run atop the pop charts.

August 5. Bing Crosby's "Swinging on a Star" (Decca 18597) commences a nine-week residence at number one. The song featured John Scott Trotter's Orchestra and the Williams Brothers Quartet (whose members included seven-year-old Andy Williams), as did the flip side, "Going My Way," which peaked at number fifteen. The single included two of the four Crosby songs from the *Going My Way* soundtrack to achieve hit status. Big Dee Irwin—with an assist from Dee Dee Sharp—would place "Swinging on a Star" back on the charts in mid-1963.

August 5. Louis Jordan & His Tympany Five ascend to the summit of the pop charts with "G.I. Jive" (Decca 8659), remaining there for two weeks.

August 21. *Song of Norway* premieres at New York's Imperial Theatre. Featuring music and lyrics by Robert Wright and George Forrest, and book by Edwin Lester, the musical would have a run of 860 performances. First presented the previous month by producer-director Edwin Lester's Los Angeles and San Francisco Civic Light Opera Association, the work is loosely based on Edvard Grieg's life and music.

September 15. Charlie Parker records with a band under the direction of guitarist Tiny Grimes. The four selections that result—two vocal pieces and two instrumentals, "Tiny's Tempo" and "Red Cross"—serve notice that Parker will be one of the driving forces of the bebop movement.

October 5. *Bloomer Girl* premieres at New York's Shubert Theatre. Featuring music by Harold Arlen, lyrics by E.Y. Harburg, and book by Sig Herzig and Fred Saidy, the musical would have a run of 654 performances. The plot flirts with social consciousness issues such as the appearance of bloomers in the early 1860s and the struggle of women for civil rights.

October 7. The Mills Brothers begin a five-week stay atop the pop charts with "You Always Hurt the One You Love" (Decca 18599).

October 14. Bing Crosby and the Andrews Sisters peak at number one on the pop charts with "A Hot Time in the Town of Berlin" (Decca 23350), remaining there for six weeks.

October 14. Dinah Shore's "I'll Walk Alone" (Victor 1586) begins a four-week run atop the pop charts. It appears in the film, *Follow the Boys*.

November. Columbia and RCA come to terms with the American Federation of Musicians demands which led to the Petrillo ban.

November 16. Frank Sinatra appears on the *Kraft Music Hall* at the invitation of Bing Crosby. Although the two singers apparently were on the best of terms, the clash between "the Swooner versus the Crooner" was hype for its box office appeal. The chief gag writer on Sinatra's own radio program, Carroll Carroll, would also work with Crosby; he was responsible for the show business characterizations supplied to each star: "Bing was the avuncular elder man who wanted to see a young man come along and make it; Frank was the impatient newcomer who wanted to push everything aside and get in there."

December. Glenn Miller's plane disappears over Europe, and is never found.

December 1. Jazz saxophonist Lester Young is inducted into the army. He is then stationed at Fort McClellan, Alabama.

December 2. Ella Fitzgerald and the Ink Spots reach number one on the pop charts with "Into Each Life Some Rain Must Fall" (Decca 23356), remaining there for two weeks.

December 9. Ella Fitzgerald and the Ink Spots remain atop the pop charts for another two week stint with the flip side of Decca 23356, "I'm Making Believe." The song appears in the film, *Sweet and Low-Down*.

December 16. Bing Crosby and the Andrews Sisters reach the top of the pop charts with the Cole Porter classic, "Don't Fence Me In" (Decca 23364), remaining there for eight weeks. The million-seller was culled from the film, *Hollywood Canteen*. The track concluded one of Der Bingle's most successful years as a recording artist. In all, he placed nineteen songs on the charts, including six number one hits. The time spent at the summit that year would add up to thirty-seven weeks overall.

December 20. Johnny Marvin dies at age forty-seven. Very popular as a band vocalist in the late 1920s, he went on to compose songs for Gene Autry films in the 1930s.

December 28. *On the Town* premieres at New York's Adelphi Theatre. Featuring music by Leonard Bernstein, and lyrics by Betty Comden and Adolph Green, the musical would have a run of 463 performances. The movie adaptation in 1949 would star Gene Kelly, Vera-Ellen, Frank Sinatra, and Betty Garrett.

1945

❄

January 17. Sidney Bechet returns to New Orleans for the first time since 1919, joining Louis Armstrong for an all-star concert in the Municipal Auditorium. Their segment together, heard on radio broadcast, is marred by competition between the two stars. Armstrong would complain at rehearsal that Bechet was attempting to play lead.

February 1. Lester Young is arrested for possession of marijuana and barbiturates while serving in the army. After barely defending himself at the court martial, he is sentenced to a year in the military barracks of Fort Gordon, Georgia.

February 10. The Andrews Sisters begin a ten-week run atop the pop charts with "Rum and Coca-Cola" (Decca 18636). The million seller adapted a 1906 Calypso melody from the song, "L'Anee' Passee'," which originated in Trinidad.

March 17. Johnny Mercer's "Ac-Cent-Tchu-Ate the Positive" (Capitol 183) reaches number one on the pop charts, remaining there for two weeks. The Mercer composition is included in the film, *Here Come the Waves*.

March 24. The *Billboard* chart of best-selling albums is published for the first time. The number one title that week was the *Nat Cole Trio: A Collection of Favorites*. Within a few years, the term "album"—which originally designated a collection of 78 rpm discs that were related in some manner within a book-like cardboard folder—would refer to a ten or twelve-inch LP vinyl record.

March 31. Les Brown & His Orchestra, featuring vocalist Doris Day, begin a seven-week stay atop the pop charts with "My Dreams Are Getting Better All the Time" (Columbia 36779). The song is included in the film, *In Society*.

March 31. Johnny Mercer, Jo Stafford, and the Pied Pipers go number one on the pop charts with "Candy" (Capitol 183).

April 14. Harry James & His Orchestra begin a two-week stint atop the pop charts with "I'm Beginning to See the Light" (Columbia 36758).

May 5. The Pied Pipers peak at number one on the pop charts with "Dream" (Capitol 185). The million seller was originally heard as the closing theme for Johnny Mercer's radio program.

May 11. Dizzy Gillespie and Charlie Parker record the seminal bebop pieces "Shaw 'Nuff," "Salt Peanuts," and the Tadd Dameron-penned "Hot House." They all replaced the emphasis on texture and harmony characteristic of swing arrangements with precision of group interplay and speed of execution.

May 12. Vaughn Monroe & His Orchestra begins a six-week run atop the pop charts with "There! I've Said It Again" (Victor 1637). The million seller will go number one again in a 1963 remake by Bobby Vinton.

May 26. Les Brown & His Orchestra, featuring vocalist Doris Day, reach number one on the pop charts with the million-selling "Sentimental Journey" (Columbia 36769), remaining there for nine weeks.

July 28. Johnny Mercer begins an eight-week run atop the pop charts with "On the Atchison, Topeka, and the Santa Fe" (Capitol 195). The Mercer composition is included in the film, *The Harvey Girls*.

August 16. Irish tenor John McCormack dies at age sixty-one. He begins recording for Edison Bell in 1904, but it is his operatic debut in Italy shortly thereafter which elevates him to superstardom. His popularity spreads to American in 1910; by 1915 he found it necessary to concentrate on concert performance and recordings. His hit recordings—largely in a sentimental vein—included "Mother Machree" (Victor 64181; 1911), "It's a Long, Long Way to Tipperary" (Victor 64476; 1915), and "All Alone" (Victor 1067; 1927).

September 15. Perry Como surges to the summit of the pop charts with "Till the End of Time" (Victor 1709), remaining there for ten weeks. The recording—which sells over two million copies—is based on Chopin's *Polonaise in A-Flat Major*, recently included in the film, *A Song to Remember*.

November 17. Sammy Kaye & His Orchestra, featuring vocalists Nancy Norman and Billy Williams, begins a four-week stay atop the pop charts with "Chickery Chick" (Victor 1726).

November 24. Harry James & His Orchestra, featuring vocalist Kitty Kallen, reaches number one on the pop charts with "It's Been a Long, Long Time" (Columbia 36838), remaining there for three weeks.

November 26. Charlie Parker and Dizzy Gillespie participate in a landmark recording session for the Savoy label. Recorded selections include multiple takes of "Billie's Bounce" and "Now's the Time," "Warming Up a Riff" (based on the chords of "Cherokee"), "Thriving on a Riff" (later renamed "Anthropology," and based on material from "I Got Rhythm"), "Meandering," and "Koko."

December 1. Lester Young is dishonorably discharged from military service.

December 8. Bing Crosby, accompanied by the Les Paul Trio, begins a two-week stint atop the pop charts with his version of "It's Been a Long, Long Time" (Decca 18708).

December 10. Charlie Parker and Dizzy Gillespie open at the Los Angeles club, Billy Berg's. Bebop receives a lukewarm reception at best from California clubgoers.

December 15. Bing Crosby, accompanied by Carmen Cavallaro's Orchestra, heads ups the pop charts with "I Can't Begin to Tell You" (Decca 23457), remaining there for six weeks. The million seller appears in the film, *The Dolly Sisters*.

December 19. Baritone Oscar Seagle dies at age sixty-nine. He recorded several hits during the World War I era, most notably, "There's a Long, Long Trail" (Columbia 245; 1918), with the Columbia Stellar Quartette, and "Calling Me Home to You" (Columbia 2452; 1918).

December 29. Bing Crosby begins a two-week stint atop the pop charts with "White Christmas" (Decca 18429), the second time the recording has accomplished this feat.

December 31. *Zodiac Suite*, a large-scale jazz composition by Mary Lou Williams, is recorded for the first time at New York's Town Hall. It is not issued commercially until 1991.

1946

❄

January 5. Freddy Martin & His Orchestra, featuring vocalist Clyde Rogers, begins a two-week stint atop the pop charts with "Symphony" (Victor 1747).

January 26. Vaughn Monroe & His Orchestra reach number one the pop charts with "Let It Snow! Let It Snow! Let It Snow!" (Victor 1759), remaining there for five weeks. It is the singer's sixth number one hit. One of the more versatile entertainers of the era, he started out as a trumpeter/bandleader, starred in a number of feature movies, and was in great demand on radio, where his rich baritone could be exploited to maximum effect.

January 28. Charlie Parker, Dizzy Gillespie, and Lester Young appear in Los Angeles as part of Norman Granz's Jazz at the Philharmonic series. Parker and Young play together for the only time; Parker is said to have been disappointed that Young's style—now more romantic and heavier in tone—was so different from the 1930s.

Although not a musician, Norman Granz was a major force within the record industry—as a producer, label head, concert promoter, and artist manager. He was widely hailed as a visionary who never abandoned his social conscience, demanding equal pay for African American musicians as well as equal rights for black concert goers.

A native of Los Angeles, Granz first made an impact organizing a series of Jazz at the Philharmonic concerts both in the United States and abroad, placing a particular emphasis on championing the bebop style. He founded four record companies: Clef (1946), Norgran (1953), Verve (1956), and Pablo (1973). As a label executive, his artist roster included Louis Armstrong, Count Basie, Eddie "Lockjaw" Davis, Duke Ellington, Ella Fitzgerald, Billie Holiday, Charlie Parker, Oscar Peterson, Zoot Sims, Art Tatum, Sarah Vaughan, and Ben Webster.

After selling Verve to MGM in 1960, Granz moved to Switzerland, concentrating on concert promotions and managing the careers of Fitzgerald and Peterson. He originally established Pablo as a mechanism for disseminating a 1972 JATP reunion concert. He built up a catalog of some 350 titles—including works by Roy Eldridge, Dizzy Gillespie, and Joe Pass—before selling the firm to Fantasy Records. He would refuse a lifetime achievement award from the National Academy of Recording Arts and Sciences in 1994, offering the rationale, "I think you guys are a little late" (*Los Angeles Times*, November 24, 2001).

February 9. Betty Hutton's "Doctor, Lawyer, Indian Chief" begins a two-week stay atop the pop charts.

March 2. Johnny Mercer's "Personality" (Capitol 230) peaks at number one on the pop charts, remaining there for two weeks. The song appears in the film, *The Road to Utopia*.

March 16. Frankie Carle & His Orchestra, featuring vocalist Marjorie Hughes, begin an eleven-week run atop the pop charts with "Oh! What It Seemed to Be" (Columbia 36892). Hughes is Carle's daughter.

March 23. Frank Sinatra ascends to the summit of the pop charts with his version of "Oh! What It Seemed to Be" (Columbia 36905), remaining there for eight weeks.

April 27. Sammy Kaye & His Orchestra, featuring vocalist Betty Barclay, go number one on the pop charts with "I'm a Big Girl Now" (Victor 1812).

May 4. Perry Como, accompanied by the Andre Kostelanetz Orchestra, begins a three-week stint atop the pop charts with the million-selling "Prisoner of Love" (RCA Victor 1814).

May 18. Dinah Shore, accompanied by Sonny Burke's Orchestra, reaches number one on the pop charts with "The Gypsy" (Columbia 36964), remaining there for eight weeks.

May 25. The Ink Spots begins a thirteen-week stay atop the pop charts with their rendition of "The Gypsy" (Decca 18817).

July 17. "Cabaret"—starring Petula Clark—is broadcast by BBC-TV for the first time. The show will remain on the air until November 2. Clark remains a fixture in films and on BBC radio, appearing in programs *Cabin in the Cotton*, *Calling All Forces*, and *Guest Night*.

July 29. Suffering from the loss of his heroin connection, Charlie Parker struggles through a couple of selections—including the ballad "Lover Man" (issued as "Loverman")—in a Dial recording session. That evening he is arrested after setting fire to his hotel bed and his disoriented behavior in the lobby. He is committed to Camarillo State Hospital (California) for six months.

August 3. Perry Como peaks at number one on the pop charts with "Surrender" (Victor 1877).

August 3. Eddy Howard & His Orchestra begin an eight-week run atop the pop charts with "To Each His Own" (Majestic 1070 & 7188).

August 31. Tony Martin & His Orchestra, featuring vocalist Stuart Wade, reach number one on the pop charts with their version of "To Each His Own" (RCA Victor 1921), remaining there for two weeks.

September 14. Frank Sinatra begins a four-week stay atop the pop charts with "Five Minutes More" (Columbia 37048). The song appears in the film, *Sweetheart of Sigma Chi*.

September 21. The Ink Spots ascend to the summit of the pop charts with their interpretation of "To Each His Own" (Decca 23615).

September 28. Minstrel show comedian George O'Connor dies at age seventy-two. He was reputed to have been the favorite White House entertainer of every president from McKinley through Franklin D. Roosevelt. Jim Walsh, longtime feature writer for *Hobbies* magazine, wrote that no important social event in the Capitol was considered complete without O'Connor. His biggest selling records were "Everybody Rag with Me" (Columbia 1706; 1915) and "Pray for the Lights to Go Out" (Columbia 2143; 1917).

October 19. Frankie Carle & His Orchestra, featuring vocalist Marjorie Hughes, begin a nine-week run atop the pop charts with "Rumors Are Flying" (Columbia 37069).

October 30. Mamie Smith dies at age fifty-six. She is considered the first blues vocalist to record, although her style was decidedly more pop in tone than successors like Ma Rainey and Bessie Smith. Although recording into the 1940s, she never equaled the success of her first hit—"Crazy Blues" (Okeh 4169; 1920).

December 14. Kay Kyser & His Orchestra, featuring Mike Douglas and the Campus Kids, climb to number one on the pop charts with "Ole Buttermilk Sky" (Columbia 37073), remaining there for two weeks. The song is included in the film, *Canyon Passage*.

December 28. Nat "King" Cole begins a six-week stay atop the pop charts with "(I Love You) For Sentimental Reasons" (Capitol 304).

December 28. Sammy Kaye & His Orchestra, featuring vocalist Billy Williams, reach number one on the pop charts with "The Old Lamp-Lighter" (RCA Victor 1963), remaining there for seven weeks.

1947

❄

January 4. Bing Crosby returns to the top of the pop charts for the third time with "White Christmas" (Decca 23778).

January 25. Albert Campbell dies at age seventy-four. The tenor balladeer's career is closely linked with Henry Burr; they recorded many duets together and were both members of the Columbia Male Quartet, Peerless Quartet, and Sterling Trio. His biggest hits as a soloist included "My Wild Irish Rose" (Berliner 0139; 1899), "Ma Blushin' Rosie" (Gram-o-Phone 219; 1900), and "Love Me and the World Is Mine" (Victor 4823; 1906).

January 31. Charlie Parker is released—looking healthy and rested—from Camarillo State Hospital.

February 8. Hoagy Carmichael, accompanied by the Chakadees and Vic Shoen's Orchestra, begins a two-week stint atop the pop charts with "Huggin' and Chalkin'" (Decca 23672).

February 22. Count Basie & His Orchestra, featuring vocals by Harry Edison and Bill Johnson, reach number one with the novelty song, "Open the Door, Richard!" (Victor 2127).

February 22. Freddy Martin & His Orchestra, featuring vocalist Stuart Wade, begin a three-week stay atop the pop charts with "Managua, Nicaragua" (RCA Victor 2026).

March 1. The Three Flames peak at number one on the pop charts with their version of "Open the Door, Richard!"

March 8. Dinah Shore, accompanied by Morris Stoloff's Orchestra, begin a two-week stint atop the pop charts with "Anniversary Song" (Columbia 37234). Based on the 1880 song, "Danube Waves," it is included the biopic, *The Jolson Story*.

March 15. Guy Lombardo & His Royal Canadians head up the pop charts with their version of "Managua, Nicaragua" (Decca 23782).

March 15. Ted Weems ascends to the summit of the pop charts with "Heartaches," remaining there for thirteen weeks.

May 10. Ray Noble & His Orchestra, featuring vocalist Buddy Clark, begin a two-week stay atop the pop charts with "Linda" (Columbia 37215). The song will be revived by Jan & Dean in 1963.

May 31. Frank Sinatra reaches number one on the pop charts with "Mam'selle" (Columbia 37343), culled from the film, *The Razor's Edge*.

June 6. S.H. Dudley (real name: Samuel Holland Rous) dies at age eighty-one. After a career singing opera (1886–1898), he became the baritone of the Edison Male Quartet and Haydn Quartet. With the disbanding of the latter group, he went on to become a Victor executive. He became famous as the editor of the Victor record catalogs and *Book of the Opera*. His biggest sellers as a soloist were "When Reuben Comes to Town" (Victor A-519/3001; 1900), "Whistling" (Victor A-706; 1901), and "Meet Me in St. Louis, Louis" (Victor 2807; 1904).

June 7. Art Lund begins a two-week stint atop the pop charts with his version of "Mam'selle."

June 21. The Harmonicats go number one on the pop charts with the instrumental, "Peg O' My Heart," remaining there for eight weeks.

June 28. Perry Como, accompanied by the Satisfiers and Lloyd Shaffer's Orchestra, begins a three-week stay atop the pop charts with the million-selling "Chi-Baba, Chi-Baba (My Bambino Go To Sleep)" (Victor 2259).

June 28. Red Ingle reaches number one on the pop charts with "Temptation (Tim-Tayshun)."

July 5. Buddy Clark begins a six-week run atop the pop charts with his version of "Peg O' My Heart."

July 12. Jazz bandleader Jimmie Lunceford dies in Oregon after collapsing during an autographing session.

August 9. The Three Suns peak at number one on the pop charts with their treatment of "Peg O' My Heart," remaining there for four weeks.

August 9. Tex Williams & the Western Caravan begin a six-week stay atop the pop charts with "Smoke! Smoke! Smoke! (That Cigarette) (Capitol American 40001). The crossover country hit would go on the sell more than two million copies. Although singer/guitarist Williams enjoyed a long career within the country field, none of his other recordings would ever dent the pop Top 20.

August 30. Francis Craig's "Near You" commences a seventeen-week run at number one. It remains the longest run at the top for a single release in U.S. pop music chart history.

September 29. Dizzy Gillespie presents congo player Chano Pozo at a Carnegie Hall concert devoted to the fusion of bebop and Afro-Cuban music.

October 24. Jazz pianist Thelonious Monk records two of his best known works for Blue Note: the ballad "Ruby, My Dear" and the uptempo "Well, You Needn't."

October 28. Charlie Parker records two virtuoso takes of George Gershwin's "Embraceable You" with his re-formed quintet, including trumpeter Miles Davis, pianist Duke Jordan, bassist Tommy Potter, and drummer Max Roach.

December 13. Vaughn Monroe & His Orchestra reach number one on the pop charts with the million-selling "Ballerina" (RCA 2433), remaining there for ten weeks.

1948

❄

February 21. Art Mooney's "I'm Looking Over a Four-Leaf Clover" begins a five-week run atop the pop charts.

February 27. Jack Kaufman dies at age sixty-five. He was often paired with his brother, Irving, in the recording studio. Their biggest hit was "Nobody Knows (and Nobody Seems To Care)" (Columbia 2795; 1920).

March 13. Peggy Lee reaches number one on the pop charts with "Mañana (Is Soon Enough For Me)" (Capitol 15022), remaining there for nine weeks.

March 20. *Collier's* publishes an article on bebop that reflects the general public perceptions of the genre. It begins: "You can't sing it. You can't dance it. Maybe you can't even stand it. It's bebop."

March 30. John Bieling dies at age seventy-nine. He first achieved recording success as first tenor of the Manhansett Quartet in the 1890s. He was frequently paired with Harry MacDonough in the studio, and became a member of both the Haydn and American Quartets during the first decade of the twentieth century. He was forced stop singing professionally in 1913 after damaging his voice in a marathon recording session for Edison allegedly overseen by studio assistant W. H. A. Cronkhite.

April 24. Bing Crosby, accompanied by the Ken Darby Choir, begins a three-week stay atop the pop charts with "Now is the Hour" (Decca 24279). The recording is based on the New Zealand traditional, "Hearere Ra."

May 8. Nat "King" Cole, accompanied by Frank de Vol's Orchestra, climbs to the summit of the pop charts with "Nature Boy" (Capitol 15054), remaining there for eight weeks.

May 22. Ken Griffin's "You Can't Be True, Dear" begins a seven-week run atop the pop charts.

June. Columbia introduces the long-playing (LP) record; it measures twelve inches in diameter, plays at 33 1/3 rpms, and features microgrooves constructed of a polyvinyl chloride compound. Previously, albums had consisted of collections of ten or twelve-inch 78-rpm. discs. During the 1950s, the format would focus on the adult marketplace, most notably, classical recordings, jazz, and middle-of-the-road pop fare.

July 3. Kay Kyser & His Orchestra, featuring vocals by Gloria Wood & the Campus Kids, peaks at number one on the pop charts with the novelty song, "Woody Woodpecker" (Columbia 38197), remaining there for six weeks.

August 14. Doris Day and Buddy Clark begin a five-week stay atop the pop charts with "Love Somebody" (Columbia 38174).

August 14. Al Trace's "You Call Everybody Darlin'" reaches number one on the pop charts, remaining there for six weeks.

August 28. Pee Wee Hunt's "Twelfth Street Rag" begins an eight-week run atop the pop charts.

September 15. Vernon Dalhart (real name: Marion Slaughter) dies at age sixty-five. Originally a light opera tenor, Dalhart started recording in 1916. His transformation into a hillbilly interpreter of narrative dirges such as "The Wreck of the Old 97" and "The Death of Floyd Collins" resulted in phenomenal sales spanning some thirty labels and dozens of pseudonyms (e.g., Al Craver, Mack Allen). His hit, "The Prisoner's Song" (Victor 19427; 1925) was allegedly the biggest-selling non-holiday record of the pre-1955 era, accounting for more than seven million units.

September 18. Charlie Parker records the celebrated blues-inflected instrumental, "Parker's Mood," in five takes with his quintet.

October 9. Margaret Whiting takes the British song, "A Tree in the Meadow" (Capitol 15122), to number one on the pop charts, remaining there for five weeks.

November 6. Dinah Shore, accompanied by the Happy Valley Boys, begins a ten-week stay atop the pop charts with "Button and Bows" (Columbia 38284). The recording appears in the film, *Paleface*.

December 19. Bing Crosby appears on television for the first time, singing in "A Christmas Carol" for NBC.

December 25. Spike Jones & His City Slickers, featuring vocalist George Rock, ascend to the summit of the pop charts with the Christmas novelty song, "All I Want for Christmas (Is My Two Front Teeth)" (RCA Victor 3177), remaining there for three weeks.

1949

❄

January 15. Evelyn Knight's "A Little Bird Told Me" begins a seven-week run atop the pop charts.

January 15. Jo Stafford and Gordon MacRae, accompanied by the Starlighters, reach number one on the pop charts with "My Darling, My Darling" (Capitol 15270), culled from the Broadway musical, *Where's Charley?*

January 21. The Miles Davis nonet—consisting of six winds arranged in pairs (trumpet and trombone, French horn and tuba, alto and baritone saxophone), and a rhythm section—makes its first recordings. Although the band as a working unit had already ceased to exist, two more sessions—April 1949 and March 1950—took place, resulting in twelve arrangements overall. Heavily influenced by bandleader/arranger Gil Evans, the group plays a vital role in the development of the cool jazz movement.

March 5. Les Brown & His Orchestra ascend to the summit of the pop charts with the million-selling "I've Got My Love to Keep Me Warm" (Columbia 38324). Culled from the 1937 film, *On the Avenue*, and recorded September 16, 1946, Joel Whitburn's *Pop Memories* terms it "the last great instrumental hit of the Big Band era.

March 5. Evelyn Knight's "Powder Your Face with Sunshine" peaks at number one on the pop charts.

March 6. Al Bernard—known as "the boy from Dixie"—dies at age sixty in New York City's St. Clare's Hospital. The vaudeville singer was a throwback to an earlier era, often appearing onstage in blackface. He would later apologize publicly for the racist content of his acoustic era recordings.

March 12. Blue Barron & His Orchestra begin a seven-week stay atop the pop charts with "Cruising Down the River" (MGM 10346).

March 26. Russ Morgan & His Orchestra, featuring vocals by the Skylarks, reach number one on the pop charts with the million-selling "Cruising Down the River" (Decca 24568), remaining there for seven weeks.

April. RCA Victor issues the first 45 rpm single—"Gaite Parisienne" by the Boston Pops Orchestra, conducted by Arthur Fiedler (#49-0100)—as a higher fidelity alternative to the 78 rpm disc, with its abrasive shellac coating. (The first pop 45, also pressed in April 1949, was "The Waltz You Saved For Me," by Wayne King and His Orchestra, label number 47-2715.) Although undermined by limited fidelity and the inconvenience of constantly changing platters, the company originally had designs on capturing the long play market created the previous year with Columbia's introduction of the 33 1/3 rpm record (generally issued in the ten and twelve-inch configurations) via the extended play format and multi-disc box. The appearance of jukeboxes in 1950 that could play 45s helped assure the dominance of the medium for the dissemination of singles until the public revealed a preference for cassettes and CDs in the 1980s.

April 7. *South Pacific* premieres at New York's Majestic Theatre. The fourth Rodgers and Hammerstein musical—adapted from a couple of stories from James Michener's *Tales of the South Pacific*—the production had a run of 1,925 performances. It would be the second longest running musical of the 1940s, and the second musical to win the Pulitzer Prize for drama. Perhaps best known for the classic song, "Some Enchanted Evening," it starred Mary Martin and Metropolitan Opera basso Ezio Pinza. The 1958 film adaptation would cast Mitzi Gaynor and Rosanno Brazzi (with Giorgio Tozzi's voice) in the lead roles.

April 30. Mel Torme's "Careless Hands" peaks at number one on the pop charts.

May 3. Bass vocalist John Meyer dies at age seventy-one. He was a member of both the Peerless Quartet (1911–1925) and American Quartet (1921–1925). He also recorded hits as a duo with Henry Burr in the early 1920s.

May 7. Perry Como, accompanied by the Fontane Sisters, tops the pop charts with "'A' – You're Adorable" (RCA 78-3381 and 45-2899), remaining there for two weeks.

May 14. "Riders in the Sky (A Cowboy Legend)" (RCA 3411), as recorded by Vaughn Monroe & His Orchestra, begins a twelve-week stay atop the pop charts, eventually selling more than a million copies. The record's success owed much to the haunting quality projected by the bandleader's deep baritone voice.

May 14. Russ Morgan & His Orchestra, featuring vocals by the Skylarks, go number one on the pop charts with "Forever and Ever" (Decca 24569).

June 1. Bing Crosby's Philco radio program is broadcast for the last time.

June 17. Without fanfare or editorial comment, *Billboard* begins referring to its Negro music charts as "rhythm and blues."

The term rhythm and blues (R&B) emerged as the most acceptable designation for the music that had developed out of pre-World War II blues styles, for the most distinctive new element in this genre was the addition of a dance beat. The expression first appeared in formal usage in the late 1940s as the name of RCA's division that served the black audience (see also Jerry Wexler); other alternatives at the time included "ebony" (MGM) and "sepia" (Decca and Capitol). Prior to the rise of rock 'n' roll, R&B had already evolved into a wide variety of subgenres, including:

1. The self-confident, assertive dancehall blues which, in turn, encompassed (a) big band blues (e.g., Lucky Millinder, Tiny Bradshaw); (b) shout, scream, and cry blues (e.g., Wynonie Harris, Joe Turner, Big Maybelle, Ruth Brown, LaVern Baker, Roy Brown); and (c) combo blues or jump blues. The latter possessed a number of regional strains in addition to the cosmopolitan style exemplified by Louis Jordan: West Coast (e.g., Roy Milton, Amos Milburn, T-Bone Walker), Mississippi Delta (e.g., Ike Turner's Kings of Rhythm), New Orleans (e.g., Fats Domino, Professor Longhair, the Neville Brothers) and Eastern Coast (e.g., Chuck Willis, Wilbert Harrison);
2. The more subdued club blues (e.g., Charles Brown, Cecil Gant, Ivory Joe Hunter);
3. The country-tinged bar blues (usually centered in either the Mississippi Delta or Chicago) whose chief exponents included Muddy Waters, Howlin' Wolf, Elmore James, Lightnin' Hopkins and John Lee Hooker;
4. Vocal group singing, which was subdivided into (a) the cool style (e.g., The Orioles, The Cardinals, The Spaniels); (b) the dramatic style (e.g., The Moonglows, The Flamingos, The Platters); (c) the romantics (e.g., The Harptones, the Flamingos); (d) the cool style with a strong blues emphasis (e.g., The Clovers, The Drifters); and (e) the sing-along novelty approach geared to mainstream pop acceptance (e.g., The Crows, The Penguins, Frankie Lymon & The Teenagers); and
5. Gospel-based styles, which possessed three major strains: (a) spiritual singing, with the focus upon the quality of the voice (e.g., Mahalia Jackson); (b) gospel singing, with its concentration on the interplay between voices, which were often deliberately coarsened to stress the emotional conviction of the singers (e.g., Rosetta Tharpe, the Dixie Hummingbirds); and (c) preacher singing, with its tendency to speak the message in an urgent near-shout which often revealed the phrasing and timing of singing minus the melodic dimension.

It soon became evident, musically speaking, that "rhythm and blues" was a less than satisfactory name for at least two of the most important stylistic innovations of the 1950s, the various vocal group styles and the gospel-based styles, which were to become increasingly popular as rock 'n' roll began to siphon off the unique spirit of previous R&B forms. For instance, the new vocal groups invariably based their approach on the style of two black ballad-singing aggregates who had proven to be successful with the easy listening audience, the Mills Brothers and the Ink Spots. Both groups sang in the close harmony "barbershop" style, accompanied by a light rhythm section. They were linked because of the ease with which they timed their harmonies, and the purity of their voices.

Of course, these characteristics were a far cry from those comprising the classic R&B style. Therefore, the term "rhythm and blues" became most useful as a market designation; i.e., an indication that the performer was black, recording for the black audience. As noted by author Charlie Gillett, there was ample justification—at least until 1956—for classifying the black market separately. The black audience was interested almost exclusively in black performers; only five recordings by white acts reached the R&B top ten between 1950 and 1955, and three of those were rock 'n' roll records (Bill Haley's "Dim the Lights" and "Rock Around the Clock," and Boyd Bennett's "Seventeen"). Few white singers had either the interest of the cultural experience necessary to appeal to the black audience's taste—until rock 'n' roll changed the equation, resulting in a new type of white performer.

Lacking the financial resources and industry connections of white pop acts, R&B artists displayed impressive persistence and creativity. The Harptones' doo-wop rendition of "The Shrine of St. Cecilia" (Rama 221; 1956) represents a case in point. Taking a well-known tune, the group overcame the shortage of studio resources by intoning the "tick-tocks" of a clock and "ding-dongs" of bells; the sincerity of the delivery managed to make dated lyrics sound relevant and meaningful.

Motown Records played the pivotal role in the development of R&B into a mainstream genre. The product of the vision of one man, owner and founder Berry Gordy, the label sculpted a mainstream pop sound out of gospel and blues roots which reflected the vision of upward mobility and wholesome fun held by young blacks in the 1960s. Motown's stars were groomed to offend no one; the songs they sang were had romantic lyrics that could appeal to practically anyone; and the music itself was rarely demanding, or even aggressive in the tradition of Southern soul. The closest thing to an overt political statement released by Motown in the mid-1960s was Stevie Wonder's "Blowing' In the Wind" (Tamla 54136; 1966).

Although the assembly-line approach employed by Motown led to criticism for monotony, the label released a remarkably diverse array of recordings, varying in sound, arrangement and feel. This diversity—reinforced by Motown's mainstream commercial success—proved to be the launching pad for many of the black music styles that evolved after the mid-sixties. Virtually all black musicians were in some way influenced by the Motown Sound.

A host of regional independent labels producing soul music in the 1960s sought to control production values and nurture available talent with an eye to the long-term payoff, including Vee-Jay and Chess/Checker (Chicago), Stax/Volt/Enterprise, Goldwax and Hi (Memphis), Philadelphia International, Philly Groove and Avco (Philadelphia) and Fame (Muscle Shoals, Alabama). Funk, disco and the dance-oriented styles of the eighties such as go-go music also owed much to Motown (see "February 11, 1961" in Table 1).

Hip-hop music—and its vocal offshoot, rap—represents the most significant innovation in African American popular music during the final decades of the twentieth century. The genre—which drew heavily from both dance club culture, black street poetry, and the dub music of reggae deejay toastmasters—remained a spontaneous underground phenomenon (largely centered in metropolitan New York City) throughout much of the 1970s. Although classic soul and disco records provided the core soundtrack for the pioneering MCs—who continually experimented with scratching and other rhythmic flourishes—much of what was preserved from hip-hop's gestation period was limited to rough audiocassette transfers. The release of "Rapper's Delight" (Sugar Hill 542; 1979; #36)—recorded by the Sugarhill Gang (a collection of session players gathered together by the record label expressly to capitalize on the street buzz being generated by hip-hop—proved to be a watershed development. While experimental work of hip-hop deejays has continued to elude mass-market acceptance, a wide array of rap styles—including the cartoon humor of the Fat Boys and DJ Jazzy Jeff with the Fresh Prince, the political diatribes of Grandmaster Flash and Public Enemy, the dance-inflected verse of Tone Loc and MC Hammer, and the gansta rap of N.W.A., Tupac Shakur, and Ice-T—have achieved crossover success.

Despite the continued cultural dominance of hip-hop at the onset of the twenty-first century, African American popular music—designated by the black contemporary moniker by some trade publications in the 1980s prior to the revival of the R&B designation—encompasses of wide range of styles, from the torch ballad tradition of Anita Baker and Whitney Houston to a kaleidoscopic succession of ambient and techno-infused dance genres. The latter forms include

1. Trip-hop, slow-motion breakbeat music melding rap, reggae dub, and Film Noir-influenced soundtrack samples, accented by audio loops and vinyl scratching;
2. Jungle (or drum and bass), a fragmented, speeded-up blend of reggae afterbeats, hardcore techno, hip-hop, soul, and jazz;
3. House, featuring insistent bass figures, looping drums, and erotic vocals (although originating in Chicago, it would—by means of incessant cross-fertilization—give rise to acid house, disco house, deep house, ambient house, progressive house, power house, pop house, handbag house, and countless other subgenres);
4. Techno, first identified with Detroit, an instrumental-based variant of electronica characterized by darting keyboards and impatient rattling drums; and

5. Trance—a late 1990s hybrid of techno, ambience, and house—consisting of processed, computer-generated extended compositions built around the repetition of keyboard arpeggios, octave-leaps, pitch-shifts, and lengthy drum breaks, and steadily rising crescendos.

The rich diversification of styles and comparatively rapid rate of change characteristic of black popular music in the post-World War II era stands in bold contrast to the chief white-dominated genre indigenous to the United States, country music. Gillett, in his book *The Sound of the City* (1970), offers the following rationale for this situation:

> This is partly because several white southern styles have never been widely popular with the national American audience, so that singers did not continually have to invent styles that would be special to their local audiences—those invented thirty or forty years ago were still special to a local area, or to the white south.

> In contrast, almost every black southern style has proved to have universal qualities that attract national and international audiences, and this situation has placed continual pressure on singers to come up with new styles that are not already widely known and that the local audience can feel to be its own. And invariably, musicians and singers have responded positively to such pressure.

This predisposition for change has proven to be at once a strength and a weakness. It has enabled the R & B to remain a dynamic genre, ever responsive to the needs and interests of its core audience. However, it has also discouraged participation on the part of the uninitiated, who are confused by the rapid succession of fads and fashions.

July 15. *Miss Liberty* premieres at New York's Imperial Theatre. Featuring music and lyrics by Irving Berlin and book by Robert E. Sherwood, the musical would have a run of 308 performances.

July 30. Perry Como's "Some Enchanted Evening" (RCA 78-3402 and 45-2896) begins a five-week run atop the pop charts. The million-seller is adapted from the Broadway musical, *South Pacific*.

August 28. Joe Belmont (real name: Joseph Walter Fulton) dies at age seventy-three. The whistling soloist, known as "The Human Bird," had a recording career reaching back to the 1890s. His biggest success was "Tell Me, Pretty Maiden" (Columbia 31604; 1901), a collaboration with Byron G. Harlan, Frank C. Stanley, and the Floradora Girls.

September 3. Bass singer Frank Croxton dies at age seventy-one. A member of the Columbia Stellar Quartet and Peerless Quartet (1919–1925), he also recorded hits—most notably, "On the Road to Mandalay" (Columbia 5441; 1913)—as a soloist.

September 3. Vic Damone's "You're Breaking My Heart" (Columbia) begins a four-week stay atop the pop charts.

September 10. Vaughn Monroe & His Orchestra ascend to the summit of the pop charts with "Someday" (RCA Victor 78-3510), remaining there for two weeks.

October 1. Frankie Laine—accompanied by pianist Carl Fischer, Judd Conlon's Rhythmaires, and Harry Geller & His Orchestra—begins an eight-week run atop the pop charts with "That Lucky Old Sun" (Mercury 5316).

October 30. *Lost in the Stars* premieres at the Music Box in New York City. Featuring music by Kurt Weill, and lyrics and book by Maxwell Anderson, the musical would have a run of 273 performances. It was made into a movie, starring Brock Peters and Melba Moore, in 1974.

November 12. Margaret Whiting and Jimmy Wakely reach number one on the pop charts with "Slippin' Around," remaining there for three weeks.

November 26. Frankie Laine's "Mule Train" (Mercury 5345) begins a six-week stint atop the pop charts, eventually selling more than a million copies. Born Frank Paul Lovecchio, in Chicago, March 30, 1930, Laine was reaching the peak of his recording career. His rendition of "That Lucky Old Son" (Mercury 5316)—which spent eight weeks at number one, also becoming a million-seller—was still on the charts, and "The Cry of the Wild Goose" (Mercury 5363) would also become a million-selling, chart-topper early in 1950.

Although he would never chart this high again, he would record five more million-sellers, his intense, melodramatic singing style forming a vital link between the big-band crooners and the rock 'n' rollers of the late 1950s.

December 8. *Gentlemen Prefer Blondes* premieres at New York's Ziegfeld Theatre. Featuring music by Jule Styne, lyrics by Leo Robin, and book by Joseph Stein and Anita Loos, the musical would have a run of 740 performances. Based on Loos' 1926 novel and play of the same name, it featured the song, "Diamonds Are a Girl's Best Friend," and made a star of Carol Channing. The 1953 film adaptation, which starred Marilyn Monroe and Jane Russell, would include a modified score.

December 13. Bing Crosby—whose interest in sports had been reflected in part-ownership of the Del Mar Turf Club and the Pittsburgh Pirates—purchases a 10 percent interest in the Los Angeles Rams National Football League franchise.

December 15. Birdland, the jazz club named after Charlie Parker, opens with a gala evening featuring stellar performers such as Lester Young.

December 25. Charlie Parker performs a landmark concert at Carnegie Hall which solidifies his status atop the jazz world.

1950

❄

January 7. Gene Autry makes his first—and only—appearance atop the pop charts with "Rudolph, the Red-Nosed Reindeer" (Columbia 38610). The single—featuring accompaniment by the Pinafores—would go on to sell more than eight million copies by the late 1980s, second only to Bing Crosby's "White Christmas" among Christmas recordings.

January 14. The Andrews Sisters, accompanied by Gordon Jenkins & His Orchestra, begin a five-week run at number one on the pop charts with "I Can Dream, Can't It? (Decca 24705). The million seller is adapted from the Broadway musical, *Right This Way*.

January 21. The Ames Brothers reach number one on the pop charts with "Rag Mop" (Coral 60140 & 60173), remaining there for two weeks.

January 21. Red Foley crosses over to the pop charts, beginning an eight-week stay atop the pop charts with the million-selling "Chattanoogie Shoe Shine Boy" (Decca 46205).

February 24. Franklyn Baur dies at age forty-six. He doubled as a solo recording artist and first tenor of the Revelers during the late 1920s. He later became the original "Voice of Firestone" on the radio.

February 25. Harry Lauder dies at age seventy-nine. The Scottish comedian and folk interpreter was popular in English-speaking countries during the decade prior to World War I. His biggest selling recordings were "I Love a Lassie" (Victor 52002; 1907) and "She Is My Daisy" (Victor 58007; 1909).

March 11. Frankie Laine ascends to the summit of the pop charts with "The Cry of the Wild Goose" (Mercury 5363), remaining there for two weeks.

March 18. Teresa Brewer, accompanied by the Dixieland All Stars, begins a four-week run atop the pop charts with "Music! Music! Music!" (London 30023).

March 25. Eileen Barton, accompanied by the New Yorkers, rockets to number one on the pop charts with the million-selling "If I Knew You Were Comin' I'd've Baked a Cake" (National 9103), remaining there for ten weeks.

April 6. Tenor George Wilton Ballard dies at age seventy-two. He recorded with Edison for fifteen years early in the century. His biggest hit was "M-O-T-H-E-R (A Word That Means the World to Me)" (Edison 50325; 1916).

April 29. Anton Karas begins an eleven-week stay atop the pop charts with the instrumental, "The Third Man Theme."

May 6. Guy Lombardo & His Royal Canadians, featuring guitarist Don Rodney, reach number one on the pop charts with the million-selling instrumental, "The Third Man Theme" (Decca 24839), remaining there for eleven weeks.

June 3. Perry Como, accompanied by the Fontane Sisters, begins a two-week stint atop the pop charts with "Hoop-Dee-Doo" (RCA Victor 3747).

June 10. The Ames Brothers peak at number one on the pop charts with "Sentimental Me" (Coral 60140). The million seller is the flip side of the chart-topping "Rag Mop."

June 24. The Andrews Sisters, accompanied by Gordon Jenkins & His Orchestra, head up the pop charts with "I Wanna Be Loved" (Decca 27115), remaining there for two weeks.

July. *Your Hit Parade*, a popular radio program providing a weekly forum for the top American hits songs since 1935, moves to the television medium. Its approach—featuring live renditions by an in-house cast of singers—would be rendered passé by the new breed of rock 'n' roll artists in the late 1950s.

July 7. Theodore "Fats" Navarro dies at age twenty-six. He was best known as a Gillespie disciple with a sweeter tone and more power in his prime.

July 8. Nat "King" Cole, accompanied by Les Baxter's Orchestra, begins an eight-week run atop the pop charts with "Mona Lisa" (Capitol 1010). Included in the film, *Capt. Carey, U.S.A.*, the single goes on to sell more than three million copies.

August 19. The Weavers, accompanied by Gordon Jenkins & His Orchestra, reach number one on the pop charts with their debut release, the Leadbelly-penned "Goodnight Irene" (Decca 27077), remaining there for thirteen weeks. The original A side, an adaptation of the Israeli song, "Tzena, Tzena, Tzena" would reach number two, remaining on the charts for seventeen weeks, helping the single sell more than two million copies. Ever mindful of criticism from the folk purist camp, the group also recorded a Hebrew version of the song, which was released on Decca 27053.

More than any other performing act, the Weavers were instrumental in making folk music a commercially viable genre. Furthermore, they helped buttress First Amendment values in the fight to stem the authoritarian policies of the U.S. government in its efforts to fight Communism. This anti-Establishment stance—combined with the messages of peace and brotherhood espoused in their songs—elevated them into the counterculture's pantheon of heroes during the 1960s.

Formed in 1948 by social activist and folk music interpreter Pete Seeger (b. 1919), the Weavers also included bass singer Lee Hays, soprano Ronnie Gilbert, and singer/guitarist Fred Hellerman. Born in Manhattan—the son of ethnomusicologist Charles Seeger and art music composer Ruth Crawford Seeger—Pete had left Harvard to master the banjo and collect folk songs on trips across the nation. He worked for a time as a folk archivist for the Library of Congress before becoming a guiding force in the populist music group, the Almanac Singers, during the early 1940s, prior to entering military service during World War II. Hays had started out singing in rural Arkansas churches, while Hellerman and Gilbert discovered a common interest in folk music when working together in New Jersey as summer camp counselors. The four of them got together while participating in the Greenwich Village hootenannies of the mid-1940s. They developed a following under the sponsorship of People's Songs before settling in for a six-month stint at the Village Vanguard. There the quartet earned $100 a week singing a wide range of folk-based material, including spirituals, ethnic songs, the blues, and contemporary Woody Guthrie compositions.

Whereas the Almanac Singers—whose constantly-shifting membership included the folk poet laureate Guthrie, writer Millard Lampell, and Hays—focused on grass roots activism relating to labor strikes, civil rights demonstrations, and other left-wing causes, the Weavers sought a broader audience, smoothing out the rough edges of traditional material deemed unpalatable to ears accustomed to crooners and easy listening big-band arrangements. Decca Records offered them a contract, with more hits following their initial smash: "The Roving Kind" (Decca 27332; 1950, #11); "So Long (It's Been Good To Know Ya)" (Decca 27376; 1951, #4); "On Top of Old Smoky" (Decca 27515; 1951; #2 8 weeks); "Kisses Sweeter Than Wine"/"When the Saints Go Marching In" (Decca 2770; 1951, #19/#27); an adaptation of the South African Zulu song, "Mbube," "Wimoweh" (Decca 27928; 1952; #14); "Around the Corner (Beneath the Berry Tree)" (Decca 28054; 1952, #19); and Leadbelly's "Midnight Special" (Decca 28272; 1952; #30).

With an ongoing string of hits and the dedicated management of Seeger's friend, Harold Leventhal, the Weavers had their choice of high-paying (more than $2,000 per week) bookings at clubs like Ciro's in Los Angeles, Manhattan's Blue Angel, Broadway's Strand Theatre, and gambling venues in Reno. However, their fortunes changed overnight when Seeger's past support of leftist causes brought him to the attention of Senator Joseph McCarthy and the House on Un-American Activities Committee. When Seeger refused to cooperate with government officials by providing details of his past activities, the Weavers were blacklisted by major media outlets, including radio, television, and the more lucrative performing outlets. The group returned to the folk circuit, performing and recording albums sparodically while Seeger focused on his solo career, recording first for Moe Asch's Folkways label and, beginning in 1963, for Columbia (one single, "Little Boxes," would graze the lower reaches of the Hot 100 at the onset of the British Invasion). The Weavers' LP releases—which included *The Weavers' Greatest Hits* (Decca); *The Weavers at Carnegie Hall* (Vanguard, 1955), an artistic mea culpa featuring stripped down renditions of many of their slickly produced pop hits; *Weavers Almanac* (Vanguard), *Weavers on Tour* (Vanguard, 1958), *Weavers Reunion at Carnegie Hall* (Vanguard, 1963)—sold moderately well to a college audience and have all been released on compact disc.

Seeger—who was cited for contempt of Congress in 1961, although his conviction would later be overturned—became the father of the folk revival, tirelessly championing new talent and writing such as classics as "If I Had a Hammer," "Where Have All the Flowers Gone," "Guantanamara," and "We Shall Overcome," all of which became anthems for the civil rights, anti-war, and human rights movements. He has also had a hand in writing numerous chronicles of his times, anthologies of collected folk songs. He spent much of the 1970s sailing his schooner, *The Clearwater*, up and down the Hudson River, advocating greater attention to environmental concerns there and elsewhere. The 1981 documentary, *Wasn't That a Time?*—made shortly before Hays' death August 26, 1981 at age sixty-eight—provided a history of the Weavers and their place in the modern folk revival. Originally released at Warner Bros. on videotape, it would be reissued on DVD early in the twenty-first century.

August 25. A *Down Beat* review of a Charlie Parker Birdland set states, "Bird has allowed his playing to generate into a tasteless raucous hullabaloo." At the time, his quintet had been augmented by a small string section and oboe. Despite his support of these musicians, they restricted his repertoire and alienated some fans.

October 23. Al Jolson dies at age sixty-four. Perhaps the most dynamic entertainer of the early twentieth century, he moved from minstrel shows and vaudeville to Broadway headliner in 1911. His singing role in *The Jazz Singer* (1927) stimulated the rise of sound in films. After a decade of decline, the 1946 motion picture, *The Jolson Story*, resurrected his career. His most notable hit recordings included "April Showers" (Columbia 3500; 1922), "Toot Toot Tootsie (Goo'bye)" (Columbia 3705; 1922), "California, Here I Come" (Brunswick 2569; 1924), "When the Red, Red Robin Comes Bob-Bob-Bobbin' Along" (Brunswick 3222; 1926), and "Sonny Boy" (Brunswick 4033; 1928).

October 28. Patti Page, accompanied by Harry Geller's Orchestra, begins a five-week stay atop the pop charts with "All My Love" (Mercury 5455). The melody of the million seller is based on Ravel's *Bolero*.

November 18. Sammy Kaye & His Orchestra peak to number one on the pop charts with "Harbor Lights" (Columbia 78-38963), remaining there for four weeks.

December 2. Phil Harris begins a five-week run atop the pop charts with the novelty, "The Thing."

December 16. Patti Page reaches number one on the pop charts with "The Tennessee Waltz" (Mercury 5534), remaining there for thirteen weeks. The single goes on to sell more than six million copies.

1951

❄

January 26. Marguerite Farrell dies at age sixty-two. The Buffalo, New York, native was a multi-faceted performer successful in vaudeville (comic acting, dancing, singing) as well as operetta and grand opera. Her recording career comprised two phases: 1916–1917, when she worked for Columbia and Victor, and 1921–1922, when her name appeared on the Edison lists. Her biggest hit was "If I Knock the 'L' Out of Kelly (It Would Still Be Kelly to Me)" (Victor 18105; 1916).

February 9. Pianist/bandleader Eddy Duchin dies from leukemia at age forty. Five years later, he will be honored in the biopic, *The Eddy Duchin Story*.

February 27. Bing Crosby appears on television for the second time, singing several songs on *The Red Cross Program* (NBC).

March 3. Perry Como begins an eight-week run atop the pop charts with a redo of the 1934 composition, "If" (RCA Victor 3997).

March 10. Mario Lanza's "Be My Love" peaks at number one on the pop charts.

April 21. Les Paul and Mary Ford begin a nine-week stay atop the pop charts with "How High the Moon" (Capitol 1451). The million seller is adapted from the Broadway musical, *Two for the Show*, and will be selected for the NARAS Hall of Fame.

Les Paul's innovations in recording studio production and electric guitar design greatly influenced the development of popular music in the post-World War II era. He invented a solid-body electric guitar (1941), which would be marketed by Gibson in 1951. He also invented the eight-track tape recorder, and made notable advances in the use of reverb.

Born Lester William Polfuss on June 9, 1915, in Waukesha, Wisconsin, he would drop out of high school to join Sunny Joe Wolverton's radio band on KMOX, St. Louis. Relocating in Chicago in 1934, he appeared on the radio as both C&W-oriented Rhubarb Red and the jazz-playing Les Paul. His first records appeared in 1936 on Montgomery Ward (as Rhubarb Red) and Decca (supporting blues singer Georgia White). Unhappy with the electric guitars available in the mid-1930s, he also began experimenting with his own designs.

In 1938, Paul moved to New York, garnering a regular spot on Fred Waring's program as a part of a trio. He lost the job when electrocuted during a jam session in his Queens basement in 1941. After a prolonged recovery, he adopted Hollywood as his home base in 1943, where he formed a second trio, recording V-Discs and transcriptions for MacGregor. Paul would perform in the inaugural Jazz at the Philharmonic concert, Los Angeles, on July 2, 1944, and worked with Bing Crosby on his radio show and in the studio; one of their collaborations, "It's Been a Long, Long Time," would top the pop charts. He also waxed jazz, country, and Hawaiian materials with his trio, and backed the Andrews Sisters, Helen Forrest, Dick Haymes, and other singers during the mid-1940s.

In 1947, Paul cut "Lover" in his garage studio featuring his own accompaniment on eight electric guitars manipulated via a dazzling array of multi-speed effects. Released by Capitol the following year, the track became a hit; however, a serious auto accident that January sidelined him for a year and a half (threatened with possible amputation, he had his right arm set at a permanent angle suitable for guitar playing). He returned to the spotlight—teamed with second wife Mary Ford (aka Colleen Summers)—with a string of state-of-the-art, multi-tracked best-selling singles for Capitol in the early 1950s, including "Mockingbird Hill," "Tennessee Waltz," "How High the Moon," and "Vaya Con Dios." The hits dried up in 1955, although Paul (divorced from Ford in 1964) continued to record for Columbia and London until going into semi-retirement in the late 1960s.

The guitarist returned to the studio to record two laid-back country-jazz LPs with Chet Atkins in 1976 and 1978 for RCA. Although later sessions proved less productive, he would continue to perform into the twenty-first century despite being slowed by arthritis. He was inducted into the Rock and Roll Hall of Fame in 1988, and is best heard on a four-CD retrospective, *The Legend and the Legacy* (Capitol; 1991).

June 23. Nat "King" Cole, accompanied by Les Baxter's Orchestra, reaches number one on the pop charts with "Too Young" (Capitol 1449), remaining there for five weeks.

July 28. Rosemary Clooney, with keyboardist Stan Freeman, begins an eight-week run atop the pop charts with "Come On-A My House" (Columbia 39467).

August 7. Baritone balladeer James F. Harrison (real name: Frederick Wheeler) dies at age seventy-three. He rose to prominence as part of a gospel duo with Harry Anthony, and enjoyed a string of hits as a soloist, paired with Reed Miller (aka James Reed), and as a member of the Knickerbocker Quartet. His biggest solo record was "Keep the Home Fires Burning" (Victor 17881; 1915).

September. 45 rpm discs are introduced in France (imported from the United States) by the French branch of EMI.

September 8. Tony Bennett reaches number one on the pop charts with the million-selling "Because of You" (Columbia 39362), remaining there for ten weeks. First published in 1940, the song is featured in the 1951 film, *I Was an American Spy*.

October. The first EMI long playing record is manufactured by Pathe-Marconi in France as international record companies race to catch up with the American advances emanating from the RCA-Columbia battle of the formats.

November 3. Tony Bennett begins a six-week stay atop the pop charts with "Cold, Cold Heart" (Columbia 39449), which goes on to achieve gold record status.

November 17. Eddy Howard & His Orchestra head up the pop charts with "Sin (It's No Sin)" (Mercury 5711), remaining there for eight weeks.

December 22. Johnnie Ray's "Cry" (Okeh 6840) begins an eleven-week run atop the pop charts, selling more than two million copies.

1952

❄

January 5. Pee Wee King's "Slow Poke" peaks at number three on the pop charts, remaining there for three weeks.

March 15. Kay Starr begins a ten-week run atop the pop charts with the million-selling "Wheel of Fortune" (Capitol 1964).

March 21. Disc jockey Alan Freed presides over his Moondog Coronation Ball, generally acknowledged as the first rock 'n' roll stage show. Held at the Cleveland Arena, the acts included leading rhythm and blues acts of the day such as the Dominoes, Tiny Grimes, the Paul Williams Orchestra, Danny Cobb, and Varetta Dillard.

May 17. Leroy Anderson & His "Pops" Concert Orchestra reach number one with "Blue Tango" (Decca 27875), remaining there for five weeks. Composed by Anderson, the instrumental goes on to sell over two million copies.

May 17. George Gibbs begins a seven-week stay atop the pop charts with "Kiss of Fire" (Mercury 5823). The million seller is adapted from the Argentine tango, "El Choclo."

May 24. Doris Day, accompanied by Paul Weston's Orchestra, ascends to the summit of the pop charts with the million-selling "A Guy is a Guy" (Columbia 39673). It is adapted from the World War II soldiers' song, "A Gob is a Slob," which itself was based on a 1719 British tune, "I Went to the Alehouse (A Knave is a Knave)."

June 7. Al Martino's "Here in My Heart" (B.B.S. 101) begins a three-week stint atop the pop charts, going on the sell a million copies.

June 21. Bing Crosby appears on television for the third time, joining Bob Hope and Dorothy Lamour in a telethon concerned with financing the American Olympic team.

July 5. Percy Faith & His Orchestra, featuring Stan Freeman on harpsichord, reaches number one on the pop charts with the instrumental, "Delicado" (Columbia 39708).

July 12. Vera Lynn's "Auf Wiederseh'n Sweetheart" begins a nine-week run atop the pop charts.

July 26. Rosemary Clooney, accompanied by Percy Faith & His Orchestra, goes number one with her million-selling remake of the Hank Williams classic, "Half as Much" (Columbia 39710), remaining there for three weeks.

September 2. The Gerry Mulligan quartet records "My Funny Valentine," which becomes their first hit. Chet Baker's trumpet solo thrusts him into stardom.

September 6. Eddie Fisher, accompanied by Hugo Winterhalter's Orchestra, heads up the pop charts with the "Wish You Were Here" (RCA Victor 4830). His adaptation of the title song to a Broadway musical sells over a million copies.

September 13. Jo Stafford begins a twelve-week run atop the pop charts with "You Belong to Me" (Columbia 39811), selling about two million copies.

September 27. Patti Page reaches number one on the pop charts with the million-selling "I Went to Your Wedding" (Mercury 5899), remaining there for ten weeks.

November 22. Johnny Standley, accompanied by Hoarce Heidt & His Musical Knights, begins a two-week stint atop the pop charts with "It's in the Book" (Capitol 2249). The million seller is a parody of fundamentalist preachers.

November 29. Joni James peaks at number one on the pop charts with the million-selling "Why Don't You Believe Me" (MGM 11333), remaining there for six weeks.

December 6. The Mills Brothers, accompanied by Hal McIntyre's Orchestra, begin a three-week stint atop the pop charts with "The Glow-Worm" (Decca 28384). The million seller is adapted—with new lyrics—from the 1908 hit song which appeared in the German operetta, *Lysistrata*, and Broadway musical, *The Girl Behind the Counter*.

December 22. The Modern Jazz Quartet—consisting of pianist John Lewis, vibraphonist Milt Jackson, drummer Kenny Clarke, and bassist Percy Heath—make their first recordings for the Prestige label. Their classical leanings and restrained deportment helped change the conditions in which jazz musicians play. Lewis Porter and Michael Ullman would refer to them as "the favorite jazz group of people who didn't like jazz" (*Jazz* 1993).

December 27. Jimmy Boyd's rendition of the Christmas classic, "I Saw Mommy Kissing Santa Claus," leaps to the top of the pop charts, remaining there for two weeks.

December 29. Fletcher Henderson dies at age fifty-four. Originally a pianist, he went on to lead one of the 1920s most important jazz ensembles. His biggest recordings were "Charleston Crazy" (Vocalion 14726; 1924) and "Sugar Foot Stomp" (Columbia 395; 1925). He was most successful as an arranger for Benny Goodman and other bands in the 1930s.

1953

❄

January 1. Honky-tonk artist Hank Williams dies of a heart attack at age twenty-nine. He recorded thirty-six Top Ten Country hits, and composed many country standards such as "I'm So Lonesome I Could Cry" and "Your Cheatin' Heart." His funeral is attended by more than twenty thousand people.

January 10. Perry Como, accompanied by the Ramblers, begins a five-week run atop the pop charts with "Don't Let the Stars Get in Your Eyes" (RCA Victor 5064).

January 22. Tom Lehrer records his first album, *Songs of Tom Lehrer*, at Trans Radio studios, Boston for a total of $15. Issued in March on Lehrer Records (TLP-1) in the ten-inch configuration, it sold an estimated 180,000 by 1957.

Tom Lehrer is revered as one of the finest socio-political satirists in the recorded sound medium. Because this activity remained secondary to his academic career, however, his legacy is based upon only three long-playing albums.

Born April 5, 1928, in New York City, Lehrer earned both bachelor's and master's degrees in mathematics from Harvard University, and continued on there until mid-1953 as a teaching fellow. His first LP, *Songs By Tom Lehrer*, issued on his own label in 1953 (reissued as Reprise 6216), collected those songs he had composed and performed during the Cambridge years. Topics receiving satirical treatment included regional pride ("I Wanna Go Back To Dixie"), the cowboy mystique ("The Wild West Is Where I Want To Be"), college football songs ("Fight Fiercely, Harvard"), hunting ("The Hunting Song", love songs ("I Hold Your Hand In Mine"), and the Boy Scouts of America ("Be Prepared"). Musically speaking, the arrangements consisted of Lehrer's relaxed, informal singing to his piano accompaniment.

Following army service based in the Washington, D.C., area in the mid-1950s, Lehrer embarked on a full-time performing career. He released a March 1959 live recording, *An Evening Wasted With Tom Lehrer* (Reprise 6199; 1966; #133). One cut, the acidic "Poisoning Pigeons in the Park," released as a single sweetened with strings, failed to garner either substantial radio play or sales. He returned to graduate work in 1960, teaching courses at Harvard and M.I.T. through much of the decade. He also found time to perform regularly on the weekly NBC-TV program, *That Was The Week That Was*. Many of the songs first heard on *TW3* were included on *That Was The Year That Was* (Reprise 6179; 1965; #18), recorded live at the Hungry I, San Francisco, in July 1965. This remains his best known set, although many of the songs require some knowledge of history (e.g., "Whatever Became of Hubert," "New Math," "Wernher Von Braun") for the biting humor to be appreciated today. Others—"National Brotherhood Week," "Smut," and Pollution"—remain timely to the present day. Furthermore, his approach has influenced many later comedians, most notably Ken Russell, Steve Martin, the Credibility Gap, and the Capitol Steps.

February 2. A *Time* review of the Gerry Mulligan quartet depicts the stylistic differences between bebop and cool jazz:

> In comparison with the frantic extremes, his jazz is rich and even orderly, is marked by an almost Bach-like counterpoint. As in Bach, each Mulligan man is busily looking for a pause, a hole in the music which he can fill with an answering phrase.

February 14. Teresa Brewer reaches number one on the pop charts with "Till I Waltz Again with You" (Coral 60873), remaining there for seven weeks.

March 21. Patti Page begins an eight-week stay atop the pop charts with "The Doggie in the Window" (Mercury 70070).

March 29. Arthur Fields dies at age sixty-four. A professional singer at eleven, he was successful in vaudeville, radio, and recording. His career peaked during the period of U.S. involvement in World War I; he composed as well as sang on a string of hits of a topical nature (including, under the pseudonym of Eugene Buckley, the very politically incorrect "Would You Rather Be a Colonel with an Eagle on Your Shoulder or a Private with a Chicken on Your Knee?").

April 11. Lita Roza tops the British charts with her cover of "How Much Is That Doggie in the Window?"

April 18. Frankie Laine begins a nine-week run atop the British charts with "I Believe."

May 15. Charlie Parker performs with trumpeter Dizzy Gillespie, pianist Bud Powell, bassist Charles Mingus, and drummer Max Roach in Toronto's Massey Hall. Although a commercial flop (only 35 percent of the tickets are sold), the brilliant concert is taped by Mingus and released on his Debut Records.

May 16. Percy Faith & His Orchestra, featuring vocalist Felicia Sanders, climbs to the summit of the pop charts with the movie title single, "Song From 'Moulin Rouge' (Where is Your Heart)" (Columbia 39944), remaining there for ten weeks.

May 23. "Crazy Man, Crazy" (Essex 321), by Bill Haley & His Comets, becomes the first rock 'n' roll record to enter the pop music charts.

July 4. Perry Como begins a seven-week run atop the pop charts with "I'm Walking Behind You" (RCA Victor 5293).

August 8. Les Paul and Mary Ford reach number one on the pop charts with "Vaya Con Dios (May God Be with You)" (Capitol 2486), remaining there for eleven weeks.

August 15. Perry Como, accompanied by Henri Rene's Orchestra, begins a four-week stay atop the pop charts with "No Other Love" (RCA Victor 5317), adapted from the Broadway musical, *Me and Juliet*. The song is based on Richard Rodgers' "Beneath the Southern Cross," which appeared in the TV documentary series, *Victory at Sea*.

September 12. Baritone Reinald Werrenrath dies at age seventy in Plattsburgh, New York. In addition to finding success in the concert, hall, he had a long recording career, stretching from 1904 with the Edison label, to a ten-inch album, *Reinald Werrenrath Favorites* (Gavotte LPG 104), produced in the spring of 1953.

September 26. The Ames Brothers go to number one on the pop charts with "You You You" (RCA Victor 5325), remaining there for eight weeks.

October 10. Stan Freberg, featuring comic narrative parts by Daws Butler and June Foray, begins a four-week stay atop the pop charts with St. George and the Dragonet" (Capitol 2596).

November 21. Tony Bennett reaches number one on the pop charts with "Rags to Riches" (Columbia 40048), remaining there for eight weeks.

November 23–24. Gene Austin re-cuts twelve of his vintage hits for RCA Victor.

1954

❄

January 2. Eddie Fisher begins an eight-week run atop the pop charts with "Oh! My Pa-Pa" (RCA Victor 5552), the English-language version of a song from the Swiss musical, *Fireworks*.

January 3. *The Bing Crosby Show*, the singer's first TV special, is broadcast on CBS.

January 4. Elvis Presley, then employed by Crown Electric as a truck driver, records a ten-inch acetate demo—"Casual Love Affair" and "I'll Never Stand In Your Way"—at the Memphis Recording Service, a sidelight operation run by Sam Records head Sam Phillips. Presley meets Phillips—his future producer—during this, his second session at the studio. In summer 1953 he'd recorded "My Happiness" and "That's When Your Heartaches Begin" as a present for his mother.

Elvis Presley transcends categorization as the most important recording artist of the rock era; he may, in fact, be the most dominant cultural figure of the twentieth century. Like the great heroes of Greek mythology, Presley's character has acquired a universality with which virtually all of us can identify. But it all began with his extraordinary voice, which fused gospel, black rhythm and blues and white country-pop sensibilities in more convincing fashion than any performer up to that point in time.

Presley was born in Tupelo, Mississippi, the only child (a twin brother, Jesse, was stillborn) of working-class parents. He was raised in Memphis, Tennessee, within a tightly knit household; indeed, strong family ties played a role in his decision to record a couple of pop ballads at the Memphis-based Sun Studios as a birthday present for his mother. Brought to the attention of owner Sam Phillips, he was encouraged to forge that synthesis of black and white pop styles soon to be known as rockabilly and, in a broader stylistic context, as rock 'n' roll.

Following an apprenticeship period cutting demos for Sun, Presley was teamed with local session players, guitarist Scotty Moore and bassist Bill Black, and caught lightning in a bottle with a rave-up rendition of Arthur Crudup's R&B hit, "That's All Right, Mama," backed with Bill Monroe's bluegrass standard, "Blue Moon Of Kentucky" (Sun 209; 1954). The A side contains many of the features that made Presley, at least in an intuitive sense, deserving of the later appellation, "King of Rock 'n' Roll": his plaintive voice—literally dripping with teenage hormonal excitement—swoops and swoons over the spare accompaniment consisting of acoustic guitar chords (strummed by Presley himself), electric guitar flourishes, and propulsive upright bass. Phillips would retain the split R&B-C&W format on the four remaining Sun releases during 1954–55, marketing Presley to a country audience (he became a regular on the *Louisiana Hayride* as well as appearing on WSM's *Grand Ole Opry*) because—as a southern white performer—no other viable options existed.

RCA's purchase of Presley's recording contract in late 1955 for the then princely sum of $35,000 can be attributed to two notable factors: (1) Sun's need for cash to pay off existing debts as well as to develop new talent (e.g., Johnny Cash, Carl Perkins, Roy Orbison), and (2) the management pact Presley signed with Colonel Tom Parker in mid-1955. Parker—whose business savvy would prove instrumental in advancing Presley's career (notwithstanding revisionist interpretations to the contrary)—had a long history of working with the label, most notably as Eddy Arnold's manager.

Boosted by a series of TV appearances in early 1956 on the *Dorsey Brothers*, *Milton Berle*, and *Ed Sullivan* shows, Presley's first RCA single, "Heartbreak Hotel" (#47-6420) reached number one on the pop charts (remaining there for eight weeks beginning April 21, 1956), as did the follow-up, "I Want You, I Need You, I Love You" (RCA 47-6540; 1956). The next single broke all existing precedents, with both sides—"Don't Be Cruel"/"Hound Dog" (RCA 47-6604; 1956)—ascending to the top position on the pop (eleven weeks), country (ten weeks), and R&B (six weeks) charts. While the RCA recordings as a whole had thus far lacked the spontaneity and unadorned directness of the Sun material (featuring studied arrangements with his performing band augmented by professional session players—generally drummer D. J. Fontana, pianist Floyd Cramer, saxophonist Boots Randolph, and guitarists Chet Atkins and Hank Garland—and the ubiquitous harmonies of the Jordanaires), the 45 rpm disc culled from Presley's film debut, "Love Me Tender" (RCA 47-6643; 1956; #1 5 weeks), introduced a maudlin element that would plague much of his future output. The problem seems to have been that Presley—unschooled in either musical technique or the concept of good taste—always mimicked—and integrated into his personal entertainment vocabulary—the influences to which he was exposed. Consequently, the boy who'd chosen to sing the sentimental boy-and-his-dog tear-jerker, "Old Shep" at the 1945 Mississippi-Alabama Fair (he placed second in the contest), grew up with the desire to reinterpret Engelbert Humperdinck, Tom Jones, and other singers diametrically opposed to the style that had made him famous in the first place.

Some popular music historians point to Presley's military stint from March 24, 1958 to March 1, 1960, as his pivotal career move. It is certainly true that the post-Army Elvis seem more predisposed to record shlocky movie songs (e.g., "Viva Las Vegas," RCA 47-8360; 1964; #29 as well as the bulk of the tracks from countless soundtrack albums) and romantic ballads (e.g., "She's Not You," RCA 47-8041; 1962; #5) perhaps better suited to middle-of-the-road performers. It wasn't that Presley interpreted such mainstream material badly—gentler items like "Can't Help Falling in Love" (RCA 47-7968; 1961; #2), "Good Luck Charm" (RCA 47-7992; 1962; #1), and "Return To Sender" (RCA 47-8100; #2) possessed a laid-back grace and charm that few popular artists of the period could have negotiated as convincingly. Because he was capable of so much more, however, the escapist fare he recorded for much of the 1960s gave the impression that he had sold out.

At the end of the decade, Presley provided a tantalizing glimpse as to what his recording career might have been. Motivated by criticism that he was out of touch with the tenor of the times—a politically mobilized era whose musical benchmarks included folk rock, psychedelia, and idiosyncratic singer-songwriters—and stabilized by his May 1, 1967, marriage and birth of a daughter early the following year, he opted out of the moviemaking rat-race and returned to live performing. Teamed with soulful session players from Memphis, he produced a string of tougher, more socially relevant hit singles, including "In the Ghetto" (RCA 47-9741; 1969; #3), "Suspicious Minds" (RCA 47-9764; 1969; #1), and "Don't Cry Daddy" (RCA 47-9768; 1969; #6).

Although the quality of Presley's releases proved uneven in the 1970s—ranging from the spirited "Burning Love" (RCA 74-0769; 1972; #2) to the perfunctory, exaggerated reading of "The Wonder Of You" (RCA 47-9835; 1970; #9)—he remained a major box office draw, with successes such as the 1972 Madison Square Garden concert and January 1973 Hawaii show telecast worldwide documented on disc: *Elvis As Recorded At Madison Square Garden* (RCA LSP-4776; 1972; #11) and *Aloha from Hawaii via Satellite* VPSX-6089; 1973; #1). The growing percentage of live and repackaged material among his album releases beginning in the 1970s owed much to his increasing tendency to avoid the studio. This aversion seems to have been related to his heavy drug use, from amphetamines to the recreational types then in vogue with many of his Hollywood associates. His physical deterioration was evident in the dramatic weight fluctuations and erratic behavior during concerts. Therefore, his sudden death—from a heart attack induced by a drug overdose—at his Memphis home, Graceland, on August 16, 1977, didn't come as a complete surprise to well-informed observers.

Beyond trying to accommodate the immediate rush on his recordings in the aftermath of his passing, RCA (sometimes in conjunction with subsidiary imprints such as Camden and Pickwick) has continued to release new Presley titles—virtually all of which have consisted of repackagings of previously issued material. However, the comprehensive retrospectives—including *The King Of Rock 'N' Roll – The Complete 50's Masters* (RCA 66050; 1992; 5 CDs), *Elvis: From Nashville To Memphis – The Essential 60's Masters I* (RCA 07863, c1993; 5 CDs), and *Walk A Mile In My Shoes – The Essential 70's Masters* (RCA 66670, c1995; 5 CDs)—aimed at collectors have earned universal raves from reviewers. Among the more dubious projects have been marketing gimmicks such as *The Elvis Presley Collection* (whose projected double-CD/cassette titles include "Country," "Rock 'N' Roll," "Love Songs," "Classics," and "Movie Magic"—each containing one "never-before-released bonus song"), leased to Time/Life Music in 2002. True rarities have surfaced over the years such as the *Louisiana Hayride* performances available on ten-inch open reel tape in the Louisiana State Library archives in addition to material from Presley's early career release on albums; e.g., *Elvis: The First Live Recordings* (Music Works/Jem; 1984) and material culled from his legendary jam sessions with Jerry Lee Lewis and Carl Perkins at Sun Studios, the *Million Dollar Quartet* (Charly; ca. 1985) and *The Complete Million Dollar Session* (Charly; 1988). But, more typically, the new material has tended to be of a documentary (or infotainment) nature, in which music is a secondary consideration; e.g., *Elvis: One Night With You* (HBO), *Elvis Presley's Graceland* (HBO), *Elvis On Tour* (MGM/UA ML100153; 1984), and *Elvis Memories* (Vestron ML 1054; 1987).

Recent conservative estimates have placed the total number of legitimate Presley sound recordings sold worldwide at 500,000,000. Given his status as an American Institution, with something to offer virtually every popular music enthusiast, it's unlikely that the selling of Elvis Presley will continue unabated for many years to come.

January 7. Muddy Waters records "I'm Your Hootchie-Coochie Man" for the Chess label. In March, it becomes his fifth consecutive R&B Top Ten single, going back to his 1951 chart breakthrough, "Louisiana Blues."

January 14. The "Rock 'n' Roll Jubilee," promoted by disc jockey Alan Freed, reflects the first usage of that phrase at a concert. The words "rock" and "roll" had been coupled together for a number of years in rhythm and blues recordings. Nevertheless, Freed, albeit unsuccessfully, tried to copyright the phrase later in the year. Within a couple of years, it would achieve universal acceptance within the media in referring to the teen-age-oriented genre built upon the commingling of R&B and country music.

January 18. WMGM-radio, New York hires Noble Sissle—actor and composer renown for collaborating with Eubie Blake on songs such as "I'm Just Wild About Harry" and "Love Will Find A Way" and the musicals *Chocolate Dandies* and *Shuffle Along*—as a disc jockey. Signing the "Mayor of Harlem" would later be interpreted by *Billboard* as "a move to capture the Negro market for potential advertisers."

January 23. WNBC, New York, announces plans to replace its all-night classical music program with pop music recordings. This move positions the radio station to challenge the audience share of WNEW.

February 6. After a price increase two weeks earlier, RCA Victor slashes the LP list price almost two dollars to $3.99. This decision is the most dramatic of a series of moves by the record industry to boost the format's market share.

February 10. *The Glenn Miller Story*, starring Jimmy Stewart, premieres in New York City. The accompanying soundtrack album, featuring Miller's original recordings, tops the January 2–August 4 installments of the pop LP charts.

February 13. Guitar Slim (aka Eddie Jones) achieves an R&B number one with his only chart hit, "The Things That I Used To Do." Jones, who worked with Huey "Piano" Smith in the 1940s, was the third artist known as "Guitar Slim"; Alexander Seward and Norman Green used the appellation in the 1930s.

February 26. In one of the earliest instances of an anti-rock'n'roll backlash, Michigan Republican Ruth Thompson proposes a bill in the House of Representatives banning the distribution of any "obscene, lewd, lascivious or filthy" record or "other article capable of producing sound." Convicted offenders would pay fines as high as $5000, be imprisoned for up to five years, or both.

February 27. Doris Day begins a four-week stay atop the pop charts with "Secret Love" (Columbia 40108). The million seller is culled from Day's film, *Calamity Jane*.

March 3. On the heels of their R&B chart-topping debut record, "Money, Honey," the Drifters' follow-up, "Such A Night," reaches number five. Both fail to cross-over to the pop charts, although "Such A Night" is covered by balladeer Johnnie Ray. Within a few weeks of its April 1954 release, the Ray version is banned nationally for the sexually suggestive lines: "Just the thought of your kiss sets me afire/I reminisce and I'm filled with desire."

March 6. The Stargazers top the British singles charts with "I See the Moon."

March 10. *The Threepenny Opera* is revived at the Theatre de Lys in New York City. It was first presented in Berlin in 1928—followed by a brief Broadway run in English translation in 1933—as an adaptation of *The Beggar's Opera* (1728), which is widely considered the first ballad opera or musical comedy. Featuring music by Kurt Weill and lyrics and book by Marc Blitzstein, it had an initial run of ninety-five performances. Terminated due to a prior booking, the production was revived September 20, 1955, running for 2,611 performances (the second longest engagement ever mounted Off Broadway). This production spurred the new hit recordings of "Mack the Knife" in the 1950s (Bobby Darin's version would be the top single of 1959).

March 11. *The Golden Apple* premieres at New York's Phoenix Theatre before moving uptown to the Alvin. Featuring music by Jerome Moross and lyrics and book by John Latouche, the musical would have a run of 173 performances. Based loosely on Homer's *Iliad* and *Odyssey*, it included the hit song, "Lazy Afternoon."

March 13. Jo Stafford's "Make Love to Me!" (Columbia 40143)—an adaptation of the 1923 jazz instrumental, "Tin Roof Blues"—begins a seven-week run atop the pop charts.

March 20. *Billboard* reports on the strides made by "high fidelity" discs, the current state-of-the-art in recorded sound. In the wake of pace-setting labels like Capitol, London, and RCA Victor, Columbia, Decca, and MGM will be introducing the technology in future releases.

March 31. One of the seminal R&B vocal groups, the Crows, peak at number six on the R&B survey with "Gee," their only charting single. Some pop music historians consider it the first true rock 'n' roll hit.

April 10. Perry Como reaches number one on the charts with "Wanted" (RCA Victor 5647), remaining there for eight weeks.

April 12. Bill Haley & His Comets record "(We're Gonna) Rock Around the Clock" (as well as the B side, "Thirteen Women") at the Pythian Temple Studio, New York City. Produced by Milt Gabler, it enjoyed modest success when released in the summer. When featured with the opening and closing credits in the film *The Blackboard Jungle* in 1955, however, it would become arguably the most successful rock 'n' roll single of all time, selling more than twenty-five million copies by 2005. See also: June 29, 1955.

April 14. The Midnighters (who originally recorded as the Royals) enjoy their first R&B hit with "Work With Me, Annie" (Federal). Penned by the group's lead singer, Hank Ballard, the single—the first installment of the "Annie" trilogy—would later generate a controversy for sexually explicit lines like "Annie please don't cheat/Give me all my meat."

April 21. The Gary, Indiana-based doo-wop group, the Spaniels, achieve their second Top Ten R&B single with the classic "Goodnite, Sweetheart, Goodnite." The group's label, Vee-Jay, was founded by their manager in order to provide them with a platform to achieve greater success.

April 22. Johnnie Ray tops the British charts with "Such a Night."

April 28. Big Joe Turner reaches number two on the R&B chart with "Shake, Rattle and Roll." Bill Haley whitewashes the original's suggestive lyrics in a cover that reaches the pop Top Ten on July 5. Regarding his bowdlerization of the song, Haley stated, "We steer completely clear of anything suggestive!"

April 30. The Music Performance Trust Fund reports to the Recording Industry Association of America (RIAA) that the previous year's record sales rose to an all-time high of $205 million; 78 rpm discs comprised 52 percent of all sales, 45s comprised 28 percent, and LPs comprised 20 percent.

April 30. The Association of New York-Area Rhythm and Blues Disc Jockeys states that its most important role is to discourage the radio broadcast of recordings felt to be racially derogatory or in bad taste.

May 1. Alan Freed puts on his first dance away from Cleveland, his original base of operations. More than ten thousand attend the Moondog Coronation Ball, held at the Newark (New Jersey) Armory, to hear Charles Brown, the Covers, the Harptones, the Buddy Johnson Orchestra, Nolan Lewis, and Muddy Waters. Thousands are denied entrance to avoid further overcrowding.

May 8. The British Broadcasting Company (BBC) blacklists Johnnie Ray's rendition of "Such A Night" following "a raft of complaints from listeners."

May 13. *The Pajama Game* premieres at New York's St. James Theatre. Featuring music and lyrics by Richard Adler and Jerry Ross, and book by George Abbott and Richard Bissell, the musical would run for 1,063 performances. Including such hit songs as "Hey There" and "Hernando's Hideaway," it would be made into a movie in 1957 (starring Doris Day).

May 15. *Billboard* announces that thirty million country & western records were sold the previous year, more than 13 percent of total record sales.

May 26. The second annual National Hillbilly Music Festival and Jimmie Rodgers Memorial Day—held in the Singing Brakeman's hometown, Meridian, Mississippi—earns more than $8,000.

May 30. *Jukebox Jury* debuts on the CBS radio network as a summer replacement for *The Jack Benny Show* and *Amos 'n' Andy*. Built around popular music, the program will later appear on television.

June 5. *Billboard* reports that the major record companies will provide radio DJs with 45s rather than 78 rpm discs beginning in July. While the recording industry never adopted the 45 as the standard for singles, the switch—which would spark considerable debate later in the year—was justified as a "money-saving move."

June 5. Kitty Kallen's "Little Things Mean a Lot" begins a nine-week run atop the pop charts.

June 17. The inaugural issue of *Record Mirror* is published. The British publication is one of the first popular music magazines aimed at a mass audience.

June 23. The Chords' "Sh-Boom" begins its successful chart run. Although the Canadian vocal group, the Crew-Cuts, takes their version of the song to number one on the pop survey for seven weeks beginning July 28, the Chords' rendition is both a crossover Top Ten hit and oldies classic, making it one of the few R&B records to surpass its white cover in overall sales.

The Chords were one of the more notable victims of covering which—in its most frequent manifestation—consisted of remakes of black R&B recordings by white pop music artists. The Bronx-based group emerged in 1951 out of the remnants of three Morris High School ensembles—lead vocalist Carl Feaster and his brother, baritone Claude Feaster, from the Tunetoppers; first tenor Jimmy Keyes of the Four Notes; and second tenor Floyd "Buddy" McRae of the Keynotes—who hooked up with bass William "Ricky" Edwards, then with an outfit called the Chords. After a failed audition for Bobby Robinson's Red Robin Records, Atlantic signed them to their Cat subsidiary in 1954.

The Chords' debut single, the group-composed "Sh-Boom" (Cat 104; 1954; #5 pop, #2 R&B), was actually the B side to their cover rendition of the Patti Page hit, "Cross Over the Bridge." Although their version was a big crossover hit, they lost a substantial number of sales to the Crewcuts' major label release on Mercury. They had trouble following up this success, due in part to the need to record under another name because a group called the Chords was already recording for Gem. As a result, many fans did not realize that the Chord Cats and Sh-Booms were the same group as the original Chords.

When Atlantic lost interest in the group, they moved to the Vik label in 1957, and Roulette in 1960. By this time, the Chords were in the midst of personnel upheavals, with McRae being replaced by Arthur Dix, Edwards by Joe "Ditto" Diaz (formerly with Dean Barlow and the Crickets, and the Bachelors), and Claude Feaster by Bobby Spencer. Keyes would go on to form the Popular Five in 1963 along with Dix.

June 29. Miles Davis and Sonny Rollins record three Rollins pieces—"Airegin," "Oleo," and "Doxy"—all of which would become jazz standards.

July 6. Elvis Presley, backed by bassist Bill Black and guitarist Scotty Moore, records his first single at the Sun Records studio in Memphis. The A side, "That's All Right," was recorded by R&B singer/composer Arthur "Big Boy" Crudup in early 1954, while the flip side, Blue Moon of Kentucky," was a country hit for bluegrass legend Bill Monroe in 1946. Released on July 19, it becomes a regional hit in the mid-South.

July 7. WHBQ, Memphis, DJ Dewey Phillips premieres Elvis Presley's "That's All Right" on his *Red, Hit and Blue* show shortly after 9:30 p.m. Later, he interviews Presley live in the studio. Phillips asks the singer what local high school he attended, leaving listeners no doubt as to his racial background.

July 10. *Billboard* announces that Alan Freed will assume a disc jockey position at WINS, New York, in September (his first day on the job was the 9th). His presence as a promoter and taste-maker in the Big Apple will play an instrumental role in the rapidly expanding appeal of R&B and rock 'n' roll.

July 15. R&B vocal group, the Treniers, record the novelty hit, "Say Hey (the Willie Mays Song)" (Okeh), in Manhattan. The recording, which incorporates the voice of the New York Giants' star center fielder, is directed by a twenty-one-year-old Quincy Jones.

July 19. Sun Records releases Elvis Presley's debut single, "That's All Right"/"Blue Moon of Kentucky." It makes the local Memphis charts.

July 24. The Four Aces peak at number one on the pop charts with "Three Coins in the Fountain."

July 24. "Oh What A Dream I Had Last Night" enters the R&B charts on its way to becoming Ruth Brown's eighth hit. Although credited with keeping Atlantic Records solvent during its early years, she never reaches the pop Top 20.

July 28. Elvis Presley's first press interview appeared in the *Memphis Press-Scimitar*.

July 30. The Midnighters record the second single in the Annie trilogy, "Annie Had A Baby." Like its predecessor, it is a major R&B hit, and generates considerable controversy.

August 6. "Gale's Rhythm & Blues Show" opens in Cleveland. The tour's headliners include the Drifters, Roy Hamilton, and the Spaniels.

August 7. The Crew-Cuts begin a nine-week run stop the pop charts with their cover of the Chords' R&B hit, "Sh-Boom" (Mercury).

August 7. Elvis Presley's debut single is featured in the "Review Spotlight on Talent," in *Billboard*'s country & western section. The reviewer touts the singer as "a strong new talent."

August 10. Elvis Presley performs unannounced at the Overton Park Shell in Memphis.

August 14. *Billboard* reports on the "Skokiaan" phenomenon. The African folk song is represented on the pop charts by four versions, including the original by Rhodesia's Bulawayo Orchestra, a vocal group arrangement featuring the Four Lads, and big band-styled takes by Ray Anthony and Ralph Marterle.

August 28. Elvis Presley's "Blue Moon of Kentucky" is included on *Billboard*'s country & western Territorial Best Sellers listing for the week ending August 18, in Memphis, at number three. The A side, "That's All Right," enters at number four on the same chart the following week.

August 29. The most popular R&B artist of the 1940s, Louis Jordan, begins a four-month tour of one-night engagements in El Paso, Texas.

September 9. Elvis Presley gives a concert at the grand opening of Katz's Drug Store, Memphis.

September 11. A National Ballroom Operators Association survey indicates earnings have fallen 54 percent in the first half of 1954 compared with previous year. Venue musicians and operators attribute this drop to record hops which feature the most popular versions of hit recordings and are less costly to mount.

September 11. Presley's "Blue Moon of Kentucky" tops the C&W Territorial Best Sellers chart for Memphis, while the flip side occupies the seventh position.

September 18. *Billboard* documents the rising popularity of syndicated R&B disc jockey programs, most notably, Alan Freed at WINS and Hunter Hancock at KVD—Los Angeles. The article is at a loss to identify the forces behind this development, although elsewhere in the same issue it is noted that teenagers desire R&B recordings so much they actively pursue them in retail outlets and juke joints.

September 25. Rosemary Clooney begins a six-week stay atop the pop charts with "Hey There" (Columbia 40266). The million seller was adapted from the Broadway musical, *The Pajama Game*.

September 25. After having his parody record, "Sh-Boom," played on *Jukebox Jury*, Stan Freberg is quoted by *Billboard* as saying, "I hope this puts an end to R&B." Los Angeles DJ Hunter Hancock responds, "It'll take more than Freberg to stop R&B."

September 25. Sun Records releases Elvis Presley's second single, "Good Rockin' Tonight" (an R&B hit for Wynonie Harris in 1947)/"I Don't Care If The Sun Don't Shine." That night, he makes his only appearance at the Grand Ole Opry. Following his presentation of "Blue Moon Of Kentucky," the Opry's talent coordinator, James Denny, tells Presley he should go back to driving trucks.

September 28. Charlie Parker commits himself to Bellevue Hospital after a stint there for the first ten days of the month. Although released on October 15, his fragile health was broken beyond recovery. Suffering from ulcers and still drinking heavily in order to blunt his craving for heroin and numbing his pain, he never makes high quality music again.

October 1. The Penguins' "Earth Angel," composed by Jesse Belvin as a tribute to his girlfriend, is released by the Dootone label. It will top the R&B charts beginning January 19, 1955, and achieve crossover success, garnering the group a recording contract with Mercury; however, they will fail to ever place a song on the charts again.

October 2. A prominently paced *Billboard* editorial criticizes the current onslaught of "obscene," "offensive," and "off-color" R&B records.

October 6. Presley's "Blue Moon Of Kentucky" falls to number six in its sixth week on the Memphis charts, while "That's All Right" disappears altogether.

October 9. With the controversy over sexually explicit lyrics heating up, George A. Miller, president of the Music Operators of America, criticizes off-color R&B recordings and the jukebox suppliers programming them into machines.

October 16. Elvis Presley performs on *The Louisiana Hayride* for the first time, singing both sides of his debut single.

October 20. Presley's "Good Rockin' Tonight" enters the Memphis charts at number five.

October 27. B.B. King—whose first hits, "Three O'Clock Blues" (1951) and "You Know I Love You" (1952), both topped the rhythm & blues charts—remains hot with his seventh R&B smash, "You Upset Me Baby."

October 30. *Billboard* reports that radio station, WDIA-Memphis, has implemented a program to screen records for "offensive" lyrics. Among the banned recordings are the Midnighters' "Work With Me, Annie" and "Annie Had a Baby," as well as the Drifters' "Honey Love."

November 5. Jazz trumpeter Oran "Hot Lips" Page succumbs to a heart attack in New York City. A prime mover in the Kansas City jazz scene a generation earlier, he was 46 years old.

November 6. Rosemary Clooney begins a three-week stint outpacing the competition on the pop charts with "This Ole House" (Columbia 40266), the flip side of her chart topper, "Hey There."

November 13. The results of a *Billboard* disc jockey poll are announced. Notable findings include:

- DJs play 42 percent pop music, eleven percent C&W, and five percent R&B;
- Perry Como and Patti Page are the most frequently played artists;
- Favorite singers include Frank Sinatra and Doris Day;
- Sinatra's "Young At Heart" is the favorite recording; and
- Bill Haley's interpretation of "Shake, Rattle and Roll" is the favorite R&B disc.

November 13. Eddie Fisher's "I Need You Now" (RCA Victor 5830) reaches number one on the pop charts, remaining there for three weeks.

November 18. When ABC blacklists Rosemary Clooney's "Mambo Italiano" on both the radio and television for what it considers to be "offensive lyrics," Columbia Records immediately shifts into damage control mode. The label issues a statement quoting both a New York University professor of romance languages and a Catholic priest, who claim that the Italian lyrics are "in no way offensive or vulgar."

November 20. WJOB DJ Len Ellis is asked by the local bartenders union in Hammond, Indiana, to cease airing "The Drunken Driver," a C&W single by Ferlin Husky, because it is undermining business. The record tells of a car crash caused by an intoxicated driver that causes the death of two children.

November 20. Singing cowboy Gene Autry, star of films and recordings, makes his debut at the Grand Ole Opry. Western music was still an important segment of the country and western genre, although it would be dropped from the nomenclature by the mid-1960s.

November 24. Old school artist, Lowell Fulson, enters the charts with his first Top Ten R&B single in more than a decade, "Reconsider Baby." He will make a brief return at the outset of the blues revival in 1966 with "Tramp."

November 24. Responding to a suit brought by a blind street singer based in New York City, Louis "Moondog" Hardin—whose uncopyrighted "Moondog Symphony" was appropriated as the theme music for Alan Freed's "Moondog Matinee" program in 1951, the New York State Supreme Court orders Freed to cease using the appellation "Moondog" (or any variation) on the air. Freed accepts the ruling, renaming his WINS slot, "The Rock and Roll Show."

December 1. Fred Rose dies of a heart attack in Nashville at age fifty-seven. He was co-founder—with singer Roy Acuff—of the most successful publisher of C&W music, Acuff-Rose Publications.

December 3. One of the most publicized benefit concerts of that era takes place at the Ellis Auditorium in Memphis. Mounted to assist crippled African American youth, the headliners include Little Walter, Rufus Thomas, Muddy Waters, and Big John Greer.

December 4. The Chordettes begin a seven-week run atop the pop charts with "Mr. Sandman" (Cadence).

December 7. Marty Robbins records a countrified version of "That's All Right." Despite the success Elvis Presley had with the song earlier in the year, the Robbins single fails to chart.

December 8. The Drifters' "White Christmas" debuts on the R&B survey, eventually rising to number two. Like the Bing Crosby version—the top-selling record of all time—it becomes a perennial hit, reaching number three the following year and making the pop charts in 1955, 1960, and 1962.

December 11. *Billboard* posits that 78 rpm discs "may fade into oblivion" in the face of the growing popularity of the smaller, more durable, better sounding vinyl 45s.

December 24. Johnny Ace shoots himself in the head while playing Russian roulette backstage at the City Auditorium in Houston, Texas. He dies the following day at age twenty-five. Named "the most programmed artist of the year" in 1954 by *Cashbox*, his most recent release, "Pledging My Love" (Duke)," tops the R&B charts for nine weeks beginning February 9.

1955

❄

January 1. According to *Billboard*'s year-end recap, the top songs of 1954 were "Little Things Mean A Lot," "Wanted," "Sh-Boom," "Oh, My Papa," and "Hey There."

January 1. The Five Keys peak at number twenty-eight on the pop charts with "Ling, Ting, Tong" (Capitol 2945).

The Five Keys followed in the footsteps of groups like the Ravens and the Dominoes, who had led the way in creating a stylistic blend of mainstream pop and rhythm and blues that possessed broad-based commercial appeal. Although failing to achieve the stratospheric success enjoyed by the Platters and post-1958 edition of the Drifters, they were one of the most professional acts of the 1950s, featuring two exceptional lead singers: Maryland Pierce, who came out of the blues shouter mold, and satin-voiced Rudy West, who specialized in romantic ballads.

The Newport News-based Five Keys began as the Sentimental Four in the late 1940s. The members included two sets of brothers: tenor Rudy (born July 25, 1933) and baritone Bernie (b. 1932) West and Ripley (b. 1933) and Raphael Ingram. They had adopted the Five Keys moniker by the time Raphael left in 1951 to join the Army; his place was filled in short order by Maryland Pierce (b. 1933) and Dickie Smith. True to their name, the line-up also included a piano accompanist, Joe Jones.

The group's first big break came when Aladdin Records executive Eddie Mesner, who had caught their performance at New York's Apollo Theater in early 1951, offered then a record contract. Although the Five Keys' debut single, "With a Broken Heart" (Aladdin), released in the spring of 1951, failed to chart, the follow-up, "The Glory of Love" (Aladdin 3099; 1951), topped the rhythm and blues charts for four weeks.

After failing to build on this early success, the group tottered on the brink of disaster when Smith and Rudy West entered the Army in 1953. They were able to find serviceable replacements, however, in Ramon Loper and Ulysses K. Hicks. Hicks would die in 1954, with West rejoining the Five Keys following his discharge from the service in 1956. In the meantime, they became consistent hitmakers after signing with the Capitol label. Their charting singles included "Ling, Ting, Tong" (#5 r&b), "Close Your Eyes" (Capitol 3032; 1955; #5 r&b), "The Verdict" (Capitol 3127; 1955; #13 r&b), "Cause You're My Lover"/ "Gee Whittakers" (Capitol 3267; 1955; #12 r&b, #14 r&b), "Out of Sight, Out of Mind" (Capitol 3502; 1956; #23 pop, #12 r&b), "Wisdom of a Fool" (Capitol 3597; 1956; #35 pop), and "Let There Be You" (Capitol 3660; 1957; #69 pop).

The group remained active for several years once their record stopped selling. Rudy West would assemble a new version of the Five Keys two decades later, their biggest moment coming on October 3, 1981, when they headlined the Royal New York Doo Wopp Show in Manhattan's Radio City Music Hall. Based in Hampton, Virginia—where they were all employed by the U.S. Postal Service—the group continued to perform on the oldies circuit in their spare time for many years.

January 1. In an attempt to stimulate record sales, RCA Victor unveils "Operation TNT." The centerpiece of the initiative consists of across-the-board price cuts: LPs from $5.95 to $3.98, 33 1/3 rpm EPs from $4.95 to $2.98, 45 rpm EPs from $1.58 to $1.49, and 45 singles from $1.16 to 89 cents.

January 5. LaVern Baker's "Tweedle Dee"—recorded in New York City on October 20 with Atlantic Records co-owners Ahmet Ertegun and Jerry Wexler producing—debuts on the R&B charts (later peaking at number four). It is the first of her thirteen R&B Top 20 singles.

One of the finest female rhythm and blues singers of the post-World War II era, LaVern Baker's greatest commercial success came from teen novelty recordings, most notably "Tweedlee Dee" (Atlantic 1047; 1955; #14, #4 r&b) and "Jim Dandy"/"Tra La La" (Atlantic 1116; 1956; #17, #1 r&b). Unable to make the transition to the adult market with any degree of lasting impact, she finally achieved widespread public acclaim in the 1990s following a twenty-year hiatus in the Philippines—where she eventually became entertainment director at the Subic Military Base—for health reasons.

Born Delores Williams on November 11, 1929, Baker first sang professionally in the nightclubs of her native Chicago billed as "Little Miss Sharecropper." Her early recordings for National, RCA, Columbia (as "Bea Baker")/Okeh, and King attracted little attention; she became an r&b chart fixture—then known as "The Countess"—after signing with Atlantic in 1953. Her hits included "Bop-Ting-A-Ling" (Atlantic 1057; 1955; #3), "Play It Fair" (Atlantic 1075; 1955; #2 r&b), the soulful waltz-tempo ballad "I Cried a Tear" (Atlantic 2007; 1958; #6, #2 r&b), the gospel rave-up "Saved" (Atlantic 2099; #34, #17 r&b), and a searing update of the Chuck Willis ballad, "See See Rider" (Atlantic 2167; 1962; #34, #9 r&b). Well aware of Baker's protean talent, the label backed the ambitious project, *LaVern Baker Sings Bessie Smith* (Atlantic 1281; 1958). Although her gospel-inflected treatment of classic blues material was every bit as effective artistically as Ella Fitzgerald's songbook series devoted to notable Tin Pan Alley composers, the album sold poorly. She moved on to the Decca subsidiary, Brunswick, in 1965. Although failing to return to the charts, she continued to perform live.

Baker's revival was spurred by her selection in 1990 to replace Ruth Brown in the acclaimed Broadway revue, *Black & Blue*. Later that year she was voted into the Rock 'n' Roll Hall of Fame and received a career achievement award from the Rhythm & Blues Foundation. A flurry of recordings for Sire, DRG, and Rhino followed complemented by numerous reissues of her classic R&B tracks. She remained active until her death on March 10, 1997.

January 8. On Elvis Presley's twentieth birthday, Sun releases his third single, "Milkcow Blues."

January 8. Carl Smith begins a seven-week run atop the country charts with "Loose Talk."

January 12. Etta James' "Wallflower" is released by Modern Records. It becomes her first R&B hit, entering the charts on February 9 (eventually peaking at number two).

January 14–15. Alan Freed oversees his first Rock 'n' Roll Ball in Harlem at the St. Nicholas Arena; according to Norm N. Nite, the more than fifteen thousand paid admissions—and $24,000 gross—for two shows (for a venue with only six thousand seats) made it the greatest advance sale in the history of American dance promotions up to that point in time. The featured performers included the Clovers, Fats Domino, the Drifters, the Harptones, the Buddy Johnson Orchestra, Ella Johnson, Nolan Lewis, the Moonglows, Danny Overbea, Red Prysock, Dakota Staton, and Big Joe Turner.

January 28. The first of a package tour of forty-two one-nighters—titled the Top Ten R&B Show—is held in New York City. Featuring Faye Adams, Charlie and Ray, the Clovers, the Bill Doggett Trio, Fats Domino, Amos Milburn, the Moonglows, and the Paul Williams Orchestra, it will cover the nation with the exception of the West Coast.

February 2. Petula Clark's "Majorca" becomes the first of her string of Top 20 hits in Great Britain and continental Europe. Success in America will elude her until "Downtown" is released stateside in late 1964.

February 5. New York City radio station WNEW announces the winners of its annual music popularity poll are Perry Como, Patti Page, the Crew-Cuts, and Ray Anthony.

February 5. The Penguins begin a three-week run at number eight on the pop charts with "Earth Angel" (Doo-Tone 348).

Named for the Kool cigarettes trademark, the Penguins—formed in Los Angeles in 1954—were comprised of lead singer Cleveland Duncan, tenor Dexter Tisby, baritone Bruce Tate, and bass Curtis Williams. They recorded perhaps the most popular doo-wop song of all time, "Earth Angel," a Williams composition which topped the R&B charts (a number eight pop hit as well) in early 1955. When Mercury Records expressed an interest in buying their contract from DooTone, manager Buck Ram insisted that the company also take on another of his clients, the less highly regarded Platters. In one of the more ironic twists in pop music annals, the Platters became one of the most popular vocal groups of that era, while the Penguins failed to chart for Mercury. They would switch to Atlantic in the late 1950s, eventually disbanding when success continued to elude them.

February 19. Pat Boone is touted as "a great new voice" in a Dot Records ad appearing in *Billboard* for his debut single, "Tra-La-La"/"Two Hearts." The latter track reaches number 16 on the pop charts, the first of Boone's thirty-eight singles to make the Top 40 through 1962.

Pat Boone was the most successful of the teen idols; only Rick Nelson came close to his thirty-eight Top 40 hits. His accomplishments are tainted, however, because many of his early hits were cleaned-up cover versions that outsold the aesthetically superior originals, including Fats Domino's "Ain't That a Shame," the El Dorados' "At My Front Door," Little Richard's "Tutti Frutti" and Long Tall Sally," Ivory Joe Hunter's "I Almost Lost My Mind," Joe Turner's "Chains of Love," and the Five Keys' "Gee Whittakers!"

Allegedly a direct descendant of frontier legend Daniel Boone, he lettered in three sports and served as student body president while attending high school in Nashville. Marrying country & western star Red Foley's daughter, Shirley, he attended David Lipscomb College in Nashville before transferring to North Texas State. While there he won a local talent show, which led to an appearance on Ted Mack's program and then a one-year stint on Arthur Godfrey's amateur hour.

In the mid-1950s Boone recorded a number of modestly successful singles for Nashville's Republic Records. He recording of "Two Hearts" (Dot 15338; 1955) was the first of fifty-nine charting singles (through late 1966) for that label. His number one hits included "Ain't That a Shame" (Dot 15377; 1955), "I Almost Lost My Mind" (Dot 15472; 1956), "Don't Forbid Me" (15521; 1956–1957), "Love Letters in the Sand" (Dot 15570; 1957), "April Love" (Dot 15660; 1957), and "Moody River" (Dot 16209; 1961). During the late 1950s, he was arguably surpassed only by Elvis Presley as a pop culture hero. He starred in fifteen films, most notably *Bernadine* (1957), *April Love* (1957), and *State Fair* (1962). In addition, he had his own television series, *The Pat Boone-Chevy Showroom* (ABC) from 1957–1960.

When the hits stopped coming, Boone continued recording for various labels, including Tetragrammaton and Curb. He continued to write books dispensing advice, including *Pray to Win* (1981) and the teen-oriented *Twixt Twelve and Twenty*, *Between You, Me and the Gatepost*, and *The Care and Feeding of Parents*. Since 1983 he has hosted a contemporary Christian radio show heard nationwide on approximately two hundred stations. In addition to appearing on many TV programs, he has starred in a number of stage productions (e.g., *The Will Rogers Follies* in Branson, Missouri).

February 23. Jimmy Reed's debut Vee-Jay single, "You Don't Have To Go," makes the R&B charts. It will peak at number nine; Reed would penetrate the R&B Top 20 a dozen more times over the next six years.

February 26. *Billboard* documents a couple of new industry developments: 45s have surpassed 78s in sales for the first time, and selected New York jukebox outlets have begun charging ten cents rather than a nickel per selection.

February 26. LaVern Baker writes Michigan Representative Charles Diggs Jr., asking that he push Congress to revise the 1909 Copyright Act to protect artists from "note-for-note copying" of previously recorded R&B songs and arrangements via the covering practice. Baker's own "Tweedle Dee" has been covered by Georgia Gibbs and Vicki Young, thereby compromising—at least in theory—her earning potential.

March 5. As the complaints over allegedly off-color or offensive R&B discs continue to escalate, music publishing giant BMI announces its commitment to upgrading surveillance of questionable lyrics. The organization notes that a number of hit singles, including Big Joe Turner's "Shake, Rattle and Roll," had not been provided clearance in the past.

March 5. Elvis Presley performs on television—albeit on a regional broadcast of "The Louisiana Hayride"—for the first time.

March 10. Ahmet Ertegun and Jerry Wexler present Ruth Brown with a gold record at Harlem's Apollo Theater, commemorating the five million plus records she has sold for the Atlantic label. Brown had been instrumental in keeping Atlantic afloat, but the company now stood on the verge of a major commercial breakthrough.

The son of the World War II-era Turkish ambassador to the United States, Ertegun—along with older brother Nesuhi—developed a lifelong love of American jazz music as a youth. His passion for the genre led to the formation of Atlantic Records in 1947 in partnership with New York jazz collector Herb Abramson. Peter Guralnick, in *Sweet Soul Music* (New York: Harper & Row, 1986, p. 55), would note that the label "was nurtured by a combination of creative enterprise, cultural sophistication, business acumen, and good taste that would have been rare in any field but that has been practically unheard of in the music industry."

Following a series of unsuccessful jazz and jump band releases, Atlantic scored the first of many rhythm and blues hits with Stick McGhee's novelty cover, "Drinkin' Wine Spo-Dee-O-Dee" (Atlantic; 1949). According to Ertegun biographer George Trow, Ahmet "did not seek to reproduce an older music exactly; rather he sought to introduce black musicians of the day to black musical modes older and more powerful than the ones they knew" (*The New Yorker*, May 29, 1978).

The label's success with R&B artists such as Ruth Brown, the Clovers, the Cardinals, the Drifters, Big Joe Turner, The Coasters, LaVern Baker, and Ray Charles owed much to Ertegun's ability to find talented associates with similar musical values, most notably engineer Tommy Dowd (who worked on most important Atlantic sessions well into the 1970s), arranger Jesse Stone, producer-executive Jerry Wexler, and songwriters-producers Jerry Leiber and Mike Stoller. Furthermore, he continued to utilize the same nucleus of New York-based session players and producers as r & b evolved into soul in the 1960s.

In addition to taking a considerable interest in artist development, Ertegun displayed great acumen as a deal maker, transforming Atlantic into one of the most powerful independent record companies through a series of distribution arrangements with recording studios and smaller labels such Stax. He also expanded into the mainstream rock field, signing both high-profile English bands (e.g., Cream, Led Zeppelin) and hip West Coast acts (e.g., Buffalo Springfield, Crosby, Stills and Nash).

On November 24, 1967, Atlantic signed a merger agreement with Warner Brothers-Seven Arts, thereby providing Ertegun even greater financial and cultural clout. His accomplishments, combined with his wit and personal charm, enabled him to become a key record industry leader. His latter day accomplishments included heading the drive for establishment of the Rock and Roll Hall of Fame Museum in Cleveland.

March 12. Saxophonist Charlie "Bird" Parker dies of heart failure in New York City at age thirty-four. Widely considered the most important innovator within the bebop genre, he last performed the previous week at Birdland, the Manhattan jazz club named in his honor.

March 15. Elvis Presley signs a management contract with Colonel Tom Parker.

March 16. Epic Records releases Roy Hamilton's "Unchained Melody." Despite competition from several other versions, the single reaches number six on the pop charts. The Phil Spector-produced revival of the song by the Righteous Brothers will become one of the most popular recordings of the rock era, enjoying even greater success in 1989 due to its inclusion on the soundtrack of the blockbuster film, *Ghosts*.

March 21. Big Maybelle records "Whole Lotta Shakin' Goin' On" for Okeh in New York City. Session players include guitarist Mickey Baker, soon to achieve success with the duo, Mickey and Sylvia. Coupled with "One Monkey Don't Stop No Show" as the A side and released September 10, the song fails to make much of an impression on the record-buying public, but is a huge crossover hit in 1957 when redone by Jerry Lee Lewis.

March 22. Alan Freed signs a two-year contract with Coral Records as an Artists & Repertoire man in the R&B field. The agreement also has him doing production work for Decca, the label's parent company.

March 26. *Billboard* notes that pop covers of R&B hits presently dominate the pop charts. This state of affairs exists despite the "scarcely veiled antagonism of many pop publishers and A&R men toward R&B material."

April. Elvis Presley and his accompanists—Bill Black and Scotty Moore—audition for *Arthur Godfrey's Talent Scouts* in New York City. They are rejected, while Pat Boone goes on to win first place.

April 1. George Martin becomes Artist & Repertoire Head for EMI's Parlophone label.

April 1. Sun releases Elvis Presley fourth single, a cover of Arthur Gunter's "Baby, Let's Play House," backed with the country chestnut, "I'm Left, You're Right, She's Gone."

April 12. The long-running radio program, *Your Hit Parade*, celebrates its twentieth anniversary.

April 17. Commodore Records releases Fats Domino's R&B chart-topper, "Ain't That A Shame." *Billboard* will mistakenly refer to the record as "Ain't It a Shame" for months.

April 27. Georgia Gibbs' "Dance With Me Henry"—a cover of Etta James' R&B hit, "Wallflower"—reaches number two on the *Billboard* pop charts. Ironically (since the lyrics and delivery represented a conscious effort to be less sexually suggestive than the original), it was deemed objectionable by radio programmers when first released with the title, "Roll With Me, Henry."

April 28. Alan Freed and Coral Records mutually agree to terminate the earlier contract making Freed a Coral A&R man and producer. Freed states he is too busy to handle such responsibilities, although he may do so in the future for Coral and other labels.

May 4. Tony Bennett reaches number one on the British charts for the only time "Stranger in Paradise."

May 12. The Gale Agency's Big R&B Show of 1955 opens in Omaha, Nebraska—the first of a six-week tour of one-nighters. Headliners include LaVern Baker, the Drifters, Roy Hamilton, and Willie Mabon.

May 13. The first documented report of a riot at an Elvis Presley concert occurs in Jacksonville, Florida.

May 14. Bo Diddley's "Bo Diddley"/"I'm A Man" (Chess) enters the R&B charts. The "A" side is credited by many rock historians with originating the "Bo Diddley" beat.

May 18. Eddie Calvert tops the British charts with his cover of "Cherry Pink and Apple Blossom White."

May 18. Perez Prado's "Cherry Pink and Apple Blossom White" begins its fifth week at the top of the pop charts. It will sell more than one million copies, more than 280,000 of which are in the foreign market. Prado—a Cuban native known as "El Rey de Mambo" (the Mambo King)—will come close to duplicating this success with "Patricia" in 1958.

May 22. Bridgeport, Connecticut, police cancel a Ritz Ballroom dance with Fats Domino scheduled to appear as the featured performer. A spokesperson justifies the action in light of "a recent near-riot at the New Haven Arena," where rock 'n' roll dances have been featured.

May 28. Although Bill Hayes' five-week run at the top of the charts with his version of "The Ballad of Davy Crockett" ended in mid-April, *Billboard* states that the song's popularity remains unsurpassed in the United States. Terming the song a "disc entity," the magazine notes that its combined sales—including renditions by Steve Allen, Rusty Draper, Tennessee Ernie Ford, Burl Ives, the Walter Schumann Voices, the Sons of the Pioneers, and the original television series soundtrack featuring Fess Parker—total more than eighteen million copies over the past six months.

June 26. Decca Records reports that sales of Bill Haley and the Comets' recordings have surpassed three million during the past thirteen months: more than one million apiece for "Rock Around the Clock" and "Shake, Rattle and Roll," and approximately five hundred thousand for both "Dim, Dim the Lights" and "Mambo Rock."

June 29. Bill Haley and the Comets' "Rock Around the Clock" becomes the first rock 'n' roll record to top the pop charts (holding down that position for eight consecutive weeks). Arguments as to the origins of the genre cover development from the 1930s to the early 1950s; however, most experts agree that Haley's music—while more mannered than the recordings of contemporaries like Bo Diddley and Little Richard—was essential in tearing down the color barrier that divided the R&B and pop genres.

July 6. Elvis Presley makes the national charts for the first time with "Baby, Let's Play House"; it occupies the number ten rung on the C&W charts.

July 13. Jackie Gleason's latest LP recording of soft background music, *Lonesome Echo*, tops the *Billboard* album charts, the first notable success of what is now referred to as the lounge style. The genre originated in prosperous 1950s suburbia; it was not so much an identifiable musical style as it was a soundtrack to the swinging lifestyle enjoyed by corporate junior executives (which explains why it was also referred to as "space age bachelor pad music") and upwardly mobile young couples. Their music had to conducive to social functions such as formal dinners, informal backyard barbeques, card games, and pool parties. It had to be upbeat, but—as background music—not too much of a distraction. It had to be a comfortable fit for people of various backgrounds attempting to fit in, while exuding a veneer of sophistication (e.g., smoothed-over exotica manufactured from countless world music traditions) in tune with one's choice of attire, car, and domicile.

The most popular strains of lounge in the post-World War II decade included in suave mood music of Gleason and Mantovani; the Latin-tinged pop of Perez Prado and Xavier Cugat; the ethnic exotica of Eva Sumac, Les Baxter, and Martin Denny; and the stereo band music recorded to capitalize on the panoramic range of this newly-emerging medium. The latter category was best exemplified by the hit recordings of Enoch Light & the Light Brigade, whose *Persuasive Percussion* (Command 800; 1960; #1 13 weeks; gold record) unleashed a long string of percussive audio effects LPs. In addition to stereo, these artists—and the countless imitators they spawned—played a key role in popularizing the record album configuration.

The more serious tone of the late 1960s signaled the demise of such patently frivolous fare. However, the nostalgia boom of the late 1980s fueled a revival of interest in lounge, or "space-age bachelor pad music," as it was sometimes termed. A host of designer record labels specializing in the genre sprang up, including Velveteen and Leisure Lab (a subsidiary of BMG). In addition to reissuing the material of obscure artists from lounge's first wave (e.g., Esquivel), these companies introduced new acts such as Combustible Edison, Semi-Gloss, and Velveteen Monster. Since the early 1990s, lounge music is been sufficiently prominent to merit its own section in high-volume record stores. Furthermore, many web sites have arisen devoted to the style, its history and culture, often including audio samples.

July 15. *Billboard* notes that "Music with an R&B beat is no longer regarded as a passing phase by major recording firms." Pop artists' interest in R&B material is attributed largely to the Crew-Cuts' success in covering the Chords' "Sh-Boom." The rush by pop acts to cover Gene and Eunice's Top Ten R&B hit, "Ko Ko Mo"—versions by Rosemary Clooney, Perry Como, the Crew-Cuts, Bill Darnell, and the Hutton Sisters—have already been released—underscores this trend.

July 16. *Billboard* publishes a couple of articles about the upsurge in popularity of R&B. One focuses on the increase of R&B records (by LaVern Baker, Sammy Davis Jr., Sarah Vaughan, and others) on the pop charts, while the other attributes the genre's "good health" to pop covers.

July 25. Columbia signs a promising duo, the Collins Kids, comprised of guitar wunderkind Larry, age ten, and lead vocalist Lorrie (13), his stunningly attractive sister. Although they enjoy modest success, they never cross-over to the pop market. Lorrie would retire a number of years later after marrying a music business entrepreneur, while Larry would continue to perform and write songs, including "Delta Dawn," a 1973 chart-topper for both Helen Reddy (pop) and Tanya Tucker (country).

July 27. Chuck Berry, one of the most distinctive guitarists and songwriters of the rock 'n' roll era, makes the R&B charts with his debut single, "Maybellene." Two weeks later, it enters the pop charts at number 23.

July 27. *Billboard* states that only two contemporary singers are guaranteed hitmakers: Nat "King" Cole (pop) and Webb Pierce (C&W).

July 29. American country balladeer Slim Whitman, best known for his yodeling flourishes, begins his eleven-week run atop the British charts with "Rosemarie." He will resurface as a media star of sorts in early 1980s via a barrage of late night cable television ads hawking a compilation of his "greatest hits."

August 3. Bill Haley sues Essex Records executive, Dave Miller, in a move to keep the early 1950s recordings he made with that label from being released. Haley's suit argues that the Essex material is "of inferior quality to said plaintiff's current releases."

August 13. The R&B/gospel independent label, Savoy, announces that anyone planning to cover its releases must obtain permission from the U.S. Copyright Office.

August 19. WINS-New York announces it will no longer broadcast "copy" recordings—that is, covers mimicking the arrangements or vocal phrasings of existing discs. The radio station provides its DJs with a list of prohibited records, including Pat Boone's "Ain't That A Shame," Georgia Gibbs' "Tweedle Dee," and Johnny Long's "Maybellene." Reinterpretations—situations where the arrangements or phrasing are widely divergent from the original recording—will not be proscribed in any manner.

September 3. Australian promoters offer Bill Haley and the Comets a guarantee of $2000 per performance for fifteen dates. The group passes on the invitation—which would have been their first foreign tour—due to fear of flying.

September 3. According to *Billboard*, independent labels—in the face of counter-moves by the majors such as signing away their most successful artists—are in the midst of a boom period. They reportedly grossed $20 million the previous year; the top-selling companies are Modern, Chess, Savoy, Peacock, Jubilee, Aladdin, and Specialty.

September 9. The J.P. Seeburg Corporation releases the Dual Music System Jukebox, the first machine capable of handling one hundred singles (although able to play only the A sides) and two-song-per-side EPs.

September 17. Capitol Records releases Les Paul's "Magic Melody, Part Two," hyping it as the shortest song ever released. Paul recorded the song—consisting of just two notes—in response to DJ complaints about his single, "Magic Melody," which ended with the familiar "shave and a haircut, two bits" musical phrase, minus the last two notes.

September 21. The Platters' first major hit, "Only You (and You Alone)," enters the pop charts at number 24. It begins a seven week run at the top of the R&B listing on October 19, and will be the first recording to sell a million copies in France (for the Barclay label).

September 28. The Robins—later to be known as the Coasters—record "Smokey Joe's Café"/"Riot In Cell Block Number Nine," featuring Leiber and Stoller songwriting/production team and engineer Bunny Robyn at Master Recorders, Los Angeles. Released on Leiber and Stoller's Spark label, the single will later be included on the Coasters' debut Atlantic LP.

The Robins are one of the more notable asterisks in rhythm and blues history. While they had limited success as a recording act, two members went on to form the core of one of the most popular doo-wop groups—and, arguably, the finest R&B-oriented comedians—of all time, the Coasters.

Formed in Los Angeles as the Four Bluebirds, in 1947, the group originally included Bobby Nunn, Ty Terrell, Billy Richards, and Roy Richard. They were offered a recording contract by the legendary Savoy label in 1949, producing their debut hit, "If It's So, Baby" (Savoy 726; 1950; #10 r&b), backed by the Johnny Otis Band, early the following year. Shortly thereafter, they would contribute vocals, along with up-and-coming chanteuse, Little Esther, to Otis' biggest hit, "Double Crossing Blues" (Savoy 731; 1950; #1 r&b 9 weeks).

As the R&B vocal group craze—which placed a premium on more sophisticated harmony arrangements—gathered momentum, the Robins added Carl Gardner and Grady Chapman in 1954. By the time they'd released the crossover hit, "Smokey Joe's Café" (Atco 6059; 1955 #79 pop, #10 r&b)—originally appearing on the Spark label (#122) in the early fall—lead singer Gardner and bassist Nunn moved on to form the Coasters.

October 5. Elvis Presley's fifth single, "I Forgot to Remember to Forget Her," reaches number two on the Memphis charts, behind Johnny Cash's "Cry, Cry, Cry."

October 12. The release of Gale Storm's "I Hear You Knockin'" (Dot) proves that a market for covers still exists. The actress—currently starring in the TV sitcom, *My Little Margie*—will reach the pop Top 5 with her rendition of the Smiley Lewis R&B hit.

Although he recorded a number of classic rhythm and blues tracks in the 1950s, Smiley Lewis labored in the shadow of fellow New Orleans musician Fats Domino (they also shared songwriter/bandleader/producer Dave Bartholomew and local session players like Huey "Piano" Smith).

Born Overton Amos Lemons on July 5, 1920, in Union, Louisiana, he moved to New Orleans in age eleven with his parents. He began recording for DeLuxe in 1947, billed as "Smiling Lewis." His first hit came with "Bells Are Ringing" (Imperial 5194; 1952; #10 r&b). Later chart smashes included "I Hear You Knocking" (Imperial 5356; 1955; #2 r&b), "One Night (Of Sin)" (Imperial 5380; 1956; #11 r&b), and "Please Listen to Me" (Imperial 5389; 1956; #9). At the height of his popularity, his "Shame Shame Shame" was included the soundtrack of the 1956 film, *Baby Doll*. Although he never had a pop hit, other artists found mainstream success with covers of his songs, most notably TV sitcom star Gale Storm with "I Hear You Knocking" (Dot 15412; 1955; #2), Elvis Presley with a sanitized reading of "One Night (Of Love)" (RCA 47-7410; 1958; #4), and British retro-rocker Dave Edmunds with yet another version of "I Hear You Knocking" (MAM 3601; 1970; #4).

Seeking to rekindle his career, Lewis signed with Okeh in 1961. When no hits resulted, he moved on to the Nashville-based Dot label, and later Loma Records (where he worked with famed producer Allen

Toussaint). He continued performing on the southern club circuit until his death from stomach cancer on October 7, 1966. His music remains available, however, via reissues such as a four-CD box set on the German Bear Family label.

October 14. Nashville talent agent Eddie Crandall catches a Bill Haley and the Comets concert in Lubbock, Texas which includes Buddy Holly—backed by Larry Welborn and Bob Montgomery—as the opening act. In the following weeks, Crandall enables Holly to make his first demo recordings for Decca in Nashville.

October 15. Buddy (Holly) and Bob (Montgomery) open for Elvis Presley at the Cotton Club in Lubbock.

October 15. ABC-TV premieres the hour-length series, *Grand Ole Opry*, broadcast live every fourth Saturday night from the Ryman Auditorium, Nashville. The guest stars are Les Paul and Mary Ford.

October 28. Johnnie Ray has become a hot commodity in Great Britain, with "Song of the Dreamer" becoming his fifth charting single there (and third in October alone).

October 28. Little Willie John makes the R&B charts for the first time with "All Around the World."

October 29. *Billboard* reviews Little Richard's "Tutti Frutti" (b/w "I'm Just a Lonely Boy"): "…cleverly styled novelty with nonsense words, rapid-fire delivery."

One of the leading pioneers of early rock 'n' roll, Little Richard's frenetic singing style helped bring down the covering phenomenon, whereby the major labels assigned mainstream singers to record smoothed-over versions (often with sanitized lyrics) of original R&B hits geared to the pop charts. Although teen crooner Pat Boone garnered comparable sales with his awkward covers of two early Little Richard songs—"Tutti Frutti" (Dot 15443; 1956) and "Long Tall Sally" (Dot 15457; 1956)—his remaining hits faced no competition in crossing over to a mainstream audience.

Born Richard Wayne Penniman on December 5, 1932, in Macon, Georgia, his primary musical influences as a youth were singing in the church choir and playing saxophone in his high school band. When bluesman Buster Brown's singer failed to show up at a local concert, Richard—then age fourteen—filled in. While touring with the band, he began wearing his trademark pompadour and was billed as "Little Richard" for the first time. He was working variety shows when Zenas Sears—a WGST, Atlanta, deejay—helped him get a contract with RCA. His first session on October 16, 1951 resulted in four recordings: "Every Hour" (a hit in the Georgia area due to on-the-air plugs by Sears), "Goin' to Get Rich Quick," "Taxi Blues," and "Why Did You Leave Me." He would cut four more tracks on January 12, 1952, but they failed to catch on with the public. He then recorded eight songs (with his group the Tempo Toppers) on February 25 and October 5, 1953 for the Houston-based Peacock label, again with negligible results.

Little Richard spent the next couple of years touring the southeast with his new backup band, the Upsetters. A tip from R&B singer Lloyd Price led him to send a demo tape to Specialty records in February 1955. Producer Bumps Blackwell sensed his potential for communicating the same kind of gospel-blues blend that had made Ray Charles a star. The first session produced "Tutti Frutti" (Specialty 561; 1955), which reached number two on the R&B chart (and number seventeen on the pop listing despite the Boone cover). Over the next three years, Little Richard recorded a prodigious number of hits (mostly his own compositions), including "Long Tall Sally"/"Slippin' and Slidin'" (Specialty 572; 1956; #6 pop, #1 r&b/#2 r&b), "Rip It Up"/"Reddy Teddy" (Specialty 579; 1956; #1 r&b/#8 r&b), "She's Got It"/"Heebie Jeebies" (Specialty 584; 1956; #9 r&b/#7 r&b), "The Girl Can't Help It" (Specialty 591; 1956; #7 r&b), "Lucille"/"Send Me Some Lovin'" (Specialty 598; 1957; #1 r&b/#3 r&b), "Jenny, Jenny"/"Miss Ann" (Specialty 606; 1957; #10 pop, #2 r&b/#6 r&b), "Keep A Knockin'" (Specialty 611; 1957; #8 pop, #2 r&b), and "Good Golly, Miss Molly" (Specialty 624; 1958; #10 pop, #4 r&b). His popularity was reinforced by appearances in three early rock 'n' roll films: *Don't Knock the Rock*, *The Girl Can't Help It*, and *Mister Rock 'n' Roll*.

Despite his wild performing antics and gender-bending lifestyle, Little Richard felt a calling to become a preacher. By the late 1950s he was only performing religious music; however, he decided to return to rock music in 1963. Subsequent recordings for a variety of labels—including Vee-Jay, Okeh, Reprise, and Green Mountain—failed to generate more than moderate sales. By the early 1970s he was appearing in rock 'n' roll revival shows and expanding into non-musical endeavors. His critically acclaimed acting role in the 1986 motion picture, *Down & Out in Beverly Hills*, represented his most notable post-1950s artistic achievement. Disney had purchased the Little Richard catalog earlier in the decade; his songs would frequently be included in other Disney films, television programs, and animation collections as part of a settlement of a dispute over back royalty payments.

October 29. King releases Joe Tex's debut single, "Davy, You Upset My Home" (b/w "Come In This House"), an answer record to the Davy Crockett craze.

November 11. *Billboard* votes Elvis Presley the most promising new Country & Western artist.

November 12. *Billboard* publishes its annual disc jockey poll results. Winners include Johnny Ace's "Pledging My Love" (most played R&B record), Chuck Berry (most promising R&B artist), Fats Domino (favorite R&B artist), and Elvis Presley (most promising C&W artist). Rock 'n' roll is barely noted within the pop category.

November 14. The reissue of Bill Haley and the Comets' "Rock Around the Clock" enters the U.K. charts for a second run. It will return three more times; in 1956, 1968, and 1974.

November 17. James P Johnson dies at age sixity-four. The influential jazz pianist had one major hit, "Carolina Shout" (Okeh 4495; 1922).

November 20. New York DJ Tommy "Dr. Jive" Smalls emcees a fifteen-minute segment of the *Ed Sullivan Show* which features R&B stars LaVern Baker, Bob Diddley, Willie "Gator Tail" Jackson, and the Five Keys. Sullivan requests that Diddley play "Sixteen Tons," providing coaching and cue cards during rehearsals when the performer claims not to know the song. Diddley nevertheless performs "Bo Diddley" during the actual show.

November 22. Steve Sholes signs Elvis Presley to RCA Victor for a reported $40,000; the money is divided between Sun Records head Sam Phillips ($25,000 as compensation for Presley's contract) and Hi-Lo Music ($15,000 for Presley's song publishing). Phillips allegedly invests his money in the Memphis-based Holiday Inn hotel chain, while Presley—who's received a $5,000 bonus—bought a new Cadillac. The deal, brokered by Presley's new manager, Colonel Tom Parker, gave RCA the rights to the five previously released Sun singles as well as an unspecified number of unreleased tracks. The label would reputedly sell a half-billion Presley records up to the singer's death alone. Although considered an outrageously high sum to pay for a largely unproven artist at the time, Phillips would spend the rest of his day defending the transaction, arguing he needed the cash outlay in order to keep Sun in business and that Presley's ascent to superstardom was by no means a sure thing.

November 23. The Cadillacs' "Speedoo" makes the R&B charts. The song celebrates the group's lead singer, Earl "Speedoo" Carroll. Paul Simon's "Was a Sunny Day" will quote the following line from the song: "Everybody calls me Speedoo, but my real name is Mr. Earl."

The Cadillacs were one of the most beloved rhythm and blues vocal groups of all time; Dave Marsh's *Rock Book of Lists* placed them number one among black doo-wop ensembles. The group's polished stage show—complete with choreographed dance steps and flashy outfits—greatly influenced acts following in their wake (particularly the Motown artists; the Temptations and Four Tops would even hire the Cadillacs' choreographer, Cholly Atkins). Although many of their classic tracks were recorded prior to the rock era and, therefore, had little chance of crossing over to a mainstream pop audience, the original recordings continue to be coveted by collectors.

The group—originally including Harlem P.S. 139 schoolmates Robert Phillips (born 1935), Laverne Drake (b. 1938), Johnny "Gus" Willingham (b. 1937), and lead singer Earl "Speedy" Carroll (b. November 2, 1937)—started performing together in 1953 as the Carnations. An audition the following year spurred manager/composer/ musical arranger Esther Navarro to sign them to a personal recording contract. She encouraged them to add another singer known as James "Poppa" Clark (b. 1937) and to change their name, ultimately deciding on the Cadillacs, after the luxury automobile, due to the preponderance of groups with bird names at the time.

In 1954, Navarro booked them into New York City's Beltone Studios to record four songs featuring backing with Rene Hall's band: "I Want to Know About Love," "I Wonder Why," "Gloria," and "Wishing

Well." The ballad "Gloria"—written by Navarro about another client, singer Gloria Smith—was released as a single on Josie, a subsidiary label of the leading R&B record companies of the early 1950s, Jubilee. Featuring an extraordinarily sensitive lead vocal by Carroll, the song became a minor R&B hit.

Despite the defections of Willingham and Clark—replaced by Charles Brooks (b. 1937) and Earl Wade (b. 1937), respectively—the Cadillacs went on to achieve even greater success with another Navarro composition, "Speedo" (Josie 785; 1956; w/Jesse Powell Orchestra; #17 pop, #3 r&b). One of the best-loved recordings of the doo-wop era, its appeal owes much to the dynamic interplay of group voices providing a backdrop for Carroll's swaggering lead, which updates a longstanding blues tradition. A novel reworking of the Christmas chestnut, "Rudolph the Red-Nosed Reindeer" (Josie 807; 1957; w/Jesse Powell Orchestra) would rise to number eleven on the R&B charts a year later. The group also had success with "Peek-A-Boo" (Josie 846; 1959; #28 pop, #20 r&b) and "What You Bet" (Smash 1712; 1961; #30 r&b).

While active well into the 1970s, the Cadillacs ceased to be an artistically important act when Carroll left in 1961 to replace Carnell Gunter in the more commercially successful Coasters. The group had already lost credibility in the late 1950s when members split into two factions, both of whom recorded and performed as the Cadillacs. After a period of inactivity in the 1970s, the Cadillacs would re-form with Carroll and Phillips in the early 1980s.

The ABC-TV program *20/20* would spotlight Carroll's life and work in the early 1990s. Despite his music activities, he worked steadily as a custodian within the New York City public school system, where he was universally loved by students and staff who knew nothing about his legacy as a musician.

December 5. Eleven of the twenty-three winners at the BMI Annual Awards Dinner in New York City are R&B songs, including "Dance with Me, Henry," "Earth Angel," "I Hear You Knockin'," "Maybellene," "Only You," "Pledging My Love," and "Sincerely."

December 15. Sun Records releases one of Johnny Cash's classic recordings, "Folsom Prison Blues." Inspired to compose the song after seeing the film, *Inside the Walls of Folsom Prison*, Cash would revive it for his bestselling 1968 Columbia LP culled from a live performance at the prison.

December 17. With "Only You" still holding down the number two position, the Platters' "The Great Pretender" enters the R&B charts at number thirteen. When the latter song begins a ten-week run atop the charts, the quintet is well on its way to becoming the most successful doo-wop group of all time.

Doo-wop, the popular name for vocal group rhythm and blues, includes the following musical qualities: group harmony, a wide range of vocal parts, nonsense syllables, a simple beat, light instrumentation, and simple music and lyrics. Above all, the focus is on ensemble singing. Single artists fit the genre only when backed by a group (the possibility that the group may not be mentioned on the record label is immaterial). Typically solo billing simply means that this individual is more prominently placed in the musical arrangement (e.g., Dion, Bobby Day, Thurston Harris) as opposed to typical group productions.

Doo-wop emerged in the urban ghettos from the blending of rhythm and blues, gospel, and popular black vocal group music in the post-World War II era. The style represented the culmination of many hours spent by teens—usually black males—practicing vocal harmonies in school gyms, street corners, and subway entrances. These young groups sought a piece of the American Dream via crossover success in the music business. From their perspective, the more direct route to success meant adapting white pop standards to contemporary black vocal styles. In other words, they attempted to replicate the formula employed a generation earlier by black groups like the Mills Brothers and the Ink Spots. The pronounced gospel and R&B traits within their work reflected the influences from childhood (church, social activities, etc.) which formed the core of their music education. Doo-wop features began emerging in African American pop music during the 1948 to 1951 period. They can be discerned in R&B hits like the Orioles' "It's Too Soon To Know" (1948) and the Dominoes' "Sixty-Minute Man" (1951). The doo-wop era began around 1952—a time when the key musical qualities of the genre were all clearly in evidence—and remained artistically and commercially viable until the early 1960s. This time frame can be subdivided into several phases of stylistic development.

Paleo Doo-Wop (1952–1954)

This subgenre retains many visible features of its stylistic ancestors; e.g., R&B in the Drifters' "Money Honey"; gospel in "The Bells of St. Mary's," by Lee Andrews and the Hearts; black pop vocal groups in the Platters' "Only You." These traits had yet to be synthesized into a truly singular style. Other notable records from this period included The Cadillacs—"Gloria" (1954), The Chords—"Sh-Boom" (1954; the cover by the Crewcuts became one of the biggest hits of that year), The Crows—"Gee" (1954), The Drifters—"Honey Love" (1954), The Harptones—"A Sunday Kind of Love" (1954), The Jewels—"Hearts of Stone" (1954), The Orioles—"Crying in the Chapel" (1953), and The Penguins—"Earth Angel" (1954).

Classical Doo-Wop (1955–1959)

This phase featured tight and sweet harmonies; however, the lead singers lost much of the smoothness typifying paleo-doo-wop recordings. Bass singers were given a more prominent role; in the past they had tended to function merely as part of the background harmony. The performers were generally quite young, featuring lyrics primarily concerned with young, idealistic love. Nonsense syllables were employed in the majority of songs. Instrumentation remained in the background, albeit with a heavy backbeat. Key recordings included The Cleftones—"Little Girl of Mine" (1956), The Del Vikings—"Come Go With Me" (1957), The El Dorados—"At My Front Door" (1955), The Five Satins—"In the Still of the Night" (1956), The Flamingos—"I Only Have Eyes For You" (1959), The Heartbeats—"A Thousand Miles Away" (1956), The Monotones—"Book of Love" (1958), The Rays—"Silhouettes" (1957), The Silhouettes—"Get a Job" (1958), and The Willows—"Church Bells May Ring" (1956).

The classical period saw the development of a wide array of spinoff styles, in part a response to newly devised marketing strategies. These included:

1. Schoolboy doo-wop. The focal point here was an ultra-high tenor, usually a male in his early teenage years. While Frankie Lymon was the definitive interpreter from the standpoint of both commercial success and singing prowess, he has many imitators, including brother Lewis Lymon (the Teenchords), the Kodaks, the Schoolboys, and the Students. Among the notable hits were Little Anthony and the Imperials—"Two People in the World" (1958), Frankie Lymon and the Teenagers—"Who Do Fools Fall in Love" (1956), and The Schoolboys—"Shirley" (1957).

2. Gang doo-wop. Lead singers studiously avoided being smooth; rather, they seemed to swagger as they sang. Likewise, harmonies, though intricate, were rough in approach. Major hits included The Channels—"That's My Desire" (1957), The Charts—"Desiree" (1958), and The Collegians—"Zoom Zoom Zoom" (1957).

3. Italo-doo-wop. Like African Americans, Italian Americans accorded music a prime place in their upbringing (through church). Although isolated white groups had appeared in the early 1950s (e.g., the Bay Bops, the Neons, the Three Friends), the first major wave of white doo-wop acts surfaced in 1958. This variant was distinguished by even tighter group harmonies, roughly-hewn tenors pushing their upper registers to produce a "sweet" sound, and the prominence of bass singers (the latter a premonition of the neo-doo-wop phase). Notable recordings included The Capris—"There's a Moon Out Tonight" (1958; 1961), The Classics—"Till Then" (1963), The Elegants—"Little Star" (1958), and The Mystics—"Hushabye" (1959).

4. Pop doo-wop. Heavily influenced by the commercial mainstream going as far back as turn-of-the-century barbershop quartets, this style had little in common with classic doo-wop other than tight harmony. Practitioners developed a number of ploys geared to making inroads into the pop market, most notably (a) cover records, (b) softening the doo-wop sound in order that it might reach a broader range of age groups, and (c) jazzing up adult-oriented standards so as to appeal to youth. Among the more popular records in this vein were The Duprees—"You Belong to Me" (1962), The Echoes—"Baby Blue" (1961), The Fleetwoods—"Come Softly to Me" (1959), The Temptations (white group)—"Barbara" (1960), and The Tymes—"So Much in Love" (1963).

Neo Doo-Wop (1960–1963)

The impetus for this phase was the oldies revival (largely focused on doo-wop) which began in 1959. Although neo-doo-wop maintained the simple melody lines and preoccupation with love lyrics typifying the classical phase, the distinctive features of doo-wop were greatly exaggerated; e.g., a greater preponderance of falsetto leads, heavier and more pronounced bass singing. Instruments also figured more prominently in song arrangements. Notable hits included Gene Chandler with the Dukays—"Duke of Earl" (1961), The Devotions—"Rip Van Winkle" (1961; 1964), Dion with the Del Satins—"Runaround Sue" (1961), Curtis Lee With the Halos—"Pretty Little Angel Eyes" (1961), The Paradons—"Diamonds and Pearls" (1960), The Reflections—"(Just Like) Romeo and Juliet" (1964), The Regents—"Barbara Ann" (1961), and The Stereos—"I Really Love You" (1961).

The absorption of new talent from a variety of backgrounds spurred the development of new stylistic subcategories, including:

1. Tin Pan Alley Doo-Wop. Exposed to doo-wop as well as schooled in music composition, young songwriters (e.g., Gerry Goffin/Carole King, Barry Mann/Cynthia Weil, Jeff Barry/Ellie Greenwich) and producers (Phil Spector) created their own formula. They melded doo-wop conventions (e.g., tight harmony, pronounced bass, nonsense syllables) with more complex melodies, augmented instrumentation, and thoroughgoing production values. Key recordings included The Chiffons—"He's So Fine" (1963), The Crystals—"Da Doo Ron Ron" (1963), The Raindrops—"The Kind of Boy You Can't Forget" (1963), Randy and the Rainbows—"Denise" (1963), and The Tokens—"Tonight I Fell in Love" (1961).
2. Distaff Doo-Wop. With few exceptions (e.g., the Chantels, the Bobbettes, the Shirelles, and fronting male groups such as the Platters), women didn't play a prominent role in doo-wop until the Tin Pan Alley variant achieved popularity. Notable hits included Patti LaBelle and the Blue Belles—"You'll Never Walk Alone" (1963), The Cookies—"Don't Say Nothin' Bad About My Baby" (1963), and Reperata and the Delrons—"Whenever a Teenager Cries" (1964).
3. Garage Band Doo-Wop. Denotes material recorded on substandard equipment. Representative examples included the Laddins—"Did It" and the Contenders—"The Clock."
4. Novelty Doo-Wop. Almost without exception, this genre encompasses humorous, uptempo material. Themes covered include fantasy (e.g., the Eternals—"Rockin' in the Jungle," the Cadets—"Stranded in the Jungle"), rebellion (e.g., the Coasters—"Yakety Yak"), fads (e.g., the Royal Teens—"Short Shorts"), and media heroes (e.g., Dante and the Evergreens—"Alley Oop").
5. Pseudo Doo-Wop. This category refers to the doo-wop style minus the vocal group format. Major strains have included solo efforts (e.g., Ron Holden and the Thunderbirds—"Love You So," Rosie and the Originals—"Angel Baby") and duos (e.g., Skip and Flip—"Cherry Pie," Don and Juan—"What's Your Name," Robert and Johnny—"Over the Mountain").

Post Doo-Wop (1964–)

For all practical purposes, the genre ceased to function in a creative sense as elements associated with it virtually disappear from recordings. With few exceptions, words replaced nonsense syllables as background responses, harmony receded into the background, falsetto appeared less frequently, the bass was used less as a separate voice, instrumentation took on much greater importance, and melodies exhibited a much greater degree of variation. A number of groups—most notably the Drifters, the Four Seasons, and Little Anthony and the Imperials—crossed over into the pop mainstream. The primary innovations in vocal group singing now took place within the *a cappella* genre.

December 19. Carl Perkins records "Blue Suede Shoes" at Sun Studios in Memphis. It will rise to number two on the pop charts, but Perkins will be unable to fully take advantage of this opportunity due to an extensive hospital stay resulting from a car accident in early 1956 while on tour.

December 23. Two high-profile rock 'n' roll shows—each spread over a week—take place during the Christmas holidays. WWRL's Dr. Jive presides over a Brooklyn Paramount extravaganza; featuring Ruth Brown and Clyde McPhatter, it grosses $85,000. The other event is held at the Manhattan Academy of Music; hosted by WINS DJ Alan Freed and starring LaVern Baker, Boyd Bennett, the Cadillacs, and Count Basie, among others, it takes in more than $100,000.

December 26. Decca releases Bill Haley and the Comets' "See You Later, Alligator." It will be his last major hit, reaching number six on the pop charts and number fourteen on the R&B listing.

December 28. Former Dominoes and Drifters lead vocalist, Clyde McPhatter makes the R&B survey for the first time as a solo artist with "Seven Days." It will go as high as number three, while stalling at number forty-four on the pop charts.

December 31. According to *Billboard*'s Honor Roll of Hits—a tabulation based upon retail sales, DJ favorites, and jukebox play—"Unchained Melody" is the top song of 1955.

1956

❄

January 2. Buddy Holly records his first session for Decca Records, in Nashville, Tennessee. Three sessions for the label would lead to just two singles, which received little attention because they didn't fit the country market mold of the day. By the end of the year, Holly—now without a record deal—decided to reinvent himself as a rock 'n' roller. He would assemble a backing group, the Crickets, in February 1957, and re-record "That'll Be the Day" (first done for Decca in 1956). Picked up by the Decca subsidiary, Brunswick, and released in May 1957, the song slowly inched up the pop music charts, reaching number one four months later (*Rolling Stone Rock Almanac* says Jan. 26).

January 6. Elvis Presley performs in the Randolph (Mississippi) High School gym—the last time he would play in a small venue of this type.

January 7. Dean Martin begins a six-week run atop the Disc Jockey charts with "Memories Are Made of This" (Capitol 3295). The record also reaches the summit of the Top 100 (five weeks), Best Seller (five weeks), and Juke Box (three weeks) charts. In 1955, thirteen of the fourteen chart-topping singles were either Tin Pan Alley material or covers of R&B songs by mainstream pop artists. The new year offers little indication that rock 'n' roll is posed to become the dominant form of popular music. Nevertheless, rock 'n' roll/R&B artists—more specifically, Elvis Presley and the Platters—will occupy the top rung for thirty-two weeks in 1956. And an increasing number of rock 'n' roll acts will populate the lower portion of the charts as well by the following year.

Although something of an anachronism during his peak period of popularity as a recording artist—from the mid-1950s to the mid-1960s—Dean Martin managed to produce a lengthy string of hit ballads during the golden age of rock 'n' roll and, later, at the height of the British Invasion when American artists at every stripe had trouble getting their songs played on the radio. While his relaxed crooning style failed to generate much critical acclaim, he enjoyed widespread public support across a wide range of media, including the record industry, the cinema, radio, television, and live performing venues.

Born Dino Crocetti, Martin (June 7, 1917–Deember 25, 1995) became interested in a singing career after finding little fulfillment working as a mill hand, gas-station attendant, and gambling casino croupier. In 1946, he teamed up with comedian Jerry Lewis; their popularity on the nightclub circuit led to a film contract with Paramount. The duo starred in sixteen movies—including *My Friend Irma* (1949), *At War with the Army* (1952), and *The Caddy* (1953)—until their breakup in 1957.

Although Martin continued to star in a wide range of film roles—in addition to being in great demand both as a host (the *Dean Martin Show* ran from 1965–1974) and guest performer on TV—he was perhaps best known for his successful sound recordings, beginning with a comic duet with Lewis, "That Certain Party" (Capitol 15249; 1948; #22). By the time he recorded "That's Amore" (Capitol 2589; 1953; #2) his suave, urbane approach was in place. He continued to chart consistently throughout the 1950s, most notably with "Memories Are Made of This," "Return to Me" (Capitol 3894; 1958; #4), and "Volare" (Capitol 4028; 1958; #12; more popular versions were recorded by Domenico Modugno in 1958 and Bobby Rydell in 1960).

Following an extended dry spell, Martin was signed by buddy Frank Sinatra's fledging Reprise label in 1962. While considering material in the studio, Martin's conductor and pianist, Ken Lane, suggested a song he'd co-written more than fifteen years earlier, "Everybody Loves Somebody" (Reprise 0281). Although Sinatra (the first to record it in 1948), Dinah Washington, Peggy Lee, and other prominent singers had failed to make it a hit, Martin's updated version reached number one on the *Billboard Hot 100* in August 1964 (it would remain atop the Adult Contemporary charts for eight weeks). He would go on to produce ten more Top 40 hits in the 1960s, including "The Door Is Still Open To My Heart" (Reprise 0307; 1964; #6) and "I Will" (Reprise 0415; 1965; #10).

Martin also became a highly successful albums artist with Reprise, placing twenty-three titles on the *Billboard* charts between 19631972, most notably, *Dream with Dean* (Reprise 6123; 1964; #15), *Everybody Loves Somebody* (Reprise 6130; 1964; #2), *The Door Is Still Open To My Heart* (Reprise 6140; 1964; #9),

Dean Martin Hits Again (Reprise 6146; 1965; #13), *(Remember Me) I'm the One Who Loves You* (Reprise 6170; 1965; #12), *Houston* (Reprise 6181; 1965; #11), *Welcome To My World* (Reprise 6250; 1967; #20), and *Gentle On My Mind* (Reprise 6330; 1969; #14).

January 10. Elvis Presley first records for RCA Victor at The Methodist Television, Radio and TV Studios in Nashville. "Heartbreak Hotel" is one of the songs to come out of this session.

January 11. The Coasters record "Down in Mexico" and "Turtle Dovin'." The group is comprised of Carl Gardner and Bobby Nunn, formerly of the Robins, as well as Billy Guy and Leon Hughes. Like the most recent material produced by the Robins, these tracks, were written and produced by Jerry Leiber and Mike Stoller, and engineered by Bunny Robyn in Hollywood, California. This combination would create a new benchmark for rock 'n' roll humor recordings, spanning satire, parody, and nonsense verse.

January 18. Little Richard's "Tutti Frutti" (Specialty)—one of the few R&B releases to outperform its white covers, in this case by Pat Boone (Dot) and Elvis Presley (Specialty)—enters the pop chart at number 26.

January 18. Bill Haley and the Comets' *Rock Around The Clock* (Decca) becomes the first rock 'n' roll record to appear on *Billboard*'s Top 15 Pop Albums chart (number 12).

January 23. Cleveland, Ohio, youth under eighteen are banned from public dancing (unless accompanied by an adult) after police announce plans to enforce a law dating back to 1931.

January 27. RCA releases its first new Elvis Presley record, "Heartbreak Hotel"/"I Was the One."

January 28. Elvis Presley first appears on national television, CBS's *Jackie Gleason Stage Show*, hosted by Tommy and Jimmy Dorsey. His performances of "Blue Suede Shoes" and "Heartbreak Hotel" play a major role in catapulting him to the top of the pop firmament. Presley will appear on the Gleason program five more times, singing "Tutti Frutti" and "I Was the One" (the B-side of his first Victor single, "Heartbreak Hotel") on February 4, followed by "Shake, Rattle and Roll," "Flip, Flop and Fly," and "I Got a Woman" on February 11; he would repeat "Tutti Frutti," "Blue Suede Shoes," and "Heartbreak Hotel" and introduce "Baby, Let's Play House" and "Money Honey" during his February 18, March 17, and March 24 appearances. One of the hosts was allegedly overheard saying, "he can't last."

January 30. Elvis Presley begins recording his first LP at RCA Victor's New York studios.

January 30. Billy Lee Riley and the Little Green Men—with Jerry Lee Lewis sitting in on piano—record what will become his biggest hit, "Red Hot," in the Sun Studios, Memphis. Previously, they'd had a local hit with "Flying Saucers Rock 'n' Roll."

February 1. Further evidence that a musical revolution is in the making, the Rock and Roll Ice Revue opens at New York City's Roxy Theater.

February 2. Atlantic Records signs the Coasters, and immediately releases a single combining their two recently recorded tracks (see: January 11, 1956), "Down in Mexico," b/w "Turtle Dovin'."

February 8. The Teen Queens' "Eddie My Love" RPM 453) enters the R&B chart on its way to becoming a Top Ten hit. The trio was the first female-dominated group with a distinctly rock or R&B-based sound to enjoy commercial success.

With the exception of the teen idols, girl groups were the only genuinely distinctive genre to peak in the early 1960s. The genre owed its success largely to the 1959 payola investigations, combined with increased attacks on rock 'n' roll's alleged bad influence on teenagers. These factors stimulated a change in image and musical focus among record companies and radio disc jockeys. Radio's efforts to clean house led to the concentration of power in the hands of the program director who, in turn, adopted national playlists and a tightened Top 40 format. There was a resulting decline in regional hits produced by small record labels; the pop music industry was driven by the ongoing search for the next big trend. Heavy reliance on proven formulas became the modus operandi as the balance of power shifted to a select group of record executives, studio producers, staff songwriters, and media personalities.

Girl groups proved to be one of the more successful formulas to be mined again and again by those labels committed to the youth market. Music historians have sometimes fallen prey to a revisionist perspective of that era which interprets the rise of girl groups—and female performers in general (e.g., Connie

Francis, Brenda Lee, Lesley Gore)—as early evidence of the increasing assertiveness of women in the workplace and within society in general. In point of fact, however, girl groups were strongly manipulated by powerful men who were well-connected within the record industry. Successful girl groups were prized in large because they were easily pliable, generally submitting to outside control with a minimal display of rebellious attitude. The younger the performers, the more likely they were to accept the strict order of the system. This at least in part explains why few groups were able to sustain a successful recording career beyond a hit recording or two.

The Chantels—the first girl group to rise above the one-hit wonder status—had limited the impact of acts such as the Teen Queens, the Paris Sisters ("I Love How You Love Me," Gregmark 6; 1956), and the Poni-Tails ("Born Too Late," ABC-Paramount 9934; 1957). The group—originally a quintet whose members were all classmates at Saint Anthony of Padua School in the Bronx, New York—were discovered backstage at an Alan Freed rock 'n' roll revue by Rama/Gee/Gone record producer Richard Barrett while waiting to meet their idol, Frankie Lymon (of the Teenagers). The Chantels' second release, "Maybe" (End 1005; 1958), proved to be a seminal event in the girl group genre featuring lead vocalist Arlene Smith in one of the most searing and honest vocal performances ever. The disc's dramatic intensity and steady sales profoundly influenced musicians and producers for years to come.

The Shirelles were the first girl group to achieve both artistic and commercial success following in the stylistic path established by the Chantels. When the Shirelles' first few releases made little impact, producer Luther Dixon decided to sweeten up their heavily R&B sound through the use of strings. He first achieved success with the West Indian-inflected "Tonight's the Night" (Scepter 1208; 1960), followed by the Carole King/Gerry Goffin composition, "Will You Love Me Tomorrow" (Scepter 1211; 1060). The latter song was a hit around the world, remaining number one for five weeks on the U.S. singles charts. The arrangement—featuring swirling strings accented by a snare drum figure which inverted the traditional rock beat and added on a slight rhythmic shuffle—spurred record industry movers and shakers to try to incorporate and enlarge upon its techniques. In addition, its success drove home the idea that the right song, combined with the right singer and right arranger and right producer, represented the best blueprint for making a pop record.

While the Shirelles were recording a long string of hit singles (most notably, "Soldier Boy" (Scepter 1228; number one, 1962), many other competitors were attempting to interpret the formula in their own ways. Producer Phil Spector was building his own roster of girl groups on the Philles label and many of Berry Gordy's biggest hits for the Motown-Tamla-Gordy (aka the Motown Sound) combine were recorded by all-female aggregates. Don Kirshner and his Aldon publishing company, located in the heart of the Brill Building complex in Manhattan, supplied songs to many record companies who, in turn, matched them up with contracted girl groups. By 1962, his firm had eighteen writers on staff, between the ages of nineteen and twenty-six, including the Barry Mann-Cynthia Weil, Gerry Goffin-Carole King, and Neil Sedaka-Howard Greenfield teams. In addition, number of record companies achieved success in large part due to girl group recordings. These included Red Bird-Blue Cat, Cameo-Parkway, Chancellor, Jamie-Guyden, and Swan.

The decline of the girl group sound was a product of a complex chain of events. Although the British Invasion dominated the media in 1964, girl-group records continued to sell well. Mary Wells, The Dixie Cups, The Supremes, and The Shangri-Las resided at the top of the charts for twenty-five percent of the year, while major hits were recorded by The Ronettes, Martha & The Vandellas, Lesley Gore, The Jelly Beans, and numerous others. More importantly, the innocent romanticism of the sound seemed out of step with an era colored by the JFK assassination, Vietnam, and the civil rights movement. With many of the key composers and producers turning to other pursuits, the public grew tired of the weak girl group recordings flooding the market. Finally, psychedelic rock, soul, Motown, the singer-songwriters, folk-rock, and the surfing sound provided stiff commercial competition.

Despite the relatively short duration of the girl group sound, its legacy continues to shine brightly. The classic songs of the genre—e.g., "The Locomotion" (Little Eva, Dimension 1000; 1962), "Will You Love Me Tomorrow," "Da Doo Ron Ron" (Crystals, Philles 112; 1963)—have regularly been revived by contemporary stars, while its stylistic features have been recreated by countless other performers. New Wave girl groups (e.g., the Go-Gos, the Bangles), the riot grrrl movement, and pop confections like the Spice Girls all represent variations of the original mold.

February 12. Screamin' Jay Hawkins records the voodoo classic, "I Put a Spell on You," for Okeh Records in New York City.

February 13. Alan Freed is resigned by Coral Records. His contract calls for him to compile and promote four dance and party LPs during his first year.

February 16. In a New York press conference, Jackie Bright, administrative secretary for the American Guild of Variety Artists, states that "DJs who put on record dances are putting musicians out of work." He adds that guild members may be forbidden to cooperate with disc jockeys in the future.

February 18. The Platters begin a two-week stay atop the singles chart with "The Great Pretender" (Mercury). At the height of their career, the Platters were an anachronism, performing classic Tin Pan Alley material updated slightly to fit the rhythmic framework of the rock 'n' roll era. Founded by Herbert Reed in 1953, the group—which also included David Lynch, Paul Robi, and lead singer Tony Williams—initially recorded in a doo-wop style for the Federal label. Failing to achieve a hit record, members were working as parking lot attendants in Los Angeles when they met music business entrepreneur Buck Ram. Initially using them to make demonstration discs of his own compositions (which tended to fall within the crooning genre), Ram insisted that Mercury Records sign them as part of a package deal involving another of his clients, the Penguins, then on the verge of stardom with the recording, "Earth Angel" (Dootone 348; 1954–1955). In one of the supreme ironies in recording history, the Penguins faded from the public eye without another pop hit, while the Platters (adding Zola Taylor in late 1955) became the top-selling vocal group of the second half of the 1950s. Their Top Ten singles included "Only You" (Mercury 70633; 1955), "The Great Pretender" (Mercury 70753; 1955–1956; #1), "(You've Got) The Magic Touch" (Mercury 70819; 1956), "My Prayer" (Mercury 70893; 1956; #1), "Twilight Time" (Mercury 71289; 1958; #1), "Smoke Gets In Your Eyes" (Mercury 71383; 1958–1959; #1), and "Harbor Lights" (Mercury 71563; 1960).

The group's decline in the early 1960s has been attributed to a number of causes, most notably the morals arrest of the male members on August 10, 1959, the departure of Williams (one of the most gifted vocalists in pop) for a solo career in 1960, and changing consumer tastes. The Platters continued to enjoy steady album sales with the release of titles such as *Encore of Golden Hits* (Mercury 20472; 1960; 174 weeks on pop charts) and *More Encore of Golden Hits* (Mercury 20591; 1960). By the early 1970s, the group—by then recording for Musicor— was considered a nostalgia act, sometimes performing in Richard Nader's rock 'n' roll revival shows. As copyright holder of the Platters' name, Ram continued to manage the official version of the group well into the 1980s. However, he was continuously forced to file lawsuits to keep pseudo groups from using the name. Greatest hits packages featuring the Mercury material have remained popular; Rhino issued a two-disc anthology and the German Bear Family label released a nine-CD box set in the late 1980s.

February 18. Kay Starr's "Rock and Roll Waltz" (RCA) begins a six-week stay atop the Juke Box survey. It will also outpace the competition on the Top 100 (four weeks), Disc Jockey (one week), and Best Seller (one week) charts. The single reflects the defensive posture presently being exhibited by the major labels. The style—Tin Pan Alley songcraft strained through a simplified waltz time signature—and the singer are old school pop, but an attempt has been made accommodate present day trends by alluding to rock 'n' roll (if only by appropriating the name itself). The other timeworn strategy being employed by the majors to cannibalize musical innovations—the covering phenomenon—is already proving less effective as record buyers—and radio listeners—are increasingly opting for the original recordings by the likes of Little Richard, Frankie Lymon and the Teenagers, Fats Domino, and the Moonglows, among others. Furthermore, the independent labels are becoming increasing adept at constructing idiosyncratic song arrangements, lyrics, and vocal mannerisms that pop artists feel uncomfortable attempting to translate to a middle-of-the-road audience.

February 22. *Billboard* reviews James Brown's first single, "Please, Please, Please," noting: "A dynamic, religious fervor runs through the pleading solo here. Brown and the Famous Flames group let off plenty of steam." The song will enter the R&B charts on April 11.

February 24. The 1931 Cleveland ordinance prohibiting anyone under age eighteen from dancing in public unless accompanied by an adult is applied by police for the first time in the rock 'n' roll era.

February 25. Elvis Presley tops *Billboard*'s Country & Western survey with "I Forgot to Remember to Forget" (RCA)—his first ever national hit.

February 25. Nelson Riddle reaches number one on the Best Seller listing with the instrumental "Lisbon Antigua," remaining there for four weeks. The single also tops the Disc Jockey survey for a week, while peaking at number two on the Top 100 and Juke Box charts.

February 25. Representative from fifteen major radio markets gather in New York City to form the National Rhythm and Blues Disc Jockey Association of America. The organization's immediate concerns include controlling offensive song lyrics and payola (i.e., rewarding DJs in some manner to play certain records).

February 27. Specialty releases Little Richard's "Slippin' and Slidin'"/"Long Tall Sally." It will become his first number one R&B recording.

March 7. Carl Perkins' "Blue Suede Shoes" enters the R&B charts, the first time a C&W artist has accomplished this feat. Genre boundaries will become increasingly blurred during the rock 'n' roll era.

March 10. RCA places a half-page ad in *Billboard* introducing Elvis Presley as "the new singing rage."

March 13. RCA releases the first Elvis Presley album and extended play discs.

March 15. Colonel Tom Parker becomes Elvis Presley's manager. Parker started out in show business organizing carny acts like the Great Parker Pony Circus and Colonel Tom Parker and His Dancing Turkeys before moving on to manage such country legends as Hank Snow, Gene Autry, and Eddy Arnold.

March 22. Trumpeter Clifford Brown makes his last studio recording. The most notable recording to come out of the session is the Sonny Rollins composition, "Pent-Up House."

March 22. Carl Perkins is seriously injuring in a car accident near Wilmington, Delaware, while traveling to New York appear on the Ed Sullivan Show.

March 25. Police arrest eleven teenagers during Alan Freed's three-day Rock 'n' Roll Show at the Stage Theater, Hartford, Connecticut. In addition, the venue's operating license is revoked. At license hearings Hartford Institute of Living psychiatrist Dr. Francis J. Braceland testifies that rock 'n' roll is "a communicable disease, with music appealing to adolescent insecurity and driving teenagers to do outlandish things…It's cannibalistic and tribalistic." Bandleader Sammy Kaye denounces these remarks in an open letter, referring to them as "thoughtless and in bad taste."

April 3. Elvis Presley performs "Heartbreak Hotel," "Blue Suede Shoes," and "Money Honey" on the *Milton Berle Show* live from the flight deck of the U.S.S. *Hancock* anchored in New York. He is paid $5,000 for his efforts, which were reputed to have been viewed by twenty-five percent of all Americans. On his final appearance of the Berle program, June 5, the host presents him with two *Billboard* Triple Crown awards for "Heartbreak Hotel," then on top of the pop, R&B, and C&W charts for sales, disc jockey, and jukebox play. He also ignites a nationwide furor over his wild gyrations while singing "I Want You, I Need You, I Love You" and "Hound Dog." One critic refers to his hip-grinding antics as "the mating dance of an aborigine." The media now begins referring to him as "Elvis the Pelvis," an appellation which greatly annoyed him.

April 6. Paramount Pictures signs Elvis Presley to a contract to make three feature films five days after he'd taken his first Hollywood screen test.

April 7. *Rock 'n' Roll Dance Party*, hosted by Alan Freed, premieres on the CBS Radio Network. It is the first regularly scheduled rock 'n' roll program to be broadcast nationwide.

April 9. Gene Vincent records "Be-Bop-A-Lula."

April 10. Nat "King" Cole is severely beaten by a number of racial segregationists during a performance at Municipal Hall in Birmingham, Alabama. WBT, Charlotte, North Carolina, DJ Bob Raiford is fired two days later for "taking an unauthorized stand on a controversial issue." Raiford's insubordination had consisted of denouncing the attack on the air.

April 11. Elvis Presley records with the Jordanaires for the first time on "I Want You, I Need You, I Love You."

April 14. The Teenagers featuring Frankie Lymon peak at number six on the pop charts with "Why Do Fools Fall in Love" (Gee 1002).

Frankie Lymon was one of the true greats of post–World War II R&B, a multi-talented singer/songwriter/actor/dancer who electrified the pop music scene as a thirteen-year-old before falling on hard times. Born on September 30, 1942 in New York City, Lymon formed his back-up group—first known as the Premiers—in the Bronx in 1955. The Teenagers—whose members included tenors Herman Santiago and Jimmy Merchant, baritone Joe Negroni, and bass Sherman Gaines—recorded a half-dozen doo-wop-styled Top Ten R&B hits in an eighteen-month span beginning in February 1956: the chart-topper "Why Do Fools Fall in Love," "I Want You to Be My Girl," "I Promise to Remember"/"Who Can Explain?", "The ABC's of Love," and "Out in the Cold Again." The group also appeared in two successful Hollywood films—"Rock, Rock, Rock" and "Mister Rock 'n' Roll"—while still a bankable commodity.

When the Teenagers lost their commercial momentum, Lymon tried to make it as a solo act. When success eluded him, he seemed to lose control of his life, dying of a drug overdose on February 28, 1968.

April 15. Eric Severeid's CBS-TV talk show features a panel discussion of rock 'n' roll. The panel includes Columbia Records A&R director Mitch Miller, DJ Alan Freed, two psychiatrists, and two teenagers. Directing his comments to "mom and dad," Freed argues that media coverage of rock 'n' roll-incited riots are "grossly exaggerated."

April 16. ABC premieres its own rock 'n' roll show, *Rhythm on Parade*. Broadcast live from Detroit's Flame Show Bar, it is hosted by Willie Bryant.

April 16. Buddy Holly's debut single, "Blue Days, Black Nights," is released.

April 23. Elvis Presley—along with sidemen Bill Black and Scotty Moore—makes his Las Vegas debut as the opening act for the Freddie Martin Orchestra and comic Shecky Greene at the New Frontier Hotel's Venus Room. The show does not go over well; he plays only a week of the two-week booking. He doesn't perform in the city again for almost thirteen years.

May 2. In a hitherto unprecedented development, five singles appear in both the pop and R&B Top Ten: Elvis Presley's "Heartbreak Hotel" (#1 pop, #6 r&b), Carl Perkins' "Blue Suede Shoes" (#4 pop, #3 r&b), Frankie Lymon & the Teenagers' "Why Do Fools Fall in Love" (#7 pop, #4 r&b), Little Richard's "Long Tall Sally" (#9 pop, #1 r&b), and the Platters' "Magic Touch" (#10 pop, #7 r&b). The Presley and Perkins records were ranked number one and two, respectively, on the C&W charts as well. This represented further evidence of the intermingling of the R&B, C&W, and pop genres that led to rock 'n' roll.

May 5. The Memphis-based Rock and Roll Trio, featuring Johnny Burnette backed by brother Dorsey on bass and guitarist Paul Burlison, cut their first record, "Tear It Up," one of rockabilly's finest hours.

May 14. Mercury releases the Platters' eponymous debut LP. Although not including the vocal group's first three hits, it goes on to sell more than fifty thousand copies, an impressive number in that era.

May 19. British pop star Lonnie Donegan, the driving force behind that nation's skiffle craze, makes his U.S. debut on NBC-TV's *Perry Como Show*, an then kicks off a month-long concert tour.

May 24. The inaugural Eurovision Song Contest takes place in Lugano, Switzerland. The brainchild of Marcel Baisoncon of the European Broadcasting Union, the event includes seven nations, each of which is allowed two songs. Switzerland wins with Lys Assia's "Refrain."

May 30. *Time* attempts to dissect the Elvis Presley phenomenon in an article entitled "Teener's Hero." While the lengthy discussion of Presley's vocal technique is inconclusive (noting, among other things, his poor diction), the author notes, "his movements suggest, in a word, sex."

June 5. See April 3.

June 6. Gene Vincent and the Blue Caps' debut single, "Be-Bop-a-Lula," is released. Vincent, who'd co-written the song with a friend, won a Los Angeles talent contest in April, and signed a recording contract with Capitol Records. It will go on to become a million seller.

June 23. Modern releases the Cadets' "Stranded in the Jungle." The Los Angeles-based doo-wop quartet will disband shortly thereafter, with Will Jones joining the Coasters, and Aaron Collins co-founding the Flares.

June 26. *Look* magazine publishes an article entitled "The Great Rock 'n' Roll Controversy. It includes the opinions of a number of observers, including Benny Goodman, who responds, "I guess it's okay, man. At least it has a beat." The writer concludes, "Going to a rock 'n' roll show is like attending the rites of some obscure tribe whose means of communication are incomprehensible."

July 1. Besieged by critics of his flamboyant image, Elvis Presley appears on the *Steve Allen Show* wearing a formal white tie and black tuxedo combination, singing "Hound Dog" to a basset hound sitting on a stool. Teenagers picket NBC the next day with signs stating, "We Want the Real Elvis." He will immediately disavow the skit, apologizing for letting his fans down.

July 2. Elvis Presley records in New York for the first time, producing the definitive masters of "Hound Dog," "Don't Be Cruel," and "Anyway You Want Me." He also uses the Jordanaires as backup singers for the first time. "Hound Dog"/"Don't Be Cruel" would become the most successful double-sided chart-topping single in rock history as well as his biggest seller ever. This is also the first Presley session to employ the Jordanaires as back-up singers. Consisting of Hoyt Hawkins, Hugh Jarrett, Neal Matthews, and Gordon Stoker, the vocal harmony group had formed in Springfield, Missouri eight years earlier with the intention of specializing in gospel music.

July 5. The New York City-based Doubleday publishes *Lady Sings the Blues*, jazz vocalist Billie Holiday's autobiography. The work, which focuses on Holiday's problems with drug addiction, racism, and other personal problems, would inspire a film in the early 1970s starring Diana Ross.

July 14. Columbia reconstitutes its one-time "race record" subsidiary, Okeh, as an R&B label. Okeh, which had had previously included Big Maybelle and Johnnie Ray on its roster, would go on to sign Smiley Lewis, the Marquees, and the Schoolboys, among others.

July 21. In addition to referring to Elvis Presley as "the most controversial entertainer since Liberace," a *Billboard* article reports that Ed Sullivan—who once stated the singer would never appear on his program—signed him for three appearances.

July 28. The Clovers peak at number thirty on the pop charts with "Love, Love, Love" (Atlantic 1094). The single's success is stymied to a degree by the Diamonds' cover version (Mercury 70889; #30 pop).

The Clovers were one of the classic 1950s vocal harmony groups, equally at home with romantic ballads and uptempo jump material. They served as a missing link between the classic post-World War II rhythm and blues sound and the newly emerging rock 'n' roll genre.

The members—dual lead tenor John "Buddy" Bailey, dual lead tenor Billy Mitchell (joined 1953), second tenor Matthew McQuater, baritone Harold "Hal" Lucas Jr., bass vocalist Harold Winley, and guitarist Bill Harris—all hailed from the Washington, D.C., and Baltimore, Maryland, metropolitan areas. Entepreneur Lou Krefetz discovered the group performing at Washington's Rose Club in the late 1940s, when they were still enrolled in high school. After signing on as manager, he garnered a recording contract with Atlantic Records in 1950.

The Clovers' first R&B hit, "Don't You Know I Love You" (Atlantic; 1951), was written by label president Ahmet Ertegun. Many more popular releases followed, including "Fool, Fool, Fool" (Atlantic; 1951), "One Mint Julep" (Atlantic; 1952), "Ting-A-Ling" (Atlantic; 1956), "Hey, Miss Fannie" (Atlantic; 1952), "I Played the Fool" (Atlantic; 1952), "Crawlin'" (Atlantic; 1953), "Good Lovin'" (Atlantic; 1953), "Lovey Dovey" (Atlantic; 1954), "I've Got My Eyes On You" (Atlantic; 1954), "Your Cash Ain't Nothin' But Trash" (Atlantic; 1954), "Blue Velvet" (Atlantic; 1955), "Nip Sip" (Atlantic; 1955), "Devil Or Angel" (Atlantic; 1956), "Love, Love, Love," and "From the Bottom of My Heart" (Atlantic; 1956). Their biggest pop hit, "Love Potion No. 9" (United Artists; 1959), followed a prolonged dry spell. They were unable to build on this success, however, and the group was relegated to the nostalgia circuit by the mid-1960s. Covers of their hits—most notably, Bobby Vee's "Devil or Angel" (Liberty; 1961), Bobby Vinton's "Blue Velvet" (Epic; 1963), and the Searchers' "Love Potion Number Nine" (Kapp; 1964)—have assured them of a place on oldies playlists. Anthologies of their best-selling singles continue to appear on a regular basis.

July 28. The Jayhawks peak at number eighteen on the pop charts with "Stranded in the Jungle" (Flash 109).

Most acts have only one bona fide shot at fame and fortune. The Jayhawks had three, each following a radically different scenario from the others. All three paths, however, stopped far short of sustained commercial success.

The Jayhawks—originally consisting of first tenor James Johnson, second tenor Carl Fisher, baritone Dave Govan, and bass Carver Bunkum (later replaced by Don Bradley)—formed in Jefferson High School, Los Angeles, in 1955. Soon thereafter, they auditioned at a local Flash Record Store, performing the Johnson-penned "Stranded in the Jungle." The proprietors liked the song enough to release it on their on label in mid-1956 (Flash 109; 1956). Although the record's commercial impact was undercut significantly by the Cadets' more polished cover version, retail sales and jukebox activity were sufficient to boost it to number nine on the R&B charts and number eighteen on the *Billboard* pop singles survey.

In an effort to secure the backing of a more established record company, the Jayhawks signed on with Aladdin, a well-known West Coast independent label. Typecast as a novelty act, the group's subsequent singles failed to achieve any notable commercial success. By 1960, the quintet (augmented by the addition of tenor Richard Owens) felt a name change was in order, signing with the Checker label—a Chess subsidiary—as the Vibrations. With the twist becoming a nationwide sensation on the heels of the chart-topping Chubby Checker hit, they came up with their own dance number, "The Watusi" (Checker 969; 1961; #25 pop, #13 r&b).

Back in the limelight, the group couldn't resist another foray into the novelty market, recording humorous tribute song, "Peanut Butter" (Arvee 5027; 1961; #20 pop, #25 r&b) as the Marathons for another label. Checker was not amused, suing Arvee for breech of contract, consequently obtaining rights to the single and releasing it on another Chess subsidiary, Argo.

Almost three years passed before the Vibrations returned to the charts during the height of the British Invasion with "My Girl Sloopy" (Atlantic 2221; 1964; #26 pop, #26 r&b). The song would fare even better the following year when reworked in a garage rock mode—and re-titled "Hang On Sloopy" (Bang 506; 1965; #1 pop)—by the McCoys. The group regained the hit-making touch intermittently throughout the 1960s with "Misty" (Okeh 7230; 1965; #63 pop, #26 r&b), the Beatles' "And I Love Her" Okeh 7257; 1966; #118 pop, #47 r&b), "Pick Me" (Okeh 7276; 1967; #39 r&b), and "Love In Them There Hills" (Okeh 7311; 1968; #93 pop, #38 r&b). They would disband in the 1970s with Owens joining the Temptations in 1971 for brief stint.

July 31. Four important R&B figures—DJ Hunter Hancock, bandleader Johnny Otis, Specialty Records head Art Rupe, and promoter Hal Zeiger—join forces in Hollywood to address the negative publicity the genre has been receiving.

August 2. A *Look* article, entitled "Elvis Presley…He Can't Be…But He Is," notes that the performer's recordings have grossed more than $6 million while he receives over three thousand pieces of fan mail each week.

August 4. The Cadets peak at number fifteen on the pop charts with "Stranded in the Jungle" (Modern 994).

Versatility defines group that recorded in the 1950s as both the Cadets and the Jacks. The original line-up—first tenor Aaron Collins, second tenor George Hollis (later replaced by Willie Davis), tenor Lloyd McCraw, baritone Ted Taylor, and bass Will "Dub" Jones—began as a spiritual quintet in Los Angeles in 1947. Signing with the RPM/Modern company as the Jacks, they initially concentrated on romantic ballads. Their reputation is based largely on one of their early releases, "Why Don't You Write Me?" (RPM 428; 1955; #82 pop, #3 r&b), which—like most material recorded by the Jacks—featured Davis, something of a throwback to the heyday of the crooners, as the lead singer.

When follow-up singles failed to chart, the group—with Prentice Moreland replacing Taylor, who went on to a solo career—opted to cover the Jayhawks' novelty hit, "Stranded in the Jungle" (#4 r&b), as the Cadets. Their reading was considered superior due to the improved production values and the animated interplay of group voices. When their version outperformed the original at retail outlets, in jukeboxes, and on the radio, they continued recording covers of contemporary R&B hits (featuring either Collins or Davis as the lead), albeit with less success.

Failing to recapture lightning in a bottle, the group fragmented in the late 1950s. Jones would become part of the reconstituted Coasters in early 1958, one of the most popular vocal groups of the Brill Building Era. Collins, Davis, and Hollis—along with bass Tommy Miller—would form the Flares, who would make a singular contribution to the early 1960s dance craze fad with "Foot Stompin' – Part 1" (Felsted 8624; 1961; #25 pop, #20 r&b).

August 11. "Flying Saucer" enters the Top 40 on *Billboard*'s Top 100. Earlier that summer, Bill Buchanan and Dickie Goodman had hit upon the idea of splicing brief snippets of then current pop hits into a rather formless narrative which simulated onsite reporting of an alien visitation along the lines of Orson Welles' 1938 radio broadcast of H.G. Wells' *The War of the Worlds*. "The Flying Saucer (Parts 1 & 2)"—accented by recognizable cameos by the likes of Fats Domino, Little Richard, the Platters, and many others—was immediately besieged by a host of lawsuits relating to copyright infringement as it raced up the charts, eventually peaking at number three. It quickly became apparent to the music business, however, that "The Flying Saucer" had stimulated a renewed interest in the songs it had appropriated as sound bites, prompting *Billboard* to note, "Several publishers are [now] piqued at not being included in the disk." Thus exonerated, the twosome proceeded to satirize their predicament in "Buchanan and Goodman on Trial" (1956). By the following year, however, with the release of "Flying Saucer the 2nd" and "Santa & the Satellite (Parts 1 & 2)"—as well as the appearance of copycats (e.g., George and Louis' "The Return of Jerry Lee"; 1958)—the formula had worn thin. Buchanan worked briefly with Bob Ancell, achieving modest success with a spoof of B-grade horror/fantasy flicks, "The Creature (Parts 1 & 2)," in late 1957. Goodman continued to mine the musical "cut-in" subgenre throughout the 1960s and 1970s, although only enjoying one major hit, the million-selling "Mr. Jaws" (#4; 1975).

Of greater significance, Buchanan and Goodman spurred a revival of interest in the novelty song genre. Such material had always been a fixture on the popular music charts, and it is likely it always will be. Acoustic era recording artists such as monologist Cal Stewart and singer Billy Murray (whose politically incorrect impressions of drunkards and darkies would be deemed incendiary today) built lasting careers around the release of a steady stream of comedy material. Spike Jones raised musical cacophony to new heights in the 1940s while helping the nation to cope with the tensions brought on by World War II. Weird Al Yankovic's satirical parodies of hit records and television soundtrack music have kept the genre fresh up to the present today.

Novelty material, however, was released with much greater frequency, and went on to achieve greater commercial success, with the onset of the rock 'n' roll era. Undoubtedly, the predominantly teen audience was inclined to be more receptive to humor in its myriad forms. Furthermore, novelties probably seemed more bankable amidst the changing tastes of popular music at the time. The "genius factor" cannot be overlooked here as well; that is, certain individual, by means of sheer talent, imposed their own stamp upon the era, irrespective of other existing trends or market conditions.

The speeded-up voice technique and sci-fi thematic material pioneered by Buchanan and Goodman continued to provide inspiration in 1958, most notably in John Zacherle's "Dinner with Drac," David Seville's "The Witch Doctor," and Sheb Wooley's "The Purple People Eater." The latter two songs spent many weeks in the number one position, inspiring a lifelong commitment to the novelty genre on the part of Seville and Wooley (the former, whose real name was Ross Bagdasarian, enjoyed a long string of hits as creator of the Chipmunk, while Wooley, employing the nom d'plume Ben Older, satirized a steady succession of 1960s pop hits a la Weird Al Yankovic).

Answer songs—this is, the practice of recording a tune which either directly answered a question posed by an earlier hit or acted as a sequel (thereby capitalizing on the popularity of the original)—almost rivaled the balance of the novelty genre's output. Two rock music scholars, Dr. Bee L. Cooper and Fred Haney, would write two substantial monographs devoted entirely to this phenomenon. Two of the more popular examples of the genre have been Jeanne Black's "He'll Have to Stay" (a response to Jim Reeves' 1959 hit, "He'll Have to Go") and Shep and the Limelites' "Daddy's Home" (1961). The latter song took the formula far beyond the follow-up stage in that it represented an ongoing installment of a series of love songs composed by James Sheppard, first as the leader of the doo-wop group, The Heartbeats (who started the cycle with "A Thousand Miles Away" in 1956), and then later with the Limelites.

By the dawn of the 1960s, song parodies had become the leading form of novelty recording. Jimmy Dean's huge hit, "Big Bad John" (#1; 1961), inspired at least five send-ups, including Phil McLean's "Small Sad Sam" (1962). Ron Dante, later the voices of the Archies ("Sugar Sugar"; #1; 1969) and the Cuff Links, reached the Top 20 with the Detergents' "Leader of the Laundromat," which applied black humor to the Shangri-Las' morbid girl-group classic, "Leader of the Pack" (#1; 1964).

Well established as a music style by this time, rock 'n' roll soon found that it was potentially lucrative to satirize itself. The Marcel's exaggeration of doo-wop conventions in "Blue Moon" (a 1934 Rodgers and Hart composition) topped the pop charts in 1961. The rhythm and blues vocal group genre had been lampooned as early as 1957 by a Canadian pop aggregate, the Diamonds. When the group's rather patronizing take-off, "Little Darlin'" (number two for eight weeks in 1957) achieved success of unforeseen proportions, they were consigned to mining the style they had viciously ridiculed well into the 1960s. Other notable doo-wop novelties included the Edsels' "Rama Lama Ding Dong" (1958; reissued in 1961), Barry Mann's "Who Put the Bomp (In the Bomp, Bomp, Bomp)," (1961), and Johnny Cymbal's "Mr. Bass Man" (1963).

Intermittent revivals of horror/science fiction themes also continued well into the 1960s as exemplified by the Ran-Dells' "Martian Hop" (1963) and Bobby "Boris" Pickett's "Monster Mash," a Karloffian exploitation of the dance craze, the Mashed Potato. The latter recording not only spent weeks perched atop the singles charts in fall 1962, but enjoyed a second Top Ten run in 1973. Novelty songs found countless other topics to address from a humorous perspective as well, including fashion—e.g., Edd Byrnes' (Kookie, Kookie (Lend Me Your Comb)"; Brian Hyland's "Itsy Bitsy Teenie Weenie Yellow Polkadot Bikini" (1; 1960)—history (Larry Verne's "Mr. Custer"; #1; 1960), and cultural stereotypes (Murray Kellum's "Long Tall Texan").

The significant drop-off in novelty tunes by 1964 appears to have been a direct result of the upsurge in creative output enjoyed by rock music with the onslaught of British beat imports and the ensuing American renaissance encompassing surf music, folk rock, soul, garage/punk, and an array of additional indigenous styles. Furthermore, the rise of social relevance in rock lyrics appears to have deflated rock's sense of humor. Songs like the Barbarians' "Are You a Boy or Are You a Girl?" (1965) and the Fraternity of Man's "Don't Bogart Me" (1968) were undeniably funny, but possessed a hard edge (the underlying message portion) which lifted them out of the novelty category.

August 14. In response to the heavily negative coverage of the singer in the mass media, including dozens of headlines calling him as "hillbilly," a Washington, D.C., DJ, Bob Rickman, creates the Society for the Prevention of Cruelty to Elvis Presley.

August 18. With Elvis Presley's cover having gone number one on the pop charts on August 8, Peacock Records re-releases Big Mama Thornton's original version of "Hound Dog," an R&B chart-topper in 1953.

August 18. Little Willie John's "Fever"—a chart-topping R&B hit for two weeks beginning July 11—enters the pop survey at number twenty-four. Cover versions of the song will become major hits for Peggy Lee (1958) and the McCoys (1965).

August 22. The Five Satins' "In the Still of the Nite" first appears on the R&B charts. It will become a doo-wop classic, and according to the *Rolling Stone Rock Almanac*, will sell over fifteen million copies by the early 1980s.

August 25. Josie Records releases the Coney Island Kids' "We Want a Rock & Roll President." Their nominees for the position include Bo Diddley, Elvis Presley, Bill Haley, and Pat Boone.

August 28. Alan Freed's second annual Rock & Roll Show, a ten-day-long event, opens at the Brooklyn Paramount Theater. Notable acts include Fats Domino and Frankie Lymon and the Teenagers.

September 1. With the record royalty payments pouring in, Elvis Presley purchases a pink Cadillac for his mother.

September 1. Howie Richmond, active for many years in the music publishing field, establishes the New York–based Roulette Records. The debut release, Bernie Knoe's "King of Nothin'," does not become a hit;

however, the label would become a doo-wop fixture in the late 1950s before moving on to pop-rock and bubblegum in the 1960s.

September 8. Harry Belafonte's *Calypso* (RCA 1248) reaches the top of the album charts, remaining there a total of thirty-one non-consecutive weeks. The roots of the brief calypso vogue can be found in the first wave of rock 'n' roll. As the music industry establishment attempted to put the latter development into perspective, attitudes such as the following were widespread:

- Elvis Presley, Little Richard, and others of that ilk were a threat to the American (read: Judeo-Christian) way of life and/or my financial security; therefore, an acceptable substitute must be found.
- Rock 'n' roll was a passing fad and, given the propensity of youth for things new and different, let's go find the next "big thing."

Calypso was hardly a new development, having been a part of the musical landscape in Trinidad since the late nineteenth century. Half-hearted efforts had even been made to sell the genre in the States in the 1930s as well as the early 1950s. It certainly had some highly saleable features; e.g., a catchy rhythm and English lyrics which were in some cases highly literate. When Harry Belafonte—an unknown folk interpreter of West Indian extraction who had languished at RCA for several years—was given calypso material to record, he quickly achieved superstar status. His "Jamaica Farewell" hit the Top 20 pop charts in late 1956, and "Banana Boat (Day-O)" peaked at number five early in the following year.

By now, the market was flooded with releases attempted to capitalize on the calypso trend. The folk camp was represented by the Tarriers' "Banana Boat Song" (number four; 1957) and Terry Gilkyson's "Marianne" (number four; 1957), while Tin Pan Alley artists came up with their inevitable cover versions. The Fontaine Sisters, Steve Lawrence, and Sarah Vaughan all reached the Top 20 in 1957 with "Banana Boat Song." The Hilltoppers scored with "Marianne," and Stan Freberg had a hit with his spoof of "Day-O."

Calypsomania ran out of steam by mid-1957 in art due to the oversaturation of the U.S. airwaves with a style that had not secured any base of support other than novelty appeal. In addition, there was a dearth of native Caribbean talent performing calypso. Reporters and tourists found that Fats Domino and other New Orleans artists were the rage in Jamaica as a result of powerful clear-channel radio stations beaming from the southern states. While other artists identified with calypso sand from public view without a trace, Belafonte continued to be successful as an album artist (e.g., *Calypso*, *Belafonte*, *An Evening with Harry Belafonte*, *Harry Belafonte at Carnegie Hall*, *Jump Up Calypso*, *The Midnight Special*), playing a major role in the commercial folk boom of the early 1960s.

September 9. Elvis Presley makes his debut on the "Ed Sullivan Show." He performs "Love Me Tender," "Hound Dog," "Don't Be Cruel," and "Ready Teddy."

September 10. Record retailers nationwide are inundated with requests for Elvis Presley's "Love Me Tender." First heard by much of the American public the previous night on the "Ed Sullivan Show," the song—slated to be the theme song in his upcoming film—is not yet available on record. By the end of the month, RCA Victor will have received over 856,327 advance orders for the song.

September 22. *Billboard* publishes a cover article with the headline, "Rock 'n' Roll in Disfavor." One passage notes, "With new experiences to their credit, such as calling riot squads and with scars such as damaged seats, some arena and auditorium operators have turned thumbs down on any more rock 'n' roll. Some nix the whole idea. Some prohibit dancing but not all concerts. Some just hire extra cops and let 'em go…"

September 26. Fats Domino's "Blueberry Hill" enters the pop charts; it will peak at number four, making it his most successful recording of all time. The record also tops the R&B charts for eight non-consecutive weeks beginning November 14.

September 26. It is Elvis Presley Day in Tupelo, Mississippi, the singer's birthplace.

September 28. Alis Lesley garners a fair amount of press coverage for her appearance in a Hollywood rock show featuring Gene Vincent and the Coasters. She is one of the first distaff rock 'n' rollers to be billed as 'The Female Presley." Nevertheless, like many other performers to be hyped in this manner, she fails to make a lasting impression.

October 6. *Billboard* notes that major Hollywood studios are itching to make rock 'n' roll-based films. Among the projects being planned are Twentieth Century Fox's *Do Re Mi* (with Fats Domino, Little Richard, and Jayne Mansfield) and *Cool It*, and Paramount's *Lonesome Cowboy*, the latter an Elvis Presley vehicle that fails to get past the planning stage.

October 13. The Five Satins peak at number twenty-four on the pop charts with "In the Still of the Nite" (Ember 1005).

The Five Satins—including Al Denby, Jim Freeman, Eddie Martin, and pianist Jessie Murphy—were formed in New Haven, Connecticut, by Fred Parris (born March 26, 1936) in early 1956. Parris had been the leader of a moderately successful recording act, the Scarletts, beginning in 1954, and liked the vocal blend achieved by the Velvets; hence, the name he gave his new group.

Parris got the inspiration of write the Five Satins' first release, "In the Still of the Nite" (#3 r&b)—one of the most celebrated R&B vocal group recordings of all time, which was, ironically, designated as the B side, backing "The Jones Girl"—while on guard duty at three a.m. with the U.S. Army. Recorded in a local church basement, the song—according to Parris, who has been involved in a seemingly endless series of lawsuits trying to received royalties due him—has remained a perennial best-seller, selling millions of copies through countless retrospective compilations.

Parris was stationed in Japan when the recording achieved hit status. In order to capitalize on this success, the Five Satins performed and recorded in the States with a substitute lead singer, Bill Baker. Baker—would possessed a lighter, sweeter voice—would be featured on the group's next hit, "To the Aisle" (Ember 1019; 1957; #25 pop, #5 r&b). Parris would return in January 1958, taking Baker's place in the Five Satins; the membership by this time included tenor Richie Freeman (born December 1940), second tenor West Forbes, baritone (b. 1937), Lewis Peoples (b. 1937), and bass Sy Hopkins (b. 1938). However, the search for further hits proved elusive; "Shadows" (Ember 1056; 1959; #87 pop, #27 r&b) represented their only return to the charts.

By the early 1960s the group had dissolved, and the ex-members resumed lives in New Haven outside of the music business. They were lured back together in 1969, however, to perform in a rock 'n' roll revival show at New York's Madison Square Garden. The experience encouraged them to continue work together intermittently both live and in the studio. In search of a more contemporary—read that, commercially marketable—sound, Parris assembled a new group in the mid-1970s consisting of Nate Marshall and ex-Five Satins Richie Freeman and Jimmy Curtis. They enjoyed one minor hit, "Everybody Stand and Clap Your Hands (For the Entertainer)" (Buddah 477; 1975; #49 r&b), before Parris returned to the nostalgia circuit with a new edition of the Satins.

October 20. Elvis Presley's "Love Me Tender" enters the pop charts at number two, the highest debut ever for this survey. The single makes a comparable splash in the C&W (number nine) and R&B (number ten) charts.

October 27. Argo Records releases Clarence Henry's "Ain't Got No Home." It will be the singer's first hit, earning him the nickname "Frogman" for the low register singing he employs in some passages.

October 28. Elvis Presley appears on the "Ed Sullivan Show" for a second time, singing "Don't Be Cruel," "Love Me Tender," "Hound Dog," and "Love Me."

November 5. Art Tatum dies of uremic poisoning at age forty-six.

November 10. *Billboard's* ninth annual DJ poll revealed a greater representation of rock 'n' roll artists and recordings than in 1955; however, mainstream pop music still dominated the survey. Among the results:

- The favorite record is Morris Stoloff's "Moonglow and Theme from *Picnic*" (the Platters' "The Great Pretender" is fourteenth, and Elvis Presley's "Don't Be Cruel," seventeenth).
- The most frequently broadcast record is Kay Starr's "Rock and Roll Waltz" ("The Great Pretender" is third; Presley's "Heartbreak Hotel," fifth; "Don't Be Cruel," seventh; Presley's "Hound Dog," nineteenth; Carl Perkins' "Blue Suede Shoes," twentieth).
- The favorite LP is Frank Sinatra's *Songs for Swinging Lovers* (*The Platters* is fifteenth; *Elvis Presley*, seventeenth).

- The favorite male vocalist is Frank Sinatra.
- The most played male vocalist is Presley (Fats Domino places ninth).
- The most played C&W artist in Presley.
- The favorite R&B artist is Domino (Presley is ranked fiftieth).

November 10. British Presley clones are already in evidence. One of the most successful, Tommy Steele, enters the British charts via "Rock with the Caveman." The number one single is Johnnie Ray's "Just Walking in the Rain," which remains there for seven weeks.

November 16. *Love Me Tender*, Elvis Presley's first film, opens in New York City. It receives mixed reviews, but nevertheless grosses almost $5 million in two months.

November 17. Alan Freed announces his next film (he has already appeared in *Don't Knock the Rock* and *Rock Around the Clock*), *Rock, Rock, Rock*. Scheduled for a December 5 premiere, in New York City, he possesses a ten percent stake in the project. He will be targeting radio with a promotional soundtrack LP, which includes such acts as LaVern Baker, Chuck Berry, Johnny Burnette's Rock and Roll Trio, the Flamingos, and Frankie Lymon and the Teenagers.

November 18. Fats Domino performs "Blueberry Hill"—the top R&B single nationwide at the time—on the *Ed Sullivan Show*.

November 21. After being nudged out of the number one position on the R&B charts by Fats Domino's "Blueberry Hill" the previous week, Bill Doggett's laid-back blues instrumental, "Honky Tonk (Parts I and II)" returns to the top slot for a fourteenth week.

November 26. Tommy Dorsey, noted swing-era trombonist and bandleader, is found dead, apparently due to an accident, in his Greenwich, Connecticut, home. Frank Sinatra first came into prominence as a lead singer in his band during the early 1940s.

December 4. Four prominent Sun artists—Elvis Presley, Johnny Cash, Carl Perkins, and Jerry Lee Lewis—participate in an impromptu recording session. They will later be dubbed the Million Dollar Quartet; their music won't be released for another quarter century.

December 4. Carl Perkins is assisted by Jerry Lee Lewis on piano for "Your True Love" and "Matchbox," an updated version of Blind Lemon Jefferson's "Matchbox Blues." Although Perkins' best days are behind him, Lewis—whose Sun debut, "Crazy Arms"/"End of the Road," failed to chart—will become a major star the following year.

December 8. *Billboard* notes that Elvis Presley records are selling at an unprecedented rate in Canada. While hit singles there typically move around 100,000 units, "Hound Dog"/"Don't Be Cruel" has sold more than 225,000 copies, and "Love Me Tender" over 135,000 copies, in sixteen weeks. Moreover, Presley is credited with stimulating record sales in general, as well as guitar sales, north of the border.

December 22. *Billboard* reports that Elvis Presley far outpaced his competitors with seventeen charting records for the year; Pat Boone follows with five, then Fats Domino, Little Richard, and the Platters with three apiece. Another article in the same issue states that records sales reached an all-time high for 1956; however, consumer preferences appear to be less predictable than ever before.

December 22. Elvis Presley places ten singles on *Billboard*'s Top 100.

1957

❄

January 1. The first British TV program devoted to rock 'n' roll, *Cool for Cats*, premieres on BBC.

January 3. Already a number one U.S. hit, Guy Mitchell's "Singing the Blues" tops the British charts; a knock-off version of the song by countrymen Tommy Steele and the Steelmen would dislodge Mitchell the following week, although he would return to the number one position on January 17.

January 4. Fats Domino records "I'm Walkin'." He is assisted by the cream of New Orleans session men, including producer Dave Bartholomew, tenor saxophonists Lee Allen and Herb Hardesty, guitarist Walter Nelson, bassist Frank Fields, and drummer Earl Palmer. It will top the R&B charts for six weeks beginning March 13 (completing a run of nineteen consecutive weeks at number one for Domino records), in addition to peaking at number four on the pop charts.

January 4. Former heavyweight boxing champion Joe Louis introduces Solomon Burke—who performs the Louis composition, "You Can Run, But You Can't Hide"—on *The Steve Allen Show*. Burke will become a pioneer of the soul music genre in the 1960s.

January 5. Elvis Presley begins a two-week stint at number two on the Disc Jockey charts with "Love Me" (RCA EP 992).

January 6. Elvis Presley performs seven songs—"Love Me Tender," "Hound Dog," "Don't Be Cruel," "Heartbreak Hotel," "Too Much," "When My Blue Moon Turns to Gold Again," and "Peace in the Valley"—in a slot lasting more than twenty minutes on Ed Sullivan's *Toast of the Town* (CBS). He would not make another television appearance until discharged from the army in 1960.

January 8. Bill Haley commences a two-week tour in Newcastle, Australia, with his newly constituted Comets. Members of the previous line-up were opposed to air travel, thereby nixing previous tour plans abroad. Supporting acts include LaVern Baker and Big Joe Turner. It is billed as the first ever "rock & roll tour" of that nation.

January 8. Elvis Presley, who turns twenty-two today, takes the U.S. Army pre-induction exam in Memphis (and passes).

January 10. The Canadian-based Crew-Cuts, make their U.S. television debut, performing on the *Dorsey Brothers Stage Show* (CBS), in Cleveland, Ohio.

January 16. Elvis Presley's "Too Much" enters the pop charts; it will become the first of his four number one singles for the year.

January 16. The Cavern Club opens in a former wine cellar on Mathew Street, Liverpool. Originally booking jazz and skiffle bands, the venue achieved legendary status after hiring the Beatles as its house band in 1961–1962.

January 19. Johnny Cash, who has been a regular on *The Jimmy Dean Show*, performs on the popular CBS television variety program, the *Jackie Gleason Show*.

January 19. Fats Domino begins a three-week run at number two on the Juke Box charts with "Blueberry Hill" (Imperial 5407), the closest he came to a chart-topping pop single during his legendary career.

January 21. Patsy Cline appears on *Arthur Godfrey's Talent Scouts* (CBS), winning with her rendition of "Walkin' After Midnight." Decca—which has brokered a deal with Four Star to obtain her recording rights— quickly releases the number (originally written for, and rejected, by Kay Starr earlier in the decade, it was cut by Cline in November 1956 with Nashville-based producer Owen Bradley). It will reach number twelve on the pop charts. Although she becomes a major country star, Cline will not enjoy another pop hit until "I Fall To Pieces" reaches number twelve on September 4, 1961.

January 23. Bill Haley and the Comets attend the world premiere of the film, *Don't Knock the Rock*, in which they make a cameo appearance.

January 31. Decca Records announces that Bill Haley and His Comets' "Rock Around the Clock" surpassed sales of one million copies in Great Britain.

February 2. Fats Domino performs two of his chart-topping R&B hits—"Blueberry Hill" and "Blue Monday"—on the *Perry Como Show*.

February 5. Bill Haley is mobbed by five thousand fans when the ocean liner *Queen Elizabeth* arrives in Southampton for his British concert debut. He becomes the first American rock star to tour the U.K.

February 9. One of the most popular doo-wop records of all time, the Del-Vikings' "Come Go with Me," enters the pop charts. It will peak at number five the following month, in addition to reaching number three on the R&B survey.

February 9. Three songs peak at number one on the Billboard pop charts: Elvis Presley's "Too Much" (RCA) on the Best Seller (three weeks) and Juke Box listings, Pat Boone's "Don't Forbid Me" (Dot) on the Top 100, and Sonny James' "Young Love" on the Disk Jockey survey.

Born into a show business family, Sonny James (real name Jimmy Loden) began performing at the age of four with his four sisters. He had his own radio show in Birmingham, Alabama, while still a teenager. While in the service during the early 1950s, he performed in the films, *Second Fiddle to a Steel Guitar*, *Nashville Rebel*, *Las Vegas Hillbillies*, and *Hillbilly In A Haunted House*.

Following military service, James signed with Capitol Records. Although a country artist by temperament, his rich baritone voice was well suited to mainstream pop market. During the late 1950s, the country charts were overwhelmed by rock 'n' roll material recorded by artists such as Elvis Presley, Jerry Lee Lewis, and the Everly Brothers. Like Johnny Cash, Marty Robbins, Johnny Horton, Jim Reeves, and other country performers, James was encouraged to record teen-oriented songs. His sixth country hit, "Young Love" (Capitol 3602) also reached number one on the pop music charts, eventually selling over one million copies. However, the pop-country hits had stopped coming by mid-1960.

In 1963, the process had reversed itself and country material was regularly crossing over to the pop charts. James' middle-of-the-road sensibilities were suddenly back in vogue. As a result, he enjoyed a string of recorded successes—often songs that had previously been pop hits by other artists—rarely equaled in country music history. Between 1964 and1975, twenty-two of his singles (at one point, sixteen in a row) reached number one on the country charts: "You're the Only World I Know" (Capitol 5280; 1964), "Behind the Tear" (Capitol 5454; 1965), "Take Good Care Of Her" (Capitol 5612; 1966), "Need You" (Capitol 5833; 1967), "I'll Never Find Another You" (Capitol 5914; 1967), "It's the Little Things" (Capitol 5987; 1967), "A World Of Our Own" (Capitol 2067; 1968), "Heaven Says Hello" (Capitol 2155; 1968), "Born To Be With You" (Capitol 2271; 1968), "Only the Lonely" (Capitol 2370; 1969), "Running Bear" (Capitol 2486; 1969), "Since I Met You, Baby" (Capitol 2595; 1969), "It's Just A Matter Of Time" (Capitol 2700; 1970), "My Love" (Capitol 2782; 1970), "Don't Keep Me Hangin' On" (Capitol 2834; 1970), "Endlessly" (Capitol 2914; 1970), "Empty Arms" (Capitol 3015; 1971), "Bright Lights, Big City" (Capitol 3114; 1971), "Here Comes Honey Again" (Capitol 3174; 1971), "That's Why I Love You Like I Do" (Capitol 3322; 1972), "When the Snow Is On the Roses" (Columbia 45644; 1972), and "Is It Wrong" (Columbia 46003; 1974).

His popularity dropped off somewhat when he switched to the Columbia label. As proponents of harder forms of country (e.g., the "Outlaw" movement, the New Traditionalist) supplanted established acts, shifts to Monument (late 1970s) and Dimension (early 1980s) did not reverse the trend. Nevertheless, James continued to perform and record through the 1990s.

February 12. On the verge of a commercial breakthrough, the Coasters record "Young Blood," written and produced by Jerry Leiber and Mike Stoller.

Jerry Leiber (born April 25, 1933) and Mike Stoller (born March 13, 1933) will be forever linked as pioneers of early rock 'n' roll. They met in New York City and, while still in their teens, wrote the classic songs "K.C. Loving"—a number one hit for Wilbert Harrison (Fury 1023; 1959)—and "Hound Dog," first a chart-topping hit for "Big Mama" Thornton (Peacock 1612; 1953), and later one of the biggest hits of the rock era for Elvis Presley (RCA 47-6604; 1956). They would become one of Presley's key sources for recording material, including the hits "Loving You" (RCA 47-7000; 1957) and "Jailhouse Rock" (RCA 47-7035; 1957).

Signing an independent production pact with Atlantic Records, Leiber and Stoller were responsible for string of chart successes by the doo-wop comedy group, the Coasters, most notably, "Young Blood" (Atco 6087; 1957), "Yakety Yak" (Atco 6116; 1958), "Charlie Brown" (Atco 6132; 1959), and "Poison Ivy" (Atco 6146; 1959). The duo would also produce many other artists (e.g., the Dixie Cups, the Drifters, Peggy Lee, Procol Harum), cutting across a wide range of musical styles. Their best material would be in a Broadway musical revue in the 1990s.

February 15. Promoter Irvin Feld launches his Greatest Shows of 1957, in Pittsburgh. The tour—which runs until May 5—spans the nation, including regions rarely, if ever, exposed to rock 'n' roll concerts. The star-studded line-up includes LaVern Baker, Chuck Berry, Charles Brown, Ann Cole, Eddie Conley and the Dimples, Bill Doggett, Fats Domino, the Five Keys, the Five Satins, Clyde McPhatter, the Moonglows, the Schoolboys, and the Paul Williams Band.

February 16. In a situation reminiscent of Tin Pan Alley's glory days, competing versions of the Ric Cartey/ Carole Joyner-penned teen ballad, "Young Love," have jockeyed for the highest position while they raced up the charts. This week, Tab Hunter's Dot single settles in for a six-week run at number one on the Top 100. He will reach the summit of the Disk Jockey (six weeks), Juke Box (five weeks), and Best Seller (four weeks) listings as well.

February 16. Elvis Presley clone, Tommy Sands, debuts on the pop charts with proto-bubblegum single, "Teen-age Crush," which eventually rises to number three. Sands' career fizzles out in short order, and today he is best remembered for his brief marriage to Nancy Sinatra.

February 22. Jerry Lee Lewis performs "Whole Lotta Shakin' Goin' On" for the first time at a small Blytheville, Arkansas club. The song—composed by Roy Hall and Dave Williams—had caught his attention when he first heard it a year ago. This is also the first documented case where Lewis added his own spontaneous lyrics to replace those he fails to remember.

February 22. The Columbia Pictures film, *Don't Knock the Rock*, makes its America premiere at the Paramount Theater, New York City. Alan Freed, playing himself, argues that rock 'n' roll has been unfairly identified with lasciviousness, delinquency, and violence, while Fats Domino, Bill Haley and the Comets, Little Richard, the Platters, and Gene Vincent also appear in the film.

February 25. The Crickets, featuring Buddy Holly, record "That'll Be the Day" during their initial session with producer Norman Petty, in the latter's Clovis, New Mexico, studio. Released May 27 (b/w "I'm Looking for Someone to Love"), it will become Holly greatest commercial success, reaching number two on the pop charts and number three in the R&B listing.

March 1. Harry Belafonte's "Banana Boat Song (Day-O)"—a Trinidad folk song culled from *Calypso*, which will top the American LP charts for thirty weeks in 1956–1967—enters the U.K. charts, eventually peaking at number three, and fueling a British calypso fad.

March 2. Mickey and Sylvia peak at number eleven on the pop charts with "Love Is Strange" (Groove 0175).

Born in New York City, Sylvia Robinson (maiden name: Vanderpool) has left an indelible mark on the record industry in a variety of roles. In 1954, she teamed with session guitarist Mickey Baker to form the duo Mickey and Sylvia; their single, "Love Is Strange" (Groove 0175; 1956; #2 R&B) remains an early rock 'n' roll classic.

She married Joe Robinson in 1956; they would found a series of rhythm and blues labels, including All Platinum, Strong, Turbo, and Vibration. After splitting with Baker, she worked as a producer—her credits included Ike and Tina Turner's "It's Gonna Work Out Fine" (Sue 749; 1961; #14), the Moments' "Love On a Two-Way Street" (Stang 5012; 1970; #3), and Shirley and Company's "Shame, Shame, Shame" (Vibration 532; 1975; 12), session musician, songwriter. She continued to record intermittently as a solo artist, her greatest success coming with "Pillow Talk" (Vibration 521; 1973; #3).

With All Platinum (soon to be reorganized as Sugar Hill) involved in Chapter 11 proceedings, Robinson was introduced to the hip-hop scene by son, Joey Jr. She formed a studio group, the Sugarhill Gang, whose first release, "Rapper's Delight" (Sugar Hill 542; 1979; #4 R&B, #36 pop), became the first mainstream rap hit. Despite efforts to add legitimate hip-hop performers to its roster—most notably, Grandmaster

Flash and Funky Four +1—Sugar Hill Records was unable to keep pace with Tommy Boy, Def Jam, Profile, and other street-smart labels, going out of business in 1985.

March 3. The head of the Catholic archdiocese centered in Chicago, Samuel Cardinal Strich, forbids the playing of rock 'n' roll in Catholic schools and "recreations" due to its "tribal rhythms" and "encouragement to behave in a hedonistic manner." Nevertheless, rock 'n' roll records continue to sell well in the area.

March 9. The Canadian-based vocal quartet, the Diamonds, make their first appearance on the pop charts with "Little Darlin'." A somewhat condescending (via exaggerated vocal mannerisms) cover of the original written and recorded by the Los Angeles doo-wop group, the Gladiolas, it rises to number two on the pop charts (#3 R&B).

March 16. Teen idol Tommy Sands begins a two-week run at number two on the Best Seller charts with "Teen-Age Crush" (Capitol 3639). Despite repeated attempts at resuscitating his career, Sands will ultimately be best remembered as Nancy Sinatra's former husband.

March 18. Bill Haley and the Comets touch down stateside following an eleven-week tour of Australia and Europe, where they performed for some five hundred thousand people.

March 19. Elvis Presley purchases a mansion in the Whitehaven section of south Memphis for $102,500. It had previously been occupied by the Graceland Christian Church.

March 30. Buddy Knox tops the Best Seller listing with "Party Doll" (Roulette); it also achieves success on the Juke Box (#2), Top 100 (#2), and Disc Jockey (#5) surveys.

March 30. Andy Williams begins a three-stint at number one on the Top 100 with "Butterfly." It also rises to number one on the Disc Jockey poll (two weeks), number two on the Juke Box survey, and number four on the Best Seller listing.

April 1. Although no longer a commercial force in the United States, Frankie Lymon and the Teenagers, begin a three-month tour of Europe with a performance at the London Palladium.

April 1. Cadence Records releases the Everly Brothers' "Bye Bye Love"; the Boudleaux Bryant composition had reputedly been rejected by thirty acts before the Don and Phil made it their second record (the Columbia single, "The Sun Keeps Shining," failed to generate much in the way of sales). It becomes a major cross-over hit, reaching number two on the pop charts, as well as going number five R&B and topping the C&W survey.

The Everly Brothers were responsible for revealing the possibilities for close, two-part harmonizing as the primary focus in rock music, thereby greatly influencing later acts such as the Beatles, the Hollies, Simon and Garfunkel, the Byrds, the Turtles, and Crosby, Stills and Nash. They also pioneered the use of country influences—not only the high-lonesome vocals, but the emphasis on melody and Appalachian-styled acoustic guitar work—within a pop-rock context. Their sound remains timeless, as evidenced by the chart-topping success of Extreme's Everlys knock-off, "More Than Words" (A&M 1552) in 1991.

Don and Phil Everly—born February 1, 1937, and January 19, 1939, respectively, in Brownie, Kentucky—began singing with their parents, well-known country performers Ike and Margaret Everly, on KMA-radio, Shenandoah, Iowa, beginning in 1945. Shortly after forming as a straight country duo in 1954, the brothers signed with Columbia. Failing to achieve success, they eventually were taken on by Cadence in part due to their photogenic good looks; label owner/producer Archie Bleyer was interested at the time in breaking into the newly emerging teen market.

The debut single, "Bye Bye Love" (Cadence 1315; 1957), featuring their aching vocals augmented by electric guitar flourishes and a lilting rock 'n' roll beat, was a smash hit, providing the direction for a long string of chart successes with the label, including "Wake Up Little Susie" (Cadence 1337; 1957; #1), "All I Have to Do Is Dream" (Cadence 1348; 1958; #1), "Bird Dog"/"Devoted to You" (Cadence 1350; #1/#10), "Problems" (Cadence 1355; 1958; #2), "('Til) I Kissed You" (Cadence 1369; 1959; #4), "Let It Be Me" (Cadence 1376; 1960; #7), and "When Will I Be Loved" (Cadence 1380; 1960; #8). In addition to the extraordinary musicality of the Everlys, the popularity of these discs owed much to high quality material (often composed by the husband-and-wife team of Boudleaux and Felice Bryant) and peerless Nashville studio musicians. The lovely echoed guitar work by Chet Atkins in the Bryants' "All I Have to Do Is Dream," for instance, all but guaranteed the song's success.

The duo switched labels when offered a lucrative contract by the fledging Warner Bros. in 1960. A number of the Warner releases—including the singles "Cathy's Clown" (Warner Bros. 5151; 1960; #1), "So Sad" (Warner Bros. 5163; 1960; #7), and "Walk Right Back" (Warner Bros. 5199; 1961; #7), and the albums *It's Everly Time!* (Warner Bros. 1381; 1960; #9) and *A Date with the Everly Brothers* (Warner Bros. 1395; 1960; #9)—represented their creative apex, thanks in part to more thorough, polished production work. However, the Everlys also exhibited a greater inclination to record middle-of-the-road, maudlin material during this period, most notably, "Ebony Eyes" (Warner Bros. 5199; 1961; #8), "Crying in the Rain" (Warner Bros. 5501; 1962; #6), and "That's Old Fashioned" (Warner Bros. 5273; 1962; #9).

By 1963, the Everly Brothers were finding it hard to crack the Top 40, despite the release of many excellent recordings. Shifting their artistic focus to albums did little to help matters; the pioneering country-rock concept LP, *Roots* (Warner Bros. 1752; 1968), considered by many to be the duo's most sophisticated effort up to that time, attracted little attention. A string of further commercial failures culminated in an acrimonious split in 1973.

A decade of futile solo projects, however, spurred a reunion in 1983. A moderately successful live album, *The Everly Brothers Reunion Concert* (Passport 11001; 1984; #162), recorded September 1983 at London's Albert Hall led to several well-crafted country-pop releases with PolyGram: *EB 84* (Mercury 822431; 1984; #8)—fueled largely by the Paul McCartney-penned single, "On the Wings of a Nightingale" (Mercury; 1984; #50) and a nostalgic video which received heavy MTV rotation, *"Born Yesterday"* (Mercury 826142; 1986; #83), and *Some Hearts* (Mercury 832520; 1989). Due to increasingly marginal sales, virtually no recordings have been released by the Everlys from 1990 onward. Nevertheless, they continue to perform, regularly receive accolades as elder statesmen of rock—including induction into the Rock and Roll Hall of Fame (1986) and treatment in musicals such as *Bye Bye Love: The Everly Brothers Musical* (1998) and *Dream, Dream, Dream* (2000)—and are well represented on compact disc by a host of album reissues and anthologies, most notably on Charly in England and Rhino in the United States.

April 4. Lonnie Donegan begins a five-week run atop the British charts with "Cumberland Gap." By late May three more skiffle songs will take up residence in the British Top 20. From its prosaic origins as sing-along jam music built around makeshift instruments like washboard drums and washtub basses, the style inspires countless British youth to form bands. Many of them—most notably, the Beatles (known at this time as the Quarrymen—will spearhead the British invasion in the mid-1960s.

April 6. Perry Como's "Round and Round" (RCA Victor) peaks at number one on the Disc Jockey poll, remaining there for a couple of weeks. The single also tops the Top 100 and Best Seller listings, and goes to number three on the Juke Box survey.

April 6. The Diamonds begin an eight-week run at number two on the Best Seller charts (seven weeks, Juke Box; six weeks, Top 100) with "Little Darlin'" (Mercury 71060).

April 12. Alan Freed's ten-day Rock and Roll Easter Jubilee begins at the Brooklyn Paramount. Headliners include the Cleftones, Bob Davies and the Rhythm Jesters, Bob Diddley, El Boy, Anita Ellis, the Harptones, the Rosebuds, and newly emerging rockabilly-pop artists Jimmy Bowen, Charlie Charlie Gracie, and Buddy Knox.

April 13. Charlie Gracie begins a two-week stint atop the Juke Box survey with his version of "Butterfly" (Cameo); it is less successful on the Best Seller (#3), Top 100 (#7), and Disc Jockey (#13) listings.

April 13. Elvis Presley zooms to the summit of the Juke Box survey with "All Shook Up" (RCA Victor), remaining there for remaining life—nine weeks—of that listing. The singles also heads up the Top 100 (eight weeks), Best Seller (eight weeks), and Disc Jockey (seven weeks) charts.

April 18. Army reserve Lieutenant Buddy Knox is called up for six months of active duty. With "Party Doll" having topped the Best Seller charts the week beginning March 30, Roulette Records A&R team, Hugo Peretti and Liugi Creatore, push him into the studio to record more than twenty songs, thereby ensuring the steady flow of product during his military stint.

April 21. Gene Austin's career enjoys a revival when NBC-TV broadcasts "The Gene Austin Story" on *The Goodyear Television Playhouse*, featuring George Grizzard in the title role and Austin dubbing the vocals. And the end of the hour show, Austin make an appearance, singing his latest composition, "Too Late." The RCA recording of the song (#20-6880) becomes his first hit—reaching number seventy-five on the *Billboard* pop singles chart—since "Ridin' Around in the Rain" (Victor 24663) in July 1934.

April 24. Verve releases Rick Nelson's first single, "Teenager's Romance"/"I'm Walking" (#10047), the latter a cover of the Fats Domino hit. It became a minor hit, selling sixty thousand copies within three days. It was followed by "Be-Bop Baby"/"Have I Told You Lately That I Love You" (Imperial 5463). Although earlier pop stars appealed specifically to teenagers, Nelson was the first artist to be marketed to this audience with notable success. Born in 1940, he began taking part in his parents' television show, the *Adventures of Ozzie and Harriet*, at age twelve. His records achieved invaluable exposure when he was allotted singing segments on the program in 1957.

The teen idol phenomenon cut across the entire American popular culture spectrum, embracing the music business, television, radio, Hollywood films, comic books, fan magazines, and general merchandising tie-ins. In all of these media, the formula consisted of selling products associated with photogenic, well-mannered young people (generally ranging in age from early teens to the mid-twenties) to teenage consumers. The process had the implicit blessing of parents and other authority figures given the alternative; that American youth would fall under the influence of more rebellious cultural icons, including juvenile delinquents feared to inhabit the street corners of every 1950s town and, of course, rock 'n' roll stars.

The first wave of rock 'n' rollers had put both parents and record industry executives on the defensive. The wild performing antics of black and white musicians alike seemed to hint at a wide array of antisocial behaviors. While Elvis Presley—hep cat clothes and surly looks, notwithstanding—was soon being portrayed by the media as a likeable mama's boy, the extra-musical escapades of many rock 'n' roll artists soon confirmed the worst fears of adult moralists. Jerry Lee Lewis defiantly defended his marriage to a thirteen-year-old second cousin, and Chuck Berry was convicted of a violation of the Mann Act for transporting an underaged girl across a state line. Even the Platters, purveyors of smooth group ballads, were embroiled in a sex and drugs scandal.

The major record companies, outflanked by smaller independent labels in signing early rock 'n' roll stars, saw an opportunity to create and promote a new musical trend in which they controlled the talent. This strategy had initially failed when calypso failed to catch on beyond a brief flurry of hits in early 1957. However, with the loss of many early rock stars due to legal problems, military service, religious convictions (Little Richard entered the seminary in 1958), fatal accidents (e.g., Buddy Holly, Ritchie Valens, the Big Bopper, Eddie Cochran), mishaps which disrupted career momentum (e.g., Gene Vincent, Carl Perkins), and the failure to find quality song material for follow-up recordings, the industry-wide push of teen idol surrogates caught on in a big way.

The ingredients of a teen idol recording included an attractive (usually white, conservatively attired, and well-groomed) young media star singing simple lyrics about typically middle-class teen concerns. Given the fact that many idols couldn't really sing, the sugary pop arrangements—exhibiting only a faint suggestion of the big beat—were vital to chart success. Many of the singers were already stars in another medium (usually TV or movies), thereby virtually assuring the success of promotional efforts on the part of the record labels.

Nevertheless, stories of teen idols literally discovered on their front porches (Fabian Forte) abounded in fan publications. If the combined forces of the industry (label promotion, trade ads, and exposure on both radio playlists and *American Bandstand*) were marshaled on behalf of a young performer (no matter how lame), anything was possible. The formula consistently worked from the late 1950s up to the mid-1960s. However, changing cultural mores (e.g., youthful rebellion was seen as more glamorous than wholesome conformity) and the British Invasion (whose artists were often marketed in teen idol fashion) rendered the genre passe.

April 27. Eddie Cochran peaks at number eighteen on the pop charts with "Sittin' in the Balcony" (Liberty 55056). Although he placed only three singles in the American Top 40, Eddie Cochran remains one of the seminal artists of the 1950s rock 'n' roll. He was particularly influential in England, where his recordings continued to chart until 1988 ("C'mon Everybody," Liberty 501; #14) in addition to being covered by the likes of Rod Stewart, The Who, Humble Pie, and the Sex Pistols.

Born October 3, 1938, in Oklahoma City, he first recorded with fellow vocalist/guitarist Hank Cochran (no relation) as The Cochrans in 1955. Following the release of several unsuccessful singles, Cochran embarked on a solo career. A cameo role performing "20 Flight Rock" in the rock 'n' roll film, *The Girl Can't Help It* (1957), help propel his debut Liberty single, "Sittin' in the Balcony," to number 18 on the *Billboard* charts. His self-penned "Summertime Blues" (Liberty 55144; 1958; #8 US, #18 UK) became an instant classic of teen rebellion. The party anthem "C'mon Everybody" (Liberty 55166; 1959; #35 US, #6 UK) and hormone-dripping "Somethin' Else" (Liberty 55203; 1959; #58 US, #22 UK) were almost as good, despite lackluster stateside sales.

Whatever greatness Cochran might have achieved became a matter of conjecture due to his premature death in a London car crash. Nevertheless, his recordings—reissued in a steady stream of anthologies—have continued to sell well to the present day.

May 2. Elvis Presley records "Jailhouse Rock," the Leiber and Stoller composition will top the pop charts for seven weeks and be the centerpiece—the strikingly choreographed convicts' dance sequence—of the MGM movie of the same name.

May 4. ABC-TV premieres the "Alan Freed Show." The featured guests include Guy Mitchell, the Del-Vikings, Screamin' Jay Hawkins, the Clovers, June Valli, Martha Carson, and the newly constituted Alan Freed Rock & Roll Orchestra, with Panama Francis, Freddie Mitchell, Big Al Sears, and Sam the Man Taylor.

May 15. Mercury Records inks a recording pact with the Del-Vikings, fresh from a Top 5 hit for the indie label, Dot.

May 27. Mercury releases Jorgen Ingmann's LP, *Swinging Guitars*. Its tracks include the rockabilly instrumental "Apache," an international hit featuring reverb-drenched lead guitar work that will influence countless rock guitarists including Duane Eddy, Hank Marvin (whose group, the Shadows, would top the British charts with their version of the song in the summer of 1960), and Matthew Ashman of Bow Wow Wow.

May 27. Johnnie Ray goes number one on the British charts with "Yes Tonight, Josephine."

June 3. Pat Boone begins a five-week run atop the Hot 100 with "Love Letters in the Sand" (Dot). The single also heads up the Disc Jockey (seven weeks) and Best Seller (five weeks) listings and pulls up at number two (behind Presley's "All Shook Up") on the last edition of the Juke Box poll.

June 3. Further evidence of the global reach of popular music: RCA Victor releases "Butter Fingers"/"Fingertips," by Cool Dip (real name: Kuldip Singh), a native of India who happens to be a rockabilly stylist.

June 3. Teenage Records releases "Angels Cried"/"The Cow Jumped Over the Moon," by the Isley Brothers, who will go on to become one of the most durable acts in popular music history. They will record a series of commercial duds up until "Twist and Shout" in 1962.

June 10. Mae Axton—a Jacksonville, Florida, schoolteacher, who wrote "Heartbreak Hotel" along with Tommy Durden—confides to *Billboard* that she permits the playing of Elvis Presley records in class when students seem unable to concentrate on learning. She exclaims, "You'd be surprised how enthusiastic they become."

June 17. The Jimmy Dorsey Orchestra return to the charts for one last hurrah, beginning a four-week run at number two on the Disc Jockey charts with "So Rare" (Fraternity 755). The Everly Brothers start a four-week run at number two on the Top 100 with "Bye Bye Love" (Cadence 1315).

June 19. Jerry Lee Lewis appears on the pop charts for the first time with "Whole Lotta Shakin' Goin' On" (Sun 267; 1957; #3); his first release, "Crazy Arms" (Sun), enjoyed moderate sales in the Memphis area. His new record, recorded at Sun Studios in one extended improvisational take, reflected a shift from his original country leanings to unrestrained rockabilly. A crossover smash, it would top both the C&W and R&B charts.

One of the great originals of 1950s rock 'n' roll, Jerry Lee Lewis was a dynamic showman possessing a lascivious vocal style underscored by revved-up boogie-woogie piano that fairly leapt from the monaural grooves of his classic Sun records. The absence of a steady source of high-quality song material, combined with personal problems, severely curtailed his ability to sustain any kind of career momentum.

Born in Ferriday, Louisiana in 1935, Lewis grew up amidst a melting pot of music styles (his cousins included gospel singer Jimmy Swaggart and country-pop star Mickey Gilley). Matriculating to Memphis, he soon signed a recording contract with the legendary Sun label. Alternating between honky tonk, rockabilly, rhythm and blues, and old folk standards in early recording sessions, Lewis struck paydirt with talking blues-derived "Whole Lotta Shakin' Goin' On", augmented by his superb improvisational gifts both as a singer and pianist as well as producer Sam Phillips' trademark echo. He stuck closely to this formula with the follow-up singles, "Great Balls Of Fire" (Sun 281; 1957; #2) and "Breathless" (Sun 288; 1958; #7). By this time, Lewis was embroiled in controversies involving alleged bigamy and marriage to his thirteen-year-old cousin, Myra Gale Brown.

Arguably one of the most stubbornly egotistical and driven artists in popular music history, he soldiered on despite being virtually banned from important promotional outlets such as radio, television, and major performing venues. Signing with Smash (distributed first by Phillips, and then by Mercury) in 1963, Lewis released material focusing on his high-voltage live act and the growing nostalgia for early rock 'n' roll—e.g., *The Greatest Live Show On Earth* (Smash 67650; 1964; #71) and *The Return Of Rock* (Smash 67063; 1965)—before cultivating a country audience. However, despite a successful run of C&W singles—most notably, "What's Made Milwaukee Famous (Has Made A Loser Out Of Me)" (Smash 2164; 1968; #2 C&W, #94 pop), "To Make Love Sweeter For You" (Smash 2202; 1968; #1 C&W), "There Must Be More To Love Than This" (Mercury 73099; 1970; #1 C&W), "Would You Take Another Chance On Me" (Mercury 73248; 1971; #1 C&W, #40 pop), "Chantilly Lace" (Mercury 73273; 1972; #1 c&w, #43 pop), and "Middle Age Crazy" (Mercury 55011; 1977; #4 C&W)—he kept on releasing albums aimed at a broader rock demographic. Moving on to Elektra in the late 1970s, and later MCA, Sire, and Warner Brothers, Lewis—still dogged by controversy (one of his wives would die under mysterious circumstances in the 1990s) and exhibiting more attitude than most rappers—has continued producing new material in the face of significantly greater demand for his vintage Sun and Smash recordings. He was inducted into the Rock and Roll Hall of Fame in 1986, and was the subject of the 1989 biopic, *Great Balls Of Fire*, starring Dennis Quaid.

June 20. Having signed Buddy Holly to a solo contract, Coral Records releases his "Words of Love"/"Mailman, Bring Me No Blues." Although it achieves limited success, the A side will be exposed to a new generation of fans when covered by the Beatles in the early days of the British Invasion.

June 21. Imperial Records releases Chris Kenner's first record, "Nothing Will Keep Me Away from You"/"Sick and Tired." It attracts little attention outside of the singer-songwriter's home base, New Orleans. He will achieve success in the early 1960s with "I Like It Like That" and "Land of 1000 Dances."

July 1. According to front-page *Billboard* article, "'Good music' may be making a comeback on the best-seller charts, but rock& roll discs continue to dominate the pop market."

July 3. In a move reflecting the growing importance of LPs within the R&B and teen markets, Atlantic Records releases six eponymously titled albums, all of which retrospectively assemble the best material of each respective artist. The works include *LaVern Baker, Ruth Brown, Ray Charles, Ivory Joe Hunter, Clyde McPhatter and the Drifters, Big Joe Turner.*

July 5. Excello Records releases Slim Harpo's sexually suggestive "I'm a King Bee," one of the most influential nonhits of all-time. Among the rock acts to cover the song are the Rolling Stones and Jimi Hendrix in the 1960s, and Brownsville Station in the 1970s.

July 6. John Lennon and Paul McCartney meet at a church picnic in the Liverpool suburb of Woolton. In the church basement, between sets featuring Lennon's band, the Quarrymen, McCartney shows Lennon how to play and sing Eddie Cochran's "Twenty Flight Rock" and Gene Vincent's Be-Bop-a-Lula." McCartney will be asked to join the Quarrymen in short order.

July 8. Elvis Presley's "Teddy Bear" (RCA Victor) begins a seven-week run atop the Top 100. It also heads up the Best Seller (seven weeks) and Disc Jockey (three weeks) listings.

July 12. Alan Freed hosts the first installment of a thirteen-week rock 'n' roll program airing Friday nights during the 10–10:30 p.m. EST time-slot. The first installment features Frankie Lymon, the Everly Brothers, Buddy Knox, Connie Francis, Ferlin Husky, and Billy Williams, among others.

July 22. Little Junior Parket peaks at number seventy-four on the pop charts with "Next Time You See Me" (Duke 164).

Although not considered to be a trailblazing artist, singer/mouth harpist Little Junior Parker was one of the most popular blues performers during the 1950s and 1960s. Born Herman Parker Jr. on March 3, 1927, in West Memphis, he first attracted attention as a member of the Howlin' Wolf Band during 1949-1950. After a brief stint with the Johnny Ace's Beale Streeters, he started his own band, Little Junior's Blue Flames, in 1951. He would tour with the Johnny Ace Revue from 1953 until Ace died of a self-inflicted gunshot wound December 24, 1954.

Parker first recorded for Modern in 1952, before making the R&B charts in a big way the following year with "Feelin' Good" (#187; #5) on Sam Phillips' legendary Sun Records. Following a dry spell during the mid-1950s, he rebounded with a string of hits for the Houston-based Duke label, including "Next Time You See Me" (#7 r&b), "Driving Wheel" (Duke 335; 1961; #85 pop, #5 r&b), "In the Dark" (Duke 341; 1961; #7 r&b), and "Annie Get Your Yo-Yo" (Duke 345; 1962; #51 pop, #6 r&b).

Parker would go on to produce modest hits for the Mercury, Blue Rock, Minit, and Capitol labels in the late 1960s and early 1970s. His career was cut short, however, by a fatal brain tumor on November 18, 1971, in Blue Island, Illinois.

July 24. The Coasters record one of their more underappreciated classics, "Idol with the Golden Head," written and produced by their long-time associates, Leiber and Stoller.

July 27. In the Art Imitates Life file, the Bobbettes' "Mr. Lee"—a tongue-in-cheek tribute to the principal of the high school where they are enrolled as students—makes the pop charts. In 1960, after a string of releases fail to click, the trio achieves minor success recording a sequel of sorts, "I Shot Mr. Lee."

July 28. Jerry Lee Lewis performs on *The Steve Allen Show*, his first ever TV appearance. With "Whole Lotta Shakin' Goin' On" racing up the pop, C&W, and R&B charts, Lewis is a hot item. He is booked to appear on the Allen show two more times, in addition to Alan Freed's Brooklyn Paramount shows, August 28–September 8.

August 4. The Everly Brothers appear on the *Ed Sullivan Show* for the second time, previewing their upcoming release, "Wake Up Little Susie."

August 5. *American Bandstand*, hosted by Dick Clark (since 1956), and originating on Philadelphia's WFIL in 1952, makes its ABC network debut. The program—first scheduled at 11:00 a.m. EST, Saturday, and later added to 3:00–4:30 p.m. weekdays slot as well—would quickly become a major catalyst behind the rise of rock 'n' roll. Its tableau consisted of local teenagers dancing to contemporary hit recordings (the show kicked off with the Crockets' "That'll Be the Day"), punctuated by guest appearances (the first guests were Billy Williams, who sang his hit, "I'm Gonna Sit Right Down and Write Myself a Letter," and the Chordettes).

August 7. The Quarrymen, featuring lead singer/guitarist John Lennon, make their Cavern club debut in Liverpool.

August 8. Further evidence of the growing acceptance of the LP: the indie label, Imperial, releases Fat Domino's first album, *This Is Fats*, which is comprised of both old hits and new material.

August 11. Nine days after his first appearance on "The Big Beat," Jerry Lee Lewis returns to again close the show with "Whole Lotta Shakin' Goin' On."

August 15. Decca issues an earlier, previously unreleased rendition of "That'll Be the Day," recorded by Buddy Holly sans the Crickets when he was still under contract to that label. However, it offers little competition to the Brunswick version that will top the pop charts in early September. Holly now has three record companies hawking his material in the marketplace.

August 19. Debbie Reynolds begins a five-week stay at number on the Top 100 with "Tammy" (Coral). The single also tops the Disc Jockey (five weeks) and Best Seller (three weeks) surveys.

September 1. "The Biggest Show of Stars for 1957" tour begins at the Brooklyn Paramount theater. Featuring Paul Anka, Chuck Berry, the Drifters, the Everly Brothers, Buddy Holly and the Crickets, Frankie Lymon and the Teenagers, Clyde McPhatter, among others, it will conclude November at the Richmond (Virginia) Mosque. The white artists would not be permitted to perform in several venues due to segregation laws banning their appearance on the same stage with blacks.

September 4. WJZ-TV, Baltimore, premieres a rock 'n' roll DJ show, *The Buddy Deane Bandstand*, which will air 3–5 p.m. EST, Monday-Saturday. Deane attracts nationwide publicity when he invites viewers to phone the station to speak to selected artists, causing the local phone lines to be swamped; phone company officials ask him to terminate this particular activity. Film clips from the program will be included in the Ramones'"Rock & Roll Radio" video a quarter of a century later.

September 5. The first flexi-disc is produced and used in a Nestle chocolate bar promotion.

September 8. Brunswick releases the Berry Gordy Jr.-penned "Reet Petite," the solo debut of Jackie Wilson, formerly with Billy Ward and the Dominoes as a replacement for Clyde McPhatter in 1953. The record resides in the lower reaches of the charts, but Wilson will make a splash with the Top Ten hit, "Lonely Teardrops," the following year.

September 9. Paul Anka's "Diana" reaches number one on the Best Seller charts (#2 Top 100, #2 DJ). It also tops the British charts with a month of its release, remaining there 9 weeks; with worldwide sales surpassing nine million, it would become one of the five biggest-selling records of all time.

September 18. "The Big Record," a record-hop-styled program, premieres on CBS-TV. Hosted by Patti Page, the first show features Tony Bennett, Sal Mineo, and Billy Ward and the Dominoes as guests.

September 20. RCA Victor hires composing-production team Jerry Leiber and Mike Stoller as independent producers and artist and repertoire directors. In this capacity, they will assist such artists as Lena Horne, Julius LaRosa, Jaye P. Morgan, and Elvis Presley. Leiber and Stoller will continue to offer their services to other labels, most notably Atlantic, which has the duo's protégés, the Coasters, under contract.

September 23. The Crickets peak at number one on the Best Seller survey (#3 Top 100, #3 Disc Jockey) with "That'll Be the Day" (Brunswick).

September 23. The premiere of *Rock Around the Clock* in Copenhagen, Denmark is marked by "violent riots led by leather-jacketed motorcycle gangs." No disturbances are reported in another part of the city where Tommy Steele made an appearance to promote his movie, *Young Man with a Guitar*.

September 23. Jimmie Rodgers begins a four-week run atop the Disc Jockey poll with "Honeycomb" (Roulette). The single also spends two weeks at number one on the Top 100 and Best Seller listings.

September 24. *Mister Rock and Roll*, a film biography of Alan Freed, premieres at Paramount in New York City. It includes cameos by rook Benton, Chuck Berry, Little Richard, Frankie Lymon and the Teenagers, Clyde McPhatter, and the Moonglows.

September 25. Roulette Records releases Frankie Lymon's debut solo single,"My Girl." However, it will soon be evident that his hit-making days are over.

October 2. Specialty Records releases Larry Williams' "Bony Maronie"/"You Bug Me, Baby." It will find crossover success (#9 R&B, #14 pop), coming close to duplicating the success of his previous single, the Top 5 pop and R&B hit, "Short Fat Fannie."

October 5. From Sydney, Australia, where he is in the midst of a tour, Little Richard tells his backing group that he intends to depart the entertainment business and enter the ministry. He cites the launch of the Russian satellite, Sputnik, the previous night, as an omen from God to give up the evils of rock 'n' roll. When his saxophonist, Clifford Burks, questioned his sincerity, Little Richard allegedly threw four diamond rings worth $8,000 into Sydney's Hunter River to underscore his intent.

October 7. According to reports, RCA Victor has already received five hundred thousand advance orders for Elvis Presley's Christmas LP; however, only two hundred thousand copies have been pressed, thus far.

October 12. After a Sydney concert, Little Richard publicly announces his intention to stop performing and recording rock 'n' roll. He stated, "If you want to live for the Lord, you can't rock & roll, too. God doesn't like it." He flew to Los Angeles the following day and was baptized a Seventh Day Adventist "to prepare for the end of the world."

October 14. The Everly Brothers begin a four-week stay atop the Disc Jockey poll with "Wake Up Little Susie" (Cadence). The single also reaches number one on the Top 100 (two weeks) and Best Seller (one week) listings.

October 16. Keen Records releases Sam Cooke's "You Send Me"/"Summertime," which will top both the pop and R&B charts, ultimately selling more than 2.5 million copies. Formerly a gospel star with the Soul Stirrers,

Cooke will become a major force in the soul music field as a songwriter, artist, producer, and record label entrepreneur.

October 18. Paul McCartney plays with the Quarrymen at the New Clubmoor Hall Conservative Club in Broadway, Liverpool.

October 21. Johnny Mathis heads up the Disc Jockey poll (#4 Best Seller, #5 Top 100) with "Chances Are" (Columbia).

October 21. Elvis Presley's "Jailhouse Rock" (RCA Victor) begins a six-week run atop the Best Seller survey. The record also reaches number one on the Top 100 (six weeks) and Disc Jockey (two weeks) listings.

October 21. Della Reese peaks at number twelve on the pop charts with "And That Reminds Me" (Jubilee 5292).

Della Reese was a polished pop-R&B stylist who appeared headed for superstardom in the late 1950s. Unable to maintain a high level of commercial consistency as a recording artist, however, Reese turned increasingly to acting, beginning in the 1960s.

Born Delloreese Patricia Early on July 6, 1931, in Detroit, she toured with Mahalia Jackson as a gospel singer between 1945 and 1949. Reese also worked with trumpeter/bandleader Erskine Hawkins in the early 1950s before going solo in 1957. She first made the charts with "And That Reminds Me." After signing with RCA, she opted for a more mainstream sound, finding immediate success with "Don't You Know" (RCA 7591; 1959; #2 pop, #1 r&b) and "Not One Minute More" (RCA 7644; 1960; #16 pop, #13 r&b). Subsequent releases, however, only reached the lower portion of the pop charts.

After acting and singing on countless television programs, Reese was offered her series, *Della*, in 1970. She was cast as Della Rogers in the popular TV series, *Chico & The Man*, from 1976 to 1978. Since appearing in *Let's Rock* (1958), Reese has landed roles in many films as well. Through it all, she has continued to perform live and occasionally make new recordings.

October 22. Tenor Harvey Hindermyer dies at age seventy-five. He was an original member of the Shannon Four, and became popular on radio as one of the "Gold Dust Twins."

October 28. Ricky Nelson peaks at number three on the Best Seller charts with "Be-Bop Baby" (Imperial 5463).

October 29. Brunswick releases the second single by Buddy Holly and the Crickets, "Oh Boy"/"Not Fade Away." The A side will reach the Top 10 in December, while the flip becomes a timeless classic covered by the Rolling Stones, the Grateful Dead, and many other rock acts.

November 3. Sun Records releases Jerry Lee Lewis' "Great Balls of Fire," backed by the Hank Williams classic, "You Win Again." The A side—co-written by celebrated composer, Otis Blackwell, along with Jack Hammer—becomes another smash for Lewis, peaking at number two on the pop charts and number three R&B, while becoming a C&W chart-topper.

November 3. ABC-Paramount releases Danny and the Juniors' "At the Hop." The recording was originally issued by the indie label, Singular, which sold seven thousand copies in Philadelphia, the group's hometown.

November 4. If any further proof is need that rock 'n' roll is completely dominating the domestic music scene, the pop, R&B, and C&W charts have the same top two songs: Elvis Presley's "Jailhouse Rock," followed by the Everly Brothers' "Wake Up Little Susie." Furthermore, positions three through six are identical on the pop & R&B charts: in descending rank order, Sam Cooke's "You Send Me," the Rays' "Silhouettes," Ricky Nelson's "Be-Bop Baby," and Jimmie Rodgers' "Honeycomb."

November 4. Jimmy Reed peaks at number thirty-two on the pop charts with "Honest I Do" (Vee-Jay 253). Jimmy Reed outsold virtually every blues recording artist of the 1950s with the exception of B.B. King. He had a considerable influence on the blues rock acts of the late 1960s, including the Rolling Stones, John Mayall, and the Steve Miller Band.

Born September 6, 1925, on a plantation in Dunleith, Mississippi, Reed learned the fundamentals of guitar and harmonica from future sidekick Eddie Taylor. Following his discharge from the Navy in 1945, he relocated to Gary, Indiana, which provided close proximity to Chicago area clubs. He first recorded for Chance in 1953, and subsequently failed an audition for Chess before catching on with the fledging Vee-Jay label, with whom he enjoyed a long string of hits between 1955 and 1965. Utilizing a distinctive mumbled, slurring vocal style with unadorned guitar/harmonica accompaniment (further assisted by the ever faithful Taylor), he not only enjoyed considerable R&B and pop crossover success with singles like "You Don't Have to Go" (Vee-Jay; 1955), "Ain't That Lovin' You Baby" (Vee-Jay), "Honest I Do," "Baby What You Want Me to Do" (Vee-Jay; 1960), "Big Boss Man"(Vee-Jay; 1961), and "Bright Lights Big City" (Vee-Jay; 1961), but issued a string of moderately popular LPs, most notably, *At Carnegie Hall* (Vee-Jay 1035; 1961), a double-disc set that was actually a studio re-creation of his live show.

Following the collapse of Vee-Jay, Reed moved on to Exodus and BluesWay in the late 1960s, but failed to sell well. Although introduced to a new audience via the American Folk Blues Festival tour of Europe in 1968 and the concurrent blues revival, his 1970s releases for a variety of labels met with public indifference. Beset with epilepsy and chronic alcoholism since early in his career, Reed died of respiratory failure on August 29, 1976, in Oakland, California. He would be inducted into the Blues Foundation's Hall of Fame in 1980 and the Rock and Roll Hall of Fame in 1991.

November 12. The film *Jamboree* is previewed in Hollywood. Jerry Lee Lewis and Fats Domino receive top billing; other performers include Frankie Avalon, Connie Francis, Carl Perkins, and Slim Whitman.

November 18. Jackie Wilson peaks at number sixty-two on the pop charts with his debut single, "Reet Petite" (Brunswick 55024).

Jackie Wilson rivaled James Brown as one of the most dynamic performers of his generation, exuding a sexy athleticism capable of working his audience into a frenzy. He was also one of the most versatile vocalists in the rock era, ranging from the soulful, gritty style of a Wilson Pickett to the smooth, gospel-inflected pop associated with Sam Cooke and Clyde McPhatter.

Born June 9, 1934, in a blue collar section of Detroit, Wilson would win his Golden Gloves weight division in the late 1940s. After high school, he began singing in local nightclubs. In 1953, Wilson joined Billy Ward and His Dominoes as a replacement for McPhatter, who'd departed to found the Drifters. During his tenure the group recorded "St. Therese of the Roses" (Decca 29933; 1956), which reached number thirteen on the pop charts.

Wilson went solo in late 1956, signing with Brunswick Records. Between 1957 and 1972 he recorded forty-nine charting singles, including "Lonely Teardrops" (Brunswick 55105; 1958; #7 pop, #1 r&b 7 weeks), "Night" (Brunswick 55166; 1960; #4 pop, #3 r&b), "Alone At Last" (Brunswick 55170; 1960; #8 pop, #20 r&b), "My Empty Arms" (Brunswick 55201; 1961; #9 pop, #25 r&b), "Baby Workout" (Brunswick 55239; 1963; #5 pop, #1 r&b 3 weeks), and "(Your Love Keeps Lifting Me) Higher and Higher" (Brunswick 55336; 1967; #6 pop, #1 r&b).

When record sales dropped off, he was relegated to playing the oldies circuit. On September 25, 1975, as part of the Dick Clark revue at the Latin Casino in Cherry Hill, New Jersey, he suffered a major heart attack while singing "Lonely Teardrops." Emerging from a coma with considerable brain damage, he never performed again, remaining in hospitals until his death on January 21, 1984. He was inducted into the Rock and Roll Hall of Fame in 1987.

November 19. WCFL, Chicago, bans Elvis Presley records from its playlists. Although picketed by the local chapter of the Elvis Presley Fan Club, the radio station stands by its decision.

November 25. "Swanee River Rock (Talkin' 'Bout That River)" becomes Ray Charles' first crossover hit, reaching number 34 on the pop charts.

November 25. *Billboard* notes that rock 'n' roll acts are less inclined to join big package shows due to their "increasingly disappointing grosses'; they are opting instead for down-sized, DJ-sponsored teen record hops, accepting smaller guarantees but receiving larger percentages of the gate.

November 25. Gene Vincent and the Blue Caps make their national television debut on the "Ed Sullivan Show," performing "Lotta Lovin'" and "Dance to the Bop."

December 1. Three acts make their national TV debut on the *Ed Sullivan Show*: Buddy Holly and the Crickets, performing "That'll Be the Day" and "Peggy Sue"; Sam Cooke ("You Send Me"); and the Rays ("Silhouettes").

December 2. Sam Cooke's "You Send Me" (Keen) begins a three-week stint at number one on the Top 100. The single also tops the Best Seller (two weeks) and Disc Jockey surveys.

December 2. Bobby Day and the Satellites peak at number fifty-seven on the pop charts with "Little Bitty Pretty One" (Class 211).

Bobby Day had only one hit record of note, but oh what a record! The double-sided single, "Rock-in Robin"/"Over and Over" (Class 229; 1958; #2 pop, #1 r&b three weeks/#41 pop), not only was a major bestseller and remains in heavy rotation on oldies radio playlists, but has been widely covered, most notably, the Dave Clark Five's "Over and Over" (Epic 9863; 1965; #1 pop) and Michael Jackson's "Rockin' Robin" (Motown 1197; 1972; #2).

He was born Robert Byrd on July 1, 1932 in Ft. Worth, Texas. Day moved to the Watts area of Los Angeles in 1948, where he formed the R&B vocal group, the Hollywood Flames—also known as The Flames, Four Flames, Hollywood Four Flames, Jets, Tangiers, and Satellites—a couple of years later. They went through many personnel changes over the years; their lineup consisted of Earl "Jackie" Nelson, David Ford, Clyde Tillis, and Curtis Williams (formerly of the Penguins and composer of the doo-wop classic, "Earth Angel") when "Buzz-Buzz-Buzz" (Ebb 119; 1957; #11 pop, #5 r&b) became a crossover hit.

Although the group continued to record into the 1960s, Day moved on to a solo career in 1957. He wrote—and recorded the original version of—"Little Bitty Pretty One," which became a Top Ten crossover hit for Thurston Harris (Aladdin 3398; 1957; #6 pop, #2 r&b). He also supplied the backing vocals for "Pretty Girls Everywhere" (Class 235; 1958; #36 pop, #6 r&b), by Eugene Church and the Fellows.

Following several more minor solo hits, Day would form a duo, Bob & Earl, with former group mate Nelson in 1960. However, he had moved into other areas of the music business (his place being taken by Bob Relf) by the time the duo released their first chart record, "Harlem Shuffle" (Marc 104; 1963; #44 pop, #44 r&b), in 1963.

December 4. Amidst reports that many radio stations have banned *Elvis' Christmas Album* due to the impropriety of having religious material interpreted by a singer for his sexually suggestive moves, CKWS-Kingston, Ontario DJ Allen Brooks plays the LP and solicits listener opinions. Eight hundred call, all but fifty-six approving of the work; those who disapprove indicate that they don't like any Presley music.

December 6. Mercury releases a cover of Chuck Willis' "The Stroll" by the Diamonds. It will eventually peak at number eight on the pop charts (#7 R&B), driving a craze for the dance of the same name.

December 7. On the heels of his huge success there with the single, "Diana," Paul Anka commences his first British tour at London's Trocadero theater.

December 8. Billie Holiday performs "Fine and Mellow" live on television; Lewis Porter and Michael Ullman, in their 1993 book, *Jazz*, would call it "one of her most famous performances."

December 11. Jerry Lee Lewis is secretly married to second cousin Myra Gale Brown in Hernando, Tennessee. She is his third wife.

December 12. KEX-Portland, Oregon Al Priddy is fired for violating the radio station's ban against airing Elvis Presley's "White Christmas."

December 15. Sammy Davis Jr. launches a Westinghouse network syndicated radio talk show; his guests—Columbia Records A&R man Mitch Miller and MGM Records president Arnold Maxim—participate in a roundtable discussion of rock 'n' roll. In response to indictments from Davis and Miller (e.g., "the comic books of music"), followed by the comment, "I don't see any end to rock and roll in the near future," Davis quips, "I might commit suicide." The following week he covers the rockabilly classic "I'm Coming Home."

December 16. Pat Boone's "April Love" (Dot) begins a six-week run atop the Disc Jockey survey. He will also outpace the competition on the Best Seller (two weeks) and Top 100 (one week) charts.

December 16. Bobby Helms' "Jingle Bell Rock" makes its debut in the pop charts. It will become a seasonal standard, returning to the best-seller lists in December 1958, 1960, 1961, and 1962.

December 30. Buddy Holly's "Peggy Sue" (Coral 61885) peaks at number three on the pop charts.

1958

❄

January 6. Danny & the Juniors' "At the Hop" (ABC-Paramount) begins a seven-week stay at number one on the Top 100. The single also tops the Best Seller (five weeks) and Disc Jockey (three weeks) surveys.

January 6. The "Flying V" electric guitar is patented by Gibson. The design will become a rock icon, utilized by countless guitarists, most notably bluesman Albert King.

January 6. Jerry Lee Lewis peaks at number two on the Top 100 with "Great Balls of Fire" (Sun 281), remaining there for four weeks.

January 13. Ricky Nelson starts a three-week run at number two on the Best Seller charts with "Stood Up" (Imperial 5483).

January 15. The Everly Brothers appear on *The Perry Como Show*—their British TV debut.

January 20. In what station manager Robert Convey terms "a simple weeding out of undesirable music," KWK concludes its "Record Breaking Week." With rock 'n' roll music banned from its airwaves, KWK deejays have been giving each of the offending discs from the station library a "farewell spin" prior to smashing it into pieces on-mike.

January 23. Brunswick releases the Crickets' "Maybe Baby"/"Tell Me How."

January 24. Coral releases Buddy Holly's "I'm Gonna Love You Too"/"Listen To Me." Holly and his band will be given the opportunity to promote their two new singles when they appear on the *Ed Sullivan Show* on January 26.

January 25. Elvis Presley's "Jailhouse Rock" enters the British pop chart in the top position, the first time this has ever happened.

January 27. Little Richard enrolls in Oakwood College, a Huntsville, Alabama, ministry run by the Seventh Day Adventist Church. During his announcement, the former singer offers a rationale for his decision: the wing of his tour plane caught fire while over the Philippines, and his prayers that the flames be extinguishes were answered. Furthermore, he dreamed that "the world was burning up, the sky melting from the heat."

January 28. Jerry Lee Lewis and Ronald J. Hargrave copyright "High School Confidential," the title song to the singer's second film.

January 29. Challenge Records releases the Champs' "Tequila" (b/w "Train to Nowhere"), the fourth most successful instrumental of the rock 'n' roll era, according to *Joel Whitburn's Pop Annual, 1955–1999*.

February 10. Michael Holliday tops the British charts with "The Story of My Life," the first Bacharach/David composition to accomplish that feat.

February 10. Elvis Presley begins a five-week run atop the Best Seller listing with "Don't" (RCA); it also heads up the Top 100 and Disc Jockey charts for a week.

February 10. Frank Sinatra begins a five-week string atop the LP charts with *Come Fly with Me* (Capitol).

February 15. The premiere of *The Dick Clark Saturday Night Show* (ABC), a half-hour rock 'n' roll revue showcasing popular recording acts of the day lip-synching their most recent hits. Broadcast live from New York City's Little Theater, the inaugural program's headliners included Johnnie Ray, the Royal Teens (performing "Short Shorts"), Jerry Lee Lewis ("Great Balls of Fire"), Connie Francis ("Who's Sorry Now"), and Pat Boone ("A Wonderful Time Up There").

February 17. Frankie Avalon peaks at number seven on the pop charts with "Dede Dinah" (Chancellor 1011).

A child prodigy of the trumpet, Frankie Avalon starred on Paul Whiteman's radio and TV programs, both of which were based in the Philadelphia area in the early 1950s. By 1957, he signed with Chancellor Records as a vocalist. The label's owners, Bob Marcucci and Peter de Angelis, also took on the management of his career.

Avalon's scored his first national hit in early 1958 with a Marcucci-de Angelis composition, "Dede Dinah" (Chancellor 1011). A prime exponent of the teen idol school, he enjoyed five Top Ten hits the following year, including three million sellers—"Venus" (Chancellor 1031), "Just Ask Your Heart" (Chancellor 1040), and "Why" (Chancellor 1045).

Although his recordings were less successful in the early 1960s, Avalon became a major Hollywood film star. His acting credits included Guns of the Timberland (1960), The Carpetbaggers (1962), and a string of beach party movies produced by American International Pictures. From the 1960s to the 1990s, he divided his time between television and film acting—most notably, Grease (1978) and Back to the Beach (1987), club appearances, and occasional recording sessions. A disco version of his number one hit, "Venus" (De-Lite 1578), was his last charting single. By the late 1970s, he became increasingly active performing on the rock and roll revival circuit.

February 17. The McGuire Sisters' "Sugartime" (Coral) begins a four-week stint atop the Disc Jockey survey. The trio's old school sound will not score as highly on the Top 100 (#5) and Best Seller (#7) charts.

February 24. The Silhouettes reach number one on the Top 100 with "Get a Job" (Ember), remaining there for two weeks. The doo-wop single also goes to number two on the Best Seller listing, and number three on the Disc Jockey poll.

One of the great one-hit wonder vocal groups, the Silhouettes—with their extraordinary vocal interplay and unerring feel for swing rhythms—deserved a better fate. The Philadelphia-based foursome formed in the mid-1950s as the Gospel Tornados. Originally comprised of lead singer Bill Horton, baritone Earl Beale, bass Raymond Edwards, and a tenor remembered only as Shorty, the group—with the encouragement of the Turbans' road manager, Richard Lewis, who took over the tenor slot in 1956—gradually began performing secular material during the week.

After a prolonged effort to obtain a recording contract from various Philadelphia and New York labels, they caught the attention of deejay Kae Williams at a local club in 1957. He became their manager and signed them to his Junior label with the proviso that they undergo a name change. Beale selected Silhouettes after a then current hit by the Rays, and "Get a Job" (Junior 391; 1957; #1 r&b 5 weeks) was released. When it began catching on with the public—thanks in part to the promotional efforts of Dick Clark on *American Bandstand*—Herald/Ember picked up national distribution rights.

The Silhouettes spent much of 1958 touring and, consequently, had little time to work on a strong follow-up record. Williams decided not to release covers of either the Impressions' "For Your Precious Love" or the Spaniels' "Stormy Weather" due to his friendship with Vee-Jay head Ewart Abner. The second Ember single, "Headin' for the Poorhouse" (#1032; 1958), received no support from Clark allegedly due to a falling out with Williams. Back on Junior, the group became disillusioned; Edwards and Horton moved on, being replaced by Cornelius Brown and John Wilson. They worked with a succession of labels—including Ace, 20th Century Fox, Imperial, and Grand (where they worked with Jerry Ragavoy, who'd formerly managed the Castelles)—through 1963. The group would ultimately disband, while Horton went on to record as Bill Horton and the Dawns for the Lawn label.

February 26. Perry Como begins an eight-week stay atop the British charts with the Bacharach/David composition, "Magic Moments."

March 2. Buddy Holly and the Crickets perform in Great Britain for the first time, at London's Trocadero. The twenty-five dates, twice-nightly package includes Ronnie Keene & His Orchestra, Ronnie Miller, Des O'Connor, and the Tanner Sisters.

March 12. Billie Holiday is sentenced to a year's probation by a Philadelphia court after being found guilty of narcotics possession.

March 13. The Recording Industry Association of America introduces its awards for record sales. As of 2005, the Beatles had garnered the most R.I.A.A. certifications, with seventy-six platinum records.

March 17. The Champs begin a five-week run at number one on the Top 100 with "Tequila" (Challenge). The single also paces the Best Seller and Disc Jockey charts for five and two weeks, respectively. A new version by the band will peak at number ninety-nine in 1962.

March 19. Big Records releases "Our Song," by a Queens, New York-based teen duo named Tom and Jerry. They would resurface in the mid-1960s as the commercial folk act, Simon and Garfunkel.

March 24. Perry Como reaches number one on the Disc Jockey listing (#3 Best Seller, #9 Top 100) with "Catch a Falling Star" (RCA).

March 24. Elvis Presley begins his service stint with the U.S. Army (as private US53310761) by reporting to Local Draft Board 86 in Memphis. His enlistment would later be hailed by rock historians as a masterstroke of public relations. Presley would emerge from the military with the image of a young patriot rather than an anti-establishment rebel in the Marlon Brando/James Dean mold. Furthermore, he'd be more committed to Parker's business leadership than ever before.

In the meantime, the rock 'n' roll genre lost its most dynamic and popular performer. Within a couple of years, other major rock 'n' roll stars would either die (e.g. Buddy Holly, Ritchie Valens, the Big Bopper, Eddie Cochran) or disappear from the public eye (e.g., Jerry Lee Lewis, Little Richard, Chuck Berry), leaving a void that would be filled by teen idols and other purveyors of soft pop.

March 25. Elvis Presley receives the regulation G.I. crew-cut from army barber James Peterson.

March 29. W. C. Handy dies at age eighty-four. The cornetist, bandleader, and music teacher first achieved success with is composition of "The Memphis Blues" in 1913. He achieved considerable recording success with his own performing ensemble, W. C. Handy's Orchestra.

William Christopher Handy has been wrongly identified as the originator of the blues by some writers. This view has been perpetuated by both the media—for example, the biopic *St. Louis Blues* (1958), starring Nat King Cole—and the city of Memphis, which has immortalized him by erecting a park (complete with a statue) bearing his name in the heart of its Beale Street blues complex and instituting the W. C. Handy Awards in 1980, recognizing achievement in blues music each year.

His actual contribution, in his capacity as co-owner of a music publishing concern in Memphis—followed by a move to New York City—early in the twentieth century, he introduced the practice of transcribing blues songs for publication. Given a middle class upbringing in his native Florence, Alabama, he began his career as a music teacher, cornetist, and bandleader. During his group's forays into southern venues, he developed a first-hand acquaintance with blues material. His formal compositions in that style—most notably, "The Memphis Blues" (1913) and "The St. Louis Blues" (1914)—began immediate standards. "The St. Louis Blues" would be recognized by Joel Whitburn's *Pop Memories, 1890–1954* (Record Research, 1986) as the most recorded American song of all time; best-selling versions were released by Prince's Orchestra (1916), Al Bernard (1919), Marion Harris (1920), the Original Dixieland Jazz Band (1921), Bessie Smith (1925), Louis Armstrong (1930), Rudy Vallee (1930), Cab Calloway (1930; 1943), the Mills Brothers (1932), the Boswell Sisters (1935), Benny Goodman (1936), Guy Lombardo (1939), and Billy Eckstine (1953). He also enjoyed success as a recording artist, his hits (credited to W.C. Handy's Orchestra) included "Livery Stable Blues" (Columbia 2419; 1919) and "St. Louis Blues" (Okeh 4896; 1923).

March 31. Chess releases Chuck Berry's "Johnny B. Goode." The single is later included in the Voyager space probe as an example of the best of human culture.

April 14. Don Gibson goes to number one on the country charts with "I Can't Stop Loving You."

April 14. British adolescent Laurie London begins a four-week run atop the Disc Jockey listing with the gospel traditional, "He's Got the Whole World (In His Hands)" (Capitol). The single will only rise as high as number two on the Top 100 and Best Seller charts.

April 14. Huey "Piano" Smith and the Clowns peak at number nine on the pop charts with "Don't You Just Know It" (Ace 545).

Due to the nature of record label credits and the marginal role of the rock press prior to the British Invasion, Bobby Marchan is virtually unknown to contemporary popular music fans. Nevertheless, he appeared on a number of seminal R&B hits in the late 1950s/early 1960s.

Born April 30, 1930 in Youngstown, Ohio, Marchan received musical training as a youth in the church choir. He began performing in the area while still attending East High School. His first recording was "Chick-A-Wa-Wa" in 1955. He was recruited to join Huey "Piano" Smith's New Orleans-based backup group, The Clowns, in 1958. He sang lead on a number of Smith's classic singles, most notably "Don't You Just Know It."

In early 1959, Marchan left The Clowns and formed the Tick Tocks. When that project failed to jell, he signed a solo recording contract with the Fire label in 1960. Shortly thereafter, he produced a smash with the soulful "There's Something on Your Mind" (Fire; 1960). Although Marchan continued to work on the periphery of the music business for many more years, he failed to have any further chart success.

April 21. The Platters peak at number one on the Top 100 (#1 Best Seller, #1 Disc Jockey) with "Twilight Time" (Mercury).

April 28. David Seville reaches number one on the Top 100 with "Witch Doctor" (Liberty), holding down that position for three weeks (#1 Best Seller two weeks, #2 Disc Jockey). Having perfected the studio technique of tape recording his voice at a slow speed, and then speeding it up during playback, Seville (aka Ross Bagdasarian) will move on to release a string of novelty singles and albums by three imaginary characters collectively known as the Chipmunks.

May 12. The Everly Brothers' "All I Have To Do Is Dream" (Cadence) begins a five-week run atop the Disc Jockey listing. Composed by Boudleaux Bryant, and featuring lyrical lead guitar work by Chet Atkins, the record will also reach number one on the Best Seller (five weeks) and Top 100 (three weeks) charts.

May 19. The soundtrack to *South Pacific* goes number one on the album charts.

June 9. Sheb Wooley surges to the summit of both the Best Seller and Top 100 listings with "The Purple People Eater" (MGM), remaining there for six weeks. The novelty also tops the Disc Jockey survey for four weeks.

June 30. Chuck Willis peaks at number nine on the pop charts with "What Am I Living For."

Although his career was tragically short due to his death April 10, 1958, from peritonitis, Chuck Willis played a key role in popularizing the teen dance, the stroll. Although an unappreciated singer featuring a restrained, but soulful delivery, he is best remembered for a handful of classic songs, including "I Feel So Bad," "It's Too Late," "Hang Up My Rock and Roll Shoes," "Close Your Eyes," "Oh What a Dream," and "What Am I Living For." They would later be covered by the likes of Elvis Presley, Ruth Brown, Buddy Holly, Jerry Lee Lewis, the Five Keys, Delbert McClinton, the Animals, Otis Redding, the Band, and Foghat.

Born January 31, 1928, Willis made a name for himself as an R&B vocalist around his native Atlanta while still a teenager. A local disk jockey, Zenus "Daddy" Sears, helped him get a record contract with Columbia in 1952. He would release a few successful singles for the label's subsidiary, Okeh, including "My Story" (#6905; 1952; #2 r&b), "'Goin' to the River" (#6952; 1953; #4 r&b), "Don't Deceive Me" (#6985; 1953; #6 r&b), "You're Still My Baby" (#7015; 1954; #4 r&b), and "I Feel So Bad" (#7029; #1954; #8).

Known as the "Sheik of the Shake" in the early 1950s because he wore turbans on stage (he admitted to owning fifty-four of them at one point), Willis joined the Atlantic roster of artists in 1956. He immediately returned to the R&B charts with "It's Too Late" (Atlantic 1098; 1956; #3 r&b) and "Juanita" (Atlantic 1112; 1956; #7 r&b). Early the following year, he cut what many consider to be the definitive interpretation of the blues standard, "C.C. Rider" (Atlantic 1130; #12 pop, #1 r&b). With its sinuous groove, the single earned him a new appellation, "King of the Stroll." One of the few black artists to successfully cross over to mainstream pop up to that point, he seemed poised for even greater success at the time of his death. He would have several posthumous hits, most notably "What Am I Living For"/"Hang Up My Rock and Roll Shoes" (Atlantic 1179; #1 r&b/#24 pop, #9 r&b). Album compilations of his work have been released on a regular basis up to the present day.

July 19. The Drifters' manager, George Treadwell, sacks the entire group, replacing them with Ben E. King and the Five Crowns.

July 21. The Coasters reach number one on the Top 100 (#2 Best Seller, #2 Disc Jockey) with the Leiber/Stoller-penned "Yakety Yak."

The Coasters were—along with the Platters and the Drifters—one of the first black rhythm and blues vocal groups (doo-wop) to find consistent success on the mainstream pop charts. Their entrée consisted of satirical commentaries on American popular culture, particularly the teen lifestyle, supplied by the legendary songwriting/production team of Leiber and Stoller.

The group formed in Los Angeles in 1947 as the Robins, finding success with the uptempo, r&b classics, "If It's So, Baby" (Savoy 726; 1950; #10 r&b) and "Smokey Joe's Café" (Atco 6059; 1955; #10 r&b). Eyeing the rapidly emerging rock 'n' roll market, the members—consisting of tenor Carl Gardner, baritone Billy Guy, tenor Leon Hughes, bassist Bobby Nunn, and guitarist Adolph Jacobs—assumed the name of the Coasters (a reference to their West Coast home base) and smoothed out the bluesy, rough edges characterizing the Robins' releases. Signing with Atlantic Records in 1956, who immediately assigned to Leiber and Stoller, the Coasters—now including tenor Cornell Gunther and bassist Will "Dub" Jones in place of Hughes and Nunn—enjoyed a long string of brilliantly arranged hit singles, including "Down in Mexico" (Atco 6064; 1956; #8 r&b); the private-eye send-up, "Searching" (Atco 6087; 1957; #3 pop, #1 r&b), backed by "Young Blood" (#8 pop, #2 r&b); a diatribe on parental authority, "Yakety Yak" (Atco 6116; #1 r&b); " Charlie Brown" (Atco 6132; 1959; #2 pop, #2 r&b), which featured—like "Yakety Yak"—an inventive sax break by King Curtis; a spoof on TV western heroes, "Along Came Jones" (Atco 6141; 1959; #9); "Poison Ivy" (Atco 6146; 1959; #7 pop, #1 r&b), and "Little Egypt" (Atco 6192; 6192; 1961. The animated vocal interplay between group members (undoubtedly a by-product of the Leiber and Stoller studio arrangements) played a large role in the success of these records. Like many teen-oriented artists of the time, their albums sold in limited quantities.

The Coasters split up in the mid-1960s after the hits dried up. However, they reunited later in the decade due to opportunities presented by the rock 'n' roll revival vogue. In addition to numerous LP reissues of their classic tracks, they returned to the studio with Leiber and Stoller to recut old material on *Sixteen Greatest Hits* (Trip; 1973). The group—featuring various personnel configurations led by Nunn, Gardner, and Hughes individually, and Guy and Jones together—has continued to perform live. They were inducted into the Rock and Roll Hall of Fame in 1987.

July 21. Elvis Presley begins a two-week stint atop the Best Seller listing with "Hard Headed Woman" (RCA). The single also spends a week atop the Disc Jockey poll, and peaks at number two on the Top 100.

July 28. Duane Eddy peaks at number six on the pop charts with "Rebel-'Rouser" (Jamie 1104).

Duane Eddy was one of the most successful instrumental recording artists during the rock 'n' roll era (mid-1950s to mid-1960s). His signature "twangy" guitar sound, built around staccato riffing on the lower (bass) strings, influenced surf music and countless British Invasion acts.

Born in Corning, New York, Eddy began playing guitar at age five. Relocated in Phoenix by his early teens, he began performing with local dance groups. Shortly after hooking up with Phoenix deejay, producer, and entrepreneur Lee Hazlewood, Eddy began releasing records on Dick Clark's Jamie label. During the 1958 to 1964 period, Eddy had twenty-seven charting singles, including the Top Ten singles "Rebel-'Rouser," "Forty Miles of Bad Road" (Jamie 1126; 1959), and "Because They're Young" (Jamie 1156; 1960). His LPs also sold very well for a teen artist, most notably the Top Five release, *Have 'Twangy' Guitar-Will Travel* (Jamie 3000; 1959), which remained on the *Billboard* pop album charts for eighty-two weeks.

Although the influx of British Invasion artists and changing public tastes ended the hits, various back-to-the-roots movements, beginning in the late 1960s, have helped keep Eddy in the public eye. He did production work in the 1970s, and has continued to perform regularly over the years (including oldies revival shows). He has attempted of comebacks as a recording artists, including a 1977 single, "You Are My Sunshine" (Asylum), produced by Hazlewood and featuring vocals by Willie Nelson and Waylon Jennings. He played on Art of Noise's industrial-dance treatment of "Peter Gunn," which reached the Top 50 in 1986. *Duane Eddy*, his first major-label album in fifteen years, was released in 1987, featuring assists from the likes of Ry Cooder, George Harrison, Jeff Lynne, and Paul McCartney. In 1995, he was inducted into the Rock and Roll hall of Fame.

July 28. Perez Prado reaches number one on the Top 100 with the Latin-flavored instrumental, "Patricia" (RCA). It also tops the Disc Jockey survey, and goes to number two on the Best Seller listing. A reworking of the song peaks at number sixty-five in 1962.

August 4. *Billboard* inaugurates its weekly Hot 100 chart for pop singles. Rick Nelson's "Poor Little Fool" (Imperial) holds down the top position for two weeks (#1 Best Seller 2 weeks, #2 Disc Jockey). For nearly fifteen years prior to this date, singles activity was tracked by a half-dozen different charts, including jukebox plays, sales, and radio plays. The consolidated, expanded listing reflected a desire to simplify chart reporting as well as the rapid growth of the music industry during the post-World War II period.

The Hot 100 has undergone a variety of changes over the years (see May 1991; December 5, 1998). Faced with criticism over its alleged bias against non-rhythmic songs, on February 12, 2005, *Billboard* introduced two new associated charts designed to track mass-appeal mainstream hits: the Pop 100 Chart and Pop 100 Airplay Chart. The Hot 100 also began taking into account paid digital downloads from websites such as Musicmatch, Napster, and Rhapsody.

August 11. Jack Scott peaks at number eleven on the Hot 100 with "Leroy" (Carlton 462). The A side, "My True Love," jumps to number three the following week.

Jack Scott followed in the tradition established by rockabilly stars like Elvis Presley, Carl Perkins, and Jerry Lee Lewis, placing singles on all three major charts: country, pop, and rhythm and blues. Born Jack Scafone Jr. on January 24, 1936, in Windsor, Ontario, the singer/songwriter/guitarist relocated to Hazel Park, Michigan in 1946. He first signed with ABC-Paramount in 1957, before debuting on the R&B charts with "My True Love"/"Leroy" (#5 r&b). Possessing a gospel quality to his vocals, Scott would also enjoy notable success with the mournful ballads "What in the World's Come Over You" (Top Rank 2028; 1960; #5 pop, #7 r&b) and "Burning Bridges" (Top Rank 2041; 1960; #3 pop, #5 r&b). Although no longer having hits after the early 1960s, he continued to perform well into the 1980s, particular in the Detroit area.

August 14. Elvis Presley's mother Gladys, dies of a heart attack complicated by hepatitis. She is buried at Graceland two days later.

August 18. Domenico Modugno rockets to number one on the Hot 100 and Best Seller listing with "Nel Blu Dipinto Di Bu (Volare)" (Decca), remaining there for five non-consecutive weeks. Bobby Rydell will reach the Top Five with an English language rendition of the song in 1960.

August 24. Buddy Holly marries Maria Elena Santiago, just two weeks after meeting her in Coral's New York office, where she was employed. Her allegedly proposed to her during that initial encounter.

August 25. The Elegants peak at number one on the Hot 100 (#2 Best Seller) with the doo-wop ballad, "Little Star" (Apt).

August 25. The Everly Brothers head up the Best Seller listing (#2 Hot 100) with "Bird Dog" (Cadence).

September 29. Tommy Edward's "It's All in the Game" (MGM) begins a six-week stay atop the Hot 100; it also spends three weeks at number one on the Best Seller list. The single was originally released in 1951, peaking at number eighteen.

October 5. Cliff Richard and the Shadows appear onstage together for the first time at the Victoria Hall, Hanley, U.K.

October 13. Little Anthony and the Imperials peak at number four on the Hot 100 with "Tears on My Pillow" (End 1027).

Few doo-wop groups had the long-term staying power of Little Anthony & The Imperials. They were able to assimilate the musical trends of three different decades—the R&B vocal group sound of the 1950s, 1960s soul, and the funk-inflected pop of the 1970s—in order to remain a commercially viable recording act.

Leader Anthony Gourdine (born January 8, 1940) first recorded as a member of the DuPonts in 1955 for the Winley label. He would form the Chesters in 1957; the Brooklyn-based group—who changed their name to The Imperials a year later—consisted of Clarence Collins, Tracy Lord, Glouster Rogers, and Ernest Wright Jr. After signing with End, The Imperials recorded three hits in the late 1950s, featuring Gourdine's tremulous lead vocals,: the classic "Tears On My Pillow" (#2 r&b), "So Much" (End 1036; 1959; #87 pop, #24 r&b), and tropical fantasy, "Shimmy, Shimmy, Ko-Ko-Bop" (End 1060; 1960; #24 pop, #14 r&b).

Although they failed to reach the charts for almost five years, The Imperials continued to find steady work as performers, particularly the night clubs across the country. The regained their hit-making touch in the mid-1960s with a more adult contemporary-oriented sound, first with the melodramatic "I'm On the Outside (Looking In)" (DCP 1104; 1964; #15 pop, #15 r&b), followed by "Goin' Out of My Head" (DCP 1119; 1964; #6 pop, #22 r&b) and "Hurt So Bad" (DCP 1128; 1965; #10 pop, #3 r&b).

When things went sour with DCP, The Imperials moved on to United Artists in the late 1960s, and Avco in the mid-1970s. Despite their failure to release any popular recordings since 1975, they have remained box-office staples, from the oldies circuit to Las Vegas, on the strength of a slick stage routine and backlog of old hits.

October 20. *Billboard*'s Best Seller listing is discontinued.

October 21. Just days from having split with the Crickets, Buddy Holly produces his last studio tracks in New York.

October 30. Art Blakey and His Jazz Messengers make what has been called the quintessential hard bop album, *Moanin'*.

November 10. Conway Twitty reaches number one on the Hot 100 with the Elvis Presley sound-alike, "It's Only Make Believe" (MGM), remaining there for two non-consecutive weeks.

November 17. The Kingston Trio climbs to the summit of the Hot 100 with a reworking of the folk standard, "Tom Dooley" (Capitol).

December 1. Phil Spector's teen trio, the Teddy Bears, begins a three-week run atop the Hot 100 with "To Know Him, Is To Love Him" (Dore).

December 20. Sidney Bechet, ill with lung cancer, performs for the last time at the Salle Wagram (France), ending his set with "Maryland, My Maryland."

December 22. David Seville's studio fabrication, The Chipmunks, begin a four-week stay at number one on the Hot 100. The Christmas single will return to the charts four more times: #41, 1959; #45, 1960; #39, 1961; #40, 1962.

December 25. Alan Freed's Christmas Rock 'n' Roll Spectacular kicks off in New York. The ten-day event features Frankie Avalon, Chuck Berry, Eddie Cochran, Bo Diddley, Dion, the Everly Brothers, and Jackie Wilson.

1959

❋

January 5. Coral Records releases Buddy Holly's "It Doesn't Matter Anymore"/"Raining in My Heart," his last release before the plane accident that took his life. Composed by Paul Anka, the A side will ultimately reach number thirteen on the Hot 100.

January 5. Eddie Cochran's "C'mon Everybody" peaks at number thirty-five (#6 UK). He begins shooting his "Teenage Heaven" sequence for the Hal Roach/Alan Freed production, *Go, Johnny Go!* His involvement in the film necessitates his withdrawal from "Winter Dance Party Tour," which features his friend Buddy Holly.

January 19. The Arbitron TV rating for the prior month reveals Dick Clark's *American Bandstand* as the most popular daytime show nationwide.

January 19. The Platters' remake of the Jerome Kern standard, "Smoke Gets in Your Eyes" (Mercury), begins a three-week stint at number one on the Hot 100. It will their last chart-topping single; by the following year, the most popular vocal group of the early rock era will no longer be a consistent hitmaker due to scandal, internal dissention, and changing fashions.

January 19. *Billboard* notes that there has been a decline in censorship of pop songs on radio and television. The article notes one notable exception, Link Wray's instrumental hit, "Rumble," because the title conjures up pictures of teen-gang violence. (Wray would relate that the title came from a concert where his band, the Wraymen, played the piece in an attempt to distract the participants of a gang "rumble.") When Dick Clark was directed not to state the song title on the air, he used the following introduction: "and now, here's Link Wray."

January 21. The Kingston Trio, a leading act in the then-evolving American folk music revival, is awarded its first gold record for the chart-topping single, "Tom Dooley." A southern folk song dating back to the Reconstruction era, it stood out at the time in its stark depiction of violence and psychological turmoil.

January 22. Buddy Holly makes his last recordings on a portable tape recorder in his New York City apartment, accompanied only by an automatic guitar. The resulting songs (some of which may have been created as much as two weeks earlier) include "Crying, Waiting, Hoping," "Learning the Game," "Peggy Sue Got Married," "That Makes It Tough," "That's What They Say," and "What to Do." His label, Coral, will over-dub the tracks posthumously and release them countless times in the upcoming years.

January 26. Specialty releases by "Bad Boy"/"She Said 'Yeah'," by Larry Williams, an artist whose best days are behind him. On the other hand, RCA issues "Almost 18"/"Jolie," by Roy Orbison, who will break out in a big way with a different label—the Nashville-based Monument Records—the following year.

February 2. Buddy Holly, Ritchie Valens, and the Big Bopper perform for the last time as part of the GAC "Winter Dance Party" tour, at the Surf Ballroom in Clear Lake, Iowa.

February 2. New entries to the Hot 100 include the Coasters' "Charlie Brown," at number sixty-nine, on its way to the Top Five, and Link Wray and His Wraymen's "Rawhide" in number ninety-eight, which falls far short of its predecessor, "Rumble." Already established as one of the most successful teen artists around, Rick Nelson appears on the LP charts at number twenty-four with *Ricky Sings Again*.

February 2. Chancellor Records releases Frankie Avalon's "Venus"; it will become the teen idol's biggest hit.

February 3. A plane, carrying Buddy Holly, Ritchie Valens, and the Big Bopper to Fargo, North Dakota, the next venue in the GAC Midwestern Winter tour, crashes during takeoff near Mason City, Iowa. "It Doesn't Matter Anymore," the orchestrated Paul Anka composition released by Holly shortly before the accident, becomes his last American hit and tops the British charts for three weeks beginning April 25.

February 7. New Orleans-based blues/R&B singer-guitarist Eddie Jones dies of pneumonia in New York City at age thirty-three. Best known as "Guitar Slim," he enjoyed his greatest success with "The Things I Used to Do; his flamboyant guitar work would influence a new generation of performers, most notably, Jimi Hendrix.

February 9. Lloyd Price's updated version of the blues classic, "Stagger Lee" (ABC-Paramount), starts a four-week run as the number one pop single. In the midst of a brief career revival, the New Orleans-based singer will enjoy almost as much success that year year with the Top Ten follow-ups, "Personality" and "I'm Gonna Get Married."

Born March 9, 1933, the Kenner, Louisiana native started his own band as a 16-year-old. His early string of hits—most notably, the R&B chart-topper "Lawdy Miss Clawdy"—was interrupted by a U.S. Army stint from 1953 to 1956. He would go on to form KRC Records in 1957 and become a major recording star with the ABC-Paramount label with crossover best-sellers into the early 1960s. When the hits became harder to come by, he founded the Double-L label, and shifted his focus to production and booking agency operations.

February 9. In *Billboard*, Irvin Feld, the package-tour promoter responsible for the GAC Winter Show, states, "after a long, hard pull in 1958…the rock & roll package-show business is looking up, with the best advance sales since the spring of '57." His most recent edition of the Biggest Show of Stars, set to kick off a seven-week tour March 29, in Richmond, Virginia, will feature the Coasters Bo Diddley, Little Anthony and the Imperials, Clyde McPhatter, and Lloyd Price, among others.

February 23. Buddy Holly's "It Don't Matter Anymore" appears in the Hot 100, at number eighty-two. Meanwhile, Mercury releases the Big Bopper's debut album, *Chantilly Lace*.

February 23. The late Ritchie Valens peaks at number two on the Hot 100 with his composition, "Donna" (Del Fi 4110).

The importance of Valens' short-lived career is largely symbolic in nature; he was the Latin recording artist to have an impact on the rock era charts. In his wake, would follow Dave "Baby" Cortez, Chris Montex, Sunny and the Sunglows, the Premiers, Cannibal and the Headhunters, and many others.

Born Richard Stephen Valenzuela on May 13, 1941, in Pacoima (outside Los Angeles), California, Valens learned to play guitar guitar as a youth and formed a band, the Silhouettes, while in high school. He signed a contract with Del-Fi Records in spring 1958, and just missed the Top Forty that fall with "Come On, Let's Go" (Del-Fi 4106). He followed with a double-sided hit, "Donna"/"La Bamba" (Del-Fi 4110; 1958–1959). Ironically, the latter track (#23), based on a traditional Mexican wedding song, has proven to be his most popular recording (a 1987 biopic based on his life, and featuring the music of Los Lobos, was entitled *La Bamba*).

At this point in time, Valens was in great demand as a performer, appearing on national television programs and package tours. On February 3, 1959, a small plane carrying Valens, Buddy Holly, and the Big Bopper (aka J. P. Richardson) crashed near Clear Lake, Iowa immediately following a concert. His studio recordings, which essentially fit on one compact disc, have been released in many editions since his death.

March 9. Frankie Avalon begins a five-week reign of the pop charts with the quintessential teen idol classic, "Venus" (Chancellor). He will have plenty of competition within the genre that year, with Fabian, Paul Anka, Ricky Nelson, Bobby Rydell, Bobby Vee, and Freddy Cannon all achieving bestsellers.

March 10. RCA releases Elvis Presley's "I Need Your Love Tonight"/"A Fool Such as I." The following day, the label sends Presley—then stationed at a West German army base—a gold disc based on advance orders of one million copies.

March 15. Legendary jazz saxophonist Lester Young succumbs to a heart attack in New York City at age forty-nine.

March 16. Just two years after enjoying his first hit—"Sittin' in the Balcony" (Liberty; #18), Eddie Cochran struggles with a recording slump; "Teenage Heaven" reached number ninety-nine for a week before disappearing from the charts. After recording a John D. Loudermilk tribute to Buddy Holy, Ritchie Valens, and the Big Bopper, "Three Stars" (which isn't released until several years following his own death), Cochran forms a road band—the Kelly Four, comprised of saxophonist Mike Henderson, drummer Gene Ridgio, bassist Dave Schreiber, and pianist Jim Stivers—and tours the United States for much of the year.

March 16. The first American rock and roll package tour geared to European audiences is announced. Featuring

Bobby Darin, Duane Eddy, Dale Hawkins, the Poni Tails, and Conway Twitty (with British artist Cliff Richard scheduled to appear in some of his homeland's venues), it will commence April 22 in London.

March 19. Massachusetts Representative Torbert McDonald introduces a bill to limit discounted postage rates for recordings to items possessing "educational or cultural value." According to the *Congressional Record*, he criticizes "postal rates which subsidize rock & roll, jazz and hillbilly musicians—that is, subsidizing musical illiterates by designating *all* phonograph records as educational material."

March 23. Hank Ballard and the Midnighters peak at number eighty-seven on the Hot 100 with "Teardrops on Your Letter" (King 5171).

One of the great rhythm and blues vocal groups of the 1950s, the Midnighters—through a combination of bad luck and ill-advised career moves—just missed the big league status attained by contemporaries like the Platters and the Drifters. Nevertheless, they played a vital role in the development of popular music prior to the British Invasion.

The Detroit-based group—whose members included lead singer and songwriter Hank Ballard (born November 18, 1936), baritone Lawson Smith (b. 1936), bass singer Norman Thrasher (b. 1936; replaced by Charles Sutton), tenor Henry Booth (b. 1935; replaced by Sonny Woods), and guitarist Billy Davis (b. 1936; replaced by Arthur Porter)—formed as the Royals in 1952. Signing with Federal Records, in Cincinnati, they first made the R&B charts with the Johnny Otis composition, "Every Beat of My Heart" (Federal; 1952), which was revived by Gladys Knight and the Pips in 1961.

Ballard—who received his first break from Otis when signed as part of the Little Esther Revue—would join the Royals in 1953. Shortly thereafter, the group became known as the Midnighters when their parent label, King Records, issued a recording contract to the "5" Royals. Their first hit following the name change, "Get It" (Federal; 1953), was banned by many radio stations due to sexually explicit lyrics. The following year, Ballard's "Work With Me Annie"—which borrowed thematically from "Get It"—achieved even greater success, spawning a best-selling answer song, Etta James's "Wallflower," and a long string of "Annie" songs (e.g., "Sexy Ways," "Annie Had a Baby") as recorded by the Midnighters.

Ballard went solo in late 1958, releasing his material on King. His composition, "The Twist"—despite being released as the B-side of "The Letter," spurred the rise of a new teen dance. *American Bandstand* MC, Dick Clark, sensing the commercial potential for the song, pitched it to the Cameo-Parkway label that ultimately brought in up-and-coming vocalist, Chubby Checker, to produce a highly derivative cover version. Although few people were aware of his role in the creation of one of the most successful recordings of the rock era, Ballard did go on to produce a few pop hits of his own, most notably, "Finger Poppin' Time" and "Let's Go, Let's Go, Let's Go."

March 24. Atlantic Records releases "There Goes My Baby," by the reconstituted Drifters, now featuring lead singer Ben E. King. The single, which will top the R&B charts for two weeks in July, will be considered a landmark in pop music production, particularly the orchestral arrangement utilized by Leiber and Stoller.

With the possible exception of the Dells, the Drifters were more successful in adapting to stylistic changes within the pop music scene than any other doo-wop group. Beginning as a rhythm and blues act in the early 1950s, they shifted to a more pop-oriented sound to remain leading hitmakers throughout the classic rock 'n' roll era, and were still regularly denting the charts at the peak of the British Invasion, folk rock, and Motown Soul.

Clyde McPhatter, formerly lead singer with Billy Ward's Dominoes, formed the Drifters in 1953 with second tenor Gerhard Thrasher, baritone Andrew Thrasher, and bass Bill Pinkney. Before McPhatter entered the Army in the mid-1950s, the group enjoyed a strong of R&B hits featuring his smooth, sexy tenor voice, most notably "Money Honey" (Atlantic 1006; 1953; #1 R&B eleven weeks), "Such A Night"/ "Lucille" (Atlantic 1019; 1954; #2/#7 R&B), "Honey Love" (Atlantic 1029; 1954; #1 R&B 8 weeks, #21 pop), "Bip Bam" (Atlantic 1043; 1954; #7 R&B), "White Christmas" (Atlantic 1048; 1954/1955/1956; #2/#5/#12 R&B), "What 'Cha Gonna Do" (Atlantic 1055; #2), "Adorable"/"Steamboat" (Atlantic 1078; 1955; #1/#5 R&B), and "Ruby Baby" (Atlantic 1089; 1956; #10).

Following a period of diminished record sales—and various personnel changes—the group disbanded in 1958. Because the Drifters had signed a multi-year contract with New York's Apollo Theater, their manager recruited another group, the Five Crowns, to fill the void. Assisted by the songwriting/production team of Leiber and Stoller, the new Drifters quickly outstripped their predecessors with releases like "There Goes My Baby" (Atlantic 2025; 1959; #2), reputedly the first R&B recording to utilize a sophisticated string arrangement, "Dance with Me" (Atlantic 2040; 1959; #15), "This Magic Moment" (Atlantic 2050; 1960; #16), "Save the Last Dance for Me" (Atlantic 2071; 1960; #1), and "I Count the Tears" (Atlantic 2087; 1960; #17).

When lead singer Ben E. King—who would record the solo hits "Spanish Harlem" (Atlantic 6185; 1960–1961; #10) and "Stand By Me" (Atlantic 6194; 1961; #4)—departed, the Drifters remained successful with recordings such as "Up On the Roof" (Atlantic 2162; 1962; #5) and "On Broadway" (Atlantic 2182; 1963; #9), which featured Rudy Lewis singing lead. Following his death in 1963, Johnny Moore became the frontman for bestsellers such as "Under the Boardwalk" (Atlantic 2237; 1964; #4) and "Saturday Night at the Movies" (Atlantic 2260; 1964; #18).

By 1967 the hits had stopped coming, although the group continued to perform well into the 1970s. The act was revived in the mid-1970s to capitalize on the oldies circuit. Releases of both new material and updated versions of the group's old hits, however, failed to compete with regular reissues of the classic Drifters recordings.

March 30. *Billboard* reports on the innovative teaching methods being employed by an Orange County Community College (Middleton, New York) professor. He recently included psychology test questions on the Coasters' "Charlie Brown," e.g., "Is Charlie Brown a conformist or a noncomformist?"; "Can you differentiate between his life-space and his environment?"

April 6. Brook Benton peaks at number three on the Hot 100 with "It's Just a Matter of Time" (Mercury 71394).

One of the premier song stylists of the late 1950s and early 1960s, Brook Benton fused the latter day crooner tradition with the mellower side of rhythm and blues best exemplified by the likes of Clyde McPhatter and Sam Cooke. His rich, velvety baritone stood out during an era dominated by higher-pitched tenor voices. Furthermore, he was a songwriter of considerable repute.

Born Benjamin Franklin Peay on September 19, 1931, in Camden, South Carolina, he sang with the Camden Jubilee Singers during his teens. He relocated to New York in 1948, joining another gospel group, Bill Landford's Langfordaires, shortly thereafter. Benton moved on to the Jerusalem Stars in 1951, before recording more secular fare under his own name for Okeh two years later. Later in the decade he teamed with songwriter Clyde Otis; their early collaborative successes included McPhatter's "A Lover's Question," the Diamonds' "The Stroll," and Nat King Cole's "Looking Back."

Benton continued to pursue a solo singing career, recording for the Vik label and then signing with Mercury in 1958. He found mainstream acceptance with "It's Just a Matter of Time" (#1 r&b nine weeks), a song he co-wrote with Otis and Belford Hendricks. He would go on to have eighteen gold records, including the Benton-Otis compositions, "Endlessly" (Mercury 71478; 1959; #16 pop, #1 r&b four weeks), "Kiddio" (Mercury 71652; 1960; #7 pop, #1 r&b nine weeks), "The Boll Weevil Song" (Mercury 71820; 1961; #2 pop, #2 r&b), "Baby (You Got What It Takes)" (Mercury 71565; 1960; #5 pop, #1 r&b ten weeks), and "A Rockin' Good Way" (Mercury 71629; 1960; #7 pop, #1 r&b four weeks), the latter two being duets with Dinah Washington.

The latter half of the 1960s, which included stints with RCA and Reprise, was a fallow period marked by few hits. He would return to prominence in 1970, however, with the Tony Joe White-penned, "Rainy Night in Georgia" (Cotillion 44057; #4 pop, #1 r&b). When follow-up releases failed to take off, he drifted into religious music, his most notable collaboration coming with the Dixie Flyers. He died April 9, 1988, of complications from spinal meningitis.

April 6. Referring to it as "the most unlikely meeting of the minds this year," *Billboard* includes an announcement by Mitch Miller—Columbia Records A&R head, producer, arranger, recording artist, and longtime spokesman against rock 'n' roll—that he is working out a number of freelance deals with the Leiber and

Stoller production team. The motivation behind this move seems to be that label's singles sales are down considerably; the article concludes that "what Columbia needs is some good, swinging rock & roll records."

April 13. The Fleetwoods begin a four-week hold on the top rung of the Hot 100 with "Come Softly To Me." The Seattle-based trio's main claim to fame consists of their ability to meld the soft vocal harmony sound of early 1950s groups like the four Aces and the Hilltoppers with an indescribable teen angst typifying the teen idol genre.

April 13. The Hot 100 features two future classics as new entries at numbers ninety-nine and one hundred: Chuck Berry's "Little Queenie" (Chess) and Wilbert Harrison's "Kansas City" (Fury), respectively. Harrison's remake of the Leiber and Stoller R&B standard, "K.C. Lovin'," will occupy the number one position on the pop charts beginning May 18. He will not enjoy another hit of note until 1969 with "Let's Work Together."

April 20. Buddy Holly tops the British charts with "It Doesn't Matter Anymore."

April 20. Dolly Parton's debut recording, "Puppy Love," is released by the Gold Band label. A *Billboard* capsule review states, "She sounds about twelve years old" (she is in fact age thirteen). It would later be a hit for Donny Osmond.

April 22. The last rock 'n' roll film to feature Alan Freed, *Go, Johnny, Go!*, premieres. A typical blend of thin plotting and engaging music, it includes staged performances by Chuck Berry, the Cadillacs, Jo Ann Campbell, Eddie Cochran, the Flamingoes, Harvey Fuqua, Ritchie Valens, and Jackie Wilson.

April 24. *Your Hit Parade* is last broadcast on television, a casualty of the rock 'n' roll craze.

May 4. With Wilbert Harrison's rendition newly positioned at the top of the Hot 100, two more versions of "Kansas City" make an appearance: Hank Ballard and the Midnighters at number seventy-three and Rocky Olson at number ninety-eight.

May 4. Dick Clark announces that the inaugural film to be issued by his recently formed production company, Drexel Films Corp., will be *Harrison High*. Based on a novel by John Farris, it will include Clark playing a high-school teacher; both Fabian and Bobby Darin are allegedly vying for the lead role. Drexel Executive VP Chuck Reeves states that the movie "will place a special emphasis on the lives of decent teenagers who make up the vast majority of today's young adult population."

May 4. The newly established National Academy of Recording Arts and Sciences announce the first annual Grammy Award winners. Ross Bagdasarian (aka David Seville) is the most feted artist, his "The Chipmunk Song" garnering trophies for Best Recording for Children, Best Comedy Performance, and Best Engineered Record. Other notable victors include Domenico Modugno's "Volare" (Record of the Year), Henry Mancini's *Peter Gunn* (Album of the Year), the Champs' "Tequila" (Best R&B Performance), and the Kingston Trio's "Tom Dooley" (Best C&W Performance).

May 9. *Melody Maker* introduces a "Juke Box Top 20" chart compiled from tw hundred machines across the United Kingdom.

May 11. Dave "Baby" Cortez claims the top spot on the pop charts for the only time in his career with the uptempo instrumental, "The Happy Organ."

May 11. George Jones peaks at number seventy-three on the Hot 100 with "White Lightning" (Mercury 71406).

George Jones has been termed the "Rolls Royce of Country Singers"; his nasal, blues-inflected style has profoundly influenced three generations of hard country song stylists. His studio work has been responsible for raising a considerable number of songs to classic status, including "She Thinks I Still Care" (United Artists 424; 1962), "The Race Is On" (United Artists 751; 1964), "Walk Through This World With Me" (Musicor 1226; 1967), "Golden Ring" (Epic 50099; 1976), and "He Stopped Loving Her Today" (Epic 50867; 1980).

Born into a musical family, Jones began performing at an early age in the Beaumont, Texas, area. Returning from a stint with the Marines in Korea, his performing skills attracted the attention of Starday

Records executive H. W. "Pappy" Dailey. He recorded four hits for the Houston-based label prior to 1957, most notably "Why, Baby, Why" (Starday 202; 1955). Shifting to Mercury, he continued to cut both rockabilly and country material, reaching number one for the first time with the up tempo novelty song, "White Lightning" (Mercury 71406), in early 1959.

Still active recording in the twenty-first century, Jones has enjoyed an unrivalled career of country chart success. According to Joel Whitburn's *Top Country Singles 1944–1988* (compiled from *Billboard* magazine), Jones charted 144 times, second only to Eddy Arnold's 145. While Jones overtook Arnold prior to the 1990s, his appeal has remained confined largely to a country audience. In contrast, country stars with comparable recording careers (e.g., Arnold, Johnny Cash, Willie Nelson) have possessed considerable crossover appeal. This can be explained by Jones' predisposition for recording material concerned with drinking and two-timing women (two timeworn country themes often ridiculed by American popular culture analysts) as well as the conviction conveyed by his peculiarly aching vocals.

Considerations of his huge body of recorded work notwithstanding, the Jones legacy was also built around the larger-than-life details of his personal life; his self-destructive drinking habits, his failed marriages (particularly to Tammy Wynette, which inspired the moniker, "Mr. and Mrs. Country Music"), record label squabbles, and a near-fatal car crash in the late 1990s. As a result, his music has acquired added stature from its perceived autobiographical dimension.

May 11. Elvis Presley goes number one on the British charts with "A Fool Such as I"/"I Need Your Love Tonight."

May 14. Jazz clarinetist/saxophonist Sidney Bechet dies on his sixty-second birthday.

May 18. Wilbert Harrison reaches number one on the Hot 100 with the Leiber/Stoller composition, "Kansas City" (Fury), remaining there for two weeks.

May 29. Herndon Stadium, Atlanta, is the scene of one of the first rock 'n' roll festivals. More than nine thousand spectators brave rainy weather to see Ruth Brown, Ray Charles, the Drifters, B.B. King, and Jimmy Reed, among others.

June 1. Johnny Horton's "The Battle of New Orleans" (Columbia) begins a six-week stay atop the pop charts. Horton will remain a hot crossover recording commodity with the best-selling singles "Sink the Bismarck" and "North to Alaska" before dying in a car accident on November 5, 1960.

June 1. *Billboard* notes that the year has seen fewer million-sellers—and more bombs—than in the immediate past, attributing this to the limits of an overly saturated marketplace. However, the tabloid also comments ominously that some teens are able to forego purchases by taping the latest singles off of the radio.

June 5. Bob Zimmerman graduates from Hibbing (Minnesota) High School. Considered something of a rebel in his hometown, he will soon be enrolling at the University of Minnesota. Rather than focusing on his studies, he will quickly make a name for himself playing at campus coffee houses as Bob Dylan.

June 12. With albums by rock 'n' roll artists still a relatively rare occurance, Chess releases two early classics, Chuck Berry's *Chuck Berry on Top* and Bob Diddley's *Go Go Bo Diddley*.

June 29. Dee Clark peaks at number eighteen on the Hot 100 with "Just Keep It Up" (Abner 1026).

Dee Clark was one of the distinctive exponents of the Chicago Soul style. An extremely versatile singer; while his warm tenor voice—very much reminiscent of Sam Cooke's early pop period—was best suited for low-key ballads, he was also convincing with more intensively dramatic material as typified by his biggest hit, "Raindrops" (Vee-Jay 383; 1961; #2 pop, #3 r&b).

Born Delectus (some sources say "Delecta") Clark, in Blythsville, Arkansas, on November 7, 1938; in 1941, he moved to Chicago with his family. In his early teens, he was a member of a vocal trio, the Hambone Kids, who recorded briefly with Okeh Records in 1952. He would move on to another group, the Goldentones (later known as the Cool Gents), the following year. After winning a Chicago talent contest in 1955, deejay Herb Kent brought them to the attention of the local Vee-Jay label. The company would credit their 1956 recordings to "the Delegates."

Vee-Jay encouraged Clark to go solo, signing him to their subsidiary, Falcon (renamed Abner Records in

1958). Despite a number of commercially unsuccessful releases, he obtained the services of The Upsetters when the band's frontman, Little Richard, entered the ministry. Shortly thereafter, Clark broke into the national spotlight in late 1958 with "Nobody But You" (Abner 1019; #21 pop, #3 r&b). He remained a consistent hit-maker until the onset of the British Invasion, most notably with "Just Keep It Up" (#9 r&b), "Hey Little Girl" (Abner 1029; 1959; #20 pop, #2 r&b), "How About That" (Abner 1032; 1960; #33 pop, #10 r&b), and the Clark-Phillip Upchurch composition, "Raindrops."

With Vee-Jay experiencing financial difficulties, Clark jumped to the Constellation label. While he remained active for a time as a performer, however, his dance number, "Crossfire Time" (Constellation 108; #92), released in Fall 1963, would be his last charting single.

June 29. Dick Clark announces plans to work with package-tour promoter Irvin Feld, forming Clark-Feld Productions; the origin of the Dick Clark Caravan of Stars live stage shows. The successful formula has Clark (who won't appear on tours) booking and rehearsing a variety of contemporary rock acts, each of which perform two or three songs per show backed by one tour band. There will be four caravans per year, with the inaugural tour focusing on the East Coast from September 18 to November 8.

July 11. Joan Baez participates in her first recording, done live—with Bob Gibson—at the Newport Folk Festival. She will soon assume a leading role in the folk music revival with a succession of Vanguard LP featuring her crystal-clear soprano voice.

July 13. Paul Anka begins a four-week stay atop the Hot 100 with his own composition, "Lonely Boy" (ABC Paramount). It is culled from the soundtrack to *Girls Town* (starring Mamie Van Doren and Mel Torme), Anka's first Hollywood film. He will go on to appear in *The Private Lives of Adam & Eve*, *Look in Any Window*, and *The Longest Day*—all featuring theme songs which he has written and recorded.

July 13. The Falcons peak at number seventeen on the Hot 100 with "You're So Fine" (Unart 2013).

The Falcons are best remembered for the later solo success of members Eddie Floyd and Wilson Pickett. Formed in early 1959 by baritone Rice, the Detroit-based group originally included tenor Joe Stubbs, the brother of Four Tops frontman Levi Stubbs, bass singer Willie Schoefield, guitarist Lance Finnie, and Floyd as lead vocalist. On the strength of their performances in local venues, they landed a recording contract in short order with Unart Records. Electing to record a Finnie-Schoefield composition, "You're So Fine" (Unart), the Falcons found themselves with a nationwide smash right out of the box.

Finding a follow-up hit proved more elusive, but the group's fortunes improved with the addition of gravelly-voiced Pickett as lead singer in late 1961. His distinctive style was evident in their next single, "I Found A Love" (LuPine), released in March 1962. Unfortunately, Pickett decided to strike out on his own later in the year, signing with the Double-L label in 1963, and ultimately achieving superstar status as an Atlantic artist in the mid-1960s. The group's commercial potential was effectively ended when Floyd also opted for a solo career, beginning a long tenure with the Stax roster in 1966.

July 13. The Flamingos peak at number eleven on the Hot 100 with "I Only Have Eyes for You" (End 1046).

The Flamingos were one of the truly great R&B vocal groups; they were without equal as ballad interpreters. The core of the group, cousins Zeke Carey (first tenor) and Jake Carey (bass), grew up in Baltimore, playing ball with neighbor Sonny Til, who went on to fame heading the seminal doo-wop ensemble, the Orioles. They relocated to Chicago around 1949, forming the Flamingos in 1952. Other members included another set of cousins, first tenor Johnny Carter and baritone Paul Wilson, and lead singer Earl Lewis. Lewis would be fired early on for, in his words, missing rehearsals, spending too much time with girls, and religious differences. He moved on to the Five Echoes and was replaced by Sollie McElroy.

In the meantime, the Flamingos began appearing regularly in nightclubs and won a series of local amateur contests. After a failed audition with United in early 1952, the group was offered a contract with the other notable Chicago R&B record company at the time, Chance. While the group allegedly never received any money, they cut six classic records for the label through 1954, most notably, "Golden Teardrops" (#1145; 1953), believed by some fans to represent a junkie's letter to his girlfriend.

With Chance in financial trouble, the Flamingos switched to Al Benson's Parrot Records, releasing three singles for the label in 1954. This amounted to a transitional period, with McElroy departing due to personal differences (he would later sing with the Moroccos, Nobels, and Chanteurs)—he was replaced by Nate Nelson, formerly with Chicago's Velvetones—and the death of manager Ralph Leon, making it necessary for group members to master his responsibilities.

They would find that Leon had been negotiating a contract with Checker, where they would enjoy their earliest chart hits, "I'll Be Home" (#830; 1956; #5 r&b), which failed to achieve major crossover sales due to Pat Boone's pop cover, and "A Kiss From Your Lips" (#837; 1956; #12 r&b). The group temporarily suspended activities when Carter and Zeke Carey (he would return in 1958) were drafted in late 1956; they regrouped early the following year, however, adding Tommy Hunt, formerly with the Five Echoes, and Terry Johnson to the line-up. In 1957-1958, they recorded at least four discs for Decca, although still legally tied to Checker as a result of Nelson's solo contract with the company.

In late 1958, the Flamingos moved to George Goldner's New York-based End label. With the sweet-voiced Hunt replacing Nelson as lead, the group enjoyed its greatest pop success with the likes of "Lovers Never Say Goodbye" (End 1035; 1959; #52 pop, #25 r&b); "I Only Have Eyes For You" (#3 r&b), with its ethereal arrangement of the 1934 Ben Selvin hit); the Sam Cooke composition, "Nobody Loves Me Like You" (#1068; 1960; #30 pop, #23 r&b), and "Mio Amore" (#1073; 1960; #74 pop, #27 r&b).

When no more hits were forthcoming, the Flamingos returned to Checker in the mid-1960s. Nelson would join the Platters in 1966; he died of a heart attack June 1, 1984. Now committed to the soul vogue, they managed to graze the charts with "The Boogaloo Party" (Philips 40347; 1966; #93 pop, #22 r&b), "Dealin' (Groovin' With Feelin')" (Julman 506; 1969; #48 r&b), and "Buffalo Soldier" (Polydor 14019; 1970; #86 pop, #28 r&b).

July 16. The Coasters record "Poison Ivy" at Atlantic's New York City studios. Written and produced, as usual, by Leiber and Stoller, it was engineered by Tom Dowd.

July 17. Jazz vocalist Billie Holiday dies at age forty-four from liver complications while in a New York City hospital on the heels of an arrest for possessing heroin in her room. Her creative period in the late 1930s and early 1940s—which greatly influenced contemporary jazz singers and instrumentalists alike—was followed by ill health, numerous drug arrests, the loss of her New York City cabaret license, and a loss of artistic direction.

July 27. Cliff Richard tops the British charts for the first time with "Living Doll."

August 6. ABC-Paramount secures the U.S. rights to release the British hit, "Livin' Doll," as recorded by teen idol Cliff Richard. However, Richard fails to make a big splash stateside, his biggest hit coming much later with "Devil Woman" (1976).

August 10. Detectives, acting on a tip from an employee of the Sheraton Gibston Hotel, Cincinnati, arrest the four male members of the Platters—Alex Hodge, David Lynch, Paul Robi, and Tony Williams— in a room with four nineteen-year-old women, all in various stages of undress. The women are charged with prostitution, lewdness, and assignation, while the men, who had wrapped up a three-day engagement at the hotel that evening, were charged with aiding and abetting the three crimes. Although all of them will be acquitted in December, the public furor—widely considered to be driven by racism—will severely undercut the group's career.

August 10. Elvis Presley climbs to the summit of the Hot 100 with "A Big Hunk O' Love" (RCA 7600), remaining there for two weeks.

August 10. Dinah Washington begins a two-week stint at number two on the Hot 100 with "What a Diff'rence a Day Makes" (Mercury 71435).

Although she failed to achieve prolonged crossover success, Dinah Washington was one of the most popular R&B singers of the post-World War II era, highly regarded for her vocal control and extraordinarily clear diction. She exerted a major influence on soul artists through her incorporation of gospel and jazz phrasing into an R&B-pop context.

Born Ruth Jones on August 29, 1924, in Tuscaloosa, Alabama, she moved to Chicago with her family as a child and first learned to sing in the St. Luke's Baptist Church choir, eventually becoming its director. She began appearing in local night clubs after an amateur contest at the Regal Theater as a fifteen-year-old.

She briefly returned to gospel music as pianist and lead singer for the Sallie Martin's Singers (1940–1941), but from that point onward remained a fixture in clubs. Jazz bandleader Lionel Hampton heard her at the Garrick Club in 1943, and immediately hired her; she took on her stage name at this time, singing with Hampton until 1946.

Washington made her earliest solo records for the Los Angeles-based Apollo in 1945, and then signed with Mercury the following year. After a number of near-misses, she broke through in the R&B market with "Am I Asking Too Much" (Mercury), achieving pop success as well with singles like "I Want to Be Loved" (Mercury), "Teach Me Tonight" (Mercury), "What a Diff'rence a Day Makes," and "Unforgettable" (Mercury; 1959). In addition to coming up big in duets with labelmate Brook Benton, she recorded jazz material on Mercury and EmArcy with a wide range of musicians, including Clifford Brown, Maynard Ferguson, Wynton Kelly, and Clark Terry.

Washington switched to Roulette Records in 1962, but garnered only a few minor pop hits. She would die of an overdose of alcohol and drugs, in Detroit, on December 4, 1963. She was inducted into the Rock and Roll Hall of Fame in 1993.

August 17. Ray Charles tops the R&B charts for two weeks (#6 pop) with his gospel-styled composition, "What'd I Say" (Atlantic). It becomes his first million seller; Jerry Lee Lewis, Bobby Darin, and Elvis Presley all record commercially successful covers of the song in the 1960s.

August 24. The Browns—veterans of the white gospel and country & western circuits—begin a four-week run at the top of the Hot 100 with unabashedly sentimental ballad, "The Three Bells" (RCA).

August 24. A *Billboard* article—bearing the headline "Rock and Roll Ain't Ready For Ol' Rockin' Chair Yet"—notes that the genre, seemingly declining in popularity the previous year, is alive and well with relative newcomers like the Brook Benton, the Drifters, Everly Brothers, and Ricky Nelson augmenting more established stars such as Elvis Presley, Fats Domino, and Lloyd Price. At present, rock 'n' roll recordings account for approximately one-half of the Hot 100.

August 31. Bobby Darin's "Mack the Knife" (Atco) enters the Hot 100. An English adaptation of "Moritat," a show-stopping number from Kurt Weill and Bertolt Brecht's *Three-Penny Opera*, the single heralds Darin's shift from teen idol to Las Vegas, post-big band pop singer. It is all part of his long-range plan to become the most successful artist in the entertainment industry.

September 4. Citing a rash of violence in New York City such as the stabbing deaths of two teenagers by a seventeen-year-old, radio station WCBS bans all renditions of "Mack the Knife."

September 7. Dick Clark's four-day stage revue at the Michigan State Fair attracts some fifteen thousand customers, the most in the fair's 110-year run. Headliners include Frankie Avalon, LaVern Baker, Freddie Cannon, the Coasters, Duane Eddy, Annette Funicello, Jan and Dean, Lou Rawls, Bobby Rydell, Santo and Johnny, and Skip and Flip.

September 21. The Canadian instrumental duo, Santo & Johnny, begin a two-week stint atop the Hot 100. Their sound is something of an anachronism, featuring a Hawaiian guitar lead in much the same style that influenced country & western music several decades earlier.

October 5. Bobby Darin reaches number one on the pop charts with "Mack the Knife," remaining there for nine non-consecutive weeks.

October 5. Nina Simone peaks at number eighteen on the Hot 100 with "I Loves You, Porgy" (Bethlehem 11021).

One of the more jazz-oriented pop artists of the 1960s, singer/pianist/composer Nina Simone brought a refined sense of style to her recorded work unrivaled among her peers. Born Eunice Waymon on February 21, 1933, in Tryon, South Carolina, she went on to attend the New York City-based Julliard School of Music. Her commercial breakthrough came with the release of "I Loves You, Porgy" (#2 r&b), culled from George and Ira Gershwin's folk opera, *Porgy and Bess*. Although she continued to enjoy periodic hit singles—most notably, "To Be Young, Gifted and Black" (RCA 0269; 1969; #76 pop, #8 r&b)—Simone more a significantly greater impact within the album sector. Her most popular LPs included *Nina at Newport* (Colpix 412; 1961; #23), *Nina Simone in Concert* (Philips 135; 1964; #102), *I Put a Spell on You*

(Philips 172; 1965; #99), and *Wild Is the Wind* (Philips 207; 1966; #110). By the 1970s she recorded less and less frequently, concentrating instead on her commitments to political activism.

October 9. Bobby Darin, age twenty-two, becomes the youngest headliner at the Sands Hotel's Copa Room in Las Vegas (Johnny Mathis had previously set the record as a twenty-three-year-old). Darin is a big success, paving the way for future bookings at gambling mecca.

October 12. Neil Sedaka's "Oh! Carol" (RCA) enters the Hot 100 at number seventy-three. Written by Sedaka for his high school friend and fellow Brill Building associate Carole King, it would peak at number nine, and remain on the charts for eighteen weeks. King would not only compose many rock standards—including "Will You Love Me Tomorrow," "The Loco-Motion," and "One Fine Day"—but help spearhead the singer/songwriter movement of the early 1970s.

October 19. Tommy Facenda debuts at number ninety-seven in the Hot 100 with "High School, U.S.A." The novelty single features dozens of differing versions, each one mentioning the high schools for a different city.

October 25. Scott Muni, a DJ at New York City's WMCA, attracts industry attention as the MC for a charity dance featuring the Four Lads, Roy Hamilton, and Clyde McPhatter, among others. The event is a sellout, attracting sixty-five hundred fans to Manhattan's New York Coliseum.

October 26. The Everly Brothers inform the media that they might leave Cadence when their current record deal expires. The duo adds that preliminary discussions have already taken place with prospective suitors RCA and Warner Bros.

October 26. The Isley Brothers peak at number forty-seven on the Hot 100 with "Shout – Part 1" (RCA 7588). It would return to the pop charts in 1962, reaching number ninety-four.

One of the more versatile and lasting soul-funk bands to achieve recording success, the Isley Brothers—like singer Sam Cooke—provided an early template for minority artists with regard to taking creative and business control of career matters. In addition to establishing their own label, T-Neck, as early as 1964, they wrote timeless classics such as "Twist and Shout" (Wand 124; 1962; #17) and the Grammy-winning "It's Your Thing" (T-Neck 901; 1969; #2) and provided a forum for developing talented young musicians like guitarist Jimi Hendrix.

The group was originally comprised of three Cincinnati-based brothers—Ronald, Rudolph, and O'Kelly Isley—all of whom had roots in gospel singing. They recorded singles for several small labels in the late 1950s before achieving a minor hit with "Shout." Stints with Atlantic, Wand (Scepter), United Artists, and Tamla (Motown)—while resulting in occasional chart successes, most notably "This Old Heart of Mine" (Tamla 269; 1966; #12 US, #47 UK)—proved problematical, with these companies attempting to make the Isleys conform a preconceived formulaic sound. As a result, the trio relaunched their own label in early 1969 and incorporated additional family members: brothers Ernie Isley (guitar, percussion) and Marvin Isley (bass, percussion) and cousin Chris Jasper (keyboards), who also composed many of their 1970s hits. Between 1973 and 1983, the Isleys released nine consecutive gold or platinum albums; their popularity was based on a seamless blend of pulsating dance rhythms, Ronald's soulful lead vocals (equally adept at silky-smooth ballads and hard-driving funk), and socially conscious lyrics, punctuated by Ernie Isley's Hendrix-inspired guitar riffs. Their most successful recordings during this period included *3 + 3* (T-Neck 32453; 1972), which featured the sexy, uptempo workout, "That Lady" (T-Neck 2251; 1973; #6 US, #14 UK); *The Heat Is On* (T-Neck 33536; 1975; #1); *Harvest For the World* (T-Neck 33809; 1976; #9 US, #50 UK); *Go For Your Guns* (T-Neck 34432; 1977; #6 US, #46 UK); and *Showdown* (T-Neck 34930; 1978; #4 US, #46 UK).

With hit recordings becoming increasingly scarce in 1983, the group reverted back to the original trio following the departure of the younger family members to form Isley, Jasper, Isley. The Isleys became a duo in early 1986 following O'Kelly's death. In late 1988, Ernie and Marvin returned to the fold; the group as now billed as the Isley Brothers featuring Ronald Isley. They were inducted into the Rock and Roll Hall of Fame in 1992, and continue to tour and record to the present day.

November. Ray Charles signs a three-year contract with ABC Paramount. Although Atlantic had wanted to retain Charles, the label had been unable to match ABC's offer of a large advance and ownership of his compositions via the establishment of the publishing company, Tangerine.

November 1. The Spacemen enter the Rhythm & Blues chart at number twenty-four with "The Clouds." Their only hit recording, it remains on the survey for eighteen weeks, peaking at number one.

November 9. RCA A&R producers/executives Hugo Peretti and Luigi Creatore offer Sam Cooke $100,000 to sign with RCA pending the expiration of his Keen Records contract.

November 9. The first day of what *Billboard* refers to as "one of the most frantic weeks in the history of the music business," as the congressional investigation of disc jockey payola gains momentum.

Payola—narrowly defined as payment (i.e., cash or gifts) for radio airplay—has been a radio fixture since the medium's inception. The practice flourished among disc jockeys playing Tin Pan Alley pop, country, rhythm and blues, and rock 'n' roll. Payola helped augment the income of a poorly paid profession; furthermore, it enabled the new music reach its intended audience, no matter how small the label on which it appeared. By the late 1950s, the proliferation of independent labels recording rock had broken the stranglehold of the majors—in particular, Columbia, RCA, and Decca—on the sales and airplay of popular records.

The American Society of Composers, Authors and Publishers (ASCAP) also had reason to be unhappy with the state of affairs at that time. The publishing house had become a dominant force in the music business through its licensing agreements regarding the sales of sheet music, piano rolls, and the recordings of Tin Pan Alley songs. A battle between ASCAP and the radio stations—whose programming had become increasingly committed to airing recorded music during the latter 1930s and early 1940s—spurred the latter to boycott ASCAP material and establish their own publishing firm, Broadcast Music Incorporated (BMI). ASCAP's history of ignoring black and country music compositions, combined with the tendency of many radio stations to target regional tastes overlooked by the major networks (ABC, NBC, and CBS) enabled BMI to secure a near monopoly on the material in these categories. The advent of rock 'n' roll, itself largely a product of the marriage of rhythm and blues and country, assured the continued dominance of BMI within the youth music market.

Therefore, it appeared to be a case of protecting vested interests when ASCAP pushed for the House Legislative Oversight subcommittee to broaden its inquiry into corrupt broadcasting practices—centered up to 1959 on television quiz programs—to cover payola practices within radio. According to the perspective held by many within the record industry, the payola investigation would assist in stamping out rock 'n' roll—already reeling from the loss of many of its top stars and faced with an onslaught of media friendly teen idols—altogether.

The music business quickly closed ranks in the face of outside political interference. ABC-TV forced *American Bandstand* host Dick Clark to unload his holdings in other music-related activities, ranging from record companies to publishing houses. In response to Federal Trade Commission directives, a number of independent record labels and distributors filed consent orders agreeing to eliminate payola. Such moves enabled the industry to withstand formal House hearings in early 1960. Clark, whose deportment under interrogation was that of a model citizen, was not found guilty of directly engaging in payola practices.

On the other hand, Alan Freed, the deejay most clearly identified with the rise of rock 'n' roll, refused to testify despite an offer of immunity. A pariah within the field he'd helped so much to nurture, he was ultimately found guilty on two counts of commercial bribery. In the end, the committee recommended anti-payola amendments to the Federal Communications Acts which prohibited the payment of cash or gifts in exchange for airplay, and required radio stations to police such activities. These amendments formally became law on September 13, 1960.

While the overall impact of the hearings remains unclear, it is clear that the general media circus surrounding them far overshadowed whatever concrete results might have taken place. The smaller independent labels had been forced to compete on more equal terms the majors and their superior publicity and distribution networks. As a result, many of the former went of business during the early 1960s. Nevertheless, new labels continued to surface—and sometimes achieve great success—in the upcoming years. Payola itself continued to be employed within the industry, giving rise to yet another scandal in the early 1970s centered around Columbia Records president Clive Davis and allegations of bribes involving money, sex, and drugs.

November 16. The Fleetwoods enjoy their second chart-topping single for the year with "Mr. Blue." Although they continue to record moderate hits through 1963, they—like many of their contemporaries—will fade from view with the onslaught of Beatlemania and subsequent British Invasion acts.

November 20. Alan Freed, after refusing to testify that he never accepted payola, is fired by WABC television in New York. On November 28, he is also fired by WNEW-TV, New York.

November 21. Following his refusal to sign an affidavit stating he never accepted payola, Alan Freed is fired by WABC radio, New York.

November 23. RCA issues a statement denying that Elvis Presley will change his style following his imminent military discharge. Addressing rumors that the artist would edge closer to the middle-of-the-road, one label official commented, "It just ain't true."

November 29. Bobby Darin garners 1959 Grammy Awards for Record of the Year ("Mack the Knife") and Best New Artist of the Year. Frank Sinatra's *Come Dance with Me* (Capitol) is named Album of the Year.

November 30. Billboard reports that the ongoing payola investigations "will substantially damage the careers of at least twenty-five DJs," including former kingmaker Alan Freed.

December 10. Municipal Court judge Gilbert Bettman acquits the four male members of the Platters of charges of aiding and abetting prostitution, lewdness, and assignation arising from their August 10 arrest in Cincinnati. Four women arrested with the group members are also acquitted.

December 14. Emile Ford and the Checkmates reach number one on the British charts with a remake of the acoustic era chestnut, "What Do You Want To Make Those Eyes At Me For?"

December 14. Tin Pan Alley veteran Guy Mitchell returns to the top of the pop charts for a final two-week hurrah with "Heartaches By the Number" (Columbia) before capitulating to the youthful acts now dominating the Hot 100.

December 14. An Ohio State University Research Center report indicates that while rock 'n' roll is the overwhelming favorite of the fourteen to eighteen age group, even more adults aged nineteen to seventy classify it at their least favorite form of music.

December 15. The Everly Brothers record outside of Nashville for the first time, waxing "Let It Be Me" in New York City. It will also be their first release to include a string accompaniment.

December 25. Ringo Starr—then an eighteen-year-old apprentice engineer—receives his first drum set as a Christmas present.

December 28. Frankie Avalon reaches number one for a second time that year with "Why" (Chancellor). With his best days as a recording artist already behind him, he will soon focus his energies on an acting career, achieving some degree of success with a series of teen-oriented beach movies.

December 29. Ray Charles records for ABC Paramount for the first time; the Hollywood session is produced by Sid Feller.

1960

❄

January 1. Johnny Cash gives the first of what will be many free concerts at San Quentin prison. Future country star Merle Haggard witnesses the show as one of the inmates.

January 4. Marty Robbins begins a two-week stint atop the Hot 100 with "El Paso" (Columbia).

January 9. Emile Ford and the Checkmates—naturalized British citizens hailing from Bahamas—first U.K. black act to top the domestic charts with "What Do You Want to Make Eyes at Me For?" Until the rise of the beat groups several years later, though, the English pop scene would continue to be dominated by American imports, middle-of-the-road home-bred singers, and bland Presley imitators.

January 10. Bill Black's Combo tops the R&B charts (#17 pop) with the instrumental, "Smokie, Part 2." The Memphis-born Black started out as session man at Sun Studios. His bass playing—seminal blend of R&B and C&W features—was an integral part of Elvis Presley's style. With Presley serving in the army, Black formed his own band in 1959 and signed with the hometown Hi label. His "White Silver Sand" would also go number one R&B (#9 pop) later in the year. His act would serve as a template for such 1960s soul-pop groups as the Mar-Keys and Booker T. and the MGs.

January 18. Johnny Preston reaches number one on the pop charts with "Running Bear" (Mercury), remaining there for three weeks. The late J. P. Richardson (aka Big Bopper) not only was the composer, but sang back-up "oom pah pah") in the studio. It would also top in British charts, and hit number three on the R&B survey.

January 18. "Baby (You've Got What It Takes)," a duet by Brook Benton and Dinah Washington, enters the R&B charts, and makes number one four weeks later. The first duet for Benton—a former gospel singer who had three R&B chart-toppers in 1959—he will team with Washington to reach number one again in June with "A Rockin' Good Way."

January 25. Jimmy Jones' "Handy Man"—written and produced by the legendary Otis Blackwell—enters the R&B charts; it will become a Top Five R&B and pop hit in short order. It is the first hit for the former lead singer of the Sparks of Rhythm, the Pretenders, and the Savoys. Revivals of the songs by both Del Shannon (1964) and James Taylor (1977) will also become pop hits.

January 25. The Original Cast Recording of *The Sound of Music* begins a sixteen-week stint atop the LP charts.

February 6. Jesse Belvin, a fixture within the 1950s West Coast R&B scene although barely in his 20s, dies in a Los Angeles car accident. His first R&B hit came with "Dream Girl" (1953) as part of the duo, Jesse and Marvin. His biggest seller was the classic "Goodnight My Love" (1956); he would enjoy additional successes both as a solo singer and as a member of the doo-wop groups The Cliques, the Sharptones, Three Dots and a Dash, and the Sheiks. He was also an accomplished composer; perhaps his greatest accomplishment in this regard was co-writing the Penguins' "Earth Angel."

February 7. Barrett Strong's "Money" makes the Hot 100; it will eventually reach number twenty-three (#2 R&B). Originally released on the Detroit-based Anna Records (owned by Berry Gordy's sister, Gwen), Berry would make it the first release of his Tamla label. It quickly acquired classic status; it would be covered by many artists, including the Beatles, the Kingsmen, Jr. Walker and the All Stars, and the Flying Lizards.

February 8. Mark Dinning climbs to the summit of the pop charts with the landmark "death disc," "Teen Angel" (MGM), remaining there for two weeks.

February 8. In the wake of the recent TV quiz show scandals, the House of Representatives Special Subcommittee on Legislative Oversight opens hearings on radio payola with testimony from Boston and Cleveland deejays.

February 12. Pat Boone is awarded a gold record for *Pat's Great Hits*. The Dot LP's material ranges from covers of R&B hits by Fats Domino and Little Richard to the Tin Pan Alley-styled "April Love" and "Love Letters in the Sand."

February 17. The Everly Brothers sign with Warner Brothers Records for $1 million.

February 17. Elvis Presley earns his first gold record for the 1956 RCA release, *Elvis*.

February 20. Jimi Hendrix makes his stage debut, playing a show at a Seattle high school.

February 22. Easy listening bandleader, Percy Faith, begins a nine-week run atop the Hot 100 with "The Theme from 'A Summer Place'" (Columbia). The instrumental's teen appeal owes much to its placement in the blockbuster film starring Sandra Dee and Troy Donahue.

February 29. Jimmy Jones peaks at number two on the hot 100 with "Handy Man" (Cub 9049). He co-wrote the song with Otis Blackwell.

One of the truly distinctive R&B singers of the early 1960s, Jimmy Jones helped popularize the falsetto style later employed by the Four Seasons and countless soul groups. Born June 2, 1937, in Birmingham, Alabama, Jones started out as a tap dancer before joining in the doo-wop act, the Sparks of Rhythm, in 1955. In 1956, he formed his own group, the Savoys (renamed the Pretenders, shortly thereafter).

Jones finally found success with the MGM subsidiary, Cub; his debut, "Handy Man" (1960; #2 pop, #3 r&b), became a classic, later returning to the charts in covers by Del Shannon in 1964 and James Taylor in 1977. After one more smash, "Good Timin'" (Cub; 1960; #3 pop, #8 r&b), follow-up releases—including minor hits "That's When I Cried" (Cub; 1960; #83) and "I Told You So" (Cub; 1961; #85)—experienced a substantial drop-off in sales. However, he had even greater success in Great Britain, topping the charts with "Good Timin'" and reaching the Top 50 with five singles.

February 29. B.B. King reaches number two on the R&B charts with "Sweet Sixteen" (it won't make the Hot 100 until reissued at the peak of the blues revival in 1972). King had fallen out of fashion following a string of bestselling singles in the early 1950s—most notably, "3 O'Clock Blues," "You Know I Love You," "Please Love Me," and "You Upset Me, Baby"—which melded the raw sensuality of the blues with sophisticated jazz guitar stylings.

March 4. The ongoing Congressional payola investigation uncovers a six-day Florida junket taken by Federal Communications Chairman John Doerfer, paid for by Storer Broadcasting.

March 5. Elvis Presley—recently promoted to sergeant—receives his Army discharge. Two days earlier, he'd left Germany en route to McGuire Air Force Base, New Jersey. From there, he is hustled to Nashville, where he records the "Stuck On You" and "Fame and Fortune." The tracks—Presley's first to utilize stereo technology—are rush-released to fans starved for new material; "Stuck On You" quickly tops the national charts.

March 10. *Record Retailer* (later renamed *Music Week*)—a British music weekly—publishes the first EP and LP tabulations in that country. The number one extended play record is "Expresso Bongo," by Cliff Richard & the Shadows, top-rated album is *The Explosive Freddy Cannon*.

March 14. Sam Cooke's begins his first West Indies tour with a concert in Jamaica's Montego Bay. He goes on to set attendance records for all venues over the next two weeks. As a result, Cooke will greatly influence a new generation of Jamaican recording stars, including Jimmy Cliff, Owen Gray, and Bob Marley. He will tour in the region two more times before his death in December 1964.

March 28. New York Representative Emanuel Celler of New York introduces two anti-payola bills in Congress, attributing "the cacophonous music called rock & roll" to the practice. The legislative proposals call for penalties of $1,000 and one year in jail for anyone found to have given or received payola.

March 30. Massachusetts Representative Thomas "Tip" O'Neill argues that the Federal Communications Commission should investigate all radio stations harboring employees known to be involved with payola, and report the findings to Congress. O'Neill refers to American youth as a "captive audience" that must be protected from both payola and rock 'n' roll, the latter being "a type of sensuous music unfit for impressionable minds."

March 31. Lonnie Donegan tops the British charts with "My Old Man's a Dustman."

April 1. In the Fountainbleau Hotel, Miami, Elvis Presley takes part in the taping of the *Frank Sinatra Timex Show* (ABC)—which will be broadcast May 12—along with Frank and Nancy Sinatra, Sammy Davis Jr.,

Dean Martin, Mitch Miller, and Joey Bishop. Under the close watch of his manager, Colonel Tom Parker, Presley takes a train from Memphis to Miami, punctuated by strategically organized "whistle stops" along the route to re-establish contact with his legions of fans.

April 2. The National Association of Record Merchants (NARM) holds its inaugural awards ceremony in Las Vegas. The most notable winners are Elvis Presley (best-selling male artist) and Connie Francis (best-selling female artist).

April 3. The Everly Brothers make their U.K. concert debut in London, the first leg of a British tour that greatly influenced British Invasion artists such as the Beatles, the Searchers, and the Rolling Stones' Keith Richards.

April 4. *Billboard* reports that RCA Victor will be the first record company to release all pop 45 rpm singles simultaneously in the mono and stereo formats. The practice begins with Elvis Presley's initial post-military single, "Stuck on You."

April 6. The Everly Brothers kick off their first British concert tour at London's New Victoria Theatre, supported by the Crickets.

April 17. In the midst of a ten-week British tour, Gene Vincent and Eddie Cochran are involved in a car crash near Chippenham, Wiltshire. Cochran later dies from brain injuries in a Bath hospital; his girlfriend, songwriter Sharon Sheeley, and Vincent are also injured. Ironically, Cochran's most recent release was entitled, "Three Steps to Heaven."

April 20. Elvis Presley's return to Hollywood—to begin filming *G.I. Blues*—is front-page news in local newspapers and entertainment publications alike.

April 21. Referred to at the time as "the single most influential person" within the popular music industry, Dick Clark appears before the Congressional committee looking into allegations of rampant payola. Despite admitting he had a financial interest in 27 percent of the records he played on "American Bandstand" over a twenty-eight-month period in the late 1950s, Clark—although ultimately required to relinquish record industry holdings constituting a conflict of interest—is not found guilty of any legal infractions. In response to his testimony, Committee Chairman Orrin Harris states, "You're not the inventor of the system or even its architect. You're the product of it. Obviously, you're a fine young man."

April 25. Elvis Presley begins a four-week stay atop the Hot 100 with "Stuck on You" (RCA).

April 30. The Everly Brothers begin a seven-week run atop the British charts with "Cathy's Clown."

May 2. Ben E. King, ex-lead singer for the Drifters, inks a solo recording deal with Atlantic subsidiary, Atco. His former group will go on to enjoy a long string of chart successes well into the mid-1960s with a succession of fronting vocalists.

May 2. *Billboard* states that many U.S. radio stations are no longer programming rock 'n' roll, opting instead for "better music" playlists. The payola hearings are cited as major force behind this trend. WNTA, Newark, is one such broadcast outlet, having recently switched to a "Golden Sound" format.

May 12. ABC-TV airs the *Frank Sinatra Timex Show*. The show features Sinatra and Elvis Presley trading off on signature songs; the former doing "Love Me Tender," and the latter, "Witchcraft." According to a *Billboard* review, "Presley needs a lot of coaching on how to stand and how to talk," while Sinatra's daughter, Nancy, "displayed great poise, charm, a pleasant singing voice and an ability to dance."

May 16. *Billboard* reports that Detroit songwriter, publisher, and producer Berry Gordy Jr. is about to launch how own record company.

May 20. DJ Alan Freed is indicted (as are seven other industry figures) for taking $30,650 in payola from six record labels. Freed—newly hired at Los Angeles radio station KDAY (whose program director, Mel Leeds, was also arrested for receiving payoffs)—would plead not guilty to the payola charges, and a trial date was set for September 19. In 1962, he would receive a suspended sentence and $300 fine.

May 20. Having failed an audition with British music entrepreneur Larry Parnes to become Billy Fury's backing band, the Silver Beetles kick off a seven-date Scottish tour in support of another Parnes artist, Johnny Gentle, at Alloa Town Hall.

May 23. The Everly Brothers begin a five-week run atop the Hot 100 with "Cathy's Clown" (Warner Bros.).

June 5. The Hollywood Argyles' novelty record, "Alley-Oop," enters the Hot 100; although competing versions are released almost overnight (most notably, a blatant carbon copy by Dante and the Evergreens, which reaches the Top 20), it will top the charts the following month. Producer Kim Fowley—having already masterminded Bumble B. and the Stingers, the Innocents, and Skip and Flip—will become an industry legend, later helping bring the Rivingtons, Paul Revere and the Raiders, and the Runaways into the public eye.

June 6. Tony Williams—who had released several solo recordings in the prior two years—leaves the Platters. He will fail to achieve much success as a solo act while his former group—with Sonny Turner filling in as lead vocalist—will continue to produce occasional hits through 1967.

June 6. In a prelude to the British Invasion, the Liverpool groups, the Silver Beetles and the Pacemakers, both perform at the Grosvenor Ballroom, Wallasey, England.

June 19. CBS radio premieres *The Kingston Trio Show*. The five-minute program—sponsored by the soft drink Seven-Up—is scheduled to be broadcast six days a week at various times.

June 24. The second annual Newport Folk Festival begins. The three-day event—hosted by writer Studs Terkel—will feature artists Joan Baez, Lester Flatt and Earl Scruggs, John Lee Hooker, Mahalia Jackson, and the Weavers.

June 27. Connie Francis begins a two-week stint atop the Hot 100 with "Everybody's Somebody's Fool" (MGM).

July 3. Ray Charles makes both the R&B and pop charts with his first ABC-Paramount release, "Sticks and Stones" (it will eventually peak at number two and number forty, respectively). Many observers had questioned Charles' move from indie powerhouse Atlantic—where he became one of the leading R&B singers of the late 1950s—to a middle-of-the-road label. However, ABC would wisely leave creative control in his hands, and Charles would make seminal recordings which fused R&B with the country & western, Tin Pan Alley, and Jazz genres.

July 11. The Hollywood Argyles peak at number one on the pop charts with novelty tribute to the cartoon caveman, "Alley-Oop" (Lute).

July 17. Lloyd Price's "Question" appears on the R&B charts (it will reach number five, his last Top 10 single); it will also be his last record to make the pop Top 20. He had been a major force behind the New Orleans Sound since breaking out with "Lawdy Miss Clawdy" (Specialty) in 1952.

July 17. Jackie Wilson's "A Woman, a Lover, a Friend" enters the R&B survey on its way to becoming his fourth chart-topper over a two-year period.

July 18. Brenda Lee begins a three-week stay atop the Hot 100 with "I'm Sorry" (Decca).

July 24. The Ventures' "Walk Don't Run" enters the Hot 100; rising to the number two position, it is the first notable hit to feature the instrumental "surf sound" built around a pulsating beat and tremolo-drenched lead guitar. With a successful string of singles (e.g., "Perfidia," "Walk Don't Run '64," "Slaughter on 10th Avenue") and albums, the group plays a key role in popularizing the lead/rhythm/bass guitar and drums format in rock music. Even when the British Invasion, and subsequent American Renaissance, render their music out-of-date, they retain a rabid following in Japan and continue to produce commercially successful instructional recordings and manuals stateside.

July 24. Duane Eddy peaks at number four (his highest position ever despite a long string of pop hits) with "Because They're Young," the title song from a teen flick starring Dick Clark and Tuesday Weld.

August 1. Having just turned eighteen earlier in the year, Aretha Franklin records popular tracks for the first time. The New York sessions—produced by the legendary talent scout John Hammond for the Columbia label—yield "Right Now," "Today I Sing the Blues," "Love Is the Only Thing," and "Over the Rainbow." The daughter of Reverend C. L. Franklin, a successful gospel artist in his own right, Aretha first recorded gospel material at age fourteen.

August 1. *Billboard* reprints the results of a recent *Seventeen* magazine survey, most notably, teenage girls as a whole listen to the radio two hours and thirteen minutes and play records two hours and twelve minutes each day.

August 3. The RCA A&R team, Hugo (Peretti) and Luigi (Creatore), convince Mickey (Baker) and Sylvia (Robinson) to reunite and try recording again. Nothing of note emerges from this comeback attempt; the duo will be remembered as the one-hit wonders responsible for "Love Is Strange" prior to embarking on solo careers in 1958.

August 6. Chubby Checker performs "The Twist" on television—*The Dick Clark Saturday Night Show* (ABC)—for the first time.

August 7. Ike and Tina Turner enter the R&B charts with "A Fool in Love," which eventually reaches number two (#27 pop). It is the recording debut for twenty-one-year-old Tina; husband Ike, on the other hand, first recorded in 1951, as leader of the Kings of Rhythm. The resulting R&B chart-topper, "Rocket 88," opened up A&R and producing gigs for the likes B.B.King, Howlin' Wolf, and Bobby "Blue" Bland.

August 8. Brian Hyland climbs to the summit of the pop charts with the novelty, "Itsy Bitsy Teenie Weenie Yellow Polkadot Bikini" (Leader).

August 8. *Billboard* reports that English Decca scrapped twenty-five copies of Ray Peterson's "Tell Laura I Love Her" because it is "too tasteless and vulgar for the English sensibility." Despite the song's morbid premise—a teenage boy's final words before dying from a car crash—it was a Top 10 hit stateside.

August 12. Drummer Pete Best passes an audition at the Wyvern Social Club, joining the Silver Beetles as they get ready to fulfill a performing commitment in Hamburg, Germany. He is the son of Mona Best, owner of the Casbah Club, where earlier editions of the group have played regularly since its opening August 29 1959.

August 15. Elvis Presley begins a five-week run atop the Hot 100 with "It's Now or Never" (RCA), a rewrite of the Italian standard, "O Solo Mio."

August 17. The Silver Beetles perform outside their native England for the first time, at the Indra Club in Hamburg, West Germany. Their show generates enough excitement to result in an ongoing three-month engagement. However, they soon break this arrangement when offered a gig at the larger, more prestigious Kaiserkeller club. They will have played 106 times by the time they make their last appearance November 30, prior to returning to England. Several more visits to Hamburg will follow through 1962.

August 20. Connie Francis begins work on her first film, MGM's *Where the Boys Are*, in Ft. Lauderdale, Florida. The soap opera treatment of college students on spring break will also star George Hamilton IV, Yvette Mimeaux, and Paula Prentiss.

August 21. Cliff Richard's backing band, the Shadows—Great Britain's answer to the Ventures—dislodge his "Please Don't Tease" from the top position on the U.K. charts with a cover of the Jorgen Ingmann instrumental, "Apache."

August 22. Brenda Lee enters *Billboard*'s Top 40 with her eponymous album (Decca 74039), which goes on to peak at number five.

Known as "Little Miss Dynamite," Brenda Lee—along with the more middle-of-the-road oriented Connie Francis—was the dominant female star during the early rock 'n' roll era. Her powerful, worldly-wise voice, capable of negotiating rave-up rockers as well as tender voice, seemed incongruous with her youth.

Born Brenda Mae Tarpley in Atlanta, she began singing by age seven on local radio and television programs. When her father died a year later, her income helped support the family. Her big break came when she met Red Foley's manager, Dub Albritten, in 1956. He booked her on Foley's shows, which led to national TV appearances. On July 30 of that year she recorded "Rockin' Around the Christmas Tree" (Decca 30776) with producer Owen Bradley in Nashville; it became her first hit. Tours of both the United States and Europe followed; to satisfy French promoters, whos thought she was an adult, Albritten started the rumor that she was a thirty-two-year-old midget.

With the release of "Sweet Nothin's" (Decca 30967; 1959; #4), Lee enjoyed a string of hits that ran through the 1960s, including "I'm Sorry"/"That's All You Gotta Do" (Decca 31093; 1960; #s 1/6), "I Want

To Be Wanted" (Decca 31149; 1960; #1), "Emotions" (Decca 31195; 1960-1961; #7), "You Can Depend On Me" (Decca 31195; 1961; #6), "Dum Dum" (Decca 31272; 1961; #4), "Fool #1" (Decca 31309; 1961; #3), "Break It To Me Gently" (Decca 31348; 1962; #4), "Everybody Loves Me But You" (Decca 31379; 1962; #6), "All Alone Am I" (Decca 31424; 1962; #3), and "Losing You" (Decca 31478; 1963; #6). By the time she was twenty-one, she had recorded 256 tracks for Decca. Recognizing that her style ran counter to pop tastes at the time, she shifted her emphasis to the country music business in the early 1970s. In addition to chart success—Top 10 recordings included "Nobody Wins" (MCA 40003; 1973), "Sunday Sunrise" (MCA 40107; 1973), "Wrong Ideas" (MCA 40171; 1974), "Big Four Poster Bed" (MCA 40262; 1974), "Rock On Baby" (MCA 40318; 1974), "He's My Rock" (MCA 40385; 1975), "Tell Me What It's Like" (MCA 41130; 1979), "The Cowgirl and the Dandy" (MCA 41187; 1980), and "Broken Trust" (MCA 41322; 1980)—she did a syndicated interview program based in Nashville and had occasional acting roles (e.g., *Smokey and the Bandit 2*).

With lifetime record sales estimated to have exceeded one hundred million, Lee has won many honors including the National Academy of Recording Arts and Sciences Governors Award.

August 29. The Ventures peak at number two with "Walk – Don't Run," a sound reminiscent of the British instrumental combo, the Shadows.

The most successful American instrumental group during the rock era, the Ventures led the way in establishing the guitar-based sound dominating popular music from 1960 onwards. Their distinctive sound—pulsing drums and metallic, twanging guitars—spanned a wide range of material (e.g., calypso, blues, Latin, psychedelia, folk rock, surf music, Merseybeat), surviving many changes in public taste. Many genres—most notably, surf music, the British Invasion, power pop, and alternative rock—have been influenced by the band.

Based in Seattle, the Ventures' first release, "Walk – Don't Run" (Dolton 25), reached number two on the pop charts in August 1960. They had fourteen hits in all during the 1960s, including the Top 10 recordings "Walk Don't Run '64" (Dolton 96; 1964) and "Hawaii Five-O" (Liberty 56068; 1969). In 1965, the band issued one of the most popular instructional records ever, Play Guitar with the Ventures (Dolton 16501). The Ventures—which included founding members Bob Bogle (guitar, bass) and Don Wilson (guitar)—continued to tour extensively through the 1990s, long after the hits stopped coming.

September 1. The Flamingos' "Mio Amore" makes the R&B charts (peaking at number 27). It will be the last notable hit for the Chicago-based doo-wop quintet until "The Boogaloo Party" enters the R&B Top 30 in 1966.

September 11. Sam Cooke's "Chain Gang" rises to number two on both the R&B and pop charts, his first major hit since signing with RCA earlier in the year. He will go on to record eleven more Top 20 hits before his death in December 1964.

September 19. Chubby Checker's "The Twist" (Parkway)—a remake of the Hank Ballard B side released on Federal in 1958)—reaches number one on the Hot 100. The artist, South Carolina native Ernest Evans, grew up in Philadelphia performing for classmates along with friends such as future teen idol Fabian Forte. The owner of the meat market, where Evans worked after school, arranged a private recording session with *American Bandstand* host, Dick Clark. As Evans completed a Fats Domino imitation, Clark's wife asked him his name. When he indicated "my friends call me Chubby," she playfully responded, "Like in Checker?" That episode of humorous word play inspired Evans' professional name.

The resulting Christmas novelty, "The Class" (which featured impressions of popular singers by Checker), attracted the attention of the Cameo-Parkway label, which decided to release the record commercially (Parkway 804; 1959). His breakthrough came when Clark advised Cameo-Parkway to record "The Twist," a dance number written by R&B singer Hank Ballard and released as the B side of "Teardrops on Your Letter" (King 5171; 1959), by Ballard and his group, The Midnighters. Checker sang his parts over an already-recorded instrumental track; released June 1959 (Parkway 811; 1960), the record took nearly fourteen months to reach the charts. Checker's nonstop itinerary of interviews, TV dates, and live appearances (he is said to have lost thirty pounds during one three-week stretch of demonstrating the Twist) ultimately paid off, however, when the single reached top of the Billboard Hot 100 in September 1960.

The Twist phenomenon inspired a rapid succession of additional dance fads. Due to his close relationship with Clark and a savvy record label, Checker was well positioned to continue as Dance King. His dance hits included "The Hucklebuck" (Parkway 813; 1960), "Pony Time" (Parkway 818; 1961), "Dance the Mess Around" (Parkway 822; 1961), "Let's Twist Again" (Parkway 824; 1961), "The Fly" (Parkway 830; 1961), "Slow Twistin'" (Parkway 835; 1962), "Limbo Rock"/"Popeye the Hitchhiker" (Parkway 849; 1962), "Let's Limbo Some More" (Parkway 862; 1963), "Birdland" (Parkway 873; 1963), and "Twist It Up" (Parkway 879; 1963).

When the dance craze subsided, Checker managed to record additional hits, most notably "Loddy Lo"/ "Hooka Tooka" (Parkway 890; 1963) and "Hey, Bobba Needle" (Parkway 907). However, his popularity was ultimately eclipsed by the British Invasion and American Renaissance styles such as surf music, soul, and folk-rock. Checker has continued to perform extensively, occasionally attempting large-scale comebacks.

September 26. Connie Francis begins a two-week stint atop the Hot 100 with "My Heart Has a Mind of Its Own" (MGM).

October 2. Maurice Williams and the Zodiacs' "Stay" enters the R&B charts (eventually reaching number three as well as topping the Hot 100). The group was earlier known as the Gladiolas; their debut release, "Little Darlin'" (1957), enjoyed moderate success until blown out of the water by the Diamonds' top-selling cover version for Mercury. "Stay" would become a signature recording for the beach music phenomenon popular at South Carolina seaside venues beginning in the 1960s. It would also be covered by countless other artists, most notably, in hit versions by the Four Seasons (Vee-Jay, 1964) and Jackson Browne (Asylum, 1978).

October 10. Larry Verne peaks at number one on the pop charts with the novelty, "Mr. Custer" (Era).

October 11. Aretha Franklin performs live in New York City for the first time at the Village Vanguard. Her selections consist largely of blues and pop standards.

October 15. Drummer Ringo Starr takes Pete Best's place when the Silver Beetles back Wally Eymond, guitarist with Rory Storm & the Hurricanes, on a recording of Gershwin's *Summertime* at Hamburg's Akustik studio.

October 16. One of the chief architects of the "Nashville Sound," Floyd Cramer, enters the Hot 100 with "Last Date." It will become his biggest hit, reaching number two (#3 R&B and #11 C&W). He would continue to punctuate solo work with studio sessions backing the likes of Chet Atkins, Elvis Presley, and Jim Reeves.

October 17. *Billboard* documents the break-up of Dion and the Belmonts with the colorful phrase, "[the members] ankled one another's scene." Dion will come close to achieving superstar status before his momentum is halted by drug addiction and the British Invasion. He will reinvent himself—much like Bobby Darin—as a folk-styled singer/songwriter before committing himself to the doo-wop nostalgia circuit where the Belmonts had begun focusing their efforts as early as the 1960s.

October 17. The Drifters reach number one on the Hot 100 with "Save the Last Dance for Me" (Atlantic), remaining there for three non-consecutive weeks.

October 17. Ike and Tina Turner peak at number twenty-seven on the Hot 100 with "A Fool in Love" (Sue 730).

Although generally mentioned in relation to his one-time wife, Tina, Ike was one of the early pioneers of rock 'n' roll in his own right. His talents—which spanned many aspects of the music industry—also play a key role in furthering the careers of many other African American artists.

Born November 5, 1931, and raised in Clarksdale, Mississippi, Turner formed a band, the Top Hatters, while still in high school. Later known as the Kings of Rhythm, they worked the small clubs throughout the Mississippi delta. He secured a recording session at Sam Phillips' legendary Sun Studios in Memphis; his band cut the R&B chart-topper, "Rocket 88," cited by many experts as the earliest rock 'n' roll recording. Due to obscure contractual considerations, however, Chess gave label credit to saxophonist

Jackie Brenston and the Delta Cats, thereby denying him a notable footnote in pop music history. He also alleged that the company paid him only $40 for writing, producing, and recording the disc.

Turner continued as a highly regarded session guitarist, producer, and talent scout during the 1950s. His collaborations with the likes of Johnny Ace, Bobby "Blue" Band, Roscoe Gordon, Howlin' Wolf, B.B. King, and Otis Rush were released on Chess, Modern, and RPM. By the mid-1950s, he was high profile club attraction based in St. Louis. One night in 1956, Annie Mae Bullock—who'd moved from Knoxville, Tennessee, to St. Louis to try to build a career as a vocalist—was given a chance to sing with his band during a club date. Impressed with her performance, Turner asked her to join the group; they would get married in 1958.

The couple's recording breakthrough came unexpectedly in 1959 when a singer tapped to record Ike's composition, "A Fool in Love," failed to appear for the scheduled session. Tina (her adopted stage name) was substituted and the track (Sue 730) reached number two on the R&B charts (#27 pop) the following year. As a result, Ike decided to focus the act on Tina, bringing in a female backing group (the Ikettes), and working out arrangements and choreography to take advantage of her dynamic voice and stage presence. They recorded a long string of R&B hits for a variety of labels—including Kent, Loma, Modern, Philles, Warner Bros., Innis, Blue Thumb, Minit, and Liberty—in the 1960s, though few—most notably, "A Fool In Love" (#2 r&b), "It's Gonna Work Out Fine" (Sue 749; 1961; #14 pop, #2 r&b), and "Poor Fool" (Sue 753; 1961; #38 pop, #4 r&b)—performed well on the pop charts. Producer Phil Spector had been particularly interested in packaging the duo for a wider audience through his renown "wall-of-sound," but the commercial failure of his reputed masterpiece, "River Deep, Mountain High" (Philles 131; 1966; #88 pop)—though it did reach number one in England—reputedly led to his decision to retire from the music business.

The late 1960s, however, brought a change of fortune as roots-based sounds once again began dominating mainstream pop. They received invaluable exposure by touring with the Rolling Stones and performing on major television programs and Las Vegas venues. Among their best-selling singles were "I Want to Take You Higher" (Liberty 56177; 1970; #34 pop, #25 r&b), "Proud Mary" (Liberty 56216; 1971; #4 pop, #5 r&b), and "Nutbush City Limits" (United Artists 298; 1973; #22 pop, #11 r&b). Their albums also regularly made the charts, most notably Outta Season (Blue Thumb 5; 1969), In Person (Minit 24018; 1969), River Deep-Mountain High (A&M 4178; 1969; recorded 1966), Come Together (Liberty 7637; 1970), Workin' Together (Liberty 7650; 1970), Live at Carnegie Hall/What You Hear Is What You Get (United Artists 9953; 1971), 'Nuff Said (United Artists 5530; 1971), Feel Good (United Artists 5598; 1972), and Nutbush City Limits (United Artists 180; 1973).

Despite their commercial success, the couple's marriage was in trouble. Tina ultimately decided to leave the act in Dallas during a 1975 tour; she obtained a divorce the following year. While she went on to both commercial and artistic success as a solo performer in the 1980s, Ike found nothing but problems. Not only did his recording activities fail to go anywhere, but he was dogged by a rash of drug and other personal problems. The one bright spot has been the public's continued interest in the classic work of the Ike and Tina Turner Revue, which has led to the release of many recorded anthologies as well as original albums such as Dance (Collectibles 5759; 1996), Don't Play Me Cheap (Collectibles 5763; 1996), Dynamite (Collectibles 5298; 1994), and It's Gonna Work Out Fine (Collectibles 5137; 1994).

October 24. Brenda Lee interrupts the Drifters' hold on the top spot of the pop charts for a week with "I Want to be Wanted" (Decca).

October 24. The Paradons peak at number eighteen on the Hot 100 with "Diamonds and Pearls" (Milestone 2003).

The Paradons, hailing from the country and western stronghold of Bakersfield, California, captured lightning in a bottle with their one notable hit, "Diamonds and Pearls" (Milestone 2003; 1960; #18). However, efforts to recapture the magic of that disc—the skewed harmonies, the catchy vocal background riffing, and plaintive lead by the song's composer, West Tyler—would all come up far short of the mark.

The Paradons—comprised of high school classmates Billy Myers, William Powers, Chuck Weldon, and Tyler—were discovered by former Louisiana rockabilly performer, Werly Fairburn, who had established

Milestone Records along with Madelon Baker, a model allegedly being groomed by General Mills in the mid-1950s to become the next Betty Crocker. In January 1960, Fairburn brought the group into Hollywood's Audio Arts Recording Studio to cut "Diamonds and Pearls." Follow-up singles like "Bells Ring." "I Had a Dream," and one Warner Bros. release, "Take All Of Me" failed to make the charts. The group disbanded, while Baker would go on to form the Audio Arts label and discover artists such as the Incredibles and Jimmy Webb.

October 27. Ben E. King records his first solo material—with producers Jerry Leiber and Mike Stoller, assisted by Phil Spector—at Atlantic Records' New York City studios. Two of the tracks—"Spanish Harlem" (#10 pop, #15 R&B) and "Stand By Me" (#4 pop, #1 R&B)—become timeless classics. Despite this fast start, however, King's solo career will soon fizzle out; he will enjoy just one other hit of note, "Don't Play That Song" (1962).

November 5. C&W crossover recording star Johnny Horton, age thirty-three, dies in a car accident near Bryan-College Station, Texas. His widow, Billy Joe, had also been married to Hank Williams at the time of his death. Ironically, both artists last performed at the Skyline in Austin, Texas.

November 7. Alvin Pleasant (A. P.) Carter—the founder and leader of the pioneering country act, the Carter Family—dies at age sixty-two in Kingsport, Tennessee.

November 10. Gregg Allman is given a guitar for his thirteenth birthday. He and his fourteen-year-old brother, Duane, learn to play it to the accompaniment of blues records. They form their first band, the Kings, a year later in Daytona Beach, Florida, followed by the Allman Joys and Hourglass (both of whom can be heard on recordings), among others. The Allman Brothers, formed in 1969, will create the template for southern rock, including a stylistic blend of roots rock, country, R&B, and jazz and lyrics built around themes of regional pride and racial brotherhood.

November 14. Ray Charles reaches number one on the Hot 100 with "Georgia on My Mind" (ABC-Paramount).

November 14. According to *Billboard*, Elvis Presley's "It's Now or Never" is now the fastest-selling single ever in Great Britain, with 780,000 copies sold during the first week following its release.

November 21. Ray Charles maintains his commercial hot hand; he now has four songs in the Hot 100: "Georgia on My Mind" (later adopted by Georgia as its state song) at number five following a week in the top position, "Ruby" at number sixty-one, "Hard Hearted Hannah at number 66, and "Come Rain or Come Shine" (selected as the theme song for the 1983 film *King of Comedy*) at number ninety-five.

November 21. *Billboard* discloses that guitarist Duane Eddy and producer (and former Phoenix DJ) Lee Hazlewood have severed a highly successful three-year partnership. It is noted that Hazlewood played a key role in creating Eddy's distinctive "twang"-oriented sound: he shared composition credits with Eddy on most of the guitarist's material, and encouraged Eddy to play his leads on the bass string and then drenched the results in reverb. Hazlewood would concentrate on running his Phoenix recording studio, punctuated by occasional attempts at launching his own solo career. Eddy went on to enjoy modest success as his own producer—most notably, with "Guitar Man" (RCA, 1962)—and would remain active as a performer into the twenty-first century.

November 21. Maurice Williams & the Zodiacs ascend to the summit of the pop charts with "Stay" (Herald).

November 28. U.S. Bonds peaks at number six on the Hot 100 with "New Orleans" (Legrand 1003).

Gary U.S. Bonds created some of the best rave-up rock 'n' roll during the Brill Building Era, a period best known for its smoothed out, or processed, interpretations of the seminal rockabilly and R&B of Elvis Presley, Jerry Lee Lewis, Little Richard, and other 1950s originators. The appeal of these recordings lies in the singer's raucous shouting, projected over a simulated party atmosphere, consisting of a murky blend of honking sax, pounding rhythms, and (seemingly) random background of youthful whooping and chattering.

He was born Gary Anderson, on June 6, 1939, in Jacksonville, Florida. His family relocated to Norfolk, Virginia, where he practiced doo-wop on street corners with a group known as the Turks. In 1960, producer Frank Guida—the new owner of a failing business, the Norfolk Recording Studios—recruited

Anderson (as a last minute substitute for another performer allegedly possessing a "bad attitude") to do the lead vocal on a song he'd co-written with a shoe salesman named Joe Royster. Anderson changed the country feel of the song to R&B, adding a chorus and thumping backbeat, and "New Orleans" (#5 r&b) became to Top 10 smash. When the single first hit the streets, Anderson was perplexed to find it credited to "U.S. Bonds." It appears to Guida got the idea from the posters in the delicatessen located next door to the studio. When Anderson insisted on the addition of his first name for future releases, fans were initially confused, thinking U.S. Bonds referred to a group.

After the second Bonds release failed to click, Guida went back to the formula established in "New Orleans." He hooked Bonds up with another Legrand act, the Church Street Five, who were having trouble getting an instrumental piece, "A Night with Daddy G," to jell. A group member, Gene "Daddy G" Barge, encouraged Bonds to write lyrics on the spot. In a matter of minutes, the verses were ready and the musicians started working out an arrangement. Sources differ as how the resulting song, "Quarter to Three" (Legrand 1008; 1969; #1 pop, #3 r&b), ended up on tape. Some rock historians state that it was recorded by accident, although Bonds would go to claim that he knowingly turn on the recorder. One critic, Dave Marsh, posits that Guida would go on to add five overdubs of party sound effects in his quest for just the right ambience. A follow-up album, *Dance 'til Quarter to Three* (Legrand 3001; 1961; #6), would do surprisingly well for a so-called teen release, remaining on the charts for twenty-eight weeks.

The Bonds-Guida team continued to mine a similar vein with success through 1962, resulting in "School Is Out" (Legrand 1009; 1961; #5 pop, #12 r&b), "School Is In" (Legrand 1012; 1961; #28), "Dear Lady Twist: (Legrand 1015; 1961/2; #9 pop, #5 r&b), "Twist, Twist Senora" (Legrand 1018; 1962; #9), "Seven Day Weekend" (Legrand 1019; 1962; #27), and the aptly named "Copy Cat" (Legrand 1020; 1962; #92). He then receded back into the club and oldies circuits (one of his songs, "Friend Don't Take Her," would be a country hit for Johnny Paycheck in 1972) until Bruce Springsteen, long an admirer of the classic Bonds recordings, offered to produce his next LP, *Dedication* (EMI America 17051; 1981; #27), along with bandmate Steve Van Zandt. The album would yield a couple of hit singles, "This Little Girl" (EMI America 8079; 1981; #11), and the reworked Cajun classic, "Jole Blon" (EMI America 8089; 1981; #65).

Following another Springsteen-Van Zandt collaboration, On the Line (EMI America 17068; 1982; #52)—including the single, "Out of Work" (EMI America 8117; 1982; #21 pop, #82 r&b)—would also achieve commercial success. Bonds then moved on to an independent label, Phoenix, producing his own LP, *Standing in the Line of Fire*. However, by then he had once again fallen out of favor with the public in the face of the new romantics and techno-pop acts then benefiting from heavy MTV rotation.

November 28. Elvis Presley begins a six-week run atop the Hot 100 with "Are You Lonesome Tonight?" (RCA).

December 1. Bobby Darin marries movie starlet Sandra Dee in a New Jersey magistrate's living room.

December 5. *Billboard* identifies five "answer records" to Elvis Presley's chart-topping "Are You Lonesome Tonight." Four of the releases represent different versions of the same tune, "Yes, I'm Lonesome Tonight," while the other is a reading of the standard, "Oh How I Miss You Tonight."

December 5. Jerry Butler peaks at number eleven on the Hot 100 with "He Will Break Your Heart" (Vee-Jay 354).

Jerry Butler's suave soul style, together with his desire to be a chef and ice sculptor while taking restaurant management courses in trade school as a youth, earned him the nickname, "The Iceman." Although only moderately successful within the pop field, chart historian Joel Whitburn rated him one of the fifteen most popular rhythm and blues recording artists during the 1942 to 1988 period.

Born in Sunflower, Mississippi, December 8, 1939, Butler moved to Chicago with his family as an infant. After graduating from high school in June 1957, he met Curtis Mayfield and Sam Gooden at the Traveling Souls Spiritualistic Church, and they performed in a series of vocal groups, most notably The Northern Jubilee Gospel Singers and the Roosters. The latter group, which also included the brothers Arthur and Richard Brooks, recruited Eddie Thomas as manager later in the year. Thomas changed their name to The Impressions, and a personal appearance shortly thereafter at a local fashion show led to recording contract with Vee-Jay's Falcon subsidiary (renamed Abner in June 1958, after Vee-Jay General Manager Ewart Abner, when it was found that a Falcon label already existed in Texas).

Butler remained with the group long enough to pen the classic, "For Your Precious Love" (Falcon/Abner 1013; 1958; #11 pop, #3 r&b), before embarking on a solo career. Although Mayfield took over lead vocals for The Impressions, he also supplied many hit songs to Butler during the 1960 to 1966 period. Their joint composition, "He Will Break Your Heart," would remain Butler's biggest success, spending seven weeks at the top of the R&B charts. During this productive run, Butler would also find success with outside material such as Felice and Boudleaux Bryant's "Let It Be Me" (Vee-Jay 613; 1964; #5 pop, #5 r&b; duet with Betty Everett), originally made popular by the Everly Brothers.

Although Butler continued to produce hits following a switch to Mercury Records in mid-1966, his releases veered ever closer to mainstream pop. His work with the Philadelphia production team of Kenny Gamble and Leon Huff—resulting in two albums, *The Ice Man Cometh* (Mercury 61198; 1969; #29 pop, #2 r&b) and *Ice on Ice* (Mercury 61234; 1969; #41 pop, #4 r&b), and best-selling singles such as "Hey Western Union Man" (Mercury 72859; 1968; #16 pop, #1 r&b), "Only the Strong Survive" (Mercury 72898; 1969; #4 pop, #1 r&b), "Moody Woman" (Mercury 72929; 1969; #24 pop, #3 r&b), and "What's the Use of Breaking Up" (Mercury 72960; 1969; #20 pop, #4 r&b)—returned him to the center of the soul constellation.

Butler was no longer a pop force by early 1970s, but continued to produce R&B hits (albeit the lower reaches of the charts) until 1983. However, he had found new challenges by this time, establishing Fountain Records in 1980 and serving four four-year terms as a Cook County Commissioner. Still active as a performer, he was inducted, along with the Impressions, into the Rock and Rock Hall of Fame in 1991, and received the Rhythm & Blues Foundation's Pioneer Award in 1994.

December 5. The annual Christmas Rock & Roll Show at Brooklyn's Paramount Theater will be hosted by WNTA, Newark DJ Clay Cole. (It had been cancelled the previous year as a result of Alan Freed's involvement in the payola scandals.) The extravaganza will run from December 23 to January 1; headliners will include Chubby Checker, Bobby Rydell, Neil Sedaka, the Drifters, Little Anthony, Bobby Vee, the Skyliners, Dion, Bo Diddley, Johnny Burnette, and Dante and the Evergreens.

December 24. Now that Chubby Checker (aka Ernest Evans) has placed three singles—"The Class," "The Twist," and "The Hucklebuck"—in the Top 40, the Philadelphia Orphan's Court raises the 19-year-old singer's weekly allowance from $150 to $200.

December 25. Cliff Richard tops the British charts with "I Love You."

December 25. 17-year-old Detroit singer Mary Wells makes the R&B charts with her debut release, "Bye Bye Baby," one of the earliest records put out by the Motown label. It eventually reaches the Top 10 (and just misses the pop Top 40). Wells, who garnered a recording contract after walking into an audition uninvited with the intent of selling a song she'd written, will record eleven Top 40 hits—most notably, the chart-topping "My Guy" in 1964.

On the strength of her cool, but sexy vocals, Mary Wells became Motown Records' first star. Born in Detroit on May 13, 1943, she arranged an audition with Berry Gordy Jr., in order to pitch a song she'd written for his client, Jackie Wilson. Gordy signed her, and that song, "Bye Bye Baby" (Motown 1003), was released as her debut single. She was placed under the guidance of Smokey Robinson, whose understated production work helped launch a string of hits: "The One Who Really Loves You" (Motown 1024; 1962), "You Beat Me to the Punch" (Motown 1032; 1962), "Two Lovers" (Motown 1035; 1962), "Laughing Boy" (Motown 1039; 1963), "You Lost the Sweetest Boy"/"What's Easy For Two Is So Hard for One" (Motown 1048; 1963), and "My Guy" (Motown 1059; 1964; #1).

At the peak of her success, Wells sued Motown, arguing that the recording contract she signed at seventeen was invalid. She received a lucrative offer from 20th Century-Fox, along with promises that she'd be provided opportunities to appear in films. However, hits eluded her and acting roles did not materialize. Later stints with Atco and Jubilee failed to resurrect her career. She retired from music business, but returned in the 1980s when a revived interest in the classic Motown Sound led to a demand for concert appearances. Wells had just completed an album for British release, *Keeping My Mind on Love*, when she discovered she had cancer of the larynx. A two-pack-a-day smoker without health insurance, a number of friends and associates within the record industry provided financial assistance prior to her death on July 26, 1992.

1961

❄

January 4. Atlantic Records—through a distribution arrangement with the Memphis-based Satellite (later Stax) label—releases Carla Thomas' debut single (and biggest hit, #10 pop, #5 r&b), "Gee Whiz (Look at His Eyes)." The teenager (daughter of Memphis deejay and R&B singer Rufus Thomas, who recorded for Sun in the early 1950s) will enjoy a long career, including a string of hit singles and albums with duo partner Otis Redding in the late 1960s.

January 9. Bert Kaempfert begins a three-week run atop the Hot 100 with the instrumental, "Wonderland By Night" (Decca).

January 15. The Supremes sign a worldwide recording contract with the Motown label.

January 30. Jerry Leiber and Mike Stoller announce plans to form Leiber and Stoller Enterprises, which will handle studio production and engineering, music writing and publishing, and talent management for various record companies. The new firm's services will be utilized by Atlantic and RCA, among other labels.

January 30. Doo-wop appears to be experiencing a revival of sorts. Two notable vocal group hits from the mid-1950s—the Five Satins' "In the Still of the Nite" and the Mello-Kings' "Tonight Tonight"—are reissued and make the Hot 100.

January 30. The Shirelles reach number one on the pop charts with the Gerry Goffin/Carole King ode to the ambiguities surrounding teen sex, "Will You Love Me Tomorrow" (Scepter), remaining there for two weeks.

February 3. Bob Dylan participates in his first recording session—held at the East Orange, New Jersey, home of friends Sid and Bob Gleason—taping "San Francisco Bay Blues" and "Jesus Met the Woman at the Well," among other songs.

February 4. Johnny Burnette undergoes an emergency appendectomy at Hollywood's Cedars of Lebanon Hospital. The Memphis-based rockabilly singer turned teen idol has to cancel Hollywood concerts valued at $10,000 as well as a twenty-eight-date British tour scheduled to begin in three days.

February 5. Gene Pitney first appears on the Hot 100 with "(I Wanna) Love My Life Away." He will go on to record sixteen Top 40 hits in the 1960s. He will also play a key role in opening up the album market to rock 'n' roll artists, interpreting a wide range of material, including teen ballads, pop standards, country & western, and opera arias.

February 12. The Miracles' "Shop Around" (#2 pop, #1 r&b seven weeks) becomes Motown's first million-seller. The group—headed by songwriter/producer/record company executive William "Smokey" Robinson—will record six more gold records for the Detroit label in the 1960s.

The premier soul music strain of the 1960s and best-known African American-owned record company, Motown was the product of Berry Gordy's vision and drive. Gordy was a prizefighter and car assembly-line employee before shifting his attentions to songwriting, record production, and artist management. After working with R&B great Jackie Wilson briefly in the mid-1950s, he began producing Detroit area singer Marv Johnson, initially for the indie firm, Kudo, and then for Tamla, a label he established in 1959.

In addition to being an excellent judge of musical talent, Gordy had the good fortune be in the right place at the right time. In short order, he hired such pivotal figures as singer/songwriters Smokey Robinson and Marvin Gaye. By 1960–1961, he had found the hit-making touch, most notably, with "Money," by Barrett Strong; "Shop Around," by Robinson's group, the Miracles; and the label's first pop chart-topper, "Please Mr. Postman," by the Marvelettes. He quickly added the Motown, Gordy, and Anna imprints; a hitherto unprecedented number of the artists he signed (many of them homegrown) went on to record hits, including Mary Wells, Stevie Wonder, Martha & the Vandellas, the Supremes, the Temptations, the Four Tops, and Junior Walker & the All Stars. Much of Gordy's success was the result of efforts to appeal to the mainstream pop marketplace. Besides maintaining songwriter/producers and a superb house band capable of consistently achieving crossover success (billed as "the Sound of Young America"), he had his acts meticulously dressed and groomed, drilled to execute polished stage routines, and provided etiquette training. The company was astute enough to weather continued changes in musical fashion, socio-political upheaval, and countless imitators within the soul field during the 1960s.

Despite signing new stars like the Jackson 5 and the Commodores (with Lionel Richie) Motown finally began losing momentum in the 1970s as established artists like Gaye, Diana Ross, and the Four Tops—dissatisfied with control being exerted over their respective careers—moved on to other labels. Other questionable moves at the included the unsuccessful attempt to launch a rock imprint (Rare Earth) and the decision to relocate to Hollywood in 1973 as Gordy began focusing on making films. By the 1980s, Motown remained solvent largely through reissues of its back catalog (particularly on the newly emerging CD and video formats) and the production of musical revues for television. Gordy sold the company to MCA in 1988; the Universal Music Group continues to operate the Motown empire to the present day.

February 13. Frank Sinatra launches his record company, Reprise, with the single, "The Second Time Around"/ "Tina." Although the label will—in keeping with his alleged antipathy for rock 'n'roll—provide a haven for easy listening artists like Dean Martin, Trini Lopez, and Sammy Davis Jr. in its early years, it will be heavily committed to rock music (as reflected by the signings of the Kinks, the Jimi Hendrix Experience, Neil Young, Captain Beefheart, Joni Mitchell, Family, and the Beach Boys) by the end of the decade.

February 13. Lawrence Welk begins a two-week stint atop the Hot 100 with "Calcutta" (Dot).

February 14. The Platters and manager Buck Ram sue Mercury in Chicago for breach of contract. The suit was precipitated by the label's refusal to accept certain recordings where Tony Williams is not the lead singer. They argue that their recording contract does not stipulate who must sing lead and that other group members have done so on about 25 percent of the Platters' prior releases. The group's future appears to be in doubt with Williams, Paul Robi, and Zola Taylor having all made solo recordings with other companies.

February 15. Jackie Wilson is shot by a mentally unbalanced fan, Juanita Jones, who had entered his New York apartment, demanding attention. Threatening suicide, Wilson attempts to disarm her and is left with a stomach wound and a bullet lodged in his back. He is rushed to Roosevelt Hospital. He will be discharged on March 31, the bullet having not been removed due to its location non-threatening, but not easily-operable spot.

February 21. The Beatles perform at Liverpool's Cavern Club for the first time; they will perform there 293 times through 1963.

February 23. Petula Clark tops the British charts for the first time with "Sailor."

February 24. Further evidence that rock 'n' roll has truly become an international phenomenon: the First French International Rock & Roll Festival is held at Le Palais des Sports, Paris. The bill includes Bobby Rydell, the U.K.'s Emile Ford, Italy's Little Tony, and French stars such as Johnny Halliday, Frankie Jordan, and Les Chausettes Noires.

February 27. Chubby Checker begins a three-week run atop the Hot 100 with "Pony Time" (Parkway).

March 1. Elvis Presley signs a five-year film deal with producer Hal Wallis.

March 6. British singer, comedian, and ukulele player George Formby dies at age fifty-seven. He appeared in more than twenty films and was closely identified with the song, "Leaning on a Lamp Post," later revived by Herman's Hermits.

March 10. Songwriter Jeff Berry, age twenty-two, signs an exclusive writing and recording contract with Trinity Music. Best known for composing the Ray Peterson death dirge, "Tell Laura I Love Her," he will team with Ellie Greenwich (they marry in 1962) to supply songs to frontline producers like Phil Spector ("Da Doo Ron Ron" and "Then He Kissed Me" for the Crystals, "Be My Baby" for the Ronettes, "River Deep, Mountain High" for Ike and Tina Turner) and Shadow Morton ("Chapel of Love" for the Dixie Cus and "Leader of the Pak" for the Shagri-Las). They will also compose such notable hits as "Do Wah Diddy Diddy" (Exciters, Manfred Mann), "Hanky Panky" (Tommy James and the Shondells), and "Cherry Cherry" (Neil Diamond).

March 17. NBC-TV premieres the weekly country show, "Five Star Jubilee." It features five performers—Snooky Lanson, Tex Ritter, Rex Allen, Carl Smith, and Jimmy Wakely—who serve as hosts on a rotating basis.

March 20. Elvis Presley climbs to the summit of the charts with "Surrender" (RCA), remaining there for two weeks. It also tops the U.K. charts as the flipside of "Wooden Heart."

March 20. KYA, San Francisco, DJ Peter Tripp goes on trial before a Special Sessions Court in New York City on 39 counts of commercial bribery (i.e., payola). Tripp, who was recently fired at WMGM, New York City, will be found guilty by the court in May.

March 25. Elvis Presley helps raise $62,000 for the U.S.S. *Arizona* memorial fund in a performance at the Block Arena, Pearl Harbor, Hawaii. It will be his last live concert for eight years as he focuses on Hollywood movies.

March 26. Gene McDaniels' first—and biggest—hit, "One Hundred Pounds of Clay," makes the Hot 100; it will eventually reach the number three position.

March 26. Elvis Presley becomes the first artist to enjoy three number one singles in a row on the British charts with "It's Now or Never," "Are You Lonesome Tonight," and "Wooden Heart."

March 27. Carla Thomas peaks at number ten on the Hot 100 with "Gee Whiz (Look at His Eyes)" (Atlantic 2086).

Prior to the rise of Aretha Franklin, Carla Thomas had been anointed the "Queen of Soul." "Gee Whiz (Look at His Eyes)" (#5 r&b), recorded while she was still a teenager, became the first Memphis Soul release to receive national attention and provided the seed money for the launching of the fabled Stax label.

Carla Thomas was born in Memphis, December 21, 1942, the daughter of noted deejay and recording artist Rufus Thomas. She grew up performing in public, joining the Teentown Singers at the age of ten. Her first record, "Cause I Love You" (1960)—released on Satellite Records, which changed its name to Stax the following year in order to avoid a trademark infringement suit with another company—consisted of a duet with her father, done during the summer break from college. Along with her father and the label's house band, Booker T. & the MG's, she was an early star on the Stax roster. Her twenty-three chart hits—often appearing on the Atlantic label due to a distribution arrangement—included "A Love Of My Own" (Atlantic 2101; 1961; #56 pop, #20 r&b), later covered by the Average White Band on the best-selling *Soul Searching* album; the answer song (to Sam Cooke's "Bring It On Home to Me"), "I'll Bring It Home to You" (Atlantic 2163; 1962; #41 pop, #9 r&b); "Let Me Be Good to You" (Stax 188; 1966; #62 pop, #11 r&b); "B-A-B-Y" (Stax 195; 1966; #14 pop, #3 r&b), the first of a string of duet with Otis Redding, "Tramp" (Stax 216; 1967; #26 pop, #2 r&b); "Knock on Wood" (Stax 228; 1967; #30 pop, #8 r&b; with Redding); and "I Like What You're Doing (to Me)" (Stax 0024; 1969; #49 pop, #9 r&b).

Although her recording career was effectively over by the time Stax went bankrupt in the mid-1970s, Thomas has remained semi-active as a club performer. She was appointed artist-in-residence for the Tennessee Arts Commission in the late 1980s, and received the Rhythm & Blues Foundation's Pioneer Award in 1993.

March 31. Instant Records releases Chris Kenner's only national hit, "I Like It Like That"/"I Like It Like That, Part Two." However, cover versions of his material will do even better; most notably, the Dave Clark Five's "I Like It Like That" (1966), and differing treatments of "Land of 1000 Dances" by Cannibal and the Headhunters (1965) and Wilson Pickett (1966).

April 1. The Beatles begin a three-month residency at Hamburg's Top Ten Club, playing seven hours a night weekdays (eight hours on weekends), with a fifteen-minute break each hour.

April 2. Paul Revere and the Raiders make their Hot 100 debut with "Like, Long Hair," which eventually reaches number thirty-eight. Their career was temporarily stalled by Revere's two-year stint "clanging bedpans in the Wilsonville asylum" as a conscientious objector. By the mid-1960s, the re-formed band would become known for wearing Revolutionary War-styled ponytails and uniforms.

April 2. Irvin Feld's Biggest Show of Stars 1961 kicks off in Philadelphia. It will much of the United States and portions of Canada as well. Headliners will include Chubby Checker, Bo Diddley, Fats Domino, the Drifters, Chuck Jackson, Ben E. King, the Shells, the Shirelles, and the Paul Williams Band.

April 3. The Marcels begin a three-week stay atop the Hot 100 with the neo-doo-wop rendition of Rodgers and Hart's "Blue Moon" (Colpix).

April 11. Bob Dylan, then age nineteen, gives his first New York City concert, at Gerde's Folk City, a small Greenwich Village Club. Opening for John Lee Hooker, he performs "The House of the Rising Son," "Song to Woody" (his own composition, a tribute to legendary folk singer Woody Guthrie), and several other tunes.

April 12. The results of the Third Annual Grammy Awards are announced; rock 'n' roll acts fail to win any awards. Ray Charles earns the spotlight, taking home trophies for Best Vocal Performance, Male; Best Performance by a Pop Single Artist ("George on My Mind"); Best Vocal Performance, Album (*The Genius of Ray Charles*); and Best R&B Performance ("Let the Good Times Roll").

April 22. The First Annual Country Music Festival begins at the Jacksonville, Florida, Colisseum. Featured performers include Patsy Cline, Lester Flatt and Earl Scruggs, the Foggy Mountain Boys, George Hamilton IV, the Louvin Brothers, Webb Pierce, Mel Tillis, Porter Wagoner, and Faron Young.

April 22. Having recovered from a February appendectomy, Johnny Burnette lauches a one-week tour of Australia and New Zealand.

April 24. Bob Dylan receives $50 for his official recording debut, contributing harmonica on the track, Calypso King," from Harry Belafonte's LP, *Midnight Special*.

April 24. Del Shannon starts a four-week run at number one on the pop charts with "Runaway" (Big Top).

May 1. The Ray Charles instrumental, "One Mint Julep"—released on Impulse, an ABC imprint specializing in jazz—peaks at number eight on the Hot 100. The big band album which it was taken from, *Genius + Soul = Jazz* (featuring Quincy Jones as arranger and a slew of respected jazz musicians), will reach number four.

May 1. The Marcels top the British charts with "Blue Moon."

May 7. Tony Orlando makes his first appearance in the Hot 100 with "Halfway to Paradise"; it will peak at number thirty-nine. The follow-up, "Bless You," will also reach the Top 40. Orlando then experiences a prolonged dry spell until resurfacing as the leader of the soft rock trio, Dawn, in the early 1970s.

May 8. On his twenty-first birthday, Ricky Nelson officially changes his first name to "Rick."

May 11. An article in the East German publication, *Freie Walt*, authored by Soviet bandleader and musicologist Alexander Utyosov, argues that the early jazz genre widely known as "Dixieland" already was being played for many years in the Odessa region before it arose in New Orleans.

May 19. The Everly Brothers launch Calliope, a label created "to discover and develop new talent." The duo's own work will still be released by Warner Brothers.

May 22. Two versions of "Every Beat of My Heart" make the Hot 100. Due to a record contract dispute, both feature the same artists: the Fury single is attributed to Gladys Knight, and the Vee-Jay release lists the Pips. The latter record will become the best-seller, reaching number six (topping the R&B charts). Gladys Knight and the Pips will become steady hitmakers first with Motown's Soul subsidiary in the late 1960s, and then with Buddah in the early 1970s.

May 22. Ernie K-Doe peaks at number one on the Hot 100 with "Mother-In-Law" (Minit 623).

Ernie K-Doe is seen by most popular music enthusiasts as a typical one-hit wonder. However, he knocked around the New Orleans rhythm and blues scene for many years, working with many of the local stars and producing a few best-selling singles under his own name.

Born Ernest Kador Jr. on February 22, 1936, in New Orleans, he was the ninth of eleven children. Although raised by his aunt on his mother's side, he sang in the New Home Baptist Church, where his father served as minister. He toured with various gospel groups as an adolescent. At the age of seventeen, he relocated briefly to Chicago, recording his first secular tracks—four in all, none of which were released—as a solo artist.

Returning to New Orleans, he recorded for the legendary Savoy label in 1954 with the Blue Diamonds, whose membership also included Huey "Piano" Smith, Billy Tate, Frank Fields, and Earl Palmer. Going solo later in the decade, he recorded for both Specialty and Ember. He would burst into national prominence with the tongue-in-cheek lament, "Mother-In-Law" (#1 r&b five weeks), featuring bass vocals by Benny Spellman. According to K-Doe, the song (composed by New Orleans producer Allen Toussaint) had special meaning to him. He allegedly retrieved it from a garbage can where Toussaint had thrown it, noting, "I was married nineteen years, and it was nineteen years of pure sorrow." Although moderately successful, his follow-up, "Te-Ta-Te-Ta-Ta" (Minit 627; 1961; #53 pop, #21 r&b), failed to establish him as a consistent hitmaker.

When his records stopped selling, K-Doe—typically wearing iridescent apparel and oversized gold rings—would continue to offer a dynamic live show. He would tell Almost Slim, author of *Walking to New* Orleans, "I don't like to brag, but I still believe I can out-perform any man in show business. Ernie K-Doe can stop any show at the drop of a hat." He did return to the charts in the late 1960s with "Later For Tomorrow" (Duke 411; 1967; #122 pop, #37 r&b) and "Until the Real Thing Comes Along" (Duke 423; 1967; #48 r&b). By 1982, K-Doe was periodically hosting an R&B radio program on WWOZ, New Orleans. He continued to make music, contributing three new tracks to the mid-1989 compilation cassette, *New Orleans: A Musical Gumbo*.

May 29. Rick Nelson tops the pop charts with "Travelin' Man" (Imperial), remaining there for two non-consecutive weeks. The record's flip side, the Gene Pitney-penned "Hello Mary Lou," does nearly as well, climbing as high as number nine (#1 U.K.).

May 29. Elvis Presley heads up the British charts with "Surrender."

May 31. Perhaps sensing the limits to a pop music career, Chuck Berry opens Berry Park, a thirty-acre amusement complex located in Wentzville, Missouri (twenty miles west of St. Louis). The facility includes a Ferris wheel and other rides, a miniature golf course, a swimming pool, a children's zoo, a ballroom, and a picnic grove complete with barbecue pits.

June 2. Two men are sentenced to a year and a day in prison (with a third receiving a suspended sentence) in Hackensack, New Jersey, for bootlegging records, the first ever successful conviction of this activity.

June 5. Roy Orbison reaches number one on the Hot 100 with "Running Scared" (Monument).

June 8. Elvis Presley's *Wild in the Country*, his seventh film, premieres in Memphis. Featuring a screenplay by the legendary Clifford Odets about a poor juvenile delinquent and the women (played by Tuesday Weld and Hope Lange) who attempt to change his life, it was originally released without any Presley songs. Its negative reception form critics and fans alike, however, led to a re-edited version featuring several numbers, including the title theme song, "I Slipped, I Stumbled, I Fell," and "In My Way."

June 12. Frankie Avalon kicks off a fifteen-day tour of South America with a concert in Buenos Aires, Argentina.

June 14. Patsy Cline is involved in a car crash near Madison, Tennessee. She receives serious head injuries and a fractured and dislocated right hip, while a passenger in another vehicle is killed.

June 19. Pat Boone heads up the pop charts for the last time with "Moody River" (Dot).

June 25. DJ Alan Freed, now affiliated with KDAY, Los Angeles, launches a tour of outdoor arenas with a Hollywood Bowl show. Headliners include the Fleetwoods, Clarence "Frogman" Henry, Etta James, Brenda Lee, Jerry Lee Lewis, Gene McDaniels, the Shirelles, Bobby Vee, the Ventures, and Kathy Young and the Innocents. Freed has received a temporary reprieve in his payola trail; originally set to start June 15, it has been postponed until October.

June 26. Gary "U.S." Bonds begins a two-week stint atop the pop charts with "Quarter to Three" (Legrand).

June 26. The Spinners make their first appearance of the Hot 100 with "That's What Girls Are Made For"; it will reach number twenty-seven (#3 r&b). The group will hit its stride early in the following decade when teamed with Philly Soul songwriter/producer Thom Bell.

July 6. The publication of the first issue of *Mersey Beat*, a fan magazine devoted to covering the Liverpool rock scene. It includes an article authored by John Lennon, "Being a Short Diversion on the Dubious Origins of Beatles."

July 10. Bobby Lewis begins a seven-week run atop the pop charts with "Tossin' and Turnin'" (Beltone 1002).

July 10. The Mar-Keys make the Hot 100 with the instrumental, "Last Night." The Memphis-based band includes guitarist Steve Cropper and bassist Duck Dunn, both of whom will become founding members of Booker T. and the MGs the following year.

July 10. The Pips peak at number six on the Hot 100 with "Every Beat of My Heart" (Vee-Jay 386).

Although never an innovator, Gladys Knight (b. May 28, 1944)—with her backing group, the Pips (originally all close family members)—has enjoyed a long, successful career, first as a pop-soul singer, and, by the late 1970s, within the adult contemporary field. The Atlanta-based act began performing in the early 1950s, recording five chart singles (including the Top 10 R&B hits, "Every Bear of My Heart" and "Letter Full of Tears") for the independent labels Huntom, Fury, and Maxx before signing with the Motown subsidiary, Soul, in 1966. While not on a par with such commercial juggernauts as Marvin Gaye, the Four Tops, the Temptations, and Stevie Wonder, the Pips recorded a string of moderately successful hits with the company, including the original rendition of "I Heard It Through the Grapevine," "The End of Our Road," "If I Were You Woman," and "Neither One of Us," which peaked at number two on the *Billboard* Hot 100 in 1973, shortly before they switched to Buddah.

With Buddah they enjoyed a brief run in the upper echelon of the charts with best-selling singles such as "Midnight Train to Georgia," "I've Got to Use My Imagination," and "Best Thing That Ever Happened to Me." Always a highly capable outfit, capable of effectively interpreting doo-wop-styled ballads, girl group novelties, R&B/gospel rave-ups, and more conventional pop-soul fare, Gladys Knight—occasionally without the Pips—gradually took on more and more easy listening material once the mainstream hits stopped coming (they managed to top the R&B charts as late as 1987 with Love Overboard"). Not surprisingly for an artist that has been active for the better part of six decades, a wealth of anthologies are available that document all phases of her career, most notably, *Anthology* (Motown, 1974), *Soul Survivors: The Best of Gladys Knight & the Pips 1973-1988* (Rhino, 1990), *The Ultimate Collection* (Motown, 1997), and *Essential Collection* (Hip-O, 1999).

July 12. Pat Boone kicks off a ten-day tour of South Africa with a show at the Ice Drome in Durban. Afterwards, he will start filming *State Fair* in southern California.

July 14. *Billboard* relates that the Twist is now being danced by adults in Philadelphia, where dance-club contests have proved immensely popular.

July 17. The Supremes' first single, "Buttered Popcorn"/"Who's Loving You," is released by Motown. While it fails to chart, the female trio—who started earlier in the year as the Primettes, opening in Detroit venues for the Primes (later known as the Temptations)—will become the most successful girl group of all time.

July 29. The Dick Clark Caravan of Stars summer tour begins at Atlantic City's Steel Pier. Headliners for the extravaganza—which concludes with a September 4 date in Detroit—will include Gary "U.S." Bonds, Freddy Cannon, Chubby Checker, Mike Clifford, Duane Eddy and the Rebels, Fabian, Chuck Jackson, Johnny and the Hurricanes, Bobby Rydell, the Shirelles, and Dodie Stevens.

August 2. The Beatles first perform at the Cavern Club, in Liverpool, where they'll appear as ongoing headliners for about three hundred engagements over the next couple of years.

August 7. The Mar-Keys begin a two-week stint at number three on the Hot 100 with "Last Night" (Satellite 107).

The Mar-Keys were one of early proponents of the Memphis Sound, a classic variant of 1960s soul that blended gritty, down-home country funk with a more urbane, uptown brand of rhythm and blues. They were also a precursor of the Memphis Horns, a loose group of studio players that placed their distinctive stamp on much of the music coming out of this recording center at the time.

The Mar-Keys formed in 1958 as a four-piece instrumental combo playing local dances in the Memphis area. Expanding to incorporate brass in 1960, the group's personnel—guitarist Steve Cropper, bassist Donald "Duck" Dunn, drummer Terry Johnson, keyboardist Jerry Lee "Smoochee" Smith, tenor saxophonist Charles "Packy" Axton, baritone saxophonist Don Nix, and trumpeter Wayne Jackson— became staff musicians for Satellite Records (owned by Axton's mother, Estelle, and rechristened Stax when threatened with a lawsuit by another similarly named label). Their first—and biggest—hit, "Last Night," with its repetitious, rock-steady brass riff, established a formula that the band milked for the better portion of the decade.

The Mar-Keys' momentum was slowed somewhat when Cropper and Dunn departed shortly thereafter to form Booker T. and the MG's with organist Booker T. Jones and drummer Al Jackson. Nevertheless, the band continued to periodically place releases—most notably, "Morning After" (Stax; 1961), "Pop-Eye Stroll" (Stax; 1962), and "Philly Dog" (Stax; 1966)—on the charts.

August 7. The Spinners peak at number twenty-seven on the Hot 100 with "That's What Girls Are Made For" (Tri Phi 1001).

Although major success eluded them at the time, the Detroit-based Spinners—as opposed to the Pittsburgh, California group of the same name—were one of the more sophisticated harmony groups of the 1960s. They emerged as one of the definitive soft soul acts of the 1970s, in a class with the best of the Gamble and Huff-produced artists, including the O'Jays and the Stylistics.

Formed in Detroit in the late 1950s, the group—originally comprised of former Ferndale High School students Bobbie Smith (tenor), George Dixon (tenor), Billy Henderson (tenor), Henry Fambrough (baritone), and Pervis Jackson (bass)—was originally known as the Domingoes. They soon came under the tutelage of Moonglows singer Harvey Fuqua, who helped create their distinctive lush vocal blend. Fuqua spurred them to record a song he'd co-written with Berry Gordy's sister, "That's What Girls Are Made For" (#5 r&b) for his Tri-Phi label. Fuqua allegedly sang lead on the Spinners' first two releases; other experts such as Marc Taylor, author of *A Touch of Classic Soul*, have argued that this misunderstanding resulted from the fact that Harvey succeeded in getting Smith to emulate the Moonglows' sound and style.

In the early 1960s Dixon had departed (to be replaced by Edgar Edwards), and Tri-Phi was subsumed by the Motown combine. From 1964-1968, the Spinners shifted to the Motown imprint, enjoying one hit of note, "I'll Always Love You" (#1078; 1965; #35 pop, #8 r&b). In 1966, Edwards left the group; his replacement, G.C. Cameron, was quickly elevated to lead vocalist. By 1969, they had been moved to Motown's V.I.P. label; the resulting hits—"It's a Shame" (#25057; 1970; #14 pop, #4 r&b) and "We'll Have It Made" (#25060; 1971; #89 pop, #20 r&b)—were produced by Stevie Wonder, then barely in his twenties.

With the group no longer a priority at Motown, they followed friend Aretha Franklin's suggestion that they sign with Atlantic. When Cameron chose to remain with Motown, Phillipe Wynne was installed at lead in 1972. They recorded thirty-three hits with the label through the mid-1980s, including the chrt-toppers, "I'll Be Around" (#2904; 1972; #3 pop, #1 r&b), "Could It Be I'm Falling In Love" (#2927; 1972; #4 pop, #1 r&b), "One of a Kind (Love Affair)" (#2962; 1973; #11 pop, #1 r&b), "Mighty Love – Pt. 1" (#3006; 1974; #20 pop, #1 r&b), "Then Came You" (#3202; 1974; #1 pop, #2 r&b; with Dionne Warwick), "They Just Can't Stop It (Games People Play)" (#3284; 1975; #5 pop, #1 r&b), and "The Rubberband Man" (Atlantic 3355; 1976; #2 pop, #1 r&b). Wynne, who died on July 14, 1984, opted for a solo career in 1977, touring with the likes of Parliament/Funkadelic. John Edwards took over his slot, with many personnel changes following over the next decade.

August 24. Solomon Burke's first hit, "Just Out of Reach (of My Two Empty Arms)," is released by Atlantic Records; it will peak at number twenty-four on the Hot 100 (#7 R&B). Burke first attracted attention as a gospel singer in the Philadelphia area at the age of nine. He hosted a gospel radio show, *Solomon's Temple*, during his teens and earned the appellation "the Wonder Boy Preacher" on the national gospel circuit. In the late 1950s, he recorded gospel, pop, and R&B sides for the Apollo and Singular labels. He will become one of the leading soul vocalists of the 1960s, and remain active as a recording artist and performer well into the twenty-firstcentury.

August 28. Joe Dowell reaches number one on the Hot 100 with "Wooden Heart" (Smash).

August 28. Motown subsidiary, Tamla, releases the Marvelettes' debut recording, "Please Mr. Postman"; it appears on the Hot 100 at number ninety-five the following week on its way to topping the pop and R&B surveys. An instant classic, the song will be widely covered in the future, most notably, by the Beatles and the Carpenters. The female vocal quintet was formed at Detroit's Inkster High School by Gladys Horton;

they were signed by Berry Gordy Jr. after winning a school talent contest. The group will remain consistent hitmakers throughout the 1960s.

September 4. The Highwaymen begin a two-week stay atop the pop charts with the gospel traditional, "Michael" (United Artists).

September 18. Bobby Vee reaches number one on the Hot 100 with "Take Good Care of My Baby" (Liberty), remaining there for three weeks.

September 26. Bob Dylan begins a two-week stint opening for the Greenbriar Boys at Gerde's Folk City, Greenwich Village.

September 29. Bob Dylan receives his first press coverage when *New York Times* music critic Robert Shelton reviews the Greenbriar Boys show at Gerde's Folk City. He refers to Dylan as "a cross between a choir boy and a beatnik" and "bursting at the seams with talent."

September 30. Bob Dylan contributes harmonica lines on three tracks being recorded for Carolyn Hester's debut Columbia LP. Producer John Hammond—who was familiar with a laudatory *New York Times* review of one of Dylan's Gerge's Folk City performances—is sufficiently impressed to sign him to a Columbia Records contract in short order. Hammond also sets up a solo recording session in October for the young folk interpreter.

Bob Dylan is arguably the most innovative—and influential—artist from the rock era. He is generally credited with melding the rhythmic energy and rebellious attitude of early rock 'n' roll with the literate poetry and social consciousness of the folk movement.

Born Robert Zimmerman in Duluth, Minnesota, he taught himself to play the guitar after developing an interest in 1950s rock 'n' roll. He enrolled at the University of Minnesota, performing for a time in Minneapolis area coffee houses. Falling under the spell of folk stylist Woody Guthrie, he relocated to New York City performing in folk venues and doing studio session work on a sporadic basis before being discovered by Columbia Records executive John Hammond. He would release a steady string of moderately popular LPs for that label into the early 1970s, most notably, *The Times They Are A-Changin'* (Columbia 8905; 1964), *Another Side of Bob Dylan* (Columbia 8993; 1964), *Bringing It All Back Home* (Columbia 9128; 1965), *Highway 61 Revisited* (Columbia 9189; 1965), and *Blonde on Blonde* (Columbia 841; 1966).

Dylan almost single-handedly pioneered the folk rock genre through a combination of inspired songwriting and ground-breaking electric folk recordings such as "Subterranean Homesick Blues" (Columbia 43242; 1965), "Like a Rolling Stone" (Columbia 43346; 1965), and "Positively 4th Street" (Columbia 43389; 1965). His influential compositions included "Blowin' in the Wind," "Don't Think Twice (It's All Right)," "Mr. Tambourine Man," "All I Really Want To Do," and "It Ain't Me Babe," which became hits for the likes of Peter, Paul and Mary, Stevie Wonder, the Byrds, Cher, the Turtles, and Johnny Cash. He remained in the vanguard of the pop music scene throughout the decade, providing the impetus for the back-to-the-roots movement (*John Wesley Harding*; Columbia 9604; 1968) and country rock (*Nashville Skyline*; Columbia 9825; 1969). Dylan is perhaps best remembered for his legendary appearance at the Newport Folk Festival in 1965, where he was allegedly booed off the stage after returning for the second set with an electric guitar in hand. If nothing else, the psychic toll of these halcyon years may explain the inexplicable release of the mediocre double-disc set, *Self Portrait* (Columbia 30050; 1970), which seemed hell-bent on de-mythologizing his preeminent status as the generation's cultural spokesperson.

Following a brief two-album hiatus with Asylum in 1973 and 1974, Dylan resigned with Columbia, where he has remained for the balance of his career to date. Although no longer the trendsetter he was in the 1960s, he has continued to produce socially relevant popular music of a high order. Produced at the outset of the 1980s evangelical revival, his so-called Christian trilogy—*Slow Train Coming* (Columbia 36120; 1979), *Saved* (Columbia 36553; 1980), and *Shot of Love* (Columbia 37496; 1981)—would attract considerable attention (in addition to provoking widespread criticism).

Dylan's new releases has had to compete against his vintage material—e.g., the five-disc retrospective box set, *Biograph* (Columbia C5X-38830; 1985) and the ongoing Bootleg series—over the last few decades. Nevertheless, he won a Grammy for his 1977 album, *Time Out of Mind* (Columbia 68556). He would garner a lifetime achievement award at the 1990 Grammies.

October 2. Vanguard Records releases Joan Baez's LP, *Volume Two*, and accompanying single, "Banks of the Ohio"/"Old Blue." The twenty-year-old singer has become a sensation among folk music devotees since appearing at the 1959 Newport Folk Festival due largely to a richness and purity of her soprano voice. Although a lightning rod for the 1960s protest movement, she will fall from favor with the advent of the singer/songwriter vogue because her repertoire is limited to traditional folk material and the compositions of contemporary songwriters.

October 9. Ray Charles begins a two-week stint atop the pop charts with "Hit the Road Jack" (ABC-Paramount).

October 19. The Beatles and Gerry & the Pacemakers combine forces, performing at Litherland Town Hall, Merseyside, as "The Beatmakers." The two bands will continue to share bills at the Cavern Club and other Liverpool venues in 1961 and 1962.

October 21. Bob Dylan records his debut album, *Bob Dylan* (Columbia), in one day with John Hammond handling production duties. With the singer supplying his own instrumental accompaniment on guitar and harmonica, recording costs come to only $400 (Rees and Crampton, *Rock Movers and Shakers*, 1992, say the 20th).

October 23. Dion climbs to the summit of the pop charts with "Runaround Sue" (Laurie), remaining there for two weeks. The single proves to have substantial staying power, also spending five weeks at number two due largely to the popularity of Jimmy Dean's "Big Bad John."

October 23. Minit Records releases Ernie K-Doe's "I Cried My Last Tear"; it fails to approach the success of his chart-topping "Mother-in-Law" earlier in the year, reaching only number sixty-nine in the Hot 100. The New Orleans-based R&B vocalist will manage to crease the charts two more times in the upcoming months before receding from public view.

October 23. Fresh from the Top 10 hit, the mildly satirical "Who Put the Bomp?," Barry Mann's follow-up, "Little Miss U.S.A."/"Find Another Fool," is released by ABC-Paramount. When it falls short of the charts, Mann—with the exception of a brief hit run as a member of the neo-doo-wop trio, the Raindrops, along with songwriting partner Cynthia Weill, 1963-1964—will focus on composing such best-sellers as the Animals' "We Gotta Get Out of This Place," the Crystals' "Uptown" and "He's Sure the Boy I Love," the Paris Sisters' "I Love How You Love Me," the Righteous Brothers' "You've Lost That Lovin' Feeling," and Paul Revere and the Readers' "Kicks."

October 30. Philles Records—a joint venture between Phil Spector and Lester Sill—releases its first record, the Crystals' "Oh Yeah, Maybe Baby"/"There's No Other (Like My Baby)"—includes many of the features of Spector's vaunted "wall of sound" production techniques: dense, Latin-tinged orchestration punctuated by a strongly accentuated beat. The B side reaches number twenty on the pop charts, eventually selling more than a million copies worldwide.

November 3. Jimmie Rodgers, the "Singing Brakeman," is unanimously elected as the first member of the Country Music Hall of Fame, located in Nashville's Music Row. Although Rodgers (1897–1933) had a relatively short recording career before dying of tuberculosis, his popularity and ability to meld a wide range of styles—including jazz, the blues, Hawaiian ballads, and Tin Pan Alley pop—within a country & western context earned him widespread recognition as the father of modern country music.

November 4. Bob Dylan makes his concert-hall debut at New York City's Carnegie Chapter Hall. Only fifty people pay the $2 admission fee—most of them are allegedly his close friends—netting the performer $20.

November 6. Country star Jimmy Dean begins a five-week run atop the Hot 100 with the spoken narrative, "Big Bad John" (Columbia).

November 6. Minit Records releases the Showmen's "It Will Stand," a modest hit which earns classic status due to its lyrics, which extol the virtues of rock 'n' roll. When the group fails to maintain this success, the members fall back into obscurity. Lead singer, General Johnson, will return in 1970 to supply the memorable scatting and hiccupping lines for the Chairmen of the Board's best-selling single, "Give Me Just a Little More Time."

November 9. Brian Epstein, the manager of several Liverpool record shops within his family's retail empire, visits the Cavern Club to see a noon-hour Beatles concert. He became curious about the band when a teen customer requested their recording of "My Bonnie." Impressed by their dynamic showmanship, he introduces himself to George Harrison and Paul McCartney; the latter tells him they provided support for Tony Sheridan on the disc in question. Epstein persuades the members to hire him as their manager before the month is out; the arrangement is formalized by contract on January 24, 1962. He will continue to serve in this capacity until his death in August 1967; while not considered the shrewdest negotiator around, his honesty and devotion to the band was never in question.

November 14. William J. Halley (real name: William J. Hanley) dies at age sixty-eight. Allegedly the only best-selling record artist to become a state legislator (New Jersey Assembly, 1917–1918) and a judge (Hoboken District Court Judge, 1923-1933), his biggest hits included "You Made Me Love You" (Victor 17381; 1913) and "Do You Take This Woman for Your Lawful Wife?" (Columbia 1497; 1914). His willingness to abandon a promising career at a relatively tender age illustrates the low esteem the recording profession.

November 20. *Billboard* provides a kaleidoscopic look at the international Twist craze: Chubby Checker is featured in a series of one- and five-minute "Twist lessons" to be aired hourly every day on WOR-TV, New York; Checker is also set to star in a British-American movie, *It's Trad Dad*; in addition to having an album, *Doin' the Twist at the Peppermint Lounge*, released by Roulette to considerable fanfare this week, Joey Dee and the Starliters are under contract to appear in the Paramount film, *Hey, Let's Twist*; Dion has been signed to star in Columbia's *Twist Around the Clock*; and there are reportedly forty-five different Twist records available in France, with two versions of "The Twist"—by Johnny Halliday and Richard Anthony, respectively—presently sharing the top position on the French pop charts.

December 2. Rock guitarist Dick Dale enters the Hot 100 for the first top with "Let's Go Trippin'" (Deltone). He would later notes the interrelationship of his music and surfing.

Surfing, which became popular with Hawaiian nobility centuries ago, caught on as a popular recreational activity along the California coast during the post-World War II period. By the early 1960s, surfing had developed into a youth subculture. The surfing lifestyle was widely disseminated by publications such as John Severson's *Surfer Magazine* and series of excellent film documentaries produced by Bruce Brown, including *Slippery When Wet* (1959), *Barefoot Adventure* (1961), and *Endless Summer*, which documented the mythological worldwide search for the ultimate wave. It encompassed fashion (surfers favored pendletons, white levis, baggies, and sun-bleached hair often helped a little by peroxide) and language. Slang surfing terms included "woodie" (a souped-up old wooden-sided station wagon used to haul surfboards), "goofy foot" (a surfer who rode with his right foot forward on the board), and "wipe-out" (resulting when a surfer lost control of the board while fighting to master a wave).

Although he failed to achieve national stardom, Dale is generally credited with introducing surf music. Backed by the Del-Tones, he developed a strong following in the Southern California area as the "Pied Piper of Balboa," most notably via weekend dances at the Rendezvous Ballroom. The essentially instrumental sound—a visceral stew of wailing saxophones and atmospheric guitar accented by a pounding twelve-bar bass beat—attempted to evoke tremendous sense of power felt through bonding with the forces of nature while surfing.

The Beach Boys almost single-handedly made the surf sound a national sensation through the addition of evocative song lyrics. Brian Wilson's compositional gifts were so fertile that he was able to give a number one hit to the comedy rock duo, Jan and Dean, while keeping his own band supplied with a steady succession of Top 10 material. That gift, "Surf City" (Liberty 55580; 1963), catapulted Jan and Dean past second echelon surf interpreters such as the Surfaris, the Chantays, the Astronauts, the Challengers, the El Caminos, the Fantastic Baggys (featuring P.F. Sloan and Steve Barrie, later to make a name in protest music), and the Marketts. Like the Beach Boys, however, Jan and Dean were savvy enough to avoid too close an identification with the surf sound, mining the car songs genre ("Drag City," Liberty 55641; 1963), new fads such as skateboarding ("Sidewalk Surfin'," Liberty 55724; 1964), and assorted novelty material ("Batman," Liberty 55860; 1966).

At its peak, between 1963 and 1965, surf music was as popular with eastern and midwestern youth as in its native Pacific Coast environment. Bands like the Minneapolis-based Trashmen, Chicago's Rivieras, and

New York's Trade Winds all climbed the upper reaches of the singles charts with surf songs. In addition, Hollywood supplied a steady stream of beach movies, most notably American International Pictures. The studio's highly successful titles—including *Beach Party, Muscle Beach Party, Beach Blanket Bingo, How to Stuff a Wild Bikini, Bikini Beach*, and *Ski Party*—helped expose many surf acts to a mainstream audience. Other popular surf films included *Surf Party, Girls on the Beach*, and *Ride the Wild Surf*. Surf music gradually lost its momentum in the mid-1960s in the face of changing fashions. The pressing social imperatives of the period (e.g., civil rights, the Vietnam War) rendered the genre irrelevant. It retreated back to its former subculture status; however, a small core of cult bands (e.g., Man or Astro-Man, Agent Orange) have continued to produce new music utilizing surf sound conventions into the new millennium.

December 4. Gene Chandler's doo-wop-styled "Duke of Earl" is released by Vee-Jay. It goes on to top the pop and R&B charts, selling more than a million copies worldwide. Forever nicknamed the "Duke of Earl," Chandler will remain a consistent hitmaker into the 1970s with such Chicago Soul staples as "Just Be True" (Constellation, 1964) and "Groovy Situation" (1970; #12 pop). He will branch out into record production (Mel and Tim's "Backfield in Motion"; 1969) and found a couple of record labels, Mr. Chan, in the early 1970s, and ChiSound later in the decade.

December 5. Ray Charles—a heroin addict since age sixteen—is charged with possession of narcotics following an arrest in a downtown Indianapolis hotel.

December 8. The Beach Boys' first recording, "Surfin'," is released by the Los Angeles indie label Candix. Written by Brian Wilson and his cousin Mike Love, the song also includes the voices of the other Wilson brothers, Carl and Dennis, and friend Alan Jardine. Instrumentation consists of Carl laying acoustic guitar, Alan on upright double bass, and Brian pounding on a garbage can.

The Beach Boys rose to fame providing the soundtrack—in four-part, Four Freshmen-styled, harmonies—to the surfing and drag racing crazes of the early 1960s; they then moved on to chronicle the carefree lifestyle of West Coast teenagers. To fans around the world, the group—originally comprised of the Wilson brother, Brian, Carl, and Dennis, their cousin Mike Love and close friend Alan Jardine—has come to symbolize the nostalgia associated with the all-too-transitory joys of the sun-drenched pleasures of youth.

Musical performances were a central activity for the Wilson family; therefore, it represented a logical progression when Dennis persuaded his associates to form a group as a vehicle for celebrating surfing, his primary passion in life. Faced with a lack of song material about the sport, Brian and Mike wrote "Surfin'" and recorded it for the local Candix label on October 8, 1961. It became a large regional hit, leading to more recordings paring surfing with car songs: "Surfin' Safari"/"409" (1962), "Surfin' U.S.A."/"Shut Down" (1963), and "Surfer Girl"/"Little Deuce Coupe" (1963), all double-sided, top ten hits on the national charts. At this point, the Beach Boys broadened their scope, addressing such concerns as school spirit, friendship, dating, insecurity, freedom and dancing.

The seeming innocence and directness of the group's lyrics was complemented by increasingly sophistication within the recording studio. Given complete production freedom by Capitol Records, Brian retired from live performing and began experimenting with new vocal and instrumental textures. After creating one of the most highly regarded rock albums ever in 1966, *Pet Sounds*, the group evolved into psychedelic drug use, fringe religious cults, the Maharishi and transcendental meditation, health foods, and other fads. Rock fans, however, had discovered new heroes. Having shed their old image, the group suffered through an identity crisis combined with weak record sales in the late 1960s. Songwriting collaborator Van Dyke Parks offered the following assessment of this period:

They've been trying to get away from the beach, you know? They don't like their image. Even when I first ran into them I could never figure out why. What's wrong with it? Get them down to the beach. Put them into trunks. The beach ain't so bad. The ocean is the repository of the entire human condition—the pollution, the solution… Steve Gaines, *Heroes and Villains*, 1986

The phenomenal success of the compilation album, *Endless Summer*, in 1974, followed by *Spirit of America*, a year later, re-established by Beach Boys' mystique in the forefront of American popular culture. The release of *15 Big Ones* in 1976 solidified the pattern which would govern the groups' career path for the next couple of decades: the release of retro pop material reminiscent of their gravy days in the 1960s (often remakes of rock classics such as "Rock and Roll Music" and "Why Do Fools Fall in Love?") as singles in contrast to albums of tepid material penned by band members. Brian no longer dominated the Beach Boys' songwriting and production; he had begun suffering from various mental and physical problems, including depression and obesity, stemming in part from the pressures of trying to top the artistic summit achieved by *Pet Sounds* and follow-up singles, "Good Vibrations" and "Heroes and Villains." For their part, the public continued to buy the group's early hits—available in endless repackagings—in large quantities; the number-one single, "Kokomo" represented their only post-1960s record to become an appreciable hit.

The Beach Boys' chart success in the United States was matched in much of Europe, Asia, and Australia. According to Dave McAleer's *Encyclopedia of Hits: The 1960s* (Blandford, 1988), the group ranked sixth overall among pop artists on the singles charts during that decade—the era encompassing all of their classic hits. In Great Britain, the Beach Boys ranked eleventh for the same period. Interestingly, their Top 10 recordings—which included "I Get Around," "When I Grow Up," "Sloop John B," "God Only Knows"—did not perform as well in the states (for example, the latter track was tucked away as a B side on the American hit, "Wouldn't It Be Nice." By the time "Good Vibrations" began its ascent to the top of the British charts, the act had supplanted The Beatles as the "World's Best Group" in that nation's music paper polls (the track would return to the UK Top 20 in 1976).

The Beach Boys have ranked equally high as a concert draw abroad from the 1960s onward despite the deaths of Dennis and Carl Wilson, and Brian Wilson's preoccupation with a solo career. Despite the temporary embarrassment of being dropped by CBS records in 1985 when their contract ran out, Steven Gaines noted,

The Beach Boys continue as a number-one concert attraction, maintaining a $50,000-a-night guarantee. They are one of the most popular live entertainment acts in the world. For millions of fans, they are, and will always be, the essence of the California dream.

December 10. The film *The Young Ones*—featuring a soundtrack by Cliff Richard—premieres in London. It goes on to become the runner-up to *The Guns of Navarone* as the top-grossing movie in Great Britain in 1962. The title song will enter the charts at number one on January 11, where it remains for eight weeks. The soundtrack album will leap-frog over Elvis Presley's *Blue Hawaii* as the top LP for a six-week run.

December 11. The Marvelettes reach number one on the pop charts with "Please Mr. Postman" (Tamla).

December 18. The Tokens begin a three-week stay atop the Hot 100 with a post-doo-wop reworking of "The Lion Sleeps Tonight" (RCA). It is the first African song to top the American charts. Although a comparatively modern work, it had been co-opted by the South African folk tradition—known both as "Mbube" and "Wimoweh"—when adapted for an American audience by Pete Seeger in the early 1950s for his group, the Weavers. It would remain a folk staple stateside until reworked into a doo-wop-tinged rock 'n' roll novelty number by the Tokens (this version would be reissued in 1994, reaching number fifty-one). Robert John would reach number three on the Hot 100 with yet another interpretation in 1972. Other artists—like David Bowie in 1976—would cover it as well.

December 25. Danny Williams tops the British singles charts with his version of "Moon River."

December 31. The Beach Boys make their first appearance under that name at the Ritchie Valens Memorial Concert, Long Beach (California) Municipal Auditorium. They earn $300. Prior names for the groups had included the Pendletones and Carl and the Passions.

1962

❄

January 1. Manager Brian Epstein arranges an audition at Decca Records for The Beatles. They perform fifteen songs, including three Lennon-McCartney originals and a cover of the Marvelettes' "Please Mr. Postman." Executive Mike Smith, who also hears Brian Poole and the Tremeloes audition the same day, opts to sign the Tremeloes. Dick Rowe, an A&R man for the label, tells Epstein, "guitar groups are on their way out!"

January 4. The Liverpool-based *Mersey Beat* publishes its first popularity poll; the Beatles come in first, followed by Gerry and the Pacemakers.

January 13. Chubby Checker's "The Twist" (Parkway) becomes the only rock era recording to go number one in two separate chart runs, remaining in the top place for a couple of weeks this time around. The twist itself also enjoys a brief revival, co-opted by adult swingers from the youth subculture.

The Twist phenomenon had its genesis in 1958 with the release of a song written by a rhythm and blues journeyman from Detroit named Hank Ballard. Ballard and his back-up group, The Midnighters, hit the pop charts for the first time that year with "Teardrops on Your Letter." The flipside of the single, "The Twist," drew its inspirations from a new dance Ballard had seen teenagers doing in Tampa, Florida.

"The Twist" went largely unnoticed until the dance spread across the country. When it became the most popular dance on *American Bandstand*, MC Dick Clark tried to get Danny and the Juniors interested in recording a cover version of the song. When they didn't come up with anything, Clark called the executives at Cameo-Parkway, Philadelphia's most successful record label, and suggested that Chubby Checker, one of its promising young artists, put out the song.

Checker's version was almost a duplicate of the original single; even the vocals, down to the final "eee-yow!," resembled Ballard's. Ballard himself, upon hearing the cover on the radio, is said to have thought he was listening to himself. Spurred by several appearances on *American Bandstand* in which Checker gave Twist lessons, the record sped up the charts, reaching number one on September 19, 1960.

After "The Twist" had run its course, Checker continued to release dance records: "The Hucklebuck," an R&B chart-topping for Paul Williams in the late 1940s; "The Pony Time," which also rose to the top of the charts; and "The Mess Around." Despite Checker's 1961 hit, "Let's Twist Again," the dance appeared on to be headed for oblivion when society columnist Cholly Knickerbocker mentioned that Prince Serge Obolensky had been observed doing it at Manhattan's Peppermint Lounge. As a result, it caught on with adults worldwide, first with the Jet Set, and later, with the rank and file. Checker appeared on the *Ed Sullivan Show* October 22, 1961 to sing "The Twist," prompting its re-release, and second successful run.

A slew of Twist songs would chart in 1962, including "Peppermint Twist – Part 1," by Joey Dee and the Starliters; "Dear Lady Twist," by Gary U.S. Bonds; "Twistin' the Night Away," by Sam Cooke; and Checker's own "Slow Twistin'." Checker and Dee went on to star in three Hollywood films: *Hey Let's Twist*, *Twist Around the Clock*, and *Don't Knock the Twist*. Checker was marketed with a line of Twist products, including Twist shirts, cuff-links, wallets, pajamas, candy, Thom McCan "Twister" shoes, and a Twist hairdo that bounced and rotated to the dance's rhythms. Newspapers and magazines provided a steady stream of pertinent news notes to help fuel the craze: for example, New York's Safety Council said that in one week during October 1961, forty-nine out of fifty-four cases of back trouble resulted from too much Twisting; in Syracuse, New York, the widow of an auto salesman who died of a heart attack after Twisting at a company party sued for workmen's compensation under the state law and won.

By 1963, however, a seemingly endless wave of new dances—the Hully-Gully, Mashed Potato, the Frug, the Watusi, the Limbo, the Monkey—all of which attempted to repeat the formula established by the Twist, rendered the original item as dated as the Lindy Hop. The dance left its impact on pop music dance styles in that couples virtually ceased dancing together for almost two decades. The dance continued to live on in cover versions of classic Twist songs such as the Beatles' "Twist and Shout" (1964; 1986) and Rod Stewart's "Twistin' the Night Away" (1972). Checker himself would enjoy a brief artistic and commercial revival via his featured role in the Fat Boys' 1988 rap remake of "The Twist."

January 13. Already a hit in Los Angeles, the Beach Boys' "Surfin'" enters *Billboard*'s "Bubbling Under the Hot 100" at number 118.

January 24. Brian Epstein formalizes a management deal with the Beatles.

January 24. Teenage recording artist, Danny Peppermint—whose single, "The Peppermint Twist," differs considerably from Joey Dee and the Starliters' competing version—barely escapes death when electrocuted by a microphone stand at the Thunderbird Hotel in Las Vegas.

January 26. Bishop Burke—who heads the Buffalo, New York Catholic Diocese—bans the Twist. This means it cannot be danced, listened to on recordings, or even sung about in any Catholic school, parish, or youth organization event. During the year, other localities will also prohibit the dance in various ways (e.g., Tampa, Florida community center dances).

January 27. Joey Dee & the Starliters begin a three-week run atop the Hot 100 with "Peppermint Twist – Part I" (Roulette), named for the favorite club hangout for the Manhattan jet set.

January 27. Elvis Presley receives his twenty-ninth gold record for "Can't Help Falling in Love" (RCA); he'd recently garnered his twenty-eighth for the soundtrack to his seventh film, Blue Hawaii (RCA).

January 29. Warner Bros. signs Peter, Paul and Mary, presently a hot ticket in Manhattan's Greenwich Village.

February 10. Enjoy Records releases the instrumental, "Soul Twist," the biggest hit for King Curtis (number seventeen on the pop charts). One of the best session players around, his honking style saxophone work graced many recordings, most notably, the Coasters' "Yakety Yak" (Atco) and "Charlie Brown" (Atco).

February 10. Henry Mancini tops the LP charts with the soundtrack to *Breakfast at Tiffany's*.

February 17. Gene Chandler's "Duke of Earl" (Vee-Jay) reaches the summit of the pop charts, remaining there for three weeks.

A prime exponent of the Chicago Soul school during the 1960s, Gene Chandler was greatly influenced by the post-World War II rhythm and blues vocal group genre. He particularly admired the Windy City-based quintet, the Spaniels, which featured the caressing lead vocals of "Pookey" Hudson.

Born Eugene Dixon on July 6, 1937, in Chicago, Chandler formed the Gaytones in 1955 while attending Englewood High School. He joined the Dukays (whose members also included tenors Shirley Jones and James Lowe, baritone Earl Edwards, and bass Ben Broyles) briefly in 1957 before serving in the U.S. Army (1957–1960). His first break came in 1960 when—back singing with the Dukays—a local talent scout, Bill Sheppard, helped them secure a recording contract with the Nat label. After hearing a group recording session in late 1961 which featured the tracks "Nite Owl" and "Duke of Earl," Vee-Jay Records executive Calvin Carter convinced Chandler to go out on his own. He re-recorded his composition "Duke of Earl" (#416; #1 r&b 5 weeks) for Vee-Jay; his distinctive post-doo-wop vocals helped drive the single to the top of both the R&B and pop charts.

While his later chart success was intermittent at best, Chandler maintained his career for decades, placing thirty-six discs on the *Billboard* R&B singles charts alone. His most popular recordings included "Rainbow" (Vee-Jay 468; 1963; #47 pop, #11; a live version, "Raindow '65 (Part I), Constellation 158, reached #69 pop, #2 r&b in late 1965), "Nothing Can Stop Me" (Constellation 149; 1965; #18 pop, #3 r&b), "I Fooled You This Time" (Checker 1155; 1966; #45 pop, #3 r&b), "To Be a Lover" (Checker 1165; 1967; #94 pop, #9 r&b), "Groovy Situation" (Mercury 73083; 1970; #12 pop, #8 r&b; duet with Barbara Acklin), and "Get Down" (Chi-Sound 2386; 1978; #53 pop, #3 r&b). In addition to performing and studio work (also for the Brunswick, 20th Century, Salsoul, and FastFire labels, among others), he directed his own record company, Mr. Chand, and was active as a songwriter and studio producer.

February 17. Billboard reports that Adam Young, Chairman of the Radio Trade Practice Committee, proposes that all pop music lyrics be screened by the National Association of Broadcasters Code Committee. Young feels such action is warranted "due to the proliferation of songs dealing with raw sex and violence beamed directly and singularly at children and teenagers."

February 18. On weekend leave from the Marines, the Everly Brothers perform their latest hit single, "Crying in the Rain" (Warner Bros.), on the Ed Sullivan Show, wearing their uniforms and regulation crewcuts.

February 28. WINS, the top-rated rock 'n' roll radio station in New York City (the home for DJ personality, Murray the K), switches to a "pretty music" format as well as reverting to its original call letters, WHN. The station will resume rock 'n' roll-based Top 40 programming within several months.

March 8. The Beatles debut on television, appearing on the BBC program, Teenager's Turn, to perform Roy Orbison's "Dream Baby."

March 10. Bruce Channel begins a three-week run atop the Hot 100 with "Hey! Baby" (Smash), which features harmonica work by roots rocker Delbert McClinton. His sound would be copied by John Lennon on the Beatles' first single, "Love Me Do," recorded later that year.

March 15. *No Strings* premieres at New York's 54th Street Theatre. Featuring music and lyrics by Richard Rodgers and book by Samuel Taylor, the musical would run for 580 performances. The work was innovative in that the orchestra was located backstage, there was no string section, musicians were placed onstage to accompany the singers, and the principals and chorus moved the scenery and props in full view of the audience.

March 17. Billboard reports that Ray Charles has established his own label, Tangerine Records, following in the footsteps of recording stars such as Sam Cooke (SAR) and the Everly Brothers (Calliope).

March 17. Blues Incorporated gives its first concert at London's Ealing Club. Personnel includes guitarist Alexis Korner, pianist Dave Stevens, mouth harpist Cyril Davies, bassist Andy Hoogenboom, saxophonist Dick Heckstall-Smith, and drummer Charlie Watts. In a short time, bassist Jack Bruce and vocalist Mick Jagger would join the group. The band would play a key role as a training ground for musicians who would guide future British Invasion acts as the Rolling Stones, Cream, and Colisseum.

March 24. Philles Records releases the Crystals' "Uptown," which goes on to sell more than one million copies. With Top 10 hits like "He's a Rebel," "Da Doo Run Run," and "Then He Kissed Me," the group would be instrumental in the development of Phil Spector's recording empire.

March 29. Gene Chandler receives a gold record for "Duke of Earl" (Vee-Jay).

March 31. Connie Francis reaches number one on the pop charts with "Don't Break the Heart That Loves You' (MGM).

April 7. Mick Jagger and Keith Richards meet Brian Jones for the first time at Ealing Jazz Club. Jones was performing as "Elmo Lewis" at the time, playing guitar with Paul Jones.

April 7. Shelley Fabares—then starring in TV's The Donna Reed Show—begins a two-week stint atop the Hot 100 with "Johnny Angel" (Colpix).

April 10. Stuart Sutcliff, the original bassist for the Beatles, dies in Hamburg, Germany of cerebral paralysis caused by a brain hemorrhage at age twenty-two. Sutcliff had met John Lennon in 1959 while both attended a Liverpool art school. After accompanying the Beatles to play in Hamburg, he departed in mid-1961 to resume painting and obtain relief for his persistent headaches. His primary legacy was the shaggy, mop-top hairstyle (created by his German girlfriend) that would become the Beatles' trademark.

April 12. Columbia Records records Bob Dylan's Town Hall (New York) concert. One selection, "Tomorrow Is a Long Time," will be included on a later retrospective album release.

April 21. Elvis Presley climbs to the summit of the pop charts with "Good Luck Charm" (RCA), remaining there for two weeks.

April 28. The National Association of Record Merchandisers (NARM) announces the best-selling artists of 1961: Elvis Presley, male vocalist category; Connie Francis, female vocalist category; and Mitch Miller and the Gang, vocal group category.

April 29. Jerry Lee Lewis gives a concert in Newcastle—his first performance in England since leaving in disgrace following news of his marriage to Myra. Fans respond favorably to the show.

May 5. Dee Dee Sharp peaks at number two on the Hot 100 with "Mashed Potato Time" (Cameo 212).

Dee Dee Sharp's classic records have not been available for decades, due to legal issues surrounding the industry practices of her one-time label, Cameo/Parkway. Nevertheless, she remained active as a recording artist well into the 1980s, occasionally placing singles on the R&B charts.

Born Dione LaRue on September 9, 1945, in Philadelphia, she caught on as a backing vocalist for Cameo by 1961. Recognizing her ample attributes—photogenic looks and a dynamic voice, combined with clear-cut diction, perfect for pop radio—the company began promoting her as a solo performer. Her debut release, "Mashed Potato Time" (#1 r&b 4 weeks), established her—along with label-mate Chubby Checker—as a leading interpreter of the dance craze fad. In addition to a rock-steady duet with Checker in "Slow Twistin'" (Parkway 835; 1962; #3 pop, #3 r&b), she produced several more best-selling dance hits over the next year: "Gravy (For My Mashed Potatoes)" (Cameo 219; 1962; #9 pop, #11 r&b), "Ride!" (Cameo 230; 1962; #5 pop, #7 r&b), and "Do the Bird" (Cameo 244; 1963; #10 pop, #8 r&b), the latter composed by Cameo/Parkway svengalis Kal Mann and Dave Appell.

By mid-1963, Sharp was a major pop star, appearing in teen films and on countless album compilations. As with many other American recording artists, however, the British Invasion—combined with Cameo-Parkway's late 1960s financial troubles—pushed her to the periphery of the music business. After two more Top 40 R&B hits, she disappeared from the charts for more than a decade. In the meantime, she married Kenny Gamble, part of the Philly Soul songwriting-record production team of Gamble and Huff, in 1967. With his assistance, she revived her moribund career as part of the Philadelphia International roster, returning to the charts with a remake of the tongue-in-cheek 10cc smash, "I'm Not in Love" (TSOP 4778; 1976; #62 r&b). She would also participate in Philadelphia International charity release, "Let's Clean Up the Ghetto" (#3627; 1977; #91 pop, #4 r&b).

May 5. The Shirelles begin a three-week stay atop the Hot 100 with "Soldier Boy" (Scepter).

May 5. The *West Side Story* soundtrack goes number one on the album charts, spending fifty-four weeks overall in that position.

May 8. *A Funny Thing Happened On The Way To The Forum* premieres at the Alvin Theatre in New York City. Featuring music and lyrics by Stephen Sondheim, and book by Burt Shevelove and Larry Gelbart, it had a run of 964 performances. Inspired by the farcical plays of Titus Maccius Plautus (254–184 B.C.), the musical starred Zero Mostel and John Carradine.

May 12. B. Bumble and the Stingers top the British charts with "Nut Rocker." The instrumental is based on the Overture to Peter Tchaikovsky's Nutcracker ballet.

May 19. Elvis Presley heads up the British charts with "Good Luck Charm."

May 26. Mr. Acker Bilk reaches number one on the pop charts with the velvety instrumental, "Stranger on the Shore" (Atco).

June 2. The Blue-Belles peak at number fifteen on the Hot 100 with "I Sold My Heart to the Junkman" (Newtown 5000).

One of the most versatile and successful—in terms of career longevity—R&B artists ever, Patti LaBelle was born Patricia Holt, on May 24, 1944, in Philadelphia. She formed the Blue-Belles, modeled after popular girl groups like the Shirelles and Ikettes, in 1962. The quartet—also consisting of Nona Hendryx, Sarah Dash, and Cindy Birdsong—recorded a half-dozen charting singles between 1962 and 1967 for the Newtown, Parkway, and Atlantic labels, most notably, the Top 20 crossover hit, "I Sold My Heart to the Junkman."

The group soldiered on as a trio when Birdsong left to join the Supremes in 1967. In 1970, they hired British manager Vicki Wickham, who encouraged them to adopt a harder-edged, funk sound as well as an updated moniker, LaBelle. Although failing to make the charts for a succession of labels—Warner Bros., RCA, and Track—in the early 1970s, they earned kudos for their collaboration with singer/songwriter Laura Nyro, *Gonna Take a Miracle* (1971).

Wickham instigated yet another makeover in 1973, with LaBelle taking on a glam-rock image accentuated by form-fitting, silver lame space suits. They exploded into the limelight at the height of the Disco era with the crossover number one smash about a New Orleans prostitute, "Lady Marmalade," which helped propel the accompanying LP, *Nightbirds* (Epic, 1974) into the Top 10. Subsequent releases, however, failed to duplicate this success and the group splintered in early 1977 over creative differences between chief songwriters LaBelle and Hendryx.

All three members enjoyed a measure of success as solo vocalists. LaBelle far outpaced her former co-horts with two dozen-odd hit singles through the 1980s, including the R&B chart-toppers "If You Only Knew" and "On My Own" (a duet with Michael McDonald, which also topped the *Billboard* Hot 100). Her best-selling album, *When a Woman Loves* (MCA, 2000), a collection of Diane Warren songs, revealed a new summit of artistic maturity, with LaBelle effectively negotiating a wide range of styles, including soul, house, and hip-hop.

June 2. Ray Charles begins a five-week run atop the Hot 100 with the Don Gibson-penned "I Can't Stop Loving You" (ABC-Paramount). It will also go number one on the U.K. charts.

June 2. Owen Gray's "Twist Baby" is the first single released by Island Records, which later included such artists as Jethro Tull, Bob Marley, Traffic, and U2 on its roster.

June 4. The Beach Boys' "409"—the B side of the Top 40 single, "Surfin' Safari" (Capitol) will actually score higher on the pop music charts, reaching number fourteen—is released, eventually peaking at number seventy-six. Although not the first rock era recording about fast cars to become a hit—earlier classics include Jackie Brenston's "Rocket '88'" (Chess; 1951), the Playmates' "Beep Beep" (Roulette; 1958), and Charlie Ryan's "Hot Rod Lincoln" (1960)—"409" created the template for a string of best-selling 45 rpm discs that continued to appear on a regular basis through the mid-1960s.

Car songs, like surf music, were largely a Southern California phenomenon. They were a by-product of the region's active hot rod scene, which had evolved from the illegal street races of the 1940s to the Bonneville Salt Flats speed weeks and drag strips of the 1960s. Hot rodding included its own crew of culture heroes, including customizer George Barris and drivers "Big Daddy" Garlits and Craig Breedlove, who set a series of land speed records in his "Spirit of America." In addition to musical tributes, the hot rod scene was lionized by Hollywood films, plastic car models available in hobby shops, and Bob Peterson's mass circulation periodical, *Hot Rod*.

Recognizing the presence of the subculture of potential consumers (not to mention the vicarious interest of middle American youth as a whole), a nucleus of talented Los Angeles-based songwriters and arrangers/producers began fueling the craze in the early 1960s, most notably Brian Wilson of the Beach Boys, Jan Berry of Jan and Dean, Roger Christian (a deejay at KFWB), Gary Usher, Terry Melcher, and Bruce Johnston. Usher—who contributed to the success of the Hondells' hits, "Little Honda" (Mercury 72324; 1964) and "My Buddy Seat" (Mercury 72366; 1964), and many the Surfaris' recordings—teamed with Christian to produce hit recordings and film soundtracks. Johnston and Melcher masterminded the success of the Ripchords (e.g., "Hey Little Cobra," Columbia 42921; 1963) and had their own hits as Bruce and Terry: "Custom Machine" (Columbia 42956; 1964) and "Summer Means Fun" (Columbia 43055; 1964).

As with surf music, the rise of folk rock and protest music, in essence, submerged the car song genre. The Beach Boys began experimenting with more progressive styles, augmented by the addition of Johnston to enable Wilson avoid touring so as to concentrate on songwriting and studio production. Jan Berry, on the brink of creating increasingly sophisticated sounds of his own, nearly died when his Corvette Stingray crashed at the fabled Dead Man's Curve. Melcher and Usher teamed up to produce the latest West Coast sensation, the Byrds.

July 7. David Rose climbs to the summit of the pop charts with the instrumental "The Stripper" (MGM).

July 14. Bobby Vinton begins a four-week stay atop the Hot 100 with "Roses Are Red (My Love)" (Epic).

August 11. Neil Sedaka reaches number one on the pop charts with "Breaking Up Is Hard To Do" (RCA), remaining there for two weeks.

August 25. Little Eva tops the Hot 100 with the Gerry Goffin/Carole King composition, "The Loco-Motion" (Dimension).

September 1. Tommy Roe commences a two-week stint at number one on the pop charts with the self-penned, Buddy Holly-styled "Sheila" (ABC-Paramount).

September 15. The Four Seasons' "Sherry" (Vee-Jay) begins a five week stay atop the Hot 100 (#1 R&B), on its way to selling more than two million copies. The record—which exploits the dynamic falsetto end of lead singer Frankie Valli's three-octave tenor range—is the culmination of a summer-long effort by producer

Bob Crewe and arranger Charles Calello to analyze the features behind the major hits of the day (and then incorporate them into the group's work). Crewe considered releasing "Sherry" on Perry (a label in which he possessed an interest), but opted for Vee-Jay when executive Randy Wood expressed the desire to purchase a lease arrangement. The single took off almost immediately following its release; the day after the group sang it on *American Bandstand*, the label received orders for 180,000 copies—a very high figure for the time.

October 3. *Stop the World – I Want to Get Off* premieres at New York's Shubert Theatre. Featuring music, lyrics, and book by Leslie Bricusse and Anthony Newley, the musical—a London hit the previous year—had a run of 555 performances. It would be adapted to film in 1966, starring Tony Tanner.

October 5. The Beatles release their first record, "Love Me Do" (Parlophone R4949), in Great Britain. Featuring John Lennon's Delbert McClinton-influenced harmonica accompaniment (from Bruce Channel's number-one hit, "Hey Baby"), it peaks at number seventeen on the English charts.

October 20. Bobby "Boris" Pickett climbs to the summit of the pop charts with the horror film parody, "Monster Mash" (Garpax), remaining there for two weeks.

November 2. Conceptualized during conversations involving Motown founder Berry Gordy, Thomas "Bean" Bowles, and Esther Gordy Edwards, the Motor Town Revue kicks off at the Boston Arena. Promoted by Supersonic Attractions head, Henry Wynne—who was initially skeptical about the tour's prospects in that only four Motown acts were proven hitmakers—it encompassed nineteen cities (largely in the Deep South) spread over twenty-three days. In addition to exposing the Motown Sound to a wider audience (especially giving exposure to little-known acts), the revue convinced Berry of the need to formally school the artists in stage presence and dance routines. Furthermore, it provided a badly needed cash infusion to cover the record company's overhead expenses.

November 3. "He's a Rebel"—written by Gene Pitney, produced by Phil Spector, and credited to the Crystals (but actually sung by Darlene Love and the Blossoms)—begins a two-week stint atop the Hot 100.

November 17. The Four Seasons go number one on the pop charts with "Big Girls Don't Cry" (Vee-Jay), remaining there for five weeks.

November 17. *Little Me* premieres at New York's Lunt-Fontanne Theatre. Featuring music by Cy Coleman, lyrics Carolyn Leigh, and book by Neil Simon, the musical would run for 257 performances. A vehicle to showcase Sid Caesar's comic talents—he would play seven difference suitors for the heroine—it would have far less successful run in the 1982 revised edition.

December 1. Marvin Gaye peaks at number forty-six on the Hot 100 with "Stubborn Kind of Fellow" (Tamla 54068).

A leading proponent of the Motown Sound, a polished variant of 1960s urban soul music, he was born Marvin Pentz Gay, Jr., on April 2, 1939, in Washington, D.C. The son of an apostolic minister, he began singing in church as a youth in addition to teaching himself piano and drums. After graduating from high school, he sang with the Rainbows and Marquees before joining Harvey Fuqua's reformed doo-wop group, the Moonglows. When Fuqua was hired as a staff writer and producer by Motown, he brought Gaye along with him in 1960 to do session work.

At Motown, Gaye—who married Anna, the sister of label president, Berry Gordy, in 1961—was encouraged to develop a career as a solo vocalist. Beginning with "Stubborn Kind of Fellow," a Top 10 R&B hit in late 1962, he had fifty-seven hits (including duets with a succession of female singers) for the label through 1981—most notably, R&B chart-toppers "I'll Be Doggone," "Ain't That Peculiar," "Ain't Nothing Like the Real Thing" (with Tammi Terrell), "You're All I Need to Get By" (with Terrell), "I Heard It Through the Grapevine," "Too Busy Thinking About My Baby," "What's Going On," "Mercy Mercy Me (The Ecology)," "Inner City Blues (Make Me Wanna Holler)," "Let's Get It On," "I Want you," and "Got To Give It Up (Pt. I)."

By the early 1970s, Gaye was chafing at the company's conservative production values. Faced with the threat of losing him to another label, Motown allowed Gaye to explore more sophisticated sociopolitical themes in his compositions. *What's Going On?* (Motown, 1971)—which addressed civil rights, environmental, and Vietnam War issues—and the sexually explicit (for its time) *Let's Get It On* (Motown, 1973) are recognized as some of the earliest R&B concept albums.

His work fell out of favor somewhat during the disco era, but he returned to the spotlight with *Midnight Love* (Columbia, 1982), which included the Grammy-winning hit single, "Sexual Healing." However, his revival was cut short when he was shot to death April 1, 1984, by his father in a family dispute.

December 10. Allan Sherman earns a gold record for his LP, *My Son, the Folk Singer* (Warner Bros. 1475).

In October 1962, after fifteen years as a successful television writer and producer, Allen Sherman achieved overnight fame as a folk singing comedian. While temporarily out of work in early 1962, Sherman approached both Capitol and Warner Brothers about recording some of his musical comedy parodies which had made him a much sought-after guest at Hollywood parties. The latter company expressed an interest, but recommended that he write travesties of folk songs—which are in the public domain—rather than parodying Broadway show tunes, which might involve copyright problems.

His debut album, *My Son, the Folk Singer*, featured folk standards with new lyrics by Sherman satirizing urban Jewish mores. For example, "Frere Jacques" became "Sara Jackman," and "The Battle Hymn of the Republic" was transformed into the saga of a cutter in Irving Roth's garment factory, who stood fast during a catastrophic fire ("trampling through the warehouse where the drapes of Roth are stored…Glory, glory Harry Lewis"). The LP became the fastest-selling item in history; over five hundred thousand copies sold in the first month alone.

Sherman quickly followed with *My Son, the Celebrity* (December 1962) and *My Son, the Nut* (1963), which included his chart-topping hit single, "Hello Muddah, Hello Faddah" (cast in the form of a complaining letter from a child in summer camp to his parents, and sung to the music of "Dance of the Hours" from the opera *La Gioconda* by Ponchielli). He also became a top concert draw as well as a frequent guest on television; in August 1963 he replaced vacationing Johnny Carson as host of the *Tonight* show. Additional hit albums were released into the mid-1960s, at which point Sherman's nonsensical brand of humor appeared to have fallen out of step with the public's demands for social relevance from its entertainers.

December 20. The Osmond Brothers appear on the *Andy Williams Show* (NBC) for the first time, singing "I'm a Ding Dong Daddy from Dumas."

December 22. The British instrumental group, the Tornadoes, begin a three-week run atop the Hot 100 with "Telstar" (London), complete with sound effects simulating space flight.

1963

❄

January 9. Former Blues Incorporated drummer Charlie Watts joins the Rolling Stones.

The Rolling Stones have been around for so long—they formed in mid-1962—and have produced such a distinguished body of work that it is easy to forget their early, and greatest, music was produced in the shadow of other musicians: initially, the American electric blues masters of the 1950s (most notably, Chess artists such as Chuck Berry, Willie Dixon, and Muddy Waters) and, as Swinging London pop icons pursuing the latest fashion, that other, more innovative—and beloved—British band, the Beatles. The group was originally comprised of Mick Jagger, vocals and harmonica; Keith Richards, rhythm guitar; Brian Jones, lead guitar; Bill Wyman, bass; Charlie Watts, drums; and Ian Stewart, piano. Because he didn't look—and behave—much like a budding rock star, Stewart was soon relegated to shadowy session man status by their Barnum-styled manager, Andrew Loog Oldham. Oldham was a publicity genius, perhaps best known for the slogan, "Would you let your daughter marry a Rolling Stone?"

Oldham's maneuvering, combined with the Stones' propulsive early singles in 1963, had them poised to follow the Beatles, the Dave Clark Five, the Searchers, and others as the latest British beat group export stateside in early 1964. The early LPs—*The Rolling Stones* (London 375; 1964; #11), *12 x 5* (London 402; 1064; #3), and *The Rolling Stones, Now!* (London 420; 1965; #5)—were earthy and soulful (for white rock of that time), comprised largely of blues and R&B covers. Following several Top 20 hits, they became superstars with the release of "(I Can't Get No) Satisfaction" (London 9766; 1965; #1), which—with its proto-acid-rock riff and angry, rebellious lyrics—is still regarded by many pop historians as one of the two or three greatest rock songs ever.

While follow-up singles and albums continued to ascend to the upper reaches of the pop charts, the Stones—like most major groups of the late 1960s—felt compelled to match the Beatles' studio experiments. Consequently, the next few years saw the release of a series of flawed masterpieces, including *Aftermath* (London 476; 1966; #2), which featured extended song compositions (by now all authored by Jagger-Richards) and Jones' exotic instrumentation; *Between the Buttons* (London 499; 1967; #2), perhaps the most eclectic collection from the band, ranging from early twentieth-century music hall to raga-rock; and *Their Satanic Majesties Request* (London 2; 1967; #2), a psychedelic tour de force that, unfortunately, comes across as a quaint relic of the flower power era.

Whether it was the example of artists like Bob Dylan and the Beatles—who released the retro recordings *John Wesley Harding* and "Get Back," respectively, in early 1968—or simply the realization that the music had strayed far from what they did best, the next album, *Beggars Banquet* (London 539; 1968; #5), was the pivotal release in the Stones oeuvre, heralding a return to roots-rock and incendiary lyrics (e.g., the raw sexuality of "Stray Cat Blues" and anti-Establishment polemic, "Street Fighting Man," the malevolent anthem "Sympathy For the Devil"). The Stones remained on top of their game by producing four more classic records in a row: *Let It Bleed* (London 4; 1969; #3), featuring chilling songs of desperation that served as an apt coda for a year marked by the controversial death of Jones in July (immediately after being replaced by guitarist Mick Taylor) and the tragic violence marring their December Altamont concert; the group's seminal live effort, recorded in November 1969 at Madison Square Garden, *"Get Yer Ya-Ya's Out!"* (London 5; 1970; #6); the dynamic *Sticky Fingers* (Rolling Stones 59100; 1971; #1), accented by its titillating zipper cover; and *Exile On Main Street* (Rolling Stones 2900; 1972: #1), an inspired double-disc set of sloppy, debauched—albeit vital and evocative—first-rate compositions (considered by some experts to be the finest LP of all time).

Widely recognized as the greatest rock band in the world by the 1970s, the Stones—despite further personnel changes: former Faces guitarist Ron Wood filling the slot vacated by Taylor, and the 1990s departures of Wyman (replaced by bassist Darryl Jones and keyboardist Chuck Leavell) and (briefly) Watts—have remained a bankable entity up to the present day. Despite their commercial success—including the number one albums *Goats Head Soup* 59101; 1973), *It's Only Rock 'N Roll* (Rolling Stones 79101; 1974), *Black and Blue* (Rolling Stones 79104; 1976), *Some Girls* (Rolling Stones 39108; 1978), *Emotional Rescue* (Rolling Stones 16015; 1980), and *Tattoo You* (Rolling Stones 16052; 1981)—the group's output has been frequently criticized for its excessive posturing and lapses into self-parody. By the late 1970s, a new generation of punk musicians had came to fore criticizing the Stones' bloated, corporate image. On occasion, however, they would tease their followers by shelving the tried-and-true formulaic approach, and releasing a truly inspired slice of rock 'n' roll such as "Start Me Up" (Rolling Stones 21003; 1981; #2), "Uncover of the Night" (Rolling Stones 99813; 1983; #9), and a re-working of the R&B classic, "Harlem Shuffle" (Rolling Stones 05802; 1986; #5).

By the 1990s, the tours and releases of newly recorded material were at least several years apart, and the individual members were devoting more attention to their solo projects. The group has operated as a quartet since the departure of bassist Bill Wyman early in the decade; the void has been filled by high-profile session men. Subsequent studio releases—*Voodoo Lounge* (Virgin 39782; 1994; #2) and *Bridges to Babylon* (Virgin 2840; 1997; #3)—were tentative and clichéd in approach. Live releases from that period managed to present the band in a better light, most notably *Stripped* (Virgin 41040; 1995; #9), which featured a no-frills, heavily acoustic format largely given over to their classic 1960s/1970s work, and *No Security* (Virgin 46740; 1998; #34), consisting of 1997 recordings spanning material representing all phases of their career. However, *A Bigger Bang* (EMI 30067 2; 2005)—a sixteen-track collection of memorable compositions driven by Watts' rock steady drumming and the snarling guitar interplay between Wood and Richards—caught even hardcore fans off guard with its unrelenting excellence.

January 11. The Beatles appear on a national television show, Thank Your Lucky Stars (BBC), miming "Please Please Me."

January 12. Steve Lawrence begins a two-week stint atop the Hot 100 with the Gerry Goffin/Carole King composition, "Go Away Little Girl" (Columbia 42601)

January 14. Charlie Watts plays with the Rolling Stones for the first time at The Flamingo Jazz Club, London.

January 19. The Exciters begin a two-run at number two on the Hot 100 with "Tell Him" (United Artists 544).

The Exciters featured one of the more dynamic soul singers of the early 1960s, Brenda Reid (born 1945). Although the group had only one hit of note, "Tell Him," it remains one of the more distinctive and popular oldies from that period.

The Exciters were formed out of the ashes of two New York City area acts. A trio of Jamaica, New York high school juniors—Carol Johnson (b. 1945), Lilian Walker (b. 1945), and lead singer Reid—began attracting attention in early 1962. In the meantime, record producer Herbert Rooney (b. 1941) was working with his own male ensemble. When Rooney's group disbanded, he hooked up with the girls to form the Exciters in mid-1962. Within a few months they had secured a contract with United Artists and recorded the Bert Russell-penned song, "Tell Him," which reached the Top 5 on *Billboard's* Hot 100 early the following year. Follow-up singles—most notably, "He's Got the Power" (United Artists; 1963), "Get Him" (United Artists; 1963), "Do-Wah-Diddy" (United Artists; 1964), "I Want You To Be My Boy" (Roulette; 1965), and a spirited reworking of the Jarmels hit, "A Little Bit of Soap" (Bang; 1966)—failed to rise above the lower reaches of the pop charts. Ironically, as the Exciters struggled to find their way back into the public consciousness, a rather limp cover of "Do-Wah-Diddy" would become a number one smash for the British Invasion band, Manfred Mann, in late 1964.

January 26. Herb Alpert & the Tijuana Brass enter the Billboard album charts with their eponymous debut (A&M 101). It will go on to reach number ten and earn gold status.

For a time in the mid-1960s, Herb Alpert's records were outselling those of the Beatles; during the week of May 21, 1966, he had five albums in the Top 20 of the *Billboard* Top LP's chart (including three of the top eight positions). However, he also made a significant impact with the record industry as a businessman, writing and producing many hits as well as forming A&M Records—one of the most successful artist-owned labels ever established—with Jerry Moss.

Born in Los Angeles, Alpert began his recording career with RCA as Dore Alpert shortly after a stint in the Army. He would then sign with Dot Records in 1959, again with no real success. Teaming up with future music business mogul Lou Adler, he helped write such best-selling recordings as Sam Cooke's "Wonderful World" and "Only Sixteen." The duo adopted the moniker Dante and the Evergreens to record a cover of the Hollywood Argyles' "Alley Oop" (1960). He would produce tracks for the likes of Jan and Dean.

In 1962, Alpert combined with Moss to found A&M Records; his group, the Tijuana Brass, recorded the firm's first hit for only $65, "The Lonely Bull" (A&M 703; 1962). A&M would go on to be recognized as the largest independent label worldwide; by the early 1970s its roster would include such artists as Joe Cocker, the Carpenters, Free, Spooky Tooth, and Sergio Mendes.

It took a few years for Alpert's own recordings with the TJB to peak commercially. His debut release, The Lonely Bull (1962), established the group's trademark sound, a light, punchy blend of mariachi music, mainstream easy listening pop, and pre-smooth jazz. Follow-up albums—Herb Alpert's Tijuana Brass, Volume 2 (A&M 103; 1963; #17), South of the Border (A&M 108; 1965; #6), and Whipped Cream & Other Delights (A&M 110; 1965; #1)—garnered increasingly greater sales. The latter LP, on the strength of the hit single, "A Taste of Honey" (A&M 775; 1965; #7), and an eye-catching cover featuring model Dolores Erickson covered only with shaving cream, elevated Alpert to the top of the pop scene. "A Taste of Honey"—with its catchy stop-and-start bass drum figure—would go on to win 1995 Grammy awards for record of the year, best non-jazz instrumental performance, best instrumental arrangement, and best-engineered record.

For the remainder of the 1960s, the TJB remained a hot commercial property, doing well with Going Places (A&M 112; 1966; #1), What Now My Love (A&M 4114; 1966; #1), S.R.O. (A&M 4119; 1966; #2), Sounds Like (A&M 4124; 1967; #1), Herb Alpert's Ninth (A&M 4134; 1967; #4), and The Beat of the Brass (A&M 4146; 1968; #1). Although public expectations limited the extent of his musical explorations, Alpert attempted some incremental variations on the group's formula, most notably the vocal ballad, "This Guy's in Love with You" (A&M 929; 1969; #1). By the late 1960s, however, his music was deemed out of step with the more serious tone of the times, and TJB albums gradually fell out of favor.

During the 1970s Alpert attempted a number of approaches to re-tool his sound, including an Afro-jazz fusion collaboration with Hugh Masekela (Herb Alpert/Hugh Masekela; Horizon 728; 1978; #65). After aborting a try at recording TJB hits disco style, he used the remaining studio time to explore material a jazz-pop mode more suited to his personal tastes. One of these takes, a slow-down dance song co-written by his cousin, "Rise" (A&M 2151; 1979), reached number one on the Billboard Hot 100.

Alpert's subsequent releases have met with mixed success, his biggest success coming with "Diamonds" (A&M 2929; 1987; #5), which featured a guest vocal by then-emerging star Janet Jackson. Since selling A&M to PolyGram in 1990 for more than $500 million, he has turned his attention to a wide range of projects. In addition to forming a new label with Moss, Almo Sounds, in 1994, he has exhibited his expressionist paintings, co-produced Broadway musicals such as Angels in America and Jelly's Last Jam, and established a philanthropic organization, the Herb Alpert Foundation.

January 26. The Rooftop Singers reach number one on the pop charts with a remake of an obscure jug band ditty dating back to the late 1920s, "Walk Right In" (Vanguard).

February 9. Paul and Paula begin a three-week stay atop the Hot 100 with "Hey Paula" (Philips), written by "Paul" (Ray Hildebrand). The pressures of stardom belie the idealization of teen love as depicted in the song's lyrics; during a tour later in the year, Hildebrand leaves the duo, forcing Dick Clark to temporarily take his place.

February 11. The Beatles record ten songs for their debut LP plus four others—which would become the next singles—in less than ten hours. The Isley Brothers hit, "Twist and Shout," is done in one take to conclude the session.

February 25. "Please Please Me" is released by Vee-Jay. It is the first release by the Beatles—the label misspells the band's name as "The Beattles"—in the United States.

March 2. The 4 Seasons' "Walk Like a Man" (Vee-Jay) reaches number one, remaining there for three weeks. It is the vocal group's third straight chart-topper (the first time any group accomplished this feat), all of which were composed by member Bob Gaudio (producer Bob Crewe shared songwriting credits on "Big Girls Don't Cry" and "Walk Like a Man"). Gaudio would go on to compose the 2006 Emmy Award-winning musical based on the group's story, Jersey Boys.

March 5. Country performers Patsy Cline, Cowboy Copas, and Hawkshaw Hawkins are killed in a plane crash at Dyersburg, Virginia. They were traveling to Nashville to appear in a benefit concert for DJ "Cactus" Jack Cal, who had died in a car crash.

March 7. Country singer Jack Anglin is killed in an auto accident while en route to Patsy Cline's funeral.

March 23. Ruby & the Romantics climb to the summit of the Hot 100 with "Our Day Will Come" (Kapp).

March 30. The Chiffons begin a four-week run atop the pop charts with "He's So Fine" (Laurie).

April 11. The Raiders record "Louie Louie" at Portland's Northwest Recorders (although CBS Records pegs the date as two weeks later), followed by the Kingsmen on April 13.

April 13. Andy Williams begins a four-week run at number four on the Hot 100 with "Can't Get Used to Losing You" (Columbia 42674).

April 27. Little Peggy March—a sixteen-year-old high school student from Lansdale, Pennsylvania, a small city thirty miles outside of Philadelphia—achieves overnight success with "I Will Follow Him" (RCA), which spends three weeks in the number one position.

April 28. The Beatles top the British charts with "From Me to You," the first of eleven consecutive singles to accomplish this feat.

May 4. Andy Williams begins a sixteen-week run atop the album chart with *Days of Wine and Roses.*

May 5. Acting upon a recommendation by George Harrison, Decca A&R Head Dick Rowe goes to see the Rolling Stones perform at London's Crawdaddy Club. The band is signed by the label within a week.

May 11. The Beatles begin a thirty-week run atop the British charts with their debut album *Please Please Me* (the longest running chart-topping LP ever by a group). Their follow-up, *With the Beatles*, replaces it at number one, remaining there for twenty-one weeks.

May 12. Bob Dylan walks out of *Ed Sullivan Show* rehearsals after being told he couldn't perform "Talking John Birch Society Blues" because it ridiculed the U.S. military.

May 17. The first Monterey Folk Festival opens. Featured artists include Joan Baez, Bob Dylan, and Peter, Paul & Mary.

May 18. Jimmy Soul starts a two-week stint atop the Hot 100 with "If You Wanna Be Happy" (S.P.Q.R.).

May 24. Blues guitarist/singer Elmore James dies of a heart attack at age forty-five. He is best remembered for the self-penned "Shake Your Money Maker" and "It Hurts Me Too."

June 1. Ray Barretto peaks at number seventeen on the Hot 100 with "El Watusi" (Tico 419).

Bandleader and percussionist Ray Barretto has been one of the most influential recording artists in Latin jazz history, having collaborated with the likes of saxophonists Gene Ammons, Lou Donaldson, Sonny Stitt, and Stanley Turrentine, trumpeters Dizzy Gillespie, Wes Garland and Clark Terry, guitarists Kenny Burrell and Wes Montgomery, and vibraphonist Cal Tjader. The first American musician to integrate the African-based conga drum into jazz, he played a key role in the fusion movement, combining his Latin heritage with orthodox bebop techniques.

Born April 29, 1929, in Brooklyn of Puerto Rican ancestry, Barretto developed his reputation performing in Tito Puente's orchestra beginning in 1957 in addition to working as a studio musician. In 1962 he formed his own ensemble, Charanga La Moderna, Best known for the pachanga-styled novelty single, "El Watusi" (Tico 419; 1963; 317). Utilizing both his own compositions and covers, he issued a series of Latin fusion LPs for Riverside, Tico, and United Artists throughout the 1960s.

In mid-1960s, he also began working closely with Fania, the New York-based record company specializing in Latin music. Both *Acid* (Fania 346; 1967) and *Hard Hands* (Fania 362; 1968)—featuring punchy Stax-like horns, sinuously hypnotic bass lines, and fiery percussive displays—are considered classic albums which anticipated the Afro-Latin funk revolution of the 1970s. He would become the music director of the label's house band, the Fania All-Stars, which included vocalists Ruben Blades and Hector Lavoe, trombonist Willie Colon, and pianist Larry Harlow. In addition to his work as a featured performer, he did session work for a wide range of artists, including the Average White Band (*Cut the Cake*; Atlantic

18140; 1975), the Bee Gees (*Main Course*; RSO 4807; 1975), Sabu Martinez (*Safari with Sabu*; RCA 1122; 1957); and Babatunde Oltunji (*High Life*; Columbia 8796; 1963).

Tiring of the stylistic limitations of salsa, he formed New World Spirit in 1992, which focused on the bebop style. He was inducted into the International Latin Music Hall of Fame in 1999.

June 1. Lesley Gore surges to the summit of the pop charts with "It's My Party" (Mercury), remaining there for two weeks.

June 7. The Rolling Stones make their British television debut when they appear in *Thank Your Lucky Stars*.

June 15. Kyu Sakamoto's "Sukiyaki" (Capitol) begins a three-week run atop the Hot 100. Previously a hit in Japan, the love song has been renamed in its U.S. release; label executives felt American listeners would be far more likely to respond favorably if the single featured a word that they were familiar with.

July 6. The Essex leap-frog to number one on the pop charts with "Easier Said Than Done" (Roulette 4494), remaining there for two weeks.

The Essex owed their existence to the U.S. Marine Corps. The earliest version of the group featured a collaboration between Walter Vickers, born 1942 in New Brunswick, New Jersey, and Rodney Taylor, also born 1942 in Gary, Indiana, while both were stationed in Okinawa in the early 1960s. They recruited Billie Hill (b. 1942; Princeton, New Jersey) and Rudolph Johnson (b. 1942; New York City) following their return to Camp LeJeune, North Carolina. Things really started to jell, however, when the foursome came across Anita Holmes (b. 1941; Harrisburg, Pennsylvania), who was then singing at the Non-Commissioned Officers' Club. In 1963, shortly after bringing her into the group, the Essex were signed by Roulette records. Their debut release, "Easier Said Than Done," became a nationwide smash while all members were still serving military terms. During their hit-making run—which spanned the follow-up singles, "A Walkin' Miracle" (Roulette 4515; 1963; #12) and "She's Got Everything" (Roulette 4530; 1963; #56)—they were granted special permission to do promotional tours, which also helped enhance the Marines' profile, as the members wore their uniforms onstage. The British Invasion, however, pushed the group back into the periphery of the entertainment business the following year.

July 20. Jan & Dean's "Surf City" begins a two-week stint atop the Hot 100. It will be the only hit to score this high for the clown princes of the California Sound. Brian Wilson writes the song to order for the duo, with an assist from Jan Berry. Fellow Beach Boy Mike Love is furious when he finds out that Wilson has been so generous to an immediate competitor; however, their recordings—most notably, "Surfin' U.S.A.," "Surfer Girl," and "Be True To Your School" are almost as successful as "Surf City."

Jan Berry (born April 3, 1941, Los Angeles) and Dean Torrence (born March 10, 1941, Los Angeles) became friends at Emerson Junior High, forming a group, the Barons, with future stars Sandy Nelson ("Teen Beat," Imperial; 1961) and Beach Boys-member Bruce Johnston. Jan, Dean, and another friend, Arnie Ginsburg, recorded a tribute to a local stripper, "Jennie Lee" (Arwin 108); the single reached number eight on the *Billboard Hot 100* in spring of 1958. Because Torrence was serving in the National Guard when the contracts were signed, the recording was credited to "Jan and Arnie."

Within a year Ginsburg had joined the U.S. Army, and Torrence—once again a civilian—resumed his partnership with Berry. Herb Alpert and Lou Adler took on management of the duo, producing the Top 10 hit, "Baby Talk" (Dore 522; 1959) for their own label. Jan and Dean's releases charted with greater consistency after signing with Liberty in 1961. With Berry exhibiting a genuine talent for songwriting and record production, the twosome's hits—most notably, "Surf City" (Liberty 55580; 1963), "Honolulu Lulu" (Liberty 55613; 1963), "Drag City" (Liberty 55641; 1963–1964), "Dead Man's Curve" (Liberty 55672; 1964), "The Little Old Lady From Pasadena" (Liberty 55704; 1964), and "Ride the Wild Surf" (Liberty 55724; 1964)—provided succinct, often humorous, commentaries on youthful California obsessions such as surfing, fast cars, and popular culture. Jan and Dean formed a close working relationship with the Beach Boys; Brian Wilson supplied them with their only number one recording, "Surf City," while Torrence, uncredited, sang lead on the Beach Boys' "Barbara Ann" (Capitol 5561; 1966). Members of the two aggregates frequently appeared on each other's recordings until their labels objected.

The duo's successful run came to a sudden end when Berry's Corvette crashed into a parked truck at 65 mph near the fabled Dead Man's Curve. Still partially paralyzed and suffering from speech difficulties, he would continue to record and perform live (sometimes with Torrence) for the remainder of the century,. Torrence focused his energies on album cover design as head of Kitty Hawk Graphics; his clients included the Beach Boys, Steve Martin, Nilsson, the Nitty Gritty Dirt Band, and Linda Ronstadt. Interest in the duo was revived by the television film bio, *Dead Man's Curve* (ABC, 1978), the release of the album *One Summer Night—Live* (1982), and their involvement with the *Back to the Beach* soundtrack (Columbia 40892; 1987).

August 3. The Tymes reach number one on the pop charts with post-doo-wop ballad, "So Much In Love" (Parkway).

August 10. Stevie Wonder—billed as the "13-year-old genius"—kicks off his recording career in auspicious fashion, beginning a three-week stay atop the Hot 100 with the live recording, "Fingertips – Pt. 2" (Tamla 54080).

Stevie Wonder is one of the truly great figures of African American popular music. Like his slightly younger contemporary, Michael Jackson, he literally grew up musically and physically in the public eye; although now approaching institutional status, he has remained a commercially successful recording artist of the better part of five decades.

Born in Detroit in 1950, he made an impact upon the music business billed as a thirteen-year-old child prodigy; hence the moniker, "Little Stevie Wonder." His first hit, "Fingertips, Pt. 2" (Tamla) was a dynamic showcase for his wide-ranging talents—singing, harmonica playing, live performing, and songwriting. As Wonder settled into the role of perennial hit-maker, however, he rapidly transcended his novelty status. While the Motown brain trust seemed hesitant to veer too far from the proven formula, his early releases displayed a surprising degree of diversity, including soul-inflected interpretations of folk-rock ("Blowin' in the Wind") and continental pop ("My Cherie Amour").

As he approached adulthood, Wonder—by now, a talented multi-instrumentalist—insisted on greater control of his career, particularly in production and less reliance of studio session players. Already threatened with the imminent defections of superstars like Marvin Gaye and Diana Ross, Motown loosened the reins somewhat, allowing him the kind of creative latitude that other labels were giving leading rock stars. If Wonder hadn't continued to produce commercially viable music, this freedom might have been short-lived. However, his singles—beginning with "Superstition"—out-performed earlier releases while his albums went from marginal hit status to major best-sellers. Of even greater significance, his 1970s output won universal critical acclaim for its artistry. His legacy was guaranteed by three LPs—*Innervisions* (1973), *Fulfillingness First Finale, Pt. 1* (1974), and the expansive *Sons in the Key of Life* (1977)—which won a combined thirteen Grammy awards.

After this peak, later releases were always somewhat unfocused and stylistically out-of-step with the prevailing trends, be it disco, punk funk, or hip-hop. By the 1980s, Wonder—just in his thirties—had assumed the mantle of elder statesman of the soul-funk nation. Mainstream pop-rock stars like Paul McCartney sought him out for collaborations and large-scale projects like USA for Africa would be considered incomplete without him. Perhaps ironically, his increasing preoccupation with film soundtrack composition was blunted by the appearance of his older, vintage recordings in a host of big budget Hollywood features. His place in the pop music pantheon assured, the extremely likeable and decidedly non-controversial Wonder—still seemingly in full possession of his creative powers—remains capable of breaking out of his commercial dormancy at any time.

August 13. Elvis Presley earns a gold record for *Elvis' Christmas Album* (RCA 1035).

August 31. The Angels jump to the summit of the pop charts with "My Boyfriend's Back" (Smash), remaining there for three weeks.

September 6. Cilla Black signs a management contract with the Beatles' manager, Brian Epstein.

September 7. Major Lance peaks at number eight on the Hot 100 with "The Monkey Time" (Okeh 7175).

One of the leading exponents of Chicago Soul in the early 1960s, Major Lance—along with Smokey Robinson and the Miracles, who recorded the hit, "Mickey's Monkey" (Tamla 54083; 1963; #8 pop, #3 r&b)—is also closely identified with the dance craze, the Monkey. Although he rarely creased the pop charts after 1965, he continued to produce rhythm and blues hits into the mid-1970s.

The Chicago native started out as a professional boxer before signing with Mercury as a singer. His career took off after switching to Columbia's re-established Okeh subsidiary (famous as a "race" label in the 1920s), and hooking up with songwriter/producer Curtis Mayfield, then a member of the Impressions. Lance's second release for the company, "The Monkey Time" (#2 r&b), with its distinctive horn-inflected orchestral arrangement, provided the template for later singles such "Hey Little Girl" (Okeh 7181; 1963; #12 pop, #12 r&b), and "Um, Um, Um, Um, Um, Um" (Okeh 7187; 1964; #5 pop, #5 r&b).

Although squeezed off the pop charts by the influx of British Invasion artists, Lance remained active within the R&B field, moving on to Dakar Records in 1968, and later Mayfield's Curtom imprint, Volt, Playboy, and Osiris. His last notable success—the last of 13 Mayfield compositions he placed on the R&B charts—was "Stay Away From Me (I Love You Too Much)" (Curtom 1953; 1970; #13). He would die of heart disease in 1994.

September 7. Randy and the Rainbows' "Denise" (Rust 5059)—the last notable doo-wop hit—drops out of the Top 10. Hailing from Queens, New York, the group consisted of brothers Dominick "Randy" Safuto (lead singer) and Frank Safuto, who'd first recorded as the Dialtones for Goldisc in 1960, Mike and Sal Zero, and Ken Arcipowski. Although doo-wop-derived material recorded by the likes of the Temptations, the Four Tops, Smokey Robinson & the Miracles, 4 Seasons, the Ad Libs, and the Brooklyn Bridge would continue to sell throughout the 1960s, the predominance of classic-styled R&B vocal groups ended with the rise of the British Invasion.

September 21. Bobby Vinton begins a three-week run atop the Hot 100 with his remake of "Blue Velvet" (Epic).

September 28. The Jaynetts peak at number two on the Hot 100 with "Sally Go 'Round the Roses" (Tuff 369).

The New York-based Jaynetts recorded only one hit, but oh, what a hit: "Sally, Go Round the Roses," with its ambiguous account of a young girl's descent into madness, delivered in chilling fashion. Songwriter Zelma "Zell" Sanders formed the group around her daughter, Johnnie Louise Richardson, formerly of R&B duo, Johnnie and Joe, whose most successful single had been "Over the Mountain, Across the Sea" (1957; #8 pop, #3 r&b). Other members included Yvonne Bushnell, Ethel Davis, Ada Ray, and Mary Sue Wells.

Richardson would leave the Jaynetts to resume her work with Joe Rivers; they performed at oldies concerts and recorded until her death on October 25, 1988. The group soldiered on, though follow-up releases such as "Keep an Eye on Her" and "Johnny Don't Cry" failed to chart. They ceased recording in 1965, and disbanded soon thereafter.

October 5. The Raiders' "Louie Louie" (Columbia) appears as a "Regional Breakout" in *Billboard*, as result of its hit status in the San Francisco area.

October 12. Jimmy Gilmer and the Fireballs—long a fixture in Texas panhandle clubs—zoom to the summit of the pop charts with "Sugar Shack" (Dot), remaining there for five weeks.

October 12. The Ronettes peak at number two on the Hot 100 with "Be My Baby" (Philles 116).

Classic exponents of the Spector Sound, the Ronettes parlayed massive beehive hairdos and an abundance of mascara to provide a tough, sultry accent to the girl group genre. All three members—sisters Veronica and Estelle Bennett and cousin Nedra Talley were born in New York City during the World War II years. They began singing together as the Darling Sisters and were performing a song-and-dance routine based on Hank Ballard and Chubby Checker's "The Twist" at the Peppermint Lounge by 1961. They went on to record for Colpix Records (1961–1962) as Ronnie and the Relatives as well as performing with disc jockey Murray the K's rock shows and singing behind of the era's top pop stars.

Signed by Phil Spector to his Philles label in 1963, the trio's first release, "Be My Baby" (Philles 116; 1963), reached number two on the *Billboard Hot 100*. Although their follow-up singles continued to feature Spector's patented Wall of Sound production, none of them broke into the Top 20. By 1966 Spector lost interest in making records and married Ronnie Bennett. After a couple of failed attempts at launching her solo career (A&M, 1969; Apple, 1971), the couple divorced in 1974.

With the other Ronettes now married, Ronnie Spector continued to work with other prominent musicians during the 1970s and 1980s, including Steven Van Zandt, Bruce Springsteen's E Street Band, and

Genya Ravan. Her greatest success came with "Take Me Home Tonight" (Columbia 06231; 1986), a duet with Eddie Money which hit number four on the pop chart.

October 19. The Kingsmen achieve "Regional Breakout" status when "Louie Louie" (originally issued as Jerden 712, but now distributed by Wand as #143) becomes a Boston hit.

October 26. Gerry and the Pacemakers top the British charts with "You'll Never Walk Alone."

October 31. The Beatles are greeted by hundreds of screaming girls at Heathrow Airport after performing in Sweden. Ed Sullivan witnesses the spectacle, which spurs him to book the band on his show.

November 2. The Kingsmen's "Louie Louie" registers as number 127—'bubbling under"—on the Hot 100. The single will leap to #83, #58, #41, #23, and then #4 over the next five weeks, effectively blowing the competing Raiders single out of the water.

November 16. Nino Tempo and his sister, April Stevens, reach number one on the Hot 100 with their reworking of the standard, "Deep Purple" (Atco).

November 23. Dale & Grace begin a two-week stint atop the pop charts with "I'm Leaving It Up to You" (Montel).

December 7. *With the Beatles* starts a twenty-one-week run atop the British album charts.

December 7. The Singing Nun—a genuine Roman Catholic nun hailing from Belgium—enjoys the biggest novelty smash of the year with "Dominique" (Philips), spending four weeks at number one. The song is sung in French, making it the second foreign language chart-topper of the year; this is the first such occurrence during the rock 'n' roll era.

December 14. The Kingsmen's "Louis Louie" peaks at number 2 on the Hot 100 (#1 on the *Cash Box* charts), remaining there for six of the next seven weeks behind Dominique," and then Bobby Vinton's "There I Said It Again." In his book, *Louie Louie* (Hyperion, 1993), Dave Marsh would write,

> Now, nobody operating in their right mind, the record business or even *Billboard*'s employ, ever believed that "Dominique" was more popular than "Louie Louie." In both the short and long run, "Louie" far outsold "Dominique" or any other record on the chart at the end of 1963. But "Dominique"…was a #1 record, and "Louie Louie"…wasn't—because *Billboard*'s Hot 100 chart measured not popularity or record sales but a combination of sales, airplay and proper decorum (and perhaps the amount of any given record label's advertising budget devoted to *Billboard*) as determined by a mystical formula comprehended by fewer mortals than grasp the essence of "Do wah diddy."

December 26, 1963. With Beatlemania raging in England, Capitol Records—exercising its first rights option as the U.S. EMI affiliate—releases "I Want To Hold Your Hand." It will surge to the top of the Hot 100 in little more than one month.

December 26. Stevie Wonder arrives in England for appearances on the BBC programs, *Ready Steady Go!* and *Thank Your Lucky Stars.*

December 31. The Kinks make their live debut at London's Lotus House Restaurant.

1964

❄

January 1. BBC-TV's *Top of the Pops* premieres. Broadcast from a Manchester church hall, DJ Jimmy Saville introduces the Dave Clark Five, the Hollies, the Rolling Stones, and the Swinging Blue Jeans, among others, all of whom mime their current hits.

January 3. *The Jack Parr Show* airs a clip of the Beatles performing "She Loves You" from *The Mersey Sound* (BBC)—the first time the band has ever been seen on U.S. television.

January 4. Bobby Vinton begins a four-week run atop the Hot 100 with "There! I've Said It Again" (Epic).

January 7. Blues Incorporated mouth harpist Cyril Davies, age thirty-two, dies of leukemia.

January 11. Johnny Cash's *Ring of Fire* (Columbia) is the first country album to top the pop charts.

January 11. Shirley Ellis peaks at number eight on the Hot 100 with "The Nitty Gritty" (Congress 202).

Born in the Bronx, New York, in 1941, Shirley Ellis split her time between singing and songwriting in the 1950s. She joined a group called the Metronomes for a time and had one of her songs, "One, Two, I Love You," recorded by the Heartbreakers for the Vik label.

In the early 1960s, Ellis met and began collaborating with songwriter Lincoln Chase, whose compositions included "Jim Dandy," a hit for LaVern Baker, and "Such a Night," which was recorded by the Drifters. Chase, who ultimately became both her manager and husband, wrote a dance song especially for her, "Nitty Gritty." Although a number of publishers passed on it—including Hal Fein of Roosevelt Music and Bobby Darin at Trinity Music—before Galico Publishing agreed to put it out. Furthermore, the Congress label, located next door to Galico and newly acquired by Kapp Records, released the Ellis recording in Fall 1963 (#8 r&b).

The follow-up, "(That's) What the Nitty Gritty Is" (Congress 208; 1964; #72 pop, #72 r&b), got lost in the initial onslaught of British Invasion acts. Later that year, however, Chase came up with "The Name Game" (Congress 230; 1964; #3 pop, #4 r&b), which would ultimately become Ellis' biggest hit. Chase supplied her with one more hit in "The Name Game" mold, "The Clapping Song (Clap Pat Clap Slap)" (Congress 234; 1965; #8 pop, #16 r&b). Despite the backing of a major label, she managed only one more minor hit, "Soul Time" (Columbia 44021; 1967; #67 pop, #31 r&b), during her lengthy entertainment career.

January 16. The Dave Clark Five top the British charts with "Glad All Over," their only recording to achieve this feat. Stateside, they are immediately anointed successors to the Beatles' in the British Invasion sweepstakes.

The Dave Clark Five were on offshoot of the Tottenham Hotspurs (suburban London) soccer team; the band was started in order to raise money for a match in Holland. The drummer, Dave Clark, soon took on the main songwriting, producing, and managing responsibilities.

The DC5, as they were frequently called, were one of the first British Invasion groups to achieve hit status in the United States. Between 1964 and1967, they placed twenty-four singles and thirteen albums on the charts. Among their notable successes were "Glad All Over" (Epic 9656; 1964; #6), "Bits and Pieces" (Epic 9671; 1964; #4), "Can't You See That She's Mine" (Epic 9692; 1964; #4), "Because" (Epic 9704; 1964; #3), "Catch Us If You Can" (Epic 9833; 1965), and the number one hit "Over and Over" (Epic 9863; 1965).

Unlike many of their British compatriots, who favored softer romantic or novelty styles, the DC5 featured a loud, dynamic sound punctuated by Denis Payton's blaring sax and Clark's taut snare drum figures. Mike Smith's gruff vocals and the densely-textured production work added to the overall sense of excitement. However, the group lacked the ability—or inclination—to develop beyond the simple formulas that had initially resulted in fame and fortune. With poor record sales and new popular music trends such as psychedelia and progressive rock, the band split up in 1970. Smith has continued to record in various projects, while Clark found success in business, including television production and releasing a double-CD retrospective of original DC5 masters in 1993.

January 16. *Hello Dolly!* premieres at New York's St. James Theatre. Featuring music and lyrics by Jerry Herman and book by Michael Steward, it would play for 2,844 performances—the record for longest running musical on Broadway until overtaken by Fiddler on the Roof. The title song would be become a chart-topping single for Louis Armstrong in the spring. A film version, starring Barbra Streisand and Walter Matthau, would be released in 1969.

January 21. Peter and Gordon record "A World Without Love" at the EMI studios in London immediately after Paul McCartney—then dating Peter Asher's sister, Jane—helps Asher finish writing the song. It will top the British charts for two weeks in March, and reach number one in ten other countries as well, including the United States.

January 23. The Kinks sign with the Pye label and—assisted by American producer Shel Talmy—record four songs within one week.

The Kinks' productive recording career has been exceeded in uninterrupted duration only by the Beach Boys and the Rolling Stones. Leader Ray Davies is also acknowledged as one of the most articulate social commentators within the rock scene.

The band was formed in the Muswell Hill section of London by brothers Ray and Dave Davies, who recruited bassist Peter Quaife from the Ravens. By the time they had signed with Pye early the following year, drummer Mick Avory had been brought in as a member. Visually, the Kinks projected a foppish, period fashion look; the early music, however, was Merseybeat-inspired power pop. Following a couple of unsuccessful singles, the Kinks broke out with "You Really Got Me" (Reprise 0306; 1964; #7 US, #1 UK), which was propelled by one of the most recognizable fuzztone-drenched guitar riffs in rock history. Follow-up singles—"All Day and All Of The Night" (Reprise 0334; 1964; #7 US, #2 UK), "Tired Of Waiting For You" (Reprise 0347; 1965; #6 US, #1 UK), "Who'll Be The Next In Line" (Reprise 0366; 1965; #34), and "See Me Free" (Reprise 0379; 1965; #23 US, #9 UK)—mined a similar vein, while LPs like *The Kinks* (Reprise 6143; 1964; #29 US, #3 UK), *Kinks-Size* (Reprise 6158; 1965; #13), *Kinda Kinks* (Reprise 6173; 1965; #60 US, #3 UK), and *The Kink Controversy* (Reprise 6197; 1966; #95 US, #9 UK)—consisted largely of forgettable, throwaway cuts, buoyed by a hit or two; in short, not a particularly auspicious beginning.

The release of "A Well Respected Man" (Reprise 0420; 1965; #13) signaled an increasing emphasis on Davies' wry audio snapshots of English society backed by a more restrained, pastoral group sound. At this stage, the Kinks seemed content to cultivate a niche audience rather than adapt to ongoing changes in pop fashion; *Face To Face* (Reprise 6228; 1966; #12 UK), their glorious final take on the British beat tradition, and concept albums like *Something Else By The Kinks* (Reprise 6279; 1967; #35 UK), *The Kinks Are The Village Green Preservation Society* (Reprise 6327; 1968), and the rock opera *Arthur (Or The Decline And Fall Of The British Empire)* (Reprise 6366; 1969), which idealized England's mythological past in contrast to its contemporary decline, represent the band's artistic summit. Although uneven in quality, *Lola Versus Powerman & The Moneyground, Part One* (Reprise 6423; 1970; #35) and *Muswell Hillbillies* (RCA 4644; 1971; #100) included material—most notably, the transvestite tribute, "Lola" (Reprise 0930; 1970; #9 US, #2 UK) and paranoid "20th Century Man" (RCA 74-0620; 1972)—ranking with their finest recordings.

With the theatrics of glitter rock becoming the rage in late 1971, the Kinks descended into self-parody, beefing up their sound by adding keyboardist John Gosling and a brass section; concept LPs like *Everybody's In Showbiz* (RCA6065; 1972; #70), *Preservation Act I* (RCA 5002; 1973), *Preservation Act II* (RCA 5040; 1974), and *Soap Opera* (RCA 5081; 1975; #51) even incorporated a female chorus at points. By the late 1970s, the band had paired back down to a basic five-piece unit; however, their brand of stadium rock continued to sound anachronistic with the rise of the punk revolution. While considered passé in Britain by the 1980s, the Kinks remained an AOR staple stateside; heavy MTV rotation helped them achieve their first Top 10 hit in thirteen years, "Come Dancing" (Arista 9016; 1983; #6 US, #12 UK). Although new releases have failed to chart since the mid-1980s, the ascendancy of Brit-pop during the 1990s inspired a renewed interest in the band's classic 1960s material.

January 25. Not yet the recluse he would become in the late 1960s, Phil Spector appears on the British television show, *Juke Box Jury*.

February 1. The Beatles' "I Want to Hold Your Hand" (Capitol 5112) begins a seven-week stay atop the Hot 100.

Catapulted by round-the-clock radio play and appearances on the *Ed Sullivan Show*, the Fab Four had gone from complete unknowns to household names in the United States in little more than a fortnight. Record companies owning the distribution rights to earlier Beatles hits rushed them back out into the marketplace. During the week of April 4, the band held down all top five positions on the *Billboard* Hot 100: "Can't Buy Me Love" (Capitol), "Twist and Shout" (Tollie), "She Loves You" (Swan), "I Want To Hold Your Hand" (Capitol), and "Please Please Me" (Vee-Jay).

These events launched the British Invasion, one of the watershed developments in American popular music history. The phenomenon involved the virtual domination of AM radio and the record industry in the United States by British artists, particularly the beat groups who had proved adept at recycling the American rhythm and blues and rockabilly songs of the 1950s.

A fortuitous convergence of historical events provided the appropriate setting for this onslaught. Perhaps of greatest importance, American rock 'n' roll had been undergoing a steady decline in quality since the major record companies—aided and abetted by other media outlets, most notably Top 40 radio and Dick Clark's "American Bandstand"—had harnessed it and begun releasing a tamer product. The pop hegemony enjoyed by teen idols such as Frankie Avalon and Fabian had driven many youth to commercial folk and jazz, while a seemingly endless stream of novelty songs—e.g., Sheb Wooley's "Purple People Eater" (MGM 12651; 1958), David Seville's "Witch Doctor" (Liberty 55132; 1958), Larry Verne's "Mr. Custer" (Era 3024; 1960) and Brian Hyland's "Itsy Bitsy Teeny Weeny Yellow Polka Dot Bikini" (Leador 805; 1960—and dance crazes proved unsuccessful in cultivating a substantial core following for rock 'n' roll.

In the meantime, the British music scene appeared incapable of producing much more than pale Elvis Presley imitators (e.g., Cliff Richard, Billy Fury, and Marty Wilde) and bland pop along the lines of Mr. Acker Bilk, whose "Stranger on the Shore" (Atco 6217; 1962) was one of the few British imports to make a substantial dent in the stateside charts prior to 1964. However, the pop underground in Great Britain was quietly brewing something far more potent starting in the mid-1950s. The skiffle music craze (a uniquely English form of folk revival music drawing heavily on American material) led by Lonnie Donegan spurred the baby boomer generation to form their own bands. The most notable of these aggregates—then known by names such as the Quarrymen and the Silver Beatles—would go on to spearhead the British Invasion.

It's hard to imagine the invasion taking place without the Beatles. Many of the bands swept along on the Fab Four's coattails to the top of the American charts possessed no more talent than the bland teen idols they had displaced. The Beatles, however, were another matter. Three of members—the songwriting team of John Lennon and Paul McCartney, and, to a lesser extent, lead guitarist George Harrison—were capable of producing first-rate material. After a brief period of covering American R&B, pop, and country standards, the group went on to compose a long string of rock classics, many of which are likely to be performed for generations to come. The band members were also all excellent musicians, thanks in large part to years spent performing in small clubs in England and Germany. Lennon and McCartney both were superb vocalists, capable of putting across rave-up rockers and introspective ballads in an equally convincing manner.

Despite the band's ability—so easy to assess in retrospect—success in the United States might easily have eluded them had not conditions proved ripe for receptiveness on the part of the American public. The Beatles, under the skilled management of Brian Epstein, had attempted a number of times in 1963 to secure a hit record on the American charts. Songs like "Love Me Do" (Tollie 9008), "From Me to You"/"Please Please Me" (Vee-Jay 581) and "She Loves You" (Swan 4152)—all hits in the U.K.—had gone nowhere when released by various labels in the states. By late 1963, however, the nation was caught up in communal sense of mourning, brought on by the assassination of popular President John F. Kennedy. The Beatles—with their cheeky wit (as evidenced in countless news interviews punctuating the whirlwind visits to the United States during the early months of 1964) and catchy, upbeat pop songs—proved to be the perfect anecdote for the nation's collective depression. In addition, the mop-top hairstyle exhibited by the band members garnered considerable attention. As had been the case with Elvis Presley's heavily greased DA hairstyle of the mid-1950s, the Beatles look engendered considered controversy on the part of the adult establishment when it first assaulted the public consciousness. It provided instant credibility with America's youth, who were always in search of culture symbols to both collectively identify with and flaunt in the face of authority figures as an act of rebellion.

These developments made a substantial impression on the British music scene. British artists of every stripe—from beat groups to purveyors of easy listening fare—were hurriedly signed up by American labels and promoted through the mass media with a vengeance. In the weeks immediately following the appearance of the Beatles on the charts, countless other U.K. recording acts—some of whom had realized very little success in their own country—enjoyed heavy radio play and print coverage stateside. The first onslaught of British performers to achieve success on the U. S. charts included Dusty Springfield, the Dave Clark Five, the Searchers, Billy J. Kramer, and Peter and Gordon. Perhaps of even greater importance, countless other British youths were inspired to become musicians, resulting in a steady stream of talent which, many would argue, has remained undiminished to the present day.

By early summer the floodgates had burst open; there seemed to be more British artists than American on the airwaves. Indeed, a considerable number of established U.S. acts—to say nothing of the more marginal recording artists—virtually disappeared from the charts in 1964 (some never to return). Stars suddenly thrust into the periphery of record industry included Dion, Fats Domino, Rick Nelson, Neil Sedaka, Connie Francis, Brenda Lee, Roy Orbison, the Everly Brothers, and Chubby Checker. Even Presley's career was sent into a tailspin. After eight years of uninterrupted success, he enjoyed only one top ten hit—"Crying in the Chapel" (RCA 447-0643); which charted in 1965 but was recorded in 1960—prior to his revival in 1969 with "In the Ghetto" (RCA 47-9741) and "Suspicious Minds" (RCA 47-9764). Only a handful of American artists continued to thrive in 1964 and beyond, most notably the Beach Boys and the Four Seasons. New home-grown talent found it necessary to incorporate elements of the merseybeat sound such as the trademark jangly guitars and seamless three-part vocal harmonies. The garage punk and folk rock movements were particularly influenced by English rock bands. Some American groups—for example, Beau Brummels and the Sir Douglas Quintet in 1965—found it expedient to ape the British Invasion look to the extent of carefully covering up their native origins.

Probably the most positive result of the British Invasion was its role in clearing away the musical deadwood which had found a home on the U.S. charts. With many of the long-established American acts—as well as countless lesser luminaries—unable to compete with the host of typically lackluster British stars, fresh stateside talent was more readily able to garner the attention of record company executives. Within a year or two of the initial British onslaught, a new wave of American musicians had already laid the groundwork for the creative renaissance in popular music during the latter half of the 1960s.

February 1. Lesley Gore begins a three-week run at number two behind "I Want to Hold Your Hand" with "You Don't Own Me" (Mercury 72206).

February 1. *Billboard* includes the page three headline: "Indiana Gov. Puts Down 'Pornographic' Wand Tune." Gil Faggen would report that Governor Matthew Welsh "told people his 'ears tingled'," after hearing the record. Welsh then sent a message to Reid Chapman, president of the Indiana Broadcasters Association, requesting that the Kingsmen's "Louie Louie" be banned from all radio stations in the state. Chapman, vice-president of WANE AM-TV, Fort Wayne, passed along this request to his membership.

February 7. The Beatles arrive at New York's John F. Kennedy Airport where an estimated twenty-five thousand fans make their first visit to the United States a major media event.

February 7. Although the Kinks' first single, "Long Tall Sally"—released in February—fails to chart in Great Britain, the group is able to parlay a massive media campaign into an appearance on ITV's *Ready Steady Go!*

February 8. The Ronettes interview the Beatles on the radio.

February 9. The Beatles make their American television debut on *The Ed Sullivan Show*.

February 11. The Beatles give their first American concert in Washington, D.C.

February 12. The Beatles play in the prestigious New York City venue, Carnegie Hall.

February 15. The Beatles begin an eleven-week stint atop the LP charts with *Meet the Beatles!* (Capitol).

February 15. The Dave Clark Five appear on the BBC program, *Thank Your Lucky Stars*.

February 15. Dionne Warwick peaks at number eight on the Hot 100 with "Anyone Who Had a Heart" (Specter 1262).

Born Marie Dionne Warwick December 12, 1940, in Orange, New Jersey, she began singing in her church choir at age six. After a stint with the Drinkard Singers, she formed the Gospelaires along with sister Dee Dee and aunt Cissy Houston. Warwick would attend the Hartt College of Music, Hartford, Connecticut, before becoming increasingly involved with studio session work in the late 1950s.

Signed to Scepter Records, she became the mouthpiece for the Burt Bacharach/Hal David songwriting and production team from 1963 to 1971, recording some notable crossover hits as "Anyone Who Had A Heart," "Walk On By," "Message to Michael," "Alfie," "I Say Little Prayer," and "This Girl's in Love With You." Warwick (who added an "e" to the end of her name for spiritual reasons) has remained successful in the performing and recording arenas up to the present day, most notably with the million sellers, "Then Came You" (with the Spinners; #1 pop), "I'll Never Love This Way Again," and "That's What Friends Are For" (with Elton John, Gladys Knight, and Stevie Wonder; #1 pop and R&B).

February 21. The New York-based band, the Echoes, take on a keyboardist named Billy Joel.

February 22. Cilla Black tops the British charts with "Anyone Who Had a Heart," the Bacharach/David song that was a U.S. hit in an interpretation by Dionne Warwick. For the first time ever, the U.K. Top 10 includes only English acts.

February 27. *What Makes Sammy Run?* Premieres at New York's 54th Street Theatre. Featuring music and lyrics by Ervin Drke and book by Budd and Stuart Schulberg, the musical would run for forty performances. Steve Lawrence, who had the starring role as movie mogul Sammy Glick, would achieve a hit with one of the show's songs, "A Room Without Windows."

March. Dick Clark transfers his *American Bandstand* operations from Philadelphia to Los Angeles.

March 2. The Beatles begin work on their first film feature, *A Hard Day's Night*.

March 14. Billy J. Kramer and the Dakotas top the British charts for the second time with "Little Children."

March 16. The Beatles set a record for advance sales with 2,100,000 copies of "Can't Buy Me Love" (Capitol).

March 19. British Prime Minister Harold Wilson present the Beatles with the Show Business Personalities of the Year award for 1963 at London' Dorchester Hotel.

March 21. The Beatles succeed themselves at number one on the pop charts with "She Loves You" (Swan).

March 22. The entire British singles Top 10 consists of homegrown acts for the first time ever.

March 23. John Lennon's *In His Own Write* is published in Great Britain.

March 25. The Beatles debut on the British TV program, *Top of the Pops*, performing "Can't Buy Me Love."

March 26. *Funny Girl* premieres at the Winter Garden in New York City. Featuring music by Jule Styne, lyrics by Bob Merrill, and book by Isobel Lennart, it would have a run of 1,348 performances. Barbra Streisand—cast as Fanny Brice, whose life was the focus of the musical—would enjoy a major hit with the show song, "People." Streisand would also star in the 1968 cinematic version as well as its 1975 sequel, *Funny Lady*.

March 27. The Beatles occupy rungs one through six on the Australian singles chart.

March 28. Madame Tussauds, London, unveils waxwork images of the Beatles, the first pop stars to be so honored.

March 28. Radio Caroline makes its inaugural broadcast from the former Danish ferry, *Fredericia*, in the North Sea.

April 3. Bob Dylan enters the British singles charts for the first time with "The Times They Are A-Changin'."

April 4. The Beatles remain atop the Hot 100, beginning a five-week run with "Can't Buy Me Love" (Capitol). At the time, their rousing rendition of "Twist and Shout" (Tollie 9001) begins a four-week run t number two.

April 7. *High Spirits* premieres at New York's Alvin Theatre. Featuring music, lyrics, and book by Hugh Martin and Timothy Gray, the musical would have a run of 375 performances. Noel Coward, whose 1941 play *Blithe Spirit* was the source of the plot, started out as the director before conflicts with star Beatrice Lillie led to his being replaced by Gower Champion.

April 11. The Searchers peak at number thirteen of the Hot 100 with "Needles and Pins" (Kapp 577).

Although overshadowed by fellow Liverpudlians, the Beatles, the Searchers were one of the most accomplished British Invasion bands. Their close, four-part harmonies and rich, jangling guitar lines presaged the commercial ascendancy of folk-rock bands such as the Byrds.

The Searchers, named after John Ford's classic 1956 film, starring John Wayne, were formed in 1961 to play behind British vocalist Johnny Sandon. The group—originally comprised of guitarist John McNally, guitarist Mike Pender, bassist Tony Jackson, and drummer Chris Curtis—later struck out on their own, playing the Star Club (Hamburg, Germany) in the wake of the successful run there by the Beatles. A residency at Liverpool's Iron Door club led A&R man Tony Hatch to offer them a record contract. After charting in the U.K. with the Drifters' "Sweets for My Sweet" (Pye; released in U.S. as Mercury 72172) in 1963, the band achieved success on both sides of the Atlantic—number one in England, number thirteen in the United States—with the million-selling "Needles and Pins" (Kapp 577; 1964). More hits—including "Don't Throw Your Love Away" (Kapp 593; 1964), "Love Potion Number Nine" (Kapp 27; 1964), "What Have They Done to the Rain" (Kapp 644; 1965), and "Bumble Bee" (Kapp 49; 1965)—and international tours followed.

When their recordings stopped charting, the Searchers continued to earn a living playing British clubs and cabarets. Signing with Sire Records, the band returned briefly to the public eye with two album releases, *The Searchers* (Sire 6082; 1980) and *Love's Melodies* (Sire 3523; 1981). Always hampered by the absence of a talented composer within the group, the inclusion of high quality material by Tom Petty, John Fogerty, Moon Martin, Alex Chilton, and other contemporary songwriters on the Sire LPs elicited critical raves. Nevertheless, both discs sold poorly and the band returned to the touring circuit.

April 16. The Rolling Stones' debut LP is released in Great Britain; it will top the charts a couple of weeks later. When issued that summer in the U.S., they are heralded as "England's newest hit sensation."

April 17. With an informal ban of the Kingsmen's "Louie Louie" in effect in Indiana, Washington, D.C., FBI lab audiologists report to the Indianapolis Special Agent in Charge: "For your information, the record…was played at various speeds but none of the speeds assisted in determining the words of the song on the record." David Marsh would later comment, in his book *Louie Louie* (1993):

> But that was a *preliminary* conclusion, and not an especially accurate one; the lyrics are only impossible to learn if you're willfully trying to hear what's not there.

April 22. The President of the National Federation of Hairdressers offers a free haircut to the next group to top the pop charts, adding "The Rolling Stones are the worst, one of them looks as if he's got a feather duster on his head."

May 9. Louis Armstrong's "Hello, Dolly!" (Kapp) breaks the Beatles' stranglehold on the Hot 100's number one position (which lasted fourteen weeks).

May 9. The Beach Boys begin a four-week stay atop the album charts with *Beach Boys Concert* (Capitol), their first LP to accomplish this feat.

May 9. Chuck Berry kicks off his inaugural British tour at London's Astoria Theatre. Supporting acts include The Animals, Karl Denver and The Nashville Teens, and The Swinging Blue Jeans.

May 16. *The Beatles' Second Album* (Capitol) heads up the album charts, pushing aside the band's American debut, *Meet the Beatles*.

May 16. May Wells begins a two-week stint atop the Hot 100 with "My Guy" (Motown).

May 17. Bob Dylan makes his live debut in the U.K. at London's Royal Albert Hall.

May 23. Ella Fitzgerald becomes the first artist to have a hit with a Beatles cover when "Can't Buy Me Love" enters the British charts.

May 30. The Beatles reach number one on the pop charts with "Love Me Do" (Tollie).

June 1. The Rolling Stones arrive at Kennedy Airport, New York City, to begin their initial U.S. tour. These shows were arranged to promote the release of their debut LP and single, the Buddy Holly-penned "Not Fade Away."

June 2. The Rolling Stones make their U.S. television debut on *The Les Crane Show*.

June 4. Suffering from acute tonsillitis, Ringo Starr collapses during a photo shoot. With a Beatles world tour imminent, session drummer Jimmy Nichol replaces him for eleven days.

June 6. The Dixie Cups begin a three-week run atop the Hot 100 with the Jeff Barry/Ellie Greenwich/Phil Spector composition, "Chapel of Love" (Red Bird).

The Dixie Cups typified the Girl Group genre: attractive teenage females with pliable voices and personalities that were molded to suit the artistic and commercial priorities of a handful of record label executives and studio producers. This trio stood apart from their peers, however, because they sang on one of the most memorable recordings—the rock steady paean to idealized romance, "Chapel of Love" (Red Bird 001; 1964; #1 pop/r&b three weeks)—of the rock era. In addition, the song was selected as the first release by Jerry Leiber and Mike Stoller's highly regarded (for its high ratio of hits to releases) Red Bird label.

The Dixie Cups—comprised of New Orleans natives Joan Marie Johnson and sisters Barbara Ann and Rosa Lee Hawkins—were introduced to Leiber and Stoller by singer Joe Jones, who'd decided to manage them after catching their act at a local talent show. Providing them with an alternative name to Little Miss and the Muffets, Leiber and Stoller placed them with the songwriting/production team of Jeff Barry and Ellie Greenwich, who had recently provided material for the Phil Spector acts, the Ronettes and the Crystals, and had recorded as the Raindrops. The couple, who married October 29, 1962, felt that "Chapel of Love"—which they co-written with Spector and placed on the *…presenting the fabulous Ronettes featuring Veronica* (Philles 4006; 1964; #96) album—possessed hit potential. Over Spector's objections, they brought in the Dixie Cups to reinterpret the song with an arranging assist from Jones.

The trio enjoyed a brief run of lesser chart entries—including "People Say" (Red Bird 006; 1964; #12 pop/r&b), "You Should Have Seen the Way He Looked At Me" (Red Bird 012; 1964; #39 pop/r&b), "Little Bell" (Red Bird 017; 1964; #51 pop/r&b), and "Iko Iko" (Red Bird 024; 1965; #20 pop/r&b)—before Red Bird went out of business in 1966. They jumped to ABC Records, but failed to record another hit.

June 27. Peter & Gordon climb to the summit of the pop charts with the Lennon/McCartney-penned "A World Without Love" (Capitol).

July 4. The Beach Boys begin a two-week stint atop the Hot 100 with "I Get Around" (Capitol).

July 11. Johnny Rivers peaks at number two on the Hot 100 with an updated version of "Memphis" (Imperial 66032).

Johnny Rivers was one of the top-selling pop-rock recording artists of the 1960s. This success owed much to the ability to discern new trends—folk rock, Motown Soul, psychedelia, the blues revival, the singer-songwriter tradition, and the rock 'n' roll revival, among others—and incorporate them into his own style. Many Rivers fans were not aware of the many facets of his talent other than the vocals and guitar work on the records; he was, in fact, a songwriter, record producer, record company executive, and music publisher of note as well.

A native of New York City, Rivers moved to Baton Rouge, Louisiana, with his family at age three. Thanks largely to the assistance of deejay Alan Freed, he obtained a recording contract with the fabled doo-wop label, Gone, during a summer trip back to New York. He departed to Nashville after graduating from high school, recording demos while attempting to break into the music industry as a songwriter. After working as a staff writer for the New York-based music publisher, Hill & Range, Rivers relocated to Los Angeles to build a performing career.

An acclaimed run as the star attraction at the Whiskey-A-Go-Go led to a contract with Imperial Records. His debut album, Johnny Rivers Live at the Whiskey a Go Go (Imperial 12264; 1964; #12)—and the Chuck Berry-penned single, "Memphis"—made him an overnight star. Rivers' engaging southern drawl and canned crowd noise endowed his recordings with a sense of live excitement, resulting in a string of hit singles—including "Mountain of Love" (Imperial 66075; 1964; #9), "Seventh Son" (Imperial 66112; 1965; #7), and "Secret Agent Man" (Imperial 66159; 1966; #3)—and albums: Here We a Go Go Again! (Imperial 12274; 1964; #38), Johnny Rivers In Action! (Imperial 12280; 1965; #42), Meanwhile Back at the Whiskey a Go Go (Imperial 12284; 1965; #21), Johnny Rivers Rocks the Folk (Imperial 12293; 1965; #91), "…and I know you wanna dance" (Imperial 12307; 1966; #52).

When his established formula began to wear thin, Rivers abruptly shifted from club and folk-blues-oriented rockers to pop-soul ballads. Singles such as "Poor Side of Town" (Imperial 66205; 1966; #1; co-written with Lou Adler), "Baby I Need Your Lovin'" (Imperial 66227; 1967; #3), and "The Tracks of My Tears" (Imperial 66244; 1967; #10), followed by the hippie-flavored LP, Realization (Imperial 12372; 1968; #5), provided the momentum to keep him on the charts well into the 1970s. By then his greatest success came with laid-back versions of rock 'n' roll-era classics such as "Rockin' Pneumonia – Boogie Woogie Flu" (United Artists 50960; 1972; #6), "Blue Suede Shoes" (United Artists 198; 1973; #38), and "Help Me Rhonda" (Epic 50121; 1975; #22; including vocals by songwriter Brian Wilson). Although his last big hit was "Swayin' to the Music (Slow Dancin')" (Big Tree 16094; 1977; #10), Rivers has continued to record in addition to performing both stateside and abroad.

In 1966, Rivers began leaving his mark on other aspects of the record industry when Imperial permitted him to establish a subsidiary label, Soul City. His efforts to build the company included a pivotal role in the career of the 5th Dimension—providing their name, finding them first-rate material, and producing and playing on their early recordings. By the late 1960s, he also owned a music-publishing firm, Johnny Rivers Music. He would remain active in running these companies into the twenty-first century.

July 18. The Four Seasons reach number one on the pop charts with "Rag Doll" (Philips), remaining there for two weeks.

July 25. Bobby Bland peaks at number forty-two on the Hot 100 with "Share Your Love With Me" (Duke 377). The song will be redone by the Band on their rock 'n' revival LP, *Moondog Matinee* (Capitol, 1973).

Born January 27, 1930, in Rosemark, Tennessee, Bland sang with the Memphis-based gospel group, the Miniatures, in the late 1940s. He was a member of the Beale Streeters—along with Johnny Ace, Earl Forest, Roscoe Gordon, B. B. King and Willie Nix—in 1949, a was a driver/valet for King and a part of the Johnny Ace Revue in the early 1950s.

Bland first recorded as a solo artist for Modern in 1952, before establishing himself as a consistent hit-maker with Duke Records. He would record forty-five hits with the label through 1972, including the R&B chart-toppers "Farther Up the Road," "I Pity the Fool," and "That's the Way Love Is." He would maintain his success with ABC/Dunhill, and then rejuvenate his career by teaming with King on a succession of recordings beginning in 1977.

July 31. Jim Reeves dies at age forty-one when his plane—en route from Arkansas to Nashville—crashes in thick fog. Possessing a smooth baritone free of southern vocal mannerisms, he was one of the first country singers to cross over to the pop market with "He'll Have to Go" in early 1960.

August 1. The Beatles begin a two-week stay atop the Hot 100 with the theme song to their debut film, "A Hard Day's Night" (Capitol).

August 1. Rockabilly cat turned teen idol Johnny Burnette—whose hits included "You're Sixteen" (#8 U.S., #3 U.K.) and "Dreamin'"—is killed in a boating accident on Car Lake, California, at age thirty.

August 6. Still years from achieving any semblance of fame and fortune, Rod Stewart performs with Long John Baldry and the Hoochie Coochie Men on *The Beat Room*, his British television debut.

August 12. *A Hard Day's Night* opens in five hundred U.S. cinemas, generally receiving rave reviews.

August 15. Dean Martin peaks at number one on the pop charts with "Everybody Loves Somebody" (Reprise).

August 19. The Beatles commence their first American tour at San Francisco's Cow Palace. The tour spans thirty shows in twenty-four cities, culminating with a charity concert at the Paramount Theater, Brooklyn, on September 20. By this time, the group's impact on American popular culture is unparalleled, with many young males emulating the "moptop" look, and countless bands utilizing the three guitars/drum lineup.

August 22. The Honeycombs reach number one on the British charts with "Have I the Right?"

August 22. The Supremes begin a two-week stint atop the Hot 100 with "Where Did Our Love Go" (Motown 1060). The breakthrough single–the first of many major hits featuring the songwriting and production talents of Brian Holland/Lamont Dozier/Eddie Holland—launches them on a trajectory to become the most successful girl group in recording history.

The three songwriter-producers, Holland-Dozier-Holland, all born in Detroit, formed a working team as part of Berry Gordy's Motown-Gordy-Tamla record company in the early 1960s. They quickly gained recognition as vital contributors to the label's polished, pop-soul output, known collectively as the "Motown Sound." From 1963 to1966, they produced an unprecedented twenty-eight Top 10 hits, including the Four Tops' "Baby I Need Your Loving" (Motown 1062; 1964), "I Can't Help Myself" (Motown 1976; 1965), "It's the Same Old Song" (Motown 1081; 1965), and "Reach Out I'll Be There" (Motown 1098; 1966); Martha and the Vandellas' Nowhere to Run" (Gordy 7039; 1965) and "Jimmy Mack" (Gordy 7058; 1967); and the Supremes' "Where Did Our Love Go" (Motown 1060; 1964), "Baby Love" (Motown 1066; 1964), "Come See About Me" (Motown 1068; 1964), "Stop! In the Name of Love" (Motown 1074; 1965), and "I Hear a Symphony" (Motown 1083; 1965).

Motivated by a desire for more creative freedom and a greater share of the profits, Holland-Dozier-Holland departed Motown in 1967 to found Invictus/Hot Wax. In addition to producing such artists as the Chairmen of the Board, Honey Cone, and Freda Payne, all three harbored solo ambitions. Whereas, Eddie Holland's success was limited to four charting singles in the early 1960s—including the Top Thirty hit, "Jamie" (Motown 1021; 1962)—his brother Brian and Dozier both released hit recordings in the 1970s. The trio disbanded in 1973 and Dozier continued his momentum as a recording artist with ABC Paramount Records.

September 1. The inaugural broadcast of ABC's *Shindig*, a weekly rock show hosted by Jimmy O'Neil. It provides vital exposure to many top recording acts of the day, most notably the Righteous Brothers who are regulars on the program.

September 4. The Animals' stateside performing debut takes place at Brooklyn's Paramount Theater. September 5. The Animals' first American single, "House of the Rising Sun" (MGM), begins a three-week run atop the pop charts.

September 19. Herman's Hermits top the British charts with "I'm Into Something Good," their only song to accomplish this feat.

September 22. *Fiddler on the Roof* premieres at New York's Imperial Theatre. Featuring music by Jerry Bock, lyrics by Sheldon Hrnick, and book by Joseph Stein, the musical would have a run of 3,242 performances—the longest running production in Broadway history until *Grease* broke the record in December 1979.

September 26. Roy Orbison surges to number one on the Hot 100 with "Pretty Woman" (Monument), remaining there for three weeks.

October 10. One of the giants of vaudeville and Broadway musical comedy, Eddie Cantor, dies.

A very successful recording artist during the 1920s, spanning both the acoustic and electronic eras, he would remain a celebrity of the first magnitude—moving on to radio, the cinema, and television—into the early 1950s.

Born Isidore Itzkowitz January 31, 1892, on the Lower East Side of New York City, he graduated from street performing to stardom in the *Ziegfeld Follies of 1917*. That show spawned his first hit recording, "That's the Kind Of a Baby For Me" (Victor 18342; 1917). He continued produce best-selling discs into the early 1930s for various labels, including Pathe, Emerson, Columbia, and Melotone. His most popular records—"You'd Be Surprised" (Emerson 10102; 1920), "Margie" (Emerson 10301; 1921), "No, No, Nora"/"I've Got the Yes! We Have No Bananas Blues" (Columbia 3964; 1923), "Charley, My Boy" (Columbia 182; 1924), "If You Knew Susie" (Columbia 364; 1925), and "Makin' Whoopee" (Victor 21831; 1929)—were typically culled from musicals and films in which he had a starring role. Occasionally self-penned, Cantor's recorded output always featured his trademark energetic verve, charm, and humor, which ranged widely from nonsense to satire.

October 10. Joe Hinton peaks at number thirteen on the Hot 100 with "Funny (How Time Slips Away)" (Back Beat 541).

Like Sam Cooke, Aretha Franklin, and many other 1960s soul singers, Joe Hinton started out singing gospel music before switching to more secular fare. He only had one bona-fide hit, but might well have gone on to greater success if he hadn't died in a Boston hospital, allegedly of "natural causes," on August 13, 1968, while still in his thirties.

Little is known about Hinton's early life. Born in 1929, he first attracted attention with the Chosen Gospel Singers. He was discovered by Don Robey, owner of he Duke and Peacock labels, while lead vocalist with the Spirits of Memphis. Robey persuaded him to record soul music.

Hinton's early singles failed to elicit much of a response. He finally made the charts with "You Know It Ain't Right" (Back Beat 537; 1963; #88 pop, #20 r&b). He followed with several more hits—"Better To Give Than Receive" (Back Beat 539; 1963; #89 pop, #89 r&b), the Willie Nelson-penned "Funny (How Time Slips Away)" (#13 r&b), and "I Want A Little Girl" (Back Beat 545; 1965; #132 pop, #34 r&b)—all of which featured his patented white hot singing. Having faded into obscurity, his death received little media coverage.

October 15. Songwriter Cole Porter—composer of such pop standards as "Night and Day" and "I Get a Kick Out of You"—dies.

October 17. Manfred Mann begins a two-week stint atop the pop charts with Jeff Barry/Ellie Greenwich-penned "Do Wah Diddy Diddy" (Ascot), formerly a minor hit with the Exciters.

October 20. *Golden Boy* premieres at New York's Majestic Theatre. Featuring music by Charles Strouse, lyrics by Lee Adams, and book by Clifford Odets and William Gibson, the musical would have a run of 569 performances.

October 31. The Supremes begin a four-week stay at number one on the Hot 100 with "Baby Love" (Motown).

November 28. The Shangri-Las top the pop charts with Jeff Barry/Ellie Greenwich/George Morton-penned teen soaper, "Leader of the Pack" (Red Bird).

December 5. *Bonanza* patriarch, Lorne Greene, reaches number one on the Hot 100 with his spoken word rendition of the western saga, "Ringo" (RCA).

December 12. Bobby Vinton goes to the summit of the pop charts with "Mr. Lonely" (Epic).

December 19. The Supremes leap to the top of the Hot 100 with "Come See About Me" (Motown), remaining there for two non-consecutive weeks.

December 24. The Yardbirds open for "The Beatles Christmas Show" at London's Hammersmith Odeon. Up-and-coming songwriter Graham Gouldman writes "For Your Love" with them in mind after seeing them perform. The new pop direction heralded by the group's recording of the song leads to Eric Clapton's departure.

December 25. The Zombies begin a ten-day stint in New York City as part of Murray the K's Christmas Show, performing along with the Shangri-Las, the Nashville Teens, and the Shirelles, among others. This follows three days of negotiations with U.S. immigration authorities, who—faced with an onslaught of British acts trying to promote their respective recordings—had attempted to circumvent an international union agreement by banning the group from working stateside.

December 26. The Beatles begin a three-week stay atop the Hot 100 with "I Feel Fine" (Capitol)—the group's sixth number one single for the year.

December 26. The Rolling Stones place an ad in the *New Musical Express* wishing starving hairdressers and their families a Happy Christmas.

1965

❄

January 8. The weekly pop music dance program, *Hullabaloo*, premieres on American television. The presence of mini-skirted go-go girls in the song sequences causes a minor stir among critics and viewing public.

January 10. In homage to his appreciation of 1950s radio comedy such as *The Goons Show*, John Lennon appears on the British TV program, *Not Only But Also*, hosted by Peter Cook and Dudley Moore.

January 11. The Righteous Brothers touch down in England to promote their recordings; they will appear on the TV programs *Ready Steady Go!*, *Scene at 6:30*, and *Discs a Go-Go*.

January 15. Charlie Watts' book tribute to jazz saxophonist Charlie Parker, *Ode to a High Flying Bird*, is published.

January 15. The Who's debut single, "I Can't Explain"—augmented by Jimmy Page's guitar work—is released by Brunswick. Although only one thousand were initially pressed, another one hundred thousand were issued as the single began climbing the charts, eventually peaking at number eight on the British charts.

January 16. The Larks peak at number seven in the Hot 100 with "The Jerk" (Money 106).

The story of the Larks is really one of two different groups that possessed one common feature: lead singer Don Julian. The earliest manifestation of the act—which formed in 1953 and included tenor Ronald Barrett (later replaced by Glen Reagan), tenor Earl Jones, and bass Randy Jones—was known as Don Julian and the Meadowlarks. Although now revered as an R&B vocal group classic, their debut single, "Heaven and Paradise" (Dootone), failed to make the charts. When it became evident that no hits were forthcoming, Julian moved on to other projects.

In the mid-1960s, Julian was inspired by the sight of a new teen dance to write "The Jerk." He recorded it in short order, naming his new group—comprised of Charles Morrison, Ted Waters, and himself—the Larks, while their back-up band became the Meadowlarks. While the single spurred a new dance craze, the Larks were unable to produce any follow-up hits. Nevertheless, the dance did inspire other best-selling records, most notably, the Capitols' "Cool Jerk" (1966) and the Miracles' "Come On and Do the Jerk" (Tamla; 1966).

January 20. Disc jockey/promoter Alan Freed dies of uremic poisoning in Palm Springs, California, aged forty-two.

January 23. "Downtown" (Warner Bros. 5494) begins a two-week stint atop the pop singles charts, making Petula Clark the first British female artist to go number one in the United States since Vera Lynn in 1952.

Although Clark (b. November 15, 1932) is best remembered in America for her string of British Invasion pop-rock hits in the mid-1960s, at age eight she was already a professional singer. Born in Epsom, England, she was appearing regularly on radio as a nine-year-old; two years later, she hosted her own program, *Pet's Parlour*. By twelve, she was performing for British troops and had appeared in her first film, *A Medal for the General*. Her acting skills were in high demand by the early 1950s, with more than twenty film credits.

Clark's first hit record, "The Little Shoemaker" (Polygon), reached number twelve on the British charts in mid-1954. More hits followed in rapid succession, including her first chart topper, "Sailor" (Pye; 1961), and million-seller, "Romeo" (Pye; 1961). After marrying Vogue Records publicity director, Claud Wolff, in 1961, and settling in France, she went on to chart success there with hits such as "Chariot" and "Monsieur."

By now a fixture in much of continental Europe, Clark breached the U.S. market with the number one hit (and Grammy Award winner for best song in 1964), "Downtown." She would go on to have twenty more stateside hits through 1972, including "I Know A Place" (Warner Bros. 5612; 19650, "My Love" (Warner Bros. 5684; 1965–1966), "I Couldn't Live Without Your Love" (Warner Bros. 5835; 1966), "This Is My Song" (Warner Bros. 7002; 1967), and "Don't Sleep in the Subway" (Warner Bros. 7049; 1967).

As the hits slowed down in the late 1960s, Clark revived her acting career. In addition to starring roles in films (e.g., *Goodbye, Mr. Chips* and *Finian's Rainbow*), she appeared in British stage productions such as *The Sound of Music*, *Candida*, and *Someone Like You* (1990; co-written with Fay Weldon). She appeared on Broadway for the first time with *Blood Brothers* (1993), costarring David and Shaun Cassidy. In the midst of these activities, she still found time to sing live and record; "Downtown '88" (PRT), a remix of "Downtown," was a Top 10 U.K. hit.

January 28. The Moody Blues reach the top of British charts for the only time in their career with "Go Now!" They will become far more popular in the United States than in their native land.

Although the bulk of their creative output appears frozen in a late 1960s progressive rock time-warp, the Moody Blues have retained strong core of followers up to the present day. During the band's innovative years, they greatly influenced the development of the classical rock genre, the integration of both symphonic instruments and synthesizers into rock music arrangements, the refinement of the concept album, and the interpretive value of cover art work and graphics.

Like many British bands beginning in the early 1960s, the Birmingham, England-based Moody Blues—comprised of vocalist/guitarist Denny Laine, vocalist/pianist Mike Pinder, vocalist/bassist Clint Warwick, drummer Graham Edge, and Ray Thomas (flute, harmonica, vocals)—were initially committed to updating American blues music. After one notable hit, the Bessie Banks cover "Go Now" (London 9726; 1965; #10 US, #1 UK), and a string of minor successes, Laine and Warwick departed in late 1966. With replacements Justin Hayward (vocals, guitar) and John Lodge (vocals, bass) in place, the group opted for a more ambitious hybrid of orchestral pop-rock and mind-expanding song lyrics. The first album with this revamped lineup, *Days Of Future Passed* (London 18012; 1967; #3 US, #27 UK), was put together while the band was making demonstration discs for British Decca's new recording process. Featuring the London Festival Orchestra, the LP was conceived as a song-cycle connected by poetic fragments and instrumental interludes; two of the tracks, "Nights in White Satin" (Deram 85023; 1967; #2—1972 reissue—US, #19 UK) and "Tuesday Afternoon" (Deram 85028; 1968; #24), would also score highly on the pop charts. Now recognized as pop-philosopher gurus much like the Beatles and Bob Dylan, the band's popular follow-up LPs—which featured the mellotron, a synthesizer derivative capable of providing thin, reedy approximation of a string choir—included *In Search Of The Lost Chord* (Deram 18017; 1968; #23US, #5 UK), *On The Threshold Of A Dream* (Deram 18025; 1969; #20 US, #1 UK), *To Our Children's Children's Children* (Threshold 1; 1969; #14 US, #2 UK; the inaugural release of the band's designer label intended, like the Beatles' Apple, to foster artistic creativity), *A Question Of Balance* (Threshold 3; 1970; #3 US, #1 UK), *Every Good Boy Deserves Favour* (Threshold 5; 1971; #2 US, #1 UK), and *Seventh Sojourn* (Threshold 7; 1972; #1 US, #5 UK).

The group took a five-year hiatus beginning in early 1973 to explore solo avenues; all members (with the exception of Edge, who concentrated on a hard rock approach) would achieve a modicum of commercial success releasing rather bland rehashes of the trademark Moodies sound. Reunited in 1978, the Moody Blues (with former Yes keyboardist Patrick Moraz replacing Pinder, who'd tired of touring) continued producing lush, albeit retro, albums which—depending on the strength of singles releases and musical fashions—achieved varying degrees of popularity. *Octave* (London 708; 1978; #13 US, #6 UK), *Long Distance Voyager* (Threshold 2901; 1981; #1 US, #7 UK), and *The Other Side Of Life* (Threshold 829179; 1986; #9 US, #24 UK), the latter featuring the autobiographical single (driven by an evocatively nostalgic MTV-friendly video clip) "Your Wildest Dreams" (Threshold 883906; 1986; #9), all earned gold or platinum awards for sales.

January 28. The Who appear on the famous BBC show, *Ready Steady Go!* for the first time.

January 30. Joe Tex begins a two-week run at number five on the Hot 100 with "Hold What You've Got" (Dial 4001).

Although his records were far more popular with rhythm and blues fans than a mainstream pop audience, Joe Tex was one of the most successful soul singers of the 1960s and 1970s—period. In fact, Joel Whitburn's *Top R&B Singles 1942–1988* rated him forty-fifth among all recording artists.

Born Joseph Arrington Jr. on August 8, 1933, in Rogers, Texas, he started out singing in local gospel groups. He won a recording contract at a talent contest held at the renowned Apollo Theater in 1954.

Although recording for King in early as 1955, he did not produce a hit until "Hold What You've Got" (#2 r&b) a decade later. He remained a chart fixture for the next fourteen years, including eleven more Top 10 R&B hits: "You Got What It Takes" (Dial 4003; 1965; #51 pop, #10 r&b), "I Want To (Do Everything For You)" (Dial 4016; 1965; #23 pop, #1 3 weeks), "A Sweet Woman Like You" (Dial 4022; 1965; #29 pop, #1 r&b), "The Love You Save (May Be Your Own)" (Dial 4026; 1966; #56 pop, #2 r&b), "S.Y.S.L.J.F.M. (The Letter Song)" (Dial 4028; 1966; #39 pop, #9 r&b), "I Believe I'm Gonna Make It" (Dial 4033; 1966; #67 op, #8 r&b), "Skinny Legs and All" (Dial 4063; 1967; #10 pop, #2 r&b), "Men Are Getting' Scarce" (Dial 4069; 1967; #33 pop, #7 r&b), "Buying a Book" (Dial 4090; 1969; #47 pop, #10 r&b), "I Gotcha" (Dial 1010; #2 pop, #1 r&b), and "Ain't Gonna Bump No More (With No Big Fat Woman)" (Epic 50313; 1977; #12 pop, #7 r&b).

Tex also recorded and toured with fellow Atlantic Records artists Solomon Burke, Arthur Conley, Don Covay, and Ben E. King in the late 1960s as part of the Soul Clan. He would convert to the Muslim faith at the peak of his career, changing his name to Joseph Hazziez in July 1972.

February 6. The Righteous Brothers climb to the summit of the pop charts with "You've Lost That Lovin' Feelin'" (Philles), remaining there for two weeks. With bass Bobby Hatfield assigned the lead vocal part, tenor Bill Medley asked producer Phil Spector what he would be doing. Spector replied to the effect that he could "take the money to the bank!"

February 6. The Rolling Stones begin a three-week stay atop the U.K. album charts with *Rolling Stones No. 2* (Decca).

February 7. A routine medical procedure becomes a major international news bulletin as George Harrison has his tonsils removed at London's University College hospital.

February 12. Pye Records sign Donovan to a contract, announcing they now had "the British Bob Dylan."

February 15. Jazz pianist and pop song stylist Nat King Cole dies of lung cancer.

February 18. The Kinks top the British charts for a second time with "Tired of Waiting for You."

February 20. Gary Lewis and the Playboys begin a two-week stint atop the Hot 100 with "This Diamond Ring" (Liberty).

February 23. Filming begins on location in the Bahamas for the Beatles' second film, tentatively titled *Eight Arms to Hold You*.

February 25. The Seekers go number one on the British charts with "I'll Never Find Another You."

February 26. Guitar virtuoso Jimmy Page's single, "She Just Satisfies," in released; it fails to make the charts.

March 5. The Mannish Boys—featuring David Bowie—have their debut single, "I Pity the Fool," released.

March 6. The Temptations peak at number one on the pop charts with "My Girl" (Gordy).

The most successful R&B vocal group of the post-World War II era, the Temptations were formed in 1960 out of two Detroit acts: the Primes, a trio including tenor Eddie Kendricks and baritone Paul Williams, and the Distants, a quintet featuring tenor Otis Williams, bass singer Melvin Franklin, and Elbridge Bryant (replaced by gospel-styled tenor David Ruffin in 1964). A successful Motown audition led to the formation of the Gordy imprint. After producing four minor R&B hits from 1962 to 1964, they hit the big time with "My Girl."

The quintet would reach the charts with forty-six more singles and thirty-three albums in the next 15 years. They won two Grammys for "Cloud Nine" in 1968, and another for "Papa Was a Rolling Stone" in 1972. Despite the departure of Ruffin (1968) and Kendricks (1971) to develop solo careers, the Temptations managed to change with the times, relying heavily on funk and psychedelic influences beginning in the late 1960s.

The group lost momentum during the disco era, but Ruffin and Kendricks returned to the fold for a reunion LP and successful tour in 1982. They have remained active to the present day—despite the deaths of Paul Williams (1971), Ruffin (1991), Kendricks (1992), and Franklin (1995)—with a line-up featuring Otis Williams.

March 7. Tom Jones goes number one on the British charts with "It's Not Unusual," the first of his sixteen Top 40 hits there during the decade.

March 8. David Bowie makes his television debut as a member of The Manish Boys. They perform "I Pity the Fool" on the British program, *Gadzooks! It's All Happening*.

Best known for his wide-ranging repertoire of alter-egos—represented in recordings by means of a dizzying array of popular music styles—the multi-talented Bowie has excelled as a songwriter, musician (most notably, on vocals, guitar, and saxophone), producer, and conceptual artist capable of communicating profound aesthetic and socio-political themes. Following his initial commercial success in the late 1960s, he managed to assume a rapid succession of personas in chameleon-like fashion, typically remaining one step ahead of prevailing cultural trends.

Born David Robert Jones January 8, 1947, in Brixton, England, he recorded briefly with several bands beginning in 1964—the King Bees, the Mannish Boys, and, as featured performer, the Lower End—before embarking on a solo career with the Bowie surname in order to avoid confusion with fellow countryman Davy Jones, later of the Monkees. After releasing about a dozen singles and an Anthony Newley-styled album, *David Bowie* (Deram 1007; 1967), without making the charts, he achieved his first taste of mass popularity with "Space Oddity" (Philips 72949; 1969; #5 UK), from the LP, *David Bowie – Man of Words, Man of Music* (Philips 7912; 1969; issued in the U.S. on RCA 4813 in November 1972 as *Space Oddity*). Two hard rock releases—*The Man Who Sold the World* (Mercury 61325l; 1971) and *Hunky Dory* (RCA 4623; 1971; #93), the latter sporting a transvestite cover (in the British edition), the FM radio staple, "Changes" (RCA 2160; 1972; #66), and the first appearance of his classic backing band, the Spiders From Mars (featuring lead guitarist Mick Ronson)—further enhanced his reputation, but *The Rise and Fall of Ziggy Stardust and the Spiders From Mars* (RCA 4702; 1972; #75 US, #5 UK), a loose concept piece about an alien invader with decidedly glam leanings.

Bowie continued to mine the sci-fi glitter rock vein with *Aladdin Sane* (RCA4852; 1973; #17 US, #1 UK), the covers tribute LP, *Pin-Ups* (RCA0291; 1973; #23 US, #1 UK), and *Diamond Dogs* (RCA 0576; 1974; #1 UK). Hiring a new band built around guitarists Carlos Alomar and Earl Slick, he moved in the direction of Philadelphia Soul and disco with *Young Americans* (RCA 0998; 1975; #9 US, #2 UK), driven by the hit single, "Fame" (RCA 10320; 1975; #1 US, #17 UK), which included backing vocals from John Lennon. Although possessing a veneer of commercial polish, *Station To Station* (RCA 1327; 1976; #3 US, #5 UK), featuring the single "Golden Years" (RCA 10441; 1975; #10 US, #8 UK), exhibited a preoccupation with stark themes such as totalitarianism and fascism. Bowie would further separate himself from the pop mainstream by recording three experimental collaborations with Brian Eno: *Low* (RCA 2030; 1977; #11 US, #2 UK), *Heroes* (RCA 2522; 1977; #35 US, #3 UK), and *Lodger* (RCA 3254; 1979; #20 US, #4 UK).

Scary Monsters (RCA 3647; 1980; #12 US, #1 UK)—which included two Top 10 British hits, "Ashes to Ashes" (RCA 12078; 1980; #1 UK), which resurrected his Major Tom character from "Space Oddity," and "Fashion" (RCA 12134; 1980; #70 US, #5 UK)—hailed a return to the mainstream. Following an extended hiatus, Bowie enlisted ex-Chic guitarist Nile Rodgers as producer of the slick, rhythm and blues-oriented LP, *Let's Dance* (EMI America 17093; 1983; #4 US, #1 UK). It was his biggest seller, due largely to the presence of several hit singles: "Let's Dance" (EMI America 8158; 1983; #1 US, #1 UK), "China Girl" (EMI America 8165; 1983; #10 US, #2 UK; best remembered for a controversial promotional video), "Modern Love" (EMI America 8177; 1983; #14 US, #2 UK), and "Without You" (EMI America 8190; 1984; #73). The next two albums, *Tonight* (EMI America 17138; 1984; #11 US, #1 UK) *Never Let Me Down* (EMI America 17267; 1987; #34 US, #6 UK), were rather tepid affairs, although the former did contain one notable single, "Blue Jean" (EMI America 8231; 1984; #8 US, #6 UK).

Although always guaranteed a substantial following, his later work—including three releases between 1989 and 1992 with his hard rock group, Tin Machine—has been uneven at best. More recent releases—most notably, the ambient-tinged collaboration with Eno, *Outside* (Virgin 30702; 1995; #21 US, #8 UK), and *Earthling* (Virgin 44944; 1997; #39 US, #6 UK), which incorporated drum-and-bass and other contemporary dance features—reflect a valiant struggle to remain artistically and commercially viable, albeit with mixed results.

March 13. The Beatles begin a two-week stay atop the Hot 100 with "8 Days a Week" (Capitol), their seventh single to accomplish this feat.

March 13. Guitarist Eric Clapton leaves the Yardbirds, allegedly due to their move in the direction of pop music, as exemplified by the soon-to-be Top 10 hit "For Your Love" (Epic).

March 13. Tom Jones makes his television debut on BBC's *Billy Cotton Band Show.*

March 14. The Rolling Stones top the British charts with for the third time with "The Last Time."

March 18. The Rolling Stones are each fined $8.50 for urinating in a public place. The incident occurred at a gas station following a Romford, Essex, England, gig.

March 19. *Tailor and Cutter* magazine publishes an article asking the Rolling Stones to wear ties to save the tie manufacturers from financial ruin.

March 20. A twice-nightly Motown package tour kicks off at London's Finsbury Park Astoria. It features Martha & the Vandellas, the Miracles, the Supremes, the Temptations, and Stevie Wonder.

March 26. The Walker Brothers make their British television debut on *Ready Steady Go!*

March 27. The Supremes reach number one on the pop charts with "Stop! In the Name of Love" (Motown), remaining there for two weeks.

April 2. The Who make their radio debut on BBC's *Joe Loss Pop Show.*

April 3. Jr. Walker and the All Stars peak at number four on the Hot 100 with "Shotgun" (Soul 35008).

Saxophonist/vocalist Walker was born Autry DeWalt II in Blythesville, Arkansas, in 1942. He formed the group—consisting of guitarist Willie Woods, organist Vic Thomas, and drummer James Graves—in South Bend, Indiana, in the early 1960s. They initially recorded for Harvey in 1962, before landing a contract with Motown's Soul imprint in the mid-1960s. The All Stars specialized in funky, sax-driven remakes of soul and pop hits like "(I'm a) Road Runner," "How Sweet It Is (To Be Loved By You)," "Come See About Me," and "These Eyes." Ironically, their biggest hits—"Shotgun" and "What Does It Take"—were originals. Although remaining active as a performing unit, their charting singles had slowed to a trickle by the early 1970s.

April 4. Unit Four Plus Two top the British charts with "Concrete and Clay."

April 9. The Rolling Stones make their live TV debut on *Ready Steady Go!*

April 10. Freddie & the Dreamers begin a two-week stint atop the Hot 100 with "I'm Telling You Now" (Tower).

April 11. *The Freewheeling Bob Dylan* heads up the British album charts.

April 11. Cliff Richard tops the British charts with "The Minute You're Gone," his eighth single to accomplish that feat.

April 19. The film, *T.A.M.I. (Teen-Age Music International)*, premieres in London. Featured artists include the Beach Boys, James Brown, the Four Tops, Smokey Robinson and the Miracles, the Rolling Stones, and the Supremes.

April 24. The Beatles manager, Brian Epstein, wins the "star prize" of an album as a result of having a letter published in *Melody Maker* which relates that Paul McCartney played lead guitar on "Ticket to Ride."

April 24. Wayne Fontana & the Mindbenders ascend to the summit of the pop charts with "Game of Love" (Fontana).

April 30. Herman's Hermits, supported by the Zombies, kick off their first U.S. tour.

Although considered to be a lightweight novelty act by many rock music critics, Herman's Hermits were one of the most successful British Invasion acts, selling more than forty million records between 1964 and 1967.

The group was formed in 1963 when Peter Noone, a Manchester School of Music student with limited stage and BBC-TV experience, hooked up with an area rock band, the Heartbeats. Famed record producer Mickie Most began working with them in 1964; their debut single, a remake of the Earl-Jean song, "I'm Into Something Good" (MGM 13280), topped the British charts and sold over a million copies worldwide. The following year, the Hermits placed more songs in the U.S. Top 10 (seven) than the

Beatles: "Can't You Hear My Heartbeat" (MGM 13310), "Silhouettes" (MGM 13332), "Mrs. Brown You've Got A Lovely Daughter" (MGM 13341), "Wonderful World" (MGM 13354), "I'm Henry VIII, I Am" (MGM 13367), "Just A Little Bit Better" (MGM 13398), and "A Must To Avoid" (MGM 13437).

The hit recordings had disappeared by early 1968 due to public interest in heavier rock styles. The group dissolved in 1971 during heated legal disputes over royalty payments. Noone tried to launch a solo career and hosted a BBC-TV series for three years in the 1970s. During the 1980s, he recorded both solo and with the Tremblers; he also appeared in the Broadway production of *The Pirates of Penzance* and hosted the VH-1 show, *My Generation*. By the 1990s, Noone had reformed the Hermits to perform in various oldies tours.

May 1. Herman's Hermits begin a three-week run atop the Hot 100 with old time music hall-styled "Mrs. Brown You've Got a Lovely Daughter" (MGM).

May 3. The Beatles enlist the British Army's Third Tank Division for filming *Help* sequences on Salisbury Plain.

May 9. Roger Miller tops the British charts with "King of the Road."

May 12. The Rolling Stones record "(I Can't Get No) Satisfaction" at RCA's Hollywood studios. The song's famous guitar riff was created by Keith Richards in the middle of the night a week earlier.

May 19. FBI agents visit Wand Records headquarters inquiring about the language on the recording, "Louie Louie," by the Kingsmen.

May 22. The Beatles reach number one on the pop charts with "Ticket to Ride" (Capitol). They are the fourth English act in a row to accomplish this feat.

May 27. Sandie Shaw heads up the British charts with "Long Live Love."

May 25. Sonny Boy Williamson (the second bluesman to use this moniker; real name: Rice Miller) dies in his sleep. The Animals, Van Morrison, the Moody Blues, The Who, and the Yardbirds were among the artists covering his material.

May 29. The Beach Boys begin a two-week stint atop the Hot 100 with "Help Me, Rhonda" (Capitol).

May 29. Bob Dylan's *Bring It All Back Home* goes number one on the British album charts.

May 31. Marianne Faithfull becomes a resident guest on BBC 2-TV's *Gadzooks! It's the In Crowd*.

June 5. Sam the Sham and the Pharaohs begin a two-week run at number two on the Hot 100 with "Wooly Bully" (MGM 13322), the first of many recording where the group flirts with nonsense syllables, sexual innuendo, and nursery rhymes.

June 12. The Beatles are included on the Queen's Birthday Honours List as recipients of the MBE (Member of the British Empire). Many protests are lodged: MP Hector Dupuis would state, "British Royalty has put me on the same level as a bunch of vulgar numbskulls."

June 12. The Supremes peak at number one on the pop charts for the fifth consecutive time with "Back in My Arms Again" (Motown).

June 19. The Four Tops surge to the top of the Hot 100 with "I Can't Help Myself" (Motown), remaining there for two non-consecutive weeks.

June 26. Folk rock becomes a national obsession when the Byrds' cover of a Bob Dylan composition, "Mr. Tambourine Man" (Columbia 43271), reaches number one on the pop singles charts. This is followed in short order by Sonny and Cher's "I Got You Babe" (Atco 6359) and Dylan's own "Like a Rolling Stone" (Columbia 43346). Simon and Garfunkel's "The Sounds of Silence" (Columbia 43396)—which topped the charts in early 1966—represents the quintessential folk rock release. Originally cut with the duo's two-part harmonies and acoustic guitar accompaniment, a version augmented by electric guitar work and a rock rhythm section received heavy radio play (and subsequent sales success).

Folk rock fused the commercial folk tradition of the early 1960s with the rock songcraft best exemplified by the Beatles. Its most notable features included the eclectic blending of strummed electric and acoustic instruments, a rock steady beat, group harmonies, and poetic—often political with a pronounced anti-establishment message—song lyrics. The genre, which reached its commercial and artistic zenith for a brief period during 1965 to 1966, was a product of experiments by young urban folk interpreters such as Dylan, Jim (later Roger) McGuinn, and Barry McGuire. These, other performers, also incorporated traditional country music the work of topical/protest singer/songwriters including Phil Ochs, Tom Paxton, Eric Andersen, Buffy Saint-Marie, Tim Hardin, Janis Ian, Leonard Cohen, Joni Mitchell, and Jackson Browne. The keynote of the movement was rebellion—rebellion against a wide range of social mores, the anti-commercial snobbery of the urban folk movement (e.g., the organizers of the Newport Folk Festival who were scandalized by Dylan's use of an electric support band in 1965), and their own pretensions regarding the moral and aesthetic values of traditional music.

The experimental inclinations of the leading folk rockers ultimately led to the eclipse of the genre's chart-topping run. For a brief moment, pop stars found they could pursue art while also cultivating monetary success and a large following. As a result, the studio experiments of the Beatles and like-minded artists pulled folk rockers toward the progressive rock vanguard. By mid-1966, folk rock was little more than a lingering memory. Nevertheless, it left a substantial imprint upon the pop world, influencing country rock, the singer/songwriter movement, the softer side of psychedelia, and various regional sounds such as San Francisco rock and Tex-Mex.

Folk rock continued to thrive abroad, in England and the Commonwealth countries. Beginning with Donovan's blend of Dylanesque lyrics and exotic instrumentation, British folk rock evolved back to an emphasis on home-grown song material framed by pop sensibilities. Spurred by the virtuostic talents of bands like Fairport Convention, Pentangle, the Incredible String Band, Lindisfarne, and Steeleye Span, British folk rock thrived for more than a decade beginning in the late1960s; many of the musicians fueling this movement remained active into the twenty-first century.

July 3. The Guess Who? peak at number twenty-two on the Hot 100 with "Shakin' All Over" (Scepter 1295).

Formed by vocalist/guitarist Chad Allan in Winnipeg as Al & the Silvertones in 1959, they would become the first Canadian rock band to achieve long-term success in the United States. With core members Randy Bachman on guitar, Bob Ashley on piano, Jim Kale on bass, and Gary Peterson on drums, the group went through a number of name changes in the early 1960s—most notably, Chad Allan & the Reflections and Chad Allan & the Expressions—before the Quality label decided to credit their rave-up American hit, "Shakin' All Over" to the Guess Who?

Although the Guess Who (sans question mark) enjoyed little commercial success over the next several years, they developed a more polished and diversified sound following the acquisition of vocalist/keyboardist Burton Cummings as a replacement for Ashley in mid-1965. The band would become a fixture on the American pop scene following the release of *Wheatfield Soul* (RCA 4171; 1969; #45), which featured "These Eyes" (RCA 74-0102; 1969; #6) and "Laughing"/"Undun" (RCA 74-0195; 1969; #10). The propulsive singles "No Time" (RCA 74-0300; 1970; #5) and "American Woman" (RCA 74-0325; 1970; #1) represented the group's commercial and creative peak.

The Guess Who continued to place singles and albums on the charts until 1975, despite the departure of Bachman—whose conversion to the Mormon faith clashed with the band's rock 'n' roll lifestyle—who went on to form Brave Belt and, later, the extremely popular Bachman-Turner Overdrive. They would disband in late 1975 with Cummings achieving a measure of solo success at the onset of the 1980s. The group has toured on a fairly regular basis since reforming in 1978, occasionally releasing records (Cummings and Bachman even returned briefly to the fold in the mid-1980s).

July 3. The Yardbirds peak at number six on the Hot 100 with "For Your Love" (Epic 9790). Although recorded with Eric Clapton on lead guitar, the band is now touring with his replacement, Jeff Beck.

More than any other guitarist, Jeff Beck (b. June 24, 1944) was responsible for defining the progressive rock genre. Combining extraordinary technique with a predisposition to expand previously defined stylistic boundaries, he blazed a path in the latter half of the 1960s that would be traveled by peers such as Jimmy Page, Mick Ronson, and Paul Kossof. His innovations included the use of dissonant chords, controlled feedback, fuzztone, and sustained notes to create emotional intensity, combined with an over-riding sense of compositional perspective, which precluded empty displays of virtuosity. Beck's later experiments with blues rock, heavy metal, jazz fusion and new wave rockabilly offered further evidence of his facility in an encyclopedic range of styles.

When blues guitar interpreter Eric Clapton professed dissatisfaction with the pop direction of the Yardbirds' first hit single, "For Your Love" (Epic 9790; 1965; #6), many observers of the British rock scene assumed he would be replaced by highly regarded session player Jimmy Page (later the founder of Led Zeppelin). Instead, the group recruited the relatively unknown Beck, who immediately positioned himself in the forefront of guitar innovators, emulating the Indian sitar by filtering his guitar through a fuzzbox in "Heart Full of Soul" (Epic 9823; 1965; #9). His restrained application of then-exotic sound effects—feedback in "Shapes of Things" (Epic 10006; 1966; #11) and the dual lead interplay with Page on "Happenings Ten Years Time Ago" (Epic 10094; 1966; #30)—enabled the Yardbirds to remain commercially viable despite a pronounced experimental orientation.

Wishing to exert greater control over the creative process, he left the Yardbirds in 1967 to form the Jeff Beck Group, which featured vocalist Rod Stewart, bassist Ron Wood (Rolling Stones), drummer Mickey Waller, and keyboardist Nicky Hopkins (Quicksilver Messenger Service). While the band's two albums—*Truth* (Epic 26413; 1968; #15) and *Beck-Ola* (Epic 26478; 1969; #15)—laid the groundwork for heavy metal, internal differences spurred Stewart and Wood to join the Faces. A new edition of the band released two well executed, if predictable, LPs, *Rough and Ready* (Epic 30973; 1971; #46) and *The Jeff Beck Group* (Epic 31331; 1972; #19), before Beck joined forces with drummer Carmine Appice and bassist Tim Bogert (both formerly with Vanilla Fudge and Cactus) to form a short-lived power trio.

Beck returned to the public eye with a highly-acclaimed fusion album, *Blow By Blow* (Epic 33409; 1975; #4). He continued in much the same vein with *Wired* (Epic 33849; 1976; #16) and *Jeff Beck with the Jan Hammer Group – Live* (Epic 34433; 1977; #23), both collaborations with Hammer, the former Mahavishnu Orchestra keyboardist.

For that point onward, Beck followed an erratic career path, retiring for lengthy periods of time before resurfacing with high profile guest contributions (e.g., Mick Jagger's *Primitive Cool*, Roger Waters' *Amused to Death*) uniformly well-received solo recordings. His LPs have included the jazz-inflected *There and Back* (Epic 35684; 1980; #21); his most polished, pop-oriented offering, *Flash* (Epic 39483; 1985; #39); "Escape" awarded the Grammy for Best Rock Instrumental), featuring Nile Rodgers' production work and bevy of vocalists; *Jeff Beck's Guitar Shop* (Epic 44313; 1989; #49), awarded the Grammy for Best Rock Instrumental Performance; *Crazy Legs* (Epic 473597; 1993), a retro tribute to Gene Vincent and his Blue Caps guitarist, Cliff Gallup; *Who Else!* (Epic 67987; 1999; #99), nominated for the Grammy for Best Rock Instrumental Performance; and *You Had It Coming* (Sony; 2001).

July 10. The Rolling Stones begin a four-week run atop the Hot 100 with "(I Can't Get No) Satisfaction" (London).

July 22. Mick Jagger, Brian Jones, and Bill Wyman are each fined five pounds plus court costs by East Ham Magistrates' Court, London, for insulting behavior on March 18. The three had been denied use of a private toilet at the Francis Service Station, Romford Road, East Ham, by mechanic Charles Keely, whereupon they urinated on the garage wall and left "making a well-known gesture."

July 29. The Beatles' second film, *Help*, debuts in London.

August 7. Herman's Hermits reach number one on the pop charts with "I'm Henry VIII, I Am" (MGM).

August 13. The Beatles arrive to New York City to kick off their third American concert tour, which will span nine cities and thirteen shows. Two days later they play before a crowd of over fifty-six thousand at Shea Stadium, Queens.

August 14. Sonny & Cher begin a three-week stay atop the Hot 100 with the Sonny Bono-penned "I Got You Babe" (Atco).

The pop-rock duo, Sonny and Cher—born Salvatore Bono, February 16, 1935, and Cherilyn Sarkasian La Pier, May 20, 1946—epitomized the hippie lifestyle in the mid-1960s with their bohemian dress and unconventional social mores. Sonny learned songwriting, arranging, and studio production working for a number of seminal record industry figures, including wall-of-sound producer Phil Spector. He met Cher when she was providing background vocals for the Ronettes. They would first record as Caesar and Cleo for the Vault and Reprise labels. Their debut LP for Reprise, along with the single, "Baby Don't Go," would make the pop charts in the summer of 1965 after "I Got You Babe" (Atco 6359) became a number one hit.

Sonny and Cher enjoyed a string of follow-up successes—both as a duo and as solo artists—until the progressive rock vogue rendered their sound passé. Following a stint as a lounge act, they rebounded with a highly rated television variety show in 1972. Their professional relationship barely outlasted a divorce in the mid-1970s. Cher would continue to enjoy major success as a solo performer and film actress (her most notable screen role came in the critically lauded *Moonstruck*). Bono would shift his attention to politics, serving a term as the mayor of Palm Springs, California, and then winning a congressional seat running as a Republican. He died in a skiing accident at age sixty-two.

August 21. The Rolling Stones start a three-week stint at number one on the album charts with *Out of Our Heads* (London).

August 27. The Beatles meet Elvis Presley—the only time they will spend time together—at the latter's Bel Air, California, home. Elvis plays bass guitar and sings with the band (Paul McCartney plays piano) in an impromptu jam. John Lennon allegedly upset Presley by asking why he didn't go back to making rock 'n' roll records.

August 28. Allen Klein joins Andrew Loog Oldham as co-manager of the Rolling Stones, who sign a 1.7 million pound contract with Decca to appear in five films.

August 31, 1965. The Beatles wrap up their latest American tour with a concert at San Francisco's Cow Palace.

August 31. Sonny and Cher arrive in England for their first promotional visit.

September 4. The Beatles peak at number one on the pop charts with "Help!" (Capitol), remaining there for three weeks. The single is the theme song to the Fab Four's second film.

September 4. Bob Dylan's "Like A Rolling Stone" (Columbia) reaches number two on the Hot 100 (#4 UK), on its way to becoming Dylan's first million-selling single. Widely considered to be the first rock single more than five minutes in length, label executives attempted to enhance its commercial potential by splitting recording into two parts; nevertheless, a considerable number of radio stations program the complete track. With FM radio just beginning to catch on, extended cuts will be heard with increasing frequency.

September 22. Great Society—featuring Darby Slick and his wife, Grace—make their live debut at The Coffee Gallery, North Beach, California.

September 25. Barry McGuire tops the Hot 100 with "Eve of Destruction" (Dunhill) despite widespread censorship of the single on American radio. McGuire will argue for years that he was also the target of a secret music industry ban.

October 2. The McCoys reach number one on the pop charts with "Hang On Sloopy" (Bang).

October 9. The Beatles begin a four-week run atop the Hot 100 with "Yesterday" (Capitol).

October 9. The Ramsey Lewis Trio peaks at number five on the Hot 100 with "The 'In' Crowd" (Argo 5506).

One of the most consistently successful jazz-pop crossover artists, Lewis has continued to produce high quality, albeit musically conservative, work for five decades. In addition to collaborating with drummer Max Roach, saxophonist Sonny Stitt, pianist Billy Taylor, trumpeter Clark Terry, vocalist Nancy Wilson, and many other established musicians, he helped nurture the careers of up-and-coming talent such as the Young-Holt Unlimited and drummer/vocalist Maurice White, who would go on to found Earth, Wind and Fire. He has received countless awards for his contributions to the record industry, including Grammies for "The In Crowd" (#2 r&b), "Hold It Right There" (from *Wade in the Water* [Cadet 774; 1966; #16]), and "Hang On Sloopy" (Cadet 5522; 1965; #11 pop, #6 r&b; received in 1973 when reinterpeted for the LP, *Ramsey Lewis' Newly-Recorded All-Time, Non-Stop Golden Hits* (Columbia 42490; 1973; #198).

Lewis was trained as a classical pianist at colleges based in his home town of Chicago, while performing jazz and rhythm and blues professionally by his mid-teens. Forming the Ramsey Lewis Trio with bassist

Eldee Young and drummer Isaac "Red" Holt in 1956, he released his debut LP, *Ramsey Lewis and His Gentlemen of Swing* (Argo; 1956). By the mid-1960s, he'd hit upon the commercial lucrative formula of reworking highly recognizable pop hits in a proto-smooth jazz style. Hits in this mode included "A Hard Day's Night" (Cadet 5525; 1966; #29 pop, #29 r&b), "Wade in the Water" (Cadet 5541; 1966; #19 pop, #3 r&b), and "Up-Tight" (Cadet 5547; 1966; #49 pop, #30 r&b). His albums from this period also sold well, most notably *The In Crowd* (Argo 757; 1965; #2), *Hang On Ramsey!* (Cadet 761; 1966; #15), and *Wade in the Water*.

With progressive rock and fusion in vogue by the 1970s, Lewis incorporated a heavy, improvisational framework into his recordings. *Sun Goddess* (Columbia 33194; 1974; #12; gold record), augmented by Stevie Wonder-influenced synthesizer touches and soaring vocals by Earth, Wind and Fire on the title track (Columbia 10103; 1975; #44 pop, #20 r&b), proved to be the biggest seller of his career. He continued to explore new musical approaches in the 1980s, most notably, orchestrated jazz in *Close Encounters with the Philharmonic Orchestra* (CBS; 1988). He has lightened his recording activities somewhat in recent years due to the demands of hosting radio and television programs, the production of commercials with son Kevyn, and teaching at Roosevelt University in Chicago.

October 29. The Rolling Stones begin a thirty-seven-date North American tour at the Montreal Forum. The final performance will take place December 5 at the Los Angeles Sports Arena.

October 30. The Toys begin a three-week run at number two on the Hot 100 with "A Lover's Concerto" (DynaVoice 209). The song was adapted by Sandy Linzer and Denny Randell from Johann Sebastian Bach's *Minuet From The Anna Magdalena Notebook*.

November 6. The Rolling Stones' "Get Off Of My Cloud" (London) tops the Hot 100 (#1 U.K.) for two weeks.

November 12. Marc Bolan (previously known as Toby Tyler) performs his first single, "Mr. Wizzard," on *Ready Steady Go!*

November 12. The Velvet Underground perform live for the first time at Summit (New Jersey) High School.

More than any rock era recording act, the Velvet Underground's best work was released well before widespread public recognition was forthcoming. Their classic late 1960s albums provided the impetus for several important postpunk genres, including white noise, the indie and alternative rock movements, goth, and grunge.

The group developed out of the collaboration of vocalist/guitarist Lou Reed and bassist/violist John Cale, who first attempted to make an impact within the record industry as the Primitives. By 1965, after recruiting guitarist Sterling Morrison and drummer Maureen Tucker, they were installed as the house band at Andy Warhol's loose assemblage of Manhattan-based pop artists, The Factory. Warhol teamed them with German model and chanteuse, Nico; their debut LP, *The Velvet Underground and Nico* (Verve 5008; 1966), attracted widespread underground attention as much for its Warhol-designed peel-away banana cover art as the music, a darkly-textured take on contemporary urban life that contrasted markedly with the prevailing flower-power values of the day, touching upon drug addiction ("Heroin"), S & M ("Venus in Furs"), and Beat era aesthetics ("European Son to Delmore Schwartz").

Free of Warhol's patronage and Nico-related entanglements, The Velvets followed with the feedback-drenched *White Light, White Heat* (Verve 5046; 1967), which featured the blistering seventeen-minute extended jam, "Sister Ray." It sold marginally, as did the considerably more subdued third album, *The Velvet Underground* (MGM 4617; 1969), with Reed now dominating the songwriting and arranging due to the departure of Cale to pursue his avant-garde leanings in a string of critically acclaimed solo releases. Augmented by the decidedly more mainstream bassist/keyboardist, Doug Yule, the band produced one more LP, *Loaded* (Cotillion 9034; 1970), a stripped-down progressive rock tour de force best remembered for the presence of the Reed classics "Sweet Jane" and "Rock and Roll." Although soldiering on with Yule and the addition several other journeymen musicians, the group effectively ended in August 1970 when Reed left for a highly successful solo career, Morrison began work on a doctorate in English, and Tucker concentrated on raising a family.

The band's seminal role in rock history would be increasingly recognized by both the media and creative artists with the appearance of a wide array of Velvet Underground recordings, including retrospective compilations—most notably, the five-disc *Box Set* (Sire 815 454-2; 1986), live concerts, authorized collections of studio outtakes, and bootlegs of every imaginable stripe. As a result, the original members reunited for a 1993 tour, documented in *Live MCMXCIII* (Sire 9362 45464-2; 1993; #70 UK). Morrison's death in 1995, however, dampened the possibility of any further group projects.

November 13. Kim Weston peaks at number fifty on the Hot 100 with "Take Me in Your Arms (Rock Me a Little While)" (Gordy 7046).

Kim Weston was one of the serviceable second-stringers within the Motown stable of artists during the 1960s. Born Agatha Natalie Weston, the Detroit native started out singing in gospel groups. Discovered by Motown songwriter/producer Eddie Holland, Weston was teamed with Marvin Gaye (whose duet partner, Mary Wells, had recently defected to the 20th Century-Fox label) when her own solo career failed to take off. Their debut single, "What Good Am I Without You" (Tamla 54104; 1964; #61 pop, #61 r&b), showed promise, but Motown shelved any further plans for the pairing when Gaye's solo recordings suddenly became consistent top sellers.

In the meantime, Weston found a measure of commercial success herself, most notably with "Take Me In Your Arms (Rock Me a Little While)" (#4 r&b), which was revived by the Doobie Brothers in the mid-1970s, and "Helpless" (Gordy 7050; 1966; #56 pop, #13 r&b). Another duet with Gaye, "It Takes Two" (Tamla 54141; 1967; #14 pop, #4 r&b), would become her only Top 20 hit. By this time, however, Weston had set her sights on a New York stage career, and Gaye hooked up with another up-and-coming singer, Tammi Terrell (they had ten chart singles before Terrell's tragic death from a brain tumor in early 1970).

Weston continued to record for a succession of labels in the 1960s and 1970s—including MGM, People, and Pride—though she rarely made the charts. Later in her career, she would organize a youth theater workshop in Detroit.

November 20. The Supremes begin a two-week stint at number one on the pop charts with "I Hear a Symphony" (Motown).

November 29. "Rolling Stones Day" is declared by Colorado Governor John A. Love; that night the band performs to a sell-out audience at the Denver Coliseum.

December 4. The Byrds begin a three-week run atop the Hot 100 with the Pete Seeger-penned "Turn! Turn! Turn! (To Everything There is a Season)" (Columbia).

December 10. The Rolling Stones' "Satisfaction" is named Best Record of the Year in the annual *New Musical Express* readers' poll.

December 25, 1965. The Beatles' *Rubber Soul* (Capitol), widely considered the first album to make an artistic statement through the inclusion of material of uniformly high quality, tops the British charts, where it enjoys a nine-week run. While *Rubber Soul*'s tracks raised the aesthetic bar with respect to lyric writing and eclectic song arrangements, the intricate studio experimentation characterizing the follow-up release, *Revolver* (Capitol; 1966), represented yet another quantum leap forward. Nevertheless, to many rock historians, the Beatles' release of *Sgt. Pepper's Lonely Heart Club Band* (Capitol 2653) remains the watershed development in the emergence of progressive rock.

In retrospect, examples of progressive rock can be identified as existing prior to that album's appearance in June 1967, ranging from Elvis Presley's early rockabilly experiments to the Byrds' folk rock classics, first recorded in 1965. However, it is significant that post-*Sgt. Pepper* works tended to exude a seriousness of purpose (i.e., the consideration of aesthetics over the commercial marketplace) hitherto relegated to the jazz and classical music sectors. The emergence of rock journalism, largely built around young intellectuals who had grown up listening to rock 'n' roll and other popular music genres, helped to spread the gospel of highbrow rock art. The youth subculture, then preoccupied with weighty social matters such as civil rights and the anti-Vietnam War movement, wholeheartedly bought into the concept.

Progressive rock implies a particular mindset in recording and performing music, a predisposition to test established limits and boundaries. Often termed "art rock," the genre owed its exploratory nature largely to psychedelia. Stylistically speaking, though, progressive rock was all over the map. From the late 1960s onward, pioneering artists, unfettered by preconceived notions of the status quo, could be found within all musical categories.

The means by which an artist would display "progressive" leanings varied according to the presence of one (or more) of the following features:

- complex—often lengthy, multi-sectional—compositions;
- virtuostic performances;
- exotic and/or eclectic instrumentation;
- frequent use of cosmic themes in the lyrics; and
- grandiosity, as opposed to earthy directness, of presentation.

The concept album represented a notable subgenre within the progressive rock movement. In view of the increased profit-making potential of the long-playing twelve-inch record (which generally included ten to fourteen songs and ranged in length from thirty to fifty minutes) over 45 rpm singles, record companies concentrated their promotional efforts toward establishing the LP as the primary mode of aesthetic expression within the rock scene. Accordingly, rock musicians began experimenting with ways of presenting a unified thematic message (both in the music and song lyrics) within the framework of a record album. Notable concept albums produced by rock artists included:

- Fairport Convention—*Babbacombe Lee* (A&M 4333; 1972)
- The Kinks—*Arthur* (Reprise 6217; 1968)
- The Moody Blues—*Days of Future Passed* (Deram 18012; 1967); *In Search of the Lost Chord* (Deram 16017; 1968); *On the Threshold of a Dream* (Deram 16025; 1969)
- Pink Floyd—*Animals* (Columbia 34474; 1977); *The Wall* (Columbia 36183; 1979)
- The Who—*Tommy* (Decca 7205; 1969); *Quadrophenia* (MCA 10004; 1973)

After a dazzlingly creative period in the late 1960s which saw even mainstream pop artists incorporating progressive rock conventions into their work, the music business split off into an extensive array of stylistic fragments. While progressive rock was marginalized in the 1970s to the extent that its artists rarely achieved mainstream success, the genre could count on the support of a relatively substantial fan base, one that was at least the equal of funk and disco. However, the emergence of the punk movement, which viciously characterized corporate rock (many read this to mean "progressive rock") as a bloated guardian of the musical equivalent of dry rot, hastened the decline of the genre. By the 1980s, the term "new wave" was being loosely applied to all rock acts displaying progressive instincts.

December 25. The Dave Clark Five reach number one on the pop charts with a remake of the Bobby Day hit, "Over and Over" (Epic).

1966

❅

January 1. Simon and Garfunkel reach the summit of the Hot 100 with an electrified mix of the folk-styled protest song, "The Sounds of Silence" (Columbia), remaining there for two non-consecutive weeks.

January 8. ABC's *Shindig* is telecast for the last time.

January 8. The Beatles begin a six-week stint at number one on the LP charts with *Rubber Soul* (Capitol), their seventh chart topper. They also top the singles charts with "We Can Work It Out" (Capitol)—their eleventh release to accomplish that feat—remaining there for three non-consecutive weeks.

January 17. NBC purchases *The Monkees* television series, scheduling it for their fall programming lineup. In an era when one mass medium can propel an artist to superstardom, the prefab band, the Monkees, ultimately benefited from the high visibility afforded by at least a half dozen—television, radio, the concert hall, magazines, sound recordings, and later, motion pictures. The desire of producers Bert Schneider and Bob Rafelson to combine the zaniness of the Beatles' *A Hard Day's Night* with the Marx Brothers in a TV sitcom provided the impetus for the formation of the group. After briefly considering the Lovin' Spoonful for the role, they placed an advertisement in the entertainment trade paper daily, *Variety*. The headline read, "Madness!! Auditions," followed by a request for "Folk and Rock Musicians-Singers for Acting Roles in a New TV Series. Running parts for four insane boys, ages 17–21."

It is alleged that 437 applicants materialized, including Danny Hutton, later a member of Three Dog Night; songwriter Paul Williams; former star of *The Donna Reed Show*, Paul Peterson; and Stephen Stills. The individuals chosen for the group had had differing degrees of involvement in show business up to that time. Mickey Dolenz had acted both as a regular (*Circus Boy*) and guest performer (*Mr. Novak, Peyton Place*) in television. He learned to play the drums only after being assigned to the instrument by Schneider and Rafelson. Davy Jones had logged time in the Broadway production of *Oliver* as well as recording some (then unreleased) tracks for Colpix Records. Michael Nesmith drifted through the folk scenes in San Antonio and Los Angeles, recording briefly for Colpix under the name of Michael Blessing. Peter Tork had been a folk music accompanist in Greenwich Village prior to checking out the L.A. scene.

The foursome proved to have a remarkable chemistry onscreen; first telecast on September 12, 1966, the free-form, youth-oriented series featured surrealistic film techniques (fast and slow motion, distorted focus, comic film inserts), one-liners, non-sequiturs, etc., all delivered at a rapid-fire pace. The basic premise had the lads cast as a rock band that got into a multitude of bizarre scrapes as they rescued maidens, ran afoul of dastardly villains and generally perpetrated pranks on unsuspecting bystanders.

Although rock critics universally despised the quartet because they were "manufactured" and had not played any instruments on their first two albums, the Monkees enjoyed an equally successful recording career. Among their many hits, "Last Train to Clarksville," "I'm a Believer," and "Daydream Believer" all reached number one on the pop charts from 1966 to 1967. During this run, the band enjoyed heavy promotion via the inclusion of a couple of songs per TV episode as well as access to material from Don Kirshner's roster of Brill Building songwriters, including Gerry Goffin-Carol King, Neil Diamond, Neil Sedaka, David Gates, Barry Mann-Cynthia Weil, and Tommy Boyce-Bobby Hart. The group's recording career stalled in the face of progressive rock and the cancellation of the TV series by NBC effective August 19, 1968. The film *Head*—scripted by Rafelson and Jack Nicholson—was a critical success but a commercial failure, confusing the Monkees' younger fans. An NBC special broadcast on April 14, 1969, "33 1/3 Revolutions Per Monkee," failed to reverse the band's decline and they ground to a halt in 1970.

The Monkees continued to live on in Saturday morning re-runs on CBS from September 1969 to September 1973. Dolenz and Jones briefly reformed the band in 1975 as Dolenz, Jones, Boyce and Hart. The 1980s would witness an explosion of interest in the group as part of a general nostalgia for the 1960s via cable TV re-runs on MTV, Nickelodeon, and other channels. Amidst the healthy sales of videotapes of the original series and compact discs of old recordings, the Monkees reformed again (sans Nesmith) as a recording and touring entity. Pegging this renaissance as largely a baby boomer phenomenon, television executives created The New Monkees for those too young to remember the real thing. Early in the twenty-first century, a compete compilation of the TV series episodes would be issued on DVD.

January 21. George Harrison marries model-actress Patti Boyd. They met on the set of the film, *A Hard Day's Night*, which included Boyd playing a schoolgirl in a train scene. She would leave him in the early 1970s after being assiduously courted by close Harrison associate, Eric Clapton.

January 29. *Sweet Charity* premieres at New York's Palace Theatre. Featuring music by Cy Coleman, lyrics by Dorothy Fields, and book by Neil Simon, the musical would have a run of 608 performances. It would be adapted to film in 1969 (starring Shirley MacLaine).

January 31. With Dunwich's release of "Gloria" (peaking at number ten on the Hot 100)—a cover of the Van Morrison-penned song first recorded by his own group, Them—by the Chicago-based Shadows of Knight, classic punk rock becomes a fixture on the pop charts. Largely driven by the inspired creations of a rash of one-hit wonders, punk rock reflected the teenage angst ensuing from confrontations involving parents, school personnel, law enforcement officers, and other authority figures combined with "the utopian dream of everyman an artist." Like all manifestations of the punk ethic over the years, the movement was not about virtuosity; indeed, its finest practitioners could barely play their instruments.

The origins of garage rock, the forerunner of mid-1960s punk, can be discerned in the instrumental groups based in California and the Pacific Northwest during the early 1960s. Within a few years a number of Mexican-American bands in southern California had begun adding vocals, most notably the Premiers ("Farmer John," Warner Bros. 5443; 1964), Cannibal & the Headhunters ("Land of 1,000 Dances," Rampart 642; 1965), and Thee Midniters ("Land of 1,000 Dances, Part 1," Chattahoochee 666; 1965). By the middle of the decade, however, the creative center of the scene had shifted back to the northern Pacific coast, home base for groups such as the Sonics (Seattle), the Kingsmen, and Paul Revere & the Raiders (the latter two hailing from Portland).

The next phase, classic punk, coincided with the rise of psychedelia in 1966. New technical breakthroughs such as fuzztone and the electric twelve-string guitar enabled young musicians possessing limited playing technique to experiment with an augmented sonic vocabulary. The genre also incorporated various fads of the moment including the drug subculture and Eastern music (e.g., ragas, sitars) and philosophy. Punk bands sprang up across the nation; the major scenes are cited below, along with those bands that had at least one moderate hit:

Boston

The Standells—"Dirty Water" (Tower 185; 1966), "Sometimes Good Guys Don't Wear White" (Tower 257; 1966), "Why Pick on Me" (Tower 282; 1966); The Barbarians—"Are You a Boy of Are You a Girl" (Laurie 3308; 1965), "Moulty" (Laurie 3326; 1966).

The Midwest, particularly the Detroit and Chicago areas

Terry Knight & the Pack—"I, Who Have Nothing" (Lucky Eleven 230; 1966); Cryan' Shames—"Sugar and Spice" (Destination 624; 1966); Shadows of Knight—"Gloria" (Dunwich 116; 1966), "Oh Yeah" (Dunwich 122; 1966); ? & the Mysterians—"96 Tears" (Cameo 428; 1966), "I Need Somebody" (Cameo 441; 1966), "Can't Get Enough Of You, Baby" (Cameo 467; 1967).

The Deep South

John Fred & His Playboy Band—"Judy in Disguise" (Paula 282; 1967), "Hey Hey Bunny" (Paula 294; 1968); The Hombres—"Let It Out" (Verve Forecast 5058; 1967); The Gentrys—"Keep on Dancing" (MGM 13379; 1965), "Spread It On Thick" (MGM 13432; 1966); The Swingin' Medallions—"Double Shot of My Baby's Love" (Smash 2033; 1966), "She Drives Me Out of My Mind" (Smash 2050; 1966).

Los Angeles

Count Five—"Psychotic Reaction" (Double Shot 106; 1966); Syndicate of Sound—"Little Girl" (Bell 640; 1966), "Rumors" (Bell 646; 1966); The Music Machine—"Talk Talk" (Original Sound 61; 1966); The Leaves—"Hey Joe" (Mira 222; 1966); The Seeds—"Pushin' Too Hard" (GNP Crescendo 372; 1966), "Can't Seem to Make You Mine" (GNP Crescendo 354; 1967).

By 1968 punk had lost its momentum, with the more adventuresome bands evolving in the direction of acid rock. The remaining holdouts had no viable options other than heavy metal. For instance, in the Michigan area, the Amboy Dukes (fronted by gonzo guitarist Ted Nugent) took the former path, whereas Grand Funk Railroad (a spin-off of Terry Knight & the Pack), the MC5, and the Stooges (lead by Iggy Pop) opted for the latter. The rebellious element of punk attitude continued to be sustained in these stylistic offshoots, ultimately to be resurrected in the second punk wave of the mid-1970s.

February 5. Petula Clark begins a two-week stint atop the Hot 100 with "My Love" (Warner Bros.), her second single to accomplish this feat.

February 7. Paul Williams publishes the premiere issue of *Crawdaddy*, the first magazine to provide serious coverage of the rock music scene, in New York City.

February 18. Brian Wilson records "Good Vibrations."

February 19. Lou Christie reaches number one on the pop charts with the falsetto tour de force, "Lightnin' Strikes" (MGM).

February 26. Nancy Sinatra climbs to the summit of the Hot 100 with "These Boots Are Made for Walkin'" (Reprise).

March 1. Gene Clark announces he is leaving the Byrds due to his fear of flying.

March 3. Neil Young, Stephen Still, and Richie Furay form Buffalo Springfield after the former is spotted by the other two while driving his hearse in Los Angeles.

March 4. The *London Evening Standard* publishes the following John Lennon statement:

Christianity will go. It will vanish and shrink. We're more popular than Jesus now. I don't know which will go first, rock 'n' roll or Christianity. Jesus was alright, but his disciples were thick and ordinary.

The public fallout (including radio station boycotts and bonfires of Beatles records in the United States) leads to a Lennon apology.

March 5. S/Sgt. Barry Sadler begins a five-week run atop the pop charts with his patriotic composition, "The Ballad of the Green Berets" (RCA).

March 7. Tina Turner records her vocal for the Phil Spector production, "River Deep Mountain High." Although it reaches number three in Great Britain, its poor U.S. performance (#88) led to Spector's temporary retirement.

March 8. Touring Poland with The Hollies, Lulu becomes the first British female singer to perform behind the Iron Curtain.

March 9. The Beach Boys begin recording "God Only Knows"; it reaches number two on the British charts and forms the cornerstone of the album, *Pet Sounds*.

March 13. Vocalist Rod Stewart departs Steampacket to begin a solo career.

March 17. The Walker Brothers top the British charts for the second time with "The Sun Ain't Gonna Shine Anymore," a song originally recorded by Frankie Valli.

April 1. Pye Records releases David Bowie's first single, "Do Anything You Say." He had previously recorded as David Jones and the Lower Third.

April 3. Peter Tork begins a solo stint at The Troubadour in Hollywood. He had recently auditioned for the TV show, *The Monkees*, and would join the cast on location shortly.

April 9. The Righteous Brothers begin a three-week stay atop the Hot 100 with "(You're My) Soul and Inspiration" (Verve).

April 11. NBC broadcasts the last edition of *Hullabaloo* (although reruns continued through August 29).

April 12. Jan Berry—a member of Jan & Dean—crashes his corvette into a parked truck in Los Angeles in the vicinity of "Dead Man's Curve," which he immortalized in a 1964 recording. His injuries eave him partially paralyzed and with permanent brain damage, effectively ending his career short of sporadic performing on the nostalgia circuit.

April 22. The Troggs' "Wild Thing" is released on both the Atco and Fontana labels.

April 23. Dusty Springfield tops the British charts for the only time with "You Don't Have to Say You Love Me."

April 30. Manfred Mann reach number one on the British charts with "Pretty Flamingo."

April 30. The Rolling Stones top the British album charts with *Aftermath*.

April 30. The Young Rascals surge to number one on the pop charts with "Good Lovin'" (Atlantic). It had been a minor hit for the Olympics the prior year.

Although best known as one of the most successful blue-eyed soul acts of the 1960s, the Rascals were also facile assimilators whose stylistic evolution mirrored the historical development of rock music. The individual band members cut their teeth on a wide range of genres, including jazz, rhythm and blues, doo-wop, pop, and rock 'n' roll. As the Rascals, they attempted to keep in step with changing fashions by veering from garage rock to soul, followed by psychedelia, progressive rock, and laid-back jazz fusion.

The band—originally called the Young Rascals—formed in New York when drummer Dino Danelli then supporting R&B artists like Willie John, hooked up with three members of Joey Dee's Starlighters—keyboardist/vocalist Felix Cavaliere, vocalist/percussionist Eddie Brigati, and guitarist Gene Cornish—to create a repertoire of songs for performance during the winter of 1964/1965. Their exciting brand of dance-oriented rock led to a contract with Atlantic Records in late 1965.

The Young Rascals' first single, the up-tempo ballad "I Ain't Gonna Eat Out My Heart Anymore" (Atlantic 2312; 1965; #52), was only a moderate seller; however, the follow-up, a cover of the Vibrations' "Good Lovin'" (Atlantic 2321; 1966), topped the charts. The band's versatility—two strong lead singers, exceptional songwriting (often featuring Cavaliere's music and Brigati's lyrics) and arrangements, and equal command of slow and high-energy number— was largely responsible for the long string of hits that followed, including the Top 20 hits "You Better Run" (Atlantic 2338; 1966; #20), "I've Been Lonely Too Long" (Atlantic 2377; 1967; #16 pop, #33 r&b), "Groovin'" (Atlantic 2401; 1967; #1 pop, #3 r&b), "A Girl Like You" (Atlantic 2424; 1967; #10), "How Can I Be Sure" (Atlantic 2438; 1967; #4), "It's Wonderful" (Atlantic 2463; 1967; #20), "A Beautiful Morning" (Atlantic 2493; 1968; #3 pop, #36 r&b), "People Got To Be Free" (Atlantic 2537; 1968; #1 pop, #14 r&b), and "A Ray of Hope" (Atlantic 2584; 1969; #24 pop, #36 r&b).

Unlike many rock bands in the 1960s, the Young Rascals' LPs sold nearly as well as their singles—whether the simple collection of songs typifying *The Young Rascals* (Atlantic 8123; 1966; #15), *Collections* (Atlantic 8134; 1967; #14), *Groovin'* (Atlantic 8148; 1967; #5), and *Time/Peace/The Rascals' Greatest Hits* (Atlantic 8190; 1968; #1)—or the later concept albums: *Once Upon A Dream* (Atlantic 8169; 1968; #9), *Freedom Suite* (Atlantic 901; 1969; #17), *See* (Atlantic 8246; 1970; #45), and *Search and Nearness* (Atlantic 8276; 1971; #198). When the hits slowed to a trickle by the 1970s, the Rascals (the moniker used beginning with the release of *Once Upon A Dream*) regrouped, with Cavaliere and Danelli bringing in guitarist/pianist/vocalist/ songwriter Buzzy Feiten, bassist Robert Popwell, and singer Ann Sutton to achieve a greater jazz orientation. The limited success of albums by the new configuration—*Peaceful World* (Columbia 30462; 1971; #122) and *The Island Of Real* (Columbia 31103; 1972; #180)—led to a breakup in 1972.

The original members have continued to work within the music industry; Danelli, Cornish, and Cavaliere got together in 1988 for a U.S. tour. However, the threesome became embroiled in litigation shortly thereafter regarding use of the band name. In 1997 the Rascals were inducted into the Rock and Roll Hall of Fame.

May. Kim Simmonds, leader of the Savoy Brown Blues Band, joins forces with his older brother, Harry, to start Kilroy's so that the group has a regular venue to perform in.

Formed in 1966, the London-based Savoy Brown has been a fixture in the United States rock scene for over forty years without the benefit of hit singles or a strong following at home. Despite frequent personnel changes in which the only constant has been lead guitarist Kim Simmonds, the band built up a loyal following through incessant touring and the release of a string of consistency high quality albums. Ever mindful of changing pop music fashions, Simmonds would shift stylistic gears from blues rock in the mid-1960s, to flirtations with acid rock by the end of the decade, to hard-rock boogie by the early 1970s. Savoy Brown reached its zenith in popularity in the late 1960s and early 1970s; best-selling albums released during that period included *Blue Matter* (Parrot 71027; 1969), *A Step Further* (Parrot 71029; 1969), *Raw Sienna* (Parrot 71036; 1970), *Looking In* (Parrot 71042; 1970), *Street Corner Talking* (Parrot 71047; 1971), and *Hellbound Train* (Parrot 71052; 1972). However, Simmonds has soldiered on in the face of diminished record sales and the unprecedented success of ex-members Lonesome Dave Preverett, Tony Stevens, and Roger Earl as Foghat.

May 1. The Beatles perform live for the last time in England at the *New Musical Express* Poll Winners' concert at Wembley Empire Pool, sharing the bill with the Rolling Stones and the Who.

May 7. The Mamas & the Papas begin a three-week run atop the Hot 100 with "Monday, Monday" (Dunhill).

May 16. Capitol releases the Beach Boys' *Pet Sounds*.

May 16. The Castiles record two songs co-written by group member Bruce Springsteen at the Bricktown Studio in New Jersey. Only five copies of the single will be pressed.

May 21. The Mamas and the Papas top the album charts with *If You Can Believe Your Eyes and Ears*.

May 24. *Mame* premieres at New York's Winter Garden. Featuring music and lyrics by Jerry Herman and book by Jerome Lawrence and Robert E. Lee, the musical ran for 1,508 performances (the fifth longest of the 1960s). It would be made into a film in 1974, starring Lucille Ball, Robert Preston, and Beatrice Arthur.

May 28. Herb Alpert and the Tijuana Brass top the album charts with "What Now My Love" (A&M 4114).

May 28. Frank Sinatra heads up the British charts with "Strangers in the Night."

May 28. Percy Sledge reaches number one on the pop charts with gospel-tinged classic, "When a Man Loves a Woman" (Atlantic 2326), remaining there for two weeks. The song plays a key role in propelling the Muscle Shoals (Alabama) Sound to the forefront of the music industry.

Sledge will be forever identified with "When a Man Loves a Woman," which he wrote along with his accompanists bassist Cameron Lewis and organist Andrew Wright. The song—which blended his intense, gospel-inflected vocal with an ethereal organ accompaniment—became the template for the Muscle Shoals Soul sound.

Sledge was born November 25, 1940 in Leighton, Alabama. Success did not come overnight for the singer; he spent the first half of the 1960s performing in the Alabama area. He was a member of the Esquires Combo when he decided to go solo in 1966. Following the release of "When a Man Loves a Woman," which reached number one on both the pop and R&B charts, he scored Top 20 hits with "Warm and Tender Love" (Atlantic 2342; 1966; #17 pop, #5 r&b), "It Tears Me Up" (Atlantic 2358; 1966; #20 pop, #7 r&b), and "Take Time to Know Her" (Atlantic 2490; 1968; #11 pop, #6 r&b).

Sledge's recording career stalled by the late 1960s, but he has continued to tour the United States, Japan, and Great Britain through the 1990s. The appearance of "When a Man Loves a Woman" in the popular film, *Platoon* (1987), spurred a revival of interest in Sledge. That same year the song was re-released in the U.K., where it reached number two on the pop charts. In 1989 he won the Rhythm and Blues Foundation's Career Achievement Award.

June 11. The Rolling Stones begin a two-week stint atop the Hot 100 with "Paint It, Black" (London).

June 12. The Dave Clark Five appear on the *Ed Sullivan Show* for the twelfth time, a record for a rock act.

June 25. The Beatles surge to the summit of the pop charts with "Paperback Writer" (Capitol), remaining there for two non-consecutive weeks.

July 2. Frank Sinatra enjoys his first number one single of the decade with "Strangers in the Night" (Reprise 1017).

July 5. Following the recommendation of Keith Richards' girlfriend, the Animals' Chas Chandler sees Jimi Hendrix play at The Café Wha? in New York. Chandler encourages Hendrix to relocate to England in order to jumpstart his career.

July 16. Tommy James & the Shondells begin a two-week stay atop the Hot 100 with "Hanky Panky" (Roulette).

A Dayton, Ohio, native, Tommy James began performing with his group, the Shondells, at school dances, auditoriums, and other area venues at the age of twelve. The outfit would occasionally cut records for small companies, including a song called "Hanky Panky" for the Snap label in 1960. More than five years later, a KDKA, Pittsburgh, disc jockey played the record on his program; it quickly became the most requested single in that radio market. Roulette Records acquired the rights to "Hanky Panky" (Roulette 4686), and it reached number one on the *Billboard Hot 100* in July 1966.

James would go on to record thirty charting singles (many co-written by him and friend, Bob King)—both with the Shondells and as a solo artist—though early 1973. His Top 10 releases included "I Think We're Alone Now" (Roulette 4720; 1967), "Mirage" (Roulette 4736; 1967), "Mony Mony" (Roulette 7008; 1968), "Crimson and Clover" (Roulette 7028; 1968-1969), "Sweet Cherry Wine" (Roulette 7039; 1969), "Crystal Blue Persuasion" (Roulette 7050; 1969), and "Draggin' the Line" (Roulette 7103; 1971). His combination of romantic innocence, catchy melodies, and hook-laden refrains provided the model for the late 1960s Bubblegum genre.

The unrelenting succession of one-night stands and drug abuse led to a breakdown in 1970. After his recovery, changing public tastes made the hits harder to come by. During a brief career revival in 1980, it was estimated that he had sold over thirty million records. The 1980s also brought success for his classic songs as covered by other artists, most notably "Crimson and Clover" (number seven, Joan Jett, Boardwalk 144; 1982), "I Think We're Alone Now" (number one, Tiffany, MCA 33147; 1987), and "Mony Mony" (number one, Billy Idol, Chrysalis 43181; 1987).

July 23. Chris Farlowe and the Thunderbirds reach the summit of the British charts with the Jagger-Richards composition, "Out of Time."

July 30. The Troggs peak at number one on the pop charts with "Wild Thing" (Atco), remaining there for two weeks. A competing release on the Fontana label also sells well.

August. *Revolver* (Capitol 2576), the first Beatles LP to display pronounced psychedelic flourishes—most notably, running tapes in reverse on "Tomorrow Never Knows," and the playful sound effects on "Yellow Submarine"—is released.

The psychedelic era evolved out of the social consciousness movement engendered by a commitment to civil rights, anti-war protest, the legalization of recreational drugs, and other youth subculture concerns. These issues were frequently addressed in rock song lyrics while the music itself often employed special effects geared to underscoring the message at hand. For example, the Doors' "Unknown Soldier" (Elektra 45628; 1968) included a marching interlude accented by a drill sergeant's shrieked commands and the discharge of rifles. The Chicago Transit Authority's "Prologue, August 29, 1968" (*Chicago Transit Authority*, Columbia 8; 1969) featured an actual recording from the 1968 Democratic National Convention which conveyed the following sequence: black militants exhorting demonstrators, "God give us the blood to keep going"; the beginning of the march; police attempting to disperse marchers; and the demonstrators chanting, "The Whole World's Watching." Pearls Before Swine's polemic on the horrors of war, *Balaklava* (ESP 1075; 1968), began with a turn of the century recording of the trumpet which was blown to commence the fabled charge of the British Light Brigade in 1856.

These spacey sound effects, however, paled in contrast to the mind expanding techniques utilized to evoke the psychedelic drug experience. Guitarist Les Paul was the spiritual godfather of studio augmentation as a result of his experiments with overdubbing and multi-tracking; his seminal 1950s recordings with vocalist Mary Ford rivaled big band and orchestral productions for fullness of sound. The unique tones he was able to coax out of his guitar within a studio environment were not equaled until Jimi Hendrix's appearance on the scene. The infancy of stereo recording in the early 1960s had witnessed a succession of sonic experiments primarily within the light pops sector. Enoch Light and the Light Brigade pioneered the spatial left-right channel ping-pong effects later employed in a spectacular manner by Hendrix in his albums, *Axis: Bold as Love* (Reprise 6281; 1968) and *Electric Ladyland* (Reprise 6307; 1968). The introduction of synthesizers into the recording process by inventors such as Robert Moog in collaboration with Morton Subotnick, Walter (Wendy) Carlos, and other avant garde artists, made available another key tool for rock production wizards.

As in so many other genres, the Beatles played a pioneering role in the evolution of psychedelic effects. The group's recording engineer, George Martin, proved extremely facile at reproducing the sounds that the Lennon-McCartney songwriting team professed to have in their heads. Martin's arsenal of studio effects included tapes run backwards, filtered voices, and the inventive use of exotic instruments (e.g., the piccolo trumpet on "Penny Lane," Capitol 5810; 1967) and ambient sounds. The critical raves and commercial success of *Revolver* and *Sgt. Pepper's Lonely Hearts Club Band* (Capitol 2653; 1967)—both of which reeked of psychedelic touches—spurred a tidal wave of imitators. The vast majority of rock acts insisted on (or were talked into) doing their own psychedelic projects. Even artists whose prior output appeared to be the antithesis of such studio excess—e.g., roots rocker Johnny Rivers, who was then enjoying a career revival with a series of soft ballads, and blues stylists, the Rolling Stones—were swept up by this new fad. Only Bob Dylan, who released a country-rock masterpiece, *John Wesley Harding* (Columbia 9604; 1968), at the peak of the psychedelic era, seemed able to run counter to prevailing fashion.

Psychedelia was sometimes referred to as "acid rock." The latter label was generally applied to a pounding, hard rock variant that evolved out of the mid-1960s garage punk movement. By late 1966, the Blues Magoos were calling their brand of wailing blues-rock "psychedelic" music. Although generally devoid of the studio gimmickry typifying the Beatles school of psychedelia, acid rock provided its own form of mind expansion by means of guitar pyrotechnics. Leading practitioners included the Cream, Blue Cheer, and the Amboy Dukes. When rock began turning back to softer, roots-oriented sounds in late 1968, acid rock bands mutated into heavy metal acts. Traces of the psychedelic era can still be found in the stylistic excesses of many third-generation metal groups.

Successive refinements of the sound, generally referred to as "neo-psychedelia," have been appearing since the rise of the new wave movement. Notable examples include the early 1980s British postpunk bands such as Echo and the Bunnymen (early 1980s), the Teardrop Explodes, and the Psychedelic Furs; proponents of the late 1980s rave scene (e.g., Stone Roses, Primal Scream, Inspiral Carpets); ambient experimentalists like Bill Nelson, Art of Noise, and Orbital; and talented eccentrics (the Lightning Seeds and XTC's side project, the Dukes of Stratosphear) positioned outside of prevailing pop music trends.

August 11. The Beatles arrive at Chicago's O'Hare Airport to begin their final American tour. John Lennon apologizes to the media for his prior comment that his group was more popular than Jesus Christ, claiming that he was misquoted and not anti-Christ. They give their last public concert on August 29, at San Francisco's Candlestick Park where they finish with Little Richard's "Long Tall Sally."

August 13. The Lovin' Spoonful begin a three-week run atop the Hot 100 with "Summer in the City" (Kama Sutra).

Founded by singer/songwriter John Sebastian and lead guitarist Zal Yanovsky, the New York-based Lovin' Spoonful evolved from jug band music to folk rock prior to its first release, the Top 10 hit "Do You Believe In Magic" (Kama Sutra 201; 1965). Due to first-rate musicianship and Sebastian's extraordinary composing skills, the band's records—dubbed "good time music" by the music press—were consistent best-sellers between 1965 and 1968. During that span, the Spoonful released eight hit albums—including the soundtracks to Woody Allen's *What's Up, Tiger Lily?* (Kama Sutra 8053; 1966) and Francis Ford Coppola's *You're a Big Boy Now* (Kama Sutra 8058; 1967)—and charted thirteen singles, most notably "Daydream" (Kama Sutra 208; 1966), "Did You Ever Have To Make Up Your Mind?" (Kama Sutra 209; 1966), and "Summer In the City" (Kama Sutra 211; 1966).

Bad publicity surrounding the arrest of Yanovsky and bassist Steve Boone for drug possession in 1967 resulted in waning popularity and the dissolution of the group the following year. Drummer Joe Butler formed a new edition of the Spoonful in the late 1960s. The resulting album sold poorly, however, and Butler moved on to Broadway acting and sound editing in Hollywood. Boosted by his Woodstock Festival performance, Sebastian enjoyed a moderately successful solo career. His "Welcome Back" (Reprise 1349; 1976), the theme song for TV's Welcome Back Kotter, reached number one on *Billboard*'s Hot 100.

The original group members reunited to perform "Do You Believe in Magic" in the Paul Simon film, *One Trick Pony* (1980). Boone, Butler, and sometime member Jerry Yester began touring as the Spoonful in 1991.

August 16. The Smothers Brothers earn a gold record for *The Funny Side of The Smothers Brothers (Think Ethnic!)* (Mercury 20777).

The Smothers Brothers—consisting of brothers Tommy (b. February 2, 1937) and Dick (b. November 20, 1939)—rose to fame in the 1960s blending comedy and urban folk music. Born on Governor's Island in New York Harbor, they attended San Jose State University (California) prior to performing in the Casual Quintet. Striking out as a duo (Tommy playing acoustic guitar, and Dick, upright bass) in 1959, they became a successful act in short order in addition to releasing a string of bestselling LPs. Their onstage antics featuring feigned arguments, with Dick assuming a superior tone, and Tommy acting dull-witted, often bursting out with the phrase, "Mom always liked you best."

They would be tapped to host a sitcom, *The Smothers Brothers Show* (1965-1966), in which Tommy played an earth-bound angel. They became major stars, however, heading a variety show, *The Smothers Brothers Comedy Hour* (1967-1969). Assisted by a talented roster of writers and cast members that included Steve Martin, Rob Reiner, Pat Paulsen, and David Letterman, they increasingly tested the limits of television satire. The program also provided a showcase for controversial artists such as JoanBaez, Harry Belafonte, Janis Ian, Peter, Paul and Mary, and Pete Seeger, whose appearance was his first on network TV since being blacklisted in the early 1950s.

CBS led CEO William Paley to unceremoniously cancel the show on April 4, 1969 due to the Smothers' refusal to meet the specified pre-air delivery dates to accommodate review by network censors. The Smothers would in turn file a successful breach of contract suit against CBS. The events surrounding this controversy were covered in the documentary film, *Smothered* (2002). The program nevertheless won the Emmy Award that year for best writing.

The Smothers Brothers would host several more television programs—*The Smothers Brothers Show* (1975), *The Tom and Dick Smothers Brothers Specials I and II* (1980), and *The Smothers Brothers Comedy Hour* (1988–1989)—with limited success. They continue to tour as well as operating the Remick Ridge Vineyards in Sonoma County, California.

August 27. Billy Stewart peaks at number ten on the Hot 100 with "Summertime" (Chess 1966).

One of the great song stylists of the 1960s, Billy Stewart's career was tragically cut short by an automobile accident In North Carolina on January 17, 1970. His ability to belt out old standards in a truly innovative manner, complete with scats and trills, earned him the nickname "Motormouth."

Born March 24, 1937, in Washington, D.C., he performed in his family's gospel group, the Stewart Gospel Singers as a teenager. He won a local amateur contest singing George Gershwin's "Summertime," which led to a series of club bookings. He also performed in a band led by his uncle, Houn' Dog Ruffin (the father of the Temptations' David Ruffin).

Bo Diddley saw Stewart perform in 1956, and promptly recruited him for his band. Diddley also recommended him to his label, Chess, although Stewart's debut single, "Billy's Blues (Parts 1 and 2)," failed to make any notable commercial impact. He would go on to sing with an R&B quartet, the Rainbows (which included future soul star Don Covay), and record briefly for Okeh Records.

His dynamic vocal style began to catch on with the public in early 1960s; he had minor success with "Reap What You Sow" (Chess 1820; 1962; #79 pop, #18 r&b) and "Strange Feeling" (Chess 1868; 1963; #70 pop, #25 R&B). "I Do Love You" (Chess 1922; 1965; #26 pop, #6 R&B) proved to be his breakthrough single, followed by a string of soul-pop hits, most notably "Sitting in the Park" (Chess 1932; 1965; #24 pop, #4 r&b); "Summertime" (#7 r&b); "Secret Love" (Chess 1978; 1966; #29 pop, #11 r&b), a former number one hit for Doris Day; and "Everyday I Have the Blues" (Chess 1991; 1967; #74 pop, #41 r&b), best known as B.B. King's signature song.

August 29. The Beatles perform in concert for the last time at Candlestick Park, San Francisco. The group would focus on studio recordings for the balance of their career, redefining the album medium in the process.

September 3. Donovan reaches number one on the pop charts with the pioneering British folk-rock single, "Sunshine Superman" (Epic).

September 10. The Supremes begin a two-week stint atop the Hot 100 with "You Can't Hurry Love" (Motown).

September 17. Jim Reeves reaches number one on the British charts with "Distant Durms," his only single to accomplish this feat.

September 24. The Association surges to the summit of the pop charts with "Cherish" (Warner Bros.), remaining there for three weeks.

October 5. Jimi Hendrix, drummer Mitch Mitchell and bassist Noel Redding play together for the first time. As a result, they form the Jimi Hendrix Experience.

October 15. The Four Tops begin a two-week stay atop the Hot 100 with "Reach Out I'll Be Three" (Motown).

October 18. *The Apple Tree* premieres at the Shubert Theatre in New York City. Featuring music by Jerry Bock, lyrics by Sheldon Harnick, and book by Bock and Harnick, with Jerome Coopersmith, it would run for 463 performances. The only triple bill (three one-act musicals) in Broadway history, Act I is based on Mark Twain's "The Diary of Adam and Eve," Act II on Frank R. Stockton's "The Lad or the Tiger?," and Act III on Jules Feiffer's "Passionella."

October 20. New Orleans-based R&B singer/songwriter Smiley Lewis dies at age forty-six. His compositions included "I Hear You Knocking" and "One Night."

October 29. ? & the Mysterians climb to number one on the pop charts with the garage band classic, "96 Tears" (Cameo).

November 5. The Monkees top the Hot 100 with their debut single, "Last Train to Clarksville" (Colgems).

November 9. John Lennon attends a "happening" at the Indica art gallery in London. He is given a catalog for Unfinished Paintings and Objects; it focuses attention on a large black bag with a "member of the audience inside," a television screen arranged to monitor the sky, and "a mirror to see your behind." The artist, Yoko Ono, appears, dressed completely in black, and hands Lennon a card with the word "breathe" printed on it. He pants at her. She guides him through the exhibition. As related by Elizabeth Partridge in her photographic biography of Lennon, *All I Want Is the Truth* (2005):

> Stopping before an empty canvas with a hammer hanging on a chain beside it, she told him that for five shillings he could hammer a nail into the canvas. John instantly understood the humor in her work, and offered her a pretend five shillings for a pretend nail. She invited him to climb a short ladder and look through a magnifying glass at the tiny letters written on a canvas on the ceiling. John climbed up and peered at the letters, which spelled out "yes."

Thus began one of the most widely chronicled relationships in rock history.

November 12. The Monkees' eponymous debut begins a thirteen-week stretch atop the album charts. It will sell more than three million copies during this run.

November 12. Formerly known for discotheque-styled rockers, Johnny Rivers reaches number one on the pop charts with the ballad, "Poor Side of Town" (Imperial).

November 19. The Supremes begin a two-week stint atop the Hot 100 with "You Keep Me Hangin' On" (Motown).

November 20. *Cabaret* premieres at New York's Broadhurst Theatre. Featurin music by John Kander, lyrics by Fred Ebb, and book by Joe Masteroff, the musical would run for 1,165 performances. The 1972 film version—starring Joel Grey (from the original cast), Liza Minnelli, Michael York, and Marisa Berenson—would incorporate notable plot modifications and go on to win the Oscar for Best Picture.

November 26. Tom Jones begins a seven-week run atop the U.K. charts with "Green Green Grass of Home" (#11 U.S.). It is Decca's first million-selling single by a British artist.

December 3. The New Vaudeville Band—the brainchild of British acoustic era revivalist, Geoff Stephens—peaks at number one on the pop charts with "Winchester Cathedral" (Fontana), remaining there for three non-consecutive weeks.

December 5. *I Do! I Do!* Premieres at New York's 46th Street Theatre. Featuring music by Harvey Schmidt and lyrics and book by Tom Jones, it would have a run of 560 performances. The cast was limited to two people, originally Mary Martin and Robert Preston, who would be followed by Carol Lawrence and Gordon MacRae. The musical included one notable song, "My Cup Runneth Over," a hit that year for Ed Ames.

December 10. The Beach Boys climb to the summit of the Hot 100 with "Good Vibrations" (Capitol).

December 26. John Lennon appears as a men's room attendant in the BBC-TV program, *Not Only...But Also*, which stars Dudley Moore and Peter Cook.

December 26. Jimi Hendrix writes the lyrics to "Purple Haze" in the dressing room of The Uppercut Club, London, where he'd perform that afternoon.

December 29. The Jimi Hendrix Experience appear on *Top of the Pops* for the first time, performing "Hey Joe."

December 31. The Monkees begin a seven-week run atop the pop charts with the Neil Diamond-penned "I'm a Believer" (Colgems).

1967

❄

January. The "Hit the Road Stax" tour is announced to the public. With their artists becoming international stars, Stax Records announced plans for a tour modeled after the popular Motown revues of the mid-1960s. The roadshow featured Al Bell as compere, with Otis Redding headlining a line-up of performers that included Booker T. & the MGs, Arthur Conley, Eddie Floyd, the Mar-Keys, and Sam and Dave. After performing in a string of European venues during late winter, the tour continued in the United States. The best-selling LP, *Hit the Road Stax* (Stax), released in April 1967, documented the label at its creative and commercial peak. Stax would never fully recover from the loss of Redding and most members of the instrumental group, the Bar-Kays, in a December 1967 plane crash en route to a Madison, Wisconsin, concert.

January 3. Carl Wilson of the Beach Boys refuses to be inducted into military service because he is a conscientious objector.

January 3. The Bee Gees top the Australian charts with "Spickes and Speckes." Plans to repeat their success in Great Britain and the United States are beginning to take form.

Many pop music artists have parlayed an eclectic blend of musical styles to achieve commercial success, but the Bee Gees are one of the few to have remained successful despite a complete image makeover. Whatever genre assayed by the group, be it British Invasion pop, Baroque ballads, rhythm and blues, disco, or adult contemporary—their recorded output has been distinguished by immaculate three-part vocal harmonies, flawless arrangements and production work, and songwriting of the highest order.

Although the group (particularly in the late 1960s) has sometimes included added personnel, the primary members have always been the three Gibb brothers, Barry (born September 1, 1947) and the twins, Robin and Maurice (born December 22, 1949). They first performed in public at an amateur talent show in Manchester's Gaumont British Theatre in 1955 as "The Blue Cats." After the family immigrated to Brisbane, Australia, in 1958, the trio began performing live as well as appearing on radio and television. Within two years the brothers had been awarded a weekly TV series and secured an eighteen-month residency at Beachcomber Nightclub in Surfers Paradise. Their popularity with Australian youth led to a contract with Festival Records in late 1962. The group's first single, "Three Kisses of Love" (available on: *Bee Gees: The Early Years, Vol. 2*; Excelsior 4402; 1980), was released in January 1963, making Australia's Top Twenty. A string of hits followed, climaxed by three number one hits in 1966: "Wine and Women," "I Was a Lover, a Leader of Men" (both on: *Bee Gees: The Early Years, Vol. 1*; Excelsior 4401; 1980), and the aforementioned "Spicks and Specks" (*Rare Precious & Beautiful*; Atco 33-264; 1968).

Primed to achieve international popularity, the family relocated to England in February 1967. The early months there were spent recording *The Bee Gees' First* (Atco 223; 1967), which included three U.S. Top 20 singles: "New York Mining Disaster" (Atco 6487; 1967), "To Love Somebody" (Atco 6503; 1967), and "Holiday" (Atco 6521; 1967). The album also earned them the "Beatles imitators" label; their father, Hugh Gibb, refuted the charge, noting, "In actual fact we began recording before the Beatles...we came from Manchester, which is only thirty miles from Liverpool. It is rubbish to say we copied the Beatles' sound, it wasn't their sound, it was an English sound that began with Tommy Steele and skiffle." (liner notes to: *Bee Gees: The Early Years, Vol. 2*)

Despite such criticisms, the group enjoyed a long run of hit singles—including "I Gotta Get a Message to You" (Atco 6603; 1968), "I Started a Joke" (Atco 6639; 1968), "Lonely Days" (Atco 6795; 1970), and "How Can You Mend a Broken Heart" (Atco 6824; 1971)—and moderate-selling LPs—most notably, *Horizontal* (Atco 233; 1968), *Idea* (Atco 253; 1968), *Odessa* (Atco 702; 1969), *Best of Bee Gees* (Atco 292; 1969), *2 Years On* (Atco 353; 1971), *Trafalgar* (Atco 7003; 1971), and *To Whom It May Concern* (Atco 7012; 1972)—interrupted only by Robin's brief departure in 1969 to pursue a solo career. By 1974, however, sales of their increasingly over-produced recordings had dropped off to the point where Atco demanded a stylistic change more in tune with the contemporary music scene. The resulting release, the R&B-disco flavored *Main Course* (RSO 4807; 1975), placed the Bee Gees squarely into the pop mainstream with the help of three Top Twenty singles (including the chart-topper, "Jive Talkin'," RSO 510). During the latter half of the 1970s, no act enjoyed greater chart success. Three of the group's contributions to the *Saturday Night Fever* soundtrack (RSO 4001; 1977)—"How Deep Is Your Love" (RSO 882; 1977), "Stayin' Alive" (RSO 885; 1977), and "Night Fever" (RSO 889; 1978)—spent a total of fifteen weeks at the top of the *Billboard Hot 100*. At one point the Bee Gees had five of their compositions in the Top Ten (including songs recorded by Samantha Sang and brother Andy Gibb). The soundtrack remained number one on the album charts for twenty-four weeks; it was estimated at the time to be the best-selling LP in history. They also earned five Grammies for their work on the film soundtrack project in 1978.

Faced with the unenviable task of trying to top their hitherto unprecedented success, the Bee Gees moved away from disco with *Spirits Having Flown* (RSO 3041; 1979), which included three number one singles: "Too Much Heaven" (RSO 913; 1978), "Tragedy" (RSO 918; 1979), and "Love You Inside Out" (RSO 925; 1979). However, album releases featuring new material from that point onward exhibited a marked decline in sales. While songs such as "The Woman in You" (RSO 813173; 1983) and "You Win Again" (Warner Bros. 7-28191; 1987) continued the group's tradition of beautiful melodies, lush harmonizing, and polished production work, they appeared predictable compared with earlier cutting-edge releases. Furthermore, Top 40 radio stations seemed less inclined to place new Bee Gees records in rotation. On the other hand, they would remain a fixture within the adult contemporary format through the 1990s. Maurice Gibb's death early in the twenty-first century effectively ended the group as an active recording and performing entity.

January 11. The Jimi Hendrix Experience record "Purple Haze." They also sign with the fledging label, Track Records.

January 14. Cliff Richard informs *The New Musical Express* that he will retire from the entertainment field in order to go into religious education in the British school system.

January 17. The *Daily Mail* publishes a report that a local council survey tabulated four thousand holes in a Lincolnshire road, thereby inspiring John Lennon's lyric in the *Sgt. Pepper* magnum opus, "A Day in the Life."

January 17. While recording a segment for Radio Luxembourg's *Ready Steady Radio*, the Jimi Hendrix Experience accumulates a $6.21 bar bill, which they lack the funds to pay off.

January 22. The Monkees make their live concert debut at San Francisco's Cow Palace to an S.R.O. crowd.

January 31. On a break from filming the "Strawberry Fields Forever" promo, John Lennon purchases an 1843 poster from a Surrey antiques shop. It becomes the source for the lyric to "Being for the Benefit of Mr. Kite."

February 3. Producer Joe Meek—producer of The Tornados' "Telstar," the first chart-topping single in the United States by a British band—fatally shoots his landlady, Violet Shenton, and then himself at his London flat.

February 4. The Monkees' eponymous debut begins a seven-week stint atop the British album charts.

February 7. The Gibb Brothers (Bee Gees) return to Great Britain after living in Australia for nine years.

February 7. Monkees Mike Nesmith and Mickey Dolenz appear on *Top of the Pops*.

February 8. Aretha Franklin completes "Do Right Woman, Do Right Man" in New York with the assistance of sisters Carolyn and Erma. Combined with the results of the one-day session at FAME studios in Muscle Shoals, Alabama back in January—"I Never Loved A Man (The Way I Love You)" and the backing track for "Do Right Woman, Do Right Man"—she now has her first Atlantic single. It will top the R&B charts for nine weeks (#9 pop), and become her first gold disc. The album of the same name also goes gold, peaking at number two. Seemingly almost overnight in eyes of most pop music fans, Franklin has become the most successful—and critically acclaimed—soul singer in the business.

February 9. The promotional video for "Penny Lane"/"Strawberry Fields Forever" is broadcast on *Top of the Pops*. It is the first single since their debut, "Love Me Do," not to top the British charts.

February 9. Conductor Percy Faith dies at age sixty-seven. His biggest hit, "Theme From a Summer Place" (Columbia), spent nine weeks atop the Hot 100.

February 13. The Monkees announce that they'll play the instruments on their recordings from now on. Some publications had criticized the band's use of session musicians on their first two albums.

February 16. Petula Clark tops the British charts with the Charlie Chaplin composition, "This Is My Song."

February 18. The Buckinghams began to two-week stint atop the Hot 100 with "Kind of a Drag" (USA).

February 27. Pink Floyd, with assistance from producer Joe Boyd, record their debut single, "Arnold Layne."

March 1. The Bee Gees secure the management services of Robert Stigwood, then an executive with the Beatles' NEMS Enterprises. Their first Atco single, "New York Mining Disaster 1941," reaches the Top Ten stateside and achieves international success.

March 4. The Rolling Stones reach number one on the pop charts with "Ruby Tuesday" (London).

March 11. Music publisher Dick James announces that 446 versions of the Lennon-McCartney song, "Yesterday," have been recorded up to that point in time.

March 11. The Supremes top the Hot 100 with "Love Is Here and Now You're Gone" (Motown).

March 17. Stax artists Booker T. and the MG's, Eddie Floyd, Otis Redding, Sam & Dave, and Carla Thomas kick off a seventeen-date British tour at London's Finsbury Park Astoria.

March 18. The Beatles surge to the summit of the pop charts with "Penny Lane" (Capitol).

March 18. Pink Floyd sign a recording contract with EMI Records.

March 25. Buffalo Springfield peak at number seven on the Hot 100 with "For What It's Worth" (Atco 6459).

Buffalo Springfield's recorded output consists of three promising studio albums released in the late 1960s. However, the group's legacy owes much to respective careers of the group members following the breakup in Spring 1968.

Buffalo Springfield, named for a steamroller manufactured in the American midwest, was formed out of a chance meeting in March 1966 between Stephen Stills (accompanied in his car by Richie Furay) and Neil Young during a Los Angeles traffic jam. The interplay between these three singer-guitarists (both on- and offstage) would supply much of the creative spark behind the band's music, best described as U.S. roots-styled offshoot of Beatles pop-rock. Young's companion, also hailing from Canadian, bassist Bruce Palmer, and drummer Dewey Martin were recruited to complete the group lineup.

Following a couple of critically acclaimed, albeit commercially unsuccessful, folk-rock singles, the band burst into the national consciousness with the release of the Stills-penned "For What It's Worth," a protest anthem documenting the L.A. police crackdown on youthful protesters opposing plans to build a business district at the expense of Sunset Strip nightlife in Summer 1966. The debut album—*Buffalo Springfield* (Atco 33-200; 1966)—was hastily reissued in February 1967 with the substitution of the group's best-selling single for the track "Don't Scold Me." Group infighting, however, undercut efforts to record a follow-up LP. One projected work, *Stampede*, was never completed, although portions would later surface both in bootleg form and on the retrospective anthology, *Buffalo Springfield Box Set* (Rhino 74324; 2001). A reassembled lineup consisting of Stills, Furay, Martin, Young (who returned after having departed in January 1967), and bassist Jim Messina would eventually complete *Buffalo Springfield Again* (Atco 33-226; 1967; #44), an ambitious album featuring extensive multi-tracking and other special effects reflecting the influence of the Beatles' *Sgt. Pepper*. The inability of the band to expand beyond a cult audience led to a final split; a third LP, *Last Time Around* (Atco 33-256; 1968; #42), which featured a group photo with a crack running down the middle, was issued several months later. Many of the song selections—including Young's folk-like "I Am A Child"; Stills' "Special Care," "Questions," and "Uno Mundo"; and Furay's country-inflected "Kind Woman"—come across as rehearsals for the individual members' subsequent musical activities.

By the end of the 1960s, all key members were well of their way to becoming superstars. Young embarked on an uneven, but distinctive, solo career; he would also have an on-and-off relationship with soft-rock trailblazers, Crosby, Stills and Nash. Furay and Messina would form one of the early country-rock acts of note, Poco. Always in demand as a record producer, Messina would move on to form a duo with Kenny Loggins in the early 1970s.

March 25. The Mamas and the Papas peak at number two on the pop charts with their remake of the Shirelles hit, "Dedicated to the One I Love" (Dunhill 4077), remaining there for three weeks.

March 25. The Turtles begin a three-week stay atop the Hot 100 with "Happy Together" (White Whale 244).

March 25. The Who make their U.S. concert debut as part of a New York rock 'n' roll show promoted by disc jockey Murray the K.

March 27. Fats Domino performs in England for the first time, at London's Saville Theatre, supported by the Bee Gees and Gerry and the Pacemakers.

March 30. Michael Cooper presides over the Chelsea Manor studios photo session that resulted in the *Sgt. Pepper* album cover.

March 31. The Jimi Hendrix Experience begin their first English tour at the Astoria theater, London; the twenty-four-date package—which includes a young Cat Stevens, the Walker Brothers, and Engelbert Humperdinck—will conclude at the Granada theater, London. Hendrix becomes a sensation pioneering hitherto unexplored areas of guitar distortion and feedback as well as employing outrageous stage devices like setting fire to his guitar at the climax of each show and playing the instrument with his teeth.

April 4. Jimi Hendrix, Kiki Dee, and Cat Stevens guest on the premiere of BBC-TV's *Dee Time*.

April 5. Hundreds of Monkee fans walk from London's Marble Arch to the U.S. Embassy to protest Davy Jones' planned call up. He will be exempted on the grounds of being responsible for supporting his father.

April 8. Sandie Shaw wins the Eurovision Song Contest, held in Vienna, with "Puppet on a String." She is the first British female to win the annual event.

April 14. The Bee Gees' "New York Mining Disaster 1941" is released by Polydor Records along with the promotional slogan "the most significant talent since the Beatles."

April 14. The Rolling Stones make their first appearance in an Iron Curtain country, causing a riot to break out at Warsaw's Palace of Culture.

April 15. Nancy and Frank Sinatra begin a four-week run atop the Hot 100 with "Somethin' Stupid" (Reprise).

April 22. *Disc & Music Echo* publishes the results of their "most popular Monkee poll": Davy Jones receives 63 percent of the votes; Mickey Dolenz, 22 percent; Peter Tork, 8 percent; and Mike Nesmith, 7 percent.

April 25. The Beatles record the theme to *Magical Mystery Tour* at Abbey Road Studios in London.

April 27. Sandie Shaw tops the British charts with "Puppet on a String."

May 1. Elvis Presley marries Priscilla Ann Beaulieu in an Aladdin Hotel private suite, in Las Vegas. Memphis Mafia member Joe Esposito is best man, and Priscilla's sister Michelle is maid of honor.

May 8. Acknowledging that they were unable to change with the rock scene, Gerry and the Pacemakers announce they are breaking up.

May 11. The Bee Gees debut on BBC-TV's *Top of the Pops*, performing "New York Mining Disaster – 1941."

May 13. *More of the Monkees* tops the British charts. It is one of only four LPs to do so that year; the others are the Monkees' debut album, *The Sound of Music*, and *Sgt. Pepper's Lonely Hearts Club Band*.

May 13. The Supremes peak at number one on the pop charts with "The Happening" (Motown); it also reached number six on the British charts. Prior to their next release, the group would be called "Diana Ross and the Supremes."

May 13. The Tremeloes top the British charts with "Silence Is Golden." The song was first recorded by the Four Seasons in 1964.

May 18. John Lennon and Paul McCartney contribute backing vocals on the Rolling Stones track, "We Love You," during a recording session at Olympic Studios, London.

May 20. *Sgt. Pepper's Lonely Hearts Club Band* is previewed on Kenny Everett's radio program, *Where It's At*. The BBC had already announced a ban on the track, "A Day in the Life," alleging it could promote drug use.

May 20. The Young Rascals reach number one on the Hot 100 with "Groovin'" (Atlantic), remaining there for four non-consecutive weeks.

June 2. The Beatles' biggest selling LP, *Sgt. Pepper's Lonely Hearts Club Band* (Capitol), is released. Although the group had been adventuresome since their initial appearance on the charts, the album managed to take many listeners by surprise. Its commercial success, even given the Beatles' exemplary track record up to that point, was astounding. Entering the *Billboard* album charts on June 24, it rose to number one a week later, remaining there for a total of fifteen weeks. During the summer of 1967, the album was heard everywhere—on the radio, in community centers, at swimming pools, wafting out of homes and college dormitory rooms, etc.

In addition, *Sgt. Pepper* became the standard by which all future recordings would be measured. Its influence spanned many areas:

- Concept albums built around a particular literary and/or sociological theme became the vogue.
- The psychedelic studio effects contained within its tracks were mirrored in the recordings of virtually every popular artist of that period.
- Performers took a greater interest in the artwork adorning their album covers. Many sought to achieve a direct correlation between cover illustrations and the nature of their music.
- Like the Beatles, other artists began spending increased amounts of time in the studio in order to maximize their chances of receiving aesthetic accolades.
- "Art for art's sake" became the prevailing motto within the rock subculture.
- The counterculture itself was aped by the music establishment.
- It was considered "hip" (even commercially imperative) to be anti-establishment in attitude.

The popularity of *Sgt. Pepper* extended beyond the fabled Summer of Love; it remained on the charts for 113 consecutive weeks. It continually re-entered the charts during the 1970s and 1980s, most notably at the time of John Lennon's assassination. The animated feature, *Yellow Submarine* (1968), employed a sizeable portion of the songs and conceptual ideas from the album.

Another film, *Sgt. Pepper's Lonely* Hearts *Club Band* (1978), starring Peter Frampton and the Bee Gees, proved to be a bust at the post office (probably due in large part to the absence of the Beatles, save the songs and the skeletal outline of the concept). The accompanying two-disc soundtrack LP was one of the most disappointing releases of the rock era, with a large percentage of the units ending up in the cut-out bins. The original album, however, was front page news again in 1987 when newspapers, magazines, radio and television stations across the nation marked the twentieth anniversary of its release. The compact disc version of *Sgt. Pepper*—released on June 2, 1987—swept to the top of *Billboard*'s CD charts. In addition, listings, albeit fanciful, of the greatest LPs of the rock era appear periodically which invariably award *Sgt. Pepper* the top spot (e.g., Paul Gambaccini's *The 200 Greatest Albums of Alltime*; "The Top 100: the Best Albums of the Last Twenty Years," *Rolling Stone*, August 27, 1987, pp. 15ff.; *The Rolling Stone Top 500 Albums*, 2005).

June 2. David Bowie's eponymous debut LP is released. It fails to make the charts.

June 3. Aretha Franklin begins a two-week stint atop the pop charts with "Respect" (Atlantic).

June 16. The Monterey International Pop Festival—featuring primary organizers (along with manager Lou Adler) the Mamas and the Papas, the Who, the Jimi Hendrix Experience, Simon and Garfunkel, Otis Redding, and the Grateful Dead, among others—begins. D.A. Pennebaker's film version will help the event to become a model for future rock festivals.

June 19. In an interview with *Life*, Paul McCartney discloses that he has taken LSD.

July 1. The Association surge to number one on the Hot 100 with "Windy" (Warner Bros.), remaining there for four weeks.

July 15. The Beatles head up the British charts with "All You Need Is Love."

July 15. Moby Grape peak at number eight on the Hot 100 with "Omaha" (Columbia 44173).

The Moby Grape will always be identified with the worst excesses of record industry hype arising from the excitement engendered by the San Francisco Sound. With the Summer of Love (1967) gathering momentum and leading Bay Area bands such as the Jefferson Airplane and Grateful Dead already enjoying impressive record sales, label rushed to sign any local bands displaying commercial potential. Columbia's signing of Moby Grape was widely viewed as a major coup; the group's popularity in the area was virtually unrivaled. The producer of the band's first two albums, David Rubinson, would later comment, "They were the closest thing to the Rolling Stones that America has produced."

The Grape's strengths included a triple guitar lineup (Peter Lewis, Jerry Miller, and Skip Spence), seamless four-part harmonies, and mature songwriting capable of incorporating country, rhythm and blues, psychedelia, and other contemporary music styles. Columbia celebrated the release of the band's *Moby Grape* (Columbia 9498; 1967) by also issuing simultaneously five singles from the debut album. Although critics agree that the LP was a classic, the public appears to have been confused by this marketing ploy. Only one of the singles, "Omaha" (Columbia 44173; 1967), would make the charts.

Although the first album peaked at number twenty-four, the media furor surrounding its release rendered this performance something of a disappointment. The label continued its grandiose promotional efforts with the Grape's next release, *Wow* (Columbia 9613; 1968), a double-album set including a psychedelic studio disc (including one track cut at 78 rpm) along with a bonus "Grape Jam" supersession featuring Mike Bloomfield, Al Kooper, and other famous guest musicians.

In the face of general public indifference and declining sales, the band recorded two more albums before splitting up, *Mody Grape '69* (Columbia 9696; 1969) and *Truly Fine Citizen* (Columbia 9912; 1969). After 1970, the various band members attempted a number of reunions. Only one album ensuing from these projects, *20 Granite Creek* (Reprise 6460; 1971) entered the charts.

July 29. The Doors begin a three-week stay atop the pop charts with "Light My Fire" (Elektra).

August 12. Aretha Franklin tops the bill at New York's inaugural jazz festival, held in Downing Stadium.

August 19. The Beatles reach number one on the Hot 100 with the flower-power anthem, "All You Need is Love" (Capitol). Mick Jagger, Marianne Faithfull, Keith Richards, Eric Clapton, Keith Moon, Graham Nash, and Gary Leeds of the Walker Brothers all contribute backing vocals.

August 19. Bunny Sigler peaks at number twenty-two on the Hot 100 with a medley of classics 1950s tunes, "Let the Good Times Roll & Feel So Good" (Parkway 153).

Bunny Sigler achieved a modicum of success as a soul journeyman at the height of the funk/disco era. Born Walter Sigler on March 27, 1941, in Philadelphia, the vocalist/multi-instrumentalist/composer/producer formed his own R&B group, the Opals, in the late 1950s. The Opals—whose membership also included Jack Faith, Ritchie Rome, and Sigler's brother James—first recorded for the V-Tone label in 1959.

By the mid-1960s, Sigler had opted for a solo career. His earliest hit, a medley of Shirley & Lee classics, "Let the Good Times Roll & Feel So Good" (#20 r&b), was followed by an extended fallow period. Signing with Philadelphia International in the early 1970s, he continued to mine oldies for singles material, including "Tossin' and Turnin'" (#3523; 1973; #97 pop, #38 r&b) and "Love Train (Part One)" (#3545; 1974; #28 r&b). He switched to Gold Mind Records in the late 1970s, were he released a string of hits through 1979, most notably "Let Me Party With You (Party, Party, Party) – Part 1" (#4008; 1978; #43 pop, #8 r&b). Although he continued to perform and work with other artists in the studio, he failed to reach the charts again.

August 26. Bobbie Gentry begins a four-week run atop the pop charts with mysterious narrative song, "Ode to Billie Joe" (Capitol). The single will peak at number fifty-four when reissued in 1976; a newly recorded version will go as high as number sixty-five that same year.

August 27. Beatles manager, Brian Epstein, aged thirty-two, is found dead in the bedroom of his London home, from an overdose of the sleeping pill Carbitrol.

September 6. Engelbert Humperdinck tops the British charts with "The Last Waltz."

September 11, 1967. The Doors earn gold records for both their chart-topping single, "Light My Fire" (Elektra 45615), and debut LP, *The Doors* (Elektra 74007). The Doors represented the darker side of psychedelic flower-power vision first identified with San Francisco bands such as the Jefferson Airplane and Quicksilver Messenger Service. Showcasing lead vocalist Jim Morrison's blatantly sexual posturing and frequently surrealistic lyrics, the band—more than three decades after its demise—has remained a highly marketable, pop culture phenomenon.

The Doors grew out of the shared musical vision of Morrison and keyboardist Ray Manzarek, both of whom were film students at UCLA. By early 1966 they had recruited drummer John Densmore and guitarist Bobby Krieger, and signed with Columbia Records. Not satisfied with their treatment by that label, they maneuvered a switch to Elektra later in the year. *The Doors* (Elektra 74007; 1967; #1), was an eclectic—and commercial—tour de force; in addition to the hit single, "Light My Fire" (Elektra 45615; 1967; shortened version), the tracks included the updated blues of "Back Door Man" and "Soul Kitchen," the German theatrical piece "Alabama Song," an eleven-minute Oedipal tone poem "The End," and the stream-of-consciousness ballad, "Crystal Ship." The second LP, *Strange Days* (Elektra 74014; 1967; #3), exhibited greater thematic unity, focusing on a nightmarish world populated by maladjusted misfits and loners.

Despite the inclusion of a number one single, "Hello, I Love You" (Elektra 45635; 1968), *Waiting For The Sun* (Elektra 74024; 1968; #1) revealed a considerable drop-off in artistic creativity. With Morrison's contribution increasingly compromised by alcohol and drug abuse, the band's work—particularly *The Soft Parade* (Elektra 75005; 1969; #6), with its pretentious title cut, an overblown attempt to reprise the epic reach of "The End"—bordered on self-parody. *Morrison Hotel/Hard Rock Café* (Elektra 75007; 1970; #4) represented something of a temporary diversion, exploring musical territory akin to roots rock 'n' roll. Perhaps heedful of widespread criticism emanating from the rock press that their best days were behind them, the Doors produced one more masterpiece—*L.A. Woman* (Elektra 75011; 1971; #9), with extended pieces like "Riders On The Storm" (Elektra 45738; 1971; #14; edited version issued as a single) and the title song exploring the jazz-rock fusion then in vogue—before Morrison died of a heart attack while residing in Paris. The remaining members released a couple of unsuccessful albums before breaking up. Although each has remained active in the music business, their greatest success has come from overseeing various archival projects involving Doors material. In 1991, Hollywood director Oliver Stone produced a feature film, *The Doors*—the soundtrack was issued on Elektra 61047, reaching number eight on the *Billboard* album charts—in response to continuing public fascination with the band. In addition to the release of many commercial video titles and a series of live recordings on their Blue Midnight label, Manzarek, Krieger, and Densmore were reportedly working with Ian Astbury—the Morrison-influenced former lead singer of the Cult—in 2002 (although Densmore would later pull out, threatening legal action if the group's name was in any way associated with this lineup).

September 23. The Box Tops leap-frog to the summit of the Hot 100 with "The Letter" (Mala), remaining there for four weeks.

September 30. BBC Radio 1 is launched; the first record spun by deejay Tony Blackburn is The Move's "Flowers in the Rain."

October 21. Lulu begins a five-week stay atop the pop charts with "To Sir with Love" (Epic).

October 31. The Stooges make their live debut at a Halloween party in Ann Arbor, Michigan.

November 4. The Soul Survivors peak at number four on the Hot 100 with "Expressway (To Your Heart)" (Crimson 1010).

The Soul Survivors were arguably the finest white soul band to make recordings between the Rascals and the Average White Band. Consisting of an expanded lineup whose members came from the New York City-Philadelphia area, the group was originally formed by Kenny Jeremiah and brothers Charles and Richard Ingui. Assisted by Philly Soul producers Kenny Gamble and Leon Huff, they surfaced with the crossover classic, "Expressway to Your Heart" (#3 r&b), which remains one of the most popular songs on oldies programming playlists. They had one follow-up hit, "Explosion in Your Soul" (Crimson 1012; 1968; #33 pop, #45 r&b), before internal conflicts led to a group break-up. The Inguis reactivated the Soul Survivors in 1972; they would crease the charts with one single, "City of Brotherly Love" (TSOP 4756; 1974; #75 r&b) before once again disappearing from view. Jeremiah would hook up with industry veteran Shirley Goodman as part of Shirley & Company in the mid-1975.

November 9. The first issue of *Rolling Stone* is published, with a John Lennon photograph (circa *How I Won the War*) adorning the cover.

November 22. Sam & Dave earn a gold record for "Soul Man" (Stax 231). Sam Moore, born October 12, 1935, in Miami, and David Prater, born May 9, 1937, in Ocilla, Georgia, were the most popular black duo of the 1960s. Both grew up singing in church, and were veterans of the southern club circuit prior to meeting at Miami's King of Hearts club in 1961. When Prater forgot the lyrics to Jackie Wilson's "Doggin' Around," at an amateur night show, Moore—who was acting as MC—coached him through the song. They went on to become a fixture in the Miami club scene, eventually singing with Roulette Records.

They switched to Atlantic in 1965, where executive Jerry Wexler loaned them out to the Stax label. Their gospel fervor was effectively captured on recordings by the Stax production/songwriting team of Isaac Hayes and David Porter. While most readily identified with the rhythm and blues market, the team known as "Double Dynamite" nevertheless crossed over to the pop charts with hits such as "Hold On, I'm Comin'" (Stax 189; 1966), "Soul Man," and "I Thank You" (Stax 242; 1968).

At the peak of their success, Moore and Prater were barely speaking to one another. Although they broke up in 1970, there were several efforts at reunification. Following the Blues Brothers' hit remake of "Soul Man" (Atlantic 3545; 1978), the duo was besieged with bookings from clubs across the country. Their last show together took place New Year's Eve, at San Francisco's Old Waldorf; Prater then began touring with Sam Daniels. In 1983 Moore would tell the Los Angeles Herald Examiner that the instigating factor in their feud was that he'd "lost respect" for his ex-partner when Prater shot his own wife during a 1968 domestic dispute. Prater would die April 9, 1988 in a Georgia automobile accident. Moore continued his career, singing on Bruce Springsteen's Human Touch (Columbia 53000; 1992). Later in 1992, Sam and Dave were inducted into the Rock and Roll Hall of Fame.

November 25. The Strawberry Alarm Clock reach the summit of the Hot 100 with the pop-psychedelic master-piece, "Incense and Peppermints" (Uni).

December 2. The Monkees begin a four-week run atop the pop charts with "Daydream Believer" (Colgems).

December 16. Gladys Knight and the Pips begin a three-week run at number two on the Hot 100 with "I Heard It Through the Grapevine" (Soul 35039). At the outset of the twenty-first century, "Grapevine" was tied for seventh among songs with the most charted versions (six in all).

December 20. Joan Baez is sentenced to forty-five days in prison after being arrested during an anti-war dem-onstration.

December 26. The Beatles film, *Magical Mystery Tour*, premieres on BBC-TV.

December 29. Dave Mason departs Traffic due to musical differences.

December 30. The Beatles peak at number one on the Hot 100 with "Hello Goodbye" (Capitol), remaining there for three weeks. Gladys Knight & the Pips hold down the number two slot with "I Heard It Through the Grapevine," followed by the Monkees at number three with "Daydream Believer."

December 31. Record label executive and producer Bert Burns suffers a fatal heart attack in a New York hotel room at age thirty-eight. He had a hand in writing "Brown-Eyed Girl," "Hang on Sloopy," and "Twist and Shout," among other songs.

1968

❄

January 1968. Bob Dylan participates in a benefit concert for Woody Guthrie (who'd died of Huntington's Chorea on October 3, 1967) at Carnegie Hall. It was his first public appearance since going into seclusion in upstate New York following his 1966 motorcycle accident.

January 1. *Billboard* reports that albums—which accounted for 192 million units in 1967—outsold singles for the first time.

January 6. The Beatles begin an eight-week run at number one with *Magical Mystery Tour* (Capitol), their eleventh chart topper.

January 13. *Your Own Thing* premieres at New York's Orpheum Theatre. Featuring music and lyrics by Hal Hester and Danny Apolinar, and book by Donald Driver, it would run for 933 performances. An adaptation of Shakespeare's *Twelfth Night* into a 1960s youth subculture contest, the musical would utilize such cotemporary props as film and slide projections.

January 18. *The Happy Time* premieres at New York's Broadway Theatre. Featuring music by John Kander, lyrics by Fred Ebb, and book by N. Richard Nash, the musical would run for 286 performances.

January 19. Duke Ellington's *Second Sacred Concert* is first performed at St. John the Divine's In New York City.

January 20. John Fred & His Playboy Band begin a two-week stint atop the Hot 100 with "Judy in Disguise" (Paula). Aretha Franklin's "Chain of Fools" (Atlantic 2464) holds down number two for both weeks.

February 1. Elvis and Priscilla Presley's only child, Lisa Marie, is born in Memphis, Tennessee. She will become a rock recording artist in her own right.

February 3. Al Green and the Soul Mates peak at number forty-one on the Hot 100 with "Back Up Train" (Hot Line 15000).

Al Green has excelled in two widely divergent genres during his lengthy career—soul/R&B and gospel. Although the former has resulted in greater commercial success and public renown, he has gone on to earn the higher honors in the latter field. The Grammies warded annually by the National Academy of Recording Arts and Sciences represent a case in point. Although rarely victorious as a pop artist ("Funny How Time Slips Away," duet with Lyle Lovett, from the LP *Rhythm, Country, and Blues*; 1994), he has consistently won within the gospel sector, including Best Soul Gospel Performance, Traditional, in 1981 for the LP *The Lord Will Make a Way* (Myrrh), and in 1982 for the LP *Precious Lord* (Myrrh); Best Soul Gospel Performance, Contemporary, in 1982 for the LP *Higher Plane* (Myrrh); Best Soul Gospel Performance, Male, in 1983 for the LP *I'll Rise Again* (Motown); Best Soul Gospel Performance by a Duo or Group, in 1984 for "Sailin' on the Sea of Your Love" (with Shirley Caeser); Best Soul Gospel Performance, Male, in 1986 for "Going Away" (Motown; album track from *Trust in God*) and in 1987 for "Everything's Gonna Be Alright" (Motown).

Influenced by Sam Cooke (then a member of the Soul Stirrers), Green—at age nine—joined a gospel group, the Green Brothers with siblings Robert, Walter, and William that earned a measure of attention over the next half-dozen years. While in a Grand Rapids, Michigan high school, he formed the pop-oriented Al Green and the Creations; after several years, the band was reconstituted as Al Green and the Soul Mates. His recording debut, "Back Up Train," just missed *Billboard*'s Top 40, but a lack of quality follow-up material resulted in a return to the Chitlin' Circuit grind of the South and Midwest.

Green's singing at a Midland, Texas, club in 1969 impressed Hi Records vice president, bandleader, and chief producer, Willie Mitchell, who signed him to a recording contract. "I Can't Get Next to You" (Hi 2182; 1970; #60 pop, #1 R&B), a cover of the 1969 Temptations chart-topper, had all the elements of his signature sound: softly caressing vocals, subdued rhythm section, and an ethereal veneer of horns and strings filling background spaces. He followed with eight million-sellers in a little more three years: "Tired of Being Alone" (Hi 2194; 1971; #11), "Let's Stay Together" (Hi 2202; 1971; #1), "Look What You Done for Me" (Hi 2211; 1972; #4), "I'm Still in Love with You" (Hi 2216; 1972; #3), "You Ought to Be with Me" (Hi 2227; 1972; #3), "Call Me" (Hi 2235; 1973; #10), "Here I Am" (Hi 2247; 1973; #10), and "Sha-La-La" (Hi 22274; 1974; #7). Much like the singles, his albums—most notably, *Al Green Gets Next to You* (Hi 32062; 1971; #58), *Let's Stay Together* (Hi 32070; 1972; #8), *I'm Still in Love with You* (Hi 32074; 1972; #4), *Call Me* (Hi 32077; 1973; #10), *Livin' For You* (Hi 32082; 1973; #24), *Al Green Explores Your Mind* (Hi 32087; 1974; #15), *Al Green/Greatest Hits* (Hi 32089; 1975; #17), and *Al Green Is Love* (Hi 32092; 1975; #28)—possessed sufficient polish to appeal to both pop and R&B listeners. His work was also acclaimed by the major trade publications; he was designated the Rock 'n' Pop Star of 1972 by *Rolling Stone*, while *Billboard*, *Cash Box*, and *Record World* all named him the Best Pop and R&B Vocalist for the year.

During the latter half of the 1970s, Green turned increasingly to his work as Pastor of the Full Gospel Tabernacle in Memphis. In 1979, he declared his intent to focus exclusively on gospel material. His 1980s Myrrh/Motown releases would include a combination of traditional hymns and self-penned religious songs, all imbued with a strong dose of Memphis soul.

Green would return to pop in the late 1980s, recording a duet with Annie Lennox for the *Scrooged* soundtrack (A&M 3921; 1988; #93), "Put a Little Love in Your Heart." He would devote an entire album, *Don't Look Back* (RCA 16310), to the exploration of his Memphis roots in 1993. Further validation of his early work came with his 1995 induction into the Rock and Roll Hall of Fame.

At the outset of the twenty-first century Green seemed as popular as ever. Not only were many of his classic soul recordings now available in CD editions, but he was touring regularly (performing a mix of gospel and pop material) and was part of the cast for the highly rated TV series, *Ally McBeal*. In Fall 2000 HarperCollins published his autobiography, *Take Me to the River*.

February 3. The Lemon Pipers peak at number one on the pop charts with the gently psychedelic "Green Tambourine" (Buddah; #7 U.K.).

February 10. The Four Tops' *Greatest Hits* goes number one on the British charts—the first Motown album to accomplish this feat.

February 10. Paul Mauriat begins a five-week run atop the Hot 100 with the instrumental "Love is Blue" (Philips).

February 15. John Lennon and George Harrison arrive in India along with their wives to study meditation with the Maharishi. The McCartney and Starr entourages arrive four days later. When Ringo makes a hasty exit, he likens the experience to attending a Butlins holiday camp.

February 15. Little Walter dies from injuries incurred in a street fight. He was the first harmonica player to use amplification, which resulted in a distorted, echo-tinged sound.

February 17. Diana Ross and the Supremes begin a three-week stint atop the British charts with *Greatest Hits* (Motown).

February 22. "The Silent Sun," the debut single by Genesis, is released.

One of the bulwarks of the 1970s progressive rock movement, Genesis is probably better known for the solo work of alumni such as Peter Gabriel, Phil Collins, Michael Rutherford, Anthony Phillips, and Steve Hackett than for their group releases. Ironically, the edition of the band achieving major commercial success in the United States was many years removed from the innovative powerhouse that won widespread critical acclaim.

Genesis was formed in Godalming, Surrey, England in 1967 when ex-Garden Wall members Gabriel (vocals) and Tony Banks (keyboards, vocals) joined forces with bassist/guitarist Rutherford, guitarist/vocalist Phillips, and drummer Chris Stewart, all formerly of The Anon. Their early releases—including the albums *From Genesis To Revelation* (Parrot 4990; 1969) and *Trespass* (Impulse 9295; 1970)—featuring lushly-textured arrangements dominated by keyboards and synthesizers, were commercial failures. Following a personnel shake-up—Hackett replacing Phillips on guitar and Collins solidifying the until then unstable percussion seat—Genesis staked out new musical territory (described by a *Stereo Review* journalist as 'the Moody Blues with teeth'), centered around Gabriel's surrealistic lyrics and theatrical flair, in a string of increasingly popular LPs: *Nursery Cryme* (Charisma 7208 552; 1971), *Foxtrot* (Charisma 7208 553; 1972; #12 UK), *Genesis Live* (Charisma 7299 288; 1973; #9 UK), *Selling England By The Pound*

(Charisma 7208 554; 1973; #70 US, #3 UK), and the rock opera *The Lamb Lies Down On Broadway* (Atco 401; 1974; #41 US, #10 UK).

When Gabriel left in 1975 for a solo career, Genesis—with Collins becoming the full-time lead vocalist—retrenched a bit artistically, opting for an overly ripe, AOR-compatible sound in *A Trick Of The Tail* (Atco 129; 1976; #31 US, #3 UK) and *Wind And Wuthering* (Atco 144; 1977; #26 US, #7 UK). Slimmed down to a trio in June 1977 with the departure of Hackett, the band's recordings—most notably, the albums *Duke* (Atlantic 16014; 1980; #11 US, #1 UK), *Abacab* (Atlantic 19313; 1981; #7 US, #1 UK), *Genesis* (Atco 80116; 1983; #9 US, #1 UK), *Invisible Touch* (Atco 81641; 1986; #3 US, #1 UK; which included the chart-topping title song), and *We Can't Dance* (Atco 82344; 1991; #4 US, #1 UK)—would acquire an additional coat of production polish, thereby ascending to the upper reaches of the charts stateside. Collins himself would leave in the early 1990s to concentrate on his acting and solo recording career (he was replaced by ex-Stiltskin vocalist Ray Wilson). Since then, the bulk of the recordings issued by Genesis have consisted of live collections and retrospective anthologies.

February 24. Married duo Esther and Abi Ofarim top the British charts with "Cinderella Rockafella."

February 28. Frankie Lymon, age twenty-five, is discovered dead of a suspected drug overdose in his mother's New York City home.

February 29. The Beatles' *Sgt. Pepper* (Capitol) dominates the Grammy Awards, winning Album of the Year, Best Cover, and Best Engineered and Recorded Album.

March 1. Elton John's first single, "I've Been Loving You Too Long," is released. It fails to make the charts.

March 8. Concert promoter Bill Graham opens the Fillmore East in New York City, modeled after the San Francisco rock theater, the Fillmore West.

March 9. Bob Dylan begins a ten-week run atop the British charts (#2 U.S.) with *John Wesley Harding* (CBS).

March 10. The late Otis Redding's "(Sittin' On) The Dock of the Bay" (Volt 157) achieves gold record status.

March 16. Otis Redding begins a four-week run atop the Hot 100 with "(Sittin' On) The Dock of the Bay."

A one-of-a-kind soul stylist equally adept at rave-up houserockers and soft, caressing ballads, Otis Redding is remembered as much for his potential as for what he actually accomplished. Toiling for years on the R&B circuit before a breakthrough performance at the 1967 Monterey Pop Festival positioned him on the verge of mainstream stardom, he would die tragically in a small plane crash at age twenty-six.

Born September 9, 1941, the Macon, Georgia-native did not seemed destined for a recording career until given an audition at Stax Records while serving as a chauffeur for an aspiring band headed by Johnny Jenkins. Redding's first release, "These Arms of Mine" (Volt 103; 1963), reached the Top 20 on the national R&B charts. Stax immediately signed him to a long-term contract, and with Booker T and the M.G.s guitarist Steve Cropper serving as arranger/producer, Redding recorded a long string of R&B hits—many self-composed—including "Mr. Pitiful" (Volt 124; 1965; #41 pop, #10 r&b), "I've Been Loving You Too Long" (Volt 126; 1965; #21 pop, #2 r&b), "Respect" (Volt 128; 1965; #35 pop, #4 r&b), "Satisfaction" (Volt 132; 1966; #31 pop, #4 r&b), "My Lover's Prayer" (Volt 136; 1966; #61 pop, #10 r&b), ""Try a Little Tenderness" (Volt 141; 1966; #4), "Tramp" (Stax 216; 1967; #26 pop, #2 r&b), and "Knock On Wood" (Stax 228; 1967; #30 pop, #8 r&b).

By the summer of 1967, when his Monterey appearance captured the imagination of white rock fans, Redding's singles were beginning to become fixtures on the pop charts. The widely acclaimed Queen of Soul, Aretha Franklin, would take one of his compositions, "Respect" (Atlantic 2403; 1967), to the top of the pop charts. Furthermore, a mere two-and-a-half weeks before his death on December 10, 1967, he recorded a song that close associates felt would propel him to mainstream success, "(Sittin' on) The Dock of the Bay" (#1 r&b).

Although only moderate sellers during his lifetime, Redding's albums—all of which have been reissued as compact discs—have remained in demand up to the present day. The material from his original LP releases—*Pain In My Heart* (Atco 161; 1964; #103), *The Great Otis Redding Sings Soul Ballads* (Volt 411; 1965; #147), *Otis Blue/Otis Redding Sings Soul* (Volt 412; 1965; #75), *The Soul Album* (Volt 413; 1966; #54), *Complete & Unbelievable...The Otis Redding Dictionary of Soul* (Volt 415; 1966; #73), *King & Queen*

(Stax 716; 1967; #36), *Otis Redding Live In Europe* (Volt 416; 1967; #32), *The Dock of the Bay* (Volt 419; 1968; #4), *The Immortal Otis Redding* (Atco 252; 1968; #59), and *Otis Redding In Person At the Whiskey A Go Go* (Atco 265; 1968; #52)—is also available through countless retrospective compilations.

March 17. The Bee Gees appear on *The Ed Sullivan Show*, their U.S. television debut.

March 20. Dave Dee, Dozy, Beaky, Mick and Tich enjoy their only U.K. chart topper, "The Legend of Xanadu."

March 23. The Beatles top the British charts with "Lady Madonna" (Parlophone), their fourteenth single to accomplish that feat.

March 25. The final episode (#58) of *The Monkees* is telecast in the United States.

March 26. Little Willie John dies in prison, where he has been serving a term for manslaughter. He co-wrote, and first recorded, "Fever" (a hit for Peggy Lee and the McCoys) and "Need Your Love So Bad," later covered by Fleetwood Mac.

April 6. Pink Floyd announce that Syd Barrett—then allegedly suffering from psychiatric disorders compounded by drug use—has officially left the group.

April 6. Virtually unknown in the United States, Cliff Richard's forty-first single, "Congratulations," becomes his ninth U.K. chart topper.

April 6. Simon and Garfunkel top the album charts with the soundtrack to *The Graduate*.

April 10. *George M!* premieres at New York's Palace Theatre. Featuring music and lyrics by George M. Cohan and book by Michael Stewart and Fran Pascal, the biographical musical celebrating Cohan's stage career would run for 427 performances. Notable songs include "Give My Regards to Broadway," "Mary's a Grand Old Name," "Yankee Doodle Dandy," "Harrigan," "Over There," and "You're a Grand Old Flag."

April 13. Bobby Goldsboro surges to the summit of the pop charts with the unabashedly sentimental "Honey" (United Artists), remaining there for five weeks.

April 19. John Lennon, George Harrison, and their wives leave the Maharishi Mahesh Yogi's ashram in Rishikesh, India two weeks early, apparently disillusioned with their mentor's worldly flaws. Bandmates Paul and Ringo have left earlier for more practical reasons—boredom and other interests.

April 20. Louis Armstrong tops the British charts with "What a Wonderful World"/"Cabaret." At sixty-nine, he is the oldest artist to accomplish this feat.

April 20. Deep Purple make their live debut in Tastrup, Denmark.

April 20. Sly & the Family Stone peak at number eight on the Hot 100 with "Dance to the Music" (Epic 10256).

Sly and the Family Stone helped pioneer one of dominant styles of the 1970s, funk music. Their variant fused the psychedelic rock of the late 1960s with classic soul; in that sense, it differed considerably from the bass-heavy grooves of mainstream funk. As popular on the pop charts as with urban black youth, the group greatly influenced the careers of later crossover giants such as George Clinton, mastermind of the Parliament/ Funkadelic collective, Rick James, and Prince.

The creative core of Sly and the Family Stone, Texas-native Sylvester Stewart, developed an impressive music business resume in Sam Francisco during the mid-1960s, excelling as a disc jockey (KSOL, KDIA), songwriter, and record producer for the likes of Beau Brummels, Bobby Freeman, and the Mojo Men with Autumn Records. His first attempt at heading a group, the Stoners, failed in 1966; however, Sly and the Family Stone—including his brother, guitarist Freddie Stone, sister Rosie Stone, who played sang and played keyboards and harmonica, and a cousin, bassist Larry Graham, who would form Graham Central Station in the early 1970s—attracted sufficient local attention in 1967 to garner a contract with Epic Records.

The group's debut LP, *A Whole New Thing* (Epic 30333; 1967) failed to attract much attention. However, the follow-up album, *Dance to the Music* (Epic 26371; 1968; #142), and the exuberant title song (Epic 10256; 1968; #8) elevated them to the forefront of the rock scene. The group maintained its momentum with a steady stream of hit singles—most notably, "Everyday People" (Epic 10407; 1968; #1), "Hot Fun in the Summertime" (Epic 10497; 1969; #2), "Thank You (Falettinme Be Mice Elf Agin)" (Epic 10555; 1970; #1), and "Family Affair" (Epic 10805; 1971; #1)—and albums: *Life* (Epic 26397; 1968; #195), *Stand!* (Epic 26456; 1969; #13), *Greatest Hits* (Epic 30325; 1970; #2), *There's A Riot Goin' On* (Epic 30986; 1971; #1), and *Fresh* (Epic 32134; 1973; #7). The uplifting, anthem-like quality of Sly and the Family Stone's early work gave way to a decidedly more negative, militant tone in *There's A Riot Goin' On*; however, the uniformly high quality of Sly's musical ideas and production work made it the most successful—artistically and commercially—of his albums.

Sly's drug problems in the 1970s led to an increasing inability to meet concert commitments and lackluster studio work. He ceased to perform or record for several years prior to attempting a comeback with the October 1979 release of *Back on the Right Track* (Warner Bros. 3303). Unfortunately, the album lacked strong material and Stone spent much of the 1980s fighting drug convictions. Sly and the Family Stone were inducted into the Rock and Roll Hall of Fame in 1993. Rumors have periodically surfaced since then that the group would soon be releasing new material. In the meantime, their classic recordings have appeared in a host of compilation releases, including *The Collection* (Castle Communications 307; 1991) and *Takin' You Higher – The Best of Sly & the Family Stone* (Sony 471758; 1992; reissued on Epic 477506; 1994).

April 24. During a birthday party, Who drummer Keith Moon drives his Lincoln automobile into a Lincoln Inn swimming pool. It becomes one of the more celebrated tales of rock star excess.

April 27. The Box Tops peak at number two on the Hot 100 with "Cry Like a Baby" (Mala 593), remaining there for two weeks.

April 29. *Hair*—billed as the "American Tribal Love-Rock Musical"—has its Broadway premiere at New York's Biltmore Theatre. Featuring the music of Galt MacDermot, and lyrics and book by Gerome Ragni and James Rado, it was first presented October 29, 1967 at Joseph Papp's New York Shakespeare Festival Public Theatre, where it continued until shifting to a Broadway nightclub, Cheetah, a month-and-a-half later.

Hair; The American Tribal Love/Rock Musical institutionalized the hippie culture of the late 1960s, incorporating large dollops of anti-war posturing, recreational drugs, and rock music. It garnered major headlines in Middle America for the inclusion of scenes in which all performers appeared naked onstage.

Following a few preview performances at a go-go club, The Cheetah, the work—featuring scripting by James Rado, music by Galt MacDermot, and lyrics by Gerome Ragni—premiered off-Broadway for the opening of the Public Theater, October 17, 1967. It shifted to Broadway' Biltmore Theater on April 29, 1968, where it ran for 1,873 performances. Stage productions were soon mounted worldwide. The Shaftesbury Theatre, London, run—which began September 27, 1968—lasted 1,998 shows until halted by a collapsing roof in July 1973. The Mexico City production, however, was terminated by government officials after one show in 1968.

In addition to the publicity generated by the nudity of performers in the Act I finale, *Hair* faced widespread suppression outside New York City for including allegedly obscene language and desecration of the American flag. The musical also attracted attention when several of its songs became Top 10 singles on the *Billboard*'s Hot 100 when adapted by mainstream pop acts: "Aquarius" (number one for six weeks in 1969 as part of a medley arrangement recorded by the 5th Dimension), "Good Morning Starshine" (Oliver; 1969), "Hair" (Cowsills; 1969), and "Easy To Be Hard" (Three Dog Night; 1969). The Broadway original cast recording did equally well on the national album charts. Approximately three dozen different soundtrack versions would be released through 2005.

The musical lost momentum in the early 1970s due largely to media saturation and the decline of the anti-war movement during the Nixon White House years. A film version—directed by Milos Forman and starring Treat Williams, Beverly D'Angelo, and John Savage—was released at the height of the disco craze in 1979, but achieved minimal success in the face of poor reviews. A number of revivals have been mounted beginning with a successful Australian production in 1992, which featured updated musical arrangements. New productions featuring script revisions also appeared on a regular basis, including three in London alone between 1993 and 2005; the latter version—with Rado's endorsement (withdrawn after attending a performance)—used the 2003 Gulf War as a reference point rather than the Vietnam War.

Hair remains highly visible to the present day. On television, *The Simpsons* has showcased four songs from the musical, and it was performed by the cast of *Head of the Class*. Two 2005 feature films also incorporated its songs: the last scene of *The 40-Year-Old Virgin* parodied "Aquarius/Let the Sunshine In," and Willy Wonka greeted children with lyrics from "Good Morning Starshine" in *Charlie and the Chocolate Factory*.

April 30. BBC-TV launches the *The Cilla Black Show*, making Black the first British female to head her own program. The theme song, "Step Inside Love," was a Paul McCartney composition.

May 3. The Beach Boys open their U.S. tour at New York's Singer Bowl; they will share featured billing with Maharishi Mahesh Yogi.

May 4. Blue Cheer's remake of the Eddie Cochran classic, "Summertime Blues" (Philips 40516), peaks at number fourteen on the *Billboard* Hot 100. It is the first hit single to combine many of the characteristics that came to be associated with heavy metal: heavily amplified electric guitars—often distorted by means of fuzz-boxes, wah-wah pedals, and a host of other accessories—slowly throbbing bass patterns, and flashy drum passages.

William Burroughs introduced the term "heavy metal" into the pop culture vernacular in his Beat novel, *Naked Lunch*. It first appeared within a musical context via the line, "heavy metal thunder," from the Steppenwolf hit, "Born To Be Wild" (Dunhill 4138; 1968). The British hard rock bands of the mid-1960s anticipated the genre, both its sound and attitude. Notable pioneers included the Who (e.g., "My Generation," Decca 31877, 1966; "I Can See For Miles," Decca 32206, 1967) and the ex-Yardbirds guitarists Eric Clapton, Jeff Beck, and Jimmy Page, all masters of fuzztone-and-feedback drenched onslaughts. Jimi Hendrix provided the link between these antecedents and the earliest practitioners of the style proper via his guitar pyrotechnics and banshee vocals.

While California bands—specifically, renegades from psychedelia (e.g., Blue Cheer) and acid rock (e.g., Iron Butterfly)—were playing heavy metal, or something close to it, by early 1968, the British scene proved more prolific at the outset of the 1970s. Three divergent movements quickly emerged there, including (1) post-psychedelic hard rock, exemplified by the cinematic guitar stylings and evocative lyric imagery of Led Zeppelin, Black Sabbath, and Robin Trower; (2) blues-derived, working class rock, built on predictable heavy riffs and the cultivation of a "bad boy" image (e.g., Deep Purple, Bad Company); and (3) aristocratic Anglo-metal, featuring the glam dress of acts like Queen and Sweet.

During this time, American bands projected a distinctly working class image; e.g., Cactus, Mountain, the Frost, Aerosmith, Kiss, Grand Funk Railroad, and Bachman-Turner Overdrive (Canada). Two subdivisions grew out of this school: American revolutionary bands, who considered rock to represent an instrument of social change (e.g., MC5); and boogie bands, dedicated to simple riffing for the sake of partying (e.g., Black Oak Arkansas, ZZ Top). In reaction to these subgenres, yet another offshoot—the American Deviates—emerged. Generally inspired by the Velvet Underground, its practitioners (e.g., Iggy and the Stooges, Alice Cooper, Blue Oyster Cult) were dedicated to, in Lester Bangs' words (*The Rolling Stone Illustrated History of Rock*. 1980 2nd ed.), "The reinforcement of whatever vestiges of primal infantalism have managed to survive into adolescence, and the glorification of adolescence as the Time of Your Life."

By the late 1970s the genre had fallen into middle-of-the-road respectability largely due to the effort of artists such as Toto, Triumph, Foreigner, Journey, Heart, Def Leppard, Van Halen, and Ted Nugent. What little flair and freshness remained was appropriated by two newly emerging genres, speed metal and punk rock. The foremost practitioners of the former—e.g., Metallica, Megadeath, Godflesh—remained viable throughout the 1990s, grudgingly appropriating the trappings of the more progressive hard rockers. Punk, however, proved to be the more important of the two, stripping heavy metal down, speeding it up, and providing some lyric content beyond the customary macho posturing. The resulting stylistic offshoot, hardcore (which itself spawned countless spinoff genres), enjoyed considerable commercial success by the early 1990s; its leading practitioners included Soundgarden, Anthrax, and the Meat Puppets.

The riot grrrl movement of the early 1990s also borrowed heavily from heavy metal. Notable distaff bands from the period included Bikini Kill and L7. Groups such as Luscious Jackson and Fluffy opted for a sound more closely aligned with the pop mainstream.

The late 1990s have seen a revival of the more traditional exponents of the genre. Reformed first generation bands such as Black Sabbath, Alice Cooper, and Grand Funk Railroad have again found success via both recordings and the stage; third generation copy bands such as Poison, Cinderella, Warrant, and Motley Crue have also enjoyed a commercial resurgence. In short, heavy metal has continued to thrive, a genre secure in the fact that its primary audience—teenaged males—will always derive immense sustenance from its manic energy and rebellious attitude.

May 4. Mary Hopkin wins within her competition group on the ITV talent show, *Opportunity Knocks*. Shortly thereafter, she is signed to the Apple label.

May 5. Buffalo Springfield dissolve. Richie Furay forms Poco; Stephen Sills becomes a founding member of Crosby, Stills and Nash; while Neil Young goes solo (eventually joining forces, on a part-time basis, with CSN)

May 13. John Lennon and Paul McCartney give a series of interviews to help launch Apple Corps in the United States.

May 15. George Harrison and Ringo Starr attend the premiere of *Wonderwall* at the Cannes Film Festival.

May 18. Archie Bell and the Drells begin the two-week stint atop the Hot 100 with "Tighten Up" (Atlantic 2478).

Archie Bell—born September 1, 1944, in Henderson, Texas—formed the Drells in the mid-1960s. The band members, who'd first sung together at Leo Smith Junior High School in Houston, included Huey "Billy" Butler, Joe Cross, and James Wise.

The group's big hit, "Tighten Up" (#1 r&b), was originally recorded as a demo in 1964. After several years of limited success, Bell received his draft notice on May 12, 1967. When bandmate—and roommate—Butler found Bell in a funk over the imminent tour of duty in Vietnam, he tried to cheer him by performing an impromptu dance called the "Tighten Up." With a studio session already scheduled for the following day in order to stockpile recordings, Bell and Butler decided to do an updated version of their old song. Bell included an introduction, stating that the group was from Houston, Texas, because "When (John F.) Kennedy was assassinated, I heard a disc say, 'nothing good ever came from Texas,' so I wanted people to know that we were from Texas and we were good."

When "Tighten Up" achieved hit status in Texas, it was picked up for national distribution by Atlantic Records. It took several months—until March 30, 1968—for the song to enter the *Billboard* Hot 100 as the label initially felt that the flip side, Dog Eat Dog," possessed the greatest potential. By that time, Bell was stuck in a West German hospital recovering from a leg wound sustained in Vietnam. While he would manage a fifteen-day pass which enabled him to record the follow-up singles, "I Can't Stop Dancing" (Atlantic 2534; 1968; #9 pop, #5 r&b), "Do the Choo Choo"/"Love Will Rain On You" (Atlantic 2559; 1968; #44 pop, #17/#25 r&b), and "(There's Gonna Be A) Showdown" (Atlantic 2583; 1969; #21 pop, #6 r&b), the group was unable to tour in support of the early Atlantic releases.

Bell received a military discharge April 19, 1969, and immediately reunited with his group, which now included Wise, Lee Bell, and Willie Parnell. However, they now found it harder to make commercially successful records. They would part with Atlantic in 1970; their last charting single for the label was "Wrap It Up" (#2768; 1970; #93 pop, #33 r&b), which was revived by the Fabulous Thunderbirds in 1986. They moved on to Glades, where they reached the mainstream charts for the last time with "Dancing To Your Music" (#1707; 1973; #61 pop, #11 r&b).

The Drells were able to regain some measure of their R&B audience after signing with Philadelphia International in 1975. Working with the renowned producers, Kenny Gamble and Leon Huff, they recorded seven more hits through 1979, including "Let's Groove" (TSOP 4775; 1976; #7). The appearance of a disco version of "Tighten Up," which generated little interest, seemed to indicate that they were running out of creative ideas. By 1981, Bell was recording on his own for the Becket label. However, the group would remain popular as part of the Atlantic Coast "beach" music scene during the 1980s.

May 18. The Intruders peak at number six on the Hot 100 with "Cowboys to Girls" (Gamble 214).

Formed in Philadelphia in 1960, the Intruders—consisting Sam "Little Sonny" Brown, Eugene "Bird" Daughtry, Phil Terry, and Robert "Big Sonny" Edwards—were one of the mainstays of the Kenny Gamble/Leon Huff stable of artists. Although the distinctive soaring tenor lead possessed by notable Philly Soul groups like the Stylistics with Russell Thompkins Jr., and Harold Melvin and the Blue Notes with Teddy Pendergrass, the Intruders—like their more successful contemporaries, the O'Jays—focused on smooth harmonies generally set to easy rocking funk-pop grooves.

The group first signed with the Gowan label in 1961. After hooking up with Gamble and Huff in the mid-1960s, the Intruders released a decade-long string of hit singles, including six Top 10 R&B hits: "Together" (Gamble 205; 1967; #48 pop, #9 r&b); "Cowboys to Girls" (#1 r&b); "(Love Is Like A) Baseball Game" (Gamble 217; 1968; #26 pop, #4 r&b); a redo of the 1961 Dreamlovers hit, "When We Get Married" (Gamble 4004; 1970; #45 pop, #8 r&b); "I'll Always Love My My Mama (Part 1)" (Gamble 2506; 1973; #36 pop, #6 r&b); and "I Wanna Know Your Name" (Gamble 2508; 1973; #60 pop, #9 r&b).

May 18. Gary Puckett and the Union Gap top the British charts with "Young Girl."

May 20. David Bowie has a dancing role in the short play, *The Pistol Shot*, aired on BBC 2.

May 25. Simon and Garfunkel top the album charts with *Bookends* (Columbia).

c. June. The release of the Maytals' "Do the Reggay" heralds the emergence of a new musical form. Jamaican music had been expanding the role of the bass for much of the 1960s; reggae brought the bass to the forefront, emphasizing the complex interrelationship between it, the trap drums, and the percussion instruments. The beat was interspersed with silences, the pulse divided as finely as sixty-four times, and cross-rhythms abound. The bass appeared to be the lead instrument, with the guitar reduced to playing "change," mere scratching at a chord. Keyboard and horns were utilized to thicken the texture.

Originally applied in 1968 to the latest in a rapidly evolving string of Jamaican dance rhythms, reggae would later become a collective term for various styles of Jamaican popular music, isolated examples of which have dented the U.S. Top 40 since the early 1960s. It is characterized by a loping beat, a strong dose of rhythm and blues, and recording techniques which have been simultaneously original in concept and primitive in execution. It has had an impact on 1970s rock that was far greater than its moderate commercial success.

The genre was a product of a diverse array of influences, including African-derived children's games, the ecstatic Christian Pocomania cult, Garveyite Rastafarians, and New Orleans rhythm and blues, which was broadcast all over the Caribbean via clear-channel radio stations in the late 1950s. These forces did not converge until the appearance of transistor radios revived Jamaican interest in popular music recordings. Out of this state of affairs emerged the "sound system man," who operated a generator-powered hi-fi rig mounted on the back of a flatbed truck that would be driven to rural areas for dances. These operators, utilizing catchy handles such as "Duke Reid," generated large audiences of fans.

In the early 1960s, the dearth of New Orleans talent (and corresponding drop-off of available imports) forced sound system men to make their own records. Primitive studios sprang up around Jamaica. The first recordings were bad copies of New Orleans music; the Jamaican musicians couldn't seem to get the New Orleans rhythm right. This "wrong" rhythm became standardized, and ska was born with its strict, mechanical emphasis on the offbeat (mm-**cha!** mm-**cha!**). One notable example of the ska style, Millie Small's "My Boy Lollipop" (Smash 1893; 1964) became a Top 10 hit in the United States.

By 1965, ska had been superseded by the slow, even more rhythmic "rock steady" genre. Sound system men began employing deejays, who would "toast" or talk over the instrumental B side of a record. The DJ—prime exponents included Prince Buster, Sir Collins, King Stitt, and U Roy—would improvise rhymes about his sexual prowess and the greatness of the sound system operator. This practice also became known as "dubbing"; some of it was "rude" (i.e., dirty—in Jamaican slang "dub" is equivalent to sexual intercourse).

Poppa-top was the final link in the evolutionary chain prior to the emergence of reggae; bubblier than rock steady, it loosened up the beat to the point where greater rhythmic division was possible. The leading exponent of the style, Desmond Dekker, reached the U.S. Top 10 with his 1969 release, "Israelites" (Uni 55129).

Despite the success of some reggae-styled material in the U.S.—e.g., Johnny Nash's "I Can See Clearly Now" (Epic 10902; 1972) and "Stir It Up" (Epic 10949; 1973), Eric Clapton's "I Shot the Sheriff" (RSO 409; 1974)—the genre remained relatively unknown to most Americans until the U.S. release of the film, *The Harder They Come*, starring Jimmy Cliff, in 1973. It became a cult favorite and opened the door to the American market for other reggae artists.

In contrast to its widespread acceptance in Europe, Africa, and South America, the genre's popularity in the United States was hampered by the scarcity of live reggae music. This was because (1) most of the records used the same pool of studio talent, and (2) most Jamaicans couldn't afford night clubs or stage show performances. The most famous reggae performer was Bob Marley, whose recordings featured protest lyrics, first-rate melodies, high quality production values, and seamless blend Jamaican roots and rock conventions (which enabled him to please both his original followers and U.S. fans). Assisted by an international distribution pact with the Island label, Marley—and his backup group, the Wailers—issued a string of critically acclaimed LPs, including *Catch a Fire* (Island 9241; 1973), *Burnin'* (Island 9256; 1973), *Natty Dread* (Island 9281; 1975), *Rastaman Vibration* (Island 9383; 1976), *Exodus* (Island 9498; 1977), *Kaya* (Island 9517; 1978), *Survival* (Island 9542; 1979), and *Uprising* (Island 9596; 1980).

Marley's promising career was abruptly cut short by his death from lung cancer in 1981. Nevertheless, reggae has left a substantial musical legacy, including hip hop (a rap-inflected spinoff, "dancehall," was popular in urban clubs during the 1990s), disco dubs with a DJ rapping over the track, and an expansion of the rhythmic possibilities in rock (as realized by artists as diverse as Jimmy Buffett, the Grateful Dead, the Clash, Police, the Flying Lizards, the Selector, Generation X, the Slits, the English Beat, Public Image Ltd., and UB40).

The genre continues to reflect the Jamaican lifestyle as well as supporting the world's most successful self-contained Third World record business. Home-grown artists such as Ziggy Marley, Musical Youth, Inner Circle, and Shabba Ranks managed to achieve international success in the 1990s within an updated reggae framework.

June 1. Simon and Garfunkel ascend to the summit of the pop charts with "Mrs. Robinson" (Columbia), remaining there for three weeks. The single's success is greatly helped by its inclusion in the smash film, *The Graduate*.

June 8. Tiny Tim enters the Hot 40 with "Tip-Toe Thru' the Tulips With Me" (Reprise 0679), peaking at number seventeen.

On the strength of his trembling falsetto, strange appearance (large nose, stringy hair, and bag-man clothes), and androgynous mannerisms, Tiny Tim (b. April 12, 1925) became a highly successful camp novelty artist in the late 1960s. Formerly billed as Herbert Khaury, among other names, he was a fixture at low-rent Greenwich Village nightclubs for years before his trilling of 1920s pop tunes to the accompaniment of his ukulele began to gather a cult audience in the mid-1960s. Bookings on *The Tonight Show* and *Rowan & Martin's Laugh-In* made him an overnight national celebrity. In spring 1968, his debut album on Reprise, *God Bless Tiny Tim*, was released; on of its cuts, a reinterpretation of the top-selling 1929 Nick Lucas hit, "Tiptoe Through the Tulips," reached the Top 20.

Tiny Tim's most notorious moment came on December 17, 1969, when he and seventeen-year-old Victoria May Budinger (known to his audience as "Miss Vicky") were married live on Johnny Carson's late night program. The couple is reputed to have spent the first three nights of their honeymoon apart in keeping with Tim's bizarre sexual code.

By early 1972, when they first filed for divorce, Tiny Tim was out of public favor and broke. He toured the backwater lounges of America for a time in the 1970s as part of a traveling vaudeville show whose other acts included Zippy the Chimp and a fireater. During their separation, it was revealed that Miss Vicky had had to work as a go-go dancer at Minnie's Lounge in Camden, New Jersey, and accept welfare in order to survive. Tim offered to take her back if she'd undergo a VD test; she refused, and the couple was divorced in 1977.

Although his shtick had paled in comparison with glitter era and postpunk gender-benders, Tiny Tim continued to perform intermittently through the 1980s before slowed by various health problems. He remained a champion of the vintage Tin Pan Alley pop fare that had always formed the bulk of his repertoire.

June 13. Cream's "Anyone for Tennis" is released. It fails to chart.

Cream began a prototypical blues-rock power trio with a decided experimental bent; through such devices as free-form jamming and extended solos, the band laid the groundrock for the progressive rock era. All three members were well-known virtuosos prior to coming together in mid-1966—drummer Ginger Baker was an alumnus of Graham Bond's Organization, bassist Jack Bruce had played with Bond and Manfred Mann, and guitarist Eric Clapton had gained a substantial following with the Yardbirds and John Mayall's Bluesbreakers. During its brief existence, the band released four best-selling albums: *Fresh Cream* (Atco 206; 1967), *Disraeli Gears* (Atco 232; 1967), *Wheels of Fire* (Atco 700; 1968), and *Goodbye* (Atco 7001; 1969).

When Cream performed its farewell concert at London's Royal Albert Hall, November 26, 1968, they were perhaps the most popular performing aggregate in popular music. Despite universal praise from the rock press and high art tastemakers such as composer/conductor Leonard Bernstein, the band had found it impossible to continue due to internal tensions. While Bruce embarked on a solo career and Clapton and Baker joined Blind Faith (before going solo as well), Atco (and, later, RSO and Polydor) continued to release live albums and compilations of previously released material.

June 22. Herb Alpert begins a four-week run atop the Hot 100 with the Bacharach/David ballad, "This Guy's in Love with You" (A&M).

June 27. Elvis Presley makes his legendary comeback TV special, referred to as the "Burbank Sessions."

July 20. Hugh Masekela reaches number one on the pop charts with the instrumental, "Grazing in the Grass," remaining there for two weeks.

Hugh Masekela is known as something of a one-hit wonder in the United States, despite a lengthy career marked by his experiments with jazz and various forms of ethnic African music within a pop context. He would later comment in *Rolling Stone* regarding his best-selling single, "Grazing in the Grass" (Uni 55066), "It was all very contrived. It happened because I came along about the time Herb Alpert was making it big with his 'South American sound,' so MCA figured that they would make me into a black Herb Alpert. I did it but it wasn't what I wanted—I wanted the fulfillment of playing something that was *me*."

Born April 4, 1939, in Wilbank, South Africa, Masekela—whose father was a noted sculptor—was raised by his grandmother prior to attending missionary schools. He began playing piano at age seven, but switched to trumpet when he saw *Young Man with a Horn* (1950), the Bix Beiderbecke biopic starring Kirk Douglas. He was a member of the Huddleston Jazz Band, until leader Father Trevor Huddleston, a priest and anti-apartheid activist, was forced to leave the country. He then formed the Merry Makers of Springs, and toured in the late 1950s with the orchestra for the opera *King Kong*, the Jazz Epistles (reputedly the first band to record jazz in South Africa), Dollar Brand, and Mariam Makeba, his wife from 1964-1966.

In 1959, Masekela received a scholarship to the Royal Academy of Music, London, with the assistance of British orchestra leader, John Dankworth. A year later—with Harry Belafonte playing the benefactor—he acquired a four-year scholarship at the Manhattan School of Music. He formed his own band in 1965, and released recordings on a designer label, Chisa. His instrumental albums were released to MCS's Uni subsidiary; *Hugh Masekela's Latest* (Uni 73010; 1967; #151), *Hugh Masekela Is Alive and Well at the Whiskey* (Uni 73015; 1968; #90), *The Promise of a Future* (Uni 73028; 1968; #17), and *Masekela* (Uni 73041; 1969; #195)—which featured the big R&B hit, "Riot" (Uni 55102; 1969; #55 pop, #21 r&b)—would become nationwide best sellers.

Masekela opted for a fusion sound in the 1970s, with *I Am Not Afraid* (Blue Thumb 6015; 1974; #149), *The Boy's Doin' It* (Casablanca 7017; 1975; #132), and a collaboration with Alpert, *Herb Alpert/Hugh Masekela* (Horizon 728; 1978; #65)—including "Skokiaan" (Horizon 115; 1978; #87)—reaching the pop LP charts. Although remaining active as a performer, his last commercial success came with the single, "Don't Go Lose It Baby" (Jive Afrika 9193; #67 r&b).

July 22. Cream earn a gold record for *Wheels of Fire* (Atco 700).

August 1968. The Byrds' *Sweetheart of the Rodeo*, released on the Columbia label (9670), becomes the first country rock album to enjoy both artistic and commercial success. Country rock represented a merging of country instrumentation with rock's beat and socially conscious attitude. Its immediate precursors included rockabilly and the Nashville crossover pop of the 1960s exemplified by singers like Skeeter Davis ("End of the World," RCA 8098; 1963), Bobby Bare ("Detroit City," RCA 8183; 1963), Johnny Cash ("I Walk the Line," Sun 241; 1956), Marty Robbins ("El Paso," Columbia 41511; 1959-60), and Jim Reeves ("He'll Have to Go," RCA 7643; 1959-60). Country rock was part of the back-to-the-roots movement instigated in the late 1960s by maturing baby boomers whose tastes were changing in favor of softer forms of pop music.

Bob Dylan's *Nashville Skyline* (Columbia 9825; 1969) brought the genre into the pop mainstream with its Top 10 single, "Lay Lady Lay" (Columbia 44926). *Nashville Skyline* also represented a symbolic synthesis of the country and rock styles with its inclusion of a Dylan-Cash duet. By the 1970s, other country artists—particularly leaders of the "outlaw" movement such as Willie Nelson, Waylon Jennings, and Kris Kristofferson—began collaborating with rock performers.

The genre's seminal artists—e.g., the Byrds, the Flying Burrito Brothers, Poco, and the Eagles—were never welcome on mainstream country radio or in the prime concert venues catering to country fans. Nevertheless, many of the leading country performers of the 1980s and 1990s, including Garth Brooks, Clint Black, and Brooks and Dunn, grew up listening to country rock.

August 3. The Doors peak at number one on the pop charts with "Hello, I Love You" (Elektra), remaining there for two weeks.

August 10. Mason Williams remains at number two on the Hot 100 with the instrumental, "Classical Gas" (Warner Bros. 7190).

August 17. Tommy James & the Shondells reach the summit of the British charts with "Mony Mony."

August 17. The Rascals begin a five-week run atop the Hot 100 with "People Got to be Free" (Atlantic).

September 21. Jeannie C. Riley climbs to the summit of the pop charts with "Harper Valley P.T.A." (Plantation).

September 28. The Beatles begin a nine-week stay atop the Hot 100 with "Hey Jude" (Apple).

November 9. Johnny Nash peaks at number five on the Hot 100 with "Hold Me Tight" (JAD 207).

Johnny Nash had been a fixture in show business for many years before he briefly became a high profile recording star in 1972. Born in 1940, in Houston, Texas, he started singing at the church attended by his Baptist parents. He had performed on a local television program at age thirteen, which led to a regular slot on Arthur Godfrey's radio and TV network shows in 1956 (which continued for seven years).

The Godfrey connection helped Nash secure a recording contract with ABC-Paramount. The eponymous debut album, released in September 1958, was followed by a steady stream of titles for label into the early 1960s. He switched to Argo before forming his own company, Joda, in the mid-1960s. Primarily a night club entertainer specializing in middle-of-the-road fare up to this point, Nash became aware of the rock steady/reggae styles based in the West Indies. He began producing recordings—the first best-seller of note being "Hold Me Tight" (1968)—that helped make this music more palatable to mainstream listeners. The breakthrough came with "I Can See Clearly Now" (Epic; 1972; #1) and "Stir It Up" (Epic; 1972), followed by the album, *I Can See Clearly Now* (Epic; 1972). Although subsequent releases sold less spectacularly, he remained a fixture in the lower reaches of the charts through much of the 1970s.

November 13. Brian Jones purchases Cotchford Farm in Sussex, once owned by *Winnie-the-Pooh* author A.A. Milne.

November 13. Hugo Montenegro tops the British charts with "The Good, the Bad and the Ugly," the theme from Clint Eastwood's spaghetti western film of the same name.

November 23. *Rolling Stone* displays a rear nude photo of John Lennon and Yoko Ono while promising "Inside: The Complete John and Yoko Record Cover."

November 26. Cream's farewell concert effectively brings down the curtain for the rock era's first true supergroup.

November 30. Diana Ross and the Supremes reach number one on the pop charts with an early Motown foray into social commentary, "Love Child" (Motown), remaining there for two weeks.

December 7. Procol Harum enter the *Billboard* Top 40 album charts for the first time with *Shine on Brightly* (A&M 4151), peaking at number twenty-four.

The roots of Procol Harum, one of leading exponents of the art rock school, lie in the Paramounts, a London band that recorded five singles between October 1963 and September 1965 and included singer/pianist Gary Brooker, guitarist Robin Trower, bassist/organist Chris Copping, and drummer B. J. Wilson. In search of a new direction, Booker was introduced to lyricist Keith Reid sometime in 1966. The two began writing songs together; several demos led to a recording contract with Deram in early 1967. Procol's first single, "A Whiter Shade of Pale" (Deram 7507; 1967)—based on the melody from Johann Sebastian Bach's *Suite No. 3 in D major*—became an international smash, selling more than four million copies overall. In the face of heightened demand for concert engagements, the group broke up. Procol's revamped lineup—featuring Brooker, Trower, Wilson, organist Matthew Fisher, and bassist David Knights—produced three critically acclaimed albums: *Procol Harum* (Deram 18008; 1967), *Shine On Brightly*, *A Salty Dog* (A&M 4179; 1969).

Artistic differences within the band, combined with disappointing sales, led to the departure of Fisher and Knights. With the addition of Copping, Procol's next two albums—*Home* (A&M 4261; 1970) *Broken Barricades* (A&M 4294; 1971)—reflected a transition from a thickly-textured keyboard sound to more guitar-based approach built around Trower's Jimi Hendrix-inspired virtuosity.

Trower's decision to embark upon a solo career led to another change in personnel: David Ball was brought in as lead guitarist and Alan Cartwright on bass, thereby enabling Copping to concentrate on organ. An offer to perform in a classical music framework led to the release of group's bestselling LP, *Procol Harum Live in Concert with the Edmonton Symphony Orchestra* (A&M 4335; 1972). The band failed, however, to capitalize on this revival in popularity, and the next four albums showed steadily declining sales.

Procol broke up in 1977, but Brooker, Fisher, Reid, and Trower reunited to record *The Prodigal Stranger* (Zoo 72445-11011-2; 1991). Brooker, Fisher, and hired hands have toured intermittently during the 1990s.

December 14. Marvin Gaye's rendition of "I Heard It Through the Grapevine" (Tamla) begins a seven-week run atop the Hot 100.

December 28. The Beatles top the LP charts with the *White Album* (Apple).

1969

❄

January 2. Led Zeppelin perform the first of a four-night stint at the Whiskey A Go Go in Los Angeles, on their way to achieving supergroup status. The support band, Alice Cooper, also stand on the threshold of stardom.

January 2. Filming of the Beatles rehearsals for the *Let It Be* album begins at Twickenham Studios. Foremost among the problems plaguing the project is George Harrison's abrupt departure on January 10.

January 3. While appearing live on *The Lulu TV Show*, Jimi Hendrix pauses after playing the opening to his latest single, then goes into "Sunshine of Your Love" in tribute to Cream, who had split up several days ago.

January 29. Fleetwood Mac go number one on the British charts with the instrumental, "Albatross"—their only single to achieve that position in the U.K.

January 30. The Beatles give a forty-minute concert on top of the Apple building—the last time they perform live as a group. A large portion of the show is included in the documentary film, *Let It Be*.

February 1. Tommy James and the Shondells begin a two-week stint atop the Hot 100 with "Crimson and Clover" (Roulette), their second chart topper.

February 5. Never commercially successful in the United States, The Move move into the top position on the British charts for the only time with "Blackberry Way."

February 15. Vickie Jones is arrested in a Fort Myers, Florida, concert for impersonating Aretha Franklin. Nobody attending the performance had requested a refund.

February 15. Sly & The Family Stone begin a four-week run atop the pop charts with "Everyday People." The recording is arguably the first funk song to top the Hot 100.

Funk was a dance-oriented offshoot of soul music that originated in the late 1960s. (The term itself had been widely used in hip urban African American circles since the early decades of the twentieth century; it carried several different off-color meanings.) It originated with James Brown's live jam sessions and by Stax groups such as Booker T. and the MGs and the Bar-Kays. Sylvester Stewart, leader of the band Sly and the Family Stone, was a notable pioneer of the genre. He developed his sound as a session musician in small San Francisco recording studios during the mid-1960s before going on to superstardom with hits such as "Everyday People" and "Dance to the Music."

By the time Sly experienced career burnout in the early 1970s, the chief features of funk were sharply delineated for the next of practitioners: (1) a polyrhythmic, syncopated dance music usually centered around a repetitious, thickly-textured bass pattern, and (2) a greater reliance on instrumental ensemble playing than had been typical of either rhythm and blues or soul. Classic exponents of the style who achieved significant success included George Clinton's Parliament/Funkadelic combine, the Ohio Players, Kool and the Gang, and Earth, Wind and Fire.

The genre dominated the black music scene throughout the 1970s, absorbing elements of disco and merging its heavy backbeat with punk's rebellious attitude to create a new stylistic offshoot, funk-punk. The most popular funk-punk artists included Prince, Rick James, and Morris Day and the Time. The innovative vanguard of funk was eventually co-opted by the rap/hip hop movement. Nevertheless, it provided the foundation for virtually every black-inspired and dance genre to emerge since 1980.

February 17. Bob Dylan and Johnny Cash record "Girl From the North Country" in Nashville's CBS Studios. The track will be included on Dylan's upcoming Nashville Skyline (Columbia) album.

February 22. Led Zeppelin's eponymous debut LP (Atlantic 8216) enters the album charts. It will peak at number ten, going on to sell in excess of four million copies.

Led Zeppelin were, far and away, the most popular rock band of the 1970s. Their immense popularity played a significant role in enabling heavy metal to cross over into the industry mainstream. In addition, guitarist Jimmy Page, who also produced the band's recordings, created a new sonic vocabulary built around virtuoso guitar riffs and special electronic effects.

Zeppelin grew out of the desire by Page, who had established a reputation as one of the top session guitarists in England during the 1960s, to explore his musical ideas within a group setting. In 1966, he jumped at an offer to play bass with the Yardbirds, a popular experimental, blue-rock act best known as the launching pad for the solo careers of guitar heroes like Jeff Beck and the previously departed Eric Clapton. Page remained in the background until Beck left the Yardbirds in 1967; he then switched to lead guitar and assumed a major voice in the band's musical direction. When the remaining members of the group decided to call it a day, Page put together his own unit, tentatively named the New Yardbirds. His recruits included a teenage lead singer, Robert Plant, bassist John Paul Jones, and drummer John Bonham. They decided to base their name on one the favorite catchphrases used by the Who's Keith Moon, "going down like a lead zeppelin."

Led Zeppelin was a straightforward blues-rock affair, accented with proto-metal touches derived from the likes of San Francisco's Blue Cheer and fellow countrymen Black Sabbath. Although inherently conservative in approach, the album stood out, driven by Page's thick, power chording, Plant's intensely-keening vocals, and Bonham's pile-driving sense of rhythm. Recorded while on tour, *Led Zeppelin II* (Atlantic 8236; 1969; #1 US, #1 UK), exudes a live feel, especially the hard-rocking "Living Loving Maid (She's Just A Woman)" and "Bring It On Home." If that LP represented, as is sometimes claimed, the birth of British heavy metal, then *Led Zeppelin III* (Atlantic 7201; 1970; #1 US, #1 UK) exhibited a masterful fusion of hard rock with more intimate, acoustic material. The next album (Atlantic 7208; 1971; #2 US, #1 UK), identified only by four runes (one selected by each group member), added ancient mysticism to the band's increasingly folk-oriented leanings. It included "Stairway to Heaven"; a study in shifting instrumental textures, the track—the most revered in the Zeppelin oeuvre—opened with aching pseudo-philosophical musings accompanied by soft strumming, and slowly builds to a frenzied climax featuring a wailing electric guitar solo by Page.

With every release now assured of mega-platinum sales, the band entered a more experimental mode, branching out into reggae and funk on *Houses of the Holy* (Atlantic 7255; 1973; #1 US, #1 UK) and following that with an eclectic double-disc set, *Physical Graffiti* (Swan Song 200; 1975; #1 US, #1 UK). However, the balance of Led Zeppelin's efforts—*Presence* (Swan Song 8416; 1976; #1 US, #1 UK), the sprawling live set, *The Song Remains the Same* (Swan Song 89402; 1976; #2 US, #1 UK), *In Through the Out Door* (Swan Song 16002; 1979; #1 US, #1 UK), and the posthumous collection of studio outtakes, *Coda* (Swan Song 90051; 1982; #6 US, #4 UK) were uneven in nature.

The group decided to disband in late 1980 following Bonham's death brought on by alcohol abuse. Since then, the remaining members explored various solo and group options, with Page and Plant reuniting in the late half of the 1990s, performing Zeppelin classics on tour and releasing *No Quarter – Unledded* (Atlantic 82706; 1994; #4 US, #7 UK), comprised of ethnically updated versions of their 1970s materials (plus four new cuts). In the meantime, all of the band's original LPs as well as various anthologies have been reissued on compact disc and DVD.

February 24. The Jimi Hendrix Experience perform at the Royal Albert Hall—their last British performance.

March 1. The Doors' lead singer Jim Morrison is arrested during a Miami concert for allegedly exposing himself on stage. While Morrison's anti-establishment behavior made him a counter-culture hero to 1960s youth, law and order authorities began a campaign of harassment that sometimes resulted in the cancellation of his group's concerts. He would be tried and found guilty of indecent exposure and profanity, receiving a sentence of eight months' hard labor (he would die in Paris while the sentence was on appeal).

March 3. Led Zeppelin record their first BBC Radio 1 session, which is later aired on *Top Gear*.

March 12. Paul McCartney marries Linda Eastman at the Marylebone registry office in London. George and Patti Harrison arrive late after a morning arrest in which they were charged with possession of 120 marijuana joints.

March 15. Cream top the British album charts with *Goodbye* (Atco; #2 U.S.), remaining there for a couple of weeks.

March 15. Tommy Roe begins a four-week stay at number one on the Hot 100 with "Dizzy" (ABC).

March 20. John Lennon marries Yoko Ono at the British Consulate Office in Gibraltar.

March 22. Marvin Gaye tops the British charts with "I Heard It Through the Grapevine."

March 25. John Lennon and Yoko Ono launch their "bed-in" at the Amsterdam Hilton hotel.

April 1. Ambrose Slade (renamed Slade in the early 1970s) debut live at Walsall (England) Town Hall.

April 1. The Beach Boys announce plans to sue their record company, Capitol, for $2,041,446.64 in outstanding royalties.

April 10. Blood, Sweat & Tears' eponymous second LP (Columbia 9720) earns a gold record. A leading force in the big band-rock vogue—which included Chicago, Lighthouse, and Colisseum—Blood, Sweat & Tears would reach number two on the Hot 100 with three singles—"You've Made Me So Very Happy" (Columbia 44776), "Spinning Wheel" (Columbia 44871), and "And When I Die" (Columbia 45008)—all of which achieved gold status that year. According to Joel Whitburn's Pop Annual series, they were the 12th most successful recording act in 1969. Just when young listeners stopped buying the album, a more mature audience began to pick up on its sophisticated arrangements, which tied together a diverse array of material, including twentieth century classical (Satie), gospel ("God Bless the Child"), and Tin Pan Alley songcraft ("Sometimes in Winter"). It would remain a solid catalog seller in the upcoming decades, gaining triple platinum recognition November 21, 1986.

April 12. The 5th Dimension reach number one on the pop charts with a medley culled from the hit musical, *Hair*, "Aquarius"/"Let the Sunshine In" (Soul City), remaining there for six consecutive weeks. It would be recognized as the top single of the year, further solidifying the black quintet's status as one of the leading soft rock acts in the business.

April 14. "The Ballad of John and Yoko" is recorded by two of the Beatles: Paul McCartney plays bass, drums, and piano, while John Lennon is responsible for the guitars.

April 16. Desmond Dekker & the Aces top the Britain singles charts with "The Israelites," the first Jamaican artist to accomplish this feat. [beginning of 1968]

April 22. In a ceremony on the roof of Apple headquarters in London, John Lennon changes his middle name from "Winston" to "Ono."

April 22. The Who perform their rock opera, *Tommy*, for the first time at the Institute of Technology, Bolton, England.

May 10. The Moody Blues begin a two-week stint atop the British charts with *On the Threshold of a Dream*; it is their first LP to accomplish this feat.

May 10. Frank Sinatra's "My Way" enters the British Top 10 for the first time; it returns to the Top 50 eight more times in the future.

May 10. The Turtles perform at the White House as guests of Tricia Nixon. Members of the group allegedly snort cocaine off Abraham Lincoln's desk.

May 23. The Grateful Dead perform outside the United States for the first time at "The Hollywood Rock Music Festival" in Newcastle-Under-Lyme, England.

May 24. The guests on BBC-TV's *33 & A Third Revolutions Per Monkee* include Fats Domino Julie Driscoll, Jerry Lee Lewis, Little Richard, and all four members of the Monkees.

May 24. The Beatles with Billy Preston begin a five-week run atop the Hot 100 with "Get Back" (Apple).

May 24. Bob Dylan goes number one on the British charts with *Nashville Skyline*.

May 25. John Lennon and Yoko Ono begin an eight-day "bed-in" promoting world peace at Montreal's Hotel La Reine Elizabeth.

May 31. Chicago Transit Authority (later shortened to "Chicago") enter the *Billboard* album charts with their eponymous debut (Columbia 8). It peaks at number seventeen, eventually achieving double platinum sales.

Chicago is widely held to be the first American rock group to include a horn section, thereby providing the impetus for the big band rock genre of the late 1960s. Although initially considered an experimental, albums-oriented recording act, only the Supremes, the Temptations and Beach Boys, among U.S. groups, have enjoyed greater success on the singles charts.

The band formed in Chicago in 1966; they were initially named the Chicago Transit Authority by manager and producer James William Guercio, then known for his work with the Buckinghams. Original members included Robert Lamm (vocals, keyboards), Terry Kath (vocals, guitar), Dan Seraphine (drums), Lee Loughnane (trumpet, vocals), James Pankow (trombone), and Walter Parazaider (woodwinds). Vocalist/bassist/organist Peter Cetera was added during the group's developmental years.

Their double-disk LP, *Chicago Transit Authority*, won critical raves for its deft blend of jazz and progressive rock styles complemented by politically leftist lyrics (penned primarily by Lamm). "Free Form Guitar," with its extended feedback-drenched jam, was as avant-garde as anything in rock during that Woodstock summer. Shortening their name to Chicago, the band followed with a string of more pop-leaning albums—*Chicago II* (Columbia 24; 1970; #4), *Chicago III* (Columbia 30110; 1971; #2), *Chicago V* (Columbia 31102; 1972; #1), *Chicago VI* (Columbia 32400; 1973; #1), *Chicago VII* (Columbia 32810; 1974; #1), *Chicago VIII* (Columbia 33100; 1975; #1), *Chicago X* (Columbia 34200; 1976; #3), *Chicago XI* (Columbia 34860; 1977; #6)—all featuring variations of their name logo on the cover. Their commercially successful approach consisted of romantic ballads (generally delivered by Cetera's high tenor)—most notably, "Saturday in the Park" (Columbia 45657; 1972; #3), "Just You 'N' Me" (Columbia 45933; 1973; #4), "(I've Been) Searchin' So Long" (Columbia 46020; 1974; #9), "Old Days" (Columbia 10131; 1975; #5), "If You Leave Me Now" (Columbia 10390; 1976; #1), and "Baby, What A Big Surprise" (Columbia 10620; 1977; #4)—punctuated by mildly uptempo rockers.

Kath's accidental death coincided with a downturn in the group's fortunes. Although sticking to their tried-and-true formula, *Hot Streets* (Columbia 35512; 1978; #12), featuring ex-Stephen Stills guitarist Donnie Dacus, suffered from mediocre song material and changing industry trends (disco and punk had both entered the pop music mainstream). Nevertheless, Chicago soldiered on, bolstered by occasional blockbuster hits like "Hard To Say I'm Sorry" (Full Moon 29979; 1982; #1) and "Look Away" (Reprise 27766; 1988; #1). Still a big concert draw, especially with the aging baby boomers, their recent studio work—e.g., the big band revival-styled *Night and Day* (Giant/RCA 24615; 1995; #90), which featured passable covers of classic Tin Pan Alley material, and *Chicago 25 – The Christmas Album* (Chicago 3035; 1998; #47)—reveals a band in the throes of a musical identity crisis.

May 31. The Plastic Ono Band record "Give Peace a Chance" (Apple) during John Lennon and Yoko Ono's "bed-in."

Although best remembered for his recorded work with the British Invasion group, the Beatles, Lennon (b. October 9, 1940) enjoyed a productive—if uneven—solo career. His studio output—while ranging widely from avant-garde experiments, to edgy political protest, to more standard pop fare—was always characterized by an uncompromising integrity and idiosyncratic richness of expression that sometimes achieved a poetic beauty unparalleled among commercial music songsmiths.

Lennon's decision to pursue a career path apart from the Beatles appears to have been at least in part the result of his personal relationship with pop artist Yoko Ono. While still with the band, he teamed with Ono to produce two free-form musical collages, *Unfinished Music No. 1: Two Virgins* (Apple 5001; 1968), packaged in a brown paper wrapping to avoid legal problems over the full-frontal nude picture of the couple which graced the cover, and *Unfinished Music No. 2: Life With the Lions* (Zapple 3357; 1969). *Life With the Lions* epitomized the problems associated with allowing full rein to self-indulgent whims, including such non-songs as "Baby's Heartbeat," a home recording depicting the death of the couple's unborn child, and "Two Minutes Silence."

Following a series of highly publicized peace activities in 1969, he released two more LPs, *Wedding Album* (Apple 3361; 1969), another collaboration with Ono featuring autobiographical snippets punctuated by amateurish electronic noodling, and pop-oriented *The Plastic Ono Band – Live Peace In Toronto 1969* (Apple 3362; 1969; #10). The latter record—which included guitarist Eric Clapton, bassist Klaus Voorman, and drummer Alan White—featured two charting singles, the flower-power anthem "Give Peace a Chance" (Apple 1809; 1969; #14 US, #2 UK) and the drug withdrawal dirge, "Cold Turkey" (Apple 1813; 1969; #30 US, #14 UK).

On the heels of the Beatles' official breakup, Lennon recorded his widely regarded masterpiece, the Phil Spector-produced *John Lennon: Plastic Ono Band* (Apple 3372; 1970; #6 US, #11 UK). Allegedly a product of his primal scream therapy, songs such as "Mother," "Working Class Hero," and "God" reflected a lifetime of resentment and barely suppressed rage. He returned to a more commercial groove with *Imagine* (Apple 3379; 1971; #1 US, #1 UK); the idealistic title track (Apple 1840; 1971; #3) remains one of the most revered compositions of the rock era. Perhaps reflecting his legal fight with U.S. immigration authorities, later releases—the double-disk live set featuring support by Elephant's Memory, *Sometime in New York City* (Apple 3392; 1972; #48 US, #11 UK), the densely-layered *Mind Games* (Apple 3414; 1973; #9 US, #13 UK), an intensely-interpreted collection of stylistically-diversified covers with Nilsson, *Pussy Cats* (RCA 0570; 1974; #60), and *Walls and Bridges* (Apple 3416; 1974; #1 US, #6 UK), which included the number one single, "Whatever Gets You Thru the Night" (Apple 1874; 1974), featuring Elton John—contained some memorable songs amidst much material of a more pedestrian nature. Although the cover LP, *Rock 'N' Roll* (Apple 3419; 1975; #6 US, #6 UK), was marketed as a loving tribute to the classic 1950s hits by the likes of Little Richard, Gene Vincent, Chuck Berry, and Buddy Holly, more than one observer speculated that Lennon's muse had deserted him.

Following a period focusing on child-rearing responsibilities, Lennon produced another collaboration with Ono, *Double Fantasy* (Geffen 2001; 1980; #1 US, #1 UK). Although the album's split format (with Lennon and Ono each fronting on seven tracks) diluted critical response, the tuneful, richly-textured singles—"(Just Like) Starting Over" (Geffen 49604; 1980; #1 US, #1 UK), "Woman" (Geffen 49644; 1981; #2 US, #1 UK), and "Watching the Wheels" (Geffen 49695; 1981; #10 US, #30 UK)—ranked with Lennon's finest work. This new creative phase was cut short by Lennon's assassination on December 8, 1980, outside his New York City co-op complex. However, previously unreleased material has continued to surface as Lennon's legacy has achieved increasing stature over the intervening years. Notable posthumous releases have included *Milk and Honey* (Polydor 817160-2; 1983; #11 US, #3 UK); a *Playboy* interview, *A Heart Play: Unfinished Dialogue* (Polydor 817238-1; 1984); 1972 concert material, *Live in New York City* (Polydor 12451; 1986; #41 US, #55 UK); a compilation of 1974-1975 studio sessions, *Menlove Ave.* (Polydor 12533; 1986); and the four-CD collection of alternative takes, live rarities, and home recordings, *John Lennon Anthology* (Polydor 8 30614-2; 1998; #99 US, #62 UK).

June 7. Blind Faith—one of the first so-called "supergroups"—make their live debut at a free concert in London's Hyde Park.

June 28. Henry Mancini peaks at number one on the pop charts with "Love Theme from Romeo & Juliet" (RCA), remaining there for two weeks.

July 3. Brian Jones, then age twenty-seven, drowns under the influence of drugs and alcohol after taking a midnight swim in his pool. His body is found by Swedish girlfriend Anna Wohlin.

July 5. The Rolling Stones give a free concert in London's Hyde Park as a tribute to Brian Jones. The estimated 250,000 attendees witness Mick Jagger's recital of an extract from Percy Bysshe Shelley's *Adonais* (followed by the release of 3,500 butterflies) and guitarist Mick Taylor's live debut with the band.

July 11. David Bowie's *Space Oddity* is released. It becomes an FM radio staple, and a steady seller for decades.

July 12. Zager & Evans head up the Hot 100 for six weeks with the sardonic sci-fi saga, "In the Year 2525 (Exordium & Terminus)" (RCA) In something of an anomaly, the single—penned by the duo's Rick Evans—would be their only recording to make the charts.

August 23. The Rolling Stones begin a four-week stay atop the pop charts with "Honky Tonk Women" (London).

August 31. Elvis Presley begins a four-week run at the Las Vegas International Hotel, his first live performances since 1961. He would reportedly gross $1.5 million overall. The venue celebrated by including an Elvis Special on the menu: polk salad with corn muffins and honey.

September 13. Creedence Clearwater Revival score their only British chart topper with "Bad Moon Rising."

September 13. Creedence Clearwater Revival begin a four-week run atop the album charts with *Green River* (Fantasy).

September 20. The Archies begin a four-week run at number one on the Hot 100 with "Sugar, Sugar" (Calendar).

September 22. The ABC weekly television show, *The Music Scene*, airs for the first time. Booked artists include James Brown, Crosby, Stills, Nash & Young, Cass Elliot, Janis Joplin, Sly & the Family Stone, and Stevie Wonder.

September 27. Creedence Clearwater Revival peak at number two with "Green River" (Fantasy). It was the band's third straight single to just miss the top spot, following on the heels of "Proud Mary" and "Bad Moon Rising." They would remain a favorite trivia question for deejays as one of the most popular acts in rock history to fail to achieve a number one hit.

September 30. Crosby, Stills & Nash earn a gold record for their eponymous debut LP (Atlantic 8229). One of the first in a wave of supergroups to populate the rock scene during the progressive rock era, each member brought a solid resume—as well as extraordinary songwriting and singing skills—to the union. Of even greater significance, the band was instrumental in returning soft rock to preeminence within the music industry.

They formed as a trio in mid-1968; David Crosby—although still actively collaborating with many West Coast artists—had recently left the Byrds, Stephen Stills had been a key member of the folk-rock ensemble, Buffalo Springfield, and Graham Nash part of the English beat group, the Hollies. The eponymous debut album (Atlantic 8229; 1969; #6) was a watershed musical event during an eventful summer that saw the first manned flight to the moon and the Woodstock Festival. Its freshness derived from ignoring many rock conventions of the day—e.g., guitar feedback, extended drum solos—in favor of close vocal harmonies and crystalline acoustic guitar textures. Recruiting Neil Young, formerly of Buffalo Springfield and already two albums into a successful solo career, the band recorded *Déjà Vu* (Atlantic 7200; 1970; #1; also featuring drummer Dallas Taylor and bassist Greg Reeves), which incorporated electric guitars and greater rhythmic energy than its predecessor. Beset by the usual ego problems, CSN&Y split up in August 1970, releasing the uneven live double-LP, *Four-Way Street* (Atlantic 2-902; 1971; #1), posthumously.

With all four principals pursuing relatively successful solo careers, the group reunited for a 1974 tour; however, no recordings were made at that time. While Young was producing a series of uncompromising albums that attempted to recast punk within the evolutionary framework of progressive rock, the original trio reformed to record *CSN* (Atlantic 19104; 1977; #2), a rather bland affair that included the hit ballad, "Just A Song Before I Go" (Atlantic 3401; 1977; #7). Yet another collaboration resulted in another slick, MOR outing, *Daylight Again* (Atlantic 19360; 1982; #8), followed by the live set, *Allies* (Atlantic 80075; 1983; #45). This edition of the band was effectively quashed by Crosby's legal difficulties due to drugs and firearms violations. While out on bail, he appeared with Stills, Nash, and Young for Live Aid; the foursome would later tour and record *American Dream* (Atlantic 81888; 1988; #16) and *Looking Forward* (Atlantic 47436; 1999; #26). Between these projects the group (sans the ever difficult Young) would release *Live It Up* (Atlantic 82101; 1990; #57) and *After the Storm* (Atlantic 82654; 1994; #98). Despite the declining public interest in Crosby, Stills & Nash's new material, continuing as a group (preferably with the dynamic counterpoint ensuing from Young's active involvement) appeared—in the face of their moribund solo careers—to be their only viable artistic and commercial option.

October 18. The Temptations' "I Can't Get Next to You" (Gordy) tops the pop charts for two weeks. The song was written by the group's producer Norman Whitfield and Barrett Strong, best known for recording one of the first Motown hits, the rock standard "Money." It was the quartet's most popular single in a year where they were surpassed only by Creedence Clearwater Revival in terms of chart success.

November 1. Elvis Presley continues his artistic and commercial revival, peaking at number one on the Hot 100 with "Suspicious Minds" (RCA).

November 8. The 5th Dimension begin a three-week stay atop the pop charts with "Wedding Bell Blues" (Soul City).

November 8. The Soul Children peak at number fifty-two on the Hot 100 with "The Sweeter He Is – Part I" (Stax 0050).

With soft rock a hot commodity in the late 1960s, Stax Records attempted to cash in on the trend with the Soul Children. Formed by the label's resident songwriting/ production team, Isaac Hayes and David Porter, the group consisted of lead singer John Colbert (born in Greenville, Mississippi and raised in Memphis), Shelbra Bennett, Anita Lewis, and Norman West. They recorded fifteen R&B hits between 1968 and 1978, most notably "The Sweeter He Is – Part I" (#7 r&b), "Hearsay" (Stax 0119; 1972; #44 pop, #5 r&b), and "I'll Be the Other Woman" (Stax 0182; 1973; #36 pop, #3 r&b). When Stax went bankrupt, the Soul Children switched to Epic Records. Colbert would go solo in the early 1980s, placing eight singles on the R&B charts as J. Blackfoot, the biggest of which was "Taxi" (Sound Town 0004; 1983; #90 pop, #4 r&b).

November 29. The Beatles reach number one on the Hot 100 with "Come Together" (Apple).

December 6. The Altamont concert takes place. It would come to symbolize the dark underside of the rock music festival movement, a bracing rejoinder to the optimism engendered by Woodstock and the flower power generation. Indeed, many cultural observers would credit it with effectively terminating the ascendancy of counterculture values and the belief in the perfectibility of American society—a society greatly changed by the civil rights movement, feminism, anti-war demonstrations, and the like during the 1960s.

The concert was the brainchild of the Rolling Stones' entourage; in the face of widespread charges of price gauging during their 1969 U.S. tour, the group embraced the idea of a free concert in the San Francisco area when their scheduled commitments had been fulfilled. After being disappointed their efforts to secure San Francisco's Golden Gate Park and—in the days immediately prior to the show—the Sears Point Speedway, concert organizers decided to hold the event on December 6 at Altamont Speedway, a hot, dry, dusty venue located in the vicinity of Livermore, California. The Stones—hoping for a public relations coup of major proportions—opened the concert to major acts based on the West Coast and sanctioned a film crew to capture the proceedings for posterity.

From the outset, the limited time to prepare the venue resulted in compromised food, water, toilet, and parking facilities. An estimated 300,000 fans would converge on the site, clogging the access road for ten miles. In retrospect, the most questionable planning decision involved hiring the Hell's Angels Motorcycle Club as the security force, payment coming in beer valued at $500. From the outset of the concert, with Santana delivering the initial set, the gang behaved aggressively, beating audience members who surged too close to the stage, and running their bikes recklessly through the crowd. During the Jefferson Airplane's performance, they seemed even more out of control, knocking vocalist Marty Balin senseless when he moved to quell one violent altercation.

The Angels seemed a bit more restrained, while the Flying Burrito Brothers and Crosby, Stills, Nash & Young performed at the peak of the afternoon heat, but lead vocalist Mick Jagger was visibly nervous from the outset of the Stones' set about the violence clearly visible in front of him. Jagger, along with guitarist Keith Richards, repeatedly implored the Angels to cease the attacks. The mayhem climaxed as the group was finishing "Under My Thumb." An eighteen-year-old African American, Meredith Hunter, was beaten and stabbed to death by gang members after he drew a handgun in self-defense. Unaware of the fatal episode, the Stones stopped playing shortly thereafter, and quickly exited via a nearby helicopter.

The mainstream and underground press alike would place the blame on the Stones and their aides as much as the perpetrators of much of the violence, the makeshift security force. The group, in turn, sued the Sears Point Speedway management for $10 million, alleging breach of contract and fraud. Large-scale outdoor concerts and festivals would continue to be held, albeit with an increasingly professional—even corporate—demeanor.

December 6. Steam begin a two-week stint at the summit of the pop charts with "Na Na Hey Hey Kiss Him Goodbye" (Fontana).

December 20. Peter, Paul and Mary climb to the summit of the Hot 100 with the John Denver-penned "Leaving on a Jet Plane" (Warner Bros.).

December 20. The Rolling Stones reach number one on the British charts with *Let It Bleed*.

December 27. *Led Zeppelin II* tops the album charts. It will sell over six million copies stateside alone.

December 27. Diana Ross and the Supremes reach number one with "Someday We'll Be Together" (Motown). It would be the trio's swan song, with Ross embarking upon a solo career immediately thereafter.

December 30. Peter Tork buys out of his Monkees contract for $160,000, which leaves him broke.

1970

❄

1970. *American Top 40*, a syndicated radio program providing a countdown of the top forty positions of the *Billboard* Hot 100 each week, makes its debut. Original host, Casey Kasem—one of the most recognizable broadcast voices in America—will remain with the show for eighteen consecutive years.

January 3. The Beatles record their last song together, "I Me Mine." It would later serve as the title for George Harrison's autobiography.

January 3. B. J. Thomas begins a four-week stay at the top of the pop charts with "Raindrops Keep Fallin' On My Head" (Scepter). Thomas—a journeyman balladeer seasoned with a dash of country intonation and attitude—enjoys far-and-away the biggest hit of his career thanks to its high profile placement in the immensely popular film, *Butch Cassidy and the Sundance Kid*, which stars Paul Newman and Robert Redford.

January 4. Keith Moon—who was not licensed to drive—accidentally runs over his chauffeur, Neil Boland, when trying to elude a gang of skin heads following an altercation in a Hatfield, England, pub.

January 6. The hottest group of the day, Crosby, Stills, Nash & Young, play in Great Britain for the first time at London's Royal Albert Hall.

January 10. The Jackson 5 burst onto the pop scene with "I Want You Back" (Motown 1157), which reaches number one on the R&B charts (four weeks), duplicating that feat three weeks later on the pop survey. Freddie Perren—who co-wrote the song with former schoolmate Fonce Mizell, with further input from Motown head Berry Gordy Jr. and producer Deke Richards—would later recount the circumstances behind the creation of the single:

[Deke] said, "here's one way to really get into things fast: Find someone who's cold and write a hit on them." Gladys Knight at the time was cold, so we wrote this song. It just started out kind of like a track that sounded really good, so we started molding it for Gladys.

[Upon hearing the track, Gordy] said, "We just signed these five brothers out of Gary, Indiana, and this sounds like a lively young track. Why don't you rewrite the song for them, to be like a young guys' group?" Adam White and Fred Bronson. *The Billboard Book of Number One Rhythm & Blues Hits*. Billboard Books, 1991.

January 14. John Lennon's erotic lithographs are formally exhibited in a London art gallery. Police close the show two days later, removing eight prints as evidence for possible prosecution under the Obscene Publications Act.

January 14. Diana Ross appears with the Supremes—at the Frontier Hotel, Las Vegas—for the last time.

January 15. Diana Ross officially leaves the Supremes for a solo career. Born in Detroit in 1944, Diana Ross first gained fame as the lead singer of the Supremes. Ross' sexy, malleable voice—combined with the group's charm school image and photogenic good looks—enabled them to cross over to the pop mainstream, a hitherto unprecedented achievement within the rhythm and blues/soul genre.

Her departure from the group seemed a foregone conclusion when, in 1967, they underwent a name change to "Diana Ross and the Supremes." Motown Records owner Berry Gordy had long felt Ross possessed sufficient star quality to warrant a solo in both a music business and motion pictures. Not only did her initial solo recordings—the singles "Reach Out and Touch (Somebody's Hand)" (Motown 1163; 1970; #20) and "Ain't No Mountain High Enough" (Motown 1169; 1970; #1) and eponymous album (Motown 711; 1970; #19)—sell well, but she garnered high Nielsen ratings for her 1971 TV special (followed by a successful soundtrack LP) and an Oscar nomination playing singer Billie Holiday in the film, *Lady Sings the Blues*. Ross maintained her momentum throughout the decade, appearing in another big-budget movie, *Mahogany* (1975), and releasing a string of best-selling, if artistically uneven, records, including *Lady Sings the Blues* (Motown 758; 1972; #1), *Touch Me In The Morning* (Motown 771; 1973; #5), *Diana Ross* (Motown 861; 1976; #5), *Diana* (Motown 936; 1980; #2), and four number one singles—the bland ballads "Touch Me In The Morning" (Motown 1239; 1973) and "Theme From Mahogany" (Motown 1377; 1975) as well as the disco-flavored "Love Hangover" (Motown 1392; 1976) and "Upside Down" (Motown 1494; 1980).

By the time her collaboration with Lionel Richie, the theme song to the film *Endless Love* (Motown 1519; 1981), had achieved a nine-week run at number one on the *Billboard* Hot 100 charts, Ross had signed a contract with RCA. Despite regular appearances on the charts over the next half-decade, she moved back to Motown (then owned by EMI London) in 1987. Despite her high visibility in the entertainment tabloids, Ross—who took a considerable amount of time off to raise a family—failed to place a recording on either the singles or albums charts from that point onward.

January 17. The soundtrack to the film, *Easy Rider*, is awarded a gold record. The LP includes tracks by top rock acts like the Byrds and Steppenwolf.

January 21. *Change of Habit*, Elvis Presley's last feature film, is released. Unlike most of his previous work, it is not a musical.

January 25. John Lennon and Yoko Ono completely shave their heads and declare 1970 to be "Year One." Their hair is donated to a North London interracial community center, which auctions it off as a fundraiser.

January 26. John Lennon writes, records, and mixes "Instant Karma"—with the assistance of producer Phil Spector—all in one day.

January 31. "I Want You Back" (Motown)—originally composed for Gladys Knight and the Pips—becomes the Jackson 5's first number one hit (#2 U.K.).

February 4. John Lennon and Yoko Ono auction off more of their hair to raise funds for the Black Power movement.

February 6. A *New York Post* reporter discloses the connection between the lyrics of five numbers from The Beatles' *White Album* and Charles Manson's role in the murder of actress Sharon Tate and others at Roman Polanski's Hollywood home.

February 7. *Led Zeppelin II* goes number one in England. It remains on the charts for 138 weeks in the United States, selling more than six million copies there.

February 7. The Dutch band, Shocking Blue, make it to the summit of the pop charts with "Venus" (Colossus). They are the first band from the Continent to accomplish this feat, thereby paving the way for an onslaught of Euro-rock acts, particularly from Germany and the Low Countries. "Venus," penned by band member Robbie Van Leeuwen, will return to number one in September 1986 via an updated post-disco arrangement by English girl group, Bananarama.

February 12. John Lennon performs "Instant Karma" on Top of the Pops—he is the first Beatle to appear on the show since 1966.

February 14. Motown Chartbusters, Vol. 3—a compilation including hits by the Four Tops, Diana Ross and the Supremes, the Temptations, and Stevie Wonder—tops the British charts.

February 14. Sly & the Family Stone begin a two-week stint atop the Hot 100 with "Thank You Falettinme Be Mice Elf Again"/"Everybody Is a Star" (Epic).

February 14. The Who perform at Leeds University, England. It is recorded for the band's next LP release, *Live at Leeds*.

February 17. Joni Mitchell announces she is retiring from live performing while onstage at London's Royal Albert Hall. She would be giving concerts again by the end of the year.

February 21. Simon and Garfunkel's LP, *Bridge Over Troubled Water*, goes number one on the British charts; it spends 41 weeks there, returning to the top eight more times. It remains on the charts for more than three hundred weeks.

February 28. Fleetwood Mac's guitarist, Peter Green, tells a *New Musical Express* interviewer that he plans to give all his money away. After being committed to a mental hospital in 1973, he restarts his music career in the 1990s.

February 28. Simon and Garfunkel's gospel-inflected "Bridge Over Troubled Water" (Columbia) tops of the Hot 100, remaining there for six weeks—the longest run of any single that year. Widely recognized as Paul Simon's greatest composition, it is awarded a gold record while still on the charts. The greatest impediment to more impressive sales figures is its presence in the chart-topping album of the same name; one of the most popular recordings of that era, it is certified 5x platinum on November 21, 1986. Having little left to prove at this point, the duo—also torn by differing career aspirations—would call it a day.

March 6. Awareness Records releases the Charles Manson LP, *Lie*. Manson was in prison at the time due to his role in the Sharon Tate murders.

March 7. Creedence Clearwater Revival begin a two-week stint at number two on the Hot 100 with "Travelin' Band" (Fantasy 637). It is the band's fourth number two hit ("Lookin' Out My Back Door" will make it five on October 3); they never make it to the top spot.

March 7. Simon and Garfunkel's *Bridge Over Troubled Water* (Columbia) begins a ten-week run atop the album charts. It becomes one of the top-selling LPs of all time.

March 8. Diana Ross performs solo for the first time in Framingham, Massachusetts.

March 11. Grammy Award winners include Joe South for Song of the Year with "Games People Play," Crosby, Stills & Nash for Best New Artist, and the Fifth Dimension for Record of the Year with "Aquarius/Let the Sunshine In."

March 14. Brook Benton—one of the most popular recording artists around a decade earlier—makes a spectacular curtain call by taking "Rainy Night in Georgia" (Cotillion 44057) to number one on the R&B charts. Arif Mardin who produced the record on November 5, 1969, at Miami's Criteria studios, would later recall that honey-toned song stylist was not initially enamored with the idea of interpreting Tony Joe White's compositions:

He said, "I don't want to sing a song about Georgia." I said, "The man isn't crazy, Brook, he wants to get out of there." Brook replied, "I see your point." White and Bronson. 1991.

March 16. Tammi Terrell dies of a brain tumor after collapsing into Marvin Gaye's arms while performing the duet "That's All You Need to Get By." She had had eight brain operations in eighteen months.

March 21. Aretha Franklin reaches number one on the R&B charts with "Call Me" (Atlantic 2706), remaining there for two weeks. The single missed the pop Top 10, although it spends more time in the Hot 100 than any of her releases since 1968's "Sweet Sweet Baby) Since You're Been Gone."

March 21. Santana peak at number nine on the Hot 100 with "Evil Ways" (Columbia 45069).

From Latin rock innovators in the late 1960s, the group—essentially guitarist Carlos Santana and a continually changing cast of rock journeymen, session players, and guest stars—has flirted with psychedelia, electric blues, jazz fusion, and pop influences within a broad progressive rock context. Relegated to commercial limbo for the better part of two decades, Santana revived his career in the late 1990s, receiving nine Grammy Awards for the best-selling LP, *Supernatural* (Arista 19080; 1999; #1).

The Mexican-born Santana formed the Santana Blues Band in October 1966 amidst San Francisco flower-power movement. After a gestation period spent largely in the Bay Area (during which time their name was shortened), the group's distinctive sound—built around Santana's fluid, lyrical guitar lines and an augmented rhythm section originally including of drummer Michael Shrieve, percussionist Jose "Chepito" Areas, and conga player Mike Carabello—captured the public's imagination during the August 1969 Woodstock Festival. The Latin-derived rhythms and psychedelic blues of the first three albums—*Santana* (Columbia 9781; 1969; #4), *Abraxas* (Columbia 30130; 1970; #1), and *Santana* (Columbia 30595; 1971; #1; commonly referred to as *Santana III*—elevated Santana to superstar status. *Caravanserai* (Columbia 31610; 1972; #8), however, signaled a shift in the direction of jazz-inflected jamming. Much of the band's 1970s output—most notably, *Welcome* (Columbia 32445; 1973; #25), *Borboletta* (Columbia 33135; 1974; #20), *Moonflower* (Columbia 34914; 1977; #10; part live/part studio), and *Inner Secrets* (Columbia 35600; 1978; #27)—continued to explore the fusion genre.

The release of *Zebop!* (Columbia 37158; 1981; #9), featuring the single, "Winning" (Columbia 01050;

1981; #17), and *Shango* (Columbia 38122; 1982; #22), which included "Hold On" (Columbia 03160; 1982; #15) and "Nowhere to Run" (Columbia 03376; 1982; #66) reflected a renewed commitment to the pop mainstream. While displaying competent musicianship and passionate social commentary, follow-up albums such as the Grammy-winning *Blues for Salvador* (Columbia 40875; 1987), *Spirits Dancing in the Flesh* (Columbia 46065; 1990; #85), and *Milagro* (Polydor 513197; 1992) experienced a sales drop-off in the face of mixed reviews. The eclectic *Supernatural*—featuring studio contributions by the likes of Dave Matthews, Everlast, Lauren Hill, Wyclef Jean, Eric Clapton, and Matchbox 20's Rob Thomas, who sang on the number one single, "Smooth" (Arista 13718; 1999; #1)—changed all that, lingering in the upper reaches of the *Billboard* LP charts for more than two years. Despite the glut of CD reissues and compilations, it was perhaps inevitable that Santana would unable to maintain such a high level of success. A member of the Rock and Roll Hall of Fame, he nevertheless remains an American institution likely to command attention for the duration of his career.

April 1. Phil Spector employs fifty musicians to record the orchestral scores to the Beatles tracks, "The Long and Winding Road" and "Across the Universe." The bill is $1914.

April 4. Brinsley Schwarz's promotion company sends 133 British journalists to see the band perform on a bill with Van Morrison at New York's Fillmore East. In addition to the $204,000 bill, the journalists—who arrived a day late in hung over condition due to mechanical problems with the plane—gneerally wrote scathing reviews. The band played poorly due to being held up until the last minute by visa problems.

April 4. Crosby, Stills, Nash & Young head up the album charts with *Déjà Vu* (Atlantic).

April 4. The Jackson 5 begin a four-week run atop the R&B charts with "ABC" (Motown 1163).

April 10. Paul McCartney issues a press statement making the breakup of the Beatles official.

April 10. Doors vocalist Jim Morrison asks a Boston audience if "anyone wants to see my genitals." The management turns of the power, bringing the concert to a premature end.

April 11. The Beatles steamroll to the summit of the Hot 100 with the title track from their last LP of original material, *Let It Be* (Apple). With the Fab Four generating maximum publicity over news surrounding their imminent breakup, the single—which holds the top spot for a couple of weeks on the way to double platinum sales—sets a record for the highest entry position in the Hot 100, making its appearance at number six on March 21.

April 11. Peter Green expresses his wish to leave Fleetwood Mac while touring in Germany. In order to avoid breach of contract, he agrees to finish the current tour.

April 14. Creedence Clearwater Revival perform in Great Britain for the first time, at London's Royal Albert Hall.

April 17. Johnny Cash performs for Richard Nixon at the White House. President Nixon requests that he play "A Boy Named Sue."

April 19. Eurovision Song Contest winner Dana heads up the British charts with "All Kinds of Everything."

April 20. The *New York Times* reports that Catholic and Protestant youth groups have adopted the Beatles' Yellow Submarine as a religious symbol.

April 26. Norman Greenbaum peaks at number one on the British charts with "Spirit in the Sky." The song repeated the feat with Doctor and the Medics in 1986 and Gareth Gates in 2003.

May 2. Tyrone Davis tops the R&B charts with "Turn Back the Hands of Time" (Dakar 616), remaining there for two weeks. According 4 Brothers record executive, Jack Daniels, "Barry [Despenza] found that soft style that Tyrone developed." Despenza himself would credit WOPA-Chicago disc jockey Big Bill Hill: "He told me I had Tyrone singing too hard. He said he'd never make it singing that way" (White and Bronson 1991).

May 4. Ohio National Guard troops kill four students and wound eleven others at a Kent State University demonstration at the escalation of the Vietnam War. The incident spurs Neil Young to write the Crosby, Stills, Nash & Young hit, "Ohio."

May 11. The soundtrack to the film documentary, *Woodstock*, is released. The triple-disc set goes gold within two weeks.

May 16. Crosby, Stills, Nash & Young go number one on the album charts with *Déjà Vu* (Atlantic).

May 16. The Moments commence a five-week stay atop the pop R&B charts with "Love on a Two-Way Street" (Stang 5012). The million seller, co-written and produced by Sylvia Robinson, would put All Platinum on the map.

May 16. The England World Cup Squad head up the British charts with "Back Home," followed (in descending rank order) by Norman Greenbaum's "Spirit in the Sky," Christie's "Yellow River," the Moody Blues' "Question," and Tom Jones' "Daughter of Darkness."

May 20. *Let It Be*, a film offering an inside look at the twilight of the Beatles' career, premieres at the London Palladium.

May 30. Ray Stevens reaches number one on the pop charts with his composition, "Everything Is Beautiful" (Barnaby), remaining there for two weeks. The flower-power ballad—along with his acidic social commentary, "Mr. Businessman"—represents something of a new career path for Stevens, who initially found success mining satirical and nonsense humor via hits like "Ahab the Arab," "Harry, the Hairy Ape," and "Gitarzan."

June 3. The Kinks' Ray Davies has to make a six thousand-mile round trip from New York to London to record "cherry cola" in place of "Coca-Cola" on the forthcoming single, "Lola," as a result of an advertising ban.

June 13. The Beatles begin a two-week stay atop the Hot 100 with "The Long and Winding Road" (Apple). It is the band's last chart-topping single. At the same time, their album, *Let It Be* (Apple), starts a four-week run atop the album charts.

June 20. The Jackson 5's "The Love You Save" (Motown 1166) peak at number one on the R&B charts, remaining there for six weeks.

June 27. The Jackson 5 begin a two-week stint atop the Hot 100 with "The Love You Save."

July 11. Three Dog Night go number one the Hot 100 with "Mama Told Me (Not To Come)" (Dunhill/ABC), remaining there for two weeks.

July 11. *Woodstock* – the soundtrack – begins a four-week stay at number one on the album charts.

July 25. The Carpenters commence a four-week run atop the Hot 100 with "(They Long To Be) Close To You" (A&M 1183).

July 25. Neil Young and Crazy Horse peak at number fifty-five on the Hot 100 with "Cinnamon Girl" (Reprise 0911).

Neil Young is one of the great talents, albeit highly idiosyncratic, within the rock music scene. An accomplishment composer and sensitive song interpreter, his material often seemed ill-suited to his singing capabilities, reducing his vocals an off-key whine. A lyrical, intense guitar player, his extended pieces could sometimes meander aimlessly. Nevertheless, it could be argued that the refusal to be predictable, even to the point of undercutting his commercial potential, has been a major factor in his retaining a substantial following since the 1960s.

Born November 12, 1945, in Toronto, Young's earliest recordings—*Buffalo Springfield* (Atco 200; 1967; #80), *Buffalo Springfield Again* (Atco 226; 1967; #44), and *Last Time Around* (Atco 256; 1968; #42)—were as a member of the short-lived folk-rock group, Buffalo Springfield. His early solo releases—*Neil Young* (Reprise 6317; 1969), *Everybody Knows This Is Nowhere* (Reprise 6349; 1969; #34), *After the Gold Rush* (Reprise 6383; 1970; #8), and *Harvest* (Reprise 2032; 1972; #1)—combined a profound melodic gift, augmented by evocative lyrics and tight ensemble playing. Young's career—which peaked commercially with the number one single, "Heart of Gold" (Reprise 1065; 1972)—was assisted by his brief association with the supergroup, Crosby, Stills, and Nash. Two best-selling LPS—*Déjà Vu* (Atlantic 7200; 1970; #1) and the live *4 Way Street* (Atlantic 902; 1971; #1—resulted from this collaboration and, while Young remained cool to later reunions, he did contribute to *American Dream* Atlantic 81888; 1988; #16).

Beginning with his tentative experimental film soundtrack, *Journey Through the Past* (Warner Bros. 6480; 1972; #45), Young seemed committed to producing an uncompromising body of recorded work, the expectations of his audience be damned. His albums have revealed a passing interest in a wide range of styles, including techno (*Trans* [Geffen 2018; 1983; #19]), country (*Old Ways* [Geffen 24068; 1985; #75]), rhythm and blues (*This Note's For You* [Reprise 25719; 1988; #61]), rockabilly (*Everybody's Rockin'* [Geffen 4013; 1983; #46]), and white noise (*Arc/Weld* [Reprise 26746; 1991; #154]). But far more disconcerting than Young's stylistic hop-scotching has been his tendency to veer between perfunctory studio exercises to inspired masterpieces; for instance, the dissonant formalism of *On the Beach* (Reprise 2180; 1974; #16) was succeeded by harrowing tension of *Tonight's the Night* (Reprise 2221; 1975; #25), the bland, folk-pop of *Comes a Time* (Reprise 2266; 1978; #7) by the revivalist rock of *Rust Never Sleeps* (Reprise 2295; 1979; #8).

One of the few 1960s generation musicians to have openly espoused the work of postpunk bands and rappers alike, Young was inducted into the Rock and Roll Hall of Fame in 1995. Still a force in the marketplace—his collaboration with alternative rockers Pearl Jam, *Mirror Ball* (Reprise 45934; 1995), reached number five on the pop albums chart—Young appears capable of producing vital recordings well into the twenty-first century.

August 1. Stevie Wonder spends six weeks at number one on the R&B charts with "Signed, Sealed, Delivered, I'm Yours" (Tama 54196).

August 12. The Carpenters earn a gold record for the Burt Bacharach/Hal David composition, "(They Long To Be) Close To You."

August 22. Bread—featuring the vocal and songwriting talents of David Gates—becomes the latest soft rock sensation when "Make It With You" (Elektra) reaches number one on the Hot 100.

August 22. Eric Burdon and War peak at number three on the Hot 100 with "Spill the Wine" (MGM 14118).

Although early frontman Eric Burdon did not last past the debut album, War remained one of the few successful interracial funk acts well into the 1980s. Although they did not record any new material for roughly a decade beginning in the mid-1980s, the band—whose work had been covered or sampled by many R&B and alternative rock artists, including Janet Jackson, TLC, Korn, and Smash Mouth—was still releasing albums at the outset of the twenty-first century.

The band, originally billed as "Eric Burdon and War," consisted of a Los Angeles-area aggregate formerly known as Nite Shift, the former Animals vocalist, and Danish harmonica player, Lee Oskar. Following several hits featuring Burdon's keening vocals—*Eric Burdon Declares "War"* (MGM 4663; 1970; #18, *The Black-Man's Burdon* (MGM 4710; 1970; #82), and the million-selling single "Spill the Wine"—the members of War decided to operate as a separate act, signing with United Artists. Emphasizing its strong rhythmic underpinning and first-rate songwriting skills, the band released a string of trailblazing recordings, including the gold singles "Slippin' Into Darkness" (United Artists 50867; 1972; #16), "The War Is a Ghetto" (United Artists 50975; 1972; #7), "The Cisco Kid" (United Artists 163; 1973; #2) "Why Can't We Be Friends?" (United Artists 629; 1975; #6), and "Summer" (United Artists 834; 1976; #7), and the albums *All Day Music* (United Artists 5546; 1971; #16; gold record), *The War Is a Ghetto* (United Artists 5652; 1972; #1; gold record), *Deliver the Word* (United Artists 128; 1973; #6; gold record), *War Live!* (United Artists 193; 1974; #13; gold record), and *Why Can't We Be Friends?* (United Artists 441; 1975; #8; gold record).

Beset by changing fashions (most notably, the rise of disco), personnel changes and varying label support—Blue Note, MCA, RCA, Priority, Lax, Virgin, and Avenue have all released new material by the band since 1977—War has failed to match the commercial success enjoyed in the early 1970s. Nevertheless, the band—now dominated by keyboardist/vocalist Leroy Jordan and producer Jerry Goldstein—has continued to produce engaging work, ranging from film soundtrack and jazz experiments in the late 1970s to the eclectic *Peace Sign* (Avenue 76024; 1994) and Hispanic-influenced *Coleccion Latina* (Avenue; 1997), both of which featuring guest contributions from the likes of Oskar and guitarist Jose Feliciano. A competing version of War—featuring four original members of the band—began recording as Guerra ("war" in Spanish) and, later, Same Ole Band, in the late 1990s.

August 29. Ronnie Dyson begins a two-week stint at number eight on the Hot 100 with "(If You Let Me Make Love to You Then) Why Can't I Touch You?" (Columbia 45110).

Although moderately successful in the R&B market, Ronnie Dyson was best known as an actor in musicals and entertainment films. Born June 5, 1950, in Washington, D.C., he spent much of his youth in Brooklyn. His big break came when he landed the lead part in the landmark Broadway musical, *Hair*, in the late 1960s. His first hit single, "(If You Let Me Make Love To You Then) Why Can't I Touch You?" (#9 r&b), was taken from an off-Broadway musical, *Salvation*.

Dyson would place a dozen more recordings on the R&B charts through 1983, most notably "I Don't Wanna Cry" (Columbia 45240; 1970; #50 pop, #9 r&b), "One Man Band (Plays All Alone)" (Columbia 45776; 1973; #28 pop, #15 r&b), and "The More You Do It "The More I Like It Done To Me)" (Columbia 10356; 1976; #62 pop, #6 r&b). He would sign with Cotillion in the early 1980s, but failed to achieve the level of sales enjoyed in the previous decade. His biggest film role came with the satire on race relations, *Putney Swope* (1970).

August 29. Edwin Starr's "War" (Gordy 7101) goes number one on the pop charts, remaining there for three weeks. A product of the songwriting/production team of Barrett Strong and Norman Whitfield—who are presently reinventing the Temptations along similar lines—the record reflects an increasing effort on the part of Motown to compete with white progressive rock and post-folk acts in the social consciousness sweepstakes.

Edwin Starr is considered something of a one-hit wonder today. However, he'd already been active throughout as a performer, recording artist, songwriter, and producer throughout much of the 1960s before making a major splash with his snarling rendition of the anti-military anthem, "War" (Gordy 7101; 1970; #1 pop, #3 r&b).

Born Charles Hatcher on January 21, 1942, in Nashville, Tennessee, he moved with his family to Cleveland at age three. He began singing doo-wop in junior high school, eventually forming the Future Tones with four friends. They would win a local television show talent contest, hosted by "Uncle Jake," five weeks in a row. Starr's musical activities were placed on hold during a two-and-a-half year military stint. When discarded, he found that his associates were no longer interested in a professional music career. R&B band leader Bill Doggett saw Starr singing in a Cleveland club shortly thereafter, and convinced him to join his tour.

Starr seemed poised to become a major star in the mid-1960s. He'd had several solo hits on the Ric-Tic label, including the spy flick parody, "Agent Double-O-Soul" (#103; 1965; #21 pop, #8 r&b). The May 7, 1966 edition of the *Billboard* Hot 100 would include the debut of three singles for which he was responsible: he recorded "Headline News" (Ric-Tic 114; #84) as a solo artist, sang lead for the Holidays on "I'll Love You Forever" (Golden World 36; #63), and wrote and produced "Oh How Happy" (Impact 1007; #12) for the Shades of Blue.

Motown's purchase of Golden World/Ric-Tic in early 1966 led to a protracted contract dispute; as a result, Starr did not record again until some of the label's staff saw him in late 1968 on a local Detroit TV show, *20 Grand*, performing a song he'd written in 1965, "Twenty-Five Miles." They encouraged them to record the song; the single (Gordy 7083; 1969; #6 pop, #6 r&b) would become his first major crossover hit. When follow-up singles failed to do as well, Motown producer Norman Whitfield asked Starr to record a Whitfield-Barrett Strong song, "War," which had originally appeared on the Temptations' LP, *Psychedelic Shack* (Motown; 1970). Many fans, especially college students, had requested that the track be released as a single, but the label was already committed to issuing "Ball of Confusion (That's What the World Is Today)" (Gordy 7099; 1970; #3 pop, #2 r&b) as the Temptations' next disc.

Starr would garner a Grammy for Best Male R&B Vocal Performance for "War," but his next release, the Whitfield-Strong composition, "Stop the War Now" (Gordy 7104; 1970; #26 pop, #5 r&b), stalled at number twenty-six, due in part to the markedly similarity with its predecessor. While he would retain a black following throughout the 1970s—placing twelve singles on the R&B charts during that decade, including "Funky Music" (Gordy 7107; 1971; #64 pop, #6 r&b), "There You Go" (Soul 35103; 1973; #80 pop, #12 r&b), and "Contact" (20th Century 2396; 1979; #65 pop, #13 r&b)—he never placed a record in the pop Top 40 again.

September 3. It is reported that the Bob Dylan bootleg LP, *Great White Wonder*, has exceeded 350,000 in sales.

September 3. Al Wilson—guitarist with Canned Heat—is found dead in fellow band member Bob Hite's garden in Topanga Canyon, Los Angeles. He was twenty-seven years old.

September 6. Jimi Hendrix plays his last concert at the Isle of Fehmarn in Germany.

September 12. Aretha Franklin heads up the R&B charts with "Don't Play That Song (I Lied)" (Atlantic 2751), staying there for three weeks.

September 16. Jimi Hendrix joins Eric Burdon during a performance at Ronnie Scott's London jazz club. It would be his last public appearance.

September 16. Led Zeppelin wins the Best Group category in the *Melody Maker* readers' poll—the first time in eight years that the Beatles failed to outpace the competition.

September 19. Diana Ross begins a three-week stay atop the Hot 100 with "Ain't No Mountain High Enough" (Motown 1169). Nickolas Ashford—who wrote the song along with Valerie Simpson—would note that Motown president Berry Gordy wanted to place the two-minute-long climatic chorus at the front of the song: "We refused to change it, and he refused to release it. He didn't release it—the disc jockeys did. They picked it up all over the country" (White and Bronson 1991).

October 3. Dawn peak at number three on the Hot 100 with "Candida" (Bell 903).

Forerunners of the Adult Contemporary genre, Tony Orlando and Dawn recorded a string of easy listening hits during the early 1970s. The group is best remembered for the anthem depicting an ex-convict's homecoming, "Tie a Yellow Ribbon Round the Ole Oak Tree" (Bell; 1973); it would be associated with the return of the Iranian hostages in 1981, while the yellow ribbon became symbolic of a homecoming, whether of a personal nature or national in scope (e.g., war).

A protégé of Aldon Music executive Don Kirshner while still in his teens, Orlando—born Michael Anthony Orlando Cassavitis, April 3, 1944, in New York City—enjoyed a brief run as a teen idol with such Carole King-penned songs as "Halfway to Paradise" (Epic 9441; 1961; #39) and "Bless You" (Epic 9452; 1961; #15). When the hits stopped coming he worked both as a song promoter and manager of April-Blackwood Music, the publishing division for Columbia Records.

Orlando's recording career was resurrected when Bell Records selected him to provide the lead vocal for a demo submitted by two Detroit-based backup singers, Telma Louise Hopkins and Joyce Elaine Vincent, who had worked with Freda Payne, Edwin Starr, Johnnie Taylor, and others. The song, "Candida," and a follow-up, "Knock Three Times" (Bell 938; 1970; #1)—both of which possessed a lilting, sing-a-long groove—became major hits. (Bell staff would claim that the two songs were recorded by Orlando with session singers.)

At this point Orlando, along with Hopkins and Vincent, signed with Bell as "Dawn, featuring Tony Orlando." For the next six years, the group became a household name with best-selling singles like "Tie a Yellow Ribbon Round the Ole Oak Tree" (Bell 45318; 1973; #1), "Say, Has Anybody Seen My Sweet Gypsy Rose" (Bell 45374; 1973; #3), "Steppin' Out" (Bell 45601; 1974; #7), and "He Don't Love You (Like I Love You)" (Elektra 45240; 1975; #1), and as hosts of a CBS-TV musical-variety show. Dawn was never an important album act; their finest chart showing came with *Greatest Hits* (Arista 4045; 1975; #16).

When Orlando unexpectedly announced his retirement from show business in July 1977, Hopkins and Vincent attempted—without much success—to continue as Dawn. The treesome reunited briefly in 1988 without any recording activity of note.

October 3. Diana Ross ascends to the summit of the R&B charts with "Ain't No Mountain High Enough."

October 10. Neil Diamond makes it to the top of the Hot 100 with "Cracklin' Rosie" (Uni). It is one of the last in a string of bare-bones, sing-a-long hits for the singer/songwriter, who begins experimenting shortly thereafter with extended compositions, heavy-handed orchestrations, and the musical stage.

October 10. The Jackson 5 begin a six-week run atop the R&B charts with "I'll be There" (Motown 1171).

October 16. James Taylor's first Warner Bros. album, *Sweet Baby James*, achieves gold status.

Taylor was the first proponent of the singer/songwriter genre to achieve superstar status. These artists—generally performing their own material (Tom Rush, who interpreted the work of other contemporary song craftsmen, was one of the notable exceptions to this rule)—often appeared as soloists, employing either a piano or guitar for accompaniment. This spare mode of presentation helped facilitate an aura of directness which differentiated them from legions of other soft rockers.

Singer/songwriters for-the-most-part evolved out of two genres: Tin Pan Alley pop and post-Dylan folk music. The former category included Carole King, Randy Newman, and Laura Nyro; the latter was represented by Taylor, Rush, Joni Mitchell, Jackson Browne, Neil Young, Leonard Cohen, and Cat Stevens. Paul Simon straddled both camps.

The appeal of these artists was largely built on the cut of personality. The most successful singer/songwriters (e.g., Browne, Simon, Taylor, Young) were able to reflect change under pressure as well as a growing awareness of inner concern. This self-absorption stood in stark contrast to the universal idealism of the preceding era's universal idealism. Many of the folk interpreters espousing the latter perspective appeared unwilling—or unable—to evolve into the confessional realm. Many of these artists (e.g., Eric Andersen, Gordon Lightfoot, Phil Ochs, Tom Paxton) lost career momentum when folk era values no longer held the attention of the mainstream pop audience. Other artists were unable to sustain a high level of conceptual creativity regarding the expression of personal feelings. Carole King and Cat Stevens both enjoyed extraordinary success in the 1971 to 1972 period, but suffered a severe dropoff in popularity shortly thereafter. King, in particular, remained a first-rate tunesmith; she simply appears to have lost the ability to hold the attention of many fans who'd found *Tapestry* to be full of fascinating insights.

Most of the singer/songwriters who tasted early stardom, however, retained a sufficiently large enough following to continue to release new material well into the twenty-first century. The genre's declining appeal during the late 1970s was largely a product of the shortfall in fresh talent.

October 17. The Jackson 5 peak at number one on the Hot 100 with "I'll Be There" (Motown 1171), remaining there for five weeks. It's the band's fourth chart-topper for the year.

October 31. The Carpenters begin a four-week run at number two on the Hot 100 with "We've Only Just Begun" (A&M 1217).

October 31. Elton John enters the *Billboard* album charts for the first time with *Elton John* (Uni 73090), eventually reaching number four.

The most popular recording artist in the United States between 1970 and 1975, Elton John would go on to become an entertainment institution (achieving knighthood in recognition of his accomplishments), appearing on Disney film soundtracks, collaborating with stage composer Tim Rice, establishing an AIDS foundation in 1992 supported in part by royalties from his recording, and reviving his 1973 composition, "Candle in the Wind," at Princess Diana's funeral. His middle-of-the-road sensibilities of recent decades obscure the fact that his ambitious early work helped cast the musical fashions of the 1970s.

Born Reginald Kenneth Dwight in Pinner, Middlesex, England, he joined Bluesology as a vocalist/pianist in the early 1960s. The band would go on to release several singles during the 1965 to 1967 period before Dwight opted for a solo career (augmented by lyricist Bernie Taupin), taking his performing name from Bluesology members Elton Dean and Long John Baldry. Following a string of unsuccessful singles and the rather bland *Empty Sky* (Uni 2130; 1969), John made a major splash on both sides of the Atlantic with *Elton John*, the first of many recordings to be produced by Gus Dudgeon. Although that album's delicate textures seemed to place it squarely within the singer-songwriter movement then in vogue, follow-up releases—most notably, *Honky Chateau* (Uni 93135; 1972; #1), *Don't Shoot Me I'm Only The Piano Player* (MCA 2100; 1973; #1), *Goodbye Yellow Brick Road* (MCA 10003; 1973; #1; double-disc set), *Caribou* (MCA 2116; 1974; #1), the loosely-structured concept LP, *Captain Fantastic And The Brown Dirt Cowboy* (MCA 2142; 1975; #1), and *Rock Of The Westies* (MCA 2163; 1975; #1)—veered in the direction of AOR rock, ideally suited as the soundtrack to his outrageously theatrical live performances. The double-LP, *Blue Moves* (MCA 11004; 1976; #3), removed much of the energy and spirited humor of John's best work, evoking instead a prevailing sense of gothic despair.

Following a brief retirement, John (sans Taupin until they reunited in 1983) experimented with a variety of styles in an attempt to return to public favor. Despite occasional hit singles and moderate album sales, he has seemed permanently out-of-sync with prevailing popular music trends. Nevertheless, his place as an elder statesman of rock seems assured as long as he remains interested in recording and touring.

November 8. In the wake of being found guilty of indecent exposure and profanity, Jim Morrison records an album of his poetry, *An American Prayer*. Although widely distributed as a bootleg recording, it would not be officially released until 1978.

November 13. The Carpenters earn a gold record for "We've Only Just Begun (A&M 1217; #2).

November 21. James Brown begins a two-week stint atop the R&B charts with "Super Bad (Parts 1 & 2)" (King 6329). It was the second recording for Brown's new band, the so-called "New Breed," teenagers who'd been working King Records sessions until he'd recruited them in March 1970.

November 21. The Partridge Family—who are presently riding the crest of a hit television program modeled after the real-life musical family, The Cowsills—go number one on the Hot 100 with "I Think I Love You" (Bell 910), remaining there three weeks.

The Partridge Family represented a marketing concept more than true performing unit. Based on actors in the television series, *The Partridge Family*—which premiered on ABC September 25, 1970, and ran until 1974—depicted the adventures of a family functioning as a touring pop band. The only actors singing on the Partridge Family recordings were David Cassidy (who also played guitar) and his stepmother, Shirley Jones, whose resumé included lead roles in many musicals. The TV family members also included Danny Bonaduce, model Susan Dey, Brian Foster, and Suzanne Crough.

Shortly after the show's debut, the group's first record, "I Think I Love You" (Bell 910; 1970), topped the charts, eventually selling four million copies. A string of hit singles—most notably, "Doesn't Somebody Want To Be Wanted" (Bell 963; 1971) and "I'll Meet You Halfway" (Bell 996; 1971)—and gold LPs—*The Partridge Family Album* (Bell 6050; 1970), *Up To Date* (Bell 6059; 1971), *The Partridge Family Sound Magazine* (Bell 6064; 1971), *The Partridge Family Shopping Bag* (Bell 6072; 1972), and *The Partridge Family at Home with Their Greatest Hits* (Bell 1107; 1972)—followed. When the program ended, Cassidy attempted, with limited success, to build a solo career begun in 1971 with the release of the Top 10 disc, "Cherish" (Bell 45150). Day achieved a degree of distinction as an actress, and Bonaduce's stints as a deejay and celebrity has-been were tainted by various legal problems.

December. T. Rex—formerly known as the eccentric British folk-rock duo, Tyrannosaurus Rex—release their eponymous debut album (Warner Bros.). Early American copies came with a separate 45 rpm disc, "Ride a White Swan," a chart-topping hit in Britain. The release revealed frontman Mark Bolan's shift to a more power-pop oriented sound, along with pronounced theatrical leanings geared to young female fans. A moderate seller stateside, *T. Rex* reflected the earliest stirrings of glitter rock within the domestic pop music scene.

The genre, sometimes termed "glam," had its origins in the early 1970s backlash against the 1960s sexual revolution. Its chief identifying features included a preoccupation with sexual ambiguity (most notably, Bolan, the Ziggy Stardust-era David Bowie) and a heightened fashion sense (e.g., Roxy Music). The performers affected a decadent look typically accented by foppish and/or futuristic clothing and tons of makeup and glitter dust.

Musically, glitter came across as a polished variant of hard rock. The leading exponents ranged stylistically from pop rock (e.g., Gary Glitter, Sweet) to punk (e.g., New York Dolls, Slade) and greatly influenced the more theatrically inclined mainstream acts of the 1970s and 1980s, including Alice Cooper, Queen, and the more androgynous new wave acts. Glitter rock lost considerable momentum when its shock value was ultimately pre-empted by genres willing to push theatrical conventions and fashion statements further to the edge. By the latter half of the 1970s most fans had defected to either the disco or heavy metal camps. Many of the leading glitter acts went on to even greater success as mainstream artists, albeit with either progressive or hard rock leanings.

December 5. The Allman Brothers Band enter the Top 40 for the first time with their LP, *Idlewild South* (Atco 342), peaking at number thirty-eight. The Allman Brothers played southern rock, sometimes termed the "Sound of the South," which became a major commercial force in the 1970s. It blended musical strains indigenous to the region—the blues, rhythm and blues, country, and gospel—into a flexible, jam-oriented style. Although jump-started by the Allmans (who first recorded in the mid-1960s as the Allman Joys, and were earning critical accolades and selling millions of records by the time guitarist Duane Allman died in a motorcycle crash in 1971), in a broader sense the genre represented a response to the progressive rock hybrids developed in northern cities during the late 1960s, most notably, the San Francisco Sound and Latin Rock. The song lyrics—indeed, sometimes even the multicultural composition of the bands—reflected the values of the "New South," including pride in one's roots (perhaps best exemplified by the 1974 Lynyrd Skynyrd anthem, "Sweet Home Alabama") and racial harmony.

Supported by a rabidly loyal fan base, many southern rock bands have enjoyed lengthy careers based on incessant touring rather than hit singles. Continued personnel changes have brought new musical ideas to the Allmans, Lynyrd Skynyrd, the Charlie Daniels Band, the Marshall Tucker Band, and other acts without any significant loss of momentum. In the meantime, new exponents of the tradition have continued to appear, most of whom have provided innovative takes on timeworn stylistic conventions such as double (even triple) lead guitar lineups, bluegrass-rock improvisation, and redneck metal fusions. Some of the promising newcomers of the mid-1990s—most notably, Government Mule, Widespread Panic, and Zero—proved successful in siphoning off legions of deadheads in the wake of Jerry Garcia's sudden death in August 1995.

December 5. Smokey Robinson & the Miracles commence a three-week stay atop the R&B charts with "The Tears of a Clown" (Tamla 54199). It originally had been an overlooked album track on *Make It Happen* (Tamla, 1967), until EMI executive John Reid released it as a single in England, where it topped the charts.

December 12. Smokey Robinson & the Miracles reach number one on the Hot 100 with "The Tears of a Clown," remaining there for two weeks.

December 26. George Harrison begins a four-week stint atop the Hot 100 with "My Sweet Lord"/"Isn't It a Pity" (Apple).

December 31. Paul McCartney sues the other Beatles to dissolve their partnership.

1971

❄

January 1. Radio Luxembourg broadcasts more than seven hours of exclusively Beatles music (singles or album tracks recorded by the group or solo members) to celebrate their tenth year in the music business.

January 2. George Harrison's three-disc album, *All Things Must Pass* (Apple), begins a seven-week stint at number one, making him the first solo Beatle to accomplish this feat.

January 9. The U.S. Jaycees name Elvis Presley as one of the ten recipients of their annual award, Outstanding Young Men of America.

January 12. The Rolling Stones' "Brown Sugar" becomes the first release on their own label, Rolling Stones.

January 17. Marvin Gaye sings the national anthem prior to Super Bowl V at the Orange Bowl, which pits the Miami Dolphins against the Baltimore Colts.

January 19. The Beatles' *White Album* is played at the Sharon Tate murder trial to try to determine what influence it might have had on Charles Manson and his followers.

January 21. *Rolling Stone* features a denim-clad John Lennon on its cover with the caption "The Rolling Stone Interview: John Lennon – Part One – The Working Class Hero."

January 23. Steel Mill perform for the last time at the Upstage Club, Asbury Park, New Jersey. The band's singer, Bruce Springsteen, experiments with several new outfits for the balance of the year: Bruce Springsteen Jam, Dr. Zoom and the Sonic Boom, and the Bruce Springsteen Band.

January 23. Dawn begins a three-week stint at number one with "Knock Three Times" (Bell). The song also tops the British charts.

January 27. David Bowie arrives in the United States for the first time. Although unable to perform due to work permit restrictions, he gains publicity by wearing a dress at a promotional appearance.

February 13. The Osmonds begin a five-week stint atop the Hot 100 with "One Bad Apple." Their fan base was initially built from regular TV appearances going back to the *Andy Williams Show*, followed by the *Jerry Lewis Show*.

February 17. James Taylor makes his television debut on *The Johnny Cash Show*. He shares the bill with Linda Ronstadt, Tony Joe White, and Neil Young.

February 18. Captain Beefheart and His Magic Band make their New York debut at Unganos.

February 18. *Rolling Stone* pictures James Taylor on its cover with the caption "The Taylors: The First Family of the New Rock."

February 20. The Original Cast Recording of *Jesus Christ Superstar* reaches the top of the album charts, remaining there for three non-consecutive weeks. It will be widely recognized as the progenitor of Christian rock, or Christian Contemporary, as it is known in radio parlance.

The genre consists of beat-oriented pop music performed by artists professing publicly to be Christian. Their song lyrics may or may not explicitly embrace Christian ideology or imagery. The music itself is not inherently "Christian," but rather reflects a wide range of stylistic influences, including heavy metal, alternative, bubblegum, pop-rock, industrial, and hip hop. Notable acts within this field had included Steven Curtis Chapman, Amy Grant, Grits, Kevin Max, Not Afraid, P.O.D., Project 86, Relient K, Soulbait, Stryper, Superchick, and Tree63.

The first documented Christian rock act appears to have been Mind Garage, who formed in 1967 and recorded *Electric Liturgy* (1970) for the RCA label. The appearance of *Jesus Christ Superstar, Joseph and the Amazing Technicolor Coat, Godspell*, and other stage works melding rock elements and Christian subject matter thrust the movement into the pop mainstream. At the same time, others—including Coldplay, Creed, Evanescence, King's X, Switchfoot, and U2—have embraced Christian ideology and had members who admit to being practicing Christians, but classify themselves as part of the general mainstream rather than Christian artists. The first mainstream act to walk this ideological tightrope was the Electric Prunes, who recorded *Mass* for Reprise in 1968.

The movement has generated some degree of criticism from both hardcore believers and the mainstream press. Some feel that the genre merely apes styles and trends within the pop mainstream. Others hold that any attempts to reach out to a general audience waters down the Christian message and content. Within the genre, there are misgivings about artists who appear to be marketing themselves to the Christian listener because the market is considered easier to penetrate.

February 20. Gordon Lightfoot begins a three-week run at number five on the Hot 100 with "If You Could Read My Mind" (Reprise 0974).

Like many commercial folk singers in the 1960s, Gordon Lightfoot adapted to changing industry trends by beefing up his song arrangements and accommodating a rock beat. Although possessing a distinctive baritone voice, he is best known as a pop music composer.

Born November 17, 1938, in Orilla, Ontario, Lightfoot studied music at Westlake College in Los Angeles before becoming interested in the work of folk revivalists like Pete Seeger and Bob Gibson. After recording for various local labels in Canada during the early 1960s, he caught the attention of Albert Grossman, then manager of Bob Dylan and Peter, Paul and Mary. Grossman added him to his stable of artists and had Peter, Paul and Mary record two of his compositions, "For Lovin' Me" (Warner Brothers 5496; 1965; #30) and "Early Morning Rain." Although a stint with United Artists was relatively unsuccessful, he became a consistent hit-maker after signing with Warner Brothers in 1969. His most popular singles included "If You Could Read My Mind," "Sundown" (Reprise 1194; 1974; #1), "Carefree Highway" (Reprise 1309; 1974; #10), and "The Wreck of the Edmund Fitzgerald" (Reprise 1369; 1976; #2). He enjoyed even greater success as an album artist, placing sixteen titles on *The Billboard 200* up through the late 1980s, most notably *Sit Down Young Stranger* (Reprise 6392; 1970; #12), *Sundown* (Reprise 2177; 1974; #1), *Cold On The Shoulder* (Reprise 2206; 1975; #10), and *Summertime Dream* ((Reprise 2246; 1976; #12). While Lightfoot has not creased the charts since the late 1980s, he continues to tour and record new music up to the present day.

February 25. BBC-TV broadcast a Led Zeppelin concert from the Paris (France) Theatre.

February 27. The posthumously released Janis Joplin album, *Pearl* (Columbia), begins a nine-week stay atop the charts.

March 4. The Rolling Stones relocate to France, becoming England's first rock tax exiles.

March 11. Jim Morrison, lead vocalist for The Doors, arrives in Paris and secures a booking at The Hotel George's. The following week he moves into an apartment at 17 Rue Beautreillis. He remains in the city until his death on July 3.

March 16. Grammy Award winners include Simon & Garfunkel (Record of the Year, Song of the Year, and Album of the Years for *Bridge Over Troubled Water* and its title track) and the Carpenters (Best New Act and Best Vocal Performance).

March 19. T. Rex heads up the British charts with "Hot Love," the first of their four singles to accomplish this feat.

March 20. Janis Joplin reaches number one on the Hot 100 with "Me and Bobby McGee" (Columbia), remaining there for two weeks.

March 20. The Rolling Stones place full-page ads in the leading British music periodicals disclaiming any connection with the release of the Decca LP, *Stone Age*, stating, "in our opinion the content is below the standard we try to keep."

March 27. WNBC-New York bans Brewer & Shipley's "One Toke Over the Line" due to its alleged drug references. More radio stations follow suit in short order.

April 3. The Temptations peak at number one on the pop charts with "Just My Imagination (Running Away With Me)" (Gordy), remaining there for two weeks.

April 14. The Illinois Crime Commission issues a list of "drug-oriented records," which includes the Beatles'

"Lucy in the Sky with Diamonds," Jefferson Airplane's "White Rabbit," and Procol Harum's "A Whiter Shade of Pale."

April 17. All four of the Beatles can be found on the latest edition of the British charts: Paul McCartney with "Another Day," John Lennon with "Power to the People," George Harrison with "My Sweet Lord," and Ringo Starr with "It Don't Come Easy."

April 17. Three Dog Night begin a six-week run atop the Hot 100 with "Joy to the World" (Dunhill/ABC). *Billboard* chart expert Joel Whitburn designates it the top single of the year.

April 23. Atlantic releases its first Rolling Stones album, *Sticky Fingers*, in England. Andy Warhol is paid $25,500 for the album sleeve artwork, complete with a working zipper.

April 29. *Rolling Stone* features Michael Jackson on its cover with the caption "Why does this eleven-year-old stay up past his bedtime?"

May 1. Ocean peaks at number two on the Hot 100 with a reworking of the gospel traditional, "Put Your Hand in the Hand" (Kama Sutra 519).

May 12. Mick Jagger marries Bianca Macias at St. Topez Town Hall. She would help him develop a greater awareness of myriad humanitarian causes worldwide prior to their separation in 1977.

May 13. Having turned 21, Stevie Wonder receives all of the professionally-related funds accrued during his childhood. Up to this point in time he'd received only $1 million of his estimated $30 million earnings.

May 15. Crosby, Stills, Nash & Young top the album charts with *4 Way Street*.

May 29. The Rolling Stones peak at number one of the Hot 100 with "Brown Sugar" (Rolling Stones), remaining there for two weeks.

May 31. Thirty-six attendees at a Grateful Dead concert receive treatment after unknowingly drinking LSD-laced cider.

June 1. Elvis Presley's birthplace—a two-room shotgun house in Tupelo, Mississippi—opens as a tourist attraction.

June 12. The Honey Cone top the charts with "Want Ads" (Hot Wax).

June 19. Carole King reaches number one on the Hot 100 with "It's Too Late"/"I Feel the Earth Move" (Ode), remaining there for five weeks. She also tops the album charts with *Tapestry*.

June 27. Bill Graham closes his New York concert venue, the Fillmore East. The headliners include the Beach Boys, the Allman Brothers, Mountain, and the J. Geils Band.

July 3. Having relocated to Paris in order to focus on writing poetry, Jim Morrison allegedly dies of a heart attack while taking a bath. The veracity of these reports would be widely questioned after his common-law wife, Pamela Morrison, succumbed to an apparent heroin overdose. With no one alive to confirm that they saw Morrison's corpse, a conspiracy theory arose that suggested he dropped out of sight to elude legal repercussions from his 1969 indecency conviction. In the meantime, books, records, and films trading on his notoriety became surefire commercial properties and his gravesite in Paris's Pere Lachaise Cemetery would be visited by a steady stream of pilgrims.

July 24. The Raiders top the Hot 100 with "Indian Reservation" (Columbia).

July 31. James Taylor goes number one on the pop charts with the Carole King composition, "You've Got a Friend" (Warner Bros.).

August 1. George Harrison presents his Concert for Bangladesh at Madison Square Garden, New York City. He is joined by such pop luminaries as Eric Clapton, Leon Russell, Ringo Starr, and Badfinger in a fundraiser for East Pakistan, then being ravaged by famine, cholera, and civil war. The event will generate a bestselling single and multi-disc album.

August 7. The Bee Gees begin a four-week run atop the Hot 100 with "How Can You Mend a Broken Heart" (Atco). It is their first number one hit; they will have nine in the 1970s, tops for the decade.

August 13. King Curtis is stabbed to death in front of his New York apartment house.

Perhaps the best known saxophone soloist in rock history, King Curtis came out of the staccato, honk-ing style of laying that evolved during the post-World War II R&B era. In addition to leaving his own recorded legacy, he worked with more than 125 other artists in the studio.

Born Curtis Ousley, on February 7, 1934, in Fort Worth, Texas, he performed in marching band and formed his own group while in high school. After graduation, he relocated to New York City, playing with such stars as Lionel Hampton and Horace Silver. He moved to a stint in Alan Freed's show band, and became a staff musician for Atlantic/Atco in 1958. There, he received wide recognition for his excit-ing solos on Coasters' singles like "Yakety Yak" (Atco; 1958) and "Along Came Jones" (Atco; 1959). Other artists wasted little time recruiting him to appear on their own recordings, including the Allman Broth-ers, Ray Charles, Sam Cooke, Eric Clapton, Bobby Darin, Delaney and Bonnie, Sam and Dave, and the Shirelles.

King Curtis balanced session work with his own prolific solo output, beginning with LP, *Have Tenor Sax, Will Blow* (Atco 33-113; 1959). He recorded a major hit, "Soul Twist" (Enjoy) in 1962 with his Noble Knights (later, the Kingpins), and returned to the charts intermittently over the next decade, most notably with "Memphis Soul Stew" (Atco; 1967) and "Ode to Billie Joe" (Atco; 1967). He became more actively involved with production work in the late 1960s, and had just been appointed to be Aretha Franklin's musical director prior to his tragic death.

August 28. John Denver's "Take Me Home, Country Roads" (RCA 0445) peaks at number two on the Hot 100, his first hit of note.

August 31. Members of the Rolling Stones—including Brian Jones' father—file a high court writ against ex-managers Andrew Loog Oldham and Easton, claiming they colluded with Decca Records to deprive the band of royalty payments.

September 4. Paul and Linda McCartney hit number one on the pop charts with the medley, "Uncle Albert/Ad-miral Halsey" (Apple).

September 4. Olivia Newton-John peaks at number twenty-five on the Hot 100 with "If Not For You" (Uni 55281).

Olivia Newton-John was one of the leading pop-rock recording artists from the early 1970s to the mid-1980s. Due to her photogenic good looks, she also made a substantial impact in the visual media. She released a number of best-selling video titles in the early 1980s, made regular appearances on television, and had starring roles in a string of films, including *Grease* (1978), *Xanadu* (1980), and *Two Of A Kind* (1984).

Born September 26, 1947, in Cambridge, England, Newton-John grew up in Australia singing folk mate-rial. Shifting to mainstream pop styles, she had become an established recording star in England by the early 1970s. Her manager, John Farrar—who had teamed with ex-Shadows guitarists Hank Marvin and Bruce Welch to form a Crosby, Stills & Nash-styled trio earlier in the decade—steered her in the direc-tion of country-pop. Several major hits—"Let Me Be There" (MCA 40101; 1973/4; #6 pop, #7 c&w), "If You Love Me (Let Me Know)" (MCA 40209; 1974; #5 pop, #2 c&w), and "I Honestly Love You" (MCA 40280; 1974; #1 pop, #1 AC, #6 c&w)—resulted in her controversial selection as the Country Music As-sociation's Entertainer of the Year in 1974. Her albums—comprised for-the-most-part of soft rock—also sold well; *If You Love Me, Let Me Know* (MCA 411; 1974) and *Have You Ever Been Mellow* (MCA 2133; 1975) both topped the charts.

While she continued to place high on the country charts for most of the decade, her music took on an increasingly smooth, middle-of-the-road feel. In fact, "Have You Ever Been Mellow" (MCA 40249; 1975; #1), "Please Mr. Please" (MCA 40418; 1975; #3), "Something Better To Do" (MCA 40459; 1975; #13), "Let It Shine" (MCA 40495; 1976; #30), "Come On Over" (MCA 40525; 1976; #23), "Don't Stop Believin'" (MCA 40600; 1976), and "Sam" (MCA 40670; 1977; #20) were all number one Adult Con-temporary hits, thereby helping broaden the appeal of that genre. By the late 1970s, her releases—most notably, "You're The One That I Want" (RSO 891; 1978; #1; with John Travolta), "Summer Nights" (RSO 906; 1978; #5; with Travolta), "Magic" (MCA 41247; 1980; #1 pop four weeks, #1 AC), and "Physical" (MCA 51182; 1981; #1 ten weeks)—had incorporated a stronger rock feel. She signed with Geffen in

1989; her first LP for the label, *Warm And Tender* (Geffen 24257; 1989; #124), a collection of lullabies, appears to have been influenced by the recent birth of her daughter. Although Newton-John had ceased being a chart fixture by the mid-1980s and oversees a retail clothing chain, she continues to intermittently tour and make new recordings.

September 4. The Undisputed Truth peak at number three on the Hot 100 with "Smiling Faces Sometimes" (Gordy 7108).

Undisputed Truth was the brainchild of Norman Whitfield, the Motown songwriter-producer who achieved major success in the early 1970s with Marvin Gaye, the Temptations and Edwin Starr. He decided to assemble a group to showcase his talents, recruiting the Delicates—Billie Rae Calvin and Brenda Joyce, then singing back-up in the studio for the Four Tops, the Supremes, and others—to complement a recent acquaintance, Joe Harris.

Harris, who would remain the core of the group's continually shifting line-up, was born and raised in Detroit; he lived in the Brewster Projects along with other future luminaries such as Martha & The Vandellas, and Diana Ross and Mary Wilson of The Supremes. While in high school, he sang with Little Joe & The Moroccos, a group best remembered for besting the Spinners in a local talent show. When a single, "Bubblegum" (Bumblebee; 1957), failed to catch on, the act broke up.

Harris then teamed up with Richard Street—who'd go on to join the Monitors and the Temptations—to form The Peps. Following a string of commercial failures on the Thelma and D-Town labels, Harris became lead singer for the Ohio Players in the late 1960s. He would co-write and produce much of their first Capitol LP, but departed when he found himself mired in an unfair production deal. After working briefly with the Stone Soul Children in Canada, he returned to Detroit and hooked up with Whitfield.

The second Undisputed Truth single, a Whitfield-Barrett Strong composition first recorded by The Temptations for their *The Sky's the Limit* album entitled "Smiling Faces Sometimes" (#2 r&b), hit pay dirt. Its underlying paranoia struck a chord with listeners during an era disillusioned with the Vietnam War and social strife emanating from the civil right movement. Follow-up singles—most notably, the original version of "Papa Was a Rollin' Stone" (Gordy 7117; 1972; #63 pop, #24 r&b)—failed to sell well; Calvin and Evans would depart on the heels of the marginally successful "Law of the Land" (Gordy 7130; 1973; #40 r&b).

Bringing in the members of a Detroit-based bar band, the Magictones (Tyrone Berkley, Tyrone Douglas, Virginia McDonald, and Calvin Stevens), Undisputed Truth took on a more rock-oriented sound reflected the influence of Jimi Hendrix and Sly Stone. The theatrical leanings of glitter rock artists and George Clinton's P-Funk collective were also evident in the group's use of silver-painted faces, brilliant sequins, and oversized white afros. These musicians would be dispatched by Harris in the late 1970s in favor of a more R&B-flavored approach built around Melvin Stuart, Marcy Thomas, Hershel "Happiness" Kennedy, and Chaka Khan's sister, Taka Boom. Although occasionally creasing the R&B charts until mid-1979, they would make their last appearance on the *Billboard* Hot 100 with "You + Me = Love" (Whitfield 8231; 1976; #48 pop, #37 r&b), later reissued as a twelve-inch single (#8306).

September 8. The National Academy of Recording Arts and Sciences gives Elvis Presley the Bing Crosby Award, which is intended for individuals who "during their lifetimes, have made creative contributions of outstanding artistic or scientific significance to the field of phonograph records." He is the sixth recipient, following Crosby, Frank Sinatra, Duke Ellington, Ella Fitzgerald, and Irving Berlin.

September 11. Donny Osmond reaches number one on the Hot 100 with "Go Away Little Girl" (MGM), remaining there for three weeks. It is the second time the song has headed up the single charts; Steve Lawrence first took it there in January 1963.

September 18. Bill Withers peaks at number three on the Hot 100 with "Ain't No Sunshine" (Sussex 219).

Bill Withers was one of the more unique singer-songwriters of the 1970s, combining his gospel-soul roots with the spare folk style popular when he began his singing career in earnest. In addition to a long and distinguished recording career, his songs have been reinterpreted by countless artists covering a wide range of styles, including Michael Bolton, Joe Cocker, Aretha Franklin, Crystal Gale, Lionel Hampton,

Michael Jackson, Mick Jagger, Etta James, Tom Jones, Johnny Mathis, Liza Minnelli, Aaron Neville, Diana Ross, Will Smith, Sting, Barbra Streisand, Grover Washington, and Nancy Wilson.

Withers was born July 4, 1938, in Slab Fork, West Virginia. His father—a coal miner—died when he was thirteen, making it necessary for him so help support the family. During a nine-year stint in the Navy, he began singing in public. He also took up songwriting in his search for suitable performance material.

Aftr moving to Los Angeles in 1967 in order to pursue a music career, Withers made the rounds with his demo tapes until landing a recording contract with Sussex Records in early 1970. His debut album, *Just As I Am* (Sussex 7006; 1971; #39), featuring production work by Booker T. Jones, propelled him to the forefront of music industry, earning a Grammy Award for songwriting with "Ain't No Sunshine" (#6 r&b). In the midst of heavy touring demands, he recorded a second LP, *Still Bill* (Sussex 7014; 1972; #4), which included the classic singles, "Lean On Me" (Sussex 235; 1972; #1 pop, #1 r&b) and "Use Me" (Sussex 241; 1972; #2 pop, #2 r&b).

Withers' career momentum was slowed by a legal battle with Sussex in 1974. He managed to get back on track the following year after signing with Columbia Records. In addition to a total of eleven charting albums, he produced a steady stream of hits into the mid-1980s, most notably "Lovely Day" (Columbia 10627; 1977; #30 pop, #6 r&b) and his collaboration with fusion saxophonist Grover Washington Jr., "Just the Two Of Us" (Elektra 47103; 1981; #2 pop, #3 r&b), the latter of which earned him four Grammy nominations (he would win for songwriting). In 1987, he would receive his ninth Grammy nomination and third Grammy as a songwriter for Club Nouveau's reworking of "Lean On Me" (King Jay/Warner Bros. 28430; #1 pop, #2 r&b).

Although no longer a chart fixture, his songs and warm vocals continue to turn up in radio and television commercials, films, and TV programs. His material is not only covered by adult contemporary artists, but also widely sampled and reinterpreted by many hip-hop acts.

October 2. Rod Stewart begins a five-week run atop the Hot 100 with "Maggie May" (Mercury 73224). The recording catapults Stewart—former lead singer for Steampacket and the Jeff Beck Group who presently divided his time between the Faces and his solo career—into the superstar bracket.

The Rod Stewart story is one of unfulfilled promise. He possesses one of the most expressive voices in rock music history, his hoarse-sounding delivery equally effective negotiating caressing ballads and exuberant rockers. However, he has frequently opted to record material of dubious quality or saddled his delivery with shallow cliches (e.g., sexual posturing in songs like "Hot Legs" and "Do Ya Think I'm Sexy?").

Born in London, Stewart's earliest recordings were made as lead singer for two John Baldry-led bands, the Hoochie Coochie Men (English Decca) and Steampacket (Columbia), between 1964 and 1967. He had his first taste of rock stardom as the vocalist on the first two albums recorded by the Jeff Beck Group, *Truth* (Epic 26413; 1968; #15) and *Beck-Ola* (Epic 26478; 1969; #15). His fame led to a contract with Mercury in 1969; his joint status as a soloist and group member for two different labels represented a unique arrangement within the rock scene at the time. When the Beck group temporarily disbanded, Stewart continued his dual career until 1975 as a member of the Faces.

Although the Faces releases—most notably—were considered uneven at best, Stewart's early solo albums—*The Rod Stewart Album* (Mercury 61237; 1969; #139); *Gasoline Alley* (Warner Bros. 61264; 1970; #27); *Every Picture Tells a Story* (Mercury 609; 1971; #1), which included "Maggie May"; and *Never a Dull Moment* (Mercury 646; 1972; #2)—all featured sensitive singing, intelligent lyrics and inspired production values. His switch to Warner Brothers, however, found him adopting a more stylized, albeit charismatic, delivery. Nevertheless, his albums—particularly, *A Night on the Town* (Warner Bros. 2938; 1976; #2), including "Tonight's the Night" (Warner Bros. 8262; 1976), which topped the singles chart for eight weeks; *Foot Loose & Fancy Free* (Warner Bros. 3092; 1977; #2); and *Blondes Have More Fun* (Warner Bros. 3261; 1978; #10), featuring the disco-oriented "Do Ya Think I'm Sexy?" (Warner Bros. 8724; 1978; #1 4 weeks)—continued to sell at platinum levels into the early 1980s.

The predictability of his material and approach in subsequent releases caused a drop-off in popularity. Now an entertainment institution, Stewart's recorded output remains highly flawed, despite occasional returns to popularity, most notably *Vagabond Heart* (Warner Bros. 26300; 1991; #10), *Unplugged...and*

Seated (Warner Bros.; 1993; #2), and, "All for Love" (A&M 0476; 1993; with Bryan Adams and Sting), the number one single from the film *The Three Musketeers*. Early in the twenty-first century, he would record several albums of pop standards, followed by softer rock material.

October 25. Hollies manager Robin Britten announces lead vocalist Allan Clarke's plans to leave the band and sign with RCA as a solo artist. Swedish singer Mikael Rickfors (whose former group, Bamboo, recently toured with the Hollies) is recruited to fill the opening.

October 30. Denise LaSalle peaks at number thirteen on the Hot 100 with "Trapped By a Thing Called Love" (Westbound 182).

A talented singer/songwriter, Denise LaSalle has also made an impact within the executive branch of the record industry. Along with husband Bill Jones, she has owned Crajon Productions since 1969.

Born Denise Craig on July 16, 1939, in LaFlore County, Mississippi, she moved to Chicago with her family in the early 1950s. LaSalle first recorded for Tarpen, a Chess subsidiary, in 1967, but switched to the Detroit-based Westbound label in the early 1970s, where she recorded her biggest hit—"Trapped By a Thing Called Love" (#1 r&b)—shortly thereafter.

LaSalle consistently scored on the R&B chart in the 1970s, although crossover success for-the-most-part eluded her. Her hits included "Now Run and Tell That" (Westbound 201; 1972; #46 pop, #3 r&b), Man-Sized Job" (Westbound 206; 1972; #55 pop, #4 r&b), "Married, But Not to Each Other" (Westbound 5019; 1976; #102 pop, #16 r&b), and "Love Me Right" (ABC 12312; 1977; #80 pop, #10 r&b). She would go to record for MCA and Malaco, among other labels, in the 1980s. After running out of steam by the mid-1980s, she chose to concentrate on the production side of the business.

October 30. The Persuaders peak at number fifteen on the Hot 100 with "Thin Line Between Love and Hate" (Atco 6822).

Formed in 1969, the New York-based soft soul group—originally consisting of lead vocalist Douglas "Smokey" Scott, James "B .J." Barnes, Willie Holland, and Charles Stodghill—struck gold shortly thereafter with the Atco single, "Thin Line Between Love & Hate," an R&B chart-topper in 1971. Plagued by large-scale personnel shifts, the Persuaders had ceased to be a hit-making entity by 1974, when the line-up consisted of Scott, Willie Coleman, Richard Gant, and Thomas Lee Hill.

November. Roxy Music is formed; members include vocalist Bryan Ferry, keyboardist Brian Eno, guitarist Phil Manzanera, saxophonist Andy Mackay, bassist Rik Kenton, and drummer Paul Thompson. The group's name is inspired by a movie theater, with the word "Music" added to avoid legal entanglements with the U.S. recording act already called Roxy.

November. Don McLean's *American Pie* LP is released. The title single—providing an idiosyncratic chronicle of pop music—clocks in at more than eight minutes, the longest chart-topper in rock history.

November 6. Cher begins a two-week run atop the Hot 100 with "Gypsys, Tramps & Thieves" (Kapp).

November 13. *Santana III* (Columbia) heads up the album charts.

November 20. Isaac Hayes reaches the summit of the pop charts with "Theme From Shaft" (Enterprise), remaining there for two weeks.

December 18. Jerry Lee Lewis and his third wife, Myra Gale Brown (his second cousin, she'd married him at age thirteen on December 11, 1957), obtain a divorce. Lewis is already preparing to marry a twenty-nine-year-old Memphis divorcee, Jaren Elizabeth Gunn Pate.

December 4. Sly & the Family Stone hit number one on the Hot 100 with "Family Affair" (Epic), remaining there for three weeks.

December 11. The Chi-Lites peak at number three on the Hot 100 with "Have You Seen Her" (Brunswick 55462).

The Chi-Lites are living proof that, if you excel at a particular style and stick with it, ever changing public tastes may eventually nudge you into the mainstream. During the 1960s, an era dominated by political rhetoric and musical experimentation, the group continued to specialize in poignant love ballads, finally breaking through to mass public acceptance with hits like "Have You Seen Her" (#1 r&b) and "Oh Girl" (Brunswick 55471; 1972; #1 pop, #1 r&b).

The group formed in 1960 out of a merger of former members of two Chicago area vocal groups, the Desideros (baritone Marshall Thompson and bass Creadel "Red" Jones) and the Chantours (tenors Eugene Record, Clarence Johnson, and Robert "Squirrel" Lester). Calling themselves the Hi-Lites, they recorded a single, "Pots and Pans," for the Chicago-based Mercury Records. When it failed to sell, however, the label nixed the deal and, to make matters worse, they were forced to give up their moniker because it was already taken.

Adding a "C" to the front of their name to emphasize their Chicago origins, Marshall and the Chi-Lites developed a regional following with a string of singles for James Shelton Jr.'s Daran and Ja-Wes labels. By the mid-1960s, they took another stab at big-time success by re-signing with Mercury; however, when two releases on the Blue Rock subsidiary flopped, the group was cut loose once again.

Things began to turn around after the group, now known simply as the Chi-Lites, hooked up with the Dakas production company, which facilitated a recording contract with music industry giant, MCA. With Record assuming a dominant role as songwriter, producer, and lead singer, they established themselves as consistent hit-makers. Although the Chi-Lites typically recorded melodic, sentimental fare featuring Record's soaring falsetto, it is somewhat ironic that their first Top 40 single was a rare excursion into social protest, the forceful "(For God's Sake) Give More Power to the People" (Brunswick 55450; 1971; #26 pop, #4 r&b).

The group peaked a year later with "Oh Girl," in which a plaintive harmonica underscore Record's stark portrayal of male vulnerability—an extremely rare approach for a male pop artist of that era. Despite such unquestioned artistry, the Chi-Lites' sometimes overdone pathos failed to click with the public following the release of the vibrant "Stoned Out of My Mind" (Brunswick 55500; 1973; #30 pop, #2 r&b). Jones would leave in 1973, while Record would detour off into a solo career with Warner Brothers three years later. The group soldiered on (re-forming with all of the original members in 1980), achieving modest success in the R&B field (forty-one charting singles in all) recording with Mercury (again!), Chi-Sound, 20th Century, Larc, and Private I up through the mid-1980s.

December 25. Melanie begins a three-week stay atop the Hot 100 with "Brand New Key" (Neighborhood).

1972

❄

January 1. Marc Bolan signs with EMI; U.K. releases appear on his T. Rex Wax Co. label.

January 15. Singer/songwriter Don McLean reaches number one of the Hot 100 with "American Pie – Parts I & II" (United Artists), remaining there for four weeks.

January 22. In an interview with reporter Michael Watts for *Melody Maker*, David Bowie admits to being bi-sexual. His sexuality will become an increasingly important part of his stage persona.

January 22. Don McLean begins a seven-week stint atop the album charts with *American Pie* (United Artists).

January 30. Paul McCartney composes and records the protest song, "Give Ireland Back to the Irish" within twenty-four hours of Bloody Sunday, when thirteen Irish Catholics are killed by British paratroopers.

February 1. Chuck Berry tops the British charts for the first time with "My Ding-A-Ling," a live recording of a song that had been a part of his repertoire for more than two decades. British morality advocate, Mary Whitehouse, tries—without success—to have the recording banned.

February 9. Wings kick off a college tour by arriving unannounced, and then performing, at Nottingham.

February 10. David Bowie kicks off his Ziggy Stardust tour at the Tolworth Toby Jug in London.

February 12. Al Green reaches number one on the Hot 100 with "Let's Stay Together"—his only recording to accomplish that feat.

February 14. John Lennon and Yoko Ono begin a week-long stint as co-hosts on the *Mike Douglas Show*.

February 18. KDAY, Los Angeles, plays two new Rolling Stones cuts non-stop all day. They are studio tapes stolen from a producer's home.

February 19. Harry Nilsson begins a four-week stay atop the Hot 100 with his interpretation of Badfinger's "Without You." The composers, Pete Ham and Tom Evans, will commit suicide following prolonged legal efforts to receive royalties for the song.

March 11. Neil Young tops the U.S. and U.K. album charts with *Harvest* (Reprise).

March 16. John Lennon lodges an appeal with the U.S. Immigration Office in New York after being served with deportation orders arising from his 1968 marijuana possession conviction.

March 18. T. Rex performs the first of two sold-out dates at Wembley's Empire Pool. The concerts are filmed by Ringo Starr for the Apple documentary, *Born to Boogie*.

March 18. Neil Young reaches number one on the Hot 100 for the only time in his career with "Heart of Gold" (Reprise), remaining there for three weeks. Fresh from a stint with the supergroup, Crosby, Stills & Nash, he seemed posed to become a major commercial force within the music industry. However, rather than consolidating or building upon his radio-friendly work on albums like *Everyone Knows This Is Nowhere* (1969), *After the Goldrush* (1970), and *Harvest* (1972), Young opted in 1973 to release a sloppy live set, *Time Fades Away*, and double-disc soundtrack to a cult film, *Journey to the Past*, that never was shown on the theatrical circuit. His somewhat cryptic explanation for these apparent acts of career suicide was that he'd tried life in the middle-of-the-road, but decided to veer off into the adjoining ditch because more interesting people could be encountered there.

March 23. The film, *The Concert for Bangladesh*—which stars George Harrison, Bob Dylan, and Eric Clapton—premieres in New York City.

March 25. America keeps "Heart of Gold" out of the top spot for three weeks with "A Horse With No Name" (Warner Bros.), a song widely accused of being a blatant Neil Young ripoff.

March 27. Elvis Presley has his last notable pop hit, "Burning Love" (#2 U.S., #7 U.K.).

March 30. *Rolling Stone* pictures Alice Cooper wrapped by a boa constrictor on its cover with the caption "Love it to Death, Alice Cooper."

March 31. The Beatles' Official Fan Club terminates operations. The band's monthly magazine ceased publication three years earlier.

April 1. The three-day Mar Y Sol festival begins on a Puerto Rican island. Headlining acts include the Allman Brothers, Alice Cooper, Dr. John, ELP, the Mahavishnu Orchestra, Osibisa, and Rod Stewart.

April 1. Paul Simon peaks at number four on the Hot 100 with "Mother and Child Reunion" (Columbia 45547).

Paul Simon's recording career has spanned a wide range of styles, from teen idol fare in the late 1950s, to folk-pop minstrelsy in the early 1960s, to continued experimentation with world music as a singer/songwriter. Although enjoying greater critical and commercial success as a member of the seminal folk-rock duo, Simon and Garfunkel, his imposing legacy as a songwriter, performer, and studio producer owes much to the decades of solo work.

Born October 13, 1941, in Newark, New Jersey, and raised in New York City, Simon hooked up with school pal Garfunkel to form Tom and Jerry. Although their first single, "Hey Schoolgirl," grazed the charts, later releases sold poorly. After attempting to make an impact under pseudonyms like True Taylor and Jerry Landis, Simon reverted to his own name, adopted England as his home base for a time. He reunited with Garfunkel in 1964; he was back in England when producer Tom Wilson overdubbed electric guitar, bass, and drums on to "The Sound of Silence" (Columbia 43396; 1965; #1), a track from their folk-styled debut album, *Wednesday Morning 3 A.M.* (Columbia 9049; 1964; #30), thereby providing their career breakthrough. His solo British LP, *The Paul Simon Songbook* (Columbia 62579; 1965), would provide material for the next couple of Simon and Garfunkel albums.

The legendary duo would split up in 1970; however, Simon maintained his career momentum with the release of the eclectic tour de force, *Paul Simon* (Columbia 30750; 1972; #4), which included the Caribbean-tinged singles, "Mother and Child Reunion" and "Me and Julio Down By the Schoolyard" (Columbia 45585; 1972; #22) and the more pop-oriented *There Goes Rhymin' Simon* (Columbia 32280; 1973; #2), featuring "Kodachrome" (Columbia 45859; 1973; #2) and gospel-inflected "Loves Me Like a Rock" (Columbia 45907; 1973; #2; with the Dixie Hummingbirds). The perfunctory *Paul Simon In Concert/Live Rhymin'* (Columbia 32855; 1974; #33) was followed by the Grammy Award-winning *Still Crazy After All These Years* (Columbia 33540; 1975; #1), whose highlights included a duet with Garfunkel, "My Little Town" (Columbia 10230; 1975; #9), and the wry "50 Ways T Leave Your Lover" (Columbia 10270; 1975; #1).

Following a long layoff, *One Trick Pony* (Warner Bros. 3472; 1980; #12)—the soundtrack to his film documentary—and *Hearts and Bones* (Warner Bros. 23942; 1983; #35) seemed out of touch with contemporary music trends such as disco and postpunk. He rebounded, though, with *Graceland* (Warner Bros. 25447; 1986; #3), which was built around African rhythms and musicians (e.g., Ladysmith Black Mambazo). *The Rhythm of the Saints* (Warner Bros. 26098; 1990; #4) took a similar approach, this time drawing inspiration from Brazilian percussion. Never a fast worker, Simon did not produce another studio LP until 1997, a soundtrack to the Broadway musical *Songs From the Capeman* (Warner Bros. 46814; #42), based on the life of Puerto Rican writer Salvador Agron. This paucity of new work, however, has been supplemented by a steady stream of reissues, including both Simon and Garfunkel and solo material.

April 8. Inspired by the Bloody Sunday massacre in Northern Ireland, Paul McCartney releases "Give Ireland Back to the Irish." Banned by the BBC and IBA, it still reaches number sixteen in Great Britain (#21 U.S.).

April 15. Roberta Flack begins a six-week run atop the pop charts with "The First Time Ever I Saw Your Face" (Atlantic). A sophisticated song stylist known for her eclectic tastes, she struck pay dirt with a composition by Irish folk interpreter Ewan MacColl, perhaps best known to American audiences as the husband Peggy Seeger.

Born February 10, 1939, in Asheville, North Carolina, Flack was raised in Arlington, Virginia. Earning a music scholarship to Howard University as a fifteen-year-old, where she met future collaborator Donny Hathaway. Signed by Atlantic Records in 1969, her velvety voice would be featured on twenty-seven hit singles through the early 1980s. She was equally adept at placing recordings on both the pop and R&B

charts; her number one pop singles included "The First Time Ever I Saw Your Face" (1972), "Killing Me Softly With His Song" (1973), and "Feel Like Makin' Love" (1974). The latter song also topped the R&B charts, as did "Where is the Love" (1972) and "The Closer I Get to You" (1978).

April 16. The Electric Light Orchestra perform live for the first time at The Fox and Greyhound, Croydon, U.K.

April 29. Roberta Flack begins a five-week run atop the album charts with *First Take*.

May 2. Bruce Springsteen auditions for Columbia A&R man, John Hammond, in the latter's New York office. Hammond is sufficiently impressed to arrange a stage audition at New York's Gaslight Club for other Columbia executives—Springsteen passes with flying colors.

May 3. Les Harley of Stone the Crows is electrocuted to death while performing at Swansea, Wales.

May 6. Joe Tex begins a two-week run at number two on the Hot 100 with "I Gotcha" (Dial 1010).

May 6. Tyrannosaurus Rex top the British charts with the double album, *Prophets, Seers and Sages and the Angels of the Ages/My People Were Fair and Had Sky in Their Hair But Now They're Content to Wear Stars on Their Brows*.

May 7. Reginald Dwight changes his name by deed poll to Elton Hercules John.

May 7. The Rolling Stones double LP, *Exile on Main Street*, is released. Many critics will call it their greatest album.

May 9. James Brown records "Get on the Good Foot" at Soundcraft Studios in North Augusta, South Carolina. The track's energy inspires Brown to rush release it in place of the previously scheduled "I Got Ants in My Pants."

May 11. *Rolling Stone* displays David Cassidy—in the buff from the navel up—on its cover with the caption "Naked Lunch Box: The Business of David Cassidy."

May 11. John Lennon appears on TV's *Dick Cavett Show*. During the interview, he claims to be under surveillance from the FBI.

May 20. T. Rex top the British charts with "Metal Guru." The band also heads up the U.K. album charts with *Bolan Boogie*.

May 26. On the verge of breaking up, Mott the Hoople are offered two songs by David Bowie: they pass on "Suffragette City" (which shows up on Bowie's *The Rise and Fall of Ziggy Stardust and the Spiders from Mars*) and record "All the Young Dudes," which becomes their biggest hit.

May 27. The Chi-Lites reach number one with "Oh Girl" (Brunswick), an extraordinarily mature ballad about male vulnerability written by lead singer Eugene Record.

June 1. Pink Floyd begin recording *Dark Side of the Moon* at Abbey Road Studios.

June 2. Dion DiMucci reunites with the Belmonts for a concert at New York's Madison Square Garden, their first performance together in more than a decade. With the oldies revival in full swing, Warner Bros. releases the show on LP.

June 3. Jethro Tull begin a two-week stint atop the album charts with *Thick as a Brick*.

Jethro Tull were one of the classic British progressive rock bands of the 1970s, notable for their use of extended song forms and eclectic mix of musical styles. Lead vocalist/flutist Ian Anderson, not only wrote most of the band's material, but supplied their visual image, with his fevered flute playing (often while hopping around on one leg) and medieval peasant costumes.

London-based Jethro Tull originated in late 1967 when fellow Scots Anderson and Glenn Cornick (bass), formerly of John Evan's Smash, recruited guitarist/vocalist Mick Abrahams and drummer Clive Bunker. Adopting the name of an eighteenth century farmer/inventor, they issued one unsuccessful English single for MGM (which mistakenly credited it to "Jethro Toe" on the label) before signing with Island in mid-1968. Their debut LP, *This Was* (Reprise 9336; 1968; #62 US, #10 UK), exhibited a strong blues-rock orientation; however, the departure of Abrahams to form Blodwyn Pig (he was replaced by guitar Martin Barrie) resulted in a shift toward progressive rock. Two rather pastoral releases—*Stand Up* (Reprise 6360;

1969; #20 US, #1 UK) and *Benefit* (reprise 6400; 1970; #11 US, #3 UK)—were followed by the extremely popular concept albums, *Aqualung* (Reprise 2035; 1971; #7 US, #4 UK) and *Thick As A Brick* (Reprise 2071; #5 UK), featuring a more propulsive thrust and Anderson biting diatribes against organized religion, government, and other institutions of the Establishment.

Beset by extensive press criticism over self-indulgent lyrics and extensive personnel changes, the group tread water with *Living In The Past* (Reprise 2106; 1972; #3 US, #8 UK), a double-disc set divided between live recordings and older studio material. As Jethro Tull's timeworn formula wore thin, the band abruptly jumped from one quick fix to another; reverting to concise song structures on *War Child* (Chrysalis 1067; 1974; #2) and *Minstrel In The Gallery* (Chrysalis 1082; 1975; #7), trying a folk-oriented approach for *Songs From The Wood* (Chrysalis 1132; 1977; #8) and *Heavy Horses* (Chrysalis 1175; 1978; #19), and adopting the trappings of techno-pop in *Walk Into Light* (Chrysalis 1443; 1983; #78 UK; Anderson's initial solo venture, assisted by Tull keyboard player Peter Vitesse) and *Under Wraps* (Chrysalis 1461; 1984; #76).

Following a three-year hiatus due to throat problems, Anderson reassembled the group in 1987. The next couple of albums—*Crest Of A Knave* (Chrysalis 1590; 1987; #32) and *Rock Island* (Chrysalis 21708; 1989; #56)—were closer to the prevailing AOR ethic than anything Tull had released since the early 1970s. The former LP won the first Grammy for the category of Best Hard Rock/Metal Performance, a choice that led to widespread criticism of NARAS. Jethro Tull continues to tour and record, although anthologies of their classic tracks have outsold the new material since the 1980s

June 3. The Staple Singers peak at number one on the Hot 100 with "I'll Take You There" (Stax 0125).

The Staple Singers—consisting of Roebuck "Pop" Staples (born December 28, 1915, in Winoma, Mississippi), along with his son Pervis and daughters Cleotha, Yvonna, and lead singer Mavis—represent one of the few acts to successfully make the transition from gospel music to secular pop fare. They were one of the most popular R&B groups of the 1970s, investing their anthems of racial pride and self actualization with a soulful spirituality clearly derived from their church music roots.

"Pop" Staples performed as a blues guitarist while in his teens, relocating to Chicago in 1935. He would join the Golden Trumpets before forming his own gospel group in the early 1950s. They first recorded for United in 1953, but didn't achieve major commercial success until opting for the pop mainstream. The group recorded an extensive string of hits with Al Bell as producer up through mid-1970s, including "Heavy Makes You Happy (Sha-Na-Boom Boom)" (Stax 0083; 1970; #27 pop, #6 r&b), "Respect Yourself" (Stax 0104; 1971; #12 pop, #2 r&b), "I'll Take You There" (Stax #1 r&b four weeks), "This World" (Stax 0137; 1972; #38 pop, #6 r&b), "Oh La De Da" (Stax 0156; 1973; #33 pop, #4 r&b), "If You're Ready (Come Go With Me)" (Stax 0179; 1973; #9 pop, #1 r&b three weeks), "Touch a Hand, Make a Friend" (Stax 0196; 1974; #23 pop, #3 r&b), and "City in the Sky" (Stax 0215; 1974; #79 pop, #4 r&b).

After enjoying two major hits from the film, *Let's Do It Again*—the title track (Curtom 0109; 1975; #1 pop, #1 r&b) and "New Orleans" (Curtom 0113; 1976; #70 pop, #4 r&b)—the group, know known as "The Staples," switched the Warner Brothers label, and later, in the mid-1980s, to Private I. Although they continued place singles on the lower reaches of the R&B charts into 1986, they had ceased to be an important pop force over a decade earlier. Mavis, who had split her time between the family project and her own solo career since 1970, remained the most active, recording hits for Stax's Volt subsidiary, Curtom, Warner Brothers, and Phono.

June 9. Columbia Records executive John Hammond signs Bruce Springsteen to a contract.

June 10. Sammy Davis Jr. begins a three-week run atop the Hot 100 with "The Candy Man" (MGM).

June 13. Clyde McPhatter dies of a heart attack while visiting friends in Manhattan.

Clyde McPhatter was a major force in the evolution of rhythm and blues toward mainstream pop music. He is also remembered for serving as lead tenor for a time in two seminal doo-wop groups: Billy Ward and the Dominoes and The Drifters.

Born November 15, 1932, in Durham, North Carolina, the son of a Baptist minister, McPhatter first sang gospel in church. Following a move to Teaneck, New Jersey, at age twelve, he developed an interest in R&B. In 1950, he was hired by an up-and-coming black vocal group, the Dominoes. His sexy, tremulous tenor elevated the Dominoes to the big leagues as steady R&B hitmakers, most notably "Sixty-Minute Man" (Federal 12022; 1951; #17 pop, #1 r&b fourteen weeks), "Have Mercy, Baby" (Federal 12068; 1952; #1 r&b ten weeks), and "The Bells" (Federal 12114; 1953; #3 r&b).

In 1953, McPhatter moved on to form his own ensemble, the Drifters, in June 1953. Signed by Atlantic Records, the group immediately began producing a string of R&B classics, including "Money Honey" (Atlantic 1006; 1953; #1 r&b eleven weeks) and widely censored "Honey Love" (Atlantic 1029; 1954; #21 pop, #1 r&b eight weeks). McPhatter's popularity was such that he was encouraged by label head Ahmet Ertegun to simultaneously embark upon a solo career. His career momentum was halted, however, when he was drafted into the army in 1954.

Discharged in 1956, McPhatter decided to focus on solo work, enjoying increasing crossover success with hits such as "Treasure of Love" (Atlantic 1092; 1956; #16 pop, #1 r&b), "Long Lonely Nights" (Atlantic 1149; 1957; #49 pop, #1 r&b), and "A Lover's Question" (Atlantic 1199; 1958; #6 pop, #1 r&b). He remained popular well into the 1960s after switching to the Mercury label, most notably with "Ta Ta" (Mercury 71660; 1960; #23 pop, #7 r&b). However, the British Invasion spearheaded by the Beatles and changing musical tastes led to his fall from commercial favor. Stints with MGM, Amy, and Bell Records in the latter half of the 1960s produced little of note, and McPhatter's skills as a live performer were eroded by an ongoing battle with alcoholism. Notable collections of his best work include *Deep Sea Ball: The Best of Clyde McPhatter* (Atlantic; 1991), *The Forgotten Angel* (2 CDs; 32 Jazz; 1998), and *A Shot of Rhythm and Blues* (Sundazed; 2000), the latter consisting of both sides of his five 1965–1967 Amy singles plus four previously unreleased alternate takes.

July 1. Neil Diamond reaches number one on the pop charts with "Song Sung Blue" (Uni).

July 8. Bill Withers begins a three-week stay atop the Hot 100 with "Lean On Me" (Sussex).

July 15. Buck Owens & His Buckaroos reach number one on the country charts with "Made in Japan" (Capitol 3314), the act's last single to accomplish this feat.

July 18. Cliff Edwards dies at age seventy-six. Better known as "Ukelele Ike," his amiable, jazz-inflected approach stimulated a nationwide craze for the ukulele in the mid-1920s. He appeared in more than fifty film musicals, and achieved immortality as the voice of Jiminy Cricket in the Disney animated feature, *Pinocchio*. His biggest hit recordings were "I Can't Give You Anything But Love" (Columbia 1471; 1928) and "Singin' in the Rain" (Columbia 1869; 1929).

July 22. Charley Pride begins a three-week run atop the country charts with "It's Gonna Take a Little Bit Longer" (RCA 0707).

July 29. Alice Cooper peak at number seven on the Hot 100 with "School's Out" (Warner Bros. 7596).

Alice Cooper—a moniker applied both to Detroit-born vocalist Vincent Furnier (b. February 4, 1948) and his backing band—came across as a straight-ahead hard rock outfit on record. Onstage, the group helped pioneer the American variant of glitter rock, with Furnier projecting a ghoulish, androgynous demeanor accented by theatrical ploys such as simulated hangings, the destruction of dolls and other props, and playing with a live snake.

The band formed as the Earwigs in 1965; comprised of lead guitarist Glen Buxton, rhythm guitarist/keyboardist Michael Bruce, bassist Dennis Dunaway, drummer Neal Smith, and Furnier (aka Cooper), they moved from Phoenix to Los Angeles, releasing a couple of singles as the Spiders on the Santa Cruz label in 1967. A couple of name changes later, they settled on Alice Cooper (allegedly a seventeenth-century witch) and signed with Frank Zappa's Straight Records. Following the release of two rather mediocre post-psychedelic LPs—*Pretties For You* (Straight 1051; 1969) and *Easy Action* (Straight 1061; 1970)—Alice Cooper moved on to Warner Brothers. Assisted by producer Bob Ezrin and exhibiting markedly improved songwriting skills, the band produced a string of proto-metal masterpieces leavened with adolescent-punk attitude: *Love It To Death* (Warner Bros. 1881; 1971; #35), *Killer* (Warner Bros. 2567; 1971; #21), *School's Out* (Warner Bros. 7596; 1972; #2), *Billion Dollar Babies* (Warner Bros. 2685; 1973; #1), and *Muscle Of Love* (Warner Bros. 2748; 1973; #10).

Feeling they had hit a creative dead end, Cooper fired his band in mid-1974, replaced them with Lou

Reed's former supporting musicians. Cooper's first solo album, *Welcome To My Nightmare* (Atlantic 18139; 1975; #5)—featuring Vincent Price as narrator and the AM radio staple, "Only Women Bleed" (Atlantic 3254; 1975; #12)—solidified his stature within the music industry. Evidently quite comfortable with celebrity life (hosting a TV show, hanging out with mainstream Hollywood stars, etc.), his retro releases remained a fixture on the lower reaches of the pop charts through the 1990s.

July 29. British balladeer Gilbert O'Sullivan goes number one on the Hot 100 with "Alone Again (Naturally)" (MAM), remaining there for six non-consecutive weeks.

August 12. Alice Cooper reaches the summit of the British charts with "School's Out" (#7 U.S.).

August 12. Freddie Hart begins a two-week stint atop the country charts with "Bless Your Heart" (Capitol 3353), his third single to accomplish this feat. He composed a fourth chart topper, "Loose Talk" as recorded by Carl Smith in late 1954.

August 26. Looking Glass enjoys a brief stretch atop the pop charts with evocative mid-tempo number, "Brandy (You're a Fine Girl)" (Epic). Despite having come upon a promising pop-rock vein, the group did little to mine it further, expressing an interest in a more hard rock-oriented direction.

August 26. Joe Simon begins a two-week stay atop the R&B charts with "Power of Love" (Spring 128). It as his second chart-topper (the first was 1969's "The Chokin' Kind") and second gold record (following the number three R&B single, "Drowning in the Sea of Love").

August 26. Jerry Wallace establishes a nonconsecutive two-week residency at number one on the country charts with "If You Leave Me Tonight I'll Cry" (Decca 32989).

September 2. Don Gibson heads up the country charts with the Gary Paxton composition, "Woman (Sensuous Woman)" (Hickory 1638).

September 2. The Hollies begin a two-week sojourn at number two on the Hot 100 with "Long Cool Woman (In a Black Dress) (Epic 10871).

September 9. The O'Jays climb to number one on the R&B charts with "Back Stabbers" (Philadelphia International 3517). It represented the first songwriting collaboration by Gene McFadden and John Whitehead (augmented by Kenny Gamble and Leon Huff's arranging and production work).

September 16. James Brown commences a four-week run atop the R&B charts with "Get on the Good Foot (Part 1) (Polydor 14139).

September 16. Sonny James peaks at the summit of the country charts with "When the Snow is on the Roses" (Columbia 45644).

September 16. Rod Stewart tops the British album charts with *Never a Dull Moment*.

September 16. Three Dog Night go number one on the Hot 100 with "Black & White" (Dunhill/ABC).

September 23. Mac Davis begins a three-week stay atop the Hot 100 with "Baby Don't Get Hooked on Me" (Columbia).

September 23. Conway Twitty rises to number one on the country charts with the Don Gibson-penned "I Can't Stop Loving You" (Decca 32988).

September 30. David Cassidy heads up the British charts with "How Can I Be Sure?"

September 30. Mel Tillis begins a two-week stint atop the country charts with "I Ain't Never" (MGM 14418).

October 14. Donna Fargo reaches number one on the country charts with her composition, "Funny Face" (Dot 17429), remaining there for three weeks.

October 14. Michael Jackson achieves his first solo chart topper with "Ben" (Motown 1207), a sentimental love song to a rat.

It appears more and more likely, with each passing year, that Michael Jackson's career will fall short of the expectations of music industry experts. By the mid-1980s, he was the most popular recording artist worldwide—his *Thriller* (Epic 38112; 1982; #1) was the top-selling album of all-time—and on the cutting edge of the rapidly expanding video medium. However, a steady barrage of bad publicity surrounding his plastic surgeries, sexual behavior, and other eccentric activities have substantially eroded his following over the years.

Raised in Gary, Indiana as part of a family of child prodigies, Michael became lead vocalist for the Jackson 5, comprised of brothers Jackie, Tito, Jermaine, and Marlon. Following the release of a couple of singles for the local Steeltown label, the group signed with Motown in 1969. The group made an immediate splash when its first four singles for the label—"I Want You Back" (Motown 1157; 1969), "ABC" (Motown 1163; 1970), "The Love You Save" (Motown 1166), and "I'll Be There" (Motown 1171; 1970)—all reached the number one position. Their early album releases—*Diana Ross Presents The Jackson 5* (Motown 700; 1970; #5), *ABC* (Motown 709; 1970; #4), *The Third Album* (Motown 718; 1970; #4), and *Maybe Tomorrow* (Motown 735; 1971; #11)—also sold extraordinarily well for a black act at the time, due largely to an engaging, effervescent sound that incorporated elements of soul, pop, and bubblegum.

It was clear out of the box, however, that Michael's impassioned singing and showmanship was the most important ingredient behind the Jacksons' success. As a result, Motown decided to issue solo material by Michael alongside group releases beginning in October 1971. Among his more notable early singles were a dynamic remake of Bobby Day's 1958 hit, "Rockin' Robin" (Motown 1197; 1972; #2) and "Ben." He continued recording and performing with his brothers, who—by now writing much of their own material—returned to top form with a proto-disco single, "Dancing Machine" (Motown 1286; 1974; #2). However, the group's fortunes would fluctuate wildly in the future as Michael would take frequent sabbaticals to pursue his solo career.

With the assistance producer/arranger Quincy Jones, Michael hit the big time with *Off The Wall* (Epic 35745; 1979; #3), powered by four Top 10 singles: the pulsating "Don't Stop 'Til You Get Enough" (Epic 50654; 1979; #1), the scintillating "Rock With You" (Epic 50797; 1979; #1), the sentimental "She's Out Of My Life" (Epic 50871; 1980; #10), and the title track (Epic 50838; 1980; #10). Despite this precedent, the unprecedented quality—and commercial staying power—of the next LP, *Thriller*, caught the industry by surprise. The record gathered momentum slowly, first making an impact in the black market, before the heavy MTV rotation of "Billie Jean" (Epic 03509; 1983; #1) and "Beat It" (Epic 03759; 1983; #1) propelled it to a thirty-seven week stretch at the top of the pop album charts; eventually, seven of its nine tracks would reach the Top 10.

Following his participation in the highly publicized *Victory* (Epic 38946; 1984; #4) album and tour with his brothers (the last time he'd work with them as a group), Michael again collaborated with Jones on *Bad* (Epic 40600; 1987; #1), which also spawned seven hit singles, five of which—"I Just Can't Stop Loving You" (Epic 07253; 1987; with Siedah Garrett)," "Bad" (Epic 07418; 1987), "The Way You Make Me Feel" (Epic 07645; 1987), "Man In The Mirror" (Epic 07668), and "Dirty Diana" (Epic 07739; 1987)—reached number one. Despite their relative popularity, subsequent releases—including *Dangerous* (Epic 45400; 1991; #1), the partial retrospective *HIStory: Past, Present And Future – Book 1* (Epic 59000; 1995; #1; double set), and a string of dance-oriented singles—have been poorly received by critics who consider anything falling short of his 1980s classics to be a letdown.

October 14. The Spinners commence a five-week run atop the R&B charts with "I'll Be Around" (Atlantic 2904). Afraid a being typecast for the sweet material he'd produced for the Delfonics and Stylisters, Thom Bell had asked to work with them after spotting the group's name on a roster of label artists.

October 16. Creedence Clearwater Revival announces that they are splitting up. In their previous three-and-a-half years together, the band netted fifteen gold discs, selling around twenty million LPs and ten million singles.

October 21. Chuck Berry reaches number one on the pop charts for the only time in career with a live novelty cut, "My Ding-A-Ling" (Chess), remaining there for two weeks.

November 3. James Taylor and Carly Simon are married in New York. Their future will include artistic collaboration.

November 4. Merle Haggard & the Strangers climb to the summit of the country charts with "It's Not Love (But It's Not Bad)" (Capitol 3419).

November 4. Johnny Nash goes to the top of the pop charts with his reggae-inflected composition, "I Can See Clearly Now" (Epic), which maintains its hegemony for four weeks. Born in Houston, Nash was already a veteran radio and television performer while in his teens. He fell in love with reggae music after visiting Jamaica; his attempts at integrating it into his own recordings, played a key role in helping to popularize the genre stateside.

November 6. The Raspberries earn a gold record for "Go All the Way" (Capitol 3348), which peaked at number five on the Hot 100 in late summer.

The Raspberries were one of the most highly regarded exponents of power-pop; however, they existed at a time when concise, melodic songs, jangly guitars, lush vocal harmonies, and mod-like dress were distinctly out of fashion. Formed in Cleveland in 1970 out of several local groups, the members—including vocalist/bassist Eric Carmen, lead guitarist Wally Bryson, rhythm guitarist Jim Bonfanti, and drummer Dave Smalley—signed a recording contract with Capitol the following year when their demos made an impression on future producer Jimmy Ienner. The first album, *Raspberries* (Capitol 11036; 1972), which included a raspberry-scented scratch-and-sniff sticker on the cover, contained the Top 5, million-selling single, "Go All the Way." Following the release of two more moderately successful LPs—*Fresh* (Capitol 11123; 1972) and *Side 3* (Capitol 11220; 1973)—Bonfanti and Smalley (who were opposed to the band's tennybopper image) left to form Dynamite. Fortified with replacements Michael McBride and Scott McCarl, the group released *Starting Over* (Capitol 11329; 1974), a concept album about the pitfalls of stardom hailed by many critics as the album of the year. Its flat sales facilitated the break-up of the band.

Eric Carmen is the only member of the Raspberries has had any kind of solo success. In addition to recording hits such as "All By Myself" (Arista 0165; 1975), "Never Gonna Fall In Love Again" (Arista 0184; 1976), "Hungry Eyes" (RCA 5315; 1987), and "Make Me Lose Control" (Arista 1-9686; 1988), he has composed the Top 10 songs for Shaun Cassidy—"That's Rock 'n' Roll" (Warner Bros. 8423; 1977) and "Hey Deanie" (Warner Bros. 8488; 1977)—and Mike Reno/Ann Wilson ("Almost Paradise," Columbia 38-04418; 1984).

November 11. Bassist Barry Oakley, age twenty-four, is fatally injured in a motorcycle accident at the same intersection where Allman Brothers bandmate Duane Allman died on a motorcycle a year earlier.

November 11. Gilbert O'Sullivan tops the British charts with "Clair."

November 11. Tammy Wynette reaches number one on the country charts with "My Man (Understands)" (Epic 10909).

November 18. Harold Melvin & the Blue Notes begin a two-week stint atop the R&B charts with the Gamble-Huff classic, "If You Don't Know Me By Now" (Philadelphia International 3520).

November 18. Cat Stevens reaches number one on the album charts with *Catch Bull at Four* (A&M), remaining there for three weeks.

Cat Stevens, born Stephen Georgiou on July 21, 1948, in London, crammed two distinctly separate music careers into his first thirty years prior to converting to Islam, adopting the name Yusaf Islam, and retiring from the music business. He is best remembered, however, for his 1970s incarnation as a singer/songwriter with a gift for socially astute lyrics.

During his early years as a recording artist, Stevens was promoted by the English Decca label as a teen idol. Although a number of his compositions (e.g., "Here Comes My Baby," "First Cut Is the Deepest") were covered by more established stars, he remained relatively unknown stateside in the 1960s. A period spent recovering from tuberculosis in 1968 enabled Stevens, who had been unhappy about Decca's overemphasis on commercial success, to think at length about his future objectives within the music industry.

Following a period of stylistic experimentation, Stevens recorded *Mona Bone Jakon* (A&M 4260; 1970; #63 UK, #164 US), which featured simple, unadorned acoustic arrangements, thereby focusing on his sensitive vocals and poetic verses. His next two albums—*Tea for the Tillerman* (A&M 4280; 1970; #20 UK, #8 US) and *Teaser and the Firecat* (A&M 4313; 1971; #3 UK, #2 US)—continued in the same vein, making him one of the most successful recording artists of the early 1970s. His singles also sold well (fourteen entered the *Billboard Hot 100* during the decade), most notably "Peace Train" (A&M 1291; 1971; #7), "Morning Has Broken" (A&M 1335; 1972; #6), "Oh, Very Young" (A&M 1503; 1974; #10), and the Sam Cooke-penned "Another Saturday Night" (A&M 1602; 1974; #6).

He maintained his popularity with the LPs *Catch Bull at Four* (A&M 4365; 1972; #2 UK, #1 US), *Foreigner* (A&M 4391; 1973; #3 UK, #3 US), and *Buddah and the Chocolate Box* (A&M 3623; 1974; #3 UK, #2 US), although arrangements were seen as increasingly cluttered. The songwriting was also noticeably less inspired in the final releases—*Numbers* (A&M 4555; 1975; #13 US), *Izitso* (A&M 4702; 1977; #18 UK, #7 US), and *Back to Earth* (A&M 4735; #1978; #33; his only 1970s album not to achieve gold status)—by which time his English audience, in particular, had become largely apathetic.

December 2. Al Green goes to the summit of the R&B charts with "You Ought to Be With Me" (Hi 2227).

December 2. The Temptations reach number one on the Hot 100 with the chilling social commentary, "Papa Was a Rollin' Stone" (Gordy). Written and produced by the group's longtime associates, Barrett Strong and Norman Whitfield, the single challenged pop song conventions of the day by clocking in six minutes and fifty-eight seconds. Along with 1965's "My Girl," it would remain their most requested recording, ultimately achieving platinum status.

December 9. Helen Reddy enjoys a week at the summit of the pop charts with the feminist anthem, "I Am Woman" (Capitol 3350).

One of the most successful female recording artists of the 1970s, Reddy remains best known as the composer and singer of the feminist anthem, "I Am Woman." Her style would provide the template for Adult Contemporary—a genre that would become a music industry fixture by the 1980s.

A native of Melbourne, Australia, Reddy moved to the United States in 1966 in order to further her singing career. The hallmarks of Reddy's future commercial success—the judicious choice of material, outstanding vocal technique, and an ingratiating delivery—were evident in her first hit, "I Don't Know How to Love Him" (Capitol 3027; 1971; #13), a selection from the then-popular rock musical, *Jesus Christ Superstar*. The ensuing LP, *I Don't Know How to Love Him* (Capitol 762; 1971; #100; gold record), included a track that was to become her signature song, "I Am Woman" (which went on earn a gold record). Released in May 1972—well after the appearance of her second album, *Helen Reddy* (Capitol 857; 1971; #167)—it would reach number one on the *Billboard Hot 100* the week of December 9, 1972, due in part to the support of women's liberation groups. The single would earn a Grammy for Best Song of 1972, and lead to her own summer 1973 TV program, *The Helen Reddy Show* (NBC).

Reddy's expanded media exposure provided an additional boost to her recording career. The Music Operators of America would name her Artist of the Year on Jukeboxes for 1973. Her Top 10 singles included "Delta Dawn" (Capitol 3645; 1973; #1; gold record), "Leave Me Alone (Ruby Red Dress)" (Capitol 3768; 1973; #3; gold record), "You and Me Against the World" (Capitol 3897; 1974; #9), "Angie Baby" (Capitol 3972; 1974; #1; gold record), and "Ain't No Way to Treat a Lady" (Capitol 4128; 1975; 1975; #8). Her albums also sold well, most notably *I Am Woman* (Capitol 11068; 1972; #14; platinum record), *Long Hard Climb* (Capitol 11213; 1973; #8; gold record), *Love Song for Jeffrey* (Capitol 1284; 1974; #11; gold record), *Free and Easy* (Capitol 11348; 1974; #8; gold record), *No Way to Treat a Lady* (Capitol 11418; 1975; #11; gold record), *Helen Reddy's Greatest Hits* (Capitol 11467; 1975; #5; double-platinum record), and *Music, Music* (Capitol 11547; 1976; #16; gold record).

The popularity of Reddy's recordings dropped off considerably in the late 1970s, perhaps due to an increasing interest in acting—she appeared in films such as *Airport 75* (1974), *Pete's Dragon* (1977), and *Sgt. Pepper's Lonely Hearts Club Band* (1978). As a result, she signed with MCA Records in 1979. Her next two LPs, *Play Me Out* (1981) and *Imagination* (1983), seemed out of touch with the MTV generation, and by the mid-1980s she was no longer affiliated with a major label. She began concentrating on theatre; *Center Stage* (Razor & Tie; 1998), comprised entirely of show music, represented her first album of new material since the early 1980s.

December 16. Billy Paul's "Me and Mrs. Jones" (Philadelphia International 3521)—a ballad treating the topic of infidelity written by Philly Soul producers Kenny Gamble and Leon Huff with the assistance of Cary Gilbert—begins a three-week run atop the Hot 100 (#1 R&B three weeks). While the single seemed to accurately reflect the ambiguous sexual mores of that era, Paul's handlers seriously miscalculated his audience on the follow-up release, the belligerent anthem, "Am I Black Enough For You?" He would attempt to regroup, but was unable to recapture the commercial momentum generated by "Me and Mrs. Jones."

1973

❄

January 6. Carly Simon begins a three-week stint atop the Hot 100 with "You're So Vain" (Elektra). The presence of Mick Jagger as a backing vocalist fuels speculation that the song is about him.

January 6. Stevie Wonder's "Superstition" (Tama 54226)—also written and produced by the Motown superstar—reaches number one on the R&B charts, maintaining a three-week hegemony.

January 9. Mick Jagger fails to obtain a Japanese visa due to a 1969 drug conviction; as a result, the Rolling Stones are forced to cancel an upcoming tour.

January 16. Still more than two years away from superstardom, Bruce Springsteen performs for twenty-five people at Villanova University.

January 26. Still virtual unknowns stateside, the Sweet go number one in the U.K. with "Blockbuster." They will score fifteen Top 40 hits in their homeland.

January 27. Roxy Music tops "the most promising new name" portion of the *New Musical Express* readers' poll.

January 27. Timmy Thomas begins a two-week stint atop the R&B charts with "Why Can't We Live Together" (Glades 1703). Backed by only a Lowrey organ and rhythm machine, the single would sell two million copies. Thomas discussed the origins of the record in the 1973 *Blues & Soul* interview:

> It was written out of my concern for the world. Not a racial trouble, but a general problem of why we can't all live together—not necessarily black and white, but take a look around the world and see al the little problems that are being experienced. And all the big ones in places such as Israel and Egypt or Vietnam.

January 27. Stevie Wonder garners his second number one pop single, "Superstition," almost a full decade following the first, "Fingertips, Part 2."

January 30. Kiss appear live for the first time at The Coventry Club, New York.

February 3. Elton John commences a three-week stint atop the Hot 100 with "Crocodile Rock" (MCA).

February 8. Max Yasgur—owner of the Woodstock farm where the legendary 1969 festival was held—dies of a heart attack at age fifty-three.

February 10. Elton John begins a six-week stay at number one on the British charts with *Don't Shoot Me, I'm Only the Piano Player*—his first LP to accomplish that feat.

February 10. The Spinners top the R&B charts with "Could It Be I'm Falling in Love" (Atlantic 2927).

February 10. Timmy Thomas peaks at number three on the Hot 100 with "Why Can't We Live Together" (Glades 1703).

Although Timmy Thomas may strike pop music enthusiasts as something of a one-hit wonder, he remained a fixture on the R&B charts for much of two decades. Born November 13, 1944, in Evansville, Indiana, the singer/songwriter/keyboardist performed with such notables as Donald Byrd and Cannonball Adderley early in his career. He was a studio musician in the mid-1960s for the Memphis-based Goldwax label.

His first hit—"Why Can't We Live Together" (#1 r&b)—would remain his biggest. While he would only creased the *Billboard* Hot 100 two more times, a dozen more of his singles reached the R&B through 1984. He also remained active as a session player, working with KC and the Sunshine Band and Betty Wright, among others.

February 11. An Auckland, New Zealand, charity raises $850 selling the sheets and pillowcases used by the Rolling Stones following a performance there.

February 14. David Bowie raises concerns following an onstage collapse at New York's Radio City Music Hall.

February 17. Merle Haggard & the Strangers reach number one on the country charts with a lament for Vietnam War POWs, "I Wonder If They Ever Think of Me" (Capitol 3455).

February 17. The O'Jays begin a four-week run atop the R&B charts with "Love Train" (Philadelphia International 3524).

February 24. The Byrds perform at The Capitol Theatre in Passaic, New Jersey—their last live show.

February 24. Robert Flack goes number one on the Hot 100 with "Killing Me Softly With His Song" (Atlantic), remaining there for five non-consecutive weeks. The recording was allegedly about Don McLean.

February 24. Loretta Lynn heads up the country charts with "Rated X" (Decca 33039). Lynn would later reflect on the genesis of the song's title,

> This was about the time that all you heard about was them movies comin' out that were rated X, and I thought, "Hmmm, I'll just write about a divorced woman," 'cause I had about eight songs banned, and every time I had a song banned, it went number one, so I didn't worry about it anymore. Roland. *The Billboard Book of Number One Country Hits*, 1991.

March 3. Grammy Award winners include Roberta Flack (Song of the Year and Record of the Year with "The First Time Ever I Saw Your Face") and Harry Nilsson (Best Pop Vocal Performance for "Without You").

March 3. Slade's "Cum On Feel the Noize" enters the British charts at number one; they are the first act to achieve this since the Beatles. It is their fourth U.K. chart topper.

March 3. Cal Smith peaks at number one on the country charts with the Bill Anderson-penned "The Lord Knows I'm Drinking" (Decca 33040).

March 5. Jimi Hendrix's former U.S. manager, Michael Jeffrey, is one of sixty-eight killed in a plane crash in France. He was on his way to London court appearance concerned with Hendrix-related issues.

March 7. CBS Records executive John Hammond suffers a heart attack at Max's Kansas City, Manhattan. The "Showcase" concert was planned to mark the signing of Bruce Springsteen.

March 8. Grateful Dead keyboardist Ron "Pigpen" Mckernan dies at age twenty-seven from liver failure induced by alcohol poisoning.

March 8. Paul McCartney is fined $170 for growing cannabis at his Campbeltown, Scotland, farm. He claimed the seeds given to him by fans, and that he didn't know what they were.

March 10. Pink Floyd's *Dark Side of the Moon* is released in the United States. Over the next fourteen years it will spend 740 weeks on the album charts.

March 10. Tammy Wynette's "'Til I Get It Right" (Epic 10940) tops the country charts.

March 17. Barbara Fairchild begins a two-week stint at number one on the country charts with "Teddy Bear Song" (Columbia 45743).

March 17. Eric Weissberg tops the album charts with *Dueling Banjos*, remaining there for three weeks. It features the theme song from the film, *Deliverance*.

March 21. The BBC bans teenybopper acts from its television show, *Top of the Pops*, due to rioting following a David Cassidy performance.

March 23. John Lennon is ordered by the immigration authorities to leave the United States within sixty days. He begins his legal battle to obtain a Green Card.

March 24. The O'Jays reach the summit of the pop charts with "Love Train" (Philadelphia International).

March 24. Alice Cooper go number one on the British album charts with *Billion Dollar Babies*.

March 27. *Rolling Stone* reports that Carlos Santana has become a disciple of Sri Chinmoy, changing his name to "Devadip," which means "the lamp of the light of the Supreme."

March 31. Donny Osmond tops the British charts with his remake of the 1957 Johnny Mathis hit, "The Twelfth of Never."

April 7. Vicki Lawrence heads up the Hot 100 with "The Night the Lights Went Out in Georgia" (Bell), remaining there for two weeks.

April 7. Diana Ross begins a two-week stay atop the album charts with *Lady Sings the Blues*.

April 14. Led Zeppelin starts a two-week stint at number one on the U.K. album charts with *Houses of the Holy*.

April 17. Pink Floyd's *Dark Side of the Moon* achieves gold record status in the United States.

April 21. Alice Cooper tops the album charts with *Billion Dollar Babies* (Warner Bros.).

April 21. "Tie a Yellow Ribbon Round the Old Oak Tree" (Bell), by Dawn featuring Tony Orlando, reaches number one on the Hot 100, remaining there for four weeks. Told from the perspective of a prisoner anticipating the reunion with his lover, the song—also a major country hit as interpreted by Johnny Carver—will come to symbolize the plight of the Iranian hostages and American servicemen involved in foreign conflicts.

April 28. Pink Floyd *Dark Side of the Moon* tops the album charts.

April 29. John Denver begins a weekly BBC 2 TV special, *The John Denver Show*.

May 1. The Carpenters perform at the White House in front of President Nixon.

May 4. Led Zeppelin kick off what is billed as the "biggest and most profitable rock 'n' roll tour in the history of the United States." The band earns more than three million dollars from the tour.

May 5. David Bowie tops the British album charts for the first time with *Aladdin Sane*, remaining there for five weeks.

May 6. Paul Simon begins his set tour without long-term partner, Art Garfunkel. The Jesse Dixon Singers serve as his backup group.

May 19. The Independents peak at number one on the R&B charts with "Leaving Me" (Wand 11252).

May 19. Stevie Wonder returns to the top spot on the pop charts with "You Are the Sunshine of My Life" (Tamla).

May 26. First Choice peak at number twenty-eight on the Hot 100 with "Armed and Extremely Dangerous" (Philly Groove 175).

Originally formed as the Debronettes, the Philadelphia trio included Rochelle Fleming, Annette Guest, and Joyce Jones. They placed a dozen singles on the R&B charts in the 1970s, beginning with "Armed and Extremely Dangerous" (Philly Groove 175; 1973; #28 pop, #11 r&b). Their other Top 40 hits included "Smarty Pants" (Philly Groove 179; 1973; #56 pop, #25 r&b), "Newsy Neighbors" (Philly Groove 183; 1974; #97 pop, #35 r&b), "The Player – Part 1" (Philly Groove 200; 1974; #70 pop, #7 r&b), "Guilty" (Philly Soul 202; 1974; #103 pop, #19 r&b), and "Doctor Love" (Gold Mind 4004; #41 pop, #23 r&b).

May 26. Barry White begins a two-week stint atop the R&B charts with "I'm Gonna Love You Just a Little Bit More Baby" (20th Century 2018), which he also composed and produced. White would refer to the song as his "national anthem," although it took a champion for his cause within the record company to issue it over the reservations of other label executives.

May 26. The Edgar Winter Group go number one on the Hot 100 with instrumental "Frankenstein" (Epic).

June 1. Former Soft Machine drummer Robert Wyatt fractures his spine after falling three stories in an attempt to leave a party via a drainpipe. Although confined to a wheelchair, he continues to make artistically lauded music.

June 2. Paul McCartney & Wings begin a four-week run atop the Hot 100 with "My Love" (Apple).

June 6. Barry White earns a gold record for "I'm Gonna Love You Just a Little Bit More Baby" (20th Century 2018; #1 R&B, #3 pop).

Born September 12, 1944, in Galveston, Texas, White was raised in Los Angeles. He got involved with recording studios at an early age, playing piano as an eleven-year-old on Jesse Belvin's 1956 hit, "Goodnight My Love." He was a member of the R&B vocal group, the Upfronts, who recorded for Lummtone in 1960. He would move on to Atlantic in 1964 as a solo act, and (as "Barry Lee") for Downey and Veep in 1965. He served as an A&R man for Mustang/Bronco from 1966 to 1967, and formed the female vocal trio, Love Unlimited, in 1969.

Completely in control of all aspects of his recorded output by the time he signed with 20th Century, White became a consistent crossover hit-maker beginning the release of "I'm Gonna Love You Just a

Little More Baby," followed by R&B chart-toppers "Can't Get Enough of Your Love, Babe" (#1 pop as well), "You're the First, the Last, My Everything," "What Am I Gonna Do with You," and "It's Ecstasy When You Lay Down Next To Me." He would attempt periodic comebacks up to his death in 2003.

June 9. The Spinners head up the R&B charts with "One of a Kind (Love Affair)," remaining there for four weeks

June 23. Manu Dibango's "Soul Makossa" (Atlantic 2971)—widely considered to be the first disco hit as well as one of the most successful Afro-rock recordings in the American scene—enters the R&B charts, peaking at number twenty-one (number thirty-five on the *Billboard* Hot 100). A funky instrumental punctuated by the interplay of vocal and saxophone riffing, "Soul Makossa" (recorded in Paris) became a dance club smash while receiving relatively little radio play. Born in Cameroon, Dibango relocated to Europe in his early teens in 1949. He first recorded in Belgium in 1952, and switched from jazz to African-styled material in the early 1960s. His home base would shift between Africa and Europe for the balance of his career.

June 30. George Harrison goes number one on the pop charts with "Give Me Love (Give Me Peace on Earth)" (Apple).

June 30. Slade head up the British charts for the fifth time with "Skweeze Me Pleeze Me."

July 7. Billy Preston begins a two-week stint atop the Hot 100 with "Will It Go Round in Circles" (A&M).

July 7. Fred Wesley and the J.B.'s step out from James Brown's shadow with the instrumental shuffle, "Doing It to Death" (People 621), which holds down the top spot on the R&B charts for two charts. Brown nevertheless provided a major assist to his backup band, writing and then producing the January 29, 1973, session from which the single emerged.

July 21. Jim Croce reaches number one on the Hot 100 with "Bad, Bad Leroy Brown" (ABC), remaining there for two weeks.

July 21. Bette Midler peaks at number eight on the Hot 100 with her remake of "Boogie Woogie Bugle Boy" (Atlantic 2964).

Although Bette Midler possessed an extraordinary voice—capable of tackling Broadway fare, big band swing numbers, torch ballads, the blues, and straight-ahead rock in equally convincing fashion—her multi-faceted talents tended to pull her in many directions, including club performing, film acting, television work (talk shows, specials, and a series), book writing (memoirs of her first world tour, *A View From a Broad*, 1980, and the children's book, *The Saga of Baby Divine*, 1983), and large-scale charity work for causes such as AIDS, restoring New York City highways and parks, and voter registration. Taken on their own merits, Midler's recordings often came across as pale facsimiles of the energy and excitement projected in her live shows.

After working musicals and other stage productions during the late 1960s, Midler decided to concentrate on singing. She developed a cult reputation doing camp comedy interspersed with a broad musical repertoire at the Continental Baths, a New York City-based gay men's club. A round of TV talk show appearances greatly expanded her fan base, and a recording contract with Atlantic followed.

The debut album, *The Divine Miss M* (Atlantic 7238; 1973; #9), achieved platinum status in addition to yielding a hit single, a cover of the Andrews Sisters' "Boogie Woogie Bugle Boy." It would also earn Midler the 1973 Grammy for Best New Artist. Although she retained her loyal concert following, LP releases—*Bette Midler* (Atlantic 7270; 1973; #6; earned gold record), *Songs for the New Depression* (Atlantic 18155; 1976; #27), *Live at Last* (Atlantic 9000; 1977; #49), *Broken Blossom* (Atlantic 19151; 1977; #51), and *Thighs and Whispers* (Atlantic 16004; 1979; #65)—underwent a steady decline in both sales and critical favor.

Midler's fortunes rebounded when her featured role in *The Rose* (1979), a film inspired by events from Janis Joplin's life, earned an Oscar nomination for Best Actress. Her dramatic reading of the title song (Atlantic 3656; 1980) reached number three, and the soundtrack album (Atlantic 16010; 1979; #12) went platinum. Her next project, a concert film and soundtrack, *Divine Madness* (Atlantic 16022; 1980; #34), also achieved considerable success.

The negative publicity ensuing from a poorly received film, *Jinxed* (1982), helped usher in another dormant career phase. Revived by a series of comedies for the Disney-owned Touchstone Pictures (*Down and Out in Beverly Hills*, 1986; *Ruthless People*, 1986; *Outrageous Fortune*, 1987; and *Big Business*, 1988), she found chart success with the triple-platinum soundtrack to *Beaches* (Atlantic 81933; 1989; #2), which included the Grammy-winning hit, "Wind Beneath My Wings" (Atlantic 88972; 1989; #1).

While Midler remained a top film draw in the 1990s (including a second Oscar nomination for her role in *For the Boys*), her recording career was considerably more erratic in nature. *Some People's Lives* (Atlantic 82129; 1990; #6)—assisted by the Grammy-winning ballad, "From a Distance" (Atlantic 87820; 1990; #2), which was heavily played during the Gulf War—achieved double-platinum status. Although Midler has failed to record a Top 40 hit since that time, she has continued to release LPs—many of them film and television soundtracks—at regular intervals. In all of them, she seems content to reprise her earlier work; for example, *Bathhouse Betty* (Warner Bros.; 1998) represents a return to the bawdy, glam style of the early 1970s club sets.

July 21. Johnnie Taylor's "I Believe in You (You Believe in Me)" (Stax 0161) begins a two-week stay atop the R&B charts.

August 4. Aretha Franklin negotiates the summit of the R&B charts with "Angel" (Atlantic 2969), holding on for a fortnight.

August 4. Maureen McGovern peaks at number one on the Hot 100 with "The Morning After" (20th Century), remaining there for a couple of weeks.

August 18. Marvin Gaye starts a six-week run atop the R&B charts with the sexually explicit "Let's Get It On" (Tama 54234).

August 18. Diana Ross goes number one on the pop charts with "Touch Me in the Morning" (Motown).

August 19. Kris Kristofferson marries Rita Coolidge in Malibu, California.

August 25. Stories begin a two-week stay atop the Hot 100 with "Brother Louie" (Kama Sutra), a paean to interracial dating. The band's Mike Brown first achieved a measure of fame and success as the frontman for The Left Banke.

September 8. Marvin Gaye reaches number one on the Hot 100 with "Let's Get It On" (Tamla), remaining there for two non-consecutive weeks.

September 15. Helen Reddy goes to the top of the pop charts with "Delta Dawn" (Capitol). Tanya Tucker duplicates the feat on the country survey.

September 19. Country rock singer/songwriter Gram Parsons—a former member of the Byrds and Flying Burrito Brothers—dies of a heroin overdose at age twenty-six. His body will be stolen from a Los Angeles funeral home and burned in the Southern California desert, allegedly in accordance with his wishes.

September 29. Grand Funk makes it to number one on the Hot 100 with "We're an American Band" (Capitol).

A populist blend of heavy metal and updated blues boogie, Grand Funk Railroad provided the template for rock band success in the 1970s: by touring constantly to large, appreciative crowds, they were able to neutralize the distaste of music critics and apathy (at least in the early years) of radio programmers. Their in-concert appeal played a major role in the transition of rock venues from smaller clubs and auditoriums to arenas and sports stadiums.

The Flint, Michigan-based Grand Funk Railroad came together in late 1968 when lead vocalist/guitarist/songwriter Mark Farner and drummer/vocalist Don Brewer—who had played with one-hit wonder, Terry Knight and the Pack—with former ? and the Mysterians bassist Mel Schacher. With Knight given complete control as manager, the band's performance in front of 125,000 people at the Atlanta Pop Festival in July 1969 led to a contract with Capitol Records.

Although the debut album, *On Time* (Capitol 307; 1969; #27), would eventually achieve gold status, the next five releases—*Grand Funk* (Capitol 406; 1970; #11), *Closer to Home* (Capitol 471; 1970; #6), *Live Album* (Capitol 633; 1970; #5), *Survival* (Capitol 764; 1971; #6), and *E Pluribus Funk* (Capitol 853; 1971;

#5; featuring a circular, silver cover imitating a U.S. coin)—went platinum, thereby validating Grand Funk Railroad's stripped-down sound, built around incessant guitar power-chords. Legal difficulties centering around the 1972 decision to fire Knight would prove temporarily disruptive, but the band rebounded with its most pop-oriented releases, including *Phoenix* (Capitol 11099; 1972; #7), augmented by the addition of organist Craig Frost, two Todd Rundgren-produced LPs, *We're an American Band* (Capitol 11207; 1973; #2; achieved double-platinum status)—which featured the chart-topping title track (Capitol 3660; 1973)—and *Shinin' On* (Capitol 11278; 1974; #5)—with the hit singles "Loco-Motion" (Capitol 3840; 1974; #1) and "Shinin' On" (Capitol 3917; 1974; #11)—and *All the Girls in the World Beware!!!* (Capitol 11356; 1974; #10), which yielded "Some Kind of Wonderful" (Capitol 4002; 1975; #3) and "Bad Time" (Capitol 4046; 1975; #4).

With internal differences coming to the fore, the band issued a lackluster live set, *Caught in the Act* (Capitol 11445; 1975; #21), and two more studio albums, *Born to Die* (Capitol 11482; 1976; #47) and the Frank Zappa-produced *Good Singin', Good Playin'* (Capitol 2216; 1976; #52). Grand Funk then disbanded, with Brewer and Schacher forming Flint, and Farner pursuing a solo career.

Farner and Brewer would re-form Grand Funk Railroad in 1981, recruiting Dennis Bellinger to play bass. The ensuing album releases, *Grand Funk Lives* (Full Moon 3625; 1981; #148) and *What's Funk* (Full Moon 923750; 1983), sold poorly, and the band would again dissolve. With classic heavy metal making a comeback, the original threesome joined forces in 1997 for a world tour that was documented by the live LP, *Bosnia* (1997). In the wake of renewed interest in the band, Capitol released a box-set anthology, *Thirty Years of Funk: 1969-1999* (Capitol; 1999). Shortly thereafter, however, Farner announced plans to return to a solo career.

October 6. Cher begins a two-week stay atop the Hot 100 with "Half-Breed" (MCA).

October 9. Priscilla Presley obtains a divorce from Elvis Presley.

October 20. The Rolling Stones reach number one on the pop charts with "Angie" (Rolling Stones).

October 23. Duke Ellington records his *Third Sacred Concert* live for RCA.

October 27. Gladys Knight and the Pips begin a two-week stint atop the Hot 100 with "Midnight Train to Georgia" (Buddah).

November 10. Former Temptations lead singer Eddie Kendricks moves into the top slot on the Hot 100 with "Keep on Truckin' (Part 1)" (Tamla 54238), remaining there for two weeks.

Eddie Kendricks really had two careers, one as lead singer of the sweet soul juggernaut, the Temptations, and another—billed as a solo performer—as a leading purveyor of 1970s funk. Within the Motown stable of artists only the great Smokey Robinson enjoyed comparable success as a recording artist in two guises.

Kendricks was born December 17, 1939, in Union Springs, Alabama, but raised in Birmingham. Relocating to Detroit in the late 1950s, he would join the Primes, who later evolved into the Temptations. He remained with the group until 1971, when he opted for a solo career.

Kendricks early records reveal a singer in search of his own trademark style; ranging from silky-smooth ballads to uptempo material, they were moderate hits at best. His breakthrough came with the propulsive dance track, "Keep On Truckin' (Part 1) (#1 r&b), followed by eight more R&B Top 10 smashes in succession, including the chart-toppers "Boogie Down" (Tamla 54243; 1973; #2 pop #1 r&b) and "Shoeshine Boy" (Tamla 54247; 1975; #18 pop, #1 r&b).

The hits tailed off in the early 1980s, but Kendrick (who by now had dropped the letter "s" from his last name) returned to the public eye with a collaborative performance—along with former Temptations mate, David Ruffin, and the blue-eyed soul duo Daryl Hall and John Oates—at the re-opening of New York's Apollo Theatre, released as an album entitled, *Live At The Apollo with David Ruffin & Eddie Kendrick* (RCA 7035; 1985; #21). A Temptations medley culled from the concert, "The Way You Do the Things You Do/My Girl" (RCA 14178; 1985; #20 pop, #40 r&b), would be his last Top 20 single on the *Billboard* Hot 100. He would continue to place duets with Ruffin on the R&B charts before succumbing to lung cancer on October 5, 1992.

November 13. Jerry Lee Lewis, Jr.—then a drummer in his father's band—is killed in a car accident near Hernando, Mississippi.

November 22. *Rolling Stone* pictures a Jerry Garcia animation figure under the caption "Welcome to the Wide Open World of the Corporate Dead."

November 24. Ringo Starr enjoys his first pop chart topper as a solo act with "Photograph" (Apple).

December 1. The Carpenters begin a two-week run at number one on the Hot 100 with "Top of the World" (A&M).

December 15. Charlie Rich reaches the summit of the pop charts with "The Most Beautiful Girl" (Epic), remaining there for two weeks. Long revered for genre-bending hits like "Lonely Weekends" (1960) and "Mohair Sam" (1965), he is the midst of an improbable comeback after disappearing from the mainstream view for close to a decade.

December 20. Bobby Darin dies from a lifelong heart condition at age thirty-seven. His career spanned teen idol rock 'n' roll, Las Vegas pop, and the singer/songwriter genre.

December 29. Jim Croce—who had perished in a late summer plane crash—makes a final appearance at number one on the Hot 100 with "Time in a Bottle" (ABC), remaining there for two weeks.

December 31. Journey make their live debut at the Winterland Ballroom in San Francisco.

1974

❄

January 3. Jim Croce's "Time in a Bottle"—which topped the Hot 100 in December—goes gold. It is the second of three posthumous Top 10 hits for the singer/songwriter. The first, "I Got a Name," was actually released shortly before his death from a plane accident, and "I'll Have to Say I Love You in a Song" will complete the hat trick later in the spring.

January 3. Bob Dylan and The Band kick off a thirty-nine-date tour of the United States. The long-awaited event spurs five million applications for the 660,000 tickets.

January 7. Carly Simon and James Taylor have their second child, Sarah Martin, in New York.

January 8. Nine years after its release, *The Early Beatles* earns a gold record. Due to its affiliation with the British EMI label, Capitol had possessed the first option to release the material comprising the album. When Capitol chose not to do so, more opportunistic indie labels quickly filled the breach. When Beatlemania swept the nation, Capitol worked hard to reassert its rights to these songs, finally issuing *The Early Beatles* during a commercial lull prior to the release the movie, *Help*.

January 12. The Steve Miller Band's "The Joker" (Capitol) reaches number one on the Hot 100. The million-selling single launched a new career path for Miller—that of an AM radio hit machine. Prior to that time, he'd been categorized as an album artist; other than "Living in the U.S.A.," which creased the pop charts, none of the tracks from his first seven LPs of original material became hit singles. "The Joker" also tops the British charts in 1990.

January 18. Bad Company is formed by ex-members of Free (Paul Rodgers and Simon Kirke), Mott the Hoople (Mick Ralphs), and King Crimson (Boz Burrell).

January 19. Al Wilson goes number one on the Hot 100 with "Show and Tell" (Rocky Road).

January 22. Carly Simon receives a gold record for *Hotcakes*. Perhaps best remembered for its naughty cover art, the album includes the Top 5 cover single, "Mockingbird" a duet with husband James Taylor.

January 22. Bob Dylan's *Planet Waves* achieves gold record status. It is his first album for Asylum, and will become his first chart-topper the following month.

January 26. Ringo Starr's "You're Sixteen" (Apple) occupies the top rung of the pop charts. As the calendar year 1974 approach, many rock fans and journalists predicted the coming of a new rock messiah. After all, 1954 had seen the emergence of Elvis Presley as a Sun recording artist, and 1964 brought the British Invasion spearheaded by the Beatles. As one *Rolling Stone* writer noted at the time, amidst speculation that the Beatles might re-form, Ringo Starr—then in the process of recording one hit after another—seemed as likely a savior as anyone. Ironically, three of the Beatles enjoyed chart-topping singles that year, and the odd man out, George Harrison, remained a consistent seller in the LP sector. The song first made the Top 10 in an interpretation by rockabilly raver-turned-teenybopper idol, Johnny Burnette.

February 2. Barbra Streisand reaches number one on the Hot 100 with "The Way We Were" (the theme to the film of the same name), remaining there for three non-consecutive weeks. It goes on to garner an Academy Award and Grammy as "song of the year."

February 9. The Barry White lounge-soul vehicle, Love Unlimited Orchestra, tops the pop charts with his instrumental composition, "Love's Theme" (20th Century).

February 13. David Bowie declines an offer from the Gay Liberation Organization to compose "the world's first Gay National Anthem."

February 14. While on a promotional tour, Daryl Dragon and Toni Tennille (Captain and Tennille) get married in Virginia City.

February 16. Bob Dylan tops the LP charts for the first time with *Planet Waves* (Asylum), remaining there for four weeks.

February 23. Suzi Quatro tops the British charts for the second time with "Devil Gate Drive."

February 27. Cher files for divorce from Sonny Bono. She would go on to marry Gregg Allman, June 27, 1975.

February 28. Bobby Bloom dies from a self-inflicted gunshot to the head at age twenty-eight. His self-composed recording, "Montego Bay," was an international hit (#8 U.S., #3 U.K.) in 1970.

March 1. Chris Difford places an ad in a shop window: Lyricist seeks musician for co-writing." Gen Tillbrook responds, and the pair go on to form Squeeze.

March 1. Queen begin their first U.K. tour as a headliner at The Winter Gardens, Blackpool.

March 2. Ex-Poppy Family member Terry Jacks begins a three-week run atop the Hot 100 with the Jacques Brel/Rod McKuen composition, "Seasons in the Sun" (Bell; #1 UK).

March 2. Stevie Wonder wins four Grammies: Album of the Year for *Innervisions*, Best R&B Song and Best Vocal for "Superstition," and Best Pop Vocal Performance for "You Are the Sunshine of My Life."

March 9. Kool and the Gang peak at number four on the Hot 100 with "Jungle Boogie" (De Lite 559).

> While mainstream pop music fans were largely unfamiliar with Kool and the Gang when their recording, "Celebration" (De-Lite 807; 1980; #1 pop, #1 r&b six weeks), topped the charts, they were the farthest thing from an overnight success. In fact, the band's core members had been working together for seventeen years prior to the release of what would be their biggest record.
>
> The origins of the group go back to frontman Robert "Kool" Bell's formation of a Jersey City-based combo, the Jazziacs, in 1964. The fourteen-year-old bassist started out doing session work and playing jam sessions on the Jersey circuit complemented by brother Ronald Bell on tenor sax, trumpeter Robert "Spike" Mullins, alto saxophonist Dennis "D. T." Thomas, drummer George Brown, and lead guitarist Charles Smith. Later in the decade, the aggregate—then known as the SoulTown Band—began leaning increasingly in the direction of R&B and funk.
>
> Shortly after renaming themselves Kool and the Gang in 1969, they garnered a recording contract with De-Lite. Their early releases—most notably, "Jungle Boogie" (#2 r&b), "Hollywood Swinging" (De-Lite 561; 1974; #6 pop, #1 r&b), "Higher Plane" (De-Lite 1562; 1974; #37 pop, #1 r&b), "Rhyme Tyme People" (De-Lite 1563; 1974; #63 pop, #3 r&b), "Spirit of the Boogie" (De-Lite 1567; 1975; #35 pop, #1 r&b)—were heavily grounded in funk rhythms. The very "blackness" of such material made crossing over to the pop charts on unlikely proposition.
>
> The onset of the disco era led to a discernable decline in their fan base; as a result, Kool opted to add lead singer James "J. T." Taylor, whose rich voice was well suited to ballads and other adult contemporary material, and smooth jazz composer/producer, Eumir Deodato. The collaboration with Deodato resulted in two best-selling albums—*Ladies Night* (De-Lite 9513; 1979; #13; platinum award), which included "Ladies Night" (De-Lite 801; 1979; #8 pop, #1 r&b) and "Too Hot" (De-Lite 802; 1980; #5 pop, #3 r&b), and *Celebrate!* (De-Lite 9518; 1980; #10; platinum award). Although the group lost commercial momentum in the last 1980s—their last chart hit was "Holiday" (Mercury 888712; 1987; #66 pop, #9 r&b)—they have continued to perform up to the present day. In all, they placed 20 LPs and 44 singles on the charts.

March 10. *Candide* is revived at New York's Broadway Theatre. Featuring music by Leonard Bernstein, lyrics by Richard Wilber and others, and book by Hugh Wheeler. The musical will run for 740 performances.

March 12. Out on a drinking binge with Harry Nilsson, John Lennon is forcibly removed from West Hollywood's Troubadour Club after yelling insults at the performers, the Smothers Brothers, and punching their manager.

March 16. Barbra Streisand begins a two-week stint atop the album charts with *The Way We Were* (Columbia).

March 23. Cher reaches number one on the pop charts with "Dark Lady" (MCA).

March 28. Arthur "Big Boy" Crudup dies of a stroke at age sixty-nine. He is best remembered for composing "That's All Right (Mama)," a regional hit for Elvis Presley in 1954.

March 30. John Denver's "Sunshine on My Shoulders" (RCA) outperforms all competition on the Hot 100.

April 6. Blue Swede reach number one on the Hot 100 with their revival of B. J. Thomas' "Hooked on a Feeling" (EMI).

April 6. The California Jam 1 festival takes place before more than two hundred thousand fans in Ontario, California. Featured artists include Black Oak Arkansas, Black Sabbath, Deep Purple, the Eagles, ELP, and Seals & Croft.

April 12. The film, *That'll Be the Day*—starring David Essex, Ringo Starr, Keith Moon, Billy Fury, and Dave Edmunds—premieres in London.

April 13. Elton John's "Bennie and the Jets" (MCA) reaches the summit of the pop charts on the strength of its appeal to both AOR and R&B fans.

April 20. Billy Joel peaks at number twenty-five on the Hot 100 with "Piano Man" (Columbia 45963). The track is an even bigger FM hit, effectively jump-starting Joel's career.

Joel's refined sense of songcraft places him squarely within the classic Tin Pan Alley mold; as a result, some pop journalists have questioned the legitimacy of his rock-styled compositions. In point of fact, he has always been more an interpreter of past traditions—his eclectic reach has encompassed light classical pastiches, boogie woogie, doo-wop, soul, protest rock, punk, and a sometimes unwieldy blend of singer/songwriter intimacy and cabaret flash—than a musical innovator. Although an accomplished singer/pianist and dynamic performer, Joel's songwriting remains the most notable feature of his extensive body of recorded work.

Born William Martin Joel in Hicksville, Long Island, he began performing in a rock vein as a member of The Echoes in 1965. He recorded a couple of albums with The Hassles in the late 1960s, followed by an eponymous LP (Epic 30030; 1970) with the hard-rock duo, Attila. Signing a solo contract with Family Productions' Artie Ripp in 1971, he produced *Cold Spring Harbour* (Family 2700; 1971), marred by a mixing fault that placed his voice in a much higher than customary register (the problem would be corrected when reissued on Columbia 32400 in 1984).

Relocating to Los Angeles, Joel signed with Columbia Records. His first LP with label, *Piano Man* (Columbia 32544; 1975; #27), proved to be a career breakthrough. The follow-up albums, *Streetlife Serenade* (Columbia 33146; 1974) and *Turnstiles* (Columbia 33848; 1976)—while enhancing his artistic reputation—failed to build on his earlier commercial success. He emerged as a superstar, however, with *The Stranger* (Columbia 34987; 1977; #2), which featured four hit singles: "Just the Way You Are" (Columbia 10646; 1977; #3), "Movin' Out (Anthony's Song)" (Columbia 10708; 1978; #17), "Only the Good Die Young" (Columbia 10750; 1978; #24), and "She's Always A Woman" (Columbia 10788; 1978; #17).

However calculated ensuing releases might appear to be, Joel has continued to experiment stylistically although never straying at any point in time beyond the boundaries of the pop mainstream. *52nd Street* (Columbia 35609; 1978; #1) was defiantly pitched to AOR sensibilities, while *Glass Houses* (Columbia 36384; 1980; #1)—which included his first chart-topping single, the retro rocker "It's Still Rock 'N' Roll To Me" (Columbia 11276; 1980)—attempted to appropriate a measure of the punk energy then gaining widespread consumer acceptance. Between a couple of perfunctory live affairs—*Songs in the Attic* (Columbia 37461; 1981; #8) and *...Live in Leningrad* (Columbia 40996; 1987; #38)—he ranged from the impassioned social commentary of *The Nylon Curtain* (Columbia 38200; 1982; #7) to the more carefree exuberance of the Brill Building-tinged *An Innocent Man* (Columbia 38837; 1983; #4) and *The Bridge* (Columbia 40402; 1986; #7).

From the mid-1980s onward, greatest hits collections (on a wide range of audio and video formats) have outnumbered releases devoted to new material. Nevertheless, Joel remains a musical chameleon, moving from energetic arena rock of *Storm Front* (Columbia 44366; 1989; #1), which included the tongue-twisting recitative, "We Didn't Start the Fire" (Columbia 73021; 1989; #1), to elegiac *River of Dreams* (Columbia 53003; 1993; #1). With only one non-retrospective album appearing since then—and another concert release, *2000 Years: The Millennium Concert* (Columbia; 2000), at that—his creative years may all be behind him.

April 20. "TSOP (The Sound of Philadelphia)" (Philadelphia International), credited to MFSB featuring the Three Degrees, begins a two-week run atop the Hot 100. MFSB—allegedly standing for "Mother Father Sister Brother"—was the house band for most Philadelphia International recordings. The song's commercial potential was enhanced by its use as the theme of *Soul Train*, the *American Bandstand*-like TV program catering to African American youth.

May 4. Abba top the British charts with "Waterloo."

May 4. Grand Funk's updated rendition of the Carole King-Gerry Goffin dance craze classic, "The Loco-Motion" (Capitol), peaks at number one on the Hot 100, remaining there for a couple of weeks. With Little Eva's original version having reached number one in August 1962, it became the only song during the rock era to do so in recordings by two different artists.

May 4. Marvin Hamlisch's film soundtrack to *The Sting* begins a five-week run atop the album charts.

May 9. Bruce Springsteen's performance at Boston's Harvard Square Theater inspires *Rolling Stone* critic, Jon Landau, to write: "I have seen rock 'n' roll's future and his name is Bruce Springsteen."

May 11. Mike Oldfield peaks at number seven on the Hot 100 with an edited short version of "Tubular Bells" (Virgin 55100).

One of the most successful progressive rock artists of the 1970s, Mike Oldfield is best remembered for the inclusion of an excerpt from his first LP, *Tubular Bells* (Virgin 105; 1973; #1 UK, #3 US), in the hugely popular horror film, *The Exorcist*. Despite the appeal of this work, it would be grossly unfair to characterize his career (as some have done) as an extended rehash of *Tubular Bells*. His experimentation with extended musical forms, Third World styles, and eclectic instrumentation significantly influenced a generation of rock musicians, many of whom would help bring these devices closer to the pop mainstream.

Born in Reading, England, Oldfield formed the folk-pop duo, Sallyangie, with his sister Sally, in the late 1960s, later performing with Kevin Ayers' band and doing session work for the Edgar Broughton Band and David Bedford. He would follow *Tubular Bells* with a succession of ambitious albums, including *Hergest Ridge* (Virgin 109; 1974; #1 UK, #87 US; his last release to chart stateside), *The Orchestral Tubular Bells* (Virgin 2026; 1975; #17 UK), *Ommadawn* (Virgin 33913; 1975; #4 UK), *Incantations* (Virgin 101; 1978; #14), and *Exposed* (Virgin 2511; 1979; #16 UK).

His work took on more of a pop-rock feel in the 1980s, highlighted by his score to the critically acclaimed film, *The Killing Fields* (Virgin 2328; 1984; #97 UK). By the 1990s, Oldfield seemed more content to capitalize on the by-then legendary debut album; his releases included *Tubular Bells II* (Reprise 2002; 1992; #1 UK), *Tubular III* (Reprise 24349; 1998; #4 UK), and *The Millennium Bell* (Reprise 80885; 1999).

May 13. Youths throw bottles and other objects outside a Jackson 5 concert at RFK Stadium in Washington, D.C., resulting in forty-three arrest and injuries to more fifty bystanders.

May 18. The Jackson 5 peak at number two on the pop charts with "Dancing Machine" (Motown 1286), remaining there for a couple of weeks.

May 18. Nashville-based singer/songwriter Ray Stevens begins a three-week run atop the Hot 100 with "The Streak" (Barnaby 600). The song parodies the current fad of streaking.

May 21. Two concert promoters are arrested by American police for selling mail order tickets for a forthcoming Elton John show. The authorities confiscate more than $12,000 in checks.

May 23. George Harrison announces the establishment of his own record label, Dark Horse.

May 24. Duke Ellington dies, revered as a true American institution.

May 28. *The Magic Show* premieres at New York's Cort Theatre. Featuring music and lyrics by Stephen Schwartz and book by Bob Randall, it was the fifth longest running Broadway musical of the 1970s, with 1,920 performances. Star Doug Henning receives comparable billing to Schwartz, as the show is centered around his role.

May 30. Fourteen-year-old Bernadette Whelan dies of heart failure four days after attending a David Cassidy concert at White City Stadium, London. More than one thousand fans were administered first aid at the show.

June 1. Ronnie Milsap heads up the country charts with the Eddie Rabbitt-penned "Pure Love" (RCA 0237).

June 1. The *New Musical Express* publishes a 100 greatest pop albums listing. It includes the Beatles' *Sgt. Pepper* at number one, Bob Dylan's *Blonde on Blonde* at number two, and the Beach Boys' *Pet Sounds* at number three.

June 8. Paul McCartney & Wings reach number one on the pop charts with "Band on the Run" (Apple).

June 8. Dolly Parton outpaces the competition on the country charts with her own composition, "I Will Always Love You" (RCA 0234).

June 15. Bo Donaldson & the Heywoods begin a two-week stay atop the Hot 100 with the tepid protest song, "Billy, Don't Be a Hero" (ABC 11435).

June 15. Charlie Rich goes number one on the country charts with "I Don't See Me in Your Eyes Anymore" (RCA 0260).

June 15. The Stylistics begin a two-week stint at number two on the Hot 100 with the falsetto tour do force, "You Make Me Feel Brand New" (Avco 4634).

June 19. The Delinquents—whose ranks include Mick Jones, soon to be a founding member of The Clash—debut at the Students' Union bar, Queen Elizabeth College, Kensington, England.

June 22. Waylon Jennings tops the country charts with "This Time" (RCA 0251).

June 29. Mickey Gilley's "Room Full of Roses" (Playboy 50056) reaches number one on the country charts. The song was originally planned as the B side of the single, "She Called Me Baby," until Houston disc jockeys, flipped the disc over, turning it into a local hit.

June 29. Gordon Lightfoot rides his composition, "Sundown" (Reprise 1194), to the summit of the pop charts.

July 6. The Hues Corporation reach number one on the Hot 100 with the soft soul classic, "Rock the Boat" (RCA Victor 0232).

The Hues Corporation helped define the disco sound as it emerged out of underground clubs and into the public mainstream. The vocal trio—consisting of soprano Hubert Ann Kelly (born April 24, 1947, in Fairchild, Alabama), baritone Bernard St. Clair Lee Calhoun Henderson (b. April 24, 1944, San Francisco), and tenor Fleming Williams (b. Flint Michigan)—formed in Los Angeles in 1969. Their debut single, "Goodfootin'" (Liberty; 1970), failed to make the charts.

The Hues Corporation's fortunes changed for the better after signing with RCA in 1973. The title track from their first LP with the label, *Freedom for the Stallion* (RCA; 1974), was modestly successful. However, the follow-up, "Rock the Boat" (#6 UK), an obscure album track brought to the attention of radio programmers by popular demand, became a worldwide smash. Another single, "Rockin' Soul" (RCA; 1974; #18), sold well, but the group failed to maintain their commercial momentum despite recording through the 1970s.

July 6. Anne Murray heads up the country charts with the Dickey Lee-penned "He Thinks I Still Care" (Capitol 3867), remaining there for a couple of weeks. The flip side, "You Won't See Me," rose as high as the Top 5 on the pop charts; it is the only time a recording artist has achieved those levels on both charts with opposite sides of the same single.

July 13. George McCrae begins a two-week stint atop the Hot 100 with "Rock Your Baby" (T.K.). Composed by KC and the Sunshine Band members, Harry Casey and Richard Finch, it will be named "single of the year" by *Rolling Stone* magazine.

July 20. Bobby Bare reaches number one for the first time with the Shel Silverstein-penned tale about witch, "Marie Laveau" (RCA 0261).

July 27. John Denver's recording career continues to crest with "Annie's Song" (RCA), which spends two weeks atop the Hot 100.

July 27. Donna Fargo heads up the country charts with "You Can't Be a Beacon (If Your Light Don't Shine)" (Dot 17506).

July 29. Cass Elliott—a founding member of the Mamas and the Papas before embarking on a solo career—dies of a heart attack while staying in Harry Nilsson's London flat.

August 3. Billy "Crash" Craddock's "Rub It In" (ABC 11437) begins a two-week stint atop the country charts.

August 10. Roberta Flack goes to number one on the pop charts with "Feel Like Makin' Love" (Atlantic).

August 17. Loretta Lynn and Conway Twitty top the country charts with "As Soon As I Hang Up the Phone" (MCA 40251).

August 17. Paper Lace climb the summit of the Hot 100 with "The Night Chicago Died" (Mercury).

August 17. The Three Degrees top the British charts with "When Will I See You Again?" The single will peak at number two on the Hot 100.

August 23. Average White Band drummer Robbie McIntosh dies of a cocaine overdose during a celebrity party attended by Cher.

August 24. Abba peak at number six on the Hot 100 with "Waterloo" (Atlantic 3035).

Parlaying catchy melodies, richly-textured four-part harmonies, and slick production values to achieve worldwide chart success, the group epitomized the Euro-pop movement of the 1970s. Although widely reviled by the rock press at the time, they achieved legendary status in the 1990s, fueled by countless reissues of their classic recordings.

The earlier configuration of Abba arose in Stockholm, Sweden when Bjorn Ulvaeus (guitar/vocals), Benny Andersson (keyboards/synthesizers/vocals), Agnetha Faltskog (vocals), and Norwegian native Anni-Frid Lyngstad-Fredriksson (vocals) began recording as Bjorn, Benny, Agnetha + Frida in 1971. Following a string of Swedish hits, the foursome—known as Abba by 1973—set their sights on international stardom. "Waterloo" (#1 UK), winner of the prestigious Eurovision Song Contest, provided the initial breakthrough. Although the first two LPs, *Waterloo* (Atlantic 18101; 1974; #28 UK) and *Abba* (Atlantic 18146; #13 UK), were limited to marginal sales, the group gradually established momentum as a hit singles machine, built around the songwriting and production talents of Ulvaeus and Andersson. Effervescent studio confections such as "S.O.S." (Atlantic 3265; 1975; #15 US, #6 UK), "I Do I Do I Do I Do I Do" (Atlantic 3310; 1976; #15), "Fernando" (Atlantic 3346; 1976; #13), "Dancing Queen" (Atlantic 3372; 1976; #1 US, #1 UK), "Knowing Me Knowing You" (Atlantic 3387; 1977; #14 US, #1 UK), "The Name of the Game" (Atlantic 3449; 1977; #12 US, #1 UK), and "Take a Chance on Me" (Atlantic 3457; 1978; #3 US, #1 UK)—while somewhat formulaic and cloying in nature—proved irresistible to a large contingency of pop music enthusiasts. Beginning with *Greatest Hits* (Atlantic 18189; 1976; #48 US, #1 UK), album releases also enjoyed greater commercial success, albeit to a considerably greater extent in Europe than in the United States.

By the late 1970s, Abba had become such a bankable commodity that they were listed on the Swedish stock exchange. While changing musical trends (first disco, then the punk revolution) diminished sales somewhat, the hits—albeit in a sadder, more reflective mode, apparently the result of the breakdown of the Ulvaeus-Faltskog (1979) and Andersson-Lyngstad (1981) marriages—continued up to the dissolution of the group in late 1982, most notably "Does Your Mother Know" (Atlantic 3574; 1979; #19), "The Winner Takes It All" (Atlantic 3776; 1980; #8 US, #1 UK), and "When All Is Said and Done" (Atlantic 3889; 1982; #27). All members remained active within the music industry; Faltskog and Lyngstad embarked on solo careers, while Ulvaeus and Andersson went on to co-write (with lyricist Tim Rice) the 1980s musical, *Chess*.

August 24. Paul Anka's "(You're) Having My Baby" begins a three-week run atop the Hot 100. With this song, Anka became the rock-era artist with the longest stretch between chart-topping singles; it has been more than fifteen years since "Lonely Boy" ended a four-week stint at #1 on August 9, 1959. During this period, however, Anka had not lacked for work, earning top dollar as a performer at adult-oriented venues in Las Vegas and elsewhere and writing songs that would be recorded by the likes of Elvis Presley and Frank Sinatra.

August 24. Merle Haggard & the Strangers head up the country charts with "Old Man from the Mountain" (Capitol 3900).

August 24. Rufus begins a three-week run at number three on the Hot 100 with "Tell Me Something Good" (ABC 11427).

A native of Great Lakes, Illinois, Chaka Khan (b. March 23, 1953) grew up on Chicago's South Side.

She first sang in a group at age eleven, and went on tour with Mary Wells with the Afro-Arts Theater troupe. She adopted her name in the late 1960s while working on the Black Panthers' breakfast program. Dropping out of high school in 1969, she knocked around with a number of bands before bursting into the public consciousness as the lead singer of the funk ensemble, Rufus. Beginning with the 1974 Top 10 single, "Tell Me Something Good," Rufus produced a string of hit singles and albums up to Khan's decision to go solo four years later.

Khan's debut, *Chaka* (Warner Bros., 1978), was a smash, propelled by popularity of the single, "I'm Every Woman." However, her next couple of albums got lost in the post-disco trauma of the early 1980s. She opted to record an assortment of jazz standards in 1982, *Echoes of an Era* (Warner Bros.), which won critical raves but left her even further from the pop mainstream. Nevertheless, she rebounded in spectacular fashion with the platinum-selling *I Feel For You* (Warner Bros., 1984), whose rap-tinged title track—a little known Prince LP cut—won a Grammy. While rarely a factor on the pop charts, she has continued to be a major force within the R&B field up to the present day, winning another Grammy in 1990 for "I'll Be Good to You," a duet with Ray Charles. With the growth of interest in Khan's classic recordings, Warner Bros. has reissued much of her legacy both in the original albums and compilations such as *Epiphany: The Best of Chaka Khan, Vol. 1* (1996) and *I'm Every Woman: The Best of Chaka Khan* (1999).

August 31. George Jones reaches number one on the country charts with "The Grand Tour" (Epic 11122).

August 31. Traffic make their last live appearance at the annual U.K. Reading Festival.

Beginning as an eclectic pop band with strong psychedelic leanings, Traffic increasingly moved toward jazz-influenced arrangements featuring extended instrumental jamming. Winwood, whose intensely soulful vocals had recently turned the Spencer Davis Group into a hit-making entity, invited woodwinds specialist Chris Wood, drummer Jim Capaldi, and guitarist Dave Mason to a countryside cottage to write material and rehearse. The resulting album, *Mr. Fantasy* (United Artists 6651; 1968), contained two Top 10 British singles, and became an FM-radio staple stateside. The artistic conflicts between Mason's pop songcraft and Winwood's jazz leanings was reflected in the stylistically divergent selections comprising *Traffic* (United Artists 6676; 1968).

Following a patchwork farewell LP in 1969 entitled *Last Exit* (United Artists 6702), Winwood joined forces Cream alumni Eric Clapton and Ginger Baker and Rick Grech (formerly of Family) to form the supergroup Blind Faith. After one album and tour followed by the brief stint with Ginger Baker's Air Force, Winwood reunited with Wood and Capaldi to record, *John Barleycorn Must Die* (United Artists 5504; 1970), Traffic's most commercially successful release, reaching number five on the pop album charts. The group's lineup was expanded to include Grech, Mason, and percussionists Reebop Kwaku Baah and Jim Gordon for the live recording, *Welcome to the Canteen* (United Artists 5550; 1971). Gordon and Grech departed after the release of the gold album, *The Low Spark of High-Heeled Boys* (Island 9306; 1971). Its laid-back, improvisational mode was continued in *Shoot Out at the Fantasy Factory* (Island 9323; 1973), which included Muscle Shoals session players bassist David Hood and drummer Roger Hawkins. Yet another Muscle Shoals musician, keyboardist Barry Beckett, was added on the live *Traffic on the Road* (Island 9323; 1973).

After *When the Eagle Flies* (Asylum 1020; 1974), which featured the Traffic's original trio plus bassist Rosco Gee, Winwood and Capaldi concentrated on solo careers. By the 1990s, Wood, Grech, and Kwaku Baah would be dead, but Winwood and Capaldi recorded one more album together under the group name, *Far From Home* (1994).

September 6. The 101 All Stars—formed by future Clash member Joe Stummer—debut at The Telegraph, Brixton Hill, London.

September 7. Ronnie Milsap's "Please Don't Tell Me How the Story Ends" (RCA 0313) begins a two-week stay atop the country charts.

September 21. Don Williams peaks at number one on the country charts with "I Wouldn't Want to Live If You Didn't Love Me" (Dot 17516).

September 22. ABC-TV premieres *The Sonny Bono Comedy Revue*.

September 28. Waylon Jennings rises to the summit of the country charts with "I'm a Ramblin' Man" (RCA 10020).

September 28. Andy Kim hits number one on the Hot 100 with "Rock Me Gently" (Capitol).

September 28. Joni Mitchell peaks at number twenty-two on the Hot 100 with "Free Man in Paris" (Asylum 11041). A huge FM hit, it will remain her most successful single.

October 5. Olivia Newton-John begins a two-week stint atop the Hot 100 with "I Honestly Love You" (MCA).

October 5. Michael Oldfield's *Tubular Bells* tops the British charts fifteen months after being released. The LP would ultimately sell more than ten million copies worldwide.

October 5. Charlie Rich's "I Love My Friend" (Epic 20006) reaches number one on the country charts.

October 12. Porter Wagoner and Dolly Parton head up the country charts with "Please Don't Stop Loving Me" (RCA 10010).

October 19. Billy Preston achieves his second pop chart topper with "Nothing from Nothing" (A&M).

October 19. Conway Twitty starts a two-week stay at number one with "I See the Want to in Your Eyes" (MCA 40282).

October 26. Lynyrd Skynyrd peaks at number eight on the Hot 100 with "Sweet Home Alabama" (MCA 40258).

One of the leading exponents of southern rock, Lynyrd Skynyrd melded the country blues roots of their native region with the free-form jamming pioneered by British bands such as the Cream, Traffic, and Free. Although most identified with Ronnie Van Zant's gritty, soulful vocals, the group also help popularize—along with regional compatriots, the Allman Brothers—the triple-pronged lead guitar format.

The band's beginnings can be traced back in 1966, when Van Zant formed the Jacksonville, Florida-based My Backyard, whose personnel included guitarists Gary Rossington and Allen Collins, drummer Bob Burns, and bassist Larry Junstrom. Initially attempting to create an American version of the Rolling Stones, Van Zant shifted his focus after hearing the Allman Brothers' music. Taking the name of a school gym teacher who had harassed them over their long hair (with slight modifications to avoid legal complications), Lynyrd Skynyrd—augmented by the additions of former Strawberry Alarm Clock guitarist, Ed King, pianist Billy Powell, and bassist Leon Wilkeson, who replaced Junstrom—caught the attention of music industry entrepreneur Al Kooper. He singed them to his MCA-backed Sounds of the South label and produced their debut album, *Pronounced Leh-nerd Skin-nerd* (MCA 363; 1973; #27). The work—powered by such AOR-friendly cuts as the blistering guitar showcase, "Free Bird," the earthy working class anthem, "Simple Man," and the barroom rave-up, "Gimme Three Steps"—established Lynyrd Skynyrd as a red-neck alternative to the Allman's hippie image. However, follow-up albums—including *Second Helping* (MCA 413; 1974; #12), *Nuthin' Fancy* (MCA 2137; 1975; #9), and *Gimme Back My Bullets* (MCA 2170; 1976; #20)—revealed the band to be a patchwork of contradictions; the reactionary polemics of "Sweet Home Alabama" served as a contrast to the anti-gun song, "Saturday Night Special" (MCA 40416; 1975; #27), and "The Ballad of Curtis Lowe," a moving tribute to a black bluesman.

Lynyrd Skynyrd would abruptly disband following an October 20, 1977, tour plane crash which claimed the lives of band members Van Zant, and Steve and Cassie Gaines. The recently released LP, *Street Survivors* (MCA 3029; 1977; #5), was reissued with a cover that removed the flames surrounding the band photograph (the original artwork remains highly collectable). Most of the remaining personnel formed the Rossington-Collins Band. Lynyrd Skynyrd re-formed in 1987 (featuring lead vocals by Ronnie's brother, Johnny, formerly of .38 Special) for a memorial tour that was documented by a live album, *Southern By the Grace of God* (MCA 8027; 1988; #68). The band got together again on a permanent basis in 1991, touring and releasing albums on a regular basis. For those feeling that the contemporary edition lacks the intensity of former group, MCA has issued a steady stream of retrospective material.

October 26. Dionne Warwicke and The Spinners climb to the summit of the Hot 100 with "Then Came You" (Atlantic).

October 31. Led Zeppelin launch their own record label, Swan Song.

November 2. Latimore's "Let's Straighten It Out" (Glades 1722) begins a two-week stint atop the R&B charts.

November 2. Stevie Wonder makes number one on the pop charts with "You Haven't Done Nothin'" (Tamla 54252). The protest song—featuring "doo-doo-wop" vocal accompaniment by the Jackson 5—would also top the R&B charts for two weeks. The album from which it was culled, *Fulfillingness First Finale*, would garner five Grammy awards the following year.

November 9. The Bachman-Turner Overdrive reach number one on the Hot 100 with "You Ain't Seen Nothing Yet" (Mercury 73622). The song was composed by former Guess Who member Randy Bachman, who originally viewed its distinctive stuttering effects as little more than a musical joke.

November 16. The B. T. Express begins a two-week stint at number two on the Hot 100 with "Do It ('Til You're Satisfied)" (Roadshow 12395).

November 16. Shirley Brown hits number one on the R&B charts with the rap-inflected "Woman to Woman" (Truth 3206), remaining there for a couple of weeks.

November 16. John Lennon's "Whatever Gets You Through the Night" (Apple) tops the Hot 100. When Elton John—who played piano on the track—told Lennon he thought it would be a number one hit, the former Beatle promised to appear onstage with him. Therefore, he appeared before twenty thousand fans at John's Thanksgiving Day concert, November 28, 1974, at Madison Square Garden. He performed the single, followed by "Lucy in the Sky with Diamonds," and "I Saw Her Standing There." The show would lead to a resumption of his close relationship with Yoko Ono, who'd been in the audience that night.

November 22. Los Angeles celebrates "Stevie Wonder Day."

November 25. Critically acclaimed singer/songwriter Nick Drake commits suicide at age twenty-six.

November 30. Gladys Knight & the Pips commences a two-week stint atop the R&B charts with "I Feel a Song (in My Heart)" (Buddah 433).

December 2. Asylum releases the Eagles' "Best of My Love"/"Ol' 55" (#45218). It becomes the band's first chart-topping single.

December 7. Carl Douglas reaches number one on the Hot 100 with his own composition, "Kung Fu Fighting" (20th Century), remaining there for two weeks.

December 14. Rufus featuring Chaka Khan reach number one on the R&B charts with "You Got the Love" (ABC 12032).

December 21. Harry Chapin's chronicle of a father-son relationship, "Cat's in the Cradle" (Elektra), goes number one on the Hot 100.

December 21. Two years before Hall & Oates have a hit with their tune, "She's Gone," Tavares take it to the top of the R&B charts.

December 28. Helen Reddy peaks at number one on the Hot 100 with "Angie Baby" (Capitol).

December 28. Stevie Wonder's "Boogie On Reggae Woman" (Tamla 54254) begins a two-week stint atop the R&B charts.

1975

❄

January 4. Elton John begins a two-week stay atop the Hot 100 with "Lucy in the Sky with Diamonds" (MCA 40344).

January 11. Carl Douglas becomes the first British-based singer to go number one on the R&B charts with his novelty composition, "Kung Fu Fighting" (20th Century 2140).

January 18. Barry Manilow climbs to the summit of the Hot 100 with "Mandy" (Arista); the song was originally titled "Brandy."

January 18. Barry White's "You're the First, the Last, My Everything" (20th Century 2133) peaks at number one on the R&B charts.

January 25. The Carpenters top the Hot 100 with a remake of the Marvelettes' 1961 hit, "Please Mr. Postman."

January 25. Gloria Gaynor peaks at number nine on the Hot 100 with "Never Can Say Goodbye" (MGM 14748).

Until the rise of Donna Summer, Gloria Gaynor carried the title "Queen of Disco" (an honor bestowed by the National Association of Discotheque Disc Jockeys in March 1975). Today, she is best known for the dance club anthem, "I Will Survive" (Polydor 14558; 1979; #1 pop, #4 r&b), featuring a woman's defiant declaration of independence from an uncaring lover.

Gaynor was born Gloria Fowles, on September 7, 1949, in Newark, New Jersey. One of seven children, she grew up preferring the records of teen doo-wop singer Frankie Lymon as well as pop stylists like Nat King Cole and Sarah Vaughan. She was an accountant briefly following high school before briefly joining a band based in Canada at eighteen. Returning to New Jersey, she was recruited by the Soul Satisfiers in 1971 after a friend persuaded her to sing with them at a local club. After touring with them for a year and a half, she formed her own group, City Life, which achieved a measure of popularity along the East Coast.

Gaynor signed with Columbia in the early 1970s, and went on to release an early disco hit, "Honey Bee" (1973; re-recorded as MGM 14706; 1974; #103 pop, #55 r&b). With the label providing minimal support, she switched to MGM, producing one of the earliest albums geared to dance clubs, *Never Can Say Goodbye* (1975). The title track (#34 r&b), previously a hit single for both Isaac Hayes and the Jackson 5, provided her commercial breakthrough, but follow-up records fared poorly.

Her fortunes reached a new peak with "I Will Survive," and the platinum-selling LP—produced by Dino Fekaris and Freddie Perren—from which it was culled, *Love Tracks* (Polydor 6184; 1979; #4). She continued to enjoy minor success through "I Am What I Am" (Silver Blue 720; 1983; #102 pop, #82 r&b, #13 UK), a song originally introduced in the Act I finale of the Broadway musical, *La Cage Aux Folles*. With her career losing momentum, she denounced her prior substance abuse habits and embraced born-again Christianity in 1982. She has remained active as a performer and recording artist (focusing on post-disco dance music and gospel), and is still extremely popular in Europe. Her autobiography, *I Will Survive*, was published in 1997.

January 25. The Ohio Players begin a two-week stint at number one on the R&B charts with "Fire" (Mercury 76343), their second single ("Funky Worm" was the first) to accomplish this feat.

February 1. Neil Sedaka returns to the top of the Hot 100 following a twelve-and-one-half-year draught with "Laughter in the Rain" (Rocket). He followed his previous chart-topper, "Breaking Up Is Hard To Do" (RCA)—which enjoyed a two-week stay at number one, beginning August 11, 1962—with a few more hits through 1963 before the British Invasion pushed him, like many other American pop artists, to the periphery of the music industry. However, Sedaka's comeback was far from complete. In 1975, alone, he would reside at the top for seven more weeks—three for "Bad Blood" (Rocket), which featured Elton John singing backup, and four as the co-writer of the Captain & Tennille's "Love Will Keep Us Together" (A&M). According to the point system employed by Joel Whitburn in his Pop Annual series, Sedaka was the fifth most successful recording artist for the year.

February 8. Bob Dylan tops the album charts with *Blood on the Tracks* (Columbia).

February 8. The Ohio Players reach number one on the pop charts with "Fire." Like most other notable funk acts, the Ohio Players kinetic mix of percussion, loping bass lines, and stabbing horn flourishes owed much to Sly and the Family Stone's progressive rock-soul fusion of the late 1960s. In terms of both recording productivity and career longevity, the group was unrivaled within the funk genre.

The band was formed in 1959, in Dayton, as Greg Webster and the Ohio Untouchables. Early on, they played behind the R&B vocal group, the Falcons, appearing on recordings such as the hit, "I Found a Love" (Lupine 1003; 1962; #6 r&b). With the addition of three members from an area band, they became known as the Ohio Players.

Although they had first recorded on their own for Lupine in 1963, their stint as the studio group for Compass Records (1967–1968) proved to be something of a breakthrough. In addition to releasing singles under their own name, they produced a number of demo tapes, one of which was released as *Observations in Time* by Capitol (#192; 1969). Moving on to Westbound Records in the early 1970s, the band enjoyed one big hit, "Funky Worm" (Westbound 214; 1973; #1 r&p, #15 pop), which revealed their penchant for tongue-in-cheek humor. They also established another tradition during this period: marketing through provocative album covers typically featuring scantily-clad women in sexually-suggestive poses.

Signing with the Mercury label in 1974, the Players began a highly successful commercial run which included the following albums: *Skin Tight* (Mercury 705; 1974; #11; featuring the single, "Skin Tight," #2 R&B, #13 pop), *Fire* (Mercury 1013; 1974; #1; featuring "Fire," #1 r&b, #1 pop), *Honey* (Mercury 1038; 1975; #2; featuring "Love Rollercoaster,: #1 r&b, #1 pop), *Contradiction* (Mercury 1088; 1976; #12), *Ohio Players Gold* (Mercury 1122; 1976; #31), and *Angel* (Mercury 3701; 1977; #41). By the time the group had switched to Arista Records in 1979, their popularity had dropped off considerably. They continued to record for a variety of labels in the 1980s—including Accord, Boardwalk, Air City, and Track—with only intermittent success. With the advent of compact discs, many of the band's classic albums were reissued (along with assorted hit collections such as PolyGram's *Funk on Fire: The Mercury Anthology*, released in 1995). Despite the death of two longtime members—saxophonist "Satch" Mitchell and trumpeter "Pee Wee" Middlebrooks—in the 1990s, the band has continued to tour up to the present day.

February 8. The Temptations peak at number one on the R&B charts with "Happy People" (Gordy 7138).

February 15. Love Unlimited climbs to the summit of the R&B charts with "I Belong to You" (20th Century 2141). The song's writer and producer, Barry White, was married to group member Glodean White.

February 15. Linda Ronstadt's "You're No Good" (Capitol) goes number one on the pop charts. Ronstadt had been a fixture on the rock scene since 1967, when her group, the Stone Poneys, surfaced with the smash single, "Different Drum." While industry observers never doubted that she possessed the talent to become a major artist; after going solo in 1968, her career languished despite enlisting the services of the band in 1971 which later became the Eagles. Ironically, she had already committed to a new record label, Asylum, when her last Capitol LP, *Heart Like a Wheel* (#11358), became a major hit, heading up the album charts the same week that "You're No Good"—originally a minor hit for Betty Everett—was the top single.

February 16. Cher premieres her weekly CBS-TV show which is built around music and comedy.

February 22. The Average White Band's "Pick Up the Pieces" (Atlantic) outpaces all competition on the Hot 100. Their debut LP, *AWB* (Atlantic), also goes number one. AWB was something of an oddity—a band consisting of six white Scotsmen that played energetic African American funk with verve and panache. Furthermore, while this instrumental would remain their best known recording, the sextet included several fine singers; in fact, the vast majority of their output would feature vocals.

February 22. Steve Harley and Cockney Rebel top the U.K. charts with "Make Me Smile (Come Up and See Me)"—their only number one single.

February 22. Labelle's "Lady Marmalade" (Epic 50048) leaps to number one on the R&B charts.

February 26. Todd Rundgren earns a gold record for the 1972 LP, *Something/Anything?* (Bearsville 2066).

Although Philadelphian Todd Rundgren has sold considerably fewer recordings than virtually any other high-profile artist with a career stretching back to the 1960s, few have had a comparable impact on the development of the music industry. Furthermore, his contributions have come in a wide range of guides, including session playing, band leader, songwriting, studio engineering and production, and conceptual video work.

After a stint as the guiding force of the 1960s cult band, Nazz, Rundgren began recording a series of solo tour de force LPs—featuring only his vocal and instrumental performances—in a mildly psyche-delic power-pop vein, including *Runt* (Ampex 10105; 1971; #185), *Something/Anything?* (Bearsville 2066; 1972; #29; achieved gold status due in part to the hit singles "I Saw the Light" (Bearsville 0003; 1972; #16) and "Hello It's Me" (Bearsville 0009; 1973; #5), *A Wizard/A True Star* (Bearsville 2133; #86), *Todd* (Bearsville 6952; 1974; #54), *Initiation* (Bearsville 6957; 1975; #86), *Faithful* (Bearsville 6963; 1976; #54; a collection of *covers*), *Hermit of Mink Hollow* (Bearsville 6981; 1978; #36), *Back to the Bars* (Bearsville 6986; #1978; #75), *Healing* (Bearsville 3522; 1981; #48), *The Ever Popular Tortured Artist Effect* (Bearsville 23732; 1983; #66), *A Cappella* (Warner Bros. 25128; 1985; #128), *Nearly Human* (Warner Bros. 25881; 1989; #102), and *2nd Wind* (Warner Bros. 26478; 1991; #118).

In the mid-1970s, Rundgren founded a keyboard-based band, Utopia. Following the release of the avant-garde oriented albums *Todd Rundgren's Utopia* (Bearsville 6954; 1974; #34), *Another Live* (Bearsville 6961; 1975; #66), *RA* (Bearsville 6965; 1977; #79), and *Oops! Wrong Planet* (Bearsville 6970; 1977; #73), he opted for a more traditional lineup featuring keyboardist Roger Powell, bassist Kasim Sulton, and drum-mer John Willie Wilcox. Although Rundgren's Spector-influenced production values and warped humor were acquired tastes, the reconstituted band enjoyed a measure of commercial success, most notably with *Adventures in Utopia* (Bearsville 6991; 1980; #32), the Beatkes parody *Deface the Music* (Bearsville 3487; 1980; #65), *Swing to the Right* (Bearsville 3666; 1982; #102), *Utopia* (Network 60183; 1982; #84), *Oblivion* (Passport 6029; 1984; #74), and *POV* (Passport 6044; 1985; #161).

Beginning in the early 1970s, Rundgren has served as engineer and producer for many notable artists, including Badfinger, the Band, Paul Butterfield, Rick Derringer, Grand Funk Railroad, Halfnelson (aka Sparks), Hall and Oates, Meatloaf, the New York Dolls, Patti Smith, the Tubes, Jesse Winchester, and XTC. With the rise of the MTV craze, he attempted to shift the focus of the video medium away from promotion in favor of conceptual art.

March 1. Bob Dylan begins a two-week stint atop the LP charts with *Blood on the Tracks* (Columbia), his first album to accomplish this feat.

March 1. The Eagles go to summit of the Hot 100 with "Best of My Love" (Asylum).

March 1. Olivia Newton-John dominates the seventeenth annual Grammy awards, winning Best Pop Vocal Performance, Female and Record of the Year for "I Honestly Love You." Her next big honor—being named the Country Music Association's Female Vocalist of the Year—creates a major furor, causing many CMA members to form the Association of Country Entertainers. She blunts the criticism somewhat by performing at various country venues and recording in Nashville.

March 1. Shirley & Company reach number one on the R&B charts with "Shame, Shame, Shame" (Vibration 532). The single was written and produced by All Platinum's Sylvia Robinson, longtime associate of the group's leader Shirley Goodman (who topped the R&B charts in September 1956 with "Let the Good Times Roll" as part of Shirley and Lee).

March 2. A Los Angeles policeman stops a Lincoln Continental—with Paul McCartney at the wheel with wife Linda—for running a red light. He finds eight ounces of marijuana in the vehicle, and arrests Linda.

March 8. The B.T. Express go to the summit of the R&B chart with the instrumental dance groove, "Express" (Roadshow 7001).

March 8. Olivia Newton-John's "Have You Never Been Mellow"—written and produced by John Farrar—reach-es number one, on its way to achieving a gold disc (her fourth single in a row to earn this distinction). The similarly named LP also tops the album charts for a week, earning gold status.

March 9. Telly Savalas—featured actor in the TV show, *Kojak*, at the time—tops the British singles charts with "If."

March 13. George Jones and Tammy Wynette obtain a divorce following six years of marriage.

March 15. After "Another Park, Another Sunday"—the first single from their LP, *What Were Once Habits Are Now Vices*—fails to crack the Top 40, the Doobie Brothers reach number one on the Hot 100 with "Black Water" (Warner Bros.).

March 15. Ben E. King celebrates his return to the Atlantic label by topping the R&B charts with "Supernatural Thing (Part 1)" (#3241).

March 15. Led Zeppelin goes number one on the British charts with the double album, *Physical Graffiti* (Swan Song).

March 15. Olivia Newton-John's *Have You Ever Been Mellow* (MCA) heads up the LP charts.

March 22. The Bay City Rollers go number one on the British charts with "Bye Bye Baby."

March 22. Led Zeppelin's *Physical Graffiti* begins a six-week run atop the album charts.

March 22. Four Seasons frontman, Frankie Valli, climbs to the summit of the Hot 100 with "My Eyes Adored You" (Private Stock), his first solo singles to accomplish this feat.

March 29. After working on the periphery of the pop mainsteam for more than a decade, Labelle top the Hot 100 with "Lady Marmalade" (Epic).

March 29. Led Zeppelin's six albums all reside in *Billboard*'s Top 100.

April 1. The TV series, *Shang-A-Lang*, starring the Bay City Rollers, premieres on Britain's ITV.

April 5. Former Rotary Connection vocalist Minnie Riperton reaches number one on the pop charts with "Lovin' You."

Despite a distinguished career during her relatively short life, Minnie Riperton seemed to be on the verge of even bigger things when she died of lymph cancer on July 12, 1979, in Los Angeles. Nevertheless, she legacy of well-crafted group and solo recordings, notable for her breathtaking vocal gymnastics which featured a five octave range.

Born in Chicago November 8, 1947, the youngest of eight children, Riperton began singing in church as a nine-year-old and enrolled at the Oakwood, Illinois, Lincoln Center to study ballet and voice a year later. She was discovered performing *a cappella* at Hyde Park High School by Raynard Miner and Rose Miller, who were then actively promoting the Gems, a girl group recently signed by Chess Records. They got her a position as receptionist for the label while she with the Gems. While attempting to make it on their own as a recording act, the group backed Chess artists like Fontella Bass and Etta James prior to breaking up in 1966.

Still under contract to Chess, Riperton released singles as Andrea Davis before becoming a lead vocalist with Rotary Connection, a progressive rock-tinged R&B band that recorded six LPs until dissolving in 1970. She did a solo album, *Come to My Garden* (#7011; #160 in 1974), later that year for Janus, a Chess subsidiary. When it went nowhere she dropped out of the entertainment field, adopting a more traditional lifestyle with husband, Richard Rudolph, until Stevie Wonder talked her into returning as a member of his backing vocal group, Wonderlove, in 1973.

After appearing on Wonder's immensely successful LP, *Fulfillingness' First Finale* (Tamla 332; 1974; #1), Riperton was recruited by Epic Records. Her initial Epic album, *Perfect Angel* (#32561; 1974; #4), included the first of nine R&B hits, "Lovin' You" (Epic 50057; #3 r&b), best known for its high-pitched vocal refrains.

Riperton first discovered she had cancer in 1976. After undergoing a mastectomy and becoming a spokesperson for the American Cancer Society, she received the organization's Courage Award in the White House ceremony in 1977. Departing Epic for Capitol in 1978, she completed one more album, *Minnie* (Capitol 11936; 1979; #29), before her death. Capitol would also release the posthumous *Love Lives Forever* (#12097; 1980; #35), featuring her taped vocals backed by various friends such as Wonder, George Benson, Peabo Bryson, Roberta Flack, Michael Jackson, and Patrice Rushen.

April 7. Ritchie Blackmore leaves Deep Purple to form his own band, Rainbow. Deep Purple replace him with Tommy Bolin.

April 12. David Bowie announces his second retirement with the words: "I've rocked my roll. It's a boring dead end, there will be no more rock 'n' roll records from me."

April 12. Art Garfunkel peaks at number one on the British charts with "Bright Eyes," remaining there for six weeks. The theme from the film, *Watership Down*, becomes the biggest-selling single of the year.

April 12. Elton John begins a two-week stint atop the Hot 100 with "Philadelphia Freedom" (MCA), a song written for that city's soccer franchise.

April 14. A Rolling Stones press release announces that Ron Wood will replace Mick Taylor as lead guitarist. Prior rumors had pegged Jimmy Page, Jeff Beck, and Chris Spedding for the job.

April 23. Badfinger's Pete Ham hangs himself. He is perhaps known for co-writing "Without You," a chart-topping single for both Nilsson and Mariah Carey.

April 26. B.J. Thomas peaks at number one on the pop charts with "(Hey Won't You Play) Another Somebody Done Somebody Wrong Song" (ABC).

May 3. The Bay City Rollers reach number one on the British album charts with *Once Upon a Star*.

May 3. "He Don't Love You (Like I Love You)" (Elektra), by Tony Orlando & Dawn, begins a three-week stay atop the Hot 100.

May 5. The Electric Light Orchestra's *Eldorado* (United Artists 339) is certified gold.

The Electric Light Orchestra had few equals in achieving a seamless blend of experimental, classically-influenced orchestration and hook-laden pop songcraft. Leader Jeff Lynne, formerly of the Idle Race and the Move, was greatly influenced by the Beatles, particularly the studio wizardry of producer George Martin.

The group was developed as a classical-rock concept in 1971 by the creative core of the surrealist British band, the Move, percussionist Bev Bevan and the multi-instrumentalists Roy Wood and Lynne. When the eccentric Wood departed in 1972 for a solo career, Lynne—as producer and chief songwriter—assumed creative control of ELO. Despite a reputation for recording highly polished, intricate recordings, ELO quickly evolved into an accomplished performing unit. At the time of the release of *ELO II* (United Artists 040; 1972; #62), the act's commercial breakthrough record, personnel included—in addition to Lynne and Bevan—Richard Tandy (Moog synthesizer, piano, harmonica, guitar), Michael De Albuquerque (bass, vocals), cellist Colin Walker, and violinists Wilf Gibson and Mike Edwards.

ELO II included the hit single, "Roll Over Beethoven" (United Artists 173; 1972; #42, #6 U.K.), which became a metaphor for the group's career. Chuck Berry's wry lyrics about the transcendence of rock 'n' roll backed by the signature motif of Beethoven's Fifth Symphony included all of the ingredients fueling ELO's popularity over the next decade: first-rate melodies, memorable hooks, and an outrageous—occasionally bizarre—sense of humor. The group's long string of chart successes would include the Top 10 singles "Can't Get It Out Of My Head" (United Artists 573; 1974; #9), "Evil Woman" (United Artists 729; 1975; #10), "Telephone Line" (United Artists 1000; 1977; #7), "Shine A Little Love" (Jet 5057; 1979; #8), "Don't Bring Me Down" (Jet 5060; 1979; #4; a rave-up rocker notable for its absence of strings), and "Hold On Tight" (Jet 02408; 1981; #10) as well as the LPs *Eldorado* (United Artists 339; 1974; #16), a concept album featuring the use of instrumental and choral interludes to tie the songs together, the disco-tinged *Face the Music* (United Artists 546; 1975; #8), the radio-friendly *A New World Record* (United Artists 679; 1976; #5), the sprawling double-disc set *Out Of the Blue* (Jet 823; 1977; #4), the mainstream pop-oriented *Discovery* (Jet 35769; 1979; #5), and the film soundtrack collaboration with Olivia Newton-John, *Xanadu* (MCA 6100; 1980; #4).

When the hits stopped coming, Lynne shifted his emphasis to record production, working with Dave Edmunds, Brian Wilson, and Tom Petty, among others. He would also release solo material and help form—along with Petty, Bob Dylan, Roy Orbison, and George Harrison—the roots-rock supergroup, The Traveling Wilburys, in the late 1980s. Bevan reformed the group as ELO Part II in the early 1990s; however, this aggregate, lacking the songwriting and production excellence contributed by Lynne, failed to achieve any semblance of chart success.

May 10. The Blackbyrds—then closely identified Donald Byrd—begin a two-week stint at number six on the Hot 100 with "Walking in Rhythm" (Fantasy 736).

One of the more commercially successful jazz-rock artists of the 1970s, Donald Byrd also left his mark as an educator and bop trumpet stylist. Born December 9, 1932, in Detroit, Michigan, he studied trumpet and composition in the early 1950s and performed during his military service. He performed and recorded with many of the most prominent bop interpreters later in the decade, including Art Blakey, Kenny Clarke, John Coltrane, and Sonny Rollins. After teaming with Pepper Adams for several years, he returned to his studies in Europe in 1961. He would begin a career as a jazz educator in the mid-1960s, serving at a number of prestigious American universities of the years such as Rutgers and Howard.

Byrd continued his recording activities in the 1960s, working extensively with saxophonist Dexter Gordon, among others. During the 1970s, he began integrating soul and funk elements into his work, most notably with a group of Howard University students who became the Backbyrds (named after the seminal 1973 Byrd LP on Blue Note, *Blackbyrd*). Their single, "Walkin' in Rhythm"—from the bestselling LP, *Flying Start* (Fantasy; 1974)—became to Top 10 crossover pop hit. Although his flirtations with fusion offended many jazz purists, he continued to garner praise for his extraordinary technique and lovely tone as a trumpeter.

May 10. Stevie Wonder performs a free concert near the Washington monument for an audience of 125,000 to celebrate Human Kindness Day.

May 17. Elton John is achieves sales of one million copies for *Captain Fantastic and the Brown Dirt Cowboy*. It is the first LP to be certified Platinum on the day of its release.

May 17. Tammy Wynette tops the British charts with her 1968 recording, "Stand By Your Man."

May 24. Earth, Wind & Fire reach number one on the pop charts with "Shining Star" (Columbia 10090). The song is culled from the group's film soundtrack album, *That's the Way of the World* (Columbia).

One of the classic funk acts of the 1970s, the Chicago-based group was created in 1969 by vocalist/percussionist Maurice White, a former member of the Ramsey Lewis Trio and session man with the Chess label. Initially known as the Salty Peppers, the band—originally consisting of Maurice's brother, bassist Verdine White, keyboardist/vocalist Wade Flemons, pianist/vocalist Don Whitehead, guitarist Michael Beal, vocalist Sherry Scott, conga player Yackov Ben Israel, tenor saxist Chet Washington, and trombonist Alex Thomas—changed their name to Earth, Wind & Fire in 1970, and released their eponymous debut LP (Warner Bros.) in March of the following year. Their follow-up, *The Need of Love* (Warner Bros., 1972), was the first in a long string of charting releases.

The Earth, Wind & Fire's fortunes took a quantum leap upward later that year with a wholesale lineup change—which featured the addition of velvet-voiced lead singer Philip Bailey, saxophonist/flutist Ronald Laws, and four other musicians to the White brothers core—and shift to the Columbia label. The group's appealing formula of positive, pseudo-spiritual lyrics and polished funk grooves resulted in a string of Top 10 albums: the film soundtrack *That's the Way of the World*, which included the chart-topping single, "Shining Star"; the largely live *Gratitude* (Columbia, 1975); *Spirit* (Columbia, 1976); *All 'n' All* (Columbia, 1978); *I Am* (Columbia, 1979), featuring the Top 10 smashes, the disco-inflected "Boogie Wonderland" (with the Emotions) and "After the Love Has Gone"; *Faces* (Columbia, 1980); and *Raise!* (Columbia, 1981).

When the hits stopped coming, the group disbanded in 1984, with Bailey and Maurice White continuing as solo performers. The White brothers and Bailey reconstituted the act in 1987, augmented by countless session players. Their periodic releases continued to crease the charts well into the 1990s; subsequently, the public—particularly in Great Britain—has exhibited a preference for reissues of the group's classic material.

May 31. After years of artistic obscurity, Freddy Fender rises to the summit of the Hot 100 with the Tex-Mex ballad, "Before the Next Teardrop Falls" (ABC/Dot).

June 7. John Denver reaches the top spot on the Hot 100 with the live track, "Thank God I'm a Country Boy" (RCA).

June 7. Elton John's *Captain Fantastic and the Brown Dirt Cowboys* goes number one in its first week on the charts—the first album ever to accomplish this feat.

June 13. John Lennon performs on television for the last time, running through the Little Richard classic, "Slippin' and Slidin'," and "Imagine" for *Salute to Sir Lew Grade.*

June 14. Asylum releases the Eagles' "One of These Nights"/"Visions" (#45257). It becomes the group's second number one single on August 2.

June 21. The Captain & Tennille (Darryl Dragon and wife, Toni Tennille) begin a four-week run heading up the Hot 100 with "Love Will Keep Us Together" (A&M 1672). The Neil Sedaka/Howard Greenfield composition becomes the top-charting single of the year.

June 21. Major Harris peaks at number five on the Hot 100 with "Love Won't Let Me Wait" (Atlantic 3248), remaining there for three weeks.

Although relatively unknown to mainstream pop enthusiasts, Major Harris has been a fixture of the R&B scene for several decades. Born February 9, 1947, in Richmond, Virginia, he sang with the Jarmels in the late 1960s before moving on to the Delfonics in 1971. Three years later, he formed the Major Harris Boogie Blues Band along with Karen Dempsey, Allison Hobbs, and Phyllis Newman.

Harris achieved his greatest success, however, as a solo performer. His Top 5 pop hit, "Love Won't Make Me Wait," gained widespread notoriety for its incorporation of sound effects depicting a woman in the throes of sexual passion. He continued to enjoy intermittent success on the R&B charts through the release of "All My Life" (Atlantic; 1983). By the late 1980s, Harris had rejoined the Delfonics, even though that group's hit-making days were long since past.

June 26. Cher divorces Sonny Bono, ending what many considered to be the quintessential 1960s hippie marriage.

June 30. Cher marries Greg Allman. They will split ten days later, divorcing after a stormy three-year relationship.

July 17. *Rolling Stone* pictures Mick Jagger and Keith Richards on its cover with the caption "The Rolling Stones 1975 Tour – World's Greatest Performing Band Bewilders the South – Baptized in Baton Rouge – Castrated in San Antone."

July 19. The Bay City Rollers top the British charts with "Give a Little Love."

July 19. Wings reach number one on the pop charts with "Listen to What the Man Said" (Capitol).

July 26. Bandleader Van McCoy makes it to the top of the Hot 100 with the disco instrumental, "The Hustle" (Avco 4653).

July 26. 10cc peak at number two on the Hot 100 with "I'm Not in Love" (Mercury 73678), remaining there for three weeks. The song's wry lyrics presented a marked contrast with the lush romanticism of the music, which allegedly featured over six hundred dubbed voices.

August 9. The Bee Gees begin a two-week stint at number one on the pop charts with funk-inflected "Jive Talkin'" (RSO 510). After having a prior LP rejected by their record label, the song signaled a stylistic change—and commercial revival—from Anglo baroque-rock to dance-oriented R&B.

August 9. Freddy Fender peaks at number one on the country charts with "Wasted Days and Wasted Nights" (ABC/Dot 17558), remaining there for a couple of weeks.

August 14. *Rolling Stone* pictures a cartoon illustration of Neil Young in a cowboy hat on its cover with a caption touting an interview conducted by Cameron Crowe.

August 23. Glen Campbell commences a three-week run atop the country charts with "Rhinestone Cowboy" (Capitol 4095).

August 23. Hamilton, Joe Frank & Reynolds reach number one on the Hot 100 with "Fallin' in Love" (Playboy).

August 30. KC & the Sunshine Band top the pop charts for the first time with "Get Down Tonight" (T.K.).

KC & the Sunshine Band epitomized the infectious, dance-floor funk ascendant in the 1970s. Based in Miami, Florida, the group's punch pop sound represented a distillation post-1960s soul (devoid of the socio-political agenda characterizing leading purveyors of the genre such as Stevie Wonder, Sly Stone, and the O'Jays) tinged with lilting Caribbean rhythms known as junkanoo.

KC—an interracial aggregate consisting of seven to eleven members—was the brainchild of vocalist/keyboardist Harry Wayne Casey and bassist Richard Finch. Together, they developed a strong regional reputation as a songwriting/ studio production team, most notably with George McCrae, whose "Rock Your Baby" (T.K. 1004; 1974; #1) was named the year's top single by *Rolling Stone*. The band released a string of top-selling hits during the latter 1970s, including "Get Down Tonight" (T.K. 1009; 1975), "That's the Way (I Like It)" (T.K. 1015; 1975; #1), "(Shake, Shake, Shake) Shake Your Booty" (T.K. 1019; 1976; #1), "I'm Your Boogie Man" (T.K. 1022; 1977; #1), "Keep It Comin' Love" (T.K. 1023; 1977; #2), and "Please Don't Go" (T.K. 1035; 1979; #1). Although not considered an album act, their long-playing catalog (as well as twelve-inch singles) were solid sellers, particularly the debut, *KC and the Sunshine Band* (T.K. 603; 1975; #4), which remained on the *Billboard Top 200* for forty-seven weeks.

Casey's involvement in a serious car accident in the early 1980s resulted in the cessation of the group's chart run. He would briefly return to the public eye billed as "KC" with the release of *KC Ten* (Meca 8301; 1984; #93), featuring the post-disco single "Give It Up" (Meca 1001; 1984; #18), before fading back into obscurity.

September 6. Glen Campbell begins a two-week stay atop the Hot 100 with "Rhinestone Cowboy."

September 6. Loretta Lynn and Conway Twitty head up the country charts with "Feelins'" (MCA 40420).

September 9. Wings kick off a thirteen-month tour at the Gaumont Theatre, Southampton, Hants, U.K. The tour will cover ten countries and be witnessed by two million people.

September 19. Queen signs a management deal with Elton John's manager, John Reid.

September 20. David Bowie tops the American pop charts for the first time with "Fame" (RCA), remaining there for two non-consecutive weeks.

September 20. Ronnie Milsap's "Daydreams About Night Things" (RCA 10335) begins a two-week stint atop the country charts

September 27. John Denver goes number one on the Hot 100 with "I'm Sorry" (RCA).

October 4. Willie Nelson begins a two-week stay atop the country charts with "Blue Eyes Crying in the Rain" (Columbia 10176).

October 7. The New York State Supreme Court rules by a 2 to 1 vote to reverse John Lennon's deportation order.

October 9. Sean Taro Ono Lennon is born in New York City. John Lennon will enter a voluntary five-year retirement to serve as househusband while wife Yoko Ono runs their business empire from an office in their Dakota Apartments home.

October 11. John Denver peaks at number two on the Hot 100 with "Calypso" (RCA 10353), remaining there for four weeks. The flip side, "I'm Sorry," topped the charts on September 27.

October 11. Neil Sedaka starts a three-week run atop the Hot 100 with "Bad Blood" (Rocket 40460).

October 18. Charley Pride's "Hope You're Feelin' Me (Like I'm Feelin' You)" (RCA 10344) peaks at number one on the country charts.

October 25. Tanya Tucker heads up the country charts with "San Antonio Stroll" (MCA 40444).

November 1. Elton John begins a three-week stay atop the pop charts with "Island Girl" (MCA).

November 1. Don Williams reaches number one on the country charts with "(Turn Out the Light and) Love Me Tonight" (ABC/Dot 17568).

November 8. John Denver's "I'm Sorry" (RCA 10353) goes to the top of the country charts (RCA 10353).

November 15. Waylon Jennings peaks at number one on the country charts with "Are You Sure Hank Done it This Way"/"Bob Wills Is Still the King" (RCA 10379).

November 22. KC & the Sunshine Band rise to the summit of the Hot 100 with "That's the Way (I Like It)" (T.K. 1015), remaining there for two non-consecutive weeks.

November 22. Dickey Lee heads up the country charts with his version of "Rocky" (RCA 10361), his only single to accomplish this feat.

November 29. Merle Haggard & the Strangers go number one on the country charts with "It's All in the Movies" (Capitol 4141).

November 29. KC's "That's the Way (I Like It)" settles into the number one position on the R&B charts.

November 29. The German studio entity, Silver Convention, begin a three-week run atop the Hot 100 with "Fly, Robin, Fly" (Midland International).

December 6. Freddy Fender climbs to number one on the country charts with "Secret Love" (ABC/Dot 17585).

December 6. The O'Jays top the R&B charts with "I Love Music (Part 1)" (Philadelphia International 3577).

December 13. Johnny Rodriguez reaches number one on the county charts with "Love Put a Song in My Heart" (Mercury 73715).

December 20. Al Green heads up the R&B charts with the disco-influenced "Full of Fire" (Hi 2300).

December 20. C. W. McCall begins a six-week run atop the country charts with "Convoy" (MGM 14839).

December 27. The Faces announce they are breaking up. Rod Stewart concentrates on his solo career, guitarist Ron Wood becomes a permanent member of the Rolling Stones, drummer Kenny Jones eventually joins The Who, and Ronnie Lane forms Slim Chance.

December 27. The Ohio Players ascend to number one of the R&B charts with "Love Rollercoaster" (Mercury 73734).

December 27. The Staple Singers outpace all competition on the Hot 100 with "Let's Do It Again" (Curtom).

1976

❄

January 3. Teenybopper idols, the Bay City Rollers, reach number one on the Hot 100 with "Saturday Night" (Arista).

January 3. Irving Kaufman dies at age eighty-five. Reputed to be the most prolific band singer ever (said to have recorded with sixty-two different orchestras between 1923 and 1933), he was also a member of the Avon Comedy Four, an extremely popular vaudeville act during the World War I era.

January 3. Former Temptation David Ruffin climbs to the summit of the R&B charts with "Walk Away From Love" (Motown 1376).

January 4. Former Beatles roadie, Mal Evans, is fatally wounded by police in his Los Angeles apartment after waving a rifle at them. They had responded to a call placed by Evans' girlfriend, who had been concerned about his agitated condition.

January 9. Pub rockers Graham Parker and The Rumour sign with their first label, Phonogram Records.

January 10. Following a British tour, Deep Purple splits up. David Coverdale goes on to form Whitesnake; Jon Lord and Ian Paice join forces with Tony Ashton.

January 10. Earth, Wind & Fire's "Sing A Song" (Columbia 10251) heads up the R&B charts, remaining there for two non-consecutive weeks.

January 10. C. W. McCall peaks at number one on the pop charts with the CB radio novelty song, "Convoy."

January 17. Singer/songwriter Barry Manilow tops the Hot 100 with a rare song he didn't compose, the Bruce Johnston-penned "I Write the Songs" (Arista).

January 17. Harold Melvin & the Blue Notes go number one on the R&B charts with "Wake Up Everybody (Part 1)" (Philadelphia International 3579), remaining there for two non-consecutive weeks..

January 19. George Harrison, John Lennon, Paul McCartney, and Ringo Starr are offered $30 million by concert promoter Bill Sargent to perform one show as "The Beatles." They unanimously refuse the proposal.

January 24. Bob Dylan begins a five-week run atop the LP charts with *Desire* (Columbia).

January 24. Diana Ross reaches number one on the pop charts with "Theme From Mahogany," her third chart topper since leaving the Supremes.

January 30. Kiss receive a platinum record award for their breakthrough release, the double-disc set, *Kiss Alive* (Casablanca).

January 31. Abba's "Mamma Mia" replaces Queen's "Bohemian Rhapsody" at the top of the British charts after the latter's nine-week run.

January 31. The Ohio Players inch to the summit of the Hot 100 with "Love Rollercoaster."

January 31. Queen dominates the annual readers' poll published by *Sounds* magazine, winning best album (*A Night at the Opera*), best single ("Bohemian Rhapsody") and best band. Mike Oldfield is named best musician; Maddy Prior, best female singer; Rainbow, best new band; Bay City Rollers, bore of the year.

January 31. Conway Twitty's "This Time I've Hurt Her More Than She Loves Me" (MCA 40492) heads ups the country charts.

February 6. Jazz pianist/composer Vince Guaraldi, forty-seven, succumbs to a heart attack in San Francisco. He won a Grammy for his instrumental recording, "Cast Your Fate to the Wind," and scored the Peanuts television specials.

February 7. Bill Anderson and Mary Lou Turner top the country charts with "Sometimes" (MCA 40488).

February 7. Tyrone Davis reaches number one on the R&B charts with "Turning Point" (Dakar 4550).

February 7. Hot Chocolate peak at number three on the Hot 100 with "You Sexy Thing" (Big Tree 16047).

Hot Chocolate were something of an anomaly in the 1970s British pop scene—whereas punk and Caribbean-based styles such as ska, rock steady, and reggae tended to dominate, they opted for more of a soul-funk direction. The interracial group was formed in 1970 by Jamaica-born, lead singer Errol Brown; members included guitarist Harvey Hinsley (b. Mitcham, England), keyboardist Larry Ferguson (b. Nassau), percussionist Patrick Olive (b. Grenada), bassist Tony Wilson (b. Trinidad), and drummer Ian King (replaced by Romford, England, native Tony Connor in 1973).

Hot Chocolate first signed with the Apple label, releasing a reggae-inflected treatment of John Lennon's "Give Peace a Chance" in 1970. With the assistance of legendary producer Mickie Most, the group recorded a string of successful U.K. singles in the early 1970s; one of their compositions, "Brother Louie" (a Top 10 English hit in 1973), would be covered by Stories later in the year, topping the U.S. charts. Other Brown-Wilson songs would be recorded by April Wine, Mary Hopkin, Peter Noone, and Suzi Quatro, among others.

Hot Chocolate would finally break into the American market with in the second half of the 1970s with "Emma" (Big Tree 16031; 1975; #8 pop), "Disco Queen" (Big Tree 16038; 1975; #28 pop, #40 r&b), "You Sexy Thing" (#6 r&b), and "Every 1's a Winner" (Infinity 50002; 1978; #6 pop, #7 r&b). Wilson would exit in 1975, with Olive switching to bass.

The group would continue to release hits in Great Britain well into the 1980s, but disbanded when Brown opted for solo career in 1987. Interest in the group was revived in the late 1990s when "You Sexy Thing" was featured in the popular films *Boogie Nights* and *Full Monty* as well as a Burger King television commercial.

February 7. Paul Simon begins a three-week stay atop the Hot 100 with "50 Ways to Leave Your Lover" (Columbia).

February 7. Donna Summer peaks at number two on the Hot 100 with her first hit, the sexually explicit "Love to Love You Baby" (Oasis 401).

Donna Summer earned considerable renown as the Queen of Disco during the later 1970s; however, few were aware of her ability to interpret a wide range of material, including pop, rock, blues, soul, and gospel. In addition, her talent encompassed acting, songwriting, and record production.

Born Adrian Donna Gaines in Boston on December 31, 1948, Summer started out singing in European musicals in 1968. Her breakthrough as a recording artist came with a Giorgio Moroder-Pete Bellote production, the "Love to Love You Baby" (Oasis 401). Despite the predominance of disco songs in her early albums—*Love to Love You Baby* (Oasis 5003; 1975; #11; gold record), *A Love Trilogy* (Oasis 5004; 1976; #21; gold record). *Four Seasons of Love* (Casablanca 7038; 1987; #29; gold record), *Once Upon A Time* (Casablanca 7078; 1977; #26; gold record), *Live and More* (Casablanca 7119; 1978; #1; platinum award), and *Bad Girls* (Casablanca 7150; 1979; #1; platinum award; featuring the hit singles "Hot Stuff" (Casablanca 978; #1; platinum award), "Bad Girls" (Casablanca 988; #1; platinum award), and "Dim All the Lights" (Casablanca 2201; #2; gold record)—she revealed an inclination to try other styles; *I Remember Yesterday* (Casablanca 7056; 1977; #18; gold record) served as a case in point, with an all-disco side and varied material on the other, including the Jimmy Webb classic, "MacArthur Park" (Casablanca 939; 1978; #1). Among her many awards were an Oscar for best movie song in 1978 with "Last Dance" (Casablanca 926; 1978; #3) and three American Music Awards that same year (Favorite Female Vocalist – Disco, Favorite LP – Disco for *Live and More*, and Favorite Single – Disco for "Last Dance").

Wishing to make a more dramatic move away from her disco image, Summer signed with Geffen Records in 1980. Since then, her albums—most notably, *The Wanderer* (Geffen 2000; 1980; #13; gold record), *Donna Summer* (Geffen 2005; 1982; #20; gold record), *She Works Hard for the Money* (Mercury 812265; 1983; #9; gold record), *Cats Without Claws* (Geffen 24040; 1984; #40)—have become increasingly diversified, with a particular emphasis on religious material. She won Grammy awards for Best Inspirational Performance in 1983 and 1984, for "He's a Rebel" and "Forgive Me," respectively.

Following a succession of disappointing LPs, Summer was relatively inactive during the 1990s. Her biggest recording success came with "Carry On," a collaboration with Moroder which won the 1997 Grammy for Best Dance Recording. She has concentrated on songwriting along with husband Bruce Sudano, particularly the country market. At the outset of the twenty-first century they were working on a musical.

February 10. Elvis Presley is named a member of the reserve force for the Memphis police.

February 12. Rolling Stone features a cover photo of David Bowie with the caption "Rolling On to Rule the World."

February 14. Natalie Cole hits number one on the R&B charts with "Inseparable" (Capitol 4193), the second single release from her debut album. Chuck Jackson, who wrote the lyrics (Marvin Yancy composed the music), would explain his feelings about the song:

> I wanted to get Nat Cole involved with his daughter, and I wanted to bring out the love between Marvin, myself, and Natalie. She could really sing these kinds of songs, because she had been singing them all the time. They set her apart from the everyday artist. (White and Bronson, 1991)

February 19. Rich Stevens—former lead singer for Tower of Power—is arrested for the drug-related murders of three men in San Jose, California. He will be found guilty in November.

February 20. Kiss place their footprints on Grauman's Chinese Theatre pavement in Hollywood.

February 21. Florence Ballard dies of cardiac arrest at age thirty-two. She left the Supremes in 1967 in frustration over not being accorded the attention she felt was her due. She later lost an $8 million lawsuit against Motown, and was reduced to living on welfare in her later years.

February 21. "Sweet Thing" (ABC 12149) becomes the second R&B chart-topping single for Rufus featuring Chaka Khan, remaining there for two weeks. Group guitarist Tony Maiden, who co-wrote the song with Khan, would later recall the origins of the song:

> We needed one more song. I had a few chords and Chaka always hums stuff when I play the guitar. She gets up and walks to the booth to sing. And we were ready to go. We just [did] a scratch thing and "Sweet Thing" was born. It was very simple. Chaka always like to do jazz. [drummer] Andre [Fischer] like strings and stuff. But I said, "No strings. Chaka's voice and the band." (White and Bronson, 1991)

February 24. In the face of rising record sales, the Recording Industry Association of America (RIAA) institutes the platinum award. Gold records have been given for singles selling one million units and an album selling five hundred thousand. The new designation applies to singles selling at least two million copies, and albums selling one million. The first platinum single went to Johnnie Taylor's "Disco Lady," and the first platinum LP was the Eagles' *Their Greatest Hits 1971–1975*. The RIAA would eventually permit record companies to obtain platinum certification for pre-1976 releases.

February 28. The Rhythm Heritage peak at number one on the pop charts with the instrumental, "Theme from S.W.A.T." (ABC).

March 6. The Eagles begin a five-week run atop the album charts with *Greatest Hits 1971–1975* (Asylum). It becomes one of the top selling LPs of all time.

March 6. The Miracles reach the summit of the Hot 100 with "Love Machine (Part 1)" (Tamla).

March 6. The Sylvers' "Boogie Fever" (Capitol 4179) tops the R&B charts. It was producer Freddie Perren's first project following a six-year stint at Motown working with the Jackson 5. Perren was attracted to the idea of producing another family act. He would note,

> There seems to be a thread that holds families together musically. There's usually a low singer, a middle singer, and a high singer. God seems to have made a person for each part that needs to be sung. The Sylvers were pure singers—they had been singing since they were little kids. (White and Bronson, 1991)

March 7. Elton John's waxwork likeness is unveiled at Madame Tussauds in London. He is the first rock star to be so honored since the Beatles.

March 13. The Four Seasons return to the number one position on the Hot 100 a final time with "December, 1963 (Oh, What a Night)" (Warner/Curb), remaining there for three weeks.

March 13. Johnnie Taylor's "Disco Lady" (Columbia 10281) begins a six-week stay atop the R&B charts (#1 pop four weeks beginning April 3). Ironically, Taylor was not impressed with the results immediately following the recording session. Producer Don Davis (who also co-wrote the song with Harvey Scales and Al Vance) remembers that the singer called, saying, "'Pete'—he called everybody Pete—'my voice is too low, the record doesn't suit me, and I think we need to go with something else'" (White and Bronson. 1991).

March 18. Nicholas Roeg's film, *The Man Who Fell to Earth*, starring David Bowie, premieres in London.

March 19. Former Free and Back Street Crawler guitarist Paul Kossoff dies of heart failure on a Los Angeles to New York flight.

March 19. Gary Thain—bassist for the Keef Hartley Band and Uriah Heep—dies of a drug overdose at age twenty-eight.

March 28. Genesis open their first U.S. tour since Peter Gabriel's departure (with drummer Phil Collins now handling vocals), performing in Buffalo.

March 30. The Sex Pistols play their first show at London's 100 Club. They begin a weekly residency there in June.

March 31. The Brotherhood of Man top the British charts with "Save Your Kisses for Me."

April 1. The Buzzcocks make their live debut at the Bolton Institute of Technology.

April 3. The Salsoul Orchestra peak at number eighteen on the Hot 100 with "Tangerine" (Salsoul 2004).

The Salsoul Orchestra epitomized the blend of sweet arrangements and sinuous dance floor rhythms typifying disco era recording acts. The brainchild of Philadelphia producer/arranger Vincent Montana Jr., the ensemble included vocalists Carl Hem, Philip Hurt, Phyllis Rhodes, and Ronni Tyson. Montana's concept was responsible for nine R&B hits from late 1952 through 1982, most notably a remake of Jimmy Dorsey's number one 1942 instrumental smash, "Tangerine" (#11 r&b) and "Nice 'N' Naasty" (Salsoul 2011; 1976; #30 pop, #20 r&b). Guest artists such as gospel/pop singer Loleatta Holloway and Cognac—were liberally employed to augment the group's sound.

April 3. Johnnie Taylor commences a four-week run at number one in the Hot 100 with "Disco Lady."

April 9. Singer/songwriter Phil Ochs hangs himself at his sister's home in Queens, New York. He was considered Bob Dylan's biggest competitor in New York's early 1960s commercial folk scene.

April 10. Peter Frampton tops the charts with *Frampton Comes Alive* (A&M), which becomes the top-selling live LP in rock history.

April 10. *Melody Maker* pans a performance by the Sex Pistols, stating "I hope we shall hear no more of them."

April 14. Motown announces the largest contract renewal up to that time, a $13 million agreement with Stevie Wonder.

April 23. The Ramones release their eponymous debut LP, considered by many to be the first true punk work.

April 24. Paul and Linda McCartney visit John Lennon at his Dakota apartment across from Manhattan's Central Park. While watching NBC's *Saturday Night Live*, they catch producer Lorne Michaels' on-the-air offer for the Beatles to play three songs live on the show. They consider taking a cab to the studio, but decide they are too tired. It will be the last time the two spent time together.

April 24. The O'Jays initiate a two-week stretch in the top rung of the R&B charts with "Livin' for the Weekend" (Philadelphia International 3587).

April 27. David Bowie is detained by customs officers on a train at the Russian/Polish border after Nazi books and mementoes are found in his luggage.

April 29. After performing in Memphis, Bruce Springsteen takes a cab to Elvis Presley's Graceland. He is apprehended by a guard after climbing over the wall of the compound.

April 30. The Who's Keith Moon pays nine cab drivers to block off both ends of the New York street so he could throw the contents of his hotel room out of the window.

May 1. The Bellamy Brothers reach number one on the Hot 100 with "Let Your Love Flow" (Warner/Curb).

May 1. Led Zeppelin begin a two-week stint atop the album charts with *Presence* (Atlantic), their fifth LP to accomplish this feat.

May 3. Paul McCartney & Wings kick off their "Wings Over America" tour in Fort Worth, Texas; it is his first concert appearance stateside in almost ten years.

May 8. Abba reach number one on the British charts with "Fernando." They also began a nine-week run atop the U.K. album charts.

May 8. The Brass Construction ascend to the summit of the R&B charts with "Movin'" (United Artists 775).

May 8. John Sebastian tops the pop charts with "Welcome Back" (Reprise), the theme song to the hit TV show, *Welcome Back, Kotter.*

May 8. BBC Radio 1 deejay Johnny Walker announces he is quitting after being told he must pretend to like the Bay City Rollers.

May 15. Diana Ross rises to number one on the R&B charts with "Love Hangover" (Motown 1392).

May 15. The Rolling Stones top the album charts with *Black and Blue.*

May 15. The Sylvers climb to the summit of the Hot 100 with "Boogie Fever."

May 16. Patti Smith performs live in the U.K. for the first time at The Roundhouse, London.

May 22. The Manhattans' "Kiss and Say Goodbye" (Columbia 10310) peak at number one on the R&B survey. It would go on to become the second single to win a platinum award, on the heels of Johnnie Taylor's "Disco Lady." Although written by the group's bass, Winfred "Blue" Lovett, he hadn't seen it as their breakout single:

> I'd never thought of it as a number for the Manhattans to record, to me it was a Glen Campbell tune. We recorded it at the same time as "Hurt" [in early 1975] but a year went by before Columbia decided to release it. I thing they were waiting for the right time: the disco thing was firmly established when we came right in there with something totally different from everything people were hearing. (White and Bronson, 1991)

May 22. Wings reach number one on the Hot 100 with "Silly Love Songs" (Capitol), remaining there for five non-consecutive weeks.

May 29. Marvin Gaye reaches number one on the R&B charts with "I Want You" (Tamla 54264).

May 29. Diana Ross begins a two-week stint atop on pop charts with "Love Hangover."

May 31. The Who earn a place in *The Guinness Book of Records* for the loudest performance of a rock band, reaching 120 decibels at the Charlton Athletic football grounds.

June 2. Wings draw 67,100 at a Seattle concert, largest attendance ever for an indoor event.

June 12. The Wurzels top the British charts with "Combine Harvester," followed by (in descending order) The Real Thing's "You to Me Are Everything," Wings' "Silly Love Songs," Our Kid's "You Just Might See Me Cry," and J. J. Barrie's "No Charge."

June 17. *Rolling Stone* pictures Paul McCartney leaning against a blonde-haired woman (presumably wife Linda) on its cover with the caption "Yesterday Today & Paul: A Beatle on the Wing, a Band on the Run…but Not Quite the Act You've Known for All These Years."

June 30. Stuart Goddard (aka Adam Ant) places the following ad in the classified section of *Melody Maker*: "Beat on a bass with the B-Sides." Andy Warren responds to the inquiry, and they go on to form Adam and the Ants.

July 10. The Starland Vocal Band reaches number one on the Hot 100 with "Afternoon Delight" (Windsong), remaining there for two weeks.

July 24. The Manhattans begin a two-week stay atop the Hot 100 with "Kiss and Say Goodbye" (Columbia 10310).

The Jersey City-based Manhattans were one of the most successful soft soul groups of all time. Comprised of lead singer George Smith (died on spinal meningitis in 1970 and replaced by Gerald Alston), tenors Edward Bivins and Kenneth Kelly, bass Winfred Lovett, and baritone Richard Taylor, they first recorded for Piney in 1962. Despite their mastery of the romantic ballad, only two of their more than forty R&B hits spanning the mid-1960s through the 1980s cracked the pop Top 30, the crossover chart-topper, "Kiss and Say Goodbye" (1976) and "Shining Star" (1980).

July 27. After years of legal wrangling with U.S. immigration authorities, John Lennon is granted his Green Card.

July 31. George Benson starts a two-week stint at number one on the album charts with *Breezin'* (Warner Bros.).

August 7. "Don't Go Breaking My Heart" (Rocket), by Elton John and Kiki Dee, begin a four-week run atop the pop charts.

August 12. *Rolling Stone* pictures Bob Marley and his guitar on its cover with the caption "Rastaman with a Bullet."

August 19. Lou Rawls earns a gold record for his recording of the Kenny Gamble/Leon Huff composition, "You'll Never Find Another Love Like Mine" (Philadelphia International 3592; #2).

Lou Rawls is a living proof that popularizing the blues, jazz, and gospel can be accomplished without sacrificing musical values and good taste. Despite the polish and sophistication characterizing his approach, however, he remains capable of displaying the hard, soulful edge that attracted listeners in the first place. Many black contemporary singers popular in the 1980s and 1990s—most notably, Peabo Bryson and Luther Vandross—were strongly influenced by his singing style.

Born December 11, 1935, in Chicago, he progressed for singing in church choirs as a youth to a stint with the famed gospel group, the Pilgrim Travellers, in the late 1950s. After the group broke up, Rawls sing the blues on the Chitlin' Circuit. He developed a unique performing style consisting of an introductory monologue that would segue into a blues song. These numbers—half soliloquy, half rap—effectively communicated the conditions faced by African Americans in the 1960s.

His vocal interplay with Sam Cooke in "Bring It On Home To Me" (RCA 8036; 1962; #13) led a contract with Capitol. Rawls released a string of albums—twenty-eight in all—over the next decade with the label. Although much of this output featured somewhat overpowering production values, the warmth of his vocals and flawless phrasing—particularly on the million sellers *Lou Rawls Live!* (Capitol 2459; 1966; #4) and *Lou Rawls Soulin'* (Capitol 2566; 1966; #7), the latter of which included the hit single "Love Is A Hurtin' Thing" (Capitol 5709; 1966; #13)—kept things interesting while consistently making the charts.

Rawls moved to MGM in 1971, immediately scoring with the single, "A Natural Man" (MGM 14262; #17). However, the company's insistence that he focus on middle-of-the-road material led to another label change, this time to Bell. When that association failed to click, Rawls asked Kenny Gamble and Leon Huff to add him to the roster of their Philadelphia International label. Their choice of material and arrangements reinvigorated his career. The up-tempo ballad, "You'll Never Find Another Love Like Mine," became his biggest crossover hit, as well as providing the impetus for seven more best-selling albums over the next five years.

The hits stopped coming following a switch to Epic Records. However, a shift to Blue Note led Rawls back to a blues-inflected approach—most notably, in the albums *At Last* (Blue Note; 1989) and *Stormy Monday* (Blue Note; 1990)—although commercial success would continue to elude him.

August 28. George Benson peaks at number ten on the Hot 100 with the Leon Russell-penned "This Masquerade" (A&M 8209).

Benson first attracted attention as a vocalist, winning a singing contest at the age of four. He would sing on the radio as "Little Georgie Benson" and with numerous rhythm and blues bands around his native Pittsburgh. Although Benson took up the guitar as an eight-year-old, he did not play in public until age fifteen. Shortly thereafter, he began playing sessions in studios outside Pittsburgh. While still a teenager, his groups, the Altairs and George Benson and His All-Stars, recorded for Amy Records. Moving to New

York in 1965, he went on to record a series of widely admired, albeit moderate selling, instrumental jazz albums for Columbia, A&M, and CTI.

Signing with Warner Bros. in late 1975, Benson was encouraged to sing for the first time as a recording artist. His debut LP for the label, *Breezin'* (Warner Bros. 2919; 1976), won three Grammy awards and reached number one on the *Billboard Hot 100*. Its triple platinum sales were driven by "This Masquerade," the first single to ever reach number one on the jazz, R&B, and pop charts. His next seven albums—*In Flight* (Warner Bros. 2983; 1977), *Weekend In L.A.* (Warner Bros. 3139; 1978), *Livin' Inside Your Love* (Warner Bros. 3277; 1979), *Give Me the Night* (Warner Bros. 3453; 1980), *The George Benson Collection* (Warner Bros. 3577; 1981), *In Your Eyes* (Warner Bros. 23744; 1983), and *20/20* (Warner Bros. 25178; 1985)—all went gold (three achieved platinum status). His easygoing pop-funk style also led to more hit singles, including "On Broadway" (Warner Bros. 8542; 1978), "Give Me the Night" (Warner Bros. 49505; 1980), and "Turn Your Love Around" (Warner Bros. 49846; 1981).

Since the 1980s, Benson has divided his time between mainstream jazz projects (including live work with Dizzy Gillespie, Lionel Hampton, and Freddie Hubbard) and the more pop-inflected recordings. His ability to navigate a middle course is reflected by chart-topping Contemporary Jazz albums such as *Tenderly* (Warner Bros. 25907; 1989), with pianist McCoy Tyner, and *Love Remembers* (Warner Bros.; 1993).

August 29. Rhythm and blues pioneer Jimmy Reed dies. Covered by the likes of Elvis Presley and the Rolling Stones, his hits included "Big Boss Man" and "Bright Lights, Big City."

August 31. George Harrison is found guilty of "subconscious plagiarism" of Ronnie Mack's "He's So Fine" when writing his own "My Sweet Lord." Earnings from the latter will go to Mack's estate. The Chiffons—who took the Mack composition to number one in 1963—go on to record "My Sweet Lord."

September 4. The Bee Gees claim the pole position on the Hot 100 with "You Should Be Dancing" (RSO).

September 4. Fleetwood Mac top the album charts for the first time with *Fleetwood Mac* (Reprise).

September 11. KC & the Sunshine Band reach number one on the pop charts with "(Shake, Shake, Shake) Shake Your Booty" (T.K.).

September 18. Wild Cherry begin a three-week stay atop the Hot 100 with "Play That Funky Music" (Epic).

October 9. Walter Murphy climbs to the summit of the Hot 100 with "A Fifth of Beethoven" (Private Stock).

October 16. Rick Dees reaches number one on the pop charts with the platinum-selling novelty, "Disco Duck (Part I)" (RSO).

October 23. Chicago begins a two-week stint atop the Hot 100 with "If You Leave Me Now" (Columbia).

November 4. *Rolling Stone* pictures Brian Wilson, wearing a bathrobe and carrying a surf board, on its cover with the caption "The Healing of Brother Brian: A Multitrack Interview with Beach Boys Brian, Dennis, Carl, Mike and Al, plus Brian's Mom, His Dad, His Wife and His Shrink."

November 6. Steve Miller goes to number one with "Rock'n Me" (Capitol).

November 13. Led Zeppelin heads up the British album charts with the video soundtrack, *The Song Remains the Same* (#2 U.S.).

November 13. Rod Stewart begins an eight-week run atop the Hot 100 with "Tonight's the Night (Gonna Be Alright)" (Warner Bros.). It reaches number five in the U.K. despite being banned by many radio stations because it addresses the seduction of a virgin.

December 1. The Sex Pistols fill in for Queen (incapacitated by Freddie Mercury's trip to the dentist) in ITV's *Today*. Guitarist Steve Jones issues a stream of profanities following interviewer Bill Grundy's request that the band say something outrageous.

One of the most revolutionary—and controversial—bands produced out of the rock subculture, the Sex Pistols are widely recognized as progenitors off the 1970s punk movement, merging a stripped-down, high energy sound with incendiary lyrics born out of economic and social inequities of post-World War II Great Britain. Although they owed much to the mid-1960s garage bands such as the Seeds and the

Standells, the anti-pop white noise of the Velvet Underground, the dumbed-down buzz saw chording of the Ramones, and the glam-tinged, street-smart hard rock of the New York Dolls, the Pistols communicated a rage and political imperative missing in the music their antecedents.

The Sex Pistols were formed in London in summer 1975 when boutique owner and would-be pop music entrepreneur Malcolm paired former Swankers Steve Jones (guitar), Glen Matlock (bass), and Paul Cook (drums) with John Lydon (aka Johnny Rotten). Rotten's green spiky hair, snarling vocals, and ill-mannered behavior made him the center of the media's sensationalized coverage of the emerging; however, raw excitement generated by the band in performance had much to do with their success in generating a strong grassroots following. Whether they were true to their nihilistic punk ethic or merely convincing poseurs, the Pistols proved to be too hot for a succession of corporate labels to handle. E.M.I. dropped the group after one widely-censored single, "Anarchy in the U.K." (E.M.I. 2566; 1976; #38 UK) and the outrage ensuing from their behavior on the British TV program, "Today." A & M likewise bailed out in March 1977 after the antics of band members (now including Sid Vicious, who'd replaced Matlock) at the post-signing party with copies of the anticipated debut release, "God Save the Queen" (A & M 7284; 1977), becoming an instant collectors item. The seminal punk anthem was reissued a couple of months later by Virgin (#181; 1977), reaching number two on the British charts, despite being banned by the BBC.

The equally vitriolic follow-ups, "Pretty Vacant" (Virgin 184; 1977; #6 UK) and "Holidays in the Sun" (Virgin 191; 1977; #8 UK), piqued interest in the long-awaited debut album, *Never Mind the Bollocks, Here's the Sex Pistols* (Warner Bros. 3147; 1977; #106 US, #1 UK). Now considered the classic statement of the British punk movement, the band—severely crippled by Rotten's departure following a brief American tour in early 1978 to form the postpunk experimental band, Public Image Ltd.—was nursed along by McLaren, releasing a string of Top 10 British singles and recycled LPs, most notably the biopic soundtrack, *The Great Rock 'N' Roll Swindle* (Warner Bros. 45083; 1979; #7 UK) and the *Some Product: Carry On Sex Pistols* (Virgin 2; 1979; #6). The Pistols were effectively terminated by the death of Vicious on February 2, 1979, due to a heroin overdose. Nevertheless, interested in the band has remained high, in part as a result of the rise of alternative rock, specifically the grunge subgenre. As a result, all the group's recordings have been reissued on compact disc, and the original lineup reassembled for a live tour in 1996, documented in the recording *Filthy Lucre Live* (Virgin America 41926; 1996; #26 UK).

December 2. *Rolling Stone* pictures Linda Ronstadt clad in red negligee on its cover with the caption "The Million-Dollar Woman."

December 25. Boston peak at number five on the Hot 100 with "More Than a Feeling" (Epic 50266). Industry experts have argued that the song was actually far more popular than this ranking would indicate, that the majority of record buyers opted for the band's first LP rather than buying the single.

Boston's success has defied many music business tenets; allowing considerable time to elapse between releases, with virtually no photo-ops to keep the group in the public eye, yet enjoying multi-platinum sales with a richly textured, power guitar sound that remains essentially unchanged since the release of the first album in 1976. That release, eponymous titled *Boston* (Columbia 34188), was the brainchild of guitarist Tom Schulz. An unlikely rock star, Schulz earned a master's degree in mechanical engineering from MIT and, as a senior product designer for Polaroid Corporation, was limited to creating his music during leisure hours. His demo tapes, produced in his own twelve-track basement studio, led to a recording contract with Epic Records. These tracks formed the core of the album, although Scholz and his supporting band—including vocalist Brad Delp, guitarist Barry Goudreau, bassist Fran Sheehan, and drummer Sib Hashian—recur some of the material on the West Coast with producer John Boylan. *Boston* was a huge success, selling more than eleven million copies; in 1995, *Billboard* called it the third-best-selling LP ever, behind Michael Jackson's *Thriller* and Fleetwood Mac's *Rumors*.

The follow-up release, *Don't Look Back* (Columbia 35050; 1978), although reaching number one, sold only six million copies. Apparently concerned about a further erosion of public interest, Scholz spent eight years working on the next album. When *Third Stage* (MCA 6188) became available in 1986, Scholz and Delp—whose soaring vocals helped define the group's intricately layered sound—were the only members left from the original lineup. Driven by the number one single, "Amanda" (MCA 52756; 1986), the album topped the charts, becoming a four-million seller. At this point, Scholz's creative focus was compromised by a series of lawsuits involving former band member Goudreau and CBS Records. He also found time to invent the Rockman, a small guitar amplifier with headphones used by many musicians. With Delp having departed in 1991 to form a band called RTZ with Goudreau, Scholz was forced to dispense, once and for all, with the fiction of group collaboration. Nevertheless, utilizing a new studio built from the money won in his successful countersuit of CBS, Scholz produced a fourth album, *Walk On* (MCA), in 1994.

December 25. Asylum releases the Eagles' "New Kid in Town"/"Victim of Love" (#45373). It becomes the band's third chart-topping single. The band also begins an eight-week run at number one on the album charts with *Hotel California* (Asylum).

December 25. Johnny Mathis heads up the U.K. charts with "When a Child is Born," his only single to accomplish this feat.

December 26. The Sex Pistols record "God Save the Queen" at Wessex Studios, London.

December 27. Blues guitarist Freddie King dies of heart trouble and ulcers at age forty-two.

1977

❄

January 1. Wings' "Mull of Kintyre," presently topping the British charts, becomes the first single to sell more than two million copies in that country.

January 6. The Sex Pistols' notoriously rude behavior causes EMI to release them from their contract; the payoff totals $68,000.

January 8. "You Don't Have To Be a Star" (ABC), as recorded by the husband-and-wife team, Marilyn Mc-Coo and Billy Davis Jr., settles into the top spot on the Hot 100. The duo were formerly members of the pop-soul vocal group, the 5th Dimension. McCoo will go on to success as the host of the long-running television show, *Solid Gold*.

January 12. The Police rehearse for the first time at drummer Stewart Copeland's London flat. Fellow musicians include Sting on bass, and guitarists Henri Padovani and Andy Summers.

January 12. EMI issues a public statement explaining that the Sex Pistols were dropped due to the negative press they had generated during the past couple of months.

January 15. The Eagles' *Hotel California* (Asylum) goes number one, their third chart-topping LP.

January 15. Leo Sayer reaches number one on the pop charts with "You Make Me Feel Like Dancing" (Warner Bros.).

January 22. Wings top the charts with *Wings Over America*, Paul McCartney's sixth number one LP since the breakup of the Beatles.

January 22. Stevie Wonder climbs to the summit of the Hot 100 with "I Wish" (Tamla).

January 23. Patti Smith fractures her spine after falling off the stage while performing in Tampa, Florida.

January 26. Blues-rock guitarist Peter Green, formerly with John Mayall's Bluesbreakers and Fleetwood Mac, is committed to a mental hospital after threatening his accountant Clifford Adams—who was attempting to give him a $51,000 royalty check—with an air rifle.

January 27. The Clash sign with the U.K. division of CBS Records.

January 29. Rose Royce—the former backing band for the Temptations—top the Hot 100 with "Car Wash" (#9 U.K.).

February 5. Mary MacGregor begins a two-week stay at number one on the pop charts with "Torn Between Two Lovers" (Ariola America).

February 10. The Clash start work on their debut LP at London's CBS studios.

February 12. The Police record their debut single, "Fall Out," for $255 at London's Pathway Studios.

February 14. Janis Ian receives 461 Valentine's Day cards after stating in the "At Seventeen" lyrics that she had never received any.

February 15. The Sex Pistols fire bassist Glen Matlock, replacing him with Sid Vicious.

February 19. Manfred Mann's Earth Band peak at number one on the Hot 100 with the Bruce Springsteen composition, "Blinded By the Light" (Warner Bros.).

February 19. Leo Sayer tops the British singles charts for the only time in his career with "When I Need You."

February 21. Fleetwood Mac's *Rumours* (Reprise) is released. It sells more than 15 million copies throughout the century, and spends thirty-one weeks atop the charts.

February 22. The *New Musical Express* readers' poll gives the "Turkey of the Year" award to the Sex Pistols.

February 25. Polydor Records UK offers The Jam $10,200 as a signing bonus.

February 26. The Eagles head up the pop charts with "New Kid in Town" (Asylum).

March 2. The Jam sign a four-year recording contract with Polydor, and then play the first of a five-week Wednesday night run at The Red Cow, Hammersmith, London.

March 4. CBS releases the Clash's eponymous debut LP in Great Britain; however, the label's U.S. branch holds off releasing it until 1979. Americans will buy more than one hundred thousand copies of the English pressing, making it one of the top-selling imports ever.

March 5. Al Stewart peaks at number eight on the Hot 100 with "Year of the Cat" (Janus 266). The British singer-songwriter will remain a popular album artist well into the 1980s.

March 5. Barbra Streisand begins a three-week run atop the Hot 100 with "Love Theme from 'A Star Is Born' (Evergreen)" (Columbia).

March 9. *The Jacksons* (CBS) is aired for the last time on television, a casualty of poor ratings.

March 10. The Sex Pistols sign a recording contract with A&M outside Buckingham Palace at 7 a.m. The agreement will be voided in just six days.

March 11. The Slits—the first all-female punk band—perform live for the first time, opening for The Clash at London's Roxy Club.

March 12. Bob Seger peaks at number four on the Hot 100 with "Night Moves" (Capitol 4369).

Bob Seger exemplified the best in American hard rock during the 1970s: melodic, yet propulsive, guitar-dominated treatments of well-crafted songs sung with raw passion. Like others in this blue collar, heartland genre—including Bruce Springsteen, John Mellencamp, and Tom Petty—Seger eschewed hype and industry image-making, developing career momentum through touring and positive word-of-mouth regarding recordings.

Michigan-native Seger first recorded for the Hideout and Cameo labels—five singles in all during the 1966-1967 period—as Bob Seger and the Last Heard. Signing with Capitol Records and changing the name of the band to the Bob Seger System, he issued *Ramblin' Gamblin' Man* (Capitol 172; 1969; #62), driven by the success of the title track (Capitol 2297; 1968; #17). When the follow-up LPs—*Noah* (Capitol 236; 1970) and *Mongrel* (Capitol 499; 1970)—achieved marginal sales, he shifted personnel, billing himself as a solo act. However, the album releases—including the oldies cover collection *Brand New Morning* (Capitol 3187; 1971), *Smokin' O.P.'s* (Capitol 2109; 1972), *Back in '72* (Capitol 2126), *Seven* (Capitol 2184; 1974), and *Beautiful Loser* (Capitol 11378; 1975)—continued to feature the same straight-ahead rock style.

Reorganizing his supporting musicians once more as the Silver Bullet Band in the mid-1970s, Seger began attracting critical raves for his mature compositions and precision performing, finding commercial success with releases such as *Live Bullet* (Capitol 11523; 1976; #34), *Night Moves* (Capitol 11557; 1977; #8), *Stranger in Town* (Capitol 11698; 1978; 4), and *Against the Wind* (Capitol 12041; 1980; #1). The later albums—the live *Nine Tonight* (Capitol 12182; 1981; #3), *The Distance* (Capitol 12254; 1982; #5), *Like a Rock* (Capitol 12398; 1986; #3), *The Fire Inside* (Capitol 91134; 1991; #7), and *It's a Mystery* (Capitol 99774; 1995; #27)—while lacking the intensity and innovative drive of his classic work, have all been workmanlike affairs which have retained his core audience.

March 12. The Sex Pistols are involved in an altercation with Bob Harris, presenter of BBC 2's *The Old Grey Whistle Test*, at London's Speakeasy Club.

March 13. Manhattan Transfer top the British singles charts with "Chanson D'amour."

March 16. The Sex Pistols are fired from A&M due to pressure from other label artists and the Los Angeles head office. The band receives the $27,500 from the arrangement.

March 18. The Clash's debut single, "White Riot," is released, peaking at number thirty-eight on the British charts.

March 20. Lou Reed is barred from performing at the London Palladium due to his punk image.

March 20. T. Rex give their last concert at The Locarno in Portsmouth, England.

March 24. *Rolling Stone* pictures Fleetwood Mac together on a mattress for its cover with the caption "True Life Confessions."

March 26. Daryl Hall & John Oates reach number one on the pop charts with "Rich Girl" (RCA), remaining there for two weeks.

April. Steve Rubell and Ian Schrager open Manhattan's Studio 54. It immediately becomes the most highly visible disco club, catering to the celebrity consciousness of that era.

April 2. Abba heads up the British charts with "Knowing Me, Knowing You," their fifth single to accomplish this feat.

April 2. Frank Sinatra enjoys a number one LP for the first time in England with *Portrait of Sinatra*.

April 8. The Damned perform at CBGB's, in New York, making them the first British punk group to appear live in the United States.

April 9. Abba ascend to the top of the pop charts for the only time with their MOR take on the disco craze, "Dancing Queen" (Atlantic). Nevertheless, the Swedish vocal quartet—who first achieved stateside success with "Waterloo" in 1973—would remain consistent hitmakers for the balance of the 1970s.

April 11. Alice Cooper draws an audience of forty thousand in Sydney, Australia, the largest crowd to ever attend a rock concert in that nation.

April 16. David Soul reaches number one on the Hot 100 with "Don't Give Up on Us" (Private Stock).

April 22. The Jam's first single, "In the City," is released. Never a force stateside, the band make the British Top 40 eighteen times, including four chart toppers.

April 23. Adam and the Ants debut at London's Roxy Club.

April 23. Thelma Houston tops the pop charts with the disco melodrama, "Don't Leave Me This Way" (Tamla).

April 25. Elvis Presley makes his last recordings live at the Saginaw, Michigan, Civic Center. Three of the songs appear on the posthumously released *Moody Blue* (RCA).

April 30. Glen Campbell goes number one on the Hot 100 with "Southern Nights" (Capitol).

May 6. The Boomtown Rats perform in England for the first time, at London's Studio 51.

May 7. "Hotel California"/"Pretty Maids All in a Row" (Asylum 45286) becomes the Eagles' fourth number one pop single.

May 12. Led Zeppelin receives the Outstanding Contribution to British Music at the second Ivor Novello Awards celebration.

May 14. Leo Sayer reaches number one on the Hot 100 with "When I Need You" (Warner Bros.). It repeats the feat on the British charts.

May 21. Rod Stewart heads up the British charts with the double-sided hit, "I Don't Want to Talk About It"/"First Cut is the Deepest."

May 21. Stevie Wonder begins a three-week stay atop the Hot 100 with "Sir Duke" (Tamla).

May 26. *Beatlemania*, a simulated Beatles concert starring four performers who look and sound like the original quartet, opens at New York's Winter Garden Theater. They will garner capacity crowds for the next several years.

May 27. Declan McManus makes his performing debut as Elvis Costello (at the Nashville in London).

May 27. The Sex Pistols' "God Save the Queen" is released. It is banned by British radio, television, and posh retailers, while record plant workers refuse to handle it. Nevertheless, it will sell two hundred thousand copies in one week, reaching number two on the U.K. charts.

May 28. Steward Copeland, Sting, and Andy Summers perform together for the first time as part of Mike Howlett's band, Strontium 90, at the Circus Hippodrome, Paris.

May 29. Warsaw, make their live debut in support of the Buzzcocks at The Electric Circus, Manchester. They will soon change their name to Joy Division.

May 31. The BBC announces a ban on the Sex Pistols' "God Save the Queen." The IBA warns radio stations that playing the single would violate Section 4:1 of the Broadcasting Act.

June 11. KC & the Sunshine Band reach number one on the pop charts with "I'm Your Boogie Man" (T.K.)

June 18. Fleetwood Mac's "Dreams" (Warner Bros.) tops the Hot 100. Although this will be the only one of the seven singles culled from the *Rumours* to achieve this level of popularity, the LP will spend thirty-one weeks at number one, beginning April 2. The band will nevertheless be the most successful singles act of 1977.

June 18. Aretha Franklin's "Break It to Me Gently" (Atlantic 3393) peaks at number one on the R&B charts.

June 25. The Emotions top the R&B charts with "Best of My Love" (Columbia 10544), remaining there for four non-consecutive weeks.

June 25. Marvin Gaye climbs to the summit of the pop charts with disco-tinged "Got to Give It Up (Pt. 1)" (Tamla).

June 25. Elvis Presley's "Way Down" (RCA 10998) debuts on the *Billboard* country survey. It will reach number one on August 20, four days after his death.

June 26. Elvis Presley appears in concert for the last time at the Market Square Arena, Indianapolis, Indiana.

June 30. Marvel Comics issues a special edition comic book built around the rock band, Kiss.

July 2. Bill Conti tops the Hot 100 with "Gonna Fly Now" (United Artists), the instrumental theme from Sylvester Stallone's Academy Award-winning film, *Rocky*.

July 2. Donna Fargo heads up the country charts with the recitation song, "That Was Yesterday" (Warner Bros. 8375).

July 9. Alan O'Day's "Undercover Angel" (Pacific) peaks at number one on the pop charts.

July 9. Charley Pride's "I'll Be Leaving Alone" (RCA 10975) tops the county charts.

July 16. Shaun Cassidy's rendition of "Da Doo Ron Ron" (Warner/Curb) reaches number one on the Hot 100. Written by Jeff Barry, Ellie Greenwich, and Phil Spector, the song reached the Top 5 in spring 1963 with Spector producing the Crystals. Cassidy, the most popular teen idol of the moment, achieved TV fame as a cast regular on *The Hardy Boys*; with his popularity on the wane in the early 1980s, he would star in the short-lived TV series treatment of the film hit, *Breaking Away*.

July 16. The Commodores climb to the summit of the R&B charts with "Easy" (Motown 1418).

July 16. Ronnie Milsap's "It Was Almost Like a Song" (RCA 10976) begins a three-week stint atop the country charts. It would also become his first crossover hit, reaching number sixteen on the Hot 100. The LP from which it was taken, *It Was Almost Like a Song*, would earn Milsap a third Country Music Association Album of the Year award. Its popularity would result in RCA presenting the first gold album inscribed in Braille to Milsap the following year.

July 16. Teddy Pendergrass peaks at number forty-one on the Hot 100 with "I Don't Love You Anymore" (Philadelphia International 3622).

A premier balladeer whose velvety vocal delivery spanned the soul, funk, disco, and black contemporary eras, Teddy Pendergrass has also survived countless personal setbacks—artistic disputes, love affairs, and a serious automobile accident on March 18, 1982, which left him partially paralyzed.

Born March 26, 1950, in Philadelphia, Pendergrass honed his performing skills working in local clubs during the 1960s. He joined the budding Philly Soul juggernaut, Harold Melvin & The Bluenotes as a drummer in 1969; he became their lead vocalist the following year. Produced by Kenny Gamble and Leon Huff, the group enjoyed considerable success in the early 1970s, recording such crossover hits as "If You Don't Know Me By Now" (Philadelphia International 3520; 1972; #3 pop, #1 r&b), "The Love I Lost (Part 1)" (Philadelphia International 3533; 1973; #7 pop, #1 r&b), "Bad Luck (Part 1)" (Philadelphia International 3562; 1975; #15 pop, #4 r&b), "Hope That We Can Be Together Soon" (Philadelphia International 3569; 1975; #42 pop, #1 r&b), and "Wake Up Everybody (Part 1)" (Philadelphia International 3579; 1975; #12 pop, #1 r&b).

Pendergrass left The Bluenotes in late 1975 under acrimonious circumstances. While it took a couple of years for his solo career to gain momentum, he ultimately established himself as a major R&B recording artist in the romantic soul-pop vein pioneered by the likes of Barry White. His chart smashes—always more popular with black listeners than the pop mainstream audience—included "I Don't Love You

Anymore" (#5 r&b), "Close the Door" (Philadelphia International 3648; 1978; #25 pop, #1 r&b), "Turn Off the Lights" (Philadelphia International 3696; 1979; #48 pop, #2 r&b), "Can't We Try" (Philadelphia International 3107; 1980; #52 pop, #3 r&b), "Love T.K.O." (Philadelphia International 3116; 1980; #44 pop, #2 r&b), "Two Hearts" (20th Century 2492; 1981; #40 pop, #3 r&b; with Stephanie Mills) "You're My Latest, My Greatest Inspiration" (Philadelphia International 02619; 1981; #43 pop, #4 r&b), "Hold Me" (Asylum 69720; 1984; #46 pop, #5 r&b; accompanied by a young Whitney Houston), "Lov 4/2" (Asylum 69568; 1986; #6 r&b), and "Joy" (Asylum 69401; 1988; #77 pop, #1 r&b). Shortly before his car mishap, Pendergrass starred in the film, Soup For *One* (1982). He also worked with a supergroup comprised of Philadelphia International artists such as Archie Bell, Dee Dee Sharp Gamble, The O'Jays, Billy Paul, and Lou Rawls; the profits of their sole hit, "Let's Clean Up the Ghetto" (Philadelphia International 3627; 1977; #91 pop, #4 r&b), were contributed to an urban charity project.

July 23. Barry Manilow goes number one on the pop charts with "Looks Like We Made It" (Arista).

July 30. Andy Gibb reaches the top of the *Hot* 100 with "I Just Want to Be Your Everything" (RSO), remaining there for four non-consecutive weeks.

July 30. Slave—a nine-member band founded in Dayton, Ohio—go number one on the R&B charts with "Slide" (Cotillion 44218).

August 6. The Brothers Johnson achieve number one on the R&B charts with "Strawberry Letter 23" (A&M 1949). George Johnson first heard the song on a Shuggie Otis LP, *Freedom Flight* (1971), given to him by the latter's cousin, who he dated for a time.

August 6. Charlie Rich reaches the summit of the country charts with "Rollin' With the Flow" (Epic 50392), remaining there for two weeks. Producer Billy Sherrill, who came across the song on the B side of a T. G. Sheppard single, would relate that he improved it by changing one word in the original:

> Not to applaud myself, but I think it was a key word. We had a real good feel on it, but the one line always bothered me. He said, "I've got a lot of crazy friends, and One forgives me of my sins," meaning Jesus. I thought, "This just don't sit with me at all." Let's just say "I've got a lot of crazy friends and *they* forgive me of my sins." Charlie said, "I like that better." (Roland, 1991)

August 12. Guitarist Henri Padovani quits The Police following a nine month stint. The Band continues as a trio.

August 13. The Floaters begin a six-week run atop the R&B charts with "Float On" (ABC 12284).

August 16. Elvis Presley dies of heart failure at Graceland, Memphis, at age forty-two. Record stores nationwide reported runs on existing Presley stock, prompting RCA to keep its Indianapolis plant open twenty-four hours a day, pressing Presley material exclusively to try to meet demand. "My Way," recorded during his June concert tour and released as a single in November, becomes his final gold record.

August 19. The Sex Pistols kick off an undercover British tour as The Spots (which stands for "Sex Pistols on tour secretly").

August 20. The Emotions reach the top of the Hot 100 with "Best of My Love," remaining there for five non-consecutive weeks.

Few acts paid more dues than the Emotions prior to reaching the upper echelons off the music charts. At the time when their biggest hit, "Best of My Love" (Columbia 10544), simultaneously topped the pop and R&B charts, the group had been active in show business for twenty years, having interpreted a variety of styles and taken on several different names in the process.

The group originated with three sisters, Sheila, Wanda, and Jeanette Hutchinson, who first sang as the Hutchinsons, and later, the Heavenly Sunbeams, in Chicago's Mt. Sainai Baptist Church. Guided by their father, Joe, they first performed on television in 1958, soon thereafter hosting a radio gospel program, followed by a Sunday morning TV series. Shifting to soul in the mid-1960s while still in high school, they recorded as Three Ribbons and a Bow for several Midwestern labels, including Vee-Jay.

The Staple Singers saw the sisters perform live, and referred them to Stax Records in 1968. They began calling themselves the Emotions at this time after a friend noted that their music was so powerfully emotionally that it elicited spinal chills. Thirteen of their singles for the Stax subsidiary, Volt, made the R&B charts, most notably the Isaac Hayes-produced "So I Can Love You" (Volt 4010; 1969; #39 pop, #3 r&b). They also appeared in the 1973 *Wattstax* documentary before the label went out of business in 1975.

The Emotions went on to sign with Kalimba Productions, fronted by Maurice White of Earth, Wind and Fire, who hooked them up with his band's label, Columbia Records. The initial product of this collaboration, *Flowers* (Columbia 34163; 1976; #45), proved to be their most successful album up to that point. The follow-up, *Rejoice* (Columbia 34762; 1977; #7), did even better, achieving platinum sales, due largely to the popularity of the funky "Best of My Love" (produced and co-written by White), which featured Wanda singing lead an octave higher than her usual register.

The Emotions would return to the Top 40 only one more time, backing Earth, Wind and Fire on the infectious dance number, "Boogie Wonderland" (ARC 10956; 1979; #6 pop, #2 R&B). They bounced around from one label to another in the 1980s, while achieving moderate success in the R&B market. The move from Red Label Records to Motown in the mid-1980s coincided with departure of Theresa (who'd previously taken a sabbatical from the group between 1970 and 1978), who was replaced by Adrianne Harris.

August 20. Elvis Presley's "Way Down/Pledging My Love" (RCA 10998) heads up the country charts.

August 27. The Floaters reach number one on the British charts with "Float On."

August 27. Crystal Gayle's "Don't It Make My Brown Eyes Blue" (United Artists 1016) begins a four-week stay atop the country charts (#2 pop). It would become Gayle's only million-selling single, net two Grammys, and bring writer Richard Leigh a second CMA Song of the Year award (the first was for "I'll Get Over You"). Gayle's *We Must Believe in Magic* is the first LP by a Nashville-based female to certified platinum by the RIAA.

September 3. Elvis Presley begins a fifteen-week run atop *Billboard*'s country album charts; *Moody Blue* accounted for the first ten weeks, followed by *Elvis In Concert*, a two-disc set culled from Presley's final live tour.

September 3. Elvis Presley tops the British charts for the seventeenth time with "Way Down."

September 16. Singer/songwriter and teen heart throb Marc Bolan dies in a car accident when his girl friend drives off an English road, hitting a tree. He had a chart-topping British single, "Hot Love" (1971) and Top 10 U.S. hit in 1972, "Bang a Gong (Get It On)."

September 22. *Rolling Stone* runs an obscure publicity photo of a mid-1950s Elvis Presley on its cover, supplemented only by the performer's name, and birth and death dates.

September 24. KC and the Sunshine Band peak at the summit of the R&B charts with "Keep It Comin' Love" (T.K. 1023), his fourth and final single to accomplish this feat.

September 24. "I've Already Loved You in My Mind" (MCA 40754) becomes Conway Twitty's ninth country chart-topper in a row (and twenty-fifth overall). Twitty would later state,

> That's one of my personal favorites, of all the things I've written. You know, President Jimmy Carter almost got kicked out of office for sayin' that. And he was just bein' truthful. There ain't a man walkin' that ain't had a thought like that cross his mind when he sees a pretty lady walk by. (Roland, 1991)

September 30. Mary Ford dies from cancer following fifty-four days in a diabetic coma. Her early 1950s recordings with guitarist/producer Les Paul revolutionized pop music recording.

October 1. Meco begins a two-week stint atop the Hot 100 with a Euro-disco treatment of "Star Wars Theme/ Cantina Band" (Millennium). The medley was adapted from the John Williams pieces appearing in the soundtrack to the Academy Award-winning film, *Star Wars*.

October 1. Kenny Rogers reaches number one on the country charts with "Daytime Friends" (United Artists 1027).

October 1. Barry White's "It's Ecstasy When You Lay Down Next to Me" (20th Century 2350) heads up the R&B charts, remaining there for five weeks.

October 8. The Kendalls—consisting Royce Kendall and daughter Jeannie—burst onto the country scene in a big way, beginning a four-week run in the top spot with their debut single, "Heaven's Just a Sin Away" (Ovation 1103). It would go on to garner a Grammy and the CMA award for "Single of the Year." Ironically, Ovation didn't envision the track as a hit, designating "Making Believe" as the duo's first release. However, when Emmylou Harris put out her own version of that song, the record quickly disappeared. The label opted for "Live and Let Live" as the second single, tucking "Heaven's Just a Sin Away" on flip side. But when deejays began playing the B side, Ovation shifted its promotional efforts.

October 8. Ted Nugent peaks at number thirty on the pop charts with "Cat Scratch Fever" (Epic 50425).

Ted Nugent was one of the more dynamic performers within the hard rock field during the 1970s, a fact that did not translate particularly well to sound recordings. Well aware of the differences between the two forms of communication, the singer/guitarist/ songwriter explained to *Circus* magazine how he used this situation to further the creative process in the studio: "There's no way anyone will ever capture a live performance on record because you just don't have all the elements. You don't have the face-to-face, body-to-body, flesh-to-flesh, volume-to-skull; but seeing how my entire inspiration comes from the stage and the intensity thereon, I secure that whole desire for that intensity in the studio and that's where [my] songs come from" (March 16, 1978).

Born in Detroit Michigan, Nugent played in a succession of rock bands in the early 1960s before forming the Chicago-based Amboy Dukes in 1966. Three releases on the Mainstream label—*The Amboy Dukes* (Mainstream 6104; 1967; #183); *Journey to the Center of the Mind* (Mainstream 6112; 1968; #74), featuring the title single (Mainstream 684; 1968; #16); and *Migration* (Mainstream 6118; 1969)—cemented their national reputation as a premier acid rock band. Later albums—*Marriage on the Rocks/Rock Bottom* (Polydor 4012; 1970; #191) and *Survival of the Fittest/Live* (Polydor 4035; 1971; #129)—suffered from internal differences as to the stylistic direction the band should take in the face of changing fashions within the music scene.

Interesting in taking greater control of his career, Nugent went solo in 1975. A key ingredient in his future success was the decision to sign with Epic Records; supporting his contention that Top 40 radio did not represent a viable promotional vehicle, the Columbia subsidiary supported an exhaustive touring schedule aimed at reaching the potential record buying audience. As a result, Nugent's high-energy, guitar-driven recordings sold consistently at platinum levels, including *Ted Nugent* (Epic 33692; 1975; #28), *Free-For-All* (Epic 34121; 1976; #24), *Cat Scratch Fever* (Epic 34700; #17), Double *Live Gonzo!* (Epic 35069; 1978; #13), and *Weekend Warriors* (Epic 35551; 1978; #24). Two more albums—*State of Shock* (Epic 36000; 1979; #18) and *Scream Dream* (Epic 36404; 1980; #13)—achieved gold status.

Personal problems (the disruption of his strong family orientation by a late 1970s divorce) and major shifts in the lineup of his backing band contributed to the declining success of Nugent's 1980s albums: the live *Intensities in 10 Cities* (Epic 37084; 1981; #51), *Nugent* (Atlantic 19365; 1982; #51), *Penetrator* (Atlantic 80125; 1984; #56), *Little Miss Dangerous* (Atlantic 81632; 1986; #76), and *If You Can't Lick 'Em...Lick 'Em* (Atlantic 81812; 1988; #11). Later in the decade, he was further distracted by celebrity appearances on television programs and other public events and car racing activities. In 1989, he linked up with former Styx vocalist/guitarist Tommy Shaw to form Damn Yankees, an attempt at refining his blunt metallic attack with the polished AOR melodicism then dominating the charts. After a measure of success with the group—*Damn Yankees* (Warner Bros. 26159; 1990; #13), featuring the single, "High Enough" (Warner Bros. 19595; 1990; #3); *Don't Tread* (Warner Bros. 45025; 1992; #22)—he returned to a solo career.

October 15. Debby Boone—the daughter of 1950s teen idol Pat Boone—reaches number one on the Hot 100 (#1 AC) with "You Light Up My Life" (Warner/Curb), remaining there for ten consecutive weeks. The theme song from the film of the same name, it will be recognized as the most successful single of the decade. It will also be Boone's only pop hit.

October 20. *Rolling Stone* publishes a punk-styled double photo of Johnny Rotten (aka John Lydon) on its cover with the caption "ROCK IS SICK AND LIVING IN LONDON: A Report on the Sex Pistols."

November 5. Don Williams negotiates the summit of the country charts with "I'm Just a Country Boy" (ABC/Dot 17717).

November 12. Peter Brown peaks at number eighteen on the Hot 100 with "Do Ya Wanna Get Funky With Me" (Drive 6258).

Vocalist/keyboardist/producer Peter Brown is closely identified with the disco era. His mastery of studio technology enabled him to function as a one-man band in the manufacture of slick, uptempo dance material.

Born on July 11, 1953, in Blue Island, Illinois, Brown attended the Art Institute of Chicago in the mid-1970s. He recorded a series of dance hits—most notably, "Do You Wanna Get Funky With Me" (#3 r&b), "Dance With Me" (Drive 6269; 1978; #8 pop, #5 r&b), "You Should Do It" (Drive 6272; 1978; #54 pop, #25 r&b), and "Crank It Up (Funk Town), Pt. 1" (Drive 6278; 1979; #86 pop, #9 r&b)—which crossed over to the pop charts at the height of the disco craze. When dance-oriented music retreated to the underground in the 1980s, Brown continued to release recordings, albeit less commercially successful, for RCA and Columbia.

December 5. Roland Kirk dies. One of most innovative musicians in jazz history, Kirk pioneered many unorthodox performing techniques, including circular breathing, playing two or three saxophones at once, and simultaneously singing and playing the flute. Beyond these novelties, his improvisational skills as a soloist and encyclopedic mastery of jazz styles, from Dixieland to free jazz, were of the highest order. In addition to incorporating many instruments rarely used within jazz (e.g., piccolo, harmonica, nose whistle), he designed the "trumpophone" (a trumpet with a soprano sax mouthpiece) and "slidesophone" (a down-scaled trombone/slide trumpet with sax mouthpiece).

Kirk lost his sight at the age of two when overmedicated by a nurse. Mastering a wide range of instruments as a youth, he cut the rhythm and blues-tinged *Triple Threat* (King 534; 1956), which featured his simultaneous playing of the tenor saxophone (fingered with the left hand), the "manzello" (a modification of the saxello, itself a curved variant on the B-flat soprano sax) with the right, and the "stritch" (a modified E-flat alto) functioning as a drone. Relocating from Louisville to Chicago, he recorded *Introducing Roland Kirk* (Argo 669; 1960), which featured saxophonist/trumpeter Ira Sullivan. Although now securely within the jazz fold, he would retain a pronounced bluesy edge for the duration of his career.

Following a stint with Charles Mingus in 1961, Kirk did sessions for a variety of notable recording artists, including Quincy Jones, Roy Haynes, Tubby Hayes, Eddie Baccus, and Sonny Stitt. His own recorded output—much of which featured his backing group, the Vibration Society—was equally prolific. Critically acclaimed releases included *I Talk with the Spirits* (Limelight 82008; 1964), an eclectic collection of material from musicals and seminal musicians like Django Reinhart and Clifford Brown; the propulsive *Rig, Rig and Panic* (Limelight 82027; 1965; and *Volunteered Slavery* (Atlantic 1534; 1968), which reflected Kirk's pronounced commitment to African-American socio-political concerns.

December 24. The Bee Gees begin a three-week stay atop the pop charts with "How Deep Is Your Love" (RSO). The single will remain on the Hot 100 for thirty-three weeks, a lengthy run for that era. It is the trio's first release from the phenomenally successful *Star Night Fever* soundtrack, which will all but solidify their position as the most successful recording act in the latter half of the 1970s.

1978

❄

January 5. The British punk trailblazers, The Sex Pistols, make their American concert debut in Atlanta in front of five hundred people.

January 10. The Sex Pistols appear on *Variety*, their American television debut.

January 13. The Police enter Surrey (U.K.) Sound Studios to record their debut album. Nigel Gray will do the production work.

January 14. Player rides "Baby Come Back" (RSO) to the summit of the pop charts, residing there for three weeks. The single exhibits extraordinary staying power, spending a total of thirty-two weeks on the Hot 100. Like many other one-hit wonders, the group was unable to capitalize on this success and maintain a successful recording career.

January 14. The Sex Pistols perform a farewell concert at the Winterland in San Francisco.

January 18. Billy Joel is awarded a platinum record for his album, *The Stranger*.

January 23. Adam and the Ants make their broadcast debut on Radio 1's *John Peel Show*.

January 23. Chicago singer/guitarist Terry Kath fatally shoots himself with his own 9mm handgun at a Los Angeles party. Witnesses say he thought the weapon was not loaded.

January 24. EMI record plant personnel refuse to press copies of the Buzzcocks forthcoming release, "What Do I Get" due to the B side title, "Oh Shit."

January 25. Bob Dylan sponsors a second benefit concert for incarcerated boxer, Rubin "Hurricane" Carter. The show, which lasts seven hours at the Houston Astrodome, includes performers such as Ringo Starr, Stephen Stills, and Stevie Wonder.

January 25. Joy Division make their performing debut at Pips in Manchester, U.K.

January 26. *Billboard* reports that Kiss and Elvis Presley share the distinction of having earned the most platinum albums in one year, three each in 1977.

January 26. *Rolling Stone* pictures Bob Dylan in shades on its cover with the caption "The Rolling Stone Interview."

January 28. Fleetwood Mac goes number one in Great Britain with *Rumours* (Warner Bros.), remaining on the charts there for more than 440 weeks. The album goes on to sell more than 15 million copies worldwide.

January 31. Talking Heads appear on *The Old Grey Whistle Test*, their British TV debut.

February 3. The made-for-TV biopic about Jan Barry and Dean Torrance, *Dead Man's Curve*, premieres on the ABC network. It movie includes Barry in a small role.

February 4. Further evidence of their international appeal, the Swedish group, Abba, begins a seven-week run atop the British charts with *The Album*, their third number one LP in the U.K.

February 4. The Bee Gees return to top spot on the Hot 100 following an absence of only three weeks with their second single from *Saturday Night Fever*, "Staying Alive" (RSO; #1 U.K.). The trio seem incapable of a wrong career move at this point in time; when Andy Gibb's "(Love Is) Thicker Than Water" (RSO)—co-written and produced by Barry Gibb—pushes them out of the number one position following a four-week stint, they reoccupy it yet again for eight consecutive weeks with the third single from the film soundtrack, "Night Fever" (RSO). According to Joel Whitburn's Pop Annual series, "Night Fever" and "Staying Alive" will rank as the first and fourth most popular singles for the year.

February 14. Dire Straits begin work on their debut LP at London's Basing Street Studios. Production costs will total $21,250.

February 18. Winners at the Grammy Awards celebration include Fleetwood Mac (Album of the Year for *Rumours*), the Eagles (Record of the Year for "Hotel California"), and the Bee Gees (Best Pop Vocal Performance for "How Deep Is Your Love").

February 22. The Police appear in a Wrigley's Chewing Gum commercial aimed at American TV. They dye their hair blonde for the film session.

February 23. Whitesnake featuring David Coverdale debuts at the Sky Bird Club in Nottingham, England.

March 4. Andy Gibb begins a two-week stint atop the pop charts with "(Love Is) Thicker Than Water" (RSO).

March 4. The Internal Revenue Service conducts dawn raid of the home of Jerry Lee Lewis, removing cars worth more than $170,000 to pay off his tax debts.

March 11. Kate Bush's debut single, "Wuthering Heights" (inspired by the Emily Bronte novel), begins a four-week stay at number one in Great Britain.

March 11. Meat Loaf enters the British charts with *Bat Out of Hell*, remaining there for 416 weeks and selling more than two million copies.

March 18. The Bee Gees head up the Hot 100 with "Night Fever" (RSO), remaining there for eight weeks.

March 19. Billy Joel performs for the first time in Great Britain at London's Drury Lane Theatre.

March 22. The Police sign with A&M Records.

March 27. BBC-TV broadcasts the Beatles parody, *All You Need Is Cash*, featuring the Rutles.

March 30. U2 win $850 and a chance to audition for CBS Ireland in a Dublin talent contest sponsored by Guinness.

April 15. Johnny Mathis and Deniece Williams begin a four-week stay atop the R&B charts with "Too Much, Too Little, Too Late" (Columbia 10693).

April 21. British folk rock chanteuse, Sandy Denny, dies following a fall down stairs at a friend's home. She first achieved fame as the lead vocalist for Fairport Convention, and then formed her own band, Fotheringay, in the early 1970s.

April 22. The Blues Brothers—featuring John Belushi and Dan Aykroyd—make their debut on NBC's *Saturday Night Live*.

April 22. Bob Marley and the Wailers perform at the "One Love Peace Concert" in Jamaica. It was Marley's first public appearance in that nation since being wounded in an assassination attempt a year and a half earlier.

April 29. P. J. Proby is fired from title role in the London stage musical, *Elvis*, after repeatedly changing his lines from the script.

April 29. The Bee Gees top the British charts with "Night Fever."

May 6. The *Saturday Night Fever* soundtrack begins an eighteen-week run atop the British album charts.

May 13. Yvonne Elliman reaches number one on the pop charts with yet another Barry Gibb/Maurice Gibb/Robin Gibb composition, "If I Can't Have You" (RSO).

May 19. Dire Straits' first major label single, "Sultans of Swing," is released. It was recorded for only $205.

May 20. *The Buddy Holly Story*, starring Gary Busey, premieres in Holly's home town, Lubbock, Texas.

May 20. The Paul McCartney-penned "With a Little Luck" (Capitol), by Wings, begins a two-week stay atop the Hot 100.

May 25. After catching The Hype—soon to be renamed U2—performing at the Project Arts Centre, Dublin, Paul McGuinness becomes their manager.

May 26. The Irish television program, *Youngline*, features The Hype (U2).

June 3. Johnny Mathis and Deniece Williams go number one on the pop charts with "Too Much, Too Little, Too Late."

June 9. Siouxsie and the Banshees sign with Polydor Records.

June 10. John Travolta and Olivia Newton-John ascend to the summit of the Hot 100 with "You're the One That I Want" (RSO), a selection from the hit film musical, *Grease*.

June 16. Frankie Lanz, Joe Contorno, and Tony De Lauro organize the first doo-wop oldies extravaganza, the Royal New York Doo-Wop Show, at the Beacon Theater, in Manhattan. Featured artists include the Chiffons, the Cleftones, Jimmy Clanton, the Earls, the Elegants, the Mello-Kings, and the Skyliners. Within the few years, the show would be presented twice annually at New York's Radio City Music Hall, with many of the top 1950s and early 1960s doo-wop groups on the bill.

June 17. Andy Gibb begins a seven-week stay atop the Hot 100 with "Shadow Dancing" (RSO). It was his third consecutive number one single, making him the most successful recording artist of the year. The record was very much a family affair, having been co-written by Gibb—along with his three brothers, Barry, Maurice, and Robin Gibb (better known as the Bee Gees)—and produced by Barry Gibb.

July 5. EMI stops pressing the new Rolling Stones LP, *Some Girls* (Rolling Stones), after celebrities (including Lucille Ball) featured in mock advertisements on the sleeve lodge complaints.

July 27. *Rolling Stone* pictures Patti Smith—sweaty and disheveled in a see-through shirt and black bra, against a wall of fire—on its cover with the caption "Patti Smith Catches Fire."

August 5. With the disco craze peaking, the Rolling Stones go number one with their own dance-oriented number, "Miss You" (Rolling Stones). If the group is, in fact, selling out, they have plenty of company. Artists as seeming far removed from the urban club scene as country singer Dolly Parton, AOR stalwart Rod Stewart, and punk/new wave pioneers like the Talking Heads and Blondie all issue rhythmically pulsating fare—complete with extended play disco mixes on twelve-inch single editions.

August 12. The Commodores begin a two-week stint atop the Hot 100 with the Lionel Richie-penned ballad, "Three Times a Lady" (Motown). It also tops the British charts, becoming Motown's biggest-selling single there.

August 19. The Commodores begin a five-week run at number one on the British charts with "Three Times a Lady."

August 26. Frankie Valli reaches number one on the pop charts with the Barry Gibb composition, "Grease" (RSO), retaining the position for two weeks. It was the second chart-topper in 1978 culled from the film version of the hit musical, *Grease*. It is also the eighth number one hit for the RSO label in 1978, seven of which featured Gibb as composer and producer.

September 9. A Taste of Honey begin a three-week run atop the Hot 100 with "Boogie Oogie Oogie" (Capitol).

September 30. Exile begin a four-week stay atop the Hot 100 with "Kiss You All Over" (Warner/Curb).

September 30. John Travolta and Olivia Newton-John reach number one on the British charts with "Summer Nights."

October 28. Nick Gilder's long climb up the pop charts with "Hot Child in the City" (Chrysalis) peaks at number one.

November 4. Barbara Mandrell's "Sleeping Single in a Double Bed" (ABC 12362) becomes her first chart topper.

November 4. Anne Murray heads up the Hot 100 with "You Needed Me" (Capitol).

November 11. The Cars release the first-ever commercially available picture disc single, "My Best Friend's Girl."

November 11. Donna Summer's rendition of "MacArthur Park" (Casablanca) begins a three-week stint atop the pop charts. The Jim Webb composition was first a hit for film star Richard Harris in 1968 before German producer Georgio Moroder transformed it into a dance floor number for the reigning disco diva. Summer also goes number one on the album charts with *Live and More* (Casablanca).

November 25. The Kendalls reach number one on the country charts with "Sweet Desire"/"Old Fashioned Love" (Ovation 1112).

December 2. Chic commence a five-week run atop the R&B charts with "Le Freak" (Atlantic 3519).

December 2. Eddie Rabbitt's "I Just Want to Love You" (Elektra 45531) reaches the summit of the country charts.

December 2. Barbra Streisand and Neil Diamond top the pop charts with "You Don't Bring Me Flowers" (Columbia), remaining there for two non-consecutive weeks.

December 9. Chic—the dance club vehicle for the producer/songwriting team of Bernard Edwards and Nile Rodgers—go number one on the Hot 100 with "Le Freak," spending six non-consecutive weeks there in all. Despite an enviable string of hit singles that stretched into the early 1980s, the duo would disband the group in order to concentrate on making records for other artists.

December 9. Charlie Rich and Janie Fricke outpace the competition on the country charts with "On My Knees" (Epic 50616).

December 16. Kenny Rogers begins a three-week run atop the country charts with "The Gambler" (United Artists 1250).

December 25. John Lydon's Public Image Ltd. Perform live for the first time at London's Rainbow Theatre.

December 28. Former Big Star guitarist, Chris Bell, dies at age twenty-seven when his car crashes into a telephone pole.

December 30. Emerson, Lake & Palmer announce their official break up.

December 30. XTC make their live U.S. debut in Philadelphia.

1979

❄

January 2. Former Sex Pistols bassist Sid Vicious goes on trial in New York for murdering girlfriend Nancy Spungen. To the popular mind, the sensationalized headlines surrounding the case are equated with the punk scene as a whole.

January 5. Charles Mingus dies at age fifty-six. He had recently collaborated with Joni Mitchell on the posthumous release, *Mingus*.

January 5. Prince debuts live at the Capri Theater, Minneapolis, Minnesota.

January 6. The Bee Gees begin a two-week stay atop the Hot 100 with "Too Much Heaven" (RSO).

January 6. Cheryl Lynn's "Got To Be Real" (Columbia 10808) reaches number one on the R&B charts. It was her debut single; her previous experience with music had been limited largely to singing in the Church of the Living God. Everything changed following an appearance on *The Gong Show*—the result of some arm-twisting by her boyfriend at the time—brought inquiries from countless record companies. Deciding on Columbia, Lynn had little trouble adapting to the studio recording process. She would later recall,

> I think it was because I was enjoying so much what I was doing. And I think success comes from being able to do something that you really like, to have a job that you really enjoy doing. It wasn't like a job to me, it was like, "I'm having fun." The atmosphere that was created in the studio for me was "Be yourself." All I did was express myself. (White and Bronson, 1991)

January 6. Don Williams ascends to the summit of the country charts with "Tulsa Time" (ABC 12425).

January 8. Rush are named Canada's official Ambassadors of Music.

January 9. The United Nations International Childrens' Emergency Fund is the beneficiary of a charity concert starting The Bee Gees; John Denver; Earth, Wind & Fire; Olivia Newton-John; Rod Stewart; and Donna Summer, among others. With each artist performing one song and donating all future rights and royalties of the song to UNICEF, more than $50 million would be raised.

January 13. John Conlee's "Lady Lay Down" (ABC 12420) tops the country charts.

January 13. Earth, Wind & Fire peak at number one on the R&B charts with "September" (ARC 10854).

January 13. Donny Hathaway falls to his death from a fifteenth-floor room at the Essex House Hotel, Manhattan. The thirty-three-year-old musician/composer/arranger had been recording a second LP with Roberta Flack earlier that day. It would never be determined whether the incident was an accident or suicide.

Donny Hathaway's musical talents spanned a wide range of fields, including songwriting, arranging, producing, and performing (both as a singer and keyboardist). Born in Chicago, on October 1, 1945, Hathaway spent most of his youth in St. Louis, where he began singing gospel at age three. He attended the Washington, D.C.-based Howard University on a fine arts scholarship; he laid the groundwork there for future collaborations with one of his classmates, Robert Flack.

Hathaway first reached the charts as part of the duo, June (Conquest) & Donnie, with "I Thank You Baby" (Curtom 1935; 1969; #45 r&b), re-released three years later (Curtom 1971; 1972; #94 pop, #41 r&b) following his early rise to prominence as a recording artist. All of his biggest hits were duets with Robert Flack, his down-home, funky style acting as a foil to her ethereal brand of soul singing. Their best-selling singles included "You've Got a Friend" (Atlantic 2808; 1971; #29 pop, #8 r&b), "Where Is the Love" (Atlantic 2879; 1972; #5 pop, #1 r&b), "The Closer I Get to You" (Atlantic 3463; 1978; #2 pop, #1 r&b), and the posthumously issued "You Are My Heaven" (Atlantic 3627; 1980; #47 pop, #8 r&b). He also earned praise during the 1970s as a producer/writer for many artists, most notably Jerry Butler, Aretha Franklin, the Staple Singers, and Carla Thomas.

January 20. Parliament begin a four-week run atop the R&B charts with "Aqua Boogie" (Casablanca 950).

January 20. Dolly Parton reaches number one on the country charts with "I Really Got the Feeling"/"Baby I'm Burnin'" (RCA 11420).

January 23. Toto are awarded a platinum record for their eponymous debut LP.

January 26. Jackson Browne and Graham Nash are featured in the first of three benefit concerts for the Pacific Alliance in its fight against nuclear power plant construction.

January 26. Bob Dylan forms his own record label, Accomplice Records.

January 26. The "Gizmo" guitar synthesizer is demonstrated in public for the first time.

January 27. Crystal Gayle begins a two-week stint atop the country charts with "Why Have You Left the One You Left Me For" (United Artists 1259).

January 29. On the heels of a poorly attended concert tour and reviews panning their latest LP, *Love Beach*, Emerson, Lake and Palmer break-up.

February 2. Sid Vicious dies of a heroin overdose during a party in his New York flat celebrating his release on $50,000 bail pending his trial for the murder of former girlfriend Nancy Spungen the previous October.

February 3. Blondie goes number one on the British charts with "Heart of Glass" (#1 U.S.), the first of five chart-topping singles in that nation.

February 3. The Blues Brothers tops the album charts with *Briefcase Full of Blues*.

February 3. The Village People peak at number two on the Hot 100 with the dance club class, "Y.M.C.A." (Casablanca 2201), remaining there for three consecutive weeks.

February 3. Wolfman Jack MCs a tribute show at the Clear Lake City (Iowa) "Surf Ballroom" to commemorate the twentieth anniversary of the deaths of Buddy Holly, Ritchie Valens, and the Big Bopper. Starring Del Shannon, Jimmy Clanton, and other stars from rock 'n' roll's early days, it is taped for cable TV broadcast.

February 4. A month-long rock memorabilia auction organized to fund the Save-the-Whales campaign kicks of in San Francisco. Items offered for sale include a Cheech and Chong bong, Alice Cooper's boa constrictor, a Paul Kantner guitar, and the black jacket worn in the filming of *Grease* by John Travolta.

February 7. Stephen Still begins work on the first digitally recorded rock album.

February 10. Eddie Rabbit begins a three-week run atop the country charts with "Every Which Way But Loose" (Elektra 45554), the title song to the blockbuster film directed by Clint Eastwood.

February 10. Rod Stewart peaks at number one on the Hot 100 with "Do Ya Think I'm Sexy?" (#1 U.K.), remaining there for four weeks. He also outlasts all LP competition for three weeks with *Blondes Have More Fun*.

February 17. Blondie start a four-week stay atop the British LP charts with Parallel Lines.

Blondie melded tuneful 1960s pop-rock with the attitude and aggression of the emerging New York City punk revolution in laying the groundwork for the new wave genre. The band's glam image—which centered around their street-smart Marilyn Monroe figure, lead singer Debbie Harry—would also provide a model for the Neo-Romantics of the early 1980s, a fashion-conscious movement encompassing the likes of Adam Ant, Bow Wow Wow, Duran Duran, the Thompson Twins, and Boy George of Culture Club.

Formed by August 1974 by former Wind in the Willows vocalist Harry and her boyfriend, guitarist Chris Stein, Blondie—whose classic lineup also included keyboardist Jimmy Destri, bassist Frank Infante, and drummer Clem Burke—separated itself from the rank-and-file punk groups identified with the New York club scene with a polished debut album, *Blondie* (Private Stock 2023; 1976), produced by Richard Gottehrer. The band's pinup poster good looks attracted a new label, Chrysalis, and with the release of *Plastic Letters* (Chrysalis 1166; 1978; #10 UK, #72 US), significantly broadened their American following while making them stars in Great Britain, where the single, "Denis" (Chrysalis 2180; 1978) reached number two on the charts.

Teamed with British power pop producer, Mike Chapman, Blondie produced the critically acclaimed *Parallel Lines* (Chrysalis 1192; 1979; #1 UK, #6 US), which yielded four hits: "Hanging on the Telephone" (Chrysalis 2366; 1978; #5 UK), "Heart of Glass" (Chrysalis 2275; 1979; #1 UK, #1 US), "Sunday Girl" (Chrysalis 2320; 1979; #1 UK), and "One Way of Another" (Chrysalis 2336; 1979; #24 US). Having penetrated the dance venues with "Heart of Glass," and the disco-inflected LP, *Eat to the Beat* (Chrysalis 1225; 1979; #1 UK, #17 US), the band enlisted electro producer, Georgio Moroder to record "Call Me" (Chrysalis 2414; 1980; #1 UK, #1 US) for the *American Gigolo* soundtrack. As disco encountered a backlash in the United States, Blondie shifted gears, topping the *Billboard* Hot 100 with the reggae number, "The Tide Is High" (Chrysalis 2465; 1980; #1 UK, #1 US), and an early attempt at mainstreaming hip-hop, "Rapture" (Chrysalis 2485; 1981; #5 UK, #1 US). The album containing the latter tracks, *Autoamerican* (Chrysalis 1290; 1980; #3 UK, #7 US), and *The Hunter* (Chrysalis 1384; 1982; #9 UK, #33 US) reflected the band's stylistic impasse, which appears to have contributed to the break-up in mid-1982.

Harry, Destri, and Burke all pursued solo careers, while Stein's plans for his own Chrysalis-backed label, Animal, were stymied by a prolonged illness. The foursome would re-form Blondie in 1998, releasing the poppy, but hardly trailblazing, LP, *No Exit* (Beyond-RCA/Logic 78003; 1999; #3 UK, #18 US), which included the hit single, "Maria" (Beyond-RCA/Logic 78040; 1999; #1 UK, #82 US).

February 17. The first go-go smash, "Bustin' Loose, Part 1" (Source 40967), written and recorded by Chuck Brown with support provided by the Soul Searchers, begins a four-week run atop the R&B charts. Brown, who incorporated the tune into his live shows around 1976, suspected he had something based on the crowd response to it.

> Anytime you play a tune for two years and people keep requesting it, that tells you. When I wrote the song, I just had that feeling. Ain't nothing out there like this, it's got to be accepted. (White and Bronson, 1991)

Nevertheless, the song might have gone unrecorded, it not for the persuasive powers of producer James Purdie. As Brown reflected,

> I was sick of records. I didn't make money off records [but] I could play seven nights a week. James talked me into recording one more time. (White and Bronson, 1991)

February 22. *Rolling Stone* pictures the *Blues Brothers* on its cover with the double caption "Blues Brothers Saturday Night Confidential"/"Dan Aykroyd: Messin' with the Kid."

February 23. Dire Straits perform in Boston—their first ever American show.

March 3. The Bee Gees top the British singles charts for the fourth time with "Tragedy" and the U.S. album charts with *Spirits Having Flown* (RSO), the second time they have achieved this feat.

March 4. Randy Jackson of the Jackson 5 is seriously injured in a car crash, breaking both legs. He almost dies in the hospital emergency room when a nurse injects him with methadone.

March 10. Gloria Gaynor reaches number one on the pop charts with "I Will Survive" (Polydor), remaining there for three non-consecutive weeks.

March 17. Gloria Gaynor begins a four-week run atop the British charts with "I Will Survive."

March 17. Instant Funk head up the R&B charts with "I Got My Mind Made Up (You Can Get It Girl)" (Salsoul 2078), remaining there for three non-consecutive weeks.

March 24. The Bee Gees begin a two-week stint atop the Hot 100 with "Tragedy" (RSO).

March 31. Sister Sledge peak at number one on the R&B charts with "He's the Greatest Dancer" (Cotillion 44245).

March 31. Barbra Streisand begins a four-week run atop the British album charts with *Greatest Hits, Vol. 2*.

April 3. Kate Bush makes her concert debut at Liverpool's Empire Theatre.

April 7. Dire Straits peak at number four on the Hot 100 with their debut American single, "Sultans of Swing" (Warner Bros. 8736).

> Dire Straits are a testament that a band can be out-of-step with prevailing fashions and still find success. Their laid-back blues-rock, accented by subtle, often sly, lyrics and Mark Knopfler's Dylanesque vocals, was nearly overwhelmed by the flood of disco and punk (later, postpunk) recordings beginning in the late 1970s. Extraordinary musicianship (highlighted by Knopfler's peerless lead guitar work) and subtle studio

production work did enable the band to find commercial success, although the success of their album releases varied to a considerable degree.

The driving force behind Dire Straits was lead singer/guitarist/songwriter Mark Knopfler, who decided to go into music full time after several years as a teacher. He assembled the band during 1976 and 1977; the final lineup included his brother, David, on rhythm guitar, bassist John Illsley, and drummer Pick Withers. After having their demo tapes rejected by virtually every label in England, Phonogram Records signed them in 1978 upon hearing "Sultans of Swing." Newly recorded (Warner Bros. 8736; 1978; #4 US), the single first became a hit in Holland, and then in much of Europe and the United States. With Warner Bros. acquiring their U.S. distribution rights, the band's first two LPs, *Dire Straits* (Warner Bros. 3266; 1978; #5 UK, #2 US) and *Communique* (Warner Bros. 3330; 1979; #5 UK, #11 US), were awarded gold records by the RIAA (the former ultimately selling for than eleven million copies worldwide). Furthermore, *Billboard* would designate them number one in its New LP Artists category for 1979.

With the release of *Making Movies* (Warner Bros. 3480; 1980; ##4 UK, #19 US) and *Love Over Gold* (Warner Bros. 23728; 1982; #1 UK, #19 US), the band's limitations—most notably, Knopfler's monochrome vocals and undistinguished melodies with an emphasis on minor keys—led to a decline in sales. Apparently considering new directions, the band treaded water with a couple of transitional releases, the retro EP, *Twisting by the Pool* (Warner Bros. 29800; 1983; #53 US), which celebrated Knopfler's love of the twangy rock 'n' roll popularized by the *Shadows and the Ventures*, and the live *Alchemy* (Warner Bros. 25085; 1984; #3 UK, #46 US).

Brothers in Arms (Warner Bros. 25264; 1985; #1 UK, #1 US) become the band's most artistically and commercially successful album, eventually selling more than twenty-six million copies on the strength of superb material—including three hit singles the MTV-friendly "Money for Nothing" (Warner Bros. 28950; 1985; #4 UK, #1 US), the Cajun-inflected "Walk of Life" (Warner Bros. 28878; 1985; #2 UK, #7 US), and reflective "So Far Away" (Warner Bros. 28729; 1986; #19 US)—pioneering digital production work tailored to the emerging compact disc medium. Perhaps recognizing the limitations of the group format as well as the futility of trying to top *Brothers in Arms*, Knopfler's decided to concentrate on outside projects, most notably, producing albums for Aztec Camera and Randy Newman, writing "Private Dancer" for Tina Turner, scoring various films (*Local Hero*, 1983; Cal, 1984; *Comfort and Joy*, 1984; *The Princess Bride*, 1987; and *Last Exit to Brooklyn*, 1989), session work for Joan Armatrading, a recorded collaboration with Chet Atkins—*Neck and Neck* (Columbia 45307; 1990; #41 UK; received three Grammy awards)—and a release as part of the country-oriented *Notting Hillbillies, Missing...Presumed Having a Good Time* (Warner Bros. 26147; 1990; #2 UK, #52 US).

Two more Dire Straits LPs—*On Every Street* (Warner Bros. 26680; 1991; #1 UK, #12 US), a return to the group's funky, laid-back style, and the live *On the Night* (Warner Bros. 45259; 1993; #4 UK)—would appear in the early 1990s. Perhaps due in part to the comparatively limited interest they generated, Knopfler has gone on to record a couple solo albums and compose for more films. In 2000 he would receive the Order of the British Empire medal for his contributions to the country.

April 7. The Doobie Brothers top the album charts with *Minute By Minute*.

April 10. The Bee Gees' "Love You Inside Out" (RSO 925) earns a gold disc, climaxing an unprecedented run of nine gold singles (four of which also were certified platinum) and six gold LPs (four platinum) in less than four years. With six consecutive chart-topping singles in the past sixteen months, the Bee Gees seemed likely to keep on cranking out hits well into the future. However, the trio would never again crack the pop Top 10, and only two future albums—*Bee Gees Greatest and Staying Alive*, both of which included classic recordings from their glory days—would be certified gold. Many theories would be put forward by industry observers regarding the reason for their fall from grace, including oversaturation, changing musical tastes, poor health, and internal distractions.

April 14. The Doobie Brothers return to number one on the pop charts after an absence of five years with "What a Fool Believes" (Warner Bros.). This edition of the band, however, specializes in polished white soul (built around lead vocalist Michael McDonald) as opposed to the hippie funk espoused by the early 1970s outfit.

April 14. GQ begin a two-week stint atop the R&B charts with "Disco Nights (Rock-Freak)" (Arista 0388). The quartet—comprised of Emmanuel Rahiem LeBlanc, Keith "Sabu" Crier, Herb Lane, and Paul Service—had previously recorded the song as the Rhythm Makers. They were renamed GQ by their manager, Tony Lopez, who thought the group should have a new image.

April 21. Amii Stewart goes number one on the Hot 100 with her reworking of Eddie Floyd's Stax classic, "Knock on Wood."

Amii Stewart recorded one of the most successful dance hits of the disco era, but never hesitated to say that her preferences leaned more towards adult contemporary fare. In the mid-1980s, she would tell *Record Mirror*, "You can't spend your life singing songs like 'Knock on Wood.' There's more melody now, you can dance as well as sit down…The disco era was a very good era for me, but it wasn't geared for melody."

Amy Stewart was born in 1956 in Washington, D.C., the fifth of six children; her father was engaged in classified activities for the Pentagon. She studied dance as a youth, and attended Howard University before joining the D.C. Repertory Dance Company, studying ballet and modern dance. Her first name was changed to "Amii" in her teens because someone with her name was already registered with Actor's Equity.

By 1975 Stewart had landed a part with the touring company of *Bubbling Brown Sugar*, which would take her to Broadway and, later, London. While in London, she hooked up with record producer Barry Long, who helped her record "Knock on Wood" (Ariola America 7736; #6 r&b), previously a gritty, Memphis Soul-styled hit for Eddie Floyd (Stax 194; 1966; #28). Promoted as a disco diva in much the same vein as Donna Summer, Stewart failed to find strong follow-up material. Only two other singles reached the American pop charts, the medleys "Light My Fire/137 Disco Heaven" (Ariola 7753; 1979; #69 U.S. pop, #36 U.S. r&b, #5 U.K.) and "My Guy/My Girl" (Handshake 5300; 1980; #63 U.S pop, #76 U.S. r&b, #39 U.K.), the latter a duet with Johnny Bristol. Remaining active in show business, she would enjoy modest success with the 1985 single, "Friends" (Emergency 4548; #46 U.S. r&b, #12 U.K.)

April 25. The Police debut on BBC-TV's *Top of the Pops*, performing "Roxanne."

April 28. Blondie's fusion of disco and new wave, "Heart of Glass" (Chrysalis), reaches the summit of the pop charts.

May 1. Elton John becomes the first pop star to perform in Israel.

May 5. Peaches and Herb begin a four-week run atop the Hot 100 (#1 R&B for four weeks beginning April 28) with "Reunited" (Polydor 14547). The act—which had their biggest hit with a throwback ballad at the height of the disco craze—had been recording since the mid-1960s, consisting of former record store employee Herb Feemster and three successive Peaches. The *Billboard Book of Number One Rhythm & Blues Hits* chronicles the duo's odyssey:

Herb and Francine [Baker] had [a string of] hits, until Francine took a break and was replaced temporarily by Marlene Mack. In 1970, Herb took an exam for the Washington, D.C. Police Department. On July 20 of that year he quit the music business and went to work for the city. But he missed singing, and in 1976 decided Peaches and Herb should be reunited. Former model Linda Greene met Herb through Van McCoy and became the third Peaches. (White and Bronson, 1991)

May 12. Instant Funk peaks at number twenty on the Hot 100 with "I Got My Mind Made Up (You Can Get It Girl)" (Salsoul 2078). It goes on to achieve gold record status.

Latter day exponents of Philly Soul, Instant Funk first attracted attention as the support band for producer/composer Bunny Sigler. Sigler helped them garner a recording deal with T.S.O.P. Records; their debut album, *Get Down with the Philly Jump* (T.S.O.P.; 1976) was a modest commercial success, driven in large part by the hit single, "It Ain't Reggae (But It's Funky)" (T.S.O.P.; 1976).

After a brief lull spanning a change of labels, they returned with *I Got My Mind Made Up* (Salsoul; 1978), which earned a gold disc, driven by the best-selling title track. Subsequent releases failed to do nearly as well, and another label switch (to Pop Art) in the mid-1980s failed to revive their plummeting fortunes.

May 19. Eric Clapton hosts a party at his Surrey home in celebration of his recent marriage to Patti Boyd. Using a small stage set up in the garden, a pick-up band—consisting of Clapton, Ginger Baker, George Harrison, Mick Jagger, Paul McCartney, and Ringo Starr—performs classic rock 'n' roll material by the likes of Eddie Cochran and Little Richard.

May 19. Supertramp top the album charts with *Breakfast in America* (A&M).

May 23. Mired in a record company dispute, Tom Petty files for bankruptcy with debts totaling $575,000.

May 26. The Isley Brothers peak at number one on the R&B charts with "I Wanna Be With You (Part 1)" (T-Neck 2279).

June 2. McFadden & Whitehead's "Ain't No Stoppin' Us Now" (Philadelphia International 3681) climbs to the summit of the R&B charts.

June 2. Donna Summer tops the Hot 100 with "Hot Stuff" (Casablanca), remaining there for three non-consecutive weeks.

June 9. The Bee Gees go number one on the pop charts with "Love You Inside Out." It is the third straight single from the album, *Spirits Having Flown* (RSO), to accomplish this feat.

June 9. Sister Sledge tops the R&B charts with "We Are Family" (Cotillion 44251).

June 16. Anita Ward begins a five-week run atop the R&B charts with "Ring My Bell" (Juana 3422).

June 30. Tubeway Army reaches the summit of the British charts with "Are Friends Electric?," remaining there for five weeks.

June 30. Anita Ward commences a two-week stint at number one on the Hot 100 with "Ring My Bell" (#1 U.K.).

July 6. Van McCoy dies of a heart attack. During his short life he enjoyed some measure of success as a singer, pianist, bandleader, A&R man, producer, and record company owner.

Born January 6, 1944, in Washington, D.C., McCoy started out singing in rhythm and blues vocal groups in the late 1950s. Following a stint with the Marylanders, he formed his own ensemble, the Starliters; they would briefly record for End in 1959. McCoy established the record company, Rock 'N, in 1960, as a means of getting his material out to the public (by the mid-1960s he would own the more successful MAXX label). He was also an A&R man for Scepter/Wand from 1961 to 1964, and produced the likes of the Shirelles, Gladys Knight, the Drifters, the Stylistics, and Brenda & the Tabulations. The demand for his services led to the creation of Van McCoy Productions in 1968. He wrote and produced most of the 1970s records for the most successful of his discoveries, *Faith, Hope & Charity*.

McCoy's own recording career took awhile to gather momentum. Following a couple of minor R&B hits in the mid-1970s, he broke through with the disco instrumental smash, "The Hustle" (Avco 4653; 1975; #1 pop, #1 r&b), backed by the Soul City Symphony. He continued to enjoy moderate success with follow-up releases—most notably, "Change with the Times" (Avco 4660; 1975; #46 pop, #6 r&b) and "Party" (H&L 4670; 1976; #69 pop, #20 r&b)—prior to his death.

July 14. Donna Summer begins a five-week stay atop the Hot 100 with "Bad Girls" (Casablanca 988).

July 21. Donna Summer reaches number one on the R&B charts with "Bad Girls," her only single to pace both R&B and pop charts.

July 23. Keith Godchaux—keyboardist and vocalist with the Grateful Dead for much of the 1970s—dies following a car crash. Afterwards, the Dead organization began referring to the band's keyboard slot as "the hot seat."

July 28. The Boomtown Rats head up the British charts with "I Don't Like Mondays," which was based on an actual shooting incident.

July 28. Chic begin a six-week run atop the R&B charts with "Good Times" (Atlantic 3584). Its central riff would be sampled by the Sugarhill Gang for their seminal rap hit, "Rapper's Delight"; Chic's songwriter/producers, Nile Rodgers and Bernard Edwards, had to take legal action to secure a share of the composer credits for that song.

August 18. Chic climb to number one on the pop charts with "Good Times."

August 18. Joe Jackson peaks at number twenty-one on the Hot 100 with "Is She Really Going Out With Him?" (A&M 2132). Jackson will move on to many other styles—including small combo jazz, postpunk, and art music—over the course of his lengthy career.

August 25. The Knack begin a six-week stay atop the Hot 100 with "My Sharona" (Capitol), a hook-laden blend of punk and power pop.

September 8. Michael Jackson reaches number one on the R&B charts with "Don't Stop 'Til You Get Enough" (Epic 50742), remaining there for five weeks.

September 16. The first commercially successful rap single, the Sugarhill Gang's "Rapper's Delight," is released by the Sugarhill label.

September 22. Two anti-nuclear benefit concerts—featuring Jackson Browne, Chaka Khan, Tom Petty, Bonnie Raitt, and Bruce Springsteen—are held at Madison Square Garden.

October 13. Michael Jackson tops the Hot 100 with "Don't Stop 'Til You Get Enough."

October 20. Herb Alpert begins a two-week stint at number one on the Hot 100 with the jazz-inflected instrumental, "Rise" (A&M).

November 3. M—the studio brainchild of Englishman Robin Scott—tops the Hot 100 with "Pop Muzik" (Sire).

November 10. The Eagles' "Heartache Tonight" (Asylum 46545)—released on October 13—becomes their fifth, and final, chart-topping single.

November 10. Donna Summer peaks at number two on the Hot 100 with "Dim All the Lights" (Casablanca 2201). Combined with her three chart-topping hits—"Bad Girls," "Hot Stuff," and "No More Tears" (with Barbra Streisand)—the record helps make her the most successful singles artist of the year.

November 17. The Commodores reach number one on the Hot 100 with the Lionel Richie-penned "Still" (Motown).

November 24. Barbra Streisand and Donna Summer begin a two-week stint atop the pop charts with "No One Tears (Enough is Enough)" (Columbia).

December 8. Moe Bandy's "I Cheated Me Right Out of You" (Columbia 11090) heads up the country charts.

December 8. Styx go number one on the Hot 100 with "Babe" (A&M), remaining there for two weeks.

December 13. *Rolling Stone* pictures Bette Midler reclining amidst dozens of flower-market roses on its cover with the caption "The Rose: Bette Midler Conquers Hollywood."

December 15. Rufus and Chaka begin a three-week stay atop the R&B charts with "Do You Love What You Feel" (MCA 41131).

December 22. Rupert Holmes tops the pop charts with "Escape (The Pina Colada Song)" (Infinity), remaining there for three non-consecutive weeks.

December 25. Conway Twitty starts a three-week run stop the country charts with "Happy Birthday Darlin'" (MCA 41335).

December 31. David Bowie performs an acoustic version of "Space Oddity" on the Kenny Everett New Year Show.

1980

❄

January 2. R&B singer Larry Williams dies from gunshot wounds at age forty-five. His songs—including the hits "Short Fat Fannie" (#5 U.S., #21 U.K.) and "Boney Maronie"—were covered by rock artists such as the Beatles and the Jam.

January 5. Michael Jackson commences a six-week stay atop the R&B charts with "Rock With You" (Epic 50797).

January 5. KC & the Sunshine Band, a hitmaking machine during the latter half of the 1970s, heads up the pop charts for the last time with "Please Don't Go" (T.K.). Group frontman/songwriter/producer KC (aka Harry Casey) will take an industry hiatus following a serious car accident, before beginning a solo career.

January 5. Kenny Rogers tops the country charts with "Coward of the County" (United Artists 1327), remaining there for three weeks.

January 12. The Sugarhill Gang peak at number thirty-six on the Hot 100 with "Rapper's Delight" (Sugar Hill 542).

The label responsible for bringing rap into the American cultural mainstream, Sugar Hill remained a dominant commercial force well into the 1980s. Prior to the release of "Rapper's Delight" (Sugar Hill; 1979; #4 R&B, #36 pop), recorded by a group of studio rappers named the Sugarhill Gang, rap was disseminated largely on cassettes. As a result, hip-hop made the transition from New York City street dances to radio airwaves and dance clubs across the nation.

A result of the Chapter 11 reorganization of Joe and Sylvia Robinson's All Platinum label, Sugar Hill's early recordings utilized house bands to approximate the breaks hip-hop deejays were using as soundbeds to frame MC raps. The later invention of sampling technology would spell the end for such warm, organic arrangements, resulting in a more synthetic feel.

The company also pioneered artistic statements and social commentary in rap recordings. Before Grandmaster Flash garnered critical raves and crossover sales for the albums *The Adventures of Grandmaster Flash on the Wheels of Steel* (Sugar Hill; 1981) and *The Message* (Sugar Hill 268; #53), the genre functioned almost exclusively to provide black party music.

Sugar Hill's early success led to many other signings, including Funky 4 +1, Grandmaster Melle Mel, Spoonie Gee, and the Treacherous 3. Poor sales, however, led to the label's demise in 1985. Its legacy, however, is widely recognized within the hip-hop community; gangsta rappers such as Ice Cube and Dr. Dre as well as more pop-oriented artists (e.g., Busta Rhymes) have sampled classic Sugar Hill tracks. *The Sugar Hill Records Story* (Rhino 72449; 1997), a five-CD compilation augmented by a twelve-inch vinyl disc featuring Grandmaster Flash & the Furious Five's "The Message" and souvenir booklet, does a thorough job of outlining the company's history.

January 15. The Ramones—one of the most guiding forces behind the punk scene—perform on BBC's *The Old Grey Whistle Test*.

January 19. Michael Jackson's "Rock with You" begins a four-week stint at number one on the Hot 100.

January 19. Pink Floyd's *The Wall* (Columbia) begins a fifteen-week run atop the LP charts, and goes on to sell more than eight million units.

January 19. The Pretenders top both the British singles and album charts with "Brass in Pocket" and their eponymous debut.

January 25. The Specials make their U.S. debut at the New York club, Hurrah.

January 26. Prince makes his television debut on *American Bandstand*.

February 2. Tom Petty and the Heartbreakers peak at number ten on the Hot 100 with "Don't Do Me Like That" (Backstreet 41138).

Petty is a rarity—one of those rare pop artists confident enough to work within a style without recourse to public opinion. His platform has always been meat-and-potatoes, FM-radio-friendly hard rock. What separates Petty from many of the genre's practitioners—besides career longevity—is his refined sense of songcraft, intelligent lyrics, and distinctive (thin and reedy, yet passionately soulful) vocals.

Emerging at the height of the progressive rock vogue exemplified by the likes of Pink Floyd and King Crimson, Gainesville, Florida-native Petty favored a sound directly descended from 1960s garage bands leavened with upwardly mobile, Byrds-accented folk rock. After obtaining a contract from Shelter in the mid-1970s, he and his band—the Mudcrutches—struggled in the studio. Taking time to regroup, Petty and new backing ensemble—consisting of keyboardist Benmont Tench, lead guitarist Mike Campbell, bassist/cellist Ron Blair, and drummer/keyboardist Stan Lynch—recorded *Tom Petty and the Heartbreakers* (Shelter 52006; 1976; #55). While the lack of label support hurt sales in the United States, favorable reviews (*Sounds* named them Best New American Band) and a 1977 U.K. tour propelled the LP to number twenty-four in Great Britain. Band momentum was further facilitated by the release of *You're Gonna Get It* (Shelter 52029; 1977; 23), and by late 1978 both albums were certified gold.

MCA's purchase of Shelter's distributor, ABC, led to protracted litigation regarding Petty's contractual status. When MCA finally agreed to let the band record for another subsidiary label, the richly-textured *Damn the Torpedoes* (Backstreet 5105; 1979; #2)—which had been financed largely by Petty himself—was released to virtually universal acclaim. However, by 1981 he was back in court due to MCA's stated intention of charging $9.98 (rather than the normal $8.98) for the next LP, *Hard Promises* (Backstreet 5160; 1981; #5). Petty justified his stance in the February 1, 1981 issue of the *Los Angeles Times*: "It's just not fair to the kids who buy records. It all comes down to greed—MCA doesn't need a new [office] tower. And if we don't take a stand, one of these days records are going to be $20."

Hard Promises and the band's fifth album, *Long After Dark* (Backstreet 5360; 1982; #9), continued to mine familiar territory with great success. However, Petty, feeling the need to map out new directions, took more than two years off while band members engaged themselves in outside projects. The resulting release, *Southern Accents* (Backstreet 5486; 1985; #71985), focused on his regional roots, augmented by the liberal use of horns and a female chorus. The promotional video for the track, "Don't Come Around Here No More" (Backstreet 52496; 1985; #13), also attracted considerable attention, winning the MTV Award for Best Special Effects and the Grand Prix for Best Video Clip at the Montreaux Golden Rose Television Festival. *Pack Up the Plantation* (Backstreet 8021; 1985; #22), the band's first live LP (also issued in various video configurations), retained the gospel/R&B touches of *Southern Accents*, even in the performance of older material.

Petty began expending more and more of his creative energy collaborating with other artists. After touring with Bob Dylan in 1986, he recorded an album, *Traveling Wilburys Volume 1* (Warner Bros. 25796; 1988; #3), with Dylan, George Harrison, Roy Orbison, and Jeff Lynne; its success inspired a follow-up (sans the deceased Orbison), *Volume 3* (Warner Bros. 26324; 1990; #11). He issued a couple of highly regarded solo LPs—*Full Moon Fever* (MCA 6253; 1989; #3) and *Wildflowers* (Warner Bros. 45792; 1994; #8)—both of which revealed greater stylistic diversity than his work with the Heartbreakers, ranging from acoustic-flavored ballads to no depression-influenced roots rockers. He also joined with the Heartbreakers to provide the backup to Johnny Cash's *Unchained* (American 39742; 1996). Through all this, Petty and the band released first-rate albums at periodical intervals, including *Let Me Up (I've Had Enough)* (Backstreet 5836; 1987; #20), *Into the Great Wide Open* (MCA 10317; 1991; #13), *Playback* (MCA 611375; 1995; a six-CD anthology including many previously unreleased tracks), *She's the One* (Warner Bros. 46285; 1996; #15; film soundtrack), and *Echo* (Warner Bros. 47294; 1999; #10).

February 20. AC/DC's lead singer, Bon Scott, is pronounced dead at King's College Hospital, London, following a wild evening of partying with a friend. The coroner states he "drank himself to death."

February 7. Pink Floyd's concert extravaganza, *The Wall*, debuts in Los Angeles before moving to New York for a second U.S. performance. The stage sets include a 120-foot-long wall, which is destroyed during the show's climax.

February 15. Prince's eponymous debut LP (Warner Bros. 3366; #22) earns a gold record. Prince—rechristened

"The Artist Formerly Known as Prince" in the late 1980s)—is widely considered the most important rhythm and blues artist of the post-disco era. He has helped popularize many musical and fashion trends in addition to nurturing countless musicians—including Sheila E., Vanity 6, Morris Day & the Time, and Andre Cymonee—at his recording studio/designer label complex, Paisley Park.

Born Prince Rogers Nelson, on June 7, 1958, in Minneapolis, he formed his own band, Grand Central, while in junior high school. He signed with Warner Bros. prior to turning 20, and soon became a chart fixture. His hits included the R&B chart-topping singles "I Wanna Be Your Lover," "When Doves Fly," "Let's Go Crazy," "Kiss," and "Sign 'O' the Times," in addition to a succession of platinum-selling LPs, most notably, the double-disk set, *1999* (Warner Bros., 1982), and the soundtrack to his first film vehicle, *Purple Rain* (Warner Bros., 1984), which spent twenty-four weeks at number one and reportedly sold more than eleven million copies.

Long at odds with Warner over his use of controversial lyrics and their attempts at slowing the prolific outpouring of Prince releases, he left to establish the NPG label (which was distributed by EMI). With his sales in a steady decline, Prince joined the Arista roster; however, sales would continue to lag well below those of his 1980s work.

February 16. The Captain & Tennille reach number one on the pop charts with "Do That to Me One More Time" (Casablanca).

February 16. Shalamar's "Second Time Around" (Solar 11709) climbs to the summit of the R&B charts.

February 17. Kenny Rogers tops the British charts with "Coward of the County."

February 18. Bill Wyman announces his intention of leaving the Rolling Stones in 1982 on the band's twentieth anniversary. He ends up postponing the date until 1993.

February 21. *Rolling Stone* pictures Tom Petty on its cover with the caption ""Damn the Torpedoes and Full Speed Ahead."

February 21. Prince's first album goes platinum just six days after being certified gold.

February 23. Queen settles into a four-week stint at the top of the Hot 100 with the neo-rockabilly number, "Crazy Little Thing Called Love" (Elektra). Penned by lead vocalist Freddie Mercury, the single will achieve gold record status on May 12, 1980, while the accompanying LP, *Play the Game*, is certified platinum October 1.

February 23. Ray, Goodman & Brown head up the R&B charts with "Special Lady" (Polydor 2033).

February 26. Island Records executives Rob Partridge and Bill Stewart watch U2 perform at Dublin's National Boxing Stadium before an audience of twenty-four hundred, and then offer them a recording contract.

February 27. The Grammy Award winners include the Doobie Brothers (Song of the Year for "What a Fool Believes"), Billy Joel (Album of the Year for *52nd Street*), Rickie Lee Jones (Best New Artist), and Gloria Gaynor (Best Disco Record for "I Will Survive").

February 29. The glasses worn by Buddy Holly at the time of his fatal plane crash are discovered in a police file in Mason, Iowa.

March 1. Blondie reach number one on the British charts with "Atomic," their third single to accomplish this feat.

March 1. The Whispers top the R&B charts with "And the Beat Goes On" (Solar 11894).

March 22. The Jam reach number one on the British charts for the first time with "Going Underground"/ "Dreams of Children." It's the first single of the decade to debut in the top spot.

March 22. Pink Floyd, one of the most acclaimed progressive rock bands of all time, reach number one with "Another Brick in the Wall, Part II" (Columbia; #1 U.K.), remaining there for four weeks. The single is culled from the double-disc concept album, *The Wall*, which would be reinterpreted as the film and, still later, as a live stage extravaganza.

March 29. Orchestra leader Mantovani dies at age seventy-four. He topped the British charts in 1953 with "The Song From Moulin Rouge," and sold millions of easy listening albums.

March 29. Pink Floyd's *Dark Side of the Moon* spends its 303rd week on the album charts, breaking the record formerly held by Carole King's *Tapestry*.

April 5. Genesis top the British album charts for the first time with *Duke*.

April 5. R.E.M. make their live debut at St. Mary's Episcopal Church, Athens, Georgia.

April 14. Gary Numan's *The Touring Principle* is released. It is the first commercially available large-scale rock video.

April 19. AC/CD replaces Bon Scott—who died during a bout of heavy drinking—with Brian Johnson, a thirty-two-year-old singer with the band, Geordie.

April 19. Blondie's "Call Me" (Chrysalis)—culled from the soundtrack to the film, *American Gigolo*, starring Richard Gere—begins a six-week run at number one on the Hot 100.

April 19. For the first tie in country music history, the first five chart positions are occupied by women: Crystal Gayle, followed by Dottie West, Debbie Boone, Emmylou Harris, and Tammy Wynette.

April 26. "Mirror in the Bathroom," by The Beat (aka English Beat), becomes the first digitally recorded single to be released in Great Britain.

April 26. Blondie's "Call Me" heads up the British charts.

April 30. The film, *McVicar*, starring Roger Daltrey, premieres in London.

May 1. Pink Floyd's "Another Brick in the Wall" is banned by the South African government after black children adopt it as they anthem to protest inferior education.

May 9. The winners at the twenty-fifth Ivor Novello Awards include the Boomtown Rats (Best Pop Song and Outstanding British Lyric for "I Don't Like Mondays") and Supertramp (Best Song for "The Logical Song").

May 18. Ian Curtis—lead vocalist for Joy Division—hangs himself at age twenty-three. When he was discovered, Iggy Pop's "The Idiot" was playing on his turntable, accompanied by a written note that stated: "At this very moment, I wish I were dead. I just can't cope anymore."

May 21. Five Jimi Hendrix gold records are stolen from Electric Ladyland Studios in Los Angeles.

May 30. Carl Radle dies of kidney failure at age thirty-eight. The bass player had been a member of Derek and the Dominoes, and had also worked with George Harrison and Delaney & Bonnie, among others.

May 31. Lipps, Inc., a studio concept masterminded by Minneapolis songwriter/producer Steve Greenberg, reaches the top spot on the pop charts with the dance floor classic, "Funkytown" (Casablanca), remaining there for four weeks.

One-hit wonders abounded during the disco era, but few enjoyed the degree of success Lipps, Inc. had with "Funkytown" (Casablanca 2233; 1980; #1 pop, #2 r&b). The group was a Minneapolis-based studio concept put together by songwriter/producer/multi-instrumentalist Steven Greenberg. "Funkytown" was more of an elongated dance club riff, featuring reverb-enhanced vocals by Cynthia Johnson, the 1976 Miss Black Minnesota U.S.A., and countless audio special effects. It spent four weeks at number one, and twenty-three weeks on the *Billboard* Hot 100 (both rare feats at the time); although it failed to do quite as well on the R&B charts, it hung on at number two for five weeks.

Greenberg did have four more modest hits: "Rock It" (Casablanca 2281; 1980; #64 pop, #85 r&b), "How Long" (Casablanca 2303; 1980; #29 r&b), "Hold Me Down" (Casablanca 2342; 1981; #70 r&b), and "Addicted to the Night" (Casablanca 812900; 1983; #78 r&b). However, disco's retreat from the pop mainstream back to the clubs, combined with postpunk's increasingly interest in dance floor beats, spelled the end of the line for Greenberg's project.

May 31. Paul McCartney heads up the British album charts with *McCartney II*.

May 31. "The Theme From M*A*S*H* (Suicide is Painless)" tops the U.K. charts a decade after it was recorded.

June 19. Donna Summer becomes the first artist to be signed by Geffen Records.

June 26. *Rolling Stone* pictures Pete Townshend doing his trademark leap in the air while playing guitar on its cover. The Townshend interview focuses on the eleven fans trampled to death at a Who concert in Cincinnati six months earlier.

June 28. Paul McCartney & Wings begin a three-week stay atop the Hot 100 with "Coming Up (Live at Glasgow)" (Columbia).

July 19. Billy Joel climbs to the summit of the pop charts with "It's Still Rock and Roll to Me" (Columbia), remaining there for two weeks.

July 19. Queen reach number one on the British album charts with *The Game*.

August 2. Olivia Newton-John begins a four-week stay atop the Hot 100 with "Magic" (MCA), a track from the soundtrack to the film, *Xanadu*.

August 30. Christopher Cross reaches number one on the pop charts with "Sailing" (Warner Bros.).

September 6. The Jam head up the British charts with "Start."

September 6. Diana Ross begins a four-week run atop the Hot 100 with "Upside Down" (Motown).

September 25. Led Zeppelin drummer John Bonham dies at Jimmy Page's home after a heavy bout of drinking with the band; the surviving members elect to disband.

October. The Bee Gees fire manager Robert Stigwood, and file a $125 million suit based upon an independent audit that turned up evidence of fraud and unfair enrichment at the group's expense. Stigwood responds in early November with a $310 million countersuit—filed in New York State Supreme Court—accusing the Bee Gees of libel, corporate defamation, and breach of contract. It is notable that the Bee Gees—who had placed six singles from their last two LPs at the top of the charts—ceased to be an artistic or commercial force. Although they remained moderately successful within the Adult Contemporary genre, few pop music artists of comparable stature ever fell so rapidly and completely from the public eye.

October 4. Queen tops the pop charts for a second time in 1980 with "Another One Bites the Dust" (Elektra). It will maintain its hegemony for three weeks, earning a platinum award in the process.

October 27. Steve Took, former percussionist for T. Rex, dies at age thirty-one.

October 25. Barbra Streisand goes number one on the Hot 100 with "Woman in Love" (Columbia), remaining there for three weeks.

November 15. Kenny Rogers begins a six-week run atop the pop charts with the Lionel Richie composition, "Lady" (Liberty).

December 6. Leo Sayer begins a five-week run at number two on the Hot 100 with "More Than I Can Say" (Warner Bros. 49565).

December 8. John Lennon is shot to death by Mark David Chapman while entering his residence, Manhattan's Dakota Apartments, after a recording session with his wife, Yoko Ono, which involved putting the final touches on her single, "Skating on Thin Ice."

December 11. *Rolling Stone* pictures Dolly Parton in a Santa costume on its cover with the caption "The Unsinkable Dolly Parton Bursts Into the Movies."

December 12. The Police earn a gold record for *Zenyatta Mondatta* (A&M 4831). The album would be certified platinum on February 27, 1981.

The Police were one of many conventional rock acts allowing themselves to be marketed under the New Wave banner in order to enhance their chances for commercial acceptance. Although the band's savvy blend of stripped-down guitar-driven pop, smoothed-over reggae rhythms, and bleached blonde poster boy looks connected with the public from the start, an abundance of infectious compositions and clever video clips—programmed round-the-clock by MTV and other cable TV channels—would elevate them to superstardom at the time of their breakup.

The original impetus for the Police was supplied by drummer Stewart Copeland, who provided its name and enlisted his brother, Miles, a talent agent and record executive, to manage their career. He added singer/bassist/composer Gordon Sumner (aka Sting) for his stage presence in 1976, and when the original lead guitarist left the following year, brought in Andy Summers, who was well known for session work and as a member of various British rock groups.

The band's debut album, *Outlandos D'Amour* (A&M 4753; 1978; #23), failed to catch on immediately due to BBC censorship of the initial singles releases—"Roxanne" (A&M 2096; 1979; #32) and "Can't Stand Losing You" (A&M 2147; 1979; #42 UK)—and the inability to fit established radio playlist guidelines in the U.S. Critics, however, were almost without exception, enthusiastic; the *New York Times'* John Rockwell would write that "no other rock band in recent memory has been able to combine intellectuality, progressivism, and visceral excitement so well" (April 5, 1979). When A&M decided to include "Roxanne" on the sampler LP, *No Wave*, the song entered the *Billboard Hot 100*.

With A&M providing greater studio and promotional support, the second album, *Regatta De Blanc* (A&M 4792; 1979; #25), earned a 1980 Grammy for Best Rock Instrumental Performance with the title track. The next release, *Zenyatta Mondatta*, did even better, reaching number five and garnering two Grammys in 1981, Best Rock Performance by a Duo or Group with Vocal ("Don't Stand So Close to Me") and Best Rock Instrumental Performance ("Behind My Camel"). *Ghost in the Machine* (A&M 3730; 1981; #2), although receiving only lukewarm endorsements from the press (due in part to its darker thematic concerns), also achieved platinum sales.

The fifth LP, *Synchronicity* (A&M 3735; 1983; #1), commercially outstripped all of the Police's earlier work by a considerable margin, largely due to the widespread appeal of the Sting-composed ballad, "Every Breath You Take" (A&M 2542; 1983; #1). The work included many other gems as well, including three more hit singles: "King of Pain" (A&M 2569; 1983; #3), "Synchronicity" (A&M 2571; 1983; #16), and "Wrapped Around Your Finger" (A&M 2614; 1984; #8). *Synchronicity* would pull all of the band's earlier albums back onto the charts as well as earning two 1983 Grammys: Best Pop Vocal Performance by a Duo or Group with Vocal ("Every Breath You Take") and Best Rock Performance by a Duo or Group with Vocal.

At this point in time the band members split off to pursue various solo projects, only getting together to perform three benefit concerts for Amnesty International in summer 1986. Although demands for an official reunion for been repeatedly dashed, A&M has continued to market the Policy legacy via a steady stream of compilation releases, most notably *Every Breath You Take – The Singles* (A&M 3902; 1986; #7), *Message in a Box: The Complete Recordings* (A&M 0150; 1993; #79), and *The Police Live!* (A&M 0222; 1995; #86).

December 20. John Lennon tops the British charts with "(Just Like) Starting Over."

December 27. John Lennon's "(Just Like) Starting Over" (Geffen) begins a five-week stay atop the Hot 100.

December 28. St. Winifred's School Choir reaches number one on the British charts with "There's No One Quite Like Grandma."

December 29. Singer/songwriter Tim Hardin dies of a heroin overdose. His compositions include "If I Were a Carpenter" and "Reason to Believe."

1981

❄

January 3. David Bowie appears in the Broadway show, *The Elephant Man*, for the last time.

January 10. John Lennon's "Imagine" begins a four-week stint atop the British charts, a decade after it was recorded. It remains a standard in that nation; the BBC-TV audience would vote it the song with the best lyrics of all time in a poll aired October 1999.

January 12. The Recording Industry Association of America donates eight hundred albums covering the broad spectrum of contemporary entertainment to the White House record library.

January 22. *Rolling Stone* pictures a nude John Lennon embracing Yoko Ono on its cover. The issue includes more photos taken during Lennon's last hours.

January 24. Adam and the Ants—who have yet to break out in the United States—begin a ten-week run atop the British charts with their debut LP, *Kings of the Wild Frontier*.

January 29. *Creem* publisher, Barry Kramer (age thirty-seven), is discovered dead in his Birmingham, Michigan, apartment. Previously, a leading mouthpiece for the punk and metal scenes, the magazine will soon cease publication.

January 31. Blondie reaches number one on the pop charts with "The Tide Is High" (Chrysalis).

February 5. *Rolling Stone*'s cover depicts Bruce Springsteen skating on a frozen New Jersey reservoir with the caption "Bruce Springsteen and the Secret of the World."

February 6. George Harrison, with studio support from Paul McCartney and Ringo Starr—records "All Those Years Ago," a tribute to John Lennon.

February 6. Hugo Montenegro—who composed and recorded the theme song to the Clint Eastwood spaghetti western, *The Good, the Bad, and the Ugly* (#2 U.S., #1 U.K.)—dies in southern California.

February 6. Yoko Ono's "Walking On Thin Ice" is released by Geffen Records. It features John Lennon on guitar and was mixed the night he was murdered.

February 7. Kool & the Gang begin a two-week stay atop the Hot 100 with "Celebration" (De-Lite).

February 7. John Lennon tops the British charts with "Woman"—his third recording to go number one in seven weeks.

February 8. R.E.M. record for the first time at Bomba Studios in Smyrna, Georgia. The tracks laid down include "(Don't Go Back To) Rockville," "Gardening at Night," and "Radio Free Europe."

February 9. Bill Haley is found dead from a heart attack at his home in Harlingen, Texas. He sold more than sixty million records over his career.

February 13. Island begins marketing "One Plus One" cassettes; one side contains a roster artist's album, and other is blank for recording purposes.

February 15. Guitarist Mike Bloomfield—formerly a member of the Paul Butterfield Blues band and Electric Flag—dies of a drug overdose in San Francisco.

February 21. Dolly Parton tops the pop charts with "9 to 5" (RCA)—her first pop number one—remaining there for two non-consecutive weeks.

February 21. REO Speedwagon outpaces the competition on the album charts with *Hi Infidelity*. It will spend fifteen non-consecutive weeks at number one.

February 21. Tierra begins a two-week stint at number two on the Hot 100 with "Together" (Boardwalk 5702).

Tierra stand as proof that movie star good looks, fortuitous timing and ceaseless promotion are not the only roads to success in the music business. The Los Angeles-based group was formed in 1972 by the Salas brothers, Rudy (guitars) and Steve (trombone/timbales), both former members of the Latin rock-oriented El Chicano. Other members included percussionist Andre Baeza, bassist Steve Falomir, keyboardist Joey

Guerra, drummer Philip Madayag, and reeds specialist Bobby Navarrete. Tierra broke through with a lush ballad, "Together" (#9 r&b), at the peak of the disco/funk era. Follow-up releases—including a remake of the Delfonics' "La La Means I Love You" (Boardwalk 129; 1981; #72 pop, #33 r&b)—did not fare as well, and the group never made the charts again after late 1982.

February 25. Grammy Award winners include Christopher Cross (Best New Artist and Best Song for "Sailing"), Bob Seger (Best Rock Performance for "Against the Wind"), and Pat Benatar (Best Female Performance for "Crimes of Passion").

February 28. Eddie Rabbitt begins a two-week stint at number one on the Hot 100 with "I Love a Rainy Night" (Elektra).

March 9. Robert Plant gives a secret performance at Keele University fronting his new band, The Honey Drippers.

March 14. Eric Clapton is hospitalized with bleeding ulcers, necessitating cancellation of a U.S. tour. He would require further medical attention when involved in the car crash five weeks later.

March 14. Roxy Music peak at number one on the British charts with John Lennon's "Jealous Guy."

March 14. "What Kind of Fool" (Columbia 11430), a duet featuring Barbra Streisand and Barry Gibb, begins a four-week stay atop the Adult Contemporary charts. The third single from Streisand's immensely successful *Guilty* album, which was co-produced by Gibb, it also reached number ten on the Hot 100. Streisand was just one of many artists profiting from the creative input of Bee Gees members as well as their production team, Albhy Galuten and Karl Richardson; others included Yvonne Elliman, Andy Gibb, Samantha Sang, Dionne Warwick, and Kenny Rogers.

March 19. Bluesman Tampa Red dies.

Although Tampa Red is generally placed within the pre-World War II country blues tradition, he was in actuality an essential link to the rhythm and blues era immediately preceding the rise of rock 'n' roll. The vocalist/guitarist (and sometimes pianist) developed an urbane style during his years in Chicago beginning in 1925, nurtured by his open-house jam sessions with the scene's leading blues musicians.

Born Hudson Woodbridge on December 15, 1903, in Smithville, Georgia, he would take on his mother's maiden name as a youth. His performing nom de plume came from a stay in Tampa during the early 1920s. Tampa Red's first recordings—done in an acoustic blues styles, featuring his vocals and guitar accompaniment—were made for the Chicago-based Paramount in 1928. He would go on to work with Georgia Tom Dorsey in the early 1930s.

He produced a series of seminal R&B singles, most successful of which included the suggestive "Let Me Play With Your Poodle" (Bluebird 0700; 1942; #4 r&b), "Detroit Blues" (Bluebird 0731; 1945; #5 r&b), "When Things Go Wrong With You" (Victor 22-0035; 1949; #9 r&b), and "Pretty Baby Blues" (RCA 0136; 1951; #7 r&b). He also was a prominent session player during this period, providing guitar accompaniment for hits like Big Maceo's "Things Have Changed" (Bluebird 0735; 1945; #4 r&b). He would retire from performing in the early 1970s; as a result, his death attracted little media attention.

March 21. The late John Lennon begins a three-week run at number two on the Hot 100 with "Woman" (Geffen 49644).

March 21. REO Speedwagon reaches number one on the Hot 100 with "Keep on Loving You" (Epic).

March 28. Blondie begin a two-week stint atop the pop charts with "Rapture" (Chrysalis), their fourth—and last—single to accomplish this feat. It is also the first chart topper to incorporate a rap sequence.

March 28. Elton John releases "I Saw Her Standing There" as a tribute to John Lennon.

April 2. Columbia Records launches the "Nice Price" series of back catalog albums.

April 5. Canned Heat vocalist Bob Hite dies of a heart attack at age thirty-six.

April 7. Bruce Springsteen and the E Street Band perform in Hamburg, Germany, kicking off their first tour (which will encompass ten countries) outside North America.

April 11. Daryl Hall and John Oates begin a three-week run atop the Hot 100 with "Kiss on My List" (RCA).

April 11. Juice Newton's cover of "Angel of the Morning" (Capitol 4976) goes number one on the AC charts (#4 pop, #22 country), remaining there for three weeks. It was Newton's "breakthough record." Her manager, Otha Young, recalled, "It was great. We actually were on the road in a broken-down motor home when we heard it was on the charts" Wesley Hyatt, 1999.

April 18. Buck's Fizz—winner of that year's Eurovision Song Contest—top the British singles chart.

April 25. Emmylou Harris peaks at number thirty-seven on the Hot 100 with a remake of the Chordettes' "Mr. Sandman" (Warner Bros. 49684).

One of the few country artists able to pull in rock listeners, Emmylou Harris has maintained a successful recording career over four decades by maintaining a steadfast allegiance to roots styles in the face of rampant technological change and media image manipulation. In addition to possessing one of the most appealing voices in popular music, her popularity has owed much to the use of first-rate backup musicians and the discriminating selection of song material from a wide range of sources, including Bill Monroe ("Scotland"), Hank Williams ("Jambalaya"), Chuck Berry ("You Never Can Tell"), Bob Dylan "I'll Be Your Baby Tonight"), the Beatles ("Here, There and Everywhere," "For No One"), Creedence Clearwater Revival ("Bad Moon Rising," "Lodi"), Paul Simon ("The Boxer"), and Leonard Cohen ("Ballad of a Running Horse").

A native of Birmingham, Alabama, Harris's first recording, the acoustic folk-styled album, *Gliding Bird* (Jubilee 0031; 1969), failed to attract much attention. She went on to duet with ex-Byrds and Flying Burrito Brothers vocalist Gram Parsons on two highly acclaimed country rock LPs, *G.P.* (Reprise; 1972) and *Grievous Angel* (Reprise; 1973). Following his fatal drug overdose, Harris secured a solo recording contract from Reprise; support was provided by Parsons's former backing musicians, The Hot Band, comprised of guitarist James Burton, rhythm guitarist Rodney Crowell, steel guitarist Hank De Vito, pianist Glen Hardin, bassist Emory Gordy, and drummer John Ware. Her early albums—*Pieces of the Sky* (Reprise 2213; 1975; #45), *Elite Hotel* (Reprise 2236; 1976; #25 US, #17 UK), and *Luxury Liner* (Reprise 3115; 1977; #21 US, #17 UK)—were divided between her own material and covers of leading pop music songwriters. By the late 1970s, Harris had begun to experiment a bit with her formula; *Quarter Moon In A Ten Cent Town* (Reprise 3141; 1978; #29 US, #40 UK) was close to straight Nashville country, *Blue Kentucky Girl* (Reprise 3318; 1979; #43) incorporated a more pervasive bluegrass approach, and *The Ballad of Sally Rose* (Reprise 25205; 1985) attempt to merge the concept album with traditional country.

Harris seemed to be treading water artistically by the late 1980s. She hired a new backing band, the roots-oriented Nash Ramblers, and recorded intermittently in a trio with Dolly Parton and Linda Ronstadt. Now approaching something akin to institutional status, she appears immune to the cyclical vicissitudes of commercial success.

April 29. Elton John pays $23,000 at a Christie's auction in London for 232 BBC *Goon Show* radio scripts broadcast during the 1950s.

May 2. Sheena Easton begins a two-week stint atop the Hot 100 with "Morning Train (Nine to Five)" (EMI America 8071). The title was changed to avoid confusion with Dolly Parton's "9 to 5."

May 2. Grover Washington Jr., with Bill Withers as featured vocalist, begins a three-week run at number two on the Hot 100 with "Just the Two of Us" (Elektra 47103). It will be the only Top 10 single for smooth jazz saxophone stylist.

May 8. Sheena Easton earns a gold record for "Morning Train (Nine to Five)." Her eponymous debut LP will be certified gold on October 12, 1981.

While working toward a degree at the Royal Scottish Academy of Drama and Art, Easton frequently performed in local nightclubs and pubs. An audition with EMI Records led to a contract in May 1979. Her debut single, "Modern Girl" (EMI America 8080) reached the Top 10 in England in early 1980.

"Morning Train" enabled Easton to capture an American audience; more stateside hits followed: "For Your Eyes Only" (Liberty 1418; 1981), "You Could Have Been With Me" (EMI America 8101; 1981-1982), "Telefone (Long Distance Love Affair)" (EMI America 8172; 1983), "Strut" (EMI America 8227; 1984), "Sugar Walls" (EMI America 8253; 1985), and "U Got the Look" (duet with Prince). The latter three releases signaled a switch from her formerly wholesome image to more sexually suggestive material.

Her pop-rock style translated well worldwide; she released a Spanish-language album, *Todo Me Recuerda a Ti*, in 1983, and earned gold records in Canada and Japan. In 1984, she received a Grammy for Best Mexican/American Performance for "Me Gustas Tal Como Eres," a duet with Luis Miguel.

Although Easton's recording career had lost momentum by the late 1980s, she continued touring on a regular basis. In the 1990s, she also appeared in films (e.g., *Indecent Proposal*), on Broadway (*The Man of La Mancha*), and on television (e.g., *Jack's Place*, *Body Bags*, *The Highlander*).

May 11. Bob Marley dies of lung cancer and a brain tumor at age thirty-six. He was the leading force in the worldwide popularity of reggae music and the Rastafarian faith.

May 15. Public Image Ltd. perform at New York's Ritz Club posing behind a video screen while music is played from tapes. They are showered with missiles and booed off the stage.

May 16. Kim Carnes reaches number one on the pop charts with "Bette Davis Eyes" (EMI America), remaining there for nine non-consecutive weeks.

May 19. Sting is named Songwriter of the Year at the twenty-sixth Ivor Novello Awards.

May 23. Smokey Robinson's "Being With You" (Tamla 54321) begins a three-week run at number two on the Hot 100.

June 1. The first issue of *Kerrang!* is issued as a special bi-weekly music periodical. AC/DC adorn the cover, with features on Girlschool, Motorhead, and Saxon. It will be widely regarded as the finest heavy metal magazine ever published.

June 2. Prince makes his British debut at London's Lyceum Ballroom. He won't perform in England again for five years.

June 13. Smokey Robinson tops the British charts with "Being with You."

June 20. The Dutch studio entity, Stars on 45, ascends to the summit of the Hot 100 with "Medley" (Radio), which features material composed by Lennon/McCartney, Jeff Barry, and Andy Kim.

July 4. George Harrison's tribute to recently murdered musical cohort, John Lennon, "All Those Years Ago" (Dark Horse 49725), reaches the top slot on the Adult Contemporary charts. It was his first single to accomplish this feat, although he'd been a AC fixture throughout the 1970s. It performed nearly as well on the Hot 100, stalling at number two on the Hot 100 for three weeks beginning July 4 due the Kim Carnes' juggernaut, "Bette Davis Eyes."

July 11. Kenny Rogers' "I Don't Need You" (Liberty 1415) begins a six-week stint at number one on the AC charts. The first single from his *Share Your Love With Me* album, produced by Lionel Richie, it also topped the country charts and went to number three on the Hot 100. Regarding his decision to work with Richie, Rogers reflected, "I just loved the way he thought. He had the innate ability to say the simplest things and put them to beautiful music and everybody can relate to them" Hyatt. 1999.

July 11. The Specials top the British charts with "Ghost Town."

July 25. Air Supply climbs to summit of the pop charts with "The One That You Love" (Arista).

August 1. Rick Springfield begins a two-week stay atop the Hot 100 with "Jessie's Girl" (RCA).

August 1. Time Warner launches the cable television channel, MTV, with programming consisting largely of music video clips. The first clip shown, the Buggles' "Video Killed the Radio Star," is more than a symbolic gesture as contemporary pop artists scramble to produce videos as a commercial vehicle to promote their latest recordings. As a consequence, the role of radio in breaking new releases is significantly diminished as the decade unfolds. Owing their success largely to the video medium include photogenic acts in the emerging genres such as techno-pop (e.g., Human League, Depeche Mode) and the New Romantics (Adam Ant, Duran Duran, the Thompson Twins, etc) as well more traditional rockers like Billy Idol and Def Leppard. Within a couple of years, even artists who had been sharply critical of the extra-musical considerations at work in video clips—including Bruce Springsteen, Tom Petty, and the Police—jumped on the MTV bandwagon with a vengeance.

Pushed into the center stage of American culture by MTV, music video clips—variously called "promo clips," "picture music," or, simply, "videos"—made a substantial impact upon the public consciousness during the early 1980s. Their influence can be discerned in a wide range of present-day institutions, including Hollywood films, television programming, broadcast journalism and documentaries, advertising, and iPods and competing MP3 players. The medium, generally consisting of concise visual presentations accompanying pop songs as opposed to the various types of full-length video programs (e.g., extended concerts, documentaries, recapitulations of movie/television appearances), is distinguished by the use of videotape (largely supplanted by digital equipment and software by theater 1990s) as opposed to the celluloid footage widely used within the entertainment film sector.

In some respects, video clips are a comparatively recent development; e.g., the form's conceptual and technical sophistication, the astronomical costs of production and burgeoning home videocassette market. If one accepts the aforementioned definition of the medium, then it can be established that they have been around far longer than the video phenomenon itself. As early as 1921, the German Oskar Fischinger started experimenting with short animated films utilizing abstract-geometrical forms dancing to jazz and classical music. He later achieved immortality for his conceptualization of the initial sequence in Walt Disney's *Fantasia* set to Bach's "Toccata and Fugue."

By the mid-1930s, visual shorts had begun incorporating plots and universally recognizable settings in order to enhance the existing musical track. Large numbers of clips were made for theatrical distribution featuring the era's big bands and other top pop artists. Michael Shore, in *The Rolling Stone Book of Rock Video*, noted, "some of them are fully as imaginative and eye-catching as anything being made today."

The appearance of the video jukebox represented a further refinement in the evolution in the evolution leading up to the modern day video clip. The Panoram Soundie would play musical movie shorts for a dime or quarter. Although the machine continued to be used throughout the 1940s, the majority of filmlets were produced in the early years of that decade, typically featuring simulated live performances by stars such as Louis Armstrong, Fats Waller, Cab Calloway, and Bing Crosby. However, a small percentage of them included primitive special effects as in the case of Mabel Todd's "At the Club Savoy" which employed the device of flashback to tell the story of the girl's guilt (set in a temperance hall no less!) over going on a bender the previous night. While soundies were the victims of neglect on the part of a generation obsessed with TV and rock 'n' roll, an updated version called the Scopitone enjoyed widespread popularity in Europe during the late 1950s and early 1960s. The clips produced during this period were gaudy and often unintentionally surreal in their attempts to visually complement the music. Neil Sedaka's "Calendar Girl" (1961) represented a case in point, featuring elaborate set and costume changes for every month of the year.

The groundwork for the present day video clip was laid in the mid-1960s as an increasing number of bands began making promotional films to send television rock shows. The rationale for the rise of this phenomenon among the pop artists of that era included (1) the lack of availability in-person, (2) the high cost—financially and physically—of constant travel (a particularly salient point of view for American acts who found a receptive market in England for their video clips via TV pop music variety programs such as *Ready Steady Go!*), (3) opposition to live performing (the Beatles—as was so often the case—set the precedent by announcing their retirement from the stage in the summer of 1966), and (4) concern with the negative implications of lip-synching as had been the modus operandi for hit artists seeker wider exposure via television since the early days of *American Bandstand*. Given the experimental climate of rock music during the psychedelic period, it was inevitable that many of these prototype videos would display a high level of aesthetic creativity and technical mastery of the medium. A classic example is the 1967 clip, "Happy Jack," available on home video as part of the 1979 film documentary on the Who's career, *The Kids Are Alright*. The clip reveals a wealth of comic invention, casting the band members as bumbling burglars in a Chaplinesque silent-movie-style caper.

Queen's "Bohemian Rhapsody" is generally recognized as a video clip most responsible for ushering in the modern era. It is felt to represent the first case in which a video played a primary role in elevating a pop song to hit status. The clip anticipates many of the cinematic techniques achieving widespread application at a later date, including split images and widely panning stage shots.

During its infancy, the video clip profited from the creative energy expended on a wide variety of fronts. Most notable sources of input were (1) the underground art community, (2) television, (3) commercial film, and (4) dance clubs.

The Underground Art Community

The underground played a vital role in broadening the medium's aesthetic reach, incorporating elements of dramatics (e.g., acting, mime, soliloquy), contemporary art music, the graphic arts, documentary journalism, filmmaking, and animation. A San Francisco-based group of conceptual artists, The Residents, pioneered the multi-media approach to video production. The group's "Land of 1000 Dances" (1975) has been characterized by Shore as "The most utterly, exuberantly original and bizarre performance video ever." The work possesses three distinct sequences: a dreamlike pixilated opening in which the group members wheel shopping carts with pointy telephone-wire conductor-like structures attached to their fronts; a cavern club setting reveals the band perverting the 1960s dance classic for which the clip is titled in mutant tribal stomp fashion; the ending features a storm trooper zapping the surreal performers with a ray gun.

Television

The tube has always been the major channel for the transmission of the video clip. Therefore, it is not surprising that a host of TV programming formats have influenced the genre, including sitcoms and serial (e.g., *Ozzie & Harriet* with Ricky Nelson, *The Donna Reed Show* with Shelly Fabares and Paul Peterson), variety shows (Elvis Presley's 1956 appearances on *The Ed Sullivan Show*, *Stage Show*, featuring the Dorsey brothers, and *The Steve Allen Show* remain lead-in snapshots in the photo album of rock history), and music concert/dance venues. The pioneering stateside shows such as *Your Hit Parade* and *American Bandstand* were duplicated in England as *Top of the Pops* and *Juke Box Jury*. The U.K.'s *Ready Steady Go!* first broadcast in August in August 1963, broke new ground in allowing artists to perform without lip-synching. ABC's *Shindig* and NBC's *Hullabaloo*, both instituted in 1965, featured rerecorded, conceptual shorts such as the Beatles' hijinks in a railroad car set. During the 1970s, *The Midnight Special* represented the prime venue for video clips, enabling the fledging form to reach a growing audience.

The Monkees deserves at least a footnote in video clip history for its attempt to blend all of the aforementioned TV formats. Modeled after the Beatles film, *A Hard Day's Night*, the program was killed by the band's lack of musical credibility at a time when progressive rock held sway as well as the rise of pallid copies such as *The Archies* and *The Partridge Family* (it would make a comeback in the 1980s via syndication on, ironically enough, MTV). The program's director, Bob Rafaelson, would note in *The Rolling Stone Book of Rock Video*:

> Almost all the effects you see in videos today, the psychedelic solarizations, the quick cutting, are things we were doing years ago.

Video Clips on Television, 1985

A. MTV/Music Television. This cable television channel pioneered the Top 40 pop music concept within a video context. After losing $50 million between 1981 and 1983, the station achieved an $8.1 million profit during the first half of 1984; during the latter time span it reached 23.5 million households, up 57 percent from 1983. On January 1, 1985, its owner Warner Amex, launched Video Hits One (VH-1), which targeted a middle-aged audience.

B. Cable Competitors
  1. Full-time Programming
     Discovery Music Network
     Cable Music Channel (Originally part of Ted Turner's communications empire, it was bought out by MTV in late 1984 after several months of lackluster impact.)
  2. Part-time Programming
     USA (Offerings have included *Night Flight*, *Radio 1990*, and *Heart Beat City*.)
     Disney Channel (*DTV* segments, usually lasting fifteen minutes apiece, several times per day.)
     BET (*Video Vibrations*)
     WTBS (*Night Tracks*)

    The Nashville Network

    Nickelodeon

C. Networks

    1. ABC (*ABC Rocks*)

    2. CBS (*Solid Gold*)

    3. NBC (*Friday Night Videos*; *Rock-N-America*, featuring Dick Clark)

D. Independent Stations

    1. *America's Top 10*, featuring Casey Kasem

    2. *N.Y. Hot Tracks*

    3. *101 Rock Place*

    4. *Solid Gold* (syndicated reruns)

Categories of Video Clips with Notable Examples

A. Live Concert. Aim: to provide an appreciation for the act as a performing unit. This represents the most cliché-ridden grouping; e.g., guitars arranged in phalanx formation, smoke bombs. A chief variant: posturing in more intimate surroundings—such as a living room or classroom—with little attempt to make it appear like the artist is really performing. Examples: Bruce Springsteen's "Glory Days"; Police's "Spirits in the Material World."

B. Dance/Theatrical Sequence. Key influence: *West Side Story*. Examples: Michael Jackson's "Beat It" and "Thriller"; Rod Stewart's "Young Turks."

C. Dramatic Action. Essence: a linear plot which may or may not conform to the song's lyrics. The visual action frequently skirts around the lyrics (they may be too vague to allow for a literal interpretation), thereby giving rise to a surrealistic frame of reference. Examples: Berlin's "No More Lies," a take-off on *Bonnie and Clyde*; Golden Earring's espionage fantasy, "Twilight one"; Greg Kihn's Oz parody, "Reunited."

D. Message Video. The typical approach consists of protesting the status quo. Hot topics include: class stratification, war, the environment, the complexities and pressures of modern society, unabashed hedonism, conformism, authoritarian leadership, and moral bankruptcy. Examples: Billy Joel's "Allentown"; U2's "Sunday Bloody Sunday"; Randyandy's "Living in the USA"; Devo's "Beautiful World." The latter clip, according to Shore, "may be the most powerful sociopolitical use of sustained, concentrated onstage since the Odessa Steps sequence of Eisenstein's *The Battleship Potemkin*." The visual reveal a protagonist tuning in on 1950s Americana, communicated via a quick-cut montage of images culled from newsreels and TV framed by the band's sardonic greeting-card verse. The video's progression from innocence to increasingly disturbing images constitutes the core of its dramatic thrust.

E. Conceptual. There are three major subheadings here: (1) art for art's sake; the clip glorifying technical virtuosity as its own end. Prime examples include Missing Person's "Surrender Your Heart," which features Peter Max art endowed with breathtaking kinetic energy, and Philip Glass' "Act III," a visual depiction of the music's thematic development. (2) Art aimed at evoking an emotional reaction. The most productive is again surrealism; David Bowie's "Ashes to Ashes" represents a production tour de force. Bowie is cast in three roles; that of a Pagliacci clown, high-tech junkie, and asylum inmate. The imagery is cryptic and evocative, featuring flamboyant costumes, Slavic figures in procession, a clown sinking into a lake, etc. Especially intriguing are the clip's deliberately overloaded direction (characterized by demented, horror-movie camera angles and neurotic cuts from supersaturated color to black and white) and the self-referential video-within-video motif, wherein each new sequence is introduced by Bowie holding up a postcard-sized video screen displaying the first shot of the next sequence. (3) Anti-art art. Artists working in this category generally cultivate the cheap look, although many are of poor quality due to limited financial resources. Clips are typified by risk-taking (high degree of subjectivity, transcending the boundaries of good taste regarding the status quo, etc.) and inclinations to excess. Avant-garde artists such as Eno and Cabaret Voltaire fall within this category.

F. Humorous/Gag Presentation. Again, three main divisions exist: (1) Black humor. This form does not refer to racial subject matter but rather to a somewhat flippant treatment of the darker sides of life, often at the risk of crossing over into the realm of what a mainstream audience would consider to be bad taste. Favored themes include marital violence and fear of the bomb a la Dr. Strangelove.

The Gap Band's "You Dropped a Bomb on Me" is a particularly clever variation on the latter theme, employing metaphor (i.e., love equated with a bombing raid) to achieve jarring visual—as well as literary—impact. (2) Satire. Examples abound here; Donald Fagen's "New Frontier" represents one of the more strikingly conceived contributions. The work comments playfully on 1950s mores, insecurities, and sense of aesthetic chic. The outwardly nostalgic plot reveals a young couple revisiting the cold war years via a deserted bomb shelter. A less successful trend within this grouping, from an artistic standpoint, would be the self-conscious, often pretentious, attempt to spoof video making itself. (3) Nonsense. Utopia's "Feets Don't Fail Me Now," a product of video wunderkind Todd Rundgren, which portrays Muppet-styled cockroaches who suspect they should be involved in anything besides their present predicament, exemplifies this type.

G. The Travelogue. A prevailing strategy here seems to be the more exotic the clime the better one's chances of holding the viewer's attention. Teen stars Duran Duran shamefully exploited this maxim, offering the same lot from one video to another merely spread across a varying palette of locales; today a jungle in Indochina, tomorrow sailing the Caribbean, or maybe the mystical rites of the Inca past. Stop-action photography represents one of the heavily used cinematic devices within this category. Jean-Luc Ponty's "Individual Choice," Randyandy's "Living in the USA," and James Brown's "America" all feature frantically speeded-up images of Americans going about their everyday activities with liberal dollops of easily recognized physical landmarks thrown in for good measure.

Commercial Films

An increasingly refined synthesis of music and plot—which became the hallmark of the conceptual video clip—evolved during the rock era. In the first true rock 'n' roll film, *Blackboard Jungle* (1955), the music functioned merely to frame the plot. Elvis Presley, as with television, inalterably changed the course of development with his steady stream of releases between 1956 and 1968, most of which featured a half dozen or so carefully choreographed song interludes. The next advance was ushered in by the jukebox musical which starred the likes of Little Richard, Chuck Berry, Chubby Checker, and Frankie Avalon. These movies typically showcased several pop acts performing within a lame, forgettable plot. The jukebox musical mutated in the 1960s into muscle beach movies, social relevance flicks, and drug-tinged surrealism. By the time nostalgia (e.g., *American Graffiti*) and dance-oriented (e.g., *Saturday Night Fever*) films became bankable commodities in the 1970s a genuinely seamless bend of music and action had been achieved, due in large part to rock's then unassailable position as the soundtrack of life in Middle America.

Dance Clubs

By the onset of the 1980s clubs had become the outlet for the viewing of video clips. While the ascendancy of club to a mass preoccupation was closely linked to the disco music craze, additional factors played a key role such as the decline of radio as an innovative medium, the AOR-preoccupation of record labels, and the expense of touring as a means of breaking acts. Video came to be seen by the industry as a one-time expense which could be viewed continuously, even in many places at the same time, and the founding of RockAmerica by Ed Steiberg in 1980 rendered the marriage complete. Largely as a result of Steiberg's awareness of the demo tapes in abundant supply made by record companies for in-house marketing meetings, company-wide conventions, etc., RockAmerica quickly became the nation's largest video pool servicing video-equipped rock clubs.

The hegemony enjoyed by the clubs disappeared almost overnight with the institution of MTV in the fall of 1981. Within a couple of years virtually every channel in the United States possessed at least one program built around videos. The video clip's importance to the record industry by then transcended its original promotional issues; MTV was lending its name to sampler albums, and the shorts functioned to cement the tie-in between films and soundtrack releases. On occasion, artists (e.g., Joe Jackson in 1984, Van Halen and Journey in 1986) rebelled against the make-a-clip-for-MTV syndrome. In addition, the channel's viewership leveled off in the mid-1980s (spurring the development of non-musical programming) and industry insiders such as Dick Clark rechristened radio as the foremost arbiter in determining chart action. Nevertheless, the video clip phenomenon has remained a force within the entertainment field up to the present day.

A preoccupation with the blatantly promotional aspects of video clips as well as their proliferation tends to obscure the high order of aesthetic creativity characterizing a notable percentage of the available product. Additional signs of the aesthetic viability of these clips include (1) the diversified range of styles, themes, and techniques developed in such a comparatively short span of time; (2) the increased involvement of first-line film directors such as Andy Warhol and Zbigniew Rybczynski with the medium; and (3) the indelible mark they have left upon our society. Videos mirror, and to some degree, influence society's values, attitudes, and belief systems. Although frequently criticized as being superficial and preoccupied with sex and violence, they have employed a bold new visual vocabulary to reflect the rich diversity of life itself. The images portrayed include:

1. Vicarious experience. Videos offer up an exciting kaleidoscope of activities such as exotic travel (e.g., Elton John on the Riviera in "I'm Still Standing," Mike Nesmith in "Rio"), spying (e.g., Glenn Frey in a *Miami Vice* segment), and war (e.g., Pat Benetar as a fighter pilot in "Shadows of the Night").

2. Nostalgia. The Alan Parsons Project's "Don't Ask Me Why" parodies Depression era films, detective novels, and comic strips. Disney Television clips offer a double dose of the past—classic rock 'n' roll songs set to familiar vintage cartoon footage spliced together in montage form.

3. Instruction. Clips may either provide one's first awareness of an idea, issue, subject, etc., or depict it more vividly by exploiting the possibilities of the medium. "We Are the World" exhorts viewers to share their wealth with the dispossessed and starving African masses while Prince's "1999" opts for enjoying life unencumbered by Puritanical hang-ups before it's too late.

4. The expression of youthful rebelliousness. Targets typically include schools (e.g., Twisted Sister's "We're Not Gonna Take It"), the law (e.g., Sammy Hagar's "I Can't Drive 55"), and a host of other institutions at the core of the Establishment.

5. The expression of regional pride; for example, Los Angeles is represented by Randy Newman's "I Love L.A." and Frank Sinatra's "L.A. is My Lady."

6. Materialism. Chief objects of devotion include cars (e.g., ZZ Top's "Gimme All Your Lovin'") and clothes (e.g., ZZ Top's "Best Dressed Man," the camp elegance of Adam Ant). Upward mobility (e.g., Joe Jackson's "Steppin' Out") represents a major variation on this theme.

7. Protest. This activity is largely the province of the message video. The high profile of a spin-off school, whose seeming praise of the status quo is overlaid with a strong ironic twist (e.g., Bruce Springsteen's "Born in the USA," John Cougar Mellencamp's "Pink Houses"), attests to the artistic depth of the better video clips.

8. Tolerance for mild deviations in behavior. America likes to view itself as the last bastion of individuality, and the skewed characterizations of some videos would appear to support this argument. Boy George, formerly with the band, Culture Club, flirted with transvestism although he made it clear that he was basically a well-adjusted, decent bloke whose father and brothers were boxers. Rod Stewart indulges in voyeurism in "Infatuation," but somehow his never-say-die attitude leaves us rooting for him to win the girl right up until the end of the clip.

In some instances, video clips might be viewed as social change agents. Viewing clips could hasten catharsis; that is, identifying with a particular message, knowing you're not alone out there. The strong emotional and intellectual benefits of this experience could in turn stimulate the viewer to take on more of an activist role; for example, to donate food and money to the hungry in Ethiopia after viewing Band Aid's "Do They Know It's Christmas?"

The medium has continued to attract both advocates and detractors during its relatively brief history. One of the biggest boosters of the form has been director Zbigniew Rybczynski, winner of a 1983 Academy Award for his film short, *Tango*. Rybczynski would decide to abandon the film medium because he considered it to have reached an aesthetic dead-end. After committing exclusively to video clips, he offered the following rationale in the January 1985 issue of *Music and Sound Output*:

> I believe now is a very interesting time. We are at the point of a big revolution in video. Music video is the beginning of something very important in culture. There is nothing more new in any other kind of art. Consider the (main) audience, young people. They don't read anymore. They have only TV screens. This I the only way to learn about the world or something about aesthetics. I don't think other art

exists for a really big audience. Nobody goes to art galleries. This is part of the past. For the younger generation throughout the whole country, their only contact with art is through music video.

Critics of the form have justified their stance with a number of arguments. They include:

1. The crass commercialism characterizing both the content of many clips as well as the mode of presentation. They have been subverted by skilled pitchmen to the point where it's hard to distinguish them—and, for that matter, much television fare—from straightforward advertisements.
2. The inclination of a significant portion of these clips to self indulgence and plain bad taste.
3. Their omnipresence within our society.
4. Eric Zorn's contention that the medium "threatens to rob us of the special images we conjure up to go with a song." He would note that many MTV viewers claimed to "play back" the video in their minds upon hearing a particular song on the radio. The proliferation of music videos, in short, seemed likely to produce "an entire generation of people who will overlook the sublime, extremely personal element of music."

In response to these claims, it should be noted that music video clips can bring out dimensions of a song otherwise lost to the listener. It would appear that this genre is merely the most recent outgrowth of the ongoing symbiotic relationship between music and the visual image. Established precedents include passion plays, opera, ballet, and incidental music for dramatic presentations. Furthermore, all media—including songs without accompanying video information—have been deployed in the service of commercial gain, with quality output inevitably overwhelmed by more pedestrian works. The controversy still rages, in part because it could be argued that these clips run the gamut, from innovative art, to artifice (skill used as a means of deception to stoke the star-making machinery of the music business) and craft (compromise creativity bolstered by ingenuous execution).

Perhaps the most notable feature of video clips as a recording medium is that they possess the power to evoke strong aesthetic reactions within a short time span. For many, such an experience might not signify anything other than light entertainment. However, they are capable of challenging the participant on far deeper levels, whether drawing upon other art forms (e.g., Todd Rundgren's manipulation of the visual symbols of Dali and Magritte on a more literal plane in "Time Heals") or developing the unique possibilities of the video medium itself. These possibilities include sensory overload (i.e., jamming as much information as possible within the time constraints of a pop song by increasing the rapidity of images, spitting the screen, etc.—a technique which has been especially influential I television ads; notable examples include Billy Joel's "We Didn't Start the Fire" and Tom Petty's "Jammin' Me"), the manipulation of predictable censoring standards (already engraved in stone for older media such as TV, the cinema, comics, radio, etc.), and dispensing with narrative demands, and, thereby, encouraging figurative forms of thinking.

August 15. Diana Ross and Lionel Richie begin a nine-week run atop the Hot 100 with "Endless Love" (Motown). The Richie composition is assisted by its inclusion in the soundtrack to the film, *Endless Love*.

One of the major forces in Black Contemporary music in the 1970s and 1980s, Richie's diversified talents—he was a gifted songwriter and record producer, and played piano and saxophone as well as singing—enabled him to achieve industry success in a number of guises. His ability to appeal to a broad-based audience was a result of an upbringing that included formal training in the classics as well as exposure to the pop, rhythm and blues, and country genres then popular in his native Alabama.

While attending Tuskegee Institute, Richie joined a group that would become known as the Commodores. Signed by Motown in 1974, they negotiated funk and tender ballads with equal verve, releasing a string of hits that stretched well into the 1980s. By 1980, Richie was in great demand outside the group, writing and producing "Lady" (Liberty 1380; 1980; #1 pop six weeks, #1 AC four weeks, #1 c&w) for Kenny Rodgers as well as the title song to the film, *Endless Love*. The latter work (Motown 1519; 1981; #1 r&b seven weeks, #1 AC three weeks), recorded with Diana Ross, would become Motown's biggest-selling single ever as well as top duet recording of all time. These growing commitments spurred him to go solo. His smooth, easy listening style immediately clicked with "Truly" (Motown 1644; 1982; #1 pop two weeks, #1

AC four weeks), which won a Grammy for Best Pop Male Vocal Performance; the accompanying album, *Lionel Richie* (Motown 6007; 1982; #3) would achieve quadruple platinum sales. The eight singles drawn from it and his second LP, *Can't Slow Down* (Motown 6059; 1983; #1; 8 million + sales), would all reach the Top 10. The latter record also earned two 1984 Grammy Awards, for Album of the Year and Producer of the Year. He would also be named Writer of the Year by the American Society of Composers, Authors and Publishers in both 1984 and 1985. While slow to appear due to Richie's full slate of activities, the third album, *Dancing on the Ceiling* (Motown 6158; 1986; #1), maintained his career momentum, selling more than four million copies.

Richie played a key role in the "USA for Africa" project, sharing writing credits with Michael Jackson and participating in the recording of both the record, "We Are the World" (Columbia 04839; 1985; #1 pop four weeks, #1 AC two weeks, #1 r&b two weeks) and accompanying video release. He would also contribute music to a number of high-profile films such as *White Nights*—most notably "Say You, Say Me" (Motown 1819; 1985; #1 pop four weeks, #1 AC five weeks, #1 r&b two weeks)—and *The Color Purple* (1985). Although perceived as dated—his last Top 10 single came in early 1987 with "Ballerina Girl" (Motown 1873; #7 pop, #1 AC four weeks)—he has continued to issue moderately successful recordings that appeal to mainstream pop, Adult Contemporary, and rhythm and blues audiences.

August 22. The Carpenters' "Touch Me When We're Dancing" (A&M) reaches number one on the Adult Contemporary charts. It is the fifteenth—and last—AC chart-topper for the duo; only Elton John has achieved more up to the present day.

August 29. The Pointer Sisters begin a three-week run at number two on the Hot 100 with "Slow Hand" (Planet 47929).

September 5. Stevie Nicks, Tom Petty and the Heartbreakers begin a six-week run at number three on the Hot 100 with "Stop Draggin' My Heart Around" (Modern 7336).

September 17. *Rolling Stone* pictures a brooding Jim Morrison on its cover with the caption "Jim Morrison: He's hot, he's sexy and he's dead."

September 19. Simon & Garfunkel reunite for a Central Park concert before four hundred thousand fans. The performance will later be issued on record and video.

September 22. Songwriter Harry Warren dies at age eighty-eight. He composed more than four hundred songs, including "I Only Have Eyes for You."

October 1. *Rolling Stone* pictures Yoko Ono wearing shades on its cover with the caption "Yoko: An Intimate Conversation."

October 10. The Four Tops go number one on the R&B charts with "When She Was My Girl" (Casablanca 2338), remaining there for two weeks.

October 17. Christopher Cross begins a three-week stay atop the Hot 100 with "Arthur's Theme (Best That You Can Do)" (Warner Bros.). The track is featured in the Dudley Moore film, *Arthur*.

October 24. Luther Vandross peaks at number one on the R&B charts with "Never Too Much" (Epic 02409), remaining there for two weeks.

October 31. The Rolling Stones begin a three-week run at number two on the Hot 100 with "Start Me Up" (Rolling Stones 21003).

November 7. Daryl Hall and John Oates begin a two-week stint atop the Hot 100 with "Private Eyes" (RCA).

November 7. Roger rises to the summit of the R&B charts with his version of "I Heard It Through the Grapevine (Part 1) (Warner Bros. 49786)," remaining there for a fortnight.

November 12. *Rolling Stone* pictures Keith Richards on its cover with the caption "No Regrets: The Rolling Stone Interview."

November 21. Kool & the Gang's "Take My Heart (You Can Have It If You Want It)" (De-Lite 815) reaches number one on the R&B charts.

November 21. Olivia Newton-John begins a ten-week run atop the Hot 100 with "Physical" (MCA).

November 21. Hank Williams Jr. reaches number one on the country charts with "All My Rowdy Friends (Have Settled Down)" (Elektra 47191).

November 28. Earth, Wind & Fire heads up the R&B charts with "Boogie Wonderland" (Columbia).

November 28. Foreigner begins a ten-week residence at number two on the Hot 100 with "Waiting for a Girl Like You" (Atlantic 3868).

November 28. Merle Haggard tops the country charts with "My Favorite Memory" Epic 02504).

November 28. Luther Vandross peaks at number thirty-three on the Hot 100 with "Never Too Much" (Epic 02409).

Vandross enjoyed a very successful career as a session singer and recording commercials prior to becoming one of the preeminent R&B stylists of his generation, widely known for his impeccable phrasing and vocal control. Born April 20, 1951, in New York City, he began playing piano at age three. One of his compositions, "Everybody Rejoice (A Brand New Day)," was included in the Broadway musical, *The Wiz*, in 1972. He became a fixture on ad jingles, from U.S. Army to Burger King spots.

His entrée to the pop music industry came when a friend, guitarist Carlos Alomar, introduced him to David Bowie. He would contribute a song, "Fascination," and sing on Bowie's highly successful LP, *Young Americans* (RCA; 1975), later touring with him as well. While continuing to sing jingles and cutting two obscure albums under the name Luther, he quickly became one of the busiest backing vocalists and arrangers around, recording with Bette Midler, Ringo Starr, Carly Simon, Donna Summer, Barbra Streisand, Chaka Khan, Chic, and Change.

With several labels expressing an interest in Vandross as a solo artist, he produced two demos, "Never Too Much" and "A House Is Not a Home." As a result, Epic Records signed him in 1981, granting him full creative control. Beginning with *Never Too Much* (Epic 37451; 1981; #1 R&B), he released a long string of platinum-selling albums, including *Forever, For Always, For Love* (Epic 38235; 1982), *Busy Body* (Epic 39196; 1983), *The Night I Fell In Love* (Epic 39882; 1985), *Give Me the Reason* (Epic 40415; 1986), *Any Love* (Epic 44308; 1988), *The Best of Luther Vandross...The Best of Love* (Epic 45320; 1989), and *Power of Love* (Epic 46789; 1991). Although his singles have had limited crossover appeal, they have consistently reached the R&B Top 10. Despite the demands ensuing from pop stardom, he would continue to write and produce for other artists, most notably Aretha Franklin, Cheryl Lynn, Dionne Warwick, Teddy Pendergrass, and Whitney Houston until his death early in the twenty-first century. He also acted in films, most notably Robert Townsend's *Meteor Man* (1993).

December 1. Vince Clarke announces that he is leaving Depeche Mode to form Yazoo with Alison Moyet.

December 5. Johnny Lee peaks at number one on the country charts with "Bet Your Heart on Me" (Full Moon 47215).

December 9. Sonny Til, lead singer of the Orioles, dies of a heart attack.

One of the seminal R&B vocal groups, the Baltimore-based Orioles (first known as the Vibra-Naires)—originally consisting of lead tenor Earlington Carl Tilghman (aka Sonny Til), tenor Alexander Sharp, baritone George Nelson, bass Johnny Reed, guitarist Tommy Gaither—were formed in 1947. In addition, to recording the chart-topping R&B classics "It's Too Soon To Know" and "Tell Me So" in the late 1940s, the million-selling "Crying in the Chapel" (1953) is widely considered to be one of the first rock 'n' roll-styled recordings. Although the hits stopped coming in 1953, the group soldiered on until Til's death.

December 12. George Jones climbs to the summit of the country charts with "Still Doin' Time" (Epic 02526).

December 19. Steve Wariner's "All Roads Lead to You" (RCA 12307) reaches number one on the country charts.

December 25. Michael Jackson phones Paul McCartney with the suggestion that they collaborate on recordings. The initial result, "The Girl Is Mine" (Columbia), reaches number two on the Hot 100 (#8 U.K.).

December 26. AC/DC begin a three-week stay atop the album charts with *For Those About to Rock We Salute You*.

December 26. Alabama heads up the country charts with "Love in the First Degree" (RCA 12288).

December 27. Singer/songwriter/bandleader Hoagy Carmichael dies at age eighty-two. He gained national prominence after composing "Star Dust" (words were later added by Mitchell Parrish) while a law student at Indiana University. He also wrote "Georgia on My Mind," "Lazy River," and "Old Buttermilk Sky."

1982

❋

January 9. Gene Watson's "Fourteen Carat Mind" (MCA 51183) reaches number one on the country charts.

January 16. Ronnie Milsap heads up the country charts with "I Wouldn't Have Missed It for the World" (RCA 12342).

January 17. Tommy Tucker, then forty-eight, succumbs to poisonous fumes while renovating the floors of his New York home. His biggest success came with his own composition, the R&B standard "Hi Heel Sneakers" (Checker), which reached number eleven on the Hot 100 at the outset of the British Invasion.

January 20. While performing in Des Moines, Ozzy Osbourne—believing it to be one of his rubber fakes—bites the head off an unconscious bat thrown onstage by someone in the audience. He is later taken to the hospital for a rabies injection.

January 30. Daryl Hall and John Oates reach number one on the pop charts with "I Can't Go for That (No Can Do)" (RCA).

January 30. Paul McCartney appears on the BBC radio program, *Desert Island Discs*. His selections include Elvis Presley's "Heartbreak Hotel," Chuck Berry's "Sweet Little Sixteen," John Lennon's "Beautiful Boy," and Little Richard's "Tutti Frutti."

February 6. After inhabiting the fringes of the rock scene for more than a decade, the J. Geils Band surge to the top of the Hot 100 with "Centerfold" (EMI America), remaining there for six weeks. At the same time, the group's *Freeze-Frame* (EMI), starts a four-week run atop the album charts. Aided by heavy rotation of promotional video clips on MTV, the band's unabashedly retro blues-rock sound will continue to sell well until lead singer Peter Wolf opts for the solo career in the mid-1980s.

February 6. Kraftwerk becomes the first German act to top the British charts with "The Model/Computer Love."

February 9. UNICEF is given $9 million by George Harrison, a decade after the charity concert for Bangladesh.

February 13. The Jam perform two numbers—"Town Called Malice" and "Precious," their double A-sided chart topper—on the same broadcast of *Top of the Pops*, the first band to do this since the Beatles.

February 13. The marble slab from Ronnie Van Zant's grave is stolen. Police locate it a couple of weeks later in a dried-up river bed.

February 21. Deejay Murray the K. dies. He is widely believed to be the first person to play a Beatles record on a U.S. radio station.

February 24. Police are named Best British Group at the Brit Awards. Adam and the Ants garner Best Album for *Kings of the Wild Frontier*.

February 24. Grammy Award winners include John Lennon and Yoko Ono (Album of the Year for *Double Fantasy*), Kim Carnes (Song of the Year for "Bette Davis Eyes"), Quincy Jones (Producer of the Year), and Sheena Easton (Best New Act).

March 6. The Go-Go's begin a six-week run atop the album charts with *Beauty and the Beat*.

March 6. Tight Fit peak at number one on the British singles charts with a remake of "The Lion Sleeps Tonight."

March 19. Ozzy Osbourne's guitarist, Randy Rhoads, is killed near Orlando when the light aircraft carrying him crashes after buzzing the band's tour bus and accidentally clipping it.

March 20. Joan Jett and the Blackhearts begin a seven-week stay at number one on the pop charts with punk-inflected "I Love Rock 'n Roll" (Boardwalk). It goes on to become a platinum seller, and is recognized as the most successful single of the year by *Joel Whitburn's Pop Annual, 1955–1999*. The song first appeared as the B side for the 1960s band, The Arrows.

March 24. Aileen Stanley (real name: Maude Elsie Aileen Muggeridge) dies at age eighty-nine. The Chicago native was perhaps the most popular female recording artist in the mid-1920s (with the possible exception of Bessie Smith). Dubbed "the Phonograph Girl," her hits included "Singin' the Blues" (Victor 18703; 1921), "Home Again Blues" (Victor 18760; 1921), and "Sweet Indiana Home" (#18922; 1922).

April 21. Joe Strummer disappears for three weeks, making it necessary for his group, The Clash, to cancel a tour. He is found living in bohemian fashion in Paris.

April 30. Rock critic Lester Bangs—best known for his work in *Creem, Rolling Stone*, and *The Village Voice*—dies of a heart attack.

May 1. Barry Manilow tops the British album charts for the first time with *Barry Live in Britain.*

May 8. Neil Bogart dies of cancer at age thirty-nine. As head of Casablanca Records, he helped nurture the careers Joan Jett, Kiss, Donna Summer, and the Village People, among other artists.

May 8. The theme song to the Academy Award-winning film, *Chariots of Fire*—as performed by Euro-pop artist, Vangelis (Polydor)—holds down the top spot on the Hot 100. The Vangelis composition will be the bestselling instrumental recording for the year.

May 15. Asia top the album charts with their eponymous debut; it will spend nine weeks in that position.

May 15. Paul McCartney, with Stevie Wonder providing harmony, reaches number one with "Ebony and Ivory" (Columbia), remaining there for seven weeks. It also tops the British charts, and is the twenty-fourth McCartney song to top the Hot 100.

May 23. Fearing that their use will put members out of work, the U.K. Musicians Union moves a resolution to ban synthesizers and rhythm machines from studio recording and live concerts.

May 28. Promoter Bill Graham stages a Vietnam Veterans benefit concert in San Francisco featuring Country Joe and the Fish, the Grateful Dead, and the Jefferson Starship.

May 31. R.E.M. signs a five-album deal with the independent label, I.R.S.

June 7. Graceland, the late Elvis Presley's Memphis home, is opened to public visitations.

June 12. Gary "U.S." Bonds, Jackson Browne, Linda Ronstadt, Bruce Springsteen, and James Taylor appear before a Central Park audience of 450,000 at a rally for nuclear disarmament.

July 3. The Human League herald the arrival of techno-pop when "Don't You Want Me" (A&M/Virgin) settles in for a three-week stay atop the Hot 100. The British trio's synthesizer-dominated sound will open the charts to Depeche Mode, OMD, and Euythmics, among others, as well as exerting a profound influence on emerging genres such as hip-hop, the New Romantics, house, and techno.

July 4. Ozzy Osbourne marries his manager, Sharon Arden. She plays a major role in ensuring the longevity of his career.

July 5. Sun Records music director, Bill Justis, dies at age fifty-six. He worked with Johnny Cash, Elvis Presley, Jerry Lee Lewis, and other legends as well as recording "Raunchy," which reached number two in 1957.

July 24. Survivor begins a six-week run at number one on the Hot 100 with "Eye of the Tiger" (Scotti Bros.).

August 5. *Rolling Stone* pictures the Go-Go's in Hanes underwear on its cover with the caption "Go-Go's Put Out."

August 21. Zapp top the R&B charts with "Dance Floor (Part 1)" (Warner Bros. 29961), remaining there for two weeks.

September 3. The three-day US Festival kicks off in San Bernardino, California. Subsidized by Apple Computers founder, Steve Wozniak, the headliners include the B-52's, Pat Benetar, Jackson Browne, the Cars, the English Beat, Fleetwood Mac, Gang of Four, Grateful Dead, Tom Petty, the Police, the Ramones, and Talking Heads.

September 4. Aretha Franklin's "Jump To It" (Arista 0699) begins a four-week stay atop the R&B charts.

September 4. "Abracadabra" (Capitol), the Steve Miller Band's last notable hit single, starts a non-consecutive two-week stretch heading up the pop charts. Switching to the Mercury label the following year, Miller would settle into the role of rock elder statesman, producing a series of moderately successful AOR LPs.

September 11. Afrika Bambaataa peaks at number forty-eight on the Hot 100 with "Planet Rock" (Tommy Boy 823). A major underground hit, it will go on to earn a gold record.

While DJ Kool Herc is widely credited with creating hip-hop, Afrika Bambaataa led the way in disseminating it worldwide. His vision incorporated deejays, rappers, singers, studio producers, break dancers, and graffiti artists into one youth culture movement.

Born Kevin Donovan on April 10, 1960, in the Bronx, New York, he took the name of a nineteenth-century Zulu chief meaning "affectionate leader." Known as the "Master of Records," due to his unrivaled disc collection, he experimented with recorded musical elements such as Latin rock. European disco, funk, punk, and the German electro bands such as Kraftwerk in order to create the ultimate dance environment. Although his primary creative medium was the club and street dances, he produced many important twelve-inch singles and albums during the 1980s, most notably "Planet Rock" with Soulsonic Force, "Renegades of Funk" with Soulsonic Force (Tommy Boy 839, 1983), "Unity" with James Brown (Tommy Boy 847; 1984), *Planet Rock: The Album* (Tommy Boy; 1986), and *Warlock and Witches, Computer Chips, Microchips and You* (Profile; 1996). While no longer in hip-hop's innovative vanguard, he has remained in high demand as an elder statesman of the genre, working parties and raves and often making radio station appearances.

September 11. Chicago begins a two-week stint atop the Hot 100 with the sentimental ballad, "Hard to Say I'm Sorry" (Full Moon).

October 2. John Cougar's second single from the platinum-selling *American Fool* album, "Jack & Diane" (Riva), reaches number one, remaining there for four weeks. The million-seller will prove to be the singer/songwriter's watershed recording, elevating him to superstar status and instilling the confidence to shed the hated show business moniker, "Cougar," in favor of his real name, "Mellencamp."

John Mellencamp has evolved from an AOR-friendly hard rocker in the Bob Seger-Bruce Springsteen mold to the critically hailed exponent of country and R&B-flavored roots rock. Born in Seymour, Indiana with a form of spina bifida, he started his first band at age fourteen. After attending community college and trying a series of blue-collar jobs, he relocated in New York City in the mid-1970s with a backlog of self-penned songs with hopes of establishing a music career. There, he signed with David Bowie's manager, Tony DeFries, who assigned him the moniker "Johnny Cougar" and help secure a reported million dollar deal with Main Man. The resulting album, *Chestnut Street Incident* (Main Man 601; 1976), was a commercial failure, and he was dropped by parent company MCA.

Signing with Riva Records in the late 1970s (to his frustration, as John Cougar), Mellencamp began building a following through well-crafted recordings—including the hit singles "I Need a Lover" (Riva 202; 1979), "This Time" (Riva 205; 1980), and "Ain't Even Done with the Night" (Riva 207; 1981)—and constant touring. His commercial breakthrough came with *American Fool* (Riva 7501; 1982, #1), driven by Grammy-winning "Hurts So Good" (Riva 209; 1982; #2), "Jack and Diane" (Riva 210), "Hand to Hold On To" (Riva 211; 1982), all of which were in heavy MTV rotation. The 1980s were a watershed decade for him, including the following Top 10 albums: *Un-Huh* (Riva 7504; 1983), *Scarecrow* (Riva/Mercury 824865; 1985), *The Lonesome Jubilee* (Mercury 832465; 1987), and *Big Daddy* (Mercury 838220; 1989). In addition to producing his own recordings, he was in demand to perform similar duties for other artists, including Mitch Ryder's *Never Kick a Sleeping Dog* (1983) and James McMurtry's *Too Long in the Wasteland* (1989).

He was a co-organizer of Farm Aid along with Willie Nelson and Neil Young in 1985; he would go on to appear at Farm Aid concerts I through VI. He has given additional concerts over the years to bring attention to the problems of the American farmer, and, in 1987, he testified before a congressional subcommittee. His strong political activism also extended criticism of beer- and cigarette-company sponsorship of concert tours and the refusal to allow his music to be employed in commercials.

By the 1990s, Mellencamp's recordings were less commercially successful, due in part to their more introspective tone and greater reliance on folk instrumentation. He was now moving into other fields, directing and acting in the film, *Falling From Grace* (1992; scripted by author Larry McMurtry), and mounting exhibitions of his paintings. He suffered a heart attack in 1994, but has continued to remain active as a performer and recording artist.

October 2. Evelyn King begins a five-week run atop the R&B charts with "Love Come Down" (RCA 13273).

October 30. Men at Work become the latest Aussie sensation, topping the pop charts with "Who Can It Be Now?" (Columbia).

November 6. Joe Cocker and Jennifer Warnes begin a three-week stay atop the Hot 100 with "Up Where We Belong" (Island).

November 6. Marvin Gaye achieves the longest-running chart topper of the R&B era with "Sexual Healing" (Columbia 03302), outpacing the competition for ten weeks.

November 6. Grandmaster Flash peaks at number sixty-two on the Hot 100 with "The Message" (Sugar Hill 584).

Grandmaster Flash, born Joseph Saddler in Barbados, West Indies, on January 1, 1958, played a major role in establishing the conventions of hip hop recordings. Named for his lightning speed in manipulating record players, he pioneered the technique of "cutting" between discs on two separate turntables, in the process creating a continuous flow of beats punctuated repetitive rhythmic "breaks."

Flash developed his skills playing records at local block parties in the Bronx during the 1970s. He was signed by the Enjoy label shortly after creating the Furious Five, a group of rappers—initially, Grandmaster Melle Mel, Kid Creole, Cowboy, Duke Bootee, and Kurtis Blow; augmented with the addition of Scorpio on electronics in 1980—to complement his deejay pyrotechnics. Following several underground rhythm & blues hits, he became an industry-wide phenomenon with the release of twelve-inch single, "The Adventures of Grandmaster Flash on the Wheels of Steel" (Sugar Hill 557; 1981; #55 r&b), a funky melage of sampling (most notably, Chic's "Good Times" and Queen's "Another One Bites the Dust"), scratching, breaks, and energetic rapping. The Sylvia Robinson/Duke Bootee-penned "The Message" (#4 r&b, #8 UK; issued in both the seven- and twelve-inch configurations), remains one of the seminal rap recordings of all-time, anticipating the gangsta subgenre with hard-hitting social commentary regarding ghetto life.

Unfortunately, Flash's career went downhill from there due to group infighting—Melle Mel, Scorpio, and Cowboy left in late 1983 to form a new version of The Furious Five—and cocaine addiction. Despite a legal victory over Melle Mel to use the group name, Flash's recordings in the mid-1980s—most notably, "Sign of the Times" (Elektra 69677; 1985; #55 r&b), "Girls Love the Way He Spins" (Elektra 69643; 1985; #54 r&b), "Style (Peter Gunn Theme)" (Elektra 69552; 1986; #54 r&b), and "U Know What Time It Is" (Elektra 69490; 1987; #57 r&b)—represented a less revelatory brand of electro-hip hop which failed to cross over to the pop charts. With his approach rendered increasingly dated by the rise of such hard-edged rappers as Public Enemy, Eric B, and KRS-One, Flash—despite a reunion with Melle Mel for a charity concert in 1987—faded into obscurity.

November 13. Eddy Grant—a former member of the Equals—heads up the British charts with "I Don't Wanna Dance."

November 13. Men at Work begin a thirteen-week run atop the album charts with *Business as Usual* (Columbia). It will go on to sell more than five million copies stateside.

November 27. Lionel Richie ascends to the summit of the pop charts with his own composition, "Truly" (Motown), remaining there for two weeks.

December 1. Michael Jackson's *Thriller* is released. It will become the biggest-selling pop album ever, with sales of more than twenty-five million (it will be overtaken in the twenty-first century by the Engles' *Greatest Hits*).

December 11. Toni Basil reaches number one with the Mike Chapman/Nicky Chinn composition, "Mickey" (Chrysalis). Basil, a veteran choreographer/actress (whose roles included a supporting role in the landmark cult film, *Easy Rider*), further assisted the single by putting together a memorable promotional video which depicted her in a series of cheerleading skits.

December 18. Daryl Hall and John Oates begin a four-week stay atop the Hot 100 with "Maneater" (RCA).

December 25. Soft Cell's "Tainted Love"/"Where Did Our Love Go" remains on the *Billboard* Hot 100 for forty-three weeks, then the longest-charting single of the rock era.

December 29. Jamaica issues a set of commemorative stamps honoring Bob Marley.

1983

✳

1983. The Nashville Network premieres on cable television.

January 5. Everything But the Girl—whose name was inspired by a used furniture store in Hull, U.K.—debuts live at London's ICA.

January 15. "The Girl Is Mine" (Epic 03288), a Michael Jackson/Pal McCartney duet, begins a three-week stay atop the R&B charts (#2 pop). It was written by Jackson, with McCartney in mind, to repay him for contributing "Girlfriend" to the *Off the Wall* LP. While it remains McCartney's only R&B chart-topper, he was the co-writer (with fellow Beatle, John Lennon) of another #1 R&B single, Earth, Wind & Fire's "Got to Get You Into My Life." Jackson would recall the circumstances surrounding its release:

> [Producer] Quincy [Jones] and I eventually chose 'The Girl Is Mine' as the obvious first single from *Thriller*. We really didn't have much choice. When you have two strong names like that together on a song, it has to come out first or it gets played to death and overexposed. We had to get it out of the way. (White and Bronson, 1991)

January 15. Men at Work's "Down Under" (Columbia)—already a U.K. chart topper—goes number one on the Hot 100, remaining there for four non-consecutive weeks.

January 22. MTV, the pioneering twenty-four-hour music video network, begins broadcasting to the West Coast after being added by Group W Cable in Los Angeles.

January 28. Billy Fury dies of heart failure. He had twenty-six Top 40 singles in the U.K.

January 29. Men at Work achieve the number one position simultaneously on the American and British singles and album charts with "Down Under" and *Business As Usual* (Columbia). The last artist to accomplish this feat was Rod Stewart in 1971.

February 4. Karen Carpenter, age thirty-two, dies of cardiac arrest complicated by anorexia nervosa at her parent's home.

February 5. Def Leppard begins a ninety-two-week run in the LP charts with *Pyromania*. Although never reaching number one, it sells more than six million units in the United States alone.

February 5. The Gap Band's "Outstanding" (Total Experience 8205) reaches number one on the R&B survey. Although the band's drummer, Raymond Calhoun, first conceived of the song while enjoying the company of his one-year-old daughter, it was adapted—at the suggestion of producer Lonnie Simmons—to address a grown woman. The engineer for the session, Rudy Taylor, noted one particular feature behind the record's appeal:

> Lonnie likes to play percussion. He had this little off-beat he was playing. We worked on that and it really paid off. I was talking to Ice Cube. He said that was his favorite part in the whole record, that little percussion thing. And he said that's what makes it happen for them now, for the rappers. I think like eight rap groups have redone 'Outstanding.' It's still got that flavor ten years later, so it must be happening. (White and Bronson, 1991)

February 5. Michael Jackson's second single from *Thriller*, "Billie Jean" (Epic 03509), starts a nine-week run as the number one R&B record. At the time, a debate raged over the true meaning of the lyrics. Jackson would later comment in his autobiography, *Moonwalk*,

> A lot of people have asked me about that song, and the answer is very simple. It's just a case of a girl who says that I'm the father of her child and I'm pleading innocence because "the kid is not my son." There never was a real "Billie Jean" (except the ones who came after the song). The girl in the song is a composite of people we've been plagued by over the years. This kind of thing has happened to some of my brothers and I used to be really amazed by it. I couldn't understand how these girls could say they were carrying someone's child when it wasn't true. (White and Bronson, 1991)

February 5. Toto tops the Hot 100 with the production tour de force, "Africa" (#3 U.K.).

February 19. Patti Austin and James Ingram reach number one on the pop charts with "Baby Come to Me" (Qwest; #11 U.K.), remaining there for two weeks.

March 2. Philips, Polygram, and Sony begin producing compact disc players and software. CDs—mostly imports—appear in retail outlets in small numbers.

March 5. Michael Jackson's "Billie Jean" begins a seven-week run atop the Hot 100.

March 12. Bonnie Tyler heads up the British charts for the only time in her career with "Total Eclipse of the Heart."

March 12. U2 enjoy their first number one LP in Great Britain with *War*, which would spend 147 weeks on the charts.

March 13. Motown's twenty-fifth anniversary show—featuring many original Motown artists—is taped at the Pasadena (California) City Auditorium. The event—which included Michael Jackson's famous moonwalk in the first public performance of "Billie Jean"—would be broadcast as a TV special, and later released in the video format.

March 14. Jon Bon Jovi, Richie Sambora, and Alec John Such form Bon Jovi.

March 17. The ARMS Concert—also known as the Ronnie Lane Appeal for Action for Research into Multiple Sclerosis—is held at London's Royal Albert Hall. The show—organized by former Small Faces guitarist Lane, who was suffering from the disease—featured Jeff Beck, Eric Clapton, Jimmy Page, Charlie Watts, Steve Winwood, Bill Wyman. It would be released on video the following year by Music Media.

March 26. Duran Duran head up the British charts for the first time with "Is There Something I Should Know?" At the time, the group is in the midst of the U.S. promotional trip.

April 5. Danny Rapp—leader of the doo-wop group, Danny and the Juniors—shoots himself to death.

April 9. David Bowie tops the British charts with "Let's Dance."

April 9. DeBarge peak at number thirty on the Hot 100 with "I Like It" (Gordy 1645).

One of the major teen groups of the 1980s, the group was on the verge of becoming a major pop phenomenon when lead singer Eldra (El) DeBarge opted for a solo career. Formed in 1978, the Grand Rapids, Michigan-based family group—consisting of a sister, Bunny, and three other brothers, James, Mark, and Randy—were signed the following year by Motown, who marketed them as the next Jackson Five.

Their debut album, *DeBarges* (Motown; 1981), did not set the world on fire; however, "I Like It," released in late 1982, became a best-seller both on the R&B and pop charts. From this point onward, DeBarge became an unstoppable force, producing one hit after another, including "All This Love" (Motown; 1983); "Time Will Reveal" (Motown; 1983); "Rhythm of the Night" (Motown; 1985; #3), from the film, *The Last Dragon*, in which they appeared; and "Who's Holding Donna Now?" (Motown; 1985).

Bunny chose to remain with Motown when the remaining three DeBarge brothers signed to Striped Horse Records in 1987. The final blow to the group's declining fortunes came when their other brothers, Chico and Bobby DeBarge, were arrested and convicted on cocaine trafficking charges in 1988.

April 16. George Clinton's "Atomic Dog" (Capitol 5201) begins a four-week run atop the R&B charts. A prime example of the increasing fragmentation of radio playlists, the single fails to make the Hot 100.

April 16. Bonnie Tyler tops the British charts with *Faster Than the Speed of Light*.

April 17. Felix Pappalardi, then age forty-three, is fatally shot by his wife during a jealous rage. He played bass for the hard rock band, Mountain, and produced the Cream albums, *Disraeli Gears* and *Wheels of Fire*.

April 23. Dexy's Midnight Runners peak at number one on the pop charts with "Come on Eileen" (Mercury).

April 30. Michael Jackson returns to the top of the Hot 100 after only a week's absence with "Beat It" (Epic 03759), remaining there for three weeks. The track is notable for Eddie Van Halen's scorching guitar solo and Jackson's tour de force dance sequence in the accompanying promotional video.

April 30. Bluesman Muddy Waters dies at age sixty-eight. His more notable compositions included "Got My

Mojo Working," "I Just Want to Make Love to You" (an early Rolling Stones hit), "I'm Your Hoochie Coochie Man," and "You Need Love" (reworked—without assigning credit—by Led Zeppelin as "Whole Lotta Love").

May 5. The Stranglers' "Golden Brown" is named the most performed work of 1982 at the twenty-eighth Ivor Novello Awards.

May 7. Aerosmith enters the album charts at number one with *Get a Grip*.

May 7. Mark Knopfler receives an honorary music doctorate from the University of Newcastle-upon-Tyne, England.

May 7. Paul Weller introduces his new group, Style Council, at an anti-nuclear benefit concert in London.

May 12. AOR heavyweight Meat Loaf files for bankruptcy with debts of more than $1 million.

May 14. New Edition's "Candy Girl" (Streetwise 1108) reaches number one on the R&B charts.

May 14. Spandau Ballet top the British album charts with *True*.

May 14. U2 peak at number fifty-three on the Hot 100 with "New Year's Day" (Island 99915).

Undeniably the most consistently popular rock band of the postpunk era, U2—much like the Beatles and other classic 1960s artists—have remained committed to musical experimentation. As a result, they defy easy categorization; radio formats embracing their recordings include AOR, Modern Rock (alternative), Adult Contemporary (easy listening), and Contemporary Hits Radio (Top 40).

Formed in Dublin, Ireland, in 1977, the band—consisting of vocalist Bono Vox (real name: Paul Hewson), guitarist/keyboardist The Edge (real name: David Evans), bassist Adam Clayton, and drummer Larry Mullen—produced a couple of successful recordings for the Irish market, the EP *U2: Three* (CBS 7951; 1979) and colored (both yellow and orange versions) single "Another Day" (CBS 8306; 1980), which led to an Island contract featuring international distribution. Their debut album, *Boy* (Island 9646; 1980; #63), produced by the highly regarded Steve Lillywhite, received extensive praise from the rock press. The follow-up LP, *October* (Island 9680; 1981) further refined the group's strikingly original formula: politically-charged lyrics passionately delivered by Bono, accented by The Edge's jagged guitar riffing, and anchored by an economically driving rhythm section.

U2 appeared destined to remain a cult favorite until the release of *War* (Island 90067; 1983; #12), aided by the extensive MTV rotation of the videos for "New Year's Day," composed in tribute to Lech Walenska's Polish Solidarity Union, the martially stirring "Sunday Bloody Sunday," and "Two Hearts Beat As One" (Island 99861; 1983). After creatively treading water with the dynamic in concert outing, *Under A Blood Red Sky* (Island 90127; 1983; #28), *The Unforgettable Fire* (Island 90231; 1984; #12), featuring Brian Eno's ambient-tinged production work, elevated the band into the superstar ranks. Another stopgap release, the partially live mini-LP *Wide Awake in America* (Island 90279; 1985; #37), was followed by arguably one of the greatest rock albums ever, *The Joshua Tree* (Island 90581; 1987; #1). Highlighted by the singles "With or Without You" (Island 99469; 1987; #1), "I Still Haven't Found What I'm Looking For" (Island 99430; 1987; #1), and "Where the Streets Have No Name" (Island 99408; 1987; #13), the work deftly ran the gamut of emotions, from exultant anthems to spiritual introspection. *Rattle and Hum* (Island 91003; 1988; #1)—the live/studio hybrid soundtrack to a rockumentary of the same name—was a commercial hit, although panned by many critics for failing to break new artistic ground.

U2 responded by incorporating pronounced dance elements into both *Achtung Baby* (Island 10347; 1991; #1) and *Zooropa* (Island 518047; 1993; #1). Following an interlude devoted to the composition and recording of film music—most notably the single from *Batman Forever*, "Hold Me, Thrill Me, Kiss Me, Kill Me" (Island 87131; 1995; #16)—the band's obsession with kitschy mainstream music culminated with the uneven *Pop* (Island 210; 1997; #1). Recent years have revealed U2 to be in a holding pattern, releasing occasional singles, remixes, and compilations amidst various collaborations with other artists.

May 21. David Bowie climbs to the summit of the pop charts with "Let's Dance" (EMI America).

May 21. Michael Jackson's "Beat It" goes number one on the R&B charts.

May 21. The Smiths head up the U.K. independent charts with their debut release, "Hand in Glove."

May 28. Irene Cara begins a six-week run atop the Hot 100 with "Flashdance...What a Feeling" (Casablanca). The song is aided immeasurably by its placement in the soundtrack to the hit film, *Flashdance*.

May 28. Gladys Knight & the Pips head up the R&B charts with "Save the Overtime (For Me)" (Columbia 03761).

June 4. Mtume begin an eight-week stay atop the R&B charts with "Juicy Fruit" (Epic 03578).

June 25. New Edition peaks at number forty-six on the Hot 100 with "Candy Girl" (Streetwise 1108).

> While New Edition had a relatively short run as a hit-making entity, the vocal quintet nurtured some of the leading rhythm and blues artists of the 1990s. The group's original members—Bobby Brown, Ralph Tresvant, Ricky Bell, Michael Bivins, and Ronnie DeVoe—met in the early 1980s as junior high school students in Boston's Roxbury district. Promoter Maurice Starr, who discovered them performing at a local talent show, secured them a recording contract with the hip-hop label, Streetwise. Following the release of two Top 10 R&B singles—"Candy Girl" and "Is This the End" (Streetwise 1111; 1983), New Edition parted ways with Starr (who would form New Kids on the Block) and signed with MCA Records. Their next album, *New Edition* (MCA 5515; 1984) crossed over to number six on the *Billboard Hot 100*, propelled by the hit singles, "Cool It Now" (MCA 52455; 1984) and "Mr. Telephone Man" (MCA 52484; 1984-1985). Succeeding albums—*All For Love* (MCA 5679; 1985), *Under the Blue Moon* (MCA 5912. 1986), and *Heart Break* (MCA 42207; 1988)—enjoyed moderate success, but the group's singles did not perform well on the pop charts.
>
> New Edition was ultimately torn apart by the loss of key personnel to solo careers, beginning with Brown in 1986. His replacement, Johnny Gill, also struck out on his own in the late 1980s, as did Tresvant. In 1988, the remaining members formed the hip-hop trio, Bell Biv DeVoe. The group members have remained close, however, often working together in the 1990s as well as considering the possibility of reuniting to produce an album.

July 9. The Police reach number one on the pop charts with "Every Breath You Take" (A&M), remaining there for eight weeks.

July 30. Donna Summer starts a three-week stint atop the R&B charts with "She Works Hard for the Money" (Mercury 812 370).

August 13. R.E.M. peak at number seventy-eight on the Hot 100 with "Radio Free Europe" (I.R.S. 9916).

> No American rock band has created a greater body of recorded work since 1980 than R.E.M. Although considered a guiding force in the "indie rock" movement, the group's jangly guitar-driven sound owed much to the Byrds and other mid-1960s folk rock artists.
>
> The band members—lead singer Michael Stipe, guitarist Peter Buck, bassist/keyboardist Mike Mills, and drummer Bill Berry—initially performed together as the Twisted Kites in spring 1980 at an Athens, Georgia party. Their debut single, "Radio Free Europe" (Hib-Tone 0001; 1981; reissued on I.R.S. 9916; 1983; #78), produced by Mitch Easter, attracted the attention of I.R.S. head, Miles Copeland, who signed them to a long-term contract. The next release, the mini-LP, the Easter-produced *Chronic Town* (I.R.S. 70502; 1982), received widespread praise from the rock press. The debut album, *Murmur* (I.R.S. 70604; 1983; #36), co-produced by Easter and Don Dixon, continued to highlight Buck's chiming guitar and Stipe's laconic vocals. While follow-up releases—*Reckoning* (I.R.S. 70044; 1984; #27), *Fables of the Reconstruction – Reconstruction of the Fables* (I.R.S. 5592; 1985; #28), and *Life's Rich Pageant* (I.R.S. 5783; 1986; #21)—did not veer appreciably from this formula, R.E.M.'s melodic invention and intelligent, albeit often obscure, song lyrics attracted an increasingly larger audience.
>
> *Document* (I.R.S. 42059; 1987; #10), driven by the band's first Top 40 single, the moody "The One I Love" (I.R.S. 53171; 1987; #9), and *Green* (Warner Bros. 25795-2; 1988; #12), which contained the uncharacteristically humorous single, "Stand" (Warner Bros. 27688; 1989; #6), lifted R.E.M. into the commercial mainstream. Exhibiting a penchant for subtle, insightful, yet catchy, material, they were able to accomplish this without losing their cult following. A nonstop touring schedule, combined with the marketing muscle of a major label, helped push the next album, *Out Of Time* (Warner Bros. 26496-2; 1991; platinum record), to the top of the charts. It also included a couple of best-selling singles, the plaintive dirge, "Losing

My Religion" (Warner Bros. 19392; 1991; #4), and unflinchingly upbeat "Shiny Happy People" (Warner Bros. 19242; 1991; #10). Now comfortably established as an American institution, the band produced yet another bittersweet masterpiece, *Automatic For the People* (Warner Bros. 45055; 1992; #2). Their patented idiosyncratic approach notwithstanding, *Monster* (Warner Bros. 45740; 1994; #1) revealed pronounced grunge influences. *New Adventures in Hi-Fi* (Warner Bros. 46320; 1996; #2) hailed a return to the group's classic 1980s sound, while *Up* (Warner Bros. 47112; 1998; #3) sold well despite its unrelentingly down-beat tone. With Berry having departed the band in the mid-1990s due to health problems and the other members active in side projects, the future of R.E.M. as an active recording and performing unit is very much in doubt.

August 20. Aretha Franklin's "Get It Right" (Arista 9043) peaks at number one on the R&B charts, remaining there for a fortnight.

September 3. Eurythmics head up the Hot 100 with "Sweet Dreams (Are Made of This)" (RCA).

September 3. Rick James begins a six-week run atop the R&B charts with "Cold Blooded" (Gordy 1687).

September 3. UB40 ascend to the summit of the British charts with a cover of the Neil Diamond song, "Red Red Wine."

September 10. Michael Sembello hits number one the pop charts with "Maniac" (Casablanca), remaining there for a two weeks. It is the second track from the *Flashdance* soundtrack to accomplish this feat.

September 20. The Talking Heads earn a gold record for *Speaking in Tongues* (Sire 23883). The album will be certified platinum on December 15, 1986.

One of the leading artists spearheading the New Wave movement of the late 1970s, the Talking Heads were instrumental in bringing an intellectual, art-rock sensibility to a genre initially built around the brash, stripped-down energy of punk. Like the more incendiary punk bands, however, they stood in opposition—both in their edgy, eccentric musical arrangements and wry song lyrics—to the corporate rock establishment then dominated by pompous AOR artists such as Foreigner, Journey, and the Doobie Brothers.

Formed May 1975 by vocalist/guitarist David Byrne, vocalist/bassist Tina Weymouth, and drummer Chris Frantz in Manhattan, the Talking Heads were shortly thereafter signed by Sire Records head, Seymour Stein, who'd seen them performing at the legendary Bowery club, CGBG's. Following an unsuccessful single release and the addition of guiatrist/keyboardist Jerry Harrison, the band's debut album, *Talking Heads '77* (Sire 6306; 1977; #97), has heralded as one of the first masterpieces of the newly emerging punk revolution. The next LP, *More Songs About Buildings and Food*, produced by avant-garde artist, Brian Eno, moved the group closer to the commercial mainstream largely due to a funky rhythmic underpinning and Byrne's soulful, albeit idiosyncratic, vocals. Never content to merely tread water, their *Fear of Music* (Sire 6076; 1979; #21), again produced by Eno, featured Third World beats and instrumentation.

The Talking Heads reached a creative apex with *Remain In Light* (Sire 6095; 1980; #19), blending punk energy with African polyrhythms and funk phrasing with the assistance of an augmented band featuring Adrian Belew on lead guitar. Sales were considerably enhanced by the MTV-driven success of the single, "Once in a Lifetime" (Sire 40649; 1981; #14 UK). Following a three-year hiatus from the studio—during which Frantz and Weymouth formed the alternative dance group, the Tom Tom Club, while Byrne explored ethnic music with Eno and composed a stage score, *Songs From "The Catherine Wheel"* (Sire 3645; 1981)—the Talking Heads released *Speaking in Tongues* (Sire 23883; 1983; #15), which included their biggest single, "Burning Down the House" (Sire 29565; 1983; #9). *Stop Making Sense* (Sire 25121; 1984; #41) featured music from a strikingly innovative concert movie directed by Jonathon Demme.

Later works—*Little Creatures* (Sire 25035; 1985; #20), something of a return to the band's stylistic roots; *True Stories* (Sire 25512; 1986; #17), an uneven soundtrack to a Byrne-produced film; and *Naked* (Sire 26654; 1988; #19), an LP long on production values and short on quality song material—suffered from a seeming lack of commitment. Byrne would continue to explore various avant-pop directions, often drawing on international music styles for inspiration. Although an official announcement was not forthcoming until 1991, individual members had long since gone on to solo projects. Harrison, Frantz and Weymouth would regroup as the Heads in 1996, releasing one album, *No Talking, Just Head* (MCA 11504), built around the contributions of alternative rock stars such as Richard Hell, ex-Blondie Debbie Harry, INXS frontman Michael Hutchence, XTC's Andy Partridge, and Concrete Blonde's Johnette Napolitano.

September 24. Billy Joel reaches number one on the Hot 100 with the retro-styled "Tell Her About It" (Columbia).

October 1. Bonnie Tyler begins a four-week run atop the pop charts with "Total Eclipse of the Heart" (Columbia).

October 8. Herbie Hancock peaks at number seventy-one on the Hot 100 with the million-selling instrumental, "Rockit" (Columbia 04054). The track's popularity was helped immeasurably by a state-of-the-art video clip, which received heavy rotation play on MTV.

Herbie Hancock is one of the seminal jazz figures of the second half of the twentieth century. But while his technical proficiency as a keyboard player and composing skills are of the highest order, he is best known as a jazz innovator, experimenting with synthesizers and electronic music in general. Furthermore, he has helped broaden the fusion movement, incorporating a wide range of pop, rock, funk, and classical music elements within a jazz framework.

Born in Chicago, Hancock studied both classical and jazz music Grinnell College (Iowa) before joining Donald Byrd's band as pianist in 1960. His debut solo LP, *Takin' Off* (Blue Note 4109; 1962) demonstrated his already well-developed songwriting talents; one of his pieces, "Watermelon Man" (Blue Note 1862; 1962), would be covered by many other musicians. Other successful releases would include *Inventions and Dimensions* (Blue Note 4147; 1963), *Empyrean Isles* (Blue Note 4175; 1964), and *Maiden Voyage* (Blue Note 4195; 1965).

Hancock became a member of Miles Davis' group in 1963; during his five-year stay, Davis encouraged him to play an electric piano. The results of this experiment—*Miles in the Sky* (Columbia 9628; 1968), *Filles de Kilimanjaro* (Columbia 9750; 1969), and the elegiac masterpiece, *In a Silent Way* (Columbia 9875; 1969)—defined the jazz-rock movement of the 1970s. During this period, he also contributed session work to other artists' recordings, made television commercials, and scored his first film, Michelangelo Antonioni's *Blow Up* (MGM 4447; 1966; soundtrack).

Hancock continued to refine his electronic arrangements in the years immediately after leaving Davis; one release, *Mwandishi* (Warner Bros. 1898; 1971), was designated one of then best albums of the year by *Time* magazine. With *Head Hunters* (Columbia 32731; 1973; #13), he employed synthesizers for the first time; its platinum sales inaugurated a wholesale trend within the jazz scene. As a host of jazz-inflected techno-funk LPs flooded the marketplace, Hancock took on new challenges; utilizing a Vocoder voice synthesizer in his first recorded vocals for *Sunlight* (Columbia 34907; 1978; #58), and incorporating disco-oriented rhythms in *Feets Don't Fail Me Now* (Columbia 35764; 1979; #38).

The 1980s found Hancock divided between genre-bending experiments—most notably, *Future Shock* (Columbia 38814; 1983), which included the Grammy-winning (Best R&B Instrumental Performance) "Rockit"—more traditional jazz fare featuring the V.S.O.P. Quintet, the Herbie Hancock Quartet, and collaborations with Chick Corea and Oscar Peterson. Further honors included a 1983 Best R&B Instrumental Performance Grammy for *Sound System* (Columbia 39478; #71), a 1987 Best Instrumental Performance Grammy for "Call Sheet Blues," and an Oscar for Best Original Score on the movie *'Round Midnight* (Columbia 40464; 1986; soundtrack).

Hancock's 1990 recordings were uneven at best. *Dis Is Da Drum* (Mercury 528185; 1995) represented a failed attempted at harnessing hip-hop within a fusion context, while his efforts to provide timeless settings for the music of the Beatles, Peter Gabriel, Prince, and others in *The New Standard* (Verve 527715; 1996) comes across as both sterile and pompous. His best recordings from this period have been the countless reissues and retrospectives put out by Blue Note, Columbia, Warner Bros., and various smaller labels.

October 8. The S.O.S. Band peaks at number fifty-five on the Hot 100 with "Just Be Good to Me" (Tabu 03955), the first hit to feature the Jam/Lewis production team.

Minneapolis native Jimmy Jam (James Harris III) and Terry Lewis, born in Omaha, first gained attention as members of The Time, headed by Morris Day. Following the release of the group's debut funk-punk LP, *The Time* (Warner Bros. 3598; 1981; #50; gold record), produced by Prince, Jam and Lewis formed Flyte Time Productions. Their first success as producer-arrangers came with tracks from the S.O.S. Band's *On the Rise* (Tabu 38697; 1983; #471983), most notably the hit "Just Be Good To Me" (Tabu 03955; 1983; 1983; #2 R&B, #55 pop).

Fired from The Time by Prince, Jam and Lewis achieved further success in the mid-1980s working with R&B artists such as Patti Austin, Thelma Houston, Gladys Knight, and Klymaxx. Their trademark sound—richly scored yet streamlined, street-smart yet sophisticated—attracted the handlers of the then relatively unknown Janet Jackson. The collaboration yielded a long string of successes, including *Control* (A&M 5106; 1986; #1; five million + sales), which earned the duo a Grammy as Producers of the Year, *Rhythm Nation 1814* (A&M 3920; 1989; #1; six million + sales), *Janet* (A&M; 1993), and *The Velvet Rope* (A&M; 1997).

Now in great demand, Jam and Lewis also worked on the Human League's "Human" (A&M 2861; 1986; #3 R&B, #1 pop), Force M.D.'s "Tender Love" (Warner Bros. 28818; 1985; #4 R&B, #10 pop), Herb Alpert's "Keep Your Eye on Me" (A&M 2915; 1987; #3 R&B, #46 pop; vocals by Lewis and Lisa Keith). The New Edition's *Heart Break* (MCA 42207; 1988; #12; platinum record), Johnny Gill's eponymous debut album (Motown 6283; 1990; #8; platinum record), Ralph Tresvant's *Ralph Tresvant* (MCA 10116; 1990; #17; platinum record), and Karyn White's *Ritual of Love* (Warner Bros. 26320; 1991; #53; gold record). In 1991, they founded the A&M-backed label, Perspective; its first release, The Sounds of Blackness' *The Evolution of Gospel* (Perspective 1000; 1991; #176), won a Grammy. The team continued to freelance, working in the 1990s with the likes of Michael Jackson, Boyz II Men, Mary J. Blige, and Vanessa Williams.

October 15. Rufus and Chaka Khan reside at number one on the R&B charts with "Ain't Nobody" (Warner Bros. 29555).

October 29. Kenny Rogers and Dolly Parton ascend to the summit of the Hot 100 with "Islands in the Stream" (RCA), remaining there for two weeks.

November 12. Lionel Richie begins a four-week stay atop the pop charts with the self-penned "All Night Long (All Night)" (Motown).

November 16. The Talking Heads earn a gold record for *More Songs About Buildings and Food* (Sire 6058; 1978; #29).

December 10. Paul McCartney and Michael Jackson begin a six-week run at number one on the Hot 100 with their joint composition, "Say Say Say" (Columbia).

December 28. Dennis Wilson drowns while swimming around his docked boat in the Los Angeles area. The only true surfer in the Beach Boys, he is given a burial at sea, an honor generally reserved for naval personnel.

1984

❄

1984. Michael Jackson is a seven-time winner at the eleventh annual American Music Awards TV show for his *Thriller* (Epic) LP.

January 1. Alexis Korner, a prime mover in the British R&B scene and founder of Blues Incorporated, dies.

January 13. BBC Radio 1 bans Frankie Goes to Hollywood's "Relax" on the heels of deejay Mike Read's accusation that it is obscene. Although BBC-TV follows suit, the single goes to number one, remaining on the British charts for forty-eight weeks.

January 14. Paul McCartney tops the British charts with "Pipes of Peace," making him the first recording artist go number one solo, in a duo (with Stevie Wonder), in a trio (with Wings), and in a group (with the Beatles).

January 21. Yes reach number one on the pop charts with "Owner of a Lonely Heart" (Atco 99817), remaining there for two weeks.

The group epitomized 1970s progressive rock, featuring meticulously crafted extended compositions, elaborate thematic concepts reinforced by Roger Dean's fantasy LP cover art, and virtuoso instrumental work. Plagued by constant personnel shifts, legal bickering, and a stylistically dated sound from the late 1970s onward, their legacy is based largely on the ambitious, albeit self-indulgent, early albums.

Formed in London in mid-1968, Yes—originally consisting of lead singer Jon Anderson, bassist Chris Squire, drummer Bill Bruford, guitarist Peter Banks, and keyboardist Tony Kaye—signed with Atlantic, releasing a workmanlike eponymous debut (Atlantic 8243; 1969) and follow-up, *Time And A Word* (Atlantic 8273; 1970; #45 UK) that only hinted at the more baroque efforts to come. With the addition of innovative guitarist Steve Howe (replacing Banks, who helped form the jam band Flash) for *The Yes Album* (Atlantic 8283; 1971; #40 US, #7 UK) and keyboardist Rick Wakeman (following the departure of Kaye) prior to the release of *Fragile* (Atlantic 7211; 1971; #4 US, #7 UK), the group's signature sound—the rich, swirling instrumental interplay punctuated by Anderson's high-pitched vocals—reached fruition. The band's commercial breakthrough was assisted by the extensive radio play of the U.S. single "Roundabout/Long Distance Runaround" (Atlantic 2854; 1972; #13), culled from the latter LP.

Yes hit its creative peak with *Close To The Edge* (Atlantic 7244; 1972; #3 US, #4 UK), featuring the atmospheric title track (which comprised all of side A); the sprawling three-disc live set, *Yessongs* (Atlantic 100; 1973; #12 US, #1 UK), which now included drummer Alan White; the conceptual double album, *Tales From Topographic Oceans* (Atlantic 2908; 1973; #6 US, #1 UK), widely criticized for the allegedly aimless improvising of its extended pieces; and impressionistic *Relayer* (Atlantic 18122; 1974; #5 US, #4 UK), built around the multi-tracked synthesizer lines contributed by Patrick Moraz, who had been recruited when Wakeman left for a solo career.

Followed a hiatus in which group members worked on solo albums, Wakeman returned for the stripped-down *Going For The One* (Atlantic 19106; 1977; #8 US, #1 UK), released at the height of the British punk revolution. *Tormato* (Atlantic 19202; 1978) and *Drama* (Atlantic 16109; 1980; #18 US, #2 UK)—the latter featuring two ex-Buggles members, vocalist Trevor Horn and keyboardist Geoff Downes, who replaced Anderson and Wakeman, respectively—revealed the band to be at a creative impasse. Yes revamped their lineup in 1983, adding South African guitarist/songwriter Trevor Rabin to the core of Anderson, Kaye, Squire, and White. The resulting release, *90125* (Atco 90125; 1983; #5 US, #16 UK), was a major hit with the MTV generation, driven by the chart-topping single, "Owner of a Lonely Heart" (#28 UK).

Yes split into two camps during the late 1980s, one including Squire, White, Kaye, and Rabin, the other consisting of Anderson, Bruford, Wakeman, and Howe. The Squire faction won rights to the name in 1989, requiring the latter combination to release an album under the moniker *Anderson, Bruford, Wakeman, Howe* (Arista 90126; #30 US, #14 UK). The two groups went on to settle their differences, combining forces to release the moribund *Union* (Arista 8643; 1991; #15 US, #7 UK). The subsequent works, featuring a rotating cast of musicians, reveal Yes to be creatively bankrupt entity content to trade on past glories.

January 21. Jackie Wilson—who'd been largely incapacitated since suffering a heart attack during a 1975 performance—dies. Ono of the most dynamic R&B singers of the post-World War II era, he was immortalized in the Van Morrison composition, "Jackie Wilson Said."

January 25. Yoko Ono donates $425,000 to the Liverpool home for aged, Strawberry Fields, immortalized in the 1967 Beatles song.

January 26. Michael Jackson is hospitalized with scalp burns as a result of a flare explosion while shooting a Pepsi commercial. A bodyguard for the Jacksons—Marlon Brando's son, Miko—gets to Jackson first to put out the fire.

January 27. Madonna appears in England for the first time, performing "Holiday" on the TV program, *The Tube*, broadcast live from Manchester's Hacienda Club.

January 28. Frankie Goes to Hollywood begins a five-week stay atop the British charts with "Relax." *Top of the Pops* can't feature the recording due to a BBC ban.

February 4. Culture Club commences a three-week stint atop the Hot 100 with "Karma Chameleon" (Virgin/Epic; #1 U.K.), their fifth Top 10 stateside hit.

February 14. Elton John marries German studio engineer, Renate Blauer, in Darling Point, Sydney, Australia.

February 16. *Rolling Stone* pictures the Beatles—in a July 1964 pose taken in London—on its cover with the caption "Special Beatles Anniversary Issue."

February 18. Simple Minds top the British album charts with *Sparkle in the Rain*.

February 18. Ricky Skaggs reaches number one on the country charts with "Don't Cheat in Our Hometown" (Sugar Hill 04245).

February 21. Michael Jackson is a double winner—Best British Album (for *Thriller*) and Best International Solo Artist—at the third annual BRIT Awards, held at London's Grosvenor House.

February 25. The Thompson Twins top the British album charts with *Into the Gap*.

February 25. Van Halen begin a five-week run atop the Hot 100 with "Jump" (#7 U.K.).

February 25. Don Williams heads up the country charts with "Stay Young" (MCA 52310).

February 28. Michael Jackson is awarded a record eight Grammys (surpassing Roger Miller's six wins in 1965) for *Thriller* at the twenty-sixth annual edition of the National Academy of Recording Arts and Sciences extravaganza. His trophies include Record of the Year and Best Pop Vocal Performance, Male for "Beat It"; Album of the Year and Best Pop Vocal Performance, Male for *Thriller*; Best R&B Vocal Performance, Male and Best New R&B Song for "Billie Jean"; Best Recording for Children for *E.T. the Extra-Terrestrial*; and Producer of the Year (Non-Classical), shared with Quincy Jones. Chaka Khan also makes a strong showing, winning Best R&B Vocal Performance, Female (*Chaka Khan*); Best R&B Performance by a Duo or Group with Vocal ("Ain't Nobody," w/Rufus); and Best Vocal Arrangement for Two or More Voices ("Be Bop Medley," w/Arif Mardin).

March 3. Exile peak at number one on the country charts with "Woke Up in Love" (Epic 04247).

March 3. The German group, Nena, top the British singles charts with "99 Red Balloons."

March 10. Lee Greenwood goes to the summit of the country charts with "Going Going Gone" (MCA 52322).

March 17. The Statler Brothers top the country charts with "Elizabeth" (814 881).

March 24. Alabama's "Roll On (Eighteen Wheeler)" (RCA 13716) reaches number one on the country charts. In January, the band's *Roll On* LP had become the first Nashville album "shipped platinum."

March 24. Lionel Richie heads up the British charts with "Hello."

March 27. Metallica perform in Great Britain for the first time at London's Marquee.

March 31. Janie Fricke tops the country chart with "Let's Stop Talkin' About It" (Columbia 04317).

March 31. Kenny Loggins begins a three-week stay at number one on the pop charts with "Footloose" (Columbia).

April 1. Marvin Gaye is fatally shot by his father during an argument at his parents' Los Angeles home. The singer's father would later be sentenced a five years for voluntary manslaughter.

April 5. Cyndi Lauper's "Girls Just Want To Have Fun" video clip named the Best Female Video at the second annual American Video Awards.

April 7. Forty British acts occupy the Hot 100, a record number up to that point in time.

April 7. Earl Thomas Conley's "Don't Make It Easy For Me" (RCA 13702) heads up the country charts.

April 14. The Kendalls reach number one on the country charts with "Thank God for the Radio" (Mercury 818 056).

April 17. Elton John kicks off a forty-four-date European tour in Sarajevo, Yugoslavia. It will end June 30, at London's Wembley Stadium.

April 21. Phil Collins begins a three-week stint atop the Hot 100 with "Against All Odds (Take a Look at Me Now)" (Atlantic). It is the theme song to the hit film starring Rachel Ward.

April 21. The film soundtrack to *Footloose* heads up the album charts.

April 21. Johnny Lee with Lane Brody peak at number one on the country charts with "The Yellow Rose" (Warner Bros. 29375), the theme song to a new NBC prime-time soap, *The Yellow Rose*.

April 24. R.E.M. begin their first British tour at Birmingham's Tin Can Club.

April 26. Mike McCartney unveils a $64,000 statue of the Beatles, created by John Doubleday, at the Cavern Walks Shopping Centre in Liverpool, England.

April 26. Count Basie dies, ending a career of some fifty years as a bandleader.

April 27. With the singer dominating the pop music scene, Philadelphia radio station WWSH holds a "No Michael Jackson" weekend.

April 28. George Strait tops the country charts with "Right or Wrong" (MCA 52337).

May 1. Fleetwood Mac drummer Mick Fleetwood files for bankruptcy.

May 5. Jim Kerr, lead vocalist for Simple Minds, marries Pretenders singer Chrissie Hynde in a horse drawn carriage at Central Park, Manhattan.

May 5. The Oak Ridge Boys head up the country charts with "I Guess It Never Hurts to Hurt Sometimes" (MCA 52342).

May 5. Lionel Richie's "Hello" (Motown 1722) starts a three-week run atop the R&B charts.

May 12. Julio Iglasias and Willie Nelson reach number one on the country charts with "To All the Girls I've Loved Before" (Columbia 04217), remaining there for two weeks.

May 12. Lionel Richie begins a two-week stint on the pop charts with "Hello."

May 19. Bob Marley and the Wailers reach number one on the British charts with the album retrospective, *Legend*, remaining there for twelve weeks. It was released to commemorate the third anniversary of Marley's death.

May 26. John Conlee's "As Long as I'm Rockin' With You" (MCA 52351) peaks at number one on the country charts.

May 26. Deniece Williams begins a two-week stint atop the Hot 100 with "Let's Hear It for the Boy" (Columbia 04417).

May 26. Yarbrough & Peoples climb to the summit of the R&B charts with "Don't Waste Your Time" (Total Experience 2400).

June 2. Ricky Skaggs goes number one on the country charts with "Honey (Open That Door)" (Sugar Hill 04394).

June 2. Wham! head up the British charts with "Wake Me Up Before You Go-Go."

June 2. Deniece Williams starts a three-week run atop the R&B charts with "Let's Hear It for the Boy."

June 9. Merle Haggard reaches number one on the country charts with "Someday When Things Are Good" (Epic 04402).

June 9. Cyndi Lauper tops the pop charts with "Time After Time" (Portrait), remaining there for two weeks.

June 16. Madonna peaks at number ten on the Hot 100 with "Borderline" (Sire 29354).

> It is easy to dismiss Madonna's superstar status as the product of her considerable flair for self-promotion. Beyond her physical allure, seemingly never-ending repertoire of fashion statements, and effective career moves, Madonna's success owed much to the irresistible pull of her dance-oriented rock recordings. In her best music, the elements—somewhat pedestrian arrangements, synthesizer lines, and programmed drum beats; competent, though not particularly distinguished singing; and hook-laden, if not profound compositions—added up to much more impressive whole, with emphasis on personality—an ingredient best showcased via the video medium.
>
> Madonna burst into the public consciousness with the "Jellybean" Benitez-produced eponymous LP (Sire 23867; 1983; #8) which heralded the return of the disco ethic (sans that *outre* label) to the pop music scene. The follow-up, *Like A Virgin* (Sire 25157; 1984; #1)—produced by former Chic guitarist Nile Rodgers, and featuring the breakthrough hits, "Like A Virgin" (Sire 29210; 1984; #1) and "Material Girl" (Sire 29083; 1984; #2)—elevated her (at this juncture, in her Boy Toy manifestation) to iconic status. Her place in the pop culture pantheon now assured, she embarked upon a series of ambitious artistic statements—the eclectic tour de force, *True Blue* (Sire 25442; 1986; #1), best remembered for the anti-abortion plea in "Papa Don't Preach" (Sire 20492; 1986; #1); the remix collection, *U Can Dance* (Sire 25535; 1987; #14), featuring material first appearing on the three earlier albums); socially conscious *Like A Prayer* (Sire 25844; 1989; #1), and hits compilation, *The Immaculate Collection* (Sire 26440; 1990; #5), which included considerable studio editing of the originals (e.g., Q-sound remastering, faster tempos, earlier fade-outs, seguing of tracks)—punctuated by forays into film acting and book production.
>
> Madonna's recorded output (and the public reception) was more uneven in the 1990s. *Erotica* (Maverick 18782; 1992; #3) was a sensual, pulsating workout; its comparatively poor commercial showing seems to have influenced her decision to produce a more intimate, low-key LP, *Bedtime Stories* (Maverick 45767; 1994; #3). Following her success in the movie adaptation of Andrew Lloyd Webber's *Evita—Selections from Evita* (Warner Brothers; 1997) featured highlights from the original two-disc soundtrack—she attempted to update her sound by enlisting techno producer William Orbit for *Ray of Light* (Maverick 46847; 1998; #2). She perfected her electronica-inspired approach in *Music* (Maverick; 2000), darting effortlessly from club grooves to trip-hop and synth-based ambient textures. Newly committed to a more domestic lifestyle in the twenty-first century, it appears likely that her future recordings will continue to incorporate contemporary trends within a seamless, beat-inflected framework, and emphasize production values over the imaging making.

June 16. Eddy Raven's "I Got Mexico" (RCA 13746) peaks at number one on the country charts.

June 23. Alabama outpace the competition on the country charts with "When We Make Love" (RCA 13763).

June 23. Duran Duran begin a two-week stay at number one on the Hot 100 with "The Reflex" (Capitol).

June 23. O'Bryan heads up the R&B charts with "Lovelite" (Capitol 5329).

June 30. Huey Lewis & the News go number one on the album charts with *Sports*.

June 30. Prince's "When Doves Cry" (Warner Bros. 29286) begins an eight-week run atop the R&B charts.

July 6. The reunited Jacksons kick off their Victory Tour in Kansas City; it will end in Los Angeles on December 9.

July 7. Prince tops the pop charts with "When Doves Cry," remaining there for five weeks.

August 4. Phil Collins marries Jill Travelman.

August 11. Ray Parker Jr. begins a three-week run at number one on the Hot 100 with "Ghostbusters" (Arista 9212).

August 12. With the Los Angeles Olympics winding down, Lionel Richie performs "All Night Long."

August 25. Ray Parker Jr. tops the R&B charts for two weeks with "Ghostbusters."

August 30. *Rolling Stone* pictures Prince on its cover with the caption "Prince Scores: A Hit Album – A Hit Movie."

September 1. Tina Turner reaches the summit of the pop charts with "What's Love Got to Do With It" (Capitol), remaining there for three weeks.

September 4. MTV sponsors its inaugural video awards show at New York's Radio City Music Hall. It is directed by ex-10cc members Kevin Godley and Lol Crème, and hosted by Dan Aykroyd and Bette Midler. With Madonna, Rod Stewart, Tina Turner, and ZZ Top performing live, Herbie Hancock's "Rockit" video tops five different categories.

November. Michael Jackson attends the unveiling of his Hollywood star on the Walk of Fame, 6856 Hollywood Boulevard, Los Angeles.

September 22. John Waite goes number one with "Missing You" (EMI America).

September 29. Prince & the Revolution begin a two-week stint atop the Hot 100 with "Let's Go Crazy" (Warner Bros.).

October 6. Sheila E. peaks at number seven on the Hot 100 with "The Glamorous Life" (Warner 29285).

Although she has performed since age three, conga drummer/vocalist Sheila E. is best remembered for her slick video clips which were broadcast in heavy rotation at the height of the MTV fad. Born Sheila Escovedo, on December 12, 1959, in Oakland, California, she joined the Latin-jazz fusion band, Azteca (lead by her father, Pete "Coke" Escovedo), while still in her teens.

Her big break came when Prince enlisted her to sing on "Erotic City," the flip side of his chart-topper, "Let's Go Crazy" (1984). The resulting exposure led to a Warner Bros. contract; her resulting LP, *The Glamorous Life* (Warner Bros.; 1984), included the title single and the UK Top 20 hit, "The Belle of St. Mark" (Warner Bros.). The second album, *In Romance 1600* (Paisley Park; 1985), sold almost as well, driven by the single, "A Love Bizarre" (Paisley Park; 1985), with Prince supplying backing vocals. When her next LP, *Sheila E.* (Paisley Park; 1987), failed to catch on with the public, she enlisted as the drummer in Prince's touring band in addition to appearing in his concert film, *Sign O' the Times*. At an extended hiatus from solo recording, Sheila E. issued *Sex Cymbal* (WEA; 1991)—self-composed and produced with an assist from brother Peter Michael and David Gamson—but again met with widespread public indifference.

October 11. *Rolling Stone* pictures Tina Turner "in extasis"—leaping, hips forward, stiletto heels sharpened, fishnet-wrapped legs parted, her animated face communicating power and uninhibited desire—on its cover with the caption "Tina Turner: She's Got Legs!"

October 13. Stevie Wonder peaks at number one on the pop charts with "I Just Called to Say I Love You" (Motown 1745), remaining there for three weeks.

November 3. Billy Ocean's "European Queen"—retitled, at his manager's suggestion, as "Caribbean Queen (No More Love on the Run)"—begins a two-week stay atop the Hot 100 (Jive; #1 R&B, #1 Dance, #6 UK). It will be renamed and re-recorded as "African Queen" for import to that continent. The album from which it is culled, *Suddenly*, will peak at number nine in the U.K., on its way to earning a platinum disc.

With minimal media hype, Billy Ocean became one of the most consistent hit-makers of the 1980s. Rather than relying on a flashy image, he parlayed the judicious selection of pop-funk material and an extraordinarily soulful voice to stake his claim on the upper reaches of the charts.

Born Leslie Sebastian Charles on January 21, 1950, in Fyzabad, Trinidad, he moved to England with his family at age eight. Ocean worked for a time as a Saville Row tailor, before gravitating to studio session work in London. His Motown-inflected "Love Really Hurts Without You" (Ariola America 7621; #22 US pop, #2 UK) put him on the map in England. He relocated to the United States in the late 1970s as part of a concerted attempt to penetrate that marketplace.

Following several years of fitful commercial progress, highlighted by the release of "Night (Feel Like Getting Down)" (Epic 02053; 1981 #103 pop, #7 r&b), Ocean hit the big time with "Caribbean Queen (No

More Love on the Run)" (#1 r&b four weeks). He continued his successful run throughout the decade, most notably with "Loverboy" (Jive 9284; 1984; #2 pop, #20 r&b), "Suddenly" (Jive 9323; 1985; #4 pop, #5 r&b), "When the Going Gets Tough, The Tough Get Going" (Jive 9432; 1985; #2 pop, #6 r&b; helped by its inclusion in the soundtrack to the film *Jewel of the Nile*), "There'll Be Sad Songs (To Make You Cry)" (Jive 9465; 1986; #1 pop, #1 r&b, "Love Zone" (Jive 9510; 1986; #10 pop, #1 r&b), and "Get Outta My Dreams, Get Into My Car" (Jive 9678; 1988; #1 pop, #1 r&b). He has continued to record up to the present day, though without scoring any hits.

November 17. Wham! surge to summit of the pop charts with "Wake Me Up Before You Go-Go" (Columbia), remaining there for three weeks.

December 8. Daryl Hall and John Oates begin a two-week stint atop the Hot 100 with "Out of Touch" (RCA).

December 17. Run-D.M.C. earn a gold record for their eponymous debut LP (Profile 1202).

Run-D.M.C. were a rare commodity when they first became successful in the mid-1980s; whereas early rap stars tended to come from economically repressed inner city areas, Queens, New York rappers Joseph Simmons (Run) and Daryll McDaniels (D.M.C.) both grew up in a comfortable middle-class environment. A direct consequence of their combined backgrounds is that Run-D.M.C.'s recorded material lacks the harsh, bitter edge (e.g., profanity, violent images, revolutionary dogma) typical of rank-and-file rap/hip-hop acts.

Simmons—a one-time protégé of hip-hop pioneer Kurtis Blow—and McDaniels became involved in the New York City by their early teens. By the early 1980s they had hooked up with a club disc jockey Jay Mizell, who adopted the moniker Jam Master Jay. Run-D.M.C.'s early records for the Profile label were popular in the New York area dance-rap scene; beginning with "It's Like That" (Profile 5019; 1983; #15 R&B), the group's singles consistently made the black charts.

Their recordings—particularly the albums *Run-D.M.C.* (1984; #53), *King of Rock* (Profile 1205; 1985; #52; achieved platinum status), *Raising Hell* (Profile 1217; 1986; #3; achieved triple-platinum status assisted in large part by hit single, "Walk This Way" (Profile 5112; #4 pop, #8 R&B; a collaboration with Aerosmith's Steve Tyler and Joe Perry), and the film soundtrack *Tougher Than Leather* (Profile 1265; 1988; #9; achieved platinum status)—often crossed over to the pop charts, still a comparatively rare occurrence in the mid-1980s. This broader appeal was based in part on positive lyrics that emphasized the importance of education and urged listeners to avoid drugs and violence.

Run-D.M.C.'s clean mainstream image would prove to be something of a credibility problem by the late 1980s when changing public tastes seemed predisposed to prefer the political militancy and raw, street-smart message largely identified with gansta rappers. The group's commercial momentum was also blunted by a protracted legal battle with Profile and its publishing company, Protoons beginning in 1987. They released only one hit single in the 1990s, "Down with the King" (Profile 5391; 1993; #21), while later albums—*Back From Hell* (Profile 1401; 1990; #81), *Greatest Hits 1983-1991* (Profile 1419; 1991; #199), and *Down with the King* (Profile; 1993)—documented their rapid fall from favor.

December 22. Madonna reaches number one on the pop charts with "Like a Virgin" (Sire), remaining there for six weeks.

December 31. Def Leppard drummer Rick Allen crashes his Corvette Stingray outside Sheffield, losing his left arm. The band encourages the development of a drum kit that enables him to remain an active member.

1985

❄

January 28. "We Are the World"—the U.S. answer to Band Aid—is recorded. Composed by Michael Jackson and Lionel Richie, it includes such performers as Ray Charles, Bob Dylan, Hall & Oates, Cyndi Lauper, Diana Ross, Bruce Springsteen, Tina Turner, and Stevie Wonder.

January 31. *Rolling Stone* pictures Billy Idol—clad only black leather belts and punk-thrift store jewelry—on its cover with the caption "Billy Idol: Sneer of the Year."

February 2. Foreigner's "I Want To Know What Love Is" (Atlantic) begins a two-week stay at the top of the Hot 100; the group's only single to accomplish this feat. Formed in England in the mid-1970s, Foreigner burst upon the American scene in 1977 with their eponymous debut LP, which featured FM radio staples such as "Feels Like the First Time" and "Cold As Ice." While their material consisted almost exclusively of straight-ahead hard rock and power ballads, "I Want to Know What Love Is" would reveal the band in an uncharacteristic overachieving mode. The song possessed a strong gospel feel, which was reinforced by the inclusion of a black church choir in a supporting role. Much like Paul Simon's "Bridge Over Troubled Water," the early portion featured somber verses within a subdued, spare arrangement that took on more and more layers of sound and steadily increasing dramatic tension as the song progressed to an almost Wagnerian climax. The intensity was relaxed by followed by gradual fade-out a la the Beatles' "Hey Jude." Perhaps due in part because the band members realized that they couldn't surpass the artistry—or commercial success—of this single, Foreigner broke up a short time later.

February 7. British balladeer Matt Munro dies at age fifty-four. He reached number four on the U.K. charts with "Walk Away" (#23 U.S.); he also had ten other Top 40 hits.

February 9. Madonna begins a three-week stint atop the album charts with *Like a Virgin*.

February 11. The Police are recognized for the outstanding contribution to British music, while Prince is named best solo artist, at the fourth annual Brit Awards.

February 11. Sade's debut LP, *Diamond Life* (CBS-Epic) named Best British Album at the fourth annual Brit Awards, held at the Grosvenor House, London.

February 16. Bruce Springsteen tops the British charts with *Born in the USA* (Columbia), his first recording to accomplish that feat.

February 16. "Careless Whisper" (Columbia 04691), by Wham! (now including the added phrase "Featuring George Michael" in recognition of his dominant role as a songwriter and producer for the group), reaches number one on the Hot 100, remaining there for three weeks. The romantic ballad would also head up the Adult Contemporary survey for five weeks.

February 23. Stevie Wonder is arrested during an anti-apartheid demonstration outside the South African Embassy in Washington, D.C. He is released after being questioned by police.

February 26. Chaka Khan wins the Best R&B Vocal Performance, Female, Grammy for "I Feel For You." "I Feel For You" also nets the Best New R&B Song Grammy for its composer, Prince.

February 28. Uriah Heep lead singer David Byron dies from a heart attack.

March 2. Wham! starts a three-week stint at number one on the album charts with *Make It Big*, which eventually sells more than five million copies.

March 3. Michael Jackson appears at Madame Tussauds in London to unveil his waxwork likeness.

March 9. Dead Or Alive head up the British charts with "You Spin Me Round (Like a Record)." It is the first record by the production team of Stock, Aitken, and Waterman—who would be responsible for more than one hundred Top 40 hits—to accomplish this feat.

March 9. REO Speedwagon begins a three-week run atop the Hot 100 with "Can't Fight This Feeling" (Epic).

March 13. Duran Duran's "The Reflex" is named International Hit of the Year at the Ivor Novello Awards luncheon in London.

March 13. Bob Geldof and Midge Ure receive the Bestselling A-Side citation at the thirtieth Ivor Novello Awards for "Do They Know It's Christmas?"

March 14. Dead Or Alive are removed from the cast of the British television program, *The Tube*, after stating they are incapable of performing live.

March 16. UTFO peak at number seventy-seven on the Hot 100 with "Roxanne, Roxanne" (Select 1182).

One of the earliest rap groups to enjoy commercial success, U.T.F.O. (which stands for UnTouchable Force Organization) created a major recording industry phenomenon with their second single, "Roxanne, Roxanne." The song's lyrics—essentially rant about a young woman who wouldn't oblige them sexually—and catchy arrangement, which producer Full Force had derived from Billy Squier's "The Big Beat," became an underground smash. Another artist, Roxanne Shante, immediately released a caustic response record, which became an even bigger hit. In short order, a slew of rappers—the Real Roxanne, the Original Roxanne, and Sparky D, among others—weighed in with their takes on the ages-old male-female standoff.

The East Wimbush, Brooklyn-based act—comprised of Whodini break dancers Doctor Ice and Kangol Kid as well as The Educated Rapper (and, later, Mix-Master Ice)—produced their own Roxanne follow-up, "Calling Her a Crab (Roxanne, Part 2)," before trying to find a fresh approach in order to remain commercially viable, including the rock/rap fusion of their third LP, *Lethal* (Select; 1987), and the raw sexual rhyming of *Bag It and Bone It* (Jive; 1991). In the face of public apathy, the group split, with Doctor Ice going on to issue several solo albums.

March 23. Philip Bailey and Phil Collins head up the British charts with "Easy Lover."

March 23. John Fogerty tops the album charts with *Centerfield*.

March 23. Billy Joel marries supermodel Christie Brinkley on a boat docked near the Statue of Liberty. They would divorce in 1993.

March 30. Phil Collins reaches number one on the pop charts with "One More Night" (Atlantic), remaining there for two weeks.

March 31. Jeanine Deckers (aka The Singing Nun) dies from an overdose of sleeping pills, the result of a suicide pact with a friend.

April 5. More than five thousand radio stations worldwide air the charity single, "We Are the World." It tops the charts in the United States and much of the Western world.

April 6. Singer/songwriter Gilbert O'Sullivan wins a lawsuit against his manager, Gordon Mills, for unpaid royalties, receiving a $2 million settlement.

April 7. Wham! perform at the workers' gymnasium in Beijing, the first Western pop act permitted to do a live show in China.

April 8. Songwriter J. Fred Coots dies. His compositions included "Santa Claus Is Coming to Town" and "Love Letters in the Sand," the latter a chart topper for Pat Boone.

April 13. Maze featuring Frankie Beverly begin a two-week stint atop the R&B charts with "Back in Stride" (Capitol 5431).

April 13. The one-off charity project, USA for Africa, starts a four-week run atop the Hot 100 with "We Are the World" (Columbia 04389). The Michael Jackson/Lionel Richie composition goes on to achieve quadruple platinum sales.

April 18. Wham! become the first Western pop act to have an album released in China.

April 27. DeBarge ascends to the summit of the R&B charts with "Rhythm of the Night" (Gordy 1770).

April 27. USA for Africa's *We Are the World* begins a three-week stint atop the album charts.

May 4. USA for Africa's "We Are the World" tops the R&B charts, remaining there for a couple of weeks. Producer Quincy Jones would reflect that, after recording the instrumental tracks, he sent demo tapes to all artists involved along with a note to

Check your egos at the door. I put that line in a letter I sent to all the artists before they got there, and everybody understood…Oh, there were little murmurs beforehand that the song "is not rock 'n' roll"…but once we got to the session, I was sure everything would totally even itself out and bring everyone into a euphoric state, and that's what happened. (White and Bronson, 1991)

May 11. Producer/keyboardist Paul Hardcastle heads up the British charts with "19." The title refers to the average age of American soldiers in the Vietnam War.

May 11. Madonna peaks at number one on the pop charts with "Crazy for You" (Geffen).

May 18. Kool & the Gang's "Fresh" (De-Lite 880623) heads up the R&B chart.

May 18. Simple Minds climb to the summit of the Hot 100 with "Don't You (Forget About Me)" (A&M). The track's popularity is enhanced by its inclusion in the soundtrack to the hit film, *The Breakfast Club*.

May 25. Dire Straits top the British charts with *Brothers in Arms* (Warner Bros.). It duplicates this feat in twenty-five other nations (including the United States), selling more than twenty million copies worldwide.

May 25. Whitney Houston's "You Give Good Love" (Arista 9274) goes number one on the R&B charts.

The daughter of soul/gospel singer Cissy Houston and cousin of pop chanteuse Dionne Warwick, Whitney was destined for singing success. In addition to possessing one of the truly distinctive voices within mainstream popular music, Houston's good looks have enabled her to secure starring film roles—most notably, *The Bodyguard* (1992), *Waiting To Exhale* (1995), and *The Preacher's Wife* (1996)—and a prominent part in the accompanying soundtrack albums.

Born August 9, 1963 in Newark, New Jersey, Houston burst onto the scene in the mid-1980s with a string of best-selling singles, including "Saving All My Love For You" (Arista 9381; 1985; #1), "How Will I Know" (Arista 9434; 1985; #1), "Greatest Love Of All" (Arista 9466; 1986; #1), "I Wanna Dance With Somebody (Who Loves Me)" (Arista 9598; 1987; #1), "Didn't We Almost Have It All" (Arista 9616; 1987; #1), "So Emotional" (Arista 9642; 1987; #1), and "Where Do Broken Hearts Go" (Arista 9674; 1988; #1). By the 1990s—despite hits like "I'm Your Baby Tonight" (Arista 2108; 1990; #1), "All the Man That I Need" (Arista 2156; 1991; #1), "I Will Always Love You" (Arista 12519; 1992; #1), and "Exhale" (Arista 12885; 1995; #1)—her career lost some momentum due to mediocre albums encumbered with insipid material and routine synthesizer-drenched production work and a slew of imitators (e.g., Mariah Carey, Toni Braxton, Brandy, and Celine Dion). Nevertheless, as the preeminent torch singer of her time, Houston's best recordings may still lie in the future.

May 25. Wham! begin a two-week stint atop the pop charts with "Everything She Wants" (Columbia).

June 1. Freddie Jackson's "Rock Me Tonight (For Old Times Sake)" (Capitol 5459) starts a six-week run atop the R&B charts.

June 1. Prince and the Revolution begin a three-week stay at number one on the album charts with *Around the World in a Day* (Paisley Park).

June 8. Tears for Fears reach number one on the Hot 100 with "Everybody Wants to Rule the World" (Mercury), remaining there for two weeks.

June 22. Bryan Adams begins a two-week stay atop the pop charts with "Heaven" (A&M).

June 29. Ronnie Milsap's "She Keeps the Home Fires Burning" (RCA 14034) climbs to the summit of the country charts.

July 6. Phil Collins goes to number one on the Hot 100 with "Sussudio" (Atlantic).

July 6. Exile tops the country charts with "She's a Miracle" (Epic 04864).

July 13. Duran Duran's "A View to a Kill" begins a two-week tenure at number one (#2 UK). It is the group's sixth million-selling single and the first James Bond film theme to top the pop charts.

July 13. Loose Ends head up the R&B charts with "Hangin' on a String (Contemplating)" (MCA 52570).

July 13. Willie Nelson's "Forgiving You Was Easy" (Columbia 04847) tops the country charts.

July 20. "Dixie Road" (MCA 52564)—recorded specifically for Lee Greenwood's first *Greatest Hits* album—peaks at number one on the country charts.

July 20. Rene & Angela begin a two-week stint atop the R&B charts with "Save Your Love (For #1)" (Mercury 880 731).

July 27. Earl Thomas Conley reaches number one on the country charts with "Love Don't Care (Whose Heart It Breaks)" (RCA 14060).

July 27. Eurythmics top the British charts with "There Must Be an Angel (Playing with My Heart)."

July 27. Paul Young ascends to the summit of the pop chart with the Daryl Hall composition, "Everytime You Go Away" (Columbia 04867).

August 3. Alabama heads up the country charts with "Forty Hour Week (For a Livin')" (RCA 14085).

August 3. Sting peaks at number three on the Hot 100 with "If You Love Somebody Set Them Free" (A&M 2738).

Feeling stylistically constrained as the frontman for the supergroup Police, Sting (aka Gordon Sumner) has opted for a solo career defined by experimentation across a wide range of genres. His work also demonstrates a literary flair and social commitment while retaining the melodic flair and slick production values that characterized Police's recordings.

Sting's celebrity status—as reflected by heavy video rotation on MTV and extensive press coverage—helped assure bestseller status for his ambitious debut release, *The Dream of the Blue Turtles* (A&M 3750; 1985; #2), and its four Top 20 singles. The work was nominated for an Album of the Year Grammy, while he shared the 1985 Song of the Year Grammy with Mark Knopfler for "Money for Nothing" (Warner Bros. 28950; #1). Most of the jazz and worldbeat musicians utilized on his LP accompanied him on a support tour; these concerts were documented on the double live set, *Bring on the Night* (A&M BRIN 1; 1986).

Although extremely active in film acting and pursuing social causes such as Band Aid, Amnesty International, and the Rainforest Foundation, he found time to record another jazz-funk album, ...*Nothing Like the Sun* (A&M 6402; 1987; #9). Its dark tone, largely evoked by thickly-textured orchestrations, was continued by *The Soul Cages* (A&M 6405; 1991; #2), a stripped-down, folk-oriented affair pervaded by religious references.

Sting's subsequent releases—the triple-platinum *Ten Summoner's Tales* (A&M 0070; 1993; #2), which included the Grammy winning "If I Ever Lose My Faith in You" (1993; #17); the chart-topping "All for Love" (A&M 0476; 1993; with Bryan Adams and Rod Stewart) from the film *The Three Musketeers*; Mercury *Falling* (A&M 0483; 1996; #5); and the engaging *Brand New Day* (Interscope 490443; 1999; #9) have been decidedly more upbeat. With the latter album winning two Grammys (Pop Album of the Year and Best Male Pop Vocal Performance for the title song), Sting appears to have found the key to balancing critical acclaim and commercial success—all on his terms and timeframe.

August 3. Tears for Fears begin a three-week run atop the Hot 100 with "Shout" (Mercury 880294).

August 10. Hank Williams Jr. outpaces the competition on the country charts with "I'm For Love" (Warner Bros. 29022).

August 12. Kyu Sakamoto dies in a plane crash. He was the first Japanese artist to top the U.S. charts with "Sukiyaki" in 1963.

August 24. Huey Lewis & the News reach number one on the pop charts with "The Power of Love" (Chrysalis), remaining there for two weeks.

August 31. Dire Straits' *Brothers in Arms* (Warner Bros.) begins a nine-week run atop the album charts. It will reach the top rung in twenty-five other nations on its way to selling more than twenty million copies.

September 7. John Parr climbs to the summit of the Hot 100 with "St. Elmo's Fire (Man in Motion)" (Atlantic), maintaining the position for a couple of weeks.

September 21. Dire Straits begin a three-week stay atop the pop charts with "Money for Nothing" (Warner Bros.). The satirical take on rock stardom is greatly assisted by an award-winning promotional video which is placed in heavy rotation on MTV.

October 5. Midge Ure—formerly with Slik and Ultravox—reaches number one on the British charts with "If I Was."

October 12. Ready for the World peak at number one on the Hot 100 with "Oh Sheila" (MCA).

October 19. The Norwegian band, A-Ha, tops the pop charts with "Take on Me" (Warner Bros.). As with "Money for Nothing," it is augmented by a tour de force animated video clip.

October 26. Whitney Houston has her first chart-topping single with "Saving All My Love for You" (Arista)

November 2. Stevie Wonder reaches number one on the Hot 100 with "Part-Time Lover" (Tamla).

November 9. Jazz keyboardist Jan Hammer climbs to the summit of the pop charts with the instrumental, "Miami Vice Theme" (MCA).

November 16. Sade's second album, *Promise* (CBS/Epic), reaches number one on the British charts, achieving a multi-platinum as well.

November 16. "We Built This City" (Grunt), the Starship's first single from the album, *Knee Deep in the Hoopla* (RCA), begins a two-week run atop the Hot 100 (#12 UK), a level of success never achieved by either Jefferson Airplane or Jefferson Starship. The album will peak at number seven.

November 23. Joe Turner dies at age seventy-four in Inglewood, California. Turner evolved from a band singer to R&B shouter who enjoyed a string of hits for Atlantic—most notably, "Shake, Rattle and Roll," "Corinna, Corinna," and "Flip, Flop and Fly."

One of the leading shout blues interpreters of the 1930s and 1940s, Big Joe Turner—he was six feet, two inches in height, and weighed three pounds—would later find a whole new audience as a rock 'n' roll trailblazer. Taken in its entirety, his career represented a synthesis of most major twentieth century styles, including gospel, blues, swing, rhythm and blues, jazz, and rock 'n' roll.

Born in Kansas City on May 18, 1911, Turner absorbed gospel singing in church, and folk, blues, and pop songs from local performers and sound recordings as a child. In addition to selling papers and junk as a youth, he earned money singing with a blind guitarist in the streets. By the late 1930s, he had become a highly regarded blues singer though limited to performing in rundown bars and theaters in the Midwest. He was also garnering attention as a songwriter; his compositions included "Cherry Red," "Hold 'Em Pete," "Lucille," "Piney Brown Blues," and "Sun Risin' Blues." His earliest known recordings—done in a boogie-woogie style which was back in vogue following his success at the December 23, 1938, Carnegie Hall "Spirituals To Swing" concert—were made for Vocalion on December 30, 1938, with Pete Johnson: "Goin Away Blues" and "Roll 'Em Pete."

The duo would work together at Café Society and Café Society Uptown in New York City for the next five years as well as recording for Decca in 1940. Turner continued to make records for the label's Race and Sepia series for the next four years, both solo and with Willie "The Lion" Smith, Art Tatum, Sam Price, and the Freddie Slack Trio. Turner cut eleven singles for National Records between 1945 and 1947, but with limited success. He spent the next few years recording for a wide variety of companies—including Freedom, MGM, Down Beat/Swingtime, Modern/RPM, Aladdin, Rouge, Imperial, and DooTone—but making little impact due to declining interest in the blues.

Sensing his potential as an updated R&B belter, Atlantic Records added him to their roster in 1951. Now referred to as the "boss of the blues," Turner enjoyed his greatest success as a recording artist with hits such as "Chains of Love" (Atlantic 939; 1951; #30 pop, #2 r&b), "The Chill Is On" (Atlantic 949; 1951; #3 r&b), "Sweet Sixteen" (Atlantic 960; 1952; #3 r&b), "Don't You Cry" (Atlantic 970; 1952; #5 r&b), "Honey Hush" (Atlantic 1001; 1953; #23 pop, #1 r&b), "Shake, Rattle, and Roll" (Atlantic 1026; 1954; #22 pop, #1 r&b), "Flip Flop and Fly" (Atlantic 1053; 1955; #2 r&b), "Hide and Seek" (Atlantic 1069; 1955; #3 r&b), and "Corrine Corrina" (Atlantic 1088; 1956; #41 pop, #2 r&b). When the singles stopped charting after 1958, he shifted his focus to albums, proving equally adept at classic blues, jazz, and R&B-inflected rock 'n' roll. Notable releases included *The Boss of the Blues* (Atlantic 1234; 1956), *Joe Turner* (Atlantic 8005; 1957), *Rockin' the Blues* (Atlantic 8023; 1958), *Big Joe Is Here* (Atlantic 8033; 1959), and *Big Joe Rides Again* (Atlantic 1322; 1960).

He continued to record up to his death for many labels, including Arhoolie, United Artists, MCA, Black and Blue, Big Town, Spivey, Muse, Savoy, and Pablo. Many of his classic recordings have been reissued on compilations such as *His Greatest* Recordings (Atco 376; 1971), The *Big Joe Turner Anthology* (Rhino 71550; 1994), and *Volume 1: I've Been to Kansas City* (Decca/MCA 42351).

November 30. Phil Collins and Marilyn Martin go number one on the pop charts with "Separate Lives" (Atlantic).

December 7. Mr. Mister's "Broken Wings" (RCA) peaks at number one on the Hot 100, remaining there for two weeks.

December 21. Lionel Richie begins a four-week stay atop the pop charts with his composition, "Say You, Say Me" (Motown).

December 28. Shakin' Stevens reaches number one on the British charts with "Marry Christmas Everyone."

December 31. Rick Nelson dies—along with his fiancée Helen Blair, his sound engineer Clark Russell, and back-up band members Andy Chapin, Rick Intveld, Bobby Neal, and Patrick Woodward—when a DC3 charter plane crashes near De Kalb, Texas, after catching fire between concert dates in Guntersville, Alabama, and Dallas. He will be buried January 6 at Forest Lawn Memorial Park, Hollywood, California, following a memorial service there in the Church of the Hills.

1986

❄

January 4. Phil Lynott, best known as the vocalist/bassist for the 1970s hard rock group, Thin Lizzy, dies of a drug overdose after spending roughly a week in a coma. When Thin Lizzy failed to achieve the commercial success many predicted for them, the group disbanded in 1983. Lynott went on to form Grand Slam, and shortly before his death enjoyed moderate sales with *Out in the Fields*, a collaboration with guitarist Gary Moore.

January 13. Former Sex Pistols John Lydon, Steve Jones, and Paul Cook—along with the mother of the deceased Sid Vicious—file a claim against Glitterbest/McLaren (their former manager) for one million pounds of past royalties due them. The case would be settled out of court in their favor.

January 18. Dionne (Warwick) & Friends begin a four-week run atop the Hot 100 with "That's What Friends Are For" (Arista).

January 20. Stevie Wonder organizes concerts in Atlanta, New York, and Washington, D.C., to celebrate the inaugural observance of Martin Luther King's birthday as a U.S. national holiday. Artists participating in the festivities included Bill Cosby, Bob Dylan, Wynton Marsalis, Eddie Murphy, and the Pointer Sisters.

January 25. A-Ha tops the British charts with "The Sun Always Shines on TV," the first Norwegian act to accomplish this feat.

January 25. The Red Wedge tour commences in Manchester, U.K. Headlining acts in support of the British Labour Party—then attempting to unseat the incumbent Conservative majority—include Billy Bragg, the Communards, Junior Giscombe, and the Style Council. These and other like-minded English activists win a small measure of support in the more politically astute elements of the U.S. postpunk subculture.

January 29. Fleetwood Mac's Stevie Nicks marries Kim Anderson to honor the dying request of the latter's former wife. She will divorce Anderson, a Warner Bros. Records promotion man, shortly.

February 1. Music publisher Dick James dies of a heart attack at sixty-seven. His portfolio at one time included Northern Songs, best known publishing the Lennon/McCartney compositions. He also formed a successful record label, DJM, which helped get Elton John established as a recording star. His business operations would be continued by son Stephen.

February 3. PIL's *Album* is released in Great Britain. The cassette release is titled *Cassette*, and its initial single would be called "Single" (although commonly known as "Rise"). At the time, John Lydon's experimental postpunk band was attracting interest with the recent acquisition of ex-Cream drummer Ginger Baker.

February 5. Bob Dylan and Tom Petty and the Heartbreakers kick off their World Tour in New Zealand.

February 6. With Feargal Sharkey on a tour stop at Sheffield, his mother, Sybil, and sister, Ursula, are kidnapped by armed terrorists for four hours while visiting friends in Londonderry, Ireland. Although believed to be an ambush of security forces at the time, the perpetrators would ultimately leave without firing a shot.

February 8. Billy Ocean begins a four-week stay atop the British charts with "When the Going Gets Tough, the Tough Get Going," a featured song in the hit film, *The Jewel of the Nile*.

February 15. Whitney Houston reaches number one on the pop charts with "How Will I Know" (Arista), remaining there for two weeks.

February 17. Sigue Sigue Sputnik's debut single, "Love Missile F1-11," is released in Great Britain. Headed by former Generation X guitarist Tony James, the band was in the midst of a major publicity hype engineered by their record label and management, as well as the fad-driven media.

February 22. MTV sets aside twenty-two hours to broadcast all forty-five episodes of the original Monkees TV series.

February 28. George Michael announces that Wham! will officially dissolve that summer.

March 1. Mr. Mister begin a two-week stint atop the Hot 100 with "Kyrie" (RCA).

March 6. The Band's Richard Manuel hangs himself from a shower curtain rod in a Florida hotel room.

March 8. Whitney Houston reaches number one on the album charts with her eponymous debut, logging fourteen weeks in that position.

March 8. Diana Ross tops the British singles charts with "Chain Reaction," written and produced by the Gibb brothers.

March 15. The Starship climb to the summit of the pop charts with "Sara" (Grunt).

March 22. Heart reach number one on the Hot 100 with "These Dreams" (Capitol).

March 29. Austrian singer/songwriter Falco begins a three-week run atop the Hot 100 with "Rock Me Amadeus" (A&M).

March 29. Cliff Richard and The Young Ones head up the British charts with a charity version of the singer's 1959 hit, "Living Doll."

March 31. O'Kelly Isley, vocalist with the Isley Brothers, dies of a heart attack at age forty-eight.

April 11. Dave Clark's musical, *Time*, starring Cliff Richard, opens at London's Dominion Theatre.

April 19. The Bangles peak at number two with the Prince composition, "Manic Monday."

The Bangles emerged from Los Angeles' "paisley underground," a brand of soft psychedelia also performed by the Rain Parade and Dream Syndicate. Following a self-released single (as the "Bangs," a name owned by another group) and EP with I.R.S., the Bangles signed with Columbia in 1983. When the original bass player left and was replaced by former Runaway Michael Steele, the band's lineup was set, including Susanna Hoffs and Debbi Peterson, both on guitar and vocals, along with drummer/vocalist Vicki Peterson.

David Kahne, a producer specializing in power-pop, was recruited to assist in recording Bangles' debut album. *All Over the Place* (Columbia 39220; 1984). The critically acclaimed LP attracted the attention of funk star, Prince, who gave the band the song, "Manic Monday' (Columbia 38-05765). Thanks in large part to MTV, which placed the promotional video of the highly photogenic girls into heavy rotation, the single reached number two on the pop charts, paving the way for the breakthrough album, *Different Light* (Columbia 40039; 1986). A string of hit recordings followed, most notably, the number one singles "Walk Like An Egyptian (Columbia 38-06257; 1986), "Hazy Shade of Winter" (Def Jam/Columbia 38-07630; 1987) and "Eternal Flame" (Columbia 38-68533; 1989). The media's increasing fascination with Hoffs fomented dissention within the group, leading to a break-up in late 1989. Hoffs has enjoyed the greatest success among the former band members; however, poor sales for her solo album and a number of undistinguished film appearances in the early 1990s led to a disappearance from public view.

April 19. George Michael tops the British charts with "A Different Corner."

April 19. Prince & the Revolution begin a two-week stint at number one on the pop charts with "Kiss" (Paisley Park).

April 26. Roxy Music's *Street Life – 20 Greatest Hits* begins a five-week run atop the British album charts.

May 1. Songwriter /producer Hugo Peretti diet at age seventy. His compositions include "Shout," Twistin' the Night Away," and "You Make Me Feel Brand New."

May 3. Robert Palmer tops the Hot 100 with "Addicted to Love" (Island; #5 U.K.). Palmer originally recorded the song as a duet with Chaka Khan, but her voice was removed due to contractual problems.

May 10. Falco heads up the British charts with "Rock Me Amadeus." He becomes the first Austrian artist to accomplish this feat on both the U.K. and U.S. surveys.

May 10. The Pet Shop Boys peak at number one on the pop charts with "West End Girls" (EMI America; #1 U.K.).

May 17. Whitney Houston begins a three-week stay atop the Hot 100 with "Greatest Love of All" (Arista).

May 17. Janet Jackon peaks at number four on the Hot 100 with "What Have You Done For Me Lately?" (A&M 2812), her first major hit.

Although Janet Jackson's musical identity owes much to the slick funk-pop production work of ex-The Time members, Jimmy Jam and Terry Lewis, her photogenic good looks and well-choreographed dancing skills have also been key ingredients in her commercial success. Now entering her third decade as a major recording artist, she has become an industry institution much like her older brother, Michael.

Born in Gary, Indiana, Janet started out singing with the Jackson 5 on their television variety show in the 1970s before garnering roles on programs like "Good Times," "Diff'rent Strokes," and "Fame." She achieved marginal success with her first two albums, *Janet Jackson* (A&M 4907; 1982; #63) and *Dream Street* (A&M 4962; 1984). However, the next LP—*Control* (A&M 5106; 1986; #1)—made her a star, driven by several Jam and Lewis-penned hit singles—"What Have You Done For Me Lately," "Nasty" (A&M 2830; 1986; #3), "When I Think Of You" (A&M 2855; #1), and "Control" (A&M 2877; 1986; #5)—and the accompanying high-energy video clips that appeared in heavy rotation on MTV, BET, and other cable TV stations.

With Jackson now sharing songwriting responsibilities and projecting a more mature sexuality, follow-up recordings—the albums *Janet Jackson's Rhythm Nation 1814* (A&M 3920; 1989; #1), *Janet* (Virgin 87825; 1993; #1), *The Velvet Rope* (Virgin 44762; 1997; #1), and *All For You* (Virgin 10144; 2001; #1) as well as a string of number one singles: "Miss You Much" (A&M 1445; 1989), "Escapade" (A&M 1490; 1990), "Black Cat" (A&M 1477; 1990), "Love Will Never Do (Without You)" (A&M 1538; 1990), "That's the Way Love Goes" (Virgin 12650; 1993), "Again" (Virgin 38404; 1993), and "Together Again" (Virgin 38623; 1997)—have cemented her place in the pop music pantheon. With the fashion spreads and glitzy dance routines are now balanced with lyrics addressing racism, inequality, and other forms of social consciousness, Jackson seems intent on maximizing her core audience.

May 17. Spitting Image peak at number one on the British charts with "The Chicken Song." At the time, *Spitting Image*, which specialized in ridiculing politicians and public figures, had become the most popular Sunday television program in the country.

June 7. Madonna reaches number one on the pop charts with "Live to Tell" (Sire).

June 14. Patti LaBelle and Michael McDonald begin a three-week run atop the Hot 100 with "On My Own" (MCA).

July 5. El DeBarge peaks at number three on the Hot 100 with "Who's Johnny" (Gordy 1842).

Born June 4, 1961, in Grand Rapids, Michigan, Eldra DeBarge was the lead singer for DeBarge—comprised of a sister and three brothers—from their formation in 1978 until he decided to go solo in 1986. His debut LP, *El DeBarge* (1986), was a hook-laden fusion of pop-R&B poured in the Michael Jackson mold. He maintained his momentum with the hit single, "Who's Johnny?" (#1 r&b), the theme song for the blockbuster film, *Short Circuit*, followed by "Real Love" (1989). In order to prolong his career, he chose to expand beyond his teen idol base, focusing on the adult contemporary market with albums like *Heart, Mind & Soul* (Warner/Reprise, 1994).

July 5. Janet Jackson starts a two-week stint at number one on the album charts with *Control* (A&M).

July 5. Billy Ocean climbs to the summit of the pop charts with "There'll Be Sad Songs (To Make You Cry)" (Jive).

July 12. Simply Red reach number one on the Hot 100 with "Holding Back the Years" (Elektra).

July 15. El Cerrito, California, declares John Fogerty Day in recognition of the accomplishments of one of its native sons. In accepting the honor, Fogerty would state,

I feel strongly about growing up in El Cerrito and living in El Cerrito. It's the small-town values. That's why I'm still here. That's why I raised my kids here. This is neat. This is really neat! This kind of thing reaffirms what this country is all about!

July 19. Genesis tops the pop charts with "Invisible Touch" (Atlantic). Former member, Peter Gabriel, is in the runner-up slot with "Sledgehammer."

July 26. Peter Gabriel reaches number one on the Hot 100 with "Sledgehammer" (Geffen).

July 26. Randy Travis heads up the country charts with "On the Other Hand" (Warner Bros. 28962).

August 2. Peter Cetera begins a two-week stint atop the pop charts with "Glory of Love" (Full Moon).

August 2. George Strait reaches number one on the country charts with "Nobody in His Right Mind Would've Left Her" (MCA 52817).

August 9. The Judds head up the country charts with "Rockin' with the Rhythm of the Rain" (RCA 14362).

August 16. Madonna begins a two-week stint atop the Hot 100 with "Papa Don't Preach" (Sire).

August 16. John Schneider peaks at number one on the country charts with "You're the Last Thing I Needed Tonight" (MCA 52827).

August 23. T. G. Sheppard tops the country charts with "Strong Heart" (Columbia 05905).

August 30. Don Williams reaches number one on the country charts with "Heartbeat in the Darkness" (Capitol 5588).

August 30. Steve Winwood climbs to the summit of the pop charts with "Higher Love" (Island).

September 6. Bananarama reach number one on the Hot 100 with their remake of Shocking Blue's "Venus" (London).

September 6. Conway Twitty's "Desperado Love" (Warner Bros. 28692) tops the country charts.

September 13. Berlin go number one on the pop charts with "Take My Breath Away" (Columbia).

September 13. Levert's "(Pop, Pop, Pop) Goes My Mind" (Atlantic 89389) tops the R&B charts.

September 20. Oran "Juice" Jones heads up the R&B charts with "The Rain" (Def Jam 06209).

September 20. Huey Lewis & the News begin a three-week run atop the Hot 100 with "Stuck with You" (Chrysalis).

September 22. The Smiths sign with EMI Records for $1.7 million.

October 7. The Judds' *Rockin' with the Rhythm* achieves platinum status—their second album to accomplish this feat.

October 11. Janet Jackson reaches number one on the pop charts with "When I Think of You" (A&M 2855), remaining there are two weeks.

October 18. Tina Turner peaks at number two on the Hot 100 with "Typical Male" (Capital 5615), remaining there for three weeks.

October 25. Cyndi Lauper begins a two-week stint atop pop charts with "True Colors" (Portrait).

October 31. Roger Waters goes to the high court to try and stop Dave Gilmour and Nick Mason from using the Pink Floyd moniker for future recording and live performances.

November 1. Anita Baker peaks at number eight on the Hot 100 with "Sweet Love" (Elektra 69557).

An exponent of traditional rhythm and blues vocalizing, Baker's restrained intensity and subtle coloring attracted widespread media attention and pop mainstream success in the mid-1980s. Born in Toledo and raised in Detroit, she began her professional career as lead singer for the R&B group, Chapter 8, from 1976 to 1984. Her moderately successful debut album, *The Songstress* (Beverly Glen 10002; 1983) was followed by the commercial breakthrough release, *Rapture* (Elektra 60444; 1986), which included Top 10 single, "Sweet Love" (Elektra 7-69557; 1986), reputed to have sold more than four million copies. Her subsequent albums, most notably the chart-topping *Give You the Best That I've Got* (Elektra 60827; 1988) and *Compositions* (Elektra 60922; 1990), have all been best sellers.

November 8. Boston begins a two-week stay at number one on the pop charts with "Amanda" (MCA).

November 22. Human League climbs to the summit of the Hot 100 with "Human" (A&M/Virgin).

November 29. Bon Jovi top the pop charts with "You Give Love a Bad Name" (Mercury).

December 5. Roxy Music earns a gold record for the 1982 LP release, *Avalon* (Warner Bros. 23686).

Roxy Music's decadent, densely-textured variant of art rock appealed far more to a European, rather than an American, audience. Factors behind the group's limited appeal stateside included a complex image—an image based as much on camp fashion (their early look blended futuristic costumes and 1950s hairstyles) and lifestyle concepts as music per se, rather arch escapist lyrics not in tune with a society grappling with the very real issues of the Vietnam War and Watergate scandal, and the tendency of the rock press to portray them as glitter rock alternative to Alice Cooper, David Bowie, and others.

Roxy Music was founded by vocalist Bryan Ferry and keyboardist Brian Eno. With the addition of saxophonist Andy Mackay, lead guitarist Phil Manzanera, and drummer Paul Thompson (although this was the classic lineup, there would be frequent personnel changes over the years), the band recorded *Roxy Music* (Island 9200/Reprise 2114; 1972; #10 UK) prior to having ever performed live. The album cover—the first of many by Roxy to feature female models in provocative poses—attracted as much attention in the United States as did the music in the grooves. Released on the heels of extensive touring in Europe and North America, *For Your Pleasure* (Warner Bros. 2696; 1973; # 4 UK, #193 US) easily outsold the debut LP.

By 1973 it was clear that Roxy was Ferry's band due to the departure of Eno (to be replaced by Eddie Jobson) over artistic differences. Although remaining members devoted a considerable amount of time and energy over the few years to solo projects—Ferry producing *These Foolish Things* (Atlantic 7304; 1973; #5 UK), *Another Time, Another Place* (Atlantic 18113; 1974; #4 UK), and *Let's Stick Together* (Atlantic 18187; 1976; #160); Manzanera, *Diamond Head* (Atco 113; 1975) and *Mainstream* (Antilles 7008; 1975; with the band Quiet Sun); and Mackay, *In Search of Eddie Riff* (1975) and *Rock Follies* (1976)—the band gained increasing critical respect and commercial success, issuing *Stranded* (Atco 7045; 1974; #1 UK, #186 US), *Country Life* (Atco 106; 1975; #3 UK, #37 US), and *Siren* (Atco 127; 1975; #4 UK, #50 US).

Following a lackluster live LP, *Viva! Roxy Music* (Atco 139; 1076; #6 UK, #81 US), the band verified suspicions that a breakup had taken place. When Ferry's solo career failed to gain momentum, however, he re-formed Roxy along with Manzanera, Mackay, and Thompson. The ensuing releases—*Manifesto* (Atco 114; 1979; #7 UK, #23 US), *Flesh + Blood* (Atco 102; 1980; #1 UK, #35 US), the unabashedly romantic *Avalon* (Warner Bros. 23686; 1982. #1 UK, #53 US; achieved platinum status), and the live EP, *Musique/ The High Road* (Warner Bros. 23808; 1983; #26 UK, #67 US)—all garnered critical acclaim and moderate sales in the United States. Ferry's disinclination to tour in support of the band's releases led to another breakup. With the exception of Eno, who went on to father the ambient and electronica genres, Ferry has remained the most prominent ex-member of the band, periodically releasing a string of stylistic diverse solo albums.

December 6. Peter Cetera and Amy Grant reach number one on the Hot 100 with "The Next Time I Fall" (Full Moon).

December 13. Bruce Hornsby & the Range settle into the top rung of the pop charts with "The Way It Is" (RCA 5023).

December 20. The Bangles begin a four-week run at number one on the Hot 100 with "Walk Like an Egyptian" (Columbia 06257).

December 20. The Housemartins top the British charts with the Jasper Isley-penned "Caravan of Love."

December 27. Wang Chung begin a two-week stint at number two on the Hot 100 with "Everybody Have Fun Tonight" (Geffen 28562).

1987

❄

January 6. Eric Clapton begins a six-day stint at London's Royal Albert Hall; it is the first year of what becomes an annual event.

January 10. Billy Joel's "This Is the Time" (Columbia 06526) tops the Adult Contemporary charts, maintaining that position for a total of three weeks. The third single from the album, *The Bridge*, it was the singer/songwriter's seventh AC chart-topper and twentieth record to make the pop Top 20 (peaking at #18). Reflecting on the song in the 1997 *Billboard* article, he noted, "One of the most difficult things to maintain is a relationship, and that's what this song is about."

January 17. Gregory Abbott reaches number one on the pop charts with "Shake You Down" (Columbia).

January 22. Steve "Silk" Hurley reaches number one in Great Britain with his only hit, "Jack Your Body," the first house recording to top the charts.

January 24. Billy Vera and the Beaters begin a two-week stint atop the Hot 100 (#1 AC, #42 country, #70 R&B) with "At This Moment" (Rhino 74403). The song had a rather usual odyssey prior to achieving such a degree of success. Written by Vera—who based the lyrics on a recent relationship he'd had with a girl—it was then recorded live at a Los Angeles club, the Roxy, in January 1981 with an eight-piece band, the Beaters. The ensuing release reached number seventy-nine on the pop charts in September 1981. In the mid-1980s, Michael Weithorn, a producer for the NBC comedy, *Family Ties*, became interested in the song after hearing a Vera club performance. He had Vera and his group re-record about thirty seconds of the song for use one of the show's scenes. When viewers overwhelmed Vera and the network with fan mail and calls after the episode's airing, Vera shopped the song around to various record companies. Rhino agreed the reissue the original version, but, with no more broadcasts of the episode planned in the immediate future, the window of opportunity appeared to have closed for good. However, when the song was played again for the season opener of *Family Ties* in September 1986, the record received a new lease on life. At result, Vera's recording career enjoyed a brief revival before he settled into acting and voiceover work for commercials, the writing of album liner notes, and occasional gigs with the Beaters in the 1990s.

January 30. Paul Simon holds a London press conference to announce that both the ANC and United Nations have ceased to blacklist him (the sanctions had been imposed when he broke the boycott on recording in South Africa).

February 7. Madonna peaks at number one on the pop charts with "Open Your Heart" (Sire).

February 7. Lionel Richie's "Ballerina Girl" (Motown 1873) begins a four-week stay at the top of the AC chart. Culled from the highly successful *Dancing on the Ceiling* LP, it was part of a double-sided hit; the B side, "Deep River Woman," a duet with Madonna, rose as high as number twenty-eight AC and number seventy-one pop. "Ballerina Girl" would be his last Top 10 pop single (#7; #5 R&B), due largely to a succession of personal setbacks (the death of his father, a divorce, and news that his friend had come down with AIDS) shortly thereafter.

February 9. Paul Simon is named Best International Solo Artist at the sixth annual Brit Awards, held at London's Grosvenor House.

February 14. Bon Jovi begin a four-week run atop the Hot 100 with "Livin' on a Prayer" (Mercury), their second number one single.

February 21. Ben E. King tops the British charts with "Stand By Me." Initially released in 1961, it had been featured in the recent film, *Stand By Me*.

February 22. Pop artist Andy Warhol dies following a gall bladder operation. He produced and managed the Velvet Underground, and designed the album covers, *Velvet Underground and Nico* (1967; featuring a "peeled banana") and the Rolling Stones' *Sticky Fingers* (1971; featuring a real jeans zipper).

March 7. The Beastie Boys become the first rap act to top the album charts with their debut release, *Licensed to Ill*, which include the hit single, "(You Gotta) Fight for Your Right (to Party!) (Def Jam 06595).

The Beastie Boys were widely attacked by the music press and the rap establishment alike at the outset, largely due to their origins as a hardcore group when formed in 1981. The group members—MCA (Adam Yauch, b. August 5, 1965), Mike D (Mike Diamond, November 20, 1966), and Ad-Rock (Adam Horowitz, October 31, 1967; replaced Kate Schellenbach and John Berry in the early 1980s)—would steadfastly protest accusations of musical piracy, arguing that rap was part of the post-punk cultural underground.

Hailing from well-to-do Jewish families in New York City, they acquired seasoning playing area youth clubs. In 1982, they recorded a seven-inch EP, *Pollywog Stew*, on the indie imprint, Rat Cage, followed in 1983 by the twelve-inch rap single, "Cookie Puss," which was based on a crank call they made to Carvel Ice Cream. They were signed by Def Jam in 1985, with their debut single for the label, "She's on It"—a track from the *Krush Groove* soundtrack that sampled AC/DC's "Back in Black"—becoming an underground hit. Some degree of national exposure was gained by opening for Madonna's Virgin Tour and RUN-D.M.C.'s Raisin' Hell trek.

Their first album, *Licensed to Ill* (Def Jam, 1986)—which combined old school rap rhythms, metal guitar riffing, and b-boy humor viewed from a satirical perspective—became Columbia's fastest-selling debut ever (and most successful rap LP of the decade), attracting considerable industry criticism. Furthermore, conservative elements censured the record's violence, sexism, rebellious posturing, and shallow party-hearty stance. With Def Jam attempting to assert greater control over the group's affairs, the Beasties relocated to California in late 1988, signing with Capitol and forming a working alliance with the British production team, the Dust Brothers, convincing them to apply their cut-and-paste sampling approach to *Paul's Boutique* (1989), a kaleidoscopic psychedelic-funk masterpiece that almost single-handedly created the alternative hip-hop genre. While media observers recognized the visionary features of the album, it experienced a considerable drop-off in sales, reaching only number fourteen on the *Billboard* Top 200.

Check Your Head (1992), released on the group's new imprint, Grand Royal, offered yet another radical innovation, that of positioning rap verses on top of lo-fi grooves built around their own performances of an eclectic blend of styles, including hardcore punk, neu metal, 1970s dinosaur rock, jazz-soul fusion, updated lounge motifs, and dance-floor funk. Now embraced by college and alternative rock radio audiences, the record would debut in the Top 10. For much of the decade, the Beasties seemed content to nurture this Gen-X following, reissuing their early indie material in *Same Old Bullshit* (Grand Royal, 1994); using *Ill Communication* to flesh out the ideas first explored in *Check Your Head*; and collecting the instrumental jams from the third and fourth LPs—enhanced with a couple of new tracks—for *The In Sound From Way Out!* (Grand Royal, 1996).

Hello Nasty (Grand Royal, 1998) found the group probing the boundaries of their tried-and-true formula, however, building densely-layered hip-hop arrangements (complete with freestyle verses, call-and-response vocal refrains, and turntable scratching) on a retro electro-funk foundation. Like *Ill Communication*, it quickly rose to the top of the charts. Recent years have found the Beasties again treading water with *The Sounds of Silence* (Grand Royal, 1999)—and exhaustive double-disc compilation encompassing not only album releases, but B sides, non-LP singles, and EPs—painstakingly documented two-DVD *Video Anthology* (Voyager, 2000).

March 14. Boy George heads up the British singles charts with the David Gates-penned "Everything I Own," replicating Ken Boothe's 1974 run with the song.

March 14. Huey Lewis & the News reach number one on the pop charts with "Jacob's Ladder" (Chrysalis).

March 21. Club Nouveau's remake of the Bill Withers classic, "Lean on Me" (King Jay), begins a two-week stint atop the Hot 100.

March 21. U2 reach number one on British charts for the third time with *The Joshua Tree* (#1 U.S.). It becomes the fastest-selling album in U.K. history.

March 27. U2 performs from the roof of a downtown Los Angeles store while shooting the video for "Where the Streets Have No Name." With thousands of spectators bringing traffic to a halt, the police intervene to end the session.

March 28. Mel and Kim top the British charts with "Respectable."

April 4. The Starship climb to the summit of the pop charts with "Nothin's Gonna Stop Us Now" (Grunt), remaining there for two weeks. The single is featured in the film, *Mannequin*.

April 13. The Rolling Stones' Bill Wyman announces his AIMS Project (Ambition, Ideas, Motivation, Success) at London's Champagne Exchange. Utilizing the band's mobile studio, he will record unknown artists throughout Great Britain.

April 18. Aretha Franklin and George Michael begin a two-week run atop the Hot 100 with "I Knew You Were Waiting (For Me)" (Arista).

April 23. Carole King sues Ode Records owner Lou Adler for breach of contract. She claims to be owed more than $400,000 in royalties. She also asks for the rights to her old recordings.

April 25. Madonna becomes the only female artist to score four number one British singles when "La Isla Bonita" outpaces the competition.

April 25. U2 begins a five-week run atop the album charts with *The Joshua Tree*.

May 2. Cutting Crew reach number one on the pop charts with "(I Just) Died in Your Arms" (Virgin), maintaining that position for a couple of weeks.

May 9. Starship start a four-week run heading up the British charts "Nothing's Gonna Stop Us Now."

May 16. U2's "With or Without You" (Island) begins a three-week stay atop the Hot 100.

June 6. Kim Wilde peaks at number one on the pop charts with her remake of the Supremes hit, "You Keep Me Hangin' On" (MCA).

June 13. Atlantic Starr top the Hot 100 with "Always" (Warner Bros.).

June 20. Lisa Lisa & Cult Jam ascend to the summit of the pop charts with "Head to Toe" (Columbia).

June 24. Jackie Gleason dies at age seventy-one.

Brooklyn native Jackie Gleason left an inestimable legacy in a wide range of entertainment fields, including standup comedy/master of ceremonies in the live theatre circuit, radio (both as a disc jockey and actor), Broadway shows, stage, film, and television, the latter including specials, variety shows, sitcoms, and numerous guest appearances. Surprisingly, his contributions to the recording industry—most notably, pioneering easy listening or mood music as well as the newly emerging album medium—are considerably less known to the contemporary public.

By the time Gleason had become a best-selling recording artist, he was already a show business legend. He was already closely identified with music, having appeared in musicals such as *Follow the Girls* and *Along 5th Avenue* beginning in the late 1930s as well as the peak years of TV's "vaudeo" format. His forays into the record studio were not merely an effort to capitalize on the high-profile Gleason name; rather, he was a talented middle-brow composer and bandleader interested in sound recordings as a powerful medium for communication.

Gleason's earliest hit recordings were the singles, "Melancholy Serenade" (Capitol 2361; 1953; #22), a self-penned million-seller, and "Terry's Theme from *Limelight*" (Capitol 2507; 1953; #30). He would go on to much greater success, though, with album releases. One of the early superstars of the genre, he placed seventeen titles on the charts between 1955 and 1969, including the Top 10 hits *Music To Remember Her* (Capitol 570; 1955; #5), *Lonesome Echo* (Capitol 627; 1955; #1), *Romantic Jazz* (Capitol 568; 1955; #2), *Music for Lovers Only/Music to Make You Misty* (Capitol 475; 1956; #7), *Music to Change Her Mind* (Capitol 632; 1956; #8), and *Night Winds* (Capitol 717; 1956; #10).

His work was easily recognizable for its dreamy, reflective feel; his studio orchestras included world-class soloists such as trumpeters Bobby Hackett and Pee Wee Erwin. Although he was most successful leading his Society Dance Orchestra, he also produced records as a pianist with bass and drums accompaniment and recreating his famous comic characterizations. While an audience has always existed for the middle-of-the-road style of music, his efforts were commercially eclipsed in the 1960s by the distinctive "cascading strings" sounds of Mantovani and more upbeat arrangements of Percy Faith, Henry Mancini, and other Hollywood-based conductors.

June 27. Whitney Houston begins a two-week stint atop the Hot 100 with "I Wanna Dance With Somebody (Who Loves Me)" (Arista). She is the first female artist to have four consecutive chart-topping singles and to enter the album charts at number one with *Whitney* (Arista).

July 11. Heart reach number one on the pop charts with "Alone" (Capitol), remaining there for three weeks.

July 19. Bruce Springsteen performs behind the Iron Curtain for the first time. The East Berlin concert—which is attended by 180,000 people—is broadcast on East German television.

August 1. "Shakedown" (MCA)—recorded for the film *Beverly Hills Cop II*—becomes Bob Seger's first chart-topping single. The song was originally intended for Glenn Frey, but the former Eagles singer/guitarist had to pass on it due to a case of laryngitis.

August 8. U2 begin a two-week stay atop the Hot 100 with "I Still Haven't Found What I'm Looking For" (Island).

August 22. Levert's "Casanova (Atlantic 89217) heads up the R&B charts, remaining there for two weeks.

August 22. Madonna peaks at number one on the pop charts with "Who's That Girl" (Sire).

August 29. Los Lobos begin a three-week run atop the Hot 100 with cinematic version of Ritchie Valens' "La Bamba" (Slash).

September 5. The Force M.D.'s go number one on the R&B charts with "Love is a Huse" (Tommy Boy 28300), remaining there for a couple of weeks.

September 12. L.L. Cool J peaks at number fourteen on the Hot 100 with "I Need Love" (Def Jam 07350).

Born James Todd Smith on January 14, 1968, in Bayshore, Long Island, New York, L.L. Cool J (which stands for Ladies Love Cool James) began recording rap demos while in high school, one of which attracted the attention of producer Rick Rubin. The ensuing 1984 single, "I Need a Beat," sold one hundred thousand units, providing the impetus for the Def Jam label and placed L.L. Cool J at the forefront of the East Coast school of rappers. His assertive, street tough style proved commercially viable on the mainstream pop charts, His debut LP, *Radio* (Def Jam, 1986), reached number forty-six on the *Billboard* Top 200, while the follow-ups, *Bigger and Deffer* (Def Jam, 1987) and *Walking with a Panther* (Def Jam, 1989), made the Top 10.

Although his collaboration with producer Marley Marl *Mama Said Knock You Out* (Def Jam, 1990), garnered a Grammy, L.L. Cool J's effort to satisfy both pop and gangsta rap fans caused his early 1990s work to vacillate between clichéd hardcore posturing and macho self parody. He revived his career, however, stripped-down funk of *Phenomenon* (Def Jam, 1997) and the chart-topping *G.O.A.T. Featuring James T. Smith: The Greatest of All Time* (Def Jam, 2000). Now something of a rap institution with a career spanning three decades, L.L. Cool J maintained his success with *The Definition* (Def Jam), ranked 125th in *Billboard*'s year-end compilation of the most popular albums in 2004.

September 19. The Fat Boys, with backing vocals by the Beach Boys, peak at number twelve on the Hot 100 with "Wipeout" (Tin Pan 885960).

The Fat Boys were the clown princes of rap in the 1980s. Their unthreatening, mass media-friendly approach helped to counteract the intimidating, gangster image with which the hip-hop genre was saddled as it attempted to cross-over to the pop mainstream.

The Brooklyn-born trio appeared on the music scene at the perfect time: the outset of the MTV-driven video age. Their humor was rooted in visual slapstick, accentuating their large size and awkward movements in a world that worshipped svelte, sexy physiques. The threesome—consisting of Darren "The Human Beat Box" Robinson, Mark "Prince Markie Dee" Morales, and Damon "Kool Rock-ski" Wimbley—allegedly tipped the scales at more than 750 pounds combined.

The Fat Boys were only modestly successful at the outset; they first made the R&B charts in mid-1984 with "Fat Boys"/"Human Beat Box" (Sutra 135; #65), billed as the Disco 3. Taking the name of this single, they consolidated their success with such releases as "Jail House Rap" (Sutra 137; 1984; #105 pop, #17 r&b), "The Fat Boys Are Back" (Sutra 144; 1985; #27 r&b), "Sex Machine" (Sutra 152; 1986; #23 r&b), "Falling In Love" (Tin Pan 885766; 1987; #16 r&b), "Wipeout" (#10 r&b), and "The Twist" (Tin Pan

887571; 1988; #16 pop, #40 r&b; with Chubby Checker)—all assisted by promotional video clips which were frequently shown and various network and cable television channels.

By now idolized by young blacks and suburban white kids alike, the Fat Boys were seen in films such as *Krush Groove* (1985; which featured them along with Run-D.M.C., Sheila E., and Kurtis Blow as the Krush Groove All Stars) *Disorderlies* (1987) as well as countless fan magazines. By the 1990s, however, they had become passé. Any hopes of a return to favor were dashed by Robinson's death from heart failure on December 10, 1995.

September 19. Michael Jackson and Siedah Garrett reach number one on both the pop and R&B charts with "I Just Can't Stop Loving You" (Epic 07253).

September 26. Whitney Houston begins a two-week stint atop the Hot 100 with "Didn't We Almost Have It All" (Arista).

September 26. LL. Cool J reaches number one on the R&B charts with "I Need Love" (Def Jam 07350).

October 3. Lisa Lisa and Cult Jam head up the R&B charts with "Lost in Emotion" (Columbia 07267).

October 5. Former Smiths guitarist Johnny Marr begins rehearsing with the Pretenders, who are scheduled to support U2 on an American tour.

October 10. Stephanie Mills peaks at number one on the R&B charts with "(You're Puttin') A Rush on Me" (MCA 53151).

October 10. Whitesnake climbs to the summit of the pop charts with "Here I Go Again" (Geffen).

October 17. Michael Jackson's Bad (Epic 07418) begins a three-week stay atop the R&B charts.

October 17. Lisa Lisa & Cult Jam reach number one on the Hot 100 with "Lost in Emotion."

October 24. Michael Jackson commences a two-week stint atop the pop charts with "Bad."

November 4. Ron Wood and Bo Diddley, calling themselves the Gunslingers, begin a North American tour at the Newport Music Hall, Columbus, Ohio. The tour will run though a November 25 show at the Ritz, in New York City.

November 7. The O'Jays head up the R&B charts with "Lovin' You" (Philadelphia International 50084).

November 7. Tiffany surges to the top of the Hot 100 with her reworking of the Tommy James & the Shondells hit, "I Think We're Alone Now" (MCA), remaining there for two weeks.

November 14. Angela Winbush's "Angel" (Mercury 888 831) begins a two-week stint atop the R&B charts.

November 21. Billy Idol goes number one with a redo of another Tommy James classic, "Mony Mony 'Live'" (Chrysalis).

November 28. "(I've Had) The Time of My Life"—by Bill Medley, formerly of the Righteous Brothers, and Jennifer Warnes—tops the Hot 100.

November 28. Stevie Wonder's "Skeletons" (Motown 1907) begins a two-week stay atop the R&B charts.

December 1. A Kentucky teacher loses her appeal in the U.S. Supreme Court after being fired for showing Pink Floyd's *The Wall* to her class. The film was determined to be inappropriate for minors due to its language and sexual content.

December 5. Ex-Go Go's lead singer, Belinda Carlisle, reaches number one on the pop charts with "Heaven is a Place on Earth" (MCA).

December 12. George Michael begins a four-week run atop the Hot 100 with "Faith" (Columbia).

December 19. The Pet Shop Boys peak at number one on the British charts with "Always on My Mind." The song was previously a hit for Brenda Lee (1972) and Elvis Presley (1973).

1988

✳

January 9. Whitney Houston reaches number one on the pop charts for the sixth consecutive time with "So Emotional" (Arista).

January 16. George Harrison goes to number one on the Hot 100 with the Rudy Clark composition, "Got My Mind Set on You" (Dark Horse).

January 22. On the verge of stardom, Faith No More make their live English debut at Dingwalls, London, the beginning of a thirteen-date tour.

January 23. Michael Jackson tops the pop charts with "The Way You Make Me Feel" (Epic).

January 28. The Sex Pistols only legitimate album, *Never mind the Bollocks, Here's the Sex Pistols*, is awarded a gold record eleven years after being released.

January 30. A court case involving lead vocalist Holly Johnson and ZIT Records discloses that Frankie Goes to Hollywood did not play on their hits, "Relax" and "Two Tribes"; leading session musicians were instead employed to make the records.

January 30. INXS climb to the summit of the Hot 100 with "Need You Tonight" (Atlantic).

February 6. Tiffany begins a two-week stay atop the pop charts with "Could've Been" (MCA).

February 15. Def Leppard are forced to cancel an El Paso concert after receiving threats that it would be disrupted. Vocalist Joe Elliot had previously referred to the city as "the place with all those greasy Mexicans."

February 20. Expose reach number one on the Hot 100 with "Seasons Change" (Arista).

February 20. Kylie Minogue heads up the British charts with "I Should Be So Lucky." Minogue first achieved fame in an Australian soap opera, *Neighbors*. When the recording was turned down by all major U.K. labels, producer Pete Waterman released it on his PWL imprint. She would place more than thirty singles in the U.K. Top 30, and just miss the number one position stateside with her update of the Goffin/King classic, "The Loco-Motion."

February 20. Salt-N-Pepa peak at number nineteen on the Hot 100 with "Push It" (Next Plateau 315). The single will go on to be certified platinum.

The first distaff rappers of note, they were instrumental in paving the way for other female acts in a male-dominated genre. They provided an assertive, more grown-up vision of African American women—in contrast to the wise-cracking, arrogant young teens most visible among the female MCs—that helped rap cross-over to mainstream pop acceptance.

Salt-N-Pepa were the brainchild of Hurby "Luv Bug" Azor, who enlisted his girlfriend, Cheryl James (Salt), and Sandra Denton (Pepa) to provide an answer song to Doug E. Fresh and Slick Rick's hip-hop hit, "The Show." The ensuing single, "The Show Stoppa (Is Stupid Fresh)" (Pop Art; 1985)—with the duo billed as "Super Nature"—constructed around a sample from the *Revenge of the Nerds* soundtrack, had little trouble garnering massive airplay due to the limited number of rap releases then available for pop consumption. Its success led to a long-term deal with Next Plateau Records for the act, now known as Salt-N-Pepa from a line in "The Show Stoppa," where they referred to themselves as "the salt and pepper MCs.

The debut album, *Hot Cool & Vicious* (Next Plateau 1007; 1987; #26; platinum record)—with the DJ, Spinderella (Pamela Greene) rounding out the group—was dominated by Azor's vision. He wrote their lyrics, was credited with the studio production, and created the b-girl-derived visual image—basketball warm-up gear, large gold bamboo earrings, rope chains, and asymmetrical haircuts—as seen on their first video, "Tramp." Ironically, the single's B side, "Push It"—built around innocuously suggestive lyrics and an engaging, go-go beat—proved to be the trio's commercial breakthrough, garnering a Grammy nomination and heavy MTV rotation. The popular follow-up LP, *A Salt With a Deadly Pepa* (Next Plateau 1011; 1988; #38; gold record), emphasized dance rhythms (best appreciated in the Salt-N-Pepa's video clips) at the expense of the verses, which contained little of literary or social import.

The third album, *Blacks' Magic* (Next Plateau 1019; 1990; #38; platinum record), featured greater creative control by the group, with four tracks produced by Salt and one by Spinderella. The music emphasized their rhythm and blues influences, including dead legends like Jimi Hendrix and Billie Holiday, while the verses covered mature themes such as self-esteem ("Expression"), predatory males ("Do You Want Me"), and loveless relationships ("Let's Talk About Sex"). *Very Necessary* (Next Plateau/London 828392; 1993; #4), which consolidated the artistic growth begun on the previous LP, elevated Salt-N-Pepa to the status of pop icons, selling more than five million copies on the strength of the hit singles "Shoop" (Next Plateau 857314; 1993; #4; gold record) and "Whatta Man" (Next Plateau 857390; 1994; #3; platinum record). Released in the wake of prolonged record label maneuvering punctuated by the trio's decision to cut ties with Azor, *Brand New* (Red Ant; 1997) sold poorly. Much of problem appeared to rest with the act, which came across as tentative, perhaps due to the rise of more youthful imitators such as TLC. At this point in time, the act's future seemed in question, with the three members (including Deirdre Roper, who had replaced Greene as Spinderella) all expressing interest in solo careers.

February 27. George Michael begins a two-week stay atop the Hot 100 with his own composition, "Monkey" (Columbia).

February 28. k.d. lang performs at the closing ceremony of the Calgary Winter Olympics.

March 10. Andy Gibb dies in a hospital at age thirty following a long battle with cocaine addiction, which severely weakened his heart.

March 12. Big-voiced British singer Rick Astley becomes the latest sensation when "Never Gonna Give You Up" (RCA) begins a two-week run as the top pop single. He does almost as well with his follow-up release, "Together Forever" (RCA), which spends a week at number one, before losing some career momentum.

March 19. Guitarist Kurt Cobain and bassist Krist Novoselic, along with drummer Dave Foster, are billed as Nirvana for the first time at a performance in the Community World Theater, Tacoma, Washington. Described at the time as a trio—Chad Channing would replace Foster as drummer in May—playing heavy rock with punk overtones, they went into Seattle's Reciprocal Recording Studios June 11, 30, and July 16 to produce the songs comprising the debut single, "Love Buzz"/"Big Cheese," and the three-EP box set Sub Pop 200 ("Mr. Moustache," "Blew," "Floyd the Barber," "Spank Thru," and the instrumental "Sifting").

The group's album—*Nevermind* (DGC), produced by Butch Vig at Sound City Studios in Van Nuys, California, and released September 24, 1991—almost single-handedly propelled the grunge sound into the commercial mainstream. Its first single, "Smells Like Teen Spirit"—built around Cobain's passionate guitar work, became a Generation X teen anthem, perhaps the most widely recognized alternative rock song of the decade. While Nirvana's promise was cut short by Cobain's April 1994 suicide, they have remained a commercial force to the present day via a string of posthumous releases. Their style has evolved in the hands of Seattle bands like Alice in Chains, Soundgarden, and the Foo Fighters, led by multi-instrumentalist, Dave Grohl, who'd taken over Nirvana's drummer slot in the fall of 1990.

March 26. Michael Jackson begins a two-week stint atop the Hot 100 with "Man in the Mirror" (Epic).

April 8. R.E.M. signs with Warner Brothers Records.

April 9. Billy Ocean reaches number one on the pop charts with "Get Outta My Dreams, Get Into My Car" (Jive), remaining there for two weeks.

April 9. Dave Prater—who enjoyed a string of hits in the 1960s with Sam & Dave—is killed when his car collides with a tree in Syracuse, Georgia. He is fifty years old.

April 11. Singer Cher wins the Best Actress Oscar for her performance in *Moonstruck*.

April 19. Sony Bono is sworn in as the Mayor of Palm Springs, California.

April 23. Whitney Houston begins a two-week stay atop the Hot 100 "Where Do the Broken Hearts Go" (Arista).

April 23. Roy Orbison celebrates his fifty-second birthday at a Bruce Springsteen concert, highlighted by the audience's rendition of "Happy Birthday."

April 23. Pebbles peaks at number five on the Hot 100 with her first pop hit, "Girlfriend" (MCA 53185).

American songwriter/producers, L. A. Reid and Babyface (born Kenneth Edmonds; nicknamed by space-funkster Bootsy Collins) have been referred to as the "Chinn and Chapman of black pop/dance" by *The Guinness Encyclopedia of Popular Music*. They first worked together in the Deele before making a splash at the controls of Pebbles' "Girlfriend."

The team's distinctive sound—characterized by strongly melodic fare framed by hard, fast rhythms—has been employed by many lead R&B artists, including Paula Abdul, the Boys, Toni Braxton, Bobby Brown, the Jacksons, and Midnight Star. Babyface, in his own right, specializes in the release of smooth, romantic recordings—including *Lovers* (Solar; 1989), *Tender Lover* (Solar; 1989), *A Closer Look* (Solar; 1991), and *For the Cool in You* (Epic; 1994)—utilizing the vocal talents of such singers as Pebbles and Karyn White.

May 7. Terence Trent D'Arby makes it to the summit of the pop charts with "Wishing Well" (Columbia).

May 14. Gloria Estefan and the Miami Sound Machine begin a two-week stint atop the Hot 100 with "Anything For You" (Epic; #10 U.K.).

May 14. Led Zeppelin reunite for the Atlantic Records fortieth anniversary party in New York. The late John Bonham's son, Jason, plays drums.

May 21. Billy Bragg and Wet Wet Wet reach number one on the British charts with "With a Little Help From My Friends"/"She's Leaving Home," recorded for the Childline charity.

May 21. Prince tops the U.K. album charts with *Lovesexy*.

May 28. George Michael begins a three-week run at number one on the pop charts with "One More Try" (Columbia).

June 18. Rick Astley tops the Hot 100 with "Together Forever" (RCA).

June 25. Debbie Gibson goes to the summit of the pop charts with her composition, "Foolish Brat" (Atlantic).

June 27. The Fat Boys sue Miller Beer for $5 million due to a TV commercial centered around three overweight rappers allegedly styled in their own image.

July 2. Michael Jackson's "Dirty Diana" (Epic) reaches number one on the Hot 100, his third single to accomplish that feat in 1988.

July 9. Cheap Trick begin a two-week stint atop the pop charts with "The Flame" (Epic).

July 23. Richard Marx makes it to number one on the Hot 100 with "Hold on to the Nights" (EMI Manhattan).

July 23. D. J. Jazzy Jeff & the Fresh Prince peak at number twelve on the Hot 100 with "Parents Just Don't Understand" (Jive 1099).

Born in Philadelphia on September 25, 1968, Will Smith (aka the Fresh Prince) first found fame as a comical pop-rapper along with partner D .J. Jazzy Jeff (Jeffrey A. Townes). The duo's crossover success enabled Smith to become the first rap artist to make the transition to television success, a result of his landing the title role in the sitcom *The Fresh Prince of Bel-Air*, which ran six seasons on NBC. A string of film roles (e.g., *Bad Boys*, *Independence Day*, *Men In Black*, *Wild, Wild West*) followed, which in turn have propelled Smith back to the top of the charts as a solo act.

D. J. Jazzy Jeff and the Fresh Prince's debut album, *Rock the House* (Jive 1026; 1987; #83), attracted considerable attention due to its innovative blend of samples (ranging from James Brown to the *I Dream of Jeannie* theme) and scratching accented by the charismatic wit of Smith's humorous anecdotes. The follow-up, *He's the D.J., I'm the Rapper* (Jive 1091; 1988; #4)—driven by the hits "Parents Just Don't Understand" and "A Nightmare On My Street" (Jive 1124; 1988; #15)—achieved unprecedented crossover popularity, ultimately selling more than two-and-a-half million copies. Subsequent LPs—*And In This Corner* (Jive 1188; 1989; #39; gold record award), *Homebase* (Jive 1392; 1991; #12; platinum record award; included singles "Summertime" (Jive 1465; 1991; #4) and "Ring My Bell" (Jive 42024; 1991; #20), and *Code Red* (Jive; 1993)—while selling well, came across as rather silly and contrived.

Although never officially disbanded, the duo hasn't recorded since 1993, apparently due to the demands of Smith's media stardom. His first solo rap recordings—two songs, including the title cut, which topped the *Billboard Hot 100*—appeared on soundtrack, *Men In Black: The Album* (Columbia 68169; 1997). The album, *Big Willie Styles* (Columbia; 1997; #1)—which included the chart-topping single, "Getting' Jiggy Wit It" (Columbia 78804; 1998)—validated efforts to place his recording career back on the front burner. The film title track, "Wild Wild West" (Overbrook 79157; 1999; #1; featuring Dru Hill and Kool Mo Dee), offered further proof that PG-rated hip-hop possesses considerable sales potential.

July 30. Steve Winwood's "Roll With It" (Virgin) begins a four-week stay atop the pop charts, making it the most successful single for the year.

August 19. Elvis Presley's "Hound Dog" is named the most played record of all time on American jukeboxes.

August 27. George Michael heads the Hot 100 with "Monkey" (Columbia), remaining there a couple of weeks. It is the fourth consecutive number one single since January for the British singer/songwriter, earning him top recording artist honors for 1988, according to *Joel Whitburn's Pop Annual, 1955–1999*.

August 27. Kylie Minogue begins a four-week run atop the British album charts with her debut LP, *Kylie*.

September 3. Rick Astley heads up the British charts with "Never Gonna Give You Up."

September 6. Elton John memorabilia is auctioned off at Sotheby's in London. The two thousand-odd items include his boa feathers, "Pinball Wizard" boots, and hundreds of pairs of spectacles.

September 10. Guns N' Roses burst onto the scene with a two-week stint at number one on the pop charts with the group composition, "Sweet Child O' Mine" (Geffen). The pop metal band will dominate the LP charts for the remainder of the decade before inner tensions lead to a breakup.

September 24. Bobby McFerrin begins a two-week stay atop the Hot 100 with the a cappella tour de force, "Don't Worry Be Happy" (EMI Manhattan 50146).

A one-of-a-kind talent, McFerrin possesses the ability to reproduce vocally virtually any musical instrument as well as many other natural sounds. Born March 11, 1950, in New York City, to opera-singing parents, he studied piano rather than voice at Julliard and Sacramento State College. Following stints playing piano with University of Utah dance workshops and singing in various journeyman bands, he was asked to join Jon Hendricks' jazz group. On the strength of highly acclaimed solo performances at the Playboy Jazz Festival (1980) and Kool Jazz Festival (1981), he was signed to a recording contract by Elektra.

From the beginning, McFerrin's releases ran contrary to traditional notions of jazz vocalizing. He performed without instrumental backup, combining his multitextured voice with rhythmic body slaps to simulate full-band accompaniment. His material—a blend of original compositions and covers—spanned the classical, jazz, soul, funk, and pop genres. After a series of moderately selling albums, he broke through with "Don't Worry Be Happy." By the late 1980s, he seemed to be everywhere, collaborating with jazz stars (Herbie Hancock, the Manhattan Transfer, Chick Corea), classical musicians (Yo-Yo Ma), film star narrators (Robin Williams, Jack Nicholson); recording the theme to *The Cosby Show*; and providing the accompaniment to a number of television commercials.

October 8. Def Leppard reaches number one on the pop charts with "Love Bites" (Mercury).

October 8. The New Kids on the Block peak at number ten on the Hot 100 with "Please Don't Go Girl" (Columbia 07700).

New Kids on the Block are widely viewed within the record industry white clones of the youthful pop-soul phenoms, New Edition. After parting with the latter act over a record contract dispute, composer/producer/promoter Maurice Starr enlisted a Boston talent agency to locate talented white singers, rappers, and dancers. The resulting group—comprised of Donnie Wahlberg, break dancer Danny Wood, Joe McIntyre, and brothers Jonathan and Jordan Knight—released an eponymous debut album, *New Kids on the Block* (Columbia 40475; 1986), which sold poorly. However, the follow-up, *Hangin' Tough* (Columbia 40985; 40985), topped the charts, propelled by the hit singles, "Please Don't Go Girl" and "You Got It" (Columbia 38-08062; 1988). Although their rhythm and blues-inflected bubblegum was generally panned by rock journalists, a string of Top 10 singles followed: "I'll Be Loving You (Forever) (Columbia 38-68671; 1989), "Hangin' Tough" (Columbia 38-68960), "Didn't I (Blow Your Mind)" (Columbia 38-

68960), "Cover Girl" (Columbia 38-69088; 1989), "This One's for the Children" (Columbia 38-73064; 1989), "Step By Step" (Columbia; 1990), and "Tonight" (Columbia; 1990). In 1991, the unit topped *Forbes* magazine's list of top-grossing American entertainers:

Professional and legal problems (e.g., allegations of brawling and arson, a lawsuit disclosing that members hadn't sung on their recordings) served to diminish the group's popularity. In 1992, they resurfaced as NKOTB; the recordings revealed a more musically ambitious approach. Although a modest seller by past standards, *Face the Music* (1994)—produced by Wahlberg, Teddy Riley, and Narada Michael Walden (known for his work with Whitney Houston and Marian Carey), among others—earned uniformly high marks from critics. By the late 1990s, however, the group had been eclipsed by newer acts catering to the youth market such as the Backstreet Boys and 'N Sync. Wahlberg turned increasingly to production work (among his clients was younger brother, Marky Mark) and Jordan Knight attempted to mount a solo career.

October 15. UB40 achieve the top pop single with "Red Red Wine" (A&M), the second chart run for this rendition of the Neil Diamond song. The British ska/bluebeat revival band took the recording to number thirty-four in 1984, albeit edited to a shorter length to appeal to radio programmers.

October 22. Phil Collins begins a two-week stint at number one on the Hot 100 with his remake of the 1966 Mindbenders hit, "Groovy Kind of Love" (Atlantic).

November 5. The Beach Boys return to the number one position following a draught of twenty-two years with "Kokomo" (Elektra). The platinum-selling single, culled from the soundtrack to the film, *Cocktail,* came as a total surprise for a band that had been relegated to reprising their classic 1960s hits since Capitol struck gold with two retrospective compilations, *Endless Summer* (1974; #1) and *Spirit of America* (1975; #8). With chief songwriter Brian Wilson more interested in launching a solo career, however, the Beach Boys were unable to build on this success.

November 12. The Escape Club peak at number one on the pop charts with "Wild, Wild West" (Atlantic).

November 12. Kylie Minogue begins a two-week stint at number three on the pop charts with the Gerry Goffin/Carole King composition, "The Loco-Motion." Two other artists—Little Eva (1962) and Grand Funk (1974) had already recorded chart-topping versions of the song.

November 19. Bon Jovi begin a two-week run atop the Hot 100 with "Bad Medicine" (Mercury).

December 3. Will to Power reach number one on the pop charts with "Baby, I Love Your Way"/"Freebird Medley" (Epic).

December 10. Chicago climbs to the summit of the Hot 100 with "Look Away" (Reprise), remaining there for two weeks.

December 24. Ziggy Marley & the Melody Makers head up the R&B charts with "Tumblin' Down" (Virgin 99299), remaining there for two weeks.

December 24. Poison begin a three-week stay atop the pop charts with "Every Rose Has Its Thorn" (Enigma).

1989

❄

January 5. The Mission is the big winner in the latest *Melody Maker* Readers Poll, sweeping best band, best live act, best single, and best album. Other winners included Morrissey, best male singer; Julianne Regan, best female singer; and House of Love, best new band.

January 7. Roberta Flack tops the R&B charts with "Oasis" (Atlantic 88996).

January 7-8. Lou Reed and John Cale reunite for two tribute shows for Andy Warhol at St. Ann's Church, New York.

January 14. Bobby Brown reaches number one on the pop charts with "My Prerogative" (MCA 53383).

By the late 1980s, Bobby Brown was widely hailed as the king of New Jack Swing. Although not a particularly gifted singer or charismatic personality, he appears blessed with sound commercial instincts and the good fortune to have worked with some of the best studio producers in the business.

Born Robert Beresford Brown, February 5, 1969, in Boston, he first made an impact as part of teen idol sensations, the New Edition. He made a rather tentative start as a solo artist with *King of Stage* (MCA; 1986), produced by Larry Blackmon and John Luongo. However, his next LP, *Don't Be Cruel* (MCA; 1988)—with Teddy Riley and LA & Babyface manning the boards—was a major smash, including the number one crossover hit, "My Perogative." Film roles (e.g., *Ghostbusters II*), video releases, a storybook marriage to singing superstar Whitney Houston, and more best-selling recordings—including *Dance...Ya Know It!* (MCA; 1989) and *Bobby* (MCA; 1992)—followed, marred only by allegations of drug abuse and marital dischord.

January 14. Karyn White starts a three-week run atop the R&B charts with "Superwoman" (Warner Bros. 27783).

January 18. The Rolling Stones officially enter the Rock 'n' Roll Hall of Fame at the fourth annual induction dinner, Waldorf Astoria, New York City.

January 21. Phil Collins begins a two-week stint atop the Hot 100 with "Two Hearts" (Atlantic 88980).

January 21. Taylor Dayne peaks at number two on the Hot 100 with "Don't Rush Me" (Arista 9722).

January 21. Just six weeks following his death, Roy Orbison begins a three-week stay atop the British charts with the LP compilation, *The Legendary Roy Orbison*.

January 25. Bobby Brown is arrested for an overtly sexually suggestive performance in Columbus, Ohio. He will be fined $652 for violating the anti-lewdness ordinance law.

January 25. Madonna restarts divorce proceedings against Sean Penn in Los Angeles County Court, and relocates to a three-bedroom home in the Hollywood Hills.

February 4. Milli Vanilli enter the Hot 100 for the first time with "Girl You Know It's True" (Arista 9781). The single will peak at number two (number one in sales for two weeks), on its way to achieving platinum status. The mastermind behind the Euro-pop act, German producer Frank Farian (who also created the hugely successful Boney M), pushed forward two photogenic models in their early twenties. With the promotional video—which featured the young men lip-synching to a slickly choreographed dance routine—in heavy rotation on MTV as well as other cable stations committed to a similar programming format, the duo became an overnight sensation.

Few acts have fallen from grace as quickly as the German-based Milli Vanilli, named after a New York night club. The duo—comprised of former orphan Rob Pilatus and Fabrice Morvan, a trampoline athlete prior to a serious neck injury caused by a fall—worked as back-up singers for an assortment of German artists before getting together to work out a blend of rap and soul. They quickly achieved stardom on the strength of the hit singles, "Girl, You Know It's True" (1988) and "Girl, I'm Gonna Miss You" (1988), both driven by slick video clips which were heavily played on MTV and a host of pop music programs.

Milli Vanilli were victims of a large-scale consumer backlash when word surfaced that they merely photogenic front-men for a studio group fabricated by producer Frank Farian, and had not sung on any of their recordings. The twosome took on a contrite public persona, returning all music awards, and expressing the desire to make a comeback on the merits of their own vocals. However, their efforts would never receive a widespread public hearing.

February 4. New Edition begins a two-week stint atop the R&B charts with "Can You Stand the Rain" (MCA 53464).

February 4. Sheriff peaks at number one on the pop charts with "When I'm With You" (Capitol).

February 7. Georgia state representative Billy Randall introduces a bill to make "Tutti Frutti"—composed by Macon native Little Richard—the state's official rock song.

February 11. Paula Abdul begins a three-week run atop the Hot 100 with "Straight Up" (Virgin).

Paula Abdul's career success had everything to do with timing—and the MTV phenomenon. She studied dance throughout her childhood, and—after attending college at California State, Northridge—became a Los Angeles Lakers cheerleader. Jackie Jackson noticed Abdul's skills in planning dance routines, and hired her to choreograph the Jacksons' "Torture" video. She went on to work in television and films as well as assisting many other artists in video production, most notably Janet Jackson, Duran Duran, the Pointer Sisters, and ZZ Top.

Abdul joined the roster of Virgin Records artists in the late 1980s. Her first album, *Forever Your Girl* (Virgin 90943; 1988), became one of the decade's bestsellers seven million copies in the United States), topping the *Billboard Top 200* chart and producing four number one singles: "Straight Up" (Virgin 7-98256; 1988), "Forever Your Girl" (Virgin 7-98238; 1989), "Cold Hearted" (Virgin 7-99196; 1989), and "Opposites Attract" (Virgin 7-99158; 1989). Despite widespread criticism of her singing, the LP succeeded due to catchy funk arrangements and flashy videos that effectively captured her stylish, energetic dance moves and girlish charm.

To capitalize on Abdul's success, Virgin released an album of dance remixes of her hit recordings entitled *Shut Up and Dance* (Virgin 91362; 1990). The next album, *Spellbound* (Virgin 91611; 1991) maintained her upward career trajectory, reaching number one and spawning five hit singles. Subsequent releases have been less successful, but Abdul remains active both as a performer and choreographer. She is best known to 21st century youth, however, as a celebrity judge on the highly-rated TV show, *American Idol*.

February 12. Aretha Franklin loses a court case to Broadway producer Ashton Springer, who initiated a $1 million suit when she didn't appear for rehearsals (due, he claimed, to her fear of flying) for the stage show, *Sing Mahalia Sing*.

February 13. Michael Jackson fires his manager, Dileo, who allegedly pursued a $60 million settlement in return for not revealing the singer's lifestyle to the media.

February 18. Fine Young Cannibals top the British charts with *The Raw and the Cooked*.

February 18. Debbie Gibson begins a five-week stay atop the LP charts with *Electric Youth*.

February 18. Tone Loc peaks at number two on the Hot 100 with "Wild Thing" (Delicious Vinyl 102). One of the first rap singles to become a major pop hit, it goes on to earn double platinum status.

February 18. Vanessa Williams goes number one on the R&B charts with "Dreamin'" (Wing 871 078), remaining there for a couple of weeks.

February 25. The Fine Young Cannibals—a Birmingham, England-based band consisting of black vocalist Roland Gift, guitarist Andy Cox, and bassist David Steele—reaches number one on the British singles charts with "She Drives Me Crazy" (I.R.S./MCA 53483). Owing much to Gift's striking looks and stagy posturing, both of which were brilliantly exploited in the trio's promotional video clips, the trio burst onto the American scene with a moderately successful remake of Elvis Presley's "Suspicious Minds." Three major hits followed in 1989: "She Drives Me Crazy," "Good Thing" (#1 pop), and "Don't Look Back" (#11 pop). However, Gift's first love appears to have been acting. The band took their name from the 1960 film, *All the Fine Young Canibals*, and would appear in the Danny Devito comedy, *Tin Men* (1987). With Gift besieged by additional film offers, the band would split up at their commercial peak.

March 1. R.E.M.'s first package of arena venues, "Green World Tour," kicks off at the Louisville Gardens, Kentucky.

March 2. Madonna begins a $5 million sponsorship deal with Pepsi Cola.

March 4. Anita Baker's "Just Because" (Elektra 69327) ascends to the summit of the R&B charts.

March 4. Debbie Gibson begins a three-week run atop the Hot 100 with her composition, "Lost in Your Eyes" (Atlantic).

March 11. Australian actor turned singer Jason Donovan heads up the British charts for the first time with "Too Many Broken Hearts."

March 11. Debbie Gibson reach number one on the album charts with *Electric Youth* (Atlantic), remaining there for five weeks.

March 11. Levert featuring Heavy D. tops the R&B charts with "Just Coolin'" (Atlantic 88959).

March 15. The Rolling Stones ink a $70 million deal to play fifty North American concerts, the largest such contract in rock history.

March 16. MTV launches a contest with Jon Bon Jovi's childhood home as the prize.

March 16. Dokken's *Tooth and Nail* (Elektra 60376) goes platinum. A more convincing argument for dominance for heavy metal during the decade would be hard to find. Dokken was a journeyman band at best, possessing little potential for producing radio-friendly, hit singles. Yet their four 1980s LPs all went platinum; *Tooth and Nail* only reaching as high as number seventy-one on the charts.

March 18. A California radio station has a steamroller run over all its Cat Stevens records in protest over the singer/songwriter's support of the Ayatollah Khomeni.

March 18. Surface begin a two-week stint atop the R&B charts with "Closer Than Friends" (Columbia 08537).

March 25. Mike & the Mechanics reach number one on the pop charts with "The Living Years" (Atlantic). The group represented a side project for Genesis keyboardist Mike Rutherford.

April 1. The Bangles climb to the summit of the Hot 100 with "Eternal Flame" (Columbia).

April 1. The Boys take up residency atop the R&B charts with "Lucky Charm" (Motown 1952).

April 6. Enya earns a gold record for her new age album, *Watermark* (Geffen 24233).

Easily the most popular Irish female singer in recorded sound history, Enya—born Eithne Ni Bhraonain in Gweadore, County Donegal—possesses an ethereal voice ideally suited to translate the mysterious beauty of her cultural heritage for worldwide consumption. After recording with her family's group, Clannad, in the early 1980s, she went solo to produce the British film soundtrack, *The Frog Prince* (Island ISTA 10; 1985). It was followed by *Enya* (Atlantic 81842; 1987), the score to a BBC television documentary, "The Celts." The album established the template for Enya's later releases, blending new age-influenced ambient textures and synthesizer washes, bits of traditional instrumentation (uilleann pipes, harps), and her Irish-language singing, placed deep within the overall mix rather than distinctly up front.

Collaborating with backing musicians, Roma and Nicky Ryan (the latter also assuming production responsibilities), on songwriting, Enya would produce a masterpiece, *Watermark* (Geffen 24233; 1988; #25 US, #5 UK). With her pure, lyric soprano voice set amidst lush arrangements built around choral-like effects and aural collages, the album made her an international star. The success of singles like "Orinoco Flow" (Geffen 27633; 1988; #24 US, #1 UK), "Evening Falls" (WEA 356; 1988; #20 UK), and "Storms In Africa" (WEA 368; 1989; #41) singled her out as one of the few so-called new age artists capable of crossing over to the pop charts, despite her apparent aversion to touring. Although, not approaching the brilliance of *Watermark*, follow-up releases—*Shepherd Moons* (Reprise 26775; 1991; #17 US, #1 UK), *The Memory Of Trees* (Reprise 46106; 1995; #9 US, #5 UK), *A Day Without Rain* (Reprise 47426; 2000; #2)—have maintained Enya's commercial and aesthetic standing within the music industry.

April 8. Today head up the R&B charts with "Girl I Got My Eyes on You" (Motown 1954).

April 8. Roxette's "The Look" (EMI) goes to the top of the pop charts.

April 10. The Academy of Country Music cites Alabama as the Artist of the Decade. During the period, the band sold forty million records, and won two Grammies, thirteen ACM trophies, and eight awards from the Country Music Association. In addition, *Billboard* named them the top country artist from 1982 to 1985.

April 12. A couple of KLOS-Los Angeles deejays ask what happened to David Cassidy? The singer calls the station and is invited onto the show. He plays three songs on the air, and is subsequently signed by a record company.

April 15. The American girl group, the Bangles, begin a four-week run atop the British charts with "Eternal Flame."

April 15. Bobby Brown's "Every Little Step" (MCA 53618) peaks at number one on the R&B charts.

April 15. Deacon Blue head up the British album charts with *When the World Knows Your Name*.

April 15. Fine Young Cannibals top the Hot 100 with "She Drives Me Crazy."

April 15. Bonnie Raitt's *Nick of Time* (Capitol), produced by Don Was, enters the album charts. It will remain there for two years, selling more than two million copies in the process.

April 22. Madonna starts a three-week run atop the Hot 100 with "Like a Prayer" (Sire).

April 22. Karyn White begins a two-week stint at number one on the R&B charts with "Love Saw It" (Warner Bros. 27538).

May 2. One of the Motown "Funk Brothers, session drummer Benny Benjamin dies. He performed on many of the hits produced by the label.

May 2. A security guard alerts the police that a man wearing a wig, fake moustache, and false teeth has entered Zales Jewellers. After detaining him, the police discover he is Michael Jackson.

May 6. Holly Johnson, formerly lead vocalist for Frankie Goes to Hollywood, peaks at number one on the British charts with his debut solo album.

May 6. Jody Watley's "Real Love" (MCA 53484) tops the R&B charts.

May 13. Bon Jovi peak at number one on the pop charts with "I'll Be There for You" (Mercury).

May 13. Skyy reach the summit of the R&B charts with "Start of a Romance" (Atlantic 88932), remaining there for a fortnight.

May 20. Paula Abdul begins a two-week stint atop the Hot 100 with "Forever Your Girl" (Virgin).

May 20. Recorded to raise funds for the Hillsbourgh Football victims, "Ferry Cross the Mersey" reaches number one on the British charts, remaining there for three weeks. The one-off group, Ferry Aid, includes the Christians, Holly Johnson, Gerry Marsden, and Paul McCartney.

May 20. Milli Vanilli's "Baby Don't Forget My Number" (Arista 9832) enters the Hot 100 on its way to number one (July 1). It becomes the group's second consecutive million-selling single.

May 20. Jody Watley begins a two-week stint at number two on the Hot 100 with "Real Love" (MCA 53484), a song she co-wrote with funk-punk pioneer Andre Cymone.

May 20. XTC peaks at number seventy-two on the Hot 100 with "The Mayor of Simpleton" (Geffen 27552).

Although rarely able to rise above cult status stateside, XTC were extremely popular in their native England during the early years of the postpunk era. Hurt by their aversion to live performing, the band's recorded work—featuring a gift for infectious melodies, tight song arrangements eschewing extended solos, and quirky, rapid-fire rhythms and instrumental flourishes revealing a pronounced punk influence—has frequently been compared with the Beatles.

Formed in Swindon in 1976, XTC—originally comprised of guitarist/singer/ composer Andy Partridge, bassist Colin Moulding, drummer Terry Chambers, and keyboardist Barry Andrews—earned a contract with Virgin Records in short order based on their gift for pop songcraft, frequently laced with wit and incisive social commentary. The decided power-pop leanings of the band's early albums—*White Music* (Virgin 2095; 1978; #34 UK), *Go 2* (Virgin 2108; 1978; #21 UK), *Drums and Wires* (Virgin 13131; 1979;

#34 UK, #176 US), *Black Sea* (Virgin 13147; 1980; #16 UK, #41 US), and *English Settlement* (Epic 37943; 1982; #5 UK, #48 US)—caused them to be largely overlooked by the rock press, then infatuated with the punk revolution.

As Partridge exercised greater control over XTC in the mid-1980s, the music in the LPs *Mummer* (Geffen 4027; 1983; #51 UK, #145 US), *Big Express* (Geffen 24053; 1984; #38 UK, #178 US), and the Todd Rundgren-produced *Skylarking* (Geffen 24117; 1986; #90 UK, #70 US; latter pressings included the controversial underground hit, "Dear God") took on a more reflective, complex tone. In keeping with Partridge's notoriously eccentric outlook, the band's alter ego, the Dukes of Stratosphear, released two tributes to 1960s psychedelia, the EP *25 O'Clock* (Virgin C 1; 1985), which outsold *The Big Express*, and *Psonic Psunspot* (Geffen 2440; 1987).

Despite various extra-musical problems (e.g., litigation against a former manager in the late 1980s, a recording strike against Geffen during much of the 1990s), XTC has continued to release engagingly eclectic albums. *Oranges & Lemons* (Geffen 24218; 1989; #44) was named the top college-radio LP of 1989, while *Nonsuch* (Geffen 24474; 1992; #97) also reached number one on the college charts. Newly signed to the indie label, TVT, the band released material stockpiled during the decade as two LPs, *Apple Venus Volume I* (TVT 3250; 1999; #42 UK), which featured acoustic material set off by lush orchestrations, and the more typical *Wasp Star (Apple Venus Volume 2)* (TVT 3260; 2000).

May 22. Public Enemy fires one of its members, Professor Griff, after his anti-Semitic remarks were published in the *Washington Post*.

May 27. Atlantic Starr heads up the R&B charts with "My First Love" (Warner Bros. 27525).

May 27. Cliff Richard's 100th single, "The Best of Me," is released. It becomes his twenty-sixth Top 3 hit on the British charts.

May 29. Former Quicksilver Messenger Service guitarist John Cipollina dies from emphysema. A June 16 tribute concert featuring many notable San Francisco rock musicians is held at the Fillmore West.

May 31. David Bowie's Tin Machine performs live for the first time at the International Music Awards in New York.

June 3. Natalie Cole's "Miss You Like Crazy" (EMI 50185) goes number one on the R&B charts.

June 3. Michael Damian tops the pop charts with a redo of the David Essex hit, "Rock On" (Cypress).

June 3. Donny Osmond peaks at number two on the Hot 100 with "Soldier of Love" (Capitol 44369).

June 10. De La Soul reach number one on the R&B charts with "Me Myself and I" (Tommy Boy 7926).

June 10. Bette Midler tops the Hot 100 with "Wind Beneath My Wings" (Atlantic).

June 12. The Elvis Presley Autoland Museum—which contains more than 20 cars once owned by 'The King"—opens at Graceland.

June 17. The New Kids on the Block climb to the summit of the pop charts with "I'll Be Loving You (Forever)" (Columbia).

June 17. The O'Jays begin a two-week stint atop the R&B charts with "Have You Had Your Love Today" (EMI 50180).

June 24. Neneh Cherry peaks at number three on the Hot 100 with "Buffalo Stance" (Virgin 99231).

In the late 1980s, Neneh Cherry surfaced with a series of edgy dance hits, helped immeasurably by heavy rotation on MTV, who recognized her street-smart demeanor and photogenic good looks as an unbeatable combination. Born March 10, 1964, in Stockholm, Sweden, the step-daughter of avant-garde jazz trumpeter Don Cherry, she sang with the British postpunk act, Rip, Rig and Panic, in the early 1980s, before forming Float Up CP with several members of that band. She next provided backing vocals for the likes of the Slits and The The ("Slow Train to Dawn," 1987)

A talented composer—she co-wrote the hits "Buffalo Stance," "Manchild" (Circa; 1989), and "Kisses on the Wind" (Circa; 1989) with husband Cameron McVey—Cherry maintained her creative momentum with a video release, *The Rise of Neneh Cherry* (1989), and a series of internationally successful LPs, including *Raw Like Sushi* (Circa; 1989), *Homebrew* (1993), and a collection of studio remixes, *Buddy X* (1993). She achieved further public attention via brisk poster sales, the use of "Buffalo Stance" in the film *Slaves of New York*, and the inclusion of her rendition of Cole Porter's "I've Got You Under My Skin" on the AIDS charity collection, *Red Hot and Blue*. Having mothered a child well before achieving stardom, Cherry has appeared content to maintain a low profile since the mid-1990s.

June 24. Richard Marx reaches number one on the Hot 100 with "Satisfied" (EMI 50189).

June 27. Tom Jones is awarded a star on the Hollywood Walk of Fame.

July 1. Peabo Bryson outpaces the competition on the R&B charts with his remake of the Al Wilson hit, "Show & Tell" (Capitol 44347).

July 1. Milli Vanilli top the pop charts with "Baby Don't Forget My Number" (Arista).

July 8. The Fine Young Cannibals surge to the summit of the Hot 100 with "Good Thing" (I.R.S./MCA).

July 8. Soul II Soul begin a two-week stay atop the R&B charts with "Keep On Movin'" (Virgin 99205).

July 15. Simply Red reaches number one on the pop charts with "If You Don't Know Me By Now" (Elektra).

July 22. Chuckii Booker settles into the top position on the R&B charts with "Turned Away" (Atlantic 88917).

July 22. Martika begins a two-week stint at number one on the Hot 100 with "Toy Soldiers" (Columbia).

July 29. Surface's "Shower Me With Your Love" (Columbia 68746) climbs to the top of the R&B charts.

August 5. Bobby Brown peaks at the summit of the R&B charts with "On Our Own" (MCA 53662). At the same time, it begins a three-week run at number two on the Hot 100.

August 5. "Batdance" (Warner Bros. 22924), culled from the soundtrack—composed and produced by Prince—to the film, *Batman*, goes number one (#2 UK). The heavily sampled house cut includes dialog excerpts featuring Michael Keaton and Jack Nicholson. The soundtrack—which topped the British charts on July 1—is in its third of six weeks atop the LP charts.

August 9. Santana's *Barboletta* (Columbia 33135) is certified gold, bandleader Carlos Santana's fourteenth album (including collaborations with Mahavishnu John McLaughlin and Buddy Miles) to achieve that distinction up till then. Unlike his LPs, however, *Barboletta* didn't sell the requisite five hundred thousand copies shortly after its release; rather, it took almost fifteen years to accomplish the feat. Although promoted as a return to Santana's roots rock beginnings, the record continued the downward spiral in popularity that commenced with the shift to a jazz-rock approach following platinum sales for his first four albums. By the early 1980s, even gold records would seem unattainable. This would set the scene for one of the more unlikely comebacks in rock history when *Superstition* propelled him back into multi-platinum territory.

August 9. Although ceasing to exist in the mid-1980s, Wham! achieve gold status for their debut LP, *Fantastic* (Columbia 38911), despite the fact that its highest chart position was number eighty-three. Nevertheless, the album continued to sell at a moderate pace long after its July 1983 release. This was due largely to the high level of success enjoyed by former Wham! lead singer/songwriter/producer George Michael.

August 12. Richard Marx begins a three-week run atop the Hot 100 with "Right Here Waiting" (EMI).

August 12. Prince's "Batdance" heads up the R&B charts.

August 19. Stephanie Mills reaches number one on the R&B charts with "Something in the Way (You Make Me Feel)" (MCA 53624).

August 26. Babyface (aka Kenny Edmonds) begins a two-week stint atop the R&B charts with "It's No Crime" (Solar 68966).

August 31. The Rolling Stones' "Steel Wheels North American Tour 1989" opens at Veterans Stadium, Philadelphia. The group is augmented by saxman Bobby Keys, keyboardists Chuck Leavell and Matt Clifford, and vocalists Cindy Mizelle, Bernard Fowler, and Lisa Fischer. Living Colour holds down the opening slot. The tour ends with a November 19 Pay-Per-View show at Atlantic City's Convention Center.

September 2. Paula Abdul reaches number one on the pop charts with "Cold Hearted" (Virgin).

September 9. The New Kids on the Block top the Hot 100 with "Hangin' Tough" (Columbia).

September 9. Teddy Riley featuring Guy head up the R&B charts with "My Fantasy" (Motown 1968). Composed by new jack swing pioneer Riley, it is used in Spike Lee's film, *Do the Right Thing*.

September 16. Gloria Estefan enjoys her first solo chart topper with "Don't Wanna Lose You" (Epic).

September 16. Eric Gable's "Remember (The First Time)" (Orpheus 72663) reaches number one on the R&B charts.

September 21. *Rolling Stone* pictures Madonna, with camera in hand, on its "Rock & Roll Photo Album" issue.

September 22. Russian-born composer Irving Berlin dies at age 101. His compositions included "Alexander's Ragtime Band," "White Christmas," and "Easter Parade."

September 23. Maze featuring Frankie Beverly begin a two-week stay atop the R&B charts with "Can't Get Over You" (Warner Bros. 22895). It was the band's first hit following twenty-one chart singles on the Capitol label and a three-year hiatus from the entertainment business.

September 23. Milli Vanilli's "Girl I'm Gonna Miss You" (Arista 9870) goes number one on the pop charts, remaining there for a couple of weeks. It is the group's second number one in a row; like their last two singles, it is awarded a gold disc.

September 23. The pop-metal band, Warrant, begins a two-week stint at number two on the Hot 100 with "Heaven" (Columbia 68985).

September 30. Tina Turner heads up the British album charts with *Foreign Affair*.

October 7. Janet Jackson starts a four-week run atop the Hot 100 with "Miss You Much" (A&M 1445).

October 7. Soul II Soul featuring Caron Wheeler rise to the summit of the R&B charts with "Back to Life (However Do You Want Me)" (Virgin 99171).

October 7. "I Got Dreams" (MCA 53665) becomes Steve Wariner's ninth chart-topping single. It is also the first country hit of that magnitude to feature scat singing, unless one counts Roger Miller's 1964 recording, "Dang Me."

October 14. Clint Black's "Killin' Time" (RCA 8945) reaches number one on the country charts.

October 14. Janet Jackson's "Miss You Much" begins a two-week stint atop the R&B charts.

October 21. Ricky Van Shelton peaks at number one on the country charts with "Living Proof" (Columbia 68994).

October 28. Alabama's "High Cotton" (RCA 8948) tops the country charts.

October 28. Regina Belle heads up the R&B charts with "Baby Come to Me" (Columbia 68969).

October 28. Tears for Fears peak at number two on the Hot 100 with the neo-psychedelic "Sowing the Seeds of Love" (Fontana 874710).

October 31. The first MTV unplugged show is recorded in New York, featuring Squeeze.

November 4. Roxette top the pop charts with "Listen to Your Heart" (EMI).

November 4. George Strait reaches number one on the county charts with "Ace in the Hole" (MCA 53693).

November 4. Surface begin a two-week stay atop the R&B charts with "You Are My Everything" (Columbia 69016). It is the third chart topper from their sophomore album, *2nd Wave*.

November 11. "When I See You Smile" (Epic), by Bad English, reaches number one on the Hot 100, remaining there for a couple of weeks.

November 11. Kathy Mattea heads up the country charts with "Burnin' Old Memories" (Mercury 874 672).

November 11. Chris Rea begins a three-week stint atop the British album charts with *The Road to Hell*.

November 11. Lisa Stansfield reaches number one on the British charts with "All Around the World."

November 18. Jermaine Jackson hits the summit of the R&B charts with "Don't Take It Personal" (Arista 9875), a song originally pitched to Milli Vanilli by label chief, Clive Davis.

November 18. Eddy Raven's "Bayou Boys" (Universal 66016) reaches number one on the country charts.

November 25. Milli Vanilli's "Blame It On The Rain" (Arista 9904) begins a two-week stint atop the Hot 100, the third chart-topper in a row for the group. It will become their second platinum disc, and fourth straight single to surpass sales of one million copies. Milli Vanilli's next single, "All or Nothing" (Arista 9923), fails to do as well, peaking at number four pop. However, Pilatus and Morvan are soon confronted with a much bigger problem: news surfaces that they didn't sing on any of the tracks comprising their debut LP. With damage control foremost on their minds, the twosome opt to come clean, and soon the public is informed that the actual vocalists for the group were John Davis, Brad Howe, and Charles Shaw. Rumored comebacks fail to get off the ground, and Milli Vanilli soon becomes an obscure footnote in the annals of show business infamy.

November 25. Stephanie Mills peaks at number one on the R&B charts with "Home" (MCA 53712). The song is taken from the finale of the black Broadway musical, *The Wiz*, which starred Mills as a fifteen-year-old in the role of Dorothy.

November 25. Dolly Parton heads up the country charts with "Yellow Roses" (Columbia 69040).

November 26. The first MTV unplugged concert, featuring Squeeze, is aired.

November 29. *Songs For 'Drella: A Fiction*—an album-length suite composed by Lou Reed and John Cale as a tribute to Andy Warhol, is performed by the duo at the Brooklyn Academy of Music.

December 2. Randy Travis goes number one on the country charts with an almost note-for-note remake of Brook Benton's "It's Just a Matter of Time" (Warner Bros. 28841). Travis would later tell *Stereo Review's* Peter Reilly,

> It's just about as close to pop as you're ever going to hear from me. [Producer Richard] Perry's purpose is to show the influence that country has had on rock. You can hear that when you listen to Hank Williams.

December 2. Luther Vandross begins a two-week stint atop the R&B charts with "Here and Now" (Epic 73029).

December 9. Garth Brooks reaches number one on the country charts with "If Tomorrow Never Comes" (Capitol 44430).

December 9. Billy Joel climbs to the summit of the pop charts with "We Didn't Start the Fire" (Columbia), remaining there for two weeks.

December 16. Miki Howard goes number one on the R&B charts with "Ain't Nothin' in the World" (Atlantic 88826).

December 16. Shenandoah head up the country charts with "Two Dozen Roses" (Columbia 69061).

December 23. Phil Collins begins a four-week run atop the Hot 100 with "Another Day in Paradise" (Atlantic).

December 23. The Gap Band's "All of My Love" (Capitol 44418) reaches number one of the R&B charts, remaining there for two weeks. The album on which the single appears, *Round Trip*, is the group's last one, due largely to Ronnie Wilson's desire to become a minister.

December 23. Ronnie Milsap's "A Woman in Love" (RCA 9027) tops the country charts. It's his thirty-fifth single to accomplish this feat, putting him third on the all-time list behind Conway Twitty (40) and Merle Haggard (38).

December 23. Linda Ronstadt and Aaron Neville begin a two-week stint at number two on the Hot 100 with "Don't Know Much" (Elektra 69261).

1990

❄

January 6. Babyface tops the R&B charts with "Tender Lover" (Solar 74003).

January 13. Janet Jackson reaches number one on the R&B charts with "Rhythm Nation" (A&M 1455).

January 19. Mel Appleby—a member of the vocal duo, Mel & Kim—dies of pneumonia. She was only twenty-three years old.

January 20. "How Am I Supposed To Live Without You" (Columbia 73017) becomes Michael Bolton's first single to top the Hot 100, holding down that slot for three weeks. It also spends a couple of weeks at number one on the Adult Contemporary survey. He would reach the Top 40 three more times in 1990 with "How Can We Be Lovers" (Columbia 73257; #3), "When I'm Back On My Feet Again" (Columbia 73342; #7), and a cover of "Georgia On My Mind" (Columbia 73490; #36).

January 20. "I'll Be Good to You" (Qwest 22697), by Quincy Jones featuring Ray Charles and Chaka Khan, begins a two-week stint atop the R&B charts.

January 23. David Bowie announces his final world tour, "Sound and Vision." Plans call for each audience—through local radio stations—helping determine the running order for an upcoming hits compilation.

January 23. Lynyrd Skynyrd guitarist Allen Collins—who survived the 1977 plane crash that decimated the band—dies of pneumonia at age thirty-seven.

January 30. Bob Dylan is named a commander in France's Order of Arts and Letters.

January 30. Taking offense at the reissue of an early single, "Sally Cinnaman," the Stone Roses destroy the offices of their former record label, Revolver FM, and splash paints over cars in the parking lot. Band members are arrested and charged with criminal misconduct.

February 3. Regina Belle's "Make It Like It Was" (Columbia 73022) heads up the R&B charts.

February 6. The day is proclaimed a national holiday in Jamaica to commemorate Bob Marley's birth.

February 8. Del Shannon dies of self-inflicted gunshot wounds. He recorded ten Top 40 singles during the 1960s.

February 10. Paula Abdul—supported by The Wild Pair—reaches number one on the Hot 100 for the fourth time in a little more than a year with "Opposites Attract" (Virgin 99158), remaining there for three weeks. It will also earn her a fourth gold disc.

February 10. Skyy reside atop the R&B charts with "Real Love" (Atlantic 88816).

February 14. The Rolling Stones perform the first of ten sellout nights scheduled for the Korakuen Dome, Tokyo. Five hundred thousand fans see the shows, netting the band $20 million.

February 17. Ruby Turner peaks at number one on the R&B charts with "It's Gonna Be Alright" (Jive 1317).

February 21. Linda Ronstadt garners Best Pop Performance by a Duo or Group with Vocal at the thirty-second Grammy Awards ceremony, while her *Cry Like a Rainstorm – Howl Like the Wind* nets the Best Engineered Recording for George Massenberg.

February 24. Stacy Lattisaw with Johnny Gill top the R&B charts with "Where Do We Go From Here" (Motown 2026).

February 24. Sinead O'Connor rises to the summit of the British charts with "Nothing Compares 2 U."

February 24. Johnny Ray—a key link between the crooning tradition and rock 'n' roll with almost two dozen Top 40 singles in the 1950s—dies of liver failure.

March 3. Janet Jackson begins a three-week run atop the Hot 100 with "Escapade" (A&M 1490).

March 8. The Rolling Stones figure prominently in the 1989 edition of the *Rolling Stone* (magazine) Music Awards, winning Artist of the Year, Best Band of 1989, Best Tour, Worst Album Cover (*Steel Wheels*), and Comeback of the Year. The Critics Award category also produces three wins: Artist of the Year, Best Tour, and Best Drummer (Charlie Watts). Cher wins Worst Dressed Female and Worst Video for "If I Could Turn Back Time," and Donny Osmond the Most Unwelcome Comeback award.

March 10. Janet Jackson's "Escapade"—a concerted effort by songwriting/production team of Jimmy Jam and Terry Lewis to capture the feel of Martha & the Vandellas' "Nowhere to Run"—reaches number one on the R&B charts.

March 14. Michael Jackson is named Artist of the Decade at the annual Soul Train Awards.

March 17. Quincy Jones—featuring Al B. Sure!, James Ingram, El DeBarge, and Barry White—tops the R&B charts with "The Secret Garden (Sweet Seduction Suite)" (Qwest 19992).

March 20. Gloria Estefan's tour bus is rammed by a tractor trailer en route to a concert. She suffers a serious back injury, which requires an operation two days later.

March 24. Alannah Myles begins a two-week stay at number one on the pop charts with "Black Velvet" (Atlantic).

March 24. Sinead O'Connor tops the British album charts with *I Do Not Want What I Haven't Got*. The album duplicates the feat twelve other countries, including a six-week run in the United States.

March 24. Lisa Stansfield hits the summit of the R&B charts with "All Around the World" (Arista 9928), remaining there for a couple of weeks.

March 25. Motley Crue drummer Tommy Lee is arrested for mooning the audience during an Augusta, Georgia concert. He would later be charged with indecent exposure.

April 7. Taylor Dayne reaches number one on the Hot 100 with "Love Will Lead You Back" (Arista).

April 7. Troop start a two-week stint atop the R&B charts with "Spread My Wings" (Atlantic 86244).

April 10. A jury awards Tom Waits $2,475,000 in punitive damages for Doritos Chips' use of a Waits sound-alike on radio ads.

April 12. The Astronomical Union's Minor Planet Center announces that Asteroids 4147-4150 will be named after Beatles members.

April 14. Tommy Page tops the pop charts with "I'll Be Your Everything" (Sire).

April 20. Janet Jackson is given a star on the Hollywood Walk of Fame at the outset of Janet Jackson Week in Los Angeles.

April 21. After 7 peak at number one on the R&B charts with "Ready or Not" (Virgin 98995), remaining there for two weeks.

April 21. Fleetwood Mac head up the British charts with *Behind the Mask*, their fourth album to accomplish this feat.

April 21. Paul McCartney's Rio audience totals 184,000, a new attendance record for a rock concert

April 21. Sinead O'Connor begins a four-week run atop the Hot 100 with her interpretation of the Prince song, "Nothing Compares 2 U" (Ensign). It also goes number one in eighteen other countries.

April 24. In the midst of constructing the set for "The Wall" concert in Potsdamer Platz, Germany, Roger Waters' road crew discovers an unexploded World War II bomb.

April 25. The Fender Stratocaster with which Jimi Hendrix played the "Star Spangled Banner" at the Woodstock Festival was auctioned off for $295,000.

April 28. Sinead O'Connor begins a six-week run atop the album charts with *I Do Not Want What I Haven't Got*.

April 28. Axl Rose, lead singer for Gun N'Roses, marries Erin Everly, daughter of the Everly Brothers' Don Everly, at Cupid's Wedding Chapel in Las Vegas. They will divorce the following January.

May 5. Bell Biv DeVoe—formerly members of New Edition—go number one on the R&B charts with "Poison" (MCA 53772), remaining there for two weeks.

May 18. The Rolling Stones Urban Jungle Europe 1990 tour kicks off in Rotterdam. The twenty-two-date set will end August 18 in Prague, the result of a formal invitation from Czech President Vlacek Havel. The group has appeared in Eastern Europe on only one other occasion, Poland, in 1964.

May 19. Another ex-New Edition member, Johnny Gill, heads up the R&B charts with "Rub You the Right Way" (Motown 1982).

May 19. Madonna begins a three-week stay atop the pop charts with "Vogue" (Sire).

May 26. En Vogue peak at number one on the R&B charts with "Hold On" (Atlantic 87984), remaining there for a fortnight.

May 26. For the first time ever, the top five rungs of the Hot 100 are occupied by female artists: Madonna remains in the top slot with "Vogue," followed (in descending order) by Heart, Sinead O'Connor, Wilson Phillips, and Janet Jackson.

May 30. Midnight Oil performs in front of Exxon's 6th Avenue office in Manhattan in protest of the *Valdez* oil spill. Police found it necessary to shut off the surrounding streets; the concert would later be released on commercial video.

June 9. Englandneworder begins a two-week stint atop the British charts with "World in Motion."

June 9. MC Hammer peaks at number one on the album charts with *Please Hammer Don't Hurt 'Em*, remaining there for twenty-one consecutive weeks—the longest uninterrupted run ever on that listing.

June 9. Tony! Toni! Tone! top the R&B charts with "The Blues" (Wing 873 994).

June 9. Wilson Phillips—a trio comprised of Chynna Phillips, daughter of John and Michelle Phillips, and Brian Wilson's daughters, Carnie and Wendy Wilson—ascend to the summit of the Hot 100 with "Hold On" (SBK).

June 16. M. C. Hammer peaks at number eight on the Hot 100 with "U Can't Touch This" (Capitol 15571).

M. C. Hammer, born Stanley Kirk Burrell in Oakland's (California) subsidized housing district, was the first rapper to cross pop crossover superstardom. An ingenious songwriter/arranger whose material featuring liberal samples of soul-funk hitmakers such as James Brown and Parliament, his considerable dance skills and expertly choreographed performances played a major role in his success. The fact that Hammer released several video titles during his peak period of popularity in the early 1990s, attests to the strong visual orientation of his work.

Burrell was nicknamed "Little Hammer" while working as a batboy for the Oakland Athletics as a result of his resemblance to home run king, "Hammerin'" Hank Aaron. Baseball player friends lent him the money to establish his own record company; his Bay Area success led to a contract with Capitol Records. His second major label album, *Please Hammer Don't Hurt 'Em* (Capitol 92857; 1990; #1 twenty-one weeks)—featuring "U Can't Touch This," based on an unauthorized sample from the Rick James hit, "Super Freak (Part 1)" (Gordy 7205; 1981; #16); a rap update of the Chi-Lites' "Have You Seen Her" (Capitol 44573; 1990; #4) and "Pray" (Capitol 44609; 1990; #2), accompanied by a promotional video clip which melded religion, hip hop, and a West Side Story-influenced dance sequence in—introduced him to the big time. High profile tours, a children's cartoon (*Hammerman*), and endorsement deals with Pepsi and Kentucky Fried Chicken followed. However, the rise of gangsta rap (which rendered his flashy, slick approach dated), bad investments (e.g., horse breeding, real estate), and uneven follow-up LPs—*Too Legit to Quit* (Capitol 98151; 1991; #2) and The *Funky Headhunter* (Giant; 1994)—caused his career to stall.

In 1996, he had to declare bankruptcy with $13.7 million in debts. Since then, Hammer has attempted to resurrect his career, while dividing time raising funds for his ministry.

June 16. Quincy Jones, featuring Tevin Campbell, reaches number one on the R&B charts with "Tomorrow (A Better You, A Better Me) (Qwest 19881). The song originally appeared as an instrumental track on the debut LP by the Brothers Johnson, *Look Out for #1* (1976); Jones had Siedah Garrett write lyrics for it as part of his *Back on the Block* project.

June 16. Roxette begins a two-week stint atop the pop charts with "It Must Have Been Love" (EMI).

June 23. M.C. Hammer zooms to the summit of the R&B charts with "U Can't Touch This" (Capitol 15571), a rap adaptation of the Rick James song, "Super Freak" (Capitol 15571).

June 30. The New Kids on the Block reach number one on the Hot 100 with "Step By Step" (Columbia), remaining there for three weeks.

June 30. Troop's "All I Can Do Is Think of You" (Atlantic 87952) heads up the R&B charts. The song was written by Michael Lovesmith and Brian Holland for the former's band, the Smith Connection, who ultimately decided against recording it. The Jackson 5 would record it for their *Moving Violation* LP; Motown released it as the flip side of a remake of the Supremes' "Forever Came Today," and then as its own A side, going as high as number fifty.

July 7. Lisa Stansfield's "You Can't Deny It" (Arista 2024) peaks at number one on the R&B charts.

July 14. Johnny Gill begins a two-week stint atop the R&B charts with "My, My, My" (Motown 2033).

July 21. "She Ain't Worth It" (MCA), by Glenn Medeiros featuring Bobby Brown, commences a two-week stay at the summit of the pop charts.

July 28. Elton John's *Sleeping with the Past* begins a five-week run atop the British album charts.

July 28. Partners in Kryme start a four-week stay at number one on the British charts with "Turtle Power," the first rap single to accomplish this feat.

July 28. Keith Sweat goes number one on the R&B charts with "Make You Sweat" (Vintertainment 64961)

August 4. After 7 heads up the R&B charts with "Can't Stop" (Virgin 98961).

August 4. After first appearing on the Hot 100 June 16 with "Vision of Love" (Columbia 73348), Mariah Carey rides the song to number one, remaining there for four weeks. Carey would go on to win the 1990 Grammy for Best New Artist.

The most successful female recording artist in the rock era, and the top recording artist of the 1990s by a substantial margin, Mariah Carey belongs to the same torch singing, ballad tradition that spawned Barbra Streisand, Dionne Warwick, and Whitney Houston. Like these singers, Carey's florid style owes more to *bel canto* stage and mainstream pop conventions than rhythm and blues, gospel, and rock influences—all of which are nevertheless discernable in her recordings.

A native of Long Island, New York, she was groomed for a singing career by her mother, Patricia Carey, a former member of the New York City Opera. Carey's rise to fame was meteoric. In addition to winning the 1990 Grammy for Best New Artist, she enjoyed eight number one singles—"Vision Of Love" (Columbia 73348; 1990), "Love Takes Time" (Columbia 73455; 1990), "Someday" (Columbia 73561; 1991), "I Don't Wanna Cry" (Columbia 73743; 1991), "Emotions" (Columbia 73977; 1991), "I'll Be There" (Columbia 74330; 1993), "Dreamlover" (Columbia 77080; 1993), and "Hero" (Columbia 77224; 1993)—during her first four years as a Columbia recording artist; fourteen in all during the decade. Her albums—particularly the eponymous debut (Columbia 45202; 1990; #1 11 weeks; 113 weeks on the charts), *Music Box* (Columbia; 1993; #1), *Daydream* (Columbia 66700; 1995; debuted at #1), and the hip hop-influenced *Butterfly* (Columbia 67835; 1997; #1)—also sold well. She was the most successful artist on the pop charts in the 1990s by a substantial margin. While Carey's vocal tools (including a seven-octave range) are considered above reproach from a technical standpoint, some critics have characterized her choice of material as bland at best. While she remains firmly in control of her career—making substantial contributions as a songwriter and producer, cracks have appeared in the firmament in recent years. After signing a lucrative recording contract with Virgin in early 2001, the disappointing performance of her first release—the *All That Glitters* soundtrack—led to rumors that the company was trying to void the deal. Furthermore, her productivity had allegedly been compromised by various personal problems. She came back strong, however, with a chart-topping album of original material in 2004.

August 11. Mariah Carey begins a two-week stint atop the R&B charts with "Vision of Love."

August 25. The Time reside at number one on the R&B charts with "Jerk Out" (Paisley Park 19750).

August 27. Guitarist Stevie Ray Vaughan is killed when the helicopter transporting him from a Wisconsin festival collides with a ski slope. Three members of Eric Clapton's entourage are also casualties of the accident.

September 1. Sweet Sensation climb to the summit of the pop charts with "If Wishes Comes True" (Atco).

September 1. Tony! Toni! Tone! begin a two-week stay atop the R&B charts with "Feels Good" (Wing 877 436).

September 6. Former Creedence Clearwater Revival guitarist Tom Fogerty dies at age forty-nine due to complications from AIDS, acquired during a blood transfusion.

September 8. Jon Bon Jovi reaches number one on the Hot 100 with "Blaze of Glory" (Mercury).

September 15. En Vogue head up the R&B charts with "Lies" (Atlantic 87893).

September 15. Wilson Phillips begin a two-week stint atop the pop charts with "Release Me" (SBK).

September 22. The Boys go number one on the R&B charts with "Crazy" (Motown 2053).

September 22. Garth Brooks enters the album charts with *No Fences*. It goes on to become the top-selling country album ever, exceeding thirteen million copies during the first five years it is available.

September 29. Nelson's "(Can't Live Without Your) Love and Affection" (DGC 19689) tops the Hot 100. It is the first hit for the Los Angeles-based mainstream rock duo, consisting of identical twins vocalist/bassist Gunnar Nelson and vocalist guitarist Matthew Nelson, then age twenty-two. They were also responsible for a more notable music business first: three generations of one family have gone number one, beginning with grandfather Ozzie Nelson in 1935, and followed by father Rick in 1958 with "Poor Little Fool."

September 29. Prince peaks at number one on the R&B charts with "Thieves in the Temple" (Paisley Park 19751).

October 6. Pebbles begins a three-week run atop the R&B charts with "Giving You the Benefit" (MCA 53891).

October 6. Maxi Priest reaches number one on the pop charts with "Close to You" (Charisma).

October 13. George Michael climbs to the summit of the Hot 100 with "Praying for Time" (Columbia).

October 20. James Ingram achieves a chart-topping pop single with "I Don't Have the Heart" (Warner Bros.).

October 27. Janet Jackson's "Black Cat" (A&M) peaks at number one on the Hot 100.

October 27. Samuelle's "So You Like What You See" (Atlantic 87864) begins a two-week stint atop the R&B charts.

November 3. Vanilla Ice tops the pop charts with "Ice Ice Baby" (SBK).

November 10. Mariah Carey's "Love Takes Time" (Columbia 73455) begins a three-week stay at number one, her second consecutive single to head up the Hot 100. Like "Vision of Love," it also tops the R&B (the week of November 10–16) and Adult Contemporary charts.

November 15. *Rolling Stone* pictures Bruce Springsteen and his guitar in front of an American flag—an outtake from Anne Leibovitz's shoot for the *Born in the U.S.A.* album—on the cover of its 1980s special issue.

November 17. Bell Biv DeVoe heads up the R&B charts with "B.B.D. (I Thought It Was Me)?" (MCA 53897).

November 21. Longtime couple Mick Jagger and ex-model Jerry Hall marry in the midst of a Bali vacation.

November 24. Al B. Sure! tops the R&B charts with "Misunderstanding" (Warner Bros. 19590).

December 1. Whitney Houston goes number one on both the pop and R&B charts with "I'm Your Baby Tonight" (Arista 2108). She will continue to outpace the competition on the R&B listing for a second week.

December 8. Stevie B begins a four-week run atop the Hot 100 with "Because I Love You (The Postman Song)" (LMR/RCA).

December 15. Ralph Tresvant reaches number one on the R&B charts with "Sensitivity" (MCA 53932), making him the last ex-New Edition member to accomplish this feat.

December 21–22. Two John Lennon tribute concerts are held at the Tokyo Dome, Japan. Performers include Natalie Cole, Miles Davis, Daryl Hall and John Oates, Linda Ronstadt, and Sean Lennon.

December 22. Tony! Toni! Tone! start a two-week stint atop the R&B charts with "It Never Rains (In Southern California)" (Wing 879 068). Composed by group members Tim Christian and Raphael Wiggins, the song is unrelated to the similarly titled hit enjoyed by Englishman Albert Hammond in 1972.

December 29. Cliff Richard peaks at number one on the British charts for the twelfth time with "Saviour's Day."

1991

❋

January 4. Paul Simon's "Born at the Right Time" tour kicks off in Tacoma, Washington.

January 5. Madonna begins a two-week stint atop the Hot 100 with "Justify My Love" (Sire).

January 18. Three fans attending an AC/DC concert in Salt Lake City, Utah, are crushed within the crowd.

January 19. Janet Jackson reaches number one on the pop charts with "Love Will Never Do (Without You)" (A&M).

January 19. Paul Simon donates at least $15,000 from the profits of his Phoenix concert toward efforts to legislate a paid holiday in Arizona honoring Dr. Martin Luther King Jr.

January 26. Cher makes *Canteen*, a special video—featuring Janet Jackson, Bonnie Raitt, Paul Simon, and Van Halen—for the Gulf War's Desert Storm troops.

January 26. Surface's "The First Time" (Columbia) begins a two-week stay atop the Hot 100.

February 9. C & C Music Factory peak at number one on the pop charts with "Gonna Make You Sweat (Everybody Dance Now)," remaining there for two weeks.

February 10. Lisa Stansfield creates a media flap when she becomes the only winner (Best British Female Artist) at the tenth annual Brit Awards ceremony to allude to the Gulf War in her acceptance speech. Status Quo demonstrate a more hollow anti-establishment gesture by discarding regulation black tie formal wear to reveal to the jeans/t-shirt uniform typifying hard rock acts when honored with Outstanding Contribution to the British Music Industry.

February 16. Queen tops the British album charts for the seventh time with *Innuendo*.

February 16. The Simpsons go number one on the British singles charts with "Do the Batman."

February 20. Bob Dylan garners a lifetime achievement award at the Grammy festivities.

February 23. Whitney Houston begins a two-week stint atop the Hot 100 with the Sister Sledge song, "All the Man I Need"—her ninth number one single in a little more than five years.

February 26. Songwriter Doc Pomus dies at age fifty-five. His compositions—which were often collaborations with Mort Shuman—included "Save the Last Dance for Me," "Sweets for My Sweet," and "A Teenager in Love."

February 27. James Brown is paroled after serving two years of a six-year prison sentence imposed for resisting arrest via a car chase spanning two states.

March 2. Mariah Carey's eponymous debut album begins an eleven-week run at number one.

March 2. Madonna's "Rescue Me" enters the Hot 100 at number fifteen, making her the highest-debuting female artist during the rock era.

March 7. George Michael is voted Best Male Singer and Sexiest Male Artist by *Rolling Stone* readers.

March 7. A white-washed head shot of Sinead O'Connor adorns the cover of *Rolling Stone*. The adjoining caption reads "Artist of the Year: Sinead O'Connor; The Rolling Stone Interview."

March 7. Lisa Stansfield is cited as Best New Female Singer in the *Rolling Stone* Critic's Picks 1990 survey.

March 9. Mariah Carey ascends to the top of the Hot 100, remaining there for two weeks, with "Someday" (Columbia 73561). Her third consecutive number one single is one of her biggest radio hits (#1 airplay four weeks).

March 9. The Clash achieve their only British chart topper with "Should I Stay or Should I Go" (CBS). First released in 1982, it receives an assist from its placement in the Levi's TV ad.

March 9. Chris Rea reaches number one on the British charts with *Auberge*, his second LP to accomplish this feat.

March 16. All seven members of country singer Reba McEntire's band are killed in a plane crash near San Diego.

March 18. U2 are fined $850 after being convicted of illegally selling condoms at Dublin's Virgin Megastore.

March 20. Eric Clapton's four-year-old son, Coner, is killed after falling from a fifty-third-floor window in Manhattan where he was staying with his mother.

March 21. Guitar innovator Leo Fender dies from Parkinson's disease.

March 23. R.E.M. top the British album charts for the first time with *Out of Time*.

March 23. Timmy T climbs to the summit of the pop charts with "One More Try" (Quality).

March 24. The Black Crowes are dropped as the support act on a ZZ Top tour after repeatedly criticizing the sponsor, Miller Beer.

March 30. Gloria Estefan begins a two-week stay atop the Hot 100 with "Coming Out of the Dark" (Epic).

April 3. Paul McCartney records his unplugged session for MTV.

April 9. Record producer Martin Hannett dies. He had worked with many Manchester bands (e.g., Happy Mondays, Joy Division, Magazine, New Order, The Smiths) as well as the Psychedelic Furs and U2.

April 11. Paula Abdul holds a press conference, denying allegations that backing vocalist Yvete Marine sang uncredited lead parts on her LP, *Forever Your Girl*.

April 12. In London, Soul II Soul's Jazzie B launches a new label, Finki Dred, under the sponsorship of Motown Records. Early signings, Kofi and Lady Levi, make little headway in the U.S. scene.

April 13. The Londonbeat reach number one on the pop charts with "I've Been Thinking About You" (Radioactive).

April 20. Steve Marriott, age forty-four, dies in a fire which ignited his sixteenth-century cottage, located in Arkesden, Essex (U.K.). He was a child actor prior to becoming lead vocalist for the Small Faces and Humble Pie.

April 20. Wilson Phillips peak at number one on the Hot 100 with "You're in Love" (SBK).

April 23. Johnny Thunders—one of the founding members of flam rockers, the New York Dolls—dies of a drug overdose.

April 27. Amy Grant begins a two-week stint atop the pop charts with "Baby Baby" (A&M).

April 30. Nirvana signs with Geffen Records.

May 2. Ireland bans R.E.M.'s "Losing My Religion" video due to its religious imagery.

May 4. Cher tops the British charts for the first time with "The Shoop Shoop Song."

May 6. *Truth or Dare in Bed with Madonna*, the singer's "warts-and-all" documentary film, premieres in Los Angeles.

May 11. Roxette reach number one on the Hot 100 with "Joyride" (EMI). The song was allegedly inspired by a Paul McCartney interview; he stated that composing songs with John Lennon was like a "joyride."

May 18. Hi-Five climb to the summit of the pop charts with "I Like the Way (The Kissing Game)" (Jive).

May 18. R.E.M. tops the album charts with *Out of Time*.

May 22. The Shamen's Will Sinott drowns when pulled under by strong currents during a break from filming a group video in Tenerife.

May 25. Mariah Carey makes it four-for-four when "I Don't Wanna Cry" (Columbia 73743) begins a two-week stay at number one on the Hot 100. It also joins her first two singles in topping the Adult Contemporary survey. However, unlike its predecessors, it fails to earn a gold record.

June 1. Former Temptations singer David Ruffin dies of a drug overdose. He reached number nine as a solo artist in 1975 with "Walk Away from Love."

June 1. Seal begins a three-week run atop the British charts with his eponymous album.

June 1. Sting appears in the premier broadcast of the Soviet television rock show, *Rock Steady*.

June 8. Extreme go number one on the pop charts with the Everly Brothers-styled "More Than Words" (A&M).

June 13. *Rolling Stone* pictures Madonna drenched in Euro-decadence on its cover with the caption "Madonna: Big-Time Girl Talk; The Rolling Stone Interview."

June 15. Paula Abdul's "Rush Rush" (Virgin 98828) begins a five-week run atop the Hot 100. A major radio favorite (#1 airplay eight weeks), it is Abdul's fifth chart-topper and million-seller. It also heads up the Adult Contemporary charts for five weeks, her only record to reach the top position.

July 20. EMF reach number one on the pop charts with "Unbelievable" (EMI).

July 27. Bryan Adams begins a seven-week stay atop the Hot 100 with "(Everything I Do) I Do It for You" (A&M).

July 28. An estimated two thousand youths riot after an MC Hammer concert in Penticon, Canada, resulting in close to one hundred arrests.

September 14. "The Promise of a New Day" (Captive/Virgin 98752) goes number one, Paula Abdul's sixth—and last—single to do so. It is also the first release on her own record label, Captive. However, her recording career begins a downslide, with only four more records making the Top 40 (the last in mid-1995). She would remain in the public eye as a result of her stormy marriage to actor Emilio Estevez from 1992 to 1994; a starring role in the TV movie, *Touched By Evil*; and an alleged cheating scandal surrounding her stint as a judge on the highly-rated television program, *American Idol*, in 2005.

September 21. Bryan Adams' "(Everything I Do) I Do It for You" begins its twelfth consecutive week at number one on the British charts, a new record.

September 21. Color Me Badd begin a two-week stint atop the Hot 100 with "I Adore Mi Amour" (Giant).

October 5. Bryan Adams heads up the British album charts with *Waking Up the Neighbors*.

October 5. Guns N' Roses begins a two-week stint atop the album charts with *Use Your Illusion II*.

October 5. Marky Mark & the Funky Bunch climb to the summit of the pop charts with "Good Vibrations" (Interscope).

October 12. "Emotions" (Columbia 73977) becomes Mariah Carey's fifth straight pop chart-topper out of the box (remaining there for three weeks), a feat never before accomplished. It is also her third number one R&B hit, and fourth million-seller. Another pattern is becoming discernable in Carey's relatively short recording career; while this song outpaces its competition on the airplay list for four weeks, it only reaches number ten in sales. Until the equation reverses itself in mid-1996, Carey singles will consistently score higher on the airplay—as opposed to sales—survey.

October 12. Metallica peak at number sixteen on the Hot 100 with "Enter Sandman" (Elektra 64857).

Since forming in 1981, Metallica have led the way in redefining the stylistic boundaries of heavy metal. While incorporating elements of punk and hardcore, the band has brought a greater energy, sonic diversity (ranging from visceral thrash and riff-heavy grinders to roots-derived rockers and melodramatic ballads), and attention to songcraft, most notably appealing melodic hooks and strong lyrics, to what was perceived as a rather tired, moribund genre.

Guided by drummer/composer Lars Ulrich and lead vocalist/rhythm guitarist/composer James Hetfield—the constants in the constantly shifting lineup of the early 1980s—Metallica emerged as one of the premier American bands on the strength of frenetically-paced, loud albums such as *Kill 'Em All* (Megaforce 069; 1983), *Ride the Lightning* (Megaforce 769; 1984; #100), and *Master of Puppets* (Elektra 60439; 1986; #29). Following the flawed *...And Justice for All* (Elektra 60812; 1988; #6)—where cluttered arrangements and poor production values blunted the visceral intensity of the material—the band entered a creative watershed period with the release of *Metallica* (Elektra 61113; 1991; #1), *Load* (Elektra 61923; 1996; #1), and *Re-Load* (Elektra 62126; 1997; #1).

Some observers have argued that Metallica's late 1990s work represented that musical equivalent of treading water. Nevertheless, the albums from this period—*Garage Inc.* (Elektra 62323; 1998; #2), an exploration of the work of seminal metal groups, and *S&M* (Elektra 62463; 1999; #2), a live greatest hits collaboration with the San Francisco Symphony Orchestra—reveal a continued commitment to innovation within a post-metal framework. It remains to be seen, however, whether Ulrich's high profile role in the music industry fight against Napster and other unauthorized downloading of mp3 files on the Internet will ultimately erode the band's popularity.

October 17. *Rolling Stone* pictures Eric Clapton framed in shadow on its cover with the caption "Eric Clapton's Blues."

October 31. *Rolling Stone* portrays Jerry Garcia in a white tuxedo shirt and (untied) black bow tie on its cover. The interview inside focus on the death of Grateful Dead keyboardist Brent Mydland and the emotional toll that touring had taken on him.

November 2. Karyn White reaches number one on the pop charts with "Romantic" (Warner Bros.).

November 9. Naughty By Nature peak at number six on the Hot 100 with "O.P.P." (Tommy Boy 988). It goes on to earn double-platinum sales.

Naughty By Nature were one of the first rap acts to enjoy major crossover hits without losing their street credibility among hardcore fans. Initially calling themselves New Style, the trio formed in 1986, while the members—MCs Treach (Anthony Criss) and Vinnie (Vincent Brown) and DJ Kay Gee (Keir Gist)—were attending the same East Orange, New Jersey high school. At the onset of the new decade, they were discovered by Queen Latifah, who brought them to her management company and the Tommy Boy label. Their eponymous debut (Tommy Boy, 1991)—featuring pulsating funk rhythms and clever wordplay—achieved platinum status out of the box, due in part Top 10 pop single, "O.P.P." (which reportedly referred to male or female genitals). Treach began receiving acting offers, appearing in the films *Juice*, *The Meteor Man*, *Who's the Man?*, and *Jason's Lyric*.

Naughty By Nature's follow-up, *19 Naughty III* (Tommy Boy, 1993), also went platinum, driven by the hit single, "Hip Hop Hooray," with its catchy "hey! Ho!" chant. Although *Poverty's Paradise* (Tommy Boy, 1995) found the group creatively treading water, it would win a Grammy for Best Ray Album. An extended recording hiatus followed, with Treach landing a ongoing role in the HBO prison series, *Oz*, and Kay Gee producing records for the likes of Aaliyah, Krayzie Bone, Next, and Zhane. Other distractions included Treach and Vinnie's 1997 arrests in Harlem for illegal weapons possession, and the former's brief marriage to Pepa (of Salt-N-Pepa).

In 1999, the trio made a comeback, albeit not breaking any new ground, with *19 Naughty Nine: Nature's Fury* (Arista). At this point, Kay Gee exited to produce full-time; Treach and Vinnie decided to carry on as a duo, releasing *IIcons* (TVT) on March 5, 2002. The album made halting attempts at updating their signature sound, opting for spare production values and a series of guest collaborators, most notably alternative rock goddess, Pink.

November 9. Prince & the N.P.G. begin a two-week stay atop the pop charts with "Cream" (Paisley Park).

November 23. Michael Bolton goes number one on the Hot 100 with a redo of the Percy Sledge chart-topper, "When a Man Loves a Woman" (Columbia).

November 30. PM Dawn ascend to the summit of the pop charts with "Set Adrift on Memory Bliss" (Gee Street).

December 7. Michael Jackson begins a seven-week run atop the Hot 100 with "Black or White" (Epic).

1992

❄

January 11. Nirvana tops the album charts with *Nevermind*, while their single, "Smells Like Teen Spirit" (DC 19050) peaks at number six on the Hot 100. They also perform on NBC's *Saturday Night Live*.

Nirvana are widely recognized as the most important band to emerge from the Seattle-based grunge scene in the late 1980s. Whereas many of their compatriots—most notably, Soundgarden, Mudhoney, and Alice in Chains—concentrated on postpunk hardcore with heavy metal accents, they also brought a melodic subtlety and strong sense of pop songcraft to the genre.

Singer/songwriter/guitarist Kurt Cobain and bassist Krist Novoselic recruited drummer Chad Channing to form Nirvana in 1987. Although based in Aberdeen, Washington, the excitement generated by their live shows soon led to a record contract with the indie label, Sub Pop, in nearby Seattle. Following the release of a highly collectible single, "Love Buzz" (Sub Pop 23; 1988), written by the 1960s Dutch group, Shocking Blue, Nirvana released the critically acclaimed *Bleach* (Sub Pop 34; 1989). A brooding, angry collection built around throbbing bass and distorted guitar, it showcased Cobain's raging vocals and rapidly maturing compositional skills. Signing with a major label, the next *Nevermind* (Geffen 24425; 1991; #1), created a sensation. Driven by the radio-friendly, power pop-punk of "Smells Like Teen Spirit," Nirvana's success caused a scramble on the part of domestic record companies to sign alternative bands. Hailed as the Bob Dylan of his generation, Cobain exhibited increasing psychological problems in coping with his success.

Although follow-up albums—an anthology of older, previously unavailable tracks, *Incesticide* (Geffen 24504; 2992; #39), and the uncompromisingly raw *In Utero* (Geffen 24536; 1993; #1)—represented something of a creative drop-off, Nirvana remained on the cutting edge of the indie rock revolution until Cobain committed suicide on March 4, 1994. Posthumous releases—particularly the live compilations, *Unplugged In New York* (Geffen 24727; 1994; #1) and *From The Muddy Banks Of The Wishkah* (Geffen 25105; 1996; #1)—have found a wide audience, while the band's legacy, albeit in a more musically conservative, polished edition, has been carried on by Dave Grohl (who'd joined Nirvana as a drummer prior to the recording of *Nevermind*), who went on to found Foo Fighters and take on the lead vocalist/guitarist/songwriting roles. The Yugoslavian-born Novoselic has been less visible, doing occasional session work and releasing an obscure band project, the eponymous *Sweet 75* (Geffen 25140; 1997).

January 14. Jerry Nolan—former drummer with glam rock pioneers, the New York Dolls—dies from a stroke.

January 16. Eric Clapton records an unplugged (acoustic) session for MTV, helping ignite a new music industry vogue.

January 21. Billy Idol is fined $2,700 and required to appear in a series of anti-drug commercials after being found guilt of assault and battery in an altercation outside a West Hollywood restaurant.

January 22. Mariah Carey's stepfather goes to court seeking redress for the costs of her Manhattan apartment, a car, and dental work, which she was supposed to repay after achieving success.

January 25. Color Me Badd's "All 4 Love" (Giant 19236) tops the pop charts, on its way to becoming the group's third consecutive million-seller. A major radio hit—it outpaces the competition on the airplay listing for four weeks—"All 4 Love" also exhibits considerable staying power, remaining in the Hot 100 for twenty-five weeks.

January 29. Willie Dixon—R&B singer/songwriter/bassist who spent much of his career as a producer for the Chess label—dies. Rock acts such as the Rolling Stones and Led Zeppelin would record his compositions, which included "I Can't Quit You Baby," :Little Red Rooster," and "You Shook Me."

February 1. British compatriots George Michael and Elton John team up to take "Don't Let the Sun Go Down On Me" (Columbia 74086) to the top of the Hot 100. It will also head up the Adult Contemporary survey for two weeks. This is the second time around for John with this song (which he co-wrote with longtime partner, lyricist Bernie Taupin, for the *Caribou* LP). It peaked at number two in August 1974 for the MCA label.

February 8. Right Said Fred begins a three-week stint atop the Hot 100 (#2 U.K.) with "I'm Too Sexy" (Charisma).

February 11. Motley Crue fires lead singer Vince Neil, who states that car racing is more important to him than the band's music. He will be reinstated in 1997.

February 14. *Wayne's World*, which stars Mike Myers and includes a cameo appearance by Meat Loaf, premieres in the United States.

February 19. *Crazy For You* premieres at New York's Shubert Theatre. Featuring music by George Gershwin, lyrics by Ira Gershwin, and book by Ken Ludwig, the work included six songs from the 1930 score of *Girl Crazy*, plus two rediscovered in a Seacaucus, New Jersey warehouse in 1982. Among the notable selections were "Someone to Watch Over Me," "Embraceable You," "I Got Rhythm," "But Not For Me," and "Nice Work If You Can Get It."

February 21. James P. Johnson's orchestra compositions are performed at Lincoln Center. Despite having written many Broadway-styled songs and shows an opera, symphony, and rhapsodies, he would remain known as "the Father of Stride Piano."

February 22. Shakespears Sister begins an eight-week stay atop the U.K. charts with "Stay." The duo includes former Bananarama member Siobhan Fahey and vocalist Marcella Detroit, co-writer (with Eric Clapton) of "Lay Down Sally."

February 24. Kurt Cobain and Courtney Love are married in Waikiki, Hawaii. They are reportedly expecting a child around September 10.

February 29. Mr. Big begins a three-week stint atop the Hot 100 (#3 U.K.) with "To Be With You" (Atlantic).

February 29. U2's "Zoo TV" tour opens at the Lakeland Civic Centre Arena, Florida.

March 5. R.E.M. dominate the *Rolling Stone* Music Awards, winning Album of the Year for *Out of Time*, Artist of the Year, Best Single and Best Video for "Losing My Religion, Best Band, Best Guitarist, and Best Songwriter.

March 21. Vanessa Williams' "Save the Best for Last" (Wing) begins a five-week stint atop the Hot 100. The ex-model's road to success has included its share of pitfalls; most notably, the notoriety arising from the disclosure that she'd posed nude for Penthouse, which led to her being forced to give up the Miss Universe crown. Although it is Williams' only number one pop hit, she will remain a steady R&B hitmaker throughout the decade.

March 22. Polygram officially announces the breakup of Tears for Fears. Roland Orzabal will continue to use the name for his releases.

March 23. Janet Jackson signs a recording contract with Virgin for $16,000,000.

March 24. A Chicago court settles a Milli Vanilli class action suit by approving rebates of up to $3 to anyone who can prove they purchased the group's music before November 27, 1990, the date the lip synching scandal broke.

March 28. Ozzy Osbourne invites the first two rows of the audience on stage at The Irvine Meadows Amphitheater, California. Other rows follow, and his band is forced to leave the stage; the celebrants cause $100,000 worth of damage

April 2. *Rolling Stone* pictures Axl Rose on its cover. The interview inside reveals a more fragile, vulnerable side to the Gun n' Roses singer than previously portrayed by the media.

April 4. Bruce Springsteen tops the British album charts for the third time with *Human Touch*.

April 8. *Five Guys Named Moe* premieres at the Eugene O'Neill Theatre in New York City. Featuring songs associated with 1940s R&B bandleader/composer Louis Jordan and book by Clarke Peters, the work would have a run of 445 performances. Selections include "Ain't Nobody Here But Us Chickens," "Choo, Choo, Ch-boogie," and "Is You Is or Is You Ain't My Baby?"

April 11. Def Leppard tops the British charts for the second time with *Adrenalize*, the long-awaited follow-up to the platinum-selling *Hysteria*.

April 14. *Guys and Dolls* is revived at New York's Martin Beck Theatre. The show utilizes the same Frank Loesser songs as the original 1950 production, including "Luck Be a Lady" and "Sit Down, You're Rockin' the Boat."

April 16. *Rolling Stone* pictures Nirvana on its cover, with the focus on Kurt Cobain's t-shirt, which displays the words "CORPORATE MAGAZINES STILL SUCK."

April 18. Def Leppard begin a five-week run atop the album charts with *Adrenalize*.

April 18. Annie Lennox heads up the British album charts with her debut solo release, *Diva*.

April 18. Right Said Fred go number one on the U.K. singles charts with "Deeply Dippy."

April 20. "A Concert for Life" is held at Wembley Stadium as a tribute to Freddie Mercury and for AIDS awareness. Performers include David Bowie, Def Leppard, Extreme, Bob Geldof, Guns N' Roses, Elton John, Annie Lennox, George Michael with Queen, and U2.

April 23. George Michael announces he is giving $500,000 in royalties from the sale of his recording of "Don't Let the Sun Go Down on Me" to various British and American charities.

April 25. Kris Kross begins an eight-week run atop the Hot 100 with the double-platinum selling single, "Jump" (Ruffhouse 74197). It helped make Jermaine Dupri—who wrote and produced the song—a superstar.

Atlanta native Jermaine Dupri (b. September 23, 1973) was one of the most successful R&B producers of the 1990s, nurturing new talent on his own label, So So Def Recordings, in addition to working with superstars like Mariah Carey and TLC. The son of talent manager/concert promoter Michael Mauldin, Dupri performed onstage with Diana Ross as a nine-year-old, and tours with the likes of Cameo and Herbie Hancock in the mid-1980s. In 1987, he produced and secured a record contract for the trio, Silk Tymes Leather.

Dupri formed So So Def Productions in 1989, and reached the top of the charts with the debut album, *Totally Krossed Out* (1992), by Kris Kross, a teen duo he'd discovered the year before in an area shopping mall. He went on to produce tracks on TLC's first two LPs, which sold a combined total of more than 15 million copies. In 1993-1994, he achieved platinum sales with the debut albums of two more So So Def acts, Xscape and Da Brat (he also assisted other label artists like Lil Bow Wow and Jagged Edge). By now, his services were in high demand; he would be recruited to work with Carey (the album, *Daydream*, which sold more than eight million units), Janet Jackson, Old School rappers Run-D.M.C. and Whodini, and up-and-coming R&B singer, Usher. The resulting LP, *My Way* (1997), surpassed double-platinum sales within three months of its release, making the teenage heart-throb a superstar.

While continuing to collaborate with such notable rap acts as Snoop Dog, OutKast, Slick Rick, NAS, and Master P, Dupri released his own single, "The Party Continues," in early 1998. The favorable response led to a debut solo album, *Jermaine Dupri Presents: Life in 1472* (So So Def, 1998), which featured a star-studded roster of guest artists. Although a polished package (as might be expected), his follow-up, *Instructions* (So So Def, 2001), was marred by mindless boasting and clichéd lyrics. As an accomplished producer and record label executive—*Billboard* ranked So So Def as the twelfth most successful R&B/Hip-Hop label of 2004 in its December 25, 2004 issue—Dupri continue to view his own solo recordings as little more than vanity projects.

April 26. *Jelly's Last Jam* premieres at the Virginia Theatre in New York City. Featuring the music of Jelly Roll Morton (adapted and augmented with additional music by Luther Henderson), lyrics by Susan Birkenhead, and book by George C. Wolfe, it would have a run of 569 performances.

April 29. *Falsettos* premieres at New York's John Golden Theatre. Featuring music and lyrics by William Finn, and book by Finn and James Lapine, the work—which combined two one-act musicals, *The March of the Falsettos* (1981) and *Falsettoland* (1990)—would have a run of 486 performances.

May 2. The British band, Nirvana, sues the Seattle-based grunge band of the same name, claiming they'd been using the moniker since 1968. The dispute is settled out of court in terms favorable to the British act.

May 5. Radiohead's debut recording, *The Drill* EP, is released.

May 9. Queen's "Bohemian Rhapsody" (Hollywood) peaks at number two on the pop charts; it is a reissue of the recording that rose to number nine in 1976.

May 29. Clifton, New Jersey's Sacred Heart School decides not to sing "We are the Champions" at their graduation ceremony out of concern that some students are identifying too closely with Queen's Freddie Mercury.

May 30. The Black Crowes top the album charts with *The Southern Harmony and Musical Companion*.

May 30. Paul Simon marries singer Edie Brickell. He will lend his songwriting and production skills in attempting to revive her flagging career.

June 13. Billy Ray Cyrus begins a seventeen-week run atop the album charts with *Some Gave All*.

June 20. After an absence of almost nine months, which saw two of her singles fall short of number one ("Can't Let Go", #2; "Make It Happen," #5), Mariah Carey returns to the top for the sixth time with a remake of the Jackson 5 smash, "I'll Be There" (Columbia 74330). Another major radio hit, it heads up the airplay listing eight weeks (in contrast to a two-week hegemony in the Hot 100). It also enjoys a two-week reign on the Adult Contemporary survey.

June 25. *Rolling Stone* pictures three of the Red Hot Chili Peppers in the buff on its cover. Guitarist John Frusciante was cut out of the shot right before the issue went to press because he'd left the band on May 7 during a Japanese tour.

July 4. Sir Mix-A-Lot begins a five-week sojourn atop the pop charts with the double-platinum seller, "Baby Got Back" (Def American).

July 11. A line of ties—eight in all—designed by Jerry Garcia go on sale. The collection grosses $10 million by the end of the year, with President Bill Clinton reportedly purchasing a set.

August 8. Madonna's "This Used to Be My Playground" (Sire 18822) reaches the summit of the Hot 100. The song is assisted by its inclusion in the film, *A League of Their Own*, in which she stars along with Geena Davis and Tom Hanks.

August 15. Boyz II Men begin a thirteen-week run atop the Hot 100 with "End of the Road" (Motown).

August 20. *Rolling Stone* pictures Ice-T in a policeman's uniform on its cover. That summer his song, "Cop Killer," had been condemned by Congress and President George Bush, and pulled from many record stores across the nation.

October 5. Former Temptations vocalist Eddie Kendricks dies of lung cancer a year after having a lung removed.

October 31. Boyz II Men top the British charts with "The End of the Road," which is culled from the film *Boomerang*.

November 14. The Heights go number one on the pop charts with "How Do You Talk To An Angel" (Capitol), remaining there for two weeks.

November 28. Whitney Houston begins a fourteen-week run atop the Hot 100 with the quadruple-platinum seller, "I Will Always Love You" (Arista).

December 20. Blues singer/guitarist Albert King dies. His raw style was something of a throwback to the post-World War II era, lacking the sophistication of contemporaries such as B.B. King and Robert Cray.

1993

❄

January 6. The media report that David Bowie recently lost $4.25 million in unpaid royalties resulting from a bootleg scam perpetrated by the Italian Mafia.

January 7. R.E.M. headlines a Greenpeace benefit show attended by five hundred people at the 40 Watt Club, Athens, Georgia. The event is recorded on a solar-powered mobile recording studio.

January 8. The U.S. Postal Service issues a commemorative stamp depicting Elvis Presley, the first rock artist to be so honored.

January 12. Van Morrison does not attend the Rock and Roll Hall of Fame induction dinner—he is the first living inductee to do so.

January 14. The Pixies announce that they have broken up.

January 19. The mid-1970s edition of Fleetwood Mac gets back together to perform at Bill Clinton's presidential inauguration. Their 1977 hit, "Don't Stop," had served as Democratic ticket's campaign theme.

February 6. Shortly after being his elected to the Rock 'n' Roll Hall of Fame, music luminaries such as Bob Dylan, Bono, Steve Winwood, and Elvis Costello participate in an impromptu tribute to Van Morrison at the Point in Dublin.

February 27. Whitney Houston's "I Will Always Love You" becomes the longest chart-topper of the rock era, having spent fourteen weeks in the number one position.

March 6. Peabo Bryson and Regina Belle reach number one on the pop charts with "A Whole New World (Aladdin's Theme)" (Columbia), culled from animated Disney film, *Aladdin*.

March 11. Oasis record their first demos at The Real People's Studio in Liverpool. The tracks include "Columbia," "Fade Away," and "Rock 'n' Roll Star."

March 13. Eric Clapton begins a three-week stay atop the LP charts with *Unplugged*.

March 13. Lenny Kravitz goes number one on the British album charts with *Are You Gonna Go My Way?* remaining there for two weeks.

March 13. Canadian rapper Snow (aka Darrin O'Brien) begins a seven-week run atop the Hot 100 with "Informer" (EastWest). He had been in prison for when the single was released.

March 16. Jerry Lee Lewis, his wife Kerrie, and son Lee move to Dublin, where he begins hanging out with the likes of Van Morrison and Ron Wood.

March 20. Dr. Dre peaks at number two on the Hot 100 with "Nuthin' But a 'G' Thang" (Death Row 53819).

Andre Young, better known as Dr. Dre, played a major role in steering rap away its preoccupation with partying, politics, and the exploration of new sonic effects to a celebratory form of gangsta rap. As a record producer, he modified the influential George Clinton school of funk into a stretched-out, lazier variation which he termed "G-funk. He was also a high-profile label executive; first with Death Row Records—co-founded in 1992 with Suge Knight, it provided the template for hip-hop aesthetics in the mid-1990s—and, in the late 1990s, Aftermath Records.

Born February 18, 1965, in Compton, California, Dr. Dre first attracted attention in the early 1980s working South Central Los Angeles house parties and clubs as part of the World Class Wreckin' Cru. By 1986, he had teamed with Ice Cube to supply compositions to Ruthless Records. The label's owner, rapper Eazy-E, together with the twosome, formed N.W.A. (aka Niggaz With Attitude). The group released two albums, *N.W.A. and the Posse* (Marcola/Rams Horn 5134; 1987) and *Straight Outta Compton* (Ruthless/Priority 57102; 1989; #37; double platinum), the latter of which attracted widespread publicity due to its incendiary lyrics, most notably on the heavily censored track, "Fuck tha Police." With the departure of Ice Cube, N.W.A. released two more records—the EP *100 Miles and Runnin'* (Ruthless/Priority 7224; 1990; #27; platinum) and *Efil4zaggin* (Ruthless/Priority 57126; 1991; #1; platinum)—featuring Eazy-E's comic-book lyrics set Dre's thickly-textured funk arrangements.

Intent on pursuing a solo career, Dre released his debut solo album, *The Chronic* (Death Row 57128; 1992; #3), which profoundly modified the hip-hop landscape with its G-funk sound. He then shifted his focus to production work, providing the music to several film soundtracks—most notably, *Above the Rim* (1994) and *Murder Was the Case* (1994)—and assisting protégé Snoop Doggy Dog with *Doggystyle* (Death Row/Interscope 92279; 1993; #1), Warren G, and Blackstreet, among others.

Alienated by the gangster behavior of Death Row partner, Knight, Dre severed all ties in summer 1996 and formed Aftermath. While the new label was not an immediate success, Dre slowly returned to public favor with a more mainstream pop approach on the LPs *Dr. Dre Presents…The Aftermath* (Aftermath/Interscope 90044; 1996; featuring his production work with various artists) and *2001* (Aftermath/Interscope 490486; 1999; #2; also issued in "clean" and "instrumental" versions).

March 24. Eric Clapton garners six Grammys, most notably for the LP, *Unplugged*, and the song, "Tears In Heaven," inspired by his four-year-old son's tragic death due to a fall from the 53rd floor window of a Manhattan where he resided with his mother.

April 3. The Bluebells top the British charts with "Young at Heart"; it was released ten years earlier, but was revived after being featured in a Volkswagen television commercial.

April 3. Depeche Mode head up the U.K. album charts for the first time with *Songs of Faith and Devotion*.

April 13. Massachusetts observes "Aerosmith Day."

April 16. The Earth Day celebration at the Hollywood Bowl features Paul McCartney, Ringo Starr, Don Henley, and Steve Miller in concert. McCartney had last performed there as a member of the Beatles in 1965.

April 22. The Who's *Tommy* opens on Broadway at the St. James Theatre.

April 27. Prince issues a statement saying he's retiring from studio recording to concentrate on filmmaking and other ventures.

April 29. Guitarist and producer Mick Ronson dies of cancer. Def Leppard's Joe Elliot would offer the following tribute: "If there's a God up there, why does he do this? It can only be because he's trying to put together the ultimate band."

May 1. George Michael, Queen, and Lisa Stansfield top the British charts with the "The Five Live EP," recorded at the Freddie Mercury tribute concert.

May 1. Silk begins a two-week stint at number one on the pop charts with "Freak Me" (Keia/Elektra).

May 14. Four "super hero" costumes worn by Kiss members are sold at a Christie's auction in London for $34,000.

May 15. Janet Jackson begins an eight-week stay atop the Hot 100 with "That's the Way Love Goes" (Virgin).

May 22. Ace of Base peak at number one on the British charts with "All That She Wants," remaining there for three weeks.

June 12. UB40 top the British charts with a remake of the Elvis Presley hit, "(I Can't Help) Falling in Love with You."

June 27. Tina Turner tops the British album charts with *What's Love Got to Do with It?*

July 10. SWV reaches number one on the pop charts with "Weak" (RCA), remaining there for two weeks.

July 24. UB40 begin a seven-week run atop the Hot 100 with "Can't Help Falling in Love" (Virgin 12653). The song—composed by Hugo Peretti/Luigi Creatore/George David Weiss—was a number two hit for Elvis Presley in early 1962.

The multiracial, English band, UB40—the first important exponent of reggae to hail from outside Jamaica—rose to popularity in the midst of the ska/bluebeat revival craze. Although they did not address the topical concerns of West Indies reggae artists (e.g., Rastafarianism, ganja rituals, European colonialism), their songs exhibited a strong socio-political bent, addressing—among other issues, the U.K.'s unemployment problems (the band's name itself was inspired by an English unemployment form), nuclear war, and the repressive policies of former British prime minister, Margaret Thatcher.

UB40's key members—lead vocalist/guitarist Ali Campbell and lead guitarist/singer Robin Campbell—were sons of Ian Campbell, a Scottish folk interpreter popular during the early 1960s. Formed in early 1979, the band—ranging in size from eight to twelve members over the years, including core members Astro, vocals/trumpet; Michael Virtue, keyboards; Earl Ralconer, bass; Brian Travers, saxophone; Jim Brown, drums; and Norman Hassan, percussion—became a fixture on the British charts with the release of the album, *Signing Off* (Graduate 2; 1980; #2 UK). UB40's popularity spread to much of Europe in the early 1980s on the strength of LPs such as—of the which featured an augmented brass section in order to provide an authentic R&B feel to arrangements.

Until the band signed with A&M Records in 1983, their recordings had only been available in the United States as imports. Pushing Ali's wholesome good looks and reggae-pop treatments of rock classics such as Sonny and Cher's "I Got You Babe" (A&M 2758; 1985; #28; w/Chrissie Hynde), Neil Diamond's "Red Red Wine" (A&M 2600; 1983; #34), the Temptations' "The Way You Do the Things You Do" (Virgin 98978; 1990; #6), Al Green's "Here I Am" (Virgin 99141; 1991; #7), and Elvis Presley's "(I Can't Help) Falling in Love with You" (Virgin 12653; 1993; #1 UK, #1 US) via video clips geared to cable television and dance clubs, UB achieved considerable success in America with the following albums: *Labour of Love* (A&M 4980; 1983; #14; consisted entirely of cover versions), *Geffery Morgan* (A&M 5033; 1984; #60), *Little Baggariddim* (A&M 5090; 1985; #40), *Rat in the Kitchen* (A&M 5137; 1986; #53), *CCCP: Live in Moscow* (A&M 5168; 1987; #121), *UB40* (A&M 5213; 1988; #44), *Labour of Love II* (Virgin 91324; 1990; #30; another collection of covers), and *Promises and Lies* (Virgin 88229; 1993; #6).

Ali's departure in 1995 for a solo career disrupted the UB40's creative and commercial momentum. With his return to the fold in 1997, the band picked up where they'd off, placing recordings high on the U.K. charts—e.g., *Guns in the Ghetto* (DEP International 16; 1997; #7 UK) and *Labour of Love III* (DEP International 18; 1998; #8 UK)—albeit enjoying less success stateside.

September 11. Mariah Carey takes over the number one position on the pop charts with "Dreamlover" (Columbia), remaining there for eight weeks.

September 16. *Rolling Stone* pictures a bare-chested Janet Jackson—with hands from an unseen person covering a portion of her breasts—on its cover with the caption "Janet Jackson: the joy of sex."

November 6. Meat Loaf begins a five-week stay atop the Hot 100 with "I'd Do Anything For Love (But I Won't Do That)" (MCA).

December 11. Janet Jackson reaches the summit of the pop charts with "Again" (Virgin), remaining there for two weeks.

December 11. Snoop Doggy Dogg tops the album charts with *Doggy Style*, remaining there for three non-consecutive weeks.

Snoop Doggy Dog (aka Calvin Broadus) was a pop culture celebrity well before the release of his first album, the platinum selling *Doggystyle* (Death Row/Interscope; 1993). He had already appeared on mentor Dr. Dre's chart-topping album, *The Chronic* (Priority/Interscope (2 57128; 1992), in addition to being arrested in connection with the murder of an alleged Los Angeles gang member. Overnight, he had become a figurehead of the controversial gangsta rap genre, his picture appearing on the covers of mass circulation magazines such as *Newsweek*, *Rolling Stone*, and *Vibe*.

Doggystyle was the fastest-selling debut LP in history, entering the pop album charts at number one and selling almost one million units alone in its first week of release. All issues of notoriety aside, the record's success owed much to Dr. Dre's funky production work and Snoop's mesmerizing treatment of both the harsher side of hood life and partying. The commercial rise of rappers 2Pac and the Notorious B.I.G., combined with a weak follow-up album, *The Doggfather* (Death Row/Interscope; 1996), minus Dr. Dre's studio support, pushed hi, into the background. Subsequent releases have resurrected his artistic credibility to some degree; however, the appearance of new creative forces—most notably, RZA, Method Man, and other members of the Wu-Tang Clan—have keep him from regaining the rap spotlight.

December 25. Mariah Carey begins a four-week run atop the Hot 100 with "Hero" (Columbia). She also hits number one on the album charts with *Music Box*.

December 28. Country singer Shania Twain marries producer Mutt Lange.

1994

❄

January 7. The avatars of Britpop, Oasis, commence work on their debut LP, *Definitely Maybe*, at Monrow Studios, South Wales, U.K.

January 15. Harry Nilsson dies in his sleep. In addition to recording the Top 10 singles, "Everybody's Talkin'" and "Without You," he composed hits for The Monkees and Three Dog Night.

January 17. Donny Osmond fights former Partridge Family member Danny Bonaduce in a charity boxing match, losing 2–1.

January 22. "All For Love" (A&M 0476), by Bryan Adams, Rod Stewart, and Sting, begins a three-week stay atop the Hot 100. The platinum seller was included in the soundtrack to the film, *The Three Musketeers*, starring Kiefer Sutherland and Charlie Sheen.

January 28. After attending the premiere of *Wayne's World II* in London, Paul and Linda McCartney are presented with a $42,500 check for the Liverpool Institute for Performing Arts by Mike Myers at the Hard Rock Café.

January 19. Queen Latifah peaks at number twenty-three on the Hot 100 with "U.N.I.T.Y." (Motown 2225).

Born Dana Owens on March 18, 1970, in Newark, New Jersey, she is widely held to be the earliest female rapper to communicate a feminist perspective in an intelligent, engaging manner. Her adopted name, Latifah, is of Arabic derivation, meaning "delicate" or "sensitive." After performing as a human beatbox with the group, Ladies Fresh, she achieved a measure of renown with the release of her assertive debut single, "Wrath of My Madness" (backed by the reggae-influenced "Princess of the Posse"), in 1988. The ensuing album, *All Hail the Queen* (Tommy Boy, 1989), was equally impressive, revealing her ability to effectively interpret soul, hip-hop, dance pop, and reggae-derived dub styles.

Queen Latifah's follow-up LPs—*Nature of a Sista* (Tommy Boy, 1991) and *Black Reign* (Motown, 1993), which included the hit single and Grammy winner (Best Rap Solo Performance), "U.N.I.T.Y."—showcased increasingly more bellicose posturing tempered somewhat by commentaries on the social inequities of inner city life. Latifah's popularity was now at a peak, due in no small part to her high profile acting career, which ranged from a regular spot on the Fox-TV sitcom, *Living Single*, to film roles like *Jungle Fever*, *Juice*, and *House Party 2*.

After a long sabbatical from the music business, she issued *Order in the Court* (Motown, 1998), which attempted to meld hip-hop with old school R&B in much the same fashion as the Fugees, Faith Evans, and others during the mid-1990s. Although no longer a trendsetter, Latifah continues to balance her music, acting, and celebrity-related activities up to the present day.

February 8. Oasis cancel their first tour abroad after being deported from Holland due their involvement in a drunken brawl on a cross-channel ferry.

February 12. Alice in Chains enters the album charts at number one with *Jar of Flies*.

February 12. Celine Dion's "The Power of Love" (550 Music 77230) reaches the pinnacle of the Hot 100, remaining there for four weeks (#1 AC 4 weeks). The song had a long history of success prior to the appearance of Dion's rendition. One of its co-writers, Jennifer Rush, topped the British charts (#57 US pop) with a version produced in Germany by two other co-writers, Candy de Rouge and Gunther Mende. Air Supply's cover reached number sixty-eight on the Hot 100 (#13 AC) in 1985, while Laura Branagan's remake went to number twenty-six on the pop charts (#19 AC) in 1987.

Celine Dion became one of the most successful singers of the 1990s, reputedly selling over one hundred million albums. Although she underwent a physical transformation in the late 1980s aimed at enhancing her marketability, Dion's magnificent voice—an instrument perfectly suited for melodramatic ballads—has been the key to her worldwide popularity.

Born March 30, 1968, in Charlemagne, Quebec, Dion grew from a regional to an international recording star while still a teenager. She finally cracked the U.S. market with the release of *Unison* (Epic 46893;

1990; #74). She would go on record sixteen Top 40 singles in the 1990s, including the number one hits "The Power of Love" (550 Music/Epic 77230; 1993), "Because You Loved Me" (550 Music/Epic 78236; 1996; from the film *Up Close & Personal*), "M Heart Will Go On" (550 Music/Epic 78825; 1998; from the film *Titanic*), and "I'm Your Angel" (Jive 42557; 1998; duet with R. Kelly). Other singles reaching number one on the Adult Contemporary charts included "If You Asked Me To" (Epic 74277; 1992), "It's All Coming Back To Me Now" (550 Music/Epic 78345; 1996), "All By Myself" (550 Music/Epic 78529; 1997), "To Love You More" (cut from album *Let's Talk About Love*), and "That's the Way It Is" (cut from album *All the Way…A Decade Of Song*). She became a fixture on movie soundtracks, also charting with songs from *Beauty and the Beast* and *Sleepless in Seattle*.

The commercial success of Dion's albums was even more impressive; she released at least three dozen titles, a substantial portion of which were either in French or geared to foreign markets. Her biggest sellers—all of which were issued in the United States—included *Celine Dion* (Epic 52473; 1992; #34; certified gold), *The Colour of My Love* (550 Music/Epic; 1993), *Falling Into You* (550 Music/Epic; 1996; #1), *Let's Talk About Love* (550 Music/Epic 68861; 1997; #1), *These Are Special Times* (550 Music/ Epic; 1998), *All the Way…A Decade of Song* (550 Music/Epic 63760; 1999; #1), and *The Collector's Series, Vol. 1* (550 Music/Epic; 2000).

Her recorded work has won numerous awards, most notably, a Grammy and Oscar for the theme song to *Beauty and the Beast* (Epic 74090; 1992; #9; duet with Peabo Bryson), Grammies for Best Pop Album and Album of the Year with *Falling Into You*, and an Oscar for Best Original Song with "My Heart Will Go On."

February 14. Van Morrison receives a special award for his Outstanding Contribution to British Music at the 1994 Brit Awards.

February 19. Mariah Carey tops the British charts for the first time with the Pete Ham/Tom Evans song, "Without You."

February 20. Tori Amos tops the British album charts with *Under the Pink*.

February 26. Toni Braxton tops the charts with her eponymous LP.

February 28. Eric Clapton performs at London's Royal Albert Hall for the one hundredth time in a charity concert for "Children in Crisis."

March 1. Nirvana play their last concert when they appear at The Terminal Einz in Munich.

March 4. Kurt Cobain is rushed to the hospital after overdosing on champagne and fifty to sixty Rohypnol pills in a Rome hotel. Internet rumors claim he is dead.

March 12. The Swedish group, Ace of Base, reach number one on the Hot 100 with "The Sign" (Arista 12653), remaining there for six weeks.

March 13. Mariah Carey begins a three-week stint atop the British album charts with *Music Box* (Columbia).

March 21. Bruce Springsteen wins an Oscar for "Streets of Philadelphia."

March 22. Producer/recording artist Dan Hartman dies. A former Edgar Winter associate, he reached number eight on the British charts with "Instant Replay" (#29 U.S.).

March 26. Richard Marx takes "Now and Forever" (Capitol 58005) to the top of the Adult Contemporary charts (#7 pop) for an eleven-week run. Although Marx wrote the song specifically about his wife, Cynthia Rhodes, former lead vocalist with the New Wave band Animotion, he would note, "There's a lot of people who can relate to parts or all of it" (Hyatt 1999).

April 8. Kurt Cobain is found dead in his Seattle home from a self-inflicted shotgun wound by electrician Gary Smith. Local radio station KXRX breaks the news at 9:40 a.m.

April 9. R. Kelly begins a four-week stint atop the Hot 100 with "Bump N' Grind" (Jive 42207). The platinum seller also spends twelve weeks at number one on the R&B charts.

Born Steven Williams in Chicago, he emerged out of the New Jack Swing movement as frontman for the East Coast-based band, Public Announcement. They released two best-selling albums, *Born into the*

90's (Jive, 1992) and *12 Play* (Jive, 1993), which skillfully blended classic funk rhythms, updated hip-hop production values, and suave soul crooning. The latter record remains his benchmark work, selling more the five million copies; driven in part by the chart-topping single, "Bump n' Grind."

Kelly opted to go solo in the mid-1990s; although comprised largely of romantic ballads, the most notable feature of his eponymous debut (Jive, 1995) was its carnal imagery. Nevertheless, it achieved sales of more than four million as well as including three platinum singles. By the time he won Grammy awards for Best Male R&B Vocal Performance, Best R&B Song, and Best Song Written Specifically for a Motion Picture or for Television with "I Believe I Can Fly," which appeared in the Michael Jordan film, *Space Jam* (1996), his crossover appeal was a foregone conclusion. In the meantime, he was in great demand as a studio producer, working with Michael Jackson, Celine Dion, and Puff Daddy, among others. One of his biggest commercial successes came with Aaliyah, who married him at age fifteen, stirring up considerable press controversy in the process.

Kelly's follow-up albums—the sprawling, experimental double-disc set, *R* (Jive, 1998), and the more radio-friendly *TP-2.Com* (Jive, 2000)—remained grounded in his core aesthetic: sinuous grooves and lush arrangements accented by soothing vocals that sugar-coat the explicit wordplay. More recent releases, however, have failed to match the success of his 1990s work. His collaboration with JAY-Z, *The Best of Both Worlds* (Universal, 2002), was something of an artistic and commercial disappointment, while the well-crafted *Chocolate Factory* (Jive, 2003) was overshadowed by the singer's legal difficulties, which included being hit with twenty-one counts of child pornography in Chicago and twelve more in Polk County, Florida, not to mention a number of other sex-related civil suits. Still, Kelly's career has displayed a resiliency that defies many industry observers; *Billboard*'s December 25, 2004, "Year in Music & Touring" issue listed him as sixteenth on its tabulation of Top Pop Artists.

April 10. More than five thousand fans attend a public memorial service for Kurt Cobain at Seattle Center's Flag Pavilion.

April 11. The first Oasis single, "Supersonic," is released in Great Britain. It peaks at number thirty-one on the charts.

April 17. Pink Floyd begins a four-week run atop the British album charts with *The Division Bell*.

April 17. Prince tops the British charts for the first time with "The Most Beautiful Girl in the World."

April 23. Pink Floyd's *The Division Bell* (Columbia 64200) debuts at number one, remaining there for four weeks and achieving double-platinum sales before the end of the year. The group had reached the top with three previous albums—*Dark Side of the Moon*, *Wish You Were Here*, and *The Wall*—but this represented the first time since they'd regrouped as a trio in 1987 following Roger Waters' departure for a solo career.

April 30. NAS peaks at number ninety-one on the Hot 100 with "It Ain't Hard to Tell" (Columbia 77385).

Born Nasir Jones on September 14, 1973, in Queensbridge, Long Island, New York, the son of a jazz musician, he began rapping at age ten in a local ensemble, the Devastin' Seven. After submitting a demo tape in the late 1980s to Main Source producer, Large Professor, he was subsequently featured on that group's album, *Breaking Atoms* (1991). His solo debut, "Half Time," was included in the film, *Zebra Head* (1992), which spurred Columbia to offer him a generous record deal. Assisted by noted producers like A Tribe Called Quest's Q-Tip and Premier (Gang Starr), he recorded the acclaimed masterpiece, *Illmatic* (Columbia, 1994).

Subsequent albums—the chart-topping *It Was Written* (Columbia, 1996) and *I Am...The Autobiography* (Columbia, 1999), followed by the less successful (albeit Top 10 best-sellers) *NAStradamus* (Columbia, 1999), and *Stillmatic* (Ill Will, 2001)—would dilute *Illmatic's* literate lyrics and rich ghetto imagery, opting instead for catchy refrains and superstar posturing. At this point, Nas had lost much of his street credibility in his single-minded quest for fame and fortune, with hardcore rapper JAY-Z dissing him onstage and in the track, "Super Ugly."

While Nas was apparently going through a bout of soul-searching, Columbia reached into the vaults for *From Illmatic to Stillmatic: The Remixes EP* (2002) and *The Lost Tapes* (2002). His next album of original material, *God's Son* (Columbia), issued at the end of 2002, found him attempting to rise above the controversy regarding prior career moves. The work exhibited a decidedly spiritual perspective while relying on the talents of fellow performers Eminem, Alicia Keys, and Tupac Shakur as well as producers Ron Browz, Salaam Remi, Chucky Thompson, and the Alchemist.

May 7. OutKast peak at number thirty-seven on the Hot 100 with "Player's Ball" (LaFace 24060). It goes on to earn gold record status.

Formed as part of Atlanta's hip-hop underground in 1993 by teenage rappers Andre "Dre" Benjamin and Antoine "Big Boi" Patton, OutKast was signed within a matter of months by the Arista imprint, LaFace. Their debut album, *Southernplayalisticadillacmuzik* (LaFace, 1994), made the Top 20 and garnered a "Best Newcomer" Gong at the 1995 Source awards. Their sophomore effort, *Atliens* (LaFace, 1996)—which featured the chart-topping rap singles, "Elevators (me & you)" and "Atliens"—rose to number two on the *Billboard* Top 200, boosted by world class production values, innovative jazz-inflected instrumentation, and jagged rhythms reminiscent of British House music.

Aquemini (LaFace, 1998) and *Stankonia* (LaFace, 2000) were widely acknowledge to be hardcore dance masterpieces, built around the duo's distinctive interplay of rap verses. Their eclectic double-CD set, *Speakerboxxx/The Love Below* (LaFace/Zomba), released in 2003 and rated the second most popular album of 2004 by *Billboard*, elevated them to superstar status. The venerable trade magazine also designated them the top duo/group (and number three pop act) of the year; two OutKast releases, "The Way You Move" and "Hey Ya!," were included in the Top 10 singles of 2004.

May 8. Stiltskin top the British charts with "Inside." Its popularity owed much to a TV jeans commercial.

May 26. Michael Jackson weds Lisa Marie Presley. They will divorce the following year.

June 11. Madonna's "I'll Remember" (Maverick/Sire 18247) begins a four-week stint atop the AC charts. The theme song for the film, *Without Honors*, starring Joe Pesci, it barely missed a comparable run in the Hot 100, spending four weeks at number two behind All-4-One's "I Swear."

May 21. All-4-One reaches number one on the Hot 100 with "I Swear" (Blitzz/Atlantic 87243), remaining there for eleven weeks and achieving platinum sales. A version by John Michael Montgomery would top the country charts.

May 28. Madonna begins a four-week run at number two on the Hot 100 with "I'll Remember" (Maverick/Sire 18247).

June 2. *Rolling Stone* pictures a close-up head shot of Kurt Cobain on its cover shortly after his suicide.

June 9. TLC vocalist Lisa "Left Eye" Lopes sets fire to the $2 million mansion owned by her boyfriend, NFL star Andre Rison. She will be charged with arson and fined $10,000 with five years probation.

June 25. Janet Jackson peaks at number two on the Hot 100 with "Any Time, Any Place" (Virgin 38435).

June 27. Aerosmith posts a new song on the Internet that can be downloaded free, the first time this has been done by a major band.

July 2. Aaliyah peaks at number five on the Hot 100 with the million-selling "Back and Forth" (Jive 42174).

Born Aaliyah Haughton January 16, 1979, in Brooklyn, New York, she was raised in Detroit around show business trappings (her mother worked for a time as a professional singer and an uncle—an entertainment lawyer—was married to Gladys Knight). Appearing in concert with Knight at age eleven, she recorded the multi-platinum-selling *Age Ain't Nothing But a Number* (Blackground/Jive, 1994), while barely a teenager. The album's success—assisted by the Top 10 pop singles, "Back & Forth" and a cover of the Isley Brothers' "At Your Best (You Are Love)"—was obscured somewhat by the news that she'd married her producer, R. Kelly, as a fifteen-year-old.

Breaking away from Kelly, Aaliyah utilized Timbaland, Missy Elliott, Jermaine Dupri, and others as producers for her follow-up, *One in a Million* (Blackground, 1996). Although not selling as well as its successor, the record's minimalist hip-hop arrangements provided the perfect setting for her polished, seductive vocals. By the onset of the new century, she seemed poised to become a major actress, having starred in *Romeo Must Die* and signed to play in the two *Matrix* sequels.

Delayed somewhat due to these added careers demands, her third album, *Aaliyah* (Blackground, 2001), was revealed a significantly increased degree of self-assurance and stylistic diversity. However, a few weeks after its release, Aaliyah died when her privately chartered plane crashed August 25, 2001, while returning from a video shoot in the Bahamas.

July 2. Warren G. and Nate Dogg begin a three-week run at number two on the Hot 100 with "Regulate" (Death Row 98280).

July 9. Elton John's "Can You Feel the Love Tonight" (Hollywood 64543) goes number one on the AC charts (#4 pop), holding the position for eight consecutive weeks. The first single from the soundtrack to *The Lion King*, which he co-wrote with Tim Rice, the accomplished lyricist for Broadway musicals such as *Jesus Christ Superstar*. The album would top the LP charts for ten weeks beginning June 16. The record won countless awards, including an Oscar for Best Song, a Grammy for Best Male Pop Vocal Performance, and a Grammy nomination for Song of the Year. The song was retained for the Broadway adaptation of *The Lion King*, which opened November 1997 and went on the garner six Tonys.

July 16. The soundtrack to the animated film, *The Lion King* (Walt Disney 60858), begins a nine-week run atop the album charts. Featuring music composed by Elton John (who also performed on the tracks) and lyrics by Tim Rice, it would achieve platinum sales seven times over by the end of the year.

August 6. "Stay (I Missed You)" (RCA 62870), by Lisa Loeb & Nine Stories, begins a three-week stint top the Hot 100. The million seller was included on the soundtrack to the film, *Reality Bites*, starring Winona Ryder.

August 12. Woodstock '94 is held in Saugerties, New York. Featured performers include Aerosmth, Green Day, Nine Inch Nails, and the Red Hot Chili Peppers.

August 25. *Rolling Stone* pictures the Rolling Stones in masks on its cover. The band were in Toronto rehearsing for their imminent *Voodoo Lounge* tour.

August 27. Boyz II Men reach number one on the Hot 100 with "I'll Make Love to You" (Motown 2257), remaining there for fourteen weeks. The platinum seller also tops the R&B (nine weeks) and Adult Contemporary (three weeks) charts.

August 31. Aaliyah and R. Kelly are secretly married at the Sheraton Gateway Suites in Rosemont. Aaliyah would never admit to being married, even though a copy of the marriage certificate is published in a magazine. The marriage will later be annulled on the grounds that she was only fifteen at the time.

September 6. Session pianist Nicky Hopkins dies. He was a member of Quicksilver Messenger Service in the early 1970s and worked with the Beatles, Jeff Beck, the Steve Miller Band, the Rolling Stones, the Small Faces, and The Who.

October 1. Luther Vandross and Mariah Carey peak at number two on the Hot 100 with their remake of the Lionel Richie-penned "Endless Love" (Columbia 77629).

October 8. Sheryl Crow begins a two-week run at number two on the Hot 100 with "All I Wanna Do" (A&M 0702).

November 26. The Eagles' *Hell Freezes Over* (Geffen 24725)—comprised of 1994 live renditions of eleven old hits along with four new studio tracks—debuts at number one, remaining there for two weeks and achieving quadruple-platinum sales by the end of the year. The album title represented a tongue-in-cheek jab at earlier Glenn Frey assessment of the possibility that the band would ever reunite following their 1982 breakup. The Eagles would go on to do exactly that for a 1994 tour; the lineup—which remained the same as in 1982—consisted of singer/guitarist Frey, singer/drummer Don Henley, guitarist Joe Walsh, guitarist Don Felder, and bassist Timothy B. Schmit.

November 26. Pearl Jam reaches number eighteen with "Tremor Christ" (Epic 77771), their highest position on the pop singles charts up to this point in time.

Although not a particularly innovative band, Pearl Jam played a key role in popularizing the grunge experiments of Seattle acts such as Mudhoney and Soundgarden. Their early work was indispensable in transforming grunge into the alternative rock mainstream.

Pearl Jam evolved out of the various configurations put together by guitarist Stone Gossard and bassist

Jeff Ament. Originally with the proto-grunge band, Green River, which pioneered a distortion-heavy blend of punk rock and heavy metal, they helped form Mother Love Bone. A tribute project arising out of the death of the group's lead vocalist, Andrew Wood, brought the twosome into contact with lead guitarist Mike McReady. The additions of vocalist Eddie Vedder and drummer Dave Abbruzzese in 1991 would complete Pearl Jam's lineup.

The debut, *Ten* (Epic 47857; 1991; #2), instantly elevated the band to superstar status on the strength of melodic hard rock material penned by Gossard and Ament and the soulful singing of Vedder (who also contributed the song lyrics). Their success unwittingly spawned a school of lumbering, sub-metal imitators and, consequently, considerable criticism from the rock press. Pearl Jam's political activism for a wide range of causes—most notably, the support of concert taping and an aborted attempt to undercut Ticketmaster's monopoly on the arena concert circuit—and willingness to collaborate with rock legends such as the Doors (sans Jim Morrison), Bob Dylan, and Neil Young helped expand their steadfastly loyal fan base. Follow-up LPs—*Vs* (Epic 53136; 1993; #1), *Vitalogy* (Epic 66900; 1994; #1; originally released in vinyl only format), *No Code* (Epic 67500; 1996; #1), and *Yield* (Epic 68164; 1998; #2)—have veered little from the band's basic formula, revealing a commitment to social consciousness verve and power rock basics.

Always a major touring attraction—in this regard, their popularity has surpassed only by a few dinosaurs such as the Grateful Dead and the Rolling Stones—fans had to search out Internet files and the underground exchange of bootleg tapes and CDs until the release of *Live On Two Legs* (Epic 69752; 1998; #15), which belied the conventional wisdom that concert recordings don't sell well. In recognition of the demand for live material in the commercial marketplace, the band issued a complete collection (forty-eight in all) of their 2000 tour dates the following year; the first series consisting of European venues, the second, their American concerts.

December 3. Boyz II Men go to number one on the Hot 100 with "On Bended Knee" (Motown 0244), remaining there for six non-consecutive weeks.

December 15. *Rolling Stone* pictures Courtney Love on its cover with the caption "Courtney Love Talks About Music, Madness and the Last Days of Kurt Cobain."

December 17. Jamaican reggae singer Ini Kamoze begins a two-week run atop the Hot 100 with "Here Comes the Hotstepper" (Columbia 77614). The platinum seller—which appears in the film, *Ready to Wear*, starring Julia Roberts—samples Bobby Byrd's "Hot Pants" and Taana Gardner's "Heartbeat," and include an interpolation of "Land of 1000 Dances."

1995

❄

January 24. David Cole, keyboardist/producer for C&C Music Factory, dies of meningitis at age thirty-two. He topped the charts in 1991 with "Gonna Make You Sweat," and produced Mariah Carey, Aretha Franklin, and Whitney Houston, among others.

January 28. TLC begin a four-week stay atop the Hot 100 with "Creep" (LaFace 24082)—their first chart-topping single. The platinum seller—which samples Slick Rick's "Hey Young World"—also spends nine weeks at number one on the R&B charts.

A calculated blend of image and studio production, the Atlanta-based TLC would, in less than a decade, became one of the most successful female recording groups in history. Founded and managed by rhythm and blues singer, Pebbles, the hip-hop trio—consisting of Tionne "T-Boz" Watkins, Lisa "Left-Eye" Lopes, and Rozonda "Chilli" Thomas—exudes a spirited verve that has enabled them to transcend their playful, cartoonish image.

TLC's first album, *Oooooohhh...On the TLC Tip* (LaFace; 1992; four-million seller), owed much of its popularity to the deft use of cutting-edge producers such as L.A. Reid, Babyface, and Daryl Simmons—"Baby-Baby-Baby" (LaFace 24028; 1992; #2; platinum award)—and Dallas Austin—"Hat 2 Da Back" (LaFace 14043; 1993; #30). Another of the LP's tracks, "Ain't 2 Proud 2 Beg" (LaFace 24008; 1992; #6; platinum award), was studio tour de force, incorporating samples from James Brown's "Escape-ism," Kool & the Gang's "Jungle Boogie," Average White Band's "School Boy Crush," Silver Convention's "Fly, Robin, Fly," and Bob James' "Take Me to the Mardi Gras."

While generally considered less accomplished from an artistic standpoint, the follow-up, *CrazySexyCool* (LaFace; 1994; #1), would sell more than ten million copies, driven by the singles "Creep," "Red Light Special" (LaFace 24097; 1995; #2; gold record), "Waterfalls" (LaFace 24107; 1995; #1; platinum award), and "Diggin' On You" (LaFace 24119; 1995; #5; gold record). The third album, *Fanmail* (LaFace 26055; 1999; #1; platinum award)—which included the million sellers "No Scrubs" (LaFace 24385; 1999; #1) and "Unpretty" (LaFace 24424; 1999; #1)—maintained the group's commercial momentum.

February 1. Manic Street Preachers guitarist, Richey James, disappears without a trace after leaving London's Embassy Hotel at 7 a.m. without taking his packed suitcase. His vehicle is found sixteen days later on the Severn Bridge in the vicinity of Bristol.

February 19. Tommy Lee—drummer for hair metal band, Motley Crue—marries *Baywatch* star Pamela Anderson, who wears a white bikini for the Cancun beach ceremony.

February 19. Roxette perform in Beijing during Chinese New Year festivities. They are the first Western act to play in China's capitol since George Michael in 1984.

February 25. Madonna begins a seven-week stay atop the Hot 100 with "Take a Bow" (Maverick/Sire 18000). She co-wrote the song with singer/producer Babyface, who supplies backing vocals. The million seller also spent nine weeks at number one on the Adult Contemporary charts.

March 10. Gareth Evans, former manager of the Stone Roses, settles his $17 million lawsuit with the band for alleged wrongful dismissal out of court for an undisclosed sum

March 12. The Spin Doctors perform at singer Chris Barron's old school in Princeton, New Jersey, raising $10,000 towards a European trip for the choir.

March 28. Country star Lyle Lovett and actress Julia Roberts announce their separation after twenty-one months of marriage.

March 31. Jimmy Page narrowly avoids being knifed while performing with Robert Plant at Auburn Hills, Michigan. The perpetrator—who was apprehended by two security guards—would state that he wanted to kill Page due to the satanic nature of the guitarist's music.

April 4. "Baby It's You" is released, the first single by the Beatles in twenty-five years.

April 15. Montell Jordan reaches the top position of the Hot 100 with "This Is How We Do It" (PMP/RAL 851468), remaining there for seven weeks. The platinum-selling single—which samples Slick Rick's "Children's Story"—spends seven weeks at number one on the R&B charts.

April 19. The Stone Roses perform live for the first time in five years at The Rockerfella Club, Oslo, Norway.

April 26. Courtney Love is reported to have turned down a million dollar offer by *Playboy* to pose in the nude.

April 29. Tupac Shakur marries Keisha Morris inside the Clinton Correctional Facility, where he has been serving a four-year term for sex abuse.

May 6. Oasis go number one on the British charts for the first time with "Some Might Say."

May 20. Robson Green and Jerome Flynn begin a seven-week run atop the British charts with "Unchained Melody"/"(There'll be Blue Birds Over) The White Cliffs of Dover."

May 20. Hootie & the Blowfish begin a four-week run at number one on the album charts with *Cracked Rear View*. The recording will go on to sell more than fifteen million copies.

May 25. The earliest known recording by Mick Jagger and Keith Richards, dating back to 1961, is sold at Christie's in London for $85,425.

June 3. Bryan Adams begins a five-week stay atop the Hot 100 with "Have You Ever Really Loved Woman?" (A&M 1028). The platinum seller—which appears in the film, *Don Juan DeMarco*, starring Johnny Depp—also enjoys a five-week run at number one on the Adult Contemporary charts.

June 13. Alanis Morissette's *Jagged Little Pill* is released. It will go on to sell more than 15 million copies, and she will become the first Canadian female to top the album charts.

June 30. Garth Brooks is given a star on Hollywood's Walk of Fame. He buries the master tapes of his *Hits* album underneath the star.

July 8. TLC reaches the summit of the Hot 100 with the platinum seller, "Waterfalls" (LaFace 24107), remaining there for seven weeks.

August 9. Jerry Garcia dies in his sleep while taking a break between tours in a detox center. Although the official cause was attributed to a heart attack, few who followed the guitarist's career back to the halcyon days of the San Francisco flower-power scene in the latter half of the 1960s doubted that the many years of substance abuse hastened his death. Deadheads circulated countless rumors of possible replacements—from Carlos Santana to Warren Haynes, an up-and-coming guitarist with Government Mule—but Grateful Dead sources revealed no inclination on the part of remaining personnel to soldier on. While the balance of the decade was given over to various solo projects and the release of vintage live and studio material by the band, the members would in fact regroup along with Haynes, Jimmy Herring, and Jeff Chimenti in the early 2000s.

August 24. "Some Might Say," by Oasis, is released. It becomes the band's first chart topper.

August 26. Seal hits number one on the Hot 100 with "Kiss From a Rose" (ZIT/Sire 17896). Culled from the film, *Batman Forever*, starring Val Kilmer, the million seller heads up the Adult Contemporary charts for twelve weeks.

September 2. The Cleveland, Ohio-based Rock and Roll Hall of Fame, housed in a futuristic building designed by world renowned architect I. M. Pei, officially opens. The facility's center attraction would be the artists being elected (and inducted at an honorary dinner) annually since the mid-1980s by the industry membership headed by Atlantic Records co-founder, Ahmet Ertegun. Other attractions included exhibits focusing on rock's history and cultural icons such as the guitars played by Les Paul, Jimi Hendrix, and other seminal performers. Considered a key ornament in the downtown revitalization of Cleveland, the museum also reflected the fact that rock and roll was now part of the Establishment spanning at least three generations of fans.

September 2. Michael Jackson reaches number one on the Hot 100 with "You Are Not Alone" (Epic 78002), his thirteenth chart-topping single. The platinum seller also heads the R&B charts for four weeks.

September 9. "Gangstas Paradise" (MCA Soundtracks 55104), by Coolio featuring L. V., begins a three-week stay atop the Hot 100. The single—a rap version of Stevie Wonder's "Pastime Paradise" which appeared in the film, *Dangerous Minds*, starring Michelle Pfeiffer—achieves triple-platinum sales.

September 30. Mariah Carey reaches number one of the Hot 100 with "Fantasy" (Columbia 78043), remaining there for eight weeks. The double-platinum seller—which samples the Tom Tom Club's "Genius of Love"—spends six weeks atop the R&B charts.

September 30. Deep Blue Something's "Breakfast At Tiffany's tops the British charts.

November 1. The Smashing Pumpkins head up the album charts with the double-disc set, *Mellon Collie and the Infinite Sadness*.

November 25. Whitney Houston occupies the top spot of the Hot 100 with "Exhale (Shoop Shoop)" (Arista 12885). The platinum seller also heads up the R&B charts for eight weeks.

December 2. "One Sweet Day" (Columbia 78074), by Mariah Carey and Boyz II Men, begins a sixteen-week run atop the Hot 100. The double-platinum single also spends thirteen weeks in the top spot of the Adult Contemporary charts.

December 14. *Rolling Stone* pictures Mick Jagger on its cover. Inside, the Jann Wenner interview—culled from three 1994–1995 sessions lasting up to four hours each and a follow-up phone call—covers the performer's entire career.

December 25. Dean Martin dies. The actor and singer recorded such hits as "Memories are Made of This" (Capitol; 1956, #1), "Return to Me" (Capitol; 1958; #2), and "Everybody Loves Somebody" (Reprise; 1964; #1).

December 30. Michael Jackson tops the British charts with "Earth Song."

1996

❄

January 2. Progressive rap act Arrested Development makes their breakup official. Their legacy includes two hit LPs and a chart-topping single, "Tennessee."

January 18. Lisa Marie Presley is granted a divorce from Michael Jackson after less than two years of marriage.

January 20. For assaulting a security guard, Bobby Brown is fined $1,000, sentenced to two years probation, and required to attend anger management classes.

January 27. Babylon Zoo's "Spaceman" begins a five-week stint atop the British charts. It is the fastest-selling non-charity single of all time in that nation, moving 420,000 copies in six days.

February 13. The most successful British band of the decade with nine number one recordings (seven singles and two albums), Take That, announce their breakup at the Manchester Hilton.

February 17. Bruce Springsteen's expired Platinum American Express card sells for $4,500 at a New York memorabilia sale. He let a Los Angeles waiter keep the card after handing it to him by mistake.

February 19. Pulp's Jarvis Cocker is arrested for allegedly attacking children performing with Michael Jackson at the Brit Awards. Because the police fail to charge him with any criminal offence, all charges are dropped on March 11.

February 28. Grammy Award winners include Alanis Morisette (Album of the Year for *Jagged Little Pill*, Best Song and Best Female Rock Vocal for "You Oughta Know"), Nirvana (Best Alternative Album for *Unplugged*), and Coolio (Best Rap Performance for "Gangsta's Paradise").

February 29. Status Quo sues Radio 1 for $425,000 arguing the BBC station is breaking the law by not placing their new record in rotation.

February 23. Celine Dion begins a six-week stint atop the Hot 100 with "Because You Loved Me" (550 Music/Epic 78237).

March 3. Take That's "How Deep Is Your Love"—their final single—starts a three-week run atop the British charts. It is their eighth record to accomplish this feat.

March 9. Oasis guitarist/songwriter Noel Gallagher deserts the stage during a performance at the Vernon Valley Gorge ski resort in New Jersey, claiming his hands are too cold to play.

March 10. Alanis Morissette dominates the twenty-fifth Juno Awards held in Hamilton, Canada, winning Best Album and Best Rock Album for *Jagged Little Pill*, Best Female Singer, Best Songwriter, and Best Single.

March 16. The Ramones' Buenos Aires, Argentina, concert is billed as their last ever performance.

March 19. The Beatles' *Anthology II* collection is released. It features "Real Love," a new Beatles recording featuring contributions of the three living members around an old demo track of John Lennon's voice.

March 23. Celine Dion tops the U.K. album chart with *Falling Into You*.

March 30. Celine Dion's dramatic ballad, "Because You Loved Me" (550 Music 78237), reaches number one on the Adult Contemporary charts, remaining there for nineteen weeks—a record that remains unbroken to the present day. Written by Diane Warren as a tribute to her father, the song was helped by its inclusion in the film *Up Close and Personal*, which starred Michelle Pfeiffer and Robert Redford. The platinum-selling single also garnered numerous industry awards, including a Grammy for Best Song Written for a Motion Picture or Television, Grammy nominations for Record of the Year and Song of the Year, and an Oscar nomination for Best Song.

April 18. Chic guitarist Bernard Edwards dies in a Tokyo hotel room. He was a very successful producer; his clients included ABC, Power Station, and Rod Stewart.

April 18. *Rolling Stone* pictures Bush singer Gavin Rossdale on its cover with the caption "Three million albums, five hit singles…Bush: Why won't anyone take Gavin Rossdale seriously?"

May 4. Mariah Carey begins a two-week stay atop the Hot 100 with "Always Be My Baby" (Columbia 78276). The platinum seller also spent a week at number one on the R&B charts.

May 4. George Michael reaches number one on the British charts with "Fastlove," remaining there for three weeks.

May 4. Alanis Morissette begins a six-week run atop the British album charts with *Jagged Little Pill.*

May 8. A Los Angeles judge denies Tommy Lee and Pamela Anderson's attempt to bar *Penthouse* from publishing still photos from an X-rated movie that was stolen from their home.

May 11. Hootie & the Blowfish go number one on the album charts with *Fairweather Johnson.*

May 18. The Cleveland-based male rap quintet, Bones Thugs-N-Harmony, reach the top of the Hot 100 with "Tha Crossroads" (Ruthless 6335), remaining there for eight weeks. The double-platinum single—which samples the Isley Brothers' "Make Me Say It Again Girl"—also enjoyed a seven-week run atop the R&B charts.

June 1. "Three Lions"—the official song of England's national soccer team as recorded by Baddiel and Skinner and The Lightning Seeds—peaks at number one on the British charts.

June 14. Van Morrison receives an OBE from the Queen of England.

June 15. Jazz singer Ella Fitzgerald dies at age seventy-eight. Her composer series of albums—which have been issued on CD separately and as a set—remain steady sellers.

July 6. Jay-Z's debut album, *Reasonable Doubt,* is released on his Roc-A-Fella label.

Born Shawn Carter on December 4, 1969, in New York City, he would become one of the most influential figures in the 1990s rap scene due to his wide array of talents. Known as "Jazzy" while hustling on the streets near Brooklyn's Marcy projects where he grew up, Jay-Z was inspired by a local rapper, Big Jaz, to start his own record company. Along with partners Kareem Burke and Damon Dash, he formed the Roc-A-Fella imprint in 1995.

While content to appropriate the gangsta conventions then in vogue on *Reasonable Doubt,* his production skills helped boost it to number twenty-three on the *Billboard* charts. Taking a decidedly pop direction, his subsequent CDs—*In My Lifetime, Vol. 1* (Roc-A-Fella, 1997), *Vol. 2: Hard Knock Life* (Roc-A-Fella, 1998), *Vol. 3: Life and Times of S. Carter* (Roc-A-Fella, 2000), *Roc La Familia – The Dynasty* (Roc-A-Fella, 2000), and *The Blueprint* (Uptown/Universal, 2001)—all topped the charts (with the exception of his sophomore effort, which peaked at number three). Utilizing the Roots as his backing band, he tried a new direction with *MTV Unplugged* (Def Jam, 2001). The double-disc set, *The Blueprint2: The Gift & the Curse* (Def Jam, 2002) found Jay-Z still trying to push the envelope. No longer content to rely on his unparalleled rhyming skills and innovative beats, he worked a wide array of guest performers (including Beyonce Knowles, Lenny Kravitz, Rakim, and Scarface) and outside producers (Dr. Dre, Heavy D, the Neptunes, Timbaland, and Kanye West) into his grand scheme.

By the late 1990s, Jay-Z had transcended musical stardom, becoming something of a cultural icon. In addition to producing some of the top R&B artists, he established his own clothing line and became a favorite subject of the paparazzi (Destiny Child's Knowles becoming his main squeeze in the early years of the new century). Obviously comfortable with the spotlight—as evidenced by the prefabricated feud with fellow New Yorkers Nas and Mobb Deep, which he instigated by ridiculing them in the song, "Takeover"—Jay-Z is unlikely to relinquish his East Coast hegemony anytime in the near future.

July 13. "How Do U Want It" (Death Row 854652), by 2 Pac (featuring KC and JoJo), begins a two-week stay atop the Hot 100. The double-platinum single—which samples Quincy Jones' "Body Heat"—also spent three weeks at number one on the R&B charts.

July 27. Toni Braxton reaches the summit of the Hot 100 with "You're Makin' Me High" (LaFace 24160), which remains in the Top 40 for thirty-nine weeks. The platinum-selling single also tops the R&B charts for two weeks.

July 28. Former Shangri-Las vocalist Marge Ganser dies of breast cancer.

August 3. The Spanish duo, Los Del Rio, begin a fourteen-week stint atop the Hot 100 with "Macarena (Bayside Boys Mix)" (RCA 64407). They wrote and recorded the original version in 1993; it became an international dance craze after being remixed by the Miami production team, the Bayside Boys.

August 10. Eric Clapton's "Change the World" (Reprise 17621) begins a thirteen-week stay in the top rung of the Adult Contemporary charts. Included in the soundtrack to the film, *Phenomenon*, the single set a record by remaining on the AC charts for eighty weeks in addition to reaching number five on the Hot 100. It was represented by three Grammy Awards: Record of the Year, Song of the Year, and Best Male Pop Vocal Performance (won by Clapton). Co-writer Wayne Kirkpatrick attributed the record's success to the broad-based coalition of talent that went into its creation: a rock star assisted by R&B producer Babyface doing a song created by three country-oriented songwriters.

August 12. The Spice Girls top the British charts with "Wannabe."

October 31. *Rolling Stone* pictures Tupac Shakur—his chest and torso tattoos in full view—on its cover with the caption "[1971–1996] Tupac Shakur: The Strange & Terrible Saga."

October 31. Slash announces his departure from Guns N' Roses. He notes that he'd spoken with Axl Rose on only two occasions since 1994.

November 9. "No Diggity" (Interscope 97007), by BLACKstreet (featuring Dr. Dre), reaches number one on the Hot 100, remaining there four weeks. The platinum seller includes a female rap by Queenpen and samples Bill Withers' "Grandma's Hands" (Interscope 97007).

November 19. Celine Dion's "It's All Coming Back to Me Now" (550 Music 78435) tops the AC charts, initiating a five-week run. Originally recorded by its writer, Jim Steinman, with his group Pandora's Box, in 1989, the cover version would stall at number two (for five weeks) on the pop charts behind Los Del Rio's "Macarena" and BLACKstreet's "No Diggity," respectively.

November 29. Tiny Tim dies of a heart attack. Known more for his eccentricities on the *Tonight Show* than for his 1968 hit, "Tiptoe Through the Tulips" (#17), he championed Tin Pan Alley pop music from the early decades of the twentieth century throughout his career.

December 4. The newly re-formed Journey begins a four-week stint at number one on the AC charts with "When You Love a Woman" (Columbia 78428; #12 pop). Lead singer Steve Perry defended criticism that the single sounded just like the group's material from more than a decade earlier, stating, "Nothing sounds more pretentious than someone being something they're not. One of the things we've always known is that there are certain musical directions that fit what [our] chemistry is about. We're going to sink or swim being what we are and not by trying to reinvent ourselves and not by trying to be the flavor of the month" (Hyatt 1999).

December 7. Toni Braxton begins an eleven-week run atop the Hot 100 with "Un-Break My Heart" (LaFace 24200). The platinum seller—featuring Shanice's backing vocal—sent fourteen weeks at number one on the Adult Contemporary charts.

December 28. The Spice Girls top the British charts with "2 Become 1."

December 31. Paul McCartney is listed as a knight on the Queen's New Year's Honours List.

1997

❄

January 5. Sonny Bono is killed after hitting a tree skiing at a Lake Tahoe area resort. The U.S. Congressman—and former mayor of Palm Springs, California—first achieved fame as the guiding force behind the hit-making duo, Sonny and Cher.

January 19. Madonna is named Best Actress at the Golden Globe Awards for her role in *Evita*.

January 21. "Colonel" Tom Parker—born Andreas van Kuijk in Holland—dies at age eighty-seven. After working as a carnival barker—one colorful anecdote relates that his dancing chickens were spurred on by a hotplate covered with straw—he graduated to managing artists such as Gene Austin, Hank Snow, Eddy Arnold, and Elvis Presley. He never applied for a green card after emigrating to the United States and lived in constant fear of deportation.

January 23. *Rolling Stone* pictures Marilyn Manson on its cover with the caption "Best New Artist."

Marilyn Manson (born Brian Hugh Warner) was the most censored musician of the 1990s. The concerted efforts of parental groups, religious leaders, politicians, and other authority figures to suppress him have focused more on his alleged stage behavior and public statements than his recordings per se (although detractors would argue that they contain material that is equally unpleasant). Manson has emerged from the controversies surrounding him as a savvy media manipulator and outspoken martyr for First Amendment rights.

Inspired by lectures about the subliminal messages allegedly embedded in rock albums he received while attending a private Christian school, Warner formed the band, Marilyn Manson and the Spooky Kids, in 1969. Each member adopted a stage name based on both a female icon and storied murderer (in Warner's case, Marilyn Monroe crossed with Charles Manson). Releasing a series of self-produced cassettes, the band impressed Trent Reznor, who signed them to his own label, Nothing Records, in 1993.

Touring with Reznor's group, Nine Inch Nails, in support of his debut LP, the industrial-hardcore *Portrait of an American Family* (Nothing/Interscope 92344; 1994), Manson made headlines over alleged sexually lewd behavior and self-mutilations onstage as well as for being named a "reverend" of the Church of Satan. His notoriety, combined with the success of the band's revved-up version of the Eurythmics' "Sweet Dreams (Are Made of This)" (Nothing/Interscope 95504; 1995), helped the *Smells Like Children* EP (Nothing/Interscope 92641; 1995; #31) go platinum.

Manson's next album, *Antichrist Superstar* (Nothing/Interscope 90006; 1996; #3), represented the first part of a "pseudoautobiographical trilogy"; its aggressive edge effectively framed the concept about a nihilistic rock god. Later installments, the David Bowie-influenced, glam-rock *Mechanical Animals* (Nothing/Interscope 98273; 1998; #1) and goth rock-oriented *Holy Wood (In the Shadow of the Valley of Death)* (Nothing/ Interscope; 2000; #13), further reinforced his status as a shock-rock American institution. Having written (with Neil Strauss) an autobiography, *The Long Hard Road out of Hell* (1997), Manson would go on to form his own label, Post Human Records, in 2000.

February 12. U2's "Popmart" world tour is launched at a Manhattan K-Mart.

February 22. The Spice Girls begin a four-week stint atop the Hot 100 with "Wannabe" (Virgin 38579).

February 24. Brit Awards winners include the Spice Girls (Best Single for "Wannabe"), Manic Street Preachers (Best Group), Prodigy (Best Dance Act), George Michael (Best Male Artist), Gabrielle (Best Female Artist), and Best Newcomer (Kula Shaker).

February 26. Songwriter Ben Raleigh dies from burns sustained from setting fire to his bathrobe while cooking. He shared composition credits for "Scooby-Doo Where Are You" and "Tell Laura I Love Her."

February 28. Death Row Records head Marion "Suge" Knight is given a nine-year prison sentence for violating his probation for a 1995 assault conviction. He will not be permitted to run his label while incarcerated.

March 1. Claiming his hearing had been irreparably damaged by a New Jersey concert featuring Motley Crue, Clifford Goldberg has his lawsuit thrown out of court. The judge claims the fan, who had sat near the front of the stage, knew the risk he was taking.

March 9. Notorious B.I.G. (aka Christopher Wallace) is fatally shot while leaving a party at the Petersen Automotive Museum in Los Angeles. The twenty-four-year-old is believed to be a casualty of an East Coast/West Coast rap feud.

March 17. The Memphis-based Elvis Presley Enterprises loses its legal challenge to stop London entrepreneur Sid Shaw from using the name "The King" on his souvenirs. Shaw, owner of a memorabilia show called Elvisly Yours, would comment, "I'm delighted. I've proved that Elvis belongs to all of us—Elvis part of our history, part of our culture."

March 17. Singer Jermaine Stewart dies of cancer. His single, "We Don't Have to…Take Our Clothes Off," reached number two on the British charts in 1986.

March 22. "Can't Nobody Hold Me Down" (Bad Boy 79083), by Puff Daddy featuring Mase, begins a six-week stint atop the Hot 100. The double platinum seller, which samples Grandmaster Flash's "The Message" and Matthew Wilder's "Break My Stride," also heads up the R&B charts for six weeks.

Born Sean Combs on November 4, 1970, in Harlem, New York, he was raised in the Mt. Vernon area. Securing employment at Uptown Records—a label on the rise via hits by Mary J. Blige and Heavy D and the Boyz—through his childhood friend, Heavy D, he worked his way up from general gofer to A&R man, and then executive producer of Father MC's hit album, *Father's Day* (1990). In 1992, however, Combs was fired due to undisclosed differences. He decided to form his own record company, Bad Boy, and by late 1993 had signed Craig Mack and the Notorious B.I.G., both of whom went on to become major hitmakers. While continuing to run Bad Boy—whose roster included Faith Evans and Total in the mid-1990s—he also remixed tracks for R&B stars like Boyz II Men and Mariah Carey.

Signed to Arista, his Puff Daddy solo project would be placed on hold in the wake of B.I.G.'s murder. He would ultimately make a splash with the assertive anthem, "Can't Nobody Hold Me Down" (featuring Mase), which reached number one on the *Billboard* Hot 100 in early 1997. He also topped the charts in mid-year with tribute to B.I.G., "I'll Be Missing You" (featuring Faith Evans, 112 & the Lox), followed by his equally successful debut LP, *No Way Out* (Arista, 1997); both of which won Grammys, for Best Performance and Best Rap Album, respectively. While garnering considerable press for his relationship with actress Jennifer Lopez, he maintained his pop ascendancy with the reflective, melodic *Forever* (Arista, 1999) and—as P. Diddy & the Bad Boy Family—the somewhat lackluster *The Saga Continues…* (Arista, 2001). He seems content at present to maintain a relatively low profile, focusing on the management of his record industry empire.

March 24. Harold Melvin dies at age fifty-seven. His biggest hit was "If You Don't Know Me By Now," which reached number three on the Hot 100.

March 24. U2 tops the album charts with *Pop*.

April 13. The Notorious B.I.G. tops the album charts with *Life After Death*.

Born Christopher Wallace on May 21, 1972, in Brooklyn, New York, he was a leading exponent of rap's East Coast school in the mid-1990s prior to his tragic death. Initially performing in the greater New York area as Biggy Smallz, he was discovered by Bad Boy Records owner, Sean "Puffy" Combs, who provided him with cameo recording spots for established R&B artists like Mary J. Blige. His major label debut, *Ready To Die* (Arista, 1994), propelled him to the forefront of the gangsta rap genre, a lifestyle he knew first-hand, having been arrested on many occasions for assault, robbery, and weapon offenses. A string of successful singles followed, most notably, the 1995 Top 10 pop hits, "Big Poppa" and "One More Chance – Stay With Me."

B.I.G. found himself caught up in the East Coast/West Coast rivalry between Bad Boy and the Los Angeles-based Death Row label. Eventually, threats exchanged in the press and on recordings led to Tupac Shakur's death at the hands of unknown gunmen in Las Vegas on September 13, 1996. Although nothing could be substantiated, it is believed that B.I.G.'s murder on March 9, 1997, may well have been motivated by a desire for revenge. Released a matter of days following his assassination, B.I.G.'s second album, *Life After Death* (Artista, 1997), went straight to the top of the pop charts, fueled both by sensationalized media coverage and the fatalistic tone characterizing many of its songs. Two chart-topping singles, "Hypnotize" and "Mo Money Mo Problems," would be released in short order, along with the equally successful tribute disc by Combs and B.I.G.'s wife, Faith Evans, "I'll Be Missing You." Although padded with the contributions of a stellar galaxy of rap stars—including Lil' Kom, Eminem, Snoop Dogg, Busta Rhymes, Missy Elliott, and Ice Cube—his final album of original material, *Born Again* (Arista, 1999), also reached number one on the *Billboard* Top 200.

April 17. *Rolling Stone* pictures a preppie looking Beck on its cover with the caption "The Rolling Stone Interview: Beck – Where It's At Now."

May. The Foo Fighters long-awaited second album, *The Colour and the Shape*, is released.

A spin-off of the Seattle-based alternative band, Nirvana, the Foo Fighters have gone on to realize the promise of the grunge movement. Their sound—a commercially successful blend of postpunk hardcore influences and melodic power-pop—has inspired an entire school of imitators (e.g., Creed, Our Lady Peace) within the 1990s alternative rock movement.

Following the suicide death of Nirvana frontman Kurt Cobain, drummer Dave Grohl created the Foo Fighters. The band's debut album, *Foo Fighters* (Roswell 34027; 1995; #3 UK, #23 US), was a one-man tour de force, comprised exclusively of Grohl's compositions and musicianship. Shortly thereafter, however, he enlisted a supporting cast—guitarist Pat Smear, bassist Nate Mandel, and drummer William Goldsmith—while retaining vocal, lead guitar, and songwriting duties.

Active touring, particularly during summer festival season, combined with a seemingly endless supply of radio-friendly tracks, helped boost the band's next two albums—*The Colour and the Shape* (Roswell 58530; 1997; #3 UK, #10 US) and *There Is Nothing Left To Lose* (RCA 67892; 1999; #10 UK, #10 US) into the upper reaches of the *Billboard Top Pop Albums* chart. The Foo Fighters' arrangements have reflected a growing subtlety and refinement over time, and Grohl—still the creative core of the band in the face of personnel shifts—has begun taking on outside recording projects (e.g., scoring the 1998 film, *Touch*).

May 3. The Notorious B.I.G. tops the Hot 100 with "Hypnotize" (Bad Boy 79092; accompanied by Pam Long), remaining there for three weeks. The platinum seller—which samples Slick Rick's "La Di Da Di" and Herb Alpert's "Rise"—also heads up the R&B charts for three weeks.

May 4. Courtney Love places the house she shared with Kurt Cobain up for sale in the *Seattle Times*. The asking price for the five bedroom, four bathroom house (the adjacent carriage house where Cobain had committed suicide had been torn down) is $3 million.

May 15. Courtney Love sells the Seattle mansion she'd shared with Kurt Cobain for $3 million.

May 15. The joint effort by Oasis and Sony to squelch unofficial Internet sites carrying the band's lyrics, audio files, and photographs becomes public.

May 20. U2 cause massive traffic flow problems in Kansas City when they pay to have the freeway system shut down to shoot the video to "Last Night on Earth." City fathers defended their decision, claiming that much favorable publicity would be gained through a video by a popular rock band.

May 24. The Tulsa, Oklahoma-based trio of brothers, Hanson, begin a three-week stay at number one on the Hot 100 with the platinum-selling "MMMBop" (Mercury 57461).

May 24. The Spice Girls top the album charts with *Spice*. They are only the third all-female ensemble to accomplish this feat (following the Supremes and the Go-Go's).

May 25. Elvis Presley is reported to be the world's bestselling posthumous entertainer, with international sales of more than $1 billion.

May 29. Singer/songwriter Jeff Buckley disappears after taking a swim in the Mississippi River while recording in Memphis.

June 4. Jeff Buckley's body is discovered after being spotted by a passenger on a sightseeing riverboat.

June 12. *Rolling Stone* pictures Jakob Dylan on its cover with the caption "The Wallflowers' Jakob Dylan: The Price of Fame & Life With Father."

June 14. "I'll Be Missing You" (Bad Boy 79097), by Puff Daddy and Faith Evans, with 112, goes number one on the Hot 100, remaining there eleven weeks. A "tribute to The Notorious B.I.G., the triple-platinum seller—which samples The Police's "Every Breathe You Take"—tops the R&B charts for eight weeks.

August 30. "Mo Money Mo Problems" (Bad Boy 79100), by The Notorious B.I.G. featuring Puff Daddy and Mase, begins a two-week stay atop the Hot 100. The platinum seller samples Diana Ross's "I'm Coming Out."

September 6. Elton John records a new version of "Candle in the Wind" after performing the song live at Princess Diana's funeral.

September 13. Mariah Carey reaches number one on the Hot 100 with "Honey" (Columbia 78648), remaining there for three weeks. The platinum seller samples Treacherous 3's "The Body Rock."

September 22. Elton John's "Candle in the Wind 1997" (a new recording of the track, featuring revamped lyrics that originally appeared on 1973's *Goodbye Yellow Brick Road Album*) is released. A musical tribute to Princess Diana, it would become the best-selling single in history, selling thirty-two million copies in only thirty-seven days.

October 4. Boyz II Men hit the top of the Hot 100 with the platinum-selling "4 Seasons of Loneliness" (Motown 0684).

October 11. Elton John begins a fourteen-week stint atop the Hot 100 with the double-sided single, "Candle in the Wind 1997"/"Something About the Way You Look Tonight" (Rocket 568108). It also heads up the Adult Contemporary charts for ten weeks.

October 12. John Denver dies when a plane he is piloting (without a legal license) crashes. He was one of the leading Adult Contemporary artists on the 1970s.

November 12. George Michael launches his Internet fan club, Members Online.

December 27. The Spice Girls top the British charts with "Too Much."

1998

❄

January 15. Blues harmonica virtuoso Junior Wells dies. He worked with early electric blues pioneers such as Muddy Waters as well as rock superstars like Van Morrison and Santana.

January 17. Savage Garden begins a two-week stay atop the Hot 100 with "Truly Madly Deeply" (Columbia 787230.

January 19. Carl Perkins, age sixty, succumbs to a series of strokes. He wrote and recorded many rockabilly classics, most notably, "Blue Suede Shoes."

January 24. Oasis tops the British charts with "All Around the World," which sets the record with the longest running time for a number one single, timing out at nine minutes and thirty-eight seconds.

January 31. Janet Jackson reaches number one on the Hot 100 with "Together Again" (Virgin 38623), remaining there for two weeks. The disc remains in the Top 40 for thirty-four weeks. It is her eighth chart-topping single.

February 6. Beach Boys guitarist Carl Wilson, age fifty-one, succumbs to lung cancer.

February 6. Austrian singer, Falco—who topped the American and British charts in 1986 with "Rock Me Amadeus"—dies in an automobile accident.

February 14. Celine Dion's "My Heart Will Go On" sets a record for radio rotations in the United States with 116 million plays in a week.

February 14. Usher begins a two-week stay at number one on the Hot 100 with "Nice & Slow" (LaFace 24290). It spends eight weeks atop the R&B charts.

David Freeland has succinctly described the qualities at the core of Usher's success:

Drawing upon old-fashioned show-biz pizzazz, Usher entertains fans through flamboyant displays of physical agility. As an artist he takes the basic qualities inherent within R&B for decades—danceable rhythm, catchy melody, convivial feeling—and updates them with his naughty buy nice personal style. Beyond his charisma and effervescent music, Usher's appeal lies in a persona that tempers sensuality with sweetness and charm.

Born Usher Raymond, in Chattanooga, Tennessee, on October 14, 1978, he started out singing in the church choir where his mother worshipped and participated in local talent shows. His mother moved the family to Atlanta when he was twelve in order to provide greater career opportunities. After winning a competition of TV's *Star Search*, Usher was signed while still in high school by Antonio "L.A." Reid to LaFace, the label he'd formed along with fellow producer Kenneth "Babyface" Edmonds.

The debut album, *Usher* (LaFace; 1994)—featuring the midtempo dance hit, Think of You" (LaFace; 1994), produced by Sean "Puffy" Combs—barely hinted at his future success. He became a major star with the release of *My Way* (LaFace; 1997), driven by seductive dance floor lament, "You Make Me Wanna" (LaFace; 1997; #1 r&b), produced by Jermaine Dupri. After taking time out to do film and television acting—during which time he fulfilled his legal obligations to LaFace by releasing *Live* (LaFace; 1999)— Usher re-emerged with *8701* (Arista; 2001), an uneven affair highlighted by the single, "U Remind Me" (Arista; 2001; #1 pop, #1 r&b), built around an attention-grabbing synthesizer figure and pounding bass line.

February 17. Bob Merrill—a songwriter whose output included "How Much Is That Doggie in the Window" and "People"—commits suicide at age seventy-seven.

February 18. The Epiphone Supernova guitar donated by Oasis' Noel Gallagher brings $7,820 at a Bonhams auction for Children in Need.

February 23. Oasis are banned from flying Cathay Pacific Airlines following "abusive and disgusting behavior" on a Hong Kong-to-Perth, Australia flight.

February 25. The winners at the fortieth Annual Grammy Awards include Shawn Colvin (Record of the Year and Song of the Year for "Sunny Came Home"), Bob Dylan (Album of the Year for *Time Out of Mind* and Best Male Rock Vocal Performance for "Cold Irons Bound"), Paula Cole (Best New Artist), Sarah McLachlan (Best Female Pop Vocal Performance for "Building a Mystery" and Best Pop Instrumental Performance for "Last Dance"), Elton John (Best Male Pop Vocal Performance for "Candle in the Wind 1997"), James Taylor (Best Pop Album for *Hourglass*), the Wallflowers (Best Rock Performance by a Duo or Group with Vocal and Best Rock Song—written by frontman Jakob Dylan—for "One Headlight"), John Fogerty (Best Rock Album for *Blue Moon Swamp*), Erykah Badu (Best Female R&B Vocal Performance for "On & On" and Best R&B Album for *Baduizm*), R. Kelly (Best Male R&B Vocal Performance and Best R&B Song for "I Believe I Can Fly"), Puff Daddy (Best Rap Performance by a Duo or Group for "I'll Be Missing You" —with Faith Evans and 112—and Best Rap Album for *No Way Out*), Trisha Yearwood (Best Female Country Vocal Performance for "How Do I Live" and Best Country Collaboration with Vocals—with Garth Brooks—for "In Another's Eyes"), Alison Krauss & Union Station (for Best Country Performance by a Duo or Group with Vocal for "Looking in the Eyes of Love," Best Country Instrumental Performance for "Little Liza Jane" and Best Bluegrass Album for *So Long So Wrong*), and Johnny Cash (Best Country Album for *Unchained*).

February 28. Cornershop reaches number one on the British charts with "Brimful of Asher." Although very successful in their native country, the band are unable to make much of an impression stateside.

February 28. Celine Dion begins a two-week stint atop the Hot 100 with "My Heart Will Go On (Love Theme From Titanic)" (550 Music/Epic 78825). It also remains number one for ten weeks on the Adult Contemporary charts.

March 13. Jedge Dread (aka Alex Hughes) dies after collapsing during a Canterbury performance. He had had ten hit singles in England during the 1970s.

March 14. Will Smith reaches number one on the Hot 100 with "Gettin' Jiggy Wit It" (Columbia 78804), remaining there for three weeks. The track samples Sister Sledge's "He's the Greatest Dancer," the Bar-Kays' "Sang and Dance," and Spoonie Gee's "Love Rap."

March 15. Madonna heads up the British charts with *Ray of Light*, her sixth LP to accomplish this feat (no other female artist has had more than three chart topping albums).

April. Mase is arrested on charges of disorderly conduct.

Born Mason Durrell Betha on August 27, 1977, in Jacksonville, Florida, he relocated to Harlem with his family at age five. Following a couple of years in Florida during his early teens (where he'd been sent due to concerns about peer pressure from unsavory elements), he started rapping in order to entertain friends on his high school basketball team. Shortly after being offered a scholarship to play basketball at the State University of New York, he adopted the name Mase Murder and joined the rap act, Children of the Corn. The group disbanded when a member died in an auto accident, and Mase hooked up with Sean "Puffy" Combs at an Atlanta music conference in 1996.

After appearing as a guest rapper on a string of Combs productions—most notably, with the Notorious B.I.G., Mariah Carey, Brian McKnight, and Busta Rhymes—he achieved superstardom with his debut album, *Harlem World* (Bad Boy, 1997), which topped the charts during the first two weeks following its release. Mase's distinctively simple, laid-back raps featured a wide array of guests, including Combs, Black Rob, DMX, Eightball & MJG, Jay-Z, Lil' Cease, Lil' Kim, the Lox, Monifah, 112, and Rhymes and production by Jermaine Dupri, the Hitmen, and The Neptunes, among others.

Prior to the release of his second album, *Double Up* (Bad Boy, 1999), Mase remained in the news through collaborations with the likes of Brandy, Cam'ron, Harlem World, Blackstreet, and Mya and the disorderly conduct episode. Although reaching number eleven and achieving gold sales, its commercial potential was severely undermined by Mase's pre-release announcement that he was retiring from the entertainment business in order to enter the ministry. He remained exclusively committed his new course—working with inner city youth, giving inspirational speeches, and writing a memoir, *Revelations: There's Light After the Lime*—until the release of the relatively subdued *Welcome Back* (Bad Boy, 2004), which was rated one of the most popular albums of the year (#152) by *Billboard*.

April 2. Milli Vanilli member Rob Pilatus is discovered dead in a Frankfurt hotel room after ingesting a lethal combination of drugs and alcohol.

April 4. K-Ci & JoJo begin a three-week stint atop the Hot 100 with "All My Life" (MCA 55420). The act consists of two brothers, Cedric and Joel Hailey. The single also heads up the R&B charts for two weeks.

April 5. James go number one on the British album charts with *The Best of James*.

April 5. Cozy Powell—drummer for both ELP and Whitesnake—dies in a car crash.

April 5. The Spice Girls make their live debut in Glasgow, Scotland.

April 6. Former Plasmatics singer, Wendy O. Williams, dies from self-inflicted gunshot wounds.

April 7. Tammy Wynette dies at age fifty-five. Best known for the 1968 country hit, "Stand By Your Man" (Epic), she sold more than thirty million records worldwide.

April 9. R&B-pop singer Brook Benton dies. He was one of the more consistent hitmakers of the late 1950s and early 1960s.

April 17. Linda McCartney dies at age fifty-six following a long battle with cancer. In addition to her involvement with music and photography, she had become a millionaire by marketing vegetarian food products.

April 19. Robbie Williams begins a two-week stint atop the British album charts with *Life Thru a Lens*.

April 25. Next reaches the summit of the Hot 100 with "Too Close" (Arista 13456), remaining there for five non-consecutive weeks through June 5. It also tops the R&B charts for three weeks. It samples Kurtis Blow's "X-mas Rappin'."

Musically, Next combined the longstanding traditions of romantic crooning as refined in the early 1990s by Boyz II Men combined with the gospel fervor of 1960s classic soul singers. Their lyrics, however, pushed raw sexuality to new levels of explicitness, which required extensive editing for dissemination in the mass media.

The Minneapolis-based trio formed in 1992 after brothers Terrance (aka T-Low; born June 7, 1974) and Raphael (aka Tweety; b. January 28, 1976) were introduced by their uncle, then a gospel choir director, to Robert Lavelle (R. L.) Huggar (b. April 2, 1977). Under the guidance of manager (and former gospel/R&B singer) Ann Nesby, Next recorded a demo at a Minneapolis studio run by the production team of Jimmy Jam and Terry Lewis. Upon hearing it, Naughty By Nature's Kay Gee signed them to his fledging Divine Mill label, part of the Arista Records family. Powered by funky dance rhythms in the singles "Butta Love" (Arista; 1997) and "Too Close" (Arista; 1997), their debut, *Rated Next* (Arista; 1997), became a major hit. However, the formula had begun to wear a bit thin following the release of *Welcome II Nextasy* (Arista; 2000) and the *Next Episode* (J-Records; 2002).

May 7. Eddie Rabbitt dies of lung cancer. In addition to recording many country and pop hits on his own, his compositions were recorded by the likes of Dr. Hook, Tom Jones, and Elvis Presley.

May 9. Jimmy Page appears on *Saturday Night Live* with rapper Sean "Puffy" Combs. He performs "Come With Me" from the soundtrack to the film, *Godzilla*; the track samples a guitar riff from Led Zeppelin's "Kashmir."

May 15. Frank Sinatra dies at age eighty-two. His recording career spanned some sixty years.

May 23. Mariah Carey's goes number one on the Hot 100 with "My All" (Columbia 78821).

May 31. Geri Halliwell announces that she has left the Spice Girls, noting, "This is because of differences between us. I am sure the group will continue to be successful and I wish them all the best."

June 6. Brandy and Monica begin a thirteen-week stay atop the Hot 100 with "The Boy Is Mine" (Atlantic 84089). It also heads up the R&B charts for eight weeks.

June 7. Songwriter/producer Wally Gold dies at age seventy. He had been a member of the late 1950s group, the Four Esquires, and wrote "It's My Party" and "It's Now or Never."

July 27. The Corrs climb to number one—following thirty weeks on the British album charts—with *Talk on Corners*.

July 11. Billie reaches the summit of the British charts with "Because We Want To." At fifteen, she is the second youngest female to accomplish this feat (Helen Shapiro did it at fourteen with "You Don't Know" in 1961).

July 25. The Beastie Boys reach number one on the album charts with *Hello Nasty*.

August 6. *Rolling Stone* pictures the Beastie Boys—in a basketball jump ball pose—on its cover with the caption "Back in the Game."

September 5. Aerosmith reach number one on the Hot 100 with "I Don't Want To Miss a Thing" (Columbia 78952), remaining there for four weeks. The song is included in the soundtrack to the film, *Armageddon*, starring Bruce Willis.

September 16. A Sotheby's auction includes a notebook belonging to Beatles' roadie Mal Evans (including the lyrics to "Hey Jude"), which sells for $189,550; a two-tone denim jacket owed by John Lennon ($15,640); and the Union Jack dress worn by Ginger Spice ($70,244).

September 19. Robbie Williams peaks at number one on the British charts with "Millennium."

October 3. Monica begins a five-week nonconsecutive run atop the Hot 100 with "The First Night" (Arista 13522). The song—which samples Diana Ross's "Love Hangover"—also enjoys a six-week stay at number one on the R&B charts.

Monica is often compared with another youthful R&B singer, Brandy; indeed the two collaborated on the mega-hit, "The Boy Is Mine" (Arista; 1998). Although she has not enjoyed Brandy's level of commercial success, Monica is felt to possess a richer, more dynamic vocal style—the result of a professional singing career started as a ten-year-old.

Born Monica Arnold, in Atlanta, Georgia, on October 24, 1980, she first attracted attention as a member of the gospel group, Charles Thompson and the Majestics. Her performance of Whitney Houston's "The Greatest Love of All" at a talent show at age twelve spurred producer/record executive Dallas Austin to offer an Arista recording contract. Monica's debut album, *Miss Thang* (Arista; 1995), revealed a mature talent, equally at home with hot dance numbers and tender ballads. The follow-up, *The Boy Is Mine* (Arista; 1998), proved to be her commercial breakthrough, including two best-selling singles, the title track and "The First Night" (Arista; 1998).

At the peak of success, Monica opted to take time off from career demands. She also spent time recovering from the harrowing experience of witnessing her boyfriend's shooting suicide in 1999. Plans for the release of the long-awaited *All Eyez on Me*, originally set for 2002, were shelved due to alleged Internet piracy. It was issued the following year, in reworked form, as *After the Storm* (J-Records), enjoying solid sales due in large part to heavy radio play for the engaging lead single, "So Long" (J-Records; 2003).

October 17. The Barenaked Ladies peak at number one on the Hot 100 with "One Week" (Reprise 17174). It also tops the Modern Rock charts for five weeks.

October 31. Cher tops the British charts with "Believe." She becomes the first female over age 50 to accomplish this feat.

November 11. Paddy Clancy—singer with the Clancy Brothers—dies at age 76. His compositions included "Carrickfergus" and "Wild Mountain Thyme."

November 14. Former Fugees member Lauryn Hill reaches the top of the Hot 100 with "Doo Wop (That Thing)" (Ruffhouse 78868), remaining there for two weeks.

November 28. The female R&B vocal trio Divine hit the summit of the Hot 100 with "Lately" (Red Ant 15316).

December 5. R. Kelly and Celine Dion begin a six-week stay atop the Hot 100 with "I'm Your Angel" (Jive 42557). It also heads the Adult Contemporary charts for twelve weeks.

December 25. Former Love guitarist Bryan MacLean dies of a heart attack at age sixty-two.

December 26. The Spice Girls reach number one on the British charts with "Goodbye."

1999

❄

January 10. Norman Cook tops the British singles charts for the third time—all under different names. His present incarnation is Fatboy Slim (having recorded the hip-hop-inflected dance number, "Praise You"); his previous hits were with The Housemartins and Beats International.

January 16. Brandy begins a two-week stay at number one on the Hot 100 with "Did You Ever?" (Atlantic 84198).

January 30. Britney Spears goes number one on both the singles and album charts with "…Baby One More Time" (Jive 42545)—remaining there for two weeks—and the album of the same name (Jive 41651), respectively.

Attractive, personable, and a born entertainer, it could be argued that Britney Spears (b. December 2, 1981, Kentwood, Louisiana) was destined to be teen idol material. Certainly, the preteen audience in the late 1990s was sufficiently well-heeled to provide elbow room for a host of competitors, including Christina Aguilera and Ricky Martin from the Latin music scene, Brandy and Monica (R&B), LeAnn Rimes (country music), Jessica Simpson (Christian Contemporary), and 'N Sync (pop-rock). As an adult, it remains to be seen whether she will be able maintain her commercial success a la Michael Jackson or fade into obscurity much like bygone stars David and Shaun Cassidy, Bobby Sherman, Leif Garrett, Tiffany, Debbie Gibson, and the New Kids on the Block.

A veteran of television commercials and the off-Broadway show, *Ruthless* (1991) prior to appearing as a regular on The New Mickey Mouse Club (1993–1994 seasons), Spears' recording career began at age fifteen when an audition for Jive Records led to a contract. To record the debut album, Jive—following the formula that had helped lift one of its other acts, the Backstreet Boys, to superstardom—sent her to Stockholm to work with producers Max Martin and Eric Foster White.

Hyped by steady touring—both as opening act for label mates 'N Sync and on her own performing to backing tapes at shopping malls—Spears' debut single, "…Baby One More Time" (Jive 42525) entered the Billboard Hot 100 at number one in October 1998. The album, …Baby One More Time (Jive 41651; 1999), repeated the feat when released the following January. Helped by three more successful singles— "Sometimes" (album cut from Jive 41651; 1999; #21), "(You Drive Me) Crazy" (Jive 42606; 1999; #10), and "From the Bottom of My Broken Heart" (2000; #14)—and her provocative blend of suggestive sexuality and youthful innocence, the LP would sell more than thirteen million copies through 2000, also earning her a Grammy nomination for Best New Artist.

Spears' follow-up album, Oops!…I Did It Again (Jive; 2000), also reached number one, selling in excess of eight million within a year of its release. She collaborated on a memoir, Heart to Heart (2000), with her mother, thereby providing an alternative to the legions of knock-off paperbacks attempting to exploit her celebrity. By now a major pop culture phenomenon, she was represented by a flood of import and non-musical releases in domestic record bins. Although her third official album, Britney (BMG; 2001), strained the credibility of her demure image, it continued her commercial hot streak.

February. Eminem's major label debut, *The Slim Shady LP*, is released by Interscope.

Born Marshall Mathers (word play on the initials behind his stage name) October 17, 1973, in St. Joseph, Missouri, he grew up poor, splitting time between the Kansas City area and Detroit. He began freestyling at age fourteen, first attracting grassroots attention as part of the Detroit-based duo Soul Intent. Eminem's early independent label releases, *Infinite* (1996), followed by *The Slim Shady EP* (1997)—while suffering from poor distribution and promotion—made a splash within the rap underground, due both to his hyperactive, nasal-voiced delivery and skin color, which earned him the moniker "great white hope."

Allegedly coming across Eminem's demo tape on the floor of Interscope label head Jimmy Iovine's garage, Dr. Dre went to see him perform at the 1997 Rap Olympics in Los Angeles, where he earned second place in the freestyle category. Dre signed him on the spot, and the resulting album, *The Slim Shady* LP— described by Stephen Thomas Erlewine as "an inspired, surrealistic parody of Jerry Springer-fueled pop culture and gangsta rap"—rose to number two, selling two million copies during its first months in the marketplace. *The Marshall Mathers LP* (Interscope, 2000) rocketed to the top of the charts, its stark—often humorous—depictions of violence, drugs, gay bashing, and the like singling him out for censure by the mainstream press and countless would-be social reformers.

Eminem played a key role in the emergence of D-12, a group vehicle in which he was supported by five black childhood friends. Their hard-edged album, *Devil's Night* (Shady/Interscope, 2001), also topped the charts, followed by the equally successful, *D12 World* (Shady/Interscope, 2004), named the thirtieth most popular LP of the year by *Billboard* in its "Year in Music & Touring" section (December 25, 2004). The rapper's next solo outing, *The Eminem Show* (Interscope, 2002), was more stridently political than prior works, focusing much of its inventive on the perceived failing of the Bush administration.

February 4. Gwen Guthrie—who collaborated with Aretha Franklin and Stevie Wonder, and composed material for Roberta Flack and Sister Sledge, among others—dies of cancer.

February 5. NSYNC appears on the television program, *Sabrina the Teenage Witch*.

February 7. Blondie go number one with "Maria"—their sixth British chart topper.

February 13. Monica begins a four-week stay atop the Hot 100 with "Angel of Mine" (Arista 13590)

February 14. Lenny Kravitz tops the British charts with "Fly Away," which had been used with a television car advertisement.

February 16. Robbie Williams is the big winner at the Brit Awards, being named Best British Solo Artist, Best Single ("Angels"), and Best Video ("Millennium"). Also cited are the Manic Street Preachers (Best British Group) and Natalie Imbruglia (Best Female Artist and Newcomer).

February 27. Britney Spears begins a two-week stay atop the British charts with "Baby One More Time," on its way to becoming the biggest-selling single of the year.

March 2. Dusty Springfield dies at age fifty-nine following a long battle against cancer.

March 3. Music professor Peter Jeffrey sues The Smashing Pumpkins, their promoters, and an earplug manufacturer, claiming his hearing was damaged at a concert in Connecticut.

March 3. Oasis agree to give their former drummer Tony McCarroll a one-off payment of $935,000 after he sued the band for millions in unpaid royalties. He was fired by the group in 1995.

March 7. Boyzone top the British singles charts for the fifth time with a remake of Billy Ocean's 1986 hit, "When the Going Gets Tough."

March 13. Cher reaches number one on the Hot 100 with "Believe" (Warner Bros. 17119), remaining there for four weeks. It is her fourth chart-topping single as a solo act; the first since early 1974.

March 13. TLC heads up the album charts with *Fanmail* (LaFace).

March 14. Stereophonics go number one on the British charts with *Performance and Cocktails* the first album for Richard Branson's V2 label.

March 21. *13* becomes Blur's fourth consecutive chart-topping album in Great Britain.

March 29. The David Bowie Internet Radio Network broadcasts its first show for Rolling Stone Radio. The program features Bowie introducing his favorite recordings.

April 2. The Black Crowes' Knoxville, Tennessee concert will cause teenager Joshua Harmon—who has a second row seat—to sue the band for $385,000 a year later, claiming significant hearing loss.

April 3. Lionel Bart—composer of the musical, *Oliver*, as well as pop songs like Cliff Richard's "Living Doll"— dies from cancer at age sixty-nine.

April 4. The Corrs' *Talk on Corners* goes number one for the tenth time on the British album charts. They also had the second ranked album with *Forgiven, Not Forgotten*.

April 10. London's Royal Albert Hall hosts a charity tribute concert for the late Linda McCartney. Featured performers include Paul McCartney, Elvis Costello, Chrissie Hynde, George Michael, and Sinead O'Connor.

April 10. TLC begins a four-week stint atop the Hot 100 with "No Scrubs" (LaFace 24385). It also tops the R&B charts for five weeks.

April 16. Drummer and singer/songwriter Skip Spence dies of lung cancer in a San Francisco hospital at age fifty-two. An original member of Jefferson Airplane and founding member of Moby Grape, he had battled schizophrenia and alcoholism for decades.

April 18. Catatonia top the British charts with *Equally Cursed and Blessed*. Their other two albums also resided in the Top 40 at the time.

April 28. Tom Petty receives a star on the Hollywood Walk of Fame.

May 8. Former Menudo member Ricky Martin reaches number one on the Hot 100 with "Livin' La Vida Loca" (C2/Columbia 79124), remaining there for five weeks.

May 9. The Backstreet Boys top the British charts with "I Want It That Way."

May 10. Author and singer/songwriter Shel Silverstein dies of a heart attack at age fifty-seven. His compositions include Johnny Cash's "A Boy Named Sue" and Dr. Hook's "Sylvia's Mother."

May 16. Boyzone top the British charts with "You Needed Me."

May 22. Country singer Tim McGraw reaches number one on the album charts with *A Place in the Sun*.

May 24. Freddie Mercury is featured on a set of millennium stamps issued by the Royal Mail (Great Britain).

May 27. At the Ivor Novello Awards, Rod Stewart receives a Lifetime Achievement citation, Robbie Williams and Guy Chambers are named Songwriters of the Year, and Chrissie Hynde garners the Outstanding Contribution to British Music.

June 5. The Backstreet Boys reach number one on the album charts with *Millennium*.

June 12. Jennifer Lopez begins a five-week run atop the Hot 100 with "If You Had My Love" (Epic/Work 79163).

July 5. From the Greenpeace boat, *Rainbow Warrior*, moored in the River Thames, Eurythmics announce that the profits to their first world tour in more than a decade would go to charity.

July 10. Ricky Martin begins a three-week run atop the British charts with "Livin' La Vida Loca."

July 17. Destiny's Child reaches number one on the Hot 100 with "Bills, Bills, Bills" (Columbia 79175). It also tops the R&B charts for nine weeks.

The Houston-based group—originally consisting of lead singer Beyonce Knowles, second lead vocalist Kelly Rowland, alto LaTavia Roberson, and soprano LeToya Luckett—came together in 1993, adopted their name from Book Of Isaiah. Beyonce's father, Music World Management's Mathew Knowles, steered the quartet from early local impact opening for best-selling rhythm and blues artists to international recognition after signing with Columbia in 1997.

Their initial success came with the inclusion of "Killing Time" in the top-grossing 1997 film, *Men In Black*. They built up further momentum with the release the eponymous debut LP (Columbia; 1998), which featured production assists from leading urban r & b/hip-hop producers R. Kelly, Timbaland, Missy "Misdemeanor" Elliott, and Wyclef Jean. The latter's collaboration with the quartet, the infectious dance number "No, No, No, Part 2)" (Columbia 78618; 1997; #3 pop), reached number one of the r & b charts. Their second album, *The Writing's On The Wall* (Columbia 69870; 1999)—while including producers Elliott, Kevin "She'kspere" Briggs, Rodney Jenkins, Chad Elliot, Dwayne Wiggins of Tony! Toni! Tone!—provided more opportunities for creative input by group members. The anti-male anthem "Bills, Bills, Bills" (Columbia 79175; 1999; #1 pop) headed up the R&B charts for nine consecutive weeks.

Despite personnel problems—Roberson and Luckett were, according to a lawsuit settled July 24, 2002, allegedly forced out by Mathew Knowles after refusing to accept his legal guardianship—Destiny's Child, bolstered by the additions of Farrah Franklin and Michelle Williams in February 2000, emerged as the leading female R&B vocal act. With Beyonce Knowles now dominating songwriting and production, the group released a steady stream of hits, most notably, the albums, *8 Days Of Christmas* (Columbia; 2001) and *Survivor* (Columbia; 2002; #1; platinum)—winner of the 2002 Grammy Award for Best R & B

Performance by a Duo or Group with Vocal—and the singles "Say My Name" (Columbia; 2001; #1 pop) and "Independent Women, Part 1" (Columbia; 2002; #1 pop eleven weeks), the latter of which appeared in the *Charlie's Angels* soundtrack. In late 2001, the group—now a trio following the departure of Franklin that August—announced a hiatus to work on solo recording projects. During the interim, they released *This Is The Remix* (Columbia; 2002), comprised largely of old hits—ranging from street-smart hip-hop to torchy R&B-tinged ballads—reworked by producers such as Timbaland, Maurice Joshua, and Neptunes. With Knowles achieving superstar status as a solo artist, actor, and model by the middle of the first decade of the 21st century, the long-term status of the group appeared in jeopardy.

July 24. "Wild Wild West" (Overbrook 79157)—by Will Smith, featuring Dru Hill & Kool Mo Dee—goes number one. Featuring samples of Kool Moe Dee's "Wild, Wild West" and Stevie Wonder's "I Wish," it is the title song for the film starring Smith and Kevin Kline.

July 31. Christina Aguilera begins a five-week stint atop the Hot 100 with "Genie in a Bottle" (RCA 65692). The platinum seller—which also reaches number one on the British charts—helps her win the 1999 Best New Artist Grammy award.

August 19. Lauryn Hill wins New Artist of the Year and Album of the Year at the Source Hip Hop Musc Awards in Los Angeles. Other winners include R. Kelly, R&B Artist of the Year; DMX, Artist of the Year and Solo and Live Performer of the Year.

August 19. The Advertising Clearance Centre bans a TV ad featuring Linda McCartney's appeal to boycott fishing.

September 4. Enrique Iglesias begins a two-week stay at number one on the Hot 100 with "Bailamos" (Overbrook 97122). Its success owes much to its inclusion in the film *Wild Wild West*.

September 18. TLC goes number one on the Hot 100 with "Unpretty" (LaFace 24424), remaining there for three weeks. It is the R&B vocal trio's fourth chart-topping single.

September 21. David Bowie's latest album of new material, *hours...*, becomes the first by a major artist to be made available by Internet download. Listing at $17.98, it is disseminated via the Liquid Audio format, and—as a marketing incentive—includes a bonus track, "No One Calls," not available on the retail release.

October 5. Roger Daltrey announces that The Who are reforming, and that their first concert would take place in Las Vegas on October 29.

October 9. "Heartbreaker" (Columbia 79260)—by Mariah Carey (featuring Jay-Z)—begins a two-week stay atop the Hot 100. The recording, which samples Stacy Lattisaw's "Attack of the Name Game," also goes number one of the R&B charts for two weeks.

October 10. Hoyt Axton dies of a heart attack, aged sixty-one. He wrote material for the likes of Elvis Presley, Glen Campbell, John Denver, Ringo Starr, and Three Dog Night, and charted with his own interpretations of "When the Morning Comes" and "Flash of Fire."

October 23. Santana's "Smooth" (Arista 13718), featuring lead vocals by Rob Thomas, moves into the top position on the Hot 100, remaining there for twelve weeks.

October 31. EMI announces that artists selling less than eighty thousand copies would be discouraged from releasing singles in the future.

October 31. In an article entitled, "New Pop Fortunes," *The (London) Sunday Times* reports that the Coors are worth $2.55 million each, Boyzone $5 million each, Jamiroquai $6.8 million, the Chemical Brothers $6.8 million each, and Norman Cook $17 million.

November 10. WEA announces that The Eagles' *Their Greatest Hits 1971–1975* (Asylum; 1975) is the biggest selling LP of the millennium in the United States, reaching twenty-six million units.

November 11. Britney Spears dominates the MTV Awards, winning Best Female Singer, Best Pop Act, Best Breakthrough Artist, and Best Song for "Baby One More Time." The Offspring garner Best Rock Act, Will Smith Best Male Act, and Bono the Free Your Mind prize.

November 13. It is announced that Cliff Richard inks a service pact with Remotemusic.com, the first deal linking a notable recording artist with an Internet firm.

December 20. Country artist Hank Snow, widely known as "The Singing Ranger," dies. He began recording in the 1930s, modeling his career after the Father of Country Music, Jimmie Rodgers.

December 26. Singer/songwriter Curtis Mayfield—formerly with the Impressions—dies at age fifty-seven.

December 29. The Smiths' *The Queen Is Dead* tops the *Melody Maker* Music of the Millennium album poll.

December 30. The Queen's Millennium Honours List includes Slade's Noddy Holder (MBE) and former Dire Straits singer/songwriter/guitarist Mark Knopfler (OBE).

2000

❄

January 12. Charlotte Church fires manager Jonathan Shalit. Shalit had been instrumental in the teenage singer's success, negotiating concert dates and a five-album deal with the Sony label which enabled her to earn more than $10 million up to that point.

January 15. Christina Aguilera begins a two-week stint atop the Hot 100 with "What a Girl Wants."

Christina Aguilera came along at the perfect time in pop music history; with pre-teens possessing more disposable income than ever before, teen idol recording stars became a hot commodity in the 1990s. Furthermore, Hispanic performers captured an increasing share of music industry revenue during this decade. Add Aguilera's striking good looks, exuberant singing style, accomplished stage skills, and a major label promotional budget, and chart success would seem to have been a foregone conclusion.

Due largely to her father's military career, Aguilera traveled widely as a youth until the family settled in Wexford, Pennsylvania. After starting out in Pittsburgh-area talent shows, she appeared on the TV series *Star Search* at age eight and garnered a cast slot on *The New Mickey Mouse Club* four years later. Her recording career commenced with a hit single in Japan, "All I Wanna Do," a duet with Keizo Nakanishi. She next recorded "Reflection" for inclusion on the soundtrack of the animated feature, *Mulan* (1998).

Signing a recording contract with RCA in 1998, her debut album—*Christina Aguilera* (RCA 67690; 1999; #1)—would sell more than ten million copies over the next year, assisted by two number one singles, "Genie in a Bottle" (RCA 65692; 1999) and "What a Girl Wants" (RCA 65960). Aguilera's superstar status was affirmed by an invitation to perform at the Super Bowl XXXIII Halftime Show and a 1999 Grammy award for Best New Artist.

With import singles and albums flooding the market, two more albums were issued domestically in 2000, *Mi Reflejo* (RCA), a Spanish-language collection geared to her huge Hispanic following, and *My Kind of Christmas* (RCA). The following year she would collaborate with Lil' Kim, Mya, and Pink in the chart-topping single, "Lady Marmalade" (Twentieth Century-Fox 497 561-2; 2001; from the film soundtrack to *Moulin Rouge*), formerly a number one hit for Labelle in 1975. With her popularity remaining at a peak level through 2001, Aguilera appears likely to sustain her storybook career well into adulthood.

January 16. The media report that Mick Jagger's chances at gaining knighthood were irreparably hurt after an affair with a Brazilian lingerie model resulted in a child born out of wedlock. Tony Blair's Labour Party apparently felt the move necessary given its commitment to a family values platform.

January 28. Motown saxophonist Thomas "Beans" Bowles dies of prostate cancer. His session credits include the Supremes' "Baby Love" and Marvin Gaye's "What's Going On."

January 29. Savage Garden top the Hot 100 with "I Kew I Loved You," remaining there for four non-consecutive weeks.

February 4. Bjorn Ulvaeus discloses that Abba members passed on a $1 billion offer from an Anglo-American consortium to reform the group.

February 11. Geri Halliwell provides testimony in a court dispute involving Aprilia Scooter Company. The firm had sued the Spice Girls for $2.72 million over lost advertising in their sponsorship of the 1998 Spiceworld tour.

February 12. Mariah Carey begins a two-week run atop the Hot 100 with "Thank God I Found You."

February 12. R&B singer Screamin' Jay Hawkins dies at age seventy. A Golden Gloves boxing champion by sixteen, he is best remembered for his macabre stage show and the rock 'n' roll standard, "I Put a Spell on You."

February 17. John Lennon's Steinway piano, on which he composed songs such as "Imagine," was displayed at Liverpool's Beatles Story Museum.

February 18. An American court orders the release of FBI files on John Lennon. They include documentation regarding his support of the Irish Republican cause and the Workers' Revolutionary Party.

February 20. All Saints begin a two-week stint atop the British charts with "Pure Shores," their fourth number one single.

February 22. The engagement ring Sid Vicious gave to girlfriend Nancy Spungen went on sale for $2,550.

February 23. Carlos Santana dominates the forty-second annual Grammy Awards ceremony, matching Michael Jackson's 1983 record of eight Grammies won in one evening. His trophies include album of the year *Supernatural*), record of the year ("Smooth," the duet with Rob Thomas), top performance by a duo/group with vocal ("Maria Maria"), pop collaboration with vocals ("Smooth"), rock performance by a duo or group ("Put Your Lights On"), rock instrumental performance ("The Calling"), and rock album (*Supernatural*). Other multiple winners included TLC (who scored on three of seven nominations, including best R&B performance by a duo or group with vocal), Sting (best pop album and best male pop vocal performance), and Dixie Chicks (best country album and best country performance).

February 25. The Spice Girls are determined to be guilty of charges by 1998 world tour sponsors, the Aprilia Scooter Company, that they knew ahead of time that Geri Hershey was leaving the group.

February 26. Lonestar begins a two-week stay atop the Hot 100 with "Amazed."

March 3. Brit Award winners include Tom Jones, Best Male Artist; Travis, Best Band and Best Album for *The Man Who*; Robbie Williams, Best Single for "She's the One"; Five, Best Pop Act; TLC, Best International Group; Beck, Best International Male Artist; Macy Gray, Best Newcomer; and the Spice Girls for Outstanding Contribution.

March 4. Lonestar begins a two-week stint atop the Hot 100 with "Amazed."

March 7. Oasis lead vocalist Liam Gallagher garners the Best Dressed Man Award from *GQ*.

March 10. The Pretenders' Chrissie Hynde is arrested in Manhattan for leading an animal rights protest against the Gap clothing retailer for the alleged use of leather from cows slaughtered "illegally and cruelly."

March 18. Destiny's Child top the Hot 100 with "Say My Name," remaining there for three weeks.

March 22. Yusuf Islam, formerly known as Cat Stevens, joins the campaign to uphold the ban on the promotion of homosexuality in British schools.

March 24. A film company pays $1,079,5000 for more than nine hours of film shots by Yoko Ono in the 1970s. The footage included Lennon smoking and addressing his political beliefs.

March 24. Elton John's *Aida* opens on Broadway. Elton John exits after fifteen minutes, complaining that his songs had been ruined.. Although he wrote the music in twenty-one days, it took five years to mount the production.

March 25. *NSYNC sell a million tickets—netting $42.5 million—in a day for their upcoming tour.

March 27. Ian Dury dies of cancer. Disabled by polio as a youth, the sometime actor formed the pub rock band, Kilburn and the High Roads, in the early 1970s, and then recorded the classic punk LP, *New Boots and Panties* (Stiff; 1979).

March 30. Mick Jagger opens the new arts center named for him at his former school, Dartford Grammar. He noted that his days there had been the worst time of his life.

April 7. A Joni Mitchell tribute concert in New York features Bryan Adams, Mary Chapin Carpenter, Shawn Colvin, Elton John, k.d. lang, Cyndi Lauper, James Taylor, and Richard Thompson.

April 8. *NSYNC reaches number one on the album charts with *No Strings Attached*.

April 8. "Maria Maria," by Santana featuring The Product G&B, begins a ten-week run atop the Hot 100.

April 9. Moby begins a five-week run atop the British album charts with *Play*.

April 12. Metallica sues Napster and three institutions of higher learning—Indiana University, University of Southern California, and Yale University—for copyright infringement.

April 28. James Brown Enterprises destroyed by fire. Memorabilia and live tapes are destroyed. An employee is later arrested for arson.

May 7. Britney Spears tops the British charts with "Oops! I Did It Again."

May 8. *U.S. News & World Report* (vol. 128, no.18, p. 45) notes that Dr. Dre has sued Napster for aiding and abetting music piracy. Attorney Howard King, who is also handling the case previously set forth by Metallica, stated, "The public should know it's not just the record labels being hurt by piracy, but artists, too." Napster's very existence appears to be in danger with the Record Industry Association of America pressing its copyright infringement case in court against the software trading site. Furthermore, another Internet-based music service, MP3.com, was found liable last week for infringing on record company copyrights.

On the other hand, however, some artists seem convinced that Napster is a harbinger of new marketing trends. Last week, alternative rock acts Limp Bizkit and Cypress Hill signed a tour deal with Napster. The former group's lead singer, Fred Durst, observed, "Nowadays you can go on Napster and hear the Limp Bizkit single. If you like it, go get it. It's a cool way to make sure your $16 is being spent well."

May 12. The ten-foot-high iron gates to Strawberry Fields, the Merseyside landmark immortalized by a Beatles song, are stolen. They are later found at a local scrap metal concern.

May 15. Britney Spears tells a German magazine that she intends to abstain from sex until her wedding night.

May 21. Whitney Houston begins a two-week stint atop the British album charts with *The Greatest Hits*.

May 21. Billie Piper reaches number one on the U.K. charts with "Day & Night."

May 22. Fran Healy—vocalist for Travis—wins Best Contemporary Song for "Why Does It Always Rain on Me?" and Songwiter of the Year for the album, *The Man Who*, at the Ivor Novello Awards.

May 22. Robbie Williams establishes a children's trust, "Give It Sum," with $3.4 million earned from a Pepsi deal. Beneficiaries will include Jeans for Genes and UNICEF.

May 28. Sonique begins a three-week stay atop the British charts with "It Feels So Good."

May 28. Britney Spears reaches number one on the album charts with *Oops!...I Did It Again*.

June 9. Sinead O'Connor—then raising two natural birth children—tells *Curve* magazine, "I am a lesbian. I haven't been very open about that, I've gone out with blokes because I haven't necessarily been terribly comfortable about being a lesbian."

June 17. Aaliyah tops the pop charts with "Try Again."

June 22. *Rolling Stone* pictures Kid Rock—wearing a vest made of aluminum beer tabs—on its cover with the caption "Kid Rock Talks Trash."

June 24. "Be With You," by Enrique Iglesias, begins a three-week stay atop the Hot 100.

July 15. Vertical Horizon reach number one on the pop charts with "Everything You Want."

July 22. Matchbox 20 top the Hot 100 with "Bent."

July 29. *NSYNC begin a two-week stint atop the pop charts with "It's Gonna Be Me."

August 3. *Rolling Stone* pictures a shirtless Blink-182 on its cover with the caption "The Half Naked Truth About Blink-182."

August 12. "Incomplete," by Sisq6, reaches number one on the Hot 100, remaining there for two weeks.

August 25. Jack Nitzche dies of a heart attack. He co-wrote such hits as "Needles and Pins" and "Up Where We Belong," and produced the Rolling Stones, the Walker Brothers, and Neil Young.

August 26. "Doesn't Really Matter," by Janet (Jackson), begins a three-week run atop the Hot 100.

September. Madonna tops the British pop charts with "Music."

September 3. Robbie Williams starts a three-week stay at number one on the British album charts with *Sing When You're Winning*.

September 16. Madonna's "Music" (Maverick) reaches number one on the Hot 100, remaining there for four weeks.

September 17. Paula Yates is found dead by her young daughter. She was known as a presenter on the British music program, *The Tube*, and her marriage to Bob Geldof. She would leave him to live with INXS vocalist, Michael Hutchence.

October 5. *Top of the Pops* issues a Top 40 listing based upon its weekly program. The most successful singles are "Relax," by Frankie Goes to Hollywood, at number one; the Beatles' "She Loves You," number two; and Frank Sinatra's "My Way," number three.

October 14. Christina Aquilera begins a four-week run atop the Hot 100 with "Come On Over Baby (All I Want Is You)."

November 11. Creed's "With Arms Wide Open" goes number one on the pop charts.

November 12. Winners at the MTV Europe Awards include All Saints (Breakthrough Artist), Natalie Imbruglia (Best Song for "Torn"), Madonna (Best Female Artist and Best Album for *Ray of Light*), the Spice Girls (Best Group), and Robbie Williams (Best Male Artist).

November 13. The Beatles launch their first official Web site (www.thebeatles.com). The band retrospective, *1*, is released that day as well.

November 18. Destiny's Child begins an eleven week run atop the Hot 100 with "Independent Women, Part I."

November 19. The Beatles begins an eleven-week run atop the British album charts with *1*.

November 20. Mel C. announces she's leaving the Spice Girls during a television interview on ITV's *Frank Skinner Show*.

December 3. Hoyt Curtin—composer of the themes to *The Flintstones*, *Yogi Bear*, *The Jetsons*, and other cartoons—dies of heart failure.

December 18. Singer-songwriter Kirsty MacColl is killed by a speedboat off the coast of Mexico. She was forty-one years old.

December 19. Roebuck "Pop" Staples—vocalist with the Staple Singers—dies at age eighty-five.

December 21. Record Industry Association of America releases sales figures that reflect the success of a new wave of teen idols. Jive Records—whose roster includes the Backstreet Boys, Britney Spears, and *NSYNC—had become a major industry player with sales of thirty-one million units for the year.

December 24. Four Season bassist Nick Massi dies.

Selected Bibliography

❄

Billboard. *Joel Whitburn's Pop Annual, 1955–1999*. Menomonee, WI: Record Research, 2000.

Black, Johnny (with contributions from Hugh Gregory and Andy Basire). *Rock and PopT imeline; How music changed the world through four decades*. San Diego, CA: Thunder Bay Press, 2001.

Dearling, Robert, and Celia Dearling (with Brian Rust). *The Guinness Book of Recorded Sound*. Guinness Books, n.d.

Dixon, Robert M.W., and John Godrich (Eds.). *Blues & Gospel Records, 1902–1943* (3rd ed.). Essex, U.K.: Storyville Publications, 1982.

Gillet, Charlie. *The Sound of the City: The Rise of Rock and Roll*. New York: Outerbridge & Dienstfrey, distr. by E.P. Dutton, 1970.

Giovannoni, David. "Dating Victor 78s," http://members.tripod.com/~Vinylville/faq-9.html. Posted August 1995.

Green, Stanley. *Broadway Musicals; Show By Show* (4th ed., revised and updated by Kay Green). New York: Hal Leonard Publishing Corporation, 1994.

Hyatt, Wesley. *The Billboard Book of Number One Adult Contemporary Hits*. New York: Billboard Books, 1999.

Laufenberg, Frank. *Rock and Pop: Day by Day; Birthdays, Deaths, Hits and Facts*. Bergisch Gladbach: Lubbe, 1980. Published in English translation by Blandford in 1992 (Astrid Mick, translator; Hugh Gregory, editor).

Nite, Norm N. *Rock On Almanac; The First Four Decades of Rock 'n' Roll: A Chronology* (2nd ed.). New York: HarperPerennial, 1992.

Rees, Dafydd, and Luke Crampton (Eds.). *Rock Movers & Shakers*. Santa Barbara, CA: ABC-Clio, 1992.

Roland, Tom. *The Billboard Book of Number One Country Hits*. New York: Billboard Books, 1991.

Rolling Stone Rock Almanac; The Chronicles of Rock & Roll, by the editors of *Rolling Stone*. Foreword by Peter Wolf. New York: Macmillan, 1983.

Schoenherr, Steven E. "Recording Technology History," http://history.acusd.edu/gen/recording/notes.html#origins. Posted 1999; revised July 6, 2005.

Smith, Steve, and The Diagram Group. *Rock Day by Day*. Guinness Books, 1987.

The Source. *Rock Chronicle*. New York: Delilah, 1982.

This Day in Music, by the editorial board, *This Day in Music*. Collins & Brown, 2005.

Tobler, John. *This Day in Rock; Day by Day Record of Rock's Biggest News Stories*. New York: Carroll & Graf, n.d.

Whitburn, Joel. *The Billboard Book of Top 40 Albums*, (3rd ed.). New York: Billboard Books, 1995.

Whitburn, Joel. *The Billboard Book of Top 40 Hits*, (8th ed.). New York: Billboard Books, 2004.

White, Adam. *The Billboard Book of Gold & Platinum Records*. New York: Billboard Books, 1990.

White, Adam, and Fred Bronson. *The Billboard Book of Number One Rhythm & Blues Hits*. New York: Billboard Books, 1991.

Compiled by Bruce Hall

Index